The Cambridge History of the English Language is the first multi-volume work to provide a full account of the history of English. Its authoritative coverage extends from areas of central linguistic interest and concern to more specialised topics such as personal and place names. The volumes dealing with earlier periods are chronologically based, whilst those dealing with more recent periods are geographically based, thus reflecting the spread of English over the last 300 years.

Volume IV deals with the history of the English language from 1776 to 1997. An extensive introduction details the changing socio-historical setting in which English has developed in response to a continuing background of diversity as it was transplanted to North America and beyond. Separate chapters on pronunciation, syntax, and vocabulary chronicle the linguistic features of the language during this period, taking as the basis for discussion the common core inherited form the sixteenth century and shared by what are now the two principal varieties, American and British English. In addition, there are chapters on English as a literary language, English grammar and usage, and onomastics.

THE CAMBRIDGE HISTORY
OF THE ENGLISH LANGUAGE

GENERAL EDITOR Richard M. Hogg

VOLUME IV 1776–1997

THE CAMBRIDGE HISTORY OF THE ENGLISH LANGUAGE

VOLUME IV *1776–1997*

EDITED BY

SUZANNE ROMAINE

*Merton Professor of English Language,
University of Oxford*

CAMBRIDGE
UNIVERSITY PRESS

PUBLISHED BY THE PRESS SYNDICATE OF THE UNIVERSITY OF CAMBRIDGE
The Pitt Building, Trumpington Street, Cambridge CB2 1RP, United Kingdom

CAMBRIDGE UNIVERSITY PRESS
The Edinburgh Building, Cambridge CB2 2RU, United Kingdom
40 West 20th Street, New York, NY 10011–4211, USA
10 Stamford Road, Oakleigh, Melbourne 3166, Australia

First published 1998

Printed in the United Kingdom at the University Press, Cambridge

Typeset in Monotype Garamond 11/13 pt   [SE]

A catalogue record for this book is available from the British Library

Library of Congress cataloguing in publication data

The Cambridge history of the English language.
Vol. 1 edited by Richard M. Hogg.
Vol. 2 edited by Norman Blake.
Vol. 4 edited by Suzanne Romaine.
Vol. 5 edited by Robert Burchfield.
Includes bibliographical references and index.
Contents: v. 1. The beginning to 1066 – v. 2. 1066–
1476 – v. 4. 1776–1997 – v. 5. English in Britain and Overseas:
origins and development.
1. English language – History.   I. Hogg, Richard M.
II. Blake, N. F. (Norman Francis)   III. Burchfield,
R. W. (Robert William)   IV. Romaine, Suzanne
PE1072.C36 1992   420'.9   91–13881
ISBN 0 521 26474 X (v. 1)
ISBN 0 521 26475 8 (v. 2)
ISBN 0 521 26478 2 (v. 5)
ISBN 0 521 26477 4 (v. 4)

CONTENTS

Contents

Contents

FIGURES

TABLES

CONTRIBUTORS

SYLVIA ADAMSON *University Lecturer in English Language, University of Cambridge*

JOHN ALGEO *Professor Emeritus, University of Georgia*

RICHARD COATES *Professor of Linguistics, University of Sussex*

DAVID DENISON *Professor of English Linguistics, University of Manchester*

EDWARD FINEGAN *Professor of Linguistics and Law, University of Southern California*

MICHAEL K. C. MacMAHON *Professor of Phonetics, University of Glasgow*

SUZANNE ROMAINE *Merton Professor of English Language, University of Oxford*

GENERAL EDITOR'S PREFACE

Although it is a topic of continuing debate, there can be little doubt that English is the most widely spoken language in the world, with significant numbers of native speakers in almost every major region – only South America falling largely outside the net. In such a situation an understanding of the nature of English can be claimed unambiguously to be of world-wide importance.

Growing consciousness of such a role for English is one of the motivations behind the History. There are other motivations too. Specialist students have many major and detailed works of scholarship to which they can refer, for example Bruce Mitchell's *Old English Syntax*, or, from an earlier age, Karl Luick's *Historische Grammatik der englischen Sprache*. Similarly, those who come new to the subject have both one-volume histories such as Barbara Strang's *History of English* and introductory textbooks to a single period, for example Bruce Mitchell and Fred Robinson's *A Guide to Old English*. But what is lacking is the intermediate work which can provide a solid discussion of the full range of the history of English both to the Anglicist who does not specialise in the particular area to hand and to the general linguist who has no specialised knowledge of the history of English. This work attempts to remedy that lack. We hope that it will be of use to others too, whether they are interested in the history of English for its own sake, or for some specific purpose such as local history or the effects of colonisation.

Under the influence of the Swiss linguist, Ferdinand de Saussure, there has been, during this century, a persistent tendancy to view the study of language as having two discrete parts: (i) synchronic, where a language is studied from the point of view of one moment in time; (ii) diachronic, where a language is studied from a historical perspective. It might therefore be supposed that this present work is purely diachronic. But this is not so. One crucial principle which guides *The Cambridge History of the English*

Language is that synchrony and diachrony are intertwined, and that a satisfactory understanding of English (or any other language) cannot be achieved on the basis of one of these alone.

Consider, for example, the (synchronic) fact that English, when compared with other languages, has some rather infrequent or unusual characteristics. Thus, in the area of vocabulary, English has an exceptionally high number of words borrowed from other languages (French, the Scandinavian languages, American Indian languages, Italian, the languages of northern India and so on); in syntax a common construction is the use of *do* in forming questions (e.g. *Do you like cheese?*), a type of construction not often found in other languages; in morphology English has relatively few inflexions, at least compared with the majority of other European languages; in phonology the number of diphthongs as against the number of vowels in English English is notably high. In other words, synchronically, English can be seen to be in some respects rather unusual. But in order to understand such facts we need to look at the history of the language; it is often only there that an explanation can be found. And that is what this work attempts to do.

This raises another issue. A quasi-Darwinian approach to English might attempt to account for its widespread use by claiming that somehow English is more suited, better adapted, to use as an international language than others. But that is nonsense. English is no more fit than, say, Spanish or Chinese. The reasons for the spread of English are political, cultural and economic rather than linguistic. So too are the reasons for such linguistic elements within English as the high number of borrowed words. This History, therefore, is based as much upon political, cultural and economic factors as linguistic ones, and it will be noted that the major historical divisions between volumes are based upon the former type of events (the Norman Conquest, the spread of printing, the declaration of independence by the USA), rather than the latter type.

As a rough generalisation, one can say that up to about the seventeenth century the development of English tended to be centripetal, whereas since then the development has tended to be centrifugal. The settlement by the Anglo-Saxons resulted in a spread of dialect variation over the country, but by the tenth century a variety of forces were combining to promote the emergence of a standard form of the language. Such an evolution was disrupted by the Norman Conquest, but with the development of printing together with other more centralising tendencies, the emergence of a standard form became once more, from the fifteenth century on, a major characteristic of the language. But processes of emigration and colonisation then gave rise to new regional varieties overseas, many of which have now achieved a high degree of linguistic independence, and one of which, namely American English, may even have a dominating influence on British English. The structure of this work is designed to reflect these different types of development. Whilst the first four volumes offer a reasonably straightforward chronological account, the later volumes are geographically based. This arrangement, we hope, allows scope for the proper treatment of diverse types of evolution and development. Even within the chronologically oriented volumes there are variations of structure, which are designed to reflect the changing relative importance of various linguistic features. Although all the chronological volumes have substantial chapters devoted to the central topics of semantics and vocabulary, syntax, and phonology and morphology, for other topics the space allotted in a particular volume is one which is appropriate to the importance of that topic during the relevant period, rather than some pre-defined calculation of relative importance. And within the geographically based volumes all these topics are potentially included within each geographical section, even if sometimes in a less formal way. Such a flexible and changing structure seems essential for any full treatment of the history of English.

One question that came up as this project began was the extent to which it might be possible or desirable to work within a single theoretical linguistic framework. It could well be argued that only a consensus within the linguistic community about preferred linguistic theories would enable a work such as this to be written. Certainly, it was immediately obvious when work for this History began, that it would be impossible to lay down a 'party line' on linguistic theory, and indeed, that such an approach would be undesirably restrictive. The solution reached was, I believe, more fruitful. Contributors have been chosen purely on the grounds of expertise and knowledge, and have been encouraged to write their contributions in the way they see most fitting, whilst at the same time taking full account of developments in linguistic theory. This has, of course, led to problems, notably with contrasting views of the same topic (and also because of the need to distinguish the ephemeral flight of theoretical fancy from genuine new insights into linguistic theory), but even in a work which is concerned to provide a unified approach (so that, for example, in most cases every contributor to a volume has read all the other contributions to that volume), such contrasts, and even contradictions, are stimulating and fruitful. Whilst this work aims to be authoritative, it is not prescriptive, and the final goal must be to stimulate interest in a subject in which much work remains to be done, both theoretically and empirically.

The task of editing this History has been, and still remains, a long and complex one. As General Editor I owe a great debt to my friends and colleagues who have devoted much time and thought to how best this work might be approached and completed. Firstly, I should thank my fellow-editors: John Algeo, Norman Blake, Bob Burchfield, Roger Lass and Suzanne Romaine. They have been concerned as much with the History as a whole as with their individual volumes. Secondly, there are those fellow linguists, some contributors, some not, who have so generously given of their time and made many valuable suggestions: John Anderson, Cecily Clark, Frans van Coetsem, Fran Colman, David Denison, Ed Finegan, Olga Fischer, Jacek Fisiak, Malcolm Godden, Angus McIntosh, Lesley Milroy, Donka Minkova, Matti Rissanen, Michael Samuels, Bob Stockwell, Tom Toon, Elizabeth Traugott, Peter Trudgill, Nigel Vincent, Anthony Warner, Simone Wyss. One occasion stands out especially: the organisers of the Fourth International Conference on English Historical Linguistics, held at Amsterdam in 1985, kindly allowed us to hold a seminar on the project as it was just beginning. For their generosity, which allowed us to hear many views and exchange opinions with colleagues one rarely meets face-to-face, I must thank Roger Eaton, Olga Fischer, Willem Koopman and Federike van der Leek.

With a work so complex as this, an editor is faced with a wide variety of problems and difficulties. It has been, therefore, a continual comfort and solace to know that Penny Carter of Cambridge University Press has always been there to provide advice and solutions on every occasion. Without her knowledge and experience, encouragement and good humour, this work would have been both poorer and later. After the work for Volume I was virtually complete, Marion Smith took over as publishing editor, and I am grateful to her too, not merely for ensuring such a smooth change-over, but for her bravery when faced with the mountain of paper from which this series has emerged.

Richard M. Hogg

EDITOR'S ACKNOWLEDGEMENTS

Given the long time this volume was in preparation, it has passed through the hands of more than a few editors at Cambridge University Press. I would like to thank, in particular, Penny Carter, Judith Ayling and Kate Brett for their help during their respective tenures as editor in charge of the Cambridge History of the English Language project. I am grateful to Richard Hogg for comments on my introduction.

Suzanne Romaine
Oxford, 1997

CONTRIBUTORS' ACKNOWLEDGEMENTS

The contributors to this volume are grateful for the help and advice they have received from friends, colleagues and students, as well as from their fellow contributors and the editors of and contributors to other volumes. We wish especially to thank the following.

James Adamson, Adele S. Algeo, Dwight Atkinson, Syd Bauman, Linda van Bergen, Douglas Biber, Norman Blake, Joe Bray, R. W. Burchfield, Colin T. Clarkson, Teresa Fanego, Anne Finell, Olga Fischer, Susan Fitzmaurice, Julia Flanders, Nik Gisborne, Sarah Hawkins, Jane Hodson, Dick Hudson, Merja Kytö, Sidney Landau, Roger Lass, Grevel Lindop, Peter Matthews, Terry Moore, Fujio Nakamura, Terttu Nevalainen, Francis Nolan, John Payne, Jackie Pearson, Allen Renear, Matti Rissanen, Alan Shelston, Barry Symonds, Mary Syner, Ingrid Tieken-Boon van Ostade, Elizabeth Traugott, Graeme Trousdale, Nigel Vincent, Anthony Warner, E. S. C. Weiner, Marcus Wood, John Woolford, students at Manchester 1994–5.

ABBREVIATIONS

~	contrasts with/ corresponds to	ME	Middle English
ø	zero form or site of gap	ModE	Modern English
AmerE	American English	NP	noun phrase
AP	adjective phrase	OE	Old English
ARCHER	A Representative Corpus of Historical English Registers	*OED*	*Oxford English Dictionary*
		p.c.	personal communication
		PDE	Present-Day English
BrE	British English	PL	plural
CHEL	*Cambridge History of the English Language*	PP	prepositional phrase
		pple	participle
CV	Cardinal Vowel	PRES	present tense
e	early	SAI	subject-auxiliary inversion
EPD	*English Pronouncing Dictionary*	SG	singular
Gen.Am.	General American	1, 2, 3	first, second third person
IPA	International Phonetic Alphabet	s.v.	*sub voce, sub verbo* 'under the/ that word'
l	late	VP	verb phrase
Lat.	Latin	WWP	Women Writers Project, Brown University
LPD	*Longman Pronunciation Dictionary*		

I   INTRODUCTION

Suzanne Romaine

1.1   From Old English to new Englishes: unity in diversity?

The final decades of the eighteenth century provide the starting point for this volume – a time when arguably less was happening to shape the **structure** of the English language than to shape **attitudes** towards it in a social climate that became increasingly prescriptive. Baugh and Cable (1993) appropriately entitle their chapter on the period from 1650 to 1800 'The Appeal to Authority', characterising the intellectual spirit of the age as one seeking order and stability, both political and linguistic. This so-called Augustan Age was one of refinement. After two centuries of effort to remedy the perceived inadequacies of English to enable it to meet a continually expanding range of functions, the eighteenth century was a time for putting the final touches on it, to fix things once and for all. In the nineteenth century and early part of the twentieth the success of England as an imperial nation combined with romantic ideas about language being the expression of a people's genius would engender a triumphalist and patriotic attitude to English. The language was now not so much to be improved but preserved as a great national monument and defended from threat in a battle over whose norms would prevail. As the demographic shift in the English-speaking population moved away from Britain, the twentieth would be declared the American century, and the Empire would strike back.

The most radical changes to English grammar had already taken place over the roughly one thousand years preceding the starting year of this volume. Certainly MacMahon's chapter makes clear how in our own period the phonology of English underwent nothing like the series of changes called the Great Vowel Shift (see Lass, volume III). It is noteworthy too that changes affecting morphology are insignificant by comparison with those of previous periods. Hence, there is no separate chapter devoted to them here. English is currently undergoing the final stages of changes begun centuries earlier, e.g. the loss of case marking in *wh*-pronouns. The use of *who* in the objective case occurs sporadically even as early as the sixteenth century among writers such as Marlowe. Even though *who* has become increasingly accepted in written English and Sapir (1921: 167) predicted the demise of *whom* within a couple of hundred years, it is still with us.

The immediately preceding period dealt with in Volume III (1476–1776) of this series, the Early Modern Period, has often been described as the formative period in the history of Modern Standard English. By the end of the seventeenth century what we might call the present-day 'core' grammar of Standard English was already firmly established. As pointed out by Denison in his chapter on syntax, relatively few categorical innovations or losses occurred. The syntactic changes during the period covered in this volume have been mainly statistical in nature, with certain construction types becoming more frequent. The continuing expansion of the progressive, in particular, its use in passives such as *the house is being built*, is a product of the late eighteenth century. By the time it appeared, the prescriptive spirit was so well established that it was condemned as an inelegant neologism and consciously avoided by many writers. As Baugh and Cable (1993: 287–8) note, the origin of the construction can be traced back to the latter part of the eighteenth century, but its establishment and ultimate acceptance required the better part of a century. The so-called *get* passive, e.g. *the vase got broken*, is also largely a nineteenth-century development.

Other changes such as the spread and regularization of *do* support began in the thirteenth century and were more or less complete in the nineteenth. Although *do* coexisted with the simple verb forms in negative statements from the early ninth century, obligatoriness was not complete until the nineteenth. The increasing use of *do* periphrasis coincides with the fixing of SVO word order. Not surprisingly, *do* is first widely used in interrogatives, where the word order is disrupted, and then later spread to negatives.

The part of the language probably most affected by change in our period is its vocabulary. Baugh & Cable (1993: 292) draw our attention, in particular, to the great increase in scientific vocabulary and the large number of new terms in common use among modern English speakers, e.g. *bronchitis, cholesterol, relativity, quark*, etc. Under James Murray's editorship of the *Oxford English Dictionary* (*OED*), scientific and technical vocabulary fell outside the range of 'common words' to which the dictionary was committed (see 1.3.1). Murray, for instance, rejected *appendicitis* as too technical only to have it quickly become part of common usage after the coronation of Edward VII was postponed in 1902 due to an inflamed appendix (Willinsky 1994:125). As time went on, citation sources drew more on science than humanities, reflecting the increasingly important role of science and technology in everyday modern life. In my own time as an academic I have witnessed the introduction and spread of computer literacy, which has given new senses to old words, e.g. *windows*, *virus*, *boot*, as well as completely new terms and acronyms, e.g. *DOS* (*Disk Operating System*), *Bitnet* (*Because it's time network*), *byte*, *micro-processor*, etc. Computer technology has also made its impact felt in research methods, where machine-readable text corpora are now indispensable tools in the study of the English language, particularly in cases where there is no possibility of examining informants' intuitions, or listening to tape recordings.

Many of the great grammarians, lexicographers and dialectologists such as Poutsma, Jespersen, and Visser, worked from manually compiled and analysed corpora. James Murray is said to have had over four million citation slips in the editing of the *OED*. The corpus grew to over eleven million during the some forty years the dictionary was being edited. Yet it would probably have been hard for Murray to imagine his successors having the possibility of working with corpora of 500 million words capable of being searched by a computer in a matter of minutes, one which is well within today's technical capabilities. While Murray and his co-workers struggled with slips of paper in proverbial shoe boxes, dictionary staff at Oxford University Press today are able to access electronic databases which they scan for new terms. The *OED* is now available on CD-ROM.

The resources for exploiting corpora and the increasing number of large corpora in existence today open up linguistic phenomena to empirical investigation on a scale previously unimaginable. Grammatical and lexicographical studies that formerly took a lifetime to complete can now be done in a relatively short time span with increasing precision. In the past three decades corpora and text banks of natural language sentences or utterances have become increasingly widely used in linguistics, lexicography, information technology and computer science research.

While the English vocabulary has grown much in size since 1776, it is difficult to say precisely how large it is today for reasons explained by Algeo in his chapter. Borrowing has recently become less important as a source for new English words than it was previously. The formation of new words in the Old English period relied heavily on compounding and affixing. English now has many formatives borrowed from French and Latin to use in its basic word formation processes. Algeo shows that French is still the major source for recent English loanwords. In addition, Greek and Latin formatives are still highly productive resources for new technical terms coined in English. The extent of borrowing and the source languages used depends, however, to a certain extent on which variety of English does the borrowing (see Romaine, volume VI). The prominence of Japanese loanwords in recent years, for example, is closely linked to the rise of Japan as a major economic power in the late twentieth century. Among the new words from Japanese noted by Algeo & Algeo (1993) are *karaoke*, *kabuki*, *karoshi*, *kenbei*, and a few others.

It has long been a commonplace that the history of words offers a window into the history of a language. Linguistic changes having their origin in social and cultural developments can be readily seen in vocabulary and semantics. When a language is transplanted to a new place, as English was to the new English colonies in North America, new names were needed for the novel flora and fauna encountered by the early explorers and settlers (see Coates's chapter for a discussion of new place names).

In my sweeping attempt to paint a broad but brief linguistic landscape for our period, I am reminded of Strang's (1970: 19) cautionary words that 'at every stage the history of a language must be studied in the light of its use in the world'. This serves to remind us that every language has what is often called an internal and external history. Scholars generally treat these two aspects of the history of languages as more or less separate enterprises and language historians have usually thought that the more important job is to track internal evolution. Traditional histories present the language as changing largely in response to internal linguistic pressures. Language history is viewed as a series of changes with little attempt to answer the question of who originated them and what motivation others might have had for adopting and spreading them. These questions about the social origins and motivations for change naturally become harder to answer the further back in time we go, but have become increasingly difficult to ignore in the context of the greater understanding modern sociolinguistic research has yielded (see Romaine 1982). External history in its broadest sense will include all the political and social events associated with the community of English speakers from the time of their first arrival in Britain to the present day.

During the roughly 1,200 years between the arrival of English speakers in the British Isles and the first permanent settlement of English colonists in the North American colonies, one can speak with some justification of only one national standard. The only other contender was Scottish English (see McClure 1994). Its period as standard was limited both chronologically and geographically to Scotland during the fourteenth to sixteenth centuries, when Scotland was independent from England (see, however, Jones 1993 for discussion of Scottish Standard English in the eighteenth century). None of the attempted revivals has succeeded in reclaiming the status of standard for any variety of Scots.

In Kloss's (1978) terms the modern varieties of Scots lack a Scottish root, but function instead as varieties of English. While the English spoken in Ireland was equally distinctive (see Kallen 1994), no standard materialised, not even with the establishment of the Irish Republic in 1922, and despite the conscious use of a literary Anglo-Irish on the part of Yeats (1865–1939), Synge (1871–1909) and others, who in the late nineteenth and early twentieth century consciously fashioned their language on that of the rural districts only then undergoing anglicisation. Because Irish was seen as the language serving a unifying nationalist function, there was no need to declare linguistic independence for Hiberno-English.

Now the history of English is quite clearly also the social history of the English-speaking world, changing in response to a continuing background of diversity in which English has ceased to be an 'English' language. The domain of English literature too has ceased to be the country England and commenced to be a language (English). The shift in focus from country to language led by authors such as Joyce, Shaw, Pound, and Eliot is now propelled even further by Achebe, Soyinka, Walcott, Narayan, and others (see 1.3.4). The singular term *English* seems no longer adequate to describe the social, regional, and other variations in a language used by millions. If anything, developments in the period from 1776, which saw the beginnings of the first major transplanted or colonial variety of English take shape, the origins of other colonial varieties of English and English-based pidgins and creoles and what was to be the most important variety in the twentieth century (American English), show that in the modern period, we are talking of the history of 'Englishes' (see Rissanen, Ihalainen, Nevalainen & Taavitsainen 1992). The preceding period saw the spread of the language through the British Isles, while this volume sees the beginning of an overseas expansion on two more continents, Africa and Australia, which resulted from the movement of English-speaking populations from the British Isles, documented in more detail in the two subsequent volumes. Volume V (Burchfield 1994) treats some of the overseas varieties spoken by native and non-native speakers and volume VI (Algeo forthcoming), the development of the English language in North America.

Considerable discussion took place in the planning stages of this volume and the *Cambridge History of the English Language* project as a whole over the question of what form(s) of English would provide the basis for volume IV. For various reasons it was obvious that volumes I to III should treat the development of the variety which came to be codified as Standard English, or in other words, Standard British English. After 1776, however, it is necessary to decide whether to continue to place primary emphasis on the British Standard.

The subsequent devolution of the British Empire into a number of independent nations linked by history, culture and language has created various national standards of English, of which British English is now just one. Moreover, as Algeo (1988a: 46) points out, 'twentieth century British English is certainly not the ancestor of any other national variety and has no special linguistic claim to be considered the norm against which other varieties are measured. Moreover, it is in as much need as any other variety of having its idiosyncrasies noted.'

Accordingly, the basis for discussion in this volume shifts to the common core inherited from the sixteenth century and shared by what are now the two principal varieties, American and British English. It is important to recognise that this common core English is not a variety in its own right and is not to be confused with Standard English (see Preisler 1995), or for that matter, the British variety. The common core is defined in terms of structural properties shared by all speakers regardless of geographical origin. Thus, each of these major varieties can be used as a norm against which to observe the deviations of the other. Up until recently, most comparisons have assumed the British variety as a norm and focused on the peculiarities of American.

I feel it is necessary to mention the editors' deliberations here since their outcome has had implications for the organisation of the project as a whole. The purpose of this volume is not to discuss the forms of American or British English as such, rather to lay a common historical foundation on which volumes V and VI may build in their discussion of regional forms of English which developed after 1776.

1.2   1776 and after: an age of revolutions and empires

Despite their emphasis on internal history, language historians have typically implicitly invoked, even if only in a gross way, external history in the customary periodisation of the language – notwithstanding the fact that most developments which left significant marks on the language such as the Great Vowel Shift spanned centuries and are therefore difficult to pinpoint within our conventional boundaries. Editors of previous volumes in this series have rightly noted the linguistic arbitrariness in our convention of demarcating the major periods in the development of English by reference to major historical events such as the Norman Conquest, usually taken as the beginning of the Middle English period. After 1066, French became the language of court and law for the next 300 years, relegating English to domestic domains. The Anglo-Saxon nobility was practically wiped out. The English which re-emerged later was much altered in structure, and the debate still continues about the extent to which change was internally or externally motivated (see the papers in Gerritsen & Stein 1992, Bailey & Maroldt 1977, and Romaine 1996).

Historians generally refer to the language used between 1500 and 1700 as early Modern English (eModE), with some suggesting that it begins as early as 1400 and continues until 1800. The structural stability of English over the late Modern English period challenges any simple-minded view of the relationship between social change and language change which might lead us to expect that language change is necessarily faster and more radical during periods of social upheaval. Kilpiö (1995), for instance, found remarkable stability from Old to early Modern English in the proportion of the functions of the verb *to be* (i.e. as copula or non-copular main verb as opposed to auxiliary in passive and active constructions). The copula uses are consistently the most frequent, although this varies according to text type.

While a major tenet of modern sociolinguistics is that language change is embedded in a social context, Finegan's chapter shows how the social changes of our period were to have a primary impact on the way that people looked at their language. Broadly speaking, one of the most important sociolinguistic developments affecting the modern period is standardisation, a process spanning centuries and still on-going. The late Modern English period consolidates the foundation laid for Modern Standard English to be codified in the grammars and dictionaries of the eighteenth century. In 1775 Dr Johnson (1709–84) published the dictionary (1755) that was to be definitive for generations to come, based on the usage of 'good' authors from Shakespeare to Addison. He furthermore insisted that the best pronunciation was that which deviated least from spelling. He found English 'copious without order and energetick without rules'. To men like Johnson, it was self-evident that English had no grammar. Throughout the century anything provincial or dialectal was heavily criticised. Among the vocabulary excluded from Johnson's dictionary were slang, dialect (including Scotticisms and Americanisms, see 1.3) and unnecessary foreign words. Yet much more was at stake than language standards (see 1.4). As Johnson noted in his preface 'Languages were the pedigree of nations.' Both needed laws because 'tongues, like governments, have a natural tendency to degeneration'.

Historian Gwyn Williams sums up well the spirit of the time when he writes (1989: xvii):

> The late 18th century was a great age for dictionaries and grammars in England. Most European states at the time were striving to standardise a national language and to eliminate dialects and minority tongues, none more so than the new French Republic with its 'language of liberty' [. . .] In [. . .] Britain, the standardisation of a national language assumed distinctive form.
>
> Towering over the torrent of grammars and dictionaries were a trinity of texts – Bishop Lowth's comprehensive grammar of 1762, James Harris's theory of universal grammar of 1751 and Samuel Johnson's Dictionary of 1755. Powerful, abundant and detailed, these governed the cultivation of 'good English' in an increasingly literate and book-reading country. They made the 'national language' into a class language. Grounded in a theory of a universal grammar which reflected qualities of the mind and in a veneration of Latin and Greek, they rigorously defined a 'refined language', strong in abstraction; it alone could be the vehicle of intellectual endeavour, including the political. Spoken English and the 'vulgar' in general was dismissed as the reflection of inferior minds, incapable of expressing anything of consequence, certainly of nothing political – 'cant' as Johnson called it. In an England where social distinctions were multiplying and intensifying as social mobility accelerated and in which the all-embracing veneration of a Glorious Constitution, dating from 1688 and enshrining a peculiar English liberty, had been strongly reaffirmed in the aftermath of American Independence, this conception of language achieved a hegemony of unparalleled power [. . .] Dissidents were trapped within the very words they had to use. If they resorted to the 'vulgar', as they often did, they simply validated their own exclusion. William Cobbett's struggle with 'grammar' was an exemplary epic. This was a 'national language' which enforced submission and dependency upon most of those who used it. It was what drove Blake to denounce 'mind-forg'd manacles' and Paine to complain of being 'immured in the Bastille of a word'.
>
> It was Thomas Paine himself [. . .] who stormed this particular Bastille [. . .] by any standards one cares to apply, the impact of Paine on the English of England was shattering.

The starting year of this volume is of course intentionally symbolic because it marks the declaration of independence of the United States of

America from Britain. Politically, it was a watershed of similar proportions to the events of 1066 and all that happened thereafter in England to culture and language. At the time our volume takes up the history of English, George III had reigned for sixteen years. Many of the leading literary persons of the eighteenth century who had left their mark on the language had already died: Alexander Pope in 1744, Laurence Sterne in 1768 and Oliver Goldsmith in 1774. Samuel Johnson was an old man of sixty-seven. A new generation of authors who were to have subsequent linguistic and literary impact had just been born: Jane Austen was a child of one year, Samuel Taylor Coleridge was four and William Wordsworth, six. New literary genres such as the novel had just made their appearance (see Watt 1957). As Thomas Paine rightly observed (1791/1969: 168), 'it was an age of revolutions'. In her chapter on the development of the literary language, Adamson documents two revolutions in poetic diction which had as their aim a return to 'common speech'.

Of course, the English language did not change overnight in response to momentous political events such as the Norman Conquest of 1066 any more than it did when the American colonies declared their independence. Its status, however, did. For it was not long after political separation that Noah Webster (1758–1843) declared linguistic independence (1789: 20):

> As an independent nation our honour requires us to have a system of our own, in language as well as government. Great Britain, whose children we are, and whose language we speak, should no longer be our standard. For the taste of her writers is already corrupted, and her language is on the decline. But if it were not so, she is at too great a distance to be our model and to instruct us in the principles of our language.

While nothing in this text is indexical of a variety which was already on its way to becoming distinct from British English, it was Webster who did much to alter spelling and propel the American variety on a different course (see Mencken 1919: chapter 8, for discussion of spelling differences between American and British English). In adopting some of the spellings that were later to become distinctly American, e.g. <or> instead of <our> in words such as *color*, <er> instead of <re> in words such as *center*, etc., Webster believed he was saving the language from the corruption by foreign influences (i.e. Latin, French, etc.) of ancient Saxon spelling. But more importantly, a 'capital advantage' of his reforms would 'make a difference between the English orthography and the American'.

Webster's vocabulary of 37,500 words in his *Compendious Dictionary of the English Language* (1806) was intended to surpass in size (by 5,000 words) and correctness the dictionaries available in London. By the time his dictionary appeared, he had already published a grammar, and a speller (1783), which was to sell over seventy million copies. His two-volume work appearing in 1828 was titled *An American Dictionary of the English Language*. In it he included not only new words in what was to become American English but also words which had taken on a different sense in their new location.

Webster sought no less than to validate linguistically the creation of a new nation and national identity in his belief that 'a national language is a band of national union'. Over time, America's linguistic independence made itself felt on the development of the English language as a whole. Indeed, Ayto (1983: 83) goes so far as to say that Webster's revision of the spelling system represents 'by far the most wide ranging reform of the English language ever successfully carried through, and there is little doubt that it owed its success to a spontaneous desire to reinforce the new national identity by means of a new national language'. By the eighteenth century a single, unified standard for English had ceased to exist.

Americans have subsequently proved themselves to be Great Britain's children none the less in their willingness to vest primary authority for linguistic matters in the privately authored dictionary. As in Britain, diction-aries became surrogates for the language academies of other countries. In view of the American ideals of freedom and prosperity, it is perhaps not surprising that the notion of a centralised decision-making institution of the kind that Swift proposed in 1712 was rejected, even in 1780 John Adams too called for an institution for the purpose of 'refining, correct-ing, improving and ascertaining the English language'. Adams, however, saw the standardisation which would come out of such a body as an American contribution to the role of English as a future world language. Webster's lexicographical tradition was carried on after his death by a succession of direct literary heirs down through until the present day. Until 1890 the title of his dictionary remained unchanged. Subsequent editions dropped the word *American* and were referred to as *International*.

While Webster's linguistic declaration of independence was unparalleled for more than two hundred years, it should come as no surprise that its repercussions would be felt in other corners of the empire. Australia would be the next to follow suit in time. The appearance of Baker's (1945) *The Australian Language*, confidently asserted in its title the autonomy of Australian English in the same way that Mencken (1919), following in Webster's footsteps, had attempted to do for American English with his book, *The American Language*. Baker (1945: 11) wrote:

we need some better starting point than Murray's Dictionary. We have to work out the problem from the viewpoint of Australia, not from the viewpoint of England and of the judgements she passed upon our language because she did not know it as well as we do.

It is tempting to dwell on the similarities, linguistic and otherwise, between Australia and the United States *vis-à-vis* Britain. However, there are also many differences. The United States revolted against Britain. Australia did not (though the movement to abolish the Queen as head of state in Australia in 1994 has been tantamount to revolution in some quarters). All Australia's major institutions of parliament, bureaucracy, education, etc., and even common language are modelled on British lines. A strong sentimental attachment to what many regarded as 'the home country' persisted for a long time. This has had linguistic ramifications.

Australia too now has its own dictionary *The Australian National Dictionary* (Ramson 1988). The 1940s also saw the initiation of Mitchell's studies of the Australian English accent in socio-historical perspective. While Mitchell (1946) declared that there was nothing 'wrong' with Australian speech, his comparison of the Australian accent with that of educated southern British English was for some an unpleasant reminder of the extent to which Australian English deviated from RP (received pronunciation), as described by Jones (1917), Gimson (1980) and other English phoneticians (see 1.3.3 and MacMahon, this volume).

In the same year that the American Revolution (or the War of Independence, as it was called in Britain) ended in 1783, another revolution of a different type was beginning in England, where James Watt invented the steam engine. This and other events are generally taken to have launched the Industrial Revolution. With it Britain became the first nation to have an industrial working class. The Industrial Revolution gave impetus for the growth of modern cities at the same time as it fuelled unprecedented expansion and consolidation of Empire during the course of the eighteenth and nineteenth centuries. Later, the application of science to industry in the twentieth century would create what C. P. Snow (1959) refers to as the 'scientific revolution'. The industrial-scientific revolution and the agrarian revolution are in his view the two major transformations in human social history.

If the eighteenth and nineteenth centuries were ones of revolutions, they were also a time for empire building. Even after its loss of face following the American Revolution, England dominated the world during the nineteenth century in what was still an age of exploration and discovery. By this time, however, centre stage had shifted to the Pacific rather than the

Atlantic. James Cook's three voyages put much of the remaining New World onto European maps and opened the way for further colonial expansion and settlement. It is one of the ironies of colonial history that the outcome of the American Revolution was instrumental in the convict settlement of Australia. While the war was in progress convicted criminals awaited transportation, but when the battle was lost and with it Britain's nascent North American empire, the government had to look elsewhere to get rid of its convicts. In July 1786 Britain decided to establish a penal colony at Botany Bay.

'At home', urbanisation and greater educational opportunities meant an increase in contact between diverse groups in society. Improved means of travel and communication brought about by the steam engine and the telegraph also helped disseminate the new standard English promoted in the schools. Even more remarkable are the technological innovations of the late nineteenth and twentieth centuries such as the telephone (invented by Alexander Graham Bell in 1876), film, television and the personal computer. Thanks to Thomas Edison's experiments with wax cylinders in the 1870s we now have sound recordings. The increased precision of phonetic transcription puts our statements about pronunciation and prosody in this period on a much firmer footing than in previous periods. One of the first executives of the BBC, the first radio broadcasting service established in 1922, likened the radio to the printing press in terms of its impact: 'The broadcasting of aural language is an event no less important than the broadcasting of the visual language [printing], not only in its influence on human relations, but in its influence upon the destinies of the English language' (cited in McCrum, Cran & MacNeil 1986: 26). With the launching of Intelsat III in 1967, for the first time in history no part of the globe was completely out of touch with any other part.

Increasingly sophisticated and rapid telecommunications brought about through computers in the late twentieth century have created a network of computers, popularly called the 'information superhighway', on which one can transcend great distances without leaving home or the office. Internet 'traffic' is increasing every year with more and more users being linked. Of course, one needn't sit at home in front of the keyboard: air travel makes it possible to circumnavigate the globe in a matter of hours rather than months.

The technology facilitating these developments originated largely in the English-speaking world, and not surprisingly, English has become its lingua franca. Until 1995 it was difficult to communicate via the Internet in any language that could not be expressed in the Standard English alphabet as defined by the American Standard Code for Information Interchange (ASCII) set down in 1982. Similarly, the corporations and financial institutions of the anglophone countries have dominated world trade and made English the international language of business. Books in the English language have dominated the publishing business. There are few countries in the world where English books cannot find a market of some kind. Other major languages such as French and German have continued to lose ground against English over the course of this century as mediums of scholarly publication. By 1966 70 per cent of the world's mail and 60 per cent of its radio and television broadcasts were already in English. Before 1600 the idea that English might be a world language was not seriously entertained since it was thought to have many flaws. At that time knowledge of English was virtually useless in travelling abroad. Nowadays, it is regarded as essential. If the medium is the message, as McLuhan (1989) tells us, then the language of his global village is indeed English.

Political and economic centralization during the two centuries preceding our starting point had made London the largest metropolis in Europe. Around 1700 London had over a half million inhabitants and its growth rate exceeded that of the whole population of England. Life in this densely populated area brought more and more people into contact. The city grew from three million people in the early 1860s to four and a half million by the turn of the twentieth century. Town life brought increasing opportunities for social advancement at the same time as it brought greater social stratification. A newly monied class of merchants in London would be eager to learn what H. C. Wyld (1920) called the 'new-fangled English', i.e. the newly codified Standard English, as a sign of their upward mobility.

The transition from a society of estates or orders to a class-based society is one of the (if not THE) great themes of modern British social history (Wrightson 1991). William Caxton's three estates of 'clerkes, knyghtes, and labourers' were differentiated in terms of social function. From the eighteenth century, however, a different perception of social structure emerged based on classes distinguished primarily in terms of economic criteria. The Industrial Revolution opened up new avenues for the accumulation of wealth, prestige and power other than those based on hereditary landed titles. As Jonathan Swift put it in *The Examiner* 1710 (cited in Corfield 1991: 106): 'Power, which according to an old maxim was used to follow Land, is now gone over to Money.'

While the nation as a whole became more affluent with the gap between rich and poor filled in by the middle classes, 'gentleman' became a term of social approval and moral approbation (see Phillips 1984), while 'ladies' were of the middle class and 'women' of the working class. Female students at Owens College in Manchester, for instance, were divided between 'ladies' (taking a single course, presumably for pleasure only) and 'women' who were registered for examinations, which they needed for career purposes. The development of the census after 1841 with its social rankings based on occupations and their titles solidified the economic bases of social stratification.

Some historians have seen the growth of London and its accompanying social and occupational stratification as the single most important feature of the social history of the late Stuart period (see Beloff 1938). London's residents were increasingly segregated into residential areas as buildings proliferated beyond the ancient limits of the twin cities of London and Westminster. The combination of physical proximity yet vast social distance is a hallmark of urbanisation. Within the confines of the city social segregation tended at first to operate vertically within buildings so that basements and attics might be divided into small flats and the intermediate floors were occupied by the wealthier. These patterns of urbanisation were being replicated in other parts of the country, such as in Edinburgh, which became an administrative and financial centre in the eighteenth century. The inhabitants of a typical Edinburgh tenement in Dickson's Close, for example, included a fishmonger on the first floor, a lodging keeper on the second, the Countess Dowager of Balcarres on the third, Mrs Buchanan of Kellow on the fourth, and milliners and manteau-makers on the fifth (Gordon 1970: 16).

Socially distinct spaces would emerge only later when the suburbs would be 'discovered' by the middle class as an ideal physical expression of their distance from the working class. In the suburb geographic distance became an icon of social separateness and class consciousness. The spatial association of low-status residential districts with industrial areas prompted the more affluent to move to the suburbs, a move facilitated by the development of suburban railway. In the US the flight to the suburbs was largely complete by the 1970s when more people lived in suburbs than elsewhere. The eventual segregation of cities into residential, manufacturing and business areas took place in the context of the by now well-established social status of merchants and bankers, who played a considerable role in determining the pattern of migration to newer residential areas.

By the latter half of the nineteenth century Britain had already become a largely urban nation. At the turn of the twentieth, 78 per cent of its population lived in towns. The social impact of urbanisation has been studied from the perspective of many disciplines, including that of sociolinguistics (see, e.g., Nordberg 1994). The growing importance of social class and the consolidation of British working-class culture in the fifty years from 1875 to 1925 are reflected in language, particularly in the creation of urban dialect, which was to become a major focus of interest to sociolinguists in the twentieth century. Thanks to the Industrial Revolution, the neighbouring countryside of the counties of Essex, Kent, Suffolk and Middlesex was becoming depopulated as thousands of impoverished farm workers came to London's East End in search of work. We now know that a number of features made their way into working-class London speech from their regional dialects, and then eventually became part of middle-class usage.

The central role of London in linguistic change is still evident from studies done by Trudgill (1986), Wells, and others. Wells (1982), for instance, summarises the influence of London in the following terms:

> Not only did its courtly and upper class speech lay the historical basis for Standard English and in many respects for R.P. [received pronunciation], but its working class accent is today the most influential source of phonological innovation in England and perhaps in the whole English-speaking world.

By contrast, the influence of major US cities has been much more regionally limited because the American colonies lacked a single centre of linguistic prestige. Even though the major port cities of Boston, New York, Philadelphia and Charleston were important points of contact with Britain and centres of diffusion for their respective hinterlands, none was London's equal with respect to the development of Standard English. London's norms, especially with regard to written English, were aspired to in the colonies. The distribution of post-vocalic /r/ in the United States in words such as *car*, *barn*, etc. reflects the history of settlement patterns of colonists from different parts of Britain and Ireland as much as it does a changing prestige norm. Nowadays, in New York City the lower one's social status (as measured in terms of factors such as occupation, education, and income, etc.), the fewer post-vocalic /r/s used, while in London the reverse is true.

At first, dialectologists did not consider these newly emergent urban speech forms of interest, but concentrated their efforts instead on documenting the rural dialects which they believed would soon disappear. Even earlier, however, these very dialects had been ignored because they were considered corrupt versions of the standard language. The popularity of the study of dialects from the early 1800s onwards is due at least to two developments, Romanticism, and the rise of comparative historical linguistics (see 1.4). As I pointed out earlier, Dr Johnson had been interested in recording in his dictionary only the words and phrases found in the works of 'polite writers', certainly not what Wordsworth called 'the very language of men'.

The sociolinguistic consequences of urbanisation are quite complex because urbanisation tends to promote linguistic diversity as well as uniformity. Urban environments are often the site of contact between languages as well as dialects because towns have typically attracted migrants from many rural areas, who speak different languages and regional dialects. In urban centres languages of wider communication and standard languages serve to unify a diverse population. A person living in an urban environment typically has exposure not only to many more individuals from diverse social and cultural backgrounds, but also to a more diverse set of communicative situations occasioned by contact with the bureaucratic institutions of urban life. Most of these encounters no longer involve face-to-face interaction with people one knows, but require the use of the telephone, fax machine, etc., with strangers. Urban residents are often members of larger, more numerous and less dense social networks than rural dwellers, particularly those employed in service positions which bring them into contact with many people. Incoming migrants from rural areas often discard marked dialect forms as part of the process of accommodation to urban speech ways. The net result is dialect levelling, at present a major force across south-east England, and seen by some as a threat to the preservation of regional dialect more generally, particularly due to the impact of mass media.

Although we frequently read or hear about teachers, parents, and others worrying about the Americanisation of English in the late twentieth century, Chambers's (1992: 679) study on dialect acquisition revealed that at least in Oxfordshire, adolescents opted for British rather than American lexical variants when tested for items such as *chips* vs. (*french*) *fries, jumper* vs. *sweater*, etc. While such Americanisms are almost a feature of daily life in British advertising as well as in other parts of the world, they have scarcely penetrated everyday use among the group where one might expect them to have the most prestige. The limited influence of popular media on actual speech behaviour suggests that what is crucial is actual social interaction rather than passive exposure. When moving from one country to another Americans and Britons make great lexical accommodation, but not, it would seem, just through passive listening. People don't talk to their televisions (at least not when I wrote this, though 'interactive cable television' currently being experimented with on a limited basis may make my remark obsolete within a short time after this volume is published).

Not coincidentally, it is in rural and working-class communities where the most local forms of speech are still most strongly preserved today, in those parts of society furthest removed from literate traditions. Residents of areas of cities which have long been typically working class are better able to preserve the strongest form of urban dialect. Sociolinguistic research in Belfast has provided a model for understanding change based on the idea of social network. Change is accounted for as speaker innovation which spreads from one network to another through weak ties. This model also makes some predictions about rate of change. More specifically, it is claimed that change is slow to the extent that the relevant populations are well established and bound by strong ties. It is rapid to the extent that weak ties exist in populations (Milroy & Milroy 1985: 375; Milroy 1992). The terms 'rapid' and slow' are of course relative. Certainly, the early Modern English and subsequent period did not experience the social upheaval which must have accompanied the Viking and Norman conquests.

A substantial body of research into changes affecting varieties of urban speech in major cities on both sides of the Atlantic such as New York, Detroit, Glasgow, Belfast, etc. have shown that social factors such as social class, ethnicity, gender, network structure, age and style and other such 'social variables' are implicated in change (see Weinreich, Labov & Herzog 1968). Major urban centres around the globe are likely to become even more fertile ground for investigation of change. The end of the twentieth century will witness an unprecedented change in patterns of human settlement world-wide, when for the first time in history more people will live in cities and towns than in rural areas. Furthermore, the rise of urbanisation is connected with an increase in social stratification which in turn is reflected in linguistic variation.

While London once provided a point of origin for the diffusion of Standard English, now it has become an increasingly diverse city through the influx of overseas migrants from the Caribbean and Asia. As many as fifty different languages may be spoken in parts of the city. Similarly, Melbourne, once primarily a monolingual town, now has the largest concentration of Greek speakers in the world. Miami is now predominantly Hispanophone.

Mass literacy as a cultural development made possible by universal schooling also has to be reckoned with as a factor having major impact on language in the modern period. The spread of literacy has taken place only in the most recent centuries of the evolution of human language. Two or three centuries ago, most speakers of English were semi- or pre-literate. Until modern times it was largely only the gentry who were educated. The introduction of compulsory schooling in England in 1870 eventually made the majority of people literate. Over time, literacy acts as a brake on linguistic change and lessens the distance between the upper and working classes. The rate of literacy was higher in London than elsewhere in the country during the early Modern English period; even 70 per cent of servants in the city could sign their names by 1700. Nevertheless, at that time it was probably only the professional and merchant classes, i.e. men who had had an education, who were fully literate. As many as 98 per cent of all books printed in England emanated from the capital. Over half the booksellers were established there and a large proportion of the reading public. The burgeoning of the magazine trade in the Victorian era with roughly 25,000 circulating periodicals has been seen as the 'verbal equivalent of urbanism' (Shattuck & Wolff 1982: xiv).

The spread of literacy also meant an increase in private correspondence in the form of letters, diaries, etc. These provide a rich source of information on less carefully monitored styles since most of these were not intended for publication. Biber and Finegan (1989) have demonstrated what historians of the language have long intuited, namely that personal letters are among the most involved and therefore oral of written genres. They constitute good evidence for what Labov (1966) calls 'change from below', i.e. below the level of conscious awareness and associated with lower classes in the social hierarchy (see Denison, this volume).

Just as Standard English once diffused out from the London merchant class, now vernacular London speech is spreading to other cities like Norwich, where many young people now say *bovver* and *togevver* instead of *bother* and *together*. Cockneys have used these forms for generations. There is evidence that the change from /th/ to /v/ is spreading by face-to-face contact rather than via the media since areas closer to London have adopted these features more quickly than areas farther away, though the television programme *East Enders* has made some features of Cockney accessible to millions. Not even the Royal Family has been immune to change from below. The British press has charged Prince Andrew with sounding like a Cockney, and Princess Anne has been accused of 'linguistic slumming'. *The Daily Telegraph* (Harris 1987), accused the Duchess of York of taking 'miwlk' rather than 'milk' in her tea and noted that the Princess of Wales believed she was married in a place called 'St. Paw's Cathedral'. Increased glottalisation has also been making headway among middle-class speakers, with the Princess of Wales heard noting, 'There's a lo? of i? abou?' (Rosewarne 1994: 3). Glottalisation has now been reported from other parts of the English-speaking world such as New Zealand (Holmes 1995). 'Change from above', by contrast, is conscious, and is associated with the middle class, supposedly more sensitive to the overt prestige norms of the standard variety.

Sociolinguistic research of modern urban areas has, if anything, given us a revealing picture of the standard's uneven diffusion as it illustrates how social-class boundaries act in similar ways to geographical ones in terms of their ability to impede or facilitate the spread of linguistic features. The spread of the 'newfangled English' was also at first uneven. The standards of the highest class of speakers were not necessarily those of the new self-constituted authorities on correctness of the seventeenth and eighteenth centuries. Wyld (1920: 283) assures Modern English speakers that we would no doubt consider that educated persons of that period spoke 'in a reprehensible manner'. He (1920: 282–3) cites, for example, the dropping of final t/d as widespread among all classes of speakers in the seventeenth and eighteenth centuries (see Romaine 1984a). Pope, for instance, rhymed *neglects* with *sex*. Similarly, Marshall (1982: 8) has noted of the late eighteenth century that 'even the gentry thought it no disgrace to speak with a provincial accent'. While the term 'King's English' was used by the end of the sixteenth century to label normative forms of English, not all royalty have been considered good exemplars of it. Actor John Kemble, for instance, advised King George IV when he was Prince of Wales that 'it would become your royal mouth much better to pronounce the word oblige, and not obleege' (cited in Bailey 1991: 3).

Thus, it was not initially the highest-ranking social groups of the day but instead the *nouveau riche* or bourgeoisie who eagerly sought the refinements the grammarians had to offer as signs of their emergent status as educated persons. As this newfangled English became available to an increasing portion of English society, the markers of upper-class linguistic etiquette shifted from syntax to accent. This change can be seen in nineteenth-century novels in which innumerable shibboleths unmask social climbers (see Phillips 1984 and Mugglestone 1995). By 1864 Henry Alford warned of the open and merciless laughter which awaited 'any unfortunate member if he strews the floor with his "aitches"'. George Bernard Shaw's *Pygmalion* (1916) and the popular musical made from it, *My Fair Lady*, attest to the English preoccupation with accent (and its power for social transformation). The Cockney flower seller, Eliza Doolittle, is trained by the phonetics professor, Henry Higgins (modelled on Henry Sweet), to speak like a 'lady' with an RP accent. Sweet (1890: vi–vii) described all too well the anxiety bound up with validating one's social place through accent when he said:

> The Cockney dialect seems very ugly to an educated Englishman or woman because he – and still more she – lives in a perpetual terror of being taken for a Cockney, and a perpetual struggle to preserve that **h** which has now been lost in most of the local dialects of England, both North and South.

H-dropping was tantamount to 'social suicide', observed Alexander Ellis (1869). Even today Wells (1982: 254) states that h-dropping operates as the 'single most powerful pronunciation shibboleth in England'. Trudgill's (1974) study of Norwich reveals that h-dropping shows the sharpest stratification of any of his phonological variables with a large gap between middle- and working-class speakers. Indeed, it functions more like some grammatical variables which are generally more sharply stratifying in the English-speaking world than phonological ones. Research done on both sides of the Atlantic again permits some interesting comparisons. Only working-class speakers, for instance, in Detroit and Norwich use non-standard third-person-singular present-tense verb forms without -*s*, e.g. *he go* with any great frequency and this is more so in Norwich than in Detroit. The gap between the middle- and working-class norms is also greater in Norwich than in Detroit reflecting the greater social mobility in the American social system.

Like many others both before and after her, Eliza Doolittle submits to remodelling her social and linguistic persona. As long as she pronounces her vowels and consonants correctly, Eliza Doolittle does not betray her working-class East London origins and is indeed received in the best of society, no matter how 'vulgar' her vocabulary or grammar are. Elocution became a public and private pursuit. Mugglestone (1995: 4) says that five times as many works on elocution appeared between 1760 and 1800 than had done so in the years before 1760. Sixpenny manuals with titles such as *P's and Q's. Grammatical Hints for the Million* and *Poor Letter H. Its Use and Abuse* under the name of the Hon. Henry H. sold thousands of copies. The title page of the Hon. Henry H.'s book shows a man with the letter H in his hand coming up to a very elegantly dressed woman and saying, 'Please, Ma'am, you've dropped something.' Alan Ross (1956), however, demonstrated that there was a lexical component to being U(pper class) as well, citing such notable pairs as *have one's bath* (U) vs. *take a bath* (non-U), *writing paper* vs. *note paper* (non-U), *table-napkin* (U) vs. *serviette* (non-U), *pudding* (U) vs. *sweet* (non-U) (see 1.3.4).

Even though, as Strang (1970: 107) points out, by 1770 English had a standard written form almost as invariable as today's, its norms were not universally embraced. Even Dr Johnson, who had a clearly thought out opinion of how English was best to be spelled and is often given credit for fixing English spelling in its modern form, used two 'standards' of spelling, one in his dictionary and another in his private writings (see Osselton 1984). Epistolary spelling of the highly educated and literate in this period is characterised by the retention of a wide variety of spellings which had already dropped out of the printed language. The letters of Addison, Defoe and Steele, for instance, contain spellings such as *cutt* and *fitt*. While such spellings are common down to 1580, they virtually disappeared by the middle of the next century. The spread of standardized spelling in informal writings and the displacement of individual and regional peculiarities is a topic that requires much further research.

Standardisation and literacy go hand in hand since the acquisition of literacy presupposes the existence of a codified written standard, and standardization depends on the existence of a written form of language. The continuing expansion of Standard English is reflected in the new text types which begin to appear in English. In the centuries preceding the time period of this volume, English took over Latin and French as the language of court proceedings, official correspondence, educational and scientific treatises. This was not accomplished without considerable accommodation of the literary language and other specialised varieties to extensive borrowing of vocabulary, syntax, and whole styles of composition. In the medieval period educated people would have been trained in Latin or Greek and used these as models for composition in English. Throughout the history of English, translation has provided a means of enrichment of both vocabulary and syntactic structures, but it has also provided rhetorical canons and is the source of most modern prescriptivism (see Finegan, this volume). By comparison with classical Latin, English was in many respects stylistically limited. Furthermore, its use was confined to England and therefore its utility as the lingua franca of science and technology it was to claim in later centuries was at this stage doubtful.

Writers such as Thomas Phaire strongly attacked the Latinism of medical treatises:

> how long would they haue the people ignorant? Why grutche they physicke to come forth in Engliyshe? Woulde they haue no man to know but onely they? (*The Boke of Chyldren*, 1545, ed. Neale and Wallis 1955)

While Mulcaster was among the first to question in 1582 why everything could not be written in English, it was not until 1700 that the tradition of writing academic texts in Latin finally died out. With the demise of Latin, models for a literary standard English are no longer found outside the language but from within its own resources. Modern literary style has increasingly drawn on colloquial English rather than classical style (see Adamson, this volume). The reaction to Inkhorn words in the sixteenth century is paralleled by the movement for Plain English in late twentieth century. Of course, the medical profession still relies heavily on a vocabulary based on Greek and Latin still largely inaccessible to the lay person.

The passing of the old style has not, however, been uniformly greeted with enthusiasm. In a speech on declining standards of English, Prince Charles singled out for special attack the modern adaptations of the King James Bible, describing it as a 'dismal wasteland of banality, cliche and casual obscenity (*Daily Mail* 20 December 1989). 'If English is spoken in heaven (as the spread of English as a world language makes more likely each year) God undoubtedly employs Cranmer as his speech-writer. The angels of the lesser ministries probably use the language of the New English Bible and the Alternative Service Book for internal memos' (*Daily Telegraph* 29 December 1989). In railing against the 'tide of pollution that engulfs our language', D. J. Enright commented: 'We don't want God sounding like a civil servant, any more than we want civil servants imagining they are God. Modern translators have achieved the miracle of turning wine into water' (*Observer* 24 December 1989).

As Blake (1992: 10) points out, these criticisms reflect most people's expectations that the language of the Bible should reflect an idealised version of English rather than current actuality. Critics of the new translations want them to be written in a language which is as elevated and literary as the older ones. The rationale behind these new translations is that they are more understandable and accessible to the modern reader. No one appears to object to the New English Bible on the grounds that it is an inaccurate translation or that it inaccurately reflects modern English culture. Blake underlines the great importance such idealised models of literary style have had on the development of English. He (1992: 20) notes that hypotaxis has been accepted as more literary and elevated largely because it was associated with Latin models.

1.3 Shifting centres of gravity and the notion of a common core

In their popular account of the history of the English language, McCrum, Cran & MacNeil (1986) mark symbolically their shift of focus by announcing their adoption of American spelling in chapter 7, which deals with American English. They (1986: 235n) predict that their decision will be greeted with 'pain or pleasure'. In the 'pain' camp are those who still see Standard British English as synonymous with Standard English, while others such as Webster confidently predicted that a language would develop in North America as different from the future language of England as Modern Dutch, Danish, and Swedish were from German or one another. Others erred on the more conservative side, like T. S. Eliot, who felt that 'America is not likely to develop a new language until its civilisation becomes more complicated and more refined than that of Britain; and there are no indications that this will ever happen. Meanwhile, America will continue to provide a small number of new words which can usefully be digested by the parent language' (cited in Burchfield 1989: 121). Commentators such as G. F. Graham (1869) opined that 'the recklessness' of American usage had already flooded English with many new and strange terms. However, in Graham's view, they were 'interlopers'. Genuine 'Americanisms' did not belong to 'our language' (cited in Crowley 1991: 168).

John Witherspoon, the Scottish President of Princeton University and one of the signers of the Declaration of Independence, was apparently the first to use the term *Americanism*. He observed in 1781 that the lower classes in America used less dialect, but that educated people more often offended against good style than their counterparts in England would. Interestingly, travellers from England to the American colonies in the eighteenth century often expressed the view that the English of the American colonies was 'better' and more homogeneous than in England. English commentators said similar things at first too about the English of New Zealand and praised it for its purity. It was not long, however, before any noticed departure from British English was condemned, almost without exception. Complaints about the 'bad' influence of American culture and language can now be found in practically all parts of the world. The author of one letter written in 1991 to the Swedish press stated that for the past ten years he had aspired to learning the 'King's English' and that American English got on his nerves. His solution was that American cultural imperialism must be forcefully resisted.

Webster's remark about British English being eclipsed by American English seems even now to give the British Council pause as they seek to guarantee the supremacy of the British variety of the language, particularly in the lucrative export market for English as a second language. In an article detailing the money to be made from teaching English as a foreign language, Sir Richard Francis, then Director General of the British Council, said 'when it comes to quality and choice, invariably what I hear is that people wish to come to Britain to learn British English, or as I would prefer to call it, standard English' (Greaves 1989:14). Similarly, Burchfield (1989: xii) assumes that all varieties other than British English are by definition not part of Standard English when he says that 'overseas varieties of English, in the United States, Australia and elsewhere, are steadily moving away, in small matters and large, from Standard English and from one another, at a somewhat accelerated rate'. The centre of gravity for this Standard English is Oxford (Burchfield 1989: 50).

In 1991 Prince Charles warned teachers of English as a foreign language in what was then Czechoslovakia to play their part in 'maintaining standards and safeguarding the language's heritage' (*Guardian* 9 May 1991). From the Prince's point of view there were dangers involved in English being the world's lingua franca. The main one was the risk of different varieties of English growing up in different parts of the world, which would lead to unintelligibility. He went on to say that this 'nightmare could possibly become a reality unless there are enduring standards, a common core of the language, and common standards of grammar'. He finished by saying that he hoped the Czech teachers would not abandon the serious study of grammar, which to a certain extent had already happened in the UK. These and other remarks seemed to suggest that the onus for maintaining standards of correct British English usage would rest more on non-native than native speakers, since it was the latter whom the Prince said appreciated the importance of being taught what he called 'real' grammar.

Certainly, the British variety is more advanced in terms of its codification, its pedigree having been established in a long line of grammars and dictionaries of great influence around the English-speaking world. Yet by the beginning of the twentieth century, Brander Matthews (1900: 239–40) had, like Webster, claimed that the centre had already shifted to the other side of the Atlantic:

> What will happen to the English language in England when England awakens to the fact that the centre of the English-speaking race is no longer within the borders of that little island? Will the speech of the British sink into dialectic corruption, or will the British resolutely stamp out their undue local divergences from the normal English of the main body of users of the language in the United States? Even now, at the end of the nineteenth century, more than half of those who have English as their mother tongue are Americans; and at the end of the twentieth century the numerical superiority of the Americans will be as

overwhelming as was the numerical superiority of the British at the beginning of the nineteenth. Will the British frankly accept the inevitable? Will they face the facts as they are? Will they follow the lead of the Americans when we shall have the leadership of the language, as the Americans followed their lead when they had it? Or will they insist on an arbitrary independence, which can have only one result – the splitting off of the British branch of our speech from the main stem of the language?

While not directly replying to Matthews's questions, an anonymous British author writing in the *New Statesman* (25 June 1927) made it clear that Britain was not yet ready to relinquish its claim (cited in Bailey 1991: 157). However, the very fact that such a possibility had to be entertained and commented on bespeaks a certain anxiety.

> The English language proper belongs to the people who dwell south of Hadrian's Wall, east of the Welsh hills and north of the English channel. . . . We obviously cannot admit that the English language contains 'Anglicisms' – because that admission would imply that our language belongs to everybody who uses it – including negroes and Middle-Westerners and Americanised Poles and Italians. That is the fundamental point. 'Anglicisms' are English tout court. And on the question of what words and idioms are to be used or to be forbidden we cannot afford any kind of compromise or even discussion with the semi-demi-English-speaking populations of overseas. Their choice is to accept our authority or else make their own language.

In 1913 the Society for Pure English was founded by the Poet Laureate of Great Britain, Robert Bridges, who (not surprisingly, given his puristic bent) was prejudiced against perceived Americanisms. As far as he was concerned, American English was a 'welter of blundering corruptions' (cited in Bailey 1991: 206). Writing in 1925, Bridges was alarmed at the threat of 'other speaking races' to 'pure bred' Englishmen settled abroad. Such puristic sentiments continue today as is evident in this statement made by Enoch Powell, a former Member of Parliament (cited in Greenbaum 1990: 15): 'Others may speak and read English – more or less – but it is our language not theirs. It was made in England by the English and it remains our distinctive property, however widely it is learnt or used.'

Dr Johnson would, of course, have had no truck with the notion of 'Anglicism' in his dictionary. In addition to excluding Scots along with other 'dialectal' usage, there are no entries for American words such as *loon* (defined, for instance, by Nathan Bailey in his *Universal Etymological English Dictionary*, 1721) and the numerous borrowings from native American languages such as *raccoon, squash* and *muskrat*, which were known to the English reading public from travellers' and explorers' accounts and well established in American written usage by 1755 (see Romaine, volume VI). Johnson did not visit America and his negative attitudes towards it and the English used there are well known. In his review of Lewis Evan's *Map and Account of the English Colonies in America* (1756), he noted, for example, that the treatise was written 'with such elegance as the subject admits tho' not without some mixture of the American dialect, a tract of corruption to which every language widely diffused must always be exposed' (cited in Read 1980: 17).

In the following sections I will assume that we can identify a common core to British and American features of a language now more correctly called International English. Nevertheless, the notion of a common core is controversial for many reasons, one of which I mentioned at the outset: namely, that it is sometimes confused with the concept of Standard English, a variety equated with a class of people, i.e. the educated upper-class elite rather than with a set of features. Just as it is not always possible to decide unequivocally what belongs to Standard English, the common core may also be difficult to delimit precisely. Now that English has spread so widely beyond its original body of native speakers to countries such as India and Singapore, it becomes even more difficult to treat English as a single language containing a common core to which all varieties can be referred. Initially, English became a common language for the elite in those countries. Now that English has diffused even more widely and is one of a few languages whose non-native speakers outnumber its native speakers, the concept of native speaker itself has become problematic.

Kachru (1980), for instance, recognises three concentric circles characterised by various functions and domains of usage as well as by modes of transmission and maintenance. In the so-called 'inner circle' English is multifunctional, transmitted through the family and maintained by governmental or quasi-governmental agencies (e.g. media, school, etc.), and is the language of the dominant culture. The 'outer' circle contains countries colonized by English-speaking powers. English is typically not the language of the home, but transmitted through the school. Norms come officially from the inner circle, but local norms also play a powerful role in dictating everyday usage. The expanding circle contains those countries where English is taught as a means of communication with the rest of the world. It has few, if any, domains of use within the respective countries. Its norms come exclusively from the inner circle. In the case of the inner circle one could also argue that its users created a new environment through English, whereas in the case of the outer circle, there was already another cultural environment in place which affected English.

In sociolinguistic terms I believe English can be best described as a 'pluricentric' language (see e.g. Clyne 1992). Such a language is one whose norms are focused in different local centres, capitals, centres of economy, publishing, education and political power. Examples of such languages include not just English but also most of the major languages of Western Europe such as French, German, Spanish and Portuguese, and non-Western ones such as Arabic and Chinese. Pluricentric languages can, however, be of different types. Some such as Swedish have one 'real' centre with one or more satellites of emigrant communities. Compare the Standard Swedish of Sweden and the varieties of Sweden spoken in Finland, which are subordinate to the norms of Swedish as used in Sweden.

The term *pluricentric* is useful since it allows us to overcome some of the difficulties in applying either the term *language* or *dialect* to varieties such as American English, Australian English, British English, etc. To use the term *dialect* suggests that the national varieties are heteronymous with respect to some other variety, while to use the term *language* suggests a much greater degree of distance, autonomy and elaboration than actually exists (see Kloss's 1967 discussion of *Abstand* ('distance') and *Ausbau* ('elaboration') and Chambers and Trudgill's 1980 discussion of *autonomy* and *heteronomy*).

The centres of pluricentric languages can shift over time, as documented in the volumes of *The Cambridge History of the English Language*. Pluricentricity during the Middle English period before the establishment of a standard meant one scribal tradition vs. another. For a brief while it was then London vs. Edinburgh. Later, it meant London vs. the rest of Britain. Now it means London vs. New York vs. Sydney, etc.

As I noted in section 1.1, our decision to address the common core of British and American English can be justified on several grounds, historical, social and linguistic. While there are many varieties of English spoken around the world today, there are from a linguistic point of view only two major types: British and American. All other varieties, such as Australian English, Canadian English, Indian English, etc., can be clearly related to one of these two by virtue of settlement history (e.g. British colonization of Australia and New Zealand vs. American colonization of Guam, Hawaii, etc.) and/or geographical proximity (e.g. the case of Canadian English *vis-à-vis* American English). While acknowledging that there are many varieties of Standard English, Trudgill & Hannah (1982), for instance, recognise two main varieties, North American and British English. They define Standard British English as that variety spoken and written by educated speakers in England, and with minor differences in Wales, Scotland, Northern Ireland, Eire, Australia, New Zealand and South Africa. Standard North American English is that variety spoken and written by educated speakers in the United States and Canada.

American and British English were also the first two national varieties to come into existence after the unity of English was broken in the eighteenth century. English was not exported to South Africa, New Zealand and Australia until much later in the eighteenth and nineteenth centuries. The main linguistic influences on these varieties seem to come from south-eastern England. These varieties are therefore similar to RP (see 1.3.3).

By virtue of number of speakers, and influence as a norm for foreign learners, British and American English are also clearly the two most important varieties. Until recently, the norm adopted for teaching English as a foreign language throughout much of Europe was Standard British English, with examiners not tolerating American forms. This was the result of a conscious policy motivated at least partly by fear that competing norms would confuse students. Now that many more Europeans study in the United States and are increasingly exposed to American media, there is a greater tolerance for Standard American English. At the same time though there is often still an intolerance of mixing the norms. Similarly, publishing houses are reluctant to accept any inconsistencies in spelling and other norms. Trudgill & Hannah (1982: 2) argue convincingly that this is an unrealistic position to adopt. A Belgian student, for instance, who has studied Standard British English at school and who later studies in the United States will most likely adopt some North American forms into her speech, just as native speakers of British English also do when they spend time in the United States. All that should matter is that students aim for native-like competence, even if that competence is an amalgam.

On a practical level, however, problems arise for teachers who, in principle, would like to be tolerant of other norms for Standard English but are not familiar with the forms which occur in those other varieties. An American teacher, for instance, is quite likely to consider a sentence such as *I'll give it him* incorrect because such sentence types are not part of the North American standard. The other variant, however, *I will give it to him* is part of the common core (see Denison, this volume, and 1.3.2).

The split between the two major varieties is somewhat neater when looked at from a lexical and grammatical standpoint. Grammatical differences, in particular, tend to be for the most part minor, at least as far as the inner circle is concerned. If no distinctive vocabulary items are used,

1 expressions for things found in Britain but not the US;
2 expressions that were common English before the separation [of] the two nations and have been retained in British use, but died [out] in the US;
3 expressions originating in Britain after 1775, e.g. *to be on the dole* (cf. American *to be on welfare*). While *dole* is common to both (cf. [OE] *da:l* 'share, portion'), with the meaning 'to dispense goods', [in] modern Britain it now has the specific meaning of 'receivin[g] unemployment benefits';
4 expressions that have a distinctive use in Britain by virtue of thei[r] meaning, grammar, pronunciation, frequency, context, situation[,] or style, e.g. *underdone* (cf. American *rare*);
5 expressions that Americans interpret for whatever reason a[s] characteristically British, e.g. *doss*.

Of course, each variety has neologisms not shared with the other and [cut] words may change in their geographical limitation, as Algeo shows, either [cut] between regional and standard national usage or between national varieties. [cut] The Scottish term *bap* for a bread roll has now become part of mainstream [cut] standard British use. The British short form *fridge* is now used by many [cut] younger Americans, although this could well be a case of independent [cut] innovation. Cockney rhyming slang *chew the fat* (<*have a chat*) has become [cut] part of the common core of colloquial English, while others have diffused [cut] into general British colloquial (but not American) English, such as *loaf* [cut] 'head' (<*loaf of bread*).

Many assume that simply because they do not know a feature it must [cut] belong to the other variety and there has been a tendency in Britain to label [cut] any innovation an Americanism. The term *jacket potato*, for instance, is [cut] widely believed to be an Americanism, but is not. Algeo cites *you know* as [cut] one instance which has been widely assumed to be an Americanism on [cut] both sides of the Atlantic. Over 150 years ago, however, Americans [cut] bemoaned it as a Briticism.

Other false Americanisms one can easily exclude as not part of the [cut] common core or peculiar to either variety, include *number phone* instead of [cut] *phone number*. The latter example comes from Dennis Baron (1990: xii), who [cut] relates how his daughter made herself unpopular by correcting her English [cut] teacher during a time when he and his family were spending a year in [cut] France. When Baron's daughter challenged the teacher on the correctness [cut] of *number phone* (cf. French *numéro de téléphone*), the teacher explained that [cut] *phone number* might be 'ok' in American English, but that in her class only

---

it is quite often not possible to tell in certain text types (apart from spelling) what nationality the author is.

1.3.1 The lexical common core

A little over a century after Johnson's dictionary appeared, the *OED* was launched under James Murray's editorship. In it the notion of a 'core' vocabulary evolved. Murray designated entries as 'Common Words of literature and conversation' as opposed to other words which were labelled 'scientific', 'foreign', 'dialectal', 'slang', technical', etc. Unlike Johnson's dictionary which was finished in a scant nine years, the *OED* was to take nearly seventy-five. Its aim was to record every word used in English literature since the year 1000 and to trace its historical development. The supplement, begun in 1957 by Robert Burchfield, was rather overambitiously planned to take only seven.

Yet by the time the *OED* was completed in 1933, it had become obvious that no one dictionary could cover the entire lexicon of English. Therefore, a number of other dictionaries were planned either to cover particular historical periods (e.g. *The Dictionary of Middle English*) or to cover geographical areas (e.g. *The Dictionary of Americanisms, The Dictionary of American English*). Subsequent editions of the *OED* have recognised that there is a lot of catching up to do with three centuries worth of words and citations to document in what has since become the leading site for the development of the English language. One of Burchfield's aims in the Supplement was to ensure that the new vocabulary of all English-speaking countries received attention. It introduced roughly 50,000 new entries into the language, a 15 per cent increase in the vocabulary recorded in the *OED*.

Willinsky's examination of a century's worth of citations in the *OED* from 1884 to 1989 reveals a shift of gravity in three respects, one from the literary to journalistic as far as genre is concerned with *The Times* becoming the leading source of citations, a second from the humanities to sciences, and a third from Britain to the United States. Most of the material searched by dictionary staff still comes from Britain and the US. The electronic database used to store citations between 1989 and 1991 shows a bias towards American sources (63 per cent), with roughly twice as many as those of British origin (33 per cent), and a small remainder from other countries such as Canada, India, Australia, etc.

Algeo's chapter in this volume shows how the vocabulary of the English-speaking world is so intertwined that it must be treated as a fundamental unity with only marginal national variation. We can take the common core of Standard International English to include all expressions in the common stock of English, for which there are no significant national variations, e.g. *nation, computer*, etc. By comparison, *outwith* is confined to Scotland, and *gotten* is confined to American English. Regional and social dialect variants in the two countries will not be taken into account here (see volume VI); nor will slang or technical jargon unless these items have passed into more general usage. Proper names are, however, the subject of Coates's chapter.

A look at various editions of The American Bible Society's *Good News Bible* (1976) gives us an impressionistic view of how minor lexical variation is in the major national standards. The Society took considerable care in its original to avoid regional peculiarities in English usage. Although this was to a large degree successful, a need was still felt for a British English version, which came out in the same year. Standard Australian English is not sufficiently different from either British or American Standard usage to have required significant changes, but nevertheless if we look at the Australian edition, there is about one alteration per chapter.

In some cases decisions were made simply to retain an American or British item according to Australian usage, e.g. American *rooster* and *store* (where the British English version has *cock* and *shop*), and British English *afterwards* and *burnt* (where the American English version has *afterward* and *burned*). Among the entirely new items of vocabulary, grammar and spelling are the following: British and American *field*, which is little used in Australia, becomes variously *land, paddock* or *pastures; shorn* is substituted for *sheared* and measurements are given in metric units. The British edition also uses metric units but seems less at ease with them (cf. American *ten pounds*, British *five kilogrammes* and Australian *five kilos*; see Tulloch 1989).

A comparison of data from the Australian English corpus with the Brown Corpus of American English and the Lancaster-Oslo-Bergen Corpus of British English has facilitated further study of lexical and spelling differences. In some instances Australian usage aligns itself with the norms of American English, preferring, for instance, *movie* over *film* and *trip* over *journey*, but in other cases, with that of British English, favouring, for example, *holiday* over *vacation* (Collins and Peters 1988). Australian English is also like American English in disfavouring the use of the suffix *-st* on *while* and *among*. With respect to spelling, there are also divergent tendencies, with <or> on the increase, e.g. *color*, but persistence of words with <re> instead of <er>, e.g. *theatre*. Delbridge (1990: 73) observes that by mid 1985 six of Australia's major urban newspapers used the American

<or> spellings. Although most Australians have learned at school to take an anti-American stance in language, especially in spelling, it is not necessarily the case that Australian English is becoming unilaterally more Americanised, as some have suggested (or indeed complained).

The preparation of a corpus of New Zealand English is facilitating similar comparisons between the lexis of New Zealand and Australia in relation to the two major national varieties of British and American English. Initial analysis has shown, for instance, that *movie* is less common in New Zealand than Australia, while the preference for *trip* over *journey* is in line with the Australian tendency towards the American variant, as is the greater use of *vacation* over *holiday*. In the latter case, however, both Australia and New Zealand favour the British variant. As far as spelling is concerned, there were no <er> spellings of *centre* or *theatre* (see Bauer 1993).

While space and time may still be reckoned from Greenwich, over the past century, the world's economic centre of gravity has clearly shifted from Europe to the United States. Almost as if in tacit recognition of Mark Twain's declaration that the King's English is a joint stock company with Americans holding most of the shares, economic reasons seem to have been to the fore in the decision to include Americanisms in the *OED*. Kenneth Sisam, who was responsible for the administration of the Oxford dictionaries, recognised somewhat reluctantly that 'USA words of a certai status and permanence' had to be included because 'one must please t Americans' (cited in Burchfield 1989: 4). Much earlier in correspondi with Henry Fowler, author of *The King's English* (1906), who was to prod for Oxford University Press the *Quarto Oxford Dictionary* (never finish Sisam worried that 'without a liberal sprinkling of Americanisms', a tionary couldn't be sold in America. He wondered if Fowler thou would 'be a sin to admit them, even with an asterisk or an obelus or other sign of disapprobation?' (cited in Burchfield 1989: 143). I replied that he had no horror of Americanisms.

Meanwhile, in the US Alan Walker Read was to begin his pio work in the 1930s on a dictionary of Briticisms, i.e. features of which are limited to or characteristic of English as spoken in th Kingdom. While investigating comments made by British travelle language of America, it occurred to him to study the com American travellers on the language of Britain as a rich source menting Briticisms. Travellers tales have of course long prov source of peculiarities of language and other customs, as I no

Algeo (1988a: 50–51) subsequently defined the notion of that it includes:

British English would do. If *number phone* was good enough for the Queen, it was good enough for her class!

The dividing line between such obvious errors as *number phone* which occur through influence from a learner's native language and other deviations found in the English spoken in India and Singapore is not so clear. What is the status of *furnitures*, for instance? On what basis does one decide whether to accept the use of such plurals not found in any native variety of English as forming part of a new standard variety? What were originally regarded as Americanisms, as we have seen, have now gained legitimacy. More importantly, who decides? The challenge to the hegemony of British English came first from the inner circle, i.e. from other native users like the Americans, New Zealanders, Australians, Canadians and South Africans but now increasingly it comes from the outer circle too, (i.e. India, Singapore, Nigeria, etc.) who claim legitimacy for their non-native varieties. Seventy million Indians who use English outnumber the entire population of Britain, yet citations from Indian publications intended for the *OED* make up less than 1 per cent. The 'outer circle' has already made contributions to International English, e.g. *savvy* (from Portuguese/Spanish 'to know' via pidgin English) and enriched literature in English (see 1.3.4).

1.3.2 The grammatical common core

While lexical items spring most readily to mind when thinking of Americanisms and Briticisms, grammatical differences are much more subtle and it is not always possible to draw a clear line between what is lexical and what is grammatical, or indeed between grammar and semantics (see Quirk, Greenbaum, Leech & Svartvik 1985 for an account of British and American grammatical differences). There are quite systematic differences, for instance, in the expression of modality between British and American English (see Kytö 1991 for historical discussion). Algeo (1988b) shows how grammatical differences between the two varieties are principally matters of the collocability and co-occurrence restrictions of particular words rather than of syntactic rules *per se* of the kind likely to attract the attention of grammar books. In terms of modern linguistic theory they are the sorts of features that would receive specification in the lexicon.

Of the differences separating Standard American and British varieties grammatical ones are perhaps the least important since they are the least numerous, the least salient and the least likely to lead to lack of understanding. Take, for instance, differences in the use of definite articles. British English sometimes lacks a determiner where American English would have one, e.g. *to be in (the) hospital, to leave (the) university.* Compare, however, *in school* common to both varieties, although *school* itself has wider reference in the US than in Britain, where one would not, for instance, refer to a university student as being still *in/at school.* Probably for speakers of each national variety the special uses of the other are obtrusive and seem to be more frequent than they are. Foreign learners increasingly want dictionaries to show both American and British variants.

Once we move beyond the confines of the standard varieties of British and American English, matters inevitably become more complex, as my earlier example of plurals such as *furnitures* shows. However, we do not have to move even that far afield before we encounter a wide range of constructions and distinctions not found in the standard varieties. Many of these differences have not received systematic treatment because both dialectologists and sociolinguists have tended to concentrate more on vocabulary and phonology (see, however, the studies in Trudgill and Chambers 1991). Indeed, one reason sociolinguists have paid less attention to syntactic variation has been the theoretical problems posed by its very existence, in particular the issue of whether a set of variants can be regarded as semantically equivalent (see Romaine 1984b). As Harris (1984) points out, an assumption of direct semantic equivalence between standard and non-standard variants involves a further assumption that the variants are embedded in identical grammars and are therefore simply surface realisations of the same underlying syntactic and semantic structure.

In some cases grammatical differences lead to miscomprehension, as shown by Trudgill (1981) in his study of some syntactic variants in dialects of English. Native speakers, for instance, were hardly better than non-natives when it came to understanding the meaning of *Don't jump off while the bus stops*, which is widely used in parts of northern England to mean 'Don't jump off until the bus stops'. Similarly, Labov (1991) found that the use of so-called positive *anymore* in certain regional varieties of American English was puzzling to speakers of other varieties, e.g. *Anymore it's hard to get coal, That's the trouble with airplanes anymore.* Here *anymore* means simply 'nowadays'.

While it could be argued that these are simply differences in the meanings of individual lexical items such as *while* and *anymore*, it is harder to accommodate within the notion of a common grammatical core the observation that a number of regional and non-standard varieties also have a richer range of aspectual distinctions than Standard English. Milroy (1984: 21), for instance, notes a major difference between the aspect systems of Hiberno-English and Standard English which leads to misunderstanding. In the following dialogue, A is a native of South-west Donegal while B and C are both Standard English speakers.

A: How long are youse here?
B: Till after Easter
    (A looks puzzled; a pause of two seconds follows)
C: We came on Sunday.
A: Ah, Youse're here a while then.

What has caused the problem is not the difference in pronouns, where Hiberno-English along with some other regional varieties has a distinct form for the second person plural, but the fact that Hiberno-English generally avoids the use of the *have* auxiliary as a marker of the perfect. Thus, B and C assume that A means 'How long will you be here for?', while A means 'How long have you both been here?' To complicate matters, Hiberno-English has no single form which corresponds in meaning to Standard English *have* + past participle. In some cases the equivalent may be a construction using *be* + *after*, e.g. *I am after seeing him*, which means 'I have just seen him'. In addition, there is a construction which makes use of have + past participle, but the participle comes after the object, unlike in Standard English where it comes before. Compare Hiberno-English: *I've it pronounced wrong* and Standard English: *I've pronounced it wrong*.

While linguists have been quick to jump to the conclusion that such constructions must have been the result of influence from Irish Gaelic on English, Harris (1991) has identified similar patterns in other regional varieties of English not influenced by Irish, as well as in earlier forms of Standard English. Compare, for example, 'Have you the lion's part written?' (*Midsummer Night's Dream* I.ii.68).

1.3.3   The phonological common core

As far as the notion of a common phonological core is concerned, matters are also complicated because it has been seen in terms of the idea of a standard, but Standard English grammar is compatible with a wide range of accent types. Even Noah Webster saw the standardisation of pronunciation as a complete impossibility. That prospect was to await more ambitious English phoneticians such as Daniel Jones and historians of the language such as Wyld (see MacMahon, this volume). I feel the term *standard* does not really apply to accent in any case, but only to grammar. Moreover, it is a concept more applicable to the written than spoken language. This is in contrast to some earlier views on the subject such as that of Abercrombie (1965: 11) who writes:

> I use the word *dialect* [emphasis in original] for any form of English which differs from Standard English in grammar, syntax, vocabulary, and of course in pronunciation too, though a difference in pronunciation alone is not enough to make a different dialect . . . Some people speak Standard English, with an accent, and some speak it without . . . This 'accentless' pronunciation . . . I shall refer to as RP.

Most linguists would now accept that Standard English is a dialect like any other, and use the term *variety* rather than *dialect*. In Britain, however, RP (received pronunciation) is sometimes considered the equivalent of a Standard English pronunciation, particularly in England. The term RP has been in use for the past century and owes its origin to A. J. Ellis (1869:23), who recognised 'a received pronunciation all over the country, not widely differing in any particular locality, and admitting a certain degree of variety. It may be especially considered as the educated pronunciation of the metropolis, of the court, the pulpit, and the bar.' At the same time, however, Ellis (1869: 630) maintained 'there is **no** standard of pronunciation' [emphasis in original].

The norms of what is today referred to as RP have been extensively documented by phoneticians such as Jones (1917), who was largely responsible for establishing the use of the term in its present sense and who based his description on his own speech. It is the norm usually taught to foreign learners of English and the kind of accent often referred to popularly as the Queen's or King's English (see, e.g., Alford 1864), Oxford English (see, e.g., Chapman 1932), BBC English, etc. This accent has its origins in the south-east of England and was spread in the public (i.e. private) schools. Wyld (1927: 149) in fact, used the term 'Public School English' to refer to that speech 'form which all would probably agree in considering the best, that form which has the widest currency and is heard with practically no variation among speakers of the better class all over the country'. While it is spoken by only about 5 per cent or less of the population (and therefore hardly has wide currency), it is nevertheless considered a prestigious accent throughout the UK and the British Commonwealth. An anecdote (possibly apocryphal) has it that upon being asked how many RP speakers there were in his department at London, Jones replied after a pause 'two'. He did not, however, reveal the identity of the second person.

The use of RP as a teaching model has been justified on the grounds that it has been more carefully described than any other accent of English and that it is widely understood (see Romaine 1997a). Wyld argued for the intrinsic superiority of its sounds saying that no other variety of English surpassed it in clarity or beauty. Departures from this norm were so distasteful to him that sixty years after his departure from the University of Liverpool to take up the Merton Chair of English Language at the University of Oxford (which he held from 1920 to 1945), Wyld was remembered for having 'reduced women students to tears by his fierce comments on their northern pronunciation' (cited in Bailey 1991: 9).

Yet, as Macaulay (1988: 115) has pointed out, RP is not necessarily the phonetically easiest of models for foreign learners to acquire. It has, for example, more vowel contrasts and diphthongs than many other accents of English such as Scots, which is radically different. Most varieties of English are rhotic, unlike non-rhotic RP, and therefore less divergent from spelling practices. Nor is RP necessarily the most socially appropriate, as is sometimes argued. Most learners who have been taught RP and then come to Britain find out very quickly that most people do not speak this way. Abercrombie (1963: 55) observes that the peculiar social position of RP makes many people hostile to it. Honey (1989: 66) comments that the present Queen, her son, as well as the Queen Mother all speak a variant of RP which is not widely admired or imitated. Indeed, he goes on to say, 'in the mouths of other speakers it is actually ridiculed'. Yet, even the Prince of Wales has been heard to pronounce *ate* in the American way /eit/ rather than as in British English, for which he was promptly reproached by the British press. Abercrombie (1963: 48–9) even suggested that the dividing line between RP and non-RP speakers is so sharp that 'one either speaks RP or one does not, and if the opportunity to learn it in youth has not arisen, it is almost impossible to acquire it in later life'. Elsewhere he comments that this 'accent bar is a little like a colour bar' (Abercrombie 1965: 15).

The second claim about its wide intelligibility has, moreover, never been systematically tested, but has simply been assumed due to the extensive broadcasting of the BBC, both in Britain and overseas through the World Service. Certainly, American audiences find it harder to understand than most Britons do American speech varieties, but this reflects the differential exposure of the two populations. The pre-eminence of RP in British broadcasting is not surprising since both Jones and Wyld were among the experts on the BBC Advising Committee on Spoken English. As a result of the Second World War and the advent of commercial radio and television the BBC no longer dominates the media to the same degree.

Until quite recently the voice of the BBC was uniformly RP. Nevertheless, the editor of the *BBC Pronouncing Dictionary of English* (Miller

1971: v) writes that 'although the BBC does not, and never did, impose pronunciations of its own in English words, the myth of "BBC English" dies hard'. Even within the UK there are now varieties of RP (see Wells 1982: 279–301) and news readers and reporters with marked regional accents can be heard. Over the course of her political career Margaret Thatcher continually modified her accent in the direction of RP, while other politicians have exploited the value of regional accents. Harold Wilson's northern counties accent and Neil Kinnock's Welsh English accent create more of an impression that they are 'of the people' than would RP (see Honey 1988).

RP is giving way abroad to localised norms in Australia and New Zealand too. When the Australian Broadcasting Corporation was created in 1932, it recommended Jones's (1917) norms for its news readers. However, in 1941 its chairman revealed that only 2 out of 450 applicants for the position of announcer could be selected. Most of those recognised as suitable were Englishmen. Due to Mitchell's influence so-called 'educated Australian speech' (which Mitchell 1946 later termed 'cultivated') was subsequently adopted as the style for national broadcasting. This variety of Australian speech, while distinctively Australian, was still close to RP, and quite different from the variety which Mitchell termed 'Broad Australian'. Nowadays, however, a cultivated accent is no longer essential for the ABC. Since 1983 it has required only 'acceptable styles of educated speech' (see Leitner 1982, 1984), and now all questions concerning pronunciation, style and usage are referred to an Australian dictionary, not a British one.

In New Zealand too RP is giving way to local norms (see Bell 1982). With the advent of the US-owned Cable News Network (CNN), now transmitted widely in Europe and around the world, one can argue that American accents are just as, if not even more, familiar to a wide audience. In addition, American television programmes are shown to an increasingly large audience.

The influence of RP as a teaching model is also on the decline. Macaulay (1988: 122) notes that it has never served as a general standard for teaching English throughout British schools, except in the private sector. He adds that its importance in teaching English as a foreign language is paradoxical when most teachers do not speak it themselves. There is less and less justification for assigning RP a special status now that English has clearly assumed the role of world language.

Although there is a close relationship between regional and social dialect in both the United States and Britain in which working-class varieties are more localised, there is nothing similar to RP in the United States (or possibly anywhere else in the world). Some writers, however, have used the term *network English* or *General American English*, as if there were a recognised standard variety of pronunciation (see Baugh & Cable 1993: 376 and also Denison and MacMahon, this volume). To the extent that there is a network standard, it has never been synonymous with a particular social class in the way that RP has in Britain, though of course, educated speakers in both countries would tend not to use non-standard grammatical features. American English has pluricentric norms for pronunciation with different regions having their own standards used by educated speakers. The idea of the 'President's English' is not one Americans would find interpretable in the way Britons would make sense of the notion of the 'Queen's' or 'King's English'. Many former American presidents have spoken with quite pronounced regional accents, John F. Kennedy (from eastern New England) and Jimmy Carter (from the south-east) being two good examples. Both were non-rhotic while the majority of Americans speak with rhotic accents (see 1.2). Both linking /r/ and intrusive /r/ were features of Kennedy's speech, while Carter did not use intrusive /r/. In some respects the accent used by Kennedy resembles RP more closely phonologically than do other varieties of North American English. There is, for example, an /æ/-/a/ split similar to the RP split, but the set of words belonging to each class is not quite the same in the two accents.

It is by appealing to such variation in the phonetic realization of vowel phonemes and to a lesser extent in the number and behaviour of phonemes themselves that linguists find it possible to describe a common phonological core. The differences between Cockney and RP, for example, are nearly all phonetic rather than phonological and most of phonological differences are variable, e.g. loss of /h/ (see 1.2). Using Scottish Standard English, RP and General American as reference points, Giegerich (1992), for example, recognises 'types' of English representing different points in an accent typology. He (1992: 44) argues that most areas of southern Britain (excluding Scotland and to some extent the north of England) share a standard vowel system that is subject to little regional variation.

The following diagram from Trudgill & Hannah (1982: 5) attempts to depict the relationships among the major varieties with respect to pronunciation. It indicates the two major types, North American and British, with the two varieties of Irish English falling somewhere between the two and Scottish English to some extent separate. Australian, New Zealand and South African English are all typologically closer to RP than to American English in that they are non-rhotic and there are no major phonemic differences between these accents and RP. The consonant system of English is relatively uniform throughout the English-speaking world.

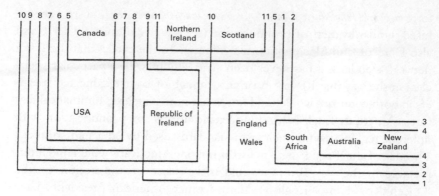

Key

1. /ɑː/ rather than /æ/ in *path* etc.
2. absence of non-prevocalic /r/
3. close vowels for /æ/ and /ɛ/, monophthongisation of /ai/ and /ɑu/
4. front [aː] for /ɑː/ in *part* etc.
5. absence of contrast of /ɒ/ and /ɔː/ as in *cot* and *caught*
6. /æ/ rather than /ɑː/ in *can't* etc.
7. absence of contrast of /ɒ/ and /ɑː/ as in *bother* and *father*
8. consistent voicing of intervocalic /t/
9. unrounded [ɑ] in *pot*
10. syllabic /r/ in *bird*
11. absence of contrast of /ʊ/ and /uː/ as in *pull* and *pool*

Figure 1.1 Pronunciation differences among varieties of English (from Trudgill & Hannah 1982: 5)

1.3.4   The literary common core

Although literature is clearly grounded in language, the notion of a common core to literary tradition is more problematic than the concept of a linguistic common core. In her chapter Adamson documents for the most part the evolution of the literary language in Britain, though the revolutions she identifies are relevant in examining the subsequent development of literatures in English around the world. In Australia, for instance, authors such as Les Murray would insist that an authentic Australia would be a vernacular republic founded on an Australian consciousness which had severed its ties to England. Similarly in New Zealand, Frank Sargeson saw his task as getting out from under the shadow of the great English novelists of the eighteenth century by inventing a literary language drawn from and representing the New Zealand subject. Later, when the Empire writes back in what Jamaican poet Louise Bennett would call 'colonization in reverse', a generation of indigenous writers would set out to break consciously with imported writing styles and to use the text as a site of resistance to European literate traditions in order to write their own emerging national literatures. The national literatures of many African countries are already written in English and many more will be.

Indeed, George Steiner (1975: 5) suggests that a major shift in gravity beyond the inner circle has occurred as far as the literary language is concerned when he noted that the 'principal energies of the English language, as if its genius for acquisition, for innovation, for metaphoric response, had also moved away from England'. As evidence, we can note how in recent years the Booker Prize for fiction, arguably Britain's most prestigious literary award, has gone to a number of writers writing in English who have never lived in England. Some of them write in non-mainstream varieties of English, including, for instance, Keri Hulme of New Zealand, 1985 prize winner for her novel *The Bone People*. Similarly, the Nobel prize for literature has included among its recent winners Derek Walcott from St Lucia (1992) and Seamus Heaney (1996) from Ireland.

Not long after Steiner's remarks, Q. D Leavis's last public lecture took as its theme the Englishness of the English novel. Speaking in 1980, she reflected on the plight of 'our run-down Britain' (cited in Singh 1983: 325):

> The England that bore the classical English novel has gone forever, and we can't expect a country of high-rise flat-dwellers, office workers and factory robots and unassimilated multi-racial minorities, with a suburbanized countryside, factory farming, sexual emancipation without responsibility, rising crime and violence, and the Trade Union mentality, to give rise to a literature comparable with its novel tradition of a so different past.

In a similar vein an article bemoaning 'Britain's lost literary horizons' (Brookman, *THES* 12 February 1993) suggests 'it is probably no coincidence that the Booker Prize for Fiction has in the past ten years been awarded mainly to writers from wider cultural backgrounds', among them several Africans. This comment came in the year that Ben Okri of Nigeria won the prize for his book *The Famished Road*.

Interestingly, in 1994 when a British author did win the prize critics were not pleased at the winning novel's use of Glaswegian dialect in its description of a week in the life of an ex-convict from Glasgow, which one judge, Rabbi Julia Neuberger, said made the novel 'completely inaccessible'. In his acceptance speech, however, Scotsman James Kelman placed his novel, *How Late It Was, How Late*, in the context of a 'worldwide process of decolonisation and self-determination'. He declared, 'My culture and my language have the right to exist' (McAfee 1994). 'The bottom line is that certain linguistic forms are not worthy of literature. It's just not true of Scotland, it's equally true of Somerset or Wales. As soon as you enter school you are informed that your culture and your language is inferior' (Smith 1994). In the novel Kelman tries to write in an authentic Scottish voice.

As the experience of writing in English in the Caribbean, India, and Africa shows, finding a voice takes time and the more recently decolonising Pacific Islands are now among the last of the anglophone colonies to develop a literature in English. Linguists, writers and literary critics have begun to concern themselves with some of the many crucial issues raised by language in post-colonial literature (see e.g. Ashcroft, Griffiths & Tiffin 1989). One key question is whether and to what extent it is possible to use the coloniser's language while rejecting the world view it offers. One 'solution' is of course to abandon the colonial language altogether and write, as Ngũgĩ wa Thiong'o now does, in an indigenous language, or other languages believed to be untainted by colonial origins. Another is to appropriate the coloniser's language and to use it as Chinua Achebe and others do around the world in innovative and distinctive ways to make it bear the burden of their experience.

Indeed, for many authors there has been no choice but to do the latter or to be silent because the very process of colonisation either wiped out indigenous languages, as it did in many parts of the Caribbean, or weakened their transmission so severely that many contemporary writers never had the opportunity to acquire them or develop their use for literary purposes. Irish poet John Montague described the painful process in his poem 'A Grafted Tongue' (Fallon and Mahon 1990: 46–7):

> To grow
> a second tongue, as
> harsh a humiliation
> as twice to be born

Similar sentiments are expressed by Antiguan author Jamaica Kincaid (1996: 7) when she observed how 'the first words I said were in the language of a people I would never like or love'.

The use of pidgin and creole languages in the quest for a distinctive voice shows how the very act of writing in a marginalised language whose status as a language is denied by the mainstream is symbolic of the appropriation of the power vested in the written word. Writing in Hawai'i Creole English or Tok Pisin becomes, in Le Page and Tabouret-Keller's (1985) terms, an 'act of identity' (see Romaine 1995). Rejecting the term *dialect* because it suggested inferiority, Edward Kamau Brathwaite (1984) argued for the use of what he called 'nation language' (Jamaican Creole English) in poetry as a way of capturing the sounds and rhythm of oral traditions of performance. Inspired by hearing a recording of T. S. Eliot reading from *The Waste Land*, Brathwaite urged poets to model their poetry on the African-derived rhythms of calypso in order to break the pentameter, which other New World poets before him such as Walt Whitman had also sought to undermine.

Dub poets such as Jean Binta Breeze would carry on the process of legitimising nation language by writing it down (Morris 1988: 29). Cooper (1995: 68) notes how in this print version of the performance 'Dubbed out', the spacing of the lines jerking to a halt enacts the beating down of sense and lyricism. When the fluidity of word moving is released from mechanical rigidity of the beat and fixity of page, poetry becomes verbal dance. Through the commercial success of performers such as Mikey Smith, Benjamin Zepphaniah or Mutabaruka the once historically devalued Caribbean popular culture has become part of multicultural Britain. As the message of protest went out from Kingston and London around the world, Mutabaruka derided the paradoxical image of the revolutionary poet as media star entertaining the masses.

> I
> search for words
>
> moving
> in their music
>
> not
>
> broken
> by
>
> the
>
> beat

Common to most post-colonial writers is the need to write from the inside out in order to counter the perspectives offered in earlier literature written primarily by Europeans as outsiders looking in. This raises some crucial questions about point of view and whether in fact some genres and techniques of narration are better suited to the task of writing from the inside out. Point of view is also linked to the question of authenticity, a major concern of indigenous writers. In his controversial first novel *Once*

Were Warriors (1990), part-Maori author Alan Duff presents his characters largely from within by narrating from the vantage point of members of the Heke family, who live in a low-income state housing project called Pine Block. Like the Hekes, most of the residents of Pine Block are Maori or part-Maori, but the housing estate is cheek by jowl with the houses of more affluent white middle-class New Zealanders. From the outset the novel focuses on the disparities between the residents of Pine Block and their Pakeha (New Zealanders of European origin) neighbours, in particular, the Tramberts, whose house can be seen from the back kitchen window of the Heke's house.

When the story begins, Beth Heke is looking at the two-storey Trambert house surrounded by large trees and pasture land and thinking to herself. The worlds of Them (the Pakeha/White) and Us (Maori/Black) are at once juxtaposed.

> Bastard, she'd think, looking out her back kitchen window. Lucky white bastard, at that glimpse of two-storey house through its surround of big old trees and its oh so secure greater surround of rolling green pasture-land, while she – Clicking her tongue, Oh to hell with him. Or good luck to him, if she wasn't in too bad a mood.
>
> Good luck to you, white man for being born into your sweet world, and bad luck to you, Beth Heke (who used to be a Ransfield but not that life was so much better then), for being married to an arsehole. And yet I *love* him. just *can't help* myself. I *love* the black, fist-happy bastard. And she'd light another smoke, and always went ahh in her mind and some-times aloud because she liked that first hit against the back of her throat, and she'd squint through the drifts. And wonder. (*OWW*, p. 7)

Since these are the opening lines of the novel, they are crucial in orient-ing the reader. While at first glance, they can be read as narration in the third person, the shifting deixis in tense and pronouns, mark changes in per-spective, indicating tension in identities and allegiances, e.g. the second person *you* addressed to her white neighbour and the *you* to herself reflect-ing on her own life. Although Beth clearly belongs to the Maori world by birth and marriage (and her residence in Pine Block), at times she gazes as an outsider on both the Maori and Pakeha worlds.

One narrative feature of Duff's prose which contributes to the difficulty of distinguishing the narrator's voice from those of his characters is the use of colloquial and at times non-Standard English, as both the language of narration and of the characters' reported speech and thought. The charac-ters' subjectivities pervade the surrounding authorial report. It becomes difficult to say whether the characters' idiom is tinged with the narrator's or whether the narrator's prose is 'contaminated' by its proximity to the thinking characters. The similarity of the language of narration, interior monologue and narrated monologue fuses, the narrative into one.

The only Pakeha characters in the novel are the Tramberts, whose function is merely to symbolise, even if only stereotypically, the Pakeha world and its privileges *vis-à-vis* the Maori one. The story is not about them and hence we do not see them from the inside out, except on one fleeting occasion when Gordon Trambert makes an appearance at the funeral of Beth's teenage daughter, Grace. From her perch in a tree from where she can see into the Trambert dining room, Grace, the oldest Heke daughter, who later hangs herself from that tree, becomes the focalising agent for reporting what goes on at the dinner party (*OWW*, p. 117). The reader never really hears what the Tramberts have to say or think about anything. The choice of the more distant deictic form *that* emphasizes the distance between Grace and the Tramberts.

> Nibble-nibble-nibble, then down'd go their knife and fork or whatever it was they were eating the course with, V-ed points in on the plate, dabdab with that bit of cloth at their dainty mouths, picking up that glass of wine, which'd started off as white and then the mother and her husband's come along and filled more glasses with red wine; it had to be red wine unless it was something else a Pine Block girl didn't know about just as she didn't know about red or white wine, only that she'd figured it from TV. Each course taking an age to eat.
>
> For hours this show went on: each person seeming to take a turn at talking (*taw*king) how they do, holding court as they'd say in English at school, then someone replying or responding or saying anything at all, just resuming their eating, their wine sipping, their dabdabs at their mouths with serviettes, which a Pine Block girl knows're called sumpthin else except she doesn't know precisely what.

Again, it is not entirely clear who thinks or reports what. Duff draws our attention to the way in which white New Zealanders of the Tramberts' social status would likely have pronounced *talking* by exaggerating its vowel. Dining in the midst of such polite conversation and other middle-class trappings such as wine and table napkins is not part of Grace's life, as indicated linguistically in the use of non-U *serviette* as well as Grace's ignorance of the U alternative. If it is the author who is speaking here, then he declines to reveal that he knows that the Tramberts would probably use the word *table napkin* (see 1.2).

Duff's technique is highly reminiscent of that of Virginia Woolf, as described by Auerbach (1968: 536), who characterised its essence as 'a multipersonal representation of consciousness', shifting between the consciousness of different characters who represent multiple points of view rather than narrating the novel from a single point of view, the consciousness of one character.

By contrast, part-Samoan author Albert Wendt wrote his first and a number of subsequent novels primarily in Standard English in the conventional third person. His first novel, *Sons for the Return Home* (1973), can be read metaphorically as a classic case of alienation. The namelessness of the characters is indicative of their lack of identity. The intellectual son of Samoan parents who migrate to New Zealand in search of work has been educated in Pakeha institutions, and thus is caught between two worlds, at home in neither. Although he is Samoan by birth, he finds he cannot live in Samoa, nor can he accept the Samoan world view. He resists assimilation to it and remains outside of it, on the margins. He is neither inside nor outside. In New Zealand too he is the outside, the Other, although there he is forced to be on the margins by the racism of a white society that prevents his full assimilation at the same time that it demands it. Indeed, they must prevent it in order to maintain the boundaries between the centre and the Other. Keeping the Other out is a means of self-preservation. After his parents have been called to the school principal's office to be congratulated on their youngest son's receipt of the School Certificate, the boy reminds them (*SRH*, p. 13): 'We've been here for nearly thirteen years and they still treat us as strangers. As inferiors . . . I speak their language, their peculiar brand of English, as well as any of them. They have to pretend I'm their equal, that I'm a New Zealander, because they can't do anything else.'

The sites of Centre and Margin are not stable throughout the novel. Paradoxically and ironically, it is Samoa (literally 'the centre') which is the centre, not just of the parents' lives and aspirations, but also from the Samoan point of view, it is the centre of the universe. As the boy sees it, (*SRH*, p. 40): 'Our whole life here is only a preparation for the grand return to our homeland. Their hopes and dreams all revolve round our return.'

African American critic Henry Louis Gates, Jr. (1992: 315) has raised many questions about the nature of the relationship between centre and margin. Although novels such as those of Duff and Wendt may appear to trade on the margin, they use the currency of English. When they write in English using genres like the novel, which, despite its modernity, has its origin in Western literate traditions, indigenous writers leave themselves open to evaluation by Western critical standards, formulated in metropolitan centres such as London and New York rather than in Apia or Kingston, or even Auckland. If, however, these standards are used we must be fully conscious of their development against particular ideological assumptions rather than take them as neutral, objective and universally valid (see Mudrooroo 1990). Some of the negative critical evaluations of the works by indigenous writers of the Pacific are based on misunderstandings of the difficulties such authors face in integrating oral historical traditions into Western modes of narration in a distinctive way while remaining faithful to the cultural values which give meaning to these traditions.

Pakeha critic C. K. Stead, for example, invoked language in questioning Hulme's authenticity as a Maori author. In characterising *The Bone People* as a 'novel by a Pakeha which has won an award [The Pegasus Award for Maori Literature] intended for a Maori', Stead (1985: 104) points out that Hulme was not brought up speaking Maori. This demand for authenticity based on language rests on a fundamental misunderstanding of the linguistic situation for many minority peoples, whose efforts to transmit their language have been undermined by policies of forced assimilation. An 1871 act prohibited Maori in schools. Even Witi Ihimaera and Patricia Grace, whose Maoriness does not seem to be questioned, speak English as their native language. Patricia Grace has argued for a national literature in English which includes the Maori point of view.

The novel as a genre constitutes a strategic site in the discourse of national identity. A number of scholars such as Anderson (1991) and Bhabha (1990) have discussed the ways in which nations may be brought into being through narration, thus attesting the critical role of written literature, in particular, the novel in the service of empire and nation. In Said's view (1993: 69), the novel and imperialism are unthinkable without one another. Authors such as Ihimaera, Grace, and Wendt are writing novels which validate an indigenous rather than a settler's view of history. Ihimaera's novel *The Matriarch* (1987), for instance, can lay a strong claim to being the novel of modern New Zealand, an epic validating a Maori version of nationhood, which threatens the very foundation and continuation of Pakeha rule in New Zealand. In his novel as well as in Albert Wendt's *Leaves of the Banyan Tree* (1978) local or vernacular histories of families stand for the colonial and post-colonial condition of the Maori and Samoan people respectively. While Frederick Jameson (1986: 69) has commented that Third World novels are 'necessarily allegorical' and should be read as 'national allegories', Third World literature has no monopoly on national allegory. The authors' choice of narrative voice and plot is to some extent dictated by the necessity to establish themselves as credible narrators of (family) history within their own cultures. Both authors also tell us that without acknowledgement and reinstatement of values authentic to the indigenous past, the modern nation-state rests on shaky foundations (Romaine 1997b). As in Joyce's Ireland, history has become a nightmare.

1.4   Language, nation, and identity: staking a claim on the past and future

Because national identity is not a permanent or static possession, it has to be continually reinvented. Although Grillo (1989: 44) has argued that there was an almost total lack of attention to any relationship between language and national identity in England, I believe he is mistaken. The role played by language in England's changing conceptions of itself can be seen in both the construction of a glorious past for the language as well as in ever increasing prognostications of a bright future as world language. English, like England, was to have its conquests. As Dean Trench wrote (1855):

> What can more clearly point out our ancestors' native land and ours as having fulfilled a glorious past, as being destined for a glorious future, than that they should have acquired for themselves and for those who came after a clear, a strong, a harmonious, a noble language?

The energetic activities of intellectuals such as James Murray, Joseph Wright, author of the *English Dialect Dictionary*, and others were central to the shaping of European nationalism in the nineteenth century, a time when, as Pedersen (1931–43) puts it, 'national wakening and the beginnings of linguistic science go hand in hand'. Historians such as Seton-Watson (1977) and Anderson (1991) have observed how nineteenth-century Europe was a golden age of vernacularising lexicographers, grammarians, philologists and dialectologists. Their projects too were conceived as children of empires.

Willinsky (1994) singles out the *OED*, in particular, as the 'last great gasp of British imperialism'. It captured a history of words that fit well with the ideological needs of the emerging nation-state. As Willinsky observes (1994: 194), the *OED* speaks to a 'particular history of national self-definition during a remarkable period in the expansion and collapse of the British empire'. Murray's tenure as editor of the *OED* coincided roughly with the period which historian Eric Hobsbawm (1987) has called the Age of Empire, 1875–1914. With the *OED*, Murray and other editors were engaged in establishing England and Oxford University Press's claim on the English language and the word trade more generally.

Britain's expansionist policy brought with it increasing exposure to other languages. The British presence in India awakened the attention of scholars to Sanskrit. In 1786 Sir William Jones gave a speech to the Philological Society which was to provide a firm basis for the comparative-historical study of language. In 1839 De Quincey called for a monument of learning and patriotism to be erected to the English language in the form of a history of English from its earliest rudiments. The Early English Text Society subsequently founded by F. J. Furnivall was to produce a canon of texts. Such works would help solidify the unity of nation and language and their continuity from the earliest times. Sentiments such as these were at least partly responsible for the replacement of the term *Anglo-Saxon* by *Old English*.

While colonial expansion was underway, there was also a need for more civil servants in the service of empire. The opening of the Civil Service to competitive examinations in English language and literature, as recommended by the Trevelyan and Northcote report of 1853 (*The Organisation of the Permanent Civil Service*), gave impetus to the institutionalisation of English studies. The History of the English Language was treated as distinct from its literature.

Such notions were instrumental in the establishment of what today we might call 'English studies', i.e. the study of English language and literature. It had taken some centuries before people were confident enough about English to deem it worthy of study as a subject for teaching and research. Now that English is so well established as a discipline, we tend to forget that even as late as the nineteenth century it was not recognised as a legitimate subject.

The increasing enlargement of the state education system made the classics-based curriculum increasingly unsuitable for the many new pupils to be encompassed within it. Women and the working classes of both sexes would find the classics too intellectually demanding and needed an easier subject. James Murray actually credited the women's movement directly for the appearance of English studies at Oxford in the nineteenth century. 'But for the movement to let women share in the advantages of a university education', he said (Murray 1900: 31), 'it is doubtful whether the nineteenth century would have witnessed the establishment of a School of English Language and Literature at Oxford.'

The English Dialect Society founded in 1873 (and its American counterpart, the American Dialect Society in 1889) were spin-offs of the increasing interest focused on the standard literary language in the curriculum. These projects were motivated by the fear that if work were not begun to record what was non-standard, it would soon disappear. Wyld argued strongly in favour of making the study of the English language a central component in secondary schools. There he believed it would be 'beyond controversy' (1906: 34). Wyld could not, of course, have foreseen just how controversial it would indeed become towards the end of the twentieth century as questions about the canon and standards became a major pre-occupation when the Conservative government launched its National Curriculum.

Cameron & Bourne (1988) see the Kingman report (1988), which emerged from the Committee of Inquiry into the Teaching of the English Language set up by the UK Secretary of State for Education as a key ideological text about the state of the English language and its relation to the state of the nation. This proposal to make the teaching of English the cornerstone of a national curriculum whose aim is to produce a common culture has to be understood in historical context as a continuation of the spirit of the earlier Newbolt Report (1921). It too had advocated mass education in English language and literature as the basis for a common national culture so that (cited in Crowley 1991: 201):

> The English people might learn as a whole to regard their own language, first with respect and then with a genuine feeling of pride and affection. More than any mere symbol it is actually a part of England; to maltreat it or deliberately debase it would be seen to be an outrage . . . Such a feeling for our native language would be a bind of union between classes and beget the right kind of national pride.

Yet the National Curriculum was also a reaction to the liberal ideas of the 1960s and 1970s as well. Kenneth Baker, Secretary for Education at the time the Kingman committee was set up, commented that while few schools taught traditional grammar, little had been put in its place. A central task for Kingman's committee was to equip teachers with a proper model of grammar. Earlier, The Swann Report (1985: 385) had challenged the ethnocentrism of common culture in order to replace it with cultural pluralism, but it made clear at the same time that this conception of culture was to be transmitted through English as the 'central unifying factor in being British'. In its concern with grammar, Kingman harked back to earlier ideology about the connection between language and nation. 'Language above all else is the defining characteristic of an individual, a community, a nation' (Kingman 1988: 43). As Cameron and Bourne point out (1988: 159), part of the meaning of Kingman is nostalgia for the good old days of imperial majesty now faded, and part of what a Conservative Party Campaign slogan called 'Making Britain Great Again'.

Thus, on numerous occasions in the past century right down to the present day, the English language would be offered as evidence of the underlying unity that held all together despite superficial differences, particularly when political and cultural crisis threatened. In an interview with Margaret Thatcher when she was Prime Minister (*Newsweek* 8 October 1990) and stood much to gain from aligning herself with then President Ronald Reagan, she very generously conceded that Shakespeare belonged as much to Americans as to Britons in characterising the 'special relationship' that exists between the United States and Britain. Speaking to an American interviewer, she observed:

> the Magna Carta belongs as much to you as it does to us; the writ of habeas corpus belongs as much to you as it does to us . . . There is such a common heritage as well as the language. Shakespeare belongs as much to you as he does to us . . . That is what unites us and has united us – rather more than a philosophy, but history as well, and language and mode of thought.

Indeed, Gramsci (1985: 183–4) observes that:

> Every time the question of the language surfaces, in one way or another, it means that a series of other problems are coming to the fore: the formation and enlargement of the governing class, the need to establish more intimate and secure relationships between the governing groups and the national-popular mass, in other words to reorganize the cultural hegemony.

Despite the fact that the Newbolt report claimed it was not advocating the 'teaching of standard English on any grounds of "social superiority"' or 'the suppression of dialect' (cited in Crowley 1991: 205), as Crowley observes, the attempt to create unity by means of a class dialect in contradistinction to other forms of speech which are branded vulgar and provincial, is doomed to defeat because it will reinforce divisions rather than make the differences between standard and non-standard 'gradually disappear' (Newbolt Report, cited in Crowley 1991: 200).

Despite democratic rhetoric from some quarters about making Standard English accessible to the population as a whole through universal education, some always wanted to maintain the exclusivity of the club of Standard English speakers. R. W. Chapman, for instance, in extolling the virtues of Oxford (= Standard) English, admitted he was 'so undemocratic as to believe that the best, in speech as in other things, can never be widely and rapidly disseminated without damage to itself' (1932: 560). Already, it was exposed to dangers from both within its ranks as well as without. 'As the speech of a very small minority of English speakers it is obviously exposed to gradual absorption by the surrounding mass and perhaps also to deliberate attack. It is well known that English vocabulary and idiom are undergoing penetration from America and elsewhere . . . Even our grammar is threatened' (1932: 562).

The division between standard and non-standard is symbolic of other fault lines as large as those of class and nation; increasingly, race and gender are at stake too. Debates about language are thus really about issues of race, gender, class or culture, as can be seen in the controversy over 'political correctness', which has also been carried out largely on the battlefield of language. While proposals for reforming sexist language are considerably older than the political correctness controversy, they have become caught up in it, as can be seen in American prescriptivist John Simon's lumping together of a variety of groups discriminated against on grounds of class, race, sexual orientation, sex and ethnicity. He (1980: xiv) objects to the 'notion that in a democratic society language must accommodate itself to the whims, idiosyncrasies, dialects, and sheer ignorance of underprivileged minorities, especially if these happened to be black, Hispanic, and later on, female or homosexual'. Simon's rejection of language reform is really a statement about keeping women (and other minority groups) accountable to white middle-class male standards by maintaining the linguistic *status quo*. A society or nation in control of itself is in control of its grammar – and in control of its women!

The *OED*'s creators had defined themselves as the white, male property-owning centre of a British Empire. The dictionary served to codify a history traced through the nation's best writers. Earlier, the act of translation of the Bible into English reflected the connection between language, nation and empire. The dissemination of the English Bible to Britain's colonies made it look as if English were the very language spoken by God. At the centre of this process of national and cultural self-definition was the act of citation. The Bible is at the top of the list of books cited in the *OED*. The dictionary derives part of its authority and power in defining the language by the process of exclusion of texts and authors. What was included authorised a view of the English language that was in line with England's hegemony in the last century.

The fact that the grammarians and lexicographers who created Standard English and set forth its rights and wrongs were male has not gone unnoticed by modern feminists such as Dale Spender (1980) and Julia Penelope (1990). A much earlier male commentator, Elias Molee, repelled by linguistic snobbery, remarked in 1888 (p. 201): 'It looks to me as if the English language were constructed by some eccentric, rich and learned bachelors who had nothing else to do but hunt up the meanings of words in dictionaries and to spell'. Bailey (1991: 274), who cites this remark, notes parenthetically that this description applied aptly to Molle's successors, the Fowler brothers! Symbolically, the first thing Becky Sharp in Thackeray's *Vanity Fair* (1848) jettisons from the coach which takes her away from school is Dr Johnson's *Dictionary*. In the twentieth century feminists such as Mary Daly (1987) would write their own dictionaries. Daly describes her *Websters' First New Intergalactic Wickedary of the English Language* as a wickedary, a dictionary for women spun by websters. She plays here on the original meaning of the word *webster* as 'female weaver' and the fact that the family name Webster is still closely associated with dictionary making in the US.

Standard English was clearly conceived of as a male norm by both H. C. Wyld and Daniel Jones. In commenting on the characteristics of what he called 'Received Standard', Wyld (1934: 614) noted that it was heard most consistently at its best among officers of the British Regular Army. 'The utterance of these men is at once clear-cut and precise, yet free from affectation; at once downright and manly, yet in the highest degree refined and urbane'. Such men had confidence in their speech without reflection on it. Fundamentally hereditary (at least in the male line!), it sufficed simply that 'their fathers have told them'. Similarly, Daniel Jones (1917: 170) in circumscribing the norms of Standard English pronunciation so narrowly that they were synonymous with the speech of the southern English families, reminds us that these were families 'whose men-folk have been educated at the great public boarding schools'.

Despite negative reactions to feminist language reform during the 1960s and 1970s many government agencies, institutions, professional organizations and publishing houses have implemented changes, in some case under legal mandate. The *New York Times*, for example, stopped using titles like *Mrs* and *Miss* with the names of women. The London *Times*, however, still uses androcentric forms such as *spokesman* and the titles, *Mrs* and *Miss*, unless a woman has asked to be referred to as *Ms*. The Linguistic Association of Great Britain rejected a proposal to amend its constitution, to remove generic masculine pronouns. The Linguistic Society of America, on the other hand, has embraced reform and issued a set of guidelines as well as established a Committee on the Status of Women in Linguistics.

Such differences in policy are signals of the social and political outlook of editors and other influential professionals, who play important roles as gatekeepers in determining which forms they will adopt and thereby help sanction and spread. Editorial policies, however, affect for the most part only written language. In everyday conversation things may be otherwise. For example, although most US airlines have publicly replaced the term *stewardess* with *flight attendant*, as I was writing this chapter, I spoke with a young woman travel agent in the US who was still using the older term *stewardess*. British usage, both public and private, lags behind American usage in most respects. For example, in the British National Corpus of 100 million words of spoken and written British English launched in 1995 the female marked form *stewardess* occurred 92 times along with *air hostess* 51 times, while the neutral *flight attendant* occurred only 8 times and *cabin crew* 13 times. I have observed many flight attendants on British Airways flights wearing name tags identifying them as *stewardesses* or *stewards*.

Usage is still in flux and where choices exist, they are symbolic of different beliefs and political positions. Compare *When Ms Johnson was the chair(person)/(woman), she insisted that everyone pay their/his or her dues* with *When Miss Johnson was the chairman, she insisted that everyone pay his dues*. While a narrow linguistic analysis would say they mean the same thing and refer to the same state of affairs and person who happens to hold a particular position, choosing one over the others reveals approval or disapproval of, for example, feminism, language reform, political conservatism or liberalism, etc. The changes brought about in the pronoun system in response to feminist activism are actually remarkable considering that there have been virtually no major changes in the English pronouns since the Middle English period.

1.5   Conclusion: a remarkable success story?

Although McCrum, Cran & MacNeil (1986) refer rather uncritically to the spread of English as a 'remarkable success story', it has not been without many paradoxes and ironies. Robert Louis Stevenson drew attention to at least one of these when he observed that

> the race that has conquered so wide an empire has not yet managed to assimilate the islands whence she sprang. Ireland, Wales, and the Scottish mountains still cling, in part, to their Gaelic speech. It was but the other day that English triumphed in Cornwall, and they still show in Mousehole, on St. Michael's Bay, the house of the last Cornish-speaking woman.
> (cited in Treglown 1988: 163)

Most English speakers take the present position and status of English for granted. Most do not realise that English was very much itself once a minority language initially in all of the places where it has since become the mother tongue of millions. It has gained its present position by replacing the languages of indigenous groups such as the American Indian, the Celts and the Australian Aborigines, and now many more.

Another paradox in the spread of English is its designation as an official language only in the outer circle and not in the inner circle of so-called native-speaking countries. No government of the major Anglophone nations has ever felt the need to declare English as its official language because English has served effectively as a *de facto* rather than *de jure* official language. Nevertheless, as the demography of both Britain and the US are changing at the close of the twentieth century due to the entry of new immigrants, the prospect of English being declared official is being discussed. A group called US English has intensified its lobby for a constitutional amendment which would make English the official language of the United States. The English Language Act, already passed in California and other states, makes English the official language for public use. US English also seeks to repeal laws mandating multilingual ballots and voting materials. It welcomes members who agree that English is and must remain the only language of the people of the United States. A similar group in Canada called APEC (Alliance for the Preservation of English in Canada) has as its motto: 'One language unites, two divide.'

In Britain similar reactions occurred after a court case in 1988 involving a British man of Pakistani descent, who requested a Panjabi interpreter because he spoke limited English. The judge made taking English lessons a condition of the man's probation commenting that anyone who lived in Britain had a duty to understand the language. A community relations worker was quoted in the press as asking, 'Where does it say that somebody has to speak English to be a British citizen?' The answer is of course 'nowhere', but from the treatment of the case in the tabloid press it would appear that many people believe there should be a connection between language and citizenship (see Cameron & Bourne 1988: 152). While Welsh obtained legal status within Wales in 1967 through the Welsh Language Act, the newer languages of immigration like Panjabi etc. have no legal status.

While there seems to be no lack of confidence in exporting native models of English as a foreign language, it is at the same time almost paradoxical to find among all the major anglophone nations such enormous linguistic insecurity about standards of English usage. The complaint tradition stretching back to medieval times is intense on both sides of the Atlantic (see Romaine 1991 on its manifestations in Australia). Ferguson and Heath (1981: xxvii), for instance, comment on prescriptivism in the US that 'quite possibly no other nation buys so many style manuals and how-to-improve your language books in proportion to the population'. In 1989 Prince Charles angered British school teachers by complaining that his staff could not write or speak English properly. Around the same time the *Times Higher Education Supplement* carried a front page article in which several Oxford professors complained about the low standards of English used by students at Oxford University and suggested the possibility of introducing remedial instruction.

It will be the task of future generations of historians and linguists to decide what in retrospect was decisive and how much upheaval there was in what we think of today as the modern period. Here I have tried to take account not just of revolutions, but also of continuity.

FURTHER READING

I am not aware of any books which relate specifically to the external history of English during the period covered by this volume. The standard histories such as Baugh and Cable (1993) are, however, helpful, as are Dick Leith's *A Social History of English* (London: Routledge & Kegan Paul, 1983) and Richard W. Bailey's *Images of English* (Ann Arbor: University of Michigan Press, 1991).

2   VOCABULARY

John Algeo

Vocabulary is central to both the system and the use of language. Words are what are pronounced and written and organised into sentences and other grammatical combinations, being the fundamental units of meaning. Words are also what ordinary users think of as language, for they are accessible and reflect more fully the whole culture and respond more quickly to changes in society than do other aspects of language.

2.1   The study of the English vocabulary

Vocabulary study has a long history, going back in the Western world to Plato's *Cratylus*. The study of English vocabulary, however, received a sharp boost with the interest of members of the Philological Society in making a New English Dictionary, eventually renamed *The Oxford English Dictionary* (Murray, Bradley, Craigie & Onions 1884–1933). In the middle of the nineteenth century, Dean Trench (1851, 1855), who had been instrumental in beginning the *OED*, was a significant contributor to the field. *Caught in the Web of Words* (Murray 1977) traces the history of this major dictionary, and *Empire of Words* (Willinsky 1994) critically analyses its strengths and weaknesses.

The most important general English dictionary of the twentieth century is *Webster's Third New International Dictionary of the English Language*, edited by Philip Babcock Gove (1961). Its history has been traced by Herbert C. Morton (1994). The most important new specialised dictionary of the century is the *Dictionary of American English* (Cassidy and Hall 1985–). The history of English language lexicography before the period covered by this volume has been treated by Starnes and Noyes (1946), and that of American lexicography during the post-1775 period by Algeo (1990).

The study of slang has been of greater popular than scholarly interest. Noteworthy treatments of slang are, for British English, the revision of Eric Partridge's *Dictionary of Slang and Unconventional English* by Paul Beale (1984) and, for American English, the revision of Harold Wentworth and Stuart Berg Flexner's work under the title *New Dictionary of American Slang* by Robert L. Chapman (1986). The artificial and literary concoctions favoured by *Time* magazine from the mid 1920s to the mid 1960s have been recorded by George Thomas Kurian (1993); they are notable chiefly as examples of word play. The most important scholarly work ever done on the subject of slang is Jonathan Lighter's (1994–) *Random House Historical Dictionary of American Slang*.

A well-developed tradition of scholarship has treated general lexicology, for example, Jan Svartvik's (1996) *Words: Proceedings of an International Symposium*. Scholarly grammars often deal with word derivation (Jespersen 1942; Kruisinga 1932: 1–174; Quirk, Greenbaum, Leech & Svartvik 1985: 1515–85; Zandvoort 1969: 277–325). Specialised studies of English word derivation are those by Hans Marchand (1969) and Herbert Koziol (1972), which are diachronic in dating the forms they cite; by Valerie Adams (1973) and Laurie Bauer (1983), which do not date forms; and by Garland Cannon (1987), which deals with recent neologisms. The reverse dictionary of Martin Lehnert (1971, reviewed by Derolez 1972) is useful for locating examples of suffixed forms.

General issues are considered in a number of treatments (Matthews 1974; Pennanen 1972, 1982; Stein 1977). Bibliographies of the subject have been made by Richard K. Seymour (1968) and Gabriele Stein (1973). A useful index to earlier treatments of lexical items is the *Words and Phrases Index* (Wall & Przebienda 1969–70), whose four volumes index word forms treated in the main periodicals devoted to the subject (see also D. Barnhart 1994).

2.1.1 Derivation: historical and contemporary

A complication for vocabulary study is that its diachronic and synchronic facts are less distinct than those of other aspects of language, such as phonology and syntax. Many words are established in the language, learned as units, and repeated. We hear some words, such as *childishness* and *dog biscuit*, before we use them; and when we use such words we are pulling them as whole units out of our memory. Other words are produced spontaneously according to the lexical patterns of English and may be nonce forms or be frequently reinvented by speakers. The person who says *yuppishness* or *puppy biscuit* has not necessarily encountered these forms earlier, but may be inventing them at the moment of use. These two sorts of words – the established and the spontaneously produced – do not differ from each other in kind, and are not recognisably different in form.

In syntax, a fairly clear distinction exists between grammatical patterns or rules, which are established as the product of past history, and sentences, which are spontaneously produced as the expressions of current competence. In vocabulary, on the other hand, words are indifferently of either kind. As a consequence of the blurring of the diachronic–synchronic axis in vocabulary, lexicologists may use the same term, such as 'derivation', to refer to either the historical origin of a form or its current pattern of production. Yet the two do not always coincide.

An excellent, thorough overview of the history of the study of word origins is *Etymology* by Yakov Malkiel (1993). Not limited to English, it provides both a survey of the general subject and much information on etymological studies of English. Among widely used etymological dictionaries are those by C. T. Onions (1966), Ernest Klein (1966–7), and Robert Barnhart & Sol Steinmetz (1988).

2.1.2   A taxonomy of word origins

The taxonomy of word origins used here is based on that defined and exemplified by Algeo (1978, 1980) and is most similar to those used by Cannon (1987) and Barnhart and Barnhart (1982–). It pays particular attention to the relationship between a word and the sources from which it is constructed, its etyma. The primary factors are (1) whether a word has an etymon – is based on any earlier words; (2) whether the word omits any part of an etymon; (3) whether the word combines two or more etyma; and (4) whether any of its etyma are from a language other than English. The intersection of those four factors defines six major etymological or historically derivational classes, as follows:

1   Creations: words not based on other words. *Vroom*, imitative of the sound of a car moving at high speed, is a noun for such a sound or a verb for such movement (1965).

2   Shifts: words that neither combine nor shorten etyma. *Read*, as in 'a good read', has been shifted from verb to noun use (1825); and *weekend*, as in 'to weekend in the country', from noun to verb (1901).

3   Shortenings: words that omit part of their etyma. *Caff* is a shortening of *café* (1931), *PC* of *police constable* (before 1904), *telly* of

television (1940), and with changed part of speech, *burgle* of *burglar* (1872).

4   Composites: words that combine two or more etyma. *Tower block* is produced by compounding (1966), and *privatize* by affixation (1948).

5   Blends: words that combine two or more etyma and omit part of at least one. *Chunnel* blends two words, *channel* and *tunnel* (1928); and *brekker*, the word *breakfast* and the suffix *-er* (1889).

6   Loanwords or borrowings: words with at least one non-English etymon. *Courgette* is from French (1931), *zucchini* from Italian (1929), and *strudel* from German (1893); *spring roll* is a translation of a Chinese term for an egg roll (late 1960s).

Classes (2)–(5) are varieties of word-formation proper, words made from other words in the language, as in the *OED2* (1989, xxvii–xxviii), which also distinguishes between two processes of borrowing – adoption and adaptation. Adoption is said to be a popular process, borrowing words with minimum change, as *sima* (a geological term for 'the continuous basal layer of the earth's crust, composed of relatively heavy, basic rocks in silica and magnesia, that underlies the sialic continental masses and forms the crust under the oceans') was adopted from German (1909). Adaptation is said to be a learned process that alters the morphological shape of the borrowed word, as *snorkel* or *schnorkel* (an underwater breathing apparatus) was adapted from German *Schnorchel* (1944). The distinction between 'adoption' and 'adaptation' is a tenuous one and often, as in these two examples, correlates poorly with popular versus learned borrowing.

The *OED* also identifies some foreign words as 'alien', not yet naturalized in English. An example is *zori*, a Japanese term used in English for what are also called *thongs* or *flip-flops* – a sandal with a thong. Like the adoption–adaptation dichotomy, the naturalized–non-naturalized one is unclear, being based on variable factors such as the italicisation of foreign words. Both these oppositions are continuums rather than discrete categorisations. Loanwords range from those like *ngwee* (a unit of Zambian currency, 1966) with exotic spellings, pronunciations, morphology, and reference to those like *street* (a prehistorical loan from Latin, doubtless made before the Anglo-Saxon invasion of Britain) which few English speakers would think of as foreign.

In addition to the preceding major six classes, there are two others used by etymologists, which are types of incomplete etymology. They are (7) native developments, words that are phonological and semantic developments of earlier words in English and are therefore not traced to another origin (like *town*, which developed from Old English *tūn* 'an enclosed place') and (8) forms of unknown origin, words about whose earlier history we have insufficient information to make statements (like *nitty-gritty*, which appeared in 1961 with the spelling *knitty-gritty* but whose beginning is mysterious).

2.2   The growth of the vocabulary

Change that is on-going in present-day English is easiest to see in the vocabulary, although it certainly exists in all aspects of language (Barber 1964; Foster 1968). In recent times, intercommunication between the UK and the US and between each of those countries and the rest of the English-speaking world has been so extensive, with consequent mutual influence of the two varieties, that an international form of English has arisen. Local and national accents remain highly distinctive, and to a small extent national grammatical differences can be identified. In vocabulary, there are national words little known elsewhere, and sometimes not even throughout the country to which they are native, for example, British *bap* 'a bread roll used for sandwiches' and American *poor boy* 'a sandwich made on a long roll of bread'. By and large, however, the vocabulary of the English-speaking world is so intertwined that it must be treated as a fundamental unity, with only marginal national variation.

2.2.1   *The size of the vocabulary*

The English vocabulary has grown much in size since 1776. Exactly how much is difficult to say even approximately because there are no accurate counts of the number of words used in English either in 1776 or today. Estimates of the size of the vocabulary based upon dictionaries are flawed by the highly selective contents of all word books. There are said to be about 616,500 forms in the second edition of *The Oxford English Dictionary* (1: xxiii). Yet it records chiefly literary vocabulary and primarily the English of England. It represents only spottily folk language, recent neologisms, colloquialisms, technical terms, and national varieties of the language other than English as spoken in England.

A complete list of present-day English words would be impossible to make; but if we had an approximation, it would surely be many times longer than the 616,500 forms of the *OED*; indeed, it is potentially unlimited in size. In thinking of the size of the English vocabulary, we must be clear about what kind of vocabulary we have in mind: the words used by almost every English speaker, the words used by an average person, the words understood by an average person, all the words used by any English speaker, all possible words, whether actually attested or not, the words most often used by many persons, and so on.

Those various vocabularies differ not only in size but also in character. One count (Finkenstaedt, Leisi & Wolff 1970) indicates that only about 5.4 per cent of the words in a dictionary are descended from Old English, whereas another (Neuhaus 1971: 39–40) indicates that, in a running text from newspapers, 74.5 per cent of the words derive from Old English. Clearly, the nature of the often used vocabulary is different from that of seldom used words.

2.2.2 Word frequency

The frequency with which words are used has implications as a practical matter in stylistics, for example in setting an appropriate reading level for school books.

The word frequencies in two standard corpuses of English, the Brown Corpus for American and the LOB Corpus for British, are reported by Hofland and Johansson (1982). In the LOB Corpus, the 100 most frequent words are, with only 8 exceptions, grammatical words. The 10 most frequent words in that corpus are *the, of, and, to, a, in, that, is, was, it*. The 8 non-grammatical words among the 100 most frequent are *said, time, Mr, made, new, man, years, people*. The analysis made by Hofland and Johansson (1982) was of word shapes; so for example, *say, says, saying, said* were each counted as separate words, whereas *time* the noun and *time* the verb were counted as the same word. A subtler analysis appears in Johansson and Hofland (1989), which deals with the LOB Corpus only, but analyses a tagged version distinguishing various classes of words. That analysis presents the frequencies of word shapes and also of forms belonging to different word classes. In addition, it gives frequencies of typical combinations of words and of word classes.

Magnus Ljung (1974) has made a study of the frequency of morphemes to be found in a list (Thorén 1959) adapted from the 8,000 most frequent words in the Thorndike–Lorge (1959) list. The last was compiled to show word frequencies for pedagogical use.

2.2.3 Gauging changes in the size of the vocabulary

Given such fluctuation in what we mean by the 'vocabulary' of English and the problems in counting it, any estimate of its increase in size since 1776 must be viewed sceptically. Yet it seems certain that the vocabulary has increased significantly. In a sample of words from the *OED* (the first shape or sense on each page of volume 1), 393 of 1,019 are first attested after 1776. Those figures suggest that the pre-1776 vocabulary (626 words in the sample) has increased by 63 per cent, but are suspect because of the selectivity of the *OED* and the sample.

The most convenient source for estimating an increase in the size of the English vocabulary is the *Chronological English Dictionary* (Finkenstaedt, Leisi & Wolff 1970; reviewed by Derolez 1972, also 1975). However, that work must be used with caution because it is based on *The Shorter Oxford English Dictionary*, a selection from the *OED*, and the latter is not reliable for the earliest dates of use of words, although it is the best record we have. Of the 80,506 dated words the *CED* covers, 5.4 per cent originated in Old English, 18.9 per cent in Middle English, and 75.7 per cent in Modern English. Of the latter, about one-third originated after 1776 (a 34 per cent increase over pre-1776 vocabulary).

An indication of the caution with which such figures must be viewed, however, is the fact that the *Chronological English Dictionary* also indicates that of the words originating after 1776, 51 per cent were coined in the mid-nineteenth century (1826–75) and only 4 per cent in the early twentieth century (1901–50). Clearly what those figures show is not the growth of the vocabulary, but the extent of the lexicographer's sources. Such a caution is applicable to almost all statistical conclusions based on *OED* materials. Nevertheless, it seems intuitively obvious that the English vocabulary has grown and continues to do so. Objective support for that obvious intuition runs into problems of documentation, continuity, and identification.

2.2.3.1 Documentation.

The problem of documentation is to find strong evidence for the origin of a word. Our major source for such documentation is the *OED*. However, the evidence of the *OED* has to be used cautiously because we know that its earliest date of attestation is frequently not the earliest documentable use of a word. The sources drawn upon by the *OED* are not evenly distributed across the centuries. The *OED* is biased in favour of literature and particularly of canonically enshrined authors. Moreover, inescapably the *OED*'s readers were inconsistent in the thoroughness with which they gathered citations.

The improved availability of scholarly sources (editions, bibliographies, indexes, concordances, and the like) since the work on the *OED* was done enables us to see how much was missed by the compilers of that great dictionary and how cautious we must be in drawing conclusions from it (Schäfer 1980). We are now aware that the *OED*'s datings are often inadequate by several decades or even more than a century. Thus, the adjectival *abominate* is first documented in the *OED* from 1850; but it was used at least as early as 1594 (Bailey 1978: 1). As electronic texts become more available, it will be feasible to estimate more accurately how cautious we need to be in using the *OED*'s evidence, and it will become easier to correct that evidence.

Several estimates of the rate of growth of the English vocabulary have been based on *The Shorter Oxford English Dictionary*, 1968 edition. There are, however, two problems with using that work as a basis for study. First, the principles on which it was abridged from the *OED* parent work are not clear; and second, the text of the parent work itself is seriously flawed, in the ways suggested above.

In particular, excerpting of eighteenth-century books for the *OED* was to have been done in America, but citation slips for that century did not reach Murray, and so, despite efforts to cover the period, it is seriously under-represented in the *OED*. Comments upon the growth of the English vocabulary based (as they generally are) on *OED* evidence, often through the medium of the *Shorter OED*, show a significant decline in the production of new words in the eighteenth century (Finkenstaedt & Wolff 1973: 29; Neuhaus 1971: 31). The temptation is to explain that decline as a consequence of the conservative temperament of the Age of Reason, a neat instance of the effect of world view on language. In fact, what the 'decline' almost certainly shows is lack of evidence due to uneven gatherings of citations. It is a fact, not about the language of the mid-eighteenth century, but about the vicissitudes of lexicography in the late nineteenth.

The neat and impressive-looking line graphs that have been drawn to show the peaking of word-making in the vigorous, language-intoxicated high Renaissance, its deep valley of decline in the eighteenth century, and its subsequent rise to a new, if lesser, high in the mid-nineteenth century show nothing about the language. What they show is the extent and assiduousness with which the *OED* volunteers read and excerpted books. Shakespeare was over-read; the eighteenth century under-read – that is what the graphs show. We have no reliable data on which to base generalisations about the growth of the English vocabulary. To get such data we need, not a computerisation of the faulty *OED* sampling, but a wholly new approach.

2.2.3.2   Continuity

The problem of continuity is a more difficult and generally an unsolvable one. After a word is coined in English, we usually assume that all later instances of the word derive from the initial coinage. But clearly there is no reason why that should be the case for many words. A word may be independently reborrowed or reformed many times.

For example, *cosmos* 'the world' was used by Orm in the spelling *cossmos* about 1200 and identified as of Greek origin in the *Middle English Dictionary* (Kurath & Kuhn 1954–   ). The first citation of the word in the *OED* is from 1650: 'As the greater World is called Cosmus from the beauty thereof', with the reference to 'beauty' echoing the Greek sense 'world, order, beauty' despite the Latinate form of the ending. The next citation is from an 1848 translation from German of *Humboldt's Cosmos*. Thereafter, the *OED* has citations illustrating several closely related senses from 1858, 1865, 1869, 1872, 1874, 1882, and 1885. This evidence suggests that *cosmos* has been borrowed into English at least three times, twice (1200 and 1650) from Greek or Latin, and once (1848) from German.

The lack of evidence for continued use of *cosmos* between 1200 and 1650 and between 1650 and 1848 suggests that the two earlier borrowings were abortive; present-day use of *cosmos* begins with its 1848 borrowing from German. The *OED*'s 1865 citation, however, has the spelling *Kosmos* and refers to the Pythagorean concept of numerical order; it is at least influenced by Greek directly and may be another independent borrowing. It appears that the word in contemporary use is not descended from an early Middle English borrowing from Greek, but from a late Modern borrowing from German reinforced by Greek.

2.2.3.3   Identification

The Latinate vocabulary is a particular problem for both analysis and etymology. English has borrowed so many Graeco-Latin words that it has imported much of the morphemic and morphophonemic patterning of those languages, thereby creating difficulties in analysing English morphemically (Ellegård 1963) and also in identifying the etymology of new classically based words.

Because the Graeco-Latin vocabulary has been influential also on other European languages and is the basis for much scientific terminology, it is often difficult to be sure of the origin of a particular new word formed from ultimate Graeco-Latin sources. Without detailed knowledge of its history, we cannot predict the origin of a word like *haploid*. *American Heritage* (1969) derives it from Greek *haploeidēs*; *World Book* (1988) derives it from

Greek *haplous* and English *-oid*; *Random House* (Flexner 1987) and *Webster's New World* (Neufeldt 1988) derive it from the English formatives *haplo-* and *-oid*; *The Oxford English Dictionary Supplement* (*OEDS*) derives it from German *haploid*. The ultimate Greek source is not in doubt, but the immediate English source is a matter of disagreement.

To meet this problem, the editors of *Webster's Third* (1961: 7a) coined the etymological label 'ISV' for 'International Scientific Vocabulary', that is, words of uncertain origin used in several languages. A comparable label was used in the *OED* (1989: xxviii): 'mod. f.' standing for 'modern formation'. These labels avoid a misstatement when exact information is lacking, but they are an acknowledgement of ignorance rather than an etymology.

2.3   Creating as a source of new words

Words that are coinages *ex nihilo* are extremely rare, if they exist at all. Words that seem to be of that type are usually words about whose history we merely have insufficient information.

An apparent exception to that generalisation is the use of computer-generated trade names, but that exception is more apparent than real. When a new name for a product is sought from a computer program, the candidates are unlikely to be randomly generated stings of letters. Instead the computer has been programmed to produce only certain patterns of letters (CVCVC, CVCCVC, etc.) and certain final sequences are prominent in the trade names selected from such lists: *-an, -ar, -el, -ex, -on*. It seems clear that the human beings who make the final selection from computer-generated lists are guided by associations in choosing a trade name. For example, even if, as reported (Praninskas 1968: 14), *Teflon* was a computer-generated name, the last part of it clearly echoes *nylon*, and the first part is consonant with *tough*, suggesting a tough, smooth surface. Such considerations are very likely to have entered into the choice of the name, which is to that extent not a pure creation.

Echoic or onomatopoeic words are a type of creation, for example, *burp, buzz, fizz, plop, zap, zip*. However, they are not pure imitations of sounds, since there are clearly conventions of imitation, and certain sounds, such as /z/ in several of the preceding examples, acquire the value of phonesthemes.

2.4   Shifting as a source of new words

Shifting may be of shape, grammar, semantics, or pragmatics.

2.4.1 Shift of shapes

Shape shifting is illustrated by the back slang *yob* from *boy*. It is a minor kind of shifting that involves neither loss nor addition, but alteration of the spelling or pronunciation of a form.

2.4.2 Grammatical shifts

English has great freedom of shifting forms from one part of speech to another. Because of the sparse morphological marking for parts of speech, almost any English word can be used as a noun, verb, or adjective-like attributive. Nonce uses are frequent, and so are established shifts.

In nonce shifts, for example of nouns to verbs (Clark & Clark 1979), the meaning of the nonce verb derives from that of the underlying noun and the context – both the immediate lexical context and the broad non-linguistic context that we call cultural knowledge. Thus, the meaning of *porch* in *to porch a newspaper* 'to deliver by throwing into the porch of a house' depends on the noun sense of *porch*, the co-occurrence with *newspaper*, and familiarity with the fact that newspapers are in some locations brought to a private house by deliverers who throw them onto the porch.

In one examination of over 8,700 converted forms (Biese 1941) the chronological distribution of the forms by percentage was as follows:

to 14c	15c	16c	17c	18c	19c
.16	.09	.20	.20	.11	.26

Except for a dip in the eighteenth century, which is probably explained by the gap in the *OED*'s resources, Modern English has a fairly consistent rate of shifted parts of speech, with some increase in more recent times.

A type of grammatical shift that has become more important in recent times is the use of a trade name as a generic. *Escalator* began as a proprietary name, but has long since ceased to be so. The second half of *Coca-Cola* likewise has become generic; the company is fighting to prevent its nickname from the first half, *coke*, from following suit. *Ziploc* (1970), a brand name for a plastic bag that fastens by sealing two interlocking strips, has become generic under the respelling *ziplock* (1982). Other trade names that are often used generically but still maintain legal status as proprietary names are *Band-Aid* (a US term for an adhesive plaster), *Biro* (a UK term for a ball-point pen), *Cellophane*, *Filofax* (a UK loose-leaf record book), *Polaroid*, US *Scotch tape* and its UK counterpart *Sellotape*. *Teflon* is likely to win out over the non-proprietary term *polytetrafluoroethylene*; it already has metaphorical use in the political term *teflon-coated* 'possessing an ability to escape the consequences of one's actions'. *Hoover* is used generically only in the UK, even though the trade name was US in origin; it and *Xerox* have further shifted into verb use.

Another highly productive type of shift in modern times is the conversion of a verb-particle combination into a noun (Lindelöf 1938, from whom the following dated examples are taken): *show-off* (1776), *cut-up* (1782), *stand-by* (1796), *knock-out* (1818), *take-off* (1826), *sit-down* (1836), *turn-back* (1847), *stick-up* (1857), *clean-up* (1866), *pull-over* (1875), *go-round* (1886), *rub-down* (1896), *play-off* (1906), *fly-past* (1914), and *check-up* (1924). The 520 nouns converted from verb–particle combinations examined by Lindelöf were chronologically distributed by percentage as follows:

to 15c	16c	17c	18c	19c	20c
0.1	.05	.05	.07	.50	.33

Lindelöf's twentieth-century examples were limited mainly to the first third of the century. If we assume that the rate of new forms remains constant through the rest of the century, the twentieth century would account for about 60 per cent of the new total, and the nineteenth century for 30 per cent. These figures suggest strongly that this type of conversion has increased strikingly in frequency in recent times.

Lindelöf (1938: 39) observed that combinations originating in America comprised 6 per cent of the eighteenth-century examples, 17 per cent of those from the first half of the nineteenth century, 33 per cent of those from the second half of the nineteenth century, and about 39 per cent of early twentieth-century ones. He concluded:

> And there is one thing which has struck me more and more while collecting and arranging my examples, namely the very prominent part which the language of America seems to play in the creation of words of our type.

This conclusion is in keeping with a widespread but largely unsubstantiated belief that American English is more innovative than British. If we suppose that the number of innovations in a language may be partly correlated with the number of persons speaking it, the increasing size of the American population might strike us as suggesting that American innovations ought to be more numerous than they have been. Such a comparison might suggest that British English is actually more innovative than American.

2.4.3 Semantic shifts

Semantic shifting is one of the commonest types of change in language, although describing it is difficult. It is often a problem to decide whether a particular use of a word should be called a new sense or its distinct meaning attributed to the context. In addition, semantic categories are often overlapping and fuzzy. Because the semantic dimension of language is treated only incidentally in this chapter, the various types of semantic shift will not be dealt with in detail. They include, however, the following:

1. Referential shift, a change in the realia that are the referents of a term, with a consequent change in the term's meaning. The technology of printing has developed from hand presses through offset to laser; as a result the reference and sense of the verb *to print* has changed.

2. Generalisation, an expansion in the range of a term's referents. *Chap* (a shortening of *chapman*) earlier meant 'a customer' but has generalised its meaning to include any person.

3. Specialisation, a contraction in the range of a term's referents. *Frock* was once a term for the garment of a monk or clergyman (hence the related verb *to unfrock*); it generalised to various outer garments and then specialised to a woman's dress.

4. Abstraction, a shift in a term's referent to something less concrete. *Zest* denoted orange or lemon peel used for flavouring, but became the more abstract 'gusto'.

5. Concretion, a shift in a term's referent to something less abstract. *Complexion* meant a combination of the qualities (hot, cold, wet, dry) but came eventually to denote the condition of facial skin.

6. Metaphor. *Kite* was a term for a bird of prey before it was used for a toy that hovers in the air like the bird.

7. Metonymy. *Tin* was the name of a metal before it was used for a container made of that metal.

8. Clang association, the acquisition by one term of the meaning of another term which it resembles in sound. *Fruition* meant 'enjoyment, pleasure' before its association with *fruit* developed the sense 'fulfilment, realisation'.

9. Hyperbole. *Horrific* has the literal sense of 'causing horror' but is used as a colloquial and journalistic exaggeration to mean no more than 'evoking indignation, distaste, or sympathy at misfortune; severe, grave'.

10   Litotes. Strictly referring to the negation of an opposite (*not bad* for 'good'), this term is sometimes extended to any instance of understatement or even euphemism, such as *terminate* 'kill'.

11   Amelioration. *Guy* (from *Guy Fawkes*) in the nineteenth century meant 'a person of grotesque appearance' but in current American use denotes any person, being the equivalent of British *chap, bloke,* or *lad.*

12   Pejoration. *Lady*, early a term for a woman head of a household, the Anglo-Saxon term for a queen, or an epithet of the Virgin Mary, is now often used condescendingly ('the little lady', 'the ladies, God bless 'em') and is therefore rejected by many feminists.

2.4.4   *Pragmatic shifts*

Pragmatics here denotes the relationship between an expression and its users, also called *usage*. Pragmatic or usage shifts are of several kinds:

1   A change in the level of formality of use. Beginning as a fairly formal word with the sense 'guide, ruler', *governor* came in the nineteenth century to be used as a highly colloquial term of address for any socially superior man (often represented as *gov'ner*).

2   A change in a word's acceptability. *Bloody* was once a strongly tabooed word, of whose use as an intensifier the *OED*1 remarked, 'now constantly in the mouths of the lowest classes, but by respectable people considered "a horrid word", on a par with obscene or profane language'. G. B. Shaw's use of the word in *Pygmalion* was intended to be sensational and is said to have achieved that effect at the play's opening. Though still highly colloquial, the word is no longer limited to the 'lowest classes' but is found among even quite 'respectable people'. Conversely, a term like *nigger*, which was once unself-consciously used by 'respectable people', is now unacceptable in polite society. Linguistic taboo has shifted from sex, elimination, and sacrilege to race and ethnicity.

3   A change in geographical limitation, either between regional and standard national use or between national varieties. The Scottish term *bap* for a bread roll has passed into mainstream standard British use. The British term *fridge* is now widely used by younger Americans with no sense that it is foreign.

4   A change in the historical status of a word. The term *ash* for a letter of the runic alphabet is attested in Anglo-Saxon times but became obsolete until it was revived as a name for the runic letter (1840)

and later by extension as a name for the Old English digraph æ (1955). It is now also used for the phonetic sound represented in the IPA by the digraph, though that sense is not in the *OED*.

The type of pragmatic shift that has received the greatest amount of popular attention, though less scholarly investigation, is usage variation, that is, fluctuation in the acceptability of a form. An informative, historically oriented handbook on usage is *Webster's Dictionary of English Usage* (Gilman 1989). It documents, for example, fluctuations in the reputation of *like* as a conjunction and summarises the history (p. 602):

> Its beginnings [about 1380 in *Cleanness*] are literary, but the available evidence shows that it was fairly rare until the 19th century. A noticeable increase in use during the 19th century provoked the censure we are so familiar with. Still, the usage has never been less than standard, even if primarily spoken.

2.5 Shortening as a source of new words

Shortening includes a variety of processes: abbreviation, alphabetism, acronymy, elision, clipping, ellipsis, and backformation.

2.5.1 Simple shortenings

The first six of these types of shortening reduce the length of a form without altering its meaning.

1   An abbreviation (as the term is used here) is a written shortening that is pronounced like the long form, as *N.Engl.* represents 'North of England' in some dictionaries.

The terms *acronym, alphabetism,* and *initialism* are used for a number of related types of shortening (Algeo 1975), of which it is useful to recognise two main varieties (2) and (3).

2   An expression may be shortened to a sequence of letters pronounced as their names, as *FM* 'frequency modulation' is pronounced 'eff em'. Special letter names, such as those of the signal alphabet, are sometimes used, as in *ack ack* for *AA* (anti-aircraft), in this case with an onomatopoetic effect. The letters are not necessarily the initials of separate words or even morphemes: *TV* from *television* and American *PJs* or *peejays* from *pyjamas*. Some forms have the appearance of shortenings, but are

really alphabetical rebuses: *IOU* for 'I owe you' and *L-train* for 'el(evated) train'.

3   Other shortenings are sequences of letters, typically the initial letters of several words, pronounced according to normal orthoepical principles: *aids* 'acquired immune deficiency syndrome'. Some forms mix the two kinds of pronunciation: *Beeb* from *BBC*, with clipping of the final *C*, and *posslq* (pronounced /'pɑsəlkju:/) from *person of opposite sex sharing living quarters*. A vowel may be inserted to facilitate pronunciation, as in the last example and also in *Wrens* from *WRNS* (Women's Royal Naval Service), with a singular *Wren* by backformation and doubtless a pun on the bird (alluding to *bird* as a slang term for a woman). Acronymous words are sometimes formed so that their letters spell out a word of appropriate meaning: *possum* is a term for an electronic device enabling a paralysed person to operate machines like telephones and typewriters; it is from *POSM* for *patient operated selector mechanism*, with a pun on the Latin verb meaning 'I am able'.

4   An elision is the omission of a sound for phonological reasons, such as aphesis, syncope, or assimilation: *'cause* (also spelled *'cos, cos, coz*) from *because*; fo'c'sle from *forecastle*; or *ice tea* from *iced tea* (in which *-ed* is pronounced /t/ but omitted because of the immediately following /t/).

5   A clipping is a shortening of a spoken or written form, either at a morpheme boundary or between such boundaries, as *curio* was clipped from *curiosity* or *bumf* from *bum fodder*.

6   An ellipsis (as the term is used here) is the omission of a word or words from a compound or phrase, as *television* in 'She bought a new television' is a clipping from *television set*.

2.5.2   Backformation

Backformation is a form of shortening in which the omitted material is or is perceived to be a formative, typically an affix. Its omission produces a new form with a meaning related to but distinct from that of the etymon. Backformation has been a surprisingly productive source of new words (Pennanen 1966, from whom the following examples and dates are taken).

Verbs are the part of speech most often backformed, and the etymon is often an agent noun in *-er*: *swindle* (1782), *edit* (1793), *commentate* (1818), *shoplift* (1820), *bushwhack* (1834), *housekeep* (1842), *scavage* (1851), *sculpt* (1864), *play-act* (1872), *typewrite* (1887), *barn-storm* (1896), *panhandle* (1904), *sleep-walk* (1923), *proof-read* (1934), *divebomb* (1944), *name-drop* (1960).

Other verbs are formed from action nouns, many with the suffixes *-ion* or *-ation* and *-ing*, but also a variety of others: *donate* (1785), *demarcate* (1816), *enthuse* (1827), *jell* (1830), *daydream* (1845), *coeducate* (1855), *extradite* (1864), *proliferate* (1873), *tongue-lash* (1887), *dry-clean* (1899), *backfire* (1906), *backform* (1913), *psychoanalyse* (1923), *window-shop* (1934), *air-condition* (1942), *automate* (1954).

Some verbs are formed from adjectives, especially participial adjectives in *-ed*: *sulk* (1781), *ill-treat* (1794), *isolate* (1807), *handpick* (1831), *ill-use* (1841), *jerry-build* (1885), *streamline* (1927), *mass-produce* (1940), *bottle-feed* (1957).

Nouns are also backformed from adjectives: *megalith* (1853), *yid* (1890), *metronym* (1904), *highbrow* (1911), *snoot* (1930), *peeve* (1952); and from other nouns: *letch* (1796), *prize-fight* (1824), *homoeopath* (1830), *lithograph* (1839), *palmist* (1886), *osteopath* (1897), *telepath* (1907). Occasionally, an adjective is formed from a noun: *gullible* (1825).

The 793 backformations examined by Esko Pennanen (1966) were chronologically distributed by percentage as follows:

to 15c	16c	17c	18c	19c	20c
.04	.09	.14	.09	.35	.29

The apparent decline in the eighteenth century is probably due, as in other instances, to inadequate data from that period. The twentieth-century evidence was primarily from the first half of the century only. With corrections made for those factors, the evidence strongly suggests a rise in productivity of backformation. Pennanen (1966: 150) also commented on the relative productiveness of British and American English in backforming new words:

> Although the coining of back-formations is at present mainly carried on in America on the various levels of spoken and written usage, it should be emphasized that the difference here is one of degree only. This means that the same experimental and creative impulses are inherent in British English as well, even if they are controlled with greater reserve and moderation in Britain than in the U.S.

Such comments are not unusual in Continental studies of change in the English language. Even if lexical innovation is more frequent in American than in British English (a generalisation for which there is little objective support), the characterisation of American as less controlled and of British as reserved and moderate is part of a wider stereotyping of the two cultures by Europeans.

2.6   Composing as a source of new words

The language of the Anglo-Saxons relied most heavily on compounding and affixing to produce new words. And so does the English of the end of the twentieth century. English now has an abundance of new formatives borrowed from Latin and French to combine into new words, but the basic process of combining them has not changed. Compounding and affixation have probably always been the most productive processes of word derivation in English. Because they are productive, they are in some ways grammatical rather than lexical phenomena.

2.6.1   *Compounding*

Compounding in particular is on the borderline between lexis and grammar – part vocabulary and part syntax. Copulative or dvandva (Sanskrit 'two-two') compounds of the types *goody-goody, secretary-treasurer,* and *Anglo-American* (Hatcher 1951) can be so freely made that they might be considered syntactic constructions formed by grammatical rules. Other kinds of compounds, however, exhibit a wide variety of semantic relationships between their elements.

Two common types were named by Sanskrit grammarians: tatpurusha ('his servant') and bahuvrihi ('[having] much rice'), both terms being examples of the sort of compound they name. Each consists of a modifier and a noun, but they differ in the way they relate to their referents. A tatpurusha compound is endocentric, that is, the noun in the compound refers to the referent that the whole compound denotes: *airlink* is a link by air and *black-board* is a board that is black (or at least was so originally). On the other hand, a bahuvrihi compound is exocentric, that is, the noun in the compound has a different referent from the compound itself: *blockhead* is someone who has a head that is a block and *high-potency* describes something that is high in potency. In both types, the possible semantic relationships between the two parts of the compound are exceedingly varied, so syntactic rules to predict them and semantic rules to interpret them are difficult to frame, although efforts to do so have been made (Lees 1960; Levi 1978; Warren 1978).

It has been said that the aspiration of the grammarian is to reduce all language to grammar – that is, to write rules for everything. Efforts to incorporate word formation into syntax or to write separate rules for the lexicon, whether for English or universal grammar, aspire to that end (Chapin 1967; Ljung 1970; Meys 1975; Aronoff 1976; Lieber 1981).

However, experiments involving the creation and interpretation of novel compounds consisting of two nouns led Pamela Downing (1977: 840–1) to conclude that 'attempts to characterise compounds as derived from a limited set of [sentential] structures can only be considered misguided. A paraphrase relationship need not imply a derivational one.'

Although nouns are the part of speech most often compounded, other parts may also be. A variety of compound adjective puts a noun before the adjective, as in *ice-cold*. In these compounds the adjective is frequently a sensory word (a colour or other term such as *cold, sharp, soft, sweet*) or an expression of deprivation (*blind, dead, deaf, drunk, mad, naked*), although others also occur. The noun serves as an intensifier. The pattern is ancient (*ice-cold* in Old English *is-calde*) but is still productive: *dirt-cheap* (1821), *stone-broke* (1886), *razor-sharp* (1921), *razor-thin* (1971). In the preceding examples, the semantic relationship is 'as X as Y' (as cheap as dirt), but other relationships occur in the pattern. *Bone-tired* (1825) is not 'as tired as a bone' but rather 'tired all the way into the bones'.

A poorly documented kind of compounding is reduplication (Thun 1963). Three main varieties can be recognised. Identical reduplications are the least frequent: *tum-tum* (1864), *goody-goody* (1871), *lulu* (1886), *hush-hush* (1916). Consonantal (or ablaut) reduplications are more frequent: *hee-haw* (1815), *wiggle-waggle* (1825), *tick-tock* (1848), *flip-flop* (1902, after a nonce use in 1661). Rhyming reduplications are the most frequent: *rumble-tumble* (1801), *ragtag* (1820 in *ragtag and bobtail*), *chock-a-block* (1840), *honky-tonk* (1894), *heebie-jeebies* (1923). As the last three examples show, there may be a linking or extending syllable after either element.

English also has several devices for freely creating reduplicating compounds. A variety of babytalk is illustrated by *doggy-woggy* and *fuzzy-wuzzy*, and Yiddish-English makes forms like *fear-shmear, courage-shmourage*. They are each an open set of true reduplications. Such playful devices are doubtless of some antiquity, but because their products are seldom recorded, we have scant documentation for their age.

2.6.2 Affixing

Affixation is also in some respects a lexis/grammar borderline phenomenon (Hirtle 1970; Hudson 1975; Ljung 1976). It is also an area of word formation particularly susceptible to vogues and oddities of use, such as the several senses of *non-* (Algeo 1971), interposing as in *in-damn-defensible* (McMillan 1980), and the *-ers* suffix in *bonkers, champers, congratters, crackers, honkers, jabbers, jeepers, lumpers, preggers, starkers* (Stein 1984). Even apparently simple affixes, such as the adjective-forming *-ed*, may have great complexities of use and history (Hirtle 1969; Hudson 1975; Beard 1976; Ljung 1976).

A study (Ljung 1970) of derivational suffixes in the Thorén (1959) word list found 199 suffixes, of which 135 are noun-forming, 52 adjective-forming, and 12 verb-forming. The eight most frequent denominal adjective suffixes, in order of frequency, were *-y, -al, -ful, -ous, -less, -ly, -ic, -ish*.

The boundary between compounding, affixing, and other forms of word derivation is sometimes unclear. *Para-* in forms like *paratroops* and *paramedic* 'medical corpsman in a parachute unit' represents *parachute*, not merely the older affix. *Tele-* in *telecamera, telecast, telecommunication, teleconference,* and *telecourse* represents *television* or *telephone*, not merely the affix meaning 'distant'. Such cases might be described as new meanings of the affixes *para-* and *tele-*, new combining forms of the nouns *parachute* and *television*, or even blends of the nouns (*telecamera= television+ camera*). Similarly, *Watergate*, the name of a building that was the site of a covert operation leading to a political cover-up and scandal, has become the source of a new combining form, *-gate*, denoting a scandalous cover-up; and *-holic* in *workaholic* and *chocoholic* is used in the sense 'one who is inordinately fond of'.

2.7   Blending as a source of new words

Blending, the combination of two (or more) etyma with omission of part of at least one etymon, is a minor, although fashionable technique for forming new words (Pound 1914; Algeo 1977). Its most obvious form is the portmanteau, which may involve the overlapping of sounds (*motel* from *motor* and *hotel*), the overlapping of letters (*smog* from *smoke* and *fog*), or no overlapping of any kind (*brunch* and *Oxbridge*).

Folk etymology and other forms of semantic crossing due to clang association are also a kind of blending, as *buxom* in the recent sense 'busty' blends the form *buxom* (whose earlier meaning was 'obedient') with the sense of *bosom*.

Blending is not limited to the combination of two specific etyma, but can also in the case of phonesthemes involve whole sets of words. Thus *bash* combines the first consonant of words like *bang, bump, blow* with the rhyme of *crash, dash, smash*; similarly, *bonk* combines the same first consonant with the rime of *conk*.

2.8   Borrowing as a source of new words

Even if borrowing has recently become less important as a source for new English words than formerly, it is still noteworthy. Unfortunately, the most comprehensive study of borrowing in English, *A History of Foreign Words in English* by Mary S. Serjeantson (1935), is now far out of date. Loanwords include a number of types (Haugen 1950; Carstensen 1968), such as the following:

1   Foreign words, which have been imperfectly assimilated into the English system in pronunciation, spelling, morphology, semantics, or otherwise (*faute de mieux*).

2   Loanwords, taken into English with no more than sound-substitution for foreign sounds, transliteration of the spelling, or an adjustment of inflectional morphology (*glasnost* from Russian, *honcho* from Japanese, *schlep* from Yiddish).

3   Loan translations, substitutions of native morphemes for foreign ones motivated by similarity of meaning (*house of tolerance* from French *maison de tolérance*).

4   Hybrid compounds, a borrowing of a complex form with loan translation for part of it (*coffee klatsch* from German *Kaffeeklatsch*).

5   Semantic loans, substitutions of foreign meanings for those of native morphemes motivated by a similarity of shape, in effect a type of loanword folk etymology (*mogul* 'a mound on a ski slope' from Norwegian *muge* with interference from English *mogul* 'prominent person').

6   Innovative borrowing, that is, a compound made of foreign elements which does not, however, occur as a compound in the source language (*bierkeller* 'a German-style beer hall', suggested by German *Biergarten* and *Ratskeller*).

7   Loan clipping (*femt(o)-* 'one quadrillionth, i.e. 10^{-15}, of any unit in the international system of measurement' from Danish or Norwegian *femten* 'fifteen').

2.8.1   Sources of loanwords

Several efforts have been made to assess the relative importance of various languages as sources for borrowing in present-day English. Garland Cannon (1987: 69–97) has described the first three of the following corpuses, totalling 1,262 loanwords; the fourth is of the loanwords entered in *The Barnhart Dictionary Companion*, volumes 1–4:

1   407 loanwords from *The Barnhart Dictionary of New English since 1963* (Barnhart, Steinmetz & Barnhart 1973).

2   332 loanwords from *The Second Barnhart Dictionary of New English* (Barnhart, Steinmetz & Barnhart 1980).

3   523 loanwords from the 1981 addenda to *Webster's Third* (1961).

4 166 loanwords, including 22 loan translations, listed in *The Barnhart Dictionary Companion Index* (D. Barnhart 1987, 53–4).

These corpuses, which are modest in size, report loanwords from a period of approximately 25 years (1963–88). The languages (or in some cases, geographical areas) from which they record borrowing and the percentage of loanwords for each language (or area) within each corpus are as follows. The ranking is an average of the four corpuses:

	(1) BDNE	(2) BDNE2	(3) 81W3	(4) BDC	Rank
French	31.4	17.5	21.2	12.0	1
Spanish	6.6	10.8	6.1	12.7	2
Russian	3.4	5.4	2.1	24.1	3
Japanese	7.9	9.3	6.3	9.0	4
African	6.1	7.2	6.7	3.0	5
Italian	4.7	4.5	10.7	2.4	6
German	5.9	5.4	4.8	5.4	7
Greek	6.9	4.8	8.0	1.2	8
Latin	5.2	5.1	9.4		9
Yiddish	5.7	2.7	5.0	3.6	10
Arabic	2.0	3.9	1.7	6.0	11
Chinese	1.7	4.2	3.6	6.0	12
Portuguese	1.0	2.7	1.0	1.8	13
Hindi	2.2	0.9	0.2	2.4	14
Hebrew	0.7	1.5	0.4	1.2	15
Sanskrit	1.7	1.2	0.8		16
Persian	0.2	1.2		1.8	17
Afrikaans	0.5	1.5	0.4		18
Dutch	0.2	0.3		1.8	19
Indonesian	0.2	0.3	0.8	1.2	20
Malayo-Polynesian		2.1	0.2		21
Norwegian	0.2		1.5	0.6	22
Swedish	1.0	0.3	1.0		23
Korean		0.6	0.8	0.6	24
Vietnamese	1.0	0.3	0.6		25
Amerindian		1.2	0.6		26
Bengali	0.5	0.9	0.2		27
Danish	0.5		1.0		28
Eskimo	0.5	0.3	0.2	0.6	29

Each of the following languages, which share ranks 30–56, represents less than 1 per cent of the total: Amharic, Annamese, Basque, Bhutanese, Catalan, Czech, Hawaiian, Hungarian, Irish, Khmer, Mongolian, Papuan, Pashto, Pidgin English, Pilipino, Polish, Provençal, Punjabi, Samoan, Scots (Gaelic), Serbo-Croatian, Tahitian, Thai (and Lao), Turkish, Urdu, Welsh, West Indian.

Although there are some discrepancies, on the whole the four corpuses tell a remarkably consistent story. The greatest discrepancy is the high percentage of Russian loanwords in *The Barnhart Dictionary Companion*. The most likely explanation for the discrepancy is that the readers for that periodical used sources with more material about Russian matters or paid greater attention to such matters than did the readers for the other corpuses. If that discrepancy is corrected, Russian would rank about twelfth place, just below Arabic and Chinese, as a source of loanwords, and that seems appropriate.

2.8.2   French

French is clearly the major source for recent English loanwords, as it has doubtless been since the Middle Ages. Yet various efforts to assess fluctuations in the influence of French on English, even when based on the *OED*, show considerable variation, depending on the methods of assessment used. Counts made by Jespersen, Koszal, Baugh, Mossé, and Herdan vary considerably, according to the way words are counted (Pennanen 1971). Pennanen's optimistic conclusion that 'a sufficiently large sample which is evenly carried out over the entire material to be studied will give a relatively correct picture of distribution according to time' is doubtless correct, provided that its conditions of the size, consistency, and distribution of the sample are met and provided that the material being sampled is itself correct and representative. Those are conditions which at the present time are impossible to meet strictly.

Today, the reasons for the continued prominence of French are several. The physical proximity of France to Great Britain is one factor. Another is the tradition of studying French in British schools. And yet another is the prominence of France in fields such as couture and cuisine, as well as the fine arts and entertainment, which are highly productive of neologisms because fashion changes and with it the vocabulary used. Recent French loanwords in those categories are *a-go-go, à l'orange, art deco, art trouvé, cinéma vérité, courgette, nouvelle cuisine, vin de pays*. French influence is stronger on British than on American English, doubtless because

Great Britain is in closer physical and cultural contact with France than is America.

2.8.3 Japanese

The prominence of Japanese is recent and is closely linked to the rise of Japan as a major economic power in the late twentieth century. This is not to say that most Japanese loans are economic terms or names for trade objects. On the contrary, they range over a wide variety of words: military slang from the period of the occupation (*honcho, hootch, mama-san*), martial arts and weaponry terms (*dojo, nunchakus*), the arts (*hanamichi*), cultural objects (*daruma*), food (*rumaki, sushi, teriyaki*), and so on. Nevertheless, the rise of Japan as an exporter and investor has focused attention on other aspects of its culture, for which English needs names and which otherwise would simply have been ignored by English speakers.

2.8.4 German

German over many years has provided English with a good many loan-words, not all easily recognisable. German has been a prolific source of words for the sciences: mathematics, physics, chemistry and biochemistry, biology including botany and zoology, geology and mineralogy; for medicine and related fields: anatomy, physiology, pathology, and pharmacology; for the social sciences: anthropology, sociology, political science, linguistics, psychology, and psychiatry; for politics and militarism; for technologies like metallurgy; for art, music, and literary criticism; for philosophy and theology; for skiing; and for foods and drinks.

German loanwords range over a continuum from the most to the least obviously German. A single German form may appear in various shapes at different places in that continuum. Thus, the same form appears in several stages of anglicisation as *Kaffeeklatsch, kaffeeklatsch, kaffee klatsch, coffee klatsch, coffee klatch,* and *coffee clutch*. The last variation seems not yet to have been recorded lexicographically, but it is used, at least jocularly. Some loans from German are obvious: *Anschluss, Autobahn, Wanderjahr,* and *Fahrvergnügen,* once an advertising slogan for Volkswagen automobiles. Others are not at all so: *academic freedom, dunk, loan word, Vaseline*.

2.8.5 Greek and Latin

Greek and Latin formatives are highly productive sources for new technical terms coined in English. Consequently, very recent words in the scientific and technical registers that look like loans from the classical languages may actually have been formed within English from morphemes abstracted from loanwords that entered English long ago. It is frequently difficult or even quite impossible to say whether a given word is a loanword (taken from a Greek or Latin dictionary), or is a coinage within English from existing morphemes of classical origin.

Until recent times, it could be assumed that educated professional people would have had schooling in Latin and often in Greek. Today such an assumption is unwarranted in either the UK or the US. To compensate for the ignorance of classical languages, a work called *Composition of Scientific Words* (Brown 1956) made its appearance. This book, described as 'a manual of methods and a lexicon of materials for the practice of logotechnics', is an 882-page synonymy referring mainly Greek and Latin formatives to general concepts, with extensive cross-references. The user can look up either a classical formative and be referred to the general concept to which it relates or a general concept and find a list of formatives related to it. The term *logotechnics* from the self-description of the book on its title-page is an example. The entry *logos* ('Gr. word, discourse; *logion*, saying') is cross-referenced to *word*, which lists 22 words, from *appositum* to *vocabulum*, with derivatives from them and other cross-references; *techno-* is similarly cross-referenced to *art*, with 27 words listed under it. The book includes a morphological sketch of Latin and Greek, information about their spelling and pronunciation, and advice about how to form scientific terms from them. The work is a DIY manual for twentieth-century Robert Cawdreys whose lack of classical education matches that of the readership the original Cawdrey was addressing.

2.8.6   Indic

Non-European languages have also been important sources of new words. Since the seventeenth century, English has been borrowing from the languages of India, especially Hindi but also the unrelated Tamil and several others. Of the more than 1,000 loanwords listed by Rao (1954), about 43 per cent were borrowed before 1775 and 57 per cent after 1776. His list does not include, however, a good many twentieth-century loans (Hawkins 1984 includes some recent ones).

Post-1776 loans include some words closely tied to Indic social customs, but widely known outside India, such as *purdah, raj, satyagraha*, and *suttee*. Linguistics has borrowed such terms as *Aryan, sandhi*, and *svarabhakti*. The popularity of Indic music in the West has spread terms like *raga, sitar*, and *vina.* Indic food is widely available in Britain today, so in addition to older culinary terms like *chutney, curry*, and *mulligatawny*, there are now others such as *puri, samosa*, and *tandoori.*

The food terms and some other Indic loanwords are better known in Britain than America. Briticisms from India include *Blighty* 'home' and *dekko* 'observation, look'. *Chukker* 'a playing period in polo' (related to *chakra* below) and *teapoy* 'a three-legged stand' or (by folk etymology) 'a teapot stand' are rare.

Recent interest in Hinduism and Buddhism has made a number of terms connected with them more familiar to English speakers: *ashram, chakra, Hare Krishna, karma, mahatma, mandala, mantra, maya, mudra, mukti, nirvana, prana, sutra, swami, Vedanta, yoga*. Several of those terms, especially *karma* and *mantra* are undergoing semantic change in English, developing uses distant from their Indic senses. *Karma* now has the sense 'atmosphere, emanations' and *mantra* the sense 'slogan'.

Indic languages have contributed also to the general vocabulary of English: *gymkhana, jodhpur, madras, polo, puttee* do not necessarily have Indic associations, and many English speakers are unaware that *bangle, cushy, jungle, khaki, loot, pajamas* or *pyjamas, Parcheesi* (a trade name for a board game derived from an Indian version called *pachisi), swastika*, and *thug* are from the languages of India.

2.9   Recent neologisms

Many older changes in the vocabulary are difficult to trace. Recent innovations are potentially easier to track, although the same problems of documentation, continuity, and identification exist also for them.

2.9.1   *The study of neology*

The study of neologisms has been of both scholarly and popular interest. The greatest and most detailed of new-word books are the four volumes of *The Oxford English Dictionary Supplement* (1972–86), edited by Robert W. Burchfield. Because its purpose was to supplement the original *OED*, the *Supplement* entered as 'new' any word not in the volumes published between 1884 and 1928. Consequently, some of its 'new' words are rather old. The *OEDS* is nevertheless the major scholarly dictionary of neologisms. It has been supplemented by the *Oxford English Dictionary Additions Series* (Simpson & Weiner 1993).

Other new-word dictionaries that are useful for scholars because they cite evidence and give full lexical entries are three products of the Barnharts: *The Barnhart Dictionary of New English since 1963, The Second Barnhart Dictionary of New English*, and *The Third Barnhart Dictionary of New English* (Barnhart, Steinmetz & Barnhart 1973, 1980, 1990). Although they do not give full illustrative citations with sources, the supplements to *Webster's Third* (Mish 1976, 1983, 1986) are based upon the extensive files of the Merriam-Webster company. These works from American lexicographers are not limited to American sources.

Comparable works tracing neology in British sources are those by Simon Mort (1986) and John Ayto (1989, 1990). A similar work drawing on Australian sources is *The Macquarie Dictionary of New Words* (Butler 1990). Popularised treatments have been made by Sid Lerner and Gary S. Belkin (1993), and Anne H. Soukhanov (1995).

Several periodical treatments of new words are noteworthy. 'Words and Meanings, New' (1944–76) was an annual article in the *Britannica Book of the Year* for thirty-three years. A periodical devoted exclusively to neology is *The Barnhart Dictionary Companion: A Quarterly to Update General Dictionaries* (Barnhart & Barnhart 1982–). The first four volumes of the periodical have a separate index that provides various types of analysis for the neologisms (D. Barnhart 1987).

In 1937 Dwight L. Bolinger (1937–40) began a column on neology, which in 1941 began to appear in *American Speech* as 'Among the New Words' (1941–). Edited by I. Willis Russell from 1944 to 1985, it is the longest running periodical treatment of the subject. *Fifty Years 'Among the New Words': A Dictionary of Neologisms, 1941–1991* (Algeo & Algeo 1991) reprints the first fifty years of the column with a glossary-index of the new words in them and an introductory essay on neology.

A useful index (in addition to Wall & Przebienda 1969–70) is *The Barnhart New-Words Concordance* (D. Barnhart 1994), which indexes new words treated in post-1960 instalments of 'Among the New Words' and in *The Barnhart Dictionary Companion*, as well as a number of new-word dictionaries.

2.9.2 Types of recent neologisms

Estimates of the relative productiveness of one or another type of word formation are subject to many variables and consequently uncertainties. Not least among those is establishing the correct etymology of a word. For example, *unconscious* 'that part of the mind not available to introspection, which nevertheless affects behaviour' might reasonably be thought to be either a shift of use from the adjective or a clipping of the collocation *unconscious mind*, or even a reformation with the prefix *un-*. The *OED*'s first citation, dated 1884, is from Mark Pattison's *Memoirs*: 'I cannot help observing the remarkable force with which the Unconscious – *das Unbewusste* – vindicated its power.' That citation suggests that the English word is a calque on German and therefore a borrowing. Such uncertainty is far from unusual.

Any single estimate of the frequency of various types of word formation will also be skewed because of the sample of words examined, the etymological categories used, and the way the categories are applied to the sample. Consequently, different estimates are seldom fully comparable, but using several estimates rather than one has the advantage of one estimate's cancelling out the idiosyncrasies of another. Below are the percentages for six estimates:

(1)   1,000 words from *The Barnhart Dictionary of New English since 1963* (Barnhart, Steinmetz & Barnhart 1973; reported by Algeo 1980), a sample of about one-fifth of the words in that dictionary;

(2)   1,220 words in *The Longman Register of New Words* (Ayto 1989), all the words in that dictionary;

(3)   393 words from *The Oxford English Dictionary*, 2nd edn. (*OED* 1989), a sample consisting of the first form or sense on each of the 1,019 pages of volume 1 (*A–Bazouki*), provided that form or sense had an earliest citation date of 1776 or later;

(4)   about 500 words beginning with the letter *A* and first attested after 1900, taken from NEWS (New English Words Series), a collection of some 5,000 words not in the *OED* or *OEDS*, as analysed by John Simpson (1988);

(5)   2688 words from volumes 1–4 of *The Barnhart Dictionary Companion* (Barnhart & Barnhart 1982–) as analysed etymologically by David K. Barnhart (1987, 53–69);

(6)   16,570 words analysed by Garland Cannon (1987), consisting of 4,927 words in Barnhart, Steinmetz & Barnhart (1973), 4,536 words in Barnhart, Steinmetz & Barnhart (1980), and 7,107 words in the addenda of the 1981 printing of *Webster's Third* (1961).

The first three samples are the smallest, but were analysed by the same set of criteria. The sixth and largest sample includes all the words analysed in the first sample, but because of the size of the sixth sample, that duplication does not seriously affect the results. The percentages of etymological types in these six samples are as follows:

	Barnhart	Longman	OED2	NEWS	BDC	Cannon
Creations	0.0	0.0	0.3	0.0	0.0	0.6
Shifts	14.2	19.4	23.4	30.8	9.6	19.7
Shortenings	9.7	10.0	1.8	17.5	9.7	17.1
Composites	63.9	54.3	52.2	37.6	73.5	53.8
(Compounds)	(29.8)	(36.3)	(19.8)	(12.0)	(57.6)	(29.6)
(Affixations)	(34.1)	(18.0)	(32.3)	(25.6)	(15.9)	(24.2)
Blends	4.8	9.8	3.3	1.1	0.5	1.0
Loanwords	6.9	4.3	18.8	6.9	6.2	7.5
Unknown	0.5	2.2	0.3	0.0	0.5	0.4
Others				6.1		

The 'others' category exists for the NEWS corpus because 6.1 per cent of its words were not reported for any of the major categories, perhaps because of discrepancies between the simple taxonomy used here and the seventy word-formation categories used for NEWS. Since the approximately 30 words represented by that 6.1 per cent should be distributed among the major etymological categories, the figures for that corpus would change slightly.

Several large variations in percentages between the corpuses are explicable.

Shifts: the NEWS corpus is above and the two Barnhart corpuses are below average in their number of shifts. Shifts of meaning and grammatical use are more likely to be recorded in the *OED* than in dictionaries of new words because they are less obvious and of less interest to many readers of the latter (Simpson 1988: 151). Shifts of sense and grammatical category are undoubtedly more frequent than most lists of new words would suggest.

Shortenings: shortened forms are markedly higher in percentage in the NEWS and Cannon corpuses, and lower in the *OED2*. It is particularly striking that the highest percentage of shortenings is in the new words collected for the *OED* (NEWS) and the lowest percentage in the *OED2* itself. To some extent that discrepancy may reflect the fact that clipping, acronyms, and alphabetisms have become increasingly fashionable in recent years. But much of the discrepancy doubtless results from the *OED*'s practice of running in acronyms and alphabetisms under the initial letter of the alphabet; they are therefore under-represented in a sample based on distribution through the pages of the book. The other corpuses treat acronyms and alphabetisms as main entries in normal letter-by-letter alphabetised order. Nearly 7 per cent of Cannon's shortenings are words that might be alternatively analysed in other ways.

Composites: compounds are markedly more numerous in *The Barnhart Dictionary Companion* for several reasons: idioms like *keep one's feet to the fire*, entered in it, have been counted as compounds here; forms like *telework, teleworker, teleworking* are listed as independent compounds in its etymological lists, whereas the analysis of other corpuses would treat them as related to one another by affixation or backformation. The *OED*'s practice of listing compounds as run-in rather than main entries has as a consequence their undercounting in a sample based on distribution through its pages. However, the exceptionally low percentage of compounds in the NEWS corpus is puzzling. Part of the explanation for it may be that the percentage of compounds reported was only for nouns of three patterns (n+n, a+n, v+n) and adjectives of two patterns (n+a, a+n). A goodly proportion of the 6.1 per cent of 'other' words may be compounds of other kinds.

On the other hand, the *OED* enters even predictable affixed forms with greater fidelity than most dictionaries of neologisms, and therefore has a larger share of them. *The Barnhart Dictionary of New English* also pays more attention to affixation than average, whereas *The Longman Register* and *The Barnhart Dictionary Companion* pay less, but such fluctuations may reflect only the lexicographers' focus.

Blends: blends are over-represented in *The Longman Register* perhaps because it includes a good many voguish and nonce forms, which favour the process of blending.

Loanwords: borrowing appears more often in the *OED* perhaps because of the longer chronological range of the sample taken from it (more than 200 years); the other corpuses report new words from a recent twenty-five year period. There is some reason to suppose that borrowing is less influential as a kind of word derivation now than it was formerly. The *OED* also, however, prefers to cite Latin and Greek etyma when the formation of a word may be accounted for by native morphemes ultimately of classical origin, and that preference exaggerates its percentage of loanwords.

For example, the *OED* derives *adscription* in the sense 'ascription' (first attested in 1857) from Latin as an adaptation of *adscriptionem*. However, there is nothing in the available evidence to suggest that the word was taken directly from Latin, rather than formed from the prefix *ad-* and the stem *scription*, both of very long standing in English. Many of the words etymologized by the *OED* as borrowings may more properly be native formations from morphemes ultimately of foreign origin. In some cases, it is likely that both processes operated simultaneously, which would in effect make blends of the words derived from both a classical etymon (*adscriptionem*) and English formatives (*ad-* and *-scription*).

Without relying on specific percentages, it seems clear that overwhelmingly the major source for new words in English is their composition from morphemes already present in the language, by compounding and affixation. A distant, but still clearly, secondary source is the shifting of old words to new senses and uses. Shortening, borrowing, and blending are relatively minor sources for neologisms. The creation of words independently of any etyma is insignificant.

2.9.3 *Recent and older neologisms*

The percentages of words formed in English and of those borrowed from other languages in the recent corpuses contrast strikingly with those in *The Shorter OED*, as reported by Thomas Finkenstaedt (1973, 118–56). In the following table, the *SOED* percentages represent the history of English over approximately 1,200 years, as recorded in that dictionary. The *OED2* percentages are of the sample from volume 1 of the second edition of the *OED* (1989), representing a slightly longer chronological range but taken from only the first one-twentieth of the alphabet. The 'Recent' percentages are an average of the five corpuses used above that recorded new words from about a twenty-five-year period, 1963–88:

	SOED	*OED2*	*Recent*
Native formations	25.6	81.0	91.7
Loanwords	70.4	18.8	6.4
Unknown origin	4.0	0.3	1.9

These figures are certainly skewed. The extraordinarily high percentage of loanwords in the Finkenstaedt statistics for the *SOED* words is belied by both a sample from the *OED2* and five recent collections, which differ among themselves comparatively little (their percentage of loanwords ranging from 4.3 to 7.5). Borrowing may well have declined in recent years as a source of new words in English, but a decline of the proportion suggested by the discrepancies between these figures is unbelievable.

A partial reason for the discrepancy is that the *SOED* data concerns only headwords, whereas the *OED2* and the recent corpuses include new senses of old words. If the percentages are adjusted by omitting all shifts (semantic and grammatical), the native/loanword ratio becomes 75/24 for the *OED2* and 90/8 for the recent collections. That is slightly closer but still far from the *SOED*'s 26/70.

Finkenstaedt (1973, 117) himself points to another possible cause of the problem. The *SOED* (and *OED*) etymologies by preference cite the earliest classical etyma. When such etymologies are reported as the sources of the English vocabulary, we have an incorrect account of the origins of English words since many words are composed in English of morphemes from classical languages. Every *OED* etymology has to be evaluated in terms of what we want to know about the origin of the form and what the *OED* editors were probably telling us. Uncritical statistical reports of *OED* etymologies are likely to be not just useless but badly misleading. The *OED* etymologies need to be reworked to clarify what they report.

It is probable that borrowing has declined in importance as a source of new words in English. That it has declined as radically as a comparison of the *SOED* figures with those of recent studies would suggest is very unlikely.

2.10   Vocabulary change as a mirror of cultural change

Change in vocabulary also involves fluctuations in the faddishness, voguishness, popularity, or centrality of words. The stylishness of words is difficult to attest objectively, but some words are clearly a mirror of the times in which they are used. They are keywords for the zeitgeist of their age. A sampling of such words follows (many suggested by Williams 1976). The dates cited are the first recorded in the *OED2* or *Webster's Ninth New Collegiate*; most are almost certainly not the real first dates of use, but only the first in our best historical records.

Radical has had its etymological sense 'pertaining to roots' since the late fourteenth century, but in 1786 the collocation *radical reform* introduced the term to political and social use, where it has remained ever since. *Radical* alone acquired the sense 'advocating radical political reform' and developed the derivative *radicalism* by 1820. The verb *radicalize* (1823) followed shortly. More recently, a variety of new collocations have come into use: *radical feminism* (1923), *radical right* (1954), *radical left* (1969), *radical chic* (1970, from the journalist Tom Wolfe), and *radical feminist* (1971).

Economics (1792), the dismal science (as Carlyle called it) concerned with the production and distribution of material wealth, had a sixteenth-century antecedent referring to household management, but the more recent sense is not a homely one. Related terms are *economist* 'student of economics' (1804), *political economist* (1825), *economic* 'pertaining to the science of economics' (1835), *economic man* (1889, from G. B. Shaw's denial of the existence of the referent), *economic system* (1898), *economic war* (1916), *economism* (1919), *economic growth* (1940), *econometrics* (1933), and *econometrician* (1947). The sixteenth-century sense re-emerged in the Americanism *home economics* (1899).

Although *nationalist* was used in the early eighteenth century, the words that cluster with it are first attested later, in senses pertaining to devotion to one's nation: *nationalize* (1800), *nationalization* (1801), *nationalism* (1844), *nationalistic* (1866), and *nationalistically* (1913). *National* 'a citizen or subject' is from 1887, preceded by *nationhood* (1850) and followed by *nation-state* (1918). In 1892 Edward Bellamy (author of the social novels *Looking Backward* and *Equality*) used *nationalism* to denote a proposed form of socialism with national ownership of industry. *Nationalize* was used in the sense 'to bring industry and land under national control' in 1869, and *nationalization* as its *nomen actionis* in 1874. The antonyms *privatize* (1948) and *privatization* (1959) did not follow until the next century. *National socialism* appeared in 1931.

The word *social* has been in use since the sixteenth century, but in more recent times has proliferated in frequency, senses, collocations, and derivatives: *social science* (1785), *socialist* (1827), *socialize* (1828), *socialism* (1837), *sociology* (1843), *socialistic* (1848), *social contract* (1849), *social service* (1851, although not as supplied by the government until 1933), *socialization* (1884), *social democracy* and *social work* (1890), *social security* (1908), *social psychology* (1909), *social insurance* and *social welfare* (1917), *social disease* (1918), *social gospel* (1920), *social climber* (1924), *social-minded* and *social studies* (1927), *socialite* (1928), *socialist realism* (1934), *socialized medicine* (1938), *social Darwinism* (1939), *sociosexual* (1940), *socializer* (1947), and *socializee* (1952).

In what is doubtless one of the many accidents of the availability of evidence, the adverb *subconsciously* (1823) is recorded before the adjective *subconscious* (1832–4). It was later in the century that the nouns *subconsciousness* (1874) and *subconscious* (1886) appeared, although it is difficult to imagine present-day thinking, much less *psychotherapy* (1892) without the concepts. *Unconscious* had been used in a general sense since the early eighteenth century, but extended to the psychological register as a noun in 1884 and an adjective in 1912.

The noun *reform* has been used since the seventeenth century in the general sense 'alteration for the better'. About the time of Victoria's birth it was used as an adjective (1819) and shortly after began to collocate in a political sense that has continued to the present time: *Reform Bill* (1831), *Reform Act* (1832), *Reform Club* (1835), *reform movement* and *reform party* (1839), *reform politician* and *reformism* (1904), *reform mayor* (1968). About the same time as the politicisation of *reform* and motivated by a like impulse to better the world, a place of confinement for young offenders came to be known hopefully as a *reformatory* (1834), later as a still more euphemistic American *reform school* (1847) and as a toponymic British *borstal* (1907), now sensitively replaced by *youth custody centre* or *juvenile detention centre*.

Evolution and *evolve* in the etymological sense of 'unfolding what was wrapped up' are seventeenth-century words, but by 1832, a generation before Darwin's 1859 use, they had acquired the sense of 'originating new species' in opposition to the doctrine of special creation. Subsequently there appeared *evolutionary* (1846), *evolutionist* (1859), *evolutional* (1862), *evolvable* (1869), *evolutive* (1874), *evolutionistic* and *evolutionize* (1883), *evolute* (1884), *evolutionally* (1922), and *evolutionarily* (1945).

Although holding all things in common was a practice of the primitive Christian church, the name for that activity, *communism*, has been used in English only since 1840, and its application to the unchristian doctrines of Marx and Lenin somewhat later, in 1850. The related *communist* is also from 1840 and *communistic* from 1851. The years of hunting *reds under the bed* (1972) during and after World War II spawned a variety of compounds: *communist-led* (1938), *communist-inspired* (1940), *communist-directed* (1945 by Winston Churchill), *communist-dominated* (1948), and *communist-controlled* (1955). The radiation of these terms is likely to fade since the collapse of East European communism.

Ecology has been used since 1858, with an early sense of the science of the economy of animals and plants, with related forms *ecologist* (1893), *ecologic* (1896), *ecological* (1899), and *ecologically* (1909). In the more activist sense of environmentalism, especially as a Green political issue, use of the term is from the 1970s, displacing *conservationist* (1870) in popularity. It has become a voguish term and developed a new combining form, *eco-*, as in *ecospecies* and *ecotype* (1922), *ecosystem* (1935), *ecosphere* (1953), *ecophysiology* (1962), *ecocatastrophe* and *ecofreak* (1970).

Consumer in the pejorative sense of 'one who or that which consumes, wastes, squanders, or destroys' (reflecting the original sense of the verb) has been in English since the fifteenth century. Its more neutral sense of 'one who purchases goods or pays for services, a customer' dates only from 1897 (first recorded, appropriately enough, in the *Sears Roebuck Catalogue*). *Consumerism* as 'protection of the consumer's interests' is from 1944 and as 'a doctrine advocating a continual increase in the consumption of goods as the basis for a sound economy' from 1960, with the related *consumerist* (1965) and *consumeristic* (1968). Some notable collocations are *consumer goods* (1890), *consumer credit* (1927), *consumer price index* (1948), and *consumer durables* (1958), denoting, for example, TV sets as contrasted with TV dinners.

Genetic was used in the broad sense of 'pertaining to origins' in 1831, and in a more specific evolutionary sense by Darwin in 1859, but it was not until the early years of the twentieth century that related forms were used with reference to genes and the science of their study: *genetically* (1902), *genetics*

(1905), *genetic* (1908), and *geneticist* (1913). The continued importance of the term is attested by its collocations: *genetic drift* (1945), *genetic marker* (1950), *genetic code* (1961), and *genetic engineering* (1966).

Welfare has been used since the early fourteenth century in the general sense 'state of being well'. Since 1918, however, it has specialised to 'the maintenance of the members of a community in a state of well-being, especially by legislation and government management' and spawned a great progeny of compounds and collocations, some of which antedate the independent use of the noun sense: *welfare work* (1903), *welfare worker* (1904), *welfare policy* (1905), *welfare centre* (1917), *welfare department* (1922), *welfare clinic* (1937), *welfare state* and *welfarist* (1941), *welfare officer* (1944), *welfare fund* and *welfare check* (1947), *welfare food* (1948), *welfarism* (1949), *welfare service* (1952), *welfare capitalism* (1960), *welfare roll* (1970), *welfare hotel* and *welfare mother* (1971), *welfare office* (1976), *welfare family* and *welfare benefit* (1977).

Throughout the history of English, like that of all other languages, developments in the vocabulary have a social and intellectual dimension, as borrowing reflects foreign contacts, standardisation reflects the rise to power of a ruling class, concern with correctness reflects a desire to maintain or change social status, terms of address reflect social hierarchy, and terms applied to a subordinate class (such as women or blacks) by the superordinate class (such as white males) reflect social power (Leith 1983). In addition, the words that are central to our discourse at any time are tokens of the way we view and respond to the world. Vocabulary, more than any other aspect of language, is inextricably connected with our total culture.

2.11   FURTHER READING

For an overview of English lexicology and word-formation, useful sources are *An Introduction to Modern English Word-Formation* by Valerie Adams (1973) and *English Word-Formation* by Laurie Bauer (1983). New words in English are surveyed in *Fifty Years 'Among the New Words': A Dictionary of Neologisms, 1941–1991* by John and Adele Algeo (1991) and in the continuing column 'Among the New Words' (1941–). Questions of usage are authoritatively and sensibly covered in *Webster's Dictionary of English Usage* by E. Ward Gilman (1989).

3   SYNTAX

David Denison

3.1   Introduction

3.1.1   *Syntactic change*

The topic of syntactic change in late Modern English is only just beginning to get its share of serious scholarly attention, and compared with the towers of published syntactic research which the Syntax chapters of volumes I–III in this series have been launched from, this chapter has had to rely rather more on its own bootstraps. All research surveys are by definition provisional, this one especially so.

By 1776 the English language had already undergone most of the syntactic changes which differentiate Present-Day English (henceforth PDE) from Old English (henceforth OE) (see *CHEL* I: 170–1). Older patterns of word order with the verb at the clause end or in second constituent position had long been replaced by an unmarked order framed by the sequence subject–verb–object or subject–verb–complement. A subject noun phrase (NP) was virtually obligatory in simple clauses other than imperatives. Great simplifications had taken place in morphology, so that the noun and adjective had already reached their present, vestigial inflectional systems, and the verb nearly so. The number and frequency of prepositions had expanded greatly, and prepositions now served to mark a variety of nominal functions. Prepositions, particles and other words frequently joined simple lexical verbs to form group-verbs like SPEAK *to*, MAKE *up*, TAKE *notice of*.[1] Such formations as the prepositional and indirect passives had become commonplace. The complexity of the English auxiliary system had grown to encompass a wide range of mood and aspect marking, and much of its present systematic structure was already in place, including the dummy auxiliary DO. Some patterns involving finite and nonfinite subordinate clauses had been rare or impossible in OE; by 1776 most of the present repertoire was available.

However, the English of 1776 was linguistically by no means the same as that of the present day. We must now focus on change *during* the late Modern English (henceforth lModE) period. (I shall often use 'lModE' as a convenient synonym for the period covered by this volume, 1776–present day.) The earlier we look, the more obvious it becomes that English syntax differs from that of our own day, even though few post-1776 usages will cause us much difficulty. Since relatively few categorical losses or innovations have occurred in the last two centuries, syntactic change has more often been statistical in nature, with a given construction occurring throughout the period and either becoming more or less common generally or in particular registers. The overall, rather elusive effect can seem more a matter of stylistic than of syntactic change, so it is useful to be able to track frequencies of occurrence from eModE through to the present day. Of course there have been substantive changes too, particularly in the verb; for two striking examples see sections 3.3.3.4 and 3.4.3.2 below.

3.1.2   Organisation of chapter

In the main in this chapter I follow (gratefully) the pattern established in the 'Syntax' chapters of *CHEL* I–III. Like my predecessors, I recognise the traditional division between NP and VP. There is no section on the verb phrase (henceforth VP) as such. Within the VP I recognise a category **Verbal group**; to repeat the definition given in *CHEL* I: 179, 'both the finite verb alone (verb plus subject–verb agreement, tense or mood marker), and verbal phrases consisting of a main verb and one or more auxiliary verbs'. After the present section 3.1, on syntactic change and the organisation of this chapter, the rest of the chapter is set out as follows.

Section 3.2 is on the noun phrase, with a discussion of the obligatory head of an NP (noun, pronoun or adjective/zero), and then in roughly linear sequence the other, mainly optional elements (determiners, adjectives, attributive nouns, and postmodifiers). The sections on genitival determiners and attributive adjectives are the occasions for general discussions of genitives and adjectives, respectively.

Section 3.3 is on the verbal group, the context for discussion of tense, perfect, progressive, subjunctive, modal verbs, voice, the expression of time, operators, and finally a reconsideration of structural change in the verbal group.

Section 3.4 deals with the (remaining, principal) elements of the clause: subject, object, and predicative, all of which have to be discussed, of course, in relation to verbs. Subject and object include material on the passive. The section concludes with a discussion of adverbials.

Section 3.5 is a wider consideration of the structure of the clause, looking at word order and other issues in declaratives, negatives, interrogatives, imperatives, and exclamatives.

Section 3.6 is on composite sentences, a term which covers both **compound** sentences (coordinated main clauses) and **complex** ones (main clause plus subordinate(s)) – in short, sentences involving more than one clause. Here the traditional headings of **co-ordination** and **subordination** are employed. After a brief look at co-ordinate clauses, subordinate clauses are discussed under the traditional headings of finite nominal, nonfinite nominal, relative, and adverbial.

Where necessary I have had to discuss some morphological changes – those which bear directly on syntax – there not being enough in the period covered by this volume for a separate chapter on morphology. The chapter concludes with suggestions for further reading, a list of textual sources, and notes.

3.1.3   *The data*

Examples are drawn mainly from informal English (as used in private letters, diaries, journalism, and so on) and literary but non-poetic English, especially dialogue in drama and novels.[2] Children's literature, notably by E. Nesbit, has often proved a convenient source. When I started there was little machine-readable corpus material dated between *c.* 1700 and *c.* 1960. To bridge the gap I constructed a 100,000-word corpus of private letters written between 1861 and 1918, the central portion of our period, which has provided many examples: portions of the *Amberley papers* and of the *Letters* of Bell, Dowson, Green and the Webbs are the texts concerned (see Textual Sources at the end of this chapter, and for details of the corpus, Denison 1994). Informal private letters not intended for publication are generally a convenient source of colloquial language. Where usage strays outside the common core of English of the period, it is likely to be in the same direction as ordinary conversational usage. I have also drawn heavily on the letters of Keats and Mrs Gaskell and, to a lesser extent, on those of Jane Austen (lately in a version supplied by the Oxford Text Archive) and Harriet Martineau.

Otherwise many examples come from the *OED* (see note 8), a few from corpora of Present-day English, and quite a few from reference works on historical syntax. For the statistical comparisons referred to in section 3.1.1 I have relied much less on my letters corpus than on (a preliminary and incomplete version of) the ARCHER corpus, which allows the same genres to be compared for the whole period 1650–1990.[3] ARCHER has also provided many examples.

It is assumed throughout that comments apply to the 'common core' of English, apart from sporadic references to the behaviour of particular dialects and registers, especially where current variation gives the clue to chronological change. Although sound recording has been possible for over a century already, the recording of ordinary, everyday speech has only become common more recently, and I have confined myself by and large to written materials.[4] Again, we assume that in syntax it is not too much of a distortion to ignore variation between speech and writing: many apparent differences are probably as much to do with formality as medium, at least in the modern period. However, at any given time the syntax of written and spoken standards may not be identical. For some recent work on the relationship between syntax and various dimensions of style, genre, register and medium see Biber & Finegan (1987, 1992) and Biber (1988). Confining attention to written material introduces another problem, however: there can be real difficulty in distinguishing between genuine changes in syntax and mere changes in conventions of decorum in written language, as we shall see, for example, with reference to contraction of negatives (*must not* vs. *mustn't*, 3.3.8.2 and 3.5.3.4 below) and number concord after *there* (*there are lots of people outside* vs. *there's lots of people outside*, 3.4.1.1); see also English Grammar and Usage in this volume.

In dealing with the most recent period of English language history we come closest to the insights of native speakers, but there is a complementary *dis*advantage too. Most, perhaps all, linguistic changes start out as 'mistakes' relative to the standards of the time (though often not noticed at first). An aberrant usage therefore represents one of three broad possibilities: an incipient change which will in the long run prove successful, a possible change which does not get generally adopted, or simple error. (See now Milroy 1993: 221–4.) With hindsight we can tell which of the three was in fact the case, but hindsight is long-sighted and unable to focus on usage too near in time. For an example see the discussion of counterfactual *may have* in section 3.3.5.3 below. Furthermore, incipient changes can be hard to spot at all, given 'the tendency of listeners to filter out linguistic signals that do not conform to their own idiolects' (Youmans 1986: 71). (An idiolect is a personal dialect.)

3.2 The noun phrase

The noun phrase (NP) is the syntactic unit which typically functions as subject or object of a clause or object of a preposition. A pronoun or proper noun usually constitutes a complete noun phrase in itself – *he, them, James, Amsterdam* – with occasional exceptions like *poor old her, you over there, the fat James who went to school with me*. However, NPs with a common noun as head[5] routinely allow or demand more complex modification:

(1)   Determiner(s) + Modifier(s) + Head + Postmodifier(s)

Various categories can fill the functional slots of (1), as in:[6]

(2)   *both the other   faded green   football   shirts   in the drawer*
       Determiners   Adjectives   Attrib. noun   (head) Noun   Prep. phrase

This overall structure holds good for the whole of our lModE period, with significant change confined to the internal structure of the Determiner position, and to greater freedom for former postmodifiers to be used in premodification. Arguably there is yet another slot to the left of the Determiners: focusing adverbs like *also* and *even*, though their membership of NP is less certain and their positional behaviour rather freer (Huddleston 1984: 232–3); they are treated under Adverbials in sections 3.4.4 and 3.5.1.3 below. Here we shall look first at the obligatory head of the NP, then at the various optional modifier slots.

3.2.1   *The noun as head*

3.2.1.1   Count versus noncount nouns

Some nouns, semantically often those which refer to an undifferentiated mass, typically lack number marking: *bread, furniture*. They are called noncount nouns. (Compare the count nouns *loaf, chair*.) The internal makeup of the Determiner slot is affected by the choice of head noun. For example, singular count nouns like *chair* require a Determiner to form a grammatical NP, whereas noncount nouns like *furniture* do not:

(3)   This chair
       **Chair   } is expensive.
       Furniture
       This furniture

It seems very likely that there is a systematic process of change from noncount to count for some nouns, but full evidence is not yet available. Let us take one example, the noun *acquaintance* used with reference

Table 3.1. Acquaintance *in nineteenth-century quotations in the* OED

Usage	Occurrences		
abstract noun			163
of NP'*s acquaintance*			25
collective noun	with explicit SG concord	2	
	with explicit PL concord	4	
	with no indication of number	18	
	subtotal		24
count noun	morphologically SG, with SG reference	37	
	morphologically PL	47	
	subtotal		84
total			296

to persons or analogous concrete referents. Readers of nineteenth-century literature will be familiar with a now-obsolete, noncount use of the noun:

(4)   She dreaded addressing *any of her former female acquaintance*
                            (1848 Gaskell, *Mary Barton* xiv.164)

In this sense *acquaintance* was a collective noun, morphologically singular, which might have singular or plural concord. In concrete use in PDE it is a count noun:[7]

(5)   His *acquaintances* thought him enviable to have so charming a
       wife   (1871–2 George Eliot, *Middlemarch* finale.835)

The *OED* has very few examples of plural *acquaintances* s.v., and they are early: the entry supports the impression that (4) was normal nineteenth-century usage and that (5) was not. The closest I can get to an overview of nineteenth-century usage is to treat the *OED*'s nineteenth-century quotations as a corpus.[8] Those which include *acquaintance(s)* paint a different picture, as shown in table 3.1. The ratio 84:24 suggests that the count noun was far more frequent than the collective noun, and that the editors' idea of the word was not perhaps a representative one even in 1884.

An apparent difference between British English and American English may be an indication that the classification of some nouns has recently changed. For example, BrE treats a number of nouns as noncount which in AmerE can be countable:

(6)   a. You'll find excellent *value* all around the shop. (BrE)
       b. You'll find excellent *values* all around the store. (AmerE)

The AmerE (6b) is virtually impossible in BrE[9] and appears to be more recent than the noncount variant. English has long had a tendency to allow the abstract (often noncount) noun X to be used as a concrete noun meaning 'instance of X', as in *acquaintance, binding (of a book), takings, government*, and that is probably what is going on here. Further work is needed to tell how systematic the dialectal variation is, and whether the process has become any more prevalent in recent years. A correspondence on the LINGUIST discussion list in September–October 1993 revealed sporadic (American) developments of count-noun usage like *homeworks* 'homework assignments/grades', *surgeries* 'surgical operations', *legos* 'pieces of [the brand-name construction toy] Lego', *emails* 'items of electronic mail'.
  Examples (7) are different:

(7)   a. Various *accommodation* is available. (BrE)
       b. Various *accommodations* are available. (AmerE)

Here the noncount form appears to be the newer variant. Type (7b) is older than (7a) and often hard to distinguish from *accommodation* 'anything which supplies a want . . .' (see *OED* s.v., 6a, 7a):

(8)   notwithstanding the excellent *accommodations* with which your
       hospitality supplied me.   (1816 Scott, *Antiquary*, 2nd edn. I.xi.233)

  Noncount nouns referring to a food or other commodity are frequently reclassified as count nouns. One context is when the noun X is used with the meaning 'variety of X', as in:

(9)   What *breads/coffees/flours/milks* can you get in your local
       supermarket?

I suspect that the luxury of consumer choice has promoted this kind of reclassification in recent years, though it is of course a productive syntactic pattern potentially available with any mass noun. Another context is when X comes to mean 'portion of X', as with *tea* in:

(10)   I'll have a *beans on toast* and two *teas*, please.

(Notice the similar reclassification in (10) of originally plural *beans (on toast)* as a countable singular.) The new Englishes (see *CHEL* VI) are characterised by countables such as *stationeries, furnitures*, etc. (Platt, Weber & Ho 1984: 50–2).

3.2.1.2 Number

Collective nouns are notoriously troublesome as to number, and there has been much fluctuation over time. Some figures on nineteenth-century usage are given by Dekeyser (1975: 42–66). In the case of collective *acquaintance*, plural seems to predate singular (at least to judge from the *OED* examples counted for table 3.1), while many historic singulars like *government* have come to be treated as plurals:

(11) a. The *acquaintance* she had already formed *were* unworthy of her.
          (1816 Austen, *Emma* i.iii.23 [*OED*])
      b. I could not make out I had *so many acquaintance*
          (1819 Keats, *Letters* 156 p. 400 (17 Sep.))

(12) a. and your *acquaintance* must almost have doubled *itself* since
          then   (1863 Gaskell, *Letters* 535 p. 714 (2 Oct.))
      b. My *acquaintance is* confined to half-a-dozen turnipy squires and
          their wives.   (1873 R. Broughton, *Nancy* I.70 [*OED*])

(13) a. The *government, which is* trying to make up *its* mind
      b. The *government, who are* trying to make up *their* mind(s)

Notice in (13) how number is not independent of 'gender', in that singular, abstract *government* requires the inanimate relative pronoun *which*, whereas plural *government*, seen as a collection of individuals, correlates with the use of the animate relative pronoun *who*.[10] Plural concord with morphologically singular collective nouns like *government, committee, (the) public* is extremely rare in AmerE but quite acceptable in BrE, as Quirk, Greenbaum, Leech & Svartvik note (1985: 5.108, 10.36).[11] With some collective nouns both numbers are found (sometimes with dialectal variation), but in others the singular is now obsolete. One would not now find *police* used as in (14):

(14) It is incredible with what spirit and firmness *the new police has*
      defeated the canaille ['rabble'].   (1830 Jekyll, *Corr.* 13 Nov. [*OED*])

On the other hand *constituency* in (15) seems to be behaving like *government* in (13b), something which is not now possible in its parliamentary sense:

(15) and getting at last returned to parliament by *a constituency who* paid
      his expenses.   (1871–2 George Eliot, *Middlemarch* finale. 836)

Another kind of noun which has tended to change number is the classical and neoclassical borrowing ending in plural *-a*, like Lat. *data, insignia, media, strata*. These are now quite widely used as singulars, the first usually as noncount. The widespread use of *phenomena*, originally a Greek plural, as an English singular is still regarded as an error by some, though for how long? Presumably these changes originate in misconstrual of *-a* as some sort of foreign singular inflection. Originally Italian plurals like *spaghetti* and other pasta nouns have become noncount singulars in English, and for some speakers *graffiti* has become an invariable count noun, plural *or* singular.

Certain plurals in *-s* may come to be abstract singulars. In the case of sciences like *mathematics, physics*, this process was largely completed before our period, but *politics* still shows variable number:

(16)   A curious Dilemma truly *my politics have* run me into.

(1777 Sheridan, *School for Scandal* II.iii 384.15)

(17)   Now, *all my politics* as yet *is* to consider what's best for the Stout Gentleman [*sc.* John Bull].   (1840 Bulwer-Lytton, *Money* V.iii p. 237)

The majority of testable citations in the *OED* show plural verb concord, though examples with singular concord are recorded as early as 1714. For the *OED*, use 'as a singular noun' is measured within the NP, as in *a/this politics*, and dates only from 1906 (s.v. *politic* n. B.3g). The later date of singular agreement in attributive elements is predictable from the agreement hierarchy of Corbett (1991).

The converse phenomenon may be illustrated by the following:

(18)   But your *whereabouts was* doubtful

(1890 Dowson, *Letters* 97 p. 147 (8 Apr.))

The usage of (18) may be old-fashioned in PDE, which would often treat *whereabouts* as an invariable plural, perhaps because popular etymology takes *-s* for a plural inflection. Jespersen has a plural example from a newspaper of 1906 (1909–49: II 160).

3.2.2   Pronouns

Pronouns typically form an NP in themselves. We shall discuss several types of pronoun here, apart from interrogative and relative pronouns, which it will be convenient to discuss with their respective clause types in sections 3.5.3.2 and 3.6.5.2 below, and likewise *it* and *there* functioning as 'dummy' pronouns, sections 3.4.1.1 and 3.4.2.6.

3.2.2.1   Demonstrative pronouns

Demonstrative pronouns are marked for deixis and number in lModE: *this, these, that, those*. An interesting asymmetry is that the plural pronouns *these* and *those* can be used in reference to humans, the singulars *this* and *that* cannot: thus, for instance, *those who* but not **that who (Jespersen 1909–49: II 406; Quirk, Greenbaum, Leech & Svartvik 1985: 6.41–2). Poussa refers the gap ultimately to the loss by ME of gender distinction in the demonstratives, with a consequential chain of morphological, syntactic and semantic changes (1992). In writing, the gap becomes evident well before our period, despite an isolated use of pronominal *this* and *that* with human reference in Browning's verse (Poussa 1992: 402). The gap once established, usage of the singular demonstratives for human reference takes on a pejorative (or at least demeaning) sense:

(19)   'Would you like to marry Malcolm?' I asked. 'Fancy being owned by *that*! Fancy seeing it every day!'

(1905 Elinor Glyn, *Vicissitudes of Evangeline* 127 [*OED*, Poussa])

The gap does not apply to formulas of introduction (*This is John*), which Poussa characterises as equative, nor to derived interrogatives. It is a curiosity that the normal response in America to an unrecognised telephone caller is *Who is this?* (*OED* s.v. *this* B.1b), in Britain *Who is that?*, a difference which can only be twentieth century in that context but which may go back to earlier differences. Conceivably it is a matter of 'positive politeness' (increased involvement) vs. 'negative politeness' (greater social distance); see Brown & Levinson on the role of deixis in politeness strategies (1987: 121, 205).

3.2.2.2   Indefinite pronouns

One can function as a generic pronoun of personal reference, always unmodified:

(20)   *One* can't be too careful.

Quirk, Greenbaum, Leech & Svartvik point out that a meaning of 'people in general' often occurs 'with particular reference to the speaker' (1985: 6.56), citing example (21a). This usage can be traced back to well before our period (*contra* Wales 1996: 82):

(21)   a. *I* like to dress nicely. It gives *one* confidence.
        b. and you know *one should* not like to have dear Sir Thomas . . . find all the varnish scratched off.

(1816 Austen, *Mansfield Park* I.vii.77 [Phillipps])

The significance of (21b) is that a third person pronoun would normally go with *would* in this meaning, yet *one* here attracts the 'first person modal' *should* (Phillipps 1970: 128, citing Jespersen 1909–49: IV 331). Possible reference to the speaker makes ModE *one* quite unlike its most obvious equivalent in earlier English, OE *man*, ME *me(n)*. Also unlike them, ModE *one* is not confined to subject function.

After generic *one* there is a choice of anaphoric continuations:

(22)   *One* is on $\left\{ \begin{array}{c} \textit{one's} \\ \textit{his} \end{array} \right\}$ guard if $\left\{ \begin{array}{c} \textit{one} \\ \textit{he} \end{array} \right\}$ is offered a free lunch.

And even together in a single sentence:

(23)   'Oh yes, the so-called music. Yes, I suppose we do hear it if we
         concentrate, but then *one* can hear *one's* own heartbeat too, if *he*
         concentrates hard enough.'

                              (1962 Kesey, *One Flew Over the Cuckoo's Nest* (Picador, 1973) 66)

BrE and some American speakers use *one*, *one's*, and *oneself*, as does Keats
(in, it may be noted, a cheerfully colloquial passage):

(24)   Writing has this disadvan<ta>ge of speaking – *one* cannot write a
         wink, or a nod, or a grin, or a purse of the Lips, or a *smile* – *O
         law!* [original emphasis] *One* can-<not> put *ones* finger to *one's*
         nose, or yerk ye in the ribs, or lay hold of your button in
         writing – but in all the most lively and titterly parts of my Letter
         you must not fail to imagine me

                              (1819 Keats, *Letters* 156 p. 417 (20 Sep.))

The forms *he*, *him*, *his* and *himself* 'were formerly usual, and are still sometimes used' as anaphoric continuations of *one* (*OED* s.v., pron. B.21) –
indeed are the more common choice in America if the rather formal *one*
has been selected at all. However, *one* is probably declining in overall frequency in everyday speech in favour of indefinite *you*. This latter option is
found throughout our period (it goes back to ME times):

(25)   a. The really delightful marriage must be that where *your*
            husband was a sort of father, and could teach *you* even
            Hebrew, if *you* wished it.   (1871–2 George Eliot, *Middlemarch* i.10)
         b. Yet *you* can't treat it like an ordinary pipe, for it is a religious
            bequest and must therefore be approached with the utmost
            circumspection.   (1918 Bell, *Letters* II.449 (6 Mar.))

Another use of *one* is as an anaphoric pronoun (*Jan found a fossil and Kim
found one too*). Already before the lModE period it was possible to use *one* as
a 'prop-word' preceded by the indefinite article or in the plural, with or

without an adjective: *such a one, a good one, good ones*. After definite determiners a premodifying adjective was needed – *thy golden one, the learned ones* (Shakespeare) – until around 1800, after which post-modification could be sufficient: *the one preferred, the one before her eyes* (1811–12 Jane Austen). In the nineteenth century it became possible to use *this one* without post-modification (e.g. 1848 Thackeray, though much earlier with stressed, numerical *one*), likewise *those ones* (e.g. 1891 Kipling), and *these ones* appears to be a twentieth-century arrival in standard:

(26) a. To cut a long tale short, the drum ruffed, and off set four of them, a black one, and a white one, and a brown one, and *the man's one*, neck and neck, as neat as you like.

(1828 Moir, *Life of Mansie Wauch* xiv.86 [ARCHER])

  b. I know they ain't loaded. But use *these ones*. Them damn things is jinxed.   (1934 J. T. Farrell, *Young Manhood* iv. 61 [*OED*])

Jespersen expresses some surprise that *one* was beginning in the late nineteenth century to be used after genitive determiners, as in 1879–80 Trollope *my one*, and early in the twentieth after genitive NPs, *her sister's one* (1909–49: II 261).[12]

In effect this *one* behaves as if it were a common noun. In recent transformational grammar, *one* has been used as evidence for a nominal unit, $\bar{\text{N}}$ or N′, intermediate between the noun phrase (NP or N″) and the noun (N):

(27) You shouldn't mix this liquid cleaner with that *one*.

In (27) *one* cannot be a substitute for a complete NP such as *this liquid cleaner*, as witness ****with that this liquid cleaner*, nor is it likely to be a substitute for the head noun *cleaner*, but rather for *liquid cleaner*, a syntagm with no particular status in traditional grammatical description. (It certainly does not have the distribution of an NP.) The existence and grammatical significance of such units are important tenets of $\bar{\text{X}}$ (= X′, X-bar) Syntax, an influential theory which proposes that all grammatical categories – whether the familiar noun, verb, and adjective or more abstract entities like I (Inflection position) – occur in parallel hierarchies of phrase structure.

As an indefinite pronoun meaning 'someone, a certain one, an individual', *one* was already obsolete before our period unless postmodified (*OED* s.v., B.20), and during our period even that usage has largely disappeared:

(28) a. for thinking of marrying *one* who might be my father

(1777 Sheridan, *School for Scandal* III.i 392.33)

    b. Horace Smith said to *one* who ask'd him if he knew Hook 'Oh yes! Hook and I are very intimate.'

                              (1819 Keats, *Letters* 156 p. 420 (20 Sep.))

    c. there was *one* in that house whom I had loved at the first sight.

                              (1840 Bulwer-Lytton, *Money* II.i p. 183)

The function has been taken over by the compound *someone*.

The compound words made up of *any-/every-/no-/some-* and *-body/-one/ -thing* are usually treated as pronouns (thus Quirk, Greenbaum, Leech & Svartvik 1985: 6.46–7), though their etymologies suggest NPs consisting of determiner and noun. Intermittently during the ModE period they have been spelled as two words – the *OED* recognises *anybody* but not *anyone* as one word – and *no one* often still is. They freely permit postmodification by adjectives (*someone new, anything nice*) but not premodification (**new someone), which differentiates them from both personal pronouns and nouns. (Examples like *a little something* should be treated as involving conversion to noun.)

In subject function all of these compound pronouns require singular concord on the verb, even where the notional reference is plural. That is, in a sentence like:

(29)   Is everybody here?

the verb form shows clearly that *everybody* is singular, even though the implication of (29) is that the presence of more than one person is being questioned. The slightly forced usage in (30), where the indefinite pronouns refer to a mixed group of boys and girls, relies on the use of *it* as a sex-neutral pronoun for reference to children, plus strict adherence to grammatical number concord, and something similar is shown in (31), while (32), which once again refers to boys and girls, uses the conventional *he/his/him* set as anaphoric continuation of *everybody*:

(30)   a. Martha's insisting on *everybody*'s washing *its* hands

                              (1902 Nesbit, *5 Children* iii.67)

    b. But when he was gone *everyone* felt as if *it* had been trying not to cry all *its* life, and that *it* must cry now, if *it* died for it. So *they* cried.   (1906 Nesbit, *Amulet* i.13)

(31)   *Every man, woman, and child* in the village fell on *its* face on the sand.   (ibid. v.78)

(32)   *Everybody* opened *his* eyes.

                  (1960 Sendak, *Sign on Rosie's Door* (Puffin, 1972) iv.36)

It is noticeable that children's books published in America between the 1960s and 1980s tend to show more careful adherence to traditional grammatical teaching, or perhaps just closer editorial supervision, than equivalent British publications, although the nonsexist language of the late 1980s and 1990s would undoubtedly rule out examples like (32).

Increasingly often, however, these compound pronouns can have the grammatically plural indefinites *they/their/them* as anaphoric continuation; indeed Jespersen gives eModE examples (1909–49: II 495). (Even example (30b) abandons *it* for the more natural *they* beyond the sentence boundary.) This is common with the indefinites of personal reference consisting of *any-/every-/no-* + *-body/-one*:

(33)   a. that he was shut up in this poor bit of a place, with *nobody* troubling *their* heads about him!

           (1782 Burney, *Cecilia* (Bell, 1890) IV.vi.308)

    b. 'Might *anybody* ask what *their* brother has been saying?' said Solomon, in a soft tone of humility . . .

       'Oh yes, anybody may ask,' said Mr Trumbull . . . 'Anybody may interrogate. *Any one* may give *their* remarks an interrogative turn,' he continued

           (1871–2 George Eliot, *Middlemarch* xxxii.310)

There is a collection of examples in Poutsma (1914–29: III 310–11). Since then it has even spread to *somebody/someone*, as in (34), and even if (34b) has been distorted for reasons of humour or political correctness (or both, if that is not an oxymoron), such examples attest to a genuine conflict in the English pronominal system:

(34)   a. I am glad that the Labour Party's science spokesman is *someone* who knows *their* way around Whitehall.

           (1993 Tam Dalyell, *New Scientist* 1898: 52 (6 Nov.))

    b. Turkeys are so dumb that when it rains, they look up to the sky and can drown. It was to be the national bird of America until *someone* came to *their* senses.

       (1992 Emily Prager, 'Letter from New York', *The Guardian Weekend* p. 47 (12 Dec.))

Furthermore, indefinite *they* in its turn may have singular *themself* rather than the standard *themselves* as corresponding reflexive; see the next section.

In the early part of our period it was still possible to use *any* by itself as a indefinite pronoun with reference to a countable singular:

(35)　　a. Here the poor boy was locked in by himself all day, without
　　　　　　sight of *any* but the porter who brought him his bread and
　　　　　　water　　　　　(1823 Lamb, *Elia*, 'Christ's Hospital' p. 37 [Visser])
　　　　b. Woe betide *any* who suddenly discovers he has to go to
　　　　　　Brussels the next morning.
　　　　　　　　　　　　　　　　　　　　　(1972 *The Guardian* 30 Dec. 13 [*OED*])

This usage was already rare by the early nineteenth century, and *anyone*, *anybody* or *anything* (as appropriate) would now be virtually obligatory here (example (35b) is surprisingly late), except perhaps in the *any but* idiom:

(36)　　It is very hard . . . for *any but* the most committed cold-warrior.
　　　　　　　　　　　　　　　　　　　　　(1969 *The Guardian* 5 Nov. 8/3 [*OED*])

See Quirk, Greenbaum, Leech & Svartvik (1985: table 6.45, 9.58), Poutsma (1914–29: IV 1052–3). Indefinite pronominal *any* remains possible with reference to countable NPs in the plural or where number is indeterminate, and to noncount NPs.

3.2.2.3　Personal pronouns

Personal pronouns have undergone some changes in distribution, but relatively few as far as available forms are concerned. We may include here the forms *I/me/my/mine, you/your/yours, he/him/his, she/her/hers, it/its, we/us/our/ours, they/them/their/theirs, one/one's*, since it is inconvenient to separate the genitive determiners like *my* from the more strictly pronominal members of the paradigm. In the inventory of most varieties the major change has been the final loss of *thou/thee/thy/thine* (formerly the subjective, objective, genitive and disjunctive genitive forms, respectively, of the 2 SG pronoun).[13] At the very start of our period a distinction was occasionally made between *you* and *thou* for singular reference. Thus in Sheridan's comedy *A Trip to Scarborough* (1777), *thou* forms are intermittently used, mainly in anger or in patronising intimacy, and never to a social superior; any character who addresses another using *thou* also addresses him or her using *you*. The later survival of the *thou* paradigm was very marginal.[14] General loss as unmarked 2 SG pronoun removed all number distinction in the second person, leaving a gap to be filled by different expedients for marking number – always plural – in certain varieties: *you all, y'all, all-you, yiz, yous(e), y'uns, you guys, you lot*, etc. The simplification of verbal morphology associated with loss of *thou* may have had syntactic consequences: see section 3.3.3.4 below.

　A few other personal pronoun forms occur here and there, though most can be regarded as dialectal, for example, *un* for *him* in a speech by a rustic old gentleman which is peppered with other signs of non-standard usage (*A Trip to Scarborough* V.ii). The form *ye* is rare in our period except as an archaism, even rarer in the historically correct paradigm of subjective *ye* vs. objective *you*. One form in very widespread use throughout lModE is unstressed and informal *'em*, regarded as a shortening of *them* (incorrectly, as it happens, since it derives from OE *heom*).

There is a special form for genitives in independent or disjunctive function: compare *this book is mine/hers* with *my/her book*. Only where the attributive genitive ends in *-s* are both forms identical. The disjunctive use of *its* is 'extremely rare' (Quirk, Greenbaum, Leech & Svartvik 1985: 6.29); the *OED*'s sole example is from Shakespeare (s.v., B). Here is one:

(37)   and his voice was about four times its usual size, just as his body
        was four times *its*   (1902 Nesbit, *5 Children* viii.154)

The area of personal pronouns is one of those where our reliance on the written form may perhaps be misleading, since pronouns have always had strong (stressed) and weak (unstressed) forms in speech; see *CHEL* I: 144 on OE, and note, for instance, the irregular development of the long vowel in *you* (*CHEL* III, forthcoming). However, the modern weak forms (e.g. /m/ *'em* 'them', /i/ 'he') do not appear to encourage confusion or syncretism.

One kind of case selection, objective ~ subjective, only affects pronominal NPs in ModE, and there has been real change here during our period in the following environments: (A) in disjunctive use (bare responses); (B) after words which may be prepositions or conjunctions: *but, except, save* and especially *as* and *than*; and (C) as subject predicative. Let us take A and B first, illustrating the variation from a set of children's stories, with the historically older usage given first:

(38)   a. 'Mr Ji-jimmy's friend will have something worth having to put
           in his article now,' said Cyril very much later indeed.
              'Not *he*,' said Robert sleepily.   (1906 Nesbit, *Amulet* ix.175)
        b. 'Not *she*,' said the Psammead a little less crossly.   (ibid. viii.146)
        c. 'Not *they*,' cried the Princess joyously.
                                          (1907 Nesbit, *Enchanted Castle* i.28)

(39)   a. 'Not *me*!' was Gerald's unhesitating rejoinder.   (ibid. i.26)
        b. 'Not *us*!' said Mabel.   (ibid. xi.221)

(40)   a. The children were as white *as he*.   (1906 Nesbit, *Amulet* v.83)
        b. But Martha was stronger *than he*. (1902 Nesbit, *5 Children* ix.184)

(41) a. '... Just because he's bigger *than me*.' (ibid. viii.151)
      b. '... And Cyril is nearer to being a man *than us*, because he is
         the eldest.' (ibid. ii.50)
      c. 'I only wish I was bigger *than him*, that's all.' (ibid. viii.151)

It is no coincidence that the person in the A examples varies between (38) and (39): Jespersen traced 1 SG *Not me!* back to 1848 Dickens, but as late as *c.* 1940 he repeated his claim that 3 SG *Not him!* was absent even from vulgar speech (1894: 251; 1909–49: VII 264).[15] It is widespread now – indeed normal in educated speech. (Quirk, Greenbaum, Leech & Svartvik 1985: 6.4 are not explicit on person-case interaction.) As for the B difference between (40) and (41), the salient contrast appears to be between the writer's own voice and her fictional children, since the variation was a well-known marker of 'correctness'. When a century earlier the fictional Harriet Smith had said:

(42) for they are quite as well educated *as me*.

(1816 Austen, *Emma* I.iv.31)

she revealed her *lack* of education by Jane Austen's lights, a delicacy of characterisation which would not work now. The majority of Jespersen's examples are 1 SG (1909–49: VII 227–36).

The newer usage in C, objective case in subject predicative function, (44), can be traced back to the end of the sixteenth century, though the older usage, (43), remains possible for some speakers in PDE:

(43) 'Oh, if it's only *I*,' he said; [original emphasis]

(1904 Nesbit, *Phoenix* x.215)

(44) a. 'It's only *me*,' said Jimmy. (1907 Nesbit, *Enchanted castle* i.17)
      b. 'I beg your pardon . . .'
         'It's *us* that beg yours,' said Cyril politely.

(1906 Nesbit, *Amulet* iii.44)

      c. 'It's *them*!' cried Robert [original emphasis] (ibid. xiv.280)

Note that the grammatically proper 1 SG subjective of (43) is spoken by an adult curate rather than by the children of most of the other speech examples. Given the long period over which this case variation is attested, it may be possible to see not just whether first person led third in adopting objective case, but where second person fitted in.[16]

In all these types the objective form is taking over, though the change has not yet gone to completion. It has been a change introduced 'from below', and as this material shows, in first person before third at least in disjunctive use.

Another environment where the objective form is taking over, this time from the genitive, is subject of an *-ing*:

(45)   a. I don't like *his being late.*
         b. I don't like *him being late.*

(The variation seen in (45) is not confined to pronouns but shows up in most singular noun-headed NPs too, as a choice between presence and absence of *'s*.) This change is discussed in section 3.6.4.3.

In many varieties, pronoun case forms in co-ordinate NPs are not always the same as elsewhere – and are a great bugbear of prescriptivists. Objective forms in subject position are common, if non-standard:

(46) $\left\{ \begin{array}{l} \textit{Him and me} \\ \textit{Me and him} \end{array} \right\}$ went to town yesterday.

Emonds even goes so far as to argue that the objective pronouns in (41), (44) and (46) are the only normal usage for any language (like ModE) that lacks morphological case-marking, and that for theoretical reasons the older standard represented by (40) and (43) 'is not part of a dialect spoken (and hence acquired) as a native language by any natural language speech community' (1986: 93).

Conversely, and perhaps not with the same groups of speakers, subjective forms may occur in object positions:

(47)   and *between you and I,* I believe we must not mention the matter to
         him
         (1795 Mrs Meeke, *Count St. Blancard* (Minerva Press, repr. Arno, 1977) I.ii.66)

Conjoined NPs like *you and I* in examples like (47) are arguably widespread enough among educated speakers in PDE to be called standard (beside the 'correct' and historically expected *you and me*).[17] Neither (46) nor (47) is all that new. Loss of case distinction in second person pronouns may have played some part in the (46) type, though in most varieties *he* and *I* are quite secure as subjective forms when not co-ordinated. If, as seems plausible, (47) is a hypercorrect reaction to the stigmatised (46) – 'Use forms *X and I*, because *X and me* is wrong' – its occurrence well before the heyday of published prescriptive grammar, e.g. in Shakespeare, is problematic. See Jespersen (1909–49: VII 238, 271–3), Visser (1963–73: section 270), and Tieken-Boon van Ostade (1994). And why (even without the certainties of current theories of formal syntax) should (46) be so common anyway?

One possibility is to see it as a symptom of a general retreat of subjective forms to ever fewer environments, with objective pronouns clearly the unmarked case (for personal pronouns: *who/whom* goes the other way). The only environment in which subjective personal pronouns seem under no threat is as subject of finite verbs, and (46) is perhaps evidence of a stricter delineation of that environment. The prototypical subject pronoun is of unambiguous person and number, constitutes the whole of its NP, and has the potential for concord with the verb.[18] Furthermore, a pronoun of the first or second person is mainly deictic in function, a pronoun of the third person anaphoric. These are the syntactic and pragmatic features of the prototypical subject pronoun. It may be that *non*-prototypical subject pronouns are increasingly defaulting to the unmarked, objective case form. Two co-ordinated NPs will often differ in person, and the resultant NP may differ in number from its constituent NPs. In some dialects, then, a pronominal NP whose overall person and/or number bears an uncertain relation to the person/number of a pronoun within it, may no longer meet the conditions for use of a subjective form. Pronouns which are modified, making them less like deictic or anaphoric elements and somewhat more like referential nouns, may likewise fail to be marked as subjective. Hence such data as (48–9), where a pronoun in subject function does not constitute the entire subject NP:

(48)   a. that *poor I* must write helter-skelter
                    (1832 Gaskell, *Letters* 2 p. 2 (*c.* 17 Sep.))
        b. **He in the corner there* is the one you need to see.
        c. I, and not I, | And *the I* is the Giver of life
                    (1875 Lewis Morris, 'Evensong' (*Works*, 1890) 121 [Jespersen])
        d. 'Suppose *we girls* take a turn,' said Jane, laughing.
                    (1902 Nesbit, *5 Children* ii.43)

(49)   a. that *poor (old) me* must write helter-skelter
        b. ?*Him in the corner there* is the one you need to see.
        c. *The miserable little me* to be taken up and loved after tearing
           myself to pieces!   (1879 Meredith, *Egoist* xlviii.606 [Jespersen])
        d. *Us girls* can always take a joke.

Somewhat similar observations, with some useful BrE and Canadian dialect data, have been made by Shorrocks (1992). Notice the third person verb in (48c) (and also potentially in (49a)). On 'substantivized' pronouns as in (48c) and (49c), see Jespersen (1909–49: II 216, VII 223). Sentence (49d) is cited by Quirk, Greenbaum, Leech & Svartvik (1985: 6.5n.[c]) as an example of familiar speech; it can be used in dialects which would never admit *them girls* (for standard *those girls*). Indeed pairs like (48d) and (49d) are presumably responsible for hypercorrect forms like:

(50) a. just in time for *we 4*, (Mr Gaskell, Marianne Meta & *I*) to go to
          Oxford   (1860 Gaskell, *Letters* 461 p. 608 (5 Apr.))
      b. Rosemary sets a shining example to *we dithering dieters*
                          (1994 *Oldham Evening Chronicle* [headline] p. 12 (9 Mar.))

Earlier the usage of (49d) was comically rustic:

(51) *Us girls* cannot go for reasons; the attention of the cows claims
      our assistance in the evening.
                     (1798 'West-Country Farmer's Daughter', in Southey, *Life* I. 344
                                                                        (15 Aug.))

Fronting of object pronouns may also lead to 'incorrect' choice of case
form, though this is probably far less common than the co-ordination
effect with personal pronouns:

(52) *He*, who had always inspired in herself a respect which almost
      overcame her affection, she now saw the object of open
      pleasantry.   (1813 Austen, *P&P* III.xix.388)

It is of more importance in the interchange of *who* and *whom* in interrogative or relative function (3.5.3.2 and 3.6.5.2 below). Example (52) illustrates
a quite different point too: that personal pronouns, especially third person
pronouns, have become increasingly rare as antecedents of relative clauses.

3.2.2.4   Reflexive pronouns

Etymologically, reflexive pronouns are compounds of a personal pronoun
(genitive for first and second person, mostly objective for third person) and
a form of *self*. Even if we neglect dialects with forms like *meself, hisself, hissen*,
etc., containing a different selection of elements from the rather arbitrary
standard set, there have been recent changes in inventory within – or at
least close to – standard usage. Most concern a conflict between formal and
notional number. Consider the following examples:

(53) because everyone overslept *itself*, as it happened
                                              (1902 Nesbit, *5 Children* iii.63)

(54) Peaseblossom seemed to pull *herself* away from Mr. Caulder's
      back like a person forcing *themselves* to wake up.
                                        (1949 Streatfeild, *Painted Garden* ii.25)

(55) You have to take the prosecution evidence because somebody
      who's defending *themself* doesn't have to prove anything to you.
                          (1991 COBUILD Bank of English Corpus S0000000328
                                                          (radio phone in, 8 Nov.))

(56)   What can we do for *ourself*? What can we do for *ourself*?

> (1855–7 Dickens, *Little Dorrit* II.xxvi.694)

Example (53) shares its oddity with (30), discussed above. In the FORCE clause of (54), it appears that *a person* has been taken as equivalent to indefinite *they* and hence given the reflexive *themselves*, since standard English requires number concord between the two morphological parts of a reflexive; more recently a form *themself* has appeared instead in similar circumstances, as in (55).[19] As for the *ourself* of Dickens's (56), this has a history almost as long as that of *we* with singular reference, going right back to ME (see *OED* s.v.).

As with other compound pronouns, the spelling of reflexives has moved from two words to one, a process largely completed by the 1730s (to judge from ARCHER), but with occasional retention of two-word forms in respectable printed usage even in the early nineteenth century.

Reflexive pronouns are normally anaphoric to another NP in the same clause, that is, they are NPs which have the same referent as (most often) the subject NP. In true reflexive use the antecedent and reflexive have different grammatical functions:

(57)   The manager gave *herself* a day off.

In (57) *the manager* is subject, while *herself* – though having the same reference – is indirect object.

Another use of reflexives is an emphatic one, where reflexive and antecedent are in apposition and share the same grammatical function:

(58)   a. The manager *herself* gave the order.
          b. The manager gave the order *herself*.

(59)   I saw the manager *herself*.

In (58) *the manager* is subject, in (59) object, but in neither example is the grammatical function of *herself* distinct.

A variant of this emphatic use has a reflexive form without explicit antecedent:

(60)   a. I have been endeavouring to wean myself from you: for to
             myself alone what can be much of a misery? As far as they
             regard *myself* I can despise all events: but I cannot cease to
             love you.   (1819 Keats, *Letters* 150 p. 383 (13 Sep.))
          b. You know I should be most happy to do anything for *yourself*.
             But the nurse . . . there are so many impostors about!

> (1840 Bulwer-Lytton, *Money* I.i p. 167)

c. There was a temporary air about their establishments, as if . . .
there was also a dissatisfied air about *themselves*, as if
(1855–7 Dickens, *Little Dorrit* I.xxvi.303)

d. by which he had tried to convey to *her* his feeling about *herself*
and the division which her fortune made between them
(1871–2 George Eliot, *Middlemarch* lxxvii.772)

e. My dearest Boy, Yr letter is such a comfort to me & I am so
glad I may write openly to *yrself* [= *yourself*]
(1873 *Amberley Papers* II.546 (20 Jun.))

All of the above examples have a reflexive in a prepositional phrase, but
there are other possibilities, as in (61) and the second *myself* of (60a), even
(occasionally) subject position, (62):

(61)　　*Themselves* at least he had never been unnatural enough to banish
from his house　　　(1871–2 George Eliot, *Middlemarch* xxxii.303)

(62)　　and therefore I should say 'put the miniature in the exhibition' if
only myself was to be hurt.　　(1819 Keats, *Letters* 118 p. 287 (29 Mar.))

There is a degree of social marking attached to the usage in PDE, at least
in Britain: Quirk, Greenbaum, Leech & Svartvik brandish the phrase
'genteel evasion of the normal personal pronoun' (1985: 6.27(b))!
Acceptability must have declined, therefore, given the authorial status of
the nineteenth-century examples (60) and others like them, and the apparent absence of adverse comment from eighteenth-century grammarians in
Sundby, Bjørge & Haugland (1991). But just before our period there is a
snobbish dismissal by Robert Baker (1770) of the phrase *of themselves and
Families* as 'mere Shopkeepers Cant' (cited by Tieken-Boon van Ostade
1994: 231 from Leonard 1929: 175). Example (61) can perhaps be taken as
free indirect speech and therefore not in the authorial voice.

3.2.3　*Adjectives as apparent head of NP*

Although the prototypical heads of NPs are nouns and pronouns, other
categories can apparently serve that function:

(63)　　dispensing relief to *the poor*　　　(1861 Green, *Letters* 78 (16 Apr.))

The phrase *the poor* in (63) appears to have as head the adjective *poor*, and
yet it is clearly an NP. That would violate a tenet of X-bar theory, where
only a (pro)noun can be head of NP, only an adjective head of AP, and so
on. One solution is to analyse the NP *the poor* as headless, its presumed

nominal head missing by ellipsis (Huddleston 1984: 326–7; Allerton 1995). For convenience I shall, however, refer to the adjective as head of the NP, following Quirk, Greenbaum, Leech & Svartvik (1985: 7.23–6) and Rissanen (*CHEL* III, forthcoming).

Rissanen shows that in eModE, adjectives acting as NP heads could still have nongeneric reference, even to individuals, though such usage was becoming infrequent (*CHEL* III, forthcoming), being replaced principally by NPs headed by the prop-word *one* (3.2.2.2 above). In our period adjectives acting as NP heads have been almost exclusively plural generics, (64a, b), though some refer to singular abstractions, (65a), or to singular individuals, (65b):

(64)   a. the poor (= 'poor people')
        b. the French (= 'French people')

(65)   a. the unknown (= 'that which is unknown')
        b. the deceased (= 'the dead person')

The singular, nongeneric types, (65), are hardly productive now, being largely confined to fixed expressions. When a nationality like *the French* is used to mean 'the French language', it is arguable whether the phrase has a noun or adjective as head. If the latter, however, its general replacement during our period by plain *French* (Quirk, Greenbaum, Leech & Svartvik 1985: 5.58n.) – which must be analysed as noun without article – is an example of loss from the (65a) type.[20] The (65b) type now includes superlatives, the fixed phrase *the Almighty*, and a group of participial adjectives like *the deceased, his intended, the accused*. In this context Jespersen gives numerous examples up to the turn of the twentieth century of singular *the dead*, though he says in 1913 that 'colloquially *the dead man* is preferred' (1909–49: II 232). By now the preference is no longer just colloquial: *the dead* (SG) is long departed.

3.2.4   *Determiners*

Most determiners are grammatical words whose functions include those of signalling number, definiteness and other general notions for the NP as a whole; on the term **Determiner** see note 6. Within the Determiner position there is a single slot for central determiners like *the, this, a*. The same slot is used for genitive NPs like *Jim's, some old people's*, and also for forms like *his, our*, which resemble both determiners and genitive NPs. All of these items are in contrastive distribution; colloquial PDE does not permit NPs like ***this my chapter, possible until the beginning of our period and later still in literary and legal usage:

(66)   a. To support with unrelaxing vigilance every right, . . . every
franchise, in *this my adopted . . . country.*

                       (1796 Burke *Letter to Noble Lord* Wks. VIII. 40 [*OED*])

    b. They are great Men doubtless but how are they to be
compared to *those our countreymen* Milton and the two Sidneys

                       (1818 Keats, *Letters* 94 p. 234 (Oct.))

    c. As brisk as bees . . . did the four Pickwickians assemble on the
morning of the twenty-second day of December, in the year
of grace in which *these, their faithfully-recorded adventures*, were
undertaken and accomplished.

                     (1836–7 Dickens, *Pickwick* xxviii.408 [Poutsma])

    d. which have already been highly approved of in *this their new
form* by my daughters   (1864 Gaskell, *Letters* 545 p. 723 (1 Jan.))

Notice how Dickens uses the locution in playfully bombastic style, and punctuating to suggest that *these* and *their* belong to parallel NPs in apposition rather than jointly filling a single determiner slot. But Mrs Gaskell's (66d) looks more straightforward.

There are limited sets of predeterminers (*all, both*, etc.) and postdeterminers (numerals, *other, many*, etc.), named transparently from their positional behaviour with respect to central determiners; each has its own section below.

Both *no* and *every* are central determiners. Early in our period, *none* could be so used too:

(67)   and now when *none such troubles* oppress me

                       (1819 Keats, *Letters* 134 p. 352 (1 Jul.))

Example (67) postdates the general divergence of *none* and *no* in the eModE period, since which they have functioned almost exclusively as pronoun and determiner, respectively.[21]

Exceptionally for a determiner, *every* can co-occur with genitives, which are also normally central determiners: *his every move* (Quirk, Greenbaum, Leech & Svartvik 1985: 5.14n.[c]). Another usage which seems to call into doubt the classification of *every* as a central determiner is the pattern *every + the +* superlative adjective, now obsolete (*OED* s.v., 1c):

(68)   Every the most minute article. (= 'even the most minute article')

                   (1806–7 J. Beresford, *Miseries Hum. Life* (1826) i. x [*OED*])

As Poutsma points out (1914–29: IV 805, 1050, 1078–9, 1137), such other quantifiers as *many, most* and *any* could also be found before a superlative NP, though never commonly:

(69)   any the most intricate accounts

> (1823 Lamb, *Elia*, 'South-Sea House' p. 10 [Poutsma])

Compare the patterns discussed under (66).

3.2.4.1   Predeterminers

The predeterminers – those determiners which can precede the central members of the class – include the quantifiers *all, both, half* and some uses of *such, what.*

All and *both* can appear to 'float off' from an assumed basic position within the NP, (70a), by a process known as Quantifier Floating:

(70)   a. *All* the sailors looked/were looking puzzled.
         b. The sailors *all* looked puzzled.
         c. The sailors were *all* looking puzzled.

There have been changes in what is permitted here. According to Quirk, Greenbaum, Leech & Svartvik (1985: 3.28, 5.16), floated quantifiers can only follow an operator in PDE, not an ordinary verb. So a floated quantifier would not be expected after SEEM (but cf. *OED* s.v. *both* a. A.2 for a late nineteenth-century view) nor, in most dialects, after modal HAVE:

(71)   a. 'Since you seem *all* to be as mad as the whole worshipful
            company of hatters,' he said bitterly

> (1902 Nesbit, *5 Children* ix.183)

         b. especially as it had *all* to be told twice

> (1904 Nesbit, *Phoenix* iv.87)

Nowadays *all* would tend to precede the first verb in (71) or even to 'split the infinitive' (though notice that with pronoun subject it could scarcely appear in the 'basic', pre-head position). For operators see section 3.3.8 below, for split infinitives 3.5.1.3.

The quantifier *all* took final position when modifying object *it* at a time when pronominal direct objects could precede indirect objects (3.5.1.2 below):

(72)   a. And then he told it her *all*

> (1860–1 Trollope, *Framley* xxxiii.324 [Poutsma])

         b. 'And give it them *all?*' ['give all of it to them'; original
            emphasis]   (1904 Nesbit, *Phoenix* vi.133)

If *all* is unambiguously a predeterminer in (70a), what is its category when floated? Poutsma calls it 'semi-adverbial' (1914–29: IV 1023). The fact that the central determiner *each* takes part in the floated (70b, c) types without having a 'basic' (70a) variant suggests that floated quantifiers become pronominal. What are undoubtedly nominal elements – usually quantifying pronouns – can do something akin to floating, though the usage is old-fashioned now:

(73)   a. I don't think we should *any of us* like it
                                            (?1846 Gaskell, *Letters* 17 p. 47)
        b. it [*sc.* the money] had *half of it* been taken from him.
                                            (1871–2 George Eliot, *Middlemarch* lxix.697)
        c. 'She doesn't mean to be silly,' Anthea said gently; 'we *none of us*
           do, whatever you may think . . .'   (1902 Nesbit, *5 Children* i.27)
        d. 'It isn't *a word of it* true . . .'   (1921 Lawrence, *Women* xxix.422)

In (73) the quantifier phrase is in apposition to the head pronoun and contains a second copy in an *of*-phrase, a sort of right dislocation. For further examples with *all* and *both* see Jespersen (1909–49: VII 338–9).

Having strayed from predeterminer to pronominal use of certain quantifiers, we might pause to consider variation between them. In PDE we choose freely between *all the books* (*all* as predeterminer) and *all of the books* (pronominal *all*), the latter quite unmarked stylistically. Near the end of the last century, however, the *OED* was claiming that *all/both of NP*, with a plural noun as head of NP, was a colloquial innovation rare in literary use (s.vv. *all* a. A6, *both* a. A6). Despite Poutsma's few literary examples of *both of NP* with plural head noun (1914–29: IV 1064), the *of* construction does seem much the less common in the nineteenth century, to judge from ARCHER, except in such instances as *all/both of which Ns*. If the *of*-construction has gained in acceptability since then, this should perhaps be related to the spread of partitive NPs of the type *X of Y*, e.g. *a lot of books*, where the notional – and increasingly, the syntactic – head of the phrase is Y rather than X (3.2.4.4 below). (Of course, with pronoun NPs the *of*-construction has been normal throughout ModE, as in *both of us*.)

Like *every* (discussed in 3.2.4 above), the determiner *such* is somewhat unstable. It can be a predeterminer (*such a pity*) or a postdeterminer (*another such disaster, no such luck*). The predeterminer uses show some losses. PDE no longer permits premodification by *much*, (74a), though *just* remains acceptable, (74c):

(74)   a. 'Yes, yes! – but then my father was in *much such a station*; at any
          rate, there was not the disparity there is between Mary and
          me.'   (1848 Gaskell, *Mary Barton* xi.147)
       b. there is not *such another young lady* in the world
                                        (1833 Gaskell, *Letters* 3 p. 4 (*c.* 16 Dec.))
       c. and the children had the highest hopes of *just such another
          holiday* for the next summer.   (1906 Nesbit, *Amulet* i.12)

Whether predeterminer *such* is still compatible with *another* in PDE, as in
(74b, c), is doubtful, though *OED* contains seventeen examples in our
period of *such another* as determiner, the most recent dated 1926.[22] The
normal PDE order is, of course, *another such*.

3.2.4.2   Articles and demonstratives

There are minor changes in the use or omission of articles. Several nouns
denoting illnesses and afflictions have recently ceased to occur with articles, so that *a sunstroke* (1902 Nesbit, *5 Children* ix.183), *the influenza*, *the
mumps* seem old-fashioned now – although *the flu* is still quite possible, and
indeed usual in AmerE, as is *the mumps*. Jane Austen's *the headach* is now
quite impossible syntactically, in standard anyway, as well as in spelling
(Phillipps 1970: 174). George Eliot wrote *without taking percentage from drug-
gists* (1871–2 *Middlemarch* xv.147) and *in literature and the drama* (ibid.
xxxi.300), where PDE would prefer *a percentage* with article but possibly
drama without.[23] In journalism, at any rate, nouns denoting political or
other office can be used in apposition to the name of the office-holder
without an article and without an intonation break, thus *Prime Minister
John Smith* rather than *the Prime Minister, John Smith*; the usage still strikes
many Britons as an Americanism. Jucker (1992) reports that it remains far
less frequent in the upmarket British press than in mid- or downmarket
papers.

   There have been minor changes in the usage of the demonstratives. The
OED records as originally American the use of *this* to denote someone or
something not previously mentioned:

(75)   Did you read about *this fellow* that went and paid a thousand
       dollars for   (1922 S. Lewis, *Babbitt* viii. 116 [*OED*])

So-called 'new-*this*' is traced by Wald as far back as the 1930s (1983: 94),
though a similarity is noted to the lME vivid narrative use of *this* at the *second*
lexical mention of a character (*CHEL* II: 218).

3.2.4.3 Genitives

One of the items which can fill the Determiner slot (and make an NP definite) is the genitive NP. For this purpose it is convenient to include both genitive determiners like *my, his, their* and genitives like *John's, the boys', the Duke of York's*. It has been persuasively argued that PDE *'s* (plural *s'* in spelling) is no longer an inflection but a syntactic word cliticised to an NP; see Huddleston (1984: 46–7). The argument is particularly strong for the so-called 'group genitive', whose origins were discussed in *CHEL* II: 229–30, so that the structure of *the Duke of York's house* would be roughly

(76)

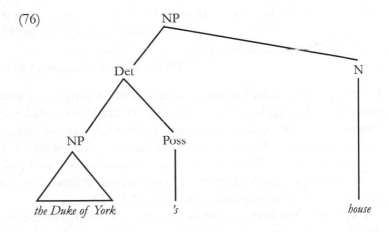

Since the ME period at least, the use of an *'s*-genitive in the Determiner slot has been in variation with an *of*-phrase in post-modifier position, thus *the book's contents* vs. *the contents of the book*. The ranges and relative frequencies of the competing constructions have varied over the course of time, with genitives of inanimates perhaps on the increase. Mossé (1947: 208) finds twentieth-century examples like *the war's duration, the cliff's edge, the car's horn* worthy of note, and Barber (1964: 132–3), cited by Strang (1970: 58), detects a revival of the *'s*-genitive at the expense of the *of*-genitive in such NPs as *biography's charm*. Conversely, however, some examples from Jane Austen, cited by Phillipps (1970: 163), are scarcely possible now:

(77)   a. and that *Mr. Elliott's idea* [= the idea of Mr Elliott] always
          produced irritation in both, was beyond a doubt.

          (1818 Austen, *Persuasion* II.xii.107)

       b. and *his sight* [= the sight of him] was so inseparably connected
          with some very disagreeable feelings, that

          (1816 Austen, *Emma* II.iv[xxii].182)

These are 'objective genitives', most clearly seen in (77b), where *his* corresponds to an object in *to see him*. What has changed – and Austen comes near the end of a long rundown – is that object relations are generally expressed in PDE by an *of*-genitive, with the *'s*-genitive confined pretty much to animate genitive followed by deverbal noun and often not even then (Quirk, Greenbaum, Leech & Svartvik 1985: 17.41–3).

Since at least the seventeenth century it has been possible to combine both constructions in patterns like *this friend of mine, an idea of the secretary's*:

(78)   a. old Rowley who . . . has, you know, never been *a Friend of mine*.
                        (1777 Sheridan, *School for Scandal* I.i 363.13)
        b. *These whipmasters of ours.*
                        (1893 K. Grahame *Pagan Papers* 96 [*OED*])

(Here, of course, we are looking at a syntagm which forms a complete NP rather than filling the Determiner slot in an NP headed by something else.) Rissanen (1993: 50–3) treats the pattern *this friend of mine* as a replacement for structures like **this my friend with double determiner (see 3.2.4 above). As Strang points out (1970: 98), the new construction allows the NP as a whole and the genitive NP to be marked independently for definiteness; see also the discussion in Jespersen (1909–49: III 15–23).

This may be the best place to mention the rise and fall of the apostrophe, almost entirely contained within our period, even though it is not a matter of syntax at all. Strang argues (1970: 109–10):

> For the genitive singular of nouns -*'s* became fairly regular by the late 17c, and in the genitive plural -*s'* not till the late 18c. This creates the curious situation that for almost all nouns the two-term system of contrast operative in speech (unmarked form without ending, form marked for case or number with sibilant ending), corresponds to a four-term system in writing.

For much of the period it has been the convention that no genitive inflection is added to proper names (and a few other nouns) already ending in /s, z/, thus *Tiberius' rule, Dickens' novels*, though this exception is now being ironed out. In our period too came the arbitrary codification of *its* and *whose* without apostrophe as the genitives of *it* and *who*, respectively, and *it's, who's* with apostrophe as the contraction of *it, who* with *is* or *has*.[24] It is hardly surprising that these conventions seem to be in rapid collapse, with what has been called 'the greengrocer's apostrophe' (*apple's 60p, Antique's, linguistic's*, and perhaps even *mean't*, all personally attested) just one symptom of what may well turn out to be the imminent demise of the apostrophe. Distressing though it is to purists, it must be admitted that genuine ambiguities caused by omission or misuse of the apostrophe are very infrequent indeed.

3.2.4.4 Partitives

It is possible to analyse an NP like *a majority of students* in two ways:

(79)   a. head noun *majority*, premodified by determiner *a* and postmodified by the prepositional phrase *of students* (cf. *a steak in breadcrumbs*)

       b. head noun *students*, premodified by complex determiner *a majority of* (cf. *a few students*)

For conflicting views see Huddleston (1984: 236–9), Quirk, Greenbaum, Leech & Svartvik (1985: 5.25, 10.43). Analysis (79a) corresponds to the syntactic origin of the pattern, while there is some semantic support for (79b), in that *a majority of students* is notionally more likely to be a partitive of *students* than a kind of *majority*. The most obvious test of structure is verbal concord: with singular *majority* or with plural *students*? For quite a number of phrases, the historical development has been a classic process of replacement: first analysis a alone, then a and b in variation, and finally b alone. The older structure is shown in:

(80)   The progress of phonetics has been so great . . . that *the great bulk of the observations* already made on living languages *is* next to useless.   (1873–4 Sweet, 'On Danish Pronunciation', *TPhS* 94)

The newer structure appears in:

(81)   *a crowd of people were arguing* with and even shoving the Guards.

                                      (1906 Nesbit, *Amulet* xi.206)

Both variants exist today in:

(82)   A group of students $\left\{ \begin{array}{c} \text{is} \\ \text{are} \end{array} \right\}$ waiting outside.

With the *majority* example already discussed, the singular variant is now somewhat pedantic and is probably obsolescent. And with *a lot of* the singular construction has disappeared entirely (and of course was never found with the plural variant *lots of*).[25] Informal English even permits concord between a plural (notional) head noun and a central determiner which, historically speaking, should be the modifier of a singular noun:

(83)   a. *These* sort of ideas

(1788 Betsy Sheridan, *Journal* 42 p. 131 (21 Nov.))

          b. *those* sort of jokes   (1949 Streatfeild, *Painted Garden* xxiii.256)

Such examples – Quirk, Greenbaum, Leech & Svartvik have a similar one with *kind of* (1985: 10.43) – give additional support to analysis (79b) over and above verbal concord, with *sort of* functioning syntactically as a kind of postdeterminer.

Nonpartitives like *a tiny stifling box of a place* (1917 Bell, *Letters* II.405) and *a/one hell of a party* (cf. also the common spelling *helluva*) may show a rather similar shift from head to part of premodifier; see here Austin (1980), Aarts (1998), *OED* s.v. *of* prep. 24.

Historically the pronoun *none* is singular (etymologically *ne* 'not' + *one*, but no longer in use as a determiner), and some careful stylists use it as such. Writers like Foster (1970: 217) assume that plural concord is becoming increasingly common when *none* is used with implicit or explicit plural partitive:

(84)   None (of them) $\left\{ \begin{array}{c} \text{is} \\ \text{are} \end{array} \right\}$ waiting outside any more.

They are mistaken to think that this is a PDE laxness. Jane Austen can use a plural verb after *none* or *neither . . . nor* (Phillipps 1970: 159). My letters corpus has only one example where concord is distinctive:

(85)   *None of his novels contain* happier sentences.

(1890 Dowson, *Letters* 83 p. 132 (27 Jan.))

– and there it is used as a plural. And preliminary corpus evidence suggests that plural *none* has been normal since long before our lModE period. The evidence is presented in table 3.2, which is confined to examples of *none* + explicit plural *of*-phrase which have a clear indication of number within the same clause or in a subordinate clause. The very small totals found in ARCHER were corroborated from *OED* citations. If these figures are good indicators of general usage, it appears that singular use became quite rare after the seventeenth century and was only revived in the twentieth; note, however, that the figures exclude a far greater number of instances indeterminate as to number.

However, Dekeyser's data for the nineteenth century (1975: 90–4) give a different picture: he finds just under 45 per cent singular use before 1850, 26 per cent after 1850, though his count has a slightly different basis, as it includes, for instance, examples without a plural *of*-phrase, as well as some

Table 3.2. *Singular and plural* none + of + NP_{PL}

| | ARCHER (British) | | | | OED quotations | | | |
| | Verbal concord | | Anaphoric pronoun | | Verbal concord | | Anaphoric pronoun | |
	SG	PL	SG	PL	SG	PL	SG	PL
1650–99	1	1	0	0	3	20	1	3
1700–49	0	0	0	0	0	13	0	2
1750–99	0	2	0	0	2	17	1	0
1800–49	0	4	0	0	3	25	0	2
1850–99	0	3	0	0	6	53	0	3
1900–49	1	3	0	0	22	30	0	0
1950–	1	3	0	0	27	26	1	1

with dummy *there*, both of which might favour singular usage. He also records – as one would expect – a greater use of singular *none* in narrative, descriptive and informative prose than in conversational English (46 per cent versus 27 per cent), though the difference is not statistically significant, and a less frequent use of singular when *none* is followed by *of* + plural NP (17 per cent versus 44 per cent).

Remembering how natural gender supplanted grammatical gender over the course of the OE and eME periods (*CHEL* II: 105–8), we might see a tendency towards 'natural number' in such developments as plural *none*, plural *government*, *public*, etc., and likewise singular *themself*.

3.2.4.5 Postdeterminers

Postdeterminers come after the central determiners. They include cardinal numerals, ordinal numerals and the general ordinals *other*, *another* (Quirk, Greenbaum, Leech & Svartvik 1985: 5.22), and quantifiers. Occasionally one hears locutions with, apparently, *another* interrupted by an adjective, typically *whole*; the main fragment may even be the nonstandard and originally jocular form *nother*:

(86)   *A whole other wife and children* all unbeknownst to Ackerley until after his father's death.
                                        (1982 *London Rev. Bks.* 20 May–2 Jun. 3 [*OED*])

(87)   but that's *a whole nother story*   (1993 Robert Stockwell, p.c. (19 Oct.))

Rather than adjective preceding determiner, which would be a major structural change in the NP, this is probably better taken as premodification within the Determiner slot.

Other can also be used pronominally, of course, and one change here has been the loss of *other* in favour of *others* where the reference is plural, with *other of* the last surviving environment:

(88)   In *other* of her Poems   (1817 Keats, *Letters* 22 p. 47 (21 Sep.))

See *OED* s.v. *other* pron. B.4, 5b, 6b.

The quantifiers show some changes of usage. Already in the eModE period, *more* had come to be used both with noncount and count nouns (*more rain, more raindrops*). *Less* has a strong tendency to behave similarly, and in fact did so between OE and the sixteenth century. Usages like *less raindrops* then became stigmatised, and in standard English a distinction has until recently been made between *less* and *fewer*: *less rain*, but *fewer raindrops*. As it happens, there are no examples either of *less* or *fewer* + plural count noun in my letters corpus, though there are some now-obsolescent usages with noncount nouns:

(89)   By-the-bye can you tell me of a good map of Somerset, of *less*
        ['smaller'] *size* than our unwieldy Ordnance Gentleman, yet
        minute enough for *my* [original emphasis] purposes?
                                        (1861 Green, *Letters* 73 (14 Mar.))

Environments where *less* was not directly followed by a plural noun were always somewhat more acceptable (e.g. *less than twenty students; twenty students, more or less*). The following example could be one such:

(90)   Capt. Goldsmith, a young Surrey officer, came with me for the
        first couple of hours, with a party of 19 mounted police – for
        honour you understand, not for safety. I could have done with
        less but in spite of them all the ride over the desert green with
        aromatic plants was delicious.   (1918 Bell, *Letters* II.451 (28 Mar.))

In (90) the modern reader is likely to interpret *less* as 'less policemen', whereas the highly educated Bell more probably understood something like 'less honour' or 'a smaller party', thus with the meaning of (89). The *OED* has a few nineteenth-century citations of *less Ns* (one erroneous); *less people* occurs in 1906 Shaw (*Doctor's Dilemma* I p. 515). Within the last generation or so, the usage has become increasingly frequent, and the current revival seems inexorable, given the strong pressure of analogy. Superlative *least* shows a similar tendency. It is tempting to see the fairly common occurrence of *amount of Ns* 'number of Ns' with plural count noun, which is non-standard at least in BrE (Quirk, Greenbaum, Leech & Svartvik 1985: 5.25), as further evidence that the count~noncount distinction is being effaced. However, the *OED* seems to regard *amount of* in the nineteenth century as equally normal with both count and noncount nouns, though with count nouns it is commonest in the idiom *any amount of Ns*.

Many had a quasi-nominal use in *a many* (*OED* s.v. B.1), a complex determiner and pronoun apparently analogous to *a few*:

(91)   You see *what a many words* it requires to give any identity to a
        thing I could have told you in half a minute.

                              (1819 Keats, *Letters* 156 p. 404 (18 Sep.))

(92)   *A many of them* played the truant   (1840 *P. Parley's Ann.* 183 [*OED*])

This usage has receded somewhat – Brook regards it as non-standard in Dickens, for instance (1970: 244) – and is now confined to the set phrase *a good/great many*, unless we relate it to another complex plural determiner and pronoun, *this/that many*. Usage here is very variable: Keats also uses *this many an N* (*Letters* 24 p. 50) and *these many Ns* (19 p. 38).

3.2.5   Adjectives

The next position or group of positions within the NP is for adjectives. Now there are three characteristic functions of adjectives, of which the one we are immediately concerned with is use in attributive position within an NP: that is, modifying a following (pro)noun. Much of our discussion will apply also to the other two: postposed adjectives within the NP (on which see also 3.2.7 below), and predicative adjectives which are independent of NPs.

3.2.5.1   Adjective order

Adjectives have mutual ordering relations which are tendencies rather than rigid rules: *big brown bag* is a more likely ordering than *?brown big bag*. Over the entire recorded history of English there have been some changes here – compare Chaucer's *the old pore mans deth* – but in our period there seems to be little chronological variation. We find such examples as

(93)   a. but indeed *that little foolish Woman* has made me very uneasy.
                          (1789 Betsy Sheridan, *Journal* 60 p. 171 (15 Jun.))
        b. *you little ungrateful puss*   (1848 Gaskell, *Mary Barton* vi.87)
        c. Mrs Lee is *a little timid woman*
                                  (1850 Gaskell, *Letters* 70 p. 112 (26 Apr.))

    d. they came into *the little interesting criss-crossy streets* that held the
    most interesting shops of all   (1906 Nesbit, *Amulet* i.18)

(94)   a. Then there is *an old curious seat* of the Marquis of
        Northampton   (1838 Gaskell, *Letters* 12 p. 28 (18 Aug.))
    b. down *some old mysterious stone steps*   (1841 ibid. 15 p. 820)

(95)   in order to find *the knitting old woman* [= some old woman who
    was famous . . . for her skill in knitting woollen stockings]
        (1851–3 Gaskell, *Cranford* xi.101)

In (93) we might expect *little* to come one place further to the right in PDE,
likewise *old* in (94), while *knitting* in (95) would probably come next to the
head noun. Of course, isolated oddities do not in themselves show a difference in the language system, since at any period there has been freedom
to violate the norms of adjectival order.

3.2.5.2 Premodifying adverbs

Certain positions in NP structure, notably the adjectival slots, permit
premodification by adverbs. The adverb is in construction with the
adjective (is part of the adjective phrase) and plays no direct part in overall
NP structure:

(96)   an *enormously* interesting molecule

In (96) *enormously* modifies not the head noun *molecule* but the adjective *interesting*. Such premodification within adjective phrases is generally possible in
all three AP functions.

A very common type of premodifying adverb is the intensifier – such
items as *very, too* – a lexical category with a high turnover because of its
expressive function. *Vastly* 'exceedingly' in (97a) was '[c]ommon in fashionable use in the 18th cent.' (*OED* s.v. 3); *monstrous* in (97b) is obsolete now
(*OED* s.v. 8b); while the evidently colloquial *frightfully* in (97c) seems peculiarly old-fashioned (and upper/middle-class British):

(97)   a. I am *vastly glad* to see you. (1779 (1781) Sheridan, *Critic* I.i 500.13)
    b. A *monstrous fine* young man!
        (1840 Bulwer-Lytton, *Money* IV.ii p. 220)
    c. '. . . I think Babylon seems *a most frightfully jolly* place to go to.'
        (1906 Nesbit, *Amulet* vi.97)

Although positionally similar to the adverbs in (97), *absolutely* in (98) is
probably a sentence adverbial (not recorded until 1851 by *OED* s.v., 8)
rather than a premodifier within the adjective phrase:

(98)   she is *absolutely fatter* since she came here

(1836 Gaskell, *Letters* 4 p. 6 (12 May))

I expect that native-speaking readers of this chapter will find particular times or places suggested to them by some of the intensifiers in *awfully kind, dreadfully nice, jolly difficult, main happy*,[26] *dead friendly, real smart, clean wrong, right fed up, sure pretty, wicked funny, pure brilliant*. The premodifier *quite* (+ e.g. *pleased*) tends to mean 'very' in America, 'somewhat' in Britain. This largely lexical matter has syntactic repercussions when an intensifier like *well*, formerly restricted to past participles, as in:

(99)   I am *well* disappointed in hearing good news from George, – for
         it runs in my head we shall all die young.

(1820 Keats, *Letters* 242 p. 530 (30 Nov.))

becomes available to younger speakers as a modifier of nonparticipial adjectives, as in *well angry* (although the usage may actually be a revival rather than an innovation).

What has seemed to some observers a recent development is the use of *that* as premodifier of adjectives:

(100)   a. Don't give me *that big* a helping.
         b. It wasn't *(all) that* good.
         c. and, as she said later, over tea and cold tongue, 'it was *that
            sudden* it made her flesh creep.'   (1906 Nesbit, *Amulet* xiv.262)

The (100b) type is mentioned by Barber (1964: 138), followed by Strang (1970: 59). However, the *OED* traces the usage back to late ME, regarding it as now just dialectal and Scottish, with a more general colloquial use in negative contexts (s.v. *that* adv. B.III.a). Such assertive examples as (100c) are evidently meant to be non-standard (and cf. Quirk, Greenbaum, Leech & Svartvik 1985: 7.56n.[e]). In (100), then, we have a change in register rather than a syntactic innovation.

The combination of 'amplifying' *quite* and 'emphasising' *too* (Quirk, Greenbaum, Leech & Svartvik 1985: 7.56n.[a], 7.57n.) is no longer idiomatic:

(101)   a. My little Frauleinchen was *quite too adorable* in her pinkest
            pinafore, & a complexion of milk & roses.

(1890 Dowson, *Letters* 105 p. 156 (25 Jun.))
         b. 'It's simply *quite too dreadfully awful*,' said Anthea.

(1902 Nesbit, *5 Children* xi.211)

Likewise only items like *much* and *far* can intensify amplifying *too* before an adjective in PDE:

(102)   we were *dreadfully too early*.   (1838 Gaskell, *Letters* 9 p. 18 (17 Jul.))

3.2.5.3   Comparison

Two premodifying adverbs are of major importance because of their use in forming comparatives and superlatives: *more* and *most*. I shall use the label **syntactic comparison** for both comparative *more narrow* and superlative *most evil*, while **morphological comparison** will cover both regular *narrower, happiest* and irregular *better, worst*, and the like. In general the two processes are in variation with each other. A rule of thumb for PDE is that monosyllabic adjectives and disyllables, especially those with primary stress on the first syllable, usually allow – and may require – morphological comparison, while others prefer syntactic comparison (Quirk, Greenbaum, Leech & Svartvik 1985: 7.81–2).[27]

Now the general tendency over the recorded history of English has been for syntactic comparison to expand at the expense of morphological comparison. Elizabethan playwrights, as is well known, frequently used morphological comparison with polysyllabic adjectives which are no longer eligible for it, e.g. *beautifulst* (*c.* 1590 Marlowe). Indeed in lME and eModE both kinds could be combined, as in *most fairest, most unkindest*, a doubling which prescriptive grammar has virtually abolished from written and at least careful spoken usage. Some examples from lModE of morphological comparison not now normal include *properer* (1821, 1852; *OED* s.v. *proper* a. 5a, 9), *playfullest* (1820 Keats), *scornfullest* (1855–7 Dickens), *sociablest* (1852 Hawthorne; *OED* s.v. *sociable* a. 2a). (A similar change was undergone by adverbs.) However, a preliminary assessment of superlatives in ARCHER does not show any clear frequency change during our period. See now also Kytö & Romaine (1997).

3.2.5.4   Transitive adjectives

Three adjective-like items in PDE have the preposition-like property of governing an NP complement: *near, like* and *worth*. Joan Maling's discussion of their history concludes that *near* remains more like an adjective, while *like* and *worth* are now best taken as prepositions (1983), whereas Quirk, Greenbaum, Leech & Svartvik treat *all* of them as prepositions but with greatest hesitation over *like* (1985: 9.4, 9.5, 15.12n.[c]). Earlier in our period the adjectives *(un)becoming, (un)worthy, next*[28] could also be transitive:

(103)   a. and any such feeling on her part was mean, ignoble, and
unbecoming the spirit with which she wished to think that she was
endowed.   (1860–1 Trollope, *Framley* xxxv.343)

           b. subjects *unworthy the notice of the Comic Muse*
                                   (1779 (1781) Sheridan, *Critic* I.i 502.9)

           c. tearing up whole handfuls of the scorched skin with the flesh
next it   (1823 Lamb, *Elia*, 'Roast Pig' p. 278 [*OED*])

The *OED* actually gives citations up to the late nineteenth century (s.vv. *unworthy* a. A.6–7, *worthy* a. A.8–10, *next* a. A.14), and in the case of *(un)worthy* labels this usage as involving ellipsis of *of*.

3.2.6   *Attributive nouns*

Whatever the internal organisation of the adjective position, adjectives as a group must precede any nouns used as attributive modifiers: *bitter coal strike*, not ****coal bitter strike*. Both *bitter* and *coal* are here attributive modifiers – they have a similar *function* – but there is no reason to conflate their grammatical categories: *coal* does not thereby become an adjective. Its distribution is quite different from that of adjectives. If reordering does occur as in (104b), it probably implies a shift of category:

(104)   a. Raves coming thick and fast for George Auld's *new powerhouse band* now at the Arcadia Ballroom, N.Y.
                              (1942 *Melody Maker* 4 July 5/4 [*OED*])

           b. The *powerhouse new bestseller* from ELIZABETH GEORGE
             (1996 Bantam Press advertisement, *The Guardian* p. 1 (3 Feb.))

An overuse of noun modifiers has often been noticed as a feature of journalese – the satirical magazine *Private Eye* likes to use the spoof headline *Shock Row Storm Probe Looms* – but in all registers there has probably been a general increase in frequency in recent years. It is common in scientific and engineering English, as in *maximum slope conductance-voltage curve*;[29] see here Varantola (1984). Foster notes the replacement of *sexual maniac* by *sex-maniac* (1970: 209). Again there may be dialectal variation: note recent Midwest American *frypan* as against more general *frying pan*, AmerE *airplane* as against *aeroplane*. (Of course, in several of these instances the N + N syntagms have been lexicalised, so that in PDE the differences are matters of lexis and morphology, not syntax, but the word formation pattern originally depends on the syntactic pattern.)

The modifying noun is usually singular:

$$(105) \quad \left.\begin{array}{l} \text{a bill} \\ \text{a note} \end{array}\right\} \text{ worth ten } \left\{\begin{array}{l} \textit{dollars} \\ \textit{pounds} \end{array}\right. \sim \text{ a ten-} \left\{\begin{array}{l} \textit{dollar} \text{ bill} \\ \textit{pound} \text{ note} \end{array}\right.$$

Quirk, Greenbaum, Leech & Svartvik, having pointed that this holds even for nouns which otherwise have no singular, as in *trouser press*, go on to suggest that nevertheless 'the plural attributive construction is on the increase, particularly in BrE where it is more common than in AmE' [American English]', citing examples like *a grants committee* (1985: 17.108). We might also compare the aurally identical variation in BrE *doll's house* vs. AmerE *doll house*.

3.2.7 Postmodification

Modifiers which follow the head belong to an enormous range of categories: quantifiers, adjectives, prepositional phrases, clauses of various sorts. Quantifiers have already been discussed in section 3.2.4.1, and for postmodifying clauses see section 3.6.

Adjectives tend to follow their head noun or pronoun in certain circumstances detailed by Quirk, Greenbaum, Leech & Svartvik (1985: 7.21–2), such as when the head is a compound indefinite pronoun (*anyone intelligent*), in certain institutionalised expressions (*heir apparent*), and when the adjective is coordinated (*soldiers timid or cowardly*) or has a complement of its own (*the boys easiest to teach*). In the last case it may be that premodification is on the increase, as in *ready-to-eat pizzas*, often when adjective + complement is partially lexicalised.

Prepositional phrases normally post-modify a head (*two singers in the front row*). Increasingly often, certain PPs can premodify the head noun, especially if they represent wholly or partially lexicalised items (*an off-the-wall suggestion*). See here Varantola (1983).

3.3 The verbal group

From noun phrase we should expect to move on to verb phrase. Now this term means different things to different scholars. In a sentence like:

(106)   Jim may not be making any money.

it could refer to *may not be making any money* (the constituent which acts as predicate), or to *making any money* (inflected lexical verb + complement), or to MAKE *any money* (stem of lexical verb + complement), or even to *may not be making* (the verbal portion of the predicate, including the negator *not*, *n't* where present).[30] As already noted above, I shall use the term 'verbal group' for the last-mentioned – which breaks up the sentence quite differently – and allow verb phrase (VP) to cover any of the others (for my purposes we do not need to define it more closely), though it will normally refer to the whole constituent which acts as predicate.

In many recent analyses the highest verb of (106) is MAY, which is therefore in effect the main verb, and which has as its complement a syntagm headed by BE (disregarding inflections), which in turn has as complement a syntagm headed by MAKE.[31] At no level of structure is there a constituent *may be making* or *may not be making*. For our purposes a more traditional view is sufficient: that (106) contains only one clause, whose VP has as its head the main or lexical verb MAKE, modified by the auxiliary verbs MAY and BE. This viewpoint fits better with the idea of the lexical verb as the most important item, and of auxiliary verbs, for example the progressive BE (together with its following *-ing* form), as grammatical words which modify its meaning: auxiliaries tend to have a more general semantics than lexical verbs while being subject to much tighter constraints of position and morphology. Our choice of analysis is made for convenience of exposition and mostly makes little difference to the detailed discussion which follows.

By contrast to (106), there are two verbal groups in either version of (107), each with its own lexical verb:

(107)   a. They want to make money.
        b. They want us to make money.

The higher clause has as its verbal group the single verb *want*, and the complement of *want* is the syntagm *(us) to make money*, which contains its own, separate verbal group *to make*.[32] We follow a now-conventional path (see here Palmer 1988) in calling WANT in (107) a catenative rather than an auxiliary. Catenatives are lexical verbs named from their ability to form chains of arbitrary length and order (subject only to semantic and pragmatic constraints):

(108)   a. Max enjoyed appearing to want to make money.
        b. Max appeared to enjoy wanting to make money.
        c. Max wanted to enjoy appearing to make money.

and so on. (All the verbs in (108) except MAKE are acting as catenatives.) The nonfinite verb which follows a catenative may have its own explicit subject, as in (107b). Various kinds of catenative will be discussed under section 3.6 below, 'Composite sentences', especially 3.6.4 and 3.6.6.6–7. Even though the auxiliary/catenative borderline has some fuzzy stretches, as we shall see, for PDE the distinction is a useful one.

We now concentrate on the recent history of auxiliary verbs and the verbal group, often regarded as the most systematic area of English syntax because it is (apparently) so tightly constrained and susceptible to neat formulation. Possible members of the finite verbal group in PDE can be represented as in (109) – the abbreviations are to be understood as <u>Perf</u>ect, <u>Prog</u>ressive, <u>Pass</u>ive – without commitment as to whether the syntagm actually forms a syntactic constituent in a given sentence:

(109) $\left\{ \begin{array}{l} \text{(Modal) (Perf = \textsc{have}) (Prog = \textsc{be}) (Pass = \textsc{be})} \\ \text{(Dummy = \textsc{do})} \end{array} \right\}$ V = Lexical verb

Round brackets surround optional items, curly brackets indicate a choice between upper and lower lines. (Conditions on the use of dummy DO are discussed in 3.3.8 below.) The formula neglects negation and inflection. In practice verbal groups with all options of the upper line selected are very rare, and I know of few genuine written examples ((172) below). The main point of formula (109) is to summarise the behaviour of pairs of verbs within the verbal group: that a modal verb, if selected, will always precede any other member of the group; that perfect HAVE will always precede passive BE if both are selected; that DO is incompatible with any other auxiliary; that the only obligatory item, the lexical verb, is always the last item; and so on. The formula also embodies the claim that each auxiliary slot has at most one filler: auxiliaries cannot generally iterate in the way that catenatives can (though see 3.3.2.3, 3.3.2.5 below, and note too that several dialects do permit double modals, e.g. Scots, *CHEL* V: 72–3). All verbs in a verbal group share the same explicit subject, so no other noun phrase can intervene. Omitted for simplicity from (109) is the fact that special properties attach to whichever selection is leftmost. It is *that* verb which carries tense, which precedes the nonverbal item *not* or the inflection *-n't*,[33] and which takes part in subject-auxiliary inversion; see section 3.5.2–3 below. And a final caveat on (109), which differs little from standard formulations in textbooks of PDE like Huddleston (1984: 129), is that it has limited historical validity. In appropriate sections below we shall follow the changing structure of the English verbal group and indeed discuss how well (109) represents PDE structure, as well as noting any special properties of untensed and nonfinite verbal groups.

3.3.1   Tense

There are, as is well known, only two morphological tenses in English, for if we look at the finite verbal group without auxiliaries – the simplest kind – only one inflectional contrast can be made on the verb:

(110)   a. The government *suppresses* dissent.
        b. The government *suppressed* dissent.

These tenses are usually called 'present' and 'past', which are tolerably good mnemonics for the associated meanings: without further information we would assume that (110b) refers to past time, while (110a) at least *could* refer to 'now' (for instance in the commentary to a television film), though a timeless meaning is perhaps more likely ('it is generally the case that . . .'). However, even past tense need not refer to past time:

(111)   It's time the government *suppressed* dissent.

In other words, the formal (morphological) terms **present** and **past tense** must not be confused with the notional (semantic) terms **present** and **past time**.

The same tense contrast is possible with auxiliaries, as in:

(112)   a. The government *has* suppressed dissent.
        b. The government *had* suppressed dissent.

(113)   a. The government *is* suppressing dissent.
        b. The government *was* suppressing dissent.

(114)   a. Dissent *is* suppressed.
        b. Dissent *was* suppressed.

Notice that (112a) probably refers to an action in past time despite the present tense inflection on HAVE. If we assume that modal verbs are likewise tensed, then we can make the general claim that the first verb — and no other — of any finite verbal group carries (present or past) tense:

(115)   a. Opposition *may* be expressed.
        b. Opposition *might* be expressed.

One usage of tenses is relatively low in notional content and more or less bound by syntactic rule, the so-called 'sequence of tenses' or **backshifting** rule, which affects reported speech and similar contexts. Thus if the direct speech of (116a) is embedded under a verb of reporting in the past tense as in (116b), it is common for the tense in the embedded clause to be 'backshifted':

(116)   a. 'I *feel* ill at this moment.'
        b. He said that he *felt* ill at that moment.

(Other changes in (116) – first → third person, proximal *this* → distal *that* – indicate that backshifting is just one of several devices for signalling deixis.)

And just like the past tense main verb FEEL in (116b), the past tense auxiliary forms in (112–15b) could serve as backshifted versions of (112–15a); see also section 3.3.5.3 below.

Tense certainly has a lot to do with time relations, but there is no one-to-one correspondence between tense and time. We see that from examples like (111); from the fact that the HAVE perfect in (112) serves in part to signal time relations; from the similar time reference of both versions of (115); from the lack of a future inflection to correspond to the notion of future time.

There has been little change in tense usage in the recorded history of English, let alone during the lModE period: what changes there have been have mostly involved alternations with periphrastic usage of one kind or another and will be dealt with under the headings of the auxiliary concerned. In the next few sections we shall see how tense interacts with individual auxiliaries, and then (3.3.7 below) we shall reverse the perspective and ask what verbal means there are for expressing the notions of time.

It is worth noting that the third person singular inflection -s,[34] found in all lexical verbs and (with minor differences) in the auxiliaries DO and HAVE, is now the only person or number distinction made in present tense inflection outside the paradigm of the highly irregular verb BE, with its forms *am/is/are*. With the effective disappearance of the old second person singular pronoun *thou* and its associated verbal inflections from most forms of English by the eighteenth century,[35] all other verbs lost their remaining person/number distinctions in the past tense, while modal verbs lost them altogether.

These are systematic changes in verbal morphology. There were also some more isolated changes in the paradigms of irregular verbs near the start of our period, the last spasms in a long-term readjustment of the OE strong verb pattern. Strong verbs were those which indicated tense by up to four 'ablaut' variants in the stem vowel. Thus OE FEOHTAN 'fight' had stem *feoht-* for most of the present (and indeed *fieht-*, with *i*-mutation, for 2 SG and 3 SG PRES), *feaht* for 1/3 SG past indicative, *fuht-* for the rest of the past tense system, and *-foht-* for the past participle. Over the ME and eModE period, all strong verbs showed reduction in the number of stem variants. Thus FIGHT itself has been reduced to two, *fight-* and *fought*, and three is the most to be found (e.g. SWIM: *swim-*, *swam*, *swum*), apart of course from BE. With potentially three past-system stem vowels being whittled down to at most two survivors, there was great uncertainty and variation in the eModE period, to which was added variation in the survival of *-en* in the past participle: BrE *got* versus *forgotten*, archaic *bounden* (as attributive adjective) versus *bound*. By lModE, standard English had settled on fixed choices for most of the doubtful cases, but Jane Austen could still in the early nineteenth century use past tense *shrunk, sprung, sunk*, past participle *ate, eat, broke*, plus others in the speech of the vulgar, e.g. past *run*, past participle *gave, took, went* (Phillipps 1970: 147). (All these variants survive to PDE in dialect.)

3.3.2   Perfect: HAVE/BE + past participle

Almost any lexical verb in English can make use of the auxiliary HAVE to form a perfect – unless, like BEWARE or for most speakers STRIDE, it simply lacks a past participle. With present tense HAVE, a verb will form a present perfect (*I have swum*), while past tense HAVE gives a past perfect, traditionally called pluperfect (*I had swum*); in addition to its tensed forms, perfect HAVE has infinitive and -*ing* form as well.[36] The syntax of the HAVE perfect has not changed significantly in the ModE period.

3.3.2.1   Perfect HAVE versus conclusive HAVE

The origins of the perfect lie in the OE period, if not earlier (see *CHEL* I: 190–2; II: 256–7), and many scholars suggest a historical relationship with the so-called conclusive perfect, the construction seen in:

(117)   'That loss hurt me more than any other in my life,' said McEnroe
recently. 'Even now I think about it. And it was my own dumb
fault. I *had it won*.'   (1992 *The Guardian* p. 18 (5 Dec.))

3.3.2.2   HAVE versus BE

In the history of English as of other European languages, HAVE has not been the only auxiliary of the perfect, and right through the ModE period it has had a rival auxiliary in BE when the lexical verb is mutative (i.e., whose meaning involves a change of state):

(118)   now they'*re* both *gone* and I can't replace them.
                                             (1917 Bell, *Letters* I.396 (2 Feb.))

With such lexical verbs the choice of perfect auxiliary is therefore a linguistic variable, and a number of scholars have plotted the history of variation, notably Fridén (1948), Rydén & Brorström (1987), and Kytö (1997). The use of BE in this context seems to have been in continuous decline ever since the OE period, and a graphical plotting of the rivalry reveals what appears to be a characteristic S-curve (Rydén & Brorström 1987: 200), with the nineteenth century the period of most rapid switchover. In the corpus of informal English used by Rydén and Brorström it is in the first few decades of that century that the use of BE with previously eligible verbs fell below 50 per cent – for the century as a whole the proportion is about one quarter – and in informal language the change was virtually complete by 1900. By the present day the residue of BE + intransitive past participle – for example, BE *swollen* – is often regarded not as a perfect but as main verb BE + predicative, or in some cases even as a passive.[37] The verb GO is one of the last verbs to permit a BE perfect, and even then many 3 SG present examples use the contracted auxiliary form *'s*, which neutralises the HAVE/BE distinction.[38] In explaining the changeover many scholars cite the neutralised auxiliary *'s* as at least a secondary contributory factor in recent centuries.

Two major reasons often cited, and applicable throughout the long decline of perfect BE, are that 'non-mutative verbs outnumbered mutative ones' (Traugott 1972: 145), in other words that the majority pattern of conjugation was extended to the minority, and that BE + past participle was more (seriously) ambiguous as a structure than HAVE + past participle and hence functionally disadvantaged. If both these explanatory factors look a little *post hoc*, they are nevertheless plausible enough. Rydén and Brorström make clear that the progress of replacement during our period was uneven in its distribution. Among the subtleties which they discuss (1987: 198–206) are the following.

They distinguish 'predominantly resultative' verbs like ADVANCE, CHANGE and especially BECOME, GROW, whose past participles are essentially stative, from verbs with nonstative past participles – for example, verbs of motion. The former were more resistant to the advance of HAVE, while focus on duration or process supported the use of HAVE. As an example of the contrast, consider the motion verb WALK, which nearly always formed its perfect with HAVE unless collocated with an adverb or prepositional phrase of direction (and sometimes even then). Rydén and Brorström's explanation is that most uses of perfect WALK are 'markedly durative' (1987: 182), and the solitary example in their corpus where WALK forms a BE perfect is clearly resultative, i.e. nondurative:

(119)   Jenny & James *are walked to Charmouth* this afternoon.

(1804 Austen, *Letters* 39 p. 143 (14 Sep.))

Outside their corpus, it seems that the BE perfect survived longer with the phrasal verb WALK *out*, which they suggest has an ingressive force (that is, emphasising an initial stage) and is therefore nondurative (1987: 22). More generally as far as semantic factors are concerned, the HAVE perfect was favoured by action contexts (which covers iteration and duration) and by unreality/uncertainty (which covers certain conditional, optative, negative and questioned contexts). A factor which looks purely morphological or syntactic is the case where the perfect auxiliary was in the infinitive: this too strongly promoted the use of HAVE. Yet it is not really independent of the semantic factors mentioned earlier. Consider a sentence like:

(120)   If it had not been so I *would have written* to tell you.

(1890 Dowson, *Letters* 98 p. 147 (16 May))

Unreality (including counterfactuality) demands a past tense modal verb in the apodosis (see 3.3.4.2 below), which in turn requires a following infinitive; past time can then only be marked by perfect aspect, hence the use of infinitive *have*. HAVE was also favoured when the auxiliary was an *-ing* form or in the past tense. Since imperatives are rare with the perfect, that really leaves the present perfect as the last bastion of the BE perfect, a point confirmed in Kytö (1997).

Loss of the BE perfect leads naturally to the obsolescence of clauses like:

(121)   I was glad to find Mrs. Ward *returned*;

(1861 Green, *Letters* 73 (14 Mar.))

where the past participle is perfect rather than passive. Only a few instances survive, often licensed by the presence of adverbs like *just* or *recently*:

(122)   The 4,500 prisoners *recently arrived at Memphis* will be sent to Indianapolis and Fort Delaware.

(1863 *The Chicago Tribune* p. 1 vol. 16 no. 294 (1 Jun.) [ARCHER])

But clauses with the participle *gone* continue to occur with some freedom.

3.3.2.3   Perfect HAVE + perfect BE

There is a kind of double perfect consisting of perfect HAVE + perfect BE + past participle. Visser has examples from ME onwards (1963–73: section 2162), and PDE still permits it with GO:

(123)   a. Cher Frere *has been gone* since four o clock this morning to a private conference.

(1788 Betsy Sheridan, *Journal* 42 p. 131 (21 Nov.))

b. I *have been returned* from Winchester this fortnight

(1819 Keats, *Letters* 161 p. 436 (?26 or 30 Oct.))

In their corpus Rydén and Brorström recorded the construction 40 times altogether with 17 different verbs (for example ADVANCE, COME, MIS-CARRY, MELT), but apart from GO they do not find it after the 1860/70s (1987: 25). (Nor do I in my corpus.) Their explanation for this curious and apparently pleonastic doubling of auxiliaries is that it stressed the resultative aspect more emphatically than the BE perfect alone, which was ambiguous between past action and resultant state. Notice that the effect of (123) in clauses with an adverbial of duration can be achieved in PDE by such expressions as:

(124)   a. He *has been away* since four o'clock.
        b. I*'ve been back* a fortnight ('two weeks')

with a predicative in place of the past participle, suggesting that the functional need has survived the general obsolescence of the BE perfect (and perhaps that *gone* in BE *gone* should now be analysed as a predicative).[39] The *to*-phrase of (123a), however, suggests that *has/had been gone* still contained verbal GO in the late eighteenth century.

3.3.2.4   Perfect of main verb BE

A peculiar use of the perfect has arisen with main verb BE, allowing the latter to behave under certain circumstances as if it were a verb of motion:[40]

(125)   *Have you been to* Paris?

This BE + *to*-phrase in the sense 'visit' cannot be used without perfect HAVE — or alternatively, can only occur in past participle form:

(126)   a. ** *Were* you ever *to* Paris. (cf. *Were* you ever *in* Paris?)
        b. **I *may be to* Paris. (cf. I *may go to* Paris.)

Warner (1993: 45, 64), following the *OED*, explicitly suggests that BE + directional phrase was grammatical with forms other than *been* until *c.* 1760, though the *OED* has only 'modern' (i.e. *c.* 1887) citations (s.v. *be* v. B6). (It is the construction of (128) which is well attested in earlier English.) Here is the modern construction:

(127)   a. '*Have* you then *been to* Sir Robert?'
        'I *have been to* Cavendish-square, but there, it seems, he has not appeared all night' . . .

                        (1782 Burney, *Cecilia* (Bell, 1890) II.v.140 [WWP])

b. '*I've been*,' says Jack, '*to Orchard-street* to-night, | To see what
   play this *Milky Dame* could write.' [original italics for
   Orchard-street and *Milky Dame*]
   (1791 Ann Yearsley, *Earl Goodwin* (Robinson), Epilogue p. 92 [WWP])

c. he *had ben to* the West-Indies
   (1795 Benjamin Dearborn, *Columbian Grammar* 114 [Sundby,
   Bjørge & Haugland])

Sundby, Bjørge & Haugland (1991: 291) quote (127c) from a usage book,
where it is apparently castigated as improper and vulgar. It is unclear to me
whether the 'impropriety' marks a recent innovation or a relic. Visser points
out that its meaning of 'go and come back' is shared with the somewhat
older construction where *to* introduces an infinitive rather than an NP
(1963–73: section 175):

(128)   To-day, after I *had been to see* additional houses taken on for the
        Armenian refugees, I dropped into the new shop of an old
        acquaintance   (1918 Bell, *Letters* II.442 (31 Jan.))

Example (127b) also contains a *to*-infinitive. Note, however, that older
occurrences like (128), especially in counterfactual use, can be hard to
distinguish from modal, BE:

(129)   I am sure *had* I *been to undergo* onything of that nature . . . I would
        hae skreigh'd ['screeched'] out at once
                                        (1816 Scott, *Antiquary*, 2nd edn. I.xi.233 [Visser])

(130)   I am glad you *were to see* the Miners' Committee: you evidently
        learn a great deal that way
                                        (1891 Sidney Webb, *Letters* 163 I.304 (18 Sep.))

However, modal BE has been confined effectively to finite use (see 3.3.5.2
below), ruling out the perfect of modal BE found in (129), while BE 'go in
order to . . . and come back', as apparently in (130),[41] is now only possible
with the perfect, so the two usages are in complementary distribution.

The *OED* implicitly relates the 'motion-verb' use of BE to the nineteenth-century BE *off/away*, 'a graphic expression for to go at once, take
oneself off' (s.v. *be* B.7b). Perhaps more recent still (because not mentioned
in the *OED*) is an obviously analogical pattern whose locative phrase does
not involve the preposition *to*:

(131)   a. *Have* you *been across the Humber Bridge?*
        b. I've never *been round Manchester Town Hall.*

And another development in colloquial BrE has *and* + past participle instead of *to* + infinitive, with connotations of criticism:

(132)   They've *been and spilled* wine on the floor.

(PDE [Quirk, Greenbaum, Leech & Svartvik])

On this see further section 3.6.6.7 below.

3.3.2.5   Unreality and double perfect

A correlation has developed between unrealised action and the use of the HAVE perfect in certain contexts. The prescriptive tradition frowns upon some of the patterns with double use of HAVE, e.g. *would have liked to have gone*, consisting of the two verbal groups *would have liked* and *to have gone*, even though each is well formed. Some examples are unreal conditionals, where HAVE may appear in the protasis, the apodosis (see 3.3.2.2 above), or both, but the usage is not confined to conditionals:

(133)   a. I intended *to have been* at Chichester this Wednesday – but on account of this sore throat I wrote him (Brown) my excuse yesterday   (1818 Keats, *Letters* 98 p. 257 (Dec.))

   b. 'Your husband, aunt? I thought *he had been dead*!'

(1849–50 Dickens, David Copperfield xlvii.587)

   c. 'I did so want *to have gone* with him,' answered she, looking wistfully towards the town.

(1850 Gaskell, Moorland Cottage iii.291)

(134)   a. if you . . . I will so dismiss you through that doorway, that you *had better have been* motherless from your cradle.

(1855–7 Dickens, Little Dorrit I.v.51)

   b. since Miss Brooke decided that it [*sc.* a puppy] *had better not have been born.*   (1871–2 George Eliot, *Middlemarch* iii.30)

In (133) the HAVE would nowadays tend to appear in the higher clause (*I had intended to be, I had thought he was dead, I had so wanted to go*); further examples like (133b) are given as (494).

   The frequent use of HAVE as a signal of unreality, always in the form of an infinitive when in an apodosis, since there has to be a modal there, can lead to a parallel use of infinitive *have* in the protasis too, even if finite HAVE is there already. The resulting double HAVE is still regarded as nonstandard, but it has been found since the fifteenth century and is very frequent in colloquial PDE. In the following literary examples it is part of the depiction of non-standard, lower-class or dialectal speech, though in

(135c) the fictional speaker is a highly educated young American and the spelling <of> may serve to contrast non-standard *I'd've been* with standard *wouldn't've noticed*:

(135)   a. and if I*'d ha known* it, I'd ha' christened poor Jack's mermaid
            wi' some grand gibberish of a name.
                                    (1848 Gaskell, *Mary Barton* xiii.159)
        b. 'I'm thankful you begin with "well!" If you*'d ha' begun* with
            "but," as you did afore, I'd not ha' listened to you . . .'
                                    (1851–3 Gaskell, *Cranford* xiv.129)
        c. . . . 'Did he notice?' I said. 'Your dad?'
            'Naw. He was three sheets to the wind. If I*'d of been* the
            *bar*tender [original emphasis on *bar*] at the Oak Room he
            wouldn't have noticed.'   (1992 Tartt, *Secret History* ii.57)
        d. 'Well, I raly would *not* [original emphasis] ha' believed it,
            unless I *had ha' happened to ha' been* here!' said Mrs. Sanders.
                                    (1836–7 Dickens, *Pickwick* xxvi.393)
        e. 'I'll swear there ain't no ring there,' she said. 'I should 'a' seen
            it if there *had 'a' been*.'   (1907 Nesbit, *Enchanted Castle* iv.87)
        f. I wish we *hadn'ta moved* so fast with the sonofabitch.
                            (1987 Wolfe, *Bonfire of the Vanities* (Cape, 1988) xix.409)

The syntagm seen in the first clause of (135a) is variously expanded as *had have Ved* and *would have Ved*, both by syntacticians and in attested instances, though it is commonest with contracted *'d* for the first verb.

Suppose we treat the construction as involving double H A V E (certainly correct for (135d-f)).[42] One analysis would treat the first H A V E as modal, since it appears to be followed by an infinitive. It is then anomalous in lacking an obligation sense and in not requiring *to*, as in the pattern

(136)   Before an X-ray they *have* to have gone without food for a whole
        day.

Example (136) shows how modal H A V E normally behaves. An alternative analysis of (135d–f), which I prefer, takes both H A V E s as perfect, the first marking anteriority (central use of the perfect) and the second unreality (secondary use): each function is separately realised. The morphological oddity then consists in the fact that the second auxiliary is an infinitive rather than a past participle despite being in the H A V E perfect, rather as Dutch auxiliaries followed by an infinitive behave when they themselves have a perfect auxiliary (Geerts, Haeseryn, de Rooij & van der Toorn 1984: 523–5).[43]

Further evidence of a strong association between unreality and the infinitive of HAVE is the kind of sentence illustrated by (137a):

(137)   a. Why couldn't you *have* done what I asked?
        b. Why couldn't you do what I asked?

Example (137a) is given by Palmer as a surprising variant of the expected (137b) and is used, he claims, to resolve a possible ambiguity between present conditional *could* and the intended meaning of past possibility, 'Why weren't you able to . . . ?' (1990: 97). As he points out, though, the form (137a) has a natural reading which is also inappropriate: 'Why wouldn't you have been able to . . . ?' He suggests that this new ambiguity may be less important. Perhaps, rather, the unreality suggested by HAVE ('You didn't do what I asked. Why not?') is what is most salient.

Finally here we must note that a new stressed form, *of*, has been created from the unstressed enclitic *'ve*:

(138)   Had I known of your illness I *should not of written* in such fiery
       phrase in my first Letter.   (1819 Keats, *Letters* 149 p. 380 (5 Sep.))

Many speakers thus apparently fail to see any connection between a non-initial, infinitival occurrence of HAVE in a verbal group and the normal auxiliary. The spelling is appearing more and more often in literary representations of dialogue, and not always – as it was in literature until the mid-twentieth century – as a mark of non-standard usage; cf. (135c).

3.3.2.6   Clipped perfect

Incomplete perfect clauses may lack subject NP and HAVE; for interrogatives the equivalent ellipsis is of HAVE and/or subject NP:

(139)   a. '*Been* pretty hot today,' he remarked.
        'Is it a record?' I asked eagerly.
            (1953 Hartley, *Go-Between* (Heinemann, 1971) viii.104 [Visser])
        b. Gerald went up to the woman.
        '*Taken* much?' he asked   (1907 Nesbit, *Enchanted Castle* iii.62)

Visser suggests that such forms 'may have been current for a long time in spontaneous conversation', but that they 'did not become common in written or printed English until the beginning of the twentieth century' (1963–73: section 2054). (His generous collection of examples includes just one from the nineteenth century and a highly dubious one from the early seventeenth.) We may add:

(140)   a. I shall insinuate some of these Creatures into a Comedy some day . . . Scene, a little Parlour . . . Ha! Hunt! *got* into you<r> new house? Ha! Mrs Novello *seen* Altam and his Wife?

                           (1818 Keats, *Letters* 98 p. 254 (18 Dec.))

      b. JACK. . . . Where is your husband?

         RACHAEL. *Gone*, as a last hope, to try to borrow.

         (1832 Jerrold, *Rent Day* II.i, in *Works* (Bradbury & Evans, 1854) VIII.23 [ARCHER])

      c. ROY. Well, father, I've done it!

         GRIFFITH. *Done* what? [Sees him] *Enlisted*!

         (1899 Herne, *Rev. Griffith Davenport* IV p. 149 [ARCHER])

Such elliptical forms are part of a broader phenomenon in which a string may be ellipted from (usually) the beginning of a clause.

3.3.3   *Progressive:* BE + *-ing*

The progressive construction, as in *I was swimming*, has undergone some of the most striking syntactic changes of the lModE period. By early in the ModE period the BE + *-ing* pattern was already well established, and its overall frequency has increased continuously ever since. Dennis (1940) estimates an approximate doubling every century from 1500, though with a slowing-down in the eighteenth century and a spurt at the beginning of the nineteenth (Strang 1982: 429). Arnaud, working from a corpus of private letters and extrapolating to the speech of literate, middle-class people, estimates a threefold increase during the nineteenth century alone (1983: 84).

3.3.3.1   Meaning and grammaticalisation

The rules for use of the progressive had already been established in the grammar before our period – in the seventeenth century, according to Strang (1982: 429) – though, as she says, 'in all generations, including the present, there are contexts in which choice is possible, and the choices of some are surprising to others' (1982: 430). Here are some instances where nonuse of the progressive is odd to my ears:

(141)   a. Now I will return to Fanny – it *rains*.

                         (1818 Keats, *Letters* 75 p. 170 (3 Jul.))

      b. if I had refused it – I *should have behaved* in a very bragadochio dunderheaded manner   (ibid. 98 p. 257 (Dec.))

      c. How is Mr. Evelyn? How *does* he *bear up* against so sudden a reverse?   (1840 Bulwer-Lytton, *Money* V.ii p. 226)

    d. 'What *do* they *say*?' asked Margaret of a neighbour in the
       crowd, as she caught a few words, clear and distinct from the
       general murmur.   (1848 Gaskell, *Mary Barton* v.72)
    e. '. . . Dover says he will take a good deal of the plate back
       again, and any of the jewellery we like. He really *behaves* very
       well.'   (1871–2 Eliot, *Middlemarch* lviii.596)
    f. Let me know how your chap. [= chapter] *proceeds* & what you
       think of no I [*sic* = number one].
            (1890 Dowson, *Letters* 105 p. 156 (25 Jun.))
    g. Suddenly he caught sight of a canvas with its face to the wall
       . . . he wondered what it *did* there.
        (1919 Maugham, *Moon & Sixpence* (Heinemann, 1955) xxxix.152)

And here are some converse examples:

(142)   a. '. . . A water-party; and by some accident she *was falling* over-
       board. He caught her.'   (1816 Austen, *Emma* viii[xxvi].218 [Phillipps])
    b. What I should have lent you ere this if I could have got it, *was*
       belonging to poor Tom   (1819 Keats, *Letters* 110 p. 277 (Feb.))

According to Strang, the use of the progressive altered in character during the eighteenth and early nineteenth centuries, at least as far as literary narrative was concerned (1982: 441–2):

> In narrative prose of the first half of the eighteenth century the construction is truly at home only in certain types of subordinate clause, especially temporal, relative or local . . . In the latter half of the eighteenth century the figures rise overall, but proportionately most in non-subordinate use [footnote omitted], so that in the century as a whole there are nearly three times as many uses in subordinate clauses, though these clauses are themselves in a minority. Taking the nineteenth century as a whole . . . the overall rate of occurrence has more than doubled, but the rate in non-subordinate clauses has nearly quadrupled. . . . In the twentieth-century [sic] the overall rate has again more than doubled, but again this conceals a near-quadrupling in non-subordinate clauses . . .

See also section 3.3.3.4 for another approach to the grammaticalisation of the progressive. Strang's analysis of the spread of the progressive is subtle. She notes that Richardson, for example, distinguishes the language of Pamela from other letter-writers in the eponymous novel by a greatly raised rate of usage of the progressive. Strang counts instances in novels around 1800 and generally finds a huge increase in the use of the progressive in past tense narrative prose between the first or early novel(s) and subsequent ones by the same author. Perhaps the progressive was not yet fully accepted in the conventions of publishing even though already common in speech, and the craft of novel-writing involved, amongst other things, developing a skill in handling this construction (1982: 448):

> The development of the [progressive] construction is of greater significance for the novelist than for any other kind of writer, and it is hardly surprising that around 1800, when all the major extensions of its functions became available, beginning novelists should experience some difficulty in coming to terms with this powerful new resource.

She goes on to speculate about developments in the *form* of the novel, including the predilection for first person and epistolary novels before the progressive was fully mature.

According to Strang (1982: 440), the combination of a modal and the progressive was rare in literature before the early nineteenth century. (It was certainly *possible* from OE times – see Denison 1993a: 383–4.) Note too her suspicion that there was more freedom to negate the progressive in the nineteenth century than previously (1982: 453). There is modest but inconclusive support for both suggestions in ARCHER.

As for the meaning or function of the progressive, Strang adopts Bodelsen's (1936/7) claim that 'the central function of the construction is to present the action of a verb as being an activity rather than an event, result or state of affairs' (1982: 443) and applies it to the eighteenth century, since then it fits in with the progressive being restricted to human or human-like subjects, and to certain verbs. With the early nineteenth-century expansion in the ranges of possible subjects and of verbs, she concludes that the progressive was becoming more temporal in function (1982: 446).

Visser takes a ruthless line against those who find a multiplicity of functions. He prefers to offer a central function which will account for most or all of its uses (1963–73: section 1806):

> The Expanded Form is that colligation [= syntactic pairing of categories] of a form of *to be* with an *-ing* which is used when the speaker chooses to focalize the listener's attention on the POST-INCEPTION PHASE of what is, was or will be going on at a point in time in the present, past or future.

Other alleged meanings are contextual, or due to adverbials, or inherent in the semantics of the lexical verb. He claims (1963–73: section 1830) that his formula covers even the use of the progressive with future meaning, as in:

(143)   We *are opening* an agency in Cuba soon.

(1958 Greene, Havana V.ii(3).204)

3.3.3.2   Restrictions on lexical verb

In general the progressive is far less often used with verbs of stative meaning like BE, HAVE, KNOW, OWN than with nonstative verbs. However, with certain stative verbs it has become possible to use a progressive to mark a transient state or behaviour:

(144)   a. He *was living* then in Park Lane, in the house Lord Woolcomb
            has now.   (1895 Wilde, *Ideal Husband* II p. 80 [ARCHER])
        b. Oh my dearest ones it's so wonderful here – I can't tell you
            how much I*'m loving* it.   (1917 Bell, *Letters* II.414 (1 Jun.))
        c. The old people *are behaving* themselves quite rational – playing
            bezique in the drawing-room.
            (1911 Besier, Lady Patricia II.i p. 96 [ARCHER])

It is difficult to be precise on dating this phenomenon, but it seems likely that frequent usage, at least, is fairly recent. In Visser's material on verbs resistant to the progressive, for instance, neither LIVE nor LOVE + inanimate object occurs in the progressive before the twentieth century (1963–73: sections 1845, 1847). Note, however, such early progressives of 'resistant' verbs as:

(145)   a. The tars *are wishing* for a lick, as they call it, at the Spanish
            galleons.   (1803 *Naval Chron.* X. 258 [*OED*])
        b. Do not live as if I *was not existing* – Do not forget me
            (1820 Keats, Letters 216 p. 490 (?May))

With the main verb BE itself, the progressive can also signal impermanence. Compare:

(146)   a. He *is* malicious.
        b. He *is being* malicious.

Apart from a couple of examples from the fifteenth century and some doubtful theological usages from various periods (see Denison 1993a: 395), the progressive of type (146b) is first recorded in the notably informal usage of Keats, as Jespersen noticed (1909–49: IV 225):

(147)   You will be glad to hear . . . *how diligent* I have been, and *am being*.

(1819 Keats, Letters 137 p. 357 (11 Jul.))

Certain reference works (Mossé 1938: section 266, Visser 1963–73: section 1834) wrongly adduce earlier examples of the following type:

(148) a. but *this is being wicked*, for wickedness sake.

                                        (1761 Johnston, *Chrysal* II 1.x.65)

      b. I ought to have paid my respects to her if possible. *It was being very deficient.*   (1816 Austen, *Emma* II.xiv[xxxii].280)

      c. and she was so happy herself, that *there was no being severe*

                                          (ibid. III.xv[li].444)

(It is Phillipps (1970: 117) who cites (148c), claiming more cautiously that by such gerundial usage, 'Jane Austen does approach the modern construction'.) Mossé and Visser ignore the fact that examples like (148) do not appear to contain a progressive verbal group *is/was being* at all: rather the verb is just copula *is* or *was*, linking (usually) an inanimate pronoun subject (*this, it, there*) to a gerundial phrase *being* + AP.[44] The subject is not an argument of the adjective phrase. A true progressive of BE would be as in (149):

(149)   I *was being* very deficient.

Given the structural assumptions of section 3.3 above, we would have very different analyses:[45]

(150) a. It [$_V$ was] [$_{NP}$ being very deficient] (for (148b))

      b. I [$_V$ was being] [$_{AP}$ very deficient] (for (149))

The date of introduction of the genuine (149) type, and the kind of text it first appeared in, have an important bearing on the progressive passive, which also contains a syntagm of the type *is being*; see section 3.3.3.4 below. Where the complement of *being* is a noun phrase rather than an adjectival phrase, we must wait until well into the nineteenth century for good examples:[46]

(151) a. I really think this illness *is being* a good thing for me.

                      (1834 R. H. Froude *Rem.* (1838) I. 378 [*OED*])

      b. One who studies *is not being* a fool

        (1871 Meredith, *Harry Richmond* (Scribner's, 1910) xxx.323 [Visser])

Visser devotes his (1963–73: section 1841) to the progressive of HAVE, a verb which in *origin* has the stative meaning 'possess'. The facts are of possible significance to the divergence of HAVE into auxiliary and nonauxiliary verbs, as we shall see in section 3.3.9. With a direct object, HAVE hardly occurs in the progressive in ModE before the nineteenth century, and then never in the meaning 'possess'. Some of Visser's citations can be predated from the quotations in the *OED*, and no doubt there are still earlier ones to be found; see Warner (1995: 546) for an example of *having fun* in 1787 Blake:

(152)   a. We *are* now *having* a spell of wind and rain.
(1808 Southey, *Life* III. 163 [*OED*, Warner])

        b. It seems the 'Goddems' *are having* some fun.
(1830 J. P. Cobbett, *Tour in Italy* 8 [*OED*])

        c. when I *was having* tea with my mater in Gattis
(1889 Dowson, *Letters* 76 p. 118 (26 Nov.))

The meanings are always more or less nonstative, though note (152a) and many similar, later examples.

Catenative uses of HAVE resist the progressive until the nineteenth century too:

(153)   a. observed that Grandcourt *was having Klesmer presented* to him by some one unknown to her
(1876 George Eliot, *Daniel Deronda*, ed. G. Handley
(Clarendon, 1984) II.xi.100 [Visser])

        b. They *were having their portraits taken* by the photogenic process.
(1842 *Blackw. Mag.* LI. 388 [*OED*])

        c. A friend now here *is having the whole lower sash of my window replaced* by a single pane of plate glass
(1844 Martineau, *Letters* p. 97 (29 Jul.))

        d. as a matter of fact, he'*s having to sell* his house.
(1927 Margaret Kennedy, *Red Sky at Morning* (Heinemann)
ii.94 [Visser])

Dates of earliest occurrences that I know of are as shown in table 3.3.[47] As auxiliary of the perfect, HAVE *never* occurs in the progressive, which is why perfect HAVE precedes progressive BE in formula (109) above.

3.3.3.3 'Passival'

Before it became possible to combine the progressive with the passive (on which see 3.3.3.4 below), certain verbs could be used in the active progressive in a sense which corresponded to a passive. Visser uses the label **passival** for this notionally but not formally passive construction:

(154)   a. Our Garden *is putting* in order, by a Man who
(1807 Austen, *Letters* 49 p. 178 (8 Feb.))

        b. But *are* there six labourers' sons *educating* in the universities at this moment?
(1850 Kingsley, *Alton Locke*, ed. van Thal (Cassell, 1967)
xiii.138 [Visser])

Table 3.3. *First occurrences of progressive of* HAVE

Type of HAVE	Pattern of VP	Earliest progressive
transitive	HAVE *something*	1787 or 1808
'passivc' (nonagentive subject)	HAVE *something done (to self)*	1842 or 1876
causative (agentive subject) + past ptcp	HAVE *something done*	1842 or 1844
causative + infinitive	HAVE *someone do something*	? (possible in PDE)
modal	HAVE *to do something*	1927

Table 3.4. *Normal versus passival progressive in the eighteenth century*

	Normal progressive	Passival progressive
intransitive verb	✓ *John was going home*	✗
transitive verb	+ object *John was preparing dinner*	− objcct *Dinner was preparing*
surface subject	agentive	nonagentive

   c. (They [*sc.* 'The Pickwick Papers'] *were* then *publishing* in parts.)

                                (1851–3 Gaskell, *Cranford* i.8)

   d. the street lamps *were lighting*

                           (1855–7 Dickens, *Little Dorrit* I.xxvii.317)

   e. Baskets, troughs, and tubs of grapes, stood in the dim village door-ways, stopped the steep and narrow village streets, and *had been carrying* all day along the roads and lanes.   (ibid. II.i.419)

   f. It's got scenes in a theatre where a ballet*'s dancing*.

                     (1949 Streatfeild, *Painted Garden* x.114)

Mossé identifies verbs of certain semantic groups – of making, building, printing, cooking, preparing and others – as particularly prone to the construction (1938: section 234–6). In all instances of the passival, the agent would have been human if expressed (which, incidentally, it rarely is, though cf. (154a)), while the surface subject is nonhuman or at least clearly nonagentive (for which (154b) is a nice example).[48] Thus at least until about 1800, there was little real danger of ambiguity; see table 3.4.

    Visser asserts that the passival increased in frequency through the eighteenth century and remained common in the nineteenth, only beginning to decline in the twentieth (1963–73: sections 1879–81) – though

Nakamura's statistics on usage in diaries and letters show a steep decline from mid-nineteenth century (1991: 126–9). Interestingly, Visser suggests that where eighteenth-century grammarians had tended to condemn it, nineteenth-century writers were 'in general, much less censorious' – perhaps because some were using it as a stick to beat a (to them) loathsome innovation, the progressive passive (3.3.3.4 below).

Two reasons can be given for the passival's decline. It has a nonagentive and therefore usually nonhuman subject. Presumably, then, it began to carry a greater risk of ambiguity (if only slightly), the more common it became for *normal* progressives to occur with nonhuman subjects. Second, with the acceptance of the new progressive passive, the passival has become increasingly redundant. Examples continue to be found sporadically.

3.3.3.4 Progressive + passive[49]

In PDE all pairs of auxiliaries are readily formed. The major and well-known exception for eModE is progressive + passive, where both use BE as auxiliary, as in:

(155) while this chapter *was being written*

Even though both kinds of auxiliary BE had been in individual use since Middle or even Old English, this combination is not found till the last quarter of the eighteenth century. Why not? People had got very close to it earlier than that,[50] but none of the following examples quite qualifies:

(156) that Miss Jervois loves to sit up late, either reading, or *being read to*, by Anne;
>   (1754 Richardson, *Grandison* III.vii.32 [*OED*, Mossé, Visser])

(157) a. There is a good opera of Pugniani's now *being acted*
>   (1769 Mrs. Harris, in *Ser. Lett. 1st Earl Malmesbury*
>   I.180 (21 Apr.) [*OED*])
>   b. Sir Guy Carlton *was four hours being examined* at the Bar of the
>   House.   (1779 J. Harris, ibid. I.410 (23 May) [*OED*])

(158) that the French . . . had been defeated, and that the Irish *were in a fair Way, of being made* quiet.
>   (1798 Woodforde, *Diary*, ed. Beresford (OUP, 1924–31)
>   V 137.19 (14 Sep.))

Examples (157) *may* be progressive passives, but they need not be, as this rewriting suggests:

(157′)   b. Sir Guy Carlton *was* four hours *in that room,* being examined
            about

That is, it is not certain that *is/was* and *being* belong to the same verbal
group, as *being* may form part of an appositive element. And (156) and (158)
lack the first BE. These precursors show that sequences like *is being* were
avoided, as confirmed later in the complaints voiced against the actual
progressive passive. And this was because it was felt that the progressive of
the verb BE itself – for the early history see section 3.3.3.2 above – was an
impossibility.

   So in the years leading up to the turn of nineteenth century, and indeed
well into that century, there was pressure *not* to use a progressive passive.
Instead two principal expedients were made use of. One was to omit
explicit passive marking, giving the passival construction already discussed
in section 3.3.3.3; the other was to omit explicit progressive marking:

(159)   he found that the coach had sunk greatly on one side, though it
            was still *dragged* forward by the horses;

(1838–9 Dickens, Nickleby v.52)

   On the other hand it must sometimes have been difficult to avoid the
progressive passive, as the following example demonstrates:

(160)   Polyxena at the moment of her sacrifice on the tomb of
            Achilles, as the bride that *was being married* to him at the moment
            of his death.   (1846 De Quincey, 'The Antigone of Sophocles',
                                              Tait's Edinburgh Magazine 13, p. 162 [Visser])

Consider the alternatives that De Quincey might have chosen:

(160′)   the bride that *was married* to him
(160″)   the bride that *was marrying* to him
(160‴)   the bride that *was getting married* to him

Here the usual omission of progressive marking, as in (160′), would
suggest that Polyxena and Achilles were already married, while the passival,
as in (160″), would be inappropriate with a potentially agentive subject, and
the GET passive, as in (160‴), was hardly known in the progressive then
(and might in any case have been interpreted as nonpassive with MARRY).
So the progressive passive had a real advantage here. Furthermore, the
adoption of the progressive passive makes the English auxiliary system
much more symmetrical. So in it came. Langacker comments that it is
'deeply entrenched' in PDE (1991: 230), but historically that is not at all

true: it is really quite young. As one of the few clearcut grammatical innovations of lModE, the progressive passive merits a full discussion.

The citations from the *OED* given as (157), respectively a probable and a possible progressive passive, have recently led to the discovery of two cast-iron examples in the same collection of informal family letters:

(161)   a. I have received the speech and address of the House of Lords; probably, that of the House of Commons *was being debated* when the post went out.

                 (1772 Mr. Harris, in *Ser. Lett. 1st Earl Malmesbury* I.264 (8 Dec.))

       b. The inhabitants of Plymouth are under arms, and everything *is being done* that can be.   (1779 Mrs. Harris, ibid. I.430 (22 Aug.))

The next and long-known example is by Robert Southey in his twenty-second year, in a jokey passage contained in a letter, not written for publication, to his old schoolfriend and longtime correspondent Grosvenor Bedford:

(162)   Never mind, 'tis only a *flash*, and you, like a fellow whose *uttermost upper grinder* [original emphasis] *is being torn out* by the roots by a mutton-fisted barber . . . will *grin* and endure it.

        Gaiety suits ill with me; the above extempore witticisms are as old as six o'clock Monday morning last, and noted down in my pocket-book for you.

                               God bless you! Good night.
                      (1795 Southey, *Life* I. 249 (9 Oct.) [*OED*])

The next recorded user is Coleridge, a close friend of Southey's and relation by marriage. There are many other examples in the writings of Southey and Colcridge. Other early users include Mary Shelley, Shelley, Keats, Lamb, De Quincey, W. S. Landor, all friends or acquaintances. I give a selection of early examples gleaned from various sources (the best collection being in Visser 1963–73: section 2158):

(163)   a.   ODE
        To a PIG, while his Nose *was being bored.*

           (1799–1800 Southey, *Annual Anthology* II.264 [*Poetry Database*])

       b. 'It [*sc.* a bill] *is being made out*, I am informed, Sir.'

                  (1801 tr. *Gabrielli's Myst. Husb.* I.125 [*OED*])

       c. The King much pleased, but would not leave the novels that *were being read* to him.

                (1808 [Ellis] Cornelia Knight, *Autobiography* II.262
                                 (9 Jun.) [ARCHER])

d. The extortionate profiteering that *is being practised* by the
tradesmen in the public market.

(1814 *Guernsey Star & Gaz.* in *New Age* (1919) 21 Aug. 278/2 [*OED*])

e. We were allowed two hours for dinner, and two more were
wasted in the evening while the coach *was being changed.*

(1817 Mary Shelley, *6 Weeks' Tour*, in *Complete Works of P. B. Shelley*,
ed. Ingpen & Peck (Gordian, 1965) VI.110)

f. While the goats *are being milked*, and such other refreshments
are preparing for us as the place affords.

(1829 Landor, *Imag. Conv., Odysseus*, etc. [*OED*])

First some scattered comments on individual examples. Example (163a)
is a title of a humorous political poem, cited here from a collection edited
by Southey himself. Interestingly, the title in Curry (1984: 159), who quotes
it from the *Morning Advertiser* of 8 July 1799, is a passival: *ODE, TO A PIG,
WHILE HIS NOSE WAS BORING.* Did Southey insist on a passive progressive which had been rejected by a newspaper editor?[51] Incidentally, it is
one of only two progressive passives prior to 1835 in the *Chadwyck-Healey
English Poetry Full-Text Database* (the other is 1800 Coleridge *is being realized*).
In (163e) notice how Mary Shelley uses the progressive passive near an
indirect passive, another construction that was probably disfavoured in
formal writing (cf. 3.4.2.3 below). Example (163f) is interesting in its use of
the new construction for an animate subject, side by side with the old one.

It seems worthwhile to examine the sociolinguistics behind early
progressive passives as represented by (160–3). Most early examples tend
to come from the pens of young people writing informally, and the vast
majority are from Southey or from writers he would have known and/or
corresponded with. Two progressive passives in the *OED*, for instance,
dated 1826 and 1828, come from a collection of reminiscences about
Samuel Parr, a sociable schoolmaster and cleric with a vast correspondence,
known by De Quincey and acknowledged by Landor for his kindness
(Denison 1993b: 27). Visser quotes one in the writings of R. H. Froude, a
divine who lived with Coleridge's elder brother as a schoolboy. Outside this
group are two early examples in Gothic novels of little literary merit.
'Gabrielli' in (163b) is probably Mrs Mary Meeke, whose novels were
apparently very popular (cf. (47), (303a)); all the reference books, for
instance, note that she was Macaulay's favourite 'bad' novelist. She was
much given to writing under pseudonyms. The other is Visser's 1802
citation from a translation by Mary Charlton, likewise a novelist and translator with the Minerva Press and conceivably the same person. There are

also the Malmesbury examples, (161) and perhaps (157), and three isolated examples from a female diarist, a provincial newspaper and a provincial (Gloucester) grammar-book, (163c, d) and (169a) below.[52] Otherwise, however, most come from a group of literary people who probably all knew each other and/or corresponded copiously. Is this significant – a kind of social network whose group identity was reinforced by common syntactic usage? (Perhaps one should posit two linked networks corresponding to the different generations involved.)

Social networks can contribute to linguistic stability (Milroy 1987: 190–207), so linguistic change may follow disruption of a social network. And even in a period of social stability, linguistic change may be initiated by the spread of some usage from one social network to another by means of individuals who are peripheral members of both. Now, members of our putative network(s) were extremely self-conscious linguistically. In the politicised English literary world of the decades around 1800, with its aggressive reviews, often highly critical about diction, it is certainly possible that consciously or otherwise, groups of literary people might have wanted to distance themselves from other, older and more conservative groups. To explain the clustering of examples, two hypotheses are open to us (the Malmesbury data make it highly unlikely that the Southey/Coleridge circle actually initiated the development of the progressive passive):

(164) a. The data are a mere accident of sampling and of the
          subsequent status of the writers.
       b. The progressive passive was already a general if
          'unrespectable' form, but was rarely written (except in private
          letters or trashy novels or newspapers?); it was seized on by
          the young iconoclasts of the Southey/Coleridge circle in a
          kind of radical experimentation.

Hypothesis (164b) is compatible with the idea of deliberate 'siding with the politically and linguistically dispossessed' (Lynda Pratt, p.c., who points out that both of my Southey examples had political and humorous applications). If we adopt it, then we can further suggest that the progressive passive spread slowly outwards from that circle at first, only later becoming acceptable in print as they themselves got older and more respectable. The 'null hypothesis' (164a) – which may, of course, turn out to be the mundane truth – would lose us our sociolinguistic insight into this important syntactic development. The next step should perhaps be further research into non-literary writings, especially perhaps vulgar forms of publishing from the southwest midlands, and work by women writers of the late eighteenth century. However, a search of some 1.8 million words of miscellaneous text dated prior to 1830, generously made available by the Women Writers Project at Brown University, has not revealed any further examples.

A widely held suspicion that the progressive passive and the progressive of main verb BE have related origins tends to be confirmed by the provenance of examples of both, though the dating shows clearly that the progressive passive was the earlier of the two. The (so far) earliest known user of progressive BE + AP is Keats, (147) above, and of progressive BE + NP is R. H. Froude, (151a) above, both of whom are among the early users of the progressive passive. And syntagms like *is being* were real neologisms in the nineteenth century, arousing what now seem the most extraordinary reactions. J. H. Newman, a friend and colleague of Froude, wrote in a letter *c.* 1871: 'but this I do know, that, rationally or irrationally, I have an undying, never-dying hatred to *is being* . . .' (Mossé 1938: section 279) (though in fact over thirty years previously he had more than once used the progressive passive himself!). For over fifty years the progressive of BE and/or the progressive passive attracted such comments as the following: 'uncouth English', 'an outrage upon English idiom, to be detested, abhorred, execrated', 'clumsy and unidiomatic', 'a monstrosity', 'an awkward neologism', containing 'an absurdity so palpable, so monstrous, so ridiculous, that it should need only to be pointed out to be scouted'. (Visser 1963–73: section 2158 gives generous coverage.) An analogy in our own time might be the reactions to *hopefully* as sentence adverb, usages like *less students* or *this criteria*, or misuse of the apostrophe. Yet now the progressive passive passes completely unnoticed as a natural and obvious possibility of English verbal usage.

As for the syntax of the progressive passive, my explanation is that what happened was a grammaticalisation of the progressive: prior to *c.* 1770 progressive BE was a main verb, from then on it could become an auxiliary, with the result that the progressive passive *was being built* was now the progressive of BUILD rather than of passive BE. The change also helps to explain the virtual disappearance at much the same time of *being Ving* (3.3.8.6 below), last regularly found in Jane Austen. Let us consider the process in a little more detail.

In semantics grammaticalisation probably involved generalisation and perhaps bleaching of meaning (but cf. Brinton 1988), while in syntax the (pre-)auxiliary changed from being head of its phrase to a modifier of the lexical head. If there has been a reanalysis of the progressive, what are the consequences of locating (the most rapid phase of) the changeover in the late ModE period? Suppose the progressive pattern

(165)   The house *was being built*.

had been normal in the eighteenth century. It would have had the analysis main verb BE + *being built*. The phrase type *being built* did exist but tended to be resultative in meaning rather than durative (see Visser 1963–73: section 1920 and cf. also section 2175 and Denison 1993a: 441). So pattern (165) would probably have had an inappropriate meaning, as the Pepys example in note 50 precisely demonstrates. However, some early *being Ved* examples *were* perhaps durative, but presumably resisted acting as predicatives to BE because of the strangeness of sequences like *is being*, a problem less evident in *there*-sentences like (157a).

Nor would a putative (165) have been supported by pattern (166), progressive BE + predicative, which was not in use before the nineteenth century (3.3.3.2 above):

(166)   Jim *was being stupid/a pest*.

Hence the semantic and syntactic oddity of the progressive passive would explain the fierceness of some people's reactions to it.

The gap left by absence of (165) could be filled by the passival (3.3.3.3 above). Although the passival, (167a), looked exactly like a normal progressive, (167b):

(167)   a. The house *was building*.
          b. Jim *was whispering*.

it was usually possible to avoid its use where the subject was open to misinterpretation as an Agent, since the progressive was not yet grammaticalised and was not generally as frequent as now. There was a partial analogy in such pairs as (168):

(168)   a. The house *was built*.
          b. Jim *was arrived*.

Just as with (167), a single surface pattern of BE + participle would be interpreted either as passive or as active according to the transitivity of the lexical verb and the potential agentiveness of the subject.

After the reanalysis, the progressive passive, (165), became possible, since it was the progressive not of passive BE but of the lexical verb. That meant that passival (167a) was no longer needed to fill the gap and furthermore was now anomalous in being a one-auxiliary form that coded both aspect and passive voice (or alternatively, the only passive verbal group not ending in a past participle). Gradually it lost productivity, with those fixed phrases that survived increasingly interpreted as ergatives (i.e. like the verb MELT in *The ice melted*).

And the possible reason for the progressive to have been reanalysed at that time? It was roughly the time when regularisation of DO went to completion, in negatives especially (3.3.8.2 below). What this meant was that there was now a glaring difference between operators (to be defined in 3.3.8 below) and others. All other operators complemented by another verb were already full-fledged auxiliaries. Perhaps this was the systemic pressure which brought progressive BE into line.

Warner (1986: 164–5) also cites the regularisation of DO as a factor in the reanalysis of constructions involving finite forms of BE, giving 1700 and 1850 as extreme limits for the reanalysis. He further suggests that loss of *thou* and associated inflections was another causal factor, and that changes in the modals would have supported changes in BE. All uses of BE belong together in Warner's intricate account, which is developed in later work into the most coherent available account of English auxiliary history (1990, 1993, 1995). Warner argues that auxiliary verbs came to differ from full verbs by having a series of forms with independent syntactic properties, rather than belonging to a paradigm with a single subcategorisation. A wide range of evidence is cited, much of which can be appreciated independently of his formal analysis, which is expressed in terms of Head-Driven Phrase Structure Grammar (whose essentials he summarises in 1993: 69ff.).

The progressive passive involves a verbal group of three members. Longer extensions opening with a modal verb and/or perfect HAVE appeared in the artificial contexts of grammars and linguistic satire during the nineteenth century, (169), but in ordinary usage they have not been found before the twentieth, (170–2):

(169)   a. I *can, may,* or *must be being conquered* [etc.]
                        (1802 Skillern, *Grammar*, paradigm of passive voice [Visser])
        b. They [= reformers who object to the passival] must say
           therefore . . . the great Victoria bridge *has been being built* more
           than two years; when I reach London, the ship Leviathan *will
           be being* built; if my orders had been followed, the coat *would
           have been being made* yesterday; if the house had then *been being
           built*, the mortar would *have been being mixed*. [italics as in
           original]   (1860 (1858–9) Marsh, *Lectures* xxix.654)
        c. Could there be a more absurd affectation than, instead of,
           The tea has been drawing five minutes, to say, The tea has

been being drawn five minutes? *Been being* – is that sense, or
English? – except to children, who say that they have been
being naughty, thereby saying only that they have been
naughty. [italics as in original]   (1871 White, *Words* xi.362)

(170)   a. She doesn't trust us. I *shall* always *be being pushed* away from
            him by her.
                        (1915 Galsworthy, *Freelands* (Scribner's, 1928) ix.95 [Visser])
        b. There's no wedding. Who *could be being married?*
                        (1918 Barrie, *Barbara's Wedding*, in *Plays of J. M. Barrie*
                                    (Hodder & Stoughton, 1931) 787)
        c. 'The solution is known and written down in certain textbooks.
            But my belief is that it *may not be being used.'*
                        (1993 *New Scientist* 1899: 13 (13 Nov.))

(171)   a. In view of the fact that the members of that class *had been*
            being educated for the previous four, five, or six winters by
                        (1929 Riddehough, *Canadian Forum* IX.107 383 [Visser])
        b. Because all these months you've been adoring him like a
            descended god, he*'s been being convinced* he is.
                        (1977 French, *Women's Room* (Sphere, 1978) IV.x.337)

(172)   a. By 1.30 I *must have been being introduced*
                        (1923 Ford Madox Ford, *Marsden Case* (Duckworth)
                                    ii.18 [Kruisinga, Visser])
        b. But he added: '. . . They *might have* all *been being used* at the
            time.'   (1993 *Daily Telegraph* 9/8 (27 Oct.))

Attempts to deny the grammaticality of such forms in PDE are untenable
on empirical grounds and on theoretical grounds too: no formal grammar
which admits the progressive passive is likely to rule out these longer but
analogous verbal groups. Though clumsy, they are occasionally needed and
used. See Denison (1993a: 429–31) for fuller discussion.

3.3.3.5 'Nominal progressive'
It is a standard assumption that the *-ing* form of the progressive is verbal
in category. However, in apparently related constructions where the *-ing* is
preceded by a preposition, (173), or governs an object NP via the preposition *of*, (174), or indeed both, (175), it shows some evidence of nominal
character:

(173)   Darkness . . . into which one ventured with grave apprehensions
        lest a 'hold-up' *might be in waiting* for him.
                                     (1885 *Harper's Mag.* Apr. 695/2 [*OED*])

(174)   'is wife *'ad been persuadin ov 'im* all night
                                     (1894 Ward, *Marcella* II.ix.227 [Visser])

(175)   'You're dirt and can't 'ardly understand what I *am a-sayin' of*, but I
        'appens to like you.'
                   (1949 Allingham, *Undertaker* (Penguin, 1986) xxiii.192 [Visser])

(Compare too the discussion of the gerund in 3.6.4.3 below.) For our
period it is appropriate to treat all such patterns as peripheral to the history
of the normal progressive. All have become marginalised. Some survive in
what are virtually set phrases like BE *in being*, BE *in hiding*, or in wholly lexicalised nouns like *lady-in-waiting*. There are literary clichés of non-standard
usage like:

(176)   They*'re* alvays *adoin'* some gammon ['humbug'] of that sort
                                     (1836–7 Dickens, *Pickwick* xxvii.404 [Visser])

And this pattern does survive in genuine dialectal use, especially with *a-*
from earlier *on* (e.g. *CHEL* V: 140 on Welsh English).

Going back to the origins of the normal progressive, whether to OE or
ME, some writers have claimed that its source was a nominal pattern with
-ing preceded by the preposition *on*, alleging a development on the lines of
he was on hunting > *he was a-hunting* > *he was hunting*. The chronology is wrong,
however, and parallel development of nominal (prepositional) and verbal
forms is more likely. Then examples like (175) and the normal progressive
would be direct descendants of the 'pure' nominal and verbal types, respectively, while examples like (174) and (176) would represent different kinds
of hybrid (Nehls 1974).

3.3.3.6   Clipped progressive

Just as with the perfect (see 3.3.2.6 above and references cited under
Further reading for that section), incomplete progressive clauses may lack
subject NP and BE; for interrogatives the equivalent ellipsis is of BE and/or
subject NP:

(177)   a. ORDEAL. . . . Where are they?
        NICHOLAS. *Running* all over the house – up stairs and down
        stairs, to and fro
                                     (1785 MacNally, *Fashionable Levities* II.iii p. 31 [ARCHER])

b. SIR C. . . . where is he now?

LITTLEWORTH. *Learning* to dance quadrilles of Sir Lennox.

SIR C. Sir Lennox, ugh – what, he's here again, is he?

LITTLEWORTH. Yes, sir, just *giving* Mr. Samuel confidence to dance before Lady Cranberry.

(1820 Serle, *Exchange No Robbery* II.i p. 25 [ARCHER])

c. '*Getting tired?*'

'Well, I'm not an atom bit sleepy,' said Kezia.

(1920 K. Mansfield, *Prelude* iii.8, in *Bliss* (Bloomsbury, 1988) [Mossé])

d. The clothes are the very best. *You buying* for your wife?

(1964 Gelber, *Square in the Eye* II.i p. 76 [ARCHER])

Now Mossé describes the usage as recent (1938: section 471) and gives no examples earlier than (177c). Visser similarly has no lModE examples before 1922, but since he has a good collection of *seventeenth*-century examples, he attributes the absence of eighteenth- and nineteenth-century attestations to mere stylistic avoidance in print (1963–73: section 1889). In fact the *OED* has eighteenth-century examples of *Coming!* 'I am coming!', 'directly!' (s.v. *come* v. B.37b), and (177a, b) show that dramatic representations of colloquial dialogue could override any possible taboo; examples also occur in elliptical echo responses. Outside drama the clipped progressive is frequent in private journals.

3.3.4   Subjunctive

In the history of English as of other Indo-European languages, there has been a choice of three moods for finite verbs: indicative, subjunctive and imperative. (We defer discussion of the imperative from the context of verbal mood to that of clause type, section 3.5.4 below.) While the indicative was the unmarked mood,[53] the subjunctive was the set of forms chosen typically to mark doubt, unreality, wishes, commands, and so on, and it was the mood selected by certain conjunctions. There were two tenses in the subjunctive just as in the indicative, but the inflections were less differentiated than those of the indicative, never distinguishing first, second and third person.

Already from OE onwards the subjunctive was losing importance for two reasons. Phonologically its forms were being reduced even faster than indicative inflections, and – perhaps in part as a consequence – syntactically its functions were being lost either to the indicative or to the modal verbs; see *CHEL* I: 150, 239–41; II: 246–8; III, forthcoming. A gradual process of loss has

Table 3.5. *Finite inflections of* BE

	Indicative				Subjunctive			
	1 SG	(2 SG)	3 SG	Plural	1 SG	(2 SG)	3 SG	Plural
present	*am*	(*art*)	*is*	*are*	*be*	(*bé*)	*be*	*bo*
past	*was*	(*wast* ~ *wert*)	*was*	*were*	*were*	(*wert*)	*were*	*were*

affected the subjunctive almost throughout the recorded history of English, though as we shall see, there have recently been signs of partial revival.

The indicative has become identical to the subjunctive throughout the past tense, and everywhere in the present tense apart from 3 SG of non-modal verbs, where the indicative has -*s*, the subjunctive -ϕ. Only the verb BE preserves fuller inflectional variety; see table 3.5. Is there still a present subjunctive? The paradigm even of the verb BE shows complete identity of infinitive, imperative and present subjunctive (under the form *be*). Since the same is true of all other verbs too, and since there is considerable overlap of function between the three forms, a persuasive analysis treats them as genuinely identical in PDE morphology, the 'base form' of the verb (see Huddleston 1984: 82–3). It must be noted, however, that historically all three have clearly been distinct forms.

The past subjunctive has a more tenuous existence. Three morphological processes have all but destroyed it. Inflectional reduction early made it indistinguishable from the indicative in the plural of strong verbs, and throughout the past tense of weak verbs. Before the ModE period strong verbs apart from *was/were* lost all singular/plural distinction in 1 and 3 past tense, and with it the possibility of explicit subjunctive marking in 1 and 3 past SG. Finally, the whole 2 SG paradigm disappeared with the loss of *thou*, leaving BE as the only verb with an explicit mood distinction in the past tense in the lModE period – and many speakers do not use the nonindicative singular form *were* at all. Furthermore, present subjunctive and past subjunctive are rather different. They are not generally in contrastive distribution; that is, there are few, if any, contexts where one can be contrasted with the other. For instance, despite varying time reference, only present subjunctives normally appear in the subordinate clauses of examples like

(178)   Max $\left\{ \begin{array}{l} \text{insists} \\ \text{insisted} \end{array} \right\}$ that the police *be* called.

(Indicative present and past do of course contrast, as in (110–15) above.) And unlike the present subjunctive, the past subjunctive behaves just like the indicative in negatives (3.3.4.1 below). Given all these facts, it is possible to argue that there is no such verbal form as 'past subjunctive' (e.g. Palmer 1988: 46, 1990: 190–1; Huddleston 1984: 83, 149–50, but cf. Quirk, Greenbaum, Leech & Svartvik 1985: 3.58). Here the case is not a watertight one even for PDE, and with our historical bias it seems appropriate to recognise a past subjunctive, however circumscribed its forms and functions.

In this section we shall concentrate mainly on subjunctives in main clauses; on choice of mood in subordinate clauses see sections 3.6.3.3, 3.6.6, 3.6.6.3 below.

3.3.4.1 Present subjunctive

In lModE the present subjunctive is morphologically distinct only with finite BE or with 3 SG of other verbs. However, negation can sometimes serve to differentiate indicative from subjunctive, in that *not* always follows an indicative in PDE but precedes a subjunctive, except *be*, which it may precede or follow, and past subjunctive *were*, which it always follows; see Quirk, Greenbaum, Leech & Svartvik (1985: 3.58):

(179)   orders that the flag *not be dipped*

(1948 *Christian Science Monitor* 4 (22 Sep.) [Kirchner, Visser])

Many subtypes of present subjunctive may be distinguished, as for instance by Visser (1963–73: sections 841–95). It occurs in expressions of the type *God grant that . . ., Long live NP, Far be it from me to VP, Suffice it to say*; in stage directions of the form *Enter NP*; and in the types *Try as he may, Say what he will*. None of them are truly productive, and some are now entirely fossilised as set phrases.

One productive syntactic pattern with a present subjunctive has as subject an indefinite pronoun:

(180)   *Take* the pipe out of his mouth, somebody.

(1841 Browning, *Pippa Passes* Poems (1905) 173 [*OED*])

From a PDE point of view, example (180) is essentially a third person imperative (section 3.5.4) with an indefinite subject. Subjunctives with definite third person subjects have been supplanted by forms involving *may* or *let* (cf. sections 3.3.5.1–2).

3.3.4.2 Past and past perfect subjunctive

As we have seen above, only clauses with a 1 or 3 SG subject and BE as finite verb have the possibility of distinguishing indicative from subjunctive in the past tense:

(181)   But it *were* better not to anticipate the comments to be made
         when   (1948 *TLS* 23 (10 Jan.) [Kirchner, Visser])

The usage of (181) is highly literary – indeed, was already a rather pompous
archaism by the early nineteenth century, according to Phillipps (1970: 155;
1978: 118) – and *would be* would be normal.

There has been a major change in apodoses (main clauses) of unreal
conditionals. Formerly a subjunctive could be found here, (182), and in
other unreal main clauses, (183):

(182)   for, if only the ladies could all have their own way in this world,
         and never be thwarted, then *were* the Millennium near at hand.
         But it is not   (1889 *Graphic* 278/2 (16 Mar.) [Visser])

(183)   a. Say it not; think it not! It *were* madness.
                                         (1840 Bulwer-Lytton, *Money* I.i p. 171)
         b. It *were* well, too, that a large number of Cossack stanitzas
            ['townships, communities'] should be intermingled with the
            new colonists.   (1895 *Daily News* 13 June 5/4 [*OED*])
         c. By 'apt use', I should say it *were* well to understand, a
            swiftness, almost a violence, and certainly a vividness.
                                         (1913 Ezra Pound, *Egoist*, in *Literary Essays*,
                                                             ed. Eliot (Faber, 1985) 52)

Examples (183b, c) are relatively late; for another turn-of-the-century
example see Denison (1993a: 313). This usage has been supplanted by
verbal groups with modal verbs, thus *should be* (first person) or, increasingly,
would be, allowing the generalisation that in the apodosis of an unreal
conditional in PDE, a past tense of a modal verb is actually obligatory
(Palmer 1988: 151–2; Denison 1993a: 312–14). Apart from modals, the
three most common finite verbs in such clauses in lModE are BE and
HAVE, partly because the past perfect is so often required, and DO.
Formerly other verbs were possible too, but Visser's collections show only
two dubious examples in our period (1963–73: section 815).

So apart from the clearly subjunctive BE, it is HAVE and DO that need
discussion. DO is not found after *c.* 1740. The use of *had been* for PDE *would
have been* is clearly related to the type seen in (182):

(184)   a. Had I yielded to the first generous impulse . . . how different
            had been my present situation!
                                         (1814 Scott, *Waverley*, ed. Lamont (World's Classics, 1986)
                                                             xxxiii[II.x].166 [Visser])

b. If he had but been a head taller, they *had never seen* a properer
man.   (1865 Kingsley, *Hereward* (Macmillan, 1889) iv.69 [*OED*])

c. It *had been* easy for me to gain a temporary effect by a mirage
of baseless opinion;   (1871–2 George Eliot, *Middlemarch* xx.201)

Here there is no formal marking of subjunctiveness in *had*, but both clauses are what Visser calls 'modal' and their verbal groups therefore 'modal pluperfects'. Visser discusses a number of subpatterns according as the protasis contains no modal *had*, contains modal *had* in an *if*-clause, contains modal *had* in inverted order, or has no expressed protasis (1963–73: sections 2034–7). He gives sporadic nineteenth- and twentieth-century examples of each, with accounts of their decline and obsolescence which differ slightly in detail, but I think it fair to say that all have become obsolescent since the eighteenth century and are now rare and pronouncedly literary. Also now obsolete, or at least obsolescent, are certain of the patterns in Visser's (1963–73: sections 2037, 2041):

(185)   a. far more than any indiscriminate praise, – I *had* almost *said*
more than any praise at all

(?1850 Gaskell, *Letters* 80 p. 131 (13 Sep.))

b. But I *had* almost *forgotten* to tell you a small piece of news.

(1891 Sidney Webb, *Letters* 172 I.319 (31 Oct.))

c. I have just driven a hundred miles and given up a morning
that *had* more profitably *been spent* with my tax accountant.

(1964 Berger, *Little Big Man* (Eyre & Spottiswoode, 1965)

Foreword.xv [Visser])

Notice that (185) contain finite *had* and not the infinitive *have* which is still productive in unreal clauses (cf. 3.3.2.5 above).

3.3.5   *Modal verbs*

Modal verbs, the most prototypical of auxiliaries,[54] do not signal aspect or voice, and have meanings typically of modality, whether **epistemic**, **deontic** or **dynamic**. Epistemic meanings concern the truth, probability, possibility, etc. of a whole proposition, deontic meanings concern permission given or obligation imposed by the speaker/writer (or in a question, the hearer/reader), while dynamic modality lacks this performative element. Examples (186) illustrate epistemic, deontic and dynamic CAN, respectively:

(186)   a. That *can't* be the time!

b. *Can* I have some sweets?

c. John *can* speak good French.

There have been considerable changes in usage of the modal verbs, and we must start by considering the inventory of items which qualify for the label. Core members include CAN (*can, could*), MAY (*may, might*), WILL (*will, would*), SHALL (*shall, should*), MUST (*must*). Palmer (1988, 1990) includes OUGHT (*ought*), DARE (*dare, durst*) and NEED (*need*) – though naturally he neglects the archaic or dialectal form *durst*. If *-n't* is analysed as an inflection, then most of the above forms have a negative counterpart. Other possible members of the category Modal are discussed in section 3.3.5.2 below.

3.3.5.1   Central modals

Here we discuss a number of changes in the meaning and usage of individual modals, starting with the modals of possibility and permission.

The verb MAY is undergoing a particularly wide-ranging set of changes. Early in our period, *might* could still be used as a deontic marked for past time:

(187 = 35a)   Here the poor boy was locked in by himself all day, without sight of any but the porter who brought him his bread and water – who *might not speak to him* [original emphasis]

(1823 Lamb, *Elia*, 'Christ's Hospital' p. 37 [Visser])

The permission-in-the-past sense is virtually obsolete, though twentieth-century examples can be found (according to Palmer 1990: 104, 'only in a very formal literary style'):

(188)   a. But father said they *might* keep the egg.

(1904 Nesbit, *Phoenix* i.18)

b. And they wanted to know whether there was permission for their crossing or what was to happen to them if they *might not* come down to the river . . . but they were not happy till I wrote them an order to say they *might* cross and continue on their way   (1918 Bell, *Letters* II.450 (17 Mar.))

See too the examples in Visser (1963–73: section 1662); the *OED* (s.v. *may* v.[1] B.4) is unhelpful here. Palmer elsewhere denies that past time can be marked at all with deontic modals in PDE, except in reported speech or in unreal or tentative contexts (1988: 100), which would apply to (188). Another unreal (though not past time) context is exemplified in (189):

(189)   Now, dearest, goodbye for today. I have a million yearnings to be
        with you: and failing that, I wish I *might* go on writing to you. But
        I must not.   (1891 Sidney Webb, *Letters* 155 I.290 (9 Sep.))

In all of these past tense functions, MAY has been largely replaced by CAN
(cf. also Collins 1988) or by BE *allowed/permitted*, HAVE *permission*, and
similar phrases:

(190)   No Officer *was permitted* to carry the newspapers out of the
        messroom.   (1811 *Sporting Mag.* XXXVII. 152 [*OED*])

Another past-time use of *might* discussed by Visser (1963–73: section 1669)
corresponds to PDE *might have*:

(191)   'But – who saw you do that?'
        'No one, I should think, since we were all in the dark.'
        'Still, they *might* hear [= 'might have heard'] it.'
                (1945 Anthony Gilbert, *Black Stage* (Chivers, 1988) v.80 [Visser])

He labels this 'eventuality in relation to the past', giving citations right
through the ModE period, and quotes the *OED* on its commonness in the
eighteenth century; see also Phillipps (1970: 121–2) on *might* for PDE *may
have*. During our period, however, it has become normal to mark the past
time element by perfect HAVE.

The relation between *may* and *might* appears to be changing too. Coates
finds little difference in meaning between epistemic *may* and *might* in her
PDE corpus: *might* 'seems no longer to be used as the tentative form of
MAY, but simply as an alternative form for the expression of the modality
"it is possible that . . ."' (1983: 153). On 'incorrect' *may* for *might* see section
3.3.5.3 below.

Other replacements of MAY by CAN, for example in deontic and epistemic use – (192) and (193), respectively – have been spread over an
extended period:

(192)   a. *May* I go now?
        b. *Can* I go now?

(193)   a. and what *may* it be?
                        (1880 Jessop, *Sam'l of Posen* II p. 167 [ARCHER])
        b. What else *can* it be?   (ibid. p. 165)

The usage in (192a) and (193a) is increasingly old-fashioned, though by no
means obsolete in all dialects.

The demise of the present subjunctive (section 3.3.4.1 above) has led to new means of expressing an exclamatory wish:

(194)   a. The devil *take* him!
        b. *May* the devil *take* him!
        c. I *hope* the devil *takes/may take/will take* him.

Thus (194a), which now survives only in formulaic utterances, was replaced mainly by (194b) in the ModE period. As Palmer observes, 'MAY is the most neutral modal' and perhaps 'the closest form in English to the subjunctive of other languages' (1990: 111). However, (194b) is now becoming rather formal, and expedients like (194c) are in turn taking over (Visser 1963–73: section 1680).

It is interesting that the negative *mayn't*, found from *c.* 1631 (Denison 1993a: 309), has become very rare in the present century. Palmer denies its very existence in PDE (later on he backtracks a little),[55] and he states that *mightn't* too is absent from many American dialects (1988: 17–18, 242). I suspect this should be related to category membership, given that being a modal is clearly a gradient rather than a clean yes/no matter: either it indicates a weakening of the membership of MAY (or perhaps just of present *may*), or it corroborates the idea that the category Modal as a whole is becoming less well-defined; see section 3.3.9 below.

Turning now to the modals which have been associated with futural meaning from OE or ME times, SHALL and WILL, we find a long tradition of differentiation according to person in certain of their uses; see *CHEL* II: 263–4, III, forthcoming. During the latter part of our period this somewhat artificial prescription has weakened considerably, and in the first person SHALL has increasingly been replaced by WILL even where there is no element of volition in the meaning. Examples which conform to the grammarians' prescription include:

(195)   a. Dearest, I fear this is a case in which I *shall* hamper you. But I
        will make up for it by my own work if I can.
                    (1891 Sidney Webb, *Letters* 169 I.313 (24 Oct.))
        b. It [*sc.* writing to Maude] *wd.* [= *would*] only lead to trouble, &
        we *shd.* [= *should*] have no right to repeat what was said
        without any intention at all of conveying censure.
                    (1872 *Amberley Papers* II.515 (16 Aug.))

There is no space to report on the history of each combination of person, clause type and meaning. Let us take one example. The *OED* (s.v. *shall* B.8c, in an entry first published 1913) reports that in categorical questions *shall* is the normal auxiliary of the future, citing the invented dialogue of (196a):

(196)   a. *Shall* you miss your train? I am afraid you will.
        b. *Shall* you go to Heaven, Mr. Green?
                                            (1862 Green, *Letters* 100 (1 Sep.))
        c. '*Shall* you let him go to Italy, or wherever else he wants to go?'
                                      (1871–2 George Eliot, *Middlemarch* ix.82)

In my letters corpus this usage actually occurs once only, (196b), though the writer repeats the quoted conversation a few lines later. On the other hand the now-normal use of *will* occurs at least twice (many other examples allow the possibility of a volitional interpretation):

(197)   a. *Will* you esteem me more or less if I tell you that I enjoyed it
                                  (1890 Dowson, *Letters* 82 p. 130 (11–12 Jan.))
        b. *Will* you be able to come here next week or *will* you prefer a
            dinner and Adélaide?   (ibid. 100 p. 150 (1 Jun.))

Examples elsewhere of the newer, general use of WILL include:

(198)   a. Now we *will* be patient.
                                  (1891 Sidney Webb, *Letters* 172 I.319 (31 Oct.))
        b. it shows that you are not well, & if you want to go to Clovelly
            or some such place for yourself we *will* do it.
                                          (1872 *Amberley Papers* II.521 (22 Aug.))

And as WILL has moved towards being the unmarked exponent of futurity, so its earlier volitional meaning has become weaker, so that examples of *would* like (199) are no longer found in PDE (except perhaps in such contexts as *would and could V*):

(199)   a. but I dare say he might ['would be able to'] come if he *would*
            ['wished'].   (1816 Austen, *Emma* I.xviii.145)
        b. and the elder ones retained some of their infantine notion
            that their father might ['would be able to'] pay for anything if
            he *would*.   (1871–2 George Eliot, *Middlemarch* xxiii.230)

Similarly, the obligation meaning of SHALL with third person subject has come to be restricted to rather formal usage.[56]

I turn now to a modal which is semantically isolated, the verb DARE. It can certainly be a modal verb syntactically, (200), though usually in nonassertive contexts. Its nonmodal doublet (found from the beginning of the seventeenth century, according to Visser 1963–73: section 1357), takes a *to*-infinitive rather than a plain infinitive, (201), and is not subject to the same restriction:

(200) a. *Dare* she risk another failure?
       b. **She *dare* risk failure.
(201) a. *Does* she *dare* to risk another failure?
       b. She *dares* to risk failure.

Visser claims tentatively that in interrogatives the nonmodal form is becoming the commoner of the two (1963–73: section 1364).

What confuses the analysis is 'mixed' usages such as the following:

(202) 'I *don't dare risk* meeting her. But I should like to talk to her very
       much.'   (1992 Tartt, *Secret history* vi.425)
(203) He began to walk back, wondering if he *dared trouble* with his
       errand a man on the verge of the grave.
                      (1932 Richard Aldington, *All Men Are Enemies* (Barker, 1948)
                                                            II.iii.153 [Visser])

In (202) the plain following infinitive is typical of modal DARE, while co-occurrence with DO implies *non*modal DARE. In confirmation that such blends are fully standard, notice *I should like* in the next sentence of (202), whose fictional speaker is a young scholar of formal manner. Example (203) shows regular verb conjugation in a context which is syntactically modal: invariable *dare* would be more common here, despite the *OED*'s strictures (s.v. *dare* v.¹ A.1c¶). There are even occasional inflected forms contracted with *n't* (3.3.8.2 below).

Modal DARE sporadically allows the following verb to be made passive ('voice-neutrality', implying transparency to subject selection) in a manner characteristic of epistemic modals but surprising for what is a dynamic modal:

(204) a. her name *dared not be mentioned* in Zelig's hearing.
                              (1916 Samuel Gordon, *God's Remnants* (Dent) i.18
                                                            [Jespersen, Warner])
       b. These two aspects of death cannot be successfully separated,
          but they *dare not be confused* or *identified*.
                      (1961 *Brown Corpus*, Religion D04:65 [Ehrman, Palmer])
       c. thus ensuring that the next time they apply for a job there is
          no way, qualified or not, that *they dare be passed over* again.
                      (1995 letter, *Oldham Evening Chronicle* 19/6 (27 Nov.))

This indication of the power of the modal stereotype has been found from time to time from OE to PDE.[57]

We move now to verbs of obligation. The verb NEED is similar to DARE in having modal and nonmodal doublets. Here, though, it is the modal usage which is the innovation, since historically NEED was not a preterite-present verb in OE like the majority of PDE modals. Up to the nineteenth century it was possible to use NEED as follows:

(205)   she saw, of course, that she *needed not to fear* me.
                (1869 Blackmore, *Lorna Doone* (Everyman, 1966) xvi.105 [Visser])

The regular past tense inflection and the following *to*-infinitive suggest that (205) has lexical (nonmodal) NEED, and while the form of negation might suggest that modal behaviour is blended in here, this is probably best taken as an archaism or a relic of the former general negation pattern (which had otherwise mostly died out by 1800); see further section 3.3.8.2 below. In modal usage NEED usually has the invariable form *need* in both present and past tenses:

(206)   a. 'Oh, I don't think we *need* have any uneasiness about that.'
                (1940 Wodehouse, *Quick Service* (Jenkins, 1960) ii.22 [Visser])
         b. There was nothing he *need* fear in a search
                (1928 Maugham, *Ashenden* (Heinemann, 1951) ii.12 [Visser])

Visser claims that in interrogatives, modal *need you V?*, etc. nowadays tends to be supplanted by *do you need to V?* (1963–73: section 1351, cf. his similar claim for DARE noted above), though Palmer's view, that the nonmodal form is more likely in formal or written texts (1990: 128), would contradict Visser's unless the change is coming from above. Until larger corpora become available it is not possible to verify either claim.

The verb OUGHT was a preterite-present in OE and has usually been treated as a modal verb, even though it normally takes a *to*-infinitive rather than the plain infinitive characteristic of core modals. However, Quirk, Greenbaum, Leech & Svartvik (1985: 3.43n.[a]) report that young people often accept and even prefer a plain infinitive after OUGHT in nonassertive contexts; in such cases it would be unambiguously a core modal. Its meaning is close to, but not identical with, *should*. Mencken, writing in the 1930s of American English (1963: 538), thought that OUGHT was replacing *should*, while Harris (1986) finds the opposite for current BrE. Historically – and arguably in PDE still (Jørgensen 1984) – the form *ought* is past tense, but the verb is now often used in nonpast contexts, or with HAVE (i.e. *ought to have Ved*) to mark past time. Visser gives full coverage of the forms *hadn't ought*, *shouldn't ought* and *didn't ought* (1963–73: sections 1722–3), non-standard but quite common, and all involving a clear past tense finite auxiliary:

(207)   'I *didn't ought* to take it,' said Eliza

(1907 Nesbit, *Enchanted Castle* iv.86)

On the negative *oughtn't* see section 3.3.8.2 below.

3.3.5.2   Peripheral modals

Here we discuss a number of verbs which belong with the modals semantically and to some extent morphosyntactically, without satisfying all of the standard criteria for modalhood.

Where a nonfinite form would be required for CAN, the verb BE *able* often acts as a suppletive – an unrelated form used to complete a paradigm – and has done so since the beginning of the ModE period:

(208)   a. What a thing it is *to be able* to talk of friendship with one's
               parents.   (1917 Bell, *Letters* II.428 (18 Oct.))
          b. but I *have not been able* quite to spot him yet.
                                                      (ibid. I.400 (10 Mar.))
          c. and I, *not being able* to bear sitting in the office any longer
                                                      (1918 ibid. II.453 (5 Apr.))

Their meanings are very similar indeed. However, the suppletion is not only used for morphosyntactic reasons, since *was able* in PDE lacks the restriction of *could* to nonassertive contexts when a single event is concerned (Palmer 1988: 117–18):

(209)   a. Yesterday she began to swallow and *was able* to gargle
                                             (1874 *Amberley Papers* II.569 (28 Jun.))
          b. ?**Yesterday she began to swallow and *could* gargle

I suspect that this restriction is of long standing, despite:

(210)   Piglet thought that they ought to have a Reason for going to
           see everybody, like Looking for Small or Organizing an
           Expotition, if Pooh could think of something.
             Pooh *could.*   (1928 A. A. Milne, *House at Pooh Corner* viii.126)

The verb HAVE in an obligation sense is close in meaning to modal MUST; differences are discussed by Palmer (1988: 129–31). This use of HAVE has a full paradigm, which allows it to act as a sort of suppletive for MUST when a nonfinite form is required:

(211)   The doctors *have had* to threaten her she shall be sent away, if she
         gives more trouble.
         (1864 Queen Victoria, *Private Correspondence* p. 289 (11 Jan.) [ARCHER])

The rise of modal HAVE predates our period; see Fischer (1994) for an account. A recent semantic development which brings modal HAVE closer to MUST is the epistemic use seen in:

(212)   a. Through the years she had sensed that something like this *had* to happen someday.

(1950 Theodore Pratt, *The Tormented* (World Distr., 1962) v.36 [Visser, Brinton])

   b. 'It *has* to be easier with two of them.'

(1961 *Brown Corpus*, Press Reportage A39:26)

   c. She was so beautiful with her rosy mouth and haughty air that she *had* to be wicked.   (ibid., General Fiction K06:179)

(In (212), especially the first example, HAVE is not unambiguously epistemic.)

The combination HAVE *got* was originally the perfect of the verb GET. In some varieties it supplements and even supplants the verb HAVE in at least two uses: as a stative main verb with meanings like 'possess', and as the quasi-modal – just discussed – with the meaning 'be obliged'. For convenience, both uses of HAVE *got* will be discussed here. As would be expected given its origins, the HAVE part always functions as an operator. Charleston dates the 'possess' sense to the second half of the eighteenth century (1941: 3.3$_2$, reference due to Warner 1993: 67), though Dr Johnson already knew of it before 1755 (Visser 1963–73: section 2011):

(213)   These Londoners *have got* a gibberage [*sc.* gibberish] with 'em, would confound a gipsey.

(1777 (1781) Sheridan, *Scarborough* IV.i 602.36)

It is now thought to be more typical of BrE than AmerE (Quirk, Greenbaum, Leech & Svartvik 1985: 3.34). During our period it has increased greatly in frequency at the expense of HAVE, though in nonassertive contexts HAVE is fighting back in its non-operator form (section 3.3.8.5).

As for the modal use, Visser dates it to the third decade of the nineteenth century (1963–73: section 2142), and Palmer asserts that it 'belongs to a more colloquial style' in current BrE (1990: 114). It does not follow from the etymology of HAVE *got* that a base form (infinitive) is ruled out – yet Palmer asserts that modal HAVE *got* is finite only (1990: 116). If true, this suggests that it is approaching full modalhood. Epistemic HAVE *got to be* 'must be' is of similar vintage to epistemic HAVE *to be*, (212) above, and has since spread from AmerE to BrE:

(214)   a. This *has got* to be some kind of local phenomenon.

           (1961 *Brown Corpus*, Science Fiction M04:165)

      b. when you have 30 of the world's best players on the field, it'*s*
         got to be a hard game.

           (1961 *LOB Corpus*, Press Reportage A33:22)

Both possession and modal uses of HAVE *got* frequently show a reduced form of HAVE, and in this century the HAVE may disappear altogether, giving a new, invariable verb form *got* (closer to standard in America, and sometimes represented together with its following *to* as *gotta*):

(215)   a. 'I don't know,' said Dickie, 'but we *got* to do it som'ow.'

           (1909 Nesbit, *Harding's Luck* v.105)

      b. If you were off there ... I'd go mad ... I *got* to be with you.

           (1925 S. Lewis, *Arrowsmith* (Grossett & Dunlap) xxxii.351)

The form HAD *better* is modal-like in semantics, morphology (finite only), and complementation (followed by base form without *to*). Compare:

(216)   a. You'*d better* go.
      b. You *should* go.

Palmer lists the negative forms as *hadn't better* or *had better not* (1990: 82). In this combination the verb HAVE can only appear in the past tense form *had*, often reduced phonetically to *'d*, or, increasingly often, to zero:

(217)   a. 'I wonder if I *better* change.'

           (1949 Streatfeild, *Painted Garden* x.111)

      b. 'I told him he *better* be careful or Julian will think he stole it.'

           (1992 Tartt, *Secret History* i.37)

Arguably we should regard (217) as exemplifying the modal verb BETTER, especially given the sporadic development of a tag question form *bett(er)n't*, at least in child language, though I have no corpus instances.[58]

Somewhat similar, except that it lacks an epistemic meaning, is HAD/WOULD (occasionally SHOULD) *rather* '(would) prefer', often reduced to *'d rather*. It is followed either by an infinitive or a finite clause. Visser has a few examples (1963–73: section 40). Negation usually follows the element *rather*, though interrogative negatives like *Wouldn't you rather ... ?* are possible (Quirk, Greenbaum, Leech & Svartvik 1985: 3.45, Palmer 1990: 167). Bolinger cites the attested (though quite non-standard) examples (218) as evidence that *rather* is on its way to becoming an auxiliary verb itself (1992: II 596):

(218)   a. You *might rather* it [= your money] be sent to a hookworm clinic.

      b. People *did rather* ['preferred to'] take that.

Possibly an auxiliary, but not an operator.

The verb BE has a modal use with various meanings (Palmer 1988: 160–1). It is always complemented by a *to*-infinitive. (Visser points out that newspaper headlines routinely omit finite BE in this construction – as elsewhere.) In ME and eModE, this usage had a full paradigm, with both participles and an infinitive, but the last generations able to use modal BE freely in this way were alive in the early decades of the nineteenth century:

(219)   a. You *will be* to visit me in prison with a basket of provisions

                           (1816 Austen, *Mansfield Park* I.xiv.135)

      b. N.B. No snuff *being* to be had in the village she made us some.

                           (1818 Keats, *Letters* 78 p. 189 (20 Jul.))

      c. None of them had been completely finished, the painting and papering *being* yet to be done.

               (1885 Sir J. Bacon in *Law Times Rep.* (N.S.) LII. 569/2 [*OED*])

      d. But new problems *may be* to come.

Although there are a few relevant later examples in Visser (1963–1973: sections 1378, 2135, 2142), most are of the fixed idiom BE *to come*. Since the early nineteenth century, then, modal BE has become to all intents and purposes finite only, bringing it close to the central modals in morphology as well as semantics.

LET can be considered as a marginal modal because it occurs with a plain infinitive, has meanings in the modal area, may commute with true modals, and requires a modal in tag questions (Palmer 1988: 171, Denison 1993a: 320):

(220)   a. *Let's* go.

      b. *Shall* we go?

      c. *Let's* go, *shall* we?

Of course its paradigm is considerably different from that of 'normal' modals. A number of variants can be distinguished, though most will be discussed under Imperatives, section 3.5.4 below. For now, note that the subject of the lexical verb can be first or third person, and if a pronoun, has objective case:

(221)   *Let me* send you a line before I fall into a little pink slumber.

                       (1889 Dowson, *Letters* 70 p. 111 (*c.* 21 Oct.))

A subjective pronoun is occasionally permitted, bringing LET rather closer to the modals:

(222)　'. . . so *let he and I* say goodnight together.'

(1838–9 Dickens, Nickleby xxx.388)

The *OED* describes this usage as 'incorrect' (s.v. *let* v.[1] 14b), and Visser adds a few more examples, some with *let's* rather than *let* (1963–73: section 2062), but it is notable that all but one of their citations involve a subjective pronoun coordinated with another NP, usually another pronoun; cf. the discussion of (47) in section 3.2.2.3 above.

Mossé (1947: 209–10) suggests that WANT is tending to take on the value of a modal auxiliary, on the evidence of commutation with modals:

(223)　a. One *wants* [= *ought*] to be very careful.
　　　　b. You *want* to [= *must*] have your teeth seen to.
　　　　c. You *don't want* to [= *must not*] overdo it for a bit.
　　　　d. You *don't want* to [= *need not*] be rude.

Unlike true modals, of course, WANT can still be an ordinary transitive verb (*She wants no discussion*) or a catenative (*I want you to come quietly*). Much has been made in the generative tradition of the possibility of phonetic contraction of *want to* (sometimes represented in print as *wanna*), and its significance for syntactic analysis; references are given in Radford (1988: 604).

At the start of our period, USE 'be in the habit of' + *to*-infinitive could convey a habitual sense in the present tense. *OED* does not state when this died out. The latest example I have found is:

(224)　The flat side [of the lute], where we *use* to carve a rose, or a
　　　　rundle　　　　(a1843 Southey *Comm.-Pl. Bk.* Ser. ii. (1849) 474 [*OED*])

The present participle *using* can be found as late as 1670; both postdate Visser's collections (1963–73: sections 1334–5). A variant with the noun *use* is seen in:

(225)　One not *in the use* to speak before his purpose was fixed.

(1825 Scott, Betrothed xxi [OED])

The past tense *used* is now the only one available, most commonly with the final [d] subsumed in the [t] of *to*, [juːstə]. The verb is sometimes an operator, with negation *used not*, or from the 1860s *use(d)n't* (*OED* s.v. *usen't*):

(226)　*Usedn't* people to have no homes and beg because they were
　　　　hungry?　　　　(1906 Nesbit, *Amulet* xii.229)

Increasingly often it is treated as a non-operator, with negative *didn't use(d)* and inverted form *did NP use(d)* . . . *?* (the spelling arouses uncertainty), though such usage has been disapproved of by prescriptivists. In some dialects *used* can follow other auxiliaries than *did/didn't*, notably *had/hadn't*, sometimes even modals, but always past tense in form:

(227)   his hands went often to his trembling lips again, as they *had used* to do when he first came in.   (1855–7 Dickens, *Little Dorrit* I.vi.64)

3.3.5.3   Modal past

Here we look at some developments in the usage of modal past tenses. On protases with inverted modal verbs – always past tense – see section 3.6.6.3 below.

In origin *must* was a past tense (OE PRES 3 SG *mot*, PAST 3 SG *moste* 'be allowed to, may'), but over the course of the ME period it came to serve also as a present tense. During the lModE period it has virtually lost the past tense use, leaving MUST with a paradigm incomplete even by modal standards, though not all grammarians of PDE recognise the obsolescence of past tense *must*, which survives best in certain backshifting contexts:

(228)   It was clear that something *must* be done at once, and I proceeded to hunt for one.   (1917 Bell, *Letters* II.406 (20 Apr.))

Palmer (1990: 184) cites from Huddleston (1977: 46):

(229)   If he had stayed in the army, he *must have* become a colonel.

with *must* as the obligatory past tense modal in the apodosis (though he claims that *must* is *present* tense here, since '*must* has no past tense form available'). If (229) is impossible for many speakers (including me), there are certainly a good many examples in the nineteenth and even twentieth centuries:

(230)   a. But it would have secured me nothing, as there would have been no funds for my maintenance at the University . . . and my career at Oxford *must have* been unfortunate.
                                    (1883 Trollope, *Autobiography* (OUP, 1950) i.10)
         b. (There are those who believe that if Hitler had invaded in 1940 he *must have* been stopped by the removal of our signposts.) (1993 John Samuel, *The Guardian Weekend* p. 70 (12 Jun.))

And there are other examples of past tense *must*:

(231)   that were it not for the assistance of Brown & Taylor I *must* be as badly off as a Man can be.   (1819 Keats, *Letters* 156 p. 398 (17 Sep.))

(232) a. and though Mrs. Philips . . . stood in too much awe of him to
          speak with the familiarity which Bingley's good humour
          encouraged, yet, whenever she *did* [original emphasis] speak,
          she *must* be vulgar.   (1813 Austen, *P&P* III.xviii.384)
       b. Therefore some re-formulation was necessitated . . . Again,
          the re-formulation *must* conform to the theory of grammar
          . . . There were no further constraints.
                              (1979 Lightfoot, *Principles of Diachronic Syntax* 407)

This, then, is a significant recent change in the paradigm of one modal.

   In Denison (1992) I discussed at length the use of *may have* for standard
might have in counterfactual contexts:

(233) a. All this *may have* come about without Hearst's Egyptian
          eruption.
                    (1960 Swanberg, *Citizen Hearst* (Scribner/Collier, 1986) IV.i.213)
       b. Had you been able to decipher these notations you *may have*
          gathered that this fact was in some way Oscar Hopkins's fault.
                         (1988 Peter Carey, *Oscar and Lucinda* (Faber, 1989) xxxv.149)
       c. relevant safety warnings were not made public. If they had
          been, action *may have* been taken and the disaster avoided.
                    (1989 *Consumer Which* (April), quoted *The Guardian* p. 20 (6 Apr.))

The usage was claimed at the beginning of the twentieth century to be
typical of Irish English, in mid-century to be typical of half-educated
American speech, and recently a strange error to be pointed out in British
English. It seems to be quite widespread in Britain and elsewhere (see also
CHEL V: 11–12), except perhaps among educated southern BrE speakers.

   Some of the various explanations I canvassed were peculiar to MAY
itself: that in non-counterfactual contexts *may have* and *might have* are wholly
or nearly synonymous and interchangeable; that *may have* is a hypercorrect
response to obsolescence, whether of *may* in favour of *might* or of the
whole MAY paradigm in favour of CAN; various sorts of blending, for
example *may have* being enabled by the familiarity of *maybe had* (adverb +
HAVE) in examples like

(234) 'This may sound crazy,' he said, 'but I'd been a little worried, you
       know? That something *maybe had* happened to her.'
                                        (1992 Tartt, *Secret History* viii.569)

Another factor considered was that unreality might now be sufficiently
marked by HAVE (cf. 3.3.2.5 above).

However, one possibility has wider importance for the modals. The use of the 'wrong' tense form could be regarded as part of an incipient loss of the general backshifting rule (3.3.1 above), at least as far as modals are concerned. There are certainly numerous instances involving MAY even without the perfect *have*:

(235)   a. If half a dozen skippers . . . were to evaporate during the approaching hot months he *may* have some small chance of tother Swab ['naval officer's epaulette'].

(1833 M. Scott, *Tom Cringle* xv [*OED*])

b. In today's violent world, people *may not* feel quite as vulnerable out of doors if they had a telephone in their pocket.

(1989 *The Independent* p. 14 (24 Oct.))

c. They were looking for the lair of a master spy who *may* be passing United States secrets to an eastern European ring, a man said in congressional hearings to have done more damage [*sc.* by computer hacking] to the Pentagon than the KGB.

They found Richard Pryce, a 16-year-old schoolboy.

(1997 *The Guardian* p. 1 (22 Mar.))

(Example (235a) is unusually early.) Rather than take examples (229–30) as relics of past tense *must*, we could conceivably regard (some of) them instead as early instances of a present tense modal in a past tense context. With the modals DARE and NEED, present tense forms have long been used in past tense contexts (see e.g. Visser 1963–73: sections 796, 1348–9, 1363):

(236)   a. I hope so soon to be with you that were it not for the selfish pleasure I take in a chat with you, I *need* hardly bc writing now.

(1861 Green, *Letters* 79 (Apr.))

b. They used to bring me nice things to eat . . . but after Ginger stood in that box, they *dare* not come, and I missed them very much.   (1877 Sewell, *Black Beauty* iv.23)

Visser reckons that *needed* was still the dominant usage in the nineteenth century (section 796). He even implies (1963–73: section 1346) that it occurs occasionally with a plain infinitive in affirmative contexts, but he gives no examples. Mine are all in negative contexts:

(237)   a. He told her she *needed not* be troubled for her minion.

(1778 Hamilton, *Munster Village* p. 75 [ARCHER])

b. He *needed not* have been jealous.

(1850 Gaskell, *Moorland Cottage* vi.341)

Examples of *dared* + plain infinitive are a little easier to find, again usually nonaffirmative (Visser 1963–73: sections 1356, 1359). I give one with ellipsis of the infinitive:

(238) 'I'll answer for it,' said Mr. Buxton in reply, 'that you'll not find any cheating has been going on. They *dared not*, sir; they know I should make an example of the first rogue I found out.'

(1850 Gaskell, *Moorland Cottage* vii.345)

But DARE and NEED are peculiar as modals.

Sporadic examples involving modals with full present~past differentiation are consonant with a weakening of backshifting, though not in themselves enough to prove anything, especially since the relevant clauses of (239a, b) are not purely counterfactual:

(239) a. The two immediate regulations to be enforced on Thames pleasure craft are disturbing. Firstly, a short safety drill . . . *cannot* realistically *be expected to have* had any significant helpful effect upon the partying and drinking people aboard the ill-fated Marchioness last weekend, given the speed with which she sank. (1989 letter, *The Guardian* p. 20 (24 Aug.))

b. And even if people like Zippe or Khan or Stemmler never left home, nothing *can* prevent a physicist in Iraq from using the world's vast technical literature to build equipment.

(1992 *New Scientist* 1844: 35 (24 Oct.))

c. With any other ruling party this sort of information *will have* cast doubts on the timing, and possibly the holding of the election. It all suggests that the Jaruzelski leadership not only prepared its own death warrant but . . .

(1989 *The Guardian* p. 23 (8 Jun.))

If this is a genuine, and persistent, tendency, it will strengthen the case of those who argue already that modals do not carry tense, or even are not verbs at all; see section 3.3.9 below.

3.3.5.4 Modal + *it/that*, and modal + *that*-clause
A usage which is somewhat archaic in standard English is the use of modal + *it/that* standing for VP material:

(240) a. 'His Mastership will do well to look to himself.' '*That* he *should*,' re-echoed Craigengelt.

(1818 Scott, *Br. Lamm.* xxi [*OED*])

b. 'You ought to have a wooden horse on wheels, *that* you *ought*!'

> (1872 Carroll, *Looking-Glass*, ed. Blackburn & White
> (Putnam's, 1934) viii.219)

c. 'We should have pulled down the screen,' whispered Arrietty.
'We *should that*,' agreed Pod.

> (1955 Norton, *Borrowers Afield* (Harcourt Brace, 1967) xviii.323)

According to Plank (1984: 336), the modal is never epistemic. Similar usage can be found for DO:

(241)   a. '. . . and I hope you like it.'
'I *do that*, and no mistake,' said the cook unexpectedly

> (1904 Nesbit, *Phoenix* iii.67)

b. And I don't go back to that nasty underground kitchen, and
me blamed for everything; *that* I *don't*, not till the dream's
finished . . .   (ibid. iii.74)

More recent examples often occur in attempts at rustic speech.

In our period modals have not been able to govern a *that*-clause, something that WILL and MAY were formerly able to do. However, we sometimes find *would* + finite clause, mostly with ellipsis of the subject pronoun *I*:

(242)   a. *Would* they & the d——d indigestions they ensure were over.

> (1889 Dowson, *Letters* 78 p. 121 (24 Dec.))

b. *Would* I had taken 'Bromo-Tablets', and never revived at all!

> (1916 W. Owen, *Let.* 3 Feb. (1967) 378 [*OED*])

See Visser (1963–73: section 814). The *OED* (s.v. *will* v.[1] B.36) describes it as archaic. As far as I know the usage is 1 SG only and thus effectively a fossilised phrase, though I have one example with a divine subject that postdates the *OED* by some three centuries:

(243)   *Would the gods* it were over.

> (1890 Dowson, *Letters* 94 p. 142 (14 Mar.))

3.3.6   *Voice: active versus passive*

Voice concerns the active~passive relationship. Generally speaking, two changes mark a passive as different from an active: first that the lexical verb is a past participle and is preceded by an auxiliary verb that is otherwise a copula, and second that the subject NP corresponds to an object in the active:

(244)   a. Max destroyed the typewriter. (active)
       b. The typewriter was destroyed (by Max). (passive)

Topics for this section are the choice of auxiliary verb, the combination of perfect and passive, and voice in nonfinite clauses. Other major developments in the passive are discussed elsewhere: combination of progressive and passive – regarded as principally a change in the progressive – in section 3.3.3.4 above, and extension of the passive to new active VPs – not a change within the verbal group – in section 3.4.1.2 below, while the relationship between passives and predicatives is discussed in section 3.4.3.1.

3.3.6.1   Auxiliaries of the passive

The principal auxiliary of the passive has always been BE. Its main competitor in the modern period is GET, which began to be used to form passives in the seventeenth century.[59] By the early years of the nineteenth century, the GET passive was reasonably common:

(245)   a. and his boy goes to the School there, where he *gets beaten*
                        (1819 Keats, *Letters* 156 p. 403 (18 Sep.))
       b. You *get entangled* in another man's mind
                        (1823 Lamb, *Elia*, 'Schoolmaster' p. 122 [*OED*])
       c. I . . . *got laughed at* pretty fairish.
                       (1836–48 B. D. Walsh, *Aristoph., Knights* i. iii [*OED*])
       d. after they *had got released* from prison.
            (1871 (1868) Collins, *Moonstone*, ed. Trodd (World's Classics, 1982)
                                      1st per., iv.22)

Many examples like (245b) allow an alternative analysis in which GET is a mutative (change-of-state) verb and the participle a stative adjective, the long-familiar pattern of:

(246)   and in spite of plumbers my room *gets very damp.*
                        (1872 *Amberley Papers* II.530 (28 Oct.))

Of course the same duality can affect the BE passive too (3.4.3.1 below).

The true GET passive is certainly on the increase. There are no unambiguous examples in my letters corpus, though ambiguous stative~nonstative examples like *gets thoroughly drenched, gets hardened, getting tired out, get rather bored* do occur. Granger even finds that they are 'extremely rare . . . and are restricted to colloquial style' in a sample of spoken material dated 1961–75, taken from the adult, educated, BrE of the Survey of English Usage (1983: 234–5). Yet Visser refers to the 'enormous popularity' of GET passives in the twentieth century (1963–73: section 1893):

(247)   a. '. . . Quite a lot of lies *get printed*, especially in newspapers.'

(1906 Nesbit, *Amulet* xiii.240)

   b. 'Murder's always dangerous, but it *gets committed* fairly
   frequently just the same . . .'

(1945 Anthony Gilbert, *Black Stage* (Chivers, 1988) v.78
[Visser])

   c. '. . . The old ladies' copy *gets delivered* before I'm home and Mrs
   B. always reads it aloud to Miss D.'

(1961 Angus Wilson, *The Old Men at the Zoo* (Secker) i.62 [Visser])

If, as would appear, they have been slower to enter the more formal registers of written English, especially BrE, a prescriptive resistance to the use of GET (in all functions) may have played some part.[60]

It is open to argument whether GET qualifies as an auxiliary. It is not an operator, and more significantly, it does not occur freely with all lexical verbs or all subject NPs. On the other hand, it is clearly subordinate semantically to the lexical verb, and in many instances it is virtually interchangeable with BE:

(248)   a. The vase *was knocked over* in the fracas.
   b. The vase *got knocked over* in the fracas.

Sometimes, especially with a subject of human reference, GET imparts a sense of volition or participation, as in the early example in note 59. Other catenatives with even more distant resemblance to the passive auxiliary BE include BECOME, FALL, GROW, REMAIN, STAY:

(249)   a. The affection of Martin now *became changed* to the vilest
   hatred.   (1789 Brown, *Power of Sympathy* xxi.36 [ARCHER])
   b. any place . . . where she could *remain concealed*
   (1791 Radcliffe, *Romance of the Forest* ix.429 [ARCHER])

Apart from GET, these verbs now tend to resist collocation with a truly verbal participle.

A clipped passive (*no sooner said than done*) is not quite the same as a clipped perfect or progressive (sections 3.3.2.6, 3.3.3.6 above), since on the one hand there is perhaps less scope for ellipsis of subject and auxiliary in independent clauses, while on the other the passive participle has always been normal as a free-standing predicative without auxiliary. But clipped passives can occur:

(250)   a. *Warned* against me, and by Winter too!

(1819 Beazley, *Steward* II.i [ARCHER])

b. *Tricked*! [*sc.* I have been tricked]

(1832 Jerrold, Rent Day II.i, in Works (Bradbury & Evans, 1854)
VIII.25 [ARCHER])

This does not seem to attract much attention from Visser, though types such as (251) which are partly similar are discussed in his (1963–73: sections 1147–57, 1925):

(251)   so I told him not to go unless expressly *sent for* by you.

(1872 Amberley Papers II.521 (21 Aug.))

3.3.6.2   Perfect + passive

It has been possible at least since eME to combine the HAVE perfect with the BE passive:

(252)   I hope the Baby *has been christened*

(1872 Amberley Papers II.527 (29 Aug.))

What is striking in the earlier part of our period is that the combination was often avoided in favour of the passive alone (as still happens in Dutch and German):

(253)   a. but that objection *is done away with*

(1818 Keats, Letters 66 p. 146 (21 May))

        b. He . . . had the croup so on Sunday that my cousins wrote
           word he *was given up*.   (1838 Gaskell, *Letters* 7 p. 13 (30 Mar.))

        c. I sent him three tragedies. They *are accepted*; and he has left me
           a note in the hall, to fix the reading – at last.

(1852 Taylor & Reade, Masks & Faces I.i p. 127)

        d. Alicia is vexed because her marriage *is postponed*;

(1863 Hazlewood, Lady Audley's Secret II.i p. 250)

        e. 'Here is an honour to your father, children,' said Mrs
           Garth . . . 'He *is asked* to take a post again by those who
           dismissed him long ago.'

(1871–2 George Eliot, Middlemarch xl.402)

(253′)   a. but that objection has been done away with
        b. he had been given up

Examples like (253) resemble the BE perfect (3.3.2.2 above) in form and in meaning too, marking the result of anterior action. Indeed there are examples ambiguous between the two analyses (passive and perfect), as Rydén and Brorström point out (1987: 24):

(254)　　Our hopes *are* again *revived* of seeing the Viceroy of Mexico.
　　　　　　　(1797 Nelson, *Letters*, ed. Naish (1958) 190 p. 328 (30 Jun.)
　　　　　　　　　　　　　　　　　　　　[Rydén & Brorström])

It seems reasonable to assume some linkage between the decline of the two forms. The effect of adding the HAVE perfect to the BE passive, as in (253'), is to draw attention to the anteriority of the action as well as to its result. Another linkage worth investigating involves the recategorisation of certain participles as adjectives rather than verbs (3.4.3.1 below): use of the sequence HAVE + *been* + participle can make clear that a participle is to be regarded as verbal.

3.3.6.3　Voice in nonfinite clauses

Our main concern here is with infinitival patterns which permit variation without significant difference of meaning between active and passive infinitives:

(255)　　a.　There is nothing *to say*.
　　　　　b.　There is nothing *to be said*.

(256)　　a.　This problem is *easy to solve*.
　　　　　b.　**This problem is *easy to be solved*.

A number of different syntactic patterns show – or have shown – such variation, all of them involving coreference between the logical object of the infinitive (in the active variant) and an NP with some function in a higher clause, usually subject or predicative complement. Fischer (1991) carefully disentangles them, giving a full discussion of their history, particularly the OE and ME phases; Jespersen's material on the later history remains useful too (1909–49: V 217–33). Type (256a) is often known as an *easy-to-please* construction or under the old Transformational Grammar label of *Tough*-Movement (from such pairs as *It is tough to solve this problem~This problem is tough to solve*).

As Fischer shows, passive forms came on the scene later than actives, though still well before our period. Change during the lModE period has largely consisted of a selective reduction of variation. Each type has a different history. Take the pattern *NP* BE *to V*, where the logical object of V is coreferential with NP. Visser's collection of active examples includes some that are surprisingly recent (1963–73: section 1384):

(257)　　a.　but they *are* all *to feed, to clothe, to rear, to settle* in life
　　　　　　　　　　　(1849 C. Brontë, *Shirley*, ed. Rosengarten & Smith
　　　　　　　　　　　　　　　(Clarendon, 1979) I.ix.171 [Visser])

b. The wet and the cold *were* now *to reckon with*

> (1902 (1909) James, *Wings of the Dove* (Scribner's, 1937)
> II.IX.ii.261 [Visser])

But throughout the ModE period the more explicit passive has been the dominant variant (Visser 1963–73: section 2151), and fossilised PDE survivals like *this house is to let* and *he is to blame* are not productive:

(258)   a. **What's to do* next?
b. What's *to be done* next?

The same applies to infinitival phrases used as noun modifiers: *a never-to-be-forgotten occasion* (Visser 1963–73: section 1922).

Consider now (259a), where the infinitive *to hear* is dependent on an adjective, *pleasant*, which is predicated of an NP, *their comments*, coreferential with the logical object of the infinitive:

(259)   a. and their comments were *pleasant to hear*

> (1862 Green, *Letters* 114 (15 Dec.))

b. In these cases there is often a great repugnancy to the taking of food, which is *very difficult to overcome*.

> (1874 *Amberley Papers* II.570 (28 Jun.))

In such cases it is generally the active rather than the passive which has triumphed. It has the advantage of being parallel to patterns in which the subject of the infinitive is expressed in a *for*-construction, and a passive infinitive is ruled out:

(259′)   a. and their comments were pleasant *for me* to hear

This may go some way to explaining the demise of the passive variant.

Fischer suggests another reason, the loss of grammatical ambiguity of *easy*-adjectives after the Latinate confusion of the eModE period (1991: 2.4.2 = 1990: 203–7). The ambiguity actually survived into our period:

(260)   This devil . . . may be alive, – for I believe some common things are *hard to die*.   (1849–50 Dickens, *David Copperfield* xlvi.574)

In (260) the adjective is predicated of an NP coreferential with the logical *subject* of the infinitive (thus more like PDE *eager* than *easy*). The latest such example for *hard* in the *OED* is from 1858 Dickens (s.v., a. A.5c), for *easy* 'not unwilling, ready' 1738 (s.v., A.12b). They were never common.

Returning to the normal situation with *easy* adjectives, coreferentiality with logical object, we find that passive infinitives took a long time to die out:

(261) a. but you know a favorite tune is *hardest to be remembered* when
    one wants it most   (1818 Keats, *Letters* 54 p. 114 (14 Mar.))
  b. books which are *rather difficult to be procured*, from having
    been privately published.
           (1850 Gaskell, *Letters* 74 p. 122 (17 Aug.))
  c. she began to be mysterious to others; and became *as difficult to
    be made out* to anybody's satisfaction, as she found the house
    and everything in it *difficult to make out* to her own.
           (1855–7 Dickens, *Little Dorrit* I.xv.182)
  d. This was *terrible to be borne*.
           (1860–1 Trollope, *Framley* xix.183)
  e. The well-educated, widely-read Conservative . . . is generally
    the pleasantest man to be met.
       (1871–2 Trollope, *Eustace Diamonds* (OUP, 1950) I.iv.34)
  f. yet something else too – something ill-assured, timid,
    incongruous – *hard to be defined*.
           (1894 Ward, *Marcella* I.x.98 [Visser])

And some adjectives not belonging to the *easy* or *pleasant* semantic groups still permit or even require a passive infinitive: thus *fit, ready*, and others.

Where the infinitive is dependent on an NP coreferential with the logical object of the infinitive, some variation remains possible. Fischer argues that the passive is more generally favoured, especially when the NP is animate and could serve as subject or object of the (active) infinitive (1991: 2.4.3 = 1990: 207–9):

(262) a. which I really think may be useful as *something to bite upon*.
           (1917 Bell, *Letters* II.410 (11 May))
  b. *The only healthy thing to do.*
        (1964 Gelber, *Square in the Eye* II.i p. 88 [ARCHER])
(263) a. there is *absolutely nothing to be done* at Box
      (1891 Beatrice Webb [Potter], *Letters* 148 I.280 (20 Aug.))
  b. I think life *too complex a thing to be settled* by these hard and fast
    rules.   (1893 Wilde, *Lady Windermere's Fan* I p. 14 [Visser])

The unmarked reading of the active equivalent of (263a) does show a subtle difference of meaning, it is true:

(263´) a. there is *absolutely nothing to do* at Box

In (262) the active is certainly favoured, perhaps by the presence of an adjective premodifying the noun in (262b) – indeed, the infinitive may be dependent on the AP rather than the whole NP – in which case that factor must be outweighed in (263b) by the presence of a *by*-phrase. The active is more common where the subject of BE is dummy *there* (Visser 1963–73: section 1385):

(264)   a. There is no more to say.
         b. There is no more to be said.

On dummy *there* see 3.4.1.1 below.

    When the NP is object within the higher clause, the infinitive is usually active:

(265)   a. I saw *nothing to retract* in them.
                           (1872 *Amberley Papers* II.519 (21 Aug.))
         b. I have *other arrangements to consider*
                    (1891 Sidney Webb, *Letters* 161 I.300 (15 Sep.))

There is an anomalous kind of passive infinitive in the complement of a catenative verb like ATTEMPT, BEGIN, HOPE, THREATEN, USE:

(266)   a. The Tuilleries, where boats *were used to be found.*
                      (1788 *London Mag.* 399 [*OED*])
         b. Whatever has to be said among us, had better *be begun to be said*, without more loss of time
                  (1855–7 Dickens, *Little Dorrit* II.xxx.745)
         c. a great amount of publicity *is being* given to this matter and a sensational atmosphere *attempted to be created.*
              (1950 *Daily Telegraph* 7/6 (17 Mar.) [Visser])

Visser traces such passives back to ME (1963–73: sections 2184–5) and notes that the prescriptive tradition condemns them for redundantly making both catenative and lower verb passive. With BEGIN, which is a raising verb (see 3.6.4.4 below), it is possible – and has become normal – to leave the catenative in the active:

(266′)   b. Whatever has to be said among us, had better *begin to be said*

but this option is not generally available in cases like (266c). Unlike other patterns discussed in this section, none of the infinitives in these anomalous patterns show active~passive variation.

    There is some voice variation in *-ing* clauses after *past* and *worth*:

(267)   but on the whole I am more & more convinced each day that there is nothing really *worth doing or having or saying.*
              (1890 Dowson, *Letters* 95 p. 144 (28 Mar.))

(268)   if the tale is judged *worth being repeated*

(1777 (1781) Sheridan, *Scarborough* V.ii 622.21)

Just as with the corresponding infinitival clauses, the active is both the older form and the main survivor in PDE; see Visser (1963–73: sections 1058). As far as *worth* is concerned, there was some variation between plain *Ving* and *the Ving*:

(269)   As soon as I received your letter I sent for Mr Angier, who could not then give me any such distinct and satisfactory answer concerning the time in which he proposed to be at Glasgow, as was *worth the communicating*.

(1789 Adam Smith, *Correspondence* 284 p. 317 (2 Feb.)
[ARCHER])

The latter reminds us that *worth* can be a transitive adjective (3.2.5.4 above), and see too the general discussion of gerunds in section 3.6.4.3 below.

3.3.7   *The expression of time in the verbal group*

In this section we review briefly the main ways of representing time by tense and/or auxiliaries, especially where there has been detectable change during lModE.

3.3.7.1   Present time

In PDE present time is typically signalled by a simple present with stative verbs (and here we may include the modals), and by a present progressive with nonstatives. During our period the progressive has become increasingly common with state verbs other than modals as a means of indicating transitory states. Modal verbs may appear in present or past tense with present time reference. With certain verbs (*I thought we might . . . , I was wondering whether you . . .*) a simple past or past progressive may serve to make a question, suggestion or request less abrupt.

3.3.7.2   Future time

Probably the most general expression of future time is the modal future formed with SHALL/WILL + infinitive. Increasingly common during our period is the use of BE *going to*, formed from the progressive of GO as follows, according to Hopper and Traugott, whose schemas I adapt (1993: 61, 88):

(270) **Stage I**   be   going   [to visit Bill]

           PROG V_{dir} [Purp. clause]

      Stage II   [be going to]   visit Bill

             TNS V_{act}

      Stage III   [be going to]   like Bill

             TNS   V

      Stage IV   [gonna] like/visit Bill

Stage I is merely the progressive of GO followed by a purpose clause. Stage II develops by syntactic reanalysis and semantic metonymy (= transfer through association), stage III – where the lexical verb can be a state verb and there is no possible purpose reading – by analogy and metaphor (= transfer through similarity), stage IV by further morphological/phonological reanalysis (especially but not exclusively in American English). The first three stages have all coexisted in the language since at least the beginning of the ModE period, and Stage III was 'fairly common by the end of the 17th century' (*CHEL* III, forthcoming). I give examples of stages III and IV:

(271)   a.   DANGLE. Nay, my dear, I *was* only *going to read*

         MRS. DANGLE. No, no; you will never read any thing that's

         worth listening to   (1779 (1781) Sheridan, *Critic* I.i 498.7)

     b.   'By God' said the cook 'he's a gona fuck us all.'

            (?1911 (1909–17) T. S. Eliot, in *Inventions of the March Hare*,

                  ed. Ricks (Faber, 1996), p.314)

OED illustrates stage IV *gonna* from 1913 (without preceding dialectal *a*, on which see 3.3.3.5 above). BE *going to* 'is rare in formal and written texts' in PDE (Palmer 1990: 142).

     Other means of signalling future time include the simple present tense, usually with a suitable adverbial. During our period the simple present with future meaning has lost ground somewhat in main clauses. Visser is correct to point out that the usage is not confined wholly to verbs of coming and going (1963–73: section 730):

(272)   She . . . *succeeds* Air Commandant Dame Anne Stephens, 50, who

        is retiring. The appointment takes effect on April 1.

                 (1962 *Daily Telegraph* 13/7 (14 Nov.) [Visser])

Nevertheless, verbs of motion and of beginning and ending are by far the most common (e.g. *takes effect* in (272)), and some nineteenth-century examples seem slightly unidiomatic now, as for instance certain of the simple present tenses in (273):

(273)   a. *Quin.* We hear you *dine* with us at Mr. Vane's.
           Soaper. We have been invited, and are here to accept.
                          (1852 Taylor & Reade, *Masks and Faces* I.i p. 125)
        b. I *leave* here tomorrow for 'The Chestnuts, Guildford', where I *stay* till Easter Tuesday
                          (1878 'Lewis Carroll', *Letters*, ed. Cohen (Macmillan, 1979)
                          I.304 (12 Apr.))
        c. I *do* definitely at last *do* the Garrick show with my mama on Wed evening.   (1890 Dowson, *Letters* 97 p. 147 (8 Apr.))
        d. I *go* to a better land – & the only regret which enters into my departure is that . . . you *don't go* with me.
                          (ibid. 109 p. 158 (18 Jul.))

Contrast *stay* in (273b) with *leave*, which remains normal PDE usage, and negative *don't go* in (273d) with positive *go*, which is still possible, if formulaic. Simple present for future time remains very widely used in dependent clauses, as in *(I'll wait) till you arrive*.

The present progressive is another possibility for expressing future meaning with nonstative verbs 'denoting activities whose performance can be "planned" or "arranged" beforehand' (Visser 1963–73: section 1830). There seems to be less semantic restriction than with the simple present, and several of (273) would be rendered more idiomatic in PDE by replacement with the progressive. Sometimes the time of arrangement needs to be distinguished from the planned activity, and one advantage of the progressive is that BE, if stressed, can be made to refer to the arrangement (and can potentially have its own adverbial):

(274)   a. I *was going* to Town *tomorrow* with Mrs D. but I though\<t> it best to ask her excuse this morning
                          (1818 Keats, *Letters* 86 p. 215 (20–21 Sep.))
        b. *A year ago* he *was coming* back as Editor to the Street.
                          (1932 *News Chron.* 11 Feb. 6/3 [*OED*])

Thus in (274a) *tomorrow* clearly belongs with GO rather than BE, whereas in (274b) *a year ago* seems to mark the time of arrangement and therefore to belong with BE.

Otherwise, for future time, WILL or SHALL can be combined with the progressive (Palmer 1990: 150).

3.3.7.3   Past time

Visser cites a number of examples where the simple present is used to refer
to states in past time up to and including the present (1963–73: section
792). Some are perhaps dialectal, and many depend on a past-time reading
of adverbials like *of late*, *lately* which may be inappropriate, but there remain
examples which suggest a standard usage now lost:

(275)   take me out of these streets, where the whole town *knows* me
          from a child!   (1849–50 Dickens, *David Copperfield* xxii.288 [Visser])

This is quite different from the **historic present** referring to past events,
which has been possible in appropriate circumstances throughout the
ModE period. The natural PDE equivalent of (275) would use the present
perfect.

   The time reference of the present perfect includes both present and past
time. We have already discussed the variation between simple present and
present perfect in passive verbal groups, and the increasing use of the latter
(3.3.6.2 above). The inclusion of a past time element means that there are
contexts in which the present perfect is in variation with the simple past.
One such is where 'current relevance' (see Palmer 1988: 48–51) – a rather
subjective notion – is involved:

(276)   a. in short, his Dissipation and extravagance exceed any thing I
             ever heard of.   (1777 Sheridan, *School for Scandal* I.i 362.25)
         b. In short, his dissipation and extravagance exceed anything I
             have ever heard of.

                                   (ibid. in *Dramatic Works of Sheridan*, ed. Knight
                                              (World's Classics, 1944) p. 193)

The choice shows some change during our period, as may be seen from the
following examples, characteristic of English up to the early part of this
century and indeed said by Jespersen to be 'more idiomatic' (1909–49: IV 64):

(277)   a. And yet I fag ['labour'] pretty well – some seven or eight
             hours per diem, and my brain *was* never more vigorous.
                                                           (1861 Green, *Letters* 89)
         b. I never *cursed* the Sabbatarian institutions of my country more
             heartily than now.   (1872 *Amberley Papers* II.525 (25 Aug.))
         c. 'What an extraordinarily fine bird!' he went on. 'I don't think I
             ever *saw* one just like it.'   (1904 Nesbit, *Phoenix* v.115)
         d. I never *saw* anything so beautiful as the kingfishers
                                              (1917 Bell, *Letters* I.400 (10 Mar.))

Simple past is now disfavoured, though still not impossible, in my dialect of BrE. It is more typical of AmerE than BrE to use the simple past in such a context as:

(278)   a. *Did* you *eat* yet?
       b. *Have* you *eaten* yet?

Does this dialectal difference reflect chronological change? Vanneck (1958) suggests that the usage of (278a) is an innovation; Visser, who gives many examples of both the (a) and (b) types, suggests that it is more likely to be a survival (1963–73: section 806). And Elsness (1989), who incidentally provides elicitation evidence in support of the transatlantic difference, finds that the present perfect is in statistical decline as measured by snapshots at 200-year intervals in a diachronic corpus.

Grammars of PDE state that the present perfect is incompatible with an adverbial expressing past time:

(279)   a. By-the-by, my dear, I*'ve had* such a letter from the doctor; *only two days ago*.   (1860–1 Trollope, *Framley* viii.72)
       b. 'This man has not only written to me, but *has* absolutely *forced* his way into my rooms *when I was dressing for dinner . . .*'
                                                  (ibid. xix.181)
       c. 'I*'ve heard* almost every single word of that,' whispered Robert, 'in Hyde Park *last Sunday*!'   (1906 Nesbit, *Amulet* xi.200)
       d. O, pooh! boating! . . . Silly boyish amusement. I*'ve given* that *up long ago*.   (1908 Grahame, *Wind in the Willows* ii.27)

See Quirk, Greenbaum, Leech & Svartvik (1985: 4.23n.[a]), where some modern instances like (279) are regarded as performance errors – that is, features of real-life utterance which do not reflect the underlying grammar of the language – and indeed the adverbials could reflect an afterthought, especially in (279a, c). Meyer (1992) argues that the present perfect is in fact compatible with past-time adverbials that are **non-rhematic** (not part of the new information in the clause). Leisi notes that the present perfect in English does not have the colloquial generality for past-time narrative that it has in German and French (1964: 128–9), but in some dialects it is possible to hear it used in a somewhat similar way. Bauer offers

(280)   I have seen it last week.

as a non-standard New Zealand usage (*CHEL* V: 401), and the present perfect has started to occur quite frequently in some spoken BrE varieties in narration of recent past events:

(281)   Det Sgt Dave Hubbard, of Slough CID, said: 'We believe that
these people *have been assaulted* by two males. They *have been*
severely *beaten*, but we do not know what kind of implements
have been used.'   (1995 *Oldham Evening Chronicle* p. 17 (13 Mar.))

I have not attested it with explicit past time adverbials, as in (279–80), but
Trudgill believes even that to be possible now in Standard English English
(1984: 42). Elsness, however, avers that examples like (279–80) are more
common in his pre-1800 material than in PDE (1989: 101).

   A common way of expressing past time is by *used to V*, originally the past
tense of USE 'be in the habit of'. The meaning combines past habitual with
the implication that the state or activity no longer obtains, and it has
probably increased in frequency, while its present tense counterpart has
disappeared (3.3.5.2 above). A variant common in the first half of our
period is BE *used to V*:

(282)   She *was used to live* thus in the house of her parents.
                         (1799 Dunlap, *False Shame* II.i p. 19 [ARCHER])

It is unclear whether this passive form has a different meaning; one might
expect more of a restriction to human subjects and a sense of habituation,
but cf. (266a) (possibly a special case because of the passive in the lower
clause). Another expedient for past habitual is *would V*.

3.3.8   *Auxiliaries and operators*

An auxiliary, as we might attempt to define the term, is a member of a
closed class of verbs which express tense, aspect or modality; which act as
modifiers to a lexical head verb; and which obey tight syntactic constraints.
We must distinguish the (rather fuzzy) set of auxiliaries from a closely
related syntactic class, the operators: those which undergo Negation,
Inversion, post-verbal ellipsis (Code), and Emphasis without the use of
DO. (Not every operator possesses every one of the NICE properties; see
Huddleston 1980 for a detailed tabulation.) The two classes overlap in large
measure, but not entirely. We shall discuss the NICE properties individually in the following sections, but let us quickly look at some crucial differences between an operator like BE and a non-operator like SEEM:

(283)   a. Jim *isn't* friendly.
        b. *Is Jim* friendly?
        c. Bill is friendly and Jim *is* too.
        d. Jim *is* friendly.

(284)   a. Jim *doesn't seem* friendly.
        b. *Does Jim seem* friendly?
        c. Bill seems friendly and Jim *does* too.
        d. Jim *dóes* seem friendly.

The NICE properties illustrated in (283) are often taken as the criterion of auxiliary status. Now in most cases the auxiliary and operator classes do coincide, so that for example progressive BE is both an auxiliary and an operator, while the lexical verb FINISH is neither. But there are operators which are not auxiliaries (e.g. BE in (283)) and – at least arguably – auxiliaries which are not operators (e.g. passive GET). And the NICE properties are significant only in lModE, not in other languages or earlier stages of English. That is why the distinction should be maintained.

    The auxiliary DO may be thought of as the 'empty' choice, selected when the syntax requires an operator but the semantics does not (hence the label 'dummy' in formula (109) above).

3.3.8.1   Affirmatives

Weak affirmatives should be impossible once the regularisation of DO is complete – though Rissanen (1991b) and others have doubted that the process *is* yet completed in spoken English. Weak affirmative DO survived into the nineteenth century in contexts where an adverb intervened between auxiliary and lexical verb (Tieken-Boon van Ostade 1987: 118ff., Warner 1993: 225), and – in writing only – in the phrase *I do assure/entreat you* (Sweet 1898: section 2180). Otherwise, examples are often either high-flown or non-standard:

(285)   No! for that sort of probity and disinterestedness which such men as Bailey possess, *does hold and grasp* the tip-top of any spiritual honors that can be paid to anything in this world.
                                 (1818 Keats, *Letters* 37 p. 79 (13 Jan.))

(286)   For when a person *does begin* thinking of one thing and thinking of another, in that manner as it's getting dark, what I say is that
                             (1855–7 Dickens, *Little Dorrit* II.ix.513)

It is difficult to collect 'ordinary' examples of weak affirmative DO – that is, unmarked either stylistically or emphatically – from written English, but the presumption should be that their frequency has continued to decline as part of the last levelling-off of the S-curve of change. They certainly occur in non-standard BrE dialects, often with aspectual meaning (*CHEL* V: 135, 226).

A special case involves adverbials of negative meaning other than *not* itself. Phillipps draws attention to Jane Austen's frequent use of DO with *by no means* (1970: 119):

(287)   and as Miss Bertram's inclination for so doing *did* by no means
         lessen   (1816 Austen, *Mansfield Park* I.x.98 [Phillipps])

In PDE, sentences with such an adverbial go with affirmatives rather than with negatives as far as DO is concerned. Note that *by no means* is Lindley Murray's sole example clearly within the VP of an adverbial 'improperly employed' to form a double negative (1795: 121).

3.3.8.2   Negatives

Old, unregularised patterns of sentence negation can only be detected with non-operators, as operators have been negated with a following *not* since the beginning of the ModE period, well before the regularisation of DO. There are traces of old negation patterns right through our period, though it was in the nineteenth century that the usage finally became effectively ungrammatical (Rydén 1979: 31):

(288)   a. for I *look not forward* with any pleasure to what is call'd being
            settled in the world   (1819 Keats, *Letters* 139 p. 362 (25 Jul.))
         b. I assume you had no plans yesterday as you *wrote not*
                                        (1890 Dowson, *Letters* 91 p. 139 (23 Feb.))
         c. I hope to see you shortly Mon. or Tues. even if, as I half fear
            from your vague remarks on Friday that we *dine not* this week.
                                        (ibid. 93 p. 141 (9 Mar.))

No doubt many instances are jocular and/or reminiscent of biblical language, and we may guess that Dowson's (288b, c) are affected archaisms. In (289) an old word order occurs with a pronominal direct object before *not*:

(289)   (I *have it not* by me, or I would copy you the exact passage)
                                        (1848 Gaskell, *Mary Barton* v.62)

Non-periphrastic negation survived longer in Scotland (*CHEL* V: 72).

   The only productive negation pattern in lModE, operator + *not*, may form a contraction. Probably normal in speech for three or even four centuries, this has only become reasonably common in published material in recent decades, at least outside dialogue. Some contractions are now non-standard, such as *ain't* or *a'n't* for *am/is/are not* or *has/have not*, *han't* for *has/have not*, *don't* for *does not*, *daresn't* or *darzent* for *dares not*, *dazzent* for *dare not*, though some of these were in more general use early in our period; for information on prescriptive attitudes in the eighteenth century see Sundby, Bjørge & Haugland (1991: 162–3), and in the nineteenth, Phillipps (1984: 69–70). An excellent, detailed history of negative contraction is Brainerd (1989[1993]).

(290)   a. but then again, *an't I* rather too smartly dress'd to look like a money-Lender?   (1777 Sheridan, *School for Scandal* III.i 389.25)

           b. I have a lively faith that yours is the very gem of all Children. *Aint* I its Unkle?   (1820 Keats, *Letters* 172 p. 448 (13 Jan.))

           c. 'But, Mary, my dear, *ain't you* old enough to know that you should not credit people's looks? . . .'

                                    (1860–1 Trollope, *Framley* xxxviii.365)

The 1 SG form *aren't* for *am not* is standard only in inversion and mainly in BrE: *aren't I*, but ***I aren't*. Jespersen explains it as a respelling of *an't*, and notes that George Eliot used it only in representations of vulgar or dialectal speech, whereas by the turn of the twentieth century it was also being put in the mouths of educated speakers (1909–49: V 432).

From the mid-eighteenth century until roughly the 1860s, *don't* was common in dialogue as negative 3 SG PRES of the auxiliary D O, with sporadic examples from the late seventeenth century (Brainerd 1989[1993]: 186) to the twentieth. Not all of the examples can be subjunctives:

(291)   a. yes your wife will say, 'here is a sum total account of Haydon again I wonder your Brother *don't* put a monthly bulleteen in the Philadelphia Papers about him . . .'

                                    (1819 Keats, *Letters* 156 p. 418 (20 Sep.))

           b. but Popkins will bet you £1,000 that he *don't* come in ['be elected'] for Groginhole.

           (1840 Bulwer-Lytton, *Money* IV.ii, in *19c plays*, ed. Rowell p. 105; omitted in Booth)

           c. Soaper praises people, *don't* he?

                          (1852 Taylor & Reade, *Masks and Faces* I.i p. 125)

           d. *Sir Michael.* Punctuality is one of my jog-trot notions; but it seems my nephew *don't* partake of that virtue

                      (1863 Hazlewood, *Lady Audley's Secret* I.i p. 240)

           e. Poor old Bill! I say, the play! Nemesis! What? Moral! Caste *don't* matter. Got us fairly on the hop.

                    (1912 Galsworthy, *Eldest Son* III, in *Plays of John Galsworthy* (Duckworth, 1929) p. 188)

For Thackeray and Trollope, the educated and upper classes could use *ain't* and 3 SG *don't* readily, but in familiar speech only (Phillipps 1978: 121, citing Clark 1975: 36–8). Other contracted forms have shown changing fortunes. Contractions involving marginal modals include *daren't* (1701), *needn't* (1775), *durs(t)n't* (1815), *oughtn't* (1836–7), *use(d)n't* (1861 non-standard, then *c.* 1863) – antedating some of the findings of Denison (1993a: 309). *Durs(t)n't*, like its positive stem *durst*, is now obsolete. As for *use(d)n't* and perhaps *oughtn't*, it looks as if they may have started off as non-standard – some early instances are put in the mouths of dialect or otherwise non-standard speakers:

(292)   a. They *oughtn't* to go at after they're married, that I'm very clear about.   (1848 Gaskell, *Mary Barton* x.131)

         b. '... I don't think it ain't constitutional for the Petty Bag to be in the Commons, Mr. Robarts. Hany ways, it never *usen't.*'

                                  (1860–1 Trollope, *Framley* xxxii.312)

In any event *oughtn't* and *use(d)n't* soon became standard colloquial:

(293)   a. 'No, don't,' said Sir Mulberry ... 'upon my life, you *oughtn't* to ...'   (1838–9 Dickens, *Nickleby* xix.241)

         b. I *oughtn't* to say that, *ought I*?   (1906 Nesbit, *Amulet* vii.111)

         c. That is a new accomplishment of Andrew's, by the way. He *usent* to drink.   (1907 Shaw, *Major Barbara* III p. 487 [*OED*])

Now, however, as they become obsolescent, they seem instead old-fashioned and therefore (by a natural, if false association), formal. At least one contraction of a central modal, *mayn't*, has also moved from colloquial normality to great rarity in the course of the twentieth century:

(294)   a. 'Oh, please, *mayn't* we have another?'

                                    (1902 Nesbit, *5 children* i.32)

         b. 'it *mayn't* be like that now ...'   (ibid. i.36)

         c. 'I'm not allowed to play in this game,' it said. 'Of course I *could* [original emphasis] find out in a minute where the thing was, only I *mayn't* ...'   (1906 Nesbit, *Amulet* xi.197)

There is a tendency in some dialects to replace *not* by *never* as general-purpose negator. See for example Cheshire (1982: 67ff.) on the dialect of teenagers in Reading (Berkshire, UK); Knowles (1973: 36ff., reference due to Graeme Trousdale), who asserts that *never* is the normal negator with (simple) past tense verbs in Liverpool; and Branford on non-standard South African English (*CHEL* V: 491). (Many speakers adopt this tactic with USED to avoid the uncomfortable *didn't use(d)* ~ *use(d)n't* choice.)

On the negation of the present subjunctive see 3.3.4.1 above; Visser argues that the order S-*not*-V is an American innovation as recent as the 1930s (1963–73: section 871).

3.3.8.3 Questions and other inversions
Inverted clauses with non-operators have always been rarer than negatives during our period. Occasional examples can be found, though most of mine look suspiciously similar:

(295)　a. but how *came you* and Mr. Surface so confidential –
　　　　　　　　　　　(1777 Sheridan, *School for Scandal* I.i 361.20)
　　　b. How on earth *came you* here?
　　　　　　　　　　　(1839 Planche, *Garrick Fever* [last scene] p. 76 [ARCHER])
　　　c. 'How *came you* to make such a mistake as this? . . .'
　　　　　　　　　　　(1871–2 Eliot, *Middlemarch* lvi.559)
　　　d. We could not love each other so well, *loved we not* our work and
　　　　duty more.　　　(1891 Sidney Webb, *Letters* 159 I.298 (14 Sep.))

That inversion of COME was somewhat formulaic is also suggested by the later survival of the idiom *How come . . . ?* (traced back to 1848 in the US by the *OED* s.v. *how* adv. A.19, with earlier variants s.v. *come* v. B.21). As for the earnest misquotation of Lovelace in (295d), that hardly counts as 1890s English. Normally, then, inversion involves an operator: hence the standard label 'Subject-Auxiliary Inversion'.

3.3.8.4 Post-verbal ellipsis and emphasis
These last two NICE properties are not as easily attested in written texts as the other two. Variation generally affects the same verbs as with the other NICE properties: HAVE and the marginal modals. I suspect that possessive HAVE resisted post-verbal ellipsis, unless negated, even in dialects where it was otherwise an operator; Visser (1963–73: section 1472n.) draws attention to the use of *did* rather than *had* in:

(296)　'Did you know that I once had a butler, two footmen, two
　　　　gardeners, a chauffeur, a lady's maid . . . ? Well, I *did*. . . .'
　　　　　　(1967 Angus Wilson, *No Laughing Matter* (Secker) IV.i.413 [Visser])

But there are examples:

(297)　he supposed she had all those feelings, but he must consider it as
　　　　very unfortunate that she *had* [original emphasis]
　　　　　　　　　　　(1816 Austen, *Mansfield Park* III.v[xxxvi].356)

Examples (298) would not generally be possible in PDE – and we must be cautious of Stevenson and Nesbit, both here inventing dialect from an earlier time:

(298)   a. I'll see him – I'll talk to him as I *used*.
                   (1844 Boucicault, *Old Heads & Young Hearts* I, ed. Thomson
                                     (CUP, 1984) p. 59 [ARCHER])
        b. He used to come here with a blind beggar, he *used*.
                  (1883 Stevenson, *Treasure Island* (Heinemann, 1922) viii.78)
        c. No one knows you have been away. You've seemed to be
           here, learning and playing and doing everything like you *used*.
                            (1909 Nesbit, *Harding's Luck* vii.164)

(299)   a. I wish his friends would propose it to him. I really think they
        ought.   (1818 Austen, *Persuasion* I.xii.102)
        b. I doubt whether I *can* [original emphasis] read it, tho' I know I
        ought   (1844 Martineau, *Letters* p. 97 (29 Jul.))

Post-verbal ellipsis is unlike the other NICE properties in that no verb follows the operator concerned, and that forms other than finite may occur:

(300)   I've missed the train and Chris may *have* too.

A difference between certain British dialects, (301a), and most other varieties, including AmerE, (301b), is that the former permit some nonfinite forms of substitute DO where the latter permit none:

(301)   a. A. Move the car! B. I *have done/might do/did do/am doing*.
        b. A. Move the car! B. I *have/might/did/am*.

(Many BrE dialects do not allow all four possibilities shown in (301a). My own, for instance, disallows *am doing* and *did do*, and even *have done* and *might do* are less natural than the plain *have* and *might* of (301b).) Butters (1983) and Kato & Butters (1987) assume that the use of nonfinite DO outside comparatives and certain other contexts is a BrE (possibly even just an English English) innovation, scarce before the First World War. There *is* a clear contrast between AmerE and BrE, but the BrE usage is hardly new. In comparatives and *as*-clauses it certainly goes back at least to ME (Visser 1963–73: sections 183, 190; Warner 1993: 117–18):

(302)   a. '. . . between a gentleman and lady of different families, who
          have known each other so short a time as we *have done*.'
                          (1860–1 Trollope, *Framley* xvi.159)

b. '... We all say that she makes herself out to be so much more ancient than she *need do*.' (ibid. xi.105)

Otherwise examples are less common, but small numbers can be found in ME, eModE and lModE:

(303)   a. but La Valette ... is the most likely to satisfy you, as he boards and sleeps in the house, and always *has done*
>
> (1795 Mrs Meeke, *Count St. Blancard* (Minerva Press, repr. Arno, 1977) II.vi.170)

      b. I ... urged him with all my eloquence to write & I hope he *has done* before this. (1838 Gaskell, *Letters* 10 p. 22 (7 Aug.))

      c. The panic among the servants still goes on, & *will do* I suppose till the fever has left the neighbourhood
>
> (1854 ibid. 195 p. 290 (17 May))

      d. by requesting me to write for the *Saturday* [original italics]. I was thunderstruck; but promised to try. I don't suppose I *shall do*. (1862 Green, *Letters* 98 (20 Aug.))

      e. BERNIE PERK: I don't think I ever heard her.
JACK PATTERSON: Well, you *mightn't have done*.
>
> (1971 Elkin, *The Dick Gibson Show* p. 147 [ARCHER])

(Indeed (303e) is American.) Mrs Gaskell seems particularly fond of the construction. For British PDE, Linda van Bergen reports six examples in the written LOB corpus but thirty-six in the spoken London–Lund corpus, which is only half as big. The data so far available are too sparse for directionality to be inferred. Note, however, that there is some disagreement as to the correct analysis of PDE DO in post-verbal ellipsis – see Huddleston (1984: 138–40) for a discussion – and dialects with few or no nonfinite forms of DO here can be said to align the DO of Code (post-verbal ellipsis) less with substitute DO and more with periphrastic (dummy) DO, making the NICE properties more coherent.

A clear diachronic change concerns ellipsis of BE after another auxiliary:

(304)   a. My Letters are in the press, and my volume *will* soon
>
> (1798 Southey, *Life* I. 347 (29 Aug.))

      b. 'He is very handsome indeed.'
'Handsome! – Yes I suppose he *may*.'
>
> (1818 Austen, *Northanger Abbey* II.i[xvi].134 [Phillipps])

Phillipps notices Jane Austen's predilection for this construction (1970: 142), and Warner notes that in this respect she comes at the end of a tradition which had lasted from the ME period (1993: 65). There are examples in Visser (1963–73: sections 1752ff.), and indeed some mid-nineteenth century, upper-class speech examples in Phillipps (1984: 74).

Now consider another ellipsis pattern (with the ellipsis site signalled by [ø]):

(305)   a. I think I could come as often again as I used *to [ø]*.

                    (1766 Abigail Adams, *Adams Family Corr.*, ed. Butterfield,
                                      I.55 (6 Oct.) [ARCHER])

    b. CÆS. But! – What, dont you like the thoughts of the Match?
       MAR. Sir, I ought *to [ø]*. (Aside. I dare not say no!)

                  (1813 H. Cowley, *Bold Stroke for a Husband*, in *Works* (1813),
                                    III.iii I.440 [WWP])

    c. 'that if every one of your clients is to force us to keep a clerk,
       whether we want *to [ø]* or not, you had better leave off
       business . . .'   (1840 Dickens, *Old Curiosity Shop* xxxiii.247 [*OED*])

    d. I didn't want to look forward to my discharge – I was afraid *to*
       [ø].   (1863 Taylor, *Ticket-of-leave Man* II.i, in *19c Plays*,
                                   ed. Booth II.106 [ARCHER])

For another example see (293a) above. This everyday construction is surprisingly recent in the written record. (Early examples are hard to come by: note that (305b) cannot be dated to the composition of the play *c*. 1783, since the passage containing it is absent from the third edition of 1784 and Inchbald's edition of 1802.) Until the mid-nineteenth century and after, most writers avoided it:

(306)   a. On Tues^y, I hope to send off the notice of it to 'D. News.' I
       fully meant *it* today; but I have not been able to read much (of
       anything) for some days past

                              (1858 Martineau, *Letters* p. 152 (4 Apr.))

    b. though I did not think nearly so ill of her as I am compelled *to*
       do now.   (1871 ibid. p. 224 (15 Mar.))

(306')   a. I fully meant *to [ø]* today

       b. as I am compelled *to [ø]* now.

From then on, however, what had been a trickle of examples soon turned into a flood. To the extent that (305) looks like post-verbal ellipsis, infinitival *to* can actually be categorised as an auxiliary verb, and Warner uses the (re)appearance of the (305) construction to date such a reanalysis of *to* (1993: 64). However, the dates in Visser cannot be relied on (1963–73: section 1000): he has some possible ME and eModE examples, mostly susceptible to different analyses, and then none at all between 1707 and 1852.

As for emphasis, I have not collected a representative set of examples. Here are possible cases with OUGHT, HAVE *got*, and modal BE:

(307)   a. They make a curtsey to the new moon when first they see it, and turn the money in their pockets, which *ought* to be doubled before the moon is out. [original emphasis]

(1838 Gaskell, *Letters* 12 p. 31 (18 Aug.))

          b. *Soaper.* Your Sir John Brute, sir, was a fine performance: you never forgot the gentleman even in your cups.
          Snarl. Which, as Sir John Brute is the exact opposite of a gentleman, he *ought* to have forgotten.

(1852 Taylor & Reade, *Masks and Faces* I.i p. 126)

          c. So long. I've *got* to go, and you've *got* to stay. [original emphases]   (1907 Nesbit, *Enchanted Castle* viii.166)

          d. 'What *are* we to do?' whispered Mabel, awestruck [original emphasis]   (ibid. viii.164)

3.3.8.5   DO periphrasis with HAVE and BE

We have already discussed (3.3.5.1–2, 3.3.8.2 above) a number of verbs which can occur in NICE contexts with and without DO. Now we consider the history of HAVE in this regard. The use of dummy DO with HAVE is fairly recent, apart from imperatives (3.5.4 below). It remains impossible with perfect HAVE, and for all other uses of HAVE there is chronological, dialectal and semantic variation. It is true that dummy DO with possessive HAVE entered AmerE before BrE (which tended to use HAVE *got* – with operator HAVE – instead), though this best-known of transatlantic distinctions in syntax is being eroded as DO + HAVE spreads in Britain. I give some examples of HAVE as an operator – thus without DO – (308), and as a non-operator, (309):

(308)   a. Now say, *haven't* you qualms?

(1829 Jerrold, *Black-ey'd Susan* I.i, in *19c Plays*, ed. Booth I.157)

          b. and I should feel quite lost if I *had not* horses to look after.

(1877 Sewell, *Black Beauty* xliii.183)

          c. I have a sort of vague fear that I may have reproduced a passage from that excellent work but *have not* the book to refer to.   (1890 Dowson, *Letters* 93 p. 141 (9 Mar.))

          d. As long as she *had not* to prepare it she did not mind a bit

(1949 Streatfeild, *Painted Garden* x.107)

e. 'We ought to have smelling salts . . . *Hasn't* your aunt any?'

(1907 Nesbit, *Enchanted Castle* viii.155)

(309)   a. 'It's time we *did have* our tea,' said Jimmy. And it was.

(ibid. v.105)

b. 'What *do you have* for breakfast?' the Fairy said impatiently,

'and who gives it you?'   (1902 Nesbit, *5 Children* i.30)

Examples (308), apart perhaps from the last, are no longer idiomatic for southern BrE. Example (309b) is consonant with Jespersen's claim (1909–49: IV.51) that *don't have X for breakfast* means 'don't (generally) eat X for breakfast', a use derived via nonstative combinations like H A V E *breakfast/dinner*, as in (309a); compare (308e), which is the normal pattern for that writer.

As for B E, the only regular co-occurrence with D O in standard is in the imperative, on which see section 3.5.4 below.[61] However, other patterns occasionally permit it, (310), rather than the expected (311):

(310)   a. ?If you *don't be careful* . . .
         b. Why *don't* you *be more careful*? (directive: 'Be more careful')

(311)   a. If you *aren't careful* . . .
         b. Why *aren't* you *more careful*? (literal meaning of question)

Typically the context is conditional or quasi-imperative, and B E forms a nonstative group-verb with its complement. The construction of (310b) at least is now normal usage (Quirk, Greenbaum, Leech & Svartvik 1985: 11.17, 11.30n):

(312)   a. 'You are happy?' Gerald asked her, with a smile.
         'Very happy!' she cried . . . 'And can you see that Rupert is happy as well?'

         . . .

         '*Why don't you be happy* as well?' she said.

(1921 Lawrence, *Women* xxvii.362)

b. 'So *why don't you be a good boy* and' – Hoag grabbed him by the shoulders.   (1961 *Brown Corpus*, Mystery & Detective L16:52)

c. If the taxi driver . . . was having a dig at me . . . *why didn't he* stop and *be a witness*?

(1995 letter, *Oldham Evening Chronicle* 26/6 (24 Jan.))

3.3.8.6   Nonfinite verbal groups

Nonfinite verbal groups show the same relative ordering patterns as finite ones, except for the position of *not* and absence of contracted negation. Combinations involving finite-only auxiliaries naturally fail to occur, and there are two additional elements to consider: the infinitive marker *to* and the *-ing* ending.

A finite verbal group can be turned into a nonfinite one by replacing tense marking on its first member by *-ing*:

(313)   a. As he *writes* mostly in the morning
          b. *Writing* mostly in the morning

(314)   a. As he *had been writing* a long book
          b. *Having been writing* a long book

PDE generally disallows this process when the finite verb is progressive BE (though not BE in other uses):

(315)   a. As he *was writing* a long book
          b. **Being writing a long book

The nonoccurrence of (315b) is often referred to more general constraints on 'double *-ing*' (Ross 1972 and subsequent writers, Quirk, Greenbaum, Leech & Svartvik 1985: 3.56n.[a]). One major change in this area is that such patterns were reasonably common from the mid-sixteenth century to the late eighteenth:

(316)   What reply she made I do not know, *being speaking* to Wildly at the same time

                    (1751 Eliza Haywood, *Betsy Thoughtless* (Pandora, 1986) xiv.85)

Jane Austen is a late exponent of this usage, as she is with several grammatical features, providing many examples in the first two decades of the nineteenth century:

(317)   we have scarcely a doubt of her *being* actually *staying* with the only Family in the place whom we cannot visit.

                        (1807 Austen, *Letters* 49 p. 180 (8 Feb.))

For examples see Visser (1963–73: 1955n.) and Phillipps (1970: 115–16). As pointed out in Denison (1985), the best-known grammar of the nineteenth century could go on reprinting the following passage at least up to 1871 without any comment on *being writing*:

(318)   The following phrases, even when considered in themselves, show that participles include the idea of time: 'The letter *being written* or *having been written;*' 'Charles *being writing, having written*, or *having been writing.*' [italics as in original]

                    (1816 Lindley Murray, *English Grammar*, 3rd edn. I 115)

Outside the works of Jane Austen, other written examples in our period that I know of are likewise incidental occurrences in grammar books (Denison 1985: 158; 1993a: 411), apart from attempts at servants' and children's usage, respectively, in (319) and the same author's *New Treasure Seekers* iii.17 (1904):

(319)   'I was a-goin' to give you warning this very day, mum, to leave at the end of my month, so I was – on account of me *being going* to make a respectable young man happy.'

(1902 Nesbit, *5 Children*, xi.208)

Such occurrences testify perhaps to the strong pattern-symmetry which the *being Ving* type satisfies, for it is a distinct oddity of PDE that it should be *un*grammatical, and PDE occurrences, genuine and invented, continue to occur (Bolinger 1979, Halliday 1980, Denison 1993a: 411):

(320)   I've often met people I know in London – you know, not because of *being going* to the same place   (attested 1994)

An important formal account is that of Warner (1993, 1995), who regards various nonfinite auxiliary forms as having their own, independent subcate-gorisations from the second half of the eighteenth century: thus *being* and *been* need not have the same subcategorisation as each other, or as *is*, *was*, etc. Without a formal analysis it is difficult to explain ungrammaticalness convincingly, but we can perhaps associate the near-complete disappearance of the *being Ving* type after *c.* 1800 with the reanalysis of the progressive postulated in section 3.3.3.4 above. In the earlier situation where BE was not an auxiliary but a copula followed by a predicative, the (315b) type was unexceptionable. After the reanalysis, the BE of *being Ving* became merely an auxiliary verb. Although there was no overwhelming reason for (315b) to become ungrammatical – and as mentioned it continues to reappear sporadically – it was now the only construction where the first auxiliary verb (the one which determines the syntax of the whole group) had the same morphology as the lexical verb. All other instances have disappeared too, for example imperative DO + imperative verb (if we assume that *keep* in *Do keep quiet* is now an infinitive), infinitive DO/modal + infinitive V. It is tempting too to relate the loss of the (315b) pattern to the obsolescence of non-finite forms of modal BE after the early nineteenth century (3.3.5.2 above).

As for *not* in PDE, '[i]n negative nonfinite clauses, the negative particle is generally positioned before the verb or the *to* of the infinitive' (Quirk, Greenbaum, Leech & Svartvik 1985: 14.6), unless a split infinitive is tolerated (3.5.1.3 below):

(321) a. It is not sufficient we know our own innocence; it is
       necessary, for a woman's happiness, *not to be* suspected.
                          (1778 Hamilton, *Munster Village* p. 75 [ARCHER])
       b. This morning Mr. Eliot *not having* received my letter, came
       personally to urge me,
                          (1869 Howells, *Selected Letters* p. 333 (28 Jun.) [ARCHER])
       c. 'I only want *not to have* my feelings checked at every turn.'
                          (1871–2 George Eliot, *Middlemarch* lxxii.736)

However, in nonfinite verbal groups with one or more auxiliary verbs, the
negator *not* may sometimes appear *after* the first verb:

(322) a. A . . . spoiled child of 30 whose mother and father *having not
       been able* to conceal from him that they think him the 8th
       wonder of the world have at last brought him to acquiesce
       in their opinion.
                          (1831 M. Edgeworth, *Let.* 20 Jan. (1971) 473 [*OED*])
       b. *Having not played* for several months, Miles had lost the
       eternally fragile trumpeters' lip.
                          (1972 *Rolling Stone* 9 Nov. 10/2 [*OED*])

Occasionally in verse this placement occurs after non-operators:

(323) With lightning eyes, and eager breath, and feet | *Disturbing not*
       the drifted snow.   (1815 Shelley *Alastor* 261 [*OED*])

3.3.9 *The verbal group revisited*[62]

In (109) above I gave a possible representation of the finite verbal group
in PDE which mentioned the categories Modal and (Lexical) Verb and the
individual auxiliaries perfect HAVE, progressive BE and passive BE. For the
beginning of our period we must allow also for perfect BE, but as discussed
in section 3.3.2.3 above, perfect HAVE and BE were not mutually exclusive,
so we cannot treat them as alternative fillers of the same Perfect slot. BE
could be used in four ways at this time:

(324) a. Jan *was arrived.*   (perfect)
       b. Jan *was singing.*   (progressive)
       c. Jan *was discovered.* (passive)
       d. Jan *was* a doctor.   (main/only verb)

All four were mutually incompatible: there could only be one occurrence
of BE in a verbal group. But perfect HAVE could be used with any of them:

(325)   a. Jan *had been arrived.*
b. Jan *had been singing.*
c. Jan *had been discovered.*
d. Jan *had been a doctor.*

These facts are easily captured by the following adaptation of the PDE (109):

(326)   Verbal group pre-1770

$$\left\{\begin{array}{l} \text{(Modal) (HAVE) (BE)} \\ \text{(Dummy = DO)} \end{array}\right\} \quad \left\{\begin{array}{l} V_{intr} \\ V_{tr} \end{array}\right\}$$

Conditions: (A) V does not include BE or HAVE (?except *had*)
(B) dummy DO is typically only chosen in NICE patterns
(C) first verb is tensed and has NICE properties in a NICE pattern

In formula (326) I have explicitly distinguished lexical verbs according to their transitivity, since BE + past participle had very different values: perfect BE with intransitive V, passive BE with transitive V. Furthermore, progressive BE also discriminated, though less reliably, between intransitive and transitive verbs (where no object was present): ordinary progressive BE with intransitive V, passival BE with transitive V (see table 3.4 above).

Notice that everything inside the curly bracket of (326) is an operator, while V represents precisely the non-operators. The diagram encapsulates relative order and absence of iteration. It captures the fact that the verb HAVE could (almost) never be preceded by BE: because there was no progressive of HAVE; the perfect of HAVE was never formed with BE; and there was a passive of nonstative HAVE though hardly of the stative verb.[63]

In fact, the English verbal group was actually approaching a pleasing symmetry and systematicity towards the end of the eighteenth century. By then the regularisation of DO had advanced almost to completion, whereas earlier in the century there was still a significant residue of unregularised forms, especially main-verb negation without DO and (but less commonly) unemphatic positives with DO.

The only problem with formula (326) is that main-verb HAVE had a perfect, and there might well have been some passives, so that sentences like:

(327)   I have *had* a very proper and a very affecting letter from the Young Lady.
        (1789 Adam Smith, *Correspondence* 284 p. 318 (2 Feb.) [ARCHER])

(328)   I have engaged no person to . . . and unless a very active and spirited man could be *had* . . .
        (1793 Washington, *Letters* p. 148 (27 Oct.) [ARCHER])

demand that, exceptionally, we treat *had* as an instance of V rather than of the operator HAVE.

However, as we have seen, there was a major reorganisation for some speakers from around 1770. The changes involved BE and to a lesser extent V. In the course of the nineteenth century BE + -*ing* ceased to discriminate between V_{intr} and V_{tr}, while BE + past participle lost the possibility of co-occurrence with V_{intr}. Increasingly the two BE auxiliaries became compatible with each other (their relationship became syntagmatic rather than paradigmatic), leading to the side-by-side position they have in (109), repeated here as (329) with a more explicit statement of conditions:

(329) $\left\{ \begin{array}{l} \text{(Modal) (Perf = HAVE) (Prog = BE) (Pass = BE)} \\ \text{(Dummy = DO)} \end{array} \right\}$ V = Lexical verb

Conditions: (A) V can include BE or HAVE
(B) main verb BE and some main verb HAVE are operators
(C) dummy DO is only chosen in NICE patterns lacking another operator
(D) first verb is tensed and has NICE properties in a NICE pattern

The upper line of the curly bracket of (329) provides a neat statement of the linear sequencing of auxiliary verbs, suggesting that there are four independent binary choices to be made: ± Modal, ± Perfect, ± Progressive, ± Passive. (There is a fifth too, marked on the first verb: present or past tense.) Thus a new symmetry in lModE verbal groups is revealed which was not there previously. There is no slot for BE or HAVE as sole verb, so these must instead be possible choices under V, having restricted co-occurrence with progressive and/or passive – just like some other lexical verbs. But main verb BE and, in British English, some instances of main verb HAVE, have the NICE properties, so we lose the neat correlation between the curly bracket and operators. If being an operator is felt to be central to an account of the verbal group, then we must resort to something like (330):

(330) $\left\{ \begin{array}{l} \text{(Modal) (Perf = HAVE)} \left\{ \begin{array}{l} \text{(Prog = BE)} \left\{ \begin{array}{l} \text{(Pass = BE)} \\ \text{(Main = BE)} \end{array} \right\} \\ \text{(some possessive/modal HAVE)} \end{array} \right\} \\ \text{(Dummy = DO)} \end{array} \right\}$ (V)

Conditions: (A) V does not include BE but does include certain uses of HAVE

(B) V is obligatory unless BE or operator HAVE are chosen

(C) dummy DO is only chosen in NICE patterns

(D) first verb is tensed and has NICE properties in a NICE pattern

By arranging the verbal group in this way, we allow the outer curly bracket to cover precisely the operators, though at some cost in our treatment of lexical verbs generally, and especially of main verb HAVE.

Looking at all the syntactic diagrams in this section, we see that there is a maximum of either four or five slots from left to right. The first four slots display two morphological generalisations. As we move from left to right within the finite verbal group, each successive position shows increasing morphological variety in nontensed forms, but decreasing variety within the tensed forms as far as polarity is concerned:

(331)   Verbal morphology in late ModE

<u>leftmost</u>   ▷▷▷▷▷▷▷▷▷   <u>rightmost</u>

tensed	tensed	tensed	tensed
	base form	base form	base form
		past pple	past pple
			-ing

tensed positive   ▷▷▷▷▷▷▷▷▷   tensed positive
tensed negative

To take two extreme cases, CAN and SING:

(332)   <u>CAN</u>   <u>SING</u>

can, can't, could, couldn't	sings, sing, sang	tensed
−	sing	base form
−	sung	past pple
−	singing	-ing

These statements would apply to English of the eighteenth century too, except that in the earlier period we sometimes find 2 SG forms of modals like *canst* and *couldst*.[64] The verbs DO, HAVE and BE are intermediate in their range of forms, apart from the exceptional person-number variation in BE.

An attractive notion is that English speakers organise their verbs around two main prototypes: an auxiliary prototype with negation in tensed forms and no untensed forms, and a nonauxiliary prototype without negation but with the full range of untensed forms. Modal BE is an interesting case in point, coming to be restricted since the early nineteenth century to finite forms only (3.3.5.2 above). Thus the auxiliary (modal) prototype has been powerful enough to attract a new member. **Tense** is the crucial concept, as might be expected in the context of finite clauses:

(333)   Verb prototypes in late ModE
        prototypical auxiliary   prototypical verb
        tensed only ± negation ◁◁◁◁▷▷▷ positive tensed and all
                                                   untensed forms

The presentation here might be compared with that in Anderson (1993).

If we try to adapt either (329) or (330) to other recent changes in the verbal group, we might replace the '(Pass = BE)' entry by simple '(Pass)', allowing the alternative exponent GET. Other quasi-auxiliaries are harder to fit in, however. For example, the form *used* belongs semantically with Tense or aspectual HAVE or perhaps Modal, and like Modal it requires a following infinitive, albeit with *to* (cf. the peripheral modal *ought*), yet for some speakers it is not mutually exclusive with Modal and DO and may even follow perfect HAVE. Other patterns which require the infinitive of a lexical verb are the TRY *and* pattern and others discussed below in section 3.6.6.7:

(334)   We should *try and give* more.

These too are compatible with modals – indeed they rarely occur *without* DO or a modal, since they are themselves virtually confined to the base form (infinitive or imperative). The double HAVE pattern (3.3.2.5 above) is impossible to fit in to (329) or (330), and the second HAVE is exclusively infinitival.

If the syntactic diagrams become unwieldy, morphology may be a more helpful organising principle. The two opposing prototypes in (333), and the range of intermediate stages between them, can serve to locate many of the new auxiliaries and quasi-auxiliaries. However, finiteness is not the only salient characteristic of auxiliaries. Another is **invariance**. Let us take modals, the prototypical auxiliaries. They never had a consonantal 3 SG PRES ending. They have lost their 2 SG forms. That leaves the four forms listed for CAN in (332). But increasingly these forms do not seem to belong to a single paradigm. With some exaggeration we can say that modal verbs are no longer marked for tense, since either a traditional present/past pair is coming to be seen as two independent verbs; or one form is used both in present tense and past tense contexts; or the verb simply lacks one or other of the two tenses. And positive~negative pairs are also tending to become divorced. In part this is because to negate the modality, it is often necessary to change the verb in addition to adding *-n't*:

(335)   a. Jan *must* be in trouble. ~ Jan *can't* be in trouble.
        b. Jan *must* try harder. ~ Jan *needn't* try harder.

Certain negative forms are obsolescent – *mayn't, usedn't, oughtn't* – and *shan't* is perhaps rare (Palmer 1990: 150).

At this point we may note a form which had all but disappeared from upper- and middle-class speech by the turn of the twentieth century: 3 SG *don't* in auxiliary use, as seen in examples (291) above. In Jespersen's useful account it is regarded as a phonetic development (1909–49: V 434–5). It too may be seen as a symptom – ultimately unsuccessful in the standard language – of the move towards invariance, since the same form is then used throughout the present tense. It also underlines the separation of positive and negative forms, since in standard speech in our period, 3 SG *don't* generally corresponded to uncontracted *does not* and positive *does*, not *do (not)*.[65] For some discussion and references see Warner (1993: 215, 265 n.22).

Other auxiliary-like verbs are also invariant, or nearly so: BETTER, GOT, TRY *and*, unreal HAVE.[66] The latter two are **nonfinite**. This is a new kind of restriction. The implicational hierarchy of (331) did not allow for items which had the base form but lacked a finite form. Actually, things may be even worse, since most speakers allow the general PRES form but not the 3 SG PRES of TRY *and*:

(336)   a. We always *try* and keep quiet.
        b. **He always *tries* and keep(s) quiet.

The universal syncretism between general present and base form in English must be playing a part here, so that **bare stem** might turn out to be the relevant category.

What I want to suggest is that we can relate the changes in the modals to many of the auxiliary-like innovations if we imagine a new opposition developing. Rather than the tense-based polarity of (333), what seems to be becoming the salient opposition is between **invariant** verbs and verbs with full conjugation:

(337)   Verb prototypes in the near future
        <u>prototypical auxiliary</u>   <u>prototypical verb</u>
        invariant   ◁◁◁◁▷▷▷▷   positive tensed and all
                                                           untensed forms

From various sources, then, verbs are appearing that are semantically like auxiliaries and which either are, or may come to be, morphologically defective. This defectiveness is, increasingly, a matter of invariance. Different items retain differing positional tendencies, of course, some occurring only in initial position in finite clauses, some only in second position, others having wider privileges of occurrence.

The power of the tensedness pattern remains strong, and if invariance is on its way in, it will have to compete for many years with tensedness before it can become the undisputed dominant morphological feature of the auxiliary prototype. But the contest has started.

3.4 Elements of the clause

In this section we consider the main clause-elements other than the verbal group.

3.4.1 Subject

In lModE all simple clauses other than imperatives require an explicit subject. Exceptions are elliptical (for instance, the clipped perfect), or set phrases, or indeed both, e.g. *Would that (we were young again!)*

3.4.1.1 Empty and anticipatory *it* and *there*

A pronominal NP can serve as dummy subject. Just as DO, a verb with little or no semantic content, can serve as dummy auxiliary in NICE contexts, so *it* and *there* can satisfy the syntactic requirement for a subject without contributing any referential meaning (though see Bolinger 1977). By and large they belong to different patterns and are not interchangeable. However, the use of *it* in Black English for standard dummy *there* is mentioned by Hench (1937), Labov (1972: 24, 270).

With identifying BE the subject can be *it* regardless of the animacy or otherwise of the complement:

(338) a. To be sure! *it is Mr. Triplet*, good Mr. Triplet of
           Goodman's Fields theatre.   (1852 Taylor & Reade,
                                                         Masks and Face I.i p. 129)

        b. Who *is it? It's* me.

With classifying BE and an NP with human referent as complement, subject *it* appears to have died out in the seventeenth century in declaratives (*OED* s.v. *it* pron. B.2d, Visser 1963–73: section 53, Poutsma

1914–29: III 328, 702, IV 731). Through the nineteenth century and even beyond, however, it was used in exclamatives:

(339)   a. What a d——d coxcomb *it* is!
                                      (1840 Bulwer-Lytton, *Money* II.ii p. 191)
        b. What a cold-blooded rascal *it* is!   (ibid. III.iii p. 208)
        c. 'What a nipper *it* is, though!'   (1909 Nesbit, *Harding's Luck* v.104)

The dummy NP *there* can be used as an empty subject, allowing the 'real' or 'logical' subject to be postponed and so altering the thematic organisation of a clause (the ordering of given and new information). In the prototypical case the verbal group contains BE, the postponed NP is indefinite. Breivik suggests that there has been no significant change since 1550 in the syntactic factors governing the use of *there*, though its pragmatic status has developed slightly in the ModE period, so that it is now less readily omitted in clauses which do not 'convey visual impact' (1983: 324). I use [ø] to indicate where *there* could be inserted in PDE:

(340)   a. Yesterday [ø] was an immense Horse fair at Dumfries
                                      (1818 Keats, *Letters* 73 p. 163 (2 Jul.))
        b. '. . . I hold it the most honourable work that [ø] is.'
                                      (1871–2 George Eliot, *Middlemarch* xl.403)
        c. First they came to a great hall in which [ø] were many ladies
            and gentlemen of the court, all dressed in rich costumes.
                                      (1911 Baum, *Wizard of Oz* xi.83)

Breivik says that dummy *there* is more frequent in speech than in the more conservative medium of writing (1983: 199, 355–6).

There has long been a tendency to use a 3 SG verb form even if the 'logical subject' that follows BE is plural:

(341)   a. '. . . If *there was going to be* Red Indians, they'd be here now.'
                                      (1902 Nesbit, *5 Children* x.192)
        b. *There's big pillars* outside   (1906 Nesbit, *Amulet* xiv.261)

Jespersen (1909–49: II. 182) and Visser (1963–73: section 84) have examples going back to lME. There were complaints already in the eighteenth century, as noted by Sundby, Bjørge & Haugland (1991: 156–8), and my examples (341) are attributed to child speakers. The usage is probably on the increase, though how far this is a grammatical change and how far a stylistic one (informal usage becoming more acceptable in written forms) is uncertain. In Dekeyser's nineteenth-century corpus, singular verb rises from nearly 6 per cent in the first half of the century to nearly 13 per cent in the second half, though he is unwilling to attribute great significance to the increase (1975: 164–8). His genre distinction makes clear that the usage was overwhelmingly a colloquial one.

Dummy *there* can be used with passives, which of course involve the verb BE, and sometimes with other active verbs. Both usages are increasingly regarded as formal and are probably on the decline:

(342)　a. *there has scar<c>e a day passed* but he has visited him
　　　　　　　　　　　　　　　　(1818 Keats, *Letters* 94 p. 236 (16 Oct.))
　　　　b. *there was one lecture prevented* here I think by an official telegram
　　　　　a short time ago　　　　(1873 *Amberley Papers* II.554 (26 Aug.))
　　　　c. To-day *there strolled in* a whole band of sheikhs from the
　　　　　Euphrates to present their respects to him
　　　　　　　　　　　　　　　　　(1917 Bell, *Letters* I.396 (2 Feb.))

3.4.1.2　Subject of the passive

The subject of a prototypical passive is an NP which would function as direct object in the corresponding active sentence. The verb is transitive in the active:

(343)　a. The entrance *was damaged* (by vandals).
　　　　b. Vandals *damaged* the entrance.

Although this remains the dominant passive type as far as subject NP is concerned, several further options have become available. First, in the ME period, came prepositional passives of the (344) type, where the subject of the passive corresponds to a prepositional object in the active. Towards the end of ME came indirect passives like (345), whose subject corresponds to an indirect object in the active:

(344)　The victim *was looked after* by a neighbour.
(345)　He *was given* painkillers.

Later still came complex prepositional passives, where the syntagm which is passivised includes another element between verb and preposition:

(346)　a. and the sale of Randalls *was* long *looked forward to*:
　　　　　　　　　　　　　　　　　　(1816 Austen, *Emma* I.ii.17)
　　　　b. delicious fruit – only too rich *to be eaten much of*
　　　　　　　　　　　　　　　　　　(ibid. III.vi[xlii].359)

For details of the origins, see *CHEL* II: 383–7, Denison (1993a: 103–62), and for further illustration and discussion of lModE changes, section 3.4.2.4–5 below. Indirect and prepositional passives are found to a limited extent in mainland Scandinavian languages but are not otherwise available in standard dialects of Germanic or other Indo-European languages. Throughout the ModE period the list of verbs (or better, VPs) which permit such passives has grown, and their frequency has tended to increase. All of these idiosyncratic passives have found less favour in formal writings, prepositional passives because they involve the shibboleth of the 'stranded preposition', indirect passives because of the ungrammaticality of corresponding passives in (above all) Latin. Of the two, indirect passives have been subject to stronger resistance, with explicit comment in grammatical works (mainly twentieth-century, according to Visser 1963–73: section 1974 and n.1) and elsewhere:

(347)   Capt. Lupton offered me a very handsome Arab mare . . . So, in the official phrase, I'm *issued* with her – Heaven prosper me for writing such horrible English.   (1917 Bell, *Letters* II.436 (13 Dec.))

Sundby, Bjørge & Haugland (1991: 240) report the correction of *I was given it* to *It was given to me* in 1777 Stubbs.

3.4.2   Object

3.4.2.1   Transitive and intransitive verbs
Rissanen remarks on the 'constant fluctuation between the transitive and intransitive use of verbs' in the history of English (*CHEL* III, forthcoming), and lModE is no exception. What is characteristic of our period as far as changes in transitivity are concerned?

The **medio-passive** is an intransitive use of a normally transitive verb:

(348)   a. That *told very well* ('that story was very successful')
                            (1779 (1781) Sheridan, *Critic* I.ii 513.15)
        b. The Welsh, I suspect, is not a language which *translates well.*
                            (1827 Southey, *Lett.* (1856) IV. 64 [Visser, *OED*])

Typical properties are that the subject of the medio-passive is nonagentive and makes a major contribution to the course or outcome of the action, and that there is a virtual requirement for certain manner adverbials in the clause (Quirk, Greenbaum, Leech & Svartvik 1985: 10.21, Kilby 1984: 46); Visser gives as an alternative to the manner adverbial the use of *will/would (not)*:

(349)   a. My Lord, if it [*sc.* the coat] had been tighter, *'twould neither have hook'd nor button'd.*
                            (1777 (1781) Sheridan, *Scarborough* I.ii 577.33 [Visser])

   b. she [*sc.* a thin woman] might be very useful as his walking-
   stick . . . let him turn farmer, she *would cut* into hurdles;
(1819 Keats, *Letters* 123 p. 310 (Mar.))
   c. the sending off of my summer clothes. The patterns are
   charming – it's to be hoped they*'ll wash*.
(1917 Bell, *Letters* II.409 (11 May))

Although quite a few of Visser's examples are eModE, most are nineteenth or twentieth century (1963–73: sections 168–9). However, as with many developments, individual possibilities may come in and drop out again, witness (348a) and (349b).

Many other transitive verbs have been used intransitively, like the previous group, with a subject corresponding to the object of transitive use, but without a manner adverbial (e.g. *a bag which tied up with strings*). Visser's lists show the ModE period as the most productive (1963–73: sections 165–7). When a transitive verb is used absolutely, i.e. without an object, the subject remains the same as it would have been in transitive use. This has been a perennial possibility (1963–73: sections 155–7), though Phillipps (1984: 71–2) argues that it was particularly favoured by the upper classes in the nineteenth century, as in *it does not answer* or *she never repeats* (*sc. an anecdote*) or *Madame de Negra receives this evening.*

A more literary usage noted by Visser (1963–73: section 142) goes the other way in making a transitive verb out of an intransitive, when verbs like GROAN and SIMPER came to be used with a direct speech object during the lModE period:

(350)   'Ah, you slug!' *groaned* Mr Jorrocks in disgust
(1845 Surtees, *Hillingdon Hall* xxviii.290 [ARCHER])

3.4.2.2   Reflexive and reciprocal use of verbs
A long-term tendency has been the alteration of reflexive verbs to intransitives. Leisi comments on this as a recent change in relation to BEHAVE, DRESS, SHAVE, WASH (1964: 152):

(351)   '. . . Suppose we go to a theatre now.'
   'Put our boots on, – and *dress*, – and *wash*?'
(1899 Kipling, *Light that Failed* viii.146 [ARCHER])

In all but BEHAVE, a reflexive explicitly marks the activity as not being performed by someone else. Conceivably the increasing rarity of personal servants has played some part here, though the process began much earlier than Leisi implies. Foster notes the loss of reflexive in ADJUST *oneself to*

Table 3.6. *Reciprocals in ARCHER corpus*

Number of individuals referred to by antecedent	Each other			One another		
	2	>2	indet.	2	>2	indet.
1700–99	32	24	18	14	16	9
1800–99	43	22	8	12	5	2
1900–	36	14	3	3	4	3
total	111	60		29	25	

sth., IDENTIFY *oneself with sth.* (1970: 213). Visser has a great deal of material in his (1963–73: sections 158, 162, 426–91).

Here is a contrasting pair of a slightly different kind:

(352)   a. when the tale *was* silently *forming itself*

                                            (?Early 1849 Gaskell, *Letters* 42 p. 71)

    b. The tale *was formed*   (ibid.)

The reciprocal pronouns *each other* and *one another* are said by Quirk, Greenbaum, Leech & Svartvik to be undifferentiated in use, though they are more common in informal and formal style, respectively (1985: 6.31). The prescriptive tradition prefers *each other* for reference to two and *one another* for more than two, though there is very little evidence of such a division in the ARCHER corpus. Once indeterminate examples have been discounted from table 3.6, the distribution reveals no significant correlation for any of the three centuries surveyed, and only a slight correlation (significant at the 10 per cent level) if the whole 300-year span is taken together.

3.4.2.3   Indirect objects and indirect passives

Definition of **indirect object** is notoriously difficult. Syntactically it tends to precede a direct object, and semantically it 'typically refers to an animate being that is the recipient of the action' (Quirk, Greenbaum, Leech & Svartvik 1985: 10.7). Many indirect objects commute with prepositional phrases headed by *to* or *for*. The indirect object, (353), shades off into what in older stages of the language can be called an ethic dative or dative of (dis)advantage, (354). There appears to have been a reduction in the range of both. The following examples illustrate usages now obsolescent or at least disfavoured in BrE (though (353b) is the norm in AmerE):

(353) a. repeat *her* some of your own Verses

(1777 Sheridan, *School for Scandal* I.i 370.11)

b. (= 133a) I intended to have been at Chichester this
Wednesday – but on account of this sore throat I
wrote *him* (Brown) my excuse yesterday

(1818 Keats, *Letters* 98 p. 257 (Dec.))

c. My latest Valueless Villanelle I enclose *you*.

(1890 Dowson, *Letters* 100 p. 150 (1 Jun.))

(354) a. It shews that TILBURINA is coming; nothing introduces *you* a
heroine like soft musick.

(1779 (1781) Sheridan, *Critic* II.ii 529.10)

b. If there were one man who would carry *you* a medical reform
and another who would oppose it

(1871–2 George Eliot, *Middlemarch* xlvi.466)

c. Could I hear *them* their lessons & take walks with them while
the Governess is away?   (1873 *Amberley Papers* II.552 (25 Jul.))

Examples like the following illustrate the difficulty of delimiting the indirect object, as they could plausibly be included with either of the preceding sets of data:

(355) a. (= 289) (I have it not by me, or I would copy *you* the exact
passage)   (1848 Gaskell, *Mary Barton* v.62)

b. and I was foolish enough to think he meant *me* marriage

(ibid. xxxii.303)

Throughout our period the indirect passive has been widely used:

(356) a. and so *I'm to be given the go-by* for any town friend of yours who
turns up and chooses to patronise us!

(1893 Pinero, *Second Mrs. Tanqueray* II.ii, in *19c Plays*, ed. Booth
II.292 [ARCHER])

b. I have, as indeed I ought to have, with *the opportunities I am
given*, a growing sense of mastery in my own work

(1917 Bell, *Letters* II.416 (29 Jun.))

A long-term process of extension of the indirect passive can be illustrated within the present century by the fact that four out of five possibilities tentatively rejected by Jespersen (1909–49: III 309) – for example, *He was sent a note* – were accepted as fully normal by Strang some sixty years later (1970: 99). Meanwhile some passives already acceptable in colloquial or non-standard speech have become increasingly frequent in writing as the bonds of the prescriptive tradition have been loosened. It is unclear to what extent the indirect passive was – and is – consciously avoided by careful stylists. Jespersen quotes one eminent editor who did (1909–49: III 309–10). The following examples may show deliberate avoidance:

(357)   a. Can you lend me 30£ for a short time? – ten I want for myself – and twenty for a friend – *which will be repaid me* by the middle of next Month   (1818 Keats, *Letters* 103 p. 272 (24 Dec.))

   b. Mark found it impossible at the moment to make any remark upon *what had been told him*   (1860–1 Trollope, *Framley* viii.73)

   c. He had fallen into the possession of a fine property . . . he had been endowed with more than average gifts of intellect; *never-failing health had been given to him, and a vision fairly clear in discerning good from evil*   (ibid. xxvii.266)

One expedient for avoiding the indirect passive is the construction sometimes known as the HAVE passive:

(358)   a. How then are these sparks which are God *to have identity given them* – . . . ?   (1819 Keats, *Letters* 123 p. 335 (Apr.))

   b. [Miss Bronte] possesses . . . a strong feeling of responsibility for the Gift, which she *has given her*.
        (1850 Gaskell, *Letters* 78 p. 128 (*c.* 25 Aug.))

   c. She *has a beautiful set of pearls, value I don't know how much, given her*.   (1852 ibid. 133 p. 200 (21 Sep.))

   d. I was always *having compliments paid me*
        (1904 Nesbit, *Phoenix* ii.35)

(358´)   a. How then are these sparks which are God to be given identity . . . ?

   b. the Gift, which she is given/has been given.

   c. She is given/has been given a beautiful set of pearls[67]

   d. I was always being paid compliments.

In Denison (1993a: 342–3) I suggested that the passive of experience (*I had my car stolen*) is essentially the same construction; see also Brinton (1994). There is some discussion in Visser (1963–73: sections 2118, 1964(3)), who in my view unnecessarily confuses the HAVE passive (*I had a present given me*) with an agentive construction, causative HAVE (*I had my house painted*). The HAVE passive dates back to the ME period. It is unclear whether it has become any less frequent as avoidance of the indirect passive becomes less necessary.

3.4.2.4 Prepositional objects and prepositional passives

The term **preposition stranding** is applied to constructions which leave a preposition in a deferred position without any immediately following object. Where there is a choice between 'pied-piping' a preposition together with its object to a fronted position,[68] as for instance in the interrogative clause of (359), and stranding it, (359'), there has been a preference for the pied-piped pattern in more formal usage:

(359)   You know *to what* I allude   (1862 Green, *Letters* 96 (24 Jul.))

(359') You know *what* I allude *to*

Since the stranding constructions are actually older, this reflects a change from above.

No new constructions have appeared in lModE, but the frequency of preposition stranding has probably increased, and some prepositions begin to permit it which previously would have resisted it even in informal speech:

(360)   There are two kinds of geniuses, the 'ordinary' and the
        'magicians'. An ordinary genius is a fellow *that* you and I would
        be just as good *as*, if we were only many times better.
                (1985 Mark Kac, *Enigmas of Chance* xxv, quoted Gleick, *Genius* 10)

One notable environment for preposition stranding is the prepositional passive. Here too the trend has been to permit passivisation more and more widely. Here are some examples of simple prepositional passives which push against the limits of tolerability:

(361)   a. In protracted expectation of the weather clearing up, the last
           evening paper from London was read and re-read . . . every
           inch of the carpet *was walked over* with similar perseverance,
           the windows *were looked out of* . . . all kinds of topics of
           conversation were started, and failed . . .
                        (1836–7 Dickens, *Pickwick* li.784)
        b. but I wd rather do *without* [original emphasis] trustees, IF
           possible. Mr Shaen . . . suggested some way in whh they *might
           be done without*   (1865 Gaskell, *Letters* 581 p. 770 (?31 Aug.))

Example (361a) is deliberately contrived by Dickens to convey the frustration of the party, since the passive prototypically suggests an active in which somebody actually does something. The now quite unremarkable passive of the prepositional verb DO *without* in (361b) is only given as 'modern', thus *c.* 1893–7, in *OED* s.v. *do* v. B.41, and as twentieth century in Visser (1963–73: section 1957).

And here are some complex prepositional passives, including some –
examples (362) – involving phrasal-prepositional verbs, those that consist
of verb + adverbial particle + preposition:

(362)   a. (= 253a) but that objection *is done away with*

              (1818 Keats, *Letters* 66 p. 146 (21 May))

      b. & perhaps things *might be got on with*.

              (1863 Gaskell, *Letters* 524 p. 703 (1 Jun.))

      c. a notion got about that I *had been bolted away with*.

              (1917 Conrad, *Lord Jim*, author's note)

      d. I don't like *being hung up on*

              (1980 Yale Udoff, *Bad Timing* [film dialogue])

(363)   a. This agreement *was* not *made a legal instrument of* because

              (1823 C. Sheridan, *letter* in Sheridan I.15 (20 Dec.))

      b. after a substantial lunch . . . *had been done ample justice to*

              (1836–7 Dickens, *Pickwick* xxx.449)

      c. boy said he wouldn't lie there *to be made game of*, and he'd tell
        his mother if they didn't begin   (ibid. xxxii.482)

      d. 'He must *be done something with*, brother Ned . . .'

              (1838–9 Dickens, *Nickleby* xxxv.456)

      e. Little Dorrit was glad *to be found no fault with*, and to see that
        Fanny was pleased   (1855–7 Dickens, *Little Dorrit* II.iii.450)

      f. we could be beat up, we could *be done anything to* and no
        one . . . was on our side.

              (1977 French, *Women's Room* (Sphere, 1978) IV.iii.295)

Jespersen describes (363d) as 'not quite natural' (1909–49: III. 317), but the
process of forming a prepositional passive is perfectly natural when the NP
which thereby becomes subject has an appropriate semantic role.

3.4.2.5   Group-verbs

I use the term **group-verb** for a multi-word lexical item with verbal function.
We have already implicitly dealt with prepositional verbs – those consisting
of a verb + preposition – in their capacity for a passive turn. A prepositional
verb like LOOK *at* is to be distinguished from a transitive phrasal verb like
LOOK *up* – verb + adverbial particle – by a well-known battery of tests:

(364)   a. She looked (carefully) at the book.

      b. **She looked the book at.

      c. She looked at it/**it at.

      d. (the book) at which she looked

Table 3.7. *Group-verbs in PDE*

Class	Label	Direct object	Prepositional object	Second particle	Examples
1	intransitive phrasal verb	−	−	−	EAT *out*, WISE *up*
2	transitive phrasal verb	+	−	−	CLEAN *sth. out*, MESS *sth. up*
3	prepositional verb	−	+	−	INSIST *on sth.*, DEAL *with sth.*
4	phrasal-prepositional verb	−	+	+	HANG *up on sb.*, GET *away with sth.*
5		+	+	+	TAKE *sth. out on sb.*, PUT *sth. over on sb.*
6		+	+	−	TAKE *sb. for sth.*, SUSPECT *sb. of sth.*
7		−	−	+	(COME *on over*, GET *back in*)
8		+	−	+	GET *sth. over with*, (READ *sth. back out*)

(365)   a. She looked (**carefully) up the number.
       b. She looked the number up.
       c. She looked ?**up it/it up.
       d. **(the book) up which she looked

For further details see Quirk, Greenbaum, Leech & Svartvik (1985: 16.2–6). I have suggested elsewhere a simple classification of verb-particle combinations in PDE (Denison 1981, 1984), reproduced as table 3.7, with classes 1–4 the most important – and having widely recognised names – and 7–8 fairly marginal.

The individual histories of group-verbs are largely matters of lexis, outside the scope of this chapter, though it is perhaps appropriate to note the growth of patterns of formation. Thus, for example, LOOK *out* is recorded in literal sense from 1390 and figuratively from 1602; in our period we first find WATCH *out* (1786), MIND *out* (1886), LISTEN *out* (1910), also KEEP *an eye out* (1889), the latter reinforced by reanalysis of KEEP *a look-out* (Denison 1981: 162–3; dates from *OED*).

The rise of the phrasal verb (classes 1 and 2) has not been uninterrupted. Here are some combinations which have fallen out of use again:

(366)   a. Hallo! . . . What's *going forward*? [= PDE *going on*]
                                    (1836–7 Dickens, *Pickwick* vii.94, sim viii.113, etc.)
        b. You have been *bred up* [= PDE *brought up*, *bred*] in the country.
                                    (ibid. xxxix.613)
        c. and *shrugging up* [= PDE *shrugging*] his shoulders with a
            constant succession of bows   (ibid. xxxv.542)
        d. And, oh, have you *mended up* [= PDE *mended*] all the old pens
            in the study?   (1840 Bulwer-Lytton, *Money* I.i p. 166)
        e. said she, hastily *checking* herself *up* [= PDE *checking*] as if
            she were afraid of having admitted too much
                                    (1851–3 Gaskell, *Cranford* xi.106)

But on the whole this is one kind of construction which does appear to be increasing in numbers and frequency.

The phrasal-prepositional verb (class 4) has been gaining ground. Those in (367) had not long been in use, as far as I know – though right from the start of our period, it had been possible colloquially to add *away at* to most intransitive verbs, e.g. 1774 *railed away at* in *OED* s.v. *tar*[1] and many examples thereafter:

(367)   a. I have not been able to do anything more but will *go away at* it
            on my return.   (1890 Dowson, *Letters* 106 p. 156 (27 Jun.))
        b. '. . . she had a father that was always *beating up on* her, she had
            to get out of the house . . .'
                                    (1977 French, *Women's Room* (Sphere, 1978) II.ix.225)

One noticeable change in lModE is that the phrasal-prepositional verb (class 4) has moved in on the territory of the transitive phrasal verb (class 2). This is in fact a fairly systematic process of replacement, or at least suppletion, which has been going on for hundreds of years: compare PUT *up* 'endure' (1573) → PUT *up with* (1755). One effect is to lessen the transitivity of the group-verb; thus, for example, BEAT *up on* need not signify actual physical attack, whereas BEAT *up* almost always does. I give some lModE examples, with the dates of earliest attestation that I have been able to find, in table 3.8.

Somewhat conversely, RUN *over* started off as a class 3 prepositional verb (RUN *over (sth./sb.)*), and with reference to road accidents increasingly functions as a class 2 phrasal verb (RUN *(sb.) over*). The reanalysis is favoured by the resultativeness typical of class 2; see Parker (1976).

Certain formations of one class can be seen as deriving from another class by a systematic process of ellipsis. Ellipsis of a direct object with a

David Denison

Table 3.8. *Spread of phrasal-prepositional verb (class 4)*

Class 2		Class 4	
GET *(sth.) away* 'succeed in removing'	*c.* 1375	GET *away with (sth.)*	1878
CATCH *(sth.) up* 'overtake'	1855	CATCH *up to (sth.)*	1888
		CATCH *up with (sb.)*	1909
CHECK *(sth.) up*	1889	CHECK *up on (sth.)*	1921
CUT *(sth.) down* 'reduce'	1857	CUT *down on (sth.)*	1939
BEAT *(sb.) up*	1907	BEAT *up on (sb.)*	1971
FOLLOW *(sth.) through* 'pursue to conclusion'	1934	FOLLOW *through on (sth.)*	1981

class 2 phrasal verb gives class 1: LAY *off (one's hands)* (?1467) → lay *off* 'desist' (1908); WIND *(sth.) up* 'conclude, sum up' (1583) → class 1 intransitive (1825). Ellipsis of a prepositional object with class 3 likewise gives a class 1 verb: DO *without (sth.)* (*c.* 1410) → class 1 intransitive (1779). From class 6 we get class 2: PUT *(sb.) out of the way* 'disturb, inconvenience, trouble' (1673)/PUT *(sb.) out of his humor* (1701)/PUT *(sb.) out of all patience* (1763) → PUT *(sb.) out* 'annoy' (1822)/'inconvenience' (1839).

Not uncommonly, earlier usage had an ordinary transitive verb – or perhaps omission of a preposition (Phillipps 1970: 152) – where PDE prefers a prepositional verb:[69]

(368) a. Enter SERVANT and *Whispers* [= PDE *whispers to*] SIR PETER.
   (1777 Sheridan, *School for Scandal* II.ii 382.19)
   b. 'There was nothing to be done, however, but to submit quietly, and *hope* [= PDE *hope for*] the best.
   (1816 Austen, *Mansfield Park* III.v[xxxvi].356)
   c. Sir Joseph Banks *joked* [= PDE *teased*] her about Otoroo.
   (1789 Mrs. Piozzi, *Journ. France* II. 28 [*OED*])
   d. 'Have you quite *recovered* [= PDE *recovered from*] that scoundrel's attack?'   (1838–9 Dickens, *Nickleby* xxxiv.435)

The converse may also occur:

(369) a. a place near Rivington which I just *glimpsed at* [= PDE *glimpsed*] lately   (1838 Gaskell, *Letters* 12 p. 32 (18 Aug.))
   b. Yet he would not *acknowledge to* [= PDE *acknowledge*] any ailment.   (1848 Gaskell, *Mary Barton* xii.148)

Compare too BrE PROTEST *at/against (sth.)* – current since the seventeenth century – with a twentieth-century use in AmerE of PROTEST *(sth.)* in the same sense of 'make formal objection to'.

Verb-particle combinations are by no means the only types of group-verb. Strang (1970: 101) suggests that various other kinds developed rapidly from about 1800: she mentions the HAVE *a try*, TAKE *a look* type (lists in Visser 1963–73: section 151), the LAUGH *one's thanks*, GROPE *one's way* type (the latter item a little later), and the FALL *flat*, COME *in useful* type. Many kinds of group-verb can be regarded as variants of the types classified in table 3.7, with a particle replaced by an element of another category. Thus GO *bad*, TAKE *place* are like class 1, MAKE *clear*, PUT *right* like class 2, GET *to grips with*, PUT *paid to*, STOP *short of*, TAKE *advantage of* like class 4, LAY *(sb.) low with (sth.)*, MAKE *(sb.) aware of (sth.)* like class 5, CATCH *(sb.) up short* like class 8.

One indication of the productive power of certain group-verb patterns is the history of GET *rid of* and LET *go of*. For the first we can imagine a historical chain of derivation of the following sort:

(370) a. Fate rid me of that nuisance.
       b. I was rid of that nuisance.
       c. I got rid ['became free'] of that nuisance.
       d. I got rid of ['removed'] that nuisance.
       e. That nuisance was got rid of.

For the second, perhaps

(371) a. I let the reins go.
       b. I let go. (elliptical)
       c. I let go of the reins.
       d. The reins were let go of.

Whatever the precise details, the histories are evidently different – after all, one contains a past participle, the other an infinitive – but the outcome has been two new group-verbs of very similar syntactic behaviour and rhythmic shape. And not long after LET *go of* is recorded in the middle of the nineteenth century comes the variant LEAVE *go (of)* (*OED* s.vv. *let* v.[1] 24b, *leave* v.[1] 13b).

3.4.2.6   Indefinite, anticipatory and anaphoric *it*

Indefinite *it* has long been used as object with transitive verbs, (372), with verbs otherwise intransitive, (373), and with verbs formed – sometimes for the nonce, sometimes more permanently – from adjectives and nouns, (374):

(372)   a. No, that which pleases me, is to think what work I'll make
when I get to London; for when I am a wife and a Lady both,
I'cod I'll *flaunt it* with the best of 'em.

(1777 (1781) Sheridan, Scarborough IV.i 602.21)

        b. There's a comment on human vanity for you! Why, *blast it*, I
was under the impression that

(1863 Twain, Selected Letters, ed. Neider p. 48 (19 Aug.) [ARCHER])

(373)   a. When I saw him taking his aim and preparing to draw the
trigger, I turned round my back, not being able to *stand it*,

(1828 Moir, Life of Mansie Wauch xiv.88 [ARCHER])

        b. a Saracenic town, built when folk had just been *crusading it* and
thought of nothing but the 'Paynim Soldan Saladin'

(1838 Gaskell, Letters 9 p. 16 (17 Jul.))

        c. The Zeppelin kept a few miles in the rear of us, and finally
hopped it.

(1915 Scotsman 13 Jan. 7/3 [OED])

(374)   a. *I*'ve [original emphasis] been used to *rough it* – before we
came into our fortune.

(1863 Taylor, Ticket-of-leave man II.i, in 19c plays, ed.
Booth II.99 [ARCHER])

        b. '. . . They can *tram it* home.'   (1904 Nesbit, Phoenix x.202)

Sometimes indefinite *it* appears to be virtually empty of meaning, *pace*
Bolinger (1977), or its reference may be merely vague and contextually determined. Visser gives a good selection of examples and points out that 'the
number of instances rapidly increases' in ModE (1963–73: sections 496–9).

Indefinite *it* has it in common with particle group-verbs (3.4.2.5 above)
that both can among other things be a means of deriving a verb from
another part of speech (cf. ROUGH *it*, ROUGH *(sth.) out*). The two often
combine, with *it* either the direct object, (375), or the prepositional object,
(376), of a group-verb in a (more or less) fixed idiom:

(375)   a. Lieutenant Thumhill is really *livin' it up*!

(1951 San Francisco Examiner 14 Feb. 12 [OED])

        b. There's nothing for it but *brazening it out*.

(1839 Planche, Garrick Fever p. 75 [ARCHER])

        c. Meanwhile he's having trouble *getting it together* and lives off the
SS [*sc.* Social Security].   (1975 New Society 20 Nov. 412/3 [OED])

        d. He '*had it in' for* more than one of the people who helped the
police. (1888 'R. Boldrewood', Robbery Under Arms II.xviii.283 [OED])

        e. Figure I might as well sign up tomorrow and *get it over with*.

(1947 R. Allen, Home Made Banners iii.18 [OED])

(On the complex origins of GET *it over with*, see Denison 1984.)

(376)   a. but, as I'*m in for it*, I may as well go it.

                         (1889 John Maddison, *Lend Me 5 Shillings* p. 16 [ARCHER])

         b. That's the message of Little Women, too . . . Its message is: *go for it*, be whoever you can be   (1995 *The Guardian 2* p. 7 (5 Jan.))

(Indefinite *it* is of high frequency: two of my examples, (375b) and (376a), even have a second occurrence.)

Object *it* may have a purely grammatical function as a 'heralding object' anticipating a finite clause. Visser describes a number of different contexts in which anticipatory object *it* may or must be used (1963–73: sections 505–26). There have been both gains and losses during our period. Some verbs which had permitted indefinite *it* before a *that*- or *how*-clause in eModE no longer do so in lModE (FIND (**it) *that* . . . , KNOW (**it) *that* . . .), though it remains normal before an *if*- or *when*-clause (LIKE *it when* . . .). In other cases *it* has become almost obligatory where before it was optional:

(377)   a. I . . . *thought best* to respect his silence.

                        (1854–5 Thackeray, *Newcomes* II.xxxvii.404 [Visser])

         b. I *think it best* to lose no time in settling

                        (1815 Austen, *Letters* 121 p. 446 (11 Dec.))

If anticipatory *it* ever could be omitted in structures like SEE *it proved that* . . . , or where a *to*-phrase intervenes between higher verb and object clause, it was before our period.[70]

Once again we find a relation with group-verbs: anticipatory *it* seems to be common when the object of a transitive phrasal verb or a prepositional verb is a *that*-clause rather than an NP (Visser 1963–73: sections 511, 519; Quirk, Greenbaum, Leech & Svartvik 1985: 16.34n.[a]):

(378)   a. And in a preceding page, 200, he *lays it down*, that 'when a part of the cargo is . . .'

                      (1838 'Bevan & others against the U.S. Bank', *Reports* . . . *Pennsylvania, E. District* IV [ARCHER])

         b. but he always *insisted on it* that the sufferer must have been the aggressor,   (1792 Belknap, *The Foresters* vii.88 [ARCHER])

With some phrasal verbs the *it* is increasingly disfavoured (GIVE *out* 'report'). With prepositional verbs it is not possible to omit *it* unless the preposition disappears too:

(378′)   b. but he always *insisted* that

Finally, we must mention anaphoric *it* used to refer to a constituent of a clause (other than one with reference to an inanimate object). Now *it* may refer to a whole clause, or – especially when used in the combination DO *it* – to part of one (Quirk, Greenbaum, Leech & Svartvik 1985: chapter 12):

(379)   a. If you don't study for the examination, you'll regret *it*.
         b. Martin is painting his house. I'm told he *does it* every four years.

These uses are of long standing. There have been subtle changes of usage here:

(380)   a. Because you hadn't cleared his father to him, and you ought to have *done it*.   (1855–7 Dickens, *Little Dorrit* I.xv.175)
         b. you can go to Latchford, or to London – which you prefer; or both if you like *it*   (1855 Gaskell, *Letters* 230 p. 334 (Feb.))
(381)   a. 'You look like the king's falconer,' said Jane . . . Robert tried to go on looking like *it*.   (1904 Nesbit, *Phoenix* iii.63)
         b. Pound himself had a long way to go: and he has gone *it*.
       (1954 T. S. Eliot, *Literary Essays of Ezra Pound* (Faber, 1985) p. xiii)

In (380) PDE would probably have used ellipsis (. . . *and you ought to have [ø]*, . . . *if you like [ø]*) rather than substitution, while it is no longer entirely natural to use *it* as anaphoric substitute for the nonobject NPs which occur in (381).

3.4.3   Predicative

It is conventional to distinguish predicatives from objects:

(382)   Jim turned out *a good teacher*.

(383)   Jim turned out *the disruptive pupils*.

Obvious differences between them include those shown in table 3.9. Example (382) illustrates a subject predicative, co-referential with the subject NP. The rivalry of different case forms in pronouns acting as subject predicative (*It is I* vs. *It is me*) has been mentioned in section 3.2.2.3 above. Both variants were already in competition at the start of our period (*CHEL* III, forthcoming), and by now the objective case has become dominant for most speakers and in most styles.

Table 3.9. *Predicative NPs versus objects*

	Predicative (e.g. *a good teacher* in (382))	Object (e.g. *the disruptive pupils* in (383))
co-referential with preceding NP	yes	not necessarily
same number as that NP	normally	not necessarily
commutes with AP	yes	no

3.4.3.1 Passive versus predicative

The borderline between a passive and BE + predicative can be a murky one:

(384) a. Jim was amused by her tirade. (passive, cf. *defeated*)
   b. Jim was amused.
   c. Jim was very amused at her tirade. (predicative, cf. *happy (with)*)

Without further information to go on, *amused* in (384b) could be analysed as either verbal or adjectival. One development in recent years has been a shift towards the latter analysis for syntagms involving certain past participles. The intensifier *much* in examples (385), which tends to collocate with verbal items, would nowadays be replaced by *very*, which collocates with adjectival items:

(385) a. I was *much disappointed.* (1818 Keats, *Letters* 72 p. 157 (27 Jun.))
   b. Lydgate was *much worried*

           (1871–2 George Eliot, *Middlemarch* lviii.586)

   c. Of course Ginger was *much excited*

           (1877 Sewell, *Black Beauty* x.46)

Visser suggests that the 'transition from participle to adjective is oftenest met with past participles denoting mental states', and he has examples of the newer usage as early as eModE (1963–73: section 1127). The process of replacement is revealed in table 3.10.[71] Visser notes that several Victorian grammarians objected to the newer usage and quotes the sarcastic response to one of them by Fitzedward Hall in 1873, which might imply that by then it was old-fashioned to resist the adjectival construal.

 An extreme example of a similar tendency is shown by:

(386) a. somebody . . . who will love you as warmly as ever *He* did
    [original emphasis], and who will so completely *attach* you,
    that you will feel you never really loved before.

         (1817 Austen, *Letters* 141 p. 483 (13 Mar.))

Table 3.10. *Some intensifiers with participial adjectives in ARCHER*

	(*Very/too*) *much*		*Very/too*	
	N	%	N	%
1650–99	27	100	0	0
1700–49	18	95	1	5
1750–99	28	97	1	3
1800–49	22	81	5	19
1850–99	11	50	11	50
1900–49	7	39	11	61
1950–	4	27	11	73

> b. It is a rare thing for a Minister to have an opportunity of so
> *attaching* & gratifying a whole people as he may now do
> (1843 Martineau, *Letters* p. 77 (28 May))

The usage in (386) shows that transitive ATTACH could be used in the sense 'make fond'; a passive-like turn existed (e.g. 1816 Austen, *Emma* III.xiii[xlix].427). However, by mid-nineteenth century the active usage had disappeared, while the participial adjective *attached* was construed with *to* rather than with the *by* of a true passive. Now, of course, it is quite normal for it to be modified by *very*.

As the balance between verbal and adjectival participles shifts, increased use of perfect + passive is another way of marking truly verbal participles (3.3.6.2 above).

3.4.3.2 Verbs with subject predicative

Visser discusses verbs occurring with subject predicatives in his (1963–73: sections 228ff.). In respect of the verb COME, he notes that it is a matter of rather unpredictable idiom as to which predicatives can occur in PDE.[72] And idiom has changed. Thus COME + past participle with *un-*, as in *came undone*, appears to be a nineteenth-century innovation (1806–7 in *OED* s.v. *undone* ppl.a.[2] 2), and conversely some eighteenth-century combinations have disappeared:

(387 = 295a)   but how *came* you and Mr. Surface *so confidential*
(1777 Sheridan, *School for Scandal* I.i 361.20)

Similarly, FALL/TURN + predicative NP, as in *fell a sacrifice, turn nun*, has become obsolete outside such set phrases as FALL *heir/victim (to)*, TURN

traitor. It is now uncommon to find CONTINUE + predicative NP, and likewise GET:

(388)   a. The Emperor Alexander it is said intends to divide his Empire
            as did Diocletian – creating two Czars beside himself, and
            continuing the supreme Monarch of the whole

                                    (1818 Keats, *Letters* 94 p. 234 (Oct.))

        b. Baby *really* [original emphasis] walks alone now & *is getting a
            sweet little thing*   (1838 Gaskell, *Letters* 9 p. 19 (17 Jul.))

In PDE when there is an NP predicative it would be more common to have
to be after CONTINUE or GET, making them catenatives.

     PDE also has a strong preference for *to be* between APPEAR, SEEM and
a verbal participle, especially an *-ing*, to the extent that grammarians often
use collocation with SEEM as a test of adjectival status; Pinker, for instance,
treats **She seemed sleeping* as quite self-evidently ungrammatical (1994: 281,
etc.). However, examples are readily found through the nineteenth century
and even into the twentieth (see Visser 1963–73: sections 1796, 1894):

(389)   a. he *seemed watching* her intently   (1816 Austen, *Emma* III.v[xli].346)

        b. there was such a fine swell of the sea that the columns *seem'd
            rising* immediat<e>ly out of the waves

                                    (1819 Keats, *Letters* 156 p. 411 (?18 Sep.))

        c. And now the mists and the storms *seemed clearing away* from his
            path   (1848 Gaskell, *Mary Barton* xiv.171)

        d. Mrs. Wilson's countenance was stamped with the anxiety of
            the last few days, although she, too, *appeared sleeping* soundly

                                                    (ibid. xxiv.257)

        e. Everyone *seemed milling around, banging* into furniture

                            (1945 Anthony Gilbert, *Black Stage* (Chivers, 1988) v.72)

(390)   a. he had fallen across the bed, and his breathing *seemed almost
            stopped*   (1848 Gaskell, *Mary Barton* xxxv.341)

        b. The Earl *seemed much annoyed.*

                                    (1877 Sewell, *Black Beauty* xxvii.113)

The date and degree of change are rather uncertain, therefore, though
change there clearly has been. Is it to be located in the higher verb or in the
participle?

     Example (390b) recalls the replacement of *much annoyed* by *very annoyed*
(3.4.3.1 above), and putting those two changes together suggests that verbs
like SEEM and APPEAR have been losing the ability to be complemented
by (truly) verbal participles. Alternatively, examples (389) could be related

to the claim that the progressive had only recently been grammaticalised (3.3.3.4 above), if verbal -*ings*, even those with their own complementation, had not yet lost as much of their nonverbal status as they subsequently have.

Another kind of variation is between predicative adjective phrase and adverbial phrase. In the early part of our period the verb LOOK showed both kinds of complementation (Visser 1963–73: section 235):

(391)   a. you look very *nicely* indeed.

(1816 Austen, *Mansfield Park* II.v[xxiii].222 [Phillipps])

        b. she looks very *neat & tidy*.

(1812 Austen, *Letters* 74.1 p. 500 (29 Nov.) [Phillipps])

Phillipps assumes that the adverbial usage in (391a) was a hypercorrect reaction to prescriptive teaching (1970: 183–4), but it can be traced back to ME. There was similar variation with FEEL and SOUND.

3.4.4   *Adverbial*

The remaining major element of the simple clause is the adverbial. Unlike the elements already discussed, adverbials are often optional elements and tend to have greater freedom of position than the obligatory elements. Nevertheless their syntax is important, if relatively poorly studied. We shall examine a handful of changes manifested in lModE, beginning with adjuncts.

The agent phrase of a passive is an adverbial adjunct. Throughout the lModE period, the productive expression has been a prepositional phrase headed by *by*, as in *He was eaten by a tiger*. Relics of older forms with other prepositions survive through to PDE as unproductive set collocations, often more adjectival than verbal: *surprised* + *at, frightened* + *of, known* + *to, filled* + *with*, and so on; see Quirk, Greenbaum, Leech & Svartvik (1985: 3.76, 16.69). Some of those which occurred earlier in our period are now obsolescent:

(392)   a. Camilla had every reason to be *satisfied of* its elegance.

(1796 Burney, *Camilla* x.463 [ARCHER])

        b. I may be again *seized with* an illness

(1809 Sheridan, *Letters*, ed. Price (Clarendon, 1966) 703 III.61

(28 May) [ARCHER])

Bare NP adverbials, that is, prepositionless NPs in adverbial function, come from a fairly restricted range: adjuncts of time (*yesterday, last time*), and in a more limited fashion adjuncts of place (*this side*) and manner (*that way*). NPs with head noun *weather* could formerly act like those with *time*, as predicatives after BE and as bare NP adverbials:

(393)   a. I have been at different times so happy as not to know *what weather it was*   (1819 Keats, *Letters* 151 p. 384 (21 Sep.))
        b. Oh! I wish you could have staid; it would have been so glorious *this weather*   (1836 Gaskell, *Letters* 4 p. 7 (12 May))

Other bare NP adverbials not now current are illustrated by:

(394)   a. We'll tell you all *another opportunity*.
                              (1777 Sheridan, *School for Scandal* I.i 370.26)
        b. Agnes Robinson was married *the beginning of this month*
                              (1833 Gaskell, *Letters* 3 p. 4 (*c.* 16 Dec.))
        c. Lady Russell's voice is at last getting better but she was *2 months* unable to talk to Ld. Russell a great privation.
                              (1872 *Amberley Papers* II.530 (28 Oct.))

Phillipps identifies adverbial *the first opportunity* as vulgar for Jane Austen, *these two months* as idiomatic (1970: 186, 169). Jespersen picks out as American and/or recent such generally accepted bare NP adverbials as *all summer* (actually found from the second half of the seventeenth century) and *all morning* (from at least 1788), and (when used of an indefinite period) *all the time* (1909–49: VII 526–7). Just as his intuitions for the early twentieth century may not have been wholly reliable, so it remains very difficult to make accurate and complete generalisations about just which PDE adverbials containing an NP must, may or cannot be used without a preposition; see Quirk, Greenbaum, Leech & Svartvik (1985: 8.52), Larson (1985). Example (394b) is perhaps still marginally possible. The AmerE indefinite adverbs of place, *some/any place*, are in origin bare NP adverbials, dated by the *OED* to the 1930s, though a little earlier in BrE and Irish dialects. The negative adverbial *no way* has come back into vogue recently from America, beginning to replace BrE *in no way*, *(in) nowise*, but the bare NP form had a continuous history from ME to at least the mid-nineteenth century (*OED* s.v. *noway* adv.).

We turn now to subjuncts, elements which 'have . . . a subordinate role . . . in comparison with other clause elements' (Quirk, Greenbaum, Leech & Svartvik 1985: 8.88). Nevalainen reports that *just, exclusively* and *uniquely* joined the list of exclusive adverbs in the eighteenth and nineteenth centuries, and that *just* replaced *but* in this function (1991):

(395) a. The disease of ennui is more frequent in the french
          metropolis, where amusement is *more exclusively* the occupation
          of higher classes, than it is in the British metropolis, where
                                  (a1847 Chalmers, *Expulsive Power* [ARCHER])
       b. but I do love to have *just* a line from you.
                                  (1891 Sidney Webb, *Letters* 164 I.306 (20 Sep.))

In some varieties *like* has become a very frequent member of the class:

(396) a. IRIS. Women are a mess, aren't they? I mean they get these
          fantastic IDEAS [original emphasis] about things, I mean life
          and all, when they're *like* three, you know.
                                  (1964 L. Hansberry, *Sign in Sidney Brustein's Window*
                                  II.i p. 253 [ARCHER])
       b. 'people are always walking up to me when I'm travelling
          and offering me a board directorship of *like* a lawn furniture
          company in Nashville and I think, "why would I want to do
          that?"'   (1995 Nick Rosen, *The Guardian OnLine* p. 3 (16 Feb.))

According to Underhill's study of a small corpus of recent American
speech (1988), it serves to mark focus, as an approximator, or as a hedge.

Finally here I discuss disjuncts, which modify a whole sentence or clause
(unlike adjuncts, which modify VPs), and which semantically are often concerned with expressing speaker attitude. The most notorious is *hopefully*,
regarded by prescriptivists as appropriate only as an adjunct (*She enquired
hopefully*), but in widespread use since the second quarter of the twentieth
century as a sentence adverbial (*Hopefully it'll be OK*), just like many other
unremarked adverbs. Many evaluative sentence adverbs derive historically
from manner adverbials or intensifiers. Toril Swan has argued that some
epistemic sentence adverbials, elsewhere called **speech act adverbs**, date
from the seventeenth century, others later, and that *c.* 1900 is a watershed
in their use (1988, 1990). The *OED* analyses the sentence adverbs *frankly*
and *seriously* as elliptical for *to speak frankly/seriously* (s.vv. *frankly* adv. 3, *seriously* adv.[2] 1), though there may not have been such a specific process of
ellipsis. For *honestly* as a sentence adverb, the *OED* has its earliest citation
from 1898 Shaw. Here are some early examples:

(397) a. GRAVES. . . . Shall we, eh? *Frankly*, now, *frankly*
          LADY FRANKLIN. *Frankly*, now, there's my hand.
                                          (1840 Bulwer-Lytton, *Money* V.iii p. 236)
       b. *Seriously*, on the whole, it is fortunate
                                  (ibid. II.ii in *19c Plays*, ed. Rowell p. 70; omitted in Booth)

c. But I want to, Papa! *Honestly*, I am restless at having been so
ignominiously overcome.

(1873 Hardy, *Pair of Blue Eyes* xviii.166 [ARCHER])

And new possibilities arise all the time:

(398)   '*Reluctantly*, a well-publicised and standard charging system may
need to be introduced . . .'   (1994 *The Guardian* p. 2 (6 Oct.))

Swan detects two positional tendencies: towards initial position, especially
for new sentence adverbials, and more surprisingly, towards late (post-
verbal) position for well-established sentence adverbs not in danger of
being mistaken for adjuncts:

(399)   *Apparently* he has now got tired of his Celtic-fringe seat.

(1908 *Westm. Gaz.* 2 June 2/2 [*OED*])

(399′)   He has now got tired of his Celtic-fringe seat, *apparently*.

3.5   Structure of the clause

The overall structure of the clause has been stable during the lModE
period. Changes have on the whole been minor. The five clause types will
be considered in turn.

3.5.1   *Declaratives*

The declarative is the most general, the least marked clause type, and our
main consideration will be word order. The unmarked order is
subject–verb–complement/object, with adverbials capable of occupying a
number of positions. Of course there are all sorts of marked variants, for
instance:

(400)   At length it was over, *the meal.*   (1921 Lawrence, *Women* ii.25)

Here the subject is postponed, leaving a pronoun copy in its place (so-
called right dislocation). We shall look at some major variants and subtypes
of the basic order.

3.5.1.1   Inversion
The principal kind of inversion is subject–auxiliary inversion (SAI), in
which the first auxiliary – an operator – precedes the subject. This kind of
inversion is largely grammatically conditioned (determined). In declaratives
it may be provoked by a negative or semi-negative in clause-initial position,

where it appears to be a late vestige of the old Verb-Second rule (see *CHEL* I: 275–7, II: 375–7, Stockwell 1984):

(401)   a. *scarcely have I* had time to vent half the malice of my
            tenderness   (1786 Cowley, *School for Greybeards* II p. 24 [ARCHER])
        b. *Not even now will I* mention a word of my affairs –
                                        (1819 Keats, *Letters* 158 p. 431 (3 Oct.))
        c. and if I once get on the scent, *never will I leave* it till the guilty
            are hunted down.
                                (1863 Hazlewood, *Lady Audley's Secret* II.ii p. 259)
        d. *Only later did he* glance at Herndon, then kneel and feel for his
            pulse.   (1953 Wright, *The Outsider* p. 220 [ARCHER])

The rather elevated tone of such noninterrogative inversions in PDE suggests that they are probably in decline; inversion can, after all, be avoided if the 'affective' element is not fronted.

Now virtually obsolete is inversion triggered by other kinds of initial adverbial:

(402)   a. SURFACE. . . . They have no malice at heart –
            MARIA. *Then is their conduct* still more contemptible . . .
                            (1777 Sheridan, *School for Scandal* II.ii 383.3)
        b. Poor Sir Fretful! *Now will he* go and vent his philosophy . . .
                                (1779 (1781) Sheridan, *Critic* I.i 509.1)
        c. And *now must I* tell you something about ourselves
                                (1838 Gaskell, *Letters* 9 p. 17 (17 Jul.))
        d. *Thus did the excellent bird* seek to occupy their minds in that first
            moment of disaster.
                            (1910 E. Nesbit, *The Magic City* (Macmillan) x.284)

SAI may also signal the protasis of a conditional:

(403)   & you say now you wd. have come *had I* answered about the
        doctor.   (1872 *Amberley Papers* II.522 (23 Aug.))

Given the formality of the (403) type in PDE as compared with an *if*-clause, it is not surprising that it has been declining in frequency, as can be seen from table 3.11 in the discussion of conditionals in section 3.6.6.3 below. SAI requires an operator. Inversion in (404) with an ordinary lexical verb is (by this time) a clear archaism:

(404 = 295d) We could not love each other so well, *loved we not* our work
              and duty more.   (1891 Sidney Webb, *Letters* 159 I.298 (14 Sep.))

A colloquial kind of SAI is illustrated by (405), one of the vocal mannerisms of the loquacious old squire, Mr Brooke:

(405)   He is pretty certain to be a bishop, *is Casaubon.*
                              (1871–2 George Eliot, *Middlemarch* vii.66)

Jespersen (1909–49: VII 66–7), Visser (1963–73: section 69) and Melchers (1983) have examples from the middle of the nineteenth century onwards, and with a range of operators in the tag. (Quirk, Greenbaum, Leech & Svartvik note this kind of right dislocation as dialectal in PDE, and as occurring only with BE (1985: 17.78n[a]).)

Another kind of inversion is not SAI at all. This is when subject and (any) verb invert after the topicalisation of some other element (indicated by italics in (406)). Topicalisation is the fronting of an item which would normally follow the verb. Apart from exclamatory sentences opening with a locative or directional adjunct (*here, there, up, off,* etc.), many such inversions are now at least rather literary in effect; see Quirk, Greenbaum, Leech & Svartvik (1985: 18.23):

(406)   a. *A similar interest* have such other tales as
                              (1927 M. Sadleir, *Trollope*, 'Anthony' IV.ii.177)
         b. and *most worthy of you* are such feelings.
                              (1816 Austen, *Mansfield Park* III.iv[xxxv].353)
         c. when *this morning* arrives a note from Freemantle telling me of
                              (1862 Green, *Letters* 112 (20 Nov.))

When the inverting verb is an operator other than DO, it is not always easy to differentiate between the inversion types represented by (402) and (406).

3.5.1.2   Placement of objects

The unmarked position of any (one) object is after the verb, of course, and has been since ME times at least. However, and again with a long history, various alternative marked positions are possible. (Sometimes a different position is grammatically determined and wholly unmarked, for example the fronting of a relative pronoun or interrogative *wh*-phrase.) We shall consider briefly first a process of leftward movement, then of rightward.

Throughout our period we find topicalisation of direct objects, used for a variety of stylistic and communicative reasons:

(407)   a. *Me* she openly petted in my brother's presence, as if I were
                too young and sickly ever to be thought of as a lover
                              (1859 George Eliot, *Lifted Veil* (Virago, 1985) i.24)

b. (= 61)   *Themselves at least* he had never been unnatural enough
to banish from his house

(1871–2 George Eliot, *Middlemarch* xxxii.303)

c. If tabloid evidence were needed of . . . [16 words omitted],
that evidence this report supplies.

(1927 M. Sadleir, *Trollope*, 'Anthony' III.ii.158)

Topicalisation of indirect objects is much rarer:

(408)   *Him* Arthur now showed, with pains and care, the state of their
gains and losses, responsibilities and prospects.

(1855–7 Dickens, *Little Dorrit* II.xxii.652)

I find no mention of it in Quirk, Greenbaum, Leech and Svartvik, though
resistance of indirect objects to other fronting processes is noted (1985:
10.7n.[b], 11.15n.[d]).

Topicalisation of prepositional objects is possible:

(409)   a. *This mischief* you may thank yourself for.

(1777 (1781) Sheridan, *Scarborough* II.i 587.20)

b. *Leigh Hunt* I showed my 1st Book to

(1818 Keats, *Letters* 41 p. 86 (23 Jan.))

Alternatively a whole prepositional phrase may be topicalised:

(410)   the Winkies gave Toto and the Lion each a golden collar; and *to
Dorothy* they presented a beautiful bracelet . . . and *to the Scarecrow*
they gave a gold-headed walking stick . . . and *to the Tin Woodman*
they offered a silver oil-can   (1911 Baum, *Wizard of Oz* xiii.111)

An important ordering principle is known as **Heavy-NP Shift**, whereby
(almost) any immediately post-verbal NP may be moved further beyond
the verb if it is 'heavy' in content and/or phonological form:

(411)   a. We are having here *the most terrible March weather imaginable*

(1866 Longfellow, *Letters* V.35 (10 Mar.) [ARCHER])

b. With that wonderfully fascinating quiet voice of his he
expounded to us *the most terrible of all philosophies*, the
philosophy of power, preached to us *the most marvellous of all
gospels*, the gospel of gold.

(1895 Wilde, *Ideal Husband* II p. 80 [ARCHER])

(Each of the shifted NPs in (411b) is further attracted by an appositive NP.)
The normal direct object position would be as in:

(411´)   a. We are having *bad weather* here
         b. expounded *a philosophy* to us, preached *the gospel* to us

Heavy-NP Shift has operated since at least OE times, and without detailed investigation of a large tagged corpus, I am not aware of any significant change in its operation during the lModE period.

What about two objects? In the nineteenth century there are numerous examples of a pronominal direct object preceding an indirect object, sufficient for that order to be accounted acceptable standard:

(412)   a. when I gave *it him*   (1805 Austen, *Letters* 44 p. 157 (21 Apr.))
         b. I sent *them* [*sc.* lines] *Mr Elmes* on Monday.
                                  (1819 Keats, *Letters* 133 p. 351 (17 Jun.))
         c. I told him that Evelyn could not pay the rest of the money,
            and he told me that . . . Mr. Sharp had just paid *it him*
                                     (1840 Bulwer-Lytton, *Money* V.i p. 225)
         d. (= 309b) 'What do you have for breakfast?' the Fairy said
                     impatiently, 'and who gives *it you?*'
                                          (1902 Nesbit, *5 Children* i.30)
         e. 'Couldn't you tell *it us* in English?' asked Anthea.
                                          (1904 Nesbit, *Phoenix* iii.63)

Indeed at the time of the First World War Poutsma still regards it as normal (1914–29: I 426). Now however, according to Quirk, Greenbaum, Leech & Svartvik (1985: 10.7, 18.38), indirect objects normally precede direct objects in PDE – meaning southern BrE and AmerE – so that *gave him it, tell us it,* and so on would be the norm, with pronouns ordered the same as full NPs, though the order of (412) is noted as a possibility for BrE only. There is both dialectal (Kirk 1985) and chronological variation here. Clearly there *has* been major change in standard varieties of English, but the number of relevant and interacting factors is large.[73]

3.5.1.3   Placement of adverbials

Light adverbs have a variety of possible positions, though probably the commonest in positive clauses in PDE is after the subject and (where there is one) the tensed operator, the 'medial medial' position of Quirk, Greenbaum, Leech & Svartvik (1985: 8.14–23):

(413)   a. when you *first* came here
                                (1863 Hazlewood, *Lady Audley's Secret* II.i p. 254)
         b. (= 401c) and if I *once* get on the scent   (ibid. II.ii p. 259)

c. A medium had *once* told him that a spirit named 'Ellen' was
present   (1873 *Amberley Papers* II.534 (19 Jan.))

The historical position is less clear. The common (414) type, no longer idiomatic, is perhaps also 'medial medial' by virtue of lexical HAVE being then an operator:

(414)   a. Speaking from within, has *always* a fine effect.
                                        (1779 (1781) Sheridan, *Critic* II.ii 534.16)
        b. Accordingly, we had *always* wine and dessert
                                        (1851–3 Gaskell, *Cranford* iii.25)
        c. he had *still* a proud way of holding his head and arching his
           neck   (1877 Sewell, *Black Beauty* xxxiii.140)
        d. besides, we had *then* time to enjoy each other's company.
                                        (ibid. xxxiii.142)

Similar examples with other verbs cannot be so analysed:

(415)   a. I wish I knew *always* the humour my friends would be in at
           opening a letter of mine   (1818 Keats, *Letters* 76 p. 175 (13 Jul.))
        b. my passion gets *entirely* the sway   (1819 ibid. 134 p. 351 (1 Jul.))

Barber claims that placement of light time-adverbs before an unemphatic auxiliary – Quirk, Greenbaum, Leech & Svartvik's 'initial medial' position – is a recent Americanism in BrE (1964: 141). Certainly that position is rare in nineteenth-century British English, though examples like (416) cast doubt on the novelty of the usage, unless all – like (416e) – involve emphatic stress on the auxiliary:

(416)   a. He *never* does appear in the least above his Profession, or out
           of humour with it   (1815 Austen, *Letters* 116 p. 433 (24 Nov.))
        b. mention to Brown that I wrote him a letter at Port<s>mouth
           which I did not send and am in doubt if he *ever* will see it.
                                        (1820 Keats, *Letters* 240 p. 525 (24 Oct.))
        c. There was one of her companions I *never* could abide
                                        (1848 Gaskell, *Mary Barton* xiv.167 [ARCHER])
        d. Up to this moment it *never* had entered my mind that it must
           be some day my fate to select a wife.
                         (1868 (1912) Stanley, *Autobiography* p. 231 (20 Aug.) [ARCHER])
        e. I question whether you ever *could* [original emphasis] do that
           well enough: it is beyond any one person's powers.
                                        (1891 Sidney Webb, *Letters* 160 I.299 (14 Sep.))

   f. 'It *always* has helped,' Robert said;

(1904 Nesbit, *Phoenix* xii.240)

Adverbials can occur in a wide range of other positions too. Here is a selection of examples with an adverbial placed abnormally by PDE standards (all are finite clauses apart from (417c)):

(417)   a. I have been *several times* thinking whether or not I should

(1818 Keats, *Letters* 98 p. 252 (17 Dec.))

        b. George is busy this morning in making copies of my verses. He is making *now* one of an Ode to the nightingale

(1820 ibid. 172 p. 451 (15 Jan.))

        c. In the hope of *soon* seeing you I remain | most sincerely yours

(ibid. 227 p. 508 (16 Aug.))

        d. a house which . . . had probably been *once* a gentleman's house

(1848 Gaskell, *Mary Barton* v.72)

        e. There was one fellow – a big chap at school – against whom I cherished an undying hate. Common injustice on M.'s part threw us *a little* together   (1861 Green, *Letters* 89)

Focusing adverbials like *even*, *also* should, in the prescriptive tradition, stand at the front or end of their NP when they are logically NP-modifiers, as in (418):

(418)   a. Most of her foibles *also* were made known to Margaret, but not all.   (1848 Gaskell, *Mary Barton* v.65)

        b. Oh . . . don't bother about the carpet. I've sold *even* that.

(1904 Nesbit, *Phoenix* iv.94)

Increasingly, however, they tend to behave like ordinary unstressed VP adverbials:

(418´)   a. Most of her foibles were *also* made known to Margaret
        b. I've *even* sold that.

Sometimes there is no conflict:

(419)   a. Mrs Green has put off her coming which is *just* the most provoking thing in the world

(1838 Gaskell, *Letters* 9 p. 19 (17 Jul.))

        b. or if it is *only* an assumed name.

(1872 *Amberley Papers* II.526 (29 Aug.))

Nevalainen discusses the positioning of *only* in detail (1991: 131–5). In her corpus a position anticipating the focused element has gone from under 10 per cent frequency in the earliest ModE to 32 per cent for the period 1840–1900. Like some of the other focusing adverbials, *like* can also precede VPs – the commonest function – and its second most common function is as NP-modifier (Underhill 1988).

A shibboleth of great potency has been the split infinitive, with speakers and especially writers taking great care to avoid interposing anything between the infinitive marker *to* and the verb itself:

(420)   a. He had not always been able *quite to follow* the conversations in the historical romances for the young.

(1902 Nesbit, *5 Children* vi.122)

      b. However, I shall just have *not to dine* out when it gets hot.

(1917 Bell, *Letters* II.412 (26 May))

According to Mossé (1947: 208–9), the split infinitive was hardly widespread before 1830. Visser's copious collection of examples goes right back to ME (1963–73: sections 977–82), but he concedes that the prejudice of grammarians in the nineteenth and twentieth centuries has kept its frequency very low until recently. The sin seems to be becoming increasingly venial:

(421)   a. This was a sign that the girls were not *to long delay* the vanishing time.   (1897 Crane, *Third Violet* p. 102 [ARCHER])

      b. 'I believe it's luckier *not to really choose* . . .'

(1906 Nesbit, *Amulet* xi.198)

      c. And now for something *to really smile about*

(1992 Royal Mail leaflet)

      d. I was too surprised *to even answer*.

(1992 Tartt, *Secret History* viii.540)

In Underhill's corpus *like* always splits an available infinitive (1988).

The position of certain conjuncts shows dialectal and therefore perhaps chronological variation. In Canada and Australia the use of *as well* as sentence-initial conjunct is common.[74] In some varieties of American English, *too* can be used likewise. None of these placings can occur in (my dialect of) BrE:

(422)   a. *As well*, its definition proves misleading in one respect.

(1994 Ian Lancashire, 'The eModE Renaissance Dictionaries Corpus', in Kytö, Rissanen & Wright 1994: 146)

      b. *Too*, the reference to Elliott Van Kirk Dobbie as 'Kirk van Dobbie' (p.124) is startling.

(1993 Randi Eldevik, book review, *Speculum* 68: 713)

c. *Too*, his framework is as coherent as they come.
(1994 Randy Allen Harris, LINGUIST 5–537 (26/22 Mar.))

3.5.2 Negatives

Our discussion of clause types moves on to negation.

3.5.2.1 Double negation

Multiple negation had been the norm throughout Old and Middle English, with *ne* prefixed or cliticised not just to the verb but to any indefinite adverb or pronoun in the clause as well. In the sixteenth century it was still common, now with *not* as the verbal negator co-occurring with such elements as *nor, never, none, nothing* (*CHEL* III, forthcoming), but by the beginning of our period multiple negation had become vanishingly rare. As Jespersen points out (1909–49: V 451–2), when it reappeared in the nineteenth century it was a clear literary marker of non-standard usage:

(423)   all he [the butler] hopes, is, he may *never* hear of *no* foreigner *never* boning *nothing* out of *no* travelling chariot
(1846–8 Dickens, *Dombey*, ed. Horsman (Clarendon, 1974)
xxxi.434 [Jespersen])

It remains non-standard but widespread.

What Jespersen calls **resumptive negation** involves a negative following on from a negative clause already completed. Here there may be variation:

(424)   'I didn't like to, *not* after what happened . . .'
(1915 Maugham, *Of Human Bondage* (Heinemann, 1937)
xc.683 [Jespersen])

(424´)   'I didn't like to, after what happened . . .'

Change is noticeable in the possibility of loosely appended *neither* after a negative:

(425)   a. But come – come it isn't fair to laugh at you *neither* my old friend   (1777 Sheridan, *School for Scandal* V.ii 432.28)
        b. I hope, sister, things are not so very bad with you *neither*
(1816 Austen, *Mansfield Park* I.iii.29)

In (425a) the speaker is Sir Oliver Surface, one of the few entirely admirable characters in the play; it may perhaps be significant, though, that he is an elderly ex-colonial. Within just a few decades, the usage of (425b) is part of the characterisation of Lady Bertram as ignorant and lazy. Jespersen shows that this usage has declined in frequency and acceptability since the eighteenth century (1909–49: V 453–4, VII 618).

3.5.2.2　Negative raising

It is characteristic of colloquial usage that a negative can be 'raised' out of the verbal group where it belongs logically, and attached instead to a higher verb:

(426)　a. You *don't seem* to believe me;

> (1863 Hazlewood, *Lady Audley's Secret* II.ii p. 258)

　　　b. 'You *didn't seem* to care much last night,' said Gerald coldly.

> (1907 Nesbit, *Enchanted Castle* iv.86)

　　　c. And I *don't think* she has much money:

> (1891 Sidney Webb, *Letters* 161 I.301 (15 Sep.))

The meaning of *don't/didn't seem to V* in (426a, b) is 'seem(ed) to not-V', just as *I don't intend to V* usually means 'I intend to not-V' (Palmer 1990: 152), and *don't think X* in (426c) means 'think that not-X'. Absence of raising may be a mere variant, perhaps more formal, (427a), or it may be necessary to express a difference of meaning, (427b):

(427)　a. you seem *not to see* how any concealment divides us.

> (1871–2 George Eliot, *Middlemarch* lxv.667)

　　　b. (= 321c) 'I only want *not to have* my feelings checked at every turn.'

> (ibid. lxxii.736)

Rissanen says that negative raising was less common in eModE than it is in PDE (*CHEL* III, forthcoming); it has been frequent at least since the late nineteenth century.

What is almost the converse process is illustrated by (428–9):

(428)　a. 'I *doubt* it is *not* so easy to turn her head, Mark . . .'

> (1860–1 Trollope, *Framley* xi.111)

　　　b. There were *doubts* that it would *not* be possible [= 'doubts that it would be possible, fears that it would not be possible'] to set up a chain reaction unless pure uranium-235 was used, but Fermi wanted to persevere with natural uranium, as making uranium-235 would be extremely [sic] difficult.

> (1992 Graham Farmelo, *New Scientist* 1849: 28 (28 Nov.))

(429)　a. I like hearing details but *miss*[,] like the children[,] *not* having the dinner specified[.]　　　　(?1854 Gaskell, *Letters* 177 p. 263)

b. 'I do *miss* Jane *not* being cross. I've nobody to fight with.'

(1949 Streatfeild, *Painted Garden* v.46)

Here a negative implicit in the semantics of the higher verb DOUBT or MISS or noun *doubt* is made explicit as an otiose *not* in the lower clause, giving a non-standard kind of double negation. By conventional rules the examples actually say the opposite of what they mean, but they are common. Rissanen has similar examples from eModE (*CHEL* III, forthcoming).[75]

3.5.3   Interrogatives

Interrogative clauses are questions (at least typically) with explicit syntactic marking (as opposed to, say, merely intonational signalling). For a careful discussion of the difference between **interrogative**, a clause type, and **question**, a meaning type, see Huddleston (1994), though I do not adopt his classification of interrogatives here.

3.5.3.1   Word order in interrogatives

Polar interrogatives or *yes/no* questions invite assent or denial by questioning the whole proposition, (430), while *wh*-questions (usually) question a single clause element in an open-ended way, (431). In main clauses, interrogatives show subject–auxiliary inversion (SAI) and – where appropriate – fronting of a *wh*-element, though the two processes cancel each other out when the *wh*-element is itself the subject, (432):

(430)   Should she be invited?

(431)   a. What is her name?
         b. What did she say?
         c. Why are we discussing this?

(432)   Who invited her?

Subordinate interrogative clauses do not normally show SAI:

(430´)   I asked whether she should be invited.

(431´)   a. I asked what her name was.
          b. I asked what she said.
          c. I asked why we were discussing that.

Sometimes they do, however. Quirk, Greenbaum, Leech & Svartvik specify certain conditions for this (1985: 15.5), such as when the clause as a whole functions as complement within a higher clause, or is appositive, both of which I would regard as semi-quotation of an original direct question. They note that in literary style a *wh*-element which is a subject complement may provoke SAI in a subordinate interrogative:

(433)   a. I shall only stay here 'till I find *what is* their determination.
                              (1788 Betsy Sheridan, *Journal* 43 p. 132 (27 Nov.))
        b. and Mr Casaubon had never himself seen fully *what was* the
           claim upon him.   (1871–2 Eliot, *Middlemarch* xxxvii.372)

One might expect a pattern marked as 'literary' to be on the decline in everyday usage. On the other hand, Quirk, Greenbaum, Leech & Svartvik also mention a more general use of SAI in subordinate clauses in Irish and other, unspecified dialects. Certainly it is normal in Ulster English for *wh*- and *yes/no* questions (Henry 1995: chapter 5), and in Welsh English for the latter (*CHEL* V: 138). It is quite common in recent American English and the New Englishes and may be becoming more respectable. I give some examples of *yes/no*-questions:

(434)   a. and seeing the ground floor windows at last open asked *had
           the Maison de Sante of Dr Delmas* arrived during the night.
                              (1939 Joyce, *Letters* p. 407 (6 Sep.) [ARCHER])
        b. '. . . he made a doll for the little girl . . . and came shyly to ask
           might he be permitted to give it to her.'
                              (1961 *LOB Corpus*, Belles lettres, biog. G10:35)
        c. 'No, sir, I asked him point blank, *was he* a traitor to his
           country.'   (1969 Weidman & Yaffe, *Ivory Tower* II.28 [ARCHER])
        d. I settled beside Poppa . . . checking to see *did he* approve.
                              (1989 A. Gurganus, *Oldest Living Confederate Widow Tells All*
                              (Faber, 1990) III.iv.414)

Further investigation of these socio-dialectal cross-currents would be welcome. Ohlander (1986: 971–3) brings in a purely linguistic factor, arguing that SAI is only possible in interrogatives subordinate to a 'question-oriented' element (e.g. *asked, wanted to know, didn't know*, imperative *tell*) rather than an 'answer-oriented' one (e.g. *knew, told*).

3.5.3.2   Interrogative *wh*-words

Wh-interrogatives are introduced by one of the familiar range of so-called *wh*-words: *who(m), what, whose, which, when, where, how, why*. The directional adverbials *whence* and *whither* have become virtually obsolete in lModE. Case-marked *whom*, (435a), became increasingly uncommon during our period, and as an obsolescent form it has long been prone to hypercorrect use, as in (435b):

(435)   a. Also *whom* do you think I have seen?
                                    (1918 Bell, *Letters* II.452 (28 Mar.))
        b. Being a Russian, he knows too *whom* is waiting in the wings for
           the pro-western ministers to fail.
                          (1993 David Hearst, *The Guardian* p. 12 (9 Dec.))

This hypercorrection runs in the opposite direction to that commonly found with fronted *personal* pronouns (3.2.2.3 above).

The same range of *wh*-words appears in subordinate clauses too, plus *whether* for subordinate polar interrogatives. That is now the main function of *whether*, which has lost several others. Already before the ModE period it had largely stopped being used for main clause polar interrogatives, and during the eModE period it ceased to appear in two related uses: introducing direct alternative questions (***Whether X *or* Y?*), and as a pronoun meaning 'which of the two'. See section 3.6.3.1 for a further narrowing of its distribution even in dependent interrogatives.

A *wh*-interrogative can be what Quirk, Greenbaum, Leech & Svartvik (1985: 11.18) call a 'pushdown element', questioning an element from an embedded clause. Here is a deeply embedded example, with the 'extraction site' indicated by [∅]:

(436)   'Why, *whom* do you mean to say that you are going to let *her marry*
        [∅]?'   (1871–2 George Eliot, *Middlemarch* vi.55)

3.5.3.3   Elliptical interrogatives

There seems to be a long tradition of elliptical questions opening with *how*, *why*, or occasionally other *wh*-words, though Visser has only a handful of examples before our period starts and a large number from then on (1963–73: section 983):

(437)   a. But *how to get out here again?* There was the rub.
                                    (1872 *Amberley Papers* II.524 (25 Aug.))
        b. *How behave?* It slapped the poor gentleman's pride in the face
           to ask.   (1879 Meredith, *Egoist* xxix.354)

In the (437) type the verb is a base form or *to*-infinitive. Compare too the grammaticalisation of *How come* as an introducer of finite clauses (3.3.8.3 above). Another variant is verbless (unless X contains a gerund):

What/How about X?, found from 1833 or 1854, respectively, in the *OED* (s.vv *mark* n.[1] 11b, *kissing* ppl.a. b.), and common from the 1880s.

3.5.3.4 Negative interrogatives

Negative interrogatives vary among the following types, where the inverted verb, V, is nowadays always an operator: (A) *V NP not* . . ., (B) *V not NP* . . ., and (C) *Vn't NP* . . . . I give some examples of each, first type A:

(438) a. But *do you not* fear lest he discover that Clara wrote the letter?
$$\text{(1840 Bulwer-Lytton, } Money \text{ II.iii p. 194)}$$
b. But *have I not* seen you with my own eyes . . . ?
$$\text{(1855 Thoreau, } Writings \text{ p. 249 (7 Feb.) [ARCHER])}$$

Then type B, with subject NPs that are pronominal, (439), or nonpronominal, (440):

(439) a. *Am not I* your wife?
$$\text{(1785 MacNally, } Fashionable\ Levities \text{ II.i p. 24 [ARCHER])}$$
b. *Shall not you* put *them* [original emphasis] into our own room?
$$\text{(1813 Austen, } Letters \text{ 82 p. 321 (15 Sep.))}$$
c. *Could not we* ensure him for Groginhole?
$$\text{(1840 Bulwer-Lytton, } Money \text{ IV.ii p. 218)}$$
d. *Do not you* think I ought to refrain, (that being the case) from reading your poetry? But I *don't*. Often is it on my desk, open before me as I work.   (1843 Martineau, *Letters* p. 78 (28 May))
e. 'Oh! do you think we may ring for tea . . .'
'Yes, surely. Why *should not we*?'
$$\text{(1848 Gaskell, } Mary\ Barton \text{ xviii.202)}$$
f. 'I had better ring the bell, my dear, *had not I*?' said Lady Glenmire, briskly.   (1851–3 Gaskell, *Cranford* viii.17)

(440) a. *Were not any other circumstances* linked with this adventure?
$$\text{(1809 Dimond, } Foundling \text{ II.i p. 33 [ARCHER])}$$
b. '*Did not your master* take any thought for you?' I said.
$$\text{(1877 Sewell, } Black\ Beauty \text{ viii.36)}$$

Then type C, with contraction:

(441) a. Oons! *haven't you* got enough of 'Em?
$$\text{(1777 Sheridan, } School\ for\ Scandal \text{ IV.i 407.21)}$$
b. but *don't you* think there is something extremely fine after sunset, when there are a few white Clouds about . . . ?
$$\text{(1817 Keats, } Letters \text{ 21 p. 42 (14 Sep.))}$$

Type B is rather formal now. With pronominal NP subjects it has become virtually obsolete, but it was not uncommon in written English up to the second half of the nineteenth century. The suspicion must arise that some instances really represented type C, at a time when contracted negatives were frowned on in print – that is what Quirk, Greenbaum, Leech & Svartvik suggest may be the case in PDE (1985: 11.7) – though examples like (439d) perhaps argue against this for the 1840s. Sundby mentions two grammarians of around 1800 who criticised the B variant as inelegant, notes that nevertheless it often seems to outnumber the A variant in Jane Austen, and speculates on the possible social marking that it may have carried (1983: 125–7). There is certainly room for more work here.

3.5.4   *Imperatives*

Imperative is a term which can be applied both to verb morphology (one use of the base form) and to clause type (covering more or less those structural possibilities seen in (442) and (448)). It is the one type effectively confined to main clause use. The main change in second person imperatives has been the disuse of the pattern with subject pronoun *you* or *thou* after a positive imperative verb, and the rise of an alternative with *you* before the verb. (Of course, nonexpression of the subject pronoun has remained another and indeed far commoner option, and this, together with loss of *thou*, has destroyed any remaining differences between 2 SG and 2 PL imperatives.) Thus in earlier usage the plain imperative, (442a), could be reinforced by *do*, by *thou/you*, or by both:

(442)   a. Go away.
        b. Do go away.
        c. Go thou/you away.
        d. You go away.
        e. Do thou/you go away.

Types (442a, b) have been available probably throughout the recorded history of English and hardly need exemplification:

(443)   a. *take* the hint and *go* away.
                    (1813 Poole, *Hole in the Wall* II p. 36 [ARCHER])
        b. *Do go* to the devil, Hetty!
                    (1851 Boker, *The World a Mask* II.i p. 19 [ARCHER])

Type (442c) likewise has a long history, though it was probably always less common and is nowadays confined to set phrases like *Mind you* and *Believe you me* (Visser 1963–73: section 24):

(444)   a. Silence. *Go you*, sirrah, and call miss Clara.
                    (1785 MacNally, *Fashionable Levities* II.iii p. 29 [ARCHER])
    b. *Come you* down again, Dyo dear.
                       (1872 Blackmore, *Maid of Sker* xi.103 [ARCHER])

Type (442d) was common in OE and early ME, became rare, and reappeared just at the beginning of our period; Visser's first valid modern example is (445a) (1963–73: section 25, and see *CHEL* III, forthcoming):

(445)   a. I take care, Missy, never *you fear*.
                (1774 Foote, *Cozeners* iii. Wks. 1799 II. 182 [*OED*, Visser])
    b. Oh, come now, *never you bother* your head about the score,
        Paddy.   (1820 Serle, *Exchange No Robbery* II.i p. 29 [ARCHER])

All the earliest lModE examples are actually negatives with *never*, a pattern now unproductive with *you* and used only with a small range of verbs. The variant that is still productive in PDE lacks *never*; some nineteenth-century examples are:

(446)   a. No! *You go* first.
                (1862 Brougham, *Duke's Motto* II.i p. 372 [ARCHER])
    b. '*You let* me alone,' whimpered the boy
           (1887 Shaw, *Unsocial Socialist* (Constable, 1930) ix.126 [ARCHER])
    c. 'Purple, *you shut* up!'
                (1897 Crane, *3rd Violet* (1970) p. 125 [ARCHER])

This type is emphatic, sometimes contrastively so.

As for type (442e), it lasted from eME till the nineteenth century (Visser 1963–73: section 1427):

(447)   a. 'Request everybody else to keep back, if you please,' said the
        physician aloud to the master; 'and *do you take* me straight to
        the place, my friend,' to the messenger.
                      (1855–7 Dickens, *Little Dorrit* II.xxv.686)
    b. I'll write down by to-night's post, and then he can meet me at
        Barchester to-morrow. Or *do you write*. There's nothing I hate
        so much as letter-writing;   (1860–1 Trollope, *Framley* xxxii.314)
    c. But *do thou put* on the mantle the while I go to prayer
          (1893 Wilkins, *Giles Corey, Yeoman* II p. 34 [ARCHER, archaistic])

The *do you X* pattern was evidently politely contrastive: 'it is *you* (not others) who are to do X', or '(while others are to do Y,) what *you* are to do is X'. It is unclear why this useful function should have been lost. Arguing solely from

PDE introspection, Davies claims that contrastive *you* is rarely needed in the same situation as what she calls 'persuasive *do*' (1983: 89–91), an explanation undermined by the many nineteenth-century examples like (447).

In negative imperatives there are equivalents of at least three of the five positive variants:

(448)   a.   Go not away.
           b.   Do not/don't go away.
           c.   ?Go you not away.
           d.   ?**You go not away.
           e.   Do not/don't thou/you go away.

Type (448a) survives only in proverbs and maxims and in archaic style (Visser 1963–73: section 1447), and (448c) is rare in lModE but probably to be found somewhere in pre-twentieth century texts, while (448b, e) have co-existed throughout our period:

(449)   *Don't provoke* me!   (1786 Cowley, *School for Greybeards* II.ii [ARCHER])
(450)   a.   Nay, now, but *don't you go* to think that I am asking for one
                           (1792 Holcroft, *Road to Ruin* II.i p. 31 [ARCHER])
           b.   *Do not you add* to the idle race.
                           (1807 A. M. Porter *Hungar. Bro.* vi. (1832) 66 [*OED*])
           c.   Imperative mood, present tense: *Do not thou go* home
                 (1861 Dickens, *Great Expectations*, ed. Caldwell (Clarendon, 1993)
                                           III.vi[xlv].365 [*OED*])

Note, however, that uncontracted (448e) has disappeared, just like the similar negative interrogative, (439d). (The combined use of DO and *you* in type (448e) does not seem to have the politely contrastive effect that it had in positive imperatives.) I have not come across type (448d).

The interaction of DO and imperative verbs differs in important ways from the behaviour of DO in NICE contexts (cf. 3.3.8.5 above and see Warner 1985: 48–9). The use of DO with HAVE and BE is attested earlier in the imperative than elsewhere. There is one example of positive imperative *do thou have* from *c.* 1525–55 Latimer in Visser (1963–73: section 1427), and, in an echo construction, negative imperative *don't have* in 1741 Richardson (1963–73: section 1447a):

(451)   a.   *Don't have* anything to say to the whiners at the gate.
                         (1832 H. Martineau *Homes Abroad* iii.47 [*OED*])
           b.   *Don't have* a thought on the matter.
                         (1958 O'Connor, *Habit of Being* 282 (17 May) [ARCHER])

For positive imperative *do be*, Visser has one example from 1749 Fielding, then 1837 Dickens. Between them comes:

(452)   Wherefore, as you are content with the property of a
          foreigner, pray *do* likewise *be* content with the privileges of a
          foreigner.

> (1796 Spence, *Meridian Sun of Liberty*, in *Pig's Meat*, ed. Gallop
> (Spokesman, 1982) Preface p. 108)

For negative imperative *do not/don't be*, Visser demonstrates a continuous history from 1590 Shakespeare onwards (1963–73: sections 1426, 1447b):

(453)   a. *Don't be* a fool, and nobody will be the wiser.

> (1832 Jerrold, *Rent Day* II.i, in *Works* (Bradbury & Evans, 1854)
> VIII.26 [ARCHER])

          b. And as for you, Mrs. Ruth, *don't you be* frightened

> (1892 Stockton, *Dusantes* II.44 [ARCHER])

Visser exaggerates when he writes that the older negative imperative *be not* 'drops into disuse after the end of the seventeenth century'. In fact it continued into the early part of our period, perhaps mainly in archaistic or high style:

(454)   a. *Be not alarmed*, miss

> (1785 MacNally, *Fashionable Levities* II.iii p. 31 [ARCHER])

          b. *Be not* then uneasy on any account

> (1803 Blake, *Letters* p. 80 (30 Jan.) [ARCHER])

          c. Oh, Martin, *be not* blind, – deaf, I mean, to our entreaties.

> (1813 Poole, *Hole in the Wall* II.i p. 28 [ARCHER])

The third person imperative is historically, perhaps still, identical to the present subjunctive:

(455)   a. (= 180) *Take* the pipe out of his mouth, somebody.

> (1841 Browning, *Pippa Passes* Poems (1905) 173 [*OED*])

          b. Someone *say* something.
          c. *Don't* anyone *say* anything.

Visser singles out a group of examples dated 1930 or later (1963–73: section 846), but he has some not dissimilar examples from early in the ModE period. Note that the pronoun in an appended tag question could be either *they* or *you*.

Several imperative-like patterns use the auxiliary LET. The subject of the lexical verb can be first or third person:

(456)   a. (= 221) *Let me* send you a line before I fall into a little pink
slumber.   (1889 Dowson, *Letters* 70 p. 111 (*c.* 21 Oct.))

        b. At this period Mrs. A read as if from a scroll in the air. 'Tell
him that he will become the Duke of Bedford *let him* regard
my words.'   (1873 *Amberley Papers* II.536 (19 Jan.))

The third person imperative with *let*, as in (456b), has become 'rather
archaic and elevated in tone' (Quirk, Greenbaum, Leech & Svartvik 1985:
11.26).

    The form *let's* or *lets* is particularly important. Hopper & Traugott (1993:
10–14) discuss the process of grammaticalisation of *lets* which permits
simultaneously in PDE a range of constructions. First there is the normal
second person imperative of the full verb LET 'allow':

(457)   a. Let us go. ('allow us to go')
        b. Let Bill go.

In (457a) *us* cannot be contracted. Then there is the 'first person imperative' (Quirk, Greenbaum, Leech & Svartvik 1985: 11.26) – that is, first
person *plural* – which is 'sometimes called an "adhortative" (involving
urging or encouraging)' (Hopper & Traugott 1993: 11):

(458)   Let's go to the circus tonight.

Here contraction is the norm. Some varieties now permit a first person singular:

(459)   Lets give you a hand.

And some even use *lets* as marker of a nonfirst-person adhortative:

(460)   a. Lets wash your hands.
        b. Lets eat our liver now, Betty.

though the cited examples are arguably still first person plurals involving
'the "phoney inclusive" *we*' (Zwicky 1977: 716) that used to be common in
hospitals (cf. *How are we feeling today?*), in which connection note the tag
question in:

(461)   'Just *swallow* it all, *shall we*, Mr Taber – just for me?'
            (1962 Kesey, *One Flew Over the Cuckoo's Nest* (Picador, 1973) 31)

    The 1 PL imperative with *let's* has three possible negations: *let's not V* and
don't let's V, both recorded from the seventeenth century, and AmerE *let's
don't V*, from 1918 (Visser 1963–73: section 1448):

(462)   a. the timid but natural suggestion, '*Don't let's!*'

                                         (1906 Nesbit, *Amulet* iv.57)

    b. An old guy . . . walked past, a placard around his neck:

        WOLVES. *Let's Don't* Breed Them. We Don't Need Them.

        (1996 E. Annie Proulx, *Accordion Crimes* (Fourth Estate, 1997) 455)

Different analogies are in conflict here: on the one hand that all negative imperatives start with *don't*, on the other that all 1 PL imperatives start with *let's*.

3.5.5   *Exclamatives*

Exclamative clauses, main or subordinate, have an initial *wh*-phrase containing *what* or *how*. (Other syntactic types with similar functions are discussed in 3.6.5.2 and 3.6.6.6 below.) *What* here is a predeterminer (*what a pity it is*) rather than the central determiner of interrogatives (*what point is there?*). Quirk, Greenbaum, Leech & Svartvik (1985: 11.31) remark on the rarity in PDE exclamatives of a whole prepositional phrase occurring as *wh*-element (pied-piping), but earlier examples are easy to find:

(463)   a. Good Heav'n! *to what an ebb of taste are women* fallen, that

                         (1777 (1781) Sheridan, *Scarborough* I.ii 577.22)

    b. *To what a sublime height will the superb edifice* attain!

                      (1789 Low, *Polititian Outwitted* II.ii p. 375 [ARCHER])

    c. *In what a slough of despond had he* come to wallow in

        consequence of   (1860–1 Trollope, *Framley* xxxiii.322)

The main change is in inversion practice. *How*-exclamatives allow subject-auxiliary inversion, (464a), though nowadays, and perhaps long since, only in literary usage, while *what*-exclamatives used to allow SAI (as in (463) and (464b)) but rarely do in PDE:

(464)   a. And you, my poor girl, *how shamefully has Robert* treated you.

                    (1863 Hazlewood, *Lady Audley's Secret* II.i p. 256)

    b. Oh *what a blessed change would it* be to her!

                     (1837 Gaskell, *Letters* 5 p. 9 (18 Mar.))

    c. *What a bore is this whooping cough.*

                     (1872 *Amberley Papers* II.512 (15 Aug.))

In subordinate exclamatives, inversion is not normally found:

(465)   a. Do you remember *how anxiously I looked* forward to the

        concomitants of my clerical life   (1861 Green, *Letters* 79 (Apr.))

b. I shudder to think *in what a depth of worldiness* [sic] *this great sorrow found* and struck me. (1862 ibid. 97 (25 Jul.))

c. I told him *what a superficial fellow I was*
(1869 Howells, *Selected Letters* I.333 (28 Jun.) [ARCHER])

There is also the possibility of what Huddleston calls subject VP inversion if the main verb is BE (1984: 373), where the whole verbal group is the pivot for inversion:

(466) *How acute must be that torture,* which seeks an asylum in suicide!
(1789 Brown, *Power of Sympathy* xxii.39 [ARCHER])

This is very much a literary usage in PDE.

3.6 Composite sentences

We can divide composite sentences – those involving more than one clause – according as the link is essentially one of co-ordination or subordination. My discussion of subordinate clauses divides them according to whether their function in the higher clause corresponds most closely to that of a noun, adjective or adverbial phrase; thus there are sections on nominal, relative and adverbial subordinate clauses, with the nominal ones further subdivided into finite and nonfinite types.

3.6.1 Coordinate clauses

Clauses linked by the co-ordinating conjunctions *and, or, but* are of equal status: both of them main clauses, or each dependent in parallel on some higher clause. Quirk, Greenbaum, Leech & Svartvik discuss co-ordination in their (1985: chapter 13). Traditionally *nor* is a co-ordinating conjunction meaning roughly 'and . . . not', or correlative with *neither*. It is now obsolete to use it with a following negative:

(467) a. 'Is that being kind . . . ?' asked Jane.
'*Nor* she is*n't* kind,' retorted Cyril. (1904 Nesbit, *Phoenix* iii.67)

b. 'I don't know that I think so *very* [original emphasis] much of that little song, Rat,' observed the Mole cautiously . . .
'*Nor* do*n't* the ducks *neither,*' replied the Rat cheerfully.
(1908 Grahame, *Wind in the Willows* ii.25)

Jespersen has a large collection of examples, with and without subject–auxiliary inversion (1909–49: VII 65–6). Example (467b) also shows loosely appended *neither,* mentioned in section 3.5.2.1 above.

For Quirk, Greenbaum, Leech & Svartvik's 'many speakers' (1985: 13.6) who allow another co-ordinating conjunction to precede *nor*, it is more like a conjunct. This, I suspect, is a recent development:

(468)   a. I don't approve of the man I've just described. *And nor*, I suspect, do you.   (1960 Rattigan, *Ross* II.i p. 72 [ARCHER])

            b. The Rhoosians couldn't stop him at Inkerman *and nor* will you.   (1974 F. Selwyn, *Cracksman on Velvet* ii.70 [*OED*])

So too is the use of *plus* as a co-ordinator:

(469)   Spanish officials said Spain would demand that the United States give up its use of the Torrejon Air Base outside Madrid and the standby Moron Air Base in southern Spain, *plus* boost both economic and military aid.

        (1975 *Atlanta Journal & Constitution* 26.1: 1, 13 (1 Jun.) [ARCHER])

And as for beginning an orthographic sentence with *And*, if that has become increasingly frequent in the twentieth century it is probably more a change in written decorum and in punctuation practice than in syntax.

The conjunct *else* 'otherwise' is usually now preceded by the conjunction *or*, but was formerly less tied to it:

(470)   Madam would look higher than Mr Ladislaw, *else* I don't know her.   (1871–2 George Eliot, *Middlemarch* liv.541)

On the combination of co-ordination and relativisation, see section 3.6.5.7.

3.6.2   *Types of nominal clause*

Nominal clauses vary in both function and form. In function they can be subject, direct (not indirect) object, complement, or appositive (*CHEL* III, forthcoming), in form they can have a verb which is finite or which is an infinitive or participle, and they may be introduced by a complementiser such as *that* (for a finite clause) or *for* (for certain infinitive clauses). First we must consider the choice between finite and nonfinite.

A long-term trend in English has been the growth of nonfinite complement clauses at the expense of finite clauses. Note the use of a contact clause (finite clause without complementiser) in (471) where (amongst other differences) modern idiom would prefer either a *to*-infinitive or object *it* + *that*-clause:

(471)   a. I only do not like *you sh^d* [= should] *marry anybody*.

                            (1817 Austen, *Letters* 140 p. 479 (20 Feb.))

    b. how I could not bear *you should be so*

                            (1819 Keats, *Letters* 138 p. 359 (15 Jul.))

    c. 'I beg *you will not do anything of the kind,*' Tertius,' said Rosamond

                    (1871–2 George Eliot, *Middlemarch* lviii.585)

Other contact clauses which are unlikely or impossible in PDE idiom include:

(472)   a. it is impossible *you should look with such eyes upon me as I have upon*

      you: it cannot be.   (1819 Keats, *Letters* 139 p. 361 (25 Jul.))

    b. I wish *you may ever be like him*.

                  (1852 Taylor & Reade, *Masks and Faces* I.ii p. 139)

Note that WISH has had many complementation types since OE or ME, including finite clauses with present or present subjunctive or *may* (*OED* s.v., 1(b)); past or past subjunctive (the usage which makes it a 'hypothesis verb' in the terminology of Quirk, Greenbaum, Leech & Svartvik 1985: 16.33); and infinitival clauses. The first, illustrated by (472b) above, has become obsolete in the twentieth century.

The string ALLOW *NP to be* was formerly ambiguous between two meanings of ALLOW, namely 'acknowledge, admit' and 'permit':

(473)   for tho' Mrs. Candour is a little talkative Everybody *allows her to be* the best natured and best sort of Woman

                (1777 Sheridan, *School for Scandal* I.i 364.23)

Here context makes clear that we have the former of the two meanings. Subsequently the ambiguity has been resolved by syntactic differentiation, the former meaning (insofar as it survives at all) occurring with a *that*-clause, and the latter only with NP + infinitive.

3.6.3   *Finite nominal subordinate clauses*

3.6.3.1   Links introducing nominal clauses

The most neutral clause connective is *that*, and all sorts of finite nominal clause have *that* as complementiser.

After a negative clause it was formerly common to use the connective *but that*, usually to imply a negative in the subordinate:

(474)   a. that I was not sure *but that* he was having [= that he was not having] a good-humoured jest with me.

                (1849–50 Dickens, *David Copperfield* xiv.173 [Poutsma])

    b. For there was no doubt *but that* Bessie was lovely
                 (1887 Rider Haggard, *Jess* (Murray, 1926) iii.26 [Poutsma])

Colloquial in the nineteenth century, but no longer standard, is *but what*:

(475)   a. who knew *but what* he might yet be lingering in the
           neighbourhood willing all sorts of awful things!
                  (1851–3 Gaskell, *Cranford* x.94 [Poutsma])
    b. Not *but what* facts might be so strong as to make it absolutely
           necessary that she should do this.
                  (1860–1 Trollope, *Framley* xliii.417)
    c. it's getting so I can't install the simplest frigging component
           but what I need a bracer.
        (1962 Kesey, *One Flew Over the Cuckoo's Nest* (Picador, 1973) 32)

Poutsma has a full discussion of the various types (1914–29 II: 609–14, V: 792–3). Some are now obsolete.

    After verbs like APPEAR, HAPPEN, OCCUR, SEEM, the normal finite clause complement is a *that*-clause, analysable as an extraposed subject:

(476)   It occurred/seemed to me *that he was lying*.
(476′)   *That he was lying* occurred/**seemed to me.

Example (476) is from Quirk, Greenbaum, Leech & Svartvik (1985: 16.60n.), though the SEEM version of (476′) shows that their analysis is problematic (even without the bizarre suggestion that the verbs are monotransitive). The following example may have *so that* as complementiser (unless there is a pause after *so*):

(477)   It happened *so that* the surliness of his liquor and his nature
        mingled at this moment with a certain exultation, a sense of
        good-luck, and a strong desire to talk and be told again of it.
               (1872 Blackmore, *Maid of Sker* xi.100 [ARCHER])

The extraposed subject clause (if that is what it is) blends with a result clause.

    That is in variation with zero in most contexts apart from nonextraposed subject clauses (Quirk, Greenbaum, Leech & Svartvik 1985: 15.4). I give examples of contact clauses – finite clauses with zero complementiser – in object position, (478), predicative complement, (479), and apposition, (480):

(478)   he suggested [∅] these could be done anytime.
               (1891 Sidney Webb, *Letters* 169 I.314 (24 Oct.))

(479)   and the result is [∅] I've applied and outlined a reasonable
          scheme for the Government of this country
                                        (1917 Bell, *Letters* II.410 (11 May))

(480)   and the fact [∅] stocks at retail are low in many lines has escaped
          attention   (1961 *Brown Corpus*, Miscellaneous H29:4)

In environments where zero is possible it is often the more colloquial
variant. Rissanen had reported a rapid increase in zero during the eModE
period, with a possible slowdown before PDE (1991a). Finegan & Biber
(1995) use the data of ARCHER to suggest tentatively that zero was preferred in Letters until 1750, but that *that* was preferred thereafter; in
Sermons and Medicine it was preferred throughout (i.e. from 1650).

    Thompson & Mulac (1991), as reported in Hopper & Traugott (1993:
201–3), discuss the grammaticalisation of strings like *I think/guess*.
Compare these pairs of examples:

(481)   a. I believe I was mistaken in *thinking that* my paper must be
             ready by the 22nd inst – there may be more time.
                                    (1891 Sidney Webb, *Letters* 145 I.277 (14 Jul.))
          b. but I *do think that* gradually you must leave it off.
                                          (1872 *Amberley Papers* II.527 (10 Sep.))
(482)   a. Fr. [= Frank] said, 'Well, *I think [∅]* you'd better not . . .'
                                                    (ibid. II.521 (21 Aug.))
          b. Bertrand, *I think*, is his granny's favourite
                                                    (1874 ibid. II.562 (26 Mar.))

In (481) THINK is clearly the higher verb, and a *that*-clause is dependent
on it. In (482), on the other hand, the phrase *I think* is more or less
conventionalised as a **parenthetical**. In such use – typically involving the
verb THINK or GUESS in a first person declarative or second person
interrogative – various changes can be detected: *that* is omitted, the phrase
takes on the positional mobility of an adverbial, it becomes possible to
regard *I think* as embedded in the other clause rather than vice versa, and
there is a reduction of certainty in the meaning of THINK. In BrE the
grammaticalisation of *I think* is well established: the phrase occurs 91
times in my letters corpus with a contact clause or parenthetically and
only once with a *that*-clause as complement.[76] *I guess* is uncommon in the
corpus (ratio 3:0 contact/parenthetical:*that*-clause), and some more frequent alternatives include *I suppose* (ratio 28:2), *I believe* (26:3), *you know*
(19:6),[77] *I hear* (4:3). All of these have been in parenthetical use since
before our period.

There are, of course, other parenthenticals; see the discussion of what Quirk, Greenbaum, Leech & Svartvik call 'comment clauses' (1985: 15.53–4). In the following unreal conditional, *I'm sure* must be treated as parenthetical if the apodosis is to have a past tense modal, here *should*, as its finite verb (cf. 3.3.4.2 above):

(483)   '. . . And I can't see him from here, and if I'd got out of bed to
         see *I'm sure* I should have fainted.'   (1904 Nesbit, *Phoenix* xii.241)

(In the letters corpus *I am sure* – never written *I'm sure*, incidentally – is an established parenthetical, ratio 10:0.)

Complementation by an appositive clause linked to an NP such as *the fact* is sometimes replaced by a plain *that*-clause:

(484)   a. We had tacitly agreed to *ignore that* any with whom we
            associated on terms of visiting equality could ever be
            prevented by poverty from doing anything that they wished.
                                            (1851–3 Gaskell, *Cranford* i.4)
         b. 'It is impossible for us to *ignore that* someone may have
            recklessly chosen to imitate . . .'
                            (1993 *The Guardian* p. 9 [American speaker] (21 Oct.))
         c. 'There's no data to *support that* these findings are related to
            dietary iron,' says Harold Sandstead, professor of preventive
            medicine and community health at the University of Texas at
            Galveston.   (1994 *New Scientist* 1919: 11 (2 Apr.))
(484´)   a. We had tacitly agreed to ignore the fact/possibility that
         b. It is impossible for us to ignore the fact/possibility/
            suggestion that
         c. There's no data to support the suggestion/claim/hypothesis
            that

The following usage is very characteristic of Mrs Gaskell:

(485)   He *named that* he had also invited his cousin, Miss Pole;
                                            (1851–3 Gaskell, *Cranford* iv.30)

There are sporadic examples throughout the period of what Warner calls CLAN-sentences, standing for clause and nominal (1982: 91–9), where a nominal element (italicised in (486)) stands in apposition to a finite clause containing a pronoun (also italicised) coreferential with part of it, such that nominal and clause together occupy only a single argument position in the structure of the higher verb:

(486)   a. Look *to Catherine Lee* how carefully *she* avoids making her
feelings the subject of her thoughts

(1825 Martineau, *Letters* p. 5 (12 May))

b. And he had thought as well *of Rudy*: how in *him* he might have
found his prophet

(1957 Buechner, *Return of Ansel Gibbs* viii.176 [ARCHER])

Sentences like (486a) are only marginally acceptable in standard; (486b)
is better because the punctuation or intonation downgrades the sense
of apposition between nominal and clause and suggests instead a fresh
start by the writer/speaker, reformulating the complement of the
higher verb.

Some verbs in the nineteenth century permitted a *whether*-clause as complement where PDE usage would not. THINK, for instance, now generally
takes a dependent interrogative clause only in nonassertive contexts:

(487)   a. (= 417a) I have been several times *thinking whether or not* I
should . . .   (1818 Keats, *Letters* 98 p. 252 (17 Dec.))

b. The porter . . . *suggested* to the gentleman, as there was so
much luggage, *whether* he would not take a second cab.

(1877 Sewell, *Black Beauty* xlvii.203)

3.6.3.2   Direct and indirect speech

Indirect speech is distinguished linguistically from the direct speech which
it reports by various deictic shifts, including backshifting of tense if the
verb of reporting is in the past tense (see 3.3.1 above):

(488)   He wrote to inform me that Mr Du Roveray *went* to Ireland
tomorrow   (1784 Betsy Sheridan, *Journal* 1 p. 28 (1 Oct.))

Modern conventions of punctuation omit overt signals of quotation –
quotation marks, dashes, indentation, or whatever – when the quotation is
anything but wholly direct, but in earlier usage it was possible to retain such
punctuation when indirect speech was particularly faithful to the idiom of
the original, as in the following examples, where I have italicised linguistic
signs of indirect speech:

(489)   a. Marianne sends 'a kiss and a love, and *wants* to come & see
you.'   (*c.* 1837 Gaskell, *Letters* 6 p. 12)

b. 'Of *himself* he *would* say nothing, though of course such a
marriage would ruin *him* in the county.' 'My dear,' said his
wife, 'that is nonsense . . .'

(1867 Trollope, *Last Chronicle of Barset* II.xlix.59)

   c. '*She had* never,' she said, 'even tried to remember what
      arrangements *had* been made by lawyers, but *she hoped* that
      Mary *might* be so circumstanced, that if her happiness *depended*
      on marrying a poor man, want of money need not prevent it.'
                  (1879–80 Trollope, *Duke's Children* (OUP, 1954) ii.10)

   d. (= 100c) and, as she said later, over tea and cold tongue, 'it
          was that sudden it made *her* flesh creep.'
                         (1906 Nesbit, *Amulet* xiv.262)

Such examples represent a sort of halfway house between direct and indirect speech, as there is no formal subordination to the verb of reporting.

They differ, however, from **free indirect speech**, where the actual words spoken (or thought) are transformed by the usual deictic shifts of indirect speech, including backshifting of tense, but without any overt subordination to, or indeed use of, a verb of reporting (and certainly no quotation punctuation). During our period this technique was developed and perfected by novelists, though a recent study by Adamson (1994) suggests that the technique was not the pure invention of Jane Austen and her contemporaries but had a longer gestation in literature and indeed in ordinary language use. Her paper gives useful references to other studies of the phenomenon.

3.6.3.3 Subjunctive in nominal clauses

Many contexts permit a present subjunctive. One such is clauses which complement an adjective, noun or verb whose meaning encompasses desire, obligation, or the like, a usage often called the **mandative subjunctive**:

(490)   a. Jerry knew it was *imperative* she *be got* some place where it was
        dry and warm.   (1947 Gallico, *The Lonely* (Joseph) i.39 [Visser])
    b. It is just as *important* that America *maintain*, if not *increase*, this
        stock-piling leadership as it is for her to develop the H-bomb.
                  (1950 *Daily Mail* 4/2 (30 May) [Visser])
    c. and Jo wrathfully *proposed* that Mr. Davis *be arrested* without
        delay   (1868 Alcott, *Little Women* (Collins, 1952) vii.89 [Visser])
    d. Many leading American professionals *ask* that the 'floater' *be*
        adopted as the official standard ball [*sc.* in golf].
                   (1927 *Daily Express* 29 Sept. 9 [*OED*])[78]
    e. If the King Street commissars were not so invincibly stupid,
        they would have *insisted* that the movement *be left* severely
        alone.   (1964 C. Driver, *Disarmers* iii. 72 [*OED*])

(491)   a. (= 179) [it was believed] that the Secretary of State gave *orders*
           that the flag *not be dipped*

                              (1948 *Christian Science Monitor* 4 (22 Sep.) [Kirchner, Visser])

        b. I respectfully *request* that I *not answer* that question.

                       (1954 *N.Y. Herald Tribune*, European edn. (23 Feb.)
                                        [Zandvoort, Visser])

The present subjunctive may be used in such clauses regardless of tense marking in the higher clause, as witnessed by this rewriting of (490c):

(490′)   *c.* and Jo wrathfully *proposes* that Mr. Davis *be arrested* without delay

A virtually synonymous construction, which in BrE has tended to supplant the present subjunctive in such patterns, is to begin the verbal group with the modal verb *should*:

(490″) *c.* . . . $\left\{ \begin{array}{l} \textit{proposes} \\ \textit{proposed} \end{array} \right\}$ that Mr. Davis *should be arrested*

Another alternative in some examples, especially in BrE, is the indicative, which does need appropriate tense marking:

(490‴) *c.* . . . $\left\{ \begin{array}{l} \textit{proposes} \\ \textit{proposed} \end{array} \right\}$ that Mr. Davis $\left\{ \begin{array}{l} \textit{is} \\ \textit{was} \end{array} \right\}$ *arrested*

Would it even be possible to have the past subjunctive here when the higher verb is past?

(490⁗) *c.* ?and Jo wrathfully *proposed* that Mr. Davis *were arrested* without delay

If so, it would be a rare context in which present and past subjunctive were in contrastive distribution. My one possible example so far is doubtful:

(492)   'I flew to the Psammead and *wished* that your infant brother *were restored* to your midst, and immediately it was so.'

                                     (1904 Nesbit, *Phoenix* xii.242)

Quirk, Greenbaum, Leech & Svartvik omit WISH from their list of 'suasive' verbs that can take a mandative subjunctive and list it only as a 'hypothesis verb' taking a past subjunctive (1985: 16.32, 33).

    In BrE the present subjunctive in examples like (490–1) has retreated to high-flown literary or legal language – indeed Mossé (1947: 208) quotes a pre-First World War writer who speaks of it as defunct – though Barber

(1964: 133–4) detects a post-Second World War revival in literary usage, which he traces to administrative language. In America, however, the present subjunctive after verbs of requesting, etc., is the norm (Algeo 1992: 61).

In clauses expressing uncertainty, a subjunctive has been rare throughout lModE outside conditional and concessive clauses (3.6.6.3 below), and the usual verb forms are *should* + *V* or, increasingly, the indicative:

(493) a. he expressed his *surprise* that the rooms *should* so long *have remained* undiscovered

(1791 Radcliffe, *Romance of the Forest* ix.422 [ARCHER])

     b. and I rather *wonder* that Eleanor *should not take* it for her own.

(1818 Austen, *Northanger Abbey* II.ix[xxiv].196 [Phillipps])

(493´) a. that the rooms had so long remained undiscovered

     b. that Eleanor does not take it for her own

Where unreality is involved, certain nominal subordinate clauses permit a past subjunctive, or a past perfect which may be regarded as subjunctive (see 3.3.4.2 above):

(494) a. I wish I *were* more worthy of you

(1891 Sidney Webb, *Letters* 153 I.288 (7 Sep.))

     b. I dined en Pologne as usual yesterday, & wished you *had been* there.   (1890 Dowson, *Letters* 91 p. 139 (23 Feb.))

     c. SNEER. Why I thought, Dangle, you *had been* an admirable linguist!

DANGLE. So I am, if they would not talk so damn'd fast.

(1779 (1781) Sheridan, *Critic* I.ii 510.22)

     d. 'I thought the Miss Musgroves *had been* ['would have been'] here . . .'   (1818 Austen, *Persuasion* I.ix.79 [Visser])

Except after WISH, WOULD/HAD RATHER, and imperative SUPPOSE, the type is now obsolete. For some more examples see Visser (1963–73: sections 2038–41). It remains normal after conjunctions expressing a rejected comparison:

(495) a. Somehow I feel *as though* I'*d known* you quite a long time already.   (1906 Nesbit, *Amulet* vii.111)

     b. I feel *as if* I *had jumped* into old age during the last two years. You would scarcely believe from outside I am the same person, but inside I am not changed.

(1918 Bell, *Letters* II.450 (6 Mar.))

3.6.4   *Nonfinite nominal subordinate clauses*

Nonfinite nominal clauses vary along at least two dimensions: whether – and if so, how – the subject of the clause is expressed, and whether the non-finite verb is a plain infinitive, a *to*-infinitive, an *-ing*, or a past participle. The following sections consider the main areas of change during our period. Another possibility, *and* + plain infinitive, is considered in section 3.6.6.7.

3.6.4.1   Complementation with *-ing* versus *to*-infinitive

In Present-Day English there are tendencies but no firm rules as to what kind of nonfinite clause a verb may take. Compare:

(496)   I *enjoy*   { *riding* / **to ride }   my bike.

(497)   I *like*   { *riding* / *to ride* }   my bike.

(498)   I *want*   { **riding / *to ride* }   my bike.

See Quirk, Greenbaum, Leech & Svartvik (1985: 16.40) for some discussion, and for changes in distribution over recent centuries, Visser (1963–73: sections 1771–96), e.g. section 1780 on TRY. Strang (1970: 100) suggests that *-ing* has been gaining ground over the *to*-infinitive, which is true with REMEMBER 'recall' and REIGN:

(499)   a.   Henry was a greater blade ['gallant'] than ever I *remember to have seen* him.   (1819 Keats, *Letters* 156 p. 419 (20 Sep.))
        b.   She *remembered to have heard* that cows . . . are susceptible to the soothing influence of the human voice.
                                           (1904 Nesbit, *Phoenix* viii.167)
        c.   with a penetrating voice that would not let him *feign to have found* it in his pocket;
                               (1876 George Eliot, *Daniel Deronda*, ed. Handley
                                           (Clarendon, 1984) VIII.lxviii.736)

It is true, too, with a number of verbs where the *to* which was formerly a marker of the following infinitive has now been reanalysed as belonging with the higher verb:

(500)   a.   since I have felt how much new Objects *contribute to keep off* a sense of Ennui and fatigue
                                           (1818 Keats, *Letters* 72 p. 157 (27 Jun.))

b. you cannot yet *accustom yourself to accuse and revile* me
  (1847 C. Brontë, *Jane Eyre*, ed. Jack & Smith (Clarendon, 1969)
  III.i[xxvii].382)

c. whether, in such a case, he was to *look forward to be disinherited*.
  (1867 Trollope, *Last Chronicle of Barset* II.xlix.59)

d. In the meantime, at the palace, Mrs. Proudie had been *reduced to learn* what was going on from Mr. Thumble.   (ibid. II.liv.127)

e. I will not *submit to be ruined* by the extravagance and profligacy of any man.   (1838–9 Dickens, *Nickleby* xxxiv.428)

Normal usage for (500) since the second half of the nineteenth century would be complementation by *to* + *Ving*, with a period of variation for each verb:

(501)   a. that Celia *objected to go*   (1871–2 George Eliot, *Middlemarch* x.87)
      b. but the signs she made of this were such as only Lydgate *was used to interpret*.   (ibid. lxxviii.777)

(502)   a. what he *objects to giving*, is a little return on rent-days to help a tenant to buy stock   (ibid. xxxviii.383)
      b. but she had *been* little *used to imagining* other people's states of mind   (ibid. lxxviii.777)

It may possibly be significant that (501a) is the author's voice and (502a) (fictional) journalism, but Eliot elsewhere in the novel uses *objection to seeing* (lxxiv.741), where the abstract noun has gone the same way as the verb; cf. the older

(503)   'I think,' faltered Mr. Winkle, 'that Sam would have no *objection to do* so . . .'   (1836–7 Dickens, *Pickwick* xliv.684)

The change in complementation reflects two long-term changes, I think. One is the rise of the prepositional verb, as OBJECT and *to* come to form a unit (and likewise the other cases exemplified in (500)). The other is the drift of the English infinitive from a nominal to a verbal character, now virtually complete, and the concomitant dissociation of the infinitive marker *to* from the homonymous preposition. An English infinitive cannot collocate with the determiner *the*, for instance, unlike its Dutch or German counterparts. Consider the effect of these changes on *to depart*:

(504)   a. Max objected to departure.
      b. Max objected to depart.
      c. Max objected to departing.

The former parallelism between (504a) and (504b) lost its force, and (504c) became necessary, since the gerund was the only form capable of combining the distribution of an NP with the possibility of its own verbal adjuncts and complements (e.g. *departing surreptitiously*).

In other cases PDE usage has *of* + *Ving*:

(505)   a. If it had not been your dreadful distance I wd have
          telegraphed but what was the *use to send* sad news
                              (1873 *Amberley Papers* II.539 (10 May))

        b. I was *in hopes* some little time back *to be able* to releive [sic] your
          dullness by my spirits   (1818 Keats, *Letters* 69 p. 150 (10 Jun.))

There are, however, some verbs which seem to have moved away from, rather than towards, complementation by *-ing*, such as FAIL, INTEND, PROPOSE, PURPOSE, since such usages as (506) seem less likely now (though in the case of (506a) it may be the obsolescence of the verb itself rather than of that usage):

(506)   a. I believe I told you I *purposed going* to Hastings next week.
                         (1890 Dowson, *Letters* 94 p. 142 (14 Mar.))

        b. and he *proposes coming* on here
                  (1871 (1868) Collins, *Moonstone*, ed. Trodd (World's Classics,
                          1982) 2nd per., 1st narr., viii.283)

        c. When Rachel *declined eating* anything   (ibid. vii.276)

Visser (1963–73: section 1779) exaggerates the success of the *-ing* construction after INTEND, which probably does still prefer the *to*-infinitive:

(507)   I had *intended to delay* seeing you till a Book which I am now
      publishing was out   (1820 Keats, *Letters* 219 p. 495 (23 Jun.))

However, the *-ing* construction has been found since at least the early eighteenth century (1706 Helsinki Corpus *intend asking*), and the two remain in competition. (In (507) the *-ing* might well have been ruled out by the infelicity of ***intended delaying seeing*.)

3.6.4.2   Indirect object + *to*-infinitive

The definition of **indirect object** is a tricky matter, and not all scholars would follow Quirk, Greenbaum, Leech & Svartvik (1985: 16.66) in including the NP of patterns like PERSUADE *NP to V* under that heading. The following example is less controversial in that regard:

(508)   The publishers . . . then *offered the author to purchase* the copyright
    for £100
                    (?1911 Thomas Seccombe, Introduction p. ix to Gaskell,
                                Mary Barton, Everyman edn.))

Since it is ungrammatical in PDE (indeed it greatly postdates *OED*'s seventeenth-century examples s.v. *offer* v. 3b), it illustrates a narrowing of complementation possibilities with OFFER. Yet without the indirect object, or with a nominal rather than infinitival direct object, (508) would correspond to normal PDE possibilities.

Conversely, perhaps, the following use of CONVINCE is fairly recent and American in origin (1958 in *OED* s.v., 3f); its novelty in BrE is perhaps demonstrated by its inclusion in Quirk, Greenbaum, Leech & Svartvik (1985: 9.2) but omission from their 16.63. It is now quite common:

(509) In the early 1980s, the observatory *convinced San Diego and other cities in the area to replace* their high-pressure sodium lights
(1993 Rosie Mestel [American], *New Scientist* 1878: 5 (19 Jun.))

In it CONVINCE becomes more like PERSUADE.

3.6.4.3 Gerunds

I shall use the term **gerund** for a nominal *-ing* form with verbal properties. I discuss them here because gerundial constructions tend to bear closest resemblance to nonfinite nominal clauses, even though combinations of preposition and gerundial construction 'can also approach (non-finite) adverbial clauses', as Rissanen points out (*CHEL* III, forthcoming). A gerundial clause is nonfinite and has a nominal function – subject, object, prepositional object, etc. – in some higher clause:

(510) a. *Eating people* is wrong.
b. I don't like *watching films alone*.
c. He objects to *being corrected all the time*.

Within its own clause the gerund may have many of the properties of an ordinary verb, such as occurrence with an object or with adverbials.

Where the subject of a gerund is expressed, there is a choice of case:

(511 = 45) a. I don't like *his* being late.
b. I don't like *him* being late.

The (511a) type is the older:

(512) a. and *his* just now refusing to pay me a part, is a proof of it.
(1777 (1781) Sheridan, *Scarborough* I.ii 580.37)
b. Sir Tunbelly Clumsey, my relation . . . is apprized of *his lordship's* being down here   (ibid. I.ii 581.4)
c. Every one laughed at the idea of *the cook's* being engaged as queen   (1904 Nesbit, *Phoenix* iii.73)

Visser has full collections of material on the rise of the form seen in (511b) (1963–73: sections 1090–1104, and further references section 1096), considerably antedating many of Jespersen's findings (1909–49: V 121–35). Nevertheless Jespersen's account of the *reasons* for the development is helpful. They include the identity in sound – and intermittently in spelling too – of the common case and genitive of most plural nouns and some names, (513), and similarly the morphological ambiguity of 3 SG feminine *her*, and the unavailability or awkwardness of any genitive for various sorts of NP, including nonpersonal pronouns, (514), co-ordinated NPs (515), or NPs with postmodifying prepositional phrase, (516):

(513)   a. and I don't wonder at *the young fellows* raving about her.
                               (1848 Thackeray, *Pendennis* xi.118 [Jespersen])
         b. William was flamingly indignant at *Mr Briggs* being too late
                               (1841 Gaskell, *Letters* 16 p. 47 (23 Dec.))

(514)   when I think of *this* being the last time of seeing you
                       (1816 Austen, *Mansfield Park* III.v[xxxvi].359 [Jespersen])

(515)   I don't think there is much likelihood, of *you and Miss Fairfax* being united.   (1895 Wilde, *Importance* II p. 138 [Jespersen])

(516)   upon *my application for her address* being refused
                       (1857 C. Brontë, *Professor*, ed. Smith & Rosengarten
                       (Clarendon, 1987) xx.185 [Jespersen])

Jespersen argues that other factors favouring the common case were for the subject NP to be indefinite or to have an inanimate referent. What is clear is that the competition between genitive and objective case had started before the lModE period, though in educated usage and outside the special circumstances exemplified by (513–16), the genitive remained the preferred option until some time in the present century. Indeed with personal pronouns a preference for the genitive form was often vociferously expressed in the prescriptive tradition, and even detected as genuinely current by more enlightened observers like Curme in 1912 and Jespersen in 1940. According to Visser, objective pronouns occurred occasionally from the end of the fifteenth century onwards, and then with ever increasing frequency 'from about the middle of the nineteenth century' (1963–73: section 1102), though Dekeyser's study shows proportions of nongenitive subject pronouns ranging only from 2.3 per cent to 6.7 per cent (1975: 180–1). By the late nineteenth century, their use was being variously recognised by observers as dialectal, vulgar, or merely colloquial. By now the balance has definitely tilted their way for nonpronominal NPs. As for pronominal NPs, Quirk, Greenbaum, Leech & Svartvik issue mixed messages on their current status, suggesting at one point that genitives like (511a) are 'preferred' with personal reference and if 'the style is formal', and at another that they are 'often felt to be awkward or stilted' (1985: 15.12, 16.42).

When the *-ing*-clause is itself sentence-initial, the genitive may still be preferable in all styles, so long as the subject is not dummy *there* (Quirk, Greenbaum, Leech & Svartvik 1985: 15.12):

(517)   a. *Our going to France* was ill-advised.
        b. ?*Us going to France* was ill-advised.

Sporadically, a subjective case may appear as subject of a gerund:

(518)   a. I recollect *Peggotty and I* peeping out at them from my little
           window   (1849–50 Dickens, *David Copperfield* ii.19 [Jespersen])
        b. But thats [*sic*] a very different thing from killing a man because
           he's a German and *he* killing you because youre [*sic*] an
           Englishman.
                          (1932 Shaw, *Too True to be Good* III p. 1161 [Jespersen])

Jespersen's collection of such examples (1909–49: V 135–6) tends to involve either hypercorrection in coordinate NPs (on which see 3.2.2.3 above), or confusion with an absolute construction, as in *He being dead, (the estate passed to his son)* (see 3.6.6.6 below).[79]

Being a nominal, a gerund may be modified by determiners and adjectives, (519), and its subject or object may be expressed in a prepositional phrase, (520):

(519)   a. I don't object so much to *the eating* as to *the excessive drinking*.
        b. *Such determined shirking of responsibilities* is typical of him.
(520)   a. They didn't like *all that shouting of/by the audience*.
        b. *The finding of the body* was the crucial breakthrough.

This behaviour is just what might be expected of an abstract action noun (cf. *the excessive consumption, the discovery of the body*). When the gerund has verbal complements and adjuncts, however, PDE usage prefers to avoid such nominal behaviour, apart from a possible genitive determiner to mark the subject of the gerund. Earlier usage was evidently more amenable to mixing nominal behaviour (a nongenitive determiner) with verbal (e.g. taking a direct object):

(521) a. I have since known no Pleasure equal to *the reducing others, to the Level of my own injured Reputation*

          (1777 Sheridan, *School for Scandal* I.i 360.14)

    b. he sought to be left alone, and spared *the being seen so subdued and weak.*   (1855–7 Dickens, *Little Dorrit* II.xxix.734)

    c. *The copying them* has been and still is my occupation . . . and I am trying to get the printing done also while I am finishing the copying.   (1873 *Amberley Papers* II.540)

    d. At least I can't fix on any tangible object or aim in life which seems so desirable as *the having got it finally over* – & *the remaining in perpetuo without desire or aim or consciousness whatsoever.*

          (1890 Dowson, *Letters* 95 p. 144 (28 Mar.))

The converse mixture was also found, with nominal behaviour (complement in an *of*-phrase) combined with verbal behaviour (e.g. adverbial modification):

(522) a. *The shutting of the gates regularly at ten o'clock* . . . had rendered our residence . . . very irksome to me.

          (1818 Mary Shelley, *Frankenstein*, ed. Rieger (Bobbs-Merrill, 1974) II.i[ix].86 [van der Wurff])

    b. then, with a more comical expression of face than before and *a settling of himself comfortably* . . . he launched into some new wonder . . .

          (1840–1 Dickens, *Master Humphrey's Clock* iii.60 [Visser])

Fanego (1996: 134) notes that the hybrid pattern seen in (521) did not become at all common until 1650. Visser claims that it was as frequent until 1900 as the equivalent pattern with *of* before the object NP, and he suggests that its subsequent rapid decline was due to successful criticism by prescriptive grammarians (1963–73: section 1124, and note also section 1040). As for (522), they too had dropped out of use by the end of the nineteenth century (Visser 1963–73: section 1120).

Varying mixtures of nominal and verbal properties in the gerund have been carefully traced through the ModE period by Wim van der Wurff, who argues that 'by 1900 . . . the construction had to be either completely nominal or completely verbal' (1993: 367). Van der Wurff doubts that Visser's explanation is adequate, since the cited grammarians are not unanimously condemnatory of (521) and fail altogether to mention other mixed types, including those like (522). Instead, or at least in addition, van der Wurff suggests that the gerund construction, originally of mixed nominal and verbal character, came to be polarised into one or other of the two: either nominal, by analogy with the increasingly frequent deverbal abstract nouns like *blockage, erasure, fulfilment*, or verbal, by analogy with the ever more frequent progressive. But note the rare PDE examples mentioned by Visser and by Quirk, Greenbaum, Leech & Svartvik (1985: 15.12n.[d], 15.14) with a determiner other than a genitive before a clausal *-ing*.

(523)   a. I'm tired of *all that feeding the animals every day.*
        b. *This smoking your pipe on every possible occasion* will ruin your
           health.
        c. There's *no making – you Serious* a Moment.
                        (1777 Sheridan, *School for Scandal* IV.i 409.1)
        d. It is *the thinking ourselves innocent.*

3.6.4.4   Raising

The subject-raising construction is one in which the surface subject of a higher verb (or other predicate) is not an argument of that verb and can be regarded instead as underlyingly the subject of a lower verb:

(524)   Nobody seems to have turned up.

(Such a claim justifies the inclusion of the construction in a section on nominal clauses, since the whole subordinate clause *nobody to have turned up* functions as an argument of the higher verb.) It can be found at least since the ME period, but the set of verbs and adjectives which permit it is subject to change. Some innovations have not prospered, for instance a raising construction with *inevitable/safe* 'certain':[80]

(525)   a. Society had better shut up shop at once, for it's *safe* to be
           'uprooted from its very foundations'.
                        (1852 Smedley, *L. Arundel* xxvii.204 [*OED*])
        b. But it is clear that here two mistakes are *inevitable* to occur.
                        (1903 Edward Carpenter, *Art of Creation* (George Allen, 1907)
                                            v.86 [Jespersen])
        c. 'You'll have a revolt of your slaves if you're not careful,' said
           the Queen.
           'Oh, no,' said Cyril; 'you see they have votes – that makes
           them *safe* not to revolt . . .'   (1906 Nesbit, *Amulet* viii.148)

Jespersen has some further examples (1909–49: III 212–13). The semantic area of certainty is apparently one with a high turnover of raising predicates. Several have moved from a subjective construction to a raising construction in which the certainty is that of the speaker/writer:

(526) He is sure to return.
   a. 'He is/feels certain that he will return.'
   b. 'It is certain that he will return.'

With *sure* the newer, raising construction, (526b), can be traced back at least to eModE, but the older construction, (526a), lingered on well into our period before being wholly replaced by other constructions (*sure that . . . , sure of Ving*).

   In the same way, verbs like HAPPEN have moved from a construction in which a personal NP is an oblique argument of HAPPEN – the norm for similar verbs in OE – to one where it is an argument only of the lower verb (Denison 1993a: 231–4). Compare:

(527) a. But, it *happened to me* the other night to be lying . . . with my
          eyes wide open;
                           (1852 Dickens, *Lying Awake*, in *Reprinted Pieces* 431)
       b. What *happened you*?
       (1993 Roddy Doyle, *Paddy Clarke Ha Ha Ha* (Minerva, 1994) p. 275)

(528) *The head-master . . . happened* to be sitting in conclave with some of
       the assistant teachers.   (1862 C. Stretton, *Cheq. Life* I. 20 [*OED*])

Examples (527) are late survivals of the older type, with (527b) probably now an Irish usage; type (528) with raising has been the norm throughout our period.

   Overall, then, the long-term trend with raising is of increase. The verb LOOK, for instance, developed a raising usage just prior to our period (Visser 1963–73: section 1254, *OED* s.v., v. 9c):

(529) The infield, or town-land . . . *looked* to be good.
                                        (1801 *Farmer's Mag.* Nov. 420 [*OED*])

As for SOUND, the PDE raising pattern is not listed by Visser or by the *OED*. Elizabeth Traugott (1997) has traced the development of PROMISE and THREATEN as raising verbs, so used from the eighteenth century. My examples (530) show transparency to subject selection, so that they must have undergone semantic change from earlier meanings which required an animate, agentive subject NP:

(530) a. Why, this adventure *promises* to be interesting!
                           (1813 H. Cowley, *A Day in Turkey* (1792), in *Works* (1813),
                                                      I.iii II.258 [WWP])

b. The parsonage slowly rises and *promises* to be as pretty as London smoke will suffer it.

   (1863 Green, *Letters* 121 (25 Apr.))

c. As he fought with the stone now, pains shot through his head, and his arms *threatened* to come away at the shoulders;

   (1891 Barrie, *Little Minister* xviii.146 [ARCHER])

As a result they can be epistemic verbs. Traugott claims to find further evidence of incipient grammaticalisation which would take them beyond mere raising verbs and towards being a kind of auxiliary.

3.6.5 Relative clauses

As a first approximation, relative clauses can be defined as post-modifying clauses. They can be classified according to the nature of their **antecedent** – the constituent which they qualify. Consider these examples, where it is the relative clause which is italicised:

(531)   a. The boy *who caused the trouble* was looking for kicks.
        b. The fire was soon put out, *which was lucky*.
        c. He got *what he wanted*.

The principal type of relative clause, (531a), is **adnominal** in that it qualifies a noun or pronoun (or, in an X-bar grammar, an $\bar{N}$), which is why our rather traditional classification of subordinate clauses implicitly classes relative clauses as adjectival (cf. *the troublesome boy*) and keeps them separate from nominal and adverbial subordinate clauses. **Sentential** relative clauses have a sentence as antecedent, (531b), are therefore less obviously adjectival, and can actually be somewhat adverbial in function (cf. *luckily*), while **nominal** or **free** relative clauses, (531c) – those which include their own antecedent – are indeed nominal, having the distribution of an NP (cf. *He got his wish*). For convenience, however, we shall discuss all of them in this section. The order of treatment will run from peculiarities of antecedent, to a long section on choice of relative marker, to relative markers that are adverbial in function, to nominal relatives, and then on to several minor types of relative clause.

3.6.5.1 Antecedents

First we look at antecedents in adnominal relatives. The obsolescence of relative clauses with personal pronouns as antecedents, especially third person pronouns, has been mentioned above (3.2.2.3). Quirk, Greenbaum,

Leech & Svartvik point out that in PDE they are confined to 'archaic or very formal contexts' (1985: 17.12). Early examples may be a little more varied stylistically, though that is not necessarily the case:

(532) a. but to attack *me who am really so innocent – and who never say an ill natured thing of anybody*

(1777 Sheridan, *School for Scandal* IV.iii 411.29)

  b. O Mr. Austin! *you who have lived, you whose gallantry is beyond the insolence of suspicion, you who are a man crowned and acclaimed, who are loved, and loved by such a woman – you who excel me in every point of advantage*, will you suffer me to surpass you in generosity?

(1884 Henley, *Beau Austin* II.iv p. 141 [ARCHER])

Verbs which cannot be marked for concord make first and second person examples seem more acceptable. Here are some third person examples:

(533) a. and *he who had seduced her from her duty and her virtue*, was the first to brand her with the disgraceful epithets, of undutiful and unchaste.   (1789 Brown, *Power of Sympathy* xxi.37 [ARCHER])

  b. What friendship with *them who take down the Court Guide to ascertain their friends' directions?*   (1861 Green, *Letters* 91 (18 Oct.))

  c. Aye your husband! – the husband of *her who now calls herself Lady Audley!*   (1863 Hazlewood, *Lady Audley's Secret* I.i p. 245)

An alternative analysis, of (533a) at least, takes the personal pronoun as part of the relative clause rather than its antecedent, in which case we have a nominal relative with marker *he who*, etc.

From OE times it has been possible to have as antecedent not the noun which precedes the relative but a genitive acting as its determiner (*CHEL* I: 224–5):

(534) a. He married in *his father's* life-time, who gave up his own apartment to him

(1778 Reeve, *Old English Baron* p. 33 [ARCHER])

  b. and deliver it [*sc.* this letter] into *the young Lady's* hand who is to be married to-morrow

(1780 Pilon, *Deaf Lover* I.i p. 15 [ARCHER])

  c. until I saw my own uneasiness reflected in *Virginia's* face, who grew alternately crimson and pale.

(1868 (1912) Stanley, *Autobiography* p. 233 (22 Aug.) [ARCHER])

This old construction, still normal for Jane Austen, is now considered awkward (Phillipps 1970: 170–1).

It is worth pointing out that sentential relative clauses need not, as in (531b), have a whole sentence or clause as antecedent. An interesting type has part of the VP as antecedent (see Quirk, Greenbaum, Leech & Svartvik 1985: 15.57), and there are examples in ARCHER from as early as the late seventeenth century:

(535) a. The Prescription supposed most likely to do good is always given first. If it fails, *which it does* nine times in ten, the second is surely likely to fail ninety nine time in a hundred.

       (1776 Adam Smith, *Correspondence* p. 201 (16 Jun.) [ARCHER])

    b. but it is over & I now defy the worst & fear not while I am true to myself *which I will be.*

       (1803 Blake, *Letters* p. 80 (30 Jan.) [ARCHER])

    c. The show, in short, is a bad show & Mrs Langtry is an éspèce de type that I should detest even if she could act *wh.* [= *which*] *she can't.*   (1890 Dowson, *Letters* 93 p. 141 (9 Mar.))

    d. What Sinead failed to understand, if she was not having a breakdown *which I think she is*, was that nobody wanted to think about 1992 and all our problems.

       (1992 Emily Prager, 'Letter from New York', *The Guardian Weekend* p. 34 (14 Nov.))

3.6.5.2 Non-adverbial relative markers

The term **relative marker** (used e.g. by Romaine 1982) or **relativiser** is a useful cover term for the traditional relative pronouns such as *who* and *which*, nonpronominal use of *which* as a determiner, and items of controversial category – pronoun or complementiser? – like *that* and *as*. All can serve to introduce relative clauses. Relativisation with a *wh*-pronoun on the one hand and with *that* or zero on the other are generally regarded as different syntactic processes. We take them in turn, then some minor patterns. Markers with an adverbial function in the relative clause are dealt with separately in the next section.

When *which* developed as a relative pronoun it was used with human and nonhuman antecedents alike (just as interrogative *which* is even now); the most familiar example to demonstrate this is the sixteenth- and seventeenth-century rendering of *The Lord's Prayer*, which opens 'Our father which art in heauen . . .'. As Rissanen explains, relative *which* began to be specialised for nonhuman reference from the sixteenth century on, with the present-day demarcation between human *who* and nonhuman *which* being reached in the course of the eighteenth century (*CHEL* III, forthcoming); Austin (1985) shows that *which* with human reference survived in uneducated usage to the end of that century. Jespersen observes that *which* rather than *who* is still normal with reference to persons when the relative is in predicative function:

(536)   To become a popular playwright, *which Shakespeare certainly was*, a man must adapt his treatment of human life to the requirements of the stage

(1907 W. A. Raleigh, *Shakespeare* (Macmillan) i.26 [Jespersen])

He compares the use of *it* rather than *he/she/they* in identifying sentences like *It was Shakespeare* (3.4.1.1 above), and note too that the appropriate interrogative would be *What was he?*, not *Who was he?*.

The relative marker *which* usually constitutes the whole of an NP, but it can sometimes act as a determiner, though much less freely than interrogative *which* (Quirk, Greenbaum, Leech & Svartvik 1985: 17.24). Outside very formal usage, nonrestrictive relative clauses with determiner *which* tend to contain prepositional phrases like *in which case*. Until the nineteenth century, relative determiner *which* was a little commoner and more varied in its use:

(537)   a. We have passed . . . from Kendal to Bownes<s> on turning down *to which place* there burst upon us the most beautiful and rich view of Winander mere

(1818 Keats, *Letters* 72 p. 157 (27 Jun.))

   b. Lady Lufton . . . had sent up a note addressed to Miss Lucy Robarts, *which note* was in Fanny's hands when Lucy stepped out of the pony-carriage.   (1860–1 Trollope, *Framley* xxxv.335)

   c. There were conjurers and jugglers and snake-charmers, *which last* Anthea did not like at all.   (1906 Nesbit, *Amulet* vii.121)

Apart from the occasional fixed phrase, it is doubtful whether it was ever anything but a literary usage (cf. *CHEL* III, forthcoming).

Case variation is found only in the *who* paradigm (apart from the apparent genitive marking in dialects with *that's~that*, to be discussed shortly). The *OED* is able to trace the use of *who* in object functions back to ME, though the editors of the first edition were reassured that relative *who* used 'ungrammatically' for *whom* was 'now' (i.e. 1924) rare or obsolete as a relative except in the indefinite sense of 'whomever'! (s.v. *who* pron. 13). If true, it suggests that prescriptivism had temporarily reversed a long-term trend; the second edition more realistically states that it is 'still common colloquially'.

The converse phenomenon, *whom* for *who*, is not uncommon in relative clauses interrupted by (what might be) a parenthetical clause:

(538)   a. but at Bailey's suggestion, *whom* I assure you *is a very capital*
                fellow, we have   (1817 Keats, *Letters* 24 p. 49 (28 Sep.))
             b. to one *whom* you understand *intends to be immortal in the best*
                points   (1818 ibid. 72 p. 159 (28 Jun.))

Jespersen has a big collection (1909–49: III 197–201), and Visser adds a few (1963–73: section 547); Dekeyser has examples and frequencies for the nineteenth century (1975: 194–202). Jespersen argues against the automatic assumption that such uses are erroneous, though hypercorrection would seem to be at work in some of them at least; cf. also sections 3.2.2.3, 3.5.3.2 on 'wrong' case choice with fronted personal and interrogative pronouns.

Historically the form *whose* is the genitive of both masculine *who* and neuter *what*, and with the reorganisation of the relative markers it has come to serve as genitive determiner corresponding to both human *who* and non-human *which*. There is, however, some resistance to the latter, especially with inanimate antecedents, presumably because interrogative *whose* is wholly human in reference, while among the *wh*-relatives there is otherwise full correlation in the standard language between forms beginning with *who*- and human antecedents. Various expedients can be used to avoid relative *whose* with a nonhuman antecedent, for instance:

(539)   a. a fragment of a Roman or Saxon teapot, the spout and
                body *of which* were lost.   (1861 Green, *Letters* 90 (18 Oct.))
             b. Yesterday afternoon I went to see one of our new primary
                schools *where* the headmaster is a friend of mine.
                                                          (1918 Bell, *Letters* II.447 (1 Mar.))

Other devices include resumptive pronouns (see 3.6.5.6 below) and the non-standard *that's* of (541). It would be interesting to test whether avoidance of *whose* with nonhuman antecedent has shown any decrease or increase during the lModE period.

Now we consider choice between a *wh*-pronoun (*who(m)* or *which* in standard) and the relative marker *that*. Here change continues, particularly in restrictive relative clauses – those which serve to identify their antecedent. There is an enormous range of relevant factors: see for instance Quirk (1957), Quirk *et al.* (1985) for PDE, and especially Romaine (1982), Biber (1988), Montgomery (1989) on the history. For example, restrictive relatives with human antecedent show a strong predilection for *who* in subject function, much less so in other functions. A reaction against the use of *that* with human antecedent took place after the end of the eighteenth century (Dekeyser 1984: 71–72). The importance of type of antecedent and grammatical function of relative marker is stressed by Ball (1996), who offers some useful pointers to these and other factors which influence choice of relative pronoun, showing that not enough variables are controlled for in most studies of relativisation. In written data for the period 1700–1900 she finds that *that* lost ground to *who* and *which*, rapidly during the eighteenth century and more gradually in the nineteenth, while in the twentieth century *who* falls back a little, *which* a little more so (1996: 248–51).

It is commonly stated that *that* does not occur in nonrestrictive relatives, but exceptions occur sporadically:

(540) a. then he brought the saddle, *that was not broad enough for my back*; he saw it in a minute and went for another, which fitted nicely.
(1877 Sewell, *Black Beauty* v.25)

b. At last the deer stopped . . . five hundred feet up the hillside. His instinct, *that had warned him of the coming slide*, told him he would be safe here.
(1895 Kipling, *Second Jungle Book*, 'Miracle of Purun Bhagat' (Macmillan, 1899) 44)

c. 'Darling!' cried Winifred, rushing to the dog, *that sat with contemplative sadness on the hearth*, and kissing its bulging brow.
(1921 Lawrence, *Women* xviii.227)

d. [The Mojave Desert] is made up of a mosaic of mountains, valleys and wide basins. The mountains, *that have uplifted in successive stages*, may be more than 100 million years old.
(1994 Bernice Wuethrich [American], *New Scientist* 1918: 30 (26 Mar.))

In earlier usage *that* was normal in nonrestrictive relatives (Strang 1970: 142), but from at least the seventeenth century it has been losing out to *wh*-pronouns (Rissanen 1984).

There is continuing controversy as to whether relative *that* should be analysed as a pronoun or as a complementiser. One piece of evidence in favour of the pronominal analysis, and which may show change in our period, is genitive *that's*, a possible alternative to *whose*:

(541) a. the house *that's* roof was damaged   ([Romaine])
b. This is the pencil *that's* lead is broken.
(1991 att. Richard Hudson [LINGUIST])

c. 'Bottom line is we want them to bring a product to market
that's time had not yet come,' said Ray Farhung, a Southern
California Edison official

(1993 Bill Vlasic, 'Cool Contest', *The Detroit News* p. 10
(10 Jan.) [Lawler, LINGUIST])

Most cited examples have *that's N* as an NP which is subject of its clause.
Relative *that's* is grammatical in Modern Scots (Romaine 1982: 95; *CHEL*
V: 74; though cf. Miller 1988: 118) and is found sporadically elsewhere. It
appears to be a new formation rather than a continuation of the OE
genitive *þæs*.[81]

A zero relative – indicated below by the symbol [∅] – is generally
regarded as a variant of the marker *that*, since they alternate as complementisers of nominal clauses. Zero is acceptable in standard only when the
function of the relative marker is an object of some kind within its clause:

(542)   a. the man [∅] we saw
        b. the man [∅] we were talking about

Visser traces the rise of the zero object relative through the history of
English, incidentally casting doubt on the proposition that it was characteristic of colloquial texts in the eModE period (1963–73: sections
627–33). But in our period it does seem to have become disfavoured in
formal writing. As Visser writes (section 630):

> In the course of the eighteenth and the nineteenth centuries a remarkable
> decline in the currency of the zero-construction becomes perceptible:
> Only writers whose style is natural and easy . . . go on freely using it,
> whereas many others, such as Johnson (who called the omission of the
> relative 'a colloquial barbarism') . . . consciously avoid it . . . The causes
> of this avoidance of the zero pattern may be seen in the influence of
> Latin syntax and in Johnson's anathema, and, perhaps, also in the fact
> that, owing to the appearance in *The Spectator* (no. 78) of the '*Humble
> Petition of* WHO *and* WHICH', in which these pronouns complain that
> the 'Jacksprat THAT' has supplanted them, and that they find themselves
> 'either not used, or used instead of another', writers had become 'relative
> pronoun-minded', and began to regard the zero-construction as too
> familiar for literary diction.

Harriet Martineau seems to be at her most natural and easy in writing to
Elizabeth Barrett:

(543)   Do you know, I don't find the obscurity *[∅] you are* (you say)
        complained of for   (1844 Martineau, *Letters* p. 104 (16 Sep.))

During the twentieth century the construction has largely regained its place in literary language. (It has long been common in colloquial language.)

In subject function a zero relative is non-standard but comes closest to standard usage in cleft sentences (clauses like (544c) split in two to focus on one element) and in existential *there* sentences (see Quirk, Greenbaum, Leech & Svartvik 1985: 17.15, 18.28n, 18.48), though it has been argued that the special properties of such clauses mean that they should not even be classified as relatives:[82]

(544) a. The first night tho' of our arrival here there was a slight
          uproar [∅] took place at about ten of the clock.
                                     (1819 Keats, *Letters* 156 p. 413 (?18 Sep.))
       b. There are an old Major and his youngish wife [∅] live in the
          next apartments to me.   (ibid. 156 p. 428 (25 Sep.))
       c. 'It really was you [∅] began it, Bobs . . .'
                                     (1902 Nesbit, *5 Children* viii.147)

Formerly the range was a little wider:

(545) a. O there is that disagreeable Lover of mine Sir Benjamin
          Backbite [∅] has just call'd at my Guardian's
                                     (1777 Sheridan, *School for Scandal* I.i 363.22)
       b. I could tell you some stories of him [∅] would make you laugh
          heartily if he wasn't your Husband   (ibid. II.ii 382.27)
       c. Why yes – here are three or four of us [∅] pass our time
          agreeably enough   (ibid. III.ii 395.16)
       d. (= 213) These Londoners have got a gibberage [*sc.* gibberish]
          with 'em, [∅] would confound a gipsey.
                                     (1777 (1781) Sheridan, *Scarborough* IV.i 602.36)

(In (545a) we have locative, not existential, *there*.) Phillipps reckons that 'the most acceptable people' in Jane Austen's novels are not given such things to say (1970: 171–2).

At this point I mention a clause type which is exclamatory in function, but with a formal structure quite different from exclamatives (3.5.5 above). It is an NP consisting of antecedent and restrictive relative clause:

(546) a. The work she did that day!
                                     (1849–50 Dickens, *David Copperfield* xxxii.391 [Jespersen])
       b. Traitors that they were . . . !
                                     (1857 Trollope, *Barchester Towers* (OUP, 1953) xviii.167 [Jespersen])

Such utterances are apparently incomplete grammatically – the higher clause has no verb – but have long been normal; see Jespersen (1909–49: III 376–7). Both zero and *that*-relatives are found.

Non-standard dialects have a range of other relative markers, some of which can occur in very limited circumstances in Standard English too, for example *as*, which marks an adnominal relative clause whose antecedent contains *such* or *same*, or a sentential, or even a nominal relative:

(547)   a. with his daughter, who read to him from time to time *such passages as he desired* from the Bible

(1847 Le Fanu, Fortunes of Col. Torlogh O'Brien xxvii.190
[ARCHER])

        b. as I was unable to go on reading & writing for *the same length of time as I had previously done.*   (1873 *Amberley Papers* II.543 (12 Jun.))

        c. I can do *just as I like.*   (ibid. II.552 (25 Jul.))

        d. I did not have my dolly *as you promised me* on my birthday.

(?1874 ibid. II.564)

The form *but* is sometimes used after a negative as the equivalent of relative pronoun + *not*:

(548)   a. *no* one of us, I suppose, *but* would [= who would not] find it a very rough defective thing

(1841 Carlyle, On Heroes (Chapman & Hall, 1898) iv.143 [Jespersen])

        b. there was *not* one *but* had been guilty of some act of oppression or barbarity.

(1888 Stevenson, Black Arrow (Heinemann, 1922)
II.i.122 [Jespersen])

        c. and *not* one of the children *but* was relieved to find that

(1902 Nesbit, 5 Children i.34)

It nearly always has subject function. As Jespersen observes (1909–49: III 180–1), similar usage occurs with *but* + personal pronoun:

(549)   *Not* one great man of them, *but he* will [= who will not] puzzle you, if you look close, to know what he means.

(1843–60 (1893) Ruskin, Selections I.172 [Jespersen])

Both have been obsolete since the early part of the twentieth century; they do not occur in my letters corpus.

Jespersen also discusses the combination *but what*, found from the beginning of the eighteenth century:

(550) a. *Not* that I think Mr. Martin would ever marry any body *but
       what* had had some education – and been very well brought
       up.   (1816 Austen, *Emma* I.iv.60 [Jespersen])
       b. till there is *no* village lane within a league *but what* offers a
       gaunt and ludicrous travesty of rural charms.
                                 (1902 Bennett, *Anna of the Five Towns* (Penguin, 1988)
                                                              i.25 [Jespersen])

His eighteenth-century examples apparently even allow it after a personal
NP antecedent, though by the early nineteenth century that had probably
become non-standard – to judge from Jane Austen's (550a), where juxtaposition with *education* in Harriet Smith's mouth looks very much like a
comic vulgarism; for more examples see Poutsma (1914–29: II 651–2),
Phillipps (1970: 171). Plain *what* is a relative marker for adnominal relative
clauses that is quite widespread in non-standard varieties of BrE (Jespersen
1909–49: III 130) but vanishingly rare in standard.

3.6.5.3   Adverbial relative markers

Many of the so-called *wh*-words are adverbial: *how, why, when, where, whence,
whither, whenever, wherever, whencever* (rare). The last three have by-forms with
-so-, and *OED* gives no alternative to *whithersoever* – except, of course, the
where(soe)ver which is now the normal choice. Whereas all the *so*-less forms
can introduce interrogatives, in relative clauses there are greater restrictions. *How* does not occur, and *why* only with the antecedent *reason*, (551a) –
and even that is frowned on in the prescriptive tradition, which prefers
(551b) (Quirk, Greenbaum, Leech & Svartvik 1985: 15.46n.[h]):

(551) a. You will see . . . *a reason why* I have not answered previously
       the letter of yours which crossed my last.
                                                    (1862 Green, *Letters* 95 (15 Jan.))
       b. *The reason [ø]* I took him out with us at Crosby was that
                                                (1872 *Amberley Papers* II.516 (17 Aug.))

A more liberal use of relative *how* and *why* occasionally turns up in earlier usage:

(552) a. O Lord! I can tell you *a way how* to perswade her to any thing.
                                               (1777 (1781) Sheridan, *Scarborough* IV.i 604.7)
       b. repeating to himself *a great many arguments why* he should be
       so satisfied.   (1860–1 Trollope, *Framley* iii.22)
       c. if it is not possible to suggest *causes why* the principle of
       analogy should have thus asserted itself.
                                                    (1894 Jespersen, *Progress* vi.175)

Without an antecedent, the relative clauses in (551a) and (552) would become fully standard interrogative clauses: *You will see why I have not answered . . . I can tell you how to persuade her . . .*

The form *whither* has been obsolescent for some time, likewise now *whence*:

(553) a. they came to the spot *whither* Louis had formerly traced his father.   (1791 Radcliffe, *Romance of the Forest* ix.429 [ARCHER])
b. I write this letter from Burslem, *whence* I depart tonight
(1900 A. Bennett, *Letters*, ed. Hepburn, II.135 (2 Aug.) [ARCHER])
c. carried back to her own room *from whence* she had been moved into the Library the day before.
(1874 *Amberley Papers* II.570 (28 Jun.))

The replacements are *where* (± *to*) and *where* + *from*, respectively; *whence* + *from* in (553c) seems to be a transitional usage (albeit of long standing).

Restrictive relative clauses may use another relativiser (*which*, *that* or zero), with or without a preposition, in a function equivalent to an adverbial relativiser:

(554) a. the window *in which* they are displayed
(1889 Dowson, *Letters* 71 p. 112 (27 Oct.))
b. the hour *that* he began to amend
(1839 Martineau, *Deerbrook* xi.207 [ARCHER])
c. the way *[ø]* you meant to treat your division [*sc.* of a book]
(1862 Green, *Letters* 94 (6 Jan.))
d. at a somewhat lower level than the one [*sc.* road] *[ø]* we were
on   (1892 Stockton, *Dusantes* II.45 [ARCHER])

It is likely that there has been an increased use of preposition stranding, and likely too that there have been changes in the distribution of forms without preposition, given our discussion of bare NP adverbials (3.4.4 above).

Both sentential and adnominal relatives may be introduced by compounds of *where* + preposition:

(555) a. Then he proceeded that a low condition of health rendered such lungs most susceptible of disease. *Whereupon I stopped him*, 'Do you mean that this low condition is connected with my present residence and work?'
(1863 Green, *Letters* 122 (28 May))
b. on whom he cast one glance – a glance *wherein the Daily Telegraph wd no doubt have read much of high import* – but I did not   (1873 *Amberley Papers* II.549 (1 Jul.))

c. I have been busily engaged on the 'Study' *whereof I told you* and which should-be [*sic*] finished to-night.
(1889 Dowson, *Letters* 77 p. 119 (29 Nov.))

Examples (555) are the *only* ones in my letters corpus (though cf. (560) below). Nonrestrictive examples, especially sentential relatives like (555a), were the longest survivors of the type. Note that with the repetition of the antecedent *glance*, (555b) is technically a restrictive relative, though its discourse function is to provide additional information rather than identification, while Dowson's (555c) is one of his mannered archaisms.

3.6.5.4   Nominal relative clauses

Our discussion of nominal relatives will begin with the matter already in hand, namely choice of relative marker. The very start of our period still showed *that* as combined antecedent and relative marker (with an alternative analysis as pronominal *that* + zero relative), though not when the relative marker had subject function in the relative clause:

(556)   a. What do you think of *that* [*sc.* the play] *you saw last night?*
(1777 (1781) Sheridan, *Scarborough* II.i 583.3)
   b. and indulging my feelings will not restore me to *that I have lost.*
(1786 Betsy Sheridan, *Journal* 23 p. 82 (8 May))

Occasional examples can be found till the end of the nineteenth century. This form was replaced by *that which* – now itself rather formal – and *what* or *whatever*, more normal for nonhuman reference, both already available at the start of our period:

(557)   a. my earliest project in the department of history was *that which Dean Hook has since carried out* – a series of lives of the 'Archbishops of Canterbury.'   (1862 Green, *Letters* 102 (11 Sep.))
   b. Don't get in a rage, and call me a coward for *what I am going to say.*   (1861 ibid. 80 (May))
   c. I have a great & unreasonable aversion to Garden though – in *whatever he plays.*   (1890 Dowson, *Letters* 83 p. 133 (27 Jan.))

These forms are not restricted to object functions.

For human reference *who(m)* ± *that* had become obsolete in nominal relatives in the nineteenth century, replaced by *he/she/they who* and recently more often by such phrases as *one who, those who.* The one exception became a fixed idiom, *as who says/should say*:

(558) The Manager inclined his head, and showed his teeth, *as who should say*, in answer to some careless small-talk, 'Dear me! Is that the case?' but said never a word.

> (1846–8 Dickens, *Dombey*, ed. Horsman (Clarendon, 1974) xxii.293 [Jespersen])

Generalising relatives have *who(m)(so)(ever)* (three optional elements makes for eight possible combinations, all attested!), now treated as singular but formerly permitting plural concord as well:

(559) *Whoever* went into this apartment *were* terrified by uncommon noises and strange appearances

> (1778 Reeve, *Old English Baron* p. 34 [ARCHER])

There are also genitival determiner forms like *whosesoever* (Jespersen 1909–49: III 67).

Quirk, Greenbaum, Leech & Svartvik observe that nominal relative *to*-infinitive clauses in PDE 'seem to be restricted to the functions of subject complement and prepositional complement' (1985: 15.8). The following types, functioning as direct objects, are now obsolete:

(560) a. Have not the foxes holes, and the birds of the air nests, and shall the children of men have not *where to lay their heads?*

> (1797 Spence, *Rights of infants*, in *Pig's meat*, ed. Gallop (Spokesman, 1982) p. 114)

   b. Think how different was the 'need' of Augustine and the 'need' of St. Louis – yet Christianity had *wherewith to supply both*.

> (1863 Green, *Letters* 118 (24 Mar.))

The curious placement of *not* after nonfinite as well as finite *have* in (560a) helps maintain the echo of Matthew 8.20 and balances the other rhetorical questions in a way that the obvious (non-relative) alternatives, *have nowhere* or *not (. . .) have somewhere/anywhere*, would not. As for (560b), compounds of *where* + preposition were anyway already somewhat uncommon by the mid-nineteenth century, and in a nominal relative clause really only appropriate to formal religious discourse and similar genres (cf. the lexicalised form *the wherewithal*).

3.6.5.5 Continuative relatives

It will be remembered that nonrestrictive relative clauses do not serve to identify their antecedent. They have a looser connection with their antecedent than do restrictive clauses, being more easily separated from them, having separate 'comma intonation', and so on. At the extreme, nonrestrictive relatives are in effect co-ordinated with, rather than subordinated to, what precedes. Such clauses are called **continuative clauses** by Jespersen (1909–49: III 105–6), 'always added after what might have been the end of the whole sentence', and 'advancing the discourse by adding new information' (Romaine 1982: 83):

(561) he had . . . seen my aunt give this person money outside the garden rails in the moonlight, *who then slunk away . . . and was seen no more* (1849–50 Dickens, *David Copperfield* xvii.214 [Jespersen])

The sentential relatives in (535) and some of the examples with determiner *which* in (537) probably belong under this heading too.

Continuative relatives may behave so much like free-standing clauses that they are punctuated as new sentences:

(562) a. and now away in search of Donamar; *whom*, from information I have received, *I expect to find in Lubeck.*
            (1819 Milner, *Jew of Lubeck* II.iii p. 20 [ARCHER])
       b. 'As the island was out of the ordinary track of vessels, I did not imagine that my bars would ever prove an obstacle to unfortunate castaways who might seek a refuge there.'
       '*Which they did n't*,' [*sic*] remarked Mrs. Aleshine, 'for under we bobbed.' (1892 Stockton, *Dusantes* II.63 [ARCHER])

This can be either colloquial or highly literary, though in the latter case it has rather lost favour.

Another effect of the semi-independence of continuative clauses is that they may themselves contain embedded wishes and questions. Jespersen cites such examples as:

(563) a. these men (*whom may Heaven pardon!*)
            (1819 Scott, *Ivanhoe* (Constable, 1820) III.vii[xxxvii].180 [Jespersen])
       b. the essential sin; *for which what pardon can there be?*
            (1841 Carlyle, *On Heroes* (Chapman & Hall, 1898) iv.151 [Jespersen])

(Both show SAI.) The idea of clauses embedded within a relative clause leads on to our next topic: syntactic strategies for dealing with relative clauses where the absent relativised NP which corresponds to the relative marker is in an embedded clause.

3.6.5.6   Resumptive pronouns and gaps
Standard PDE places constraints on extraction of elements – which includes relativisation – from deeply embedded subordinate clauses; see

Kroch (1981), Quirk, Greenbaum, Leech & Svartvik (1985: 17.63), and (with caution) *CHEL* I: 231–2. The following examples show awkward extraction from a conditional protasis; I italicise the most deeply embedded clause and mark the extraction site (the normal position for that element had it not been relativised) by [∅]:

(564)   a. I shall . . . proceed to these two points, which *if you can theme [∅] out in sexions and subsexions, for my edification,* you will oblige me.   (1819 Keats, *Letters* 153 p. 392 (22 Sep.))
       b. *Triplet.* . . . I have here three tragedies.
       Woffington. . . . Fifteen acts, mercy on us!
       Triplet. Which *if I could submit [∅] to Mrs. Woffington's judgement*
         (1852 Taylor & Reade, *Masks and Faces* I.i p. 128)

The blending of relative and conditional is somewhat akin to the combination of co-ordination and relativisation discussed below (3.6.5.7). Visser collects some similar examples of extraction from various kinds of clause, including *if-*, *when-*, and *while*-clauses (1963–73: section 535). He finds it to be well represented from the sixteenth to eighteenth centuries but to become rare in the nineteenth. Here are some examples, nonrestrictive and restrictive, showing extraction from a deeply embedded clause:

(565)   a. But as you know, there are others of whom I think incessantly, and *whom my promotion would enable me to do more for [∅]*.   (1862 Green, *Letters* 111 (20 Nov.))
       b. I send you the names & directions of the two London doctors, *one of whom he strongly recommends you to consult [∅]*
         (1873 *Amberley Papers* II.548 (26 Jun.))
       c. and as he ended the incantation which contained no words *that* it seemed likely *the Egyptian had ever heard [∅]*
         (1906 Nesbit, *Amulet* xi.204)
       d. '. . . Charles had a bloody bite-mark on his arm *that* he had no idea *how he'd got [∅]*, but it wasn't a human bite . . .'
         (1992 Tartt, *Secret History* iv.197)

Note that – the admittedly non-standard – (565d) seems to require 'unbounded *Wh*-movement' (across more than one finite clause boundary) in some generative analyses; see Radford (1988: 488, 569–76, 593).

Rarer overall but lasting into the nineteenth century is the type where the relative marker is subject of its own clause while object of the embedded clause (Visser 1963–73: section 536):

(566) Sir, there is a villain at that Maypole . . . that *unless you get rid of [ø], and have [ø] kidnapped and carried off* at the very least . . . [ø] will marry your son to that young woman

(1841 Dickens, Barnaby Rudge xxiv.186 [Visser])

In subsequent sections Visser reviews some other, similar constructions showing slight syntactic variations. A number, like (566), have not just one extraction site but a second, 'parasitic' gap, most clearly seen when both are object positions:

(567) a. After they were seated, several young Indians entered with baskets of green maize in the ear, which, *having roasted [ø] before the fire*, they distributed [ø] among the company.

(1797 Bleeker, History of Maria Kittle p. 4
[ARCHER])

   b. the while I request the loan of a £20 and a £10 – which *if you would enclose [ø] to me* I would acknowledge [ø] and save myself a hot forehead. (1817 Keats, *Letters* 17 p. 35)

   c. a written card, which *Mr. Pickwick not wishing to hurt the man's feelings by refusing [ø]*, courteously accepted [ø] and deposited [ø] in his waistcoat pocket.

(1836–7 Dickens, Pickwick xl.622 [Visser])

Such examples, probably never common, are a delight to the theoretical syntactician.

Given the complexity of their syntax, it is not surprising that speakers and writers, having once embarked on such a structure, often clarify it by inserting a personal pronoun at the site of what might otherwise have been a gap. An additional pronoun coreferential with the relative marker is called a **resumptive** pronoun. Sometimes the use of a resumptive pronoun is clearly non-standard, other times the construction is so convoluted that judgement is very insecure, but either way the phenomenon is quite well attested:

(568) a. and Hilliard [is] just one of those young Men *that* in your *wicked* [original emphasis] days you would have found pleasure in turning *his* head (1785 Betsy Sheridan, *Journal* 14 p. 63 (6 Aug.))

   b. some of them . . . write their sins, – *which*, however, they cannot deliver on paper to the confessor, but must read *them* aloud.

(1885–9 Ruskin, Præterita (George Allen, 1899) II.xi.333
[Jespersen, Visser])

   c. 'I just shoved a paper under the man's door – the one [*sc.* man]
that I knew where *he* lived – to tell him to lie low.'

                                     (1907 Nesbit, *Enchanted Castle* vi.119)

Visser reports that the usage 'passed into obsolescence after the first half
of the eighteenth century' (1963–73: section 604) – in standard English,
anyway. Note that (568b), his only post-1776 example, has the resumptive pronoun in a co-ordinate relative clause lacking its own relative
pronoun, while Betsy Sheridan's usage in (568a) may be an Irishism –
Jespersen has that construction down as being usual in Ireland. Jespersen
gives a number of lModE examples from vulgar and dialect speech
(1909–49: III 110–13).

   When *which* is used in combination with a resumptive pronoun in the
relative clause, its pronominal function becomes subservient to its role as
subordinator. A further development turns *which* into a pure connective
when there is no possible antecedent for a relative clause (*OED* s.v., B.14b):

(569)   a. '*Which* he warn't strong enough, my dear, fur to be surprised,'
        said Joe.

                (1861 Dickens, *Great Expectations*, ed. Caldwell (Clarendon, 1993)
                                      III.xix[lviii].474)

    b. '*Which* he couldn't have said anything else,' Jane told Bee,
       'because it's true.'   (1949 Streatfeild, *Painted Garden* xxiii.254)

Such usage remains non-standard.

3.6.5.7   Co-ordination + relativisation

Jespersen writes as follows (1909–49: III 78):

> It is a natural consequence of the adjunct nature of the relative clause
> that there is a tendency in many languages to use *and* before a clause if
> the [head] has another adjunct. This is the regular idiom in French, but is
> generally looked upon as a fault when it occurs in English . . . It is,
> however, frequently heard in colloquial English, and is by no means rare
> in literature, though probably not so much used now as in the 18th c.

Here are a couple of examples:

(570)   a. A large mansion-house stood in the centre of it [*sc.* the farm],
       very much out of repair, *and which*, in consequence of certain
       reports, *had received the appellation of the Haunted House.*

               (1822 W. Irving, *Bracebridge Hall* 'Dolph Heyliger', in *Complete
                 Works IX, ed. H. F. Smith (Twayne, 1977) p. 258 [Poutsma])

b. At this moment his devotion is chiefly absorbed, however, by
the comparative stranger, Lily Romilly, here for a few days, *and
on whom he lavishes compliments & attention*
(1873 *Amberley Papers* II.539 (6 May))

Jespersen has a few early nineteenth-century ones, Poutsma some
more (1914–29: II 642). In my letters corpus there are one each with
whom, (570b), and *which*. It is easier to find examples where one relative
clause is co-ordinated with another (eight examples in the letters
corpus):

(571) a. Isabella, whose marriage was now within a week to take place,
and who had
(1793 C. Smith, *Old Manor House*, ed. Ehrenpreis (OUP, 1969)
III.viii.319)

b. the severe illness of Mrs. Ward, who . . . was attacked with a
severe internal seizure, whose nature the doctors can hardly
tell, *but which was of a most agonising character.*
(1861 Green, *Letters* 87 (16 Sep.))

This, presumably, has always been sanctioned.

3.6.5.8   Nonfinite relative clauses

Ordinary nonfinite relative clauses require little discussion. There is only
one kind of nonfinite restrictive relative clause, where the verb is a *to*-infini-
tive and the relative is a prepositional object and shows 'pied-piping'
(fronting of the whole prepositional phrase):

(572) a. She has no arms *with which to contend against that foe.*
(1799 Brown, *Ormond* xv.127 [ARCHER])

b. but it was just what we both needed, an end *to which to work*
(1861 Green, *Letters* 76 (Apr.))

Stranding of the preposition is not found when the relative marker is
present (**an end which to work to*). Instead there are alternative forms which
are not relative clauses:

(572′) a. She has no arms to contend against that foe with.
b. an end to work to

Such post-modifying infinitive clauses go right back to OE (where the
preposition typically preceded the clause-final infinitive); for a discussion
of voice in such clauses see section 3.3.6.3 above.

Earlier usage occasionally permitted a nonrestrictive, nonfinite clause with subject relative:

(573)   They conversed in English, *which displeasing the Indian*, he ordered
        them to return to the wigwam,
                        (1797 Bleeker, *History of Maria Kittle* p. 3 [ARCHER])

(This bears close resemblance to the absolute clauses discussed in 3.6.6.6 below.) Normally, though, the relative marker has a *non*subject function within its clause. Now nonsubject relative markers usually show *wh*-fronting, but here they rarely do: that is, they occur in normal object/complement position rather than in the typical fronted position of a *wh*-element:

(574)   a. must I confess . . . that He it is for whom I am thus anxious
            and malicious *and to gain whom* I would sacrifice – everything?
                        (1777 Sheridan, *School for Scandal* I.i 361.16)
        b. you will not wonder at the serious cast of my countenance
            to remedy which, the lady who took my likeness, frequently
            desired me to laugh.
                        (1799 Ellicott, *Life and Letters* p. 166 (17 Feb.) [ARCHER])
        c. and she resumed a sway over his house, *to shake off which* had
            been the object of his life, and the result of many battles.
                        (1848 Thackeray, *Little Dinner at Timmins's* v.330 [Poutsma])
        d. her little sister . . . whom she had not seen . . . for five years,
            and *to bring whom* to that place on a short visit, she had been
            saving her poor means all that time.
                        (1840–1 Dickens, *Old Curiosity Shop* xxxii.241 [Poutsma])
(575)   'Now, my man,' said he, as he broke the twigs off, 'we'll see who's
        to be master – you or I'; *saying which*, Mr. Jorrocks turned
        sideways in his saddle, and gave Dickey a good lamming in the
        ribs.   (1845 Surtees, *Hillingdon Hall* xxviii.289 [ARCHER])

(I take it that the italicised relative clause in (574a) is nonrestrictive, but the distinction is a murky one.) In (574) we find subjectless, nonfinite, nonrestrictive adnominal relatives which are themselves subordinate to a following clause in which they have a nominal, (574c), or adverbial function! The complexity of the syntax makes them very much a literary usage.

Before our period a similar construction did occur with fronted relative (1700 Farquhar *the beauties of this play . . . which not to be proud of were the height of impudence*), and lModE examples can be found with difficulty:

(576) a. Misery, fun, folly, fame, honour . . . and all the host of
propulsives, *which to name even* would be to fill divers pages.

(1834 *Tait's Mag.* I. 38 [*OED*])

b. Dr. Middleton took his arm and discharged a volley at the
crotchety scholarship of Professor Crooklyn, *whom to confute by
book*, he directed his march to the library.

(1879 Meredith, *Egoist* xxxii.395)

(577) young persons of the female sex . . . who have fixed on two or
more double seats, *which having secured*, they proceed to eat apples

(1857 Oliver Wendell Holmes, *Autocrat of the Breakfast-Table*
(Strahan, 1859) ix.207 [Jespersen, Visser])

See Visser (1963–73: section 535), also Jespersen (1909–49: III 183–4),
who calls participial constructions like (577) 'not natural'. There is brief
discussion of the infinitival type, (576), in Poutsma (1914–29: V 1007–8),
who lumps them in with the syntactically very different type seen in (565a,
b), where the infinitive is in the embedded rather than the relative clause.

3.6.6   Adverbial clauses

To introduce this section I adapt two paragraphs from Rissanen (*CHEL*
III, forthcoming). Adverbial clauses are traditionally classified on a semantic basis analogously to other adverbials. Typical classes are clauses of time,
place, manner, purpose, result, condition, concession and comparison. As
will be shown below, these distinctions are in no way clearcut; many conjunctions introduce clauses of more than one semantic class. In most
instances, however, the subordinators have one central and one or more
peripheral meanings; thus, for instance, the core meaning of *when* is temporal; its causal, concessive and conditional meanings are secondary.

Adverbial clauses can function either as arguments of a higher verb or
as (optional) adjuncts. (I am uncomfortable with Quirk, Greenbaum, Leech
& Svartvik's use of **adjunct** for both functions, 1985: 15.22.) In the former
case they normally occur in the same positions as subject complements or
prepositional phrase complements, that is, final or late in the higher clause:

(578) a. It was *because I knew she wd. not wish it* that I told you not to go

(1872 *Amberley Papers* II.518 (21 Aug.))

b. I shall remain *where I am*   (1862 Green, *Letters* 112 (20 Nov.))

Most often, however, the adverbial clause functions as an adjunct, whether
to the VP or to the sentence; the majority of examples quoted in the

following discussion will be of that type. When they are sentence adjuncts they are relatively mobile, though initial and final positions in the higher clause are commonest (Quirk, Greenbaum, Leech & Svartvik 1985: 15.22). As for the internal structure of adverbial clauses, we now consider two general points about the form of conjunction and verb.

The demise of compound conjunctions consisting of preposition + *that* has taken place at different times in the history of English; the following illustrate nineteenth-century losses:

(579) a. for *besides that* the circumstance did not in her opinion justify such lasting amazement . . . her wonder was otherwise disposed of.   (1811 Austen, *S&S* I.xiv.71 [Phillipps])
  b. I w^d send it, *but that* I am sure you could not read half of it.
                    (1859 Martineau, *Letters* p. 180 (20 May))
  c. assurances . . . that it is well that I am dying, – though hell awaits me – *for that* I 'have done mischief enough' &c &c,
                    (1867 Martineau, *Letters* p. 213 (16 Jun.))

Replacing forms are the preposition used alone, therefore as a conjunction, or preposition + abstract noun (*besides the fact that*, etc. – cf. (484) above for a change in the opposite direction).

Much of our discussion of adverbial clauses will concern the choice of finite verb form: subjunctive or indicative. Visser quotes a number of eighteenth- and nineteenth-century grammarians on the choice of mood in such clauses (1963–73: section 837), suggesting that maintenance of the present subjunctive in appropriate cases was an artificial crusade of grammarians against the realities of conversational usage. In conditional and concessive *if*-clauses in my letters corpus, for instance, there are only 8 present subjunctives (as against 64 present indicatives and 110 indeterminate presents), and all (apart from Bell's lone *if you please*, a set phrase) are used by Green, a clergyman; see 3.6.6.3 below.[83] In general the present subjunctive after conjunctions, including *if*, is now high-flown and probably obsolescent.

3.6.6.1 Final and consecutive clauses

I borrow again from Rissanen (*CHEL* III, forthcoming):

> The clauses indicating purpose (final) and result (consecutive) are close to each other in meaning and the links introducing them are partly the same. The main distinction is that, unlike consecutive clauses, final clauses normally indicate action which has not taken place, i.e. they are less factual. For this reason, the mood of the final clauses is mostly expressed by subjunctive forms or by modal periphrasis

The main changes here during lModE are in the inventory of subordinating conjunctions and in the increasing disuse of the (present) subjunctive. The subjunctive is by no means obsolete:

(580) a. She . . . kept putting up the hand, that held the stone, first closing it carefully *that* the precious stone *he not lost*

> (1923 Sherwood Anderson, *Many Marriages* IV.iii.241
> [Visser])

  b. Loath though he was to encourage his employer in any way *lest* he *get* above himself, Joss was forced to drop a word of approval.

> (1940 Wodehouse, *Quick Service* (Jenkins, 1960) ii.22 [Visser])

What *is* at least archaic about (580) is the conjunctions *that* 'in order that' and *lest* 'in order that not, for fear that'. These two important conjunctions introduce purpose clauses now only in very formal registers, and certain special circumstances: *What have I done, that you should insult me?* (Quirk, Greenbaum, Leech & Svartvik 1985: 15.49). The comparatively recent conjunction *in order that* (recorded from 1711 in *OED*) occurs only with modals in my letters corpus (*may* ×1, *might* ×1) and in ARCHER (*may* ×4, *should* ×1). There is not one subjunctive. Quirk, Greenbaum, Leech & Svartvik say that in PDE a modal is obligatory with finite clauses of purpose – though an infinitival clause is a much commoner choice (1985: 15.48).

The conjunction *so (that)* may introduce a purpose clause or a clause of result, in the latter case without necessity for a subjunctive or modal, since the clause is factual. Both kinds are juxtaposed in the following example:

(581) One of the reasons for this silence might well be the fact that she was holding her black rosary crushed in her hand. *So that it would not chink. So that it had not chinked.*

> (1977 Antonia Fraser, *Quiet as a Nun* xi.108 [ARCHER])

The 'revived' use of *so* without *that* is stated by the *OED* to be originally American (s.v. *so* adv. and conj. B.23(a)).

3.6.6.2   Causal clauses

There has been much obsolescence here. Rissanen observes that *for (that)* is the most common eModE causal conjunction, but in pre-position it is hardly possible at all in PDE, and even following the main clause it is beginning to sound somewhat formal:

(582)   a. Her Husband said, he was sorry too – *for that* he thought you were a good kind of young man.

> (1813 H. Cowley, *The Town Before You*, in *Works* (1813), III.iv II.377 [WWP])

      b. and every one went to bed, and, *for* crying is very tiring, to sleep.   (1910 Nesbit, *Magic City* (Macmillan) viii.218)

      c. Your mother told us of the name chosen – & I was infinitely relieved *for* I had heard a rumour about *Galahad* [original emphasis]   (1872 *Amberley Papers* II.527 (29 Aug.))

Rissanen shows how *because* was already beginning to catch up with *for* in frequency during the seventeenth century, and in our period it has taken the lead; *because* in the first edition of 1795 was actually replaced by the *for that* of (582a)! (The form *because that* has only been archaic or dialectal in lModE; it was already uncommon after the fifteenth century.) Other conjunctions in causal clauses which have gained in importance include *since* and *as* (rare in this function in eModE), although these uses date back to the ME period. One that has been lost, in standard at least, is *being (as/that)*, whose last citation in the *OED* is already evidently old-fashioned:

(583)   With whom he himself had no delight in associating, '*being that* he was addicted unto profane and scurrilous jests.'

> (1815 Scott, *Guy Mannering* ix [*OED*])

Change here seems to be largely lexical, namely in the meaning (and frequency) of conjunctions. Rissanen discusses the grammaticalisation of various verbal *-ing* forms as conjunctions (*concerning, according*, etc.); one that is closely parallel in every way to *being (as/that)* is *seeing (as/that)*, which remains in informal usage. Nonfinite clauses are discussed further in section 3.6.6.6 below.

3.6.6.3   Conditional and concessive clauses

To quote Quirk, Greenbaum, Leech & Svartvik conditional clauses 'convey that the situation in the matrix clause is contingent on that in the subordinate clause', while the main role of concessive clauses 'is to imply that the situation in the matrix clause is unexpected in the light of that in the concessive clause' (1985: 15.32). (The matrix clause is the next higher clause minus the subordinate clause in question; see Quirk, Greenbaum, Leech & Svartvik 1985: 14.4.)

Here are some examples with a subjunctive in the subordinate clause:

(584)   a. no matter how empty the adytum ['inner sanctum'], *so that* ['so long as, if only'] the veil *be* thick enough.

(1859 George Eliot, Lifted Veil (Virago, 1985) ii.43)

    b. But *if* Georgina *do* indeed release him – if she has already done so – what will he think?

(1840 Bulwer-Lytton, Money V.ii, in 19c Plays, ed. Rowell p. 111; omitted in Booth)

    c. Is it a counter protest? Tell me very frankly if it is – if it is likely even to be taken so. *If* it *be* I will have nothing to do with it, much as I love and reverence the man.

(1861 Green, Letters 80 (May))

    d. *If* there *be* any truth in our veriest instincts God must ever be beyond us, beyond our power, our knowledge, our virtue . . . Yes, the Church, like its Head, groweth daily 'in wisdom and stature, and in favour with God and Man.' . . . And what *if* this progress which we see in the Future *be* visible in the Past? *If* Man *seem* but an outcome of the advance of the animal world, 'a monkey with something non-monkey about him,' what if Science confirms the Apostle's grand hint of the unity of the world about us with our spiritual selves, 'the whole creation groaneth and travaileth in bondage,' etc. If there are hints of a purpose to be wrought out in them as it has been wrought out in us?   *(1863 Green, Letters 119 (24 Mar.))*

The alternatives to the subjunctive are as for nominal clauses (3.6.3.3 above), including the present indicative:

(585)   and poor old women shivering to the Union . . . won't be particular if they have a covering of many colours, *so that* it *is* warm.   *([undated] Gaskell, Letters 609 p. 794 (4 Dec.))*

Notice how Green uses two indicative protases in each of (584c, d) quite close to the subjunctive ones, despite the highly sermonistic style of (584d).

    With certain subjunctive examples, *may/might* rivals *should* as the possible modal alternative:

(586)   a. And I judge that this must ever be a condition of human progress, *except* some religion *appear* which can move forward with the progress of man.   *(1863 Green, Letters 118 (24 Mar.))*

    b. Reason never comes too late, *though* it *be* midnight when she knocks at the door.

(1799 Dunlap, False Shame II p. 20 [ARCHER])

c. There is nonetheless considerable argument against the clause, softened *though* it *be*, on the grounds that Federal aid is so necessary to the public schools.

(1961 *Brown Corpus*, Learned J48:83)

Nowhere is the present subjunctive obligatory.

In the protasis of an unreal conditional the past subjunctive is optional after *if*, (587–8), with the indicative increasingly often used in standard:

(587) *If* Everest *was* only 300 metres higher, it would be physically impossible to reach the summit without bottled oxygen.

(1993 Ed Douglas, *New Scientist* 1875: 23 (29 May))

(588) Obviously, it is not easy to be a great poet. If it *were*, many more people would have done so.

(1913 Ezra Pound, *Egoist*, in *Literary Essays*, ed. Eliot (Faber, 1985) 48)

The past subjunctive is virtually obligatory in the, generally more formal, inverted protasis:

(589) Ah! *were* she a little less giddy than she is

(1843–4 Dickens, *Chuzzlewit*, ed. Cardwell (Clarendon, 1982) xviii.305 [Visser])

Only a few verbs, all past tense in form, can invert to form conditional protases without *if*, namely *were*, *had*, *did*, and past tense modals. We should note, however, that *was* was occasionally found instead of *were*:

(590) The manor of Selborne, *was* it strictly *looked after* . . . would swarm with game.

(1787 G. White, *Selborne* v. (1789) 11 [Visser, *OED*])

Visser reproduces the *OED*'s statement that this 'was common in the 17–18th centuries'.

Let us look now at the modals in inverted protases:

(591) a. *Could I* have dated [*sc.* a letter] from my Palace in Milan you would have heard from me

(1819 Keats, *Letters* 158 p. 431 (3 Oct.))

  b. And *could I* read yours [*sc.* face], I'm sure I should see

(1863 Hazlewood, *Lady Audley's Secret* I.i p. 241)

  c. *Should you* by any chance see Smith or Davies while calling here please be diplomatic.

(1890 Dowson, *Letters* 110 p. 159 (?late Jul.))

For *would*, Visser states that inversion is 'rather archaic', for *could* 'at present
... restricted to literary style', for *might* 'poetical' (1963–73: sections 1615,
1642, 1671). Quirk, Greenbaum, Leech & Svartvik suggest that *might* and
could 'require an adverb such as *but* or *just* before the lexical verb' in PDE
(1985: 15.36). Only *should* is at all common nowadays among the modals in
this pattern.

As for inverted protases with *did* as finite verb, Visser lists a number of
examples in his (1963–73: sections 819b, 1437), describing them as 'a
typical favourite with writers of "literary" English' (and Dickens in (592a)
is clearly playing on this):

(592)   a. *Did an elderly gentleman essay* to stop the progress of the ball, it
            rolled between his legs, or slipped between his fingers. *Did a
            slim gentleman try* to catch it, it struck him on the nose
                                            (1836–7 Dickens, *Pickwick* vii.102 [Visser])

        b. My dear friend, *did I want* your aid I would accept it
                                    (1840 Bulwer-Lytton, *Money* V.iii, in *19c Plays*, ed. Rowell p. 112;
                                                                                    omitted in Booth)

        c. As he lay there he thought of what he would do *did Markovitch*
            really *go* off his head.
                                            (1919 Sir Hugh S. Walpole, *Secret City* (Macmillan, 1934)
                                                                                        III.404 [Visser])

        d. 'I wish I had said that,' we might be tempted to say admiringly,
            did we not of course *remember* that this was how one legendary
            wit left himself open to perhaps the most famously crushing
            retort of all: 'You will, Oscar, you will.'
                                            (1993 'Centipede', *The Guardian 2* p. 11 (12 Aug.))

The fact that *had* and *did* pattern with subjunctive *were* (and modals) in
inverted protases, and also, as we have seen in section 3.3.4.2, in apodoses,
might justify calling them past subjunctive in such instances, although it can
also be referred merely to the normal properties of operators. There is,
however, no need for us to get involved in argument as to whether, say, *took*
in (593) is indicative, because formally indistinguishable from indicative
took, or subjunctive, on analogy with *were* in (588):

(593)   If Jim *took* more care than he does

For discussion see Visser (1963–73: section 834).

Some idea of frequency of inverted protases is given by table 3.11,
based on the more informal genres of ARCHER (British texts only).
Inversion shows a general decline over time.[84] After 1850 the total number

Table 3.11. *Inverted protases and* if-*clauses in ARCHER*

	Had (perfect auxiliary only)		*Were*		*Should*		*Could*	
	Inverted	*If*	Inverted	*If*	Inverted	*If*	Inverted	*If*
1650–99	28 (57%)	21	11 (41%)	16	10 (38%)	16	1 (25%)	3
1700–49	21 (51%)	20	17 (57%)	13	6 (25%)	16	4 (17%)	19
1750–99	13 (41%)	19	12 (43%)	16	2 (10%)	19	2 (13%)	13
1800–49	9 (38%)	15	7 (30%)	16	13 (46%)	15	6 (26%)	17
1850–99	11 (30%)	26	0 (0%)	20	3 (60%)	2	0 (0%)	8
1900–49	2 (17%)	10	0 (0%)	9	2 (67%)	1	0 (0%)	12
1950–	2 (7%)	28	1 (5%)	19	0 (0%)	3	0 (0%)	15

of occurrences of *should* is low and the percentages therefore of little value. The forms *did* (2 inverted examples altogether), *would* (3), *might* (1), *must* (0) were not worth tabulating, while for practical reasons *was* was not counted at all. In my letters corpus the overall figures are 6 inverted protases (5 per cent) to 108 *if*-clauses. Inversion nearly always involves unreal conditionals; (592a) is a rare exception.

It was formerly possible for the two clauses of an unreal conditional to have verbal groups of parallel structure:

(594)   a. But were your eyes the only things that were inquisitive? *Had* I *been* in your place, my tongue, I fancy, *had been* curious too.

(1777 (1781) Sheridan, *Scarborough* II.i 583.16)

   b. Ah! Miss Vesey, if that poor woman *had not closed* the eyes of my lost mother, Alfred Evelyn *had not been* this beggar to your father.

(1840 Bulwer-Lytton, *Money* I.i, in *19c plays*, ed. Rowell p. 54; Booth p. 167 prints *would not have been*)

As unreal conditional apodoses have moved towards an obligatory modal verb, it seems at least possible that the protases will restore the parallelism by following suit. Certainly, non-standard examples like the following are not uncommon, especially where there is some trace of a volitional meaning in *would*, (595a), or a non-English substratum, though Fillmore (1990: 153) regards it as common in current American usage:

(595)   a. I think if he *would have let* me just look at things quietly . . . it *would have been* all right   (1877 Sewell, *Black Beauty* xxix.123)

   b. If I *would have known* that, I *would have acted* differently.

See further section 3.3.2.5 above.

The protasis of a conditional, then, may be marked by a subordinating conjunction, most commonly *if*, or by subject-auxiliary inversion, and perhaps also by the use of a subjunctive verb. It is noteworthy that the imperative may also be used in certain circumstances:

(596) a. '*Stir* a whisker, Lungri, and I ram the Red Flower [*sc.* fire] down thy gullet!'

(1894 Kipling, *Jungle book*, 'Mowgli's Brothers' (Macmillan, 1895) 28)

b. *Try* to be nice and people walk all over you.

This pattern is semantically similar to a conditional (*If you stir a whisker...*). The imperative is morphologically the base form of the verb and identical to the present subjunctive. In some examples the imperative clause does retain some directive force as well as approximating to a conditional protasis:

(597) *Give* me some money and I'll help you escape.

The conjunction *or* is similarly used to imply a negative condition, as in (630c) or:

(598) *Give* me some money or I'll shoot.

See Quirk, Greenbaum, Leech & Svartvik (1985: 13.25, 13.30).

A new kind of conditional structure has no formal marking of the protasis at all: the structure is in form merely a co-ordination of main clauses corresponding to protasis and apodosis, with normal tensed verbs in both:

(599) a. You *dare* smack me in the face again, my girl, and I'll lay you out flat (1932 Shaw, *Too True to be Good* II p. 1145)

b. He *catches* that pass and the game is tied. (*c.* 1990 att. Langacker)

(600) a. 'You*'re* a man, you *want* to do a thing, you do it . . .' [spoken to a woman] (1921 Lawrence, *Women* iv.41)

b. You *keep* smoking those cigarettes, you're gonna start coughing again. (PDE [Hopper & Traugott])

c. ' . . . Next, it's like, "save Bangladesh". You *take* that burden on, you'll lose your mind.'

(1994 Ice-T [Tracey Marrow], *The Guardian Weekend* p. 7 (13 Aug.))

In fact, Langacker actually offers (599b) as a **counterfactual** example – the pass has already been dropped – in the speech of American sports announcers (1991: 268). It is not clear whether the (characteristically

American?) (600) type is a normal conditional with ellipsis of *if* (thus Lawler, LINGUIST 4–121, citing Thrasher 1974), or an asyndetic co-ordination – one without any conjunction – that is otherwise like (599). As for (599a), which seems to be the oldest, the mixed use of DARE is interesting, as that partially modal form is normal in nonassertive contexts, including conventional *if*-protases, but rare in a positive declarative, so it is not quite a 'normal' tensed verb.[85] The similarity to an *if*-protasis is consonant with a historical derivation of the (600) type by clipping of initial *if*, but it could merely be that the verbal syntax is determined by the semantics of conditionals. A curiosity of these developments is that *and* can now introduce the clause corresponding to the apodosis of the conditional, whereas in earlier English *an(d)* could be used as the subordinating conjunction which introduced the protasis; see *CHEL* III, forthcoming.

The range of conjunctions has shown some alteration. The group *in case (that)* noted in *CHEL* III (forthcoming) no longer occurs with *that* (cf. 3.6.6 above); in formal AmerE usage – common in linguistics – it retains the meaning 'in the event that, on condition that':

(601)   a. no cellar – except a small hole, dug in the ground, called a cyclone cellar, where the family could go *in case* one of those great whirlwinds arose, mighty enough to crush any building in its path.   (1911 Baum, *Wizard of Oz* i.9)
        b. the old wooden bed up there was unsafe: it was wobbly and the heavy headboard would crash down on father's head *in case* the bed fell, and kill him.

   (1933 Thurber, *The Night the Bed Fell*, in *Vintage Thurber*
   (Hamish Hamilton, 1963) II.161)

However, this meaning is no longer available in normal BrE usage; the *OED* marks it as obsolete (s.v. *case* n.[1] 10a). In BrE the subordinate clause of:

(602)   I'll take an umbrella *in case* it rains.

could only mean 'in provision against the case that it might rain' (thus *OED* 10c), not 'on condition that it does rain'; see also Quirk, Greenbaum, Leech & Svartvik (1985: 15.35n.[g], 15.46). In this meaning *in case* has virtually replaced *lest* in clauses which combine reason with contingency. Somewhat similar, though perhaps involving reason and time, is *against* in:

(603)   a. a voluntary partner secured *against* the dancing began
                    (1816 Austen, *Mansfield Park* II.x[xxviii].274 [Phillipps])

b. *You* [original emphasis] had better be getting a new gown or two I think, but not a third carmelite *against* this gets dirty.

(1852 Gaskell, *Letters* 134a p. 853 (1 Oct.))

Another usage of related meaning, *for* 'as a precaution against, for fear of' + *-ing*, is recorded in isolated examples *c.* 1800, though otherwise only up to the early eighteenth century (*OED* s.v., prep. A.23d; Visser 1963–73: section 1064).

An earlier use of *so* in the sense 'provided that' is illustrated by:

(604)   Love him! Why do you think I love him, Nurse? I'cod, I would not care if he was hang'd, *so* I were but once married to him.

(1777 (1781) Sheridan, *Scarborough* IV.i 602.20)

The *OED* has examples until the mid-nineteenth century (s.v. *so* adv. and conj. B.26a). *So as* was also used (Phillipps 1970: 197):

(605)   I take any part you choose to give me, *so as* it be comic.

(1816 Austen, *Mansfield Park* I.xiv.131 [Phillipps])

The *OED*'s last citation is from 1853 Dickens, but this usage, like the previous one, is not marked as obsolete (B.30).

The following conditional-concessive use of *though* is archaic:

(606)   And he had plenty of unsettled subjects to meditate upon, *though* he had been walking to the Land's End. (= 'And he had – and would have had – plenty . . . even if he had been walking . . .')

(1855–7 Dickens, *Little Dorrit* I.xvi.183)

Even if would be a more likely conjunction in PDE; furthermore the conditional aspect of the meaning would nowadays be signalled by *would have Ved* in the apodosis.

Except was formerly used as a conjunction in the sense 'unless':

(607)   The heat which all bodies radiate into space can have no influence in moving them, *except* there be something in the nature of a *recoil* [original emphasis] in the act of emitting radiation. And even should there be such a recoil . . .

(1875 (1876) William Crookes, 'On repulsion . . .', *Philos. Trans.* 165 p. 523 [ARCHER])

Phillipps cites a similar use from Jane Austen and contrasts it with nonoccurrence as a conjunction in PDE (1970: 197). The *OED* notes another conjunction use too, in clauses of exception (where it is a synonym of 'only'), but states that since the seventeenth century this usage has only occurred in the full form *except that* (s.v. *except* conj. C.1). However, Quirk, Greenbaum, Leech & Svartvik cite both uses for PDE, the former labelled as 'informal AmE' (1985: 15.34 n.[b], 15.44), and the latter is common enough:

(608)   'I know it's none of my business, Dot, *except* I rather like him.'
                        (1951 Marquand, *Just a Little Dutch Girl* xxi.321 [ARCHER])

The disagreements suggest at least some changes in acceptability and stylistic level. As for conjunction *without* 'unless' followed by a finite clause, the *OED* traces its decline from literary through colloquial to illiterate register (s.v., C.2):

(609)   'He means,' said Jimmy, 'that we can't take you into an exploring party *without* we know what you want to go for.'
                        (1907 Nesbit, *Enchanted Castle* xi.232)

3.6.6.4   Temporal clauses

There is relatively little to report on temporal clauses in lModE. Even in eModE '[t]he mood of the temporal clauses is mostly indicative; subjunctive forms appear when uncertainty, non-factuality or prospect are indicated' (*CHEL* III, forthcoming). If this was often the case in eModE in clauses referring to future time, introduced by *till, before*, etc., it becomes increasingly rare through the lModE period:

(610)   The Rustic sits waiting *till* the river *run* dry
                        (1837 Carlyle, *French Revolution*, II, *Constitution* (Chapman & Hall),
                                                        IV.i.185 [Visser])

One conjunction lost to any but poetic use is *ere* 'before'.

3.6.6.5   Clauses of comparison

In clauses of comparison the structure *so . . . as*, always less common that *as . . . as*, is now only archaic or dialectal in affirmative clauses (*OED* s.v. *so* adv. and conj. B.21b), and uncommon even in negative clauses:

(611)   a. a young lady *so* well brought up *as* Miss Grantly
                        (1860–1 Trollope, *Framley* xxix.283)
         b. they were none of them nearly *so* large and brave *as* you.
                        (1911 Baum, *Wizard of Oz* xxi.159)

(612)   a. These Philadelphians seem to me *as* well calculated to excel in commerce *as* to triumph in war.
                        (1787 Markoe, *Algerian Spy*, Letter xii p. 2 [ARCHER])

b. 'In the first place they're not nearly *as* pointed *as* they once were . . .'   (1960 Coward, *Pomp & Circumstance* p. 125 [ARCHER])

The *but what* variant appeared in clauses of comparison after a negative, just as in relative clauses (3.6.5.2 above):

(613)   Bradford is not *so far away but what she might*. [*sc.* come to Manchester]   (1850 Gaskell, *Letters* 72 p. 118 (14 May))

This is no longer standard.

In clauses of similarity, *like* is increasingly often found as a conjunction instead of *as*. It is conceivable that (614a) is meant to signal moral hypocrisy through 'substandard' (i.e. non-standard) grammar, while (614b) is intended to be unliterary and somewhat childlike:

(614)   a. but an open-hearted creature *like* I am, has little talent for concealment.   (1863 Hazlewood, *Lady Audley's Secret* II.i p. 253)
         b. 'I'm taking care of it – *like* you told us to.'
                                              (1906 Nesbit, *Amulet* iv.56)

The entry in the *OED* (s.v. *like* adv. (conj.) B.6a) makes clear that the usage is an old one which came to be 'generally condemned as vulgar or slovenly', although condemnation is probably less and less general.

Other recent uses of *like* are moving away from the sense of comparison. One is the 'approximator' usage, discussed in 3.4.4 above. Another introduces (more-or-less) direct speech or thought, where *I'm like 'X'* (usually present tense of BE) is slightly less explicit than *I go 'X'* in the sense 'I say/think roughly "X"':

(615)   And I'*m like*, 'Oh.' And *I go*, 'Is that where the redwoods are?'
                                    (*c.* 1990 att. Blyth, Recktenwald & Wang)

BE *like* is also newer: Blyth, Recktenwald & Wang (1990) cite what they regard as an early report of the usage, dated 1982. For a treatment in terms of grammaticalisation see Romaine & Lange (1991).

3.6.6.6   Nonfinite and verbless adverbial clauses

Adverbial clauses without a finite verb can be cross-classified by the form of verb (bare infinitive, *to*-infinitive, *-ing*, past participle, or indeed no verb at all), by whether the subject is expressed, and by whether there is a subordinator. Of twenty permutations, most are possible, many showing little change over our period. Meanings can belong to any of the semantic categories used above for finite adverbial clauses, or to more than one, especially when there is no subordinator.

Absolute constructions have no subordinator, and an expressed subject different from the subject of the higher clause, so there is no explicit syntactic link between the clauses (Quirk, Greenbaum, Leech & Svartvik 1985: 15.58):

(616) a. but *the great point once decided* I don't let trifles trouble me much.
       (1786 Betsy Sheridan, *Journal* 29 p. 97 (2 Sep.))

       b. so that at the end of the year, *all things deducted* I get almost nothing.   (1858 Tennyson, *Letters* II.194 (3 Feb.) [ARCHER])

       c. The magistrate was very considerate, and *the boy appearing really to have been misled by a fellow-apprentice*, dismissed him with a reprimand.   (1862 Green, *Letters* 114 (15 Dec.))

Pronominal subjects – fairly rare, about 1 per cent of Kortmann's PDE corpus (1992: 22) – were normally in subjective case, at least until the end of the nineteenth century (Visser 1963–73: sections 985, 994, 1076, 1078, 1154). Absolute constructions grew in popularity from ME and through the eModE period with support from Latin analogues (*CHEL* III, forthcoming). Participial absolutes have now declined noticeably, except in stereotyped expressions:

(617) Tomorrow we dine with Russell, the Scotsman, *weather permitting*.
       (1872 *Amberley Papers* II.515 (16 Aug.))

One replacement involves the subordinators *with* and *without*:

(618) a. 'You don't mean to say you took 'em down, rings and all, *with him lying there*?' said Joe.
       (1843 Dickens, *Christmas Carol* iv.63 [Visser])

       b. *With Sir Percy away*, I have even more visitors than before
       (1918 Bell, *Letters* II.449 (6 Mar.))

       c. *With his shirtsleeves rolled up* and wearing a pair of khaki pants, Tripp sat up then, holding his knees to his chest.
       (1957 Buechner, *Return of Ansel Gibbs* ix.200 [ARCHER])

       d. *With tears filling his eyes*, the Texas Democrat told his colleagues . . . that   (1989 *Los Angeles Times* p. 1 (1 Jun.) [ARCHER])

(619) a. *Without any regard for rest-room protocol*, the hulking stranger almost knocked Herford off his pins.
       (1961 *Brown Corpus*, Belles Lettres G40:17)

       b. and she could be burned to a crisp *without anybody knowing it*.
       (ibid., Romance P02:87)

The subject is always in the objective case, reflecting the prepositional origin of *with(out)*. *With* is easily the most common introducing word, and frequency appears to have increased greatly in the present century. Note too *what with*, which introduces nonfinite and verbless clauses of cause, found since the eModE period:

(620)   We had a very bad harvest this year, *what with lack of rain and neglect of canals.*   (1917 Bell, *Letters* II.135 (7 Dec.))

Absolute clauses can be introduced by *and*, (621), sometimes making a rounding-off formula, and it is not a great step to certain kinds of independent minor clause, commonly used as an exclamatory question or echo response, (622). The former can have any nonfinite verb form (or none), the latter tend to have a base form or *to*-infinitive:

(621)   a. Why didnt you say so before? *and us losing our time listening to your silliness!*   (1912 Shaw, *Pygmalion* I p. 719 [Visser])
         b. I dont know what I shall do when you are gone, with no one but Ann in the house; *and she always occupied with the men*!
                                                        (1903 Shaw, *Man & Superman* IV p. 402 [Visser])
         c. Oh, the bad times we've had, *and no one know*!
                                                        (1894 Ward, *Marcella* II.xi.258 [Visser])

(622)   She! – she talk of social reform and 'character'; she give her opinion, as of right, on points of speculation and of ethics . . . !
                                                        (ibid. III.vi.378 [Visser])

Change here again consists in the colloquial substitution of objective for subjective where the subject of the verb is a case-marked pronoun.

The so-called unattached participle has an implicit subject that is not – as it 'should' be – made explicit as subject of the higher clause:

(623)   a. but, *after calling several times for poison*, and *requesting some lady or gentleman to blow his brains out*, gentler feelings came upon him, and he wept pathetically.
                                                        (1838–9 Dickens, *Nickleby* xxi.263 [Visser])
         b. *Taken by surprise*, his scant affection for his brother had made a momentary concession to dishonour.
                                                        (1877 James, *The American* xxi.251 [ARCHER])
         c. She stood in the old yard of the inn, *smelling of straw and stables and petrol.*   (1921 Lawrence, *Women* xxxiii.304 [Visser])
         d. *Having said that*, it must be made clear to every interested person that   (1961 *LOB Corpus*, Press: editorial B11:67)

Surprisingly, 1863 is the earliest criticism of this now much-vilified usage that Visser can find (1963–73: section 1072). My examples are of various sorts, and only (623c) stands in any real danger of putting the reader on a false scent. The participles of (623a) are unattached in relation to the *gentler feelings* clause, but not if the next clause (which Visser omits) is counted. The subject of *taken by surprise* in (623b) is probably meant to be *his scant affection* rather than *he*, since Henry James seems an unlikely author to leave a participle dangling. As for (623d), *having said that* is routinely left unattached nowadays, perhaps by analogy with style disjuncts like *to say the least* or *talking of X*, or with absolute constructions like *that said*; if now standard – a moot point – it contradicts Visser's claim that 'established' uses of unattached *-ing* never involve *having* + past participle (1963–73: section 1075).

A clause type which is increasingly common is illustrated by:

(624)   a. Why, Commodore, *as far as a few barrels of biscuits and beer*
                        (1776 T. Francklin, *Contract* II p. 49 [ARCHER])
        b. *As far as whether I could attend this sort of a function in your church*
           . . . then I could attend.
        (1960 J. F. Kennedy in *U.S. News & World Report* 26 Sept. 76/1 [*OED*])

As far as X 'concerning X' (where X is usually an NP or a gerund clause and the phrase serves to limit the topic of the sentence) appears to be a shortening of such finite clauses as *as far as X is/are concerned* or *as far as X go(es)*, possibly with a contribution from *as for/to X*. It must already have been noticeably common in 1926 to have attracted condemnation (citation in *OED* s.v. *far* adv. 6b). (The very early (624a) is interrupted by another speaker and so not a certain example.) Rickford, Wasow, Mendoza-Denton & Espinoza (1995) regard ellipsis after a simple NP as essentially a (late) twentieth-century phenomenon.[86] We might compare the similar shortening in Modern German of *von X her gesehen/betrachtet* to *von X her* (Lehmann 1991: 2.4.1). In English the effect is to create a new compound preposition used for disjuncts.

We conclude this section with some patterns involving infinitives with subject unexpressed. Now, nonfinite clauses without expressed subject generally share their underlying subject with the higher verb, as in *Jim wishes to make a statement*. They have always been common and will not be discussed further – though if they were, it probably ought to be under the heading of nominal clauses. The infinitive clauses to be covered do belong, more or less, in the present section. We look first at infinitives whose unexpressed subject (represented in (625) by [ø]) *differs* from that of the higher verb; see here Fischer (1990), Denison (1993a: chapter 8), *CHEL* III (forthcoming). Few verbs in our period permit such structures compared to the range available in OE, ME or eModE. The few examples in Visser's (1963–73: sections 1195–1249) are in archaistic works or translations:

(625) a. Herluin *bade [∅] light* the peat-stalk [*sc.* peat-stack] under me
               (1865 Kingsley, *Hereward* (Macmillan, 1889) i.34 [Visser])
     b. Will you not go or *send [∅] to say* that we are come?
               (1954 Tolkien, *Two Towers* III.vi.113 [Visser])
     c. When she had no company at home, he would *urge [∅] to go*
       and seek it abroad.
               (1804 *Something Odd, a Novel, by Gabrielli* I, 130 [Visser])

Exceptions of wider occurrence are largely fossilised set phrases involving higher verb LET and such infinitives as *drive, fly, go, live,* HEAR *say/tell,* and MAKE *believe,* though at least three new ones have arisen, including LEAVE *go* in mid-nineteenth century (mentioned already in 3.4.2.5 above), and MAKE *do* in the twentieth. At least two of the older combinations have spawned derived nouns: eModE *hearsay,* lModE *make-believe.* Two further exceptional types are just plain anomalous:

(626) 'The man in the shop *said to come* over the trestle and rap on this
     window.'   (1955 Goyen, *In a Farther Country* vi.103 [ARCHER])

(627) a. one of the people who can *help to comfort* them.
               (1918 Bell, *Letters* II.454 (18 Apr.))
     b. I was just into Dublin to *help take* care of her little brothers
       and sisters.   (1968 Donleavy, *Beastly Beatitudes* xviii.193 [ARCHER])

According to Visser, SAY *to* V only goes back to the 1920s and is perhaps of Irish or American origin (1963–73: section 1242). But HELP *(to)* V is much older. It is a very interesting construction, for two reasons. One is that the (unexpressed) subject of the lower verb is arguably not wholly different from the subject of the higher verb, so that a sentence like *I helped Jim to take care of them* blurs a well-known distinction in transformational grammar between 'object control' (*I told Jim to take care of them*) and 'subject control' (*I promised Jim to take care of them*). On the basic distinction see e.g. Radford (1988: 320–4). The second claim on our notice comes from the marking of the infinitive: subjectless plain infinitives are not normally found after catenatives, only after modals.

Now we come on to infinitives whose unexpressed subject is the same as that of the higher verb, the normal case, but lacking the infinitive marker *to,* which – as just noted – is *ab*normal. The following examples are now characteristically American or north or north-east Midlands BrE dialect:

(628) a. Visitors are welcome to *come see* what these dedicated mothers can do. (1961 *Brown Corpus*, Press: Editorial B18:67)

b. 'I'll just *run say* hello to him and I'll be right back,'
(1992 Tartt, *Secret History* iii.156)

c. First Francis, and then Charles and Camilla, moved to *go stand* with him (ibid. vii.495)

Visser has examples with GO from OE through to the present day, none American prior to the twentieth century (1963–73: sections 1318, 1320); see also *CHEL* III (forthcoming) and Orton, Sanderson & Widdowson (1978: S4 GO AND). It is characteristic of this semi-auxiliary use of COME, GO, etc. that the first verb is always a bare stem (cf. 3.3.9 above), despite one implausible rogue example with *went look* cited by Visser.

3.6.6.7 Pseudo-coordination: *and* instead of *to* after catenatives
A modern-looking construction uses *and* rather than *to* to introduce a verb in the complement of another verb, a link called **pseudo-coordination** in Quirk, Greenbaum, Leech & Svartvik (1985: 13.98):

(629) a. *Come and enjoy* your repute at the Parsonage.
(1862 Green, *Letters* 96 (15 Jan.))

b. he was forced *to* leave at last, and *go and do* his duty.
(1848 Gaskell, *Mary Barton* xv.178 [ARCHER])

(630) a. but I know you are very happy & get much loved where you are so I *will try & not be* unhappy without you.
(1873 *Amberley Papers* II.559 (20 Dec.))

b. I really *must try* this time *& work* a réunion between you.
(1890 Dowson, *Letters* 94 p. 142 (14 Mar.))

c. and *do* for goodness' sake *try and realize* that you're a pestilential scourge, or you'll find yourself in a most awful fix.
(1898 Grahame, *The Reluctant Dragon* 19)

(631) a. but if I think of anything more, I *will be sure and tell* you.
(1850 Gaskell, *Moorland Cottage* iv.310)

b. *Mind & come.* (1890 Dowson, *Letters* 87 p. 135 (?10 Feb.))

The first verb is almost always a base form (infinitive or imperative), though certain constructions may permit the general present if it is identical to the base form.[87] The second verb is a base form. Although they retain much of their normal meanings as lexical verbs, the two verbs do not head independent predicates with potentially independent reference. The general informality of these patterns may have limited their frequency in writing: prescriptive grammar tends to recommend *to* for *and*, or in the case of (631b) a finite clause.

In origin most of the constructions actually date from before our period. For COME Visser has examples from lME, for GO from 1600 Shakespeare, for TRY from 1671 Milton (1963–73: sections 1316, 1319, 1321, 1193). Jespersen has examples of some less usual combinations (1909–49: V 210–11).

Another type is illustrated by:

(632)   a. 'I'*m going* back *and tell* Terry and Gottlieb they can go to the devil . . .'
                    (1925 S. Lewis, *Arrowsmith* (Grossett & Dunlap) xxvii.300)
        b. I'*m going* out *and get* a girl for my picture.
                    (1933 J. Creelman, R. Rose, *King Kong* [film dialogue])
        c. I'*m taking* him to the Sheriff *and make sure* he's destroyed.
                    (1939 N. Longley, F. Ryerson, E. A. Woolf, *Wizard of Oz*
                    [film dialogue])

This characteristically American pattern allows the first verb to be in the progressive, though the second verb remains in the base form. The first two examples – (632a) is called 'slipshod' by Jespersen (1909–49: V 211)! – seem to be more widely acceptable to American ears than (632c).

What looks like yet another variant, especially common with GO, seems to relax the morphological constraint on the verbs, only requiring that both verbs have the same tense or nonfinite part. Writers such as Visser (1963–73: section 2019) concentrate on the perfect. In fact *any* part of GO can show the same bleached, derogatory meaning:

(633)   a. 'she . . . *goes and tells* the people on board ship that it is all my fault.'
                    (1888 Rider Haggard, *Mr. Meeson's Will* (Longmans Green,
                    1921) vi.72 [Poutsma])
        b. Poor Harriet! But of course if her grey matter *went and got* watery   (1908 Jones, *Dolly Reforming Herself* II p. 56 [ARCHER])
        c. So sorry to have offended him by *going and getting* wounded.
                    (1925 S. Lewis, *Arrowsmith* (Grossett & Dunlap) xxvi.290)
        d. Louise *has* actually *gone and taken* a step which I consider dreadful.   (1871 Daly, *Divorce* II p. 99 [ARCHER])

Since there is no clear syntactic demarcation from true co-ordination, the usage of (633) is essentially a semantic change in GO – to what Carden & Pesetsky call an '"unexpected event" reading' (1977: 89). Formerly non-standard, it is increasingly part of colloquial standard. In the perfect, *been* commutes with *gone*, as it does in other uses (3.3.2.4 above); the doubled *been and gone and V* marking comically vulgar English is a literary cliché:

(634)　　a. and he *has been and tipped* me this.

(1879 Meredith, Egoist xlvii.592)

　　　　　b. 'There now, you*'ve been and gone and strook* my Poll parrot right in the fevvers – strook 'im something crool, you 'ave.'

(1904 Nesbit, Phoenix v.108)

Other verbs such as COME show similar propensities, though rarely with such striking semantic change as GO. The morphological variety and the fact that *to* cannot be substituted for *and* in (633–4) make it a rather different kind of pseudo-coordination from the preceding types. And with that, this potentially endless survey concludes on *and*.

NOTES

I am grateful for financial assistance in the compilation of my letters corpus from the University of Manchester Research Support Fund and from the Faculty of Arts.

1　I follow the practice of Palmer (1988), Denison (1993a), among others, of indicating lexemes by SMALL CAPITALS. It is with verbs above all in lModE that the practice is useful: 'HAVE', for instance, can be cited where inflectional variation is irrelevant, to subsume all of the forms *have, has, had,* and *having,* and indeed also *'ve, 's, 'd, haven't, hasn't, hadn't.* Verbal lexemes are cited under the form of the infinitive, where it exists, and otherwise of the 3 SG present.

2　Examples found in corpora or secondary sources are acknowledged briefly in square brackets with '*OED*', 'ARCHER', 'Jespersen', 'Visser', and so on. Acronyms occurring here are: ARCHER = A Representative Corpus of Historical English Registers (see note 3), LOB Corpus = The Lancaster–Oslo/Bergen Corpus of British English, WWP = Women Writers Project, Brown University, all included in the list of Textual sources, and *OED* = *Oxford English Dictionary*, 2nd edition on CD-ROM (see note 8), under Simpson & Weiner (1992) in the Bibliography. Scholars' names point to stan-dard reference works like Jespersen's *Modern English Grammar*, Poutsma's *Grammar* and Visser's *Historical Syntax*, or to works on particular topics – full details in the Bibliography. In nearly all cases the source is mentioned close by in the text. Those examples taken from the *OED* have not generally been verified separately, but as many as possible of the others have been checked in good editions.

Italics in examples are generally added by me to draw attention to the relevant words. Where italics are original this is explicitly noted.

3 ARCHER was generously provided by Edward Finegan and Douglas Biber, to whom I am most grateful; it is described in Biber, Finegan, Atkinson, Beck, Burges & Burges (1994). The version available to me contains over 1.7 million words and has little usable tagging. I must also thank Linda van Bergen for her considerable help in preparing and investigating ARCHER and other corpora, for the figures for table 3.2, table 3.6, table 3.10, and table 3.11 and, for certain datings in table 3.8, for help with checking, and for helpful criticism.

4 It is not practical for me, with current technology and limited resources, to analyse a large spoken corpus. It would have been desirable, however, and before long I expect it to be a routine academic procedure. (On corpus linguistics generally see the Introduction to this volume) In this chapter there are a mere handful of examples from speech, several of those from scripted movie dialogue. On early cylinder recordings see this volume: p. 12.

5 Here I take the traditional view that the noun and not the determiner is head.

6 Strictly speaking, the same label should not be used both for a category (word class) and for a functional class. Unfortunately, Huddleston (1984) uses **Determiner** as a functional label and **Determinative** as a category, while Quirk, Greenbaum, Leech & Svartvik (1985) do just the opposite! Since in this instance there is a reasonably good correlation between category and function, I shall use **determiner** indiscriminately for both purposes.

7 I except the phrase *of NP's acquaintance*, which neutralises the distinction between abstract and collective senses.

8 The *OED*'s collection may be unsystematic, but it is large, wide-ranging, accurate and accurately dated, electronically-readable in the CD-ROM version of the *Dictionary*, and there! These advantages seem to me overwhelming, and I have used the quotations as a corpus at several points in this chapter. It is interesting that earliest attestations and relative frequencies of usage do not always match what appears in the actual entry of a word.

The figures for *acquaintance* which appear in table 3.1 have a small margin of error for the handful of examples whose status could only be guessed at in the absence of fuller context.

9 There is, of course, a BrE use of *value* as a count noun, as in *Moral values are important*, but the contrast in (6) depends on the sense 'good value, bargain'. Langacker has an example containing the words *This car . . . is a great value for the money* (1991: 500). Compare too the word *fruit* on, say, a supermarket sign, possible in BrE and AmerE, as against *fruits*, impossible in BrE.

10 Dekeyser finds this rule violated just twice (once each way: *who* + singular concord, *which* + plural) in his extensive nineteenth-century material (1975: 53).

11 It is also reported as less common in Australian English (*CHEL* V: 303). Bauer has some interesting historical statistics on use of the noun *government* in editorials in the London *Times* 1900–85 (1990: 21–2). He finds 'plural concord rather more frequent than singular concord' up to about 1935, then 'a marked tendency for plural concord to appear with *government* when it denotes the British government, and singular concord to appear with *government* when it denotes some other government' from about 1940 to 1965, and thereafter mainly singular concord throughout. So in this sample the trend is if anything *away* from plural concord.

12 Discussion concerns NPs consisting of just a determiner and *one*. With intervening adjectives the patterns are much older, e.g. *all my pretty ones* 1605 Shakespeare; *these young ones c.* 1840 (*OED* s.v. *tucker* v.).

   Notice too that although the relevant clause of (26b) appears perfectly normal for standard PDE, the clauses on either side are distinctly non-standard in various ways. Example (26a) is from a text that is markedly Scottish in dialect.

13 I use the terms **subjective** (*he*, etc.) and **objective** (*him*), as do Quirk, Greenbaum, Leech & Svartvik (1985) and Rissanen in *CHEL* III. Rodney Huddleston made a persuasive case (p.c., 12 Dec. 93) for the use of **nominative** and **accusative** instead, given that subjective form correlates only imperfectly with subject function and likewise objective form with object function, but the Latin-based terms are opaque, and **accusative** in particular is highly counter-intuitive for, say, indirect objects (while **dative** has no support at all in ModE morphology). I have, however, retained the Latinate **genitive** (*his*) rather than use the notional – and very imprecise – term **possessive**. **Disjunctive genitive** refers to independent use without a following noun (*mine*, etc.).

14 Strang suggests (1970: 139–41) that the originally plural *ye/you* had become the unmarked second person pronoun by about 1600, and that from the late eighteenth century *thou/thee* and associated verbal inflections survived only peripherally – mainly in dialects and in the heightened archaistic languages of literature and religion. (See Sundby, Bjørge & Haugland 1991: 220–1 for some eighteenth-century comments on the use of *thou*, and also *CHEL* V: 229.)

15 The *not me* usage is probably older still, although the following gapped construction is not quite the same:

a.   The truth is this – that my pen governs me – not me *my* pen.
                              (1767 Sterne, *Letters* 749 (19 Sep.) [ARCHER])

   In corroboration of the claim that the third person subjective was much more resilient, note that a minor character in *Middlemarch* (1871–2), Mrs Dollop, the pub landlady, whose speech is comically non-standard, nevertheless says *Not they, Mr Jonas!* (lxxi.723). And from a youth we find, in a different construction, *The more spooneys they!* (finale.833), cf. PDE *The more fools them*.

16 Jespersen suggests that the order of adoption was not so much conditioned (determined) by person as by phonetic patterning: objective *me*, *thee* rhyme with subjective *he*, *she*, *we*, *ye* and so get used in traditionally subjective contexts where *him*, *her*, *us* would not be found (1894: 247–52). In fact, though, he tends to contrast 1 SG with 3 SG only, perhaps because 1 SG is the most commonly found person, and there is little hard evidence for the crucial items which would distinguish phonetic conditioning from the factor of person which I have suggested, namely 1 PL. If my Nesbit material on the *Not X* pattern is a safe indicator, though, person overrides any phonetic influence.

Further work is needed on occurrence of objective pronouns after a copula verb. In Visser's collection (1963–73: section 266), 1 SG and 2 SG occur from about 1600, 1 PL not until 1816 – though the *OED* has one dated 1713 s.v. *singularity* 3. The 3 SG occurs from about 1700, 3 PL once 1654–66, then 1850.

I note that Stageberg (1965: 171) gives the following examples without comment among a list of PDE predicatives:

a.   This is *shé*.
b.   It's *mé*.

(I owe this reference to Gareth Jones.)

17 The point that (47) is now effectively standard was made to me by Edward Finegan (p.c., 10 Nov. 93), and confirmed in Dillard (1992: 227–8); eighty years ago Poutsma expressed surprise to find that it was 'not, apparently, confined to vulgar English' (1914–29: IV 1345).

Bolinger writes of an incipient rule 'for personal pronouns as objects of prepositions, where – by dint of generations of hyperurban education – the only fairly secure spot for the objective case is with *one* preposition followed by *one* pronoun; the slightest show of any more complex affinity is apt to trigger the nominative' (1992: II 598, original emphasis).

Here is one example where the co-ordinate NP may be regarded as in loose apposition to the object *us*:

a.   Then W<m> saw *us M.A. M.E., Eliz. and I* off into an Omnibus
(1838 Gaskell, *Letters* 11 p. 26 (17 Aug.))

18 Among dialects which normally use the inflection -*s* throughout the present tense (*Birds sings*, etc.), there are some which use -∅ when the verb is immediately preceded by a subject pronoun (the 'Northern subject rule', *CHEL* V: 221–2). This suggests that subject–verb concord may operate differently with pronouns than with other NPs. Incipient loss of concord may be implicated both in pronominal case marking and in the tendency towards verbal invariance discussed in section 3.3.9.

19 Compare the *itself* of (53) with the same author's

a.   *Everyone* repeated *himself* several times

(1906 Nesbit, Amulet vii.119)

This concerns the same group of two boys but only one of the two girls!

Themselves as anaphor to a singular NP, as in (54), is common in PDE; Furness (1992: 649) gives three newspaper examples from 1988. As for *themself*, its use in recent examples like (55) is actually a *re*appearance: the *OED* says that 'in Standard Eng. *themself* was the normal form to *c.* 1540, but disappeared *c.* 1570'. The *OED* has no modern examples, but I have attested a few, and there are at least seven in the COBUILD corpora (HarperCollins/ University of Birmingham, School of English, accessed on demonstration basis). The *English Dialect Dictionary* lists *themself* as a Scotticism (I owe this last reference to Pat Poussa).

20 The usage survives best in obsolescent fixed phrases like *borrowed/translated from the French*. (The same goes for other language names, of course, as in *the Welsh* of (348b).)

21 The last example of determiner *none* in the *OED* is dated 1801 (s.v., B.1a). There are some later nineteenth-century examples of *none* placed after and separated from its noun, plus 1827 *none other Lord*. Another possible late survival is *none such*, if the head is (pronoun) *such* with determiner *none*, but it may equally well be taken as head (pronoun) *none* postmodified by *such* – thus Quirk, Greenbaum, Leech & Svartvik (1985: 6.44n.[b]).

22 The *OED* also has five citations containing *such another* without any following noun; in fact that usage was described as 'modern' in 1884 (s.v. *another* a., pron. 1c). But *such* in a pronominal NP is in any case rather formal.

23 In fact, to judge from the *OED*, *percentage* was never much used without article: in over 350 citations I find only 1862 *Draw all the profits without discount or percentage* and 1857 *South-Sea dreams and illegal percentage*, the latter written by George Eliot! As for 'the dramatic branch of literature, the dramatic art', only *the drama* (with article) is recognised in the *OED* entry s.v.

24 For example, Sundby, Bjørge & Haugland quote grammarians of 1766 and 1793 who still 'regard *it's* as the proper genitive form of *it*' (1991: 164), a spelling found occasionally in letters of Mrs Gaskell, who furthermore routinely writes *its* for *it is*. In my letters corpus Gertrude Bell frequently confuses the two spellings.

25 Note, however, a converse type:

a.   *Lots of the stuff is going* to waste.

This informal example, from Quirk, Greenbaum, Leech & Svartvik (1985: 10.43), involves a singular mass noun rather than a plural countable.

26 This adjective phrase occurs in 1852 Taylor & Reade, *Masks and Faces* I.ii, conforming to the *OED*'s statement that after the seventeenth century this intensifier occurs 'chiefly in representations of rustic or illiterate speech' (s.v. *main* adv.).

27 The actual distribution is far more subtle, of course. For instance, derivatives may pattern the same way as their stems – thus *unhappier*– while certain clause structures require syntactic comparison even with short adjectives:

  a.   But he was *more brave than* he was *frightened*, which is the essence of bravery, after all.   (1909 Nesbit, *Harding's Luck* ii.45)

There are some indications in Bauer (1990) of changing behaviour in disyllabic adjectives.

28 Etymologically, *next* is derived from the superlative, and *near*the comparative, of OE *neah*, ModE *nigh* 'near'.

29 I owe this example, from *Transactions of the Royal Society*, to Edward Finegan.

30 These analyses by no means exhaust the list of those available. In Langacker's system, for instance, a constituent consisting of all nonmodal auxiliaries plus lexical verb would be separated from the modal *may*, though the term **verb phrase** is not used (1991: chapter 5).

31 For a recent nontechnical discussion see Warner (1993: chapter 1); see also Huddleston & Pullum (in prep.). Within the more formal accounts there is disagreement as to whether the embedded syntagms should be regarded as clauses (S or S̄) or as verb phrases (VP), or indeed inflection phrases (IP).

32 We need not concern ourselves with the legitimate arguments as to whether *to make money* in (107a) is a clause or merely a verb phrase: the point is that it has its own verbal group. In (107b), *us to make money* clearly has the normal subject + predicate structure of a clause.

33 On *-n't* as an inflection see Zwicky & Pullum (1983), Huddleston (1984: 87–8).

34 By '*-s*' I mean the inflection spelt <s> or <es> and pronounced in many dialects as [s], [z] or [ɪz]; see Phonology and Morphology (*CHEL* III, forthcoming).

35 There was a contrast from the sixteenth to the eighteenth century between past sg. *you was* and pl. *you were* (erroneously stated by Strang as between *you is* and *you are*, 1970: 140), subsequently lost from standard English; see *OED* s.v. *be* v. A6¶, Phillipps (1970: 159). See also Warner (1986).

36 There is a marginal perfect formed with imperative HAVE:

  a.   ?*Have finished* your homework before you go out.

37 Quirk, Greenbaum, Leech & Svartvik's unfortunate label 'pseudo-passive' for the pattern *her friend was gone* (1985: 3.79n.[a]) is dropped in Greenbaum & Quirk (1990).

38 Rydén and Brorström (1987: 32) show that *'s* could be a shortening of *has* as well as *is* almost from the start of the eighteenth century, antedating the *OED*. As a consequence they omit examples with *'s* from their statistics.

39 Jespersen (1909–49: IV 36) records a non-GO example from 1906 which is both comparatively late and without durative adverbial: *if his appointed time had been come.*

40 Quirk, Greenbaum, Leech & Svartvik even rank HAVE *been* alongside HAVE *gone* as perfective constructions of GO (1985: 4.22n.[b])! Romaine notes *He's a been to* (i.e. 'He is someone who has been to England') as a nominalisation found in varieties of African English (p.c., 22 Jan. 1993).

41 Example (130) would considerably postdate the *OED*'s last citation of this type, 1760 Goldsmith (s.v. *be* v. B.6), if it does indeed mean 'have been to see' rather than 'had arranged to see'.

42 I have based this section on Denison (1993a). The *had have* derivation is argued for by Allen for American English (1966: 175) – I owe this reference to Steven Yoell – and in *CHEL* V: 303 for Australian English, though both it and *would have* are mentioned in *CHEL* V: 399–400.

43 For example:

   a.   Ik   had het   moeten   zien.
       I   had it   must (infinitive for past pple)   see (infinitive)
       'I ought to have seen it.'

   b.   Ik   ben   wezen   kijken.
       I   am   be (infinitive for past pple)   look (infinitive)
       'I have been to have a look.'

   Wezen is a special infinitive form – differing from the normal infinitive *zijn* – used colloquially to replace the past participle *geweest* in this construction (Geerts, Haeseryn, de Rooij & van der Toorn 1984: 578).

44 It is highly unlikely that Austen, even with her general predilection for the progressive, would have put such a novel construction as the progressive of BE into the mouths of 'careful' speakers like Eliza Bennet – the speaker in one of Mossé's examples – and especially the fussy, old, prim Mr Woodhouse, the speaker in (148b).

   Nakamura (1981: 150) cites *he is being so dogmaticall* (1665 Pepys, *Diary* (9 Mar.)) as a very early occurrence, but I remain doubtful. If the reading is correct, the meaning here would lack the normal lModE sense of temporary behaviour. But the text is expanded from Pepys's shorthand, and in context the nonprogressive *he being so dogmaticall* makes much better sense (and is the reading of earlier editions).

45 On the alternative assumption that the first (finite) BE is the highest verb in both cases – which is now the more conventional analysis – the difference would probably be not so much in structure as in category:

   a.   It [$_V$ was] [$_{NP}$ being very deficient] (for (148b))
   b.   I [$_V$ was] [$_{VP}$ being very deficient] (for (149))

46 Having stated that the pattern 'appeared for the first time in print at the end of the nineteenth century' and adduced valid examples beginning with (151b) – our (151a) antedates it – Visser confusingly goes on to discuss other groups of examples, some of them much earlier still, of the type:

a. *That's being a spunger*, sir, which is scarce honest:

(1697 Vanbrugh, *Provok'd Wife* III.i.198 [Visser])

These are quite irrelevant in exactly the same way as (148) above: there is no verbal group *is being*.

47 I am grateful to Dr Fujio Nakamura for example (153c), and to Anthony Warner for pointing out that an apparently much earlier example was in a portion of text 'calendared' [summarised] by its editor. 1842 is the date of example (153b), which can be taken as 'passive' HAVE or causative HAVE, depending whether *they* is nonagentive or agentive.

48 There is, I suppose, a slight risk of circularity here, since only the most prototypical examples may get recorded as passival. Nevertheless the generalisation seems to hold good for a great many examples. In his (1963–73: section 1880), Visser notes the exceptionality of a human subject in (154b) and one earlier example, to which we might add at least three more in his section 1879: *regiments of foot were levying* (1704–7), *his children were breeding up* (1724), and *she was taking to account* (1787) – unless we regard *regiments* and *children* as surface subjects which are not prototypically human.

49 This section and 3.3.3.2 draw heavily on work discussed in papers at a number of universities between 1992 and 1995, and published as Denison (1993a: chapters 13–14, 1993b). I am grateful for comments from the audiences concerned, particularly Sylvia Adamson's research seminar at Cambridge, and to Lynda Pratt, Marcus Wood and Prof. René Arnaud.

50 In Denison (1993a: 432–3) I explain why I discount the following, which looks superficially like an excellent – and very early – example of the progressive passive:

a. thinking to see some cockfighting, but it was just *being done*; and therefore back again   (1667 Pepys, Diary VIII 249 (3 Jun.))

Its meaning is clearly resultative.

51 Lynda Pratt cites a precedent where a newspaper publisher altered the subtitle of Southey's *Hannah* from *Plain tale* to *Plaintive tale* (p.c., 18 Oct. 94). I am grateful for her clarification of the political background.

52 Examples (161) were found by Roger Higgins, a referee for Warner (1995); I am indebted to both of them. Example (163c) comes from diary entries added to the autobiography (1861) of a woman who had spent most of her adult life abroad. Examples (169a), together with simpler progressive passives like *I am being conquered*, are quoted by Visser (1963–73: 2427n.2) as 'avowedly being inserted by the author for the sake of theoretical completeness' in his *Grammar*.

It would be pleasing if a connection could be found between (163d) and W. S. Landor, who spent some time on the neighbouring island of Jersey in 1814. On the other hand, Visser (1963–73: section 2158) quotes a complaint of 1822 against the recent use of progressive passives in newspapers and minor publications, which suggests that (162d) might not be unusual in its provenance.

I am very grateful to John Paterson of the *OED* and especially Dr H. Tomlinson of the Priaulx Library, St. Peter Port, for their help in trying to track down – unsuccessfully, alas – the original newspaper containing (163d) in order to verify the example. Dr Tomlinson suggests that *is being practised* might have been a rendering of French *se pratiquent*; the phrase *les fraudes qui pourroient se pratiquer* occurs in the *Guernsey Gazette* number 22 of 28 May 1814.

53 Reflecting the unmarked nature of the indicative, 'present/past tense' throughout this chapter means 'present/past *indicative*' unless otherwise stated.

54 Modals are not, however, 'primary' auxiliaries in the nomenclature of Quirk, Greenbaum, Leech & Svartvik (1985), Palmer (1988).

55 Notice that *mayn't* is phonologically the only negative where the *-n't* is syllabic and follows a vowel in hiatus.

56 LINGUIST carried a lively correspondence on SHALL (September 1993). While some averred that it was effectively dead in AmerE, others countered that in certain uses it was still very much alive. In Scots '[t]he loss of *sall* from contemporary speech is fairly recent' (*CHEL* V: 71).

57 To the examples quoted in Denison (1993a: 295) may be added:

a.   To sponge his cloak *durst not be done*. It hurte the woole, and
           wrought it bair, Puld off the mottes, and did no mair.
                        (1583 *Leg. Bp. St. Androis* 779 in *Satir. Poems Reform.* [OED])

See also Duffley (1994: 222).

58 James Sully noted *bett(er)n't* in childish speech in 1895 (Jespersen 1909–1949: V 436); Visser (1963–73: section 1726) gives a reference to it dated 1947; I have attested it in my own children's speech; and other attestations are reported in LINGUIST 6–435 (26 Mar. 1995). It is not in the *OED*, but cf. apparent nonnegative verbal use s.v. *better* a. A.4b(b).

59 For discussion see Denison (1993a: 419–21, 434–7). As noted there, the seventeenth-century example in the *OED* is dubious, but this one is better:

a.   I am resolv'd *to get introduced* to Mrs. Annabella;
                (1693 Powell, *A Very Good Wife* II.i p. 10 [ARCHER])

60 The crumbling of such resistance may even account for a general spread of GET, witness:

a.   I am safe at Southampton – after having ridden three stages
           outside and the rest in for it *began to be* very cold.
                       (1817 Keats, *Letters* 12 p. 16 (15 Apr.))

PDE usage would prefer *began to get* or just *got*.

61 Dr Fujio Nakamura has drawn my attention to sporadic examples of DO + BE from eModE, for example *does not be delayed* in 1713 Swift.

62 The material in this section was developed in papers read at the second conference of the European Society for the Study of English (Bordeaux, Sep. 1993), the University of Amsterdam (Oct. 93), the Oxford University Linguistics Circle (Mar. 94), and the Philological Society (May 94). I am grateful to all four audiences for comments.

63 Visser has no examples of progressive HAVE between *c.* 1500 and 1837 (1963–73: section 1841), but see section 3.3.3.2 above.

   He has no eighteenth-century examples of passive HAVE at all (1963–73: section 1928). Example (219b) in 1818 contains an early nineteenth-century instance, and the *OED* provides many other eighteenth- and nineteenth-century examples of HAVE in the passive, most often with the meaning 'acquire' and in such patterns as *may be had* and *are to be had.*

64 I was unaware that 2 SG inflections could be combined with contracted negation in writing, but Brainerd (1989[1993]: 188) gives copious evidence of it from the *English Dialect Dictionary*. Professor F. R. Palmer (p.c.) assures me that *casn't* (= *canst* + *not*) was current in southern Gloucestershire in his youth, and Ihalainen notes *cassn* in Somerset in 1970 (*CHEL* V: 229–30).

65 The character Sir Fretful Plagiary in Sheridan's *The Critic* (1779) uses within a few lines *how does it strike you?* and *it certainly don't fall off* (I.i); similarly Puff has *does it?* and *don't she . . . ?* (III.i). And Queen Victoria in the letter quoted in (211) uses *Alix don't like her* and *Alix does not sleep well* within a couple of lines of each other.

66 The verb BE is, of course, famously variable, but in Black English Vernacular and other dialects there is some use of invariant BE; Dillard cites *They don't be jokin'* (1992: 80).

67 Notice how the HAVE passive allows present tense *has* in (358b, c) even more readily than a normal passive; see section 3.3.6.2 on avoidance of the perfect passive.

68 This whimsical term was coined by J. R. Ross to embody an analysis in which a preposition is attracted, rat- or child-like, to join a fronted *wh*-pronoun (reference in Radford 1988: 497).

69 As for (368c), transitive JOKE is not possible in my dialect, though it is certainly current in others, e.g. Liverpool, while JOKE + preposition has a different meaning.

70 Visser has very few cases with omitted *it* (1963–73: section 515), and the only one from our period is probably faulty:

a.   she *owed to herself* to be a gentlewoman
      (1854–5 Gaskell, *North & South*, ed. Collin (Penguin, 1970) I.vii.100 [Visser])

The wording is *owed it to herself* in *Household Words* (1854), the first book edition (1855), and the Tauchnitz copyright edition (1855), as in most modern editions. (I have not been able to see Collin's base text, the second edition.)

71 Table 3.10 uses only the genres of journals, letters, drama, fiction and news, and only British texts in our preliminary version of ARCHER. (American texts showed the same chronological change but with rather small figures.) Not counted: instances with *so/as much*; potential perfect rather than passive participles; those prefixed by *un-* where there is no corresponding verb; compound forms like *self-centred, richly-coloured*; the forms *fit, wet, crooked, learned, inexperienced.*

72 Jespersen and others note that COME + predicative often implies that things are getting better, whereas GO + predicative is associated with things getting worse, as in the contrast *it has gone wrong, but it will come right in the end* (1909–49: III 386).

73 The availability of a *to*-phrase complicates the order question, of course. Angus Easson informs me that where the first edition of 1853 Gaskell, *Ruth* has *I'll give it you* (ed. Shelston, 1985, xxvi.331), later editions have *I'll give it to you* (p.c., 24 Jan. 1995).

74 My conviction that sentence-initial *as well* was typical of Canadian English was apparently confirmed by finding example (422a), though dented somewhat when I found the same usage in a paper by (the originally Northern Irish) Jane Roberts in the same volume (Kytö, Rissanen & Wright 1994: 155)!

75 Alternatively, (428a) can be taken to illustrate the *OED*'s *doubt* v. 5b 'to fear, be afraid', marked as archaic and dialectal.

76 The ratio 91:1 simply ignores instances of THINK with irrelevant kinds of complementation: *of*-phrase, NP + object predicative, *wh*-clause, even once direct speech. The numbers would have been higher but just as skewed had I counted the many instances where *I think* is interrupted by other words: strings like *I do (not/n't) think, I should think, I rather think* can also be used wholly parenthetically, and all show an overwhelming aversion to complementiser *that*; (481b) is exceptional.

77 The rough-and-ready nature of such counts is shown by this example, where *you know* is clearly not a parenthetical and yet takes a contact clause:

a.   Usually this rough peasant pottery is undatable; *you know* it isn't of yesterday, however, when you find masses of it in places which have not been irrigated for the last 400 years.

(1917 Bell, *Letters* II.437 (21 Dec.))

I simply omitted it.

78 It is noteworthy that the *OED*'s quotations include numerous examples of ASK *that* 'make a request' + present subjunctive like (490d), many of them nonBritish, even though the *OED* does not recognise the pattern s.v. *ask* v. Both citations for INSIST 'make a demand' *that* which the *OED* gives s.v. *insist* v. 4b have the modal *should*; cf. (490e).

79 For various patterns, including some like (518b), Klemola and Filppula even raise the possibility of origin in a Celtic substratum (1992: 315–17). Their concerns are with the use of *and*, however, and not with case usage.

80 It is interesting that William Gaskell cites *He is safe to do it* as a dialectal usage where *safe* 'sure' has, as he puts it, 'not quite the meaning of the word in common English' (1854 *First Lecture on the Lancashire Dialect*, in [Mrs] Gaskell, *Mary Barton*, p. 368).

81 According to a useful survey of the literature made by Elise Morse-Gagne and transmitted to LINGUIST (4–82, 8 Feb. 1993). Note too that if genitive *that's* had been standard 200 years ago, it would presumably have been spelled without apostrophe like *its* and *whose*; cf. 3.2.4.3 above.

82 For example, Radford (1988: 493) observes of normal relatives that antecedent + relative clause forms a constituent, and that a proper noun cannot be antecedent to a restrictive relative; yet both conditions are violated by an *it*-cleft like *It is John that she really loves*. However, Ball (1994) presents statistics to show that both kinds of clause have changed in parallel, implying that they *are* related.

83 I have not counted verbless protases. Rydén and Brorström mention in passing (1987: 203) that the letters of Edward Fitzgerald and George Eliot, dated 1830–83 and 1836–80, respectively, are very conservative for their time in their use of the subjunctive.

84 The anomalous 26 per cent inversion in protases with *could* in the period 1800–49 involves six examples: four from a single play, three of them containing the idiom *could I but* . . ., plus another instance of the idiom, plus one other.

85 It seems to me that *dare* in (599a) is a 'mixed' modal/nonmodal usage, as in (202). Note the possibility of negation with *don't*, and the archaicness of *dare* with 3 SG subject.

86 After a complex NP they adduce just three nineteenth-century examples. Two have *so far as* + gerund clause (1816 Austen, *Emma* III.xvi[lii].460, III.xvii[liii].465), but both retain some possibility of construal as extent phrases rather than topic-limiters.

87 On the significance of the 'bare stem' condition see Carden & Pesetsky (1977), Zwicky (1991). The present subjunctive – another use of the base form – is rather unlikely here, since its formality clashes with the informality of pseudo-co-ordination.

TEXTUAL SOURCES

Listed here are editions from which four or more citations have been quoted, though with no implication that the whole text has been searched. Not listed are editions cited only sporadically.

19c Plays, ed. Booth = M. R. Booth (ed.) (1969–76). *English Plays of the Nineteenth Century*, 5 vols. Oxford: Clarendon.

19c Plays, ed. Rowell = G. Rowell (ed.) (1953). *Nineteenth Century Plays*. (World's Classics, 533.) London: Oxford University Press.

Amberley Papers = B. Russell & P. Russell (eds.) (1937). *The Amberley Papers: the Letters and Diaries of Lord and Lady Amberley*, 2 vols. London: Leonard & Virginia Woolf at the Hogarth Press.

ARCHER = A Representative Corpus of Historical English Registers, compiled by D. Biber & E. Finegan. Incomplete version, 1994.

Austen = R. W. Chapman (ed.) (1933–4). *The Novels of Jane Austen*, 5 vols., 3rd edn. London: Oxford University Press.

Austen, *Letters* = R. W. Chapman (ed.) (1952, repr. 1969). *Jane Austen's Letters: to her Sister Cassandra and Others*, 2nd edn. London: Oxford University Press.

Baum, *Wizard* = L. Frank Baum (1911). *The Wizard of Oz*. Harmondsworth: Puffin, 1982.

Bell, *Letters* = Lady Bell (ed.) (1927). *The Letters of Gertrude Bell*, 2 vols. London: Ernest Benn.

Brown Corpus = W. N. Francis & H. Kucera (1961). *A Standard Corpus of Present-Day Edited American English*. Providence RI: Brown University. Included on ICAME CD-ROM. Bergen: Norwegian Computing Centre for the Humanities.

Bulwer-Lytton, *Money* = Edward Bulwer-Lytton, *Money*, in *19c Plays*, ed. Booth; a few examples cited from *19c Plays*, ed. Rowell.

Dickens, *David Copperfield* = N. Burgis (ed.) (1981). Charles Dickens, *David Copperfield*. Oxford: Clarendon Press.

Dickens, *Dombey* = A. Horsman (ed.) (1974). Charles Dickens, *Dombey and Son*. Oxford: Clarendon Press.

Dickens, *Little Dorritt* = H. P. Sucksmith (ed.) (1979). Charles Dickens, *Little Dorritt*. Oxford: Clarendon Press.

Dickens, *Pickwick* = J. Kinsley (ed.) (1986). Charles Dickens, *The Pickwick Papers*. Oxford: Clarendon Press.

Dickens: novels cited without an editor are quoted from the Oxford Illustrated Dickens.

Dowson, *Letters* = D. Flower & H. Maas (eds.) (1967). *The Letters of Ernest Dowson*. London: Cassell.

Eliot, *Middlemarch* = R. Ashton (ed.) (1994). George Eliot, *Middlemarch*. London: Penguin.

Gaskell, *Cranford* = E. P. Watson (ed.) (1972). Elizabeth Gaskell, *Cranford*. London: Oxford University Press.

Gaskell, *Letters* = J. A. V. Chapple & A. Pollard (eds.) (1966). *The Letters of Mrs Gaskell*. Manchester University Press.

Gaskell, *Mary Barton* = A. Easson (ed.) (1993). *Mary Barton: a Tale of Manchester Life*. Halifax: Ryburn Publishing.

Gaskell, *Moorland Cottage* = Elizabeth C. Gaskell, *The Moorland Cottage*, in *Cranford, etc.* (World's Classics, 110, 1963) London: Oxford University Press.

Green, *Letters* = L. Stephen (ed.) (1901). *Letters of John Richard Green*. London: Macmillan.

Hazlewood, *Lady Audley's Secret* = C. H. Hazlewood (1863). *Lady Audley's Secret*, in *19c Plays*, ed. Rowell.

Keats, *Letters* = M. B. Forman (ed.) (1952). *The Letters of John Keats*, 4th edn. London: Oxford University Press (with a few dates as corrected in World's Classics, 541, 1954).

Lamb, *Elia* = Lamb, Charles (1823). *The Essays of Elia*. London: Taylor and Hesscy. (facsimile repr. Menston: Scolar, 1969).

Lawrence, *Women* = D. H. Lawrence (1921). *Women in Love*. London: Heinemann, 1975.

LOB Corpus = *The Lancaster–Oslo/Bergen Corpus of British English, for Use with Digital Computers* (1961). Included on ICAME CD-ROM. Bergen: Norwegian Computing Centre for the Humanities.

Martineau, *Letters* = V. Sanders (ed.) (1990). *Harriet Martineau: Selected Letters*. Oxford: Clarendon.

Meredith, *Egoist* = George Meredith (1879). *The Egoist: a Comedy in Narrative*. London: Constable, 1915.

Nesbit, *Amulet* = E. Nesbit (1906). *The Story of the Amulet*. Harmondsworth: Penguin, 1959.

Nesbit, *Enchanted Castle* = E. Nesbit (1907). *The Enchanted Castle*. Harmondsworth: Penguin, 1986.

Nesbit, *5 Children* = E. Nesbit (1902). *Five Children and It*. Harmondsworth: Penguin, 1959; minor correction to (319) taken from edition by S. Kemp (World's Classics, 1994).

Nesbit, *Harding's Luck* = E. Nesbit (1909). *Harding's Luck*. London: T. Fisher Unwin, 1923.

Nesbit, *Phoenix* = E. Nesbit (1904). *The Phoenix and the Carpet*. Harmondsworth: Penguin, 1959.

Ser. Lett. 1st Earl Malmesbury = [3rd] Earl of Malmesbury (ed.) (1870). *A Series of Letters of the First Earl of Malmesbury, his Family and Friends, from 1745 to 1820*, 2 vols. London: R. Bentley.

Sewell, *Black Beauty* = Anna Sewell (1877). *Black Beauty: His Grooms and Companions*. London: Victor Gollancz, 1988.

Shaw = *The Complete Plays of Bernard Shaw*. London: Odhams, 1934.

Sheridan = C. Price (ed.) (1973). *The Dramatic Works of Richard Brinsley Sheridan*, 2 vols. Oxford: Clarendon.

Betsy Sheridan, *Journal* = W. LeFanu (ed.) (1960). *Betsy Sheridan's Journal: Letters from Sheridan's Sister 1784–1786 and 1788–1790*. London: Eyre & Spottiswoode.

Southey, *Life* = C. C. Southey (ed.) (1849–50). *The Life and Correspondence of Robert Southey*, 6 vols., 2nd edn. London: Longman, Brown, Green, and Longmans.

Streatfeild, *Painted Garden* = Noel Streatfeild (1949). *The Painted Garden: the Story of a Holiday in Hollywood*. London: Collins.

Tartt, *Secret History* = Donna Tartt (1992). *The Secret History*. London: Penguin Books, 1993.

Taylor & Reade, *Masks & Faces* = Tom Taylor & Charles Reade (1852). *Masks and Faces*, in *19c Plays*, ed. Rowell.

Trollope, *Framley* = Anthony Trollope (1860–1). *Framley Parsonage*. (Everyman's Library, 181.) London: Dent.

Ward, *Marcella* = Mrs H. Ward (1894) *Marcella*. (Virago Modern Classics.) London: Virago.

Webb, *Letters* = N. Mackenzie (ed.) (1978). *The Letters of Sidney and Beatrice Webb*, vol. 1, *Apprenticeships 1873–1892*. Cambridge University Press in co-operation with The London School of Economics and Political Science.

Wilde = R. Ross (ed.) (1969). *The First Collected Edition of the Works of Oscar Wilde 1908–1922*, 15 vols. London: Dawsons (originally published by Methuen).

WWP = Women Writers Project, Brown University.

FURTHER READING

General

Quirk, Greenbaum, Leech & Svartvik (1985) remains a convenient, copious and up-to-date descriptive survey of PDE syntax. More careful methodologically is Huddleston (1984), and Huddleston & Pullum (in prep.) is likely to combine methodological clarity with descriptive fullness on PDE. Older works which include a mass of useful information on lModE syntax generally are Jespersen (1909–49) and Poutsma (1914–29). Visser (1963–73) is the standard and indispensable reference work on English verbal syntax throughout the historical period, though it is wise to check quotations for accuracy and relevance. It is often worth looking in studies of individual authors such as Phillipps (1970, 1978), Brook (1970), among others. Current change is discussed by Mossé (1947), Barber (1964), Leisi (1964), Foster (1970), Strang (1970), Trudgill (1984), Barber (1985). The remaining suggestions are keyed to sections of the chapter.

3.2.1.1 There is brief discussion of the count-noun status of *acquaintance* in Jespersen (1909–49: II 104–5).

3.2.2 On pronouns in PDE see now Wales (1996).

3.2.2.2 On the 'prop-word *one*' see Jespersen (1909–49: II 245–71, 501–4), summarised and developed by Strang (1970: 96–7), *CHEL* II: 222–4, and now Rissanen (1997). On X-bar Theory and the category N̄ see Radford (1988: 175, 186–7, etc.). There is a discussion of indefinite *they* in Bodine (1975), with references to Poutsma (1914–29: IV 310–12), Visser (1963–73: section 89).

3.2.2.3 On the *it's I~it's me* choice see Visser (1963–73: sections 263–8), Harris (1981), Kjellmer (1986). For recent research and references on subjective~objective variation see also Denison (1996) (which overlaps with the account given above) and Chapman (1998).

3.2.2.4 Tieken-Boon van Ostade (1994) argues that the use of *myself* without antecedent instead of *I/me* may have been a 'modesty device' in the eighteenth century. A recent study of 'locally free reflexives', particularly in Jane Austen's writings, is Baker (1995).

3.2.4 The *this my country* construction is discussed in Rissanen (1993: 50–53), based on Kytö & Rissanen (1993). See also Poutsma (1914 29: IV 805–6).

3.2.4.2 On use of the article see Christophersen (1939).

3.2.4.5 On *less Ns* see Foster (1970: 217–18), Quirk, Greenbaum, Leech & Svartvik (1985: 5.24), *OED* s.v. *less* A.1c.

3.2.5.1 For discussions of adjective order in PDE see Goyvaerts (1968), Bache (1978), Quirk, Greenbaum, Leech & Svartvik (1985: 7.45, 17.113–16).

3.2.5.3 On comparison of adjectives see the discussion in Jespersen (1909–49: VII 342–56). On prescriptive attitudes to double comparison and superlatives see Sundby, Bjørge & Haugland (1991: 341–54).

3.2.6–7 There is brief discussion of the rise of the attributive noun and of premodification generally in Sørensen (1980).

3.3 The history of auxiliaries is covered extensively in Warner (1993), Denison (1993a).

3.3.2.2 On BE~HAVE variation in the perfect see Rydén and Brorström (1987), Kytö (1997).

3.3.2.5 On the non standard use of *would/had have Ved* for unreality see Visser (1963–1973: section 2157), Wekker (1987), and also some comments in Denison (1992, 1993a: 355–8). Coates (1989) gives an account of non-standard *of* for *have*, while Boyland (1998) has interesting material on incipient morphologisation of *would have*.

3.3.2.6 On clause-initial ellipsis see Jespersen (1909–49: III 225–7, VII 115–17), and for PDE Akmajian, Demers & Harnish (1979: 184–208), Quirk, Greenbaum, Leech & Svartvik (1985: 12.47–50). A dissertation mentioned by Lawler on LINGUIST is Thrasher (1974), not seen

3.3.3 Useful studies of the progressive include those of Mossé (1938), Nehls (1974), Scheffer (1975), Strang (1982). On the origins see *CHEL* II: 250–6.

3.3.3.2 A further, recent development of the progressive of BE is use with inanimate subjects, on which see Hirtle & Bégin (1990).

3.3.3.4 Syntactic change via linked social networks has been explored elsewhere in the history of English by Wim van der Wurff (1990, 1992). The politics of language around 1800 has been tackled by many writers, notably Butler (1981), Smith (1984), Wood (1994).

3.3.3.5 There are discussions of the nominal progressive (with *on*, etc. before the *-ing*) in Mossé (1938: sections 176–215), Denison (1993a: 387–8), *CHEL* I: 189–90, II: 253, III, forthcoming.

3.3.5.1 For further details of the long-term process of replacement of MAY by CAN, see Simon-Vandenbergen (1983, 1984), Kytö (1991a, 1991b). For discussions of modal vs. nonmodal usage with DARE and NEED in PDE from a semantic point of view, of blends between them, and of the general significance of use or non-use of *to* before infinitives, see Duffley (1994, 1992a, 1992b).

3.3.6.1 On use and meaning of the GET passive see now Downing (1996) and references.

3.3.6.2 There is some discussion of resistance to perfect + passive in Jespersen (1909–49: IV 102–4), Visser (1963–73: sections 793, 1909).

3.3.7.3 The explanatory value of current relevance is criticised in Klein (1992).

3.3.8.4 On retention of nonfinite DO in post-verbal ellipsis see Poutsma (1914–29: IV 757), Visser (1963–73: sections 199, 1753), Butters (1983: 4–5).

3.4.1.1 For a full study of the history and present-day features of the dummy NP *there* see Breivik (1983, 1990), and for PDE also Lakoff (1987).

3.5.1.1 See Tieken-Boon van Ostade (1987) on inversion in protases and after (semi-)negatives in the eighteenth century.

3.5.2.2 Negative raising is discussed under the heading **transferred negation** in Quirk, Greenbaum, Leech & Svartvik (1985: 14.36), Bublitz (1992). The latter treats it as in part a politeness strategy.

3.5.5 There is some discussion of eighteenth-century exclamatives in Tieken-Boon van Ostade (1987).

3.6.3.1 On contact clauses see Dekeyser (1986), Rissanen (1991a).

3.6.3.2 Additional data on free indirect speech can be found in Karpf (1933).

3.6.4.3 An analysis of gerunds which could usefully be compared with that of van der Wurff (1993) is that of Pullum (1992), although his focus is very largely on PDE. For further references on lModE usage see also Fanego (1996: 135n.).

3.6.5 On the history of relative clauses see Romaine (1982).

3.6.5.2 Nonrestrictive *that*-relatives are discussed and exemplified from PDE by Jacobsson (1994). The categorial status of relative *that* is discussed in van der Auwera (1985), who gives a good review of the main arguments, and Miller (1988). The history of zero relative markers in subject function (subject contact clauses) is discussed in Erdmann (1980), van der Auwera (1984).

3.6.5.5 For continuative relative clauses see Jespersen (1909–49: III 105–6), Reuter (1936), Romaine (1982: 83–8).

3.6.5.6 See Poutsma (1914–29: V 969–70), Jespersen (1909–49: III 111), Brook (1970: 246), Phillipps (1978: 108, 120) for further examples of non-standard *which* as connective.

3.6.3.3 Commentators who remark on a transatlantic difference in the use of the subjunctive include Foster (1970: 220–2), Traugott (1972: 181), Jespersen (1909–49: IV 162–3), Mencken-McDavid (1963: 300); see especially the survey in Visser (1963–73: section 870), and Algeo (1992), who summarises a number of elicitation experiments.

3.6.5.6 See van der Wurff (1989[1991]) on parasitic gaps.

3.6.6.6   On unattached participles see Visser (1963–73: sections 1072–5, 1149) and Quirk, Greenbaum, Leech & Svartvik (1985: 15.52). For a recent study of PDE absolutes and free adjuncts, see Kortmann (1992). On *go visit*, etc., see Shopen (1971), Carden & Pesetsky (1977), Zwicky (1991). The *as far as* construction has now been studied in detail by Rickford, Wasow, Mendoza-Denton & Espinoza (1995).

3.6.6.7   On pseudo-co-ordination see Poutsma (1914–29: II 562–4), Carden & Pesetsky (1977), Zwicky (1991).

4   ONOMASTICS

Richard Coates

Preamble

The term *proper name* deserves some theoretical discussion, as it is not uncontroversial. For the purposes of this chapter, it can be understood in an entirely traditional way; but needs to be elucidated with great care when discussing the ways in which ordinary expressions of a language become proper names. I shall define the term as meaning a species of noun phrase intended, on a particular occasion of use, to achieve individual reference to some person, object, place, institution, etc. Proper names differ from other noun phrases in achieving such reference independently of the semantic characteristics of the words out of which they may appear to be constructed. In short, proper names have no *sense* (as defined by e.g. Lyons 1977: 197–206), or, to use the term taken from a tradition begun by J. S. Mill and used by Cecily Clark in the corresponding chapter of volume II, they have no *connotation*. The theoretical issues surrounding these remarks are dealt with more fully in a related paper (Coates 1990). The distinction between *denotation* and *reference* should be clearly maintained if confusion is to be avoided. Proper names are often said to be 'names for individuals'; whilst it is true to say that they are typically used to refer to individuals (i.e. on particular occasions of use), it is quite false of the most typical ones to say that they denote individuals. For brevity, the word *name* will mean 'proper name' throughout.

The business of this chapter is to discuss English *names* (as defined above) since 1776. The English language has been used for onomastic purposes far outside its original heartland, most notably in formerly Celtic Britain, Ireland, the United States and Canada, the other former British Dominions, the surviving British colonies, to some extent in the New Commonwealth (especially the Caribbean islands), in Antarctica, and on the ocean floor. I have reluctantly concluded that it is impossible for one scholar to be the master of English onomastic practices on such a wide front; or at least, for me. I shall therefore concentrate on the area I know best, namely England, and try to cover the matters of substance in a systematic way for this one region. A very great deal of the work in English onomastics currently being done is by American scholars, especially in relation to American place-naming and in relation to the analysis of names applied to new or hitherto unstudied categories of nameables. I shall not ignore this material or similar output from other countries, but I shall relate it to an overall structure that is conceived primarily with England in mind.

The intention of this chapter is a historical one – to discuss the names of a particular historical period, 1776 to the present day. We should make an attempt to distinguish two separate sorts of linguistic fact as we try to do this. First, we need to discuss names coined since 1776. Studying such objects will be a contribution to knowledge of lexical creativity during this period. Specifically, it will be about the nature of creativity in that special name-lexicon, which we will call the ONOMASTICON, which is not unequivocally part of the language on which it draws. Individuals' onomasticons are loosely associated with the lexicons of particular languages, or with particular languages; and this is what will be meant by shorthand expressions like *the English onomasticon* or *English names* (more on which below). In syntactic terms, the objects created may be individual lexical nouns, or phrasal items, which function in context as noun phrases, with the special meaning-characteristic of REFERRING ONOMASTICALLY (i.e. without the mediation of the meaning of the elements of which they consist), rather than semantically. Second, we need to discuss the treatment, during this period, of names as classes, including pre-existing ones: what kinds of systematic or idiosyncratic relations hold between members of the class – to a large extent a matter of morphology; and what changes affect proper subsets of names – a matter of phonology and/or spelling, for the most part, though there may be relevant grammatical changes. The set of pre-existing, institutional names (i.e. those which always refer onomastically) is the name-STOCK. Additionally, it is legitimate to examine changes affecting individual names, since such piecemeal changes are characteristic of names. Naturally this could not be done in a comprehensive way for the many millions of names which exist, even if my knowledge of English names were total. But individual cases will be mentioned anecdotally as we go along, to the extent that they are of linguistic interest or throw light on name-BESTOWAL practices. Something further will be said about the socio-cultural dimension of naming below.

Talking of *English names*, as I have just done, raises a whole further problem to which there is no easy answer. What is an English name? A name like that of *Athens*, Georgia, is an English name in the sense that it was bestowed by English-speakers, and preserved as institutionalised in an English-speaking community. In that sense it is hard to call it a Greek name, whilst (ignoring changes during the transmission of the name via Latin and French to modern English) there is a more obvious sense in which that of *Athens*, Greece, is Greek. (This is reflected by differential translatability; *Athens*, Greece, is translatable into French (etc.) whilst *Athens*, Georgia, is not.) For the purposes of this chapter, I shall define an English name as one coined using English-language material; allowing for the fact that namers make use of *borrowed* onomastic elements (e.g. in place-names *-ville*, *-burg*; in given-names *-ine*, *-ette* – see below). But I shall want to mention *English-transmitted names* such as the *Athens* just mentioned, at least in passing, because their usage tells us something about the English language during the period in question: namely what the naming strategies of English-speakers were.

I doubt whether the notion 'English name' can ever be made fully coherent, and still embrace all the names bestowed by English-speakers and used in an English-language context; but the above will serve as a guide to my intentions in the pages which follow.

4.1   Sources for British names

In 1776 we are on the threshold of the information explosion. The records of this period are thus too numerous by far to catalogue exhaustively, but some prime sources for the earlier years can usefully be mentioned.

In England, personal names are recorded in parish registers (as they had been for the most part since 1538, though not all early registers survive) and in the centralised and systematised *General Register of Births, Marriages and Deaths*, which was begun in 1837, and resides at St Catherine's House in London. Derived from these pre-1837 parish and post-1837 general registers is the monumental *International Genealogical Index* of baptisms and marriages before 1900, prepared by the Church of Jesus Christ of Latter Day Saints and made freely available by the Church, on microfiche, for genealogical research. Other church records, both established and dissenting, are valuable, as are probate documents. Mentions in written records other than parish registers are, by 1776, no longer so heavily biased towards those of relatively high social status (e.g. landlords, merchants, freeholders) and arraigned wrongdoers. Poor Law records are relatively detailed, especially after the creation of Union workhouses in 1834. It is commonly said that these enable the descent of paupers to be established more exactly than that of many a person with more social pretensions. Local directories become common in the mid-nineteenth century, the first *Kelly's* having been published in London in 1799. Such name-sources proliferate almost *ad infinitum* through to modern electoral registers and telephone directories. All these records are principally of use for genealogical or other historical research, though they allow much of interest to be gleaned about patterns and fashions in the application and invention of given-names, changes of surname and (to a considerably lesser extent) the incidence and types of nicknaming; all matters which will be returned to below in sections 4.3 and 4.4. Genealogical research may apply numerical and statistical techniques to the data in these sources to determine the current distribution of some surname (e.g. the pioneering Guppy 1890, Brett 1985, Hanks 1993), the place of origin of some surname (e.g. Titterton 1990) or, inversely, the pattern of diffusion (e.g. Porteous 1985, Ecclestone 1989, Leaver 1990); all of which matters may be of interest to sociolinguistic onomastics.

Place-names are, of course, recorded aplenty in the documents just mentioned. But, with exceptions to be discussed below, there is little of interest to say about the post-1776 treatment of established names, except that by this time they regularly appear in something like their present orthographic form. Their vernacular phonological forms, if any different from the standard forms, have undergone during our period a decline in usage pretty well in step with that of the dialects with which they are associated. For instance, place-names ending in orthographic -*sham*, usually from OE genitive -*es* plus *hām* or *hamm*, are now regularly pronounced /ʃm/ (thus *Horsham* and the sham *Gravesham*, invented as a blend in 1974). Local pronunciations such as /deintri/ (*Daventry*) are at best obsolescent. The most frequent modern pronunciations are phonetic interpretations of standard written forms. The focus of our interest is therefore on the innovatory onomastic habits of 1776–1997. In principle, we need to distinguish sharply between names coined prior to 1776 but appearing in documentary records only after this date, and names coined after 1776. This is in practice a very delicate matter. The names of larger places were for the most part fixed centuries before our period, and the names of most interest to us are therefore those of relatively small agriculturally based settlements in relatively marginal land, industrial settlements and suburbs (including their streets). These arise to a considerable extent as consequences of a threefold expansion of population in England and Wales, and a consequent migration in search of work, between *c.* 1750 and 1851, and a further threefold and more by the mid-twentieth century.

After 1776 many fields and minor topographical features are documented for the first time. The documents recording such names differ qualitatively from those of most relevance for earlier times. Systematic mapping begins, in effect, with the Ordnance Survey from 1805 onwards (though charts and county maps, as well as maps of all Britain, are known from before then). Practically the whole of England had been mapped at *c.* 25 inches to the mile by 1896. The first edition of the OS 1-inch series is now generally available again, usually with revisions of major features such as railways through to the 1880s, with J. B. Harley's editorial apparatus of 1980; this is of much value in place-name research. Accurate local maps are pretty much a novelty of the post-Renaissance period. Before then, the most detailed land records had been either prose enumerations of names or descriptive phrases identifying boundary marks in sequence, or unadorned statements of hideages and acreages unlocalised within the parish or manor.

Street maps of the larger towns appear in the seventeenth century, and professionally surveyed estate maps begin to supplement terriers (catalogues of landholdings) and to become common in the eighteenth. The most important wide-ranging rural surveys are the Inclosure Awards and the Tithe Awards. Enclosure, or the redistribution of the scattered holdings of individuals into compact blocks and the hedging or fencing of the resulting territory, had taken place piecemeal since *c.* 1500. The process continued with gathering momentum for 250 years from *c.* 1600–1850, though some parishes, e.g. North Hayling (Hampshire), survived unenclosed till the 1860s. Laxton (Nottinghamshire) was never enclosed at all. In 1836 a General Inclosure Act was passed which made it possible to enclose without troubling Parliament with a private Inclosure Bill such as had been typical of the eighteenth century. The bulk of the enclosures coincided with the rise of the movement for more efficient and scientific farming, from *c.* 1750–1850, though there were no doubt enclosures for less disinterested reasons. The schedules and maps of Inclosure Awards are a prime source of local names, and many field-names are known for the first time from such documents. From what has just been said, it will readily be concluded that many of the field-names recorded in such documents are new ones. Sometimes the names of medieval (open) fields or of the furlongs (cultivation strips) within them persisted, modified or unmodified, in the names of the new enclosures. After Inclosure Awards, the next important source of local names is the Tithe Awards. The medieval and post-medieval system of support for the church involved the payment of a tenth (tithe) of the produce of unexempted land to the *rector* (the person or institution holding the advowson, i.e. the right to present to the ecclesiastical authorities a cleric as a candidate for parish priest; if the rector himself did not enter the living a deputy or *vicar* was appointed who had the right to only a certain fraction of the tithe). From the seventeenth century onwards, the custom began of replacing payment in kind to rectors with money rents (*commutation*). Enclosure was often accompanied by such commutation, and other commutations were also effected by private Acts of Parliament. Payment in kind was formally abolished by the Tithe Commutation Act of 1836. The tithe commissioners' awards to tithe-holders in each parish were set out in schedules and accompanied by good quality large-scale maps. These are together a prime source of local place-names and their physical location. In many areas, these documents are of special value, since changes in farming conditions are causing the loss of the old names for fields; sometimes these are being replaced by the Ordnance Survey's field numbers. As already noted, a significant amount of field-naming in England probably dates from the beginning of our period, and there are a good number of studies, especially by John Field, about various categories of field-name.

In our period we find a steady flow of gazetteers and topographical dictionaries which provide both name-sources and valuable topographical descriptions; the best known are Samuel Lewis' *Topographical Dictionaries* of the 1830s and 1840s, the *Parliamentary* (1847), and its successor from the house of Fullarton, the *Imperial* (Wilson 1870), Anderson's bibliographical *Book of British topography* (1881), Brabner's *Comprehensive Gazetteer* (1894–5), Hudson's *Commercial Gazetteer* (1957), the Post Office's list of approved *Postal Addresses* (1976), *Bartholomew's* (1977) and the *Ordnance Survey Atlas* (1982). Others are mentioned by Room (1983: xxxix). The main source of early American place-names is the regularly updated *List of Post-offices in the United States*, first published in 1803. We now also have the handlist edited by Coulet du Gard & Western (1981). The interior was surveyed before colonisation, and surveyors have often been as instrumental as frontiersmen in placing names on the map. Surveyors' and explorers' reports are often prime sources of first mentions. It has been noted that the act of surveying has itself been responsible for the selection of certain place-names (Rohe 1988).

The only other systematic source of new place-nomenclature in Britain since 1776, I believe, has been the Ordnance Survey's field-name books. For previously unpublished material from the post-1776 period, the interested scholar should consult the most recent volumes of the Survey of English Place-Names. Only those published since about 1970, on

Berkshire, Cheshire, Dorset, Lincolnshire, Norfolk, Shropshire and Rutland, can claim to take a proper interest in names of modern origin; names dating from after 1800 were largely ignored by earlier editors.

4.2   Scholarship

Names in England coined since 1776 have attracted relatively little scholarly attention, as compared with those coined in more remote periods; though, evidently, almost all the place-names surveyed in books on the Midwest and west coast of North America and on Australia are of post-1776 origin. One obvious class of exceptions to this general statement is the class of *English-transmitted names* first formed in languages other than English and adopted by English speakers as names of persons and (especially) places. In the US, for instance, there are numerous local studies of the type of Huden (1962) and Read (1984), and similarly in New Zealand, South Africa, Canada, Australia. These may often be construed as books designed to interpret non-English names for the descendants of English-speaking conquerors and settlers, and we shall follow this viewpoint by not discussing them, except in so far as they provide evidence for what English-speakers were prepared to do in selecting names. They are not *English names* as defined above.

For names formed out of English-language material since 1776, the etymological kind of study frequently alluded to by Cecily Clark in vols. I and II of the *Cambridge History of the English Language* is rarely necessary, the names still being to a considerable degree transparent. Interest in such names focuses largely on their morphology (see 4.3) and on the sociology, and/or microtopography, of their application and dispersal, in the case of place-names. Thus there is something of interest to say about even such apparently banal place-names as *Mount Pleasant, Happy Valley, Mount Noddy* and so on, though in many cases, so far as I am aware, it has not been said in print before.

Typical modern categories of study include:

1   'semantic' differential analyses, i.e. social-psychological studies of the connotational/affective differences among names, usually personal names, potentially applicable to the same individual (e.g. *William, Will, Wills, Willie, Bill*, etc.); see especially Lawson (1971, 1973, 1974, 1980, 1985, 1987), Lawson & Roeder (1986), as typical applications of the technique devised by the 'behavioural' psycholinguist Charles Osgood. A general study of child and adult

nicknaming, and the relations between them, is Morgan, O'Neill & Harré's social-psychological work (1979), though this has been criticised for excessive generalisation on the basis of the child data (McClure 1981b). McClure (1981a) also deals with the sociolinguistics of nicknaming, providing a useful typology of such names and including a plea for the study of subcultural nicknaming practices before they disappear in an increasingly homogeneous society. This last article also draws attention to the relevant social-psychological literature. Occasionally one finds particular local studies of nicknaming practices, e.g. Busse (1983), and Clark (1981) is an important work drawing attention to sources of evidence for nicknaming.

2   studies designed to ascertain where, when and by whom some individual name (especially given-name) was first applied, e.g. *Vanessa, Fiona, Demelza*; or who was the leading light in the upsurge in popularity of some name, whether brand-new or not, e.g. *Byron, Norman, Marlene, Scarlett, Gary, Michelle*. Such studies are often subsumed in larger dictionaries (e.g. Withycombe 1977, Dunkling & Gosling 1991) or books of serious intent written for a popular readership (e.g. Smith 1950, Dunkling 1977, Lassiter 1983). A related question is the matter of the effect of newly coined names both on the bearer and on other people, and there is a largeish social-psychological literature on the matter (stemming from the seminal paper by Ellis & Beechley (1954)), as may be seen in Lawson's bibliography (1985).

3   studies of fluctuation in the usage of personal-names, of which there is a range from solid academic studies to the annual counts of names appearing in birth announcements in *The Times* and other newspapers; many of these are collated and summarised by Dunkling (1977) and he adds material of his own collecting.

4   family-historical studies, including one-name studies. There is a vast literature on these matters, both professional and amateur. The interest of the authors of even the more serious of these is rarely directed towards the names themselves, but to their bearers, and we will not discuss this category below. Some non-linguistic studies related to these questions are mentioned briefly below.

5   studies recording for the first time a previously unascertained corpus of names, which may, of course, pre-date the time of their first record by a considerable margin (e.g. Binns 1981).

6   studies of the emergence of and the lexical and morphological characteristics of names in categories which had previously excited little linguistic interest (e.g. beauty salons, pets, storefront churches in the US).

7   studies of the place-names of regions settled, or named largely, since 1776.

8   street-name studies.

9   literary onomastics studies, i.e. explorations of authors' reasons for the choice of character-names; about which I shall say nothing in this chapter.

Studies of categories (2) and (3) are backed by a large number of name-your-baby books of very variable quality. Most of these purport to give historical analyses of a substantial range of current and defunct names, thereby making them 'comprehensible' to a name-giving public. These are mentioned here because they now form an appreciable contribution to the name-bestowal process in a way in which place-name dictionaries do not.

There are numerous studies of type (7), especially from the US, and to catalogue vast numbers of individual ones would not be very profitable. They range from article-length studies of fairly small areas like Kingsbury (1981) on Michigan's Upper Peninsula or larger ones such as Raup (1982) on Ohio or Seary (1982) on Newfoundland, to full-scale books such as Hixon & Hixon (1980) on the White Mountains district of Maine and state-level ones as catalogued in section 3 of the bibliography of Room (1989), and to Goff's collected essays (1975) on the state of Georgia. Representative of the longest historical perspective it is possible for an English-oriented scholar to have in North America is the study by Miller (1983) of the northern neck of Virginia. The major bibliography of this literature is by Sealock, Sealock & Powell (1982), with a recent update in the periodical *Names* for 1990, which covers both Canada and the US. The most general texts on the US which are readily available are Stewart (1945, 1970), which have been invaluable to me in the relevant sections below. The latter also contains an extensive bibliography of onomastic studies in the US. Stewart gives his own views on the adequacy of earlier studies of place-naming state by state (1970: xv–xvi). The pages of *Names* now keep the reader up to date with reviews and reports of new area studies.

General books about the place-names of other at least partly anglophone countries include Armstrong (1930) and Hamilton (1978) for Canada, Nienaber (1972) and Raper (1987) for South Africa, and Reed (1973) for Australia. Sections 4 and 5 of the bibliography of Room (1989) catalogue other works dealing with Canada and Australia at a more local level. At present the sole representative in its field is Hattersley-Smith's double report on the names in British territories in the South Atlantic and Antarctica (1980, 1989).

As for scholarly literature specifically on modern English place-names in England and the British Isles, Room (1983) is a unique but selective catalogue of some new names for reasonably large places; though the period of interest in this book goes back further than 1776. It conveniently brings together a considerable amount of widely dispersed material, and it has been very helpful in writing this chapter. Room's other major gazetteer (1980), of place-name changes since 1900, is conceived on a world scale but includes material from the British Isles and other anglophone countries. Note also the wide-ranging, but still Britain-centred, overview by Matthews (1972). Dealing with place-name transfer, but cast as a dictionary, is Room's *Dictionary of World Place-names Derived from British Names* (1989). An important general bibliography of English place-name studies, including those on modern names, is Spittal & Field (1990), a supplement to which is scheduled for publication in 1998. In Britain, street-name studies, except those of large medieval cities whose early street-names demand the attention of those qualified in English philology, have traditionally been the province of the amateur scholar and local historian, and some excellent studies have been produced. A first general overview of the topic is that by Room (1992), with a useful select bibliography. Field's series of articles on field-names (e.g. 1977, 1979, 1987a, 1987b), his dictionary of 1972, and his outstanding general survey of 1993 are an invaluable resource.

Very little literature exists on the external syntactic relations entered into by names. The only recent piece known to me is Margaret Berry's functional analysis (1987) which explores the statistical relation between the appearance of place-names in grammatical-subject position and the centrality of the place-name information to the subject-matter of the discourse. As for text-structure, Carter (1987) examines the typical forms of narrative openings with a view to discovering what expectations exist about the positioning of the proposition introducing the name(s) of the participant(s).

4.3 Personal names

4.3.1 *Some preliminaries*

It is often said that the modern corpus of English personal names is essentially that of the high Middle Ages. For many centuries this was true, but a brief history of naming-practices prior to 1776 is in order here, because names were introduced into the English STOCK between 1485 and 1776 which rose to popularity only in the later period which is our concern. Due reservation must be made for the aberrant onomastic practices of certain puritanical pastors in the seventeenth century, the single enduring result of which was to popularise certain Old Testament given-names such as *Abraham, Aaron, Esther, Ruth* among non-Jews. Latin and Greek names were in vogue, understandably enough, from the Renaissance onwards, though dates of first usage are not always easy to establish and it cannot positively be asserted that some particular name of this type was never used in medieval times. Among those found early are *Alethea, Caesar, Julia/-us, Lavinia, Paul* (virtually absent in the Middle Ages; popular more for its New Testament pedigree than for its Latin origin), and *Virgil*. The afflux of Greek, Latin and Italian names provided the source of the modern-day typical female name in *-a*. Some classical doublets for established names came into vogue, e.g. *Lucia* for *Luce, Lucy*. This set a pattern which continues to the present day, for we find such pairs as *Anne/Anna, Helen/Helena*, (the precise rationale and the detail of spelling-transformation differing from case to case), where the statistical relation between the names fluctuates as the wind of fashion veers. Some names of this classical type were introduced into the English name-stock because influential members of the upper classes were addicted to the amusement Arcadia of pastoralism. *Silvia* seems to be found for the first time in Shakespeare, and *Anthea* and *Julia* in Herrick.

In the early eighteenth century, there was a literature-based vogue for female names in *-inda* (*Belinda, Dorinda*). As for individual names rather than 'morphological' types, other originally literary creations or applications can be traced at all periods and well into modern times. *Pamela* is due to Sidney, but its popularity (with the present pronunciation /pamələ/) to Richardson; *Lucasta* to Lovelace; *Juliet* to Shakespeare; *Vanessa* was invented by Swift; *Lorna* by Blackmore; and *Fleur* borrowed and turned into a name by Galsworthy. The literary coined-names, especially in later centuries, are almost exclusively female.

The arrival of the house of Hanover on the throne of England gave rise to a fashion for names preferred by the German royals which persisted for over a century. Not all the relevant names were of Germanic origin, of course, but the German connection accounts for the popularity, especially at first among the upper classes, of e.g. *George, Caroline, Charlotte*, and *Albert*.

I will not try to tell the story of changes of fashion in any great detail here; that is done by Dunkling (1977). Any assertions about the relative popularity of names made below rest on Dunkling's systematic work or on unsystematic personal observation.

4.3.2   Personal-naming since 1776

The state of personal-naming in the English-speaking world in 1776 can therefore be characterised as follows. The bulk of the population used a rather restricted stock of names which closely resembled that in use in the later Middle Ages, especially the male names. To this medieval legacy was added a sprinkling of names of Biblical import, more popular with some sectaries than with others. Such names had tended to replace those of saints who were non-scriptural and/or of dubious authenticity, like *Bennet, Christopher, Catherine,* and *Margaret,* all of which had enjoyed huge popularity in medieval times; the present-day popularity of some of these is due to revival rather than continuity. The medieval practice of unisex naming (often disguised by latinisation in the documentary record) was all but gone in favour of sex-specific names. The well-to-do used a certain number of fancy names of foreign origin, and a certain number of unusual ones were traditional in some identifiable families or godparental networks.

In Elizabethan times, it had become fashionable for surnames to be used as given-names, especially to mark connections of family or sponsorship. This practice filtered slowly down the social scale without ever becoming systematic. It was preferred for second given-names (see 4.3.3). It is still common in certain parts of the English-speaking world, especially the US, though it has long extended beyond its original function of personal commemoration, as can be seen from a list of surnames which are now recognised as members of the stock of given-names and have in the last hundred years or so been freely applied to males: *Dudley, Clifford, Percy, Byron, Sidney, Stanley, Gordon, Leslie, Keith, Stuart, Graham, Scott, Craig, Ashley, Todd, Wayne,* etc.; and in the US, *Washington, Lincoln, Wesley, Dwight, Grant,* etc. Some of these clearly owe their popularity to famous individuals (*Byron, Stanley, Washington, Wayne, Wesley,* etc.) and others to families, especially the Scottish ones of *Stuart, Graham* and *Keith*. Some original surnames are now female given-names, notably *Shirley, Trac(e)y, Hayley, Kell(e)y* (though the last case is more complex, see below; and the second and fourth are unisex at least in the US). The first two at least have changed sex since their first given-name applications, for obscure though no doubt partly phonological reasons. The first and third shot to prominence by being borne by child film stars Shirley Temple and Hayley Mills, the latter being the first person to have this as a first given-name, as far as I know. It is a recurrent feature of modern personal-naming that media stars are commemorated, much as military heroes, empire-extenders and royals were commemorated in earlier times. As a result there is a rapid turnover in the fashion for such names. Relatively few pass into the common stock which maintains its popularity over long periods at modest levels – perhaps only *Stuart* and *Graham (Graeme)* among those mentioned have achieved this status, but for many of those of celluloid or TV origin it is too early to tell.

In the eighteenth century began the conscious revival of defunct names, though this fashion did not reach its full vitality till the nineteenth century (Withycombe 1977: xlv). The main impetus was literary, and the dominant source for revived names before about 1840 is the historical novels of Walter Scott, who gave us (back), for instance, *Cedric* (mistakenly for *Cerdic*), *Guy, Nigel* (both relatively slow to catch on in England) and *Wilfred* (*sic* for *Wilfrid*). Other medievalist revivals included *Arthur, Edith, Hugh, Maud, Alfred* and *Roger*. Among other minor vogues was the late-nineteenth-century fashion for neglected saints' names, under the influence of the Tractarian movement. Characteristic names from this time include *Bernard, Benedict, Edmund* (long popular in the Middle Ages, however, before declining), *Kenelm, Aidan, Mildred* and *Theodore*. Few if any of these ever became wildly popular, but *Bernard* and *Edmund* have perhaps remained the most frequent in England, and *Theodore* in the US.

As ever, the commemoration of prominent individuals by child-namers continued. We have noted above some cases of surnames being adopted as given-names; and in numerous cases the upsurge in popularity of some given-name, previously of flagging or ordinary fortunes, can be attributed to the doings of identifiable people. In this group, in the nineteenth century, may be placed *Albert* (from the Prince Consort), *Bertie* (briefly fashionable around 1900 from the pet-name of the Prince of Wales), *Cecil* (from Cecil Rhodes), and the staggeringly successful novelty *Florence* (from Florence Nightingale; though found sporadically 200 years earlier). More recent instances of the same phenomenon are *Marie* (originally with initial stress, probably from Marie Lloyd), *Marilyn* (from Marilyn Monroe), *Audrey* (from Audrey Hepburn) and *Gary* (from Gary Cooper).

Characters of small screen and popular song have also left their mark: for instance *Samantha* (apparently due to the heroine of the TV comedy show *Bewitched*) and *Michelle* (often pronounced with initial stress; due to the Beatles' song of that title).

A major feature of present naming is the facility with which names have been borrowed from other cultures, or where such borrowed names have partly supplanted similar and/or cognate established ones. We have already seen the origins of this phenomenon when considering Renaissance doublets. More recently, items in this category include the French *Josephine, Louise,* Danish *Karen* (Swedish *Karin*), Gaelic or pseudo-Gaelic *Catriona, Fiona,* and Russian *Natasha.* Cases of supplementing or supplanting include *Julia* (for *Julie*), *Maria* (for *Marie* (itself for *Mary*)), *Diane* (for *Diana,* since 1997 being reversed). This double trend is exceptionally well marked in female names.

The fact that English is a written language has had some repercussions in the given-name stock. Some alternative spellings – originally no doubt just alternative spellings due to the absence of, or lack of knowledge of, an agreed standard English – have become established as separate names, e.g. *Laurence/Lawrence, Geoffrey/Jeffrey, Rach(a)el, Den(n)is/Denys.* (Some of these may well represent instances of choice among originally foreign names competing for popularity, and may therefore be evidence for a fashion for foreign things; but not all can be explained in this way.) In recent years some fancy spellings, which can be taken as attempts to spell an existing name in a distinctive way without ceasing to represent the traditional pronunciation, have come to serve as distinct names: *Jayne, Kathryn, Martyn, Jonathon.* It is a recurrent finding in modern anglophone culture that namers are more innovative and experimental with female names than with male; a glance through Dunkling & Gosling (1991) will confirm this. And it has been noted that White (especially middle-class) males appear to feel handicapped when stuck with an untypical or unique name (Ellis & Beechley (1954) and papers building on this work, e.g. Hartmann, Nicoley & Hurley (1968)); but for a more positive view see Zweigenhaft (1983).

It has been possible, since it became usual to have two or more given-names (see more fully below), for originally simplex names to be morphologically reinterpreted as consisting of two names. The impetus for this may have been there right at the outset of double-naming: the popular *Mary Anne* was doubled by the French *Marianne,* and any name ending in /an/ (or, by reinterpretation of the spelling, /ən/) could be taken as containing *Anne.* Some recent spellings suggest that the namer intended a simplex name to gain an etymology in two pre-existing names, among which I have found *Leeanne* (among other spellings) for *Liane,* and *Jo-Anne* for *Joanne.* Some 'older' names have retained some currency by being reinterpreted as abbreviated forms of newer – or more newly fashionable – names. The most striking example may be *John,* whose popularity as a given-name has at last collapsed after many centuries near the top of the tree (Dunkling 1977: 194), and is now no longer among the top 50 boys' names in England and Wales (Dunkling & Gosling 1991). But its phonological form, usually spelt *Jon*, has been drafted in as a pet-form for the resurgent *Jonathan*, popular in the 1970s especially. This may account also for the renewal of interest in *Nathan*.

Blends have occasionally been noted. *Jancis* may represent (*Jane(t)* x *Frances*), semi-phonemically spelt (made popular by the character in Mary Webb's *Precious Bane*). Practically all such blends are bestowed on females.

Many given-names originating as pet-forms now have a secure status as independent names. These include the abbreviations *Kate (Katherine), Jill (Gillian), Alec (Alexander)*, most being formed by apocope. In some cases, no doubt, the large phonetic distance between the original and the pet-form contributed to the separation. Extended pet-forms now considered independent include *Alison* (from *Alice*), *Marian/Marion (Mary), Janet (Joan/Jane)*; though it is unlikely that any of these were ever used as functioning diminutives by speakers whose first language was English. There are, however, names which appear to be extensions of existing names with no clear morphological import and certainly no hypocoristic function, like *Marilyn* and *Janice*.

Successful outright inventions include *Wendy* (created by J. M. Barrie) and *Cheryl* (by an unknown person in the 1920s; no connection with *Cherry* has been demonstrated). Such cases of the bestowal of novel names remind us of the essential function of naming identified in the opening paragraphs of this chapter: individual reference. Especial freedom seems to be found in the female names of anglophone Black communities (though with some recurrent features like first-syllable *Sha-* or *La-*), and to some degree also among males. Novel names appear to be far more frequent in the US in general than in Britain. It has long been noted, in addition, that such naming freedom has been observed among American Blacks ever since the end of the Civil War (Algeo 1973: 56); such freedom also extended to surnames, and individuals were frequently reported to change their name at will, often incorporating etymological novelties into the new name (cf. Dillard 1976: 25).

Some new trends in English hypocoristic naming can be discerned. One is in the reduction of (especially male) given-names to their first syllable (including single interlude consonants), and the morphophonemic replacement of any /r/ which finishes up in final position: hence /l/ in *Del, Tel* for *Derek, Terence;* /z/ may also fulfil a similar function, as in *Daz, Gaz, Shaz,* for *Darren, Gary, Sharon*. The impetus for this is, of course, the lack of syllable-final /r/ in relevant dialects of British English. At the sociolinguistic level, there appears to be a tendency for the traditional male *-y* suffix, as in *Johnny*, to be used less as the automatic hypocoristic for the relevant names, but rather to carry the significance of in-group acceptance, especially in sporting contexts. The reason for this may be connected with the facts mentioned in the next paragraph. The older pet-forms with initial consonant mutation (*Dick (Richard), Bill (William), Peggy (Margaret)*), and indeed many of those with an irregular morphophonemic relation to the basic name (*Jack (John), Jim(my) (James), Mick (Michael), Sally (Sarah), Kate (Katherine)*) are undergoing something of a decline by comparison with phonologically more transparent derivatives such as *Rick/Rich, Will, Rob, Jamie, Mike, Kathy*, except in so far as they are revivified as names in their own right (*Jack, Sally, Kate*).

A point of interest is the great popularity, from about 1970 onwards, of new female names (less often revivals) representing a particular phonological type. Many satisfy the formula (C)XRY, where C is any consonant, X a short vowel, R a resonant (usually /r, l/, sometimes a nasal), and Y /i/ or occasionally /ə/. Some of such items are appropriations of earlier names of various types (*Kelly, Kerry, Shelley*); and some are of hypocoristic origin: *Annie, Carrie, Polly, Tammy, Terri*) or of ordinary lexical words (*Holly, Merry, Sherry*): and some are cultural borrowings (*Cherie, Donna, Gemma*; as to the last, note the concurrent fashion for *Emma*). An alternative involves a long vowel at X (*Carly, Hayley, Joni, Julie, Keeley* and in the US *Lori*). A preference for final /i/ in female names is underscored by the huge recent success as independent names of *Jodi, Kirsty, Lucy, Melanie, Natalie, Tracy, Zoe*, and to a lesser extent *Amy, Kimberley, Naomi, Sally, Sophie, Stacey*. (For a phonological study of American given-names, see Feinman & Slater (1985); also Cutler, McQueen & Robinson (1990).)

As noted above, in medieval times the recording of personal names in Latin obscured the fashion for men and women to bear the same name, say *Philip, Nicol* (to select arbitrary spellings for the vernacular form). In later times, when fashion had decreed the abandonment of sexually ambiguous names, a trend arose which is still in evidence to some extent: the renewal of contact between male and female names by morphological means. In almost every case, this meant the creation of female names by the suffixation of feminine elements to male names. *Thomasine* may serve as an example, dating back to the sixteenth century and recently popular in its Cornish-English form *Tamsin*. Other frequent suffixes have been a pseudo-Latin or -Romance version of *-ine*, namely *-ina (Georgina, Davina), -ette* (*Georgette* – though often the names are borrowed from French, such as *Bernadette, (Ni)Colette*), and *-a (Philippa, Roberta, Paula)*, which has become almost the default ending for female names.

It has been noted above that, at more than one period in the history of English, names have emerged which were bestowed on either males or females. Studies by Barry & Harper (1982, 1993) provide evidence for a 'universal' tendency for unisex names to become specialised as female ones (e.g. *Evelyn, Shirley*).

4.3.3 Number of personal names

Prior to Stuart times, it was vanishingly unusual for a person to have more than one given-name. King James I was baptised *Charles James*, according to a fashion emanating from the French court (and therefore redolent of Roman Catholicism). It was an aristocratic affectation, and practically all seventeenth-century instances can be traced to royal models where they do not include *Posthuma* or *Posthumus*, which originally named a person whose father had died before their birth (and was therefore not strictly a FULLY ONOMATIZED (i.e. senseless) name, see Preamble). But two names for males became common only from the late eighteenth century onwards. In the earlier part of the eighteenth century, the double female names *Mary Anne, Anne (Anna) Maria, Mary Jane* and *Sarah Jane* were often met. Despite their etymology, they were typically treated as single names in that the bearer would be addressed using the full form. During the nineteenth century they became stereotyped as the names of serving-girls and fell out of fashion. An interesting instance of double-naming – though I am not sure whether it indicates a pattern or whether it is just a freak – is mentioned by Elizabeth Ham in her autobiography, dating from the turn of the eighteenth century. A country acquaintance in Dorset had two pairs of female twins, who were named *Caroline Lucy* and *Lucy Caroline*, and *Maria Catherine* and *Catherine Maria*. These combinations do not appear to have been widely-used fixed collocations, however, and may properly be thought of as *paired* rather than *double*, i.e. the names are not regarded as elements of a single one. Paired names apart from fixed double ones had become normal in Victorian times, and this pattern remains very frequent in the late twentieth century. But address by one of the names alone was the Victorian norm, except when scolding, and remains so. The common justification nowadays offered by parents for saddling their child with two names is that the child can always fall back on the second one if he or she doesn't like the first one. This childcentred rationale has replaced the family-tie centred rationale of earlier days where the second name would typically allude to the bearer's descent or other family connections. To have more than two given-names is still relatively infrequent, and there seems to be a correlation between higher social status and the incidence of three or more names.

To the rise of double-names mentioned above, there was a parallel development in the US, the present-day results of which include the southern double (fused) types (a) with a hypocoristic first or second element (*Peggy Sue, Mary Beth, Sue Ellen* – see also above), and (b) a hypocoristic male first element (*Tommy Sue, Bobbie Ann, Billie Jean*).

4.3.4   Change of personal name

Change of given-name was traditionally viewed as a very serious matter, and could not be undertaken without the authority of the ecclesiastical courts. Even today, the baptismal name of Christians of more conservative denominations enjoys a privileged role: it may be added to, e.g. at confirmation, but not altered. The established church ignores surnames, e.g. in the christening and wedding services. As if echoing this, there is little in UK secular law to restrain persons wishing to change their surname (see below), but the secular law allows latitude for given-names too. A little flexibility has been introduced into the system now that many Christians have two given-names; they may choose to be known by either name, since both were given at the font. In other anglophone cultures, however, the adoption of alternative names (both 'Christian' and surnames) was taken much more lightly. American Blacks had slave-names, threw them off, and exercised careful choice both over their new name and over the extent to which it remained fixed (Paustian 1978; Black 1996). Recent figures in Black politics are well known to have changed their names, especially those influenced by the Black Muslim movement; but in a longer historical perspective these persons are simply further examples of Black people's individual exercise of control over their own onomastic practices. Part of the reason for such flexibility of naming is to be found in traditional West African (nick)naming practices (Dillard 1976: ch. 1), and part no doubt in reaction to the type of name foisted onto slaves by slave-masters; the ridiculously grandiose was a favourite, as in the case of the West African writer Olaudah Equiano (died 1797), known in his lifetime by the name of the Swedish king *Gustavus Vassa*. (For a wider range of reading on legal aspects of name-change, see the items in sections 7 and 20 of Lawson's bibliography (1985).)

4.3.5   Regional variety

Regrettably, it is hard in a chapter of this length to give a proper flavour of dialectally different naming practices. Most of the above would be totally irrelevant from the perspective of those Oklahomans and Floridians whose naming is of the highly inventive kind (for both sexes) discussed by Pyles (1986), Algeo & Algeo (1983); few of the names in the latter part of Pyles's article (83–8) are taken from a name-stock, and the only constraint on their form appears to be the phonology of the possible English word. Many are, in addition, applied as unisex names. All areas which share in some degree the name-stock that has formed the subject matter of most of section 4.3 have, in addition, some regionally coloured names or naming-patterns: e.g. Australia with the female names *Craigette, Rayleen* and other morphologically unusual ones, and the notorious lexical speciality *Kylie* (said to mean 'boomerang' in an unidentified aboriginal language (?Western Desert)) which achieved great popularity in the 1970s, according to figures presented by Dunkling (1977); and Wales with monolingual English speakers bearing Welsh names such as *Bronwen, Teleri, Ieuan* and *Iestyn*. There is also a class-dialect dimension to the bestowal of given-names, of that we can be reasonably sure; but there is little evidence available beyond comparisons of figures compiled from the birth announcements in newspapers with readerships of different social profiles.

4.4   Surnames

The most intense period of the creation of hereditary surnames in England was the high Middle Ages. In some areas, such as Scotland and Wales, the establishment of hereditary surnames out of partly English linguistic material proceeded rather later (McKinley 1989: 39–47), but in any event we can safely say that the English-language surname canon was complete by the beginning of our period, with the exception of the process of trans-forming some of the Scots Gaelic patronymics into English forms where any material might provide the basis for the reformation, e.g. *Mac Ambrois* 'son of Ambros' to *MacCambridge* – to be laid at the door of English-speak-ing clerks with no Gaelic.

Assuming that it is possible to identify 'English surnames' with confidence, we can say the stock has scarcely been added to since 1776. Very occasionally, a new one may have been deliberately formed and adopted by deed poll; but more often the adoption of a different surname to one's inherited one involved taking a pre-existing one, usually at the behest of a relative bearing it, in order to come into an inheritance (and occasionally for other legal reasons such as adoption or transfer to the care of a stepfather). (For an American perspective on this matter, see Scherr (1985).) I have noticed some fabrication of surnames in American usage, of which the most striking is the improbable-looking Zzzyzzx, said to have been coined deliberately to allow the bearer to be last in the phone book.

Some modern transformations of existing names can be noted. I am not aware of any academic studies on the matter, but I have noticed frequent stress-shift to the final syllable of names spelt with final -ell, -ett (Bodell, Cavell, Mantell, Twaddell, Ovett). In some cases, this is presumably in order to avoid some unwanted effects of the unchanged pronunciation, e.g. homophony with words having ridiculous or negative connotations in the cases of Twaddell, Diddell. (I actually came across the latter in the spelling Did-Dell, where the new stress pattern is enforced by the 'double-bar-relling'.) Perhaps the existence of French -elle, -ette has been an influence here. Other surnames felt to be infra dig. have been massaged by some of their bearers; familiar ones include O'Nions for Onions, De'Ath for Death and (Rams-)botham with its pronunciation transmuted from /bɒtəm/ to /bəuθm/.

The onomastic syntax of full personal names, i.e. the order of elements, has seen no change of fundamental importance in our period. Titles still precede all personal names, both given-names and surnames (in that order), except for the unique Esq., whose status as a title may be queried. People on the whole have more personal names than they did before 1776 (see above, 4.3.3), and where they have more than one given-name it is over-whelmingly normal for the first to be the one by means of which they self-refer and are addressed and referred to.

A custom emerged during the eighteenth century of using two surnames as a single entity, which came to be called a double-barrelled surname. Its origins are partly to do with the removal of any sign of aliasing in the case where a person was known by more than one separate surname, and partly to do with pleasing rich or influential relatives. In the latter case, adoption of an extra surname could be made a condition of coming into a bequest. As such, it was an upper-class phenomenon in origin, but by the mid-nine-teenth century it had come to be seen as an affectation, and is pilloried by Thackeray in his Book of Snobs (1848). Numerous instances remain in the late twentieth century. Some people have allowed the tactic to be used over and over again, resulting in the terribly grand but hardly practical Temple-Nugent-Chandos-Brydges-Grenville (the current record holder in the Guinness Book), for instance. (On some issues in surnaming related to status, see Robson (1988).)

The whole patrilineal basis of English surnaming has been called into question by the diffusion of anti-sexist ideas through society at large, espe-cially among the educated. Why should the woman, if she chooses to marry, take the man's surname; and why should their children bear the man's surname? Unorthodox surnaming practices are by no means widespread yet in England, though some practical responses to these philosophical concerns have been as follows: (1) the woman retains her 'maiden' name (whilst the children *may* bear the man's); (2) the woman adopts the man's surname in addition to her own (whilst the children *may* also bear both); (3) both partners adopt each other's surname in addition to their own (a tactic adopted by some gay men too), though so far as I know no consensus about the order of names has emerged; (4) the partners fuse their surnames and create a new one (though there may be phonological and orthographic difficulties about this in individual cases). The law has not enshrined these developments, and legally speaking the *status quo ante* is presumed; but it is not obligatory for a woman to change her surname on marriage. How retention of one's surname or adoption of one's husband's might be viewed in present-day America is explored in Duggan, Cota & Dion (1993) and Murray (1997). No one has, to my knowledge, taken up C. L'E. Ewen's suggestion, made in the 1930s, for men and women to keep their own names at marriage and pass their surname on to children of the same sex as themselves.

It has been possible since 1919, with the amendment of a wartime provision aimed at enemy aliens, for foreigners to change their names only by royal licence or with the express permission of the Home Secretary (FitzHugh 1988: 281). But change of surname has always been possible for born and bred Britishers, and the legal instruments for doing so have included seeking a private Act of Parliament (last done in 1907), or a royal licence in cases where arms had also to be changed; deed poll (plus enrolment in Chancery or Supreme Court documents, depending on the period); statutory declaration before certain law officers; or placing a public notice in the press. The vast majority of legally accepted surname changes between 1760 and 1901 are indexed by Phillimore & Fry (1905); see also Josling (1974).

4.5 Place-names

4.5.1 Preamble

The administrative structure of England has changed considerably in recent decades, as has the map which depends upon it. Following the convention of the Survey of English Place-Names, the English counties referred to below (and the Scottish and Welsh ones too) are those of before 1974 (except that the existence of the 1930s' creation the London County

Council and the Greater London Council that followed it has never been acknowledged). The county boundaries assumed are those of the earlier period also. This may lead to slightly puzzling county assignations for well-known places (e.g. Birmingham, Warwickshire). Reference to post-1974 counties and boundaries is signalled explicitly when necessary. American states are referred to by the two-letter abbreviations conventionally used, for instance, in modern zip codes.

4.5.2 Developments of older place-names in England

An issue of sociolinguistic importance is the growing standardisation of the spellings of names in the types of document we discussed in section 4.2. From Tudor times onwards, where traditional – and variable – spellings of names, especially place-names, had got out of kilter with the spoken forms, it became typical to find aliased mentions, e.g. Kirtling (Cambridgeshire) is *Kirtling quae et Catlidg nominatur* in William Camden's *Britannia* (printing of 1594). Aliasing was essentially a legal device to help ensure clear descent of landholding rights. Rarely, a place might come to have more than one etymologically unrelated name; surviving instances include *Iwerne Courtney or Shroton* (Dorset), and *West Quantoxhead or St Audries* (Somerset). Where variants of a single name were involved, the need for aliasing declined as mentions became steadily less variable in form; with the result that in modern times there may be quite wide disparity between (fairly fixed) pronunciations and fixed spellings, as in the cases of *Slaithwaite* [sluit] (Yorkshire, West Riding), and *Happisburgh* [heizbrə] (Norfolk). In some of these cases, as noted above, spelling-pronunciations have asserted themselves, and the traditional pronunciations of e.g. *Pershore* [paːʃə(r)] (Worcestershire) and *Birmingham* [brumədʒəm] (Warwickshire) are disappearing in line with the disappearance of the broad local dialects of the areas in question. (Forster (1980) is a useful catalogue, if used knowledgeably, of current and obsolescent pronunciations.) Occasionally the aliases have both survived and now name either different places or the same place in administratively or legally different aspects. A spectacular instance is *Hornsey/Harringay/Haringey* (Middlesex; *PNMx* pp. 121–3). *Harringay* survived as the (documentarily transmitted) name of the manor-house, and, from that, of an arena and a railway station; whilst the settlement including them continued to go by the vernacular development of the ancestor of this name, namely *Hornsey*. *Haringey*, an alternative medieval spelling, has been revived as the name of the London borough containing the places. Vacillation in spelling, at least in informal writing, may still commonly be met in names where it is no longer understood without philological knowledge whether the form originated in OE *tūn* preceded by a noun in the genitive case in *-es* or in *stān*, e.g. *Humberston(e)* (Lincolnshire, incorporating *stān*), *Bishopston(e)* (Sussex, incorporating *tūn*). Pronunciation may accordingly also be variable, in accordance with a modern trend to place secondary stress on (and spawn a full vowel in) a final syllable where an amphimacer pattern ('x') can be so produced.

Revivals of defunct spellings are quite common on maps these days. A favourite ploy is to apply the *Domesday* spelling of the parish name as a name for a house in the parish. This accounts for the *Esseborne* in Hurstbourne Tarrant (Hampshire). Antiquarian knowledge of ancient documents has allowed defunct older names to be fed back into the naming process, witness *Lindum Hill* in Lincoln (Lincolnshire), incorporating the Romano-British name for the city. 'Lost' names have been applied to whole areas, e.g. the *West Mercia* which names a police operational division and the *Wessex* recently applied for (mainly) touristic purposes to an area centred on Dorset, west Hampshire and southern Wiltshire. This latter is a popular adoption of Thomas Hardy's literary creation; Hardy was the 'onlie begetter' of modern Wessex (cf. Pelham 1964).

4.5.3 New place-names

Onomastic syntax, i.e. here the element-order in newly created name-forms, has remained fundamentally unchanged for a long period. The middle centuries of the second millennium saw the introduction, over a long period, of individual elements (almost all borrowed from French) which entered into generic-first constructions, such as *Lake, Mount, County, Port, Cape* (contrast the traditional English order with *-mere, Hill/-hill, -shire, -port/-haven, -head/Point*, i.e. with the specifier first). The history of onomastic syntax in our period has been little more than minor, sometimes merely dialectal, changes in the list of items which induce one order or the other. In England, the situation remains static. In the US, *River* typically takes a preposed specifier (*Hudson River*), as may *Lake (Moosehead Lake*, MN), but not necessarily (*Lake Placid*, NY). Outside England and the US, *Port X* has been the generally favoured order (*Portstewart*, (Ireland), *Port Swettenham* (Malaysia), *Port Moresby* (Papua New Guinea)), possibly in imitation of French models; whilst *X-port* may commonly be found in 'older' English areas (*Maryport* (Cumberland), *Hyannisport* (MA)). No single order is exclusive in our period in any area, however. There has been minor variation in the presence or absence of the definite article, but nothing that can be generalised; there is no definitive study of this.

Within Great Britain, relatively few new names have been coined to replace older English names. Wholesale renaming such as that seen in other political climates has never visited these shores (cf. Room 1980). Some names have changed more or less by accident: *Sibertswold* (Kent) became *Shepherdswell*, promoted through the efforts of the East Kent Railway Co., either through mistaken etymological zeal or partial deafness on the part of an employee. Occasionally a little trivial window-dressing is noted; the site of the nuclear power station at *Windscale* (Cumberland) is now generally called *Sellafield*; both of these were names predating the atomic age, drafted in as the name of the installation. Such major renaming as there has been testifies to the advance of English culture to the detriment of the Celtic ones; something is said below about this. In Ireland, the process has been reversed, and some names of the Plantation have been replaced by (usually their previous) Irish names, or anglicisations of them. There are few instances of total change as spectacular as that of *Hot Springs* (NM) in 1950 to *Truth or Consequences*, in deference to a TV show and the glory and/or money it promised to the community; but replacement and formal instability of names were very typical of the frontier zone as it moved westward, and renaming continues through to modern times throughout the US. Some diverse instances are given by Stewart (1945: 372–81).

Some new names for new places or new administrative units in England have been coined, including units superordinate to existing towns, for which, in their various ways, models are *Milton Keynes* (Buckinghamshire, the name of a small village elevated to include in its denotatum other towns within the framework of a new town), *Torbay* (Devon, a new name, in so far as it refers to an inhabited place, to cover Torquay and Paignton), *Telford* (Shropshire; used to cover Oakengates, Wellington, Dawley, etc.), and some district and county names alluded to below. Where the name is actually coined afresh, this often takes place with a fair degree of sensitivity to existing onomastic patterns, as in the case of *Camberley* (Surrey, in an area with numerous place-names in *-ley*; previously *Cambridge Town*, 1862, which was often confused postally with the Cambridgeshire *Cambridge* and therefore changed) and *Telford* (actually an application of the surname of the famous engineer Thomas Telford, which resembles a type of place-name, but which really has a quite different origin). The new county names dating from 1974 are largely applications of older names, transferred, like *Torbay*, from their original denotata; rivers in the case of *Avon* and *Tyne and Wear*, and ill-defined geographical areas of varying ethnopsychological importance in the case of *Cumbria*, *West Midlands*, *Cleveland*, and *Merseyside*. *Tyne and Wear* is the only one which, strictly speaking, is a new name-form. As for smaller administrative units: it appears to have been policy not to inflame townspersons by giving districts the names of towns whose implied pre-eminence might be resented; hence the topographical name *Rushmoor* (Hampshire; neutral between the claims of Farnborough and Aldershot, giving prominence to the name of a minor locality). On modern, in the sense of recently coined, English place-names in England, there are practically no studies at all (but note Room's dictionary of 1983), though there are studies of modern linguistic developments in pre-existing name-stocks (Coates 1980) and dictionary collections of current and obsolescent pronunciations (Forster 1980).

Modern English place-names abroad have excited rather more attention, especially since such names constitute all of, or a very significant element in, the English-language names in such countries as Canada, the west coast and Midwest of the US, South Africa, Australia, New Zealand, and to a lesser degree Ireland and northern Scotland. Matters to be noted below include the reapplication of existing place-names, the application of personal names as place-names, and the use of special, often new, place-name-forming elements. The translation of indigenous names is taken to be irrelevant to the scope of this chapter, though its existence as a tactic available to English-speaking name-givers should be noted and its relative lack of importance, both in terms of social psychology and weight of numbers, should be appreciated.

4.5.4   Strategies in creating new place-names: transfer

The older place-name record shows sporadic importation of names from the continent or from wider afield. But within England, transfer is not found irrefutably as a general place-naming strategy till late Tudor times. From *c.* 1590–1776, certain names for minor places appear to be treated as ready-made, and appear in massive numbers right through to the present day. These include *Little London* (occasionally of earlier origin), *Coldharbour* and *Mockbeggar*. There is little doubt that these names represent happy inventions that caught the public ear and eye and were transferred. In the case of Coldharbour an original trigger for the massive spread can be established (Coates 1984); and the (smaller) success of Mockbeggar is known to derive from a literary conceit of Taylor the water-poet (1622).

By the eighteenth century, name-transfer has become to some degree institutionalised. Smaller, and presumably newly founded, places (hamlets, farms, smallholdings) very often bear the names of foreign countries or of places in foreign countries (cf. Field 1987b). They are often datable precisely, because the name was applied when the original of the place in question was in the news (and that very often because of English military success). Such names include *America, Blenheim, Botany Bay, Bunker's Hill, Canada, Gibraltar, New England, New York, Portobello, Quebec* from the eighteenth century onwards, and *Alma, Maida, Odessa, Sebastopol, Waterloo* from the nineteenth. A flavour of what such names connoted to the namers may be gained from a letter of July 1736 by Rev. William Clarke, who, in relation to the construction of low houses, writes: 'I suppose this was a necessary precaution against storms, that a man should not be blown out of his bed into New England, Barbary or God knows where.' The eighteenth-century names are often for remote places at the furthest end of their parishes, i.e. those to which new settlers were 'emigrating'; the nineteenth-century ones sometimes allude to intended destinations which the namer never reached (anecdotal evidence for this may readily be found), but usually appear more generally or vaguely commemorative in character.

The years that concern us saw the expansion of many a single building or tiny cluster of cottages into a village of some consequence. A result of this is that some names which during our period became village- or suburb-names carry their etymology transparently. Inns, originally often isolated coaching establishments, sprouted hamlets at *King of Prussia* (Cornwall), and *Nelson* (Lancashire, where the ancient name of *Marsden* was displaced). An inn was established at the railway junction near Stokesay (Shropshire) and grew into the village of *Craven Arms*. Other 'promotions' are not so instantly obvious, but many an inhabited place bears the transferred name of an early-modern-period farmstead, smallholding or industrial site. Let the examples of *Chalk Farm* (Middlesex) and *Etruria* (itself obviously a transferred place-name), the pottery site in Stoke-on-Trent (Staffordshire), suffice.

Fashionable places were commemorated less often by direct transfer in our period than by usage in construction with *New. New Brighton* features, for instance, in Hampshire and Cheshire, Flintshire and Denbighshire. Watering-places abroad sometimes lend a lustre to those at home, e.g. *Montpelier [sic]* in street-names in Brighton and Dublin and *Spa* in the names of Leamington Spa (Warwickshire) and Boston Spa (Yorkshire, West Riding).

Transfer of place-names from England was the norm in the early years of the American colonies, especially Massachusetts (cf. Green 1982), and from the British Isles in general later in the southern Atlantic states, even after the War of Independence (Gulley 1995; noting that later borrowings tend to be applied to commercial and residential entities rather than urban and administrative ones). Some consequences of this mass transfer are noted below in section 4.5.6. It is of interest that some such transferred names could be structurally reinterpreted and serve as models for yet other names. A strong contender is the popular *Farmington* (CT, from a village in Gloucestershire), which has now been duplicated in well over twenty states of the Union. It wore an etymology (not the real one, of course) on its sleeve, and provided a model for names with a gerundial (or possibly adjectival of participial form) first element such as *Huntingburg* (IN) and *Bloomington* (IL and IN). Transfer has remained normal, though no longer exclusively from English places, in all anglophone overseas territories including Australia, New Zealand, and South Africa.

In the 250 years or so before 1776, ready-made place-names of literary origin could be found. Naturally the 1611 authorised version of the Bible was the source of many topographical expressions and true place-names in favourite stories that could be applied at will, hence the frequency of such minor names as *Jacob's Ladder* (Genesis 28: 12–13) – tediously predictable for steep ascents or actual stairs, *Land of Nod* (Genesis 4: 16), and *Beulah* (Isaiah 62: 4).

The Mount on which Jesus delivered his most famous sermon, coupled with the usage of the French reborrowing *mount* in Biblical place-names like *Mount Ephraim, Mount of Olives*, seems to be responsible for a rash of names in *Mount* with postposed specifier in England, though a few instances are earlier. Fashionable Tunbridge Wells (Kent) of the late seventeenth century had its *Mount Pleasant, Mount Sion* and *Mount Ephraim*, and the first of these, being not so specifically redolent of the Holy Land (and therefore of the sectarian strife of the times) as the other two, caught on in an astonishingly big way. It can be found all over England, and in North America, in locality- and street-names. (I only know of a mere handful of other cases of *Mount Ephraim* in England, by contrast.) In common with other Puritan-inspired names, *Mount* occurs frequently as a toponymic element in the US (e.g. *Mount Rushmore, Mount McKinley*).

As for names from literary sources: right at the beginning of our period, Johnson located his Abyssinian prince in *Rasselas* (1772) in *The Happy Valley*, and this name has also proliferated from Llandudno to Brighton to Hong Kong. The effect of other popular writers such as Scott, Tennyson and Dickens is negligible. Dickens on the whole used existing place-names of a non-intensional kind, which did not lend themselves to ready popularisation. (A marked exception, his town of *Eatanswill (Pickwick Papers)*, has not left copies in the real world, though *Dingley Dell* occasionally appears in minor names. On Dickens's names in general see Harder (1982).) Scott was fond of onomastic satire, and it is ironical that his parodic Scots *Tillietudlem* has now been used as a genuine place-name in the region of Craignethan Castle (Nicolaisen 1983: 218).

4.5.5   Fashions in place-name selection

In the US, there are several distinct place-naming fashions which overlap in time to some extent. The longest-established general tactic was the transfer of existing names, and this procedure never really lost its popularity, though the source of the transfer became ever more varied. Within the specifically English-language community, incident-names assumed a far greater importance than in the English homeland (cf. 4.5.9). Names borrowed from French and native American languages multiplied rapidly especially after the Revolution; and of course the heroes of this and other revolutions were commemorated in large numbers. A notable curiosity was the bunch of classically derived names in western New York State, beginning in *c.* 1790. Stewart (1945: 184–6) suggests that *Seneca Lake* (itself having a very involved, ultimately Mohegan etymology) was the spur to formulate large numbers of names sanctioned by Roman history and Latin literature, though not all the individuals commemorated were republicans. We now find *Tully, Ovid* and *Cincinnatus* among the towns of the region. *Troy*, on the Hudson River, named in 1789, provides the model for upstate *Ithaca, Utica*, and, at the end of the fashion, *Syracuse*, all place-names recorded in classical literature (though having nothing more in common); see also Zelinsky (1967). From the early decades of the nineteenth century, the fashion arose for the transfer of exotic place-names, resulting for instance in *Memphis* (TN), *Canton* (frequent; the first in MA); but the map of the US gained its present general appearance through the importation of European place-names, with frequent instances of *Berlin, Frankfort, Athens, Warsaw, Paris*, and the like. The recurrent immigration of Protestant sectaries of many kinds reinforced the tradition of Biblical place-naming which has some parallels in Britain, especially in the naming of Welsh chapels that eventually became the centre of villages (cf. Room 1983: xxii–xxiii), but which in the US accounts for up to 2 per cent of named places in some states (Leighly 1986).

4.5.6   Genericless place-names from personal names

Commemoration of individuals (or sometimes families) in place-names is universal in western European toponymy, and is very well represented in older English. A notable development in the post-1776 period, however, is the use of commemorative names with no generic place-name element, i.e. in most cases a bare surname or, more rarely, a bare given name. It is very striking that this naming-tactic is hardly ever found in England. A recent oddity for which there are few parallels is *Peterlee* (Co. Durham), a place-name application of the given-name plus surname of a trade union leader, but whose form could suggest an authentic place-name containing the element *lee (lea, leigh)*. *Peterlee* was the arbitrarily chosen name of the new town designated in 1948 (see Room 1983: 91). In the US, there are numerous instances of this kind of name, almost always where the surname is identical with, or suggests, a topographical word. Among these are *Robert Lee* (TX), from the Confederate general, *Maryhill* (WA), from the wife of the namer, and *Lilypons* (MD), enshrining the name of a singer, but with the final syllable suggesting *ponds*.

Outside England, the pattern of personal name → place-name is very frequent indeed. Its evolution may be traced fairly clearly in the toponymy of the US; my account follows the richly entertaining account by Stewart (1945), buttressed by his dictionary (1970). One of the most typical methods for forming New England place-names was by transfer from England (hence *Plymouth, Boston, Cambridge* and so on; and in spellings obsolete in England, *Lexington, Hartford, Beverly*). So predominant was the feeling that this was the proper way to go about place-naming that some non-transferred names were replaced by names duplicating those back in the old country (Stewart 1945: e.g. 47). In the early years of settlement the Massachusetts General Court had a policy forbidding the naming of places after persons. However, since vanity will out, it was not long before people tried to get personal names accepted as place-names, and this could succeed only if the surname or title in question had the recognisable form of a place-name (but even then might fail). This log-jam was broken with the acceptance in 1635 of *Saybrook* (MA), whose name was put together from the aristocratic titles of two patent-holders; but of course the place-name appearance of the new name is undeniable. Since names like *Cumberland, Wilmington, Halifax* and so on were ambiguous in reference between place-names and titles derived from those places, bows in the direction of real people were possible even within the Massachusetts system. In 1715 *Hopkinton*, commemorating a man named *Hopkins*, was accepted. Note the composition with a name-element, not an English word; a contrast is afforded by *Trenton* (NJ), originally (1714) *Trent's Town*. The historical accident of George Washington's having a surname derived from a place-name opened the floodgates (see also Baldwin & Grimaud 1992). The modern capital city was so called as early as 1791, and immediately established the model for the use of surnames, whether or not they had a toponymous appearance, as place-names. *Lafayette, Franklin, Decatur, Scranton* and hosts of others followed. During the same early post-Revolutionary period, compositional commemorative names, i.e. those containing a generic word, were still being coined, and these are dealt with in section 4.5.7 below.

Given-names are also combined in ways noted above, but may also stand alone, as in the case of *Elizabeth* (NJ), and this has remained a favourite tactic. American toponymy also knows place-names formed of the bald merger of two given-names: *Juliaetta* (ID), *Annada* (MO), *Annarose* (TX). The first two of these commemorate two persons, the third a single person with paired names. They are very often named after the family and friends of the local landowner or postal official; the latter is a person with far greater impact on American toponymy than British. Transformations of personal names are found, but are too many and varied to note in detail, and have too random a character for us to systematise.

The complete breakdown of the traditional onomastic grammar of English is represented by the vast range of post-1776 place-names which not only have no place-name generic, but violate the 'rules' in other ways too. Nouns of no topographical significance could be used as place-names. These very often were abstract nouns with political significance in the broadest sense: *Independence* (frequent), *Equality* (AL and KY), *Freedom* (NB and elsewhere); religious significance: *Praise* (KY), *Advent* (WV); or economic or moral significance in general: *Enterprise* and *Commerce* (frequent), *Plain Dealing* (LA). In the end oblique (metonymic) references to the economic function of the place were permitted in the guise of a noun: *Galena* was mined at the place of that name in IL (and in Western Australia), and *Bauxite* likewise in AR, whilst *Electron* (WA) was the site of a powerplant and *Gasoline* (TX) had a petrol refinery. Eventually, practically anything went: *Dispatch* (KS), in 1891, a mail-forwarding depot, *Worry* (NC), said to be so called when the citizens were worried about choosing a name, and *Enough* (MO), pro-NP or quantifier, for which any explanation is equally unlikely. Adjectives also came to stand as names, unadorned by generics: *Liberal* (KS), *Superior* (NB), *Odd* (WV) and *Scenic* (SD), for all of which the transparent etymology can apparently be validated.

4.5.7   *New place-name elements: habitative*

The most striking innovation of the early part of our period is the use of *-ville*, from the French *ville* 'town', and probably on the basis of French models like *Deauville* (a resort fashionable at the time); but not from contemporary French onomastic practice, which postposed any specifying element. A notable instance is *Waterlooville* (Hampshire), commemorating the battle of 1815. But the earliest use of *-ville* is in the names of (originally) select developments on the periphery of fashionable resorts, e.g. *Pittville* (Cheltenham, Gloucestershire), *Pentonville* (London, in its time remote from the City) and *Cliftonville* (Hove, Sussex, Margate, Kent and Belfast). The heyday of this name-element was *c.* 1790–1860, and the original impetus may have come from the US (see below). (Its use was rather rare outside proper names.)

Possibly related to the phenomenon of *-ville* usage is the special use of *town* which can be noted from late eighteenth century. It is often commemorative of prominent persons (cf. *Somers Town, Camden Town* in London in the late eighteenth century, and later *Canning Town* too, *Princetown* in Devon after the Prince Regent in *c.* 1813, *Kemp Town* in Brighton in the 1820s, and, rather late in the day, *Dormanstown* (Yorkshire, North Riding), planned in 1918 as a company town for the engineers Dorman Long). In some cases, such a name may enshrine the name of an individual local industrial magnate in e.g. textiles, steel or coal. One of the rather few successfully established cases of an analogical name in *-ton* in England is *Carterton* (Brize Norton, Oxfordshire, of 1901). Some areas in South Wales show this phenomenon, however, and interesting nineteenth-century onomastic dialect boundaries (on which concept see Nicolaisen 1980) may be found. Whilst the namers of Gwent and east Glamorgan favoured *town (Dukestown, Phillipstown, Wattstown)*, those of west Glamorgan favoured *-ton (Manselton, Morriston,* the later *Gowerton* (renamed in 1885 from *Gower-road*) and the defunct *Bowrington* in Maesteg). The element *-ton* was no doubt extracted from the early medieval English names of the heavily anglicised Pembrokeshire and south Carmarthenshire coast adjacent to west Glamorgan and used analogically. The word *village* is rarely found as a toponymic element, perhaps because constructions using it demand phrasal stress, perhaps because it has two syllables, and perhaps because analogical patterns of naming are preferred. Instances include *(the) Park Villages*, established around Regent's Park, London, in 1824, and *(Royal) British Legion Village* (Kent, 1921 – the *Royal* was acquired in 1971). The third of these may typify a modern minor recurrent pattern: the use of *village* in the names of institutionally founded settlements, such as *Botton Village* (Danby, Yorkshire North Riding), one of Karl König's Camphill Communities. The element may also be used to distinguish either the historical nucleus of former rural communities which have become suburbs, and/or the present commercial centre of such communities (e.g. *Chislehurst Village* (Kent)).

In Scotland, other elements have been used in the names of new developments; not surprisingly in view of the linguistic differences between Scots and English English, and the differences in tenure and legal institutions. The Scots equivalent of *town*, the monophthongal *toun*, is found in *Dennystoun*, in Dumbarton, named after a local shipbuilder; but tends to give way to *town*, at least in the written form. An instructive pair is *Gordonstoun* (Morayshire), named in 1638, and *Gordonstown* (Banffshire), named in 1770. *Burgh* was once used in Scotland in ways compatible with the special legal and administrative status of burghs, as in the case of *Fraserburgh* (Aberdeenshire), chartered as a free burgh of barony in *c.* 1600; but by our period it had come to be used more vaguely of any newly founded settlement, whatever its legal status, as in the cases of *Helensburgh* (Dunbartonshire), a naming of *c.* 1776, and *Salsburgh* (Lanarkshire), of *c.* 1839 (Johnston 1934). In previous centuries it was relatively normal for places, on being created burghs of barony, to be renamed either by or in honour of the grantee of the burgh charter (or both); typical instances being the *Campbeltown* (Argyll) which replaced *Lochhead* in 1667 and the *Castle Douglas* (Dumfriesshire) which replaced *Carlingwark* in 1792. It will be noted that such renamings were mirrors of what was going on in the English-speaking world in general (except for England itself, where these naming trends are discernible though rather more muted). It will be no surprise, therefore, that the occasional place-name consisting of a bald surname or aristocratic title is found, e.g. *Macduff* (Banffshire, 1793).

Much of the relentless anglicisation of the Highlands of Scotland after the Jacobite risings of 1715 and 1745 can be traced in place-names. Most obvious are the names of the forts placed to enforce Hanoverian sway: *Fort William, Fort Augustus* (Inverness-shire), and so on, enshrining a name-element otherwise unknown on the mainland of Great Britain, though characteristic of many a place beyond the sea (cf. below). More subtle are cases where new names are coined out of purely English material for settlements which had no military purpose; the *Covesea* founded in 1810 near Lossiemouth (Morayshire) shows how far the tendency had gone by then, for it foreshadows a significant trend in modern naming in being morphologically English whilst failing to respect existing onomastic grammar; its name was intended to suggest 'cove of the sea', a fact which does not emerge from its structure. In recent years, some bows appear to have been made in the direction of both the Scots and the Gaelic lexicon and of Gaelic word order; both may be seen to have influenced the name of the new town *Glenrothes*, designated in Fife in 1948, and of the post-1975 district of *Inverclyde* in the region of Strathclyde.

It is beyond the scope of this chapter to discuss anglicisation of the wide spectrum of names across the world, coined in great numbers of languages, except to note that it happens, and that its processes and results are akin to those operating in lexical borrowing more generally (including analogical reformation).

The practice of using a word for the now prototypical element *town*, or a toponomastic equivalent, for inhabited places is unsurprising in itself, but the variety achieved within this type of usage in English-language settings perhaps *is* surprising. In the United States and the Caribbean, names modelled on pre-existing English place-names containing lexically obsolete elements arose early (*Charleston, Kingston*), during the same general period as the earliest new creations in *-town* (*Jamestown, Georgetown*; some of these later became *-ton* (Stewart 1945: 196)). *-ville* was strongly represented in English names in the US, as was the German/Dutch equivalent *-burg* (sometimes in the apparently anglicised form *-burgh* (*Pittsburgh*)). It must be emphasised that these are *English* name-elements at this time, and have been used in countless modern place-names. There are very large numbers of names in *-ville* (paralleling the tradition in England noted above, and for a while probably reinforcing it there), *-boro, -burg* (standardised as such, in some cases replacing earlier *-borough, -burgh*, and so on), and the preposed generic *Fort* in the names of frontier towns. Instances include *Nashville* (TN), *Greensboro* (NC), *Harrisburg* (PA), *Fort Wayne* (IN). These names usually dispense with any indication of the genitive case, but note especially *Pittsburgh* and *Robertsville* (OH). Eventually *-ville* could be added to elements other than personal names, witness *Farmville* (VA), *Pleasantville* (NJ), *Rockville* (MD). *-ville* may be still in use in name-creation; certainly *Reminderville* (OH, from a surname) dates from as recently as 1955.

More recent than creations in *town* in the US are those with *City* as second element, which retain phrasal stress (*Jersey City* (NJ), *Rapid City* (SD), *Dodge City* (KS), and countless others); the first element is almost invariably a topographical word or a name.

In Ireland, *town* was the typical generic name-element of the English and Scots plantation, usually with a surname as the preposed specifier (*Andersonstown* and *Jordanstown* (Belfast), *Bagenalstown* (Co. Carlow; now renamed *Muine Bheag*)). Compare the very frequent *Newtown*, as in *Newtownhamilton* (Co. Armagh) and *Newtownbarry* (Co. Wexford). *Bally-*, from Irish *baile* 'town(ship)', is used in names almost certainly coined in English (*Ballymacarett* in Belfast, *Ballyjamesduff* in Co. Cavan).

In the US especially, it became customary to form place-names in *-(i)a*, in imitation of classical, or perhaps in some places Italian or Spanish, models. The spur, if not exactly the prototype, was no doubt the *Columbia* originally advocated as a name for the US, deriving from the name of Columbus. But names of this type could have been constructed by anyone with a classical education. Where classical suffixal alternation patterns were absent, -(i)a could be directly affixed to a personal name, as in *Ansonia* (CT, PA), which derives from a surname used as a given-name. Suffixation to other words, sometimes of historically dubious morphology, is found in the frequent *Fredonia* from *freedom* (with some concessions to Latin orthography and morphology), *Ponta* (TX – from bridges), *Pomaria* (SC – from apples) and the bizarre coaling-station *Coalinga* (CA) and debatable post office *Disputanta* (KY, VA). *Indianola* is a common place-name trading on the same sort of formation.

The only other morphologically bound suffix to gain a great deal of currency was -*polis*, from the Greek for 'city', as in *Annapolis, Indianapolis, Minneapolis, Coraopolis* (PA), *Kanopolis* (KA).

4.5.8   Other new place-name elements

Naturally, elements were taken into English topographical vocabulary from local languages where English was felt not to have an appropriate descriptive term. In turn, these could be used in place-names. Relatively familiar US examples include *kill* 'channel' (from Dutch *kil*), *bayou* 'creek' (from Choctaw *bayuk* via Cajun French), *sierra* 'mountain ridge of jagged appearance' (from Spanish), *key* 'island' (from Spanish *cayo*). Names, as opposed to elements, could also be transferred on the grounds of what they were supposed to mean in the source language. *Tioga* is a name in many states now, having been transferred from PA. It is Iroquoian for 'at the forks', but was widely held to mean 'gate' and was planted accordingly. Occasionally one suspects that English-speakers have had a go at naming places in local languages; for instance, *Loosahatchie*, a river-name in TN, has the elements ('black' + 'river') in an order which is not that of their source language, Chickasaw. H. R. Schoolcraft (see under *Schoolcraft* in Stewart (1970)) is said to have been an exponent of this art.

Other elements are applications of English words whose usage in this way is unknown in England, e.g. *run* 'stream' in the American Middle Atlantic states, *rapids* and *gulch* (whose precise pedigree is unknown, though apparently English), and the originally more recherché *defile*.

A small amount of onomastic dialectology has been done in relation to settlement patterns in the US, for instance Campbell (1991) on elements in stream-names; and words for physical aspects of the Oklahoma landscape are studied by Milbauer (1996).

4.5.9   The lexical content of American place-names: general

A striking feature of American place-naming practice is the frequency of incident-names, some of very banal origin. *Massacre Rocks* (ID) commemorates the killing of emigrants there in 1862; *Hatchet Lake* (AK) was so called because a surveyor cut his knee on a hatchet there in 1954; *Peanut* (CA) was named by the postmaster, who, when asked for his views on a possible name, happened to be eating his favourite peanuts at the time; at *Kettle Creek* (CO and OR) kettles were lost; and at *Man-Eater Canyon* (WY) a reputed murderer and cannibal was finally arrested. Place-name study has gone about its business in England with scarcely a thought that some English place-names may have such trivial or arbitrary origins. The fact that such names survive aplenty as the names of communities on the map of North America has to do with several factors. First, naming is often carried out by persons in the course of their official functions or duties (e.g. surveyors and postmasters), and their pronouncements are therefore more likely to be accepted by the official Board on Geographical Names, which, since 1906, has overseen place-naming in the US. Second, settlement of the US by English-speakers has been remarkably swift over a huge area, and this, coupled with the prevailing ethos of individual freedom, has meant that the settlers' own choice of names has gone largely unchallenged, especially in the Midwest and further west. The impact of the Lewis and Clark exploratory expedition may be noted; and for Alaska, note the explorer Robert Marshall's legacy on the map, in both English and Inuit (Cole 1992). Third, and in inverse relation to the last point, recent naming in England has taken place in an already anglophone landscape, which provides analogical pressures for new names to conform in various ways to older patterns. And fourth, that anglophone landscape is already regulated by a framework of ownership, tenure and other legal and administrative restraints, which has a decisive dampening effect on onomastic exuberance. Names, as soon as they are coined, are quasi-official, and this breeds a certain solemnity around the act of naming. This 'incident' type of name, then, appears in England only for places at the furthest remove from administrative and other formal pressures; for instance in field-names, which, generally speaking, were enshrined in no official documents till the eighteenth and nineteenth centuries, by which time a certain element of whimsy could be detected. Recognisable relatives of the American names just noted might include *Deadmans Field* (Acton, Cheshire – the site of a Civil War burial pit), *National Patent* (Wharton, Cheshire), from the introduction of patented farm machinery (mainly between 1788 and 1816), *Experiment Field*

(Adderbury, Oxfordshire), from agricultural experimentation in the late eighteenth century. But it will be noted that the range of 'incidents' responsible for such names is very restricted, and often of direct relevance to the function of the land in question, unlike the American cases noted. It is significant that Field (1972, 1993) recognises no category of incident-names for fields.

Arbitrary coinings are also plentiful in American names, e.g. *Romeo* (MI), which was named by a settler expressly to have a name that was out of the ordinary, and *Dinuba* (CA), which does not even have the same shred of culture-historical support as *Romeo*. Blending is a process which is, at least from the morphological viewpoint, arbitrary; such things are relatively uncommon in England (but NB *Gravesham* (Kent) noted above from *Gravesend/Meopham*), but are a way of life in the US. At state boundaries we may find *Latex, Oklarado, Kenvir, Texarkana* (the last of these having a place-name forming -*a* suffix); at the international boundary are *Mexicali, Calexico*. This tactic was sufficiently general to allow names to be manufactured out of pairs of personal-names, as in *Idana* (KS, from *Ida/Anna*), and out of the elements out of which company-names were constructed, as in *Latexo* (TX, from *Louisiana-Texas Orchards*). This type of construction is common in the names of company towns. More generally, the whole lexicon, rather than just pre-existing names, could be so treated; where uranium and vanadium were mined in 1936 in CO, we find *Uravan*, and where oaks and magnolias grew in proximity in LA in 1911 are the roots of *Oaknolia*.

4.6   Street-names

As towns expanded rapidly in Britain (especially in the English north and Midlands, London, south Wales and the Forth–Clyde valley in Scotland) in the late eighteenth century and the first decades of the nineteenth century, it was usual to find the tactics that had given rise to the previous generation of farm and smallholding names being used to name streets and terraces (e.g. the transfer of the names of Napoleonic and Crimean War battles). No systematic work had been done specifically on this matter until the book by Room (1992), so far as I know, but the phenomena are easy enough to spot.

Streets had borne names in the medieval towns of Britain. The dominant structural type was, and remains, [specifier+generic] (but for recent departures from this pattern, see below). The specifier was often locational or (less often) directional in character or descriptive of the street in some way, either of its physical appearance or of the commercial or other activity which took place there. Some individuals were commemorated.

Naturally all these naming possibilities survived into the modern era, and do not require comment or interpretation; but new strategies based on them were required to cope with the huge expansion of towns involving the creation of whole clutches of streets at once. Only the briefest and most selective survey is possible here. Most importantly, we find the emergence of a kind of systematicity in naming. Since so much land was in private ownership, and was developed by private landlords (often aristocratic), it is common to find collections of streets with names commemorating the family, friends, other estates or family seat of the owner. In London the technique began to be used from *c.* 1710 (cf. Reaney 1960: 239), but good examples include the late eighteenth-century bunch in Bloomsbury, London, with names connected with the Dukes of Bedford, and those relating to the Dukes of Devonshire in nineteenth-century Eastbourne (Sussex). Other landlords nailed their colours to the mast; many a town has a development of streets named after assorted people all deemed to be reformist or liberal, from Luther and Cromwell to Cobden and Carlyle. Some towns have wholesale name-transfer, mainly of London street-names (e.g. certain areas of Brighton and Liverpool); but many towns of this period have at least some London names, as with *Ludgate Hill, Fleet Street,* in Birmingham. Many contain swarms of names with royal and aristocratic connections, including the ubiquitous nineteenth-century *Victoria Street.* (For some Dublin counterparts, see Mac Aodha 1993.) Military heroes and explorers abound. The turn of the twentieth century produced familiar sets of Boer War names, the list being led by the transferred South African place-names *Ladysmith* and *Mafeking,* where victories considered stirring at the time were won, and by the surnames of prominent soldiers such as *Buller* and *Baden Powell.* Less common examples include the streets named after metals and heavenly bodies in mid-nineteenth century Cardiff (Cottle 1983: 177). When responsibility for large-scale development passed to local authorities, street-naming policies were also evolved, and have occasionally been made explicit, as in Harris's (1969) explanation of policy in Bristol and Goepel's (1983) in Crawley (Sussex). Local worthies, artists, authors, pretty villages, great houses or castles, rivers: such groups of things and people are the stock-in-trade of the local authority namer.

Some variation is found in the rather mechanical set of tactics sketched above; some alternative styles have the appearance of desperation. We find back-spellings like *Senrab Street* in London E1 (one of the heartlands of backslang, of course); the source appears to be a surname. Acronyms are occasionally met, the most depressing known to me being *Ecmod Road,* from the initials of the former Eastbourne Corporation Motor Omnibus Department. Both these tactics are employed with great freedom in the names of settlements in the US.

Sometimes we find namers ringing the changes by lighting on a particular specifier and varying the generic; a paradigm case of this is the twentieth-century development in Girton (Cambridgeshire) with streets called *Thornton Road, Way, Close* and *Court*. Various spots in Edinburgh supply an astonishing number of good examples, many having been built on place-names pre-existing at the relevant spot (unlike the Girton case). Thematic unity has sometimes been achieved by splitting a pre-existing name and applying its constituents, as in *Oliver Close* and *Cromwell Court* in Carlton Colville (Suffolk). A fashion originating in Philadelphia, PA, at the hand of William Penn himself (Stewart 1945: 105), and well known in the United States before being brought to England between the wars, was that of numerical naming (*First Avenue* and the like), specially suitable for the grid pattern of planned American towns but less easily grafted onto the periphery of places of medieval origin. It is nevertheless found fairly frequently in England in places where rapid suburban mass development made it possible (e.g. Walthamstow (Essex) and Enfield (Middlesex)).

As the twentieth century has progressed, we have seen the demise of the neutral unstressed generic *street* in street-names, supplanted in new names by *road, avenue, drive, way, gardens*, etc. (the last following in the wake of the garden-city movement in the town planning of the 1920s, a less direct consequence of which is the widespread and much-satirised use of names of flowers and trees in suburban development). *Way* is common for major thoroughfares built to relieve traffic congestion, as in *Mancunian Way* in Manchester (Lancashire). The invention of the housing-estate cul-de-sac has given new life to the country word *close* '(enclosed) field'. More varied generics are met than in former times; *precinct* and *mall* have had some vogue in city centres, but many appear to be still relatively isolated in the register of street-names, such as *ravine* (*Columbus Ravine*, Scarborough (Yorkshire North Riding)), and *circle* (*St Nicholas Circle*, Leicester). The latter is rather well represented in modern street-names in the US (cf. Algeo 1986).

A matter possibly related to the spread of *close* mentioned above has been the appropriation of a field-name, without addition or modification, as a street-name. This may have provided the impetus for the increasing frequency of genericless street-names. The ramifications of this development have not received any serious study, so far as I know, and a few examples of what I mean will have to suffice. One fairly common twentieth-century pattern is the use of the definite article with a topographical element, which often comes to serve as a generic (*The Rise, The Grove, The Avenue*). The material in the generic slot comes to be diversified, as in the unusual group in Grimsby (Lincolnshire) consisting of *The Roundway, The Cresta* and *The Berea*, the folksy neighbours *The Westering* and *The Homing* in Cambridge, and the arcane *The Cenacle* in the same city. Plural forms are also fashionable, as in *The Graylings, The Brindles* and *The Eddies* in Lowestoft (Suffolk). (The question of the source of the head, where not a true generic, in such names is far too vast to be discussed here, and may be indeterminate.) Hybrid instances may be found, as in *The Linkway* in Barnet (Hertfordshire) with the 'generic' phonologically and orthographically demoted to being the second element in a compound. Another type resembles the 'manorial' medieval place-name in form, and may be exemplified by the *Loriners, Wainwrights* of Crawley New Town. A tendency may also be noted to draft in pre-existing place-names (in the broadest sense) to serve as street-names without a generic or any other dressing-up. In Oulton (Suffolk), for instance, I have noted *The Weald, The Trossachs* and *Pennine Way* (the latter, of course, with the appearance of containing a street-name generic; the street is a mere close).

Some names are recurrent, suggesting that they were once – not always for obvious reasons or with an obvious model – applied as names *tout fait* and without local allusion. These include such obvious and well-known ones, already hinted at above in the mention of name-transfer, as the *Piccadilly* in Manchester, York and elsewhere, transferred from the seventeenth-century London name; and instances of unprepossessing *Grand Parades*, as in Hayling Island. Not all the once immensely fashionable *Elm Grove* (etc.) names can actually have marked elm (etc.) groves.

New elements in use as generics tend to be close semantic and/or phonological relatives of existing ones. *Hill* has been supplemented successively by *mount, rise* and occasionally *ascent. Drive*, originally for streets suitable for the passage of horse-drawn carriages, has, in towns, spawned *drove* and *drift* (partly depending on dialect), neither of which preserves any appropriate application of their original sense of 'way suitable for the driving of animals'. *Drove* may have owed its rapid uptake to the previous existence of *drive* and *grove*. Others derive from known originals, e.g. *crescent* from the early-eighteenth-century planned feature in Bath (Somerset).

Especially characteristic of the twentieth century (though of course not exclusively) are street-names suggesting the desirability of the place in question on account of its view or climate. Where earlier centuries had their *Prospect X (passim)*, our century has applied *view* as a generic (*Mount View, Sunny View* in Mill Hill and The Hyde, Middlesex, respectively) or more often as a frequent element in the specifier (there is a compact group of such names in Woodingdean, Brighton, e.g. *Channel View Road*). Local maps are laden with inter-war developments carrying names like *Sunnyside Road, Sunny Bank* and so on. Reference to leisure activities becomes frequent, and the element which proliferates perhaps more than others, both as a generic and as a specifier, is *park*, now construed as a place devoted to public use (unlike its pre-nineteenth-century usage). (The trigger for this pattern was the select development of the area known as *Bedford Park* in Chiswick (Middlesex) in the late nineteenth century.) More specific sporting references are embodied in such things as *Archery Road* (Eltham, Kent), *Golf Road* (Mablethorpe, Lincolnshire), and *The Fairway (passim)*. More generally, the vast majority of the street-names involving flowers, trees, etc., may be construed as attempts to suggest a desirable spot to live. The prettification of naming, and one of its consequences – the detachment of acts of naming from specifically local reference – has been one of the most significant distinguishing features of twentieth-century toponomastics.

Still other elements have been applied in new ways to the extent of supplying ordinary English words with new lexical meanings. A striking example concerns *Parade*, originally applied as a street-name in fashionable resorts for places where the well-born and rich turned out at certain times to be viewed. This was reapplied in planned towns to rows of shops (where originally I do not know), and the expression *parade of shops* is now lexical for many English users. Other such developments have resulted in the creation of true onomastic elements. In modern England, *Court* is used with great frequency in names of blocks of flats, without having come to *mean* 'block of flats'.

Older naming patterns may occasionally be revived after having lost their productivity. Modern street-names in various Danelaw towns may be formed with *-gate*, of Danish origin. The lost *Saltergate* in Lincoln seems to have been deliberately revived in 1831 (*PNLi*, p. 96), and *Mountergate* in Norwich apparently created out of medieval material in the late 1880s (*PNNf*, pp. 118–20). *Arundel Gate* and *Furnival Gate* in Sheffield (Yorkshire, West Riding) are entirely new analogical creations, based on e.g. *Far Gate, Waingate*, recorded from *c.* 1700; though these were not ancient town street-names, seeing that modern Sheffield is a scion of the industrial revolution.

I have no expertise to offer in the matter of street-naming outside Britain, but refer the reader to Stewart (1945: 244–9) for a brief account of the partially systematised naming that characterises many American towns, and to Algeo (1986) for some modern tendencies. The US has acquired newly fashionable generics just as Britain has, including *piazza, plaza* for squares, and the word *trail* corresponding in its specifically American sense to the English *drove* discussed above. *Run* is not found in England; in its topographical sense, it denotes an animal-run.

4.7   Other categories of nameables

In the virtual absence of scholarship on other categories of nameables than those covered in sections 4.2–6 above, much of our knowledge on particular onomastic questions relies on anecdote. There are potentially interesting things to say about animal-naming, for example (cf. Room 1993). There exist names which are prototypically applicable to particular genuses of animal, e.g. dog-names, cat-names. Those professionally involved with the breeding of these animals often use elaborate name-constructions which are instanced by the 'official', show-ring names for them. Some popular books have been devoted to animal-naming of this kind, e.g. A. MacGregor's *Cat-calls* of 1988. Some advertising campaigns have traded on public knowledge of which names are typical of which genus, e.g. the one in Britain featuring a dog declaring that it has changed its name to *Tiddles* to qualify for a certain brand of cat food. Horse-naming, especially the naming of racehorses, has long been partially systematised, in the sense that some namers will try to mirror the blood-line by selecting names which combine, or allude to, the names of the sire and/or the dam of the foal in question.

The names of commercial firms have received some attention, e.g. the historical account of American business names by Boddewyn (1986) in which the author puts forward eight conclusions about the development of such names, perhaps the most interesting of which is the prediction that corporations will adopt names with etymologies relatable to decreasingly specific denotations. Other commercial concerns with naming-practices striking enough to excite academic linguists have included electricity supply companies (Walasek 1983), hairdressing salons and beauty parlours (Wilhelm 1988).

American churches, especially those of Protestant fundamentalist sects, have come in for name-analysis, first, I believe, by Fairclough (1986). Special attention has been given to the so-called 'storefront' churches, e.g. by Stronks (1964), Noreen (1965) and Dillard (1976: ch. 3, 1986).

Popular accounts of modern house-names are to be found (e.g. Miles 1982, resting on her academic study of 1979), and there is a small related academic literature, including Koegler's article (1986) on apartment-names in the US. Carroll's study (1984) of the various naming strategies applicable to a single building should also be noted. Pub-names are covered by Cox (1994) on the basis of a study of the former county of Rutland; Mac Aodha (1995) deals with English-language pub-names in Ireland; and there is a general book on the topic by Dunkling & Wright (1994).

The opening paragraphs of this chapter will make it clear that section 4.7 has not, and could not have, exhausted the class of objects nameable in English; we have not touched on musical bands, army regiments, railway locomotives or other vehicles, or clubs and societies; we have confined ourselves to those about which the academic literature has had something to say. Only chapter 4 of Cottle (1983) gives a hint of the joys of widening our horizons.

4.8   Academic writings on names

The principal journal in the field of general onomastics that has a strong Modern English component or bias is *Names*. Historical or philological studies of modern names may occasionally be found in *Nomina*, and of place-names in the *Journal of the English Place-Name Society*. Other journals visiting English amidst other languages include *Onoma, Beiträge zur Namenforschung, Naamkunde, Namn och Bygd* and *Namenkundliche Informationen*, but most articles deal with earlier periods. As far as journals are concerned, surname research is largely the province of the *Genealogists' Magazine* and local family history society publications. Literary onomastics is represented by *Literary Onomastics Studies*. By and large, other onomastic pieces are carried by anglistic journals rather than by specialist journals of name-study, and these pieces tend very strongly to be about the names of earlier periods than the one in question here. Lawson (1992) offers a list of journals carrying onomastic material.

A final point to note is that surname research has come to be a legitimate activity for those interested in population dynamics, social mobility and gender rôles; accordingly there are statistical papers in recent issues of *Human Biology*, historical cluster analyses such as that by Lasker & Kaplan (1983), and culture-historical papers in *Sex Roles*.

FURTHER READING

This article is the only one I know devoted entirely to the topic of naming in English after 1776. There are also no books on the topic. All material suitable for further reading covers part of the range of this chapter and is mentioned at the appropriate points in the text. A few are mentioned here again as suitable starting points:

For theoretical background:
Algeo, J. (1973). *On Defining the Proper Name*. Gainsville (FL): Florida University Press.

On given-names:
Dunkling, L. A. & W. Gosling (1991). *The Book of First Names*. 3rd edn. London: Dent.

On modern place-names in Britain:
Room, A. (1983). *A Concise Dictionary of Modern Place-Names in Great Britain and Ireland*. Oxford: Oxford University Press.

On local place-names in Britain:
Field, J. (1993), *A History of English Field-Names*. Harlow: Longmans.

On place-names in America:
Stewart, G. R. (1945). *Names on the Land: Historical Account of Place-naming in the United States*. New York: Random House. [4th edn. San Francisco: Lexikus (1982).]

On English place-names world-wide:
Matthews, C. M. (1972). *Place-Names of the English-speaking World*. London: Weidenfeld & Nicolson.
Room, A. (1989). *Dictionary of World Place-Names Derived from British Names*. London: Routledge & Kegan Paul.

5 PHONOLOGY

Michael K. C. MacMahon

5.1 The soundscapes of the eighteenth and nineteenth centuries

5.1.1

Superficially, the period under consideration might appear to contain little of phonetic and phonological interest, compared with, for example, earlier changes such as the transition from Old to Middle English, and the Great Vowel Shift (see *CHEL* III, forthcoming). Thus, Millward claims that 'by 1800, the [consonant] system was identical to that of today' (Millward 1989: 215), and that 'the PDE vowel inventory was achieved by the end of the EMnE period, although there have been some allophonic and distributional changes since 1800' (Millward 1989: 219). Jespersen draws attention to a limited number of changes: for example, /n/ being used sometimes for /ŋ/ in unstressed position (SINGIN', BRINGIN', etc.), the use of intrusive /r/ from the end of the eighteenth century, the growing instability of the phonemic contrast between /ʍ/ and /w/ (e.g. WHERE and WEAR), variability in the use of word-initial /h/ (e.g. in HUMOUR, HOSPITAL, HUMBLE), the loss of /j/ (e.g. in TUNE), and, for some speakers, the substitution of /w/ for /v/ in words like VERY and SORRY (Jespersen 1909: 355 *et seq.*). Similarly, Wyld notes comparable examples which show that a number of relatively small changes (systemic, structural,

---

[1] The term 'rhotic' is used in this chapter to describe a *phonotactic* feature (i.e. the distribution of /r/); not, as in IPA, a phonetic feature.

[2] The vowel-height terms 'close-mid' and 'open-mid' are equivalent to the older terms 'half-close' and 'half-open'.

[3] The phonetic symbol [я], which is not IPA, is used e.g. in section 5.12.6. It refers to a 'bunched' or 'velar' or 'rhotacized' /r/.

[4] [ ] brackets enclose phonetic transcriptions, of varying degrees of narrowness. / / brackets enclose phonemic transcriptions. ( ) brackets, used by earlier phoneticians e.g. Ellis and Sweet, enclose direct quotations from their work.

[5] Where appropriate, older phonetic/phonemic transcriptions have been converted into IPA. This applies particularly to those in Bell's 'Visible Speech' alphabet. They appear in the text in the form [IPA[. . .]].

lexical-incidental, and realisational)[1] had been in progress between about the middle of the eighteenth century and the First World War (Wyld 1914: 133–60. See also Horn & Lehnert 1954: *passim*).

5.1.2

And yet, there is other evidence to show that the pronunciation of English more than 150 years ago was *noticeably* different, for reasons mainly of phonotactics (structure and lexical incidence), from what it is today, both in the USA and Britain; and, secondly, that the summaries by Millward, Jespersen, Wyld, and Horn/Lehnert have tended to conceal this fact. In 1874, the English phonetician and philologist Alexander Ellis (born in 1819) commented that 'the pronunciation of the XVIIIth century is peculiarly interesting as forming the transition to that now in use [= 1874], and as being the "old-fashioned" habit of speech which we may still hear occasionally from octogenarians'. He goes on to say that 'those who, like the author, can recollect how very old people spoke forty or fifty years ago [i.e. in the 1830s and 1840s] will still better understand the indications, unhappily rather indistinct, which are furnished by the numerous orthoepists of the latter half of the XVIIIth century' (Ellis 1874: 1040). The sort of pronunciations Ellis could recall from the 1840s were of the words CHAIR, STEAK, BREAK, GREAT, OBLIGE pronounced with an /iː/ vowel, and CARD and GUARD with prevocalic /kj-/ and /gj-/ respectively (Ellis 1869: 89).[2]

A still more vivid phonetic description of the pronunciation of the late eighteenth and early nineteenth centuries was given in 1902 by the British art critic, Charles Eastlake: 'Men of mature age can remember many words which in the conversation of old fellows forty years ago [i.e. of people born towards the end of the eighteenth century] would sound strangely to modern ears. They were generally much *obleeged* for a favour. They referred affectionately to their *darters*; talked of *goold* watches, or of recent visit to *Room*; mentioned that they had seen the *Dook* of Wellington in Hyde Park last *Toosday* and that he was in the habit of rising at *sivin* o'clock. They spoke of *Muntague* Square and St. *Tummus's 'Ospital*. They would profess themselves to be their hostess's *'umble* servants, and to admire her collection of *chayney*, especially the vase of *Prooshian* blue' (Eastlake 1902: 992–93).[3]

5.1.3

Further examples of the degree of difference between today's pronunciations of English and those of 150 and more years ago – especially of individual words – can be extrapolated from the pages of the contemporary pronouncing dictionaries. Thus, by taking individual words from Benjamin Smart's *The Practice of Elocution* (1842: 22–24) and calculating their phonemic content (in terms of English English 150 years ago), one can evoke a sense of the change that has been caused to English by phonotactic alterations. Smart has /iː/ in PROFILE, BREVIARY; /ɪ/ in CLEF, VISOR; /eɪ/ in PLACABLE, BRAVADO; /ɛ/ in FEOFF, EPOCH, PANEGYRIC; /æ/ in RAILLERY; /ʌ/ in HOUSEWIFE, SYRUP; /ɔː/ in GROAT; /ʊ/ in RUTHLESS; and /uː/ in BEHOVE.

With material from over 200 years ago, namely some of the entries in Thomas Sheridan's *A General Dictionary of the English Language* of 1780, one can calculate the pronunciation not only of individual words but of entire sentences, in what might loosely be described (for the moment – see sections 5.4.6–9) as Southern English English. Differences of segmental distribution, in terms both of structure and lexical incidence, are very noticeable. (It is impossible to be dogmatic about the quality and quantity of the individual allophones; hence only a broad phonetic (i.e. phonemic) transcription is given.)

/ðɪ ʌmbl jɛmən læft əz ðə hʌzwɪf suːnd/
The humble yeoman laughed as the housewife swooned

/ðə sɒdər frəm tʃeːniː pleːd ə kwæntɪtiː əv səneːtəz fɛrsliː/
The soldier from China played a quantity of sonatas fiercely

/ðə kwɪrɪstər sɔː ðɛ bwiː niːr ðə keː/
The chorister saw the buoy near the quay.

5.2 The historical sources and their interpretation

5.2.1

Even though a sufficient quantity of information exists in print about the pronunciation of English over the last 220 years (supplemented for a century and more by audio recordings), much of it must be used with circumspection, especially for the period 1760 to about 1860. Until about the middle of the nineteenth century, few of the people who wrote about the pronunciation of English, either in the British Isles or the USA, could be described as phoneticians, in the sense of persons with an objective appreciation of pronunciation and the necessary technical knowledge for describing it. The two most influential writers, both during their lifetimes and after, were Thomas Sheridan (1719–88) and John Walker

(1732–1807). Sheridan was born in Dublin but spent a few years at a London school before returning to Dublin. His later, professional career was as an actor on the Dublin and London stages. As well as lecturing on elocution in various cities in England and Scotland, he was also the author of several works, three of which are directly relevant to pronunciation: *British Education* (1756), *A Course of Lectures on Elocution* (1762) and a *General Dictionary of the English Language* (1780).[4] He established a reputation as an authority on English English pronunciation. Yet, the anonymous author of a tract was warning the public about the 'vicious', 'deformed' and 'ridiculous' pronunciations that Sheridan was advocating, including /tʃ/ in NATURE, instead of the /tj/, and /ɪ/ in ENJOY, instead of /ɛ/(Anon. 1790)!

John Walker (1732–1807) lived in or near London all his life. His career paralleled that of Sheridan in many ways: he was an actor, an elocutionist, and an author of works on pronunciation. His seminal work was the *Critical Pronouncing Dictionary* (1791), with revisions and many reissues, which, as well as listing the pronunciations of words, also included a lengthy (and valuable) discussion of the 'Principles of English Pronunciation'.

In America, the first major author of this period was the lexicographer Noah Webster (1758–1843). His influence can be gauged from the pronunciations he gave in his *Dictionary* of 1828 (and reprints) as well as from his comments on pronunciation in his much earlier *Dissertations on Language* (1789).

5.2.2

Considerable caution is needed, nevertheless, when interpreting the pronunciations given for the period from the mid-eighteenth century until the time of Alexander Ellis in the 1860s. The main sources of information are the pronouncing dictionaries, grammar books (which contained information about pronunciation),[5] and more general works on the English language. Both in Britain and America, a number of writers attributed to themselves the status of 'orthoepists', that is self-appointed 'authorities' on current, but, usually more specifically, 'correct', pronunciation. The list of such people includes Thomas Batchelor, James Buchanan, James Elphinston, Benjamin Franklin, Robert Nares, Thomas Sheridan, Benjamin Smart, William Thornton, John Walker, Noah Webster, and Joseph Worcester. It should also be noted that works first published in Britain were sometimes reprinted without alteration of content in America.

5.2.3

The question of the reliability of the testimony of the eighteenth- and early nineteenth-century orthoepists requires to be examined in more detail (cf. Sundby 1976: 45; Rohlfing 1984: 4; Jones C. 1989: 280). One would wish to know whether an individual orthoepist was aware of differences between putative standard and non-standard forms. Could he or she[6] have been deliberately selective and have suppressed information about certain pronunciations? For example, for various British speakers in the eighteenth century, the first phoneme in CHART was /k/, not /tʃ/, yet only a handful of authors draw attention to this. Was the orthoepist aware of register differences within social groups or individual speakers? Is it possible that the orthoepist could have had some phonetic training, or was he or she self-taught? (One assumes that acting, the profession of, for example, Thomas Sheridan and John Walker, contributed to their understanding of English pronunciation, and hence of phonetics.) Even if an orthoepist had acquired this expertise, then he or she presumably lacked sophistication in one critical area, namely the methodology for describing with any degree of accuracy the precise differences between vowel-sounds. Being able to devise, or simply know how to use, a set of vowel-*symbols* was no substitute for being able to infer the configurations of the vocal tract, especially of the tongue and lips, in the production of vowel-*sounds*. (Daniel Jones's Cardinal Vowel system, the basis of most modern descriptions of vowel-sounds, was not developed until about the time of the First World War.)[7] To what extent did an orthoepist use another author's work as a source, perhaps uncritically? Did the orthoepist have a deferential attitude to orthography, and regard that as the arbiter of the pronunciation of particular words? Was the resulting pronouncing dictionary (or introduction to pronunciation contained within a grammar book) a response to a desire to be descriptive, prescriptive or proscriptive? Because of commercial pressures to produce a particular sort of 'manual' of phonetic etiquette, it is feasible that some authors at least may have suppressed their own accent in favour of the one their prospective readership wished to see being encouraged. In general, little is known about the precise background of each orthoepist (particularly in Britain), although London (or one of the neighbouring counties) plays a part in many of their biographies.[8]

5.2.4

The later nineteenth-century phoneticians were heavily critical of the orthoepists of the earlier period. In America, Samuel Haldeman commented that orthoepists 'blind themselves to the genius and tendencies of the language, and represent a jargon which no one uses but the child learning to read from divided syllables' (Haldeman 1860: 122; cf. Ellis 1874: 1187). In Britain, Ellis was adamant that their pronouncements could not be relied upon: 'all pronouncing dictionary writers and elocutionists give rather what they think ought to be given than what they have observed as most common' (1874: 1208).[9]

5.2.5

There is much evidence to show that John Walker was sometimes prone to adopt an authoritarian and highly prescriptive view of what constituted an acceptable current English English pronunciation of certain words. For example, he objected to ANY, MANY and THAMES with /ɛ/, maintaining that the vowel should be /æ/. The words GEOGRAPHY and GEOMETRY with initial /dʒɒ-/ were, he said, 'monsters of pronunciation'. (All such examples are contradicted by entries in other, contemporary, pronouncing dictionaries.) Yet his influence on the pronunciation of particular words in English was wide and long-lasting – 'immeasurable far down into the nineteenth century' (Sheldon 1938: 380; cf. also Sheldon 1947: 130). Six later editors were to revise the contents of his *Critical Pronouncing Dictionary*, allegedly bringing it into line with current pronunciations (Wrocklage 1943: 15; cf. also Sheldon 1947: 130).

Even so, Ellis reserved his strongest criticisms for Walker and his 'usherism', the 'constant references to the habits of a class of society to which he evidently did not belong [and] the most evident marks [in the *Dictionary*] of insufficient knowledge, and of that kind of pedantic self-sufficiency which is the true growth of half-enlightened ignorance' (Ellis 1869: 624–5). A German commentator, Voigtmann, had also recognised that the pronunciation given in one of the many reprints of Walker's 1791 *Dictionary* was fundamentally out of line with the current pronunciation of the language fifty years later.[10] See also the first edition of Noah Webster's *Dictionary of the English Language* in 1828, which contains a long and withering critique of Walker's English English pronunciation (Webster 1828: xxxii–ix).

5.2.6

Walker himself – not surprisingly – was critical of some of his immediate contemporaries: perhaps more as a means of justifying his own *Dictionary* than on account of any genuine defects he had noticed in their notations of individual words. Of Thomas Sheridan, he said that there are 'numerous instances of impropriety, inconsistency, and want of acquaintance with the analogies of the language' (Walker 1791: iii). And Robert Nares, despite 'clearness of method and an extent of observation', was criticised for being 'on many occasions mistaken [about] the best usage' (1791: iv).

5.2.7

In many cases, then, it is impossible to be certain whether pronunciations of particular words given in any of the orthoepical dictionaries represented actual current usage, a minority usage that carried with it a certain social cachet, or an as yet unspoken fantasy form that the author, for whatever reason, would like to have heard being used. It must be remembered too that, given the relatively limited geographical movement of speakers of English, more so in Britain than in America, up until at least the mid-nineteenth century, very few people would have had access to a genuinely varied set of pronunciations of the language upon which to base their generalisations.

5.2.8

Other sources of information on pronunciation before about the mid-nineteenth century include a miscellaneous group of people, who, more by accident than design, reveal something of current pronunciation. For example, the famous London printer Philip Luckombe attached a list of homophones to his *History and Art of Printing* (1771: 477–86). He rhymes ALOUD and ALLOWED, and FREES, FREEZE, and FRIEZE, and AN ODE and A NODE – the latter is perhaps, incidentally, the first example of phonetic juncture in English to which specific attention is drawn in print. But he also lists ADAPT, ADEPT, and ADOPT as homophonous; similarly, EMERALDS and HAEMORRHOIDS. It is unlikely that a late eighteenth-century educated accent, or even a Cockney accent, would have treated these word-sets as homophones.

Other potentially useful sources of information include letters on linguistic matters to the daily press and periodicals – usually from academics – reformed spelling and shorthand systems, and poems and hymns. For example, John Keats rhymed THOUGHTS and SORTS in 1816 (Mugglestone 1991: 58); and John Keble rhymed POOR and STORE in a hymn he wrote in 1820.[11] Data of this sort has, however, to be used with equal caution since it is not always possible to distinguish unequivocally between eye rhymes and those ear rhymes which had a restricted regional and/or social distribution, as well as between ear rhymes and eye rhymes in general.[12]

5.2.9

The list of reliable authorities on nineteenth- and early twentieth-century pronunciation contains the names of about a dozen phoneticians. In Britain, it included Alexander Ellis, Alexander Melville Bell, and Henry Sweet; in the USA, Samuel Haldeman, William Dwight Whitney, and Charles Hall Grandgent. Without exception, they were well aware of the problems surrounding the objective validity of statements about pronunciation, both those deriving from a person's attempts to report his or her own speech-patterns, and, secondly, from socially induced attempts to argue the correctness – even the very existence – of particular pronunciations. Indeed, as early as the end of the eighteenth century, William Thornton, a scholar who had lived in England, Scotland and, finally, America,[13] had remarked in the specific context of speech analysis that 'some of the most learned men are men of the least knowledge – take away their school learning, and they remain children' (1793: 269). A century later, Sweet was to warn that 'the statements of ordinary educated people about their own pronunciation are generally not only value-less, but misleading' (Sweet 1890a: viii); and that 'there are not 100 people in England capable of writing down their own pron[unciation]' (Sweet to Storm 18 Feb. 1889). Ellis too said much the same thing: 'I have an idea that professed men of letters are the worst sources for noting peculiarities of pronunciation; they think so much about speech, that they nurse all manner of fancies, and their speech is apt to reflect individual theories' (1874: 1209). In America, Thomas Lounsbury warned similarly that 'on this subject ... there is no ignorance so profound and comprehensive as that which envelops the minds of many men of letters' (Lounsbury 1903: 582).

5.2.10

Since the First World War, the number of phoneticians (and university-level courses in phonetics) has grown considerably, and there is no lack of expert commentary on the state of English pronunciation from that time onward.[14] In Britain, the descriptive bias has been towards RP, a minority accent in terms of the number of its speakers (about 3 per cent of the

British population). In the USA, General American (henceforth GenAm.) pronunciation (used, however, by the majority of the population) has been accorded most attention. Much has also been written about other educated accents (e.g. Southern and Eastern American).

5.3 Methods of phonetic/phonological analysis

5.3.1

Before Ellis in the late 1860s, very few authors indicate that they were aware of any of the phonetics literature which had been published in Britain from the sixteenth century onwards and which could have aided them in their descriptions of pronunciation.[15] Even so, there is considerable evidence that many of them had intuitively developed a phonemic approach to the analysis of sounds, as a result of comparing the pronunciation with the spelling. Thus, for example, John Walker's analysis of the phonology (and some of the phonetics) of late eighteenth-century English (Walker 1791) bears obvious similarities, allowing for differences of terminology, to a present-day 'place-and-manner' analysis of consonant sounds.[16]

Indeed, there are several striking similarities between the type of phonetic/phonological analysis undertaken by various authors, particularly during the second half of the eighteenth century, and certain twentieth-century procedures for phonemic analysis. For example, many writers consciously use the minimal-pair principle, which results variously in 'chimers' (cf. Elphinston 1790: 33), 'contrasted examples' (cf. Batchelor 1809: 22), and 'precise pairs' (cf. Ellis 1869: 57).[17] And Edward Search's list of practice sentences for vowel contrasts (1773: 12) has its counterpart in practically every modern EFL textbook: 'I can't endure this cant', 'Sam, sing me a psalm', and 'Look at Luke.' The analysis of word-accent, moreover, is generally sophisticated, and derives from an appreciation of the technicalities of classical Greek and Latin prosody.

5.3.2

By the time of Whitney and Sweet in the 1870s, a well-developed system of phonetic and (sometimes) phonemic analysis was in existence. Whitney's study (1875) of his own idiolect benefits from his knowledge of phonetic procedures – his background as an orientalist is observable in some of his remarks. Particularly noteworthy are his statements about the distributional rules for several consonant and vowel phonemes, as well as his close attention to phonetic detail: see, in particular, his comments on the allophones of /r/, /s/, /k/, and /h/ (Whitney 1875: *passim*).

Sweet's analysis of English phonology (Sweet 1877) is similar, despite differences of terminology and symbology, to a comparable twentieth-century phonetic/phonological one. But his most obviously theoretical analysis of English phonology, or what he called 'the process of fixing the elementary distinctive sounds', is his virtually unknown paper of 1882 (cf. MacMahon 1985: 107). It anticipates the work sixty years later of phonologists such as George Trager, Bernard Bloch and Henry Smith with its argument that the number of 'elementary distinctive vowel-sounds' can be reduced from twenty to nine (see especially 1882: 14).

5.3.3

Most authors use some sort of phonetic notation, usually based on respelling of English.[18] For example, Walker, like many other orthoepists, uses a system of traditional orthographic characters with superscript numbers, pioneered by Sheridan (1780). He transcribes the /eː/ of FATE as $\overset{1}{a}$, the /aː/ of FAR as $\overset{2}{a}$, the /ɔː/ of FALL as $\overset{3}{a}$, and the /æ/ of FAT as $\overset{4}{a}$. However, he retains some 'silent' letters: e.g. PSALM is sȧm, but SAME is $\overset{2}{a}$me. Ellis uses one or other of his own phonetic notations (Glossic, Palaeotype, and variants thereof). Sweet and later writers tend to use a transcription which is either IPA or similar to it.

5.4 Standards and styles of pronunciation

The British Isles

5.4.1

Until the mid-eighteenth century, the pronunciation of English had generally been regarded as of secondary importance to matters of grammar and style. It was Thomas Sheridan who was to ask that correct pronunciation be put onto the intellectual agenda, by arguing that it was the variability of pronunciation, more than any other linguistic feature, which signalled the 'decline' of English as a language. In his *British Education* (1756) and *Lectures on Elocution* (1762) he outlined the problem. Variant pronunciations of the same word were rife; English appeared to be 'ruleless' in its pronunciation; certain 'letters' were being lost ('wh' was being replaced by 'w', and initial 'h' was being dropped, for example); unstressed syllables were not being given their full, stressed, values. The solution, he said, had to be a conscious movement towards imitating the speech patterns of 'people of education at court'; otherwise 'our language, in point of sound', would continue to 'relaps[e] into it's first state of barbarism' (Sheridan 1756: 221). By 1780, and the publication of his *General Dictionary of the English Language*, his analysis was even more dispiriting:

> The greatest improprieties … are to be found among people of fashion; many pronunciations, which thirty or forty years ago were confined to the vulgar, are gradually gaining ground; and if something be not done to stop this growing evil, and fix a general standard at present, the English is likely to become a mere jargon, which every one may pronounce as he pleases. It is to be wished that such a standard had been established during the reign of Queen Anne, [i.e. 1702–14, the time of Addison, Pope, Steele, and Swift], as it is probable that English was then spoken in its highest state of perfection'. (Sheridan 1780: Preface; cf. Danielsson 1948: 417–18)

Part of the problem lay, he claimed, in the variant pronunciations used by different professions within the higher echelons of English society:

> There is a great diversity of pronunciation of the same words, not only in individuals, but in whole bodies of men. That there are some adopted by the universities; some prevail at the bar, and some in the senate-house. That the propriety of these several pronunciations is controverted by several persons who have adopted them. (Sheridan 1780: Preface; cf. Danielsson 1948: 417–18)

5.4.2

His calls for speakers of English to imitate court speech, if only to 'fix' the language, coincided with the continuing growth in the power and prosperity of the middle classes. They in turn, conscious of their material and social strengths, did not wish their speech to betray the working-class origins of many of their forebears. A receptive audience existed – or could be created – for works on the 'correct' pronunciation of English, which would show people how to rid their speech of any unfortunate 'vulgarisms' or, equally importantly, any pedantries arising from a simplistic imitation of upper-class speech. Sheridan's role, as he saw it, was to identify the various sociolinguistic and stylistic factors; he left to his immediate successors the challenge of producing appropriate manuals of correct pronunciation which would cater for the middle classes' needs.

5.4.3

However, an alternative, and rather different, interpretation of the range of contemporary pronunciations of English was put, a few years later, in 1791, by John Walker. He had the advantage over Sheridan of having been brought up close to London and having spent all his professional life as an actor and elocutionist in the city. (Sheridan, despite having spent some time at a London school, had an Irish background, and his accent was Irish.) In Walker's opinion, the notion of extensive variant pronunciations had been overstated:

> The fluctuation of our Language, with respect to its pronunciation, seems to have been greatly exaggerated. Except for a few single words, which are generally noticed in the following Dictionary, and the words where *e* comes before *r*, followed by another consonant, as *merchant*, *service*, &c., the pronunciation of the Language is probably in the same state in which it was a century ago. (Walker 1791: vi)

He could call to mind only a small number of cases where the pronunciation reflected variability, or else socially unacceptable forms: an indistinct pronunciation of /s/ after /st/ e.g. in POSTS (Walker 1791: xii); the use of /v/ for /w/ and vice-versa 'among the inhabitants of London, and those not always of the lower order' (Walker 1791: xii–xiii); the loss of /ʍ/ 'particularly in the capital, where we do not find the least distinction of sound between *while* and *wile*, *whet* and *wet*, *where* and *were*, &c.' (1791: xiii); and /h/-dropping (and /h/-insertion) in certain words. Not only HEIR, HONEST, HONOUR, etc, had no initial /h/, but so too did HERB, HOSPITAL, HUMBLE, HUMOUR, and certain others (see further, 5.10.8) (Walker 1791: xiii). Almost all of these variants had been noted earlier by Sheridan.

5.4.4

Evidence of the type of variability that Sheridan emphasises, but Walker downplays, can be found, slightly later, in the anonymous *A Vocabulary of Such Words in the English Language as Are of Dubious or Unsettled Pronunciation* (1797), which lists just over 900 words which had fluctuating pronunciations. Leaving aside about 200 of them which by any criterion would be counted as belonging to specialist registers, e.g. GELABLE, MYROBALAN, PAROQUET, and SARDONYX, there still remain about 700 whose pronunciation varied. The author quotes the opposing views of the leading orthoepists of the day to prove the point: words like ALMOND pronounced with or without an /l/; BRACELET with stressed /æ/ or /eː/; the first syllable of CUCUMBER pronounced either as COW or QUEUE; DUKE with or without a /j/; MOBILE with the stress on the second or the first syllable; SHONE with the vowel of either GONE or MOAN; and WEAPON with either /iː/ or /ɛ/ as the stressed vowel.

5.4.5

The effect of the awareness, from about the mid-eighteenth century onwards, of variable pronunciations led several authors to try to stabilise and, where necessary, reform the pronunciation of English. The movement gathered pace in the 1770s and continued until the turn of the century. It seems to have been an explicitly book-based movement; there is no evidence of meetings etc. having been held to further the cause. A variety of explanations (not necessarily logical reasons) were put forward in justification.

Any change in language (as reflected in the variability) was seen as evidence of corruption; the pace of change was too fast; the population at large were bad speakers; the mixing of regional and London accents was producing new pronunciations; some speakers were introducing deliberate affectations into their speech; the fusion of socially inferior accents with more superior ones ('vulgar' speech and 'proper' speech) was creating pronunciations in which the social markers between classes were being blurred; discrepancies between the orthography and the pronunciation were becoming more and more obvious. (This latter point might not have mattered, had it not been for the continuing shadow cast by Dr Johnson and his famous dictum in the *Dictionary* of 1755 that as a model of pronunciation, 'the best general rule is to consider those as the most elegant speakers who deviate least from the written word'.) Finally, some authors felt that the so-called 'euphonic' genius of the language was being violated (cf. Sheldon 1938: 412–20).

5.4.6

If a standard form of English pronunciation was to be established, what should it be? There was no disagreement amongst the orthoepists that the only regional form of English that could count as 'proper' pronunciation within the British Isles was that of London, but with allowances for certain 'educated' pronunciations of particular speakers reasonably close to the capital. As James Beattie put it in 1783,

> the language ... of the most learned and polite persons in London, and the neighbouring universities of Oxford and Cambridge, ought to be accounted the standard of the English tongue, especially in accent [= intonation] and pronunciation, syntax, spelling, and idiom, having been ascertained by the practice of good authors and the consent of former ages ... the most enlightened minds must be supposed to be the best judges of propriety in speech. (Beattie 1783: 129–30)

Within London speech, however, a social standard could not be so dogmatically specified. Up until 1750, it was the speech of the Court that had been accepted unquestioningly as the standard for the language as a whole. Between 1750 and the end of the eighteenth century, however, and despite what Sheridan in particular had said, the speech of the socially secure and the learned, rather than the genteel speech of the Court, became increasingly recommended:

> the standard of these sounds ... is that pronunciation of them, in most general use, amongst people of elegance and taste of the English nation, and especially of London. (Johnston 1764: 1; cf. Danielsson 1948: 416)

> the actual practice of the best speakers; men of letters in the metropolis (Kenrick 1773: vii; cf. Sheldon 1938: 272)

> By being properly pronounced, I would be always understood to mean, pronounced agreeable to the general practice of men of letters and polite speakers in the Metropolis. (Kenrick 1784: 56)[19]

5.4.7

It was left to John Walker, in 1791, to ask pertinent questions about the social and stylistic complexities of speech patterns, as well as about the problems they posed for a standard pronunciation and its function in society. He could not accept that a person's position in relation to the Court or to education was a guarantee of the 'standard' quality of their speech:

> Neither a finical pronunciation of the court, nor a pedantic Græcism of the schools, will be denominated respectable usage, till a certain number of the general mass of speakers have acknowledged them; nor will a multitude of common speakers authorise any pronunciation which is reprobated by the learned and polite. (1791: vii–viii)

And he was clearly aware of the need to assess objectively the part that 'good usage' played amongst 'learned and polite' speakers, before deciding on any standard form of pronunciation:

> As those sounds ... which are the most generally received among the
> learned and polite, as well as the bulk of speakers, are the most legitimate,
> we may conclude that a majority of two of these states ought always to
> concur, in order to constitute what is called good usage. (1791: viii)

Slightly ironically, however, he would not hesitate to consult the
orthoepical dictionaries to determine 'the general current of custom', since
'an exhibition of the opinions of orthöepists about the sound of words
always appeared to me a very rational method of determining what is called
custom'. He admitted that he had 'sometimes dissented from the majority
... from a persuasion of being better informed of what was the actual
custom of speaking, or from a partiality to the evident analogies of the language' (1791: viii).

In a revealing passage from the 1806 and later editions of his *Critical
Pronouncing Dictionary* (it did not appear in either the 1791 or the 1797 editions), Walker again showed himself to be well aware of the difficulties of
determining the pronunciation of certain words; but he had a strategy for
achieving this:

> To a man born, as I was, within a few miles of the Capital, living in the
> Capital almost my whole life ... the true pronunciation of the language
> must be very familiar . . . But this vernacular instinct [for the pronuncia-
> tion] has been seconded by a careful investigation of the analogies of the
> language ... It can scarcely be supposed that the most experienced
> speaker has heard every word in the language, and the whole circle of sci-
> ences, pronounced exactly as it ought to be ... he must sometimes have
> recourse to the principles of pronunciation ... These principles are those
> general laws of articulation which determine the character, and fix the
> boundaries of every language; as in every system of speaking, however
> irregular, the organs must necessarily fall into some common mode of
> enunciation. (Advertisement to Walker 1806: n.p.; cf. also Walker
> 1819a: 11)

5.4.8

Several instances can be cited from the orthoepical and related literature of
the years between 1750 and 1850 to show that writers were well aware of
the existence of style-switching – although its implications for determining a 'standard' pronunciation were rarely assessed. For example:

> In living languages, the modes of prosaic pronunciation are fluctuating
> and arbitrary, whilst those of poetic composition are more fixed and
> determinate. (Ausonius 1798: 290)

And from John Witherspoon, the Scots-born Principal of Princeton College:

> I shall also admit, though with some hesitation, that gentlemen and scholars in Great Britain, speak as much with the vulgar *in common chit-chat*, as persons of the same class do in America; but there is a remarkable difference in their public and solemn discourses. (quoted by Pickering 1828: 207)

5.4.9

The retention of specific regional features (i.e. from outside London) in educated accents was regarded as perfectly normal. (The concept of a completely non-regional form of standard English pronunciation within the British Isles (later to be called RP) was not yet in existence.) Indeed, any educated speaker's pronunciation was likely to contain certain regional features:

> The best educated people in the provinces, if constantly resident there, are sure to be strongly tinctured with the dialect of the county in which they live. Hence it is, that the vulgar pronunciation of London, though not half so erroneous as that of Scotland, Ireland, or any of the provinces, is, to a person of correct taste, a thousand times more offensive and disgusting. (Walker 1791: xiv)

5.4.10

From about the beginning of the nineteenth century, however, the defining feature of a acceptable pronunciation shifted more and more to the appropriate use of *analogical* patterns of pronunciation. The essence of this principle had been well illustrated by Walker in his *Rhetorical Grammar* of 1785. The word PRONUNCIATION was often heard, he said, as if it were spelled PRONOUNCIATION – on the analogy of PRONOUNCE. Yet, says Walker, the key to how it *should* be pronounced is the operation of a 'rule' which states that <c>, <s>, and <t> are pronounced as a [ʃ] if they are followed by '*ea, ia, io*, or any similar diphthong'. Since PARTIALITY and ESPECIALLY, amongst other words, have a [ʃ], then this 'obliges us' to pronounce PRONUNCIATION also with a [ʃ] (cf. Sheldon 1938: 342–43). By a similar token, the word ASIA should be pronounced not with a [ʃ], but with a [ʒ], since the word follows the same stress and rhyme patterns of ARPASIA and EUTHANASIA (cf. Sheldon 1938: 371).

5.4.11

Questions about the nature of a standard pronunciation of English begin to recede once the nineteenth century is underway. Anon. (1813: n.p.) writes only of 'the proper pronunciation', and Anon. (1817: iii) of 'what is termed in Good Company, familiar Conversation'. Benjamin Smart (1819: 41) presumes that his reader will be 'politely educated, and pronounce ... the words of his language like other well-bred people'.[20]

In 1836, Smart was advising his readers to imitate the speech of the 'well-educated Londoner' or the 'well-bred Londoner' (Smart 1836: iv), even if such pronunciations led to a divergence from the orthography. (The remark was probably inserted by Smart as much to alert his readers to how English pronunciation had diverged from the orthography as to signal any belief on his part that English pronunciation was still in line (more or less) with the orthography.) For him, 'a good pronunciation is the use of these elements [= of pronunciation as described] exactly where the custom of good (that is well-bred) society places them, however at variance such custom may often be with the rules of orthography' (Smart 1836: xi, section 80).

He clearly distinguishes between the pronunciation he is recommending from 'familiar and consequently negligent utterance' (Smart 1836: xviii, fn. 99), and this leads, in 1842, to his invoking a specific phonological criterion, namely that 'nothing more distinguishes a person of a good, from one of a mean education, than the pronunciation of the unaccented vowels' (Smart 1842: 25). Sheridan, too, many years previously, had said virtually the same thing. To us today, this remark may seem opaque, if not pretentious. But it reflected a feature of English English pronunciation of the nineteenth century, whereby the unstressed vowels in a word like ADHER-ENT were not necessarily /ə/, but, for many speakers, still /æ/ and /ɛ/; (see further, section 5.6.6).

Smart's stipulations had their followers. In 1850 William Spurrell admitted that Smart's 'elaborate and comprehensive work is undoubtedly the best reflex of the customary pronunciation of educated English speakers, the true criterion of correct English orthoepy' (Spurrell 1850: title page). Another lexicographer, P. Austin Nuttall, was clearly thinking of Smart with his recommendation that his readers should follow 'the present usage of literary and well-bred society ... [in] London' (Nuttall 1863: v). In the majority of publications, however, no specific statement is made (or discussed) about what constituted the 'best' form of English.

5.4.12

It is in the publications of Alexander Ellis that one not only finds much more objective evidence about pronunciation (including discussions of some of the phonetic minutiae of English), but, for the first time, something approaching a sociolinguistic categorisation of the characteristic differences of pronunciation; this went far beyond the by now ingrained distinction between 'polite' and 'vulgar' speech.[21]

Ellis sets up six categories of pronunciation: (1) 'Received Pronunciation', (2) 'Correct Pronunciation', (3) 'Natural Pronunciation or Untamed English', (4) 'Peasant Speech', (5) 'Vulgar and Illiterate Speech', and (6) 'Dialect Speech' (Ellis 1869: 624–30; 1874: 1085–90, 1208–17, 1243–4; 1889). It is the first three that are of concern here.

5.4.13

'Received Pronunciation' he describes as follows: 'In the present day we may … recognise a received pronunciation all over the country, not widely differing in any particular locality, and admitting a certain degree of variety. It may be especially considered as the educated pronunciation of the metropolis, of the court, the pulpit and the bar', with some regional variation (1869: 23). He later added to the list the categories of 'the stage, the universities – and, in a minor degree, parliament, the lecture room, the hustings and public meetings' (Ellis 1874: 1216). Stylistic differences within r.p. (Ellis's abbreviation) were twofold: 'studied' and 'unstudied', corresponding to 'formal' and 'informal' styles of speaking.

There are two important caveats, however. One is the regional colouring that Ellis noticed in most r.p. speakers' speech: 'But in as much as all these localities and professions are recruited from the provinces, there will be a varied thread of provincial utterance running through the whole' (Ellis 1869: 23; see also Ellis 1874: 1215–16). In this respect, Ellis's views were precisely the same as those of his American contemporaries (see below 5.4.30).

The other caveat is that he had serious reservations about the naturalness of r.p.: whether it really was the result of historical speech patterns, rather than a somewhat uneasy amalgam of particular synchronic phonetic and phonological features. As he confessed privately in 1882 to James Murray, the editor of the *OED*, 'received speech is altogether a *made* language, not a natural growth, constantly made in every individual even now' (see MacMahon 1985: 79).

His second category was 'Correct Pronunciation', defined as the 'usage of large numbers of persons of either sex in different parts of the country, who have received a superior education' (Ellis 1869: 630.)

'Natural Pronunciation or Untamed English' was a pronunciation unaffected by, for example, 'orthoepists, classical theorists, literary fancies, [and] fashionable heresies' (1874: 1243–44).

5.4.14

Ellis was far more of an objective observer of speech phenomena than many of his contemporaries (and predecessors). He also knew that to try to extrapolate from the various strands of English pronunciation a 'standard' form was illogical:

> If orthoepists of repute inculcate such sounds, for which a tendency already exists, their future prevalence is tolerably secured. As to the 'correctness' or 'impropriety' of such sounds I do not see on what grounds I can offer an opinion. I can only say what I observe, and what best pleases my ear, probably from long practice. Neither history nor pedantry can set the norm. (Ellis 1874: 1152)

Whilst acknowledging the growth of a 'uniform pronunciation' of English, he was quick to point out that variations do still exist within it: 'there never has been so near an approach to a uniform pronunciation as that which now prevails, and … that uniformity itself is not likely to be so great as might have been anticipated' (Ellis 1869: 626).

Various factors had been at work to help ensure the growth of uniformity: contact between urban and rural communities; speakers with different accents being educated together within a university setting; the pronunciation used in Church services by the clergy being imitated by their parishioners; and the role played by primary school teachers in teaching particular pronunciations to young children. (The part played by the British Public School system in smoothing the development of RP was a slightly later development – see below, 5.4.19.)

5.4.15

The inexorable conclusion, for Ellis, was that 'there is no such thing as educated English pronunciation. There are pronunciations of English people more or less educated in a multitude of other things, but not in pronunciation' (Ellis 1874: 1214). He noted 'the marked varieties' and 'considerable divergences of pronunciation' to be found amongst 'educated speakers of all classes, even when speaking with the greater care usually taken in public delivery' (1870: 110; see also 1874: 1214). Nearly a hundred pages of Part IV (1874) of his major diachronic study of English, *On Early English Pronunciation*, are given over to a close socio-phonetic analysis of received pronunciation and other accents: 'the physician' who used /ə'krɒs/ rather than /ə'krɔːs/; the 'noble M.P.' with his /aɪ'dɪər/; the 'man of science's' /stæf/ as well as /stɑːf/; the 'professional man' with his [æb'steːn], not [æb'steɪn]; and the 'young educated London girl' who used [miːj] and [æːd], instead of [miː] and [æd] (Ellis 1874: 1208–14).[22]

5.4.16

Even so, a considerable degree of uniformity was to be found in 'educated London' speech: 'the general speech of educated London differs only in certain minute points, and in a few classes of words … from that which I have given as my own' (1874: 1209). And when comparing his own speech with that of Henry Sweet, his junior by more than twenty-five years, Ellis noted that 'his [i.e. Sweet's] pronunciation differs in many minute shades from mine, although in ordinary conversation the difference would probably be passed by unnoticed, so little accustomed are we to dwell on differences which vex the phonologist's spirit' (Ellis 1874: 1196).[23]

5.4.17

The form of English that Henry Sweet himself described in his various works was his own idiolect, with slight modifications. He never referred to it as 'standard English', but variously as an 'educated southern pronunciation' (1877: 15), or 'the educated speech of London and the district round it' (1890a: v).[24] And in his *Sounds of English* (1908), he was careful to point out that his transcribed texts were 'of a natural as opposed to an artificially normalised pronunciation, and are not intended to serve as a rigorous standard of correct speech – a standard which in our present state of knowledge it would be impossible to set up' (Sweet 1908: 89). Sweet never used the term RP (or its predecessor r.p.) for the type of English he described, but he does hark back to Ellis's categories of pronunciation when he noted the sociolinguistic and stylistic factors that could affect a person's pronunciation: age, region of origin, class, and speed of speaking (cf. Sweet 1890a: vi–viii).

5.4.18

The influence of short-lived fashions of pronunciation amongst educated London speakers was commented on by Richard Lloyd, a phonetician, towards the end of the nineteenth century:

> Even educated London English is subject to gusts of fashion which leave the general body of good English-speakers totally untouched. At the present moment it is thought in certain circles to be the 'correct thing' to change final *-ng* into *n*. There are a dozen such vagaries, which come and go, for one which makes any permanent impress on the language. (Lloyd 1894: 52)[25]

5.4.19

Lloyd was the first phonetician to draw attention to the emergence of a type of acceptable educated English pronunciation which revealed hardly any regional characteristics – i.e. even fewer than in Ellis's 'r.p.': 'the perfect English is that which is admittedly correct, while giving the least possible indication of local origin' (Lloyd 1894: 52). This assumes that, between the time of Ellis in the late 1860s and Lloyd in the mid-1890s, the amount of regional content in 'educated' speech must have been reduced. The explanation lies in the part played from about the 1870s onwards by the Public Schools (i.e. fee-paying boarding schools) in England in altering young boys' speech patterns. Before that date, any conformist influence exerted by them on speech patterns seems to have been slight – if only because educated adult society used regional accents; consequently, there was no pressure for a different accent to be adopted within the schools themselves. Honey (1991: 213) quotes the example of 'a good number of later Victorian public school headmasters, as well as leading Oxford and Cambridge dons, who had attended their public schools before 1870, [and who] retained marked traces of regional accent'.

5.4.20

The role played by this non-regional, but heavily marked social, pronunciation, in conjunction with other social characteristics, helped within a short time to reinforce the concept of the 'public-school man'. The accent was not confined to the public schools, however. The universities of Oxford and Cambridge, because of their policy of accepting almost exclusively public-school boys, provided the mechanism whereby those students who had not attended a public school would, predictably, come under the linguistic influence of those who had. The result was a yet wider dissemination of the accent. Post-University positions, e.g. in Government service, either in Britain or the Empire, or in the Anglican Church, created further opportunities for the public to hear RP and react to it – usually favourably. For example, in 1910, Marshall Montgomery set up as his phonetic role-model for non-native learners of English the accent of those 'well-educated people in London and the South of England generally; for example, at the Universities of Oxford and Cambridge and at the Great Public Schools' (Montgomery 1910: 3). He pointed out that the term 'Standard English' implied 'no absolute rigidity in the pronunciation of Modern English', and that different styles of speaking might be employed for different purposes. By this he meant only that within RP there were different styles, not allowable regional variations: 'elaborate' (for declaiming Wordsworth, Keats, and Swinburne), 'normal' (for declaiming Tennyson and Charles Lamb), and 'rapid' (for declaiming Kipling).

5.4.21

Because of its strong association with the public schools, Daniel Jones in 1917 gave the label 'Public School Pronunciation', abbreviated to PSP, to the type of English that he was to describe in all the editions of his *English Pronouncing Dictionary*, namely 'that most usually heard in everyday speech in the families of Southern English persons whose men-folk have been educated at the great public-boarding schools [in the English sense, not in the American sense]'. He points out that this pronunciation is also used by 'a considerable proportion of those who do not come from the South of England, but who have been educated at these schools', and that 'it is probably accurate to say that a majority of those members of London society who have had a university education, use either this pronunciation or a pronunciation not differing very greatly from it' (Jones, D. 1917: viii). The importance of PSP (subsequently re-named RP by Jones in 1926) in British (especially English) society, was underlined by its role as the sole accent of English which could be used on air by broadcasters working for the BBC (see Juul, Nielsen & Sørensen 1988 for details of the policy and the reactions to it). That same year, 1926, the BBC set up an Advisory Committee on Spoken English, to advise and where necessary adjudicate on the pronunciations that were to be used for particular words during broadcasts: words such as GARAGE, PEJORATIVE, QUANDARY, etc. (see Pointon 1988). The Committee was disbanded in 1939, but it was not until the

1960s that the policy of employing only RP speakers was changed, and – at least as far as news broadcasts were concerned – non-RP accents began to be heard. To an outside observer, the essence of RP was probably well summarised in 1927 by the British orientalist, Sir Denison Ross, who opined that 'the true guardians of the best-spoken English' were 'the middle-aged clubmen of London' (quoted by Fuhrken 1932: 18).

5.4.22

Jones's conception of RP as a form of English moulded by boyhood patterns of speech behaviour has been moderated to a great extent over the last thirty years. Thus, Gimson notes only the historical, not the present-day, role of the public schools in RP (Gimson 1962: 82–3; 1970: 84–5; 1980: 89; 1989: 85). The RP of the last thirty or so years is, in his opinion, 'basically educated Southern British English' (Gimson 1962: 83; 1970: 85; 1980: 89; 1989: 85), of which there are three main types: *conservative* RP used by the older generation and, traditionally, by certain professions or social groups; *general* RP most commonly in use and typified by the pronunciation adopted by the BBC;[26] and *advanced* RP mainly used by young people of exclusive social groups – mostly of the upper classes, but also, for prestige value, in certain professional circles. In its most exaggerated variety, this last type would usually be judged 'affected' by other RP speakers (Gimson 1962: 85; 1970: 88; 1980: 91; 1989: 88).

5.4.23

Wells glosses RP as the accent 'generally taken as a standard throughout England and perhaps Wales, but not in Scotland' (Wells 1982: 117); 'widely regarded as a model for correct pronunciation, particularly for educated formal speech ... a social accent associated with the upper end of the social-class continuum' (Wells 1990a: xii). Unlike Gimson, however, he associates it with a narrower social grouping and range of occupations: upper and upper-middle class, a public-school background, and a barrister, stockbroker, or diplomat. He too distinguishes between different forms of RP.

5.4.24

Phoneticians in Britain generally agree that RP is spoken by about 3 per cent, possibly slightly more, of the population of Britain (cf. Ramsaran

1990: 190) – although hard statistical evidence is lacking. This means that about one and three-quarter million people out of a total British population of about 58 million use this particular accent.

The United States

5.4.25

From the late eighteenth century onwards, in the United States, considerable differences of opinion emerged over the desirability of regarding a form of English English pronunciation as a standard which Americans should acknowledge (tacitly if necessary). This in turn raised questions about the reliability of Walker's pronunciation as an accurate reflection of current English English usage.

In 1789, the lexicographer Noah Webster's opinions were diametrically opposed to those of his contemporaries in England. He was adamant that 'Great Britain, whose children we are, and whose language we speak, should no longer be *our* standard; for the taste of her writers is already corrupted, and her language on the decline' (1789.I: 20), despite the fact that 'in many parts of America, people at present attempt to copy the English phrases and pronunciation – an attempt that is favored by their habits, their prepossessions and the intercourse between the two countries' (1789.I: 23). Indeed, in his view, there was no such thing as a standard pronunciation of English in England: 'the English themselves have no standard of pronunciation, nor can they ever have one on the plan they propose. The Authors, who have attempted to give us a standard, make the practice of the court and stage in London the sole criterion of propriety in speaking. An attempt to establish a standard on this foundation is both unjust and idle' (1789.I: 24).

The quality of the work produced by the English orthoepists did not meet with his approval: 'the pronunciation has been neglected till a few years ago; when Sheridan and Kenrick, with several compilers of less note, attempted to give us a standard. Unluckily they have all made the attempt on false principles; and will, if followed, multiply the anomalies, which already deform the language and embarrass the learner [*Footnote:* We may except Kenrick, who has paid some regard to principles, in marking the pronunciation]' (1789.I: 78). Not surprisingly, Webster was also conscious of the strong prescriptive tone of much of the discussion of pronunciation within the British Isles: that 'instead of examining to find what the English language is, [most writers] endeavor to show what it ought to be according to their rules' (Webster 1789.I: 37).

5.4.26

Like some of his contemporaries in England, Webster had also drawn up similar, though less extensive, lists of 'Differences of Pronunciation and Controverted Points Examined' and 'Modern Corruptions in the English Pronunciation' (Webster 1789.II & III: 103–79). Over a hundred words are noted as varying in their pronunciation (either within the same social class or between different regions of the country). Alternatively, they had pronunciations to which Webster personally took exception: HUMAN without the /h/ – 'a gross error'; WHIP and WHITE pronounced with /w/, not /ʍ/ – 'a foreign corruption'; SAUCE with /aː/ – 'the most general pronunciation'; PATRON with /æ/, not /eː/; EUROPEAN with stress on the second, not the third, syllable, i.e. EU'ROPEAN. For the 1829 American edition of Webster's *Dictionary*, Joseph Worcester produced a 'Synopsis of Words Differently Pronounced by Different Orthoëpists', which was subsequently revised by Chauncey Goodrich for the 1847 edition. The latter version runs to 672 words, whose pronunciation varied in terms either of segments or suprasegmental features, or both. Specialist words like CAMELOPARD, FALCHION, PLICATURE, PTISAN, and SCIOMACHY inevitably had no stable pronunciations; but a large number of 'everyday' words seemed just as variable: AGAIN with either /ɛ/ or /eː/, BALCONY with initial-syllable stress or second-syllable stress, DESIGN with /s/ or /z/, GOLD with /oː/ or /uː/, HOSPITAL with or without an /h/, and QUALM with /aː/ or /ɔː/.

5.4.27

Webster, like Walker, had serious reservations about whether a standard could indeed be established, given the practical difficulties in determining what the current usage was. But he introduced a new factor into the argument: the political appropriateness of allowing a small minority to dictate their phonetic behaviour to the majority: 'an attempt to fix a standard on the practice of any particular class of people is highly absurd' (1789.I: 25). And he asked 'what right have a few men, however elevated their station, to change a national practice? They may say, that they consult their own ears, and endeavor to please themselves' (Webster 1789.III: 165–6). In monarchical societies, 'customs of the court and stage, it is confessed, rule without resistance .... But what have we to do with the customs of a foreign nation?' (Webster 1789.III: 173).

His solution to the apparent dilemma was the eminently more democratic one of letting the usage of the nation as a whole, tempered where necessary by the application of analogical rules, be the final arbiter and creator of a standard pronunciation: 'if a standard therefore cannot be fixed on local and variable custom, on what shall it be fixed? If the most eminent speakers are not to direct our practice, where shall we look for a guide? The answer is extremely easy; the *rules of the language itself*, and the *general practice of the nation ... universal undisputed practice*, and the *principle of analogy*' (Webster 1789.I: 27–8). He went on: 'Where such principles cannot be found, let us examin [*sic*] the opinions of the learned, and the practice of the nations which speak the pure English, that we may determine by the weight of authority, the *common law* of language, those questions which do not come within any established rules' (1789.I: 79).

Webster was well aware of the various social consequences of pronunciation-differences existing within America: 'a sameness of pronunciation is of considerable consequence in a political view; for provincial accents are disagreeable to strangers and sometimes have an unhappy effect upon the social affections ... Thus small differences in pronunciation at first excite ridicule – a habit of laughing at the singularities of strangers is followed by disrespect – and without respect friendship is a name, and social intercourse a mere ceremony' (Webster 1789.I: 19–20). Equally, he recognised that the academic task of establishing a series of phonetic norms for American English would be worthless unless the nation as a whole could be informed of them: 'if the practice of a few men in the capital is to be the standard, a knowledge of this must be communicated to the whole nation' (1789.I: 25).

5.4.28

The arguments about the need for and the choice of a standard pronunciation rumbled on. A different perspective, however, was introduced by a handful of commentators who remarked on the striking similarity between some accents of American English and certain (unspecified) English English ones. Thus Timothy Dwight, who travelled in New England and New York over a twenty-year period (1796–1815) noted that the inhabitants of Boston 'with very few exceptions ... speak the English language in the English manner' (Dwight 1821–2, quoted in Krapp 1925.II: 15; see also Read 1933/1980: 23). The implication was simple: should not English

English be a standard for America as well? An American writer, known to us only as Xanthus (1826), did indeed think so, on the grounds that 'the [American] public ... have awarded to Walker nearly the same place in [orthoepy] which [Lindley] Murray and [Samuel] Johnson hold in [grammar and orthography]' and that 'the literati of this country have decided that it consists perfectly with our independence to adopt the English standards of orthoepy as well as of philology' (Xanthus 1826: 379). He did, however, acknowledge that the whole question of a standard of American pronunciation was regarded 'by many of our literati as quite unimportant, and that not a few of the presidents and professors of our colleges, and other public seminaries, render no assistance, either by precept or example, to those of their pupils who wish to pronounce correctly' (Xanthus 1826: 441). Noah Webster was considerably more critical (and realistic) than Xanthus, with his counter-view that 'there is no standard in England, except the pronunciation which prevails among respectable people; and this, though *tolerably uniform*, is not precisely the same' (Webster 1826, quoted by Pickering 1828: 204).

Support for the idea of London pronunciation as the standard for America came also from the lawyer-cum-linguist John Pickering. He argued on the grounds of a shared literary heritage: 'London is ... also the metropolis of English literature; and the usage of her polite speakers is of higher authority, generally, to the numerous and widely dispersed people who speak the English language, than that of any other city' (Pickering 1828: 202). In almost the same breath, he admitted that the usages of both England and America should be taken into account, since 'we cannot but consider our two nations, as forming but one people, so far as respects language; and the usage of the whole body of the learned and polite portion of this one people must be the standard' (Pickering 1828: 202).

This, in turn, re-opened the question of whether Walker reflected actual London usage. Joseph Worcester, one of the editors of Webster, felt that 'in this respect, no one has been more favourably situated than *Walker*; and in the pronunciation of the great mass of words in the language, he is supported by subsequent writers' (Worcester, quoted by Pickering 1828: 202–03. See also Pickering 1828: 192, 203; Xanthus 1826: 442–3). For at least some Americans, then, the notations in Walker paralleled their own intuitions (and those of their assumed co-speakers in London) about a form of pronunciation which was shared by both America and England.

It was left to Webster to strike the necessarily discordant note and point out that Walker did not in fact reflect current usage: '*Walker's scheme does not give this usage*; it deviates from it as much as Sheridan's, and even more' (Webster, 14 March 1826, quoted by Pickering 1828: 204); 'Walker's Dictionary is full of inconsistencies from beginning to end; and the attempt to make it a standard, *has done more to corrupt the language*, than any event that has taken place for five hundred years past . . . Walker's pronunciation is *so erroneous*' (Webster, December 1827, quoted by Pickering 1828: 204). However, for the *Dictionary* in 1828, he acknowledged that there could well be occasions when the 'usage of respectable people in England and the United States', which was 'identical in the two countries' and which was 'settled and undisputed', would coincide (Webster 1828: xl). To that extent, a common British–American standard of pronunciation could be said to exist for certain parts of the lexicon.

Even so, the contrast could not, in general, be clearer between England, where there was agreement that a socially superior London pronunciation was a *de facto* standard, and America where many intellectuals regarded the question of even having a standard of pronunciation as irrelevant to everyday living. Put another way, England preferred the genteel solution – at least initially; America the democratic one.

5.4.29

For the next century, most American dictionary-writers and orthoepists skirted round the question of the precise characterisation of a standard American pronunciation, using, instead, phrases like 'that pronunciation of the English language which is supported by the greatest number of competent authorities' (Smalley 1855: iii), or the 'prevailing usage of correct writers and speakers' (Cooley 1861: iii). William Dwight Whitney, when introducing his analysis of his own phonology (1875), humbly describes his accent as 'a fair specimen of that of the ordinarily educated New Englander from the interior' (Whitney 1875: 205). But behind this facade of generality and independence there lurked, in the school-rooms at least, a cramping spirit of prescriptivism. For example, an Act was passed by the New Hampshire State Legislature in 1808 to provide for teaching of the 'various sounds and powers of the letters in the English language'; and the *Common School Journal* began publishing lists of mispronunciations from 1839 onwards (Bronstein 1954: 419–20). A typical mid-century publication, aiming to teach children the 'correct pronunciation of their mother tongue', is Stearns (1858). He rails against pronunciations which he deems to be 'vulgar', 'shocking', 'affected', 'wholly destitute of authority', 'improper', and 'wrong'.

5.4.30

Up until the beginning of the twentieth century, there was little discussion of a standard form of American English evolving as a result of one particular area of the country being chosen (or choosing itself) to represent the country as a whole. Admittedly, as early as 1828, James Fenimore Cooper had pointed out that the 'distinctions in speech between New England and New York, or Pennsylvania, or any other State, were far greater twenty years ago than they are now' (Cooper 1828, quoted by Krapp 1925.I: 14) – with the implication that a supra-regional form of pronunciation was emerging.[27] By the end of the nineteenth century, regionally distinct forms of American pronunciation were well-established, but no one type was regarded by its speakers as inherently superior to any other. Even so, details of their precise forms were lacking. For this reason, Grandgent's survey, in the early 1890s, focused on 'educated Americans in various parts of the country' (Grandgent 1891: 82), and, more specifically, on 'the familiar speech of highly educated persons' (Grandgent 1891: 459; cf. also Grandgent 1895: 443), or, in different words, 'the usual speech of educated native Americans – the pronunciation that our teachers, doctors, clergymen, lawyers use (or think they use) in their ordinary conversation' (Grandgent 1893a: 273). The results of his survey showed, as expected, considerable diversity, but no one area which had achieved pre-eminence to the ears of all Americans. Eliza Andrews's analysis, albeit brief, at the same time as Grandgent's survey, of certain pronunciations from 'men and women who may, perhaps, be regarded as the representatives of the most cultured thought in America' (Andrews 1896) convinced her that there was no such thing as a standard pronunciation. If Americans were looking for phonetic role-models, they should follow the practices of 'ordinarily well bred and well educated people' (Andrews 1896: 596). Thomas Lounsbury, Professor of English at Yale, argued too for 'the usage of the educated body' (Lounsbury 1903: 261).

5.4.31

The more scholarly regional classification of American pronunciation began in 1919, when George Krapp argued that despite 'American cultivated speech' being 'extraordinarily mixed', a division into 'Eastern', 'Western' and 'Southern' was appropriate (Krapp 1919: viii). If from this there was to be a 'standard' accent, then it was 'perhaps best described ... as the speech which is least likely to attract attention to itself as being peculiar to any class or locality' (1919: ix). And, as if to emphasise the different social implications of RP and American English, he adds that Americans 'do not move in mutually exclusive and self-centered circles in their habits of speech' (1919: ix). By 1925, he was prepared to be more specific about these categories of accent. His tripartite division remains, but with clarifications. 'Eastern' is, in the terminology of the 1990s, non-rhotic and with /ɑː/ (rather than /æ/) before most voiceless fricatives (as in RP); 'Southern' is similarly non-rhotic, but with /æ/ rather than /ɑː/ before the same fricatives; 'Western', which he also calls 'General', has 'attained an unusual degree of currency', with the important proviso that it is 'a composite type, more or less an abstraction of generalised speech habits' (Krapp 1925.I: 37, 45–6). (The term 'General American' was coined by Krapp, and first used by him in this work in 1925.)

It is clear that he did not regard his 'General' accent as a standard, since 'speech is standard when it passes current in actual usage among persons who must be accounted as among the conservers and representatives of the approved social traditions of a community. In American life such persons have always been distinguished by a certain amount of literary culture' (Krapp 1925.II: 7). And, of course, 'Good English in America has always been a matter of the opinion of those who know, or think they know, and opinion on this point has always been changing' (Krapp 1925.I: 8). He did, nevertheless, recognise a growing uniformity of pronunciation 'among standard speakers, that is, among members of good standing in the community' (Krapp 1925.I: 8). John Kenyon too (1924, quoted in Kenyon 1946: vi) explicitly pointed out that 'no attempt is made to set up or even to imply a standard of correctness based on the usage of any part of America'. Instead, he chose to base his observations on the 'cultivated' pronunciation of his own locality, namely the Western Reserve of Ohio (Kenyon 1946: vi). By contrast, Hans Kurath was adamant that 'the cultured groups in each of the three areas [West, East, South]' had their own 'more or less flexible standard of pronunciation' (Kurath 1928: 281).

5.4.32

It was at about this time, during the 1920s and early 1930s, that there was a resurgence of interest in the idea of English English (i.e. RP) being accorded the status of the standard accent of American English, a move that was roundly condemned by Kurath in particular: 'It is nothing short of foolhardy to advocate the adoption of the British standard of pronunciation, as some enthusiasts have done' (Kurath 1928: 282). The leader of the enthusiasts was Miss E. M. De Witt, the author of various works on the subject, including *Euphon English in America* (1925).

5.4.33

During the last sixty years, GenAm. has taken on the role of the phonetic representative of American English – solely on the grounds of its relative homogeneity and number of speakers. Thus, Prator describes it as 'the language which can be heard, with only slight variations, from Ohio through the Middle West and on to the Pacific Coast. Some 90,000,000 people speak this General American ... they undeniably constitute the present linguistic center of gravity of the English-speaking world, both because of their numbers and their cultural importance' (Prator 1951: xi; cf. also Prator & Robinett 1972, quoted by Wells 1982.I: 118). Note Wells's caveat that because of the variability that exists in GenAm., the term itself is nowadays looked at somewhat askance (Wells 1982: 118).

Bronstein (1960: 4) has favoured a standard which is 'the socially acceptable pattern of speech as used by the educated persons of any community', and Edward Artin, in his 'Guide to Pronunciation' in the Third *Webster* (Gove 1971), opts instead not to concentrate on American English but instead to try to encompass in his notations 'as far as possible the pronunciations prevailing in general cultivated conversational usage, both informal and formal, throughout the English-speaking world' (Gove 1971: 6a; 40a).[28]

5.5   Vowel systems

5.5.1

In the 1780s, from the evidence of the pronouncing dictionaries etc., the vowel system of 'polite' Londoners consisted of sixteen phonemes. For American speakers, the number was the same. (Evidence for more or fewer vowel phonemes is discussed below.)

Using a notation which provides a good deal of information about each phoneme (see 5.8 for the realisational details), the following system can be set up for London English of the late eighteenth century (Kenrick 1784):

/iː ɪ eː ɛ æ aː ʌ ə ɒ ɔː oː ʊ uː ʌɪ ɔɪ ɔʊ/

This may be compared with the late twentieth-century system of RP (Wells 1990a):

/iː ɪ eɪ ɛ æ ɑː ʌ ə ɒ ɔː əʊ ʊ uː aɪ ɔɪ aʊ ɪə ɛə ʊə ɜː/

The only difference systemically between late eighteenth-century London English and that of America (New England) is the absence in New England of a contrast corresponding to /ʌ/ and /ə/.

	Kenrick 1784	Webster 1789	Smart 1842	RP	GenAm.	Wells 1990[29]
iː	MEET	FEET	ME	iː	iː	FLEECE
ɪ	FIT	FIT	PIT	ɪ	ɪ	KIT
eː	BAY	LATE	FATE	eɪ	eɪ	FACE
ɛ	MET	LET	PET	ɛ	ɛ	DRESS
æ	HAT	HAT	PAT	æ	æ	TRAP
aː	HEART	HALF	PATH	ɑː	æ	BATH
ʌ	BLOOD	TUN	CUB	ʌ	ʌ	STRUT
ə	EVERY		DATA	ə	ə	COMMA
ɒ	NOT	HOT	NOT	ɒ	ɑ	LOT
ɔː	CALL	HALL	ALL	ɔː	ɔː	THOUGHT
oː	NO	NOTE	NO	əʊ	oʊ	GOAT
ʊ	BULL	PULL	PULL	ʊ	ʊ	FOOT
uː	POOL	POOL	MOVE	uː	uː	GOOSE
ʌɪ	WHY	FIGHT	TIME	aɪ	aɪ	PRICE
ɔɪ	TOIL	VOICE	OIL	ɔɪ	ɔɪ	CHOICE
ɔʊ	TOWN, NOUN	ROUND	LOUD	aʊ	aʊ	MOUTH
				ɪə	ɪr	NEAR
				ɛə	ɛr	SQUARE
				ʊə	ʊr	CURE
				ɜː	ɝ	NURSE

5.5.2

In both the orthoepical and the later phonetic literature, there are comments which indicate that other vowel phonemes than those listed above may have existed over the 200-year period – at least for some speakers and at certain times. The relevant items are discussed in turn.

5.5.3   [ɪu] and [ɪuː]:/ɪuː/ or /juː/?

The notation [ɪuː] obscures a number of slightly different pronunciations. In a word like YOU, and depending on the speed at which it is said, the /juː/ sequence might be analysed *phonetically* as a rising *or* a falling diphthong: i.e. [ĭuː] or [ɪŭː]. Furthermore, sub-types of both of these can be set up, depending on the quality and timing of the diphthong's trajectory. No clear picture emerges from the literature about the precise *phonetic* characteristics of the sequence.[30] For this reason, it has been phonemicised in all cases for the purposes of discussion as /juː/. This has implications for the phonotactics: e.g. Webster's TRUTH would have been phonemically /trjuːθ/, but phonetically either [trĭuːθ] or [trɪŭːθ].[31] By the end of the seventeenth century (at least in London), an earlier [ĭu] had been replaced by [ɪŭː] (Wells 1982: 207).

In GenAm. speech, a distinction has been maintained by some speakers between /ju/ and /ɪu/. Kenyon quotes the contrast between 'Jacob used it' (/dʒekəb juzd ɪt/ and 'Jake abused it' /dʒek əbɪuzd ɪt/ (Kenyon 1946: 211).[32]

5.5.4   /ɪi/ ≠ /iː/ ≠ /eː/

John Walker, in his entries for EACH and several other words, implies that some words containing <ea> virtually contrast with others containing <ee> or <ie>: BEACH, he says, forms a 'nearly perfect rhyme' with BEECH; PEAL with PEEL; CEASE with PIECE; etc. (Walker 1774: 5–6). Certainly, up until the end of the seventeenth century, the distribution of /iː/ and /eː/ did allow such words to be contrasted (e.g. SEEM was /siːm/ and SEAM could be /seːm/). Even so, the contrast depended on a distributional characteristic of two well-established phonemes, not on an extra phoneme.

It appears unlikely that there existed in London speech in the last quarter of the eighteenth century an additional front(ish), close(ish) vowel, phonemically distinct from both /iː/ and /eː/. Ward, from his examination of the works of ten orthoepists, concludes that only William Tiffin (c.1695–1759) is likely to have had such a vowel in his idiolect (Ward, A. 1952: 143–76). Whether his accent was 'standard' rather than regionally marked – Ward suspects Norfolk features in his speech – makes any firm conclusion difficult.[33] If Tiffin's system had contained /ɪː/, then he would have contrasted MEET /miːt/, HIT /hɪt/, MEAT /mɪːt/, and MATE /meːt/.

5.5.5   /eɪ/ ≠ /eː/

The existence of another vowel phoneme, similar to /eː/, and symbolised here as /eɪ/ (but not to be entirely equated with RP/eɪ/), is discussed by Walker in the third edition of his *Dictionary*.[34] 'When *gh* comes after this diphthong [i.e. orthographic *ei*], though there is not the least remnant of the Saxon guttural sound, yet it has not exactly the simple vowel sound as when followed by other consonants; *ei*, followed by *gh*, sounds both vowels like *ae*;

or if we could interpose the *y* consonant [= IPA [j]] between the *a* and *t* in *eight*, *weight*, &c, it might, perhaps, convey the sound better' (Walker 1802: 47; see also the entry for EIGHT). This would indicate that there still existed, at least in London and to the ears of John Walker, a small group of words, deriving from ME /ai/, not ME /aː/, which had not yet fallen together with the reflexes of /aː/. The qualities of the vowel's allophones could well have involved a more open starting-point, in the region of [ɛ], perhaps more precisely [ɛ̞] (cf. Dobson 1968: 769). Such a diphthong, although no longer in RP – if indeed it ever existed in educated Southern English speech – remains as part of the phonemic system of some speakers in the North of England (cf. Wells 1982: 357). Horn/Lehnert (1954: 329) attribute Walker's comments to either an awareness of a diphthongal realisation of /eː/ induced by the orthography, or the assumption of a phonemic distinction because of the orthography. Ward, in his detailed analysis of the occurrences and transcriptions of words containing <ea> and <ee> in Walker's writings, concludes that Walker was incorrect in supposing that a phonemic contrast still existed in the last quarter of the eighteenth century (Ward, A. 1952: 177–203). Walker may have been reacting to a diphthongal, not a monophthongal, realisation of <ea> (/iː/), i.e. [ɪi], possibly because of the spelling and also any recollections from his own childhood of the speech of elderly persons born in the seventeenth century, who might indeed have contrasted /iː/, /eː/, /ɪ/, and /ɪː/. Even so, one of Walker's contemporaries, Thomas Batchelor, regarded such a distinction as 'fanciful' and induced solely by the orthography (Batchelor 1809: 63). No other contemporary writer notes such a distinction, and the balance of probability is that such a distinction no longer existed by the end of the eighteenth century.[35]

5.5.6   /æ/ and /eə/

A development in some forms of American English, first noticed towards the end of the nineteenth century, is an /eə/ phoneme, used in words such as BAD, PASS, and MAN. It contrasts with the /æ/ of BATH and SANG, as well as with the /ɛ/ of MERRY (Wells 1982: 477–79).[36] Its usage is restricted to certain areas east of Chicago; slightly different paths of change have been noticed.

5.5.7   /æ/ and /aː/

Sheridan (1762, 1780) fails to distinguish between the vowels of HAT and HEART, using the same vowel notation for both. In this respect he is out of line with all the other orthoepists, who do make the distinction; they often quote explicit minimal pairs such as SAM and PSALM to prove their point. Even Sheridan's Irish origin cannot be the explanation, since then, as now, such a distinction existed. The only explanation is that Sheridan may have recognised two phonetically different vowel qualities in HAT and HEART and concluded, subjectively, that they represented the 'same sound', i.e. the same phoneme. Had he considered other words (SAM and PSALM, for example), he would surely have recognised the need for a notational distinction.

5.5.8   /æ/ and /æː/

This is a relatively recent development in RP and educated pre-RP. Neither Walker (1791) nor Smart (1836), in their respective appendices on pronunciation, makes any mention of it. Ellis (1874) has no reference to it in his discussion of the /æ/ of LAMP (1874: 1147–8), but he does quote a single example of it under the heading of 'Young Educated London' (Ellis 1874: 1214). The word is ADD, pronounced variably as (æd) and (ædd) [= IPA [ɛ̞ːd] and [ɛ̞dː]] and taken down by Sweet.[37] More than forty years later, in 1917, Jones gives [æd] as the *only* pronunciation, but BAD and GLAD both have the long vowel as the more frequently occurring form, alongside versions with the short vowel (cf. *EPD1*). In 1911, Coleman had drawn attention to the long [æː] in his own pronunciation of MAD 'and ... other adjectives', which differed from the short [æ] used in HAD, PAD 'and ... other nouns' (Coleman 1911: 108). Jones's later comment that 'in the South of England a fully long æː is generally used in the adjectives ending in -*ad* ... and is quite common in some nouns' (Jones, D. 1960: 235) is repeated by Gimson: 'the traditionally short vowel appears to be lengthened in RP especially ... in CAB, BAD, BAG, BADGE, JAM, MAN' (Gimson 1980: 109). Together with Wells's reference to [æː] being 'marginally contrastive' with [æ] (Wells 1982: 288–9), there is sufficient evidence to show that a new phoneme has begun to emerge in RP, albeit slowly and with a highly restricted distribution.[38]

5.5.9   /ɑː/ ≠ /ɒ/ in American English

The evidence which would allow a rigorous assessment to be made of the earlier history of GenAm.'s back open and back open-mid vowels is sporadic. The following discussion must, therefore, be taken as tentative. Interpretation of the older literature is often made difficult by writers discussing sounds (and, tacitly, phonemes) in terms of orthography, or the extended orthography used by philologists (e.g. ǫ,ó), or modifications of IPA. Usually, no clear distinction is made between features which are systemic and those which have to do with phonotactics and/or realisation. In addition, GenAm. at the present time (and the accents on which it impinges, particularly in the east) contains, unlike RP, at least three sub-types from the viewpoint of open and back open-mid (half-open) vowel phonemes. When phonotactic matters are then taken into account – e.g. the vowels in LOG, ON, or WASH – further differentiation can be achieved. All this raises questions about the extent to which the earlier history of such accents can be accurately traced.

The three sub-types can be illustrated thus:

Type A: /æ/   FATHOM
         /ɑː/ FATHER, COT, CAUGHT, FODDER, BALM, BOMB
               (The realisation of /ɑː/ varies between [ɑ] and [ɔ] (with
               varying degrees of length) and is dependent on phonological
               context.)

Type B: /æ/   FATHOM
         /ɑː/ FATHER, COT, FODDER, BALM, BOMB
         /ɔː/ CAUGHT

Type C: /æ/   FATHOM
         /ɑː/ FATHER, BALM
         /ɒ/   COT, FODDER, BOMB
         /ɔː/ CAUGHT

Webster, a New Englander, writing in 1789, distinguished between the vowels of HAT, HALF, HOT, and HALL, thereby implying a four-way systemic distinction between /æ/, /ɑː/ (perhaps with a backer quality), /ɒ/, and /ɔː/ (Type C). However, a slightly earlier remark of his, in the *American Spelling Book* of 1783, to the effect that the 'short *o*' was 'nearly like' the '*u* in *shun*' (i.e. the orthographic *-tion*)[39] suggests that the vowel was unrounded, and hence the distinction that Webster was noting in 1789 between HALF and HOT may have been allophonic, and not phonemic (Type B). The comment some forty years later by William Russell in his *Lessons in Enunciation* (1830) that a 'common error' was to make the *o* of NOT 'too much like' the *a* of FAR, so that words like GOT and CLOCK sounded like GAT and CLACK (quoted by Neumann 1924: 38) is further evidence of an /ɑː/, but no /ɒ/, in the system.

Whitney's analysis of his own accent (Whitney 1875), though remarkably perceptive, is difficult to generalise from, if only because his own regional background – he was born in Northampton – straddles the line of what is now the GenAm./Eastern American isogloss. His discussion of the vowel of NOT and WHAT does, however, offer some potential evidence in favour of /ɑ/, but no /ɒ/ (Type B). In his discussion of the pronunciation of NOT and WHAT, he points out that 'the sound occupies so nearly a medial position between the *a* of *far* and that of *war* that it might with equal propriety be regarded as the short sound of either' (Whitney 1875: 214). Note also how he attributes the rounding in the vowels of WHAT, WAS, WAN, QUARRY, and SQUAD to the preceding 'labial semivowel', which 'has communicated a slight labial tinge to its successor' (1875: 214).

Towards the end of the nineteenth century, the survey instituted by Grandgent into 'educated American speech' (Grandgent 1891–2, 1893a, 1893b, 1895) provides further useful evidence. This revealed that 'in the greater part of the United States *o* [= IPA [ɒ]] (as in 'hot') ... is usually unrounded' – in other words, it would have been [ɑ] (1891: 84). In the 'western' States of Illinois, Indiana, Iowa, Kansas, Michigan, Missouri, and Ohio, 84 per cent of the speakers surveyed used [ɑ], not [ɒ]. This conclusion was supported by O. F. Emerson (1892: 38), but disputed by Porter (1892: 240). In his definitive summary, in 1895, Grandgent claimed that 'in New York all the region west of that state a short α [= IPA [ɑ]] is generally used instead of ǫ (*hot* = *hɑt, quarrel* = *kwɑɹil*)' (1895: 445).

If it is legitimate to generalise about a putative 'General American' accent from the eighteenth and nineteenth centuries, given the many imponderables and contradictions in the orthoepical accounts – particularly the lack of definitive information about which variety of American speech is being discussed – then the weight of evidence would be *against* the existence of an /ɑ/≠/ɒ/ contrast in *non*-New England speech from at least the late eighteenth century onwards. Type B would seem to have been the expected form, with Type C restricted to some parts of New England.

5.5.10   /ɒː/≠/ɔː/

Walker comments on a 'middle sound' (e.g. in BROTH) which, phonetically at least, contrasted with the 'short sound' (e.g. in GOT) and the 'long sound' (e.g. in NAUGHT and SOUGHT) (Walker 1797: 17).[40] In a little-noticed comment, Eustace presents the admittedly slim evidence in favour of this contrast having existed in Alexander Ellis's speech (Eustace 1969: 48–51). OFTEN (equivalent to current RP /ɔːfn/) was, for Ellis, (ɔɒf'n) [= IPA [ɒːfn]], whereas ORPHAN was – Eustace assumes – (ɑɒf'n) [= IPA [ɔːfn]. Other words containing /ɒː/ were ACROSS, LOST, and (sometimes) CROSS and OFF. Words with /ɔː/ were WRATH, COST, OFFICE ('not uncommon'), BECAUSE, OFF, and (sometimes) CROSS. There may be some further evidence from the *OED*'s transcription of such words although the evidence is not conclusive.[41]

5.5.11   [ʌ] and [ʊ]

Thomas Spence (1775) does not recognise the distinction between /ʌ/ and /ʊ/ (in e.g. DONE and PUT); this is most likely attributable to his regional background – he was from Newcastle-upon-Tyne. He assigns words like YOUNG, TUN, MONK, FUR, and HER to the same vowel category. On the basis of our knowledge of nineteenth- and twentieth-century Tyneside speech (cf. Shields 1974), a notation such as /ə/(alternatively /ɵ/) would be appropriate. It is also worth pointing out that Spence could publish a dictionary which included 'English pronunciation', whose regional, non-Metropolitan, character was so distinctive.[42]

5.5.12   [ʌ] and [ə]

A distinction between the /ʌ/ of CUT and the /ə/ of COMMAND is noted by less than a quarter of the writers for the period 1770 to 1880. This leads to three possible conclusions. First, such a distinction was not firmly established in the phonology of London English at this time. Second, there were some phonologies which did not have the distinction. And third, some writers were not aware of the distinction in their own speech.[43] According to Dobson (1968: 827), the historical evidence from the period before the mid-eighteenth century indicates that a [ə] sound was in use in unaccented syllables. A separate issue, however, which he does not address, is the phonemic distinctiveness of [ə] in relation to other, more open vowels, e.g. [ʌ] or [ɐ].[44] There is sufficient evidence from the late eighteenth century onwards to show that the distinction /ʌ/≠/ə/ was still unstable (or non-existent) in some forms of London speech. Walker (1785: 25) is quite adamant that the weak forms of OF, FROM, FOR, and BY contain 'the vowel *o*' which has '[slid] into the sound of the vowel *u*, and the word [OF] may be said to rhyme with *love*, *dove*, &c'. Search too (1773: 15) uses a special vowel symbol *u* for both the stressed and the unstressed vowels in LONDON (he transcribes the word 'L*u*n*u*n'); see also his transcriptions of COVER'D, FOR, OR, SOOT, and WOMAN. Odell (1806: 4), having discussed the quality of /ʌ/ (see 5.8.7), goes on to say that 'It is this same short imperfect vowel that we hear . . . in many of our final syllables, and others ... such as ovĕr, undĕr

... pilŏt ... jealŏus ... pillŏry ... thundĕrĕr, pillăr'. And, much later, Anon (1830: 17) writes that 'the vowel *o* in *from*, slides into the sound of the vowel *u*' – copying the phraseology of Walker (1785). More than forty years later, Henry Sweet did not distinguish between /ʌ/ and /ə/, using (ə) for both (Sweet 1877: 110). By 1888 and the description of 'Living English', i.e. post-1800 English, /ʌ/ and /ə/ were now distinguished, as (a) and (ə). All later writers on British English, specifically RP, make the distinction.

The only writers, whose accent being non-London, did not require an /ʌ/≠/ə/ distinction, were Spence (1775) from Tyneside, Thornton (1793),[45] and the American orthoepists.

In words like AGO, BAKER, SAILOR, and LATERAL Spence (1775) uses the symbol for /ɪ/. Thornton (1793), too, does not have a special symbol for /ə/: words like ZEPHYR and MAJESTY have the same symbol for their unstressed <y> and <e> vowels as SUN and RUFF.

The evidence that the contrast between [ə] and [ʌ] was indeed phonemic comes from several sources. Kenrick (1784), in his transcriptions, places a number over each stressed vowel, but leaves what is putatively the /ə/ vowel unmarked. Nares (1784: 11) draws attention to final unaccented vowels as in ADVANTAGE and BALLAD where there is 'an obscure sound, not clearly referable to any class of vowel sounds'; cf. also Elphinston, who comments that '*e* rapid is the feeblest of human sounds, and the shortest *e* of all tongues, from the hebrew *Scheva* ... to the french *e* feminine' (1765: 13; cf. also Rohlfing 1984: 184). Nares also points out that in a word like COLLAR, the unaccented vowel before /r/ 'resembles most that of short *u*, as if it were *collur*'. Transcriptions for BALLAD and COLLAR would, then, be /bæləd/ and /kɒlʌr/ – the latter differing from today's RP. Earnshaw (1818) too notes '*a* obscure' and '*o* obscure' in ABOMINABLE and ACTOR. Smart (1842) clearly distinguishes between the /ʌ/ of CUB and the /ə/ of ABASE and DATA.

For American English, Webster 1789 does not set up a separate unstressed vowel from that in stressed TUN (1789: 88). In his *American Spelling Book* of 1787, the rule that 'in unaccented terminating syllables, almost all vowels are pronounced like *i* and *u* short' (quoted by Neumann 1924: 56) would indicate that he regarded the [ə] in words like PROPHET and PROFIT – they were homophonous for Webster – as an allophone of /ʌ/.

5.5.13 /oː/≠/oʊ/

According to Ellis, there were some speakers in his day who distinguished between NO and KNOW by means of a monophthongal≠diphthongal contrast – in his notation, (noo) *versus* (noou) (Ellis 1869: 602). The explanation lies in their maintaining a distinction between /oː/ and /ou/ which had otherwise merged in the seventeenth century. (NO descended from OE /nɑː/ via ME /ɔː/ and seventeenth century /oː/; KNOW was from OE /knɑːwən/ via ME /ɔu/ and seventeenth century /ou/.) No other nineteenth-century writer draws attention to this distinction, and it is not commented on later. A similar distinction, however, but with different realisations, does exist today in popular London English (i.e. an accent between RP and Cockney): words like ROLLER (with /ɒə/) and POLAR (with /ʌʊ/) are distinguished (Wells 1982: 312–13). It is unlikely that Ellis's NO ≠ KNOW distinction is related to this, especially in view of the transcription he gives.

5.5.14   /ʊ/, /uː/ and /ʉː/

The distinction between the /ʊ/ of FULL and the /uː/ of FOOL is sometimes lacking. Several of the orthoepists were Scottish in origin, as can be determined from their biographies or from the internal evidence of their transcriptions. Thus Buchanan (1766), Herries (1773), Barrie (1794), Smith (1795) make no distinction between the vowel of FULL and FOOL – a characteristic Scottish feature, both then (cf. Jones, C. 1993: 113) and now.[46] Carrol 1795 also fails to note the distinction, though other evidence indicates that his background was American.[47]

It appears that Jespersen (1909/1961: 384–5) is one of the few phoneticians to draw attention to the existence of a third, more centralised, phoneme. He notes that 'some speakers' distinguish between ROOD and RUDE, ROOM and RHEUM, BROOM and BRUME, THROUGH and THREW, SOOT and SUIT: the first item in each pair has /uː/, the second /ʉː/. Daniel Jones and Wells regard such a distinction as restricted to some forms of American English (Wells 1982: 208).[48]

5.5.15   /ʌɪ/ ≠ /aɪ/

Granville Sharp (from Durham) contrasts the vowels of SIGH'D and SIDE (Sharp 1767: 23). This distinction exists today in the popular speech of the area north of Durham, namely Tyneside. It seems reasonable to conclude, then, that the distinction was in use, further south in Durham itself, 200 or more years ago. However, there is no evidence whatever to indicate that it existed as far south as London.[49]

5.5.16   /ʌɪ/ and /ɔɪ/

A noticeable feature of some late eighteenth century pronunciations is the use of /ʌɪ/ where one would expect /ɔɪ/; this could indicate the lack of a phonemic distinction between words such as BOIL and BILE, TOIL and TILE. According to Sweet (1888), the contrast between /ʌɪ/ and /ɔɪ/ resulted from the conscious awareness in the second half of the eighteenth century of <oi> in the orthography being realised in the same way as <i ... e>. Pronunciations such as [bəil] and [pəizən] (Sweet's 1888 notation) were altered to [bɔil] and [pɔizən] (Sweet 1888: 245). Historically, as a result of the gradual merging of the reflexes of ME /iː/ and /ʊɪ/, both phonetic realisations, by the seventeenth and eighteenth centuries, were diphthongs with [ə]-ish starting-points. This was to lead to the loss of a phonemic distinction, which was subsequently reversed.[50]

For the post-1770 period, one must countenance the possibility of three types of speaker: (i) those with /ɔɪ/≠/ʌɪ/; (ii) those with /ɔɪ/≠/ʌɪ/, but with /ʌɪ/ assuming a heavier functional load; and (iii) those with no /ɔɪ/, only /ʌɪ/.

The bulk of the evidence points to the existence by the end of the eighteenth century and well into the nineteenth century of – or at least a prescriptivist's desire for – the first type of speaker, with an /ɔɪ/≠/ʌɪ/ contrast: see Herries 1773, Spence 1775, Walker 1775, Sharp 1777, Anon. 1784, Elphinston 1790, Perry 1793, Adams 1794, Carrol 1795, Perry 1795, Smith 1795, Fulton & Knight 1800, Mitford 1804, Dyche 1805, Odell 1806, Hornsey 1807, Anon. 1813, Duponceau 1818, Smart 1819, Gilchrist 1824, Fulton 1826, Angus 1830, Knowles 1837, Smart 1842, Comstock & Mair 1874.

The second type of speaker, with the /ɔɪ/≠/ʌɪ/ contrast, but who assigned greater functional load to /ʌɪ/, is well instanced. Kenrick 1784 has JOIN with /ʌɪ/, but his other <oi> words have /ɔɪ/; Nares 1784 has BOIL and JOINT with /ʌɪ/; Fogg 1792 has BUY with /ɔɪ/. Hare, writing in 1832, notes that 'the diphthong in *boil, broil, spoil, join, joint, point, poison*, is no longer pronounced, at least by the bulk of educated persons, as it used to be in the last century, with the sound of the long *i*' (Hare 1832: 653). Traces of this older pronunciation have lingered on into a modern, albeit elderly, form of RP: cf. Wells (1982: 293) on the pronunciation [bʌɪ] for BOY.

The only evidence for the third type of speaker in British English is sporadic: there are no /ɔɪ/ words in Sheridan 1762 and 1781, and Buchanan 1766 notes that the vowel in BOIL, BOY and JOY '*resembles* long i' (my italics). In other words, it was probably /ʌɪ/. The possibility that other orthoepists may simply have copied Sheridan's or Buchanan's examples, without first analysing objectively their own, as well as their contemporaries', usages, makes an accurate analysis of the situation difficult. Consequently, one can do no more than note the absence of a contrast between /ɔɪ/ and /ʌɪ/ in Kenrick 1773, Barrie 1792, Anon. 1797, Mackintosh 1799, Anon. 1812, Anon. 1817, and Earnshaw 1818. As late as 1837, Knowles (1837: 7) was transcribing the diphthong in ICE as consisting of the vowels of ALL and EVE, i.e. [ɔi].

For specifically American English, there is comparable evidence of accents which lacked the distinction. For example, Anthony Benezet's word-list of 1779 rhymes BILE and BOIL, FILE and FOIL, HIGH and HOY, RIAL and ROYAL, etc. (cf. Krapp 1925.II: 197–8).

5.5.17 /ɔə/

/ɔə/ has had a relatively short life in the vowel system of RP. It began to appear in educated London speech during the eighteenth century, being the reflex of four ME vowel + /r/ sequences: [ɔr] (e.g. HORSE), [ɔːr] (e.g. BOARD), [oːr] (e.g. SWORD), and [uːr] (e.g. MOURN) (cf. Horn/Lehnert 1954.I: 502). By the early 1770s, poets were rhyming words like LAWN and MORN, DAWN and SCORN (Mugglestone 1991: 64–5). The distinction in pronunciation between HORSE and HOARSE, noted in the nineteenth century by e.g. Smart (1836), reflected either the distribution of /ɔː/ in HORSE and /oː/ in HOARSE, or, in view of his respelling of HOARSE as (hō'uarce), an emerging /ɔə/ phoneme. Such evidence is not sufficiently clear for a generalisation to be made. Ellis noted the falling-together of /ɔː/ and /ɔə/ in London speech (1874: 1122), but Sweet retained the contrast (e.g. SAW ≠ SOAR) in all of his publications, whilst admitting that its distribution was unstable. He gives, for example, alternative pronunciations of POUR and LORE with both vowels (Sweet 1885: xxix; Sweet 1890a: 7). A more precise statement about its use in the later part of the nineteenth century can be found in his letter to Alois Brandl (5 Jan. 1882) where he says that 'there's really no difference in sound between "laud" and "lord", both (laod), but many, perhaps most, make this distinction finally, as in *law* and *lore* (lao, loə) when they speak slowly. (oə) is, of course, only a shorter way of spelling *aoə*'. The American phonetician Grandgent noted in 1895 that in southern England there was no audible difference between HOARSE and HORSE (and similar words) (Grandgent 1895: 460).

From the evidence of twentieth-century British phoneticians, it is clear that the phoneme is now practically dead – at least in RP. In 1906,

Rippmann (1906: 65–6) allowed it only under specific stylistic conditions. D. Jones noted in 1909 that 'some speakers' used it, in the sense of being able to contrast words like SOAR and SAW (Jones, D. 1909: 40–1 ; cf. his later statement in Jones, D. 1958: 39), despite later listing it as one of the 'centring diphthongs of RP' (1958: 24, 65). The first edition of the *EPD* (*English Pronouncing Dictionary*) in 1917 pointed out that pronunciations with /ɔə/ could still be heard, in e.g. COURSE and LORE. According to Bridges (1919), however, the words OAR, ORE, OR, O'ER, and AWE were all homophonous. Nicklin (1920) retained /ɔə/: see his list of contrasts (1920: 51).[51] Ward regarded it as a minority pronunciation in 'South-eastern English' (Ward, I.C. 1945: 121). By 1980, it was restricted to 'conservative RP' (Gimson 1980: 117; see also Gimson 1964: 135), or the speech of elderly speakers (Wells 1982: 287). Its demise has lasted well over a century.

5.5.18 Nasalised vowels

For the pronunciation of certain foreign words, the existence of certain additional phonemes was noted. Walker (1791: 35) points out that MANOEUVRE was 'generally pronounced, by those who can pronounce French, in the French manner' – i.e. with a vowel in the area of [œ] and presumably with nasalisation as well. By contrast, Nares (1784) gives this word with the 'English' /uː/. Ellis lists a number of French sounds which some educated speakers utilised in their pronunciation of English: CAMP (as in AIDE-DE-CAMP) with (aʌ) [= IPA [ɑ̃]] (Ellis 1869: 594), MAIN (as in COUP-DE-MAIN) with (eʌ) [= IPA [ɛ̃]] (Ellis 1869: 597), BON with (oʌ) [= IPA [ɔ̃]] (Ellis 1869: 602).

5.5.19 The development of /ɜː/

The ME ancestors of /ɜː/ were three ME vowels + /r/:/ɪ/ (e.g. BIRTH), /ɛ/ (e.g. FERN), and /ʊ/>/ʌ/ (e.g. SPUR). There is continuing debate, however, about when the phoneme developed. Gimson maintains that it was 'incipient in the London region in the sixteenth century and general in the late seventeenth century … [and with] the loss of /r/ in post-vocalic positions in the eighteenth century, the PresE central long /ɜː/ was reached' (1989: 124; cf. also Dobson 1968: 914–15, 992–3; Mugglestone 1988: 137–8). Ward goes so far as to claim that there is no 'satisfactory evidence' for the continuation of the older contrast between the reflexes of ME /ɪr/, /ɛr/, and /ʊr/ after about the middle of the eighteenth century (Ward, A. 1952: 266). Yet, there is indeed some evidence to indicate that the merger was not complete until well into the nineteenth century – at least, one assumes, for particular forms of educated southern English English speech.

The discussion of this topic can be obfuscated by a failure to consider different phonetic and phonological possibilities. The notation <r>, if it is equated with /r/, tells one nothing about the quality of the realisation. If /r/ had been realised as [ɹ], i.e. a postalveolar approximant, and not an alveolar (or postalveolar) tap, trill or fricative, then the acoustic quality (or qualities) of [ɹ] would have made the sound similar to that of [ə]. Using as a parallel the situation in modern rhotic accents of Scottish English, which conveniently illustrate both the retention of the ME 3–vowels + /r/ pattern as well as fewer vowels + /r/ (and with different phonotactic rules), one can surmise that eighteenth- (and possibly even nineteenth-century) educated Southern English English *may* have contained the following sorts of speakers:

Type A (3-vowel contrast)
BIRTH /ɪr/   FERN /ɛr/   SPURN /ʌr/

But certain words (e.g. DIRTY) would contain either /ɪr/, /ɛr/, or /ʌr/. With the precise phonological contexts stated, a number of different sub-types of Type A are established (A1, A2, etc.).

Type B (2-vowel contrast)
BIRTH /ʌr/   FERN /ɛr/   SPURN /ʌr/
DIRTY etc. would be /ʌr/. There are no occurrences of accented /ɪr/.

Type C (1 vowel)
BIRTH /ɜr/   FERN /ɜr/   SPURN /ɜr/[52]

These examples from Scottish English illustrate the results over time of both systemic and phonotactic changes (all within a rhotic accent). Once educated Southern English English had become fully non-rhotic (see below, 5.10.6), three further possible phonological patterns would have arisen (of which the last, Type F, is now the current form of RP):

Type D (3-vowel contrast)
BIRTH /ɪə/   FERN /ɛə/   SPURN /ɜː/

Type E (2-vowel contrast)
BIRTH /ɜː/   FERN /ɛə/   SPURN /ɜː/

Type F (1 vowel)
BIRTH /ɜː/   FERN /ɜː/   SPURN /ɜː/

In addition, one should note that phonemic transcriptions such as /ʌr/ are not intended to specify the phonetic detail of the realisations. For this, see section 5.8.

A three-way distinction, reflecting the ME situation [Type A], is, by the end of the eighteenth century, relatively rare. One example is Spence (1775), who contrasts BIRD (/bɪrd/), EARTH (/ɛrθ/), and FUR (/fər/) – admittedly for Newcastle speech. Search , a competent phonetic observer, hints that a three-way distinction might just still exist under certain circumstances: '"ir" is almost always turned into "*ur*," as in "fir, f*ur*; dirty, d*u*rty ... ĕr is so like to "*ur*" that you cannot distinguish them unless when accented' (Search 1773: 14). A solitary mid-nineteenth-century example comes in a comment from America on English speech: Goodrich, in his revision of Webster's *Imperial Dictionary*, notes that 'some English speakers' try to keep the three vowels apart (Webster 1847: xxiii).

Almost all the orthoepists maintain a two-way distinction between /ɛr/ and /ʌr/: e.g. THIRD ≠ HERD [Type B] (Thornton 1793), FIR ≠ ERR (Smart 1842), even though the absence of /ɪr/ means that the allocation of words to particular categories alters the relation between pronunciation and orthography. Thus, Hornsey (1809) has BIRTH with /ɛr/ and DIRT with /ʌr/ [Sub-type of A]. (See also Sharp (1767: 26) and the comments on Sheridan (1786) below.) This could, of course, be counted as evidence, given the confusing situation, of orthoepy attempting to retain an orthography-based distinction when normal colloquial speech no longer recognised it.

A few orthoepists, but only until the late eighteenth century, recognise a single vowel, namely /ʌ/, + /r/ in words of this type: WORD, BIRD, HER (Sheridan 1762, Kenrick 1784), SERVICE, FIRST, WORD (Johnston 1764), CUR, SIR, HER (Adams 1794), WORD, PEARL, CIRCLE (Nares 1784). In 1786, Sheridan was deriding the single phoneme + /r/ pronunciation. Commenting on Garrick's stage accent, which was tinged with certain Staffordshire features, he noted that words like GIRD, BIRTH, HEARD, and INTERRED were all pronounced with /ʌr/ – 'a very improper pronunciation ... this impropriety' (Sheridan 1786: 28–9). Whether this reflected an aspect of phonological reality – not just in Staffordshire but also in London – rather than some socially induced pretence is impossible to judge. It is noticeable, though, that in his 1786 work, Sheridan reverts to the situation of two vowels + /r/: he contrasts BIRD (/bʌrd/) with BIRTH (/bɛrθ/), and SPIRT (/spʌrt/) with SKIRT /skɛrt/) (Sheridan 1786: 57). Another writer, Anon., some years after Sheridan, also noted the socially inferior pronunciation of EARTH with /ʌr/: a word which was 'very often liable to a coarse vulgar sound, as if written *Urth*' (Anon. 1797: n.p.).

Apart from Sheridan's data (1786), there is insufficient evidence to show whether or not there was a return to the possibility of Types A or B, before

/ɜː/ (with or without a following /r/) became the norm. A reasonable conclusion, given the varied transcriptions in the pronouncing dictionaries etc., is that this period (the last forty or so years of the eighteenth century) was one of considerable phonological change, which, in turn, led to a variety of different, and possibly unstable, pronunciations.

The evidence for considerable variability at this time (and hence evidence that a change was imminent or already in progress) comes not only from the lack of agreement amongst the orthoepists, but also from the listing of words whose phonemic composition looks suspect. Hornsey (1807) has GIRT and GIRD with /ɪr/, but DIRT, BIRD and THIRD with /ʌr/. Anon. (1812) has SKIRT with /ɛr/, but DIRT and SPIRT with /ʌr/ – perhaps simply imitating Sheridan (1786). Fulton (1826) maintains a distinction between 'e shut', 'ĕ obscure' and 'u shut', which leads to putative distinctions between DIRGE (with 'e shut'), THIRD (with 'e obscure') and BIRD (with 'u shut').

Ellis in 1869 comments that the distinction between SERF and SURF 'is frequently neglected in speech', thus leaving open the possibility that there were indeed speakers who still maintained a distinction. (Whether it was /ɛr/≠/ʌr/ or /ɛə/≠/ɜː/ is, of course, unclear (Ellis 1869: 8).) However, later in the same work, he more or less denies that such a contrast could be considered any longer to be a feature of normal English phonology: 'a distinction of course can be made ... by those who think of it, and is made by those who have formed a habit of doing so; but the distinction is so rarely made as to amount almost to pedantry when carefully carried out, like so many other distinctions insisted on by orthoepists, but ignored by speakers whose heart is in the thought they wish to convey, not in the vehicle they are using' (Ellis 1869: 201–2). Taken with the evidence from Sweet a few years later in the 1870s, it does seem that, by the late 1860s, any attempt to maintain an /ɛr/≠/ʌr/ distinction would have been looked upon as pretentious and flying in the face of the phonological realities of the day.[53]

5.6   Vowel phonotactics (structural)

5.6.1

In his analysis of unaccented vowels from 1500 to 1700, Dobson (1968) laments the difficulty in reaching firm conclusions because of the unreliability of the opinions of the orthoepists; furthermore, there appears to have been considerable variation amongst the educated population in how the unaccented vowels were realised (cf. Dobson 1968: 838–60). For the period from the late eighteenth century onwards, an objective analysis can be similarly difficult. The problem derives from the absence of any formal marker of an unaccented vowel in the orthography of English. As a result, speakers, both now and certainly during the last two centuries, have, in general, had difficulty in accepting the existence of any vowel sounds other than those associated with vowel 'letters' in stressed position. In 1874, Ellis noted the absence of conclusive evidence on the pronunciation of unaccented syllables of English. He disagreed, for example, with Melville Bell's analysis, which was already in print;[54] and he had received no responses to a questionnaire that he had made available which might have provided the necessary data.[55] He therefore devoted considerable space (1874: 1158–71) to an analysis of his own pronunciation of such vowels, with some further remarks on what he considered to be normal usage amongst other speakers.[56] His analysis reveals several interesting phonological features: for example, a contrast between the unaccented vowels in CARRIAGE and MARRIAGE; and a contrast between EMERGE and IMMERGE (Ellis 1874: 1164, 1165).[57] An additional source of information about variant forms of unaccented vowels is the correspondence between Sweet, Storm and Murray: this is referred to below.

5.6.2

Ellis's analysis is based on the orthography ('*-and, -end, -ond*' etc); the data below (on post-tonic syllables), however, has been re-organised phonologically. Ellis identifies a variety of different vowel sounds that can occur in unaccented position. In his *phonetic* notation (and with an IPA interpretation) they are: (ah) [a], (æ) [æ], (ɐ) [ə], (ʌ) [ɔ̞], (e) [e̝], (ə) [ɘ], (ə*i*) [ɘe̝], ('h) [voice], (*i*) [e̝], (o) [ɔ], (*o*) [o], (ɔ) [ɐ̝], (u) [u], (*y*) [ɪ].[58] They have been set alongside the (phonemic) transcriptions in Walker 1791 and Wells 1990.[59] Walker's and Ellis's transcriptions have been converted into IPA for ease of comparison. (Only Ellis's transcriptions are strictly phonetic: both Walker and Wells use the possibility inherent in a vowel notation which consciously indicates length (e.g. Wells's /iː/) to allow for a more precise phonetic notation on occasion: i.e. /i/ to represent [i] rather than [iː]. Walker, similarly, 200 years ago, had used single and double vowel notations for the same purpose (e.g. $\overset{1}{e}$ as the last vowel of COUNTRY, but $\overset{1}{e}\overset{1}{e}$ in SEE) to indicate the same fact).

5.6.3

Care is needed when attempting a phonetic interpretation of Walker's phonemic symbols for unaccented vowels. His /æ/ in a word like FRIGATE may appear erroneous and to be based solely on the orthography. However, a range of allophones can be detected in any speaker's pronunciation of unaccented vowels, depending on the style of speaking being used. Walker's /æ/ could, then, have included an articulation like [ɐ̈], which would not seem impossible in a slow pronunciation today of the /ə/ of FRIGATE.

5.6.4

Two aspects of unaccented vowel phonology have been chosen for exemplification: word-initial pre-tonic vowels and word-final post-tonic vowels.

5.6.5

From the admittedly limited data (based on Ellis's lists of words), it is possible to draw certain tentative conclusions about the redistribution of certain vowels in *word-initial pre-tonic* contexts over the last 200 years – see figure 5.1:

1. With words beginning with <a>, Walker's /æ/ has, by Ellis's time, given way in general to a central vowel. The exceptions are those words which orthographically have a <#VCCV ...> structure (ACCEPT etc), and a few others (such as AMONG). By 1990, /æ/ still lingers on as an optional form in some words (e.g. ACCEPT), but re-emerges as an option in AFFIX. The process of replacing a front vowel with a central vowel, we will call 'centralling'.

2. Of the seven words in Ellis's list which begin with <b> (BEGIN etc.), four have retained the equivalent of Walker's /ʌɪ/, with a period of change in the nineteenth century, but now reversed, as evidenced by Ellis's list. The other words show a laxing of /i/ to /ɪ/ (BEGIN, DEBATE etc.). Evidence that the change from /ɪ/ to /ə/ (in e.g. BEGIN, DEPEND) has its roots in the nineteenth century comes from Ellis, although the list of words containing /ə/ is now much greater than in Ellis's day. On Sweet's evidence (1878), /i/ would no longer be used in a word like REFLECT: instead the quality would be '(e¹) [= IPA [ẹ]] &, perhaps, sometimes (ɪh) [= IPA [ɪː]] as in other cases. No one says (riiflekt), as far as I know' (Sweet to Storm 29 Sept. 1878).

3. The distribution of vowels in <for ...> words (e.g. FORBID) in Walker is paralleled in both Ellis and Wells: cf. Walker's /ɔ/ with Wells's /ə~ɔː/, and Walker's /o/ with Wells's /ɔː/ (with the 'intermediate' forms given by Ellis).

4. The centralling change is also noticeable in words beginning with
<o ...> and <p ...> in the list (e.g. OBLIGE, PRODUCE), although this has
taken place post-1874. Note also Sweet's comment (1884) that 'I always
have (ə) in *Aurora, auricula, Augustan, Araucaria*' (Sweet to Murray 3 Nov.
1884).

5. The conscious *avoidance* of a central vowel, however, is noted by
Sweet: '[Certain] words seem to keep (ǫ) [= IPA [ɔ:]] for the sake of distinctness, as in *audacious* (liable to be confused with *edacious*), *audition* (con-
fusable with edition), *Augean* (with *Egean*), *authentic*'; similarly: 'I do not
think any says (kə'zeiʃən) [for CAUSATION]', and 'We never seem to have
(ə) before more than one consonant, never in *augment, austere,
auxiliary*'(Sweet to Murray 3 Nov. 1884); and '(nəwiidzən) – ludicrous'
(Sweet to Storm 7 April 1889).

6. Variation between /ɔ:/ and /ə/ is noted by Sweet: 'I fluctuate between
(ǫ) and (ə) in *Augustus, Augustan, Aurelia, auricular, authority*, according to
speech and emphasis.' For Sweet at least, there was a distinction between 'the
English name *Augustus* with (ə), [and] that of the Roman emperor with (ǫ)'
(Sweet to Murray 3 Nov. 1884). Note also: his remark on the effect of speaking style on the choice of vowel: 'I unround (ǫ) into (ə), as in *authority*, especially in quick speaking'; and his identification of a rounded central vowel in
AUSTRALIA – 'an indefinite round-mixed vowel [= IPA [əʷ]]'. For comparison, *EPD*1 (1917) has both pronunciations of AUGUSTUS, but makes no
distinction between an English and a Roman one. For AURELIA, *EPD*1
gives both /ɔ:/ and /ɒ/ (not /ə/) pronunciations. Similarly, in AURICULAR,
there is a choice between /ɔ:/ and /ɒ/. And for AUTHORITY, *EPD*1 gives
three possible vowels:/ɔ:/, /ɒ/, and /ə/.

Figure 5.1 Word-Initial Pre-Tonic Vowels

	Walker 1791 / /in IPA	Ellis 1874 [ ] in IPA	Wells 1990 / /in IPA
ABUSE	æ	ə~ə	ə
ABYSS	æ	ə~ə	ə~æ
ACCEPT	æ	æ 'generally' ~ə~ə	ə~æ~ɪ
ADAPT	æ	ə~ə	ə
ADMIRE	æ	æ 'generally' ~ə~ə	ə
ADVANCE	æ	æ 'generally' ~ə~ə	ə
AFFIX (v)	æ	ə~ə	ə~æ
ALAS	æ	ə~ə	ə

CONSONANTS (PULMONIC)

	Bilabial	Labiodental	Dental	Alveolar	Postalveolar	Retroflex	Palatal	Velar	Uvular	Pharyngeal	Glottal
Plosive	p b			t d		ʈ ɖ	c ɟ	k ɡ	q ɢ		ʔ
Nasal	m	ɱ		n		ɳ	ɲ	ŋ	ɴ		
Trill	ʙ			r					ʀ		
Tap or Flap				ɾ		ɽ					
Fricative	ɸ β	f v	θ ð	s z	ʃ ʒ	ʂ ʐ	ç ʝ	x ɣ	χ ʁ	ħ ʕ	h ɦ
Lateral fricative				ɬ ɮ							
Approximant		ʋ		ɹ		ɻ	j	ɰ			
Lateral approximant				l		ɭ	ʎ	ʟ			

Where symbols appear in pairs, the one to the right represents a voiced consonant. Shaded areas denote articulations judged impossible.

CONSONANTS (NON-PULMONIC)

Clicks		Voiced implosives		Ejectives	
ʘ	Bilabial	ɓ	Bilabial	ʼ	Examples:
ǀ	Dental	ɗ	Dental/alveolar	pʼ	Bilabial
ǃ	(Post)alveolar	ʄ	Palatal	tʼ	Dental/alveolar
ǂ	Palatoalveolar	ɠ	Velar	kʼ	Velar
ǁ	Alveolar lateral	ʛ	Uvular	sʼ	Alveolar fricative

VOWELS

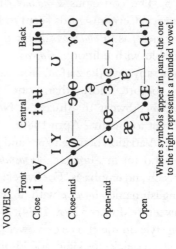

Where symbols appear in pairs, the one to the right represents a rounded vowel.

OTHER SYMBOLS

ʍ Voiceless labial-velar fricative	ɕ ʑ Alveolo-palatal fricatives
w Voiced labial-velar approximant	ɺ Alveolar lateral flap
ɥ Voiced labial-palatal approximant	ɧ Simultaneous ʃ and x
ʜ Voiceless epiglottal fricative	Affricates and double articulations can be represented by two symbols joined by a tie bar if necessary.
ʢ Voiced epiglottal fricative	k͡p t͡s
ʡ Epiglottal plosive	

DIACRITICS   Diacritics may be placed above a symbol with a descender, e.g. ŋ̊

̥	Voiceless	n̥ d̥	̤	Breathy voiced	b̤ a̤	̪	Dental	t̪ d̪
̬	Voiced	s̬ t̬	̰	Creaky voiced	b̰ a̰	̺	Apical	t̺ d̺
ʰ	Aspirated	tʰ dʰ	̼	Linguolabial	t̼ d̼	̻	Laminal	t̻ d̻
̹	More rounded	ɔ̹	ʷ	Labialized	tʷ dʷ	̃	Nasalized	ẽ
̜	Less rounded	ɔ̜	ʲ	Palatalized	tʲ dʲ	ⁿ	Nasal release	dⁿ
̟	Advanced	u̟	ˠ	Velarized	tˠ dˠ	ˡ	Lateral release	dˡ
̠	Retracted	e̠	ˤ	Pharyngealized	tˤ dˤ	̚	No audible release	d̚
̈	Centralized	ë	̴	Velarized or pharyngealized	ɫ			
̽	Mid-centralized	e̽	̝	Raised	e̝ (ɹ̝ = voiced alveolar fricative)			
̩	Syllabic	n̩	̞	Lowered	e̞ (β̞ = voiced bilabial approximant)			
̯	Non-syllabic	e̯	̘	Advanced Tongue Root	e̘			
˞	Rhoticity	ɚ a˞	̙	Retracted Tongue Root	e̙			

SUPRASEGMENTALS

ˈ	Primary stress	ˌfoʊnəˈtɪʃən
ˌ	Secondary stress	
ː	Long	eː
ˑ	Half-long	eˑ
̆	Extra-short	ĕ
ǀ	Minor (foot) group	
‖	Major (intonation) group	
.	Syllable break	ɹi.ækt
‿	Linking (absence of a break)	

TONES AND WORD ACCENTS

	LEVEL			CONTOUR	
e̋ or ꜛ	Extra high		ě or ꜜ	Rising	
é ˥	High		ê ˥	Falling	
ē ˧	Mid		e᷄ ˩	High rising	
è ˨	Low		e᷅	Low rising	
ȅ ˩	Extra low		e᷈	Rising-falling	
ꜜ	Downstep		ꜛ	Global rise	
ꜛ	Upstep		ꜜ	Global fall	

Figure 5.1 The International Phonetic Alphabet (revised to 1993, corrected 1996)

Figure 5.1 (*cont.*)

	Walker 1791 / /in IPA	Ellis 1874 [ ] in IPA	Wells 1990 / / in IPA
ALCOVE [60]	æ	æ 'generally' ~ɘ~ə	"æ
ALERT	æ	ɘ~ə	ə
AMONG	æ	ə~a~æ~ɘ	ə
ANNOUNCE	æ	ɘ~ə~æ	ə
APPEND	æ	ɘ~ə ~æ	ə
ASTRIDE	æ	ɘ~ə	ə
AVERT	æ	ɘ~ə	ə
BEGIN	i	e̞~ɛ̞~ə	ɪ~ə
BESET	i	e̞~ɛ̞~ə	ɪ~ə
BIENNIAL	ʌɪ	ɘe̞~e̞	aɪ
BILINGUAL		ɘe̞~e̞	aɪ
BINOCULAR	ʌɪ	ɘe̞~e̞	aɪ~ɪ~ə
BISECT	ʌɪ	ɘe̞~e̞	aɪ
COMBINATION	ɒ	ɒ̞	ɒ
COMBINE	ɒ	ɒ̞	ə
DEBATE	i	e̞	ɪ~ə
DEPEND	i	e̞~ɛ̞~ə	ɪ~ə
DESCENT	i	i:	ɪ~ə
DESPITE	i	e̞~ɛ̞	ɪ~ə
DESTROY	i	e̞~ɛ̞	ɪ~ə
DIRECT	i	e̞~ɘe̞	ə~ɪ~aɪ(ə)
DISSENT	ɪ	e̞	ɪ~ə
DIVERSION	i	e̞~ɘe̞	aɪ~ɪ~ə
DIVERSITY	i	e̞~ɘe̞	aɪ~ɪ~ə
DIVEST	i	e̞~ɘe̞	aɪ~ɪ~ə
DIVIDE	i	e̞	ɪ~ə
ECLIPSE	i	e̞~ɛ̞	ɪ~ə~i:
ELOPE	i	e̞~ɛ̞~i:~i	ɪ~ə
EMERGE	i	e̞ 'usually' ~i:	ɪ~ə~i:
EMIT	i	e̞	ɪ~ə~i:
EVENT	i	e̞~ɛ̞~i: ~i	ɪ~ə
FORBID	ɔ	ɔ̞	ə~ɔ:
FOREGO	o	ɔ: ~ɔ̞	ɔ:
FORETELL	o	ɔ: ~ɔ̞	ɔ:
FORGIVE	ɔ	ɔ̞	ə~ɔ:
IMMERGE	ɪ	ɛ̞m 'usually' ~ɛ̞m:	
OBLIGE	o	o~ɒ̞	ə~əʊ
OCCASION	ɒ	ɒ̞	ə
OPPOSE	ɒ	ɒ̞	ə
PRECEDE	i	e̞	ɪ~ə~i:

Figure 5.1 (*cont.*)

	Walker 1791 / /in IPA	Ellis 1874 [ ] in IPA	Wells 1990 / / in IPA
PRODUCE (v)	ɒ	o~ɒ̣	ə
PROMOTE	o	o~ɒ̣	ə
PROPOSE	o	o~ɒ̣	ə
REPOSE	i	ę̣	ɪ~ə
TOGETHER	o	u~ọ~ə	ə~u
TOMORROW		u~ọ~ə	ə~u

5.6.6

Certain conclusions can be drawn about *word-final post-tonic* vowels from the data based on Ellis and the equivalent forms in Walker and Wells, as well as from words discussed by Walker in his 'Principles of English Pronunciation' (appended to Walker 1791) – see Figure 5.2.

1. Wells maintains (1982: 257–8) that the [i] pronunciation of the final vowel in HAPPY etc. 'has probably been in use in provincial and vulgar speech for centuries' and suggests that 'it was already prevalent in the local accents of south-east England by the early nineteenth century'. The evidence from Walker (1791) and Ellis (1874) provides some confirmation of this. Indeed, its use would seem to have been much more extensive than may be supposed from the RP transcriptions with /ɪ/, rather than /i/, that have been commonplace in phonetics texts until very recently. One might even conclude that RP has, over the last century and for whatever reason(s), followed a pattern that has been out-of-line with the traditional educated speech of the London area, as evidenced by the transcriptions of Walker and Ellis.[61]

2. The use of certain front and back vowels in some words in Walker's pronunciation (e.g. /æ/ in SLUGGARD, /ɛ/ in SWEETNESS, and /ɒ/ in BANNOCK) had, by Ellis's day, all but disappeared, to be replaced by, variously, [ə] or a closer front vowel, etc. Note, in any case, that within the same phonological category in Walker's day there could be different vowels: cf. BANNOCK with /ɒ/ and PADDOCK with /ə/, and BACKWARD with /ə/ but FORWARD with /ɔː/ – evidence that a realignment of vowel phonotactics was already underway towards the end of the eighteenth century. The use, in particular, of unaccented /ɛ/ continuing until late in the nineteenth century is evidenced by comments by Murray, Storm and Sweet: 'don't most educated people say *onest* with open *e* (as in *pen, nest, guest*)?' (Storm to Murray 12 April 1888).[62] Sweet's response to the same question was that in words like HONEST, ALFRED, FOREST, RABBIT, etc., the unaccented vowel was lower than [ɪ], not [ɪ] itself (Sweet to Storm 21 Jan. 1889). Similarly, 'it is

perfectly indifferent whether you write (glaasiz) or (glaasez), the sound being between [IPA [ɪ]] and [IPA [ɛ]]' (Sweet to Storm 21 Jan. 1889).

3. Ellis's phonetic transcriptions of front vowels, in particular his distinction between a vowel raised from CV [e] and one lowered from it, lead to problems of phonemic identification. Is his [ẹ] (in e.g. PULPIT, PITIED, and RABID) to be associated with /i/ or with /ɪ/?

4. In Walker, the distribution of pre-pausal /iː/, /ɪ/, and /ə/ follows a specific pattern – although he, like later phoneticians, seems to have been well aware intuitively of the difficulties in notating them. In word-final position, e.g. in words such as QUALITY, SUNDAY, MONDAY, VANITY, EPITOME, and SIMILE, he uses the <e̅> notation, i.e. /iː/, or, more accurately, [i] rather than [iː].[63]

In the context /— dʒ,z,t,n,l,d, the vowel is /ɪ/ (e.g. CABBAGE, FACES, MARRIES, POET, LINEN, DUEL, MARRIED). But in words like CHAGRIN, PROFILE and INVALID, the vowel is /iː/.

5. There is variability in the distribution of /ə/ and /ɪ/ after a postalveolar affricate and before word-final /n/: SURGEON, STURGEON, and DUNGEON (1819: section 259) have /ə/, but PIGEON, SCUTCHEON, ESCUTCHEON and WIGEON (1819: section 259) have /ɪ/.

6. An example of a later nineteenth-century hypercorrection may be the pronunciation of EXTRA with final /ɪ/ noted by Sweet: '(extri) [is] known to me' (Sweet to Storm 15 May 1879).

Figure 5.2 Word-Final Post-Tonic Vowels

		Walker 1791 / /in IPA	Ellis 1874 [ ] in IPA	Wells 1990 / / in IPA
1	— V#			
	HARMONY	iː	ẹ	i
	MERCY	iː	ẹ̣	i
	PITY	iː	ẹ	i
	TRULY	iː	ẹ̣	i
2	— Vt#			
	FRIGATE	æ	ẹ~ẹ̣	ə~ɪ
	LAUREATE	eː	e	ə~ɪ
	PULPIT	ɪ	ẹ	ɪ
	RABBIT	ɪ	ẹ	ɪ
3	— Vk#			
	BANNOCK	ɒ	ə	ə
	HADDOCK	ə	ə	ə
	LILAC	æ	ə	ə
	PADDOCK	ə	ə	ə
	STOMACH	ə	ə	ə

Figure 5.2 (*cont.*)

		Walker 1791 / /in IPA	Ellis 1874 [ ] in IPA	Wells 1990 / / in IPA
4	— Vd#			
	AWKWARD	ə	ə	ə
	BACKWARD	ə	ə	ɔ
	DOWNWARD	ə	ə	ə
	FORWARD	ɔː	ə	ə
	FROWARD	ɔː	ə	ə
	HAGGARD	æ	ə ~ ə̞	ə
	HALBERD	ə	ə	ə
	LEOPARD	ə	ə	ə
	NIGGARD	ə	ə	ə
	PITIED		e̞̽	i̧
	PITTED		e̞̽	ɪ
	RABID	ɪ	e̞̽	ɪ
	RENARD	æ	ə	
	SHEPHERD	ə	ə	ə
	SLUGGARD	æ	ə	ə
	TOWARD	ə	ə	ə
	UPWARD	ə	ə	ə
5	— Vf#			
	SHERIFF	ɪ	e̞̽	ɪ~ə
6	—Vs#			
	PLENTEOUS	ə	ə	ə
	PRECIOUS	ə	ə	ə
	PRODIGIOUS	ə	ə	ə
	RIGHTEOUS	ə	ə	ə
	SWEETNESS	ɛ	e̞̽	ə~ɪ
7	—Vʃ#			
	PARISH	ɪ	e̞̽	ɪ
8	—Vv#			
	RESTIVE	ɪ	e̞̽	ɪ
9	—Vz#			
	CHURCH(')S		e̞̽	ɪ~ə
	PRINCE(')S		e̞̽	ɪ~ə
10	—Vdʒ#			
	CABBAGE	ɪ	e̞̽	ɪ
	CARRIAGE	ɪ[64]	e̞̽	ɪ
	GREENWICH		e̞̽	ɪ
	IMAGE	ɪ	e̞̽	ɪ
	IPSWICH		e̞̽	ɪ
	MANAGE	ɪ	e̞̽	ɪ~ə
	MARRIAGE	ɪ	e̞̽	ɪ

Figure 5.2 (*cont.*)

	Walker 1791 / /in IPA	Ellis 1874 [ ] in IPA	Wells 1990 / /in IPA
NORWICH		ę̆	ɪ
PRIVILEGE	ɪ	ę̆	ɪ
VILLAGE	ɪ	ę̆	ɪ
WOOLWICH		ę̆	ɪ

11 —Vm#

CLAPHAM		ə	ə~Ø
FATHOM	ə	ə	ə~Ø
FREEDOM	ə	ə	ə
IRKSOME	ə	ə	ə~Ø
MADAM	ə	ə[65]	ə
MEDDLESOME	ə	ə	ə~Ø
QUARRELSOME	ə	ə	ə~Ø
QUONDAM	æ	ə	æ~ə
SELDOM	ə	ə	ə
VENOM	ə	ə	ə

12 —Vn#

CAPTAIN	ɪ	ę̆~ę̆	ɪ~ə~Ø
CERTAIN	ɪ	ɪ~ę̆	ə~Ø~i
CHILDREN		ɪ	ə~Ø
CHRISTIAN	ə	ə	ə
COUNTRYMAN	æ	ə~æ	ə
DEACON	Ø	Ø	ə~Ø
EASTERN	ɛ	ə	ə~Ø
FASHION	ə	ə	ə~Ø
FELON	ə	ə	ə
GARDEN	Ø	Ø	ə~Ø
HISTORIAN	æ	ə	ə
LEGION	ə	ə	ə~Ø
LINEN	ɪ	ɪ	ɪ
LOGICIAN	ə	ə	ə~Ø
MENTION	ə	ə	ə~Ø
METROPOLITAN	æ	ə	ə~Ø
MINION	ə	ə	ə
OCCASION	ə	ə	ə~Ø
QUESTION	ə	ə	ə~Ø
PARDON	Ø	Ø	ə~Ø
PASSION	ə	ə	ə~Ø
SUBURBAN	æ	ə	ə~Ø
VOCATION	ə	ə	ə~Ø
WATCHMAN	æ	ə~æ	ə
WOMAN	ə	ə	ə
WOOLLEN	ɪ	ɪ	ə

Figure 5.2 (*cont.*)

	Walker 1791 / /in IPA	Ellis 1874 [ ] in IPA	Wells 1990 / / in IPA
13 **—Vl#**			
APPAREL	ɛ	ɛ	ə~Ø
CAMEL	ɛ	ɯ	ə~·Ø
CAROL	ə	ə~ɒ	ə~Ø
CYMBAL	æ	ə	ə~Ø
CYNICAL	æ	ə	ə~Ø
DEVIL	Ø	ə~e̞[66]	ə~Ø~ɪ
EVIL	Ø	Ø	ə~Ø~ɪ
LINEAL	æ	ə	ə
LOCAL	æ	ə	ə~Ø
LOGICAL	æ	ə	ə~Ø
MEDIAL		ɔ	ə
METRICAL	æ	ə	ə~Ø
MOUTHFUL		ọ	ʊ
OFFICIAL	æ	ə	ə~Ø
PANEL	ɪ	ə	ə~Ø
PARTIAL	æ	ə	ə~Ø
POETICAL	æ	ə	ə~Ø
PRINCIPAL	æ	ə	ə~Ø
PRINCIPLE	Ø	ə	ə~Ø
RADICAL	æ	ə	ə~Ø
SORROWFUL		ọ~ə 'rarely'	ɔ~Ø~ʊ
SYMBOL	ə	ə	ə~Ø
VICTUAL(S)	Ø	ə	ə~Ø
WITTOL	ɒ	ə	
14 **—Vst#**			
BETTERMOST		ə	
FOREMOST	ɔː	ə	əʊ
HINDMOST	ɔː	ə	əʊ
UTMOST	ɔː	ə	əʊ~ə
15 **—VsV#**			
OBSTINACY	æ—iː	e̞—e̞	ə—i
POLICY	iː—iː	ə—e̞	ə—i
PRELACY	æ—iː	ə—e̞	ə—i
16 **–VnV#**			
HARMONY	ɔː—iː	ə—e̞	ə—i
MATRIMONY	ʌ—iː	ə—e̞	ə—i
TESTIMONY	ʌ—iː	ə—e̞	ə—i
17 **–Vnt#**			
ASSISTANT	æ	ə	ə~Ø
INFANT	æ	ə	ə~Ø
INNOCENT	ɛ	ə	ə~Ø

Figure 5.2 (*cont.*)

	Walker 1791 / /in IPA	Ellis 1874 [ ] in IPA	Wells 1990 / / in IPA
PENDANT	æ	ə	ə
PRESIDENT	ɛ	ə	ə~Ø
QUADRANT	æ	ə	ə~Ø
QUIESCENT	ɛ	ə	ə~Ø
SERGEANT	æ	ə	ə~Ø
TRUANT	æ	ə	ə
18 −Vnd#			
ALMOND	ʌ	ə	ə
BRIGAND		ə	ə~Ø
DIAMOND	ʌ	ə	ə
DIVIDEND	ɛ	ɪ~ɛ̣	ɛ~ə~Ø
HEADLAND	æ	ə	ə~æ
HUSBAND	ʌ	ə	ə
JOCUND	ʌ	ə	ə~Ø~Ø
LEGEND	ɛ	ə~ɛ̣	ə~Ø
MIDLAND		ə	ə
RUBICUND	ʌ	ə	ə~Ø~Ø
19 −Vns#			
ABUNDANCE	æ	ə	ə~Ø
CLEARANCE	æ	ə	ə~Ø
CONFIDENCE	ɛ	ə	ə~Ø
DEPENDENCE	ɛ	ə	ə~Ø
GUIDANCE	æ	ə	ə~Ø
IGNORANCE	æ	ə	ə~Ø
LICENCE	ɛ	ə	ə~Ø
PATIENCE	ɛ	ə	ə~Ø
RESISTANCE	æ	ə	ə~Ø
TEMPERANCE	æ	ə	ə~Ø
20 −VrV#			
BEGGARY	ʌ—iː	ə—ɛ̣	ə—i~Ø—i
BRIBERY	ʌ—iː	ə—ɛ̣	ə—i~Ø—i
CURSORY	o—iː	ə—ɛ̣	ə—i~Ø—i
GRANARY	æ—iː	ə—ɛ̣	ə—i~Ø—i
GUNNERY	ʌ—iː	ə—ɛ̣	ə—i~Ø—i
HISTORY	ʌ—iː	ə—ɛ̣	ʌ—i~ə—i
LITERARY	æ—iː	ə—ɛ̣~ə—ɛ̣	ə—i~Ø—i
LUXURY	ʌ—iː	ə—ɛ̣	ə—i~Ø—i
NOTARY	æ—iː	ə—ɛ̣	ə—i~Ø—i
ORATORY	ʌ—iː	ə—ɛ̣	ə—i~Ø—i
PRIORY	ʌ—iː	ə—ɛ̣	ə—i
ROBBERY	ʌ—iː	ə—ɛ̣	ə—i~Ø—i
SUMMARY	æ—iː	ə—ɛ̣	ə—i~Ø—i
USURY	u—iː	ə—ɛ̣	ə—i~Ø—i
VICTORY	ʌ—iː	ə—ɛ̣	ə—i~Ø—i

Figure 5.2 (*cont.*)

	Walker 1791 / /in IPA	Ellis 1874 [ ] in IPA	Wells 1990 / / in IPA
21 −VnsV#			
CONSTANCY	æ—iː	ə—ę̆	ə—i~Ø—i
CURRENCY	ɛ—iː	ə—ę̆	ə—i~Ø i
DECENCY	ɛ—iː	ə—ę̆	ə—i~Ø—i
INFANCY	æ—iː	ə—ę̆	ə—i~Ø—i
TENANCY	æ—iː	ə—ę̆	ə—i
TENDENCY	æ—iː	ə—ę̆~ę̆-ę̆	ə—i~Ø—i
22 −Vbl#			
POSSIBLE	iː~Ø	ę̆~ə 'common custom'	
			ə—ə~ə—Ø~
			ɪ—ə~ə—Ø
23 −VfV#			
SIGNIFY	iː—ʌɪ	ę̆—əę̆	ɪ—aɪ
TERRIFY	iː—ʌɪ	ę̆—əę̆	ə—aɪ~ɪ—aɪ
24 −VlVz#			
CIVILIZE	ɪ—ʌɪ	ę̆laɪz	ə~ɪ—aɪ

5.6.7

Various orthoepists note the existence of weak forms, but there is little evidence to indicate any changes that have taken place over the past 200 or more years. A typical statement is that by Search (1773), illustrating the pronunciation of A, FROM, AS, AN, OR, A, and OF: 'The very small particles spoken hastily scarce ever retain their original sound … *u* hog won't stray so f*u*r fr*u*m home *uz un* ox *ur u* flock *u* sheep' (1773: 15).[67] See also e.g. Walker 1785: 26, Odell 1806: 47, Anon. 1830: 17. Grandgent, however, notes the absence in American English of a weak form for SAINT; in almost all other respects, American and English usage would appear to be the same (Grandgent 1895: 461–2).

5.6.8

The insertion of /ə/, humorously parodied in spellings like HENARY and 'ENARY, was a feature of at least some educated speakers' pronunciations. In 1889, Sweet was telling Storm: 'I pronounce (ambərelə) & (dzibəroltə) … with a very slight voice-glide between the b and r. It is an effort for me to leave it out & say (ambrelə, dzibroltə)' (Sweet to Storm 21 Jan. 1889). The slightness of Sweet's /ə/ in UMBRELLA is further commented on: 'My ə in ambərelə is so slight that I am certain you would not recognize it instantly' (Sweet to Storm 7 April 1889). That the insertion of /ə/ was not uncommon in educated speech is also shown by Soames's remark, in 1899, that such pronunciations were 'common mistakes' (Soames 1899: 91). *EPD*1 (1917) gives only the /ə/-less pronunciations.

5.6.9

The use of syllabic consonants rather than vowel + consonant, is noted by several writers. Walker (1791: 14) points to the absence of /ə/ in e.g. GARDEN, NAVEL, SHOVEL, and WEASEL. Odell (1806: 47) comments similarly on APPLE, ABLE, STIFLE, EVIL, etc. The older V + /l/ sequences involving vowels other than /ə/ were gradually being displaced during the nineteenth century. Sweet, for example, comments that his father 'said (sivil) = my (sivl) = civil', and '[IPA vɐəɛl], for VOWEL] with distinct (-el)' (Sweet to Storm 18 Feb. 1889). Such pronunciations were still to be heard, nearly thirty years later in 1917: *EPD*1 gives /sɪvɪl/ and /sɪvl/, /vauəl/, /vauɛl/ and /vauɪl/. By 1990, the /vauɛl/ and /vauɪl/ pronunciations were no longer in use, but /sɪvɪl/ and /sɪvl/ (together with the newer form /sɪvəl/) have been retained (Wells 1990a).

5.6.10

'Smoothing' of a diphthong + monophthong sequence (to monophthong + monophthong) is noticed as a development amongst younger speakers in the last quarter of the nineteenth century. Newman writes of words like TOWER and POWER being 'clipped into monosyllables' (Newman 1878: 701), and Sweet tells Storm that 'Lecky thinks I am rather behind the younger generation in obscuring unaccented vowels. Thus he finds they now pronounce (vaul, taul) ... with no (ə) as in my (vauəl) but with length-ening of the (l) instead. I believe he is right. I am not sure that I don't often say (taull) myself' (Sweet to Storm 18 Feb. 1889).

5.6.11

'Pre-Fricative Lengthening'[68] of earlier Modern English <a> and <o>, such that the vowels in words like FAST and LOST moved from /æ/ and /ɒ/ to /ɑː/ and /ɔː/, has been discussed by various scholars (e.g. A. Ward 1952, Mugglestone 1988). From a close examination of the incidence of words containing 'short a' and 'short o' (and potentially 'long a' and 'long o') in the works of ten orthoepists from the mid-eighteenth century to the early nineteenth centuries, Ward draws three main conclusions (Ward, A. 1952: 95–7):

1   The lengthened vowels became more and more common in 'good' speech, until by 1784 and the publication of Nares' *Elements of Orthoepy*, they were regarded as the norm. However, Sheridan's usages (1780) differ markedly from those of Nares.

2   By the end of the century, there was a limited tendency to revert to the short sounds – possibly to achieve, or avoid, a sense of affectation.

3   There was a difference in the contexts in which the lengthened vowels occurred. Lengthening was frequent before word-final /f/, /θ/, and /fC#/, /sC#/. Less common was lengthening before inter-vocalic /f/, /θ/ and /s/.

5.6.12

Using Ward's conclusions as starting-points, and widening the scope of the data to extend well beyond the end of the eighteenth century, it is possible to detect certain emerging patterns for the period 1770 to 1990:

/ɒ/ and /ɔː/

Despite the lack of any clear preference for /ɒ/ or /ɔː/ before voiceless fricatives – with few exceptions, both phonemes can occur in the same context – it is still possible to discern a certain number of patterns in the distribution of /ɒ/ and /ɔː/. But in the absence of a fully comprehensive survey of all available sources, the following results should be treated as provisional.

Monosyllabic Words

1a. In the context —f# (COUGH, OFF, TOFF, TROUGH), there is a preference for /ɒ/ between 1775 and 1842. For about ten years, between 1792 and 1804, /ɔː/ competes with /ɒ/.

ɒf	COUGH	(Walker 1775, Sharp 1777, Fulton & Knight 1800, Hornsey 1807, Smart 1842)
ɔːf	COUGH	(Fogg 1792)
ɒf	OFF	(Walker 1775, Hornsey 1807, Anon. 1813)

ɔːf	OFF	(Adams 1794, Mitford 1804)
ɒf	TOFF	(Hornsey 1807)
ɔːf	TROUGH	(Fogg 1792)

1b. In the context —ft# (LOFT, OFT, SOFT), the preference is for /ɔː/.

ɔːf	LOFT	(Hornsey 1807)
ɒf	OFT	(Carrol 1795)
ɔːf	OFT	(Kenrick 1784, Hornsey 1807)
ɔːf	SOFT	(Kenrick 1784, Nares 1784, Fogg 1792, Hornsey 1807)

2. In the context —θ# (BROTH, CLOTH, FROTH, GOTH, MOTH, WRATH and WROTH), /ɔː/ is used from 1764 to 1807. Starting in 1792, /ɒ/ competes with /ɔː/, until from 1807 onwards only /ɔː/ is used.

ɒθ	BROTH	(Mackintosh 1799)
ɔːθ	BROTH	(Anon. 1784, Nares 1784)
ɔːθ	CLOTH	(Johnston 1764, Kenrick 1784, Mitford 1804)
ɒθ	FROTH	(Barrie 1794)
ɔːθ	FROTH	(Mitford 1804)
ɒθ	GOTH	(Fogg 1792)
ɒθ	MOTH	(Smart 1842)
ɒθ	WRATH/WROTH	(Fogg 1792, Smart 1842)
ɔːθ	WRATH	(Anon. 1784, Hornsey 1807)

3a. In the context – s# (CROSS, LOSS, MOSS, TOSS), /ɒ/ predominates from 1784 to 1837, with a single appearance of /ɔː/ in 1804.

ɒs	CROSS	(Hornsey 1807, Fulton 1826, Angus 1830, Knowles 1837)
ɒs	LOSS	(Fogg 1792, Perry 1795)
ɔːs	LOSS	(Mitford 1804)
ɒs	MOSS	(Anon. 1784)
ɒs	TOSS	(Angus 1830)

3b. In the context – sp# (WASP), /ɔː/ is used.

| ɔːs | WASP | (Hornsey 1807) |

3c. In the context – st# (COST, FROST, LOST, TOST), there is a preference for /ɒ/, although examples of both phonemes can be found over approximately the same time-scale.

434

ɒs	COST	(Sheridan 1781, Anon. 1784, Thornton 1793, Adams 1794, Perry 1795, Hornsey 1807, Smart 1842)
ɔːs	COST	(Knowles 1837)
ɒs	FROST	(Adams 1794)
ɔːs	FROST	(Johnston 1764)
ɒs	LOST	(Sheridan 1781, Fogg 1792, Adams 1794, Carrol 1795, Hornsey 1807, Anon. 1812, Fulton 1826)
ɔːs	LOST	(Mitford 1804)
ɒs	TOST	(Barrie 1794)

3d. In the context – sk# (MOSQUE), /ɒ/ is used.

ɒs	MOSQUE	(Anon. 1813)

Disyllabic Words

There is a preference for /ɔː/ as the stressed vowel in a disyllabic, first-stressed, word. With disyllabic words with second stress, the limited data makes a generalisation impossible.

ɔːf	COFFEE	(Nares 1784)
ɔːθ	HOSPITAL	(Nares 1784)
ɔːf	LOFTY	(Mitford 1804)
ɔːf	OFFER	(Mitford 1804)
ɒf	OFTEN	(Perry 1795)
ɔːf	OFTEN	(Search 1773, Anon. 1784, Nares 1784)
ɔːs	PROSPER	(Mitford 1804)
ɒs	AUSTERE	(Duponceau 1818)
ɔːs	AUSTERE	(Dyche 1805)

Note in addition the use of /ɔː/ before /n/ where today's RP would have /ɒ/:

FOND (Herries 1773), GONE (Mitford 1804), WAN (Smart 1819)

Distribution of tautosyllabic /ɒr/ and /ɔː(r)/

1. There is no systematic preference over time for /ɔːr/: examples of /ɒr/ occur between 1784 and 1842; of /ɔː/ between 1773 and 1840.[69] An obvious reason is the transition from rhotic to non-rhotic structures in the exemplifying accents.

2. Instead, a number of parallel developments appear to be underway.

(a) Competing:

ɒr	CORD (Elphinston 1790, Mackintosh 1799, Gilchrist 1824)
ɔː(r)	CORD (Sheridan 1781, Anon. 1812, Angus 1830)
ɒr	WAR (Kenrick 1784, Elphinston 1790, Hornsey 1807)
ɔː(r)	WAR (Fogg 1792, Harvey 1793, Adams 1794)

(b) Chronological: /ɔː/ replacing /ɒ/

ɒr	LORD (Sharp 1777)
ɔː(r)	LORD (Sheridan 1781, Fulton 1826)
ɒr	NORTH (Carrol 1795)
ɔː(r)	NORTH (Fulton 1826)
ɒr	SHORT (Thornton 1793)
ɔː(r)	SHORT (Sheridan 1781, Fulton 1826)

(c) Widening contexts

/ɒr/ occurs before tautosyllabic (post)alveolars and dentals, with one example of an occurrence before /f/. /ɔː/ occurs more widely, including the above, bilabials and a velar.

5.6.13   /æ/ and /aː/

There is no clear, single pattern in the distribution of /æ/ and /aː/ (later /ɑː/) before voiceless fricatives and nasals. Rather, one sees over a period of about fifty years a gradual shift in favour of /aː/ (later /ɑː/) but without the full-scale distribution of today's RP.[70]

Patterns:

1. Before /f/, the preference is for /aː/. This is noticeable from as early as 1766:

cf.	LAUGH	(/æ/)	Spence 1775, Adams 1794
	LAUGH	(/aː/)	Buchanan 1766, Sheridan 1781, Kenrick 1784, Mitford 1804, Odell 1806, Hornsey 1807, Smart 1842

2. Before /ft/, both vowels are found, though there is a slight preference for /aː/ once the nineteenth century is reached:

cf.	DRAUGHT	(/æ/)	Anon. 1784, Anon. 1797
	DRAUGHT	(/aː/)	Buchanan 1766, Mitford 1804, Hornsey 1807
	RAFT	(/æ/)	[No examples]
	RAFT	(/aː/)	Barrie 1794, Odell 1806

3. Before /θ/, /æ/ is found alongside /aː/ until the end of the eighteenth century. Thereafter, /aː/ is the only quoted form.

4. Before /s/, /æ/ is generally retained, with no clear preference for /aː/, even well into the nineteenth century. It is noticeable, for example, that in none of the works surveyed were FAST, LAST and MAST quoted as having /aː/.

5. Before /nt/, a clearer pattern of distribution is apparent. Words containing orthographic 'ant' (e.g. GRANT) retain /æ/ beyond the turn of the eighteenth century:

cf.	GRANT	(/æ/)	Walker 1775, Anon. 1813, Angus 1830
	GRANT	(/aː/)	Carrol 1795, Perry 1795
	PLANT	(/æ/)	Angus 1830
	PLANT	(/aː/)	[No examples]

Words containing orthographic 'aunt' (e.g. HAUNT) generally have /aː/.

cf.	AUNT	(/æ/)	Walker 1775, Adams 1794
	AUNT	(/aː/)	Buchanan 1766, Sheridan 1781, Carrol 1795, Anon. 1812, Duponceau 1818, Gilchrist 1824, Angus 1830, Smart 1842
	HAUNT	(/æ/)	Anon. 1813
	HAUNT	(/aː/)	Hornsey 1807, Gilchrist 1824, Angus 1830, Smart 1842
	JAUNT	(/æ/)	[No examples]
	JAUNT	(/aː/)	Buchanan 1766, Perry 1793, Hornsey 1807, Anon. 1812, Duponceau 1818

One can speculate that later in the nineteenth century when /ɔː/ began to take over from /aː/ (/ɑː/) in the '-aunt' words, the shift then took place of /aː/ replacing /æ/ in the '-ant' words.

6. Before /nd/, the clear preference was for /aː/

cf.	COMMAND	(/æ/)	Walker 1775
	COMMAND	(/aː/)	Buchanan 1766, Sharp 1777, Perry 1795, Mackintosh 1799

DEMAND	(/æ/)	[No examples]
DEMAND	(/aː/)	Sharp 1777
GRAND	(/æ/)	Barrie 1794
GRAND	(/aː/)	[No examples]

7. Before orthographic <-aunch>, /æ/ is found (e.g. HAUNCH, Anon. 1784), but two examples of /aː/ (LAUNCH, Elphinston 1790, Anon. 1812) suggest a move to /aː/. A similar shift is perceptible in other <-aun-> words like JAUNDICE and LAUNDRY.

If at least most of the available sources can be considered reliable indicators of actual (as distinct from desirable) pronunciation practices, then the last decade of the eighteenth century and the first two decades of the nineteenth must be regarded as the critical period of change when the major phonotactic restructuring of /æ, aː, ɒ, ɔː/ took place.

5.6.14   American /aː/ and /ɔː/

The distribution of these two phonemes in GenAm. about 100 years ago can be tentatively established from the data provided by Grandgent in his survey of these vowels in educated American speech (Grandgent 1893b). Part of what now constitutes GenAm. was represented by 58 speakers in Grandgent's 'North' category (Vermont, western Massachusetts, Connecticut, Ontario, New York, New Jersey, Philadelphia, Michigan, Wisconsin, Ohio, Illinois).[71] Between 91 and 100 per cent of the speakers used /aː/ before /ʃ/ (SLOSH), /d/ COD, /g/ JOG, /m/ TOM, /n/ JOHN, /l/ MOLLY; this parallels the late twentieth-century pattern (Wells 1990a). However, the use of /ɔː/ by between 91 and 100 per cent of Grandgent's speakers before /f/ OFF, /θ/ CLOTH, /s/ MOSS, and /ŋ/ LONG has since given way to co-variability of /aː/ and /ɔː/ (Wells 1990a).

5.7   Vowel Phonotactics (lexical-incidental)

5.7.1

Numerous examples can be found of words in which the choice of vowel phoneme is different from what is heard in late twentieth-century RP; a selection are quoted below. They arise not from any structural realignment of the phonotactic resources of the language, but rather from the use of a particular phoneme in specific words. (Some, it must be said, do have their origins in earlier, i.e. pre-1770, structural changes, but synchronically they are to be counted as examples of lexical incidence.)

5.7.2

/iː/~/eː/ PLAIT Walker 1791; FLAY Walker 1791; GREAT Walker 1791

5.7.3

/iː/~/ɛ/ FEARFUL Walker 1791; LEISURE Walker 1791

5.7.4

/iː/~/ɪ/~/ɛ/ AESTHETICS and APOTHEGM can have either /iː/ or /ɛ/ (Sweet to Storm 23 Dec.1878; cf. also Storm 1879: 68). Western (1902: 56) has four pronunciations of AESTHETIC – deriving, one assumes, from the four such entries in *OED*1.

LEISURE had 3 pronunciations: 'I vary between lezhə and lizhə, some say liizhə – I think lezhə is commonest' (Sweet to Storm 29 April 1877). Western (1902: 65) also quotes all three as possible pronunciations. *EPD*1 (1917) gives only the /ɛ/ version, regarding the /iː/ version as 'old-fashioned'.

5.7.5

/iː/~/aɪ/ EITHER Walker 1791; NEITHER Walker 1791

In 1880 (Sweet to Storm 10 Oct.1880) and 1890a: viii, Sweet maintains that his own pronunciation of EITHER as /aɪðə/ was in a majority compared with /iːðə/. Western 1902: 65 and *EPD*1 give both.

5.7.6

/ɪ/~/aɪ/ IRASCIBLE Walker 1791; BITUMEN Walker 1791; TYPOGRAPHY Walker 1791; GUILD Walker 1791

5.7.7

/eː/~/ɛ/ SAID Walker 1791; ATE Walker 1791; LEISURE Sharp 1767

5.7.8

/eː/~/ɔɪ/ ALLOY Walker 1791

5.7.9

/æ/~/eː/ (/eɪ/) RAILLERY Walker 1791. The possibility of BADE being pronounced /bɑːd/ is ruled out by Sweet (Sweet to Storm 24 Oct. 1878): it is 'always (bæd) or (beeid)'. This is also the view of *EPD*1; Western gives only (bæd) (Western 1902: 55).

5.7.10

/æ/~/ɑː/ Sweet gives no examples – thereby suggesting that the changes which had taken place since the late eighteenth century had stabilised. Soames, however, notes the alternation in PATH (Soames 1899: 84), and Ellis (1874: 1210–13) quotes several words (CLASSES, TASK, PAST, STAFF) in which either phoneme was used.

In Boston, between 1830 and 1850, /ɑː/ replaced /æ/ in certain words – Grandgent's description was that 'it ran riot' (Mencken 1937: 336) – even being used in APPLE, MATTER, CATERPILLAR, SATISFACTION, SATUR-DAY, PRACTICAL, HAMMER, PANTRY, and HANDSOME. The origin of this temporary phonotactic change was the continuing authoritative influence of Webster. The use of /ɑː/ in such words continued until at least the end of the nineteenth century for some New England speakers (Krapp 1925.II: 73).

5.7.11

/æ/~/ɒ/ According to Walker (1791: 12), QUANTITY 'ought to be pro-nounced as if written *kwontity*, and *quality* should rhyme with *jollity*; instead of which we frequently hear the *w* robbed of its rights of proxy, and *quality* so pronounced as to rhyme with *legality*, while to rhyme *quantity*, according to this affected mode of pronouncing it, we must coin such words as *plan-tity* and *consonantity*'. Within a century, the pronunciation of EQUALITY with /æ/ was deemed 'oldfashioned & rare' (Sweet to Storm 29 April 1877). *EPD*1 (1917) has only the /ɒ/ pronunciation.

5.7.12

/ɑː/~/ɔː/ The degree of variation in the use of these two phonemes is noted by various phoneticians of the period, including Sweet, Soames (1899: 84), Wagner (1899: 41), Western (1902: 53, 57) and Storm (1879: 63 fn.1, 68, fn.2). (The latter relies on Sweet's views, made known in corre-spondence, as source.)

ALMANAC: 'I only hear (aomənæk), not (aam)' (Sweet to Storm 29 April 1877). *EPD*1 has only versions with /ɒ/ and /ɔː/.

BLANCMANGE: '(bləmaɑnzh) with French nasality but (ao*n*) [= IPA [ɔ̃]] & (oq) [= IPA [õ]] are common' (Sweet to Storm 16 Feb. 1878). *EPD*1 has equivalent pronunciations.

DAUNT: Wagner 1899: 41 gives both /ɑː/ and /ɔː/.

GAUNTLET: Western 1902: 57 has only /ɑː/.

HAUNCH: Wagner 1899: 41 gives both /ɑː/ and /ɔː/. Western 1902: 53 has only /ɑː/.

HAUNT: Wagner 1899: 41 gives both /ɑː/ and /ɔː/. Western 1902: 53 has only /ɑː/.

LAUNCH: 'I pronounce (laansh) ... but ao is not uncommon' (Sweet to Storm 29 April 1877). Western 1902: 57 has only /ɑː/. *EPD*1 has both the /ɔː/ and /ɑː/ pronunciations.

LAUNDRESS: 'I pronounce (laandres) ... but ao is not uncommon' (Sweet to Storm 29 April 1877). Western 1902: 57 has only /ɑː/. *EPD*1 has both the /ɔː/ and /ɑː/ pronunciations.

SAUCY: 'saucy etc. has mid-wide (aa)' (Sweet to Storm 23 Feb. 1880). *EPD*1 however has only the /ɔː/ pronunciation.

VASE: '(vaoz) = (vaaz) ... may still be heard' (Sweet to Storm 24 Oct. 1878). Western 1902: 53 has only /ɑː/, noting that /veɪz/ is used particularly in America. *EPD*1 gives both. Gimson, as late as *EPD*14 (1977), notes the existence still of an 'old-fashioned' /ɔː/ pronunciation; Wells (1990a) comments that this was a 'former' pronunciation. The three American pronunciations /veɪz/, /vɑːz/ and /vɔːz/ (the latter 'now only humorous') are discussed by Krapp (1925.II:123–4).

VAUNT: Wagner 1899: 41 gives both /ɑː/ and /ɔː/.

5.7.13

/ɑː/~/ɜː/ FAR: '(fəə) is known to me ... due to the analogy of (fəəðə)' (Sweet to Storm 18 May 1879). Western 1902: 53 and *EPD*1 give only the /ɑː/ pronunciation.

5.7.14

/ɒ/~/ɔː/ The only example commented on by Sweet is of the word SAUSAGE, with three pronunciations: (sɔsidzh) [= IPA [sɒsɪdʒ]], (saosidzh) [= IPA [sɔːsɪdʒ]], and (sæsidzh) [= IPA [sæsɪdʒ]] (Sweet to Storm 18 May

1879). *EPD*1 gives only the /ɒ/ pronunciation. The pronunciation with /æ/ is found in e.g. Walker 1791.

5.7.15

/ɒ/~/oː/ KNOWLEDGE Walker 1791

5.7.16

/ʊə~ɔː/ At one time, Sweet pronounced OF COURSE with an /ʊə/ – the result of the influence on his speech of his mother's Scottish accent (Sweet to Storm 20 March 1879).[72]

The use of /ʊə/ in MOURNING is discussed by Sweet. He notes that it still contrasts with MORNING for the Scots and 'archaic speakers in London', but he is emphatic that 'it is certainly extinct in the younger generation of southern speakers' (Sweet to Storm 29 April 1877). The same is confirmed some nine years later (Sweet to Storm 24 Sept. 1888), where he adds that 'I really think it is time for 'the old-fashioned *o* in mourning' to be decently buried & forgotten' (Sweet to Storm 2 Oct. 1888). By 1917, *EPD*1 noted that MOURNING with /ʊə/ was 'rare' – although it continues to be heard very occasionally still in RP.[73]

5.7.17

/ʊə~ɔə/ 'I'm sure is always pronounced (ɑim shuuə) . . . (shaɔə) is the regular vulgar form, as in (pɑoə) = poor, etc' (Sweet to Storm 27 Nov. 1879). *EPD*1 gives /ʊə/ as the main pronunciation, but [ɔə], /ɔə/, /ɔː/ and /ɜː/ as alternatives. (Jones's [ɔə] indicates more precisely the starting-point of this particular allophone of /ʊə/.)

5.7.18

/oː/~/ɔʊ/ PROW Walker 1791; SNOWDEN Walker 1791

5.7.19

/uː/~/ɔː/ CHEW Walker 1791; EWE Walker 1791

5.7.20

/uː/~/ɔʊ/ WOUND Walker 1791

5.7.21

/ɜː/~/æ/~/ɛə/ The pronunciation of GIRL has attracted attention from both phoneticians and certain members of the general public. Sweet, for example, was aware of three pronunciations: (gəəl) ('the regular pronunciation' (Sweet to Storm 16 April 1879; 18 May 1879)), (gæl) and (gææl). (In IPA transcription, these would be [gɜːl], [gæl], and [gæːl].) The last was Sweet's father's pronunciation (Sweet to Storm 18 May 1879). It is this one, with its [æː], that merits further comment.[74]

There are two problems of interpretation: what is the precise phonetic quality of the vowel, and what should be its phonemic form? [æː] could be the realisation of /ɛə/, with a lower, monophthongal realisation before /l/; the extent to which the [g] influences it is not certain. It could be that the auditory effect has become out of line with the articulatory position: i.e. the velarisation of the /l/ may have affected the /ɛə/. Second, the [æː] could be a realisation of /aː/, i.e. a predecessor of PDE /ɑː/. Comments by Soames towards the end of the nineteenth century are useful, as they indicate that the articulatory and auditory quality of the vowel was considered unusual: 'It is a curious fact that in the word *girl* a sound is often heard intermediate between **êa** [= IPA [ɛə]] and **oe** [= IPA [ɜː]] ... I myself aim at, but my friends tell me I really pronounce it differently, something like **êa** in pear. And certainly this intermediate sound is the prevailing one amongst cultivated people, whilst some of them definitely pronounce it **êa**, as if it were spelt *gair*' (Soames 1899: 66).

*EPD*1 gives four pronunciations: gəːl, gɛəl, giəl, geəl, which in a more obviously comparative transcription would be [gɜːl], [gɛəl], [gɪəl], and [geəl]. Of these, only the first appears to be current in late twentieth-century RP (Wells 1990a).

5.7.22

Below are listed comments on individual words, taken from Sweet, which reflect both chronological and stylistic changes that had been taking place during nineteenth-century English. They involve lexical incidence of consonants as well as vowels.

> FOREHEAD: 'always (forid)' (Sweet to Storm 24 Oct. 1878). *EPD*1 gives both /fɒrɪd/ and /fɒrɛd/.
> FORTUNE: 'generally (faotshən), but may well be a vulgar (faotn) & perhaps (faotin) (Sweet to Storm 23 Feb. 1880). *EPD*1 has both /fɔːtʃ(ə)n/ and /fɔːtjuːn/, but no other.

HEAR: Sweet disapproved strongly of Laura Soames's /jɜː/ pronunciation. *EPD*1 gives /hiə/, /hjɜː/, and [çɜː], the latter being closest to Soames's pronunciation.

MOMENT: '(moumənt) is specifically Irish, not English English' (Sweet to Storm 23 June 1889). *EPD*1 gives only the form with /ə/.

PHAETON: '(= feitn)' (Sweet to Storm 24 Sept. 1888). Similarly, *EPD*1.

RIBBON: '(ribin)' (Sweet to Storm 18 May 1879). *EPD*1 gives only /ribən/.

SIRRAH: 'sirrah is (sirə) but ... certainly obsolete' (Sweet to Storm 23 Dec. 1878). Similarly, *EPD*1.

TOWARDS: 'I say tə'waodz' (Sweet to Storm 29 April 1877); '(tə'waodz) or (taodz), never (tow'aodz)' (Sweet to Storm 24 Oct. 1878); 'tɛwards is, I think, only used when it comes immediately before its substantive etc., and is then pronounced (taoədz)' (Sweet to Storm 10 Jan. 1880); '(təwɔdz) [= IPA /təwɒdz/] I fear was a real vulgarism which I have now quite got rid of' (Sweet to Storm 18 Feb. 1889). *EPD*1 has five possibilities:/tɔːdz/, /tɔədz/, /tə'wɔːdz/, /tʊ'wɔːdz/, and /'twɔːdz/. The pronunciation with word-initial stress, noted by Sweet, is not given by *EPD*1. Wells (1990a) quotes three:/tə'wɔːdz/,/tu'wɔːdz/, and /tɔːdz/. A /twɔː(r)dz/ pronunciation is now regarded as American, not British, English.

5.7.23

Below are listed examples of lexical-incidental distributions, mainly from the late eighteenth century, which are not found in today's RP.

iː			
	W*I*NTER	Herries	1773
	L*E*ISURE	Anon	1784
	T*E*NURE	Anon	1784
	R*A*ISIN	Walker	1791
	TURQ*UO*ISE	Walker	1791
	OBL*I*GE	Fogg	1792
	SH*I*RE	Anon	1813
	BR*E*VIARY	Smart	1842
	OB*E*ISANCE	Smart	1842
	PROF*I*LE	Smart	1842

ɪ	YE S	Sharp	1767
	YE S	Sharp	1777
	YE S	Nares	1784
	YE STERDAY	Nares	1784
	OTHERWISE	Walker	1791
	PRIMER	Walker	1791
	SERVILE	Walker	1791
	SUICIDE	Walker	1791
	TORTOISE	Walker	1791
	LIEUTENANT	Fogg	1792
	YE S	Fogg	1792
	YE STERDAY	Fogg	1792
	YE	Thornton	1793
	JUVENILE	Carrol	1795
	VOLATILE	Carrol	1795
	YE S	Anon.	1812
	CHORISTER	Angus	1830
	CLEF	Smart	1842
	VISOR	Smart	1842
	FUTILE	Ellis	1869: 5
	PENKNIFE (/penɪf/ – 'many speakers')	Ellis 1869: 55	
	GROATS	Ellis	1869: 599
e:	LEISURE	Buchanan	1766 <Ellis 1869: 129
	UNCERTAIN	Franklin	1768 <Ellis 1869: 129
	SATIRE	Anon.	1784
	CHINA	Anon.	1784, Anon. 1817
	VARIEGATE	Walker	1791
	ANY	Mackintosh	1799
	QUEAN	Hornsey	1807
	VASE	Anon.	1813 (alternate:/ɔ:/)
	PLACABLE	Smart	1842
	BRAVADO	Smart	1842
ɛ	SERGEANT	Buchanan	1766
	FIERCE	Buchanan	1766, Fogg 1792
	PIERCE	Buchanan	1766, Fogg 1792
	MISTEACH	Sharp	1767
	TEAT	Sharp	1767, Sharp 1777
	VILLAIN	Sharp	1767
	YEAST	Sharp	1767, Sharp 1777
	BEARD	Barrie	1794
	FEOFFMENT	Duponceau	1818
	FEOFF	Smart	1842
	EPOCH	Smart	1842
	PANEGYRIC	Smart	1842
	WAINSCOT	Smart	1842

æ	YELLOW	Sharp	1767, Adams 1794
	SQUAT	Perry	1793
	PLAID	Walker	1791, Gilchrist 1824
	SAUSAGE	Walker	1791, Carrol 1795
	LAWRENCE	Carrol	1795
	CELERY	Anon.	1817
	RAILLERY	Gilchrist	1824, Smart 1842
aː	GROAT	Buchanan	1766
	WASP	Herries	1773
	DAUB	Spence	1775
	GAPE	Anon.	1813
	CHAMBERLAIN	Buchanan	1766 <Ellis 1869: 129
	BACON 'old pronunciation … in use at Bath'		Ellis 1869: 67
ʌ	QUESTION	Buchanan	1766
	SOOT	Buchanan	1766, Anon. 1784, Nares 1784, Dyche 1805
	BOMB	Sharp	1767, Sharp 1777, Nares 1784, Walker 1791, Anon. 1797, Anon. 1813[75]
	TORTOISE	Sharp	1767, Sharp 1777
	WOMAN	Sharp	1777
	HOUSEWIFE	Walker	1791, Smart 1842, Ellis 1869: 599
	JOUST	Walker	1791
	LENGTH	Thornton	1793
	VERY	Thornton	1793
	CONDUIT	Dyche	1805
	SYRUP	Smart	1842
ɒ	ROMISH	Spence	1775
	PROCESS	Anon.	1784
	OATMEAL	Nares	1784, Walker 1791
	PUPPET	Nares	1784
	ONE	Sheridan	1786 (cf. Ellis 1874: 1091, who notes it and similar pronunciations with back-rounded vowels as still in use amongst 'elderly educated people'.)
	OPEN	Thornton	1793
	FRONT	Anon.	1813 ('solemn' pronunciation)
	CHAPS	Smart	1842
ɔː	WANT	Buchanan	1766
	GROAT	Sharp	1767, Nares 1784, Perry 1793, Adams 1794, Dyche 1805, Smart 1842

	CAB*A*LS	Fogg	1792
	V*A*SE	Anon.	1813 (alternate:/e:/)
oː	STR*EW*	Nares	1784, Fulton 1826
	PR*O*VE	Walker	1791
	*E W*E (alternate /uː/)	Perry	1793
	G*O*LD (alternate uː)	Adams	1794, Anon. 1812, Hare 1832 ('regaining its legitimate full sound'), Smart 1842
ʊ	*U*VULA	Thornton	1793
	TH*EW*	Thornton	1793
	BL*OO*D	Anon.	1812
	BE*AU*TY	Duponceau	1818
uː	R*O*ME	Buchanan	1766, Sharp 1767, Nares 1784, Walker 1791, Adams 1794, Anon. 1812, Anon. 1813, Hare 1832 – but 'regaining its legitimate full sound'
	Y*EO*MAN	Sharp	1767, Sharp 1777
	GALL*EO*N	Walker	1791, Fogg 1792, Carrol 1795, Duponceau 1818, Ellis 1869: 605
	G*O*LD	Sharp	1767, Walker 1791, Fogg 1792, Adams 1794 (alternate /oː/)
	*E W*E (alternate /oː/)	Perry	1793
	T*OO*K	Thornton	1793
	H*OO*K	Thornton	1793
	W*OU*LD	Thornton	1793 (/wuːld/)
	B*UO*Y	Duponceau	1818 (/buːɪ/), Ellis 1869: 133
	BEH*O*VE	Smart	1842
	R*U*SSIAN (as in 'Russian War' < 'rouge et noir'), 'still occasionally heard'	Ellis 1869: 597	
ʌɪ	J*OI*N	Kenrick	1773, Anon. 1817
	J*OI*NT	Nares	1784,
	B*OI*L	Nares	1784, Anon. 1817
	GELAT*I*NE	Walker	1791
	OBL*I*QUE	Walker	1791
ɔɪ	B*UY*	Fogg	1792
	BOURGE*OI*S	Ellis	1869: 602
ɔʊ	C*U*CUMBER	Sharp	1767, Sharp 1777, Adams 1794, Anon. 1817, Angus 1830
	S*OU*THERN	Walker	1791
	S*OU*THERLY	Walker	1791
	PRON*U*NCIATION	Anon.	1817

5.8 Vowel realisations

5.8.1 /iː/

The evidence points to a realisation similar to that in late twentieth-century RP and GenAm.: i.e. a set of allophones lowered and retracted from CV [i]; diphthongal variants are noted by one commentator, Thomas Batchelor (see below).

The only articulatory description of /iː/ is by Thornton (1793: 281):[76] 'the mouth rather more contracted than for *e*, but the under lip so low as to shew the insertion of the lower teeth; the corners of the mouth a little extended; the tongue pressing gently upon the edges of the lower teeth'. His description of the position of the lower lip is unusual; furthermore, he produces precisely the same overall description for /ɪ/. Buchanan equates the vowel with the French /i/, thus indicating that the realisations of the two phonemes were closer together than they are now (1766: xvii). An alternative explanation, however, is that, since Buchanan was Scottish by birth and upbringing, it is likely that his realisation of /iː/ was closer (and hence nearer the French /i/) than a pre-RP /iː/ version. Mitford's comment that /iː/ was the 'precise' long equivalent of /ɪ/ (1774/1804: 27) very probably refers to the common assumption in the eighteenth century (and later) that the five vowels (i.e. vowel-letters) of English had both short and long forms. Hence /iː/ would automatically be aligned with /ɪ/ (phonologically, but not necessarily phonetically).

Batchelor analyses the /iː/ of TREE as diphthongal, pointing out that 'the tongue makes a nearer approach towards the palate in the termination of that diphthong, than happens in the beginning of it' (Batchelor 1809: 52). This would indicate a pronunciation like [ɪi]. In his reformed spelling system for English (one of Batchelor's aims), the word SEEN is re-spelled (siyn), thereby indicating the diphthongal quality. (The late twentieth-century RP form does have diphthongal variants, but only in word-final position: e.g. SEE.) It may be of significance that Batchelor hailed from a village in Bedfordshire, about 65 miles north-west of central London; his analysis may refer to his own accent, not specifically to a more southerly one.

Later writers agree on both the articulatory quality of /iː/, as well as on the use of diphthongal variants: see e.g. Sweet 1877: 27, 73; 1908: 28.

5.8.2 /ɪ/

Thornton's description (1793: 281) is exactly the same as for /iː/: 'the mouth rather more contracted than for *e*, but the under lip so low as to shew the insertion of the lower teeth; the corners of the mouth a little extended; the tongue pressing gently upon the edges of the lower teeth', and, as indicated above (5.8.1), raises some problems of interpretation. Two other descriptions are those by Buchanan (1766: xv) and Sharp (1777: 8). The former says that /ɪ/ 'approaches to the diphthong [ee] or French [i]', and Sharp points out that the length of the sound is shorter than in French /i/ (Sharp 1777: 8).

Comparisons with French vowels are a feature of many writers' attempts to analyse English vowels during the eighteenth century. Unfortunately, little is known about the precise articulatory qualities of French of this period.[77]

Nineteenth- and twentieth-century descriptions of /ɪ/ agree on its being lower and more retracted than /iː/. The most detailed analysis of its quality before the twentieth century, especially in unstressed positions, is by Sweet. His discussion of the /ɪ/ vowels of PRETTY, using Narrow Romic notation, is as follows: '(*pre*[1]*te*[1]) [= IPA [preṭe̯]] or perhaps with (*ih*) (high-mixed-wide) [= IPA [ɪː]] in the first syllable. Many say (*prite*[1]) [= IPA [prɪṭe̯]] with the regular short (*i*)' (Sweet to Storm 16 Feb. 1878; cf. also Sweet 1877: 111; Sweet to Storm 21 Jan. 1889).

5.8.3   /eː/ > /eɪ/

The history of /eː/ up to the beginning of the eighteenth century is clear. According to Dobson, an [ɛː] pronunciation, the reflex of ME /aː/, was established after 1650, but [eː] began to emerge in some forms of Southern English even earlier, at the beginning of the seventeenth century (Dobson 1968: 594, 602). By the early eighteenth century, the [eː] pronunciation was 'normal in StE'.

Two different questions need to be asked about the post-1770 period: was the vowel monophthongal or diphthongal, and what was its precise quality? Up until the turn of the nineteenth century, and thereafter rather more sporadically, most evidence points to a monophthongal realisation of /eː/,[78] with explicit parallels being drawn with the monophthongal qualities of equivalent French, German, and Italian vowels: see Sharp 1767/1777: 4, 8, 23; Nares 1784: 3; Walker 1791: 10; Thornton 1793: 289; Smith 1795: 9; Mackintosh 1799: opp. 47; Moberg 1801 (quoted in Nohlgren 1981: 36); Henslowe 1840: 16.

Walker's /eː/ is the 'long slender *a*' (of SPADE, PAIN, 'and sometimes in the [orthographic] diphthong *ea* [of BEAR])'. It corresponds, he says, 'to the sound of the French *e* in the beginning of the words *être* and *tête*'

(1791: 10). (This would suggest a sound at least nearer to CV [ɛ] rather than CV [e].) The parallel with French ÊTRE and TÊTE, however, is contradicted by his quoting French FÉE and ÉPÉE in the same work (1791: xvi).This would indicate a vowel closer to CV [e].[79] His comment (in 1791) that 'the short sound of the long, slender *a* ... may be perceived by comparing *mate* and *met*' (Walker 1791: 10) indicates that the realisations of both /eː/ and /e/ were more open than CV [e], i.e. similar to the modern RP /ɛ/ (i.e. [ẹ], and a long equivalent [ẹː]. This is confirmed by evidence from Swedish books on English of the eighteenth and, later, nineteenth centuries (cf. Nohlgren 1981: 36), especially that by Peter Moberg (1801).

The first mention of a diphthongal realisation ('Mid Long Diphthonging')[80] had been noted as early as 1711, in the Gildon-Brightland *Grammar of the English Tongue*: 'The Diphthongs ... *ai* ... *ay* ... *ey* ... *oi* ... when they are truly pronounc'd, are compounded of the foregoing or prepositive Vowel, and the Consonant[] *y*' (reproduced in Zettersten 1974: xxxii). Zettersten shows that this quotation has its source in Wallis's *Grammatica Linguae Anglicanae* of 1653 (Zettersten 1974: xxx). It is, of course, not inconceivable, that different varieties of Southern English English used both monophthongal and diphthongal realisations respectively – this was certainly the situation later, in the 1860s and 1870s, according to the evidence of Ellis (see below 5.8.3).

From the 1800s onwards, further explicit descriptions of a diphthongal pronunciation begin to appear.[81] The first is by Thomas Batchelor in 1809, who transcribes BAIL and WADE as 'beyl' and 'weyd' (Batchelor 1809: 53). (His overriding interest was in creating a reformed spelling of English which would reflect the pronunciation of early nineteenth-century English.) Critically, he accepts the difficulty of recognising a (phonetic) diphthong in cases like these: 'The motions of the tongue can neither be seen nor felt, in some cases, without more attention than grammarians generally think proper to devote to that purpose' (1809: 53). But he is adamant (as the re-spelling indicates) that the sounds are not monophthongal: 'the uniformity of error so regularly transferred frome [*sic*] one author to another, which respects the simplicity of the sounds of the long vowels in *seen* and *bail*. For the fact of their being diphthongs, which cannot be properly pronounced without moving the tongue towards the palate before they are completed, admits of proofs which are not short of demonstration' (Batchelor 1809: 53–4; see also Chomsky & Halle 1968: 283–4). Smart, writing in 1836, noted that the vowel was 'not quite simple, but finishes more slenderly than it begins, tapering, so to speak, towards the sound' of *e* in the word ME (Smart 1836: 294).

Similar comments appear about American English pronunciation. Rush says that in the pronunciation of DAY, the 'last [sound] is the element *e* heard in *eve*, and is a gradually diminishing sound' (Rush 1827: 40; quoted by Ellis 1874: 1109; see also similar comments in Rush 1855: 87). Further evidence comes from a comment by another American, Henry Day, that 'some of the English vowels are diphthongal. Of these one [= /aɪ/] is always so; others only occasionally ... The elements occasionally diphthongal are *a* in *fame*, which commences with a sound peculiar to itself, and terminates with that of *e* in *mete*' (Day 1843: 445). Notice the caveat of 'occasional', which surfaces again in Ellis' commentary on /eː/ (Ellis 1874: 1108–11). However, Haldeman identifies the <ay> of PAY etc. with the quality, but not the quantity, of the German monophthong in WEH /veː/ (Haldeman 1860: 88). Whitney, on the other hand, draws explicit attention to his own diphthongal realisation: 'It is not, however, a pure vowel-sound; it only begins with *e*, and slides off into *i* (*pin, pique*)' (Whitney 1875: 210). (His mention of PIQUE as well as PICK probably indicates that the end-point of the diphthong lay between the two monophthongs.)

For Ellis, the whole question of the phonetics of /eː/ was 'a hotly-disputed point of English pronunciation', one result of which was that he had 'very carefully and frequently examined [his] pronunciation of this letter [i.e. (*ee*) = IPA [eː]], the orthoepists' 'slender a'] (Ellis 1874: 1109). He surveys the evidence and concludes that both monophthongal and diphthongal pronunciations were in regular use: 'Londoners, or persons living in London, who dispute the possibility of prolonging (*ee*), and who certainly immediately glide away towards (*i*) ... the audibility of this (-*i*) differs with different speakers, and even with different words for the same speaker' (Ellis 1874: 1109; see also Ellis 1869: 129).

For Sweet, Ellis's junior by more than twenty five years, the only realisation was diphthongal (see e.g. 1877: 110, 1890a: 7), but he draws attention to a different change in the character of the phoneme, namely the lowering of the starting-point: 'I find that boys under twelve speak a different language from mine: they broaden the vowels, making *take* almost into *tike*, *no* almost into *now*, *see* almost into *say*' (Sweet to Sayce 3 April 1880). By 1888, Sweet regarded the 'broadening' of /eɪ/ (as well as of /ou/ and /iː/) as being more and more a feature of 'educated speech' (Sweet 1888: 277), and, critically, a relatively recent change: 'The broadening of (ei, ou) to (əi, au) is not old: it was almost unknown thirty years ago, but is now beginning to push its way into educated speech.' Ellis had noted a lower starting-point for /eɪ/, but only for the lowering (in his terminology, 'widening') of /eː/ before /r/: 'Such words as (meeɹ, mooɹ) [= IPA [meːɹ, moːɹ]] have a very peculiar effect, either antiquated or illiterate, and are replaced by (meeɹ, mooɹ) [= IPA [mẹːɹ, mọːɹ]] *mare, more* (Ellis 1869: 202; see also 596).

According to Horn/Lehnert, as late as the 1950s, the vowel was monophthongal (again) in the speech of younger RP speakers: 'in der normierten Hochsprache . . . bei der jüngeren Generation' (Horn/Lehnert 1954.I: 325); cf. also Gimson 1964: 133–4. Wells, on the other hand, finds that such an 'almost monophthongal' realisation is restricted to a particular type of U-RP (Wells 1982: 293).

5.8.4 /ɛ/

According to Ekwall (1975: 27), the quality of /ɛ/ in the early Modern period was 'usually fairly close'. One can interpret this as indicating a vowel or vowels nearer to Cardinal [e] than Cardinal [ɛ]. By 1767, however, Sharp maintained that <e> in words like BED and FED was 'exactly the sound of the Italian or French é' (Sharp 1767: 8, 1777: 8).[82] Mackintosh, too, equates it with the 'the French é acute, short, in fesse, jette' (Mackintosh 1799: opp. 47). The word FESSE (buttocks) would have been pronounced then, as now, with /ɛ/, not /e/; similarly, the word JETTE. An articulatory description, suggesting a vowel in the area of CV [ɛ], is given by Thornton,[83] who says that 'the mouth [is] a little more shut than for *a*, but the lower lip exposing still more the lower teeth, and the tip of the tongue gently pressing the under teeth' (Thornton 1793: 281).

Statements by various phoneticians and writers in the nineteenth century indicate not only the amount of variation to be heard in the realisations of /ɛ/ but also (in Britain at least) the social implications of particular realisations. In 1801, the Swedish author, Peter Moberg considered the British vowel to be the same as the short Swedish <ä>, thus making it closer to Cardinal [ɛ] than Cardinal [e] (Nohlgren 1981: 56). Later, in 1874, Ellis was adamant that his own vowel (symbolised as (e), and interpretable as IPA [ẹ],[84] was much commoner than (ᴇ), a vowel marginally closer than Cardinal [ɛ], and the sound used by Scottish speakers such as Melville Bell and James Murray.[85] Furthermore, says Ellis, there is the '*tendency* of educated pronunciation, which affects thinness . . . towards (e) rather than (ᴇ)' (Ellis 1874: 1108). Sweet, whilst not commenting on the social implications of the various realisations, states categorically that 'it is impossible to determine whether (*e*) [IPA [ẹ]] or (æ) [IPA [ɛ̣]] is the commoner sound in such words as "head", "then" &c.' (Sweet 1877: 24). Not only has this range of realisations (from approximately Cardinals [ɛ] to [e]) continued throughout the RP of the twentieth century (cf. Jones 1962: 64; Gimson 1994: 102), but the social and, as far as one can judge, the regional implications of a closer pronunciation have remained the same.

Potentially, the most explicit description of /ɛ/ in nineteenth-century American English is to be found in Haldeman (1860: 78–9; cf. also Ellis 1874: 1190–1), who measured the precise gap between the front teeth – he calls it 'jaw aperture' – in the production of /ɛ/. His figure of a quarter of an inch would make the vowel – assuming there is no retraction of the tongue body – about half way between Cardinals [ɛ] and [e]. At the same time, this information confirms the correctness of Ellis's view that Haldeman's /ɛ/ was not as open as a French, German or Italian /ɛ/ (Ellis 1874: 1190). If one can accept Thornton's and Haldeman's descriptions as both accurate and representative, then the range of American realisations was rather less than those of RP, and was centred more around Cardinal [ɛ] than comparable pronunciations in British English.

5.8.5   /æ/

There is almost an apologetic note in the earlier comments on /æ/, suggesting that the writers had difficulty in saying precisely what its quality was. Nares (1784: 3) can only remark that it 'seems to be the same in other languages as with us', and Sharp (1767: 8; 1777: 8) attempts to describe it as like the 'short articulation of the English *aw*' – which would, however, have made it a backer vowel; this seems very unlikely – 'or rather of the Italian *a*'. That would indicate a central rather than a front or a back vowel. Fortunately, Smith (1795: 32) is more precise: /æ/ is 'a small degree narrower than the French *date* . . . and not quite so narrow as the German *hätte*'. This is the clearest evidence we have that the vowel was higher than CV [a]. The French vowel would have been very close to CV [a], and the German vowel to CV [ɛ], thus making the /æ/ about halfway between [a] and [ɛ] (or, less specifically, [æ]).[86] Walker too (1791: 11) points out that the short version of /aː/ 'is generally confounded with the short sound of the slender *a*' (i.e. /eː/), which would support Smith's statement that /æ/ was realised by a closer vowel than CV [a]. This is also given some credence, albeit some twenty or more years later, by the comment from Duponceau that 'the English alphabet has no powers to express the French sound of the vowel *a* [in CAR and PAR] . . . nor can the French alphabet represent the short sound of the English *a* in *hat, fat*' (Duponceau 1818: 229). Nevertheless, Mackintosh had equated it with the French '*ă* short' (Mackintosh 1799: opp. 47).

On the other hand, Mitford (1804/1804: 17) is adamant that the /æ/ of

FATHOM, PASSIVE and AMPLE is the 'same sound, short' as in FATHER, PASSING, EXAMPLE – which would argue for a realisation possibly retracted from CV [a].[87] Smart too notes that the vowel of AT is 'nearly the same as the open vowel in *far*' (Smart 1819: 34). Yet, a few years later, he points out that a Londoner 'has even a narrower sound' in FAT than a French speaker would have in the French word FAT (= coxcomb) (Smart 1836: v).

The only clear articulatory description of /æ/ comes from Thornton (1793: 281) – whose accent may have been some form of British English.[88] He says that 'the mouth must be still more open than for [IPA [ɔː]], the lower lip descends a little below the tips of the under teeth, and the tongue must lie flat'. This suggests more of a back than a front vowel – the tongue would have to be noticeably humped for a front vowel. Thornton's evidence is, however, ambiguous because of uncertainty as to what variety of English he was describing. If, because of his years in Scotland, the accent (presumably his own) was Scottish, then he would probably not have had a SAM ≠ PSALM contrast. Thus, his realisation of a single open phoneme could indeed have been further back.[89]

Perhaps the explanation for the varying opinions lies in a changing preference: in the 1770s an [a]-ish vowel, by the turn of the century and later an [æ]-ish one, but with some authors still preferring the older pronunciation. On the other hand, there is some evidence of socially conditioned variability in the 1770s, whereby the realisations of /æ/ acted as indicators of aspects of speakers' personalities. Kenrick says this: 'But who, except flirting females and affected fops pronounce *man* and *Bath*, as if they were written *maen*, *baeth*, or like *Mary*, *fair*, &c' (Kenrick 1773: 40; cf. Sheldon 1938: 278). He was presumably implying realisations which were close to the /ɛ/ of MANY and the /eː/ of FAIR, as well as those which were diphthongal, albeit starting from the general area of /æ/ and moving towards /ɛ/ (not the other way round). A comment by Ellis, almost 100 years after Kenrick, again emphasises the role that /æ/ played as a social marker. (æ) [= CV [a] or perhaps IPA [æ]],[90] was 'also used by very delicate speakers, especially educated ladies from Yorkshire, in such as words as: b*a*sket, st*a*ff, p*a*th, p*a*ss, *au*nt, in which (ah, a) [= IPA [ɐ, ʌ] and (ææ, aah, aa) [= IPA [aː, ɐː, ʌː] are also heard' (Ellis 1869: 594). The accompanying comment about /æ/ being 'the despair of foreigners' would well suggest, in the light of twentieth-century pronunciations, that the sound was (with specific exceptions such as the one above) closer to CV [ɛ] than to CV [a]. Parallels to these types of /æ/ can be heard in some current forms of RP (cf. Wells 1982: 281).

Taking all the comments into account, one can reasonably conclude that /æ/ had different realisations – at least during the fifty years from the 1770s: a vowel between CV [ɛ] and CV [a], and other vowels open and retracted from CV [a]. Thereafter from about 1830 onwards, the realisation was between CV [a] and CV [ɛ]. The lowering of RP /æ/ towards CV [a] is a relatively recent, late twentieth-century development (cf. Wells 1982: 291–2, Bauer 1994: 115–21, esp. 119).

5.8.6 /aː/ > /ɑː/

As with /æ/, determining the quality of /aː/ with any precision is not straightforward. However, one very useful description comes from Herries, who sets up two categories of vowel on articulatory criteria: those in which the sound is 'broader and fuller . . . arising from the flat posture of the tongue' (i.e. /ɔː, oː, ʊ, ʌ/) and, second, those in which 'the tongue reaches forward, and gradually ascends towards the arch of the palate . . . and renders the sound more *acute*' (i.e. /aː, æ, ɛ, eː, iː/) (Herries 1773: opp. 25). This would indicate that /aː/ had more of a kinaesthetically fronter 'feel' to it than /ɔː/. According to Walker (1791: 10), /aː/ is the 'middle sound of *a*, as between the *a* in *pale*, and that in *wall*'. An attempt can be made to calculate more precisely its quality by taking into account that its short equivalent was 'generally confounded with the short sound of the slender *a*' (1791: 11) – thus suggesting a vowel close to the open-mid quality of [ɛ] – and, second, by replicating the sense of equidistance between vowels. If articulatory equidistance is used, then the result is a central vowel between open and open-mid [ä̞ː]. If auditory equidistance is calculated from the second formants of the vowels (by whispering them), then the result will be a vowel half-way between /eː/ (assumed to be [e̝ː]), and /ɔː/ ([ɔ̝ː]). This gives another non-open vowel, but further forward, raised and retracted from CV4, i.e. [æ̞ː]. A compromise between the two calculations gives [a̝ː].[91]

That the vowel was not close to the front line of the vowel chart is evidenced by other comments. Sharp notes that it is a 'medium sound between *aw* [= IPA [ɔː]] and the English *a*', which is 'sounded like the Italian *a*, only somewhat longer' (Sharp 1767: 9; 1777: 5, 9). Smith, nevertheless, would have it nearer to the front than the back line, with his comment that it is 'the German *a*, exactly in . . . *hart*' (Smith 1795: 5); see the similar comments in Gilchrist (1824: 263). Further evidence for a fronter rather than a backer realisation comes from Adams, a good speaker of French, who had lived in the country for many years and who was well aware of the /a/ ≠ /ɑ/ distinction in French. He provides a social comment on what happens if

/aː/ is realised with too back an articulation: '*â* ouvert et grand est trop dur, et grossier, [qui] imite plûtôt le ris des paysans, ou des ivrognes, que le ris doux et poli du beau monde' (Adams 1794: 93). This would indicate, even so, that a backer vowel was in use at this time, though restricted to lower sections of society. Ekwall (1975: 23) maintains that during the first half of the nineteenth century the realisation 'in the standard language' was further back than CV [a],[92] which derived from 'the usual pronunciation in popular speech' during the last few years of the eighteenth century. Ellis (1869) has a similar remark to Adams's about the social marking of the realisation of /aː/: (*aa*) [= IPA [ɑː]: it is 'by some recognised as the common London sound meant for (aa) [= IPA [ӓː] or [ʌː]]' (Ellis 1869: 593).

Certainly, by the late 1860s, however, a fully back open-mid or centralised open articulation seems to have become generally acceptable: 'the sounds (aant) [= IPA [ʌːnt] or [ӓːnt] (laaf) [= IPA [lʌːf] or [lӓːf],[93] 'which are now extremely prevalent' (Ellis 1869: 149).

Other socially marked allophones which Ellis draws attention to are (aah) [= IPA [ɐː],[94] 'occasionally heard from "refined" speakers . . . while (ææ) [= IPA [aː]] used by others is too "mincing"' (Ellis 1869: 593). He elaborates by saying that (ææ) [= IPA [aː]] is the sound heard 'especially from ladies, as a thinner utterance of (aa) [= IPA [ʌː]] than (aah) would be' (Ellis 1869: 594).

Sweet draws attention to the diphthongal pronunciation of /aː/ (Sweet 1877: 111), with the tongue moving in the direction of the 'mid-mixed position' (i.e. IPA [ə]); however, he points out that it is 'not marked enough to be written' – presumably, the intensity level of the diphthong decreases rapidly during the glide itself. And this is paralleled by a later (private) comment that there is a 'very slight voice murmur' between /aː/ and /m/ in ARMS and ALMS – he writes the vowel (aaᵊ) – but the pure [ɑː] is used in PART (Sweet to Storm 18 May 1879). (In ARMS and ALMS, the 'slight voice murmur' could be the change in vowel quality by anticipatory nasalisation of the vowel before the /m/. Alternatively, in the first word it could be residual rhotacisation: see section 5.10.6.

5.8.7 /ʌ/

Herries' articulatory description indicates a back vowel: the tongue is 'pulled backwards, and much depressed, to render the cavity of the mouth as wide as possible' (Herries 1773: opp. 25). Thornton's articulatory description is less transparent: 'opening the mouth a very little, just sufficient to shew the edges of the upper teeth . . . and suffering the tongue and lips to remain at rest' (Thornton 1793: 280). This produces a variety of vowel-sounds because, critically, Thornton omits any mention of the position of the lower jaw.

Comparisons with other languages are noticeable in many of the attempts to describe the articulation of /ʌ/. The phonetic quality of the vowel followed by /r/ is described by Kenrick (1784: 56), in terms which allow one to calculate with some precision what the vowel sound was. With reference to the vowel in the words SIR, HUR, CUR, he says that it 'bears a near, if not exact, resemblance to the sound of the French *leur, coeur,* &c. if it were contracted in point of time'. Hence, a short, central to front, open-mid vowel. There is no evidence that it had the rounding of the French vowel.

Smith says that the Parisian pronunciation of SOTTE (i.e. /sɔt/ with a centralised [ɔ̈] allophone) comes nearest to it – 'but still not near enough'. German words like HOLL, BOLL, DOLL, similarly, do not convey the sound as an English /ʌ/ (Smith 1795: 49). Odell notes that it is close to the quality of the Italian *o chinso* or the *e* in the French words *je, me,* etc, or 'in the final syllables of the words gloirĕ, victoirĕ, &c. when they occur in poetical composition' – which would indicate a vowel closer to [ə] than to CV [ʌ] or to [ɐ] (Odell 1806: 4). Duponceau's remark that his 'ear discriminates between the sounds of the English word *buff* and the French word *boeuf*, though they are both the same as to quantity' (1818: 240) might be used as evidence that /ʌ/ was closer to front than back, and open-mid. (Curiously, he does not mention the difference in lip-rounding.)

Much later in the century, Sweet's comparison of English /ʌ/ and French /ɔ/, together with his remarks on different varieties of /ʌ/, allow one to establish with some accuracy the qualities of the realisations: 'when I round *but* I get a vowel sumthing like the French in *dot*' (Sweet to Storm 18 Feb. 1889). Similarly, 'the polite sound is [IPA [ɐ̈]]' (Sweet to Storm 18 Feb. 1889). This contrasts with the realisation of /ʌ/ in Cockney, [IPA [ɐ]], and the 'pure back (ɐ) [= IPA [ʌ]] in the West of England and Scotland (Sweet to Storm 18 Feb. 1889; see also Sweet 1888: 275).

During the course of the twentieth century, the RP realisation has moved gradually forward towards CV [a], although the backer articulations typical of the nineteenth century can still be heard (cf. D. Jones 1962: 86; Wells 1982: 131–2; Gimson 1964: 136, 1994: 105).

5.8.8   /ɒ/

Henslowe equates the vowel of WATCH and DOG with that of the French BANC and SANG (Henslowe 1840: 1). If he is correct, then (at least his) /ɒ/

had no lip-rounding and may not have been fully open. This feature is found in many of today's accents in the British Isles.

5.8.9   /ɔː/

Sharp states that /ɔː/ is 'pronounced like the French *a* in *Ame*' (Sharp 1767: 18; 1777: 18). Similarly, Nares regards /ɔː/ as equivalent to the 'legitimate sound of the long *a* in the French language' (Nares 1784: 7). Both quotations present difficulties of interpretation: the absence of any reference to rounding, and, secondly, an open rather than an open-mid tongue position. Duponceau's remark, if it refers to British rather than American English,[95] that the '*a* in *all* and *o* in *cottage* ... differ in nothing but quantity' (Duponceau 1818: 239), further obscures the situation.

According to Thornton, for /ɔː/ 'the mouth must be more open than for [/ʌ/], but the lower lip must not discover the lower teeth ... the tongue is drawn back, the tip of it resting on the bottom of the mouth' (Thornton 1793: 280). The comment about the lower lip 'not discover[ing] the lower teeth' clearly indicates that the lower lip (or at least most of it) must be clear of the front of the lower teeth: this can only happen if there is lip-rounding. From the remark about the position of the tip of the tongue, it is not possible to gauge whether Thornton's /ɔː/ had more of an open [ɒː] quality or an open-mid [ɔː] quality, or a position somewhere between these two. But later, in his description of /oː/, he gives an important clue: 'the sound resembles the *oo* [= IPA [ɔ]], but the *o* [= IPA [o]] is made more in the mouth than in the throat' (1793: 281–2). The strong retraction and lowering of the tongue for [ɒ] could, then, be responsible for the muscular sensation of a 'throat' sound. On Thornton's evidence, at least the /ɔː/ that he was describing appears to have been more open than open-mid.

The evidence for an open, not an open-mid, vowel comes from John Herries: the tongue is 'pulled backwards, and much depressed, to render the cavity of the mouth as wide as possible' (Herries 1773: opp. 25). Ellis's description in 1869 also suggests that the phoneme had allophones which were open, but he allows for the possibility of three vowels altogether: open, between open and open-mid (half-open), and slightly above open-mid: in London speech 'the drawl of short (ɔ) [= IPA [ɒ]] is only heard in drawling utterance, as (ɔɔd) [= IPA [ɒː]] for (ɔd) *odd*, as distinct from *awed*. Preachers often say (ɢɔɔd), but seldom or ever (ɢᴀᴀd) [= IPA gɔːd] for *God*' (Ellis 1869: 602).[96]

The study of American speech instituted by Grandgent (see e.g. Grandgent 1895) revealed that the majority of American speakers towards the end of the nineteenth century used unrounded, not rounded, realisations of /ɔː/ (Grandgent 1895: 452). Thirty years later, Krapp noted the same feature, but considered it to be more typical of New England than of America generally (Krapp 1925.II: 141).

5.8.10 /oː/ > /oʊ/ > /əʊ/

Most commentators simply note the existence of /oː/ without going into detail. Sharp, for example, regards it as 'like the French *o* or *au*' (Sharp 1777: 4). Evidence for it having been a distinctly rounded vowel – at least at the beginning of the period under consideration – is provided by Herries. The lip-posture, he says, is 'narrow and circular' (Herries 1773: opp. 25). Walker's only comment is that it is a long monophthongal sound (Walker 1791: 21).

The first explicit reference to a diphthongal quality is in the work of William Smith in 1795: 'The English long *o* has in it a shade towards the *oo*, or 6th sound [i.e. the vowel of woo, food etc.] (Smith 1795: 20). (Being Scottish, Smith would have had a monophthongal realisation of his Scottish English /o/ (equivalent to English English /oː/), and would very probably have noticed without difficulty the difference between a Scottish and an English pronunciation.) He does not specify any contexts in which the diphthong occurs, thus suggesting that in all contexts the realisation was diphthongal. A much earlier reference to dipthongisation could, however, be the Gildon-Brightland *Grammar of the English Tongue* (1711: 32): 'The Diphthongs ... *ou* ... or, *ow*, when they are truly pronounc'd, are compounded of the foregoing or prepositive Vowel, and the Consonant[] *w*' (see also Zettersten 1974: xxxii). However, this category of <ou> and <ow> words could refer to items such as noun and gown, which certainly contained a diphthong. The evidence is, therefore, not wholly convincing for a diphthongal pronunciation before the end of the eighteenth century.

From the early nineteenth century onwards, the diphthongal realisation is frequently referred to as becoming the normal (or near-normal) pronunciation. Smart (1836: v) points out that in London speech, the vowel 'is not always quite simple, but is apt to contract toward the end, finishing almost as oo in *too*'. A few years later, Henry Day comments that 'some of the English vowels are 'occasionally' diphthongal, one of which is '*o* in *bone*, which commences with the sound of *o* in *colt*, and ends with that of *oo*' (Day 1843: 445). (Day was a speaker of American English, and his remarks, especially since they appeared in an American publication, refer presumably only to American English.) The force of his 'occasionally' qualification is unclear.

Some of the most perceptive comments on /oː/(or /ou/) are provided by Ellis (cf. 1874: 1152). Discussing his own pronunciation he makes various points (the first of which has already been referred to: see above, 5.5.13). In an open syllable, e.g. KNOW, his /oː/ 'regularly' had diphthongisation; in NO, his /oː/ 'often' had diphthongisation. This should be compared with his comment five years earlier (1869: 602) that there were still some speakers who contrasted NO and KNOW by means of a monophthongal ≠ diphthongal contrast: in his notation, (noo) versus (noou). However, pronunciations such as the one he describes for KNOW, SOW, etc, 'especially when the sound is forcibly uttered' are 'exaggerations, and I believe by no means common among educated speakers'. But, he asks, what causes the diphthongisation? 'In really raising the back of the tongue . . . or in merely further closing or 'rounding' the mouth . . . or in disregarding the position of the tongue, and merely letting labialised voice, of some kind, come out through a lip aperture belonging to (u) . . . ?' He is obviously discussing a closer type of lip-rounding which does not involve associated tongue raising. The conditions under which the vowel is diphthongal are pre-pausal and before 'the (k) and the (p) series'. The tendency is 'least before the (t) series . . . Before (t, d) I do not perceive the tendency . . . The sound (bóut) is not only strange to me, but disagreeable to my ear and troublesome to my tongue. Even (boo'ʉt) sounds strange . . . Mr Bell's [i.e. Alexander Melville Bell] consistent use of (. . . óu) as the only received pronunciation thoroughly disagrees with my own observations . . . As to the "correctness" or "impropriety" of such sounds I do not see on what grounds I can offer an opinion. I can only say what I observe, and what best pleases my ear' (Ellis 1874: 1152).

The fronting of the first element to a centralised or central element (e.g. [ə] or [ɜ]) was noticed towards the end of the nineteenth century: Sweet remarks on the stylistically conditioned central starting-point of the diphthong (Sweet 1890b: 76), adding that 'the constant use of [IPA [əw]] gives a character of effeminacy or affectation to the pronunciation'. Phipson (1895) writes of 'the fashionable London pronunciation' of ONLY as 'əunli', and compares it with the 'vulgar hounli' (Phipson 1895: 217). In 1909, Daniel Jones noted that the starting-point was 'slightly rounded' – i.e. not the full rounding that would be associated with a vowel transcribed with an [o] (Jones, D. 1909: 86). [97] The comment by Henry Alexander in 1939, who remarked on a sudden (and unexpected) change in the starting-point during the mid to late 1930s, suggests that this particular pronunciation was becoming more frequent (Alexander 1939: 23). The result was the possibility of homophones developing such as BODE, BIRD; SOWED, SURD; WHOLE, HURL; OWNED, EARNED.

The source of the change from [oʊ] to [əʊ] could be, firstly, the influence of the less prestigious south-eastern form [ʌʊ] – used, for example, by one of Montgomery's 'educated' speakers (Montgomery 1910: 48)[98] – followed, secondly, by a socially derived reaction to such a pronunciation, leading, in turn, to the use of a closer starting-point.

5.8.11   /ʊ/

Herries draws attention to the specific lip-position: 'narrow and circular' (Herries 1773: opp. 25), and Gilchrist notes that 'the sole difference' between FULL and FOOL is the length of the vowel in FOOL (Gilchrist 1824: 262). See below, section 5.8.12, for further discussion of this latter point. From the second half of the twentieth century, there is evidence to show that the realisation of this phoneme has already begun to shift forwards and to unround – at least in younger forms of RP (see e.g. Henton 1983, esp. 358).

5.8.12   /uː/

Thornton's description in 1793 of /uː/ indicates very close rounding: 'the organs are continued in the same position as in pronouncing [IPA [o]], except that the lips are so much contracted as to leave only a very narrow aperture, and are much protruded' (Thornton 1793: 282).

Gilchrist (1824: 262) notes that 'the sole difference' between FULL and FOOL is the length of the vowel in FOOL. This characteristic is discussed later by Sweet, who writes of (fuul), with a 'pure narrow (uu)' being 'simply a drawled (ful) . . . which is very common' (Sweet to Storm 24 Oct. 1878). The 'usual sound', however, is the 'diphthongic (uw) or (uw)'. Sweet adds, in emphasis of the diphthongal realisation, that 'Englishmen imitate the pure (uu) and (ii) of foreign languages with (uw) and (ij), never with homogeneous (ii), (uu)' (Sweet to Storm 24 Oct. 1878). An even more precise description of the difference between the central and the finishing points of the diphthong is: '[the] lips [are] almost completely closed at the end' (Sweet to Storm 10 Jan. 1880).

Gradual fronting of RP /uː/ towards [ʉː] has been noted by various phoneticians, including Wells (1982: 294), Henton (1983) and Bauer (1994:

115–121). The latter describes this change as 'probably one of the most dramatic' in late twentieth-century RP.

5.8.13 /ɜː/

Lepsius's description, in 1863, that the <u> of CURTAIN is 'pronounced more closed than [the <u> of] *cut*' (Lepsius 1863: 50–1) shows that a realisation close to, if not identical to, a close-mid central vowel had already developed.

5.8.14 /ə/

Little is said that leads to anything other than a very general appreciation of the quality of /ə/. Comments abound regarding the 'obscureness' of the sound, sometimes referred to as the 'natural vowel', and its use particularly in weak forms in English (see e.g. Smart 1819: 36, Smart 1842: 26–7)[99] and in certain monosyllables in French (Perry 1795: x). In 1767, Sharp described the final <a> of PAPA as 'a medium sound between *aw* and the English *a*' (Sharp 1767: 5), thus suggesting a vowel approximately central and open-mid. Fifty years later, Smart is careful to point out that speakers may not use quite the [ə] sound: it can be 'a sound that wavers between that in *at* and that in *ut*', as in COMBAT, NOBLEMAN, and ABJURE (Smart 1819: 36–7). Such comments, taken with those much later in the nineteenth century by James Murray and others in connection with the phonetic notation for the *OED*,[100] show that speakers had a range of unaccented vowel sounds that they could call upon, apart from /ɪ/ and /ə/. It is only later in the nineteenth century that /ə/ acquires even greater frequency of usage.

In 1889, Johan Storm queried the use of the 'obscure *ä* [= IPA [ə]] as in America', to which Sweet replied that he knew 'nothing of such a sound' (Sweet to Storm 21 Jan. 1889). If Storm was referring to the stressed vowel (as seems most likely), then he had obviously noticed a pronunciation with stressed /ə/ – which is in use today in some forms of RP.

5.8.15 /ʌɪ/ > /aɪ/

During the twentieth century, the phonemic notation of the first element of this diphthong has consistently been with either an [a] or an [ɑ], despite the firm evidence that most of the realisations, which can be counted as coming within the ambit of RP, have a starting-point which is neither of these two sounds. Sweet's notation (ai) [= IPA [ʌɪ]] in e.g. his *Primer of*

Spoken English (1890a) has given superficial credence to a realisation which starts on or close to CV [a], even though Sweet's notation (ai) does not represent a diphthong with a starting-point on or even near this vowel: Sweet's (a) is equivalent to IPA [ʌ].

The majority evidence from about the 1770s to the present day is that the starting-point has been noticeably more centralised. Sharp considers it 'like the Greek $\varepsilon\iota$ or something like the French i long before n in *Divin, Prince, Enfin*' (Sharp 1767: 4) – which could be construed as indicating a starting-point which is not even close to CV [a]. Herries, in 1773, by contrast, gives more convincing evidence of its pronunciation with his comment that it is a like a vowel beginning with that of RUN and ending with that of SEE. This would make it approximately [ʌɪ] (Herries 1773: opp. 25).[101] Odell, too, implies much the same, although his finishing-point is closer to /ɪ/ than /i/, hence /ʌɪ/ (Odell 1806: 13).

In 1836, Smart provides a useful comparison between three different possible pronunciations: (1) a sound 'begin[ning] with the sound heard in ur, but without sounding the r, and taper[ing] off into $\overset{1}{e}$' – this is the version heard from 'well-bred Londoners'; (ii) a sound starting with $\overset{3}{a}$ and moving to $\overset{1}{e}$ – 'but this is northern'; and (iii) a sound starting with $\overset{4}{aw}$ and moving to $\overset{1}{e}$ – 'which is still more rustic' (Smart 1836: iv).

A few years later, in 1843, Day says that the vowel (in American English) starts 'from a position near that in which the *a* of *father* is formed' and going to 'that in which short *i* is produced' (Day 1843: 445). This would make it [äɪ]. Sweet's notation in 1888 in the Revised Organic Alphabet (his modified version of Visible Speech) implies an open, central starting-point (which he elsewhere notates phonemically as (ai)). A back, open-mid starting-point characterises the 'vulgar' pronunciation (Sweet 1888: 275).

There are exceptions to this view that /aɪ/ in the late eighteenth and well into the nineteenth century was [ʌɪ] ish in quality. Sharp, as we have seen, likens the diphthong to 'the Greek $\varepsilon\iota$ or something like the French i long before n in *Divin*' (Sharp 1767: 4). Adams, too, by his re-spelling of THIGH as (thei), strongly suggests a starting-point which is not only front but in the area of open-mid, perhaps [θɛɪ] (Adams 1794: 85). Ellis, in a long discussion of /aɪ/, which includes a consideration of how the contrast in Greek between $\chi\varepsilon\acute{\iota}\rho$ and $\chi\alpha\hat{\iota}\acute{\rho}$ is pronounced – at least at Eton College – notes the different realisations of /aɪ/ (Ellis 1869: 107–8). The transcriptions by Walker and Melville Bell would be equivalent to IPA [ʌɪ]; Walker also allowed for the equivalent of IPA [ai] (Ellis 1869: 117). Smart's transcription was equivalent to IPA [ɐi], whereas Ellis hears 'Londoners' saying IPA [ai] (Ellis 1869: 108). He does accept, though, that a diphthong starting from the equivalent of IPA [ɐ] is heard from some speakers (Ellis 1869: 594).

What evidence we have indicates that sometime between about the end of the eighteenth century and 1870, the starting-point must have moved further forward – at least for some speakers. One hears still in conservative forms of RP a starting-point well retracted from CV [a] (Gimson 1989: 132). Jones, commenting in 1956 on this diphthong, uses the equivalent to /ɑɪ/ in his transcriptions and adds that the /ʌɪ/ transcription, with a 'rather open central vowel' [= IPA [ɐ]] as its starting-point, is sometimes regarded as being 'commoner than any other in the South'; he personally doubts it (Jones, D. 1958: 57).[102]

As early as 1767, the allophonic difference between the diphthong in STRIFE and the same (phonemic) one in STRIVE ('Pre-Fortis Clipping')[103] had been noticed by Sharp, who commented: 'There are 2 ways of sounding the long *i* and *y* [though both long] the one a little different from the other, and requiring a little more extension of the mouth . . . but this difference, being so nice, is not to be attained but by much practice, neither is it very material' (Sharp 1767: 23). His list of items is not uncontroversial, however. He instances I and AYE, HIGH and HIGH-HO, BY'T (= BY IT) and BITE, and SIGH'D and SIDE. It is doubtful if AYE did indeed differ phonetically from I. BY'T and BITE, HIGH and HIGH-HO, and SIGH'D and SIDE might have been slightly different, but depending on prosodic (and, particularly in the last pair of words, on grammatical) factors.[104]

5.8.16   /ɔi/ > /ɔɪ/

Perry (1793: xvi-xvii) and Smith (1795: 79) make the distinction between /ɔi/ and /ʌɪ/, and indicate by their notations and commentary that the realisation of /ɔi/ was [ɔːi], not [ɔɪ]. Knowles, however, has [ɪ] as the finishing-point (1837: 7). The evidence is too slim for one to make a judgement about a phonetic change between 1795 and 1837. Ellis, writing in 1874, includes no discussion of /ɔɪ/ (since none of his key-words contains this phoneme), but his own pronunciation of ENJOINED begins with a vowel closer to CV [ɒ] than CV [ɔ] (Ellis 1874: 1172). Sweet, in 1888, comments specifically on this: 'boy with *o* of n*o*t sounds peculiar to me. The diphthong begins in my pronunciation with the mid-wide German short *o*' (Sweet to Storm 16 May 1888).

The question of the durational values of different parts of the diphthong are discussed by Sweet. In 1877, he had analysed both /ɔɪ/ and /aʊ/ as consisting of two perceptibly different elements of duration: short + long

(Sweet 1877: 67). By 1888, however, he had modified his view: both elements in the diphthong were treated as being of equal length, with a glide element between them (Sweet to Storm 24 Sept. 1888). These remarks bear some relationship to the late eighteenth-century notations which implied [ɔːi] as the pronunciation (see above). Sweet's 'long' second element of 1877 may be the reflex of the late eighteenth-century [i], not [ɪ], of Herries, Perry, and Smith. If this is correct, then one might conclude, albeit tentatively, that this pronunciation began to become less noticeable during the period 1877–88, when Sweet next comments on the diphthong.

Twentieth-century transcriptions of this diphthong vary. Ward's /ɔɪ/ starts closer to CV [ɒ] than to CV [ɔ] (Ward, I.C. 1945: 112). Jones's /ɔi/ (despite the fact that his ɔ is equivalent to IPA [ɒ] in a comparative transcription) starts 'with a sound near in quality to that of long ɔː' (Jones, D. 1956: 62). Gimson, however, notes the existence of a range of sounds, starting close to CV [ɑ] ('some conservative speakers') and almost as close as CV [o] ('popular London') (Gimson 1980: 133).

5.8.17 /ɔʊ/ > /aʊ/

The quality of /ɔʊ/ requires comment, since it has been assumed that it was either /aʊ/ or /ɑʊ/ in quality by this time (cf. Gimson 1989: 138). Its distant source is ME /uː/.

In seventeenth century London English, the pronunciation was [ʌʊ], though one phonetician (Isaac Newton) gives it as [aʊ] (Dobson 1968: 684). Even so, Dobson is too hasty in stating that the 'final transition to PresE [au] is slight and easy' (Dobson 1968: 685). There is considerable evidence that, at least in the later part of the eighteenth century and well into the nineteenth century, the starting-point of the diphthong was equatable more with the vowel of BALL (and sometimes CUT), rather than SAM or PSALM.

Search's special notation of an italic *u* for the first element in ICE is used again for the first part of the diphthong in NOUN, thus suggesting that an earlier [ʌʊ]-ish articulation, characteristic of the seventeenth century, still persisted, at least for some speakers (Search 1773: 16). By now, this was probably a minority pronunciation.

Elphinston typifies most of the writers when he notes that the 'ou' of HOW, LOUD, etc. consists of 'au rapid', i.e. [ɔː], followed by 'oo' or 'w' (Elphinston 1765: 13–14).[105]

Very detailed descriptions of /ɔʊ/ in Walker (1791) allow one to calculate with considerable precision how the diphthong would have sounded.

Walker says explicitly that it 'is composed of the *a* in *ball*, and the *oo* in *woo*, or rather the *u* in *bull*' (Walker 1791: 36). His description of the *a* of *ball*, *wall* is: 'The German *a* . . . is formed by a strong and grave expression of the breath through the mouth, which is open nearly in a circular form, while the tongue, contracting itself to the root, as if to make way for the sound, almost rests upon the under jaw' (Walker 1791: 5). The 'circular form' in the word *wall* could, of course, derive from the rounding of the /w/; but in *ball*, any rounding of the /b/ should derive, instead, from the vowel. (The reference to a 'German *a*' is amplified somewhat in 1791: 11: 'the deep broad German *a*'; and 'the . . . sound . . . which we more immediately derive from our maternal language, the Saxon', section 83.) A more specific articulatory description of the 'German *a*' is found in the 1797 edition: 'The German *a*, heard in *wall*, not only opens the mouth wider than the former *a* [i.e. the *a* of *father*], but contracts the corners of the mouth so as to make the aperture approach nearer to a circle, while the *o* [of COT etc.] opens the mouth still more, and contracts the corners so as to make it the *os rotundum*, a picture of the letter it sounds' (Walker 1797: 4). Note also (1797: 11) in connection with the /ɔ:/ of LAUD, SAW: 'though it must here be noted, that we have improved upon our German parent, by giving a broader sound to this letter . . . than the Germans themselves would do'. This could be interpreted as /ɔ:/ with a more noticeably lowered F_2 than the sound that begins /ɔʊ/.

The dating of a transition to (or gradual preference for) an open and unrounded starting-point is not easy. Adams (1794: 114) aligns the 'ou' of PLOUGH with the 'au' of Italian PLAUTO, and Duponceau, writing in the United States (but born and brought up in France until his late teens),[106] states that the starting-point of the diphthong was 'no other in fact than that of the French *a* which is not . . . to be found singly in our language' (Duponceau 1818: 258). An interpretation of this would be [äʊ].

Ellis appears to suggest that the expected form in London in the late 1860s would have been (əu) [= IPA [əu]] – again not with an open starting-point (Ellis 1869: 136). Furthermore, a front, but still half-open, starting point (eu) [= IPA [ɛu]] was 'very common among Londoners, even of education' (Ellis 1869: 136). He instances DOWN TOWN pronounced as (deun teun (Ellis 1869: 597). In all, he lists five different realisations of /aʊ/: in IPA transliteration, [əu], [ɤu, [ou], [ʌu], [ɐu] (Ellis 1869: 597; see also 594).

By the last quarter of the nineteenth century, there is no doubt that the starting-point was still open-mid and the end-point still unrounded: 'a̅u̅ in *house* with length distributed over both elements and the glide between them' (Sweet to Storm 24 Sept. 1888). In IPA notation, Sweet's vowel would have been [ʌ·ʊ·]. Martin's suggestion that the better notation would be /ɔu/ ('with a very short quantity of ɔ') (Martin 1889: 83) could be taken as confirmation of the still rounded quality of (at least some) pronunciations of the diphthong.

The transition to [aʊ] or [ɑʊ] appears to have been a twentieth-century development. Ward writes of 'Southern speakers tending towards Cardinal a' (Ward, I. C. 1945: 118). Jones notes that some speakers of RP begin the diphthong with CV [ɑ] (Jones, D. 1962: 107). Gimson implies that [ɑʊ] may be a reaction to the fronter starting-point of the diphthong in various regional forms of English, especially in the London area (Gimson 1980: 137–8). In the absence of extensive sets of data, one can only surmise that the fronter starting-point (at least in RP) may be the result of regional influences.

5.9   Consonant systems

5.9.1

The consonant system during and after the late 1770s was as it is today: /p t k b d g tʃ dʒ f θ s ʃ h v ð z ʒ l r w j m n ŋ/,[107] except that two additional phonemes, /ʍ/ and /x/, were in limited use. Both were in the process of undergoing change. Walker's notation (1791) typifies a popular method of transcribing the 25 phonemes (including /ʍ/, but not /x/): <p, t, k, b, d, g, tsh, j, f, *th*, s, sh, h, hw, v, TH, z, zh, l, r, w, y, m, n, ng>.

5.9.2   /ʍ/

/ʍ/, contrasting with /w/, is retained, apparently by most speakers of educated Southern English, until at least the second half of the nineteenth century; thereafter its use becomes more infrequent.[108] One finds in Spence (1775), for example, transcriptions of words such as WHICH and WITCH, WHINE and WINE, which show that the contrast was still in existence (Spence 1775: n.p.). Dyche, however, later points out that 'the *h* is quiescent' in words like WHEEL, WHERE and WHEN (Dyche 1805: 82). On the other hand, Sweet, in his publications more than a century later, from 1877 until 1908, uses /ʍ/ without exception – and, critically, never flags it as requiring special attention; other phoneticians and language-teachers of the period, however, are more circumspect.[109] Even though Sweet lists (wh) as a consonant separate from (w) (e.g. Sweet 1888: 277), and transcribes those 'wh-' words which can have /ʍ/ with (wh) (e.g. in WHICH, 1877: 115,

WHISPER, 1888: 300), he does admit that his (wh) is 'an artificial sound for the natural (w) of South English' (Sweet 1877: 112). By 1888 he was saying that 'generally in Southern StE (wh) is levelled under (w)' (Sweet 1888: 278). He continues to use it, however, as late as 1908 (e.g. in WHAT, WHICH). Montgomery maintains that the use of /ʍ/ is restricted to females (Montgomery 1910: 13–14).

Further evidence that the phoneme was beginning to be lost from English English during the period from the late eighteenth to the late nineteenth centuries comes from various sources. The printer Philip Luckombe, in 1771, expressly claimed that the contrast no longer existed. He lists WEAR, WARE, WERE, and WHERE as homophones; similarly WEIGH and WHEY, WETHER and WHETHER (Luckombe 1771: 486). As indicated earlier (5.2.8), considerable caution is needed when accepting such statements at face-value – Luckombe maintains no contrast, for example, between MOTH and MOUTH! An early nineteenth-century writer who hints that a change was in progress (but not yet completed) is Hornsey with his remark that '*h*, though not quite mute, sinks' in words like WHILE, WHET and WHERE (Hornsey 1807: 168). Ellis notes that the name of the American phonetician and philologist Whitney would 'certainly . . . generally in London' be with a /w/, not a /ʍ/ (Ellis 1874: 1142), and that 'by far the greater number of educated people in London say (w)' in the word WHEAT (Ellis 1874: 1144–5).[110] Additional evidence that it was beginning to drop out comes from Francis Newman, writing in 1878 at the age of 72, who thundered that 'W for Hw is an especial disgrace of Southern England' (1878: 692).[111] Twentieth-century observations show that it has been used sporadically in RP – and still is.[112] In North America, the phoneme (or its analytical counterpart /hw-/) has been retained much longer than in RP (Wells 1982: 229–30). Grandgent (1893a: 277; 1895: 448), from his survey of American English pronunciation a century ago, concluded that the loss of /hw-/ was 'comparatively rare'.

5.9.3   /x/

In 1888, Sweet listed this as one of the three consonant 'sounds' that had been lost between ME and ModE (the others were [ç] and [ɤ]) (Sweet 1888: 278). The only eighteenth-century writer to comment specifically on the absence of /x/ from English English is Sheridan, himself an Irishman. (/x/ still remains today in Scottish and Irish varieties of English.) He notes that the 'peculiar guttural sound in the Irish pronunciation is not suited to English organs' (Sheridan 1781: 43–4). Carrol (1795), however, does quote words in which /x/ is used in English English, but they are 'foreign' words like ACHILLES, ARMAGH, GROENINGEN, and UTRECHT. For Scottish and Irish words like LOCH and LOUGH, most earlier writers choose to use either /f/ or /k/ word-finally, with the /k/ forms becoming dominant.[113]

5.10   Consonant phonotactics (structural)

5.10.1   /kn-/

According to Yeomans, the cluster /kn-/ (as in KNIFE) was still in use in Scotland – but presumably by speakers of Scots, not English (Yeomans (1759: 43).

5.10.2   /tl-/ and /dl-/

The use of /tl-/ and /dl-/ in place of word-initial /kl-/ and /gl-/ had been remarked upon in the seventeenth century by e.g. Robert Robinson and Simon Daines (cf. Dobson 1968: 951). The process appears to have gone unnoticed by the eighteenth- and nineteenth-century orthoepists – if indeed it was still in use. Of the later phoneticians and linguists, Sweet never mentioned it; Max Müller (1891: 199) maintained that it was not used; but several commentators disagreed. Ellis, on the other hand, regarded /tl-/ and /dl-/ as 'very usual' in England (Ellis 1874: 1219; cf. also 1874: 1165). Another phonetician, Thomas Hallam, also noted its extensive use in educated speech in the second half of the nineteenth century (cf. MacMahon 1983). He heard consistent pronunciations of GLAD, GLIMPSE, GLORY, GLORIOUS and GLADSTONE with /dl-/; of CLEARER, CLOSE and DECLARE with /tl/. However, with other speakers, the consistency was not maintained, and word-initial /kl-/ and /gl-/ were used somewhat variably (cf. Ellis 1869: 95).

A Londoner, F. Chance, writing to *Notes & Queries* in 1872, quoted /dl-/ as his 'habitual pronunciation', adding that he felt 'pretty sure that the great majority of Englishmen do as I do' (Chance 1872: 124). His letter elicited three replies, all of which seriously doubted whether it was used to any great extent (H. 1872, R. 1872, Sergeant 1872). Ellis commented on the use of /tl-/ in the speech of an American visitor from Virginia (Ellis 1874: 1218). The matter was raised again fifteen years later, in 1887, specifically with reference to American English, when Albert Tolman, of Ripon College, Wisconsin, claimed that three-quarters of his University students pronounced GLADNESS with /dl-/, not /gl-/ (Tolman 1887). Rippmann, in 1906, noted the use of /kl-/ for /tl-/ in AT LAST in 'careless speech' (Rippmann 1906: 31); /tl-/ for /kl-/was used (?only) 'in Somerset'. Wright noted the use of both /tl-/ and /dl-/ as 'individualism[s] among educated people in all parts of England' (Wright 1905: 246, 251). At about the same time, Jespersen gave both a /kl-/ and a /tl-/ pronunciation of CLYDE (Jespersen 1909/1961: 409).[114] Word-initial /tl-/ and /dl-/ can still occasionally be heard in RP.[115]

5.10.3 /-ŋ#l-/~/-ŋ#gl-/

ENGLAND and ENGLISH, for Sweet, were 'always (iqglənd) [= IPA [ɪŋglənd]], (iqglish) [= IPA [ɪŋglɪʃ]], as far as I know' (Sweet to Storm 27 Nov. 1879). That is, the option of /-ŋ#l-/ in these words did not exist (cf. RINGLET with /-ŋ#l-/). Western (1902: 58) and *EPD*1 (1917) have only the /-ŋ#gl-/ forms.

5.10.4 /pw-/, /bw-/ *and* /kw-/

POT and BOIL, with the optional pronunciations /pwɒt/ and /bwɔɪl/, had been noted in the seventeenth century by Wallis (Kemp 1972: 208; also quoted by Nares 1784: 138). /bw-/ in BUOYANT and BUOYING are found in Angus (1830: 62); BUOY is noted by Smart 1836 and Knowles; the pronunciation lived on until at least the 1870s (Ellis 1869: 602, Newman 1878: 695). The extension of /kw-/ (in words like QUEEN) to QUOIN /kwɔɪn/ appears to be a late eighteenth- or early nineteenth-century development: see Hornsey 1807; and similarly *Q*UOIT /kwɔɪt/ (Anon. 1796; Smart 1836).

5.10.5 /j/

With few exceptions, the eighteenth- and early nineteenth-century writers regarded the /juː/ sequence in words such as YOU, FEW, and VIEW as a diphthong (because of the influence of the orthography), and classified it with the other vowels.[116] Regardless of the method of classification, what is of interest is the distribution of /juː/: there was slightly greater freedom of occurrence than there is today in RP – and considerably more so than in today's GenAm. Thus a #CCC cluster with /j/ as the third element is nowadays restricted in RP to /spj-/, /stj-/, and /skj-/. In the eighteenth and early nineteenth centuries it could occur – or rather one can analyse the phonetic sequence in this way – in other contexts.[117] Furthermore, two

#CC clusters, /kj-/ and /gj-/ had a higher functional load than in today's accents. Examples are:

/#plj-/:	PLUME (Anon. 1812)
/#blj-/:	BLEW (Fulton & Knight 1800, Anon. 1812, Knowles 1837); BLUE (Elphinston 1790, Angus 1830, Knowles 1837; Hornsey 1807: 134 is ambiguously worded). (For Knowles 1837, the pronunciation of BLUE as /blu:/ was 'affected'; he preferred /blju:/). The yod-insertion in the word BLUE is noted by Sweet (Sweet to Storm 21 Jan. 1889): it is still heard, he says, but the yod-less pronunciation is more frequent.
/#krj-/:	RECRUIT (Buchanan 1766)
/#glj-/:	GLUE (Anon. 1812)
/#slj-/:	SLEW (Anon. 1812, Angus 1830); SLUICE (Buchanan 1766, Fogg 1792)
/#tʃj-/:	CHEW (Anon. 1812)
/#dʒj-/:	JUNE (Anon. 1812)
/#rj-/:	RUE (Anon. 1812), RUDE (Webster 1847)[118]

Furthermore, according to one writer (Kenrick 1784: 54), there was considerable freedom in the presence or absence of /j/: speakers could choose to use /u:/ or /ju:/ in words such as SHOE, DO, RUE, RULE, TUNE 'and many others'. The use of /dju:/ for DO and /ʃju:/ for SHOE, if indeed they were correctly quoted, is noteworthy.

The clusters /#kj-/ and /#gj-/ already existed for words such as QUEUE and GULES, which contained a following /u:/. The extension of the process to words containing two different vowels appears to have originated in the early seventeenth century – Robert Robinson, a Londoner, was the first to note it, in the word GUARDED, in 1617 (cf. Dobson 1968: 210, 952; see also Horn 1905: 42 for the reference to Richard Hodges, 1644). John Wallis, probably also from the London area, and writing in 1653, refers to the frequent insertion of /j/ in CAN, GET, and BEGIN (1653: 40; cf. Kemp 1972: 206). By the latter part of the eighteenth century, however, its use was diminishing: Sheridan 1781: 56 restricts it to GUIDE and GUILE; Nares (1784: 28–9) thought KIND with a /kj-/ a 'monster of pronunciation', fortunately heard only on the stage.[119] Later, he says that 'this strange corruption is now . . . quite abolished' (Nares 1784: 138). The evidence from Webster (1789) contradicts this with his comment on the 'very modern [English stage] pronunciation of *kind, sky, guide*, &c.' used as 'the elegant pronunciation of the fashionable people both in England and America'. (His personal view, however, was that it was 'barbarous') (Webster 1789.II: 109).

Indeed, as Walker's (1791) transcriptions indicate, the use of epenthetic /j/ was by the end of the eighteenth century restricted to fewer vowels than in Wallis's day. It continued, however, to be a feature of some forms of English until at least the last quarter of the nineteenth century.[120] Sweet attributed its occurrence to the front realisation of /aː/ – although he fails to note that this alone will not explain its occurrence before the central vowel at the beginning of /ʌɪ/.

Walker 1819 has it in KIBE, KIND, KINDLY, KINDNESS, KINE, and KITE – all the words that would have had /#k( )ʌɪ- / – but not in any words with /#kaː- /(e.g. CARD). Similarly, there is /gaːrd-/ for GARDEN, but the editor[121] points out that 'polite speakers' interpose a /j/ between the /g/ and the vowel. For GUARD, then, the pronunciation can only be /gjaːd/. Words with initial /g/ and /ʌɪ/ as the vowel (e.g. GUILE) are transcribed consistently with /gjʌɪ-/.

Angus, in his dictionary of 'words difficult to spell or pronounce', gives the 'C + j' pronunciations for GUARANTEE, GUARANTY, GUARDIAN, GUIDANCE, GUILEFUL, GUISE, KILE, and KINDNESS (Angus 1830: 84, 89). But Smart regards the /kj-/ and /gj-/ pronunciations generally as being 'affected' (Smart 1836: ix, section 55; xi, section 76). Knowles follows Walker's distributions (Knowles 1837: 7); but Smart, despite his earlier antithesis to the use of such clusters, extends the process to allow /gj-/ before the vowel of GIRL and GIRT (Smart 1842: 25).

By the 1860s and later, the /kj-/ and /gj-/ forms were reverting to their older /k-/ and /g-/ pronunciations.[122] Ellis comments, in 1869, that the forms were 'now antiquated' and 'dying rapidly out' (Ellis 1869: 206; see also 1869: 600 where they are described solely as 'antiquated . . . but still heard').[123] Confirmatory evidence is provided by Sweet, who, in 1877, commented that the process was old-fashioned: his father, born in 1814, used it (Sweet to Storm 29 April 1877; see also Sweet 1888: 270). In Sweet's own generation – he himself was in his mid-thirties at the time – he thought 'it must be quite extinct' (Sweet to Storm 18 May 1879; see also Sweet 1877: 48–9). However, the Hallam Papers indicate otherwise: Queen Victoria's second son, the Duke of Edinburgh (1844–1900) was heard, in 1881, to say CASE with /kj-/; and her fourth son, Prince Leopold (1853–84), again in 1881, had /gj-/ in AGAINST. Earlier, in 1868, the Earl of Harrowby[124] used /gj-/ and /kj-/ in GUIDANCE and KIND. George Anson (1821–98), in 1882, did the same in AGAIN and GUIDANCE.

A rather more subtle distribution of /j/ is noticeable in the speech of the Wesleyan minister George Osborn (1808–91) in 1865: CAN and GATES have the inserted /j/; but CAST and REGARD have not. (If CAST had the back vowel /aː/, then the rule would be: k, g + j /— [front vowel]). By comparison, the Bishop of Manchester and a near-contemporary of

Osborn's, James Lee (1804–69), pronounced AGAINST and AGAIN without an inserted /j/.

Equivalent pronunciations were in use in the USA until well into the twentieth century. Grandgent's survey of the 'familiar speech of highly educated persons' (Grandgent 1895) revealed /kj-/ and /gj-/ pronunciations in only a very small number of informants, of whom most were from the South. He concluded that these pronunciations had nearly died out, except in eastern Virginia (Grandgent 1891: 460). Krapp, however, noted their use, albeit infrequent, in Southern, especially Virginian, speech in 1925. The field-workers for the Linguistic Atlas of the Eastern United States (Kurath & McDavid 1961) found examples of them between 1934 and 1948 (Kurath & McDavid 1961: 175).

Sweet's pronunciation of MILK, with /mj-/ and a syllabic /l/ as the vowel element deserves attention. In Sweet (1880), he gives both (mjlk) and (mjulk) (Sweet 1880–1: 210). Later, he noted only the (mjlk) pronunciation (Sweet 1885: xxv). His explanation for the pronunciations was that the rounded vowel (presumably /ʊ/) had influenced the /l/, which had become syllabic. The vowel had then unrounded and become a 'glide-vowel'.

ENTHUSIASM could be pronounced, said Sweet, with either a /j/ after the /θ/ or not (at least in Sweet's own speech); similar variation was noted by Western (1902: 81). A yod-less pronunciation of NEWS was regarded by Sweet as 'vulgar' (Sweet to Storm 21 Jan. 1889), although Ellis (1869: 601) had noted the pronunciation, alongside /juː/, without adverse comment. A synchronic comparison of mainly three varieties of late twentieth-century English (RP, GenAm., Australian) by Bauer (1994: 103–10) illustrates the degree of variability to be heard today in the distribution of /j/, as well as the emergence of patterns of stability and potential change.

5.10.6   /r/

Evidence can be found of some types of Southern English English which were either non-rhotic or nearly so before the end of the eighteenth century. For example, Walker (1791) makes the important observation that English speakers, especially Londoners, say the /r/ so 'soft' that the pronunciations of STORM and FARM are 'nearly as if written *staum, faam*' (Walker 1791: 50).[125] Yet, he does *not* omit post-vocalic <r> (/r/) in his Dictionary entries. Whatever the reason for this latter – a desire not to confuse the reader? the acceptability of post-vocalic /r/? – he is clearly indicating that the articulation of the vowels in these words was either a type of diphthong ([ɔə], [ɑə]), or, with a faster gliding action, ([ɔ˟], [ɑ˟], or else practically monophthongal [ɔː] and [ɑː].[126] Carrol, in 1795, is explicit about the absence of /r/ in WORSTED, but also, critically, in the first syllables of NORTHERN and NORTHERLY (Carrol 1795: 54).

Further evidence that non-rhoticity had generally been achieved – certainly by the first half of the nineteenth century – comes from re-spellings. Anon. (1813: 1–2), for example, re-spells GAPE and SALVE as 'garp' and 'sarve' and rhymes them with HARP and STARVE; he or she also re-spells CALM as KARM. If /r/ had been present pre-consonantally, this rhyme pattern would not have been possible. Parallel to this is his or her re-spelling of TALK as 'tawk' to rhyme with HAWK. If TALK had still contained /l/, HAWK would not have rhymed with it – unless the putative /l/ of TALK and /w/ of HAWK had both been realised as velar approximants. Writing in 1840, Henslowe is adamant that English is non-rhotic: 'the English pronounce ə̂ [= IPA [ʌ]] instead of r: thus 'not og-r, och-r, but og-ə̂, och-ə̂' (Henslowe 1840: 16–17, 68). In the work of Smart (1842), /r/ is a 'trilled dental consonant', noted, for example, in the words RAY and PRAY. But in the words REGULATOR, EARS, ASUNDER, THUNDER, BEAR, ARMED, and STARTS, the post-vocalic <r> is not marked in the same way as the <r> of RAY and PRAY. This appears to indicate non-rhoticity (Smart 1842: 17–18). His 'untrilled r' (1842: 18), presumably refers to the <r> which has a vocalic realisation. On the other hand, he clearly confirms the existence of rhoticity in 'well-bred London society' with the observation of 'the tongue being curled back during the progress of the vowel preceding it, the sound becomes guttural, while a slight vibration of the back part of the tongue is perceptible in this sound' (Smart 1836: vii).[127]

An interesting observation by Sweet, in his private correspondence but not in his published descriptions of English, indicates that a diphthongal realisation of /ɑː/ lingered on well into the nineteenth century. There is, he says, a 'very slight voice murmur' between /ɑː/ and /m/ in ARMS and ALMS , i.e. [ɑəmz], which contrasts with the 'pure' [ɑː] in PART (Sweet to Storm 18 May 1879).

The otherwise observant comment by Search (1773: 14) suggesting that the phonetic transition from some vowels to a putative /r/ was accompanied by a [ə]-like glide ('This short "ʊ" . . . is commonly inserted between "ē, ī, ō ū" and "r", as in "there, beer, fire, more, poor, pure, our," which we pronounce "theʊr, bɪʊr, fʊɪʊr, moʊr, puʊr, ʊuʊr"') cannot be taken at face value to confirm the existence of post-vocalic /r/ in these pronunciations.[128] He could just as well have been referring to the pronunciation of the words under conditions of liaison to any following words beginning with a vowel.

Ellis, Sweet, Soames, Montgomery, Rippmann and all later phoneticians describe a non-rhotic accent of 'RP'. Sweet, questioned by Storm in 1880, explicitly ruled out the possibility of pre-consonantal /r/: 'I make no r-glide in liberty, & judging from the incapacity of Englishmen in general to do so, I doubt whether any of them do so, except provincials' (Sweet to Storm 23 Feb. 1880). However, a possible explanation for the belief that an /r/ was present comes from a remark by Sweet in 1878 to the effect that the realisation of /ɑː/ was slightly diphthongal, both in an 'r'-full word like ARMS, as well as in the less common word ALMS: 'alms and arms should be both (ɑɑmz), both, however, being really an approach to (ɑɑə), the (ɑɑ) not being absolutely monophthongic', and with 'a very slight voice murmur' between the end of the vowel and the /m/ (Sweet to Storm 18 May 1878). A year later, he had convinced himself that the transcription should be (ɑɑəmz) (Sweet to Storm 18 May 1879). Yet, his Visible Speech transcription of PART in the same letter (Sweet to Storm 18 May 1879) contains no /r/ realisation whatever.

It is the existence of this 'very slight voice murmur' which may lie at the root of the assumption made by other, competent phoneticians such as Hallam[129] that rhoticity (as well as semi-rhoticity) did exist amongst educated speakers. Hallam quotes examples such as Prince Leopold, Queen Victoria's fourth son, and younger than Sweet by eight years, pronouncing SURE and HEAR with a 'faintly uttered' /r/, and BEFORE with a definite /r/. The politician Benjamin Disraeli (1804–81), whose background was London, was heard in 1872, to say (dɑˈrˑbi) [= IPA [ˈdäˑɹbɪ]]; his pronunciation of LANCASHIRE also had word-final /r/. Charles Dickens (1812–70) in 1866 used (mɑˈsˑtɛr) [= IPA [ˈmästəɹ]] – his background, however, included a rhotic area of the South of England, Portsea. Stafford Northcote (1818–87), heard in 1875, had a similarly 'faintly uttered' /r/ in BEFORE and GOVERN. George Edward Yate (1825–1908) in 1882 pronounced an /r/ in COURSE. Lovelace Tomlinson Stamer (1829–1908), in 1874, had /r/ in CONCERNING, LORD, WORD. Emily Faithfull (1835–95), in 1878, was rhotic in DAUGHTERS, but used no /r/ in HORSE. By contrast, Joseph Lycester Lyne, perhaps better known as Fr. Ignatius (1837–1908), was consistently non-rhotic; Hallam, in 1883, recorded no /r/ in his HEARD, LORD and POOR. The evidence for considerable variation between rhoticity and non-rhoticity, with intermediate semi-rhoticity, especially during the later nineteenth century in the educated South of England, is, clearly, very strong.[130] The phonetic transcription by Eustace (1969), together with a tape-recording, of the speech of an elderly aristocratic lady, Flora Russell (born in 1867), highlights the semi-rhotic nature of her accent: see especially 1969: 75.

5.10.7   Intrusive /r/

The first example of this occurs in Sheridan (1762), who notes that in Cockney speech proper names ending in <a>, such as BELINDA, are pronounced with a word-final /r/ (Sheridan 1762: 34). The transcription of COLONEL with an intervocalic /r/ (see e.g. Sharp (1767: 30; 1777: 30 and further references in Ellis 1874: 1074) derives from the earlier, sixteenth- and seventeenth-century spelling, 'coronel', which lingered on into the eighteenth century. James Elphinston (1786–7) is the first writer to draw specific attention to intrusive /r/ in colloquial educated speech: IDEAR and WINDOWR are his examples (Elphinston 1786–7.I: 116). He also has the spellings FELLOR and WINDOR for the speech of the 'low Londoner' (Elphinston 1786–7.II: 35). By 1817, Anon. was pointing out that 'many people are guilty of this [same] error', and goes on to recommend that 'great pains should be taken to avoid' it (Anon. 1817: 15–16). Less dogmatically, perhaps, Anon. is content to point out (to schoolchildren) that they 'must be careful not to let 'the *w* go into the consonant sound of *r* in the words *saw* and *law*' (Anon. 1830: 13). Anon. notes that 'in London, the Babel of all kinds of dialects . . . [and] Cockney blunders . . . [speakers] add R to all words ending with the open sound of the vowel A, as in *idear*' (Anon. 1834: 346).

Ellis regarded intrusive /r/ as a characteristic of 'illiterate' speech, quoting the examples 'drawing, law of the land, window of the house' (Ellis 1869: 201). Later in the same work, however, he restricts the regional focus of it to Norfolk, where there is 'a great tendency among all uneducated speakers . . . in Norfolk' to say DRAWING and SAWING with the intrusive /r/ (1869: 603).[131]

Sweet's opinions on the incidence of intrusive /r/ (as in IDEA(R) OF IT) varied. In 1885, he had noted that it was very frequent ('**sehr häufig**') (Sweet 1885: xxix); by 1888 he was saying that in Standard English it occurred 'often', whilst in Vulgar English it was mandatory (Sweet 1888: 278). The following year, however, he was rather more dogmatic, albeit in private, about its prevalence in Standard English: 'I have made special observations on this point, & I am now certain that the insertion of the *r* . . . is *absolutely universal* in educated southern English speech & has been for the last 50 years. I hear it from old as well as young . . . Yet they all deny it' (Sweet to Storm 7 April 1889). Two months later, he had modified this opinion: 'I know as a fact that most people say (ɑidiər əv) in rapid speech' (Sweet to Storm 23 June 1889). The stylistic factor of rapid speech is noted again: 'most educated speakers of English ... in rapid speech' (Sweet 1890a: viii). It also occurred, he said, in 'careless speech' (Sweet 1890a: 12). A decade later, he was less certain, stating merely that it was 'widely spread ... not universal' and generally occurring 'only in rapid speech and in closely connected groups of words' (Sweet 1899: 41). Western, in 1902, noted its high frequency of occurrence in educated speech, as well as its universal occurrence in vulgar speech (Western 1902: 110).

In the first edition of the *EPD* in 1917, Daniel Jones stated that the majority of (educated) speakers did not use it. Nearly thirty years later, Ward found that it was 'heard among educated speakers' and that it was spreading: 'even in districts and among classes where it has not been known, the younger generation is using it' (Ward, I. C. 1945: 147). By 1960, it was used by a 'very large number of people, educated as well as uneducated' (Jones, D. 1960: 197). Wells notes that it is 'apt to occur in RP' (Wells 1982: 223).

5.10.8   /h-/ ~ Ø

The history and pronunciation of words with initial <h> in accented position is somewhat complex. The existence of /h/ in the phonology of Old English, but not of Anglo-Norman French (whence some of the <h>-ful words have entered English), together with loans from Latin with initial <h>, have all contributed to the current situation in which some words in educated English English are subject to variation between /h/ and Ø; e.g. HOTEL.[132] In other respects, speakers of RP will generally agree on the allocation or otherwise of /h/ to words with initial <h>.

The period from the late eighteenth to the mid-nineteenth century was one in which a change occurred in the distribution of /h/ in some of these words. The pattern can best be seen in the following, based on an examination of several works:

	With /h/	Without /h/
HERB	1795, 1836	1764, 1767, 1784(b), 1785, 1791, 1793, 1796, 1807, 1828
HERBACEOUS	1791, 1813	
HERBAGE		1775, 1785, 1791, 1796
HERBAL	1791	1775, 1785, 1796
HERBALIST	1791	1775

	With /h/	Without/h/
HOMAGE	1791, 1828, 1836	1764
HOSPITAL	1828, 1836	1764, 1775, 1781, 1784(a), 1784(b), 1785, 1791, 1792, 1796
HOSPITABLE	1775, 1791	
HOST	1791, 1828	1775, 1784(a)
HOSTESS	1791	1775
HOSTLER		1764, 1767, 1775, 1784(a), 1784(b), 1785, 1791, 1792, 1795, 1796, 1781, 1828, 1836
HOTEL	1813	
HUMAN	1791, 1836	1784(a)
HUMBLE	1764, 1793, 1828	1781, 1784(a), 1785, 1791, 1792, 1793, 1836
HUMBLY	1785	1781, 1785, 1791
HUMOUR(-)	1764, 1793, 1836	1767, 1775, 1781, 1784(a), 1784(b), 1785, 1791, 1792, 1795, 1796, 1828, 1836

Sources:

> 1764 Johnston; 1767 Sharp; 1775 Spence; 1781 Sheridan; 1784(a) Anon.;
> 1784(b) Nares; 1785 Walker; 1791 Walker; 1792 Fogg; 1793 Perry; 1795 Smith;
> 1796 Anon.; 1807 Hornsey; 1813 Anon.; 1828 Jameson; 1836 Smart.

A comment on /h-/-less pronunciations in the later nineteenth century concerns the word HUMBLE. Viëtor (1904: 25) had noted that by the beginning of the twentieth century, /ʌmbl/ was old-fashioned ('veraltet'); Sweet, writing some twenty-five years earlier, in 1877, had thought that /hʌmbl/ was 'commoner' than /ʌmbl/ (Sweet to Storm 29 April 1877). These two remarks indicate the gradual loss of /ʌmbl/ in favour of /hʌmbl/.

5.10.9   /p/~/f/

DIPHTHONG in Sweet (1890a: viii) has a /p/ (his own pronunciation); but in correspondence twelve years earlier, he gives equal place to a pronunciation with an /f/. Western points out that Sweet's /dɪpθɒŋ/ is not the 'usual' pronunciation (Western 1902: 109).

5.10.10   /-mb/

This cluster is exemplified by the single word RHOMB (Nares 1784, Walker 1791, Hornsey 1807).

5.10.11   /-ns/~/-nts/; /-nʃ/~/-ntʃ/

No examples have been noticed in print of /-nts/ rather than /-ns/ in words like PRINCE and ABSENCE until 1917.[133] Ellis, in 1874, in a discussion of the pronunciation of <-ance> and <-ence> makes no mention of it (Ellis 1874: 1161), nor does it appear in the transcription of SUBSTANCE in Ellis's own pronunciation (Ellis 1874: 1171). Sweet, however, was questioned on it by Johan Storm, the Norwegian phonetician and philologist, in the 1870s, which suggests that he had noticed it in educated English speech. Sweet is quite adamant that 'we never sound the (t) of (ts) after (n) in (æbsns), (prezns) etc' (Sweet to Storm, 29 April 1877, 18 May 1879). All of this is circumstantial evidence that the pronunciations with epenthetic /t/ and /d/ came into use sometime in the second half of the nineteenth century. By 1917, Jones was noting that FENCE and FRENZY with post-nasal /t/ and /d/ could be heard in Public School Pronunciation (i.e. RP) (*EPD*1: xix).

5.10.12   /-nʒ/ ~ /-ndʒ/; /-nʃ/ ~ /-ntʃ/; /-lʃ/ ~ /-ltʃ/; /-lʒ/ ~ /-ldʒ/

The variability in the distribution of /n/ or /l/ followed by either /ʃ/ or /tʃ/ (/bɛnʃ/ ~ /bɛntʃ/, /bʌlʒ/ ~ /bʌldʒ/) became a matter of comment only later in the nineteenth century. However, analysis of the available evidence from the pronouncing dictionaries from the period 1775 to 1836 reveals something of the emerging unsteadiness, which was later to become a matter for comment.[134]

Several generalisations can be made:

1   Through the period 1775 to 1836, the dominant preference is /-ndʒ/ (Spence 1775, Sheridan 1781, Fogg 1792, Smith 1795, Jameson 1828, Smart 1836). The only example of /-nʒ/ is Anon. 1796, but even (s)he varies between this and /-ndʒ/: cf. CHANGE and HINGE with /-nʒ/, but RANGE and SINGE with /-ndʒ/. Storm's remark in 1888 to James Murray (the editor of *OED*1) that Sweet's omission of a post-nasal plosive in DANGER, CHANGE and CENTURY seemed to be a minority usage (Storm to Murray, 12 April 1888) is added confirmation of the dominance of the /-ndʒ/ cluster. On the other hand, Laura Soames quotes it as a variant (Soames 1899: 85). One of the non-native observers, Western (1902: 102), also notes the variability, as does *EPD*1 (1917). Wagner (1899: 95) gives only a /t/-less pronunciation of BENCH, LUNCH, INCH, BELCH.

2   There is a slight preference for /-ntʃ/ rather than /-nʃ/ in the 1790s (cf. Elphinston 1790, Carrol 1795, Anon. 1796 with /-ntʃ/, and Spence 1775 and Nares 1784 with /-nʃ/. Smith 1795 uses

both patterns, and they appear to be phonologically conditioned, with /-nʃ/ following /ʌ/ (BUNCH, PUNCH), and /-ntʃ/ following /ɪ/ (CLINCH, FLINCH, INCH, WINCH).

3   There is no discernible pattern in the distribution of /-lʃ/ and /-ltʃ/. Spence 1775, Nares 1784, Smith 1795 and Jameson 1828 have /-lʃ/, and Elphinston 1790, Carrol 1795 and Smart 1836 have /-ltʃ/. Only Anon. 1796 uses both: FILCH with /-lʃ/, and SQUELCH with /-ltʃ/.

4   /-lʒ/ is restricted to Smith 1795 and Anon. 1796.

5   If /-nʃ/, then /-ndʒ/ (e.g. Spence 1775, Jameson 1828).

6   If /-lʃ/, then /-ldʒ/ (e.g. Spence 1775).

5.10.13   /-lt/ ~ /-t/

The loss of /l/ in words like TALK and HALF is an early Modern English phenomenon (cf. Dobson 1968: 988–91). The retention of /l/ in words like VAULT and SALT (containing word-final /t/) has continued in RP and GenAm. up until the present day. Anon. notes its optional use in 1797 in ALMOND (Anon. 1797: n.p.).

Examples of FAULT without /l/ (i.e. /fɔːt/) can be found up until about the end of the eighteenth century (cf. Nares 1784, Elphinston 1790, Fogg 1792, Anon. 1796); thereafter pronunciations with /l/ (/fɔːlt/), which had existed earlier (cf. Spence 1775, Nares 1784, Smith 1795), predominate: cf. Anon. 1813, Jameson 1828, Smart 1836. (Incidentally, Nares 1784 notes that both pronunciations could be heard.)

The word VAULT follows a similar pattern to FAULT. Forms without /l/ can be found in Johnston 1764, Elphinston 1790, and Fogg 1792. Nares 1784 makes an important grammatical point: VAULT as a noun is sometimes pronounced with, as well as without, the /l/; but VAULT as a verb can only be with the /l/. Pronunciations of VAULT with obligatory /l/ are to be found in Spence 1775, Smith 1795, Anon. 1796, Jameson 1828 and Smart 1836.

One can conclude, then, that from about the turn of the nineteenth century, pronunciations with /l/ in FAULT and VAULT become the norm.

5.10.14   *Unaccented /-n/ ~ /-ŋ/*

Walker observed that the 'best speakers' used /n/, not /ŋ/ in the unaccented syllables of words like SINGING, BRINGING, although his personal preference was clearly for the /ŋ/ form (Walker 1791: 49).[135] According to Wyld, who based his conclusion on 'field-work' amongst a large number of his relatives, the early nineteenth-century form was with /-n/, and the restoration of the /-ŋ/ pronunciation took place amongst educated speakers during the 1820s and 1830s (Wyld 1913: 21). Ellis, however, quotes a noble lord's 'Ain't yer goin' to have some puddin'?' in 1874 to show that 'vulgar and illiterate English' might still be classed as part of educated English, and adding that 'the so-called vulgarities of our Southern pronunciation are more frequently remnants of the polite usages of the last two centuries, which have descended, like cast-off clothes, to lower regions' (Ellis 1874: 1243).

5.10.15   Elision

The following indicates the types of elision which late eighteenth-century authors felt they needed (for whatever reason) to point out to their readers. Some, in the categories of *Elision of* C_2 *in* C_1C_2, *Elision of* C_1 *in* C_1C_2, and *Elision of C in VC#*, would be regarded as impossible in today's RP; they are marked with a *. Larger data-sets, however, are required before a clearer picture can emerge about the scale of such diachronic phonotactic changes.

5.10.16   Elision of C_2 in Word-Medial $C_1C_2C_3$

ftn	OF(T)EN Nares 1784, Adams 1794, Carrol 1795
	SOF(T)EN Nares 1784, Fogg 1792, Carrol 1795
spb	RASPBERRY Smith 1795
stb	WRIS(T)BAND Carrol 1795
stk	WAIS(T)COAT Carrol 1795
stl	HUS(T)LER Carrol 1795
	OS(T)LER Nares 1784, Smith 1795
stn	CHES(T)NUT Nares 1784, Fogg 1792, Smith 1795
	FAS(T)EN Fogg 1792
sθm	AS(TH)MA Sharp 1767, Carrol 1795
mpt	ATTEMPT Yeomans 1759, Nares 1784, Smart 1836
	EXEMPT Anon. 1784
	PROMPT Carrol 1795, Hornsey 1807
	TEMPT Sharp 1767, Anon. 1784, Fogg 1792, Hornsey 1807
	EMPTY Yeomans 1759, Adams 1794
ndb	BAN(D)BOX Nares 1784
nds	GRAN(D)SON Nares 1784
	HAN(D)SOME Johnston 1764, Nares 1784
	LAN(D)SCAPE Nares 1784

ndl	LAN(D)LORD Nares 1784
ldl	WORL(D)LY Johnston 1764, Nares 1784
lvp	TWEL(VE)PENCE* Fogg 1792
lvm	TWEL(VE)MONTH* Nares 1784, Smith 1795
rtg	MOR(T)GAGE Anon. 1784, Nares 1784, Fogg 1792, Smith 1795, Carrol 1795
rnm	GOVER(N)MENT Carrol 1795

5.10.17 Elision of C_2 in C_1C_2

kw	AWK(W)ARD* Nares 1784
dw	ED(W)ARD* Anon. 1784
	MID(W)IFE* (pronounced /midif/) Anon. 1784
sw	S(W)OON* Sharp 1767, Adams 1794
rw	FOR(W)ARD* Anon. 1784
ln	KIL(N)* Carrol 1795

5.10.18 Elision of C_1 in C_1C_2

kt	PERFE(C)T* Elphinston 1790
	VERDI(C)T* Elphinston 1790
dn	WE(D)NESDAY Mackintosh, Mackintosh & Mackintosh 1799
vp	FI(VE)PENCE* Smith 1795,
ðz	CLOA(TH)S Nares 1784, Fogg 1792, Mackintosh, Mackintosh & Mackintosh 1799
lk	FA(L)CON Johnston 1764, Sharp 1767

5.10.19 Elision of C in VC#

BRISTO(L)* Johnston 1764, Carrol 1795[136]

5.10.20 Elision of C_2V in $C_1C_2VC_3$

EXTRAOR(DI)NARY* Nares 1784
OR(DI)NARY* Nares 1784

5.10.21 Assimilations: /tj/ > /tʃ/

Kenrick, like many of his contemporaries, was uneasy about assimilations producing /tʃ/ in CREATURE, NATURE, QUESTION – even though 'a very general custom prevails, even among the politest speakers' (1784: 50). Cf. also: 'The colloquial expressions *can't you*, *won't you*, which fall upon the ear like *can't tshoo*, *won't tshoo*' (Pickering 1828: 211).

5.11 Consonant phonotactics (lexical-incidental)

Most of the following examples are taken from the period 1759–1830.

5.11.1 Fricative~Fricative

/f/~/v/:
Only /f/: VAT Carrol 1795, VENEER Carrol 1795
Only /v/: CALF's HEAD Nares 1784, Smith 1795
HOUSEWIFE (/'hʌzɪv/) Mackintosh, Mackintosh & Mackintosh 1799
PHIAL Sharp 1767, Anon. 1784, Nares 1784, Fogg 1792, Carrol 1795
WIFE's-JOINTURE Smith 1795
VIAL Smith 1795

/θ/~/ð/
Only /θ/: WITH Sheridan 1781 ('generally aspirated', but /wɪð/ before a vowel),
Anon. 1784, Perry 1793 (before a consonant), Anon. 1796
WITHOUT Perry 1793
WITHSTAND Sheridan 1781
Only /ð/: BATHS Hornsey 1807
BENEATH Johnston 1764, Sharp 1767, Sheridan 1781, Anon. 1784, Nares
1784, Fogg 1792, Carrol 1795, Anon. 1796, Jameson 1828
PATHS Hornsey 1807
SHEATH (vb.) Sheridan 1781
UNDERNEATH Sheridan 1781, Fogg 1792, Carrol 1795, Anon. 1796,
Jameson 1828
WITH Jameson 1828
WITH 'before a vowel' Anon. 1784, Anon. 1796
WITHOUT Sheridan 1781
WREATH Johnston 1764, Sharp 1767, Sheridan 1781 Anon. 1784, Fogg
1792, Anon. 1796

/s/~/z/
Only /s/: CRISIS EPD1 (1917)
DECEMBER Anon. 1784
DESIGN Nares 1784
NASAL Nares 1784
US Johnston 1764, Anon. 1784, Nares 1784, Carrol 1795
Only /z/: DISARM Fogg 1792
DISCERN Nares 1784
EVASION (/ɛ've:zjən/) Carrol 1795
GREASY 'Always (griizĭ), I think' (Sweet to Storm 29 April 1877)
HOUSEWIFE (/'hʌzwɪf/) Smart 1836
MEASURE (/'mɛzjər/) Carrol 1795
SACRIFICE Nares 1784, Smith 1795
SUFFICE Smith 1795, Mackintosh, Mackintosh & Mackintosh 1799
Both CRISIS 'is (kraisis) ... Some say, perhaps, (kraizis)' (Sweet to Storm 23 Dec.
1878)

PHTHISIS 'The following are all possible, & may all be heard, for all I know: (tisis, taisis, thisis, thaisis, tizis, taizis, thizis, thaizis)' (Sweet to Storm 23 Dec. 1878)

TRANSITION '(trɑns·izhən) or (trɑnz·ishən) . . . never (trænsishən)' (Sweet to Storm 29 April 1877)

/s/~/ʃ/
Only /s/: LEAꜱH Fogg 1792
           WINCH Fogg 1792
Only /ʃ/: NAUꜱEATE Nares 1784
           PINCERS Nares 1784

/z/~/ʃ/
Only /ʃ/: TRANꜱIENT Nares 1784

/z/~/ʒ/
Only /ʒ/: CROꜱIER Sheridan 1781
           HOꜱIER Sharp 1767, Sheridan 1781, Kenrick 1784
           OꜱIER Sharp 1767, Sheridan 1781, Anon. 1784, Smart 1836

5.11.2   *Fricative~Fricative + C*

/s/~/sk/
      Both: SCEPTIC Sheridan 1781, Nares 1784, Fogg 1792
/s/~/sj/
      Only /ʃ/: IꜱꜱUE Sharp 1767
                   TIꜱꜱUE Sharp 1767
/ʃ/~/sk/
      Only /ʃ/: ꜱCEPTIC Yeomans 1759
                   ꜱCHEDULE Johnston 1764, Sharp 1767, Spence 1775, Smith 1795, Anon. 1796, Mackintosh, Mackintosh & Mackintosh 1799, Smart 1836,
                   ꜱCHISM Yeomans 1759, Johnston 1764, Sharp 1767, Spence 1775, Smith 1795, Anon. 1796, Jameson 1828, Smart 1836
      Only /sk/: 'The regular American' one (Sweet to Storm 10 Jan. 1880)
      Both: ꜱCHISM Adams 1794, Jameson 1828

5.11.3   *Fricative~Plosive (or Ø)*

/f/~/p/:
      Both: HICCOUGH Anon. 1813
/θ/~/t/
      Only /t/: AUTHENTICK Observator 1789
                   AUTHORITY Observator 1789
/ʃ/~/k/
      Only /k/: MACHINIST Nares 1784
/x/~/k/
      Only /x/: ACHILLES Carrol 1795
                   UTRECHT Carrol 1795

/x/~/g/
    Only /x/: GROENINGEN Carrol 1795
/x/~ Ø
    Only /x/: ARMAGH Carrol 1795
/h/~ Ø
    Only /h/: CHATHAM Carrol 1795
            CLAPHAM Carrol 1795
            DISHONEST Carrol 1795
            DISHONOUR Carrol 1795
            GRESHAM Carrol 1795

5.11.4 Fricative~Approximant

/v/~/w/
    Only /w/: VEAL Webster 1789.II: 113
            VESSEL 'The pronunciation of *w* for *v* is a prevailing practice in England and America. It is particularly prevalent in Boston and Philadelphia . . . Vast numbers of people in Boston and the neighbourhood use *w* for *v*, yet I never once heard this pronunciation in Connecticut' (Webster 1789.II: 112–13).

5.11.5 Plosive~Affricate

/k/~/tʃ/
    Only /k/: CHALDRON Fogg 1792
      Both: CHART Nares 1784, Hornsey 1807, Jameson 1828, Anon. 1813, Jameson 1828
            CHIVALRY C.— 1830
/g/~/dʒ/
    Only /g/: GIBBERISH Johnston 1764, Sharp 1767,
            GIMLET Carrol 1795,
            GYRATION Perry 1793

5.11.6 Plosive~Plosive + C

/k/~/kw/
    Only /k/: QUADRILLE Nares 1784, Fogg 1792
            QUINT Hornsey 1807
            QUOTA Fogg 1792, Anon. 1796
            QUOTATION Anon. 1796
            QUOTH Nares 1784
      Both: QUOTE Nares 1784

5.11.7 Plosive~Ø

/g/ ~ Ø
    Only /g/: SUGGEST (/sʌgdʒest/) Carrol 1795

5.11.8 Affricate~Affricate

/dʒ/~/tʃ/
Only /dʒ/:   NORWICH Adams 1794
              OSTRICH Yeomans 1759, Nares 1784

5.11.9 Nasal~Nasal + C

/ŋ/~/ŋg/
Only /ŋ/:   WRONGER Sheridan 1781

5.12 Consonant realisations

5.12.1 /t/

An interesting observation by Sweet concerns the precise positioning of the front half of the tongue for the /t/ in NATURE, and 'also generally' for NET: not only the 'point but also the flat of the tongue just behind the point' are used, giving 'an approximately palatal character' to the sound (Sweet to Storm 29 April 1877). This is the source of the same comment in Sweet 1890b: 101. In addition, the passive articulator could be further forward than alveolar: 'often point-palate outer' (i.e. the very front edge of the alveolar ridge). The same, more forward articulation he noted as well for /d, s, l, n/. In his published works, however, he opts for a more general description, where /t, d, n, l/ 'are formed in the medium position' (cf. Sweet 1908: 44).

The use of a 'tapped' realisation of /t/ (and /d/) in certain phonological contexts in GenAm. appears to be a twentieth-century innovation. Haldeman (1860) makes no reference to it, not even in his lengthy transcriptions of American pronunciations (1860: 127–9); nor does Whitney (1875: 244, 249). Similarly, Ellis (1874: 1218–19), in his transcriptions of two American speakers, does not refer to it, but he does transcribe a Californian pronunciation of PARTNER with a /d/ (1874: 1230). Grandgent (1895: 456) simply states that the word ATOM contains a /t/.

Various writers from the late nineteenth century onwards note the use of the glottal plosive (glottal stop), but not as an allophone of /t/: only as the reinforcing element of initial accented vowels (see Eijkman 1909: 443–4 for a summary of the comments). Rippmann (1906: 32) notes that in 'uneducated southern English speech', [t] is 'occasionally dropped between vowels, in such words as *water, butter*'. By 1945, the glottal plosive's existence as an allophone of /t/ under certain phonological conditions had been acknowledged by Ward (1945: 135–6), although her wish to hear it less used ('it certainly makes for indistinctness') is apparent! D. Jones (1960: 151) acknowledges its existence among some speakers of RP in certain phonological contexts, as does Gimson (1962: 164). Wells (1990b: 6) also notes its increasingly frequent use, particularly in 'casual RP speech'. The conclusion must be, then, that the occurrence of [ʔ] as an allophone of /t/ in RP is very much a twentieth-century development, and the the degree of its use is increasing.[137]

In a passage which is not easy to interpret unambiguously, Yeomans (1759) appears to be trying to describe both voice onset time (thereby creating aspiration) and devoicing: 'The inward sound to *g*, as it is pronounced in *gave*, *give*, &c. at the endings of words, whispers or speaks a *k* . . . that whispering, dying afflation of the breath, which is breathed immediately after the *g* is sounded, the same as *t* after *d*, and *p* after *b*. It is in fact the aspirate *h*, stopt by the linguist in different places of the mouth' (Yeomans 1759: 36–7).

5.12.2   /θ/

Sweet, in 1880, noted that three different types of /θ/ could be heard: apico-interdental, apico-dental, and apico-gingival (Sweet to Storm 23 Feb. 1880); the last two were the commoner pronunciations. Both Lloyd and Jespersen regarded the apico-dental realisation as the norm (Jespersen 1909/1961: 401). Further differences, between present-day British (English and Scottish) apico-dental and Californian lamino-interdental articulations, are noted by Ladefoged & Maddieson (1996: 143). The precise histories of these two articulations are not yet known.

5.12.3   /ð/

In the word CLOTHES, the /ð/ is 'evanescent' (presumably an approximant) (Sweet to Storm 29 April 1877), a process which continues still in RP.

5.12.4   /ʃ/

Although the sound was 'generally point-palate inner' (Sweet to Storm 23 Feb.1880), Sweet had already noticed that in (neitʃə) 'the *sh* seems to be nearer the teeth (more "forward") than in *she* etc' (Sweet to Storm 29 April 1877). There are precise parallels to this in late twentieth-century RP.

5.12.5 /n/

Double articulations of /n/ are noted by Sweet. In 1877, he pointed out that in his pronunciation of OPEN there was a bilabial-alveolar nasal (Sweet 1877: 213). Similarly, 'I often pronounce (kq/nd·ishən) [= IPA [kɳ̂ŋ'dɪʃən]] with simultaneous (q) [= IPA [ŋ]] and (n) whispered, but this I am not quite certain of yet' (Sweet to Storm 19 Feb. 1879).

5.12.6 /r/

Any attempt to reconstruct the precise phonetic qualities of /r/ must take into account the wide range of sounds heard in late twentieth-century English as allophones of /r/, either within idiolects or across group-accents. All have presumably existed in equivalent or near-equivalent forms during the last 200 years. To expect a single '*r* sound' in the eighteenth and nineteenth centuries, rather than a series of sounds,[138] would be equivalent to expecting present-day English to have but one realisation of /r/. A further caveat must be that stylistically exaggerated allophones of /r/ may have been used by earlier authors for purposes of demonstration and analysis.

Kenrick's description suggests that his (everyone's?) typical /r/ was a postalveolar or retroflex sound: 'turning up the tip of the tongue to the palate, bending it back as it were towards the throat, emitting at the same time a strong breath through the mouth; which causes a trepidation of the tongue so suspended; and of course a jarring, tremulous sound' (Kenrick 1784: 48). 'Trepidation', meaning tremulous or vibrating movement, could refer either to a trill or, perhaps, also to a fricative. The 'jarring, tremulous sound' could be the result of e.g. creaky voiced air resonating, like a vowel sound, in the mouth. In other words, the 'jarring' may have had nothing whatever to do with the interruption of air-flow which would be caused by a tap or a trill. The phonetic possibilities would seem to be then: a postalveolar or retroflex approximant, an alveolar trill, and a postalveolar (perhaps even a retroflex) fricative.

Equally, Sheridan may have been describing an approximant rather than what, from his wording, looks like a trill ('*Er* is formed by a vibrating motion of the tip of the tongue between the upper and lower jaw, without touching either') (Sheridan 1786: 67). Had it been a trill, then he would not have expressly mentioned the lack of contact between the tip of the tongue and the roof of the mouth. The 'vibrating motion' may be the same as Kenrick's 'trepidation'. Perhaps in this context then, 'trepidation' did not involve a noticeable movement of the tongue-tip: only a sensation of semi-turbulent airflow around the tongue.

Of all the various contemporary remarks on late eighteenth- and early nineteenth-century /r/, that by Walker is the most important. In 1791, he expressly distinguished between two types of /r/ in accents of English: 'rough' and 'smooth' (Walker 1791: 50). The 'rough' sound, which 'marks' Irish English, involves 'jarring the tip of the tongue against the roof of the mouth near the fore teeth'; the 'smooth' sound is a 'vibration of the lower part of the tongue, near the root, against the inward region of the palate, near the entrance of the throat'. The latter is the typical English English sound, he says, except in word-initial position where the trill is acceptable. His examples, apparently confirming non-rhoticity in the accents of English English he was examining, imply a non-fricative, non-trill quality to the 'English' /r/. In other words, the sound appeared to be an approximant: 'In England, and particularly in London, the *r* in *lard, bard, card, regard*, &c. is pronounced so much in the throat as to be little more than the middle or Italian *a*, lengthened into *laad, baad, caad, regaad*' (Walker 1791: 50).[139]

This entire section (419) in the 'Principles of English Pronunciation' is a critical one for understanding not only the phonetics of /r/ but also the transition to non-rhoticity. Walker's pre-/d/ element in LARD etc. could be analysed as an underlying /r/ with a surface vocalic realisation; or, alternatively, as an underlying vowel – in which case, reference to /r/ in this context is not appropriate. His comments on the acceptability of a trill in word-initial position may also throw light on other writers' descriptions; they could be referring solely to the pronunciation of word-initial /r/. An additional factor, which cannot be substantiated definitely, is that Walker, like many of his fellow authors on pronunciation, may have had in mind certain specific pronunciations used on the stage and in other public-speaking contexts.

Walker's comment about /r/ being 'pronounced so much in the throat' does, in any case, require an explanation since it probably holds the key to an understanding of the process whereby rhotic accents became non-rhotic. Either he was referring simply to a vocalic articulation (lengthening of the previous vowel), or he was indicating a different sort of sound altogether. An /r/ sound, still used by some speakers of English today, is the 'bunched' or 'rhotacised' or 'velar' /r/. The tongue is raised to a back close or central close-mid vowel position – without lip-rounding, but with hollowing of the mid-line (cf. Eustace 1969: 73, Catford 1988: 170, Ladefoged & Maddieson 1996: 234–5). The phonemic and phonetic analysis of Walker's LARD etc. might well have been /laːrd/, pronounced [laːʁd]. (The non-IPA symbol [я] is used here, as in Eustace 1969, for the 'bunched' /r/.)

If this interpretation of Walker's paragraph is correct, then it allows a much clearer picture to emerge of the process whereby non-rhoticity gradually developed in English English. Stage 1 would be the change from an approximant realisation of /r/ to a rhotacised sound (analysed variously as a vowel (vocoid) or approximant with rhotacisation). Stage 2 would be the falling-together of the rhotacised realisation of /r/ with the previous vowel, leaving only a long vowel sound.

Smith's view (1795) that 'R has uniformly one sound, as in the English word *rear*, and is pronounced exactly as the French word *rare*, and German *rar* (rare). It is never silent' (Smith 1795: xliii)[140] is understandable only if one takes his 'one sound' to be an approximant, and also recognises that his accent was Scottish (and therefore rhotic).[141] (The /r/ which he claims to hear at the end as well as the beginning of <rear> – assuming he is describing English English and not Scottish English – could not be anything other than an approximant or (possibly) a fricative. Its precise connection with the French and German fricative pronunciations of /r/, however, is not clear.)

By 1842 and the work of Smart, /r/ is a 'trilled dental consonant', noted, for example, in the words RAY and PRAY. He does, however, refer to 'the untrilled r' (1842: 18), which, presumably, refers to the <r> which has a vocalic realisation, e.g. in ARMED, STARTS (Smart 1842: 18).

The distinction between two allophones, one (perhaps) trilled, the other an approximant (on the basis of the phonology of nineteenth-century English containing underlying post-vocalic /r/ which has a surface realisation as a vowel) is set out clearly in Richard Lepsius' *Standard Alphabet* (Lepsius 1863: 50–1). His 'double pronunciation of *r*' includes a pre-vocalic sound 'pronounced as a dental consonant with the top of the tongue'; examples are STARRY, ABHORRENT, SWEARING. In word-final, pre-consonantal contexts, 'it changes its nature and becomes a vowel . . . The tongue and soft palate are put, at the guttural point, into a slight sound vibration without friction. The dental *r* thus becomes a guttural vocalic *r*'. Numerous examples include ABHOR, FUR, HER, SIR, STAR, SWEAR, WAITER, and WORD. One could argue that his pre-vocalic /r/ may not have been a trill, since he mentions only the 'dental sound pronounced with the top of the tongue': there is no mention of 'trepidation' or 'jarring'. Tentatively, this could be read as evidence for a predominantly approximant realisation (still possibly with rhotacisation of the second half of the vowel) by the early 1860s.

By the late 1860s and early 1870s, different phoneticians had noted different types of /r/ in English. Alexander Melville Bell (1867: 52) described 'English' r as being a 'buzz', not a 'trill'. Ellis, on the other hand, is adamant that in pre-vocalic position, the /r/ is a trill — 'a continually repeated "make and break" of sound' (Ellis 1874: 1098). The other allophone or allophones, 'the untrilled (ɹ)', which can be either 'buzzed' or 'hissed' [= IPA 'approximant' and 'fricative'] has, says Ellis, 'a great tendency to fall into (ə) [= IPA [ə]], or some such indistinct sound' (Ellis 1874: 1098).[142]

Sweet has little to say that throws light on the precise phonetic characteristics of /r/: the sound is 'generally point-palate inner' (Sweet to Storm 23 Feb. 1880); later, he expressly rules out a fricative as a typical pronunciation: 'The English r is vowellike in sound, being quite free from buzz' (Sweet 1908: 43). This is firm evidence that, to his ears, the typical allophone was an approximant. Defective and affective pronunciations to which he draws attention include [β] or [ɓ] (defective), and [ɹw] or [w] (affective). In connection with the latter, he noted that 'vewy is no longer a "swell" pronunciation' (Sweet to Storm 24 Sept. 1888). A further defect is 'trilling' the /r/ – except in 'declamation' (Sweet 1908: 43).

American speech of the late nineteenth century used two different allophones of /r/: a voiced approximant 'formed with the tip of the tongue turned up towards the front part of the hard palate, in such a way as to leave an irregular triangular opening about 6 millimetres high and 15 wide'; and the other 'similar to the one just described, but produced further back and with a larger opening' (Grandgent 1895: 453). These clearly refer to [ɹ] and either [ɻ] or [я].[143] Whitney's /r/, 'with the tip of the tongue reverted into the dome of the mouth' was obviously [ɻ] (Whitney 1875: 235).

Twentieth-century descriptions of English English /r/ include Ward and Jones's 'postalveolar fricative' as the most usual English sound, with an alveolar tap as a contextually-conditioned allophone (Ward, I.C. 1945: 144–5; Jones, D. 1960: 195; cf. also Jespersen 1909/61: 411). For other speakers in England, a postalveolar approximant articulation is the norm (Jones, D. 1960: 195–6, 205). Gimson's analysis of the various allophones of /r/ in RP, where the norm in a postalveolar approximant, not a fricative (Gimson 1980: 205–07), may be taken as evidence that there has been a slight allophonic change during the course of the twentieth century.[144]

5.12.7 /l/

Noticeable differences in the realisations of /l/ between America and England can be found in Grandgent (1895: 451). Somewhat surprisingly, in view of what is known of /l/ in RP and GenAm. during the twentieth century, he regarded the usual allophone in England to be velarised, i.e. the dark [ɫ], with an '*u*-like quality', whereas in America such a pronunciation 'does not seem to be common'. Whitney noted that contextually conditioned realisations of /l/ occur, but did not provide details (Whitney 1875: 238).

5.13   Lexical Stress

5.13.1

Changes that have taken place in the lexical stress patterns of English over the last 200 years have been noted by several authors. Strang (1970), for example, draws attention to the use of word-initial stress on e.g. 'TRAFAL-GAR and 'SUCCESSOR, and second-syllable stress on COM'PENSATE, CON'CENTRATE, CON'TEMPLATE, and BAL'CONY; both patterns lasted well into the nineteenth century before moving over to the present-day second-syllable and initial-syllable patterns respectively (Strang 1970: 87). Of all the phonetic/phonological observations made by the orthoepists and later writers, those on lexical stress are generally the most reliable. The reason has to do with a sharp awareness of the concept of prosody (albeit mainly in relation to Greek and Latin) and how it may be applied to the analysis of English. See, for example, the comments of Ash (1775: 24), Nares (1784: 185–7), Walker (1791: 62–3), and Smart (1849: section 81).

5.13.2

For the analysis of lexical stress patterns over the past 200 years, three degrees of stress can be established: primary, secondary and zero, abbreviated here as 'p', 's', and 'z'. A word's stress pattern can then be specified as e.g. 'pzsz' (EDUCATED), 'pzz' (QUANTITY). However, there are numerous cases where no distinction is made in the pronouncing dictionaries etc. between secondary and zero stress – both being counted as less prominent than primary – and so the 'p–s–z' pattern is reformulated in terms of only two categories: 'p' and 'x' (where 'x' is unspecific as to secondary or zero stress). EDUCATED is then expressed as 'pxxx', and QUANTITY as 'pxx'. Danielson's classical and neo-classical terminology for some of the patterns ('proparoxytone', 'hebdomotone' etc.; Danielsson 1948: 232) has been avoided here as being too cumbersome and opaque. Instead, abbreviations such as 'xpx' will be used, alongside more familiar terminology such as 'penultimate' and 'antepenultimate'. Note that the stress-mark will be placed before the first segment of the stressed syllable; e.g. <be'fore>; many works from the eighteenth century onwards place an acute accent *after* the stressed vowel; e.g. <befo're>.

5.13.3

The list of words for analysis is based mainly on that in Nares (1784: 147–96), as being indicative of words which, for whatever reason, were susceptible to lexical-stress variation towards the end of the eighteenth century.[145] Nares argued that accent appeared to be 'the most unstable part of the English language' and added that 'we can all remember words differently accented from the present practice; and many might be collected which still are fluctuating, with their accent unsettled' (Nares 1784: 147).

5.13.4

On the basis of the data examined, six general patterns of variation and change can be established. They are set out as tables 5.1–5.6.

Type 1:	Zero or limited variability; no change
Type 2:	Competing forms (A~B)
Type 3:	Shorter-term changes (A>B>A)
Type 4:	Clear change, with little or no reverting to an older form (A>B)
Type 5:	Multi-stage process of change (A > B > C . . .)
Type 6:	Variation and ultimately reversal to an older form (A>B~A>A).

The dividing-lines between the six types is not always clear-cut – indeed, with further data, a more sophisticated analysis would undoubtedly result.[146] However, as the following examples indicate, there is evidence that considerable variability, leading sometimes to eventual change, existed in the lexical stressing of words during the period under consideration, as well as considerable consistency in stress-allocation. The examples below illustrate the six different types. See tables 5.1–5.6 for the data.

5.13.5   Type 1:

COMPROMIZE and EXPURGATORY have retained the same stress patterns since at least 1764. SUBSTANTIVE has had the pattern pxx until very recently (1990–LPD: British) when the alternative xpx has come into (greater) use. ENTERPRISE has retained the pattern pxx from at least 1791.

Table 5.1. *Lexical stress pattern 1*

	1764 Johnston	1781 Sheridan	1784 Anon	1784 Nares	1791 Walker	1792 Fogg	1793 Perry	1794 Adams	1795 Smith	1796 Anon	1817 Anon	1830 Angus	1835 Knowles
2-Syllable													
Ally (v)													
Annex (v)					xp								xp
Cement (v)					xp		xp						
Research (n)					xp								
Research (v)					xp								
Saline (n)													
Surcharge (v)					xp								xp
Turmoil (n)					px								px
Turmoil (v)					xp								xp
3-Syllable													
Compromize	pxp				pxx								
Contrary	pxx				pxx		pxx				pxx		pxx
Contrary ('different')													
Enterprise					pxx								
Envelope (v)					xpx		xpx						xpx
Quadruple (adj)					pxx								pxx
Quadruple (v)													ppx
Sinister ('insidious' etc)				pxx									
Sinister (left)				xpx									
Substantive	pxx				pxx	pxx	pxx						pxx
4-Syllable													
Enterprising									xxpx				pxpx
Executer					xpxx				pxxx				pxpx or xpxx
Formidably					pxxx		pxxx		pxxx				ppxx
Intumescence		xxpx	xxpx		xxpx								xxpx
Menagerie												xxxp	xxpx
Predicament	pxxx				xpxx		xpxx						xpxx
Untowardly					xpxx		xpxx	xpxx					xpxx
5-Syllable													
Aphrodisiac					xxpxx				xxxpx				xxxpx
Commendatory	xpxxx				xpxxx		xpxxx		xpxxx				xpxxx

1836 Smart	1838 Walker	1848 Craig	1853 Boag	1880 Ogilvie	1908 Afzelius	1917 EPD	1945 MacCarthy	1949 Pitman	1990 LPD Amer	1990 LPD Brit	1992 OED2	
	xp		xp	xp		xp	xp	xp	xp	xp	xp	Ally (v)
xp	xp		xp	xp		xp	xp	xp	xp	xp	xp	Annex (v)
xp	xp		xp	xp	xp	xp	xp	xp	xp	xp	xp	Cement (v)
		xp	xp	xp			xp		xp or px	xp or px		Research (n)
			xp	xp					xp or px	xp or px		Research (v)
				xp	xp	xp						Saline (n)
xp		xp		xp	xp				xp	xp		Surcharge (v)
px	px		px	px			px					Turmoil (n)
xp	xp		xp	xp								Turmoil (v)
	pxx			pxx			pxx	pxx	pxx	pxx	pxx	Compromize
pxx	pxx	pxx	pxx		pxx	pxx or xpx					pxx	Contrary
				pxx			pxx	pxx	pxx	pxx		Contrary ('different')
	pxx			pxx			pxx	pxx	pxx	pxx	pxx	Enterprise
xpx	xpx	xpx	xpx	xpx	xpx	xpx	xpx	xpx	xpx	xpx	xpx	Envelope (v)
		pxx										Quadruple (adj)
				pxx								Quadruple (v)
pxx												Sinister ('insidious' etc)
xpx												Sinister (left)
pxx	pxx	pxx	pxx	pxx	pxx	pxx	pxx	pxx	pxx	xpx or pxx	pxx	Substantive
		pxxx	pxxx	pxxx	pxxx	pxxx		pxxx	pxxx	pxxx	pxxx	Enterprising
pxxx		pxxx	pxxx	pxxx	pxxx	pxxx			pxxx	pxxx	pxxx	Executer
pxxx	pxxx	pxxx	pxxx	pxxx		pxxx		pxxx	pxxx	pxxx or xpxx	pxxx	Formidably
xxpx	xxpx	xxpx	xxpx	xxpx		xxpx			xxpx	xxpx	xxpx	Intumescence
xxpx	xxxp	xxpx	xxpx	xxpx	xxpx	xxpx		xxpx	xxpx	xxpx	xxpx	Menagerie
xpxx	xpxx	xpxx	xpxx	xpxx	xpxx	xpxx	xpxx	xpxx			xxpx	Predicament
xpxx	xpxx	xpxx	xpxx	xpxx	xpxx	ppxx or xpxx or xxpx or pxpx			xpx	xxpx		Untowardly
	xxpxx	xxpxx	xxpxx	xxpxx		xxpxx			xxpxx	xxpxx	xxpxx	Aphrodisiac
xpxxx	xpxxx	xpxxx	xpxxx	xpxxx		xpxxx			xpxxx or xxpxx	xpxxx or xxpxx	xpxxx	Commendatory

Table 5.1. (*cont.*)

	1764 Johnston	1781 Sheridan	1784 Anon	1784 Nares	1791 Walker	1792 Fogg	1793 Perry	1794 Adams	1795 Smith	1796 Anon	1817 Anon	1830 Angus	1835 Knowles
Dehortatory					xpxxx		xpxxx		xpxxx				xpxxx
Exhortatory	xpxxx				xpxxx		xpxxx		xpxxx				xpxxx
Expurgatory	xpxxx				xpxxx		xpxxx		xpxxx				xpxxx
6-Syllable													
Hypochondrical					xxxpxx		xxxpxx		xxxpxx				xxxpxx

Table 5.2. *Lexical stress pattern 2*

	1764 Johnston	1781 Sheridan	1784 Anon	1784 Nares	1791 Walker	1792 Fogg	1793 Perry	1794 Adams	1795 Smith	1796 Anon	1817 Anon	1830 Angus	1835 Knowles
3-Syllable													
Confessor	xpx	pxx			pxx	pxx	xpx						xpx or pxx
Decorous					xpx		xpx					xpx	pxx or xpx
Imbecile					xpx or xxp							xpx	xxp
Obdurate	pxx			xpx	pxx or xpx		xpx						xpx
Recusant	xpx			xpx	pxx or xpx		xpx						pxx
Supervise	pxp			xxp	xxp		pxp		xxp				pxp
Vertigo				xpx	xpx or pxx		pxx						xpx
4-Syllable													
Aristocrat												xxxp	pxxx or xpxx
Capillary	xpxx			pxxx	xpxx								pxxx
Consistory	pxxx	pxxx			pxxx		xpxx						pxxx

1836 Smart	1838 Walker	1848 Craig	1853 Boag	1880 Ogilvie	1908 Afzelius	1917 EPD	1945 MacCarthy	1949 Pitman	1990 LPD Amer	1990 LPD Brit	1992 OED2	
xpxxx	xpxxx	xpxxx	xpxxx	xpxxx							xpxxx	Dehortatory
xpxxx	xpxxx	xpxxx	xpxxx	xpxxx		xpxxx			xpxxx	xpxxx	xpxxx	Exhortatory
xpxxx	xpxxx	xpxxx	xpxxx	xpxxx	xpxxx	xpxxx			xpxxx	xpxxx	xpxxx	Expurgatory
xxxpxx	xxxpxx	xxxpxx	xxxpxx	xxxpxx	xxxpxx	xxxpxx					xxxpxx	Hypochondriacal

1836 Smart	1838 Walker	1848 Craig	1853 Boag	1880 Ogilvie	1908 Afzelius	1917 EPD	1945 MacCarthy	1949 Pitman	1990 LPD Amer	1990 LPD Brit	1992 OED2	
pxx	pxx	pxx or xpx	xpx	xpx (formerly pxx as King's cognomen)	xpx	xpx	xpx	xpx	xpx or pxx	xpx	xpx	Confessor
xpx	xpx	pxx or xpx	pxx or xpx	xpx	pxx or xpx	pxx or xpx		xpx	pxx	pxx (formerly xpx)	xpx or pxx	Decorous
xxp	xpx or xxp	pxx or xxp	pxx or xxp	pxx	pxx or xxp	pxx		pxx	pxx	pxx	pxx or xxp	Imbecile
pxx	pxx or xpx	pxx	pxx	pxx (formerly xpx)	pxx or xpx	pxx or xpx		pxx or xpx	pxx	pxx	pxx or xpx	Obdurate
pxx	xpx or pxx	pxx	xpx or pxx	pxx	pxx or xpx				pxx or xpx	pxx or xpx	pxx or xpx	Recusant
xxp	xxp	xxp	xxp	xxp	xxp	pxx or xxp	pxx or xxp	pxx or xxp	pxx	pxx	xxp	Supervise
xpx	xpx or or pxx	xpx	pxx or xpx	xpx pxx	pxx	pxx or xpx		pxx	pxx	pxx	pxx or xpx	Vertigo
pxxx	xxxp	xpxx	pxxx	pxxx or xpxx	pxxx or xpxx	pxxx or xpxx	pxxx	pxxx	xpxx	pxxx or xpxx	pxxx or xpxx	Aristocrat
pxxx	pxxx	xpxx	pxxx	pxxx or xpxx	pxxx or xpxx	xpxx		xpxx	pxxx	xpxx	pxxx or xpxx	Capillary
pxxx	xpxx	xpxx	xpxx	pxxx	pxxx or xpxx	xpxx			xpxx	xpxx	pxxx or xpxx	Consistory

Table 5.2. (*cont.*)

	1764 Johnston	1781 Sheridan	1784 Anon	1784 Nares	1791 Walker	1792 Fogg	1793 Perry	1794 Adams	1795 Smith	1796 Anon	1817 Anon	1830 Angus	1835 Knowles
Controversy	pxxx			pxxx	pxxx		pxxx						pxxx
Corollary	pxxx				pxxx		xpxx		pxxx				pxpx
Despicable	pxxx												
Disputable	xpxx				pxxx	pxxx	xpxx			pxxx			xpxx or pxxx

Table 5.3. *Lexical stress pattern 3*

	1764 Johnston	1781 Sheridan	1784 Anon	1784 Nares	1791 Walker	1792 Fogg	1793 Perry	1794 Adams	1795 Smith	1796 Anon	1817 Anon	1830 Angus	1835 Knowles
2-Syllable													
Caprice	xp			px or xp	px		xp						xp
Champagne (wine)	xp			xp	xp								PP
Florin	px			xp	px		px						px
Grimace	xp			xp	xp		xp						PP
Sherbet	px			xp	xp		xp						px
Survey (v)					xp		xp						
Turmoil	px			xp									
3-Syllable													
Advertise	pxp			xxp	xxp		xxp		xxp				xxp
Commonwealth	pxp			xxp	pxx or xxp		pxx	xpx					pxx
Concordance				xpx or pxx	xpx		xpx						xpx
Excavate	pxx				xpx		xpx						
Exquisite	pxx												
Financier	xpxx				xxp		xpxx		xxp				xxp

1836 Smart	1838 Walker	1848 Craig	1853 Boag	1880 Ogilvie	1908 Afzelius	1917 EPD	1945 MacCarthy	1949 Pitman	1990 LPD Amer	1990 LPD Brit	1992 OED2	
pxxx	pxxx	pxxx	pxxx	pxxx	pxxx	pxxx	pxxx or xpxx	pxxx or xpxx	pxxx	pxxx or xpxx	pxxx	Controversy
pxxx	pxxx	xpxx	pxxx	pxxx	xpxx or pxxx	xpxx	xpxx	xpxx	pxxx	xpxx	xpxx or pxxx	Corollary
				pxxx			pxxx or xpxx	pxxx or xpxx	xpxx or pxxx	xpxx or pxxx		Despicable
pxxx	pxxx or xpxx	pxxx	pxxx	xpxx	pxxx or xpxx	pxxx or xpxx			xpxx or pxxx	xpxx or pxxx	pxxx or xpxx	Disputable

1836 Smart	1838 Walker	1848 Craig	1853 Boag	1880 Ogilvie	1908 Afzelius	1917 EPD	1945 MacCarthy	1949 Pitman	1990 LPD Amer	1990 LPD Brit	1992 OED2	
xp	xp or px	xp	xp	xp	xp	xp	xp	xp	xp	xp	xp	Caprice
	xp	xp	xp	xp	xp	xp	xp	xp	xp	xp	xp	Champagne (wine)
px	px	px	px	px	px	px	px	px	px	px	px	Florin
xp	xp	xp	xp	xp	xp	xp	xp	xp or px	xp or px	xp	xp	Grimace
px	px	px	px	px	px	px	px	px	px	px	px	Sherbet
px	xp	xp	xp	xp	xp	xp	xp	px	xp or px	xp or px	xp	Survey (v)
		px			px	px	px	px	px	px	px	Turmoil
pxx	xxp	xxp	xxp	xxp (formerly xpx)	pxx or xxp	pxx	pxx	pxx	pxx	pxx	xxp or pxx	Advertise
pxx	pxx or xxp	pxx	pxx	pxx	pxx	pxx		pxx	pxx	pxx	pxx	Commonwealth
xpx	xpx	xpx	xpx	xpx	xpx	xpx			xpx	xpx	xpx	Concordance
pxx	pxx			pxx	pxx		pxx	pxx	pxx	pxx	pxx	Excavate
				pxx			pxx or xpx	pxx or xpx	xpx or pxx	pxx or xpx	pxx or xpx	Exquisite
xxp	xxp	xxpx	xxp	xpx	xpx or xxpx	xpx or xxpx	xpx	xpx	xxp	xpxx	xpxx	Financier

Table 5.3. (*cont.*)

	1764 Johnston	1781 Sheridan	1784 Anon	1784 Nares	1791 Walker	1792 Fogg	1793 Perry	1794 Adams	1795 Smith	1796 Anon	1817 Anon	1830 Angus	1835 Knowles
Recognize	pxx			xxp or pxx	pxx		xpx		xxp				pxp
Rendezvous	pxx	xxp		xxp	xxp	pxx	pxx	xxp				xxp	pxx
Retinue	pxx			xpx or pxx	pxx or xpx		pxx						pxx
Satellite				xpx	pxx		xpx						pxp
Scrutinize	pxx				pxx		pxx		xxp				pxp
Splenetic	xpx	pxx	pxx		pxx	pxx	pxx						xpx
Successor	xpx				pxx or xpx		xpx					pxx	xpx
4-Syllable													
Advertisement	xpxx			xpxx	xpxx or xxpx	xpxx or xxpx	xxpx						xpxx or xxpx
Celibacy	pxxx			xpxx or pxxx	pxxx		pxxx						pxxx
Coadjutor	pxpx			xxpx	xxpx		xxpx						xxpx
Commentator	pxpx				xxpx		pxpx		xxpx				pxpx
Compromizing									xxpx				pxpx
Consecutive				pxxx	xpxx		xpxx						xpxx
Diocesan	xpxx			xxpx or xpxx	xpxx		xxpx						xpxx
Inopportune					xxxp				xxxp				xxxp
Judicature	pxxx	pxxx			pxxx		pxxx						pxpx
Mediator	pxpx			xxpx	xxpx		xxpx						pxpx
Peremptory	pxxx				pxxx or xpxx		xpxx		pxxx or xpxx				pxxx
Superflous	xpxx				xpxx		xpxx				xpxx or xxpx		
Topography	xpxx				xpxx		xpxx				xpxx or xxpx		xpxx
5-Syllable													
Aristocracy	pxpxx				xxpxx		xxpxx				xxxpx ('some-times improperly')		xxpxx

1836 Smart	1838 Walker	1848 Craig	1853 Boag	1880 Ogilvie	1908 Afzelius	1917 EPD	1945 MacCarthy	1949 Pitman	1990 LPD Amer	1990 LPD Brit	1992 OED2	
pxx	pxx	pxx	pxx	pxx	pxx	pxx	pxx	pxx	pxx	pxx	pxx	Recognize
pxx	xxp	xxp or pxx	pxx	pxx	pxx	pxx	pxx	pxx	pxx	pxx	pxx	Rendezvous
	pxx or xpx	pxx	pxx	pxx (older xpx)	pxx	pxx		pxx	pxx	pxx	pxx	Retinue
pxx	pxx	pxx	pxx	pxx	pxx	pxx	pxx	pxx	pxx	pxx	pxx	Satellite
pxx	pxx	pxx	pxx	pxx	pxx	pxx	pxx	pxx	pxx	pxx	pxx	Scrutinize
pxx	pxx	xpx	pxx	xpx	xpx	xpx			xpx	xpx	xpx	Splenetic
xpx	pxx or xpx	xpx	xpx	xpx	xpx	xpx		xpx	xpx	xpx	xpx	Successor
xpxx	xpxx or xxpx	xpxx	xpxx	xpxx	xpxx	xpxx	xpxx	xpxx	xxpx or xpxx	xpxx	xpxx	Advertisement
pxxx	pxxx	pxxx	pxxx	pxxx	pxxx	pxxx or xpxx		pxxx	pxxx	pxxx	pxxx	Celibacy
xxpx	xxpx	xxpx	xxpx	xxpx	xxpx	xpxx			xpxx	xpxx	xpxx	Coadjutor
pxxx	xxpx	pxxx	xxpx	pxxx	pxxx	pxxx	pxxx	pxxx	pxxx	pxxx	pxxx	Commentator
		pxxx		pxxx	pxxx	pxxx			pxxx	pxxx	pxxx	Compromizing
xpxx	xpxx	xpxx	xpxx	xpxx	xpxx	xpxx	xpxx	xpxx	xpxx	xpxx	xpxx	Consecutive
xpxx	xpxx	xpxx	xpxx	xpxx or pxxx	xpxx	xpxx		xpxx	xpxx	xpxx	xpxx	Diocesan
xpxx	xxxp			xpxx	xxxp	xpxx or ppxx or xxxp or pxxp		xpxx	xxxp	xpxx or xxxp	xxxp or xpxx	Inopportune
pxxx	pxxx	pxxx	pxxx	pxxx	pxxx	pxxx or xpxx			pxxx or xpxx	pxxx or xpxx	pxxx	Judicature
pxxx	xxpx	xxpx	xxpx	pxxx	pxxx	pxxx		pxxx	pxxx	pxxx	pxxx	Mediator
pxxx	pxxx or xpxx	pxxx	pxxx	pxxx	pxxx			xpxx or pxxx	xpxx or pxxx	xpxx or pxxx	xpxx or pxxx	Peremptory
xpxx	xpxx	xpxx	xpxx		xpxx	xpx	xpx	xpxx	xpxx	xpxx	xpxx	Superfluous
xpxx	xpxx	xpxx	xpxx	xpxx	xpxx	xpxx		xpxx	xpxx	xpxx	xpxx	Topograhy
xxpxx	xxpxx	xxpxx	xxpxx	xxpxx	xxpxx	xxpxx	xxpxx	xxpxx	xxpxx	xxpxx	xpxxx	Aristocracy

Michael K. C. MacMahon

Table 5.3. (*cont.*)

	1764 Johnston	1781 Sheridan	1784 Anon	1784 Nares	1791 Walker	1792 Fogg	1793 Perry	1794 Adams	1795 Smith	1796 Anon	1817 Anon	1830 Angus	1835 Knowles
Hypochondriac	pxxpx				xxpxx		xxpxx		xxxpx				xxpxx
Indisputable	pxpxx				xpxxx		xxpxx		xxpxx or xpxxx				xpxxx or xpxxx
6-Syllable													
Pacificatory					xpxxxx				xpxxxx	xpxxxx			xpxpxx
Sacrificatory					xpxxxx				xpxxxx				pxxpxx

Table 5.4. *Lexical stress pattern 4*

	1764 Johnston	1781 Sheridan	1784 Anon	1784 Nares	1791 Walker	1792 Fogg	1793 Perry	1794 Adams	1795 Smith	1796 Anon	1817 Anon	1830 Angus	1835 Knowles
2-Syllable													
Access	xp		xp		xp or px		xp						px
Access (n)					xp								
Alcove	xp			xp	xp		xp						xp
Almost	xp			px or xp	xp							xp	xp
Bombast	xp			xp	xp		px						xp
Carbine	xp			xp	px		xp						pp
Cement (n)		px			px	px	px						px
Construed			px										px
Landau												xp	xp
Pretext	xp			xp	xp		xp						pp
Profile	px			xp	xp		xp						
Profile (n)													xp
Profile (v)													xp
Saline (adj)													
Surcharge (n)					xp								
Traverse (adj prep, adv, n)					xp								
Traverse (v)													

1836 Smart	1838 Walker	1848 Craig	1853 Boag	1880 Ogilvie	1908 Afzelius	1917 EPD	1945 MacCarthy	1949 Pitman	1990 LPD Amer	1990 LPD Brit	1992 OED2	
xxpxx	xxpxx	xxpxx	xxpxx	xxpxx	xxpxx	xxpxx			xxpxx	xxpxx	xxpxx	Hypochondriac
xpxxx or xxpxx	xpxxx or xxpxx	xpxxx	xpxxx or xxpxx	xpxxx	xpxxx or xxpxx	xpxxx or ppxxx or xxpxx			xxpxx	xxpxx or xpxxx xxpxx	xpxxx or xxpxx	Indisputable
xpxxxx	xpxxxx	xpxxxx	xpxxxx	xpxxxx	xpxxxx	xpxxxx or pxxxxx					xpxxxx	Pacificatory
xpxxxx	xpxxxx	xpxxxx	xpxxxx	xpxxxx								Sacrificatory

1836 Smart	1838 Walker	1848 Craig	1853 Boag	1880 Ogilvie	1908 Afzelius	1917 EPD	1945 MacCarthy	1949 Pitman	1990 LPD Amer	1990 LPD Brit	1992 OED2	
xp or px	xp or px (ought to be avoided)	xp		px	px	px or xp	px					Access
			px					px	px	px	px	Access (n)
xp	xp			px	px or xp	px	px	px	px	px		Alcove
px	px	px	px	px	px	px	px	px	px	px	px	Almost
xp	xp	xp	xp	xp	px	px		px	px	px	px	Bombast
px	xp	xp	xp	px	px	px	px	px	px	px	px	Carbine
xp	pz		px	xp	xp	xp	xp	xp	xp	xp	xp or px	Cement (n)
px			px		px or xp	px or xp		xp	xp			Construed
px	xp	px	px	xp	px	px		px	px	px	px	Landau
xp	xp	xp	xp	px or xp	px or xp	px	px	px	px	px	px	Pretext
	px or xp	px	px		px	px	px	px	px	px	px	Profile
xp				px								Profile (n)
xp				px								Profile (v)
				px	px	px						Saline (adj)
				px	px					px	px	Surcharge (n)
px				px								Traverse (adj, prep, adv, n)
xp				px (t) or xp (l)			px					Traverse (v)

Table 5.4. (*cont.*)

	1764 Johnston	1781 Sheridan	1784 Anon	1784 Nares	1791 Walker	1792 Fogg	1793 Perry	1794 Adams	1795 Smith	1796 Anon	1817 Anon	1830 Angus	1835 Knowles
3-Syllable													
Avant-garde					xpx		xpx					xpx	xpx
Balcony	xpx		xpx	xpx	xpx		xpx				pxx or xpx		pxx
Commodore	pxx				xxp or pxx		pxp		xxp				pxp
Compensate	xpx			xpx or pxx	xpx		xpx						pxx or xpx
Confiscate	xpx			xpx	xpx		xpx						xpp or pxp
Consummate (v)	pxp					xpx							
Contemplate	xpx			xpx or pxx	xpx		xpx						xpp
Coquetry	pxx				xpx		pxx					xpx	xpx
Corridor					xxp							xxp	pxx
Demonstrate	xpx			xpx	xpx		xpx						xpp
Enervate	xpx			xpx	xpx		xpx						xpx
Envelope (n)					xxp		xxp						xpx
Illustrate	xpx			xpx	xpx		xpx						xpp
Magnetize									xxp				pxp
Matador					xxp		pxx		xxp				pxp
Orchestra				xpx	xpx		pxx						
Orchestre	xpx												
Perfected			pxx										pxx
Promulgate	xpx			xpx	xpx		xpx						xpp
Quintessence					pxx							pxx	xpx
Reservoir				xxp	xxp		xxp						
Utensil	pxx			pxx	pxx		xpx						pxx
4-Syllable													
Academy	pxxx or xpxx	pxxx or xpxx			xpxx or pxpx	pxxx or xpxx	xpxx						xpxx

1836 Smart	1838 Walker	1848 Craig	1853 Boag	1880 Ogilvie	1908 Afzelius	1917 EPD	1945 MacCarthy	1949 Pitman	1990 LPD Amer	1990 LPD Brit	1992 OED2	
xpx	xpx		xpx						xxp	xxp		Avant-garde
pxx	xpx	xpx or pxx	xpx	pxx	pxx	pxx	pxx	pxx	pxx	pxx	pxx (xpx till c. 1825)	Balcony
pxx	xxp or pxx (depends on syntax)	xxp	pxx	pxx	pxx	pxx		pxx	pxx	pxx	pxx	Commodore
xpx	xpx	xpx	xpx	xxp or pxx	pxx	pxx	pxx	pxx	pxx	pxx	pxx	Compensate
xpx	xpx	xpx	xpx	xpx or pxx	pxx	pxx	pxx	pxx	pxx	pxx	pxx	Confiscate
xpx	xpx			pxx		pxx		pxx	pxx	pxx	pxx	Consummate
xpx	xpx	xpx	xpx	xpx or pxx	pxx or xxp	pxx	pxx	pxx	pxx	pxx	pxx or xpx	Contemplate
xpx	xpx	xpx	xpx	pxx	pxx	pxx			pxx or xpx	pxx	pxx	Coquetry
xxp	xxp	xxp	xxp	pxx	pxx	pxx	pxx	pxx	pxx	pxx	pxx	Corridor
xpx	xpx	xpx	xpx	xpx	pxx or xpx	pxx	pxx	pxx	pxx	pxx	xpx or pxx	Demonstrate
xpx	xpx	xpx	xpx	xpx	pxx (n); xpx (adj)	pxx	pxx	pxx	pxx	pxx	pxx	Enervate
px	xxp	pxx	px	pxx	pxx	pxx	pxx	pxx	pxx	pxx	pxx	Envelope (n)
xpx	xpx	xpx	xpx	xpx	pxx or xpx	pxx	pxx	pxx	pxx	pxx	pxx or xpx	Illustrate
pxx		pxx	pxx	pxx	pxx	pxx	pxx		pxx	pxx	pxx	Magnetize
pxx	xxp	xxp	xxp	pxx	pxx	pxx			pxx	pxx	pxx	Matador
pxx	pxx	pxx	pxx	pxx	pxx	pxx	pxx	pxx	pxx	pxx	pxx	Orchestra
pxx	pxx		pxx								pxx (formerly xpx, eg in Byron)	Orchestre
		pxx							xpx	xpx		Perfected
xpx	xpx	xpx	xpx	xpx	xpx	xpx		pxx	pxx or xpx	pxx or xpx	pxx	Promulgate
xpx	xpx	xpx	xpx	xpx	xpx	xpx		xpx	xpx	xpx	xpx	Quintessence
pxx	xxp	pxx	xxp	pxx	pxx	pxx	pxx	pxx	pxx	pxx	pxx	Reservoir
xpx	xpx	xpx	xpx	xpx or pxx	xpx	xpx	xpx	xpx	xpx	xpx	xpx	Untensil
xpxx	xpxx or pxxx	xpxx ('anciently pronounced' pxxx)	xpxx	xpxx	xpxx	xpxx	xpxx	xpxx	xpxx	xpxx	xpxx	Academy

Table 5.4. (*cont.*)

	1764 Johnston	1781 Sheridan	1784 Anon	1784 Nares	1791 Walker	1792 Fogg	1793 Perry	1794 Adams	1795 Smith	1796 Anon	1817 Anon	1830 Angus	1835 Knowles
Accessory	pxxx			pxxx	pxxx		xpxx						pxxx
Advertising					xpxx		xxpx						xxpx
Aerial	xpxx				xpxx		xpxx		xpxx			xpxx	xpx
Amphitheatre	pxpx				xxpxx		xxpx					xxpx	pxxxx
Commendable					pxxx		xpxx				pxxx ('generally')		xpxx
Dandelion	pxpx			xxpx	xxpx		xxpx					xxpx	pxpx
Despicable	pxxx												
Excavated												xpxx	xppx
Exemplary	xpxx			pxxx	pxxx				pxxx				xpxx
Gladiator	pxpx			xxpx	xxpx		xxpx						pxxx
Legislator	pxpx			xxpx	pxxx		xxpx						pxpx
Moderator	pxpx			xxpx	xxpx		xxpx						pxxx
Operator	pxpx			xxpx	pxxx		xxpx						pxpx
Procurator	pxpx			xxpx	xxpx		xxpx						pxpx
Ragamuffin	pxpx			xxpx	xxpx		pxpx						xxpx
Undertaker				xxpx			xxpx		xxpx				pxpx
Ventilator	pxpx			xxpx	pxxx		xxpx						xxpx
5-Syllable													
Administrator	pxxpx			xxxpx	xxxpx		xxxpx		xxxpx				xpxpx

Table 5.5. *Lexical stress pattern 5*

	1764 Johnston	1781 Sheridan	1784 Anon	1784 Nares	1791 Walker	1792 Fogg	1793 Perry	1794 Adams	1795 Smith	1796 Anon	1817 Anon	1830 Angus	1835 Knowles
3-Syllable													
Complaisance	pxx				xxp		xxp					xpx	xxp

1836 Smart	1838 Walker	1848 Craig	1853 Boag	1880 Ogilvie	1908 Afzelius	1917 EPD	1945 MacCarthy	1949 Pitman	1990 LPD Amer	1990 LPD Brit	1992 OED2	
pxxx	pxxx	pxxx	pxxx	pxxx	pxxx or xpxx	xpxx	xpxx	xpxx	xpxx	xpxx	pxxx or xpxx	Accessory
pxxx	xxpx	xxpx	xxpx	xxpx (formerly xpxx)		pxxx			pxxx	pxxx	xxpx	Advertising
xpxx	xpxx	xpxx	xpxx	xpxx	xpxx	xpxx or pxx	px	pxx	pxx or xpxx	pxx – (formerly xpxx)	pxx ('now in general use except in poetry')	Aerial
xxpxx	xxpxx	xxpxx	xxpx	xxpxx	xxpxx	pxxx	pxxx	pxpx	pxxx	pxxx	xxpx	Amphitheatre
xpxx	pxxx or xpxx	xpxx	xpxx	xpxx	xpxx	xpxx		xpxx	xpxx	xpxx	xpxx	Commendable
xxpx	xxpx	xxpx	xxpx	pxxx	pxxx	pxxx	pxxx	pxxx	pxxx or pxx	pxxx	pxxx	Dandelion
			pxxx				pxxx or xpxx	pxxx or xpxx	xpxx or pxxx	xpxx or pxxx		Despicable
			pxxx			pxxx			pxxx	pxxx		Excavated
pxxx	pxxx	pxxx	pxxx	pxxx	pxxx or xpxx	xpxx	xpxx	xpxx	xpxx	xpxx	xpxx or pxxx	Exemplary
pxxx	xxpx	pxxx	pxxx	pxxx	pxxx	pxxxp	pxxx		pxxx	pxxx	pxxx	Gladiator
pxxx	pxxx	pxxx	pxxx	pxxx	pxxx	pxxx		pxxx	pxxx	pxxx	pxxx	Legislator
pxxx	xxpx	xxpx	pxxx	pxxx	pxxx	pxxx			pxxx	pxxx	pxxx	Moderator
pxxx	pxxx	pxxx	pxxx	pxxx	pxxx	pxxx	pxxx	pxxx	pxxx	pxxx	pxxx	Operator
pxxx	xxpx	pxxx	pxxx	pxxx	pxxx	pxxx			pxxx	pxxx	pxxx	Procurator
pxxx	xxpx	xxpx	xxpx	xxpx	xxpx	pxxx		pxxx	pxxx	pxxx	pxxx	Ragamuffin
xxpx	xxpx	xxpx	xxpx	xxpx	pxxx or xxpx	pxxx	pxxx	pxxx	pxxx	pxxx	pxxx	Undertaker
pxxx	pxxx		pxxx	pxxx	pxxx	pxxx	pxxx	pxxx	pxxx	pxxx	pxxx	Ventilator
xpxxx	xxxpx	xxxpx	xxxpx	xpxxx	xpxxx or xxxpx	xpxxx	xpxxx	xpxxx	xpxxx	xpxxx	xpxxx	Administrator

1836 Smart	1838 Walker	1848 Craig	1853 Boag	1880 Ogilvie	1908 Afzelius	1917 EPD	1945 MacCarthy	1949 Pitman	1990 LPD Amer	1990 LPD Brit	1992 OED2	
xpx	xxp	xxp	xxp	pxx	pxx or xxp	xpx			xpx or xxp	xpx	pxx	Complaisance

Table 5.6. *Lexical stress pattern 6*

	1764 Johnston	1781 Sheridan	1784 Anon	1784 Nares	1791 Walker	1792 Fogg	1793 Perry	1794 Adams	1795 Smith	1796 Anon	1817 Anon	1830 Angus	1835 Knowles
2-Syllable													
Ally (n)													
Annex (n)													px
Archduke	xp			xp	xp		PP						PP
Belles lettres					xpx		xpx					pxx	pxx
Canine	xp			xp	xp		xp						xp
Champaign (open country)				px	px		xp						PP
Construe	px				px or xp		px						
Koran												px	px
Mishap	xp			xp	xp		xp						xp
Pantheon	xpx				xpx		xpx						xpx
Saline	xp			xp	xp		xp						xp
Survey (n)					xp		px						
Toupee					xp		xp					xp	xp
Vibrate	px			px	px		px						PP
3-Syllable													
Abdomen	xpx			xpx	xpx		xpx						xpx
Acetose					xxp		xpx					xxp	pxx
Acumen				xpx	xpx		xpx		xpx				pxx
Advertise	pxp			xxp	xxp		xxp	xxp					xxp
Anchovy	xpx			xpx	xpx		xpx						xpx
Arbutus				xpx or pxx									
Bitumen	xpx			xpx	xpx		xpx						xpx
Consummate (adj)					xpx								pxp
Contemplate	xpx			xpx or pxx	xpx		xpx						xpp

1836 Smart	1838 Walker	1848 Craig	1853 Boag	1880 Ogilvie	1908 Afzelius	1917 EPD	1945 MacCarthy	1949 Pitman	1990 LPD Amer	1990 LPD Brit	1992 OED2	
	xp			xp		xp or px	xp	px	px	xp or px	xp or px	Ally (n)
xp				xp		px or xp	xp	px	px	px	px or xp	Annex (n)
xp	xp		xp	xp	px	pp	pp	xp	xp	px	px	Archduke
xpx	xpx	pxx	xpx			ppx			xpx	xpx	xpx	xpx	Belles lettres
xp	xp	xp	xp	xp	xp or px	px	px	px	px	px	px or xp	Canine
	px	xp	xp	xp	px or xp	px	px				px	Champaign (open country)
	px			px			xp or px	xp	xp	xp	px or xp	Construe
px			px	px	px or xp	xp		xp	xp	xp	xp or px	Koran
xp	xp	xp	xp	xp	xp	px or xp	xp or px	px or xp	px or xp	xp or px	xp or px	Mishap
xpx	xpx	xpx	xpx	xpx	pxx	xp(x) or px		pxx or xpx	pxx or xpx	xpx or pxx	xpx or pxx	Pantheon
	xp or px	px	xp				px or xp	px	px	px	px or xp	Saline
px	xp or px	px	px	px or xp	px or xp	px or xp	px	px or xp	px or xp	px or xp	px or xp	Survey (n)
xp	xp	xp	xp	xp or px	xp	px		xp	px or xp	xp or px	xp or px	Toupee
px	px	px	px	px	px	xp or px	px or xp	px	xp	xp	xp or px ('older')	Vibrate
xpx	xpx	xpx	xpx	xpx or pxx	xpx or pxx	xpx or pxx	pxx or xpx	pxx or xpx	pxx or xpx	pxx or xpx	pxx or xpx	Abdomen
	xxp	xxp	pxx	xpx or xxp		pxx					xxp	Acetose
xpx	xpx	xpx	xpx	xpx	xpx	xpx		xpx	xpx or pxx	pxx or xpx	xpx or pxx	Acumen
pxx	xxp	xxp	xxp	xxp (formerly xpx)	pxx or xxp	pxx	pxx	pxx	pxx	pxx	xxp or pxx	Advertise
	xpx	pxx	xpx	xpx	pxx or xpx	xpx or pxx		xpx or pxx	pxx	pxx or xpx	xpx or pxx	Anchovy
		pxx		pxx		xpx		xpx	xpx	xpx	pxx	Arbutus
xpx	xpx or pxx	pxx or xpx	pxx or xpx	xpx	pxx or xpx	xpx or pxx		pxx	xpx	pxx	xpx or pxx	Bitumen
xpx	xpx			xxp		xpx		xpx	pxx	xpx or pxx	xpx or pxx	Consummate (adj)
xpx	xpx	xpx	xpx	xpx or pxx	pxx or xxp	pxx	pxx	pxx	pxx	pxx	pxx or xpx	Contemplate

Table 5.6. (*cont.*)

	1764 Johnston	1781 Sheridan	1784 Anon	1784 Nares	1791 Walker	1792 Fogg	1793 Perry	1794 Adams	1795 Smith	1796 Anon	1817 Anon	1830 Angus	1835 Knowles
Contrary ('obstinate')													
Decorous					xpx		pxx					xpx	pxx or xpx
Elongate				xpx	xpx		xpx						xpx
Inculcate	xpx			xpx	xpx		xpx						xpp
Inexpert					xxp		xxp		xxp				xxp
Inn holder	pxx				pxx		xpx		xpx				pxx
Interstice	xpx				xpx		xpx					pxx	xpx
Quadruple	pxx	pxx					xpx						
Remonstrate	xpx			xpx	xpx		xpx						xpp
Splenetic	xpx	pxx	pxx		pxx	pxx	pxx						xpx
Untoward	xpx												
4-Syllable													
Acceptable	xpxx				pxxx	pxxx	xpxx					pxxx	xpxx
Demonstrably					xpxx		xpxx		xpxx				xpxx
Exigency	pxxx				pxxx		pxxx		pxxx				pxxx
Exquisitely					pxxx		pxxx					pxxx	pxxx
Hospitable	pxxx						pxxx						
Hospitably					pxxx		pxxx		pxxx				pxxx
Miscellany	pxxx				pxxx		pxxx					pxxx	pxxx
5-Syllable													
Deprecatory	pxpxx				pxxxx				pxxxx				pxpxx
Despicableness		pxxxx			pxxxx		pxxxx						pxxxx

1836 Smart	1838 Walker	1848 Craig	1853 Boag	1880 Ogilvie	1908 Afzelius	1917 EPD	1945 MacCarthy	1949 Pitman	1990 LPD Amer	1990 LPD Brit	1992 OED2	
				pxx		xpx		xpx	xpx or pxx	xpx		Contrary ('obstinate')
xpx	xpx	pxx or xpx	pxx or xpx	xpx	pxx or xpx	pxx or xpx		xpx	pxx	pxx (formerly xpx)	xpx or pxx	Decorous
xpx	xpx	xpx	xpx	xpx	pxx or xpx	pxx		pxx	xpx	pxx	pxx or xpx	Elongate
xpx	xpx	xpx	xpx	xpx	pxx or xpx	pxx or xpx		pxx	xpx or pxx	pxx or xpx	pxx or xpx	Inculcate
xxp	xxp	xxp	xxp	xxp	xxp	xpx or pxp			xpx or xxp	xpx or xxp	xpx or xxp	Inexpert
pxx		pxx	pxx	pxx							pxx	Inn holder
xpx	pxx or xpx	xpx	pxx or xpx	xpx	xpx or pxx	xpx			xpx	xpx	xpx or pxx	Interstice
pxx	pxx		pxx	pxx	pxx	pxx		pxx	xpx or pxx	pxx or xpx	pxx	Quadruple
xpx	xpx	xpx	xpx	xpx	xpx	xpx or pxx		xpx or pxx	pxx or xpx	pxx or xpx	pxx or xpx ('older')	Remonstrate
pxx	pxx	xpx	pxx	xpx	xpx	xpx			xpx	xpx	xpx	Splenetic
				xpx				xpp	xp	xxp or xpx	xxp	Untoward
xpxx	pxxx	pxxx	pxxx	xpxx	xpxx	xpxx		xpxx	xpxx	xpxx	xpxx or pxxx	Acceptable
xpxx	xpxx	xpxx	xpxx	xpxx		pxxx			xpxx	xpxx or pxxx	xpxx	Demonstrably
pxxx	pxxx	pxxx	pxxx	pxxx	pxxx	pxxx		pxxx	pxxx or xpxx	pxxx or xpxx	pxxx	Exigency
pxxx	pxxx	pxxx	pxxx	pxxx	pxxx	pxxx		pxxx	xpxx or pxxx	xpxx or pxxx	pxxx	Exquisitely
				pxxx			pxxx or xpxx	pxxx	pxxx or xpxx	xpxx or pxxx	pxxx	Hospitable
pxxx	pxxx	pxxx	pxxx	pxxx	pxxx	pxxx or xpxx		pxxx	pxxx or xpxx	xpxx or pxxx	pxxx	Hospitably
pxxx	pxxx	pxxx	pxxx	pxxx	pxxx or xpxx	pxxx or xpxx		xpxx	pxxx	xpxx or pxxx	pxxx or xpxx	Miscellany
pxxxx	pxxxx	pxxxx	pxxxx	pxxxx	pxxxx	pxxxx			pxxxx or xxpxx	pxxxx or xxpxx	pxxxx	Deprecatory
pxxxx	pxxxx	pxxxx	pxxxx	pxxxx	pxxxx	pxxxx or xpxxx			xpxxx or pxxxx	xpxxx or pxxxx	pxxxx	Despicableness

Table 5.6. (*cont.*)

	1764 Johnston	1781 Sheridan	1784 Anon	1784 Nares	1791 Walker	1792 Fogg	1793 Perry	1794 Adams	1795 Smith	1796 Anon	1817 Anon	1830 Angus	1835 Knowles
Illustratively					xpxxx		xpxxx		xpxxx				xpxxx
Imprecatory									xpxxx				
Indissoluble	xpxxx						xpxxx						
Indissolubly					xpxxx				xpxxx				xpxxx
Inexplicable	xpxxx				xpxxx		xpxxx		xpxxx				xpxxx
Irreparable	xpxxx				xpxxx		xpxxx				xpxxx or xxpxx		xpxxx
Laboratory	pxxx			pxxxx	pxxxx		pxxxx		pxxxx				xpxxx
Peremptorily							xpxxx		pxxxx				pxxxx
Peremptoriness							xpxxx		pxxxx				pxxxx

However, ENTERPRISING has been subject to some variability (cf. xxpx in 1795).

5.13.6   *Type 2:*

The controversy over the stressing of CONTROVERSY appears to be relatively recent. From 1764 to at least 1917, the pattern is consistently pxxx. The competing form xpxx appears in 1945.

5.13.7   *Type 3:*

Distinctions can be drawn here on the basis of the duration of the changes. Thus, only Nares (1784) stresses FLORIN as xp – thereby raising questions

1836 Smart	1838 Walker	1848 Craig	1853 Boag	1880 Ogilvie	1908 Afzelius	1917 EPD	1945 MacCarthy	1949 Pitman	1990 LPD Amer	1990 LPD Brit	1992 OED2	
xpxxx	xpxxx	xpxxx	xpxxx	xpxxx		pxxxx or xpxxx			xpxxx or pxxxx	pxxxx or xpxxx		Illustratively
				pxxxx					pxxxx or xpxxx	pxxxx or xxpxx	pxxxx or xxpxx	Imprecatory
				xpxxx					xxpxx	xxpxx	xpxxx or xxpxx	Indissoluble
xpxxx	xpxxx	xpxxx	xpxxx	xpxxx		xxpxx or pxpxx or xpxxx			xxpxx	xxpxx	xpxxx or xxpxx	Indissolubly
xpxxx	xpxxx	xpxxx	xpxxx	xpxxx	xpxxx	xpxxx or ppxxx or pxpxx		xpxxx	xxpxx or xpxxx	xxpxx or xpxxx	xpxxx	Inexplicable
xpxxx	xpxxx	xpxxx	xpxxx	xpxxx	xpxxx	xpxxx or ppxxx	xpxxx or ppxxx	xpxxx	xpxxx or xxpxx	xpxxx	xpxxx	Irreparable
pxxxx	pxxxx	pxxxx	pxxxx	pxxxx	pxxxx or xpxxx	pxxxx or xpxxx	xpxx or xpxxx or pxxx	xpxx or pxxx	pxxxx	xpxxx (formerly pxxxx)	xpxxx or pxxxx	Laboratory
pxxxx	pxxxx	pxxxx	pxxxx	pxxxx	pxxxx	xpxxx		xpxxx	xpxxx or pxxxx	xpxxx or pxxxx	pxxxx or xpxxx	Peremptorily
pxxxx	pxxxx	pxxxx	pxxxx	pxxxx		xpxxx			xpxxx or pxxxx	xpxxx or pxxxx	pxxxx or xpxxx	Peremptoriness

about whether this was a nonce pronunciation which he personally favoured or a pronunciation which had enjoyed some currency (cf. the stressing of CHAMPAGNE as pp, Knowles 1835). Longer-term changes include CAPRICE with the alternates px and xp between 1784 and 1835, and SHERBET with xp, rather than px, between 1784 and 1793 (with one isolated, later example in 1838).

5.13.8 Type 4:

Many of the changes took place during the nineteenth century – in certain cases, apparently, suddenly: cf. ALMOST with xp up until 1835, to be followed by px from 1836 onwards; cf. also QUINTESSENCE: pxx up until

1830, then xpx from 1835 onwards. More gradual changes include CON-STRUED, which was px up until at least 1880; between 1908 and 1917, variation occurred, between px and xp; from at least 1945, if not before, the stressing changed to xp.

5.13.9   *Type 5:*

The several stress patterns of COMPLAISANCE over the last 230 years encapsulate the variability that rarely-used words can be subject to.

5.13.10   *Type 6:*

Words in this category have been subject to bouts of change over 200 years, but the evidence indicates a gradual return to older patterns.

5.13.11

A comparison of the stress patterns in the vocabulary selected for analysis, from Walker (1791) and Wells (1990a), reveals something of the changes (and lack of change) in lexical stress over a period of 200 years.

5.13.12   *2-syllable words:*

Stress has remained *unchanged* in:

(px)	CARBINE, FLORIN
(xp)	ANNEX (v), BELLES LETTRES, CEMENT (v), CHAMPAGNE, GRIMACE, SURCHARGE (v)

Stress has moved *backwards* in:

(xp > px)	ALMOST, ACCESS (n), BOMBAST, CANINE, PRETEXT, PROFILE, SALINE, SHERBET, SURCHARGE (n)

Stress has moved *forwards* in:

(px > xp)	CAPRICE, CEMENT (n), VIBRATE

5.13.13   *3-syllable words:*

Stress has remained *unchanged* in:

(pxx)	COMPROMIZE, ENTERPRISE, OBDURATE, RECOGNIZE, RETINUE (alt: (1791) xpx), SATELLITE, SCRUTINIZE, SINISTER, SUBSTANTIVE (alt: (1990) xpx)

(xpx)   CONCORDANCE, ENVELOPE (v), INCULCATE (alt: (1990) pxx), INEXPERT (alt: (1990) xxp), INTERSTICE, REMONSTRATE, SUCCESSOR (alt: (1791) pxx)

Stress has moved *backwards* in:

(xxp > pxx)   ADVERTISE, COMMODORE, COMMONWEALTH, COMPENSATE, CORRIDOR, ENVELOPE (n), IMBECILE, MATADOR, OBDURATE, RENDEZVOUS, RESERVOIR, SUPERVISE

(xpx > pxx)   BALCONY, BITUMEN, CONFISCATE, CONSUMMATE (adj & v), CONTEMPLATE, COQUETRY, DECOROUS, DEMONSTRATE, ELONGATE, ENERVATE, EXCAVATE, ILLUSTRATE, IMBECILE, ORCHESTRA, PROMULGATE, REMONSTRATE (alt: (1990) xpx), RETINUE (alt: (1791) pxx), VAGARY, VERTIGO (alt: (1791) pxx)

(xxp > xpx)   COMPLAISANCE, FINANCIER

Stress has moved *forwards* in:

(pxx > xpx)   CONFESSOR, CONTRARY (alt: (1990) pxx), QUINTESSENCE, SPLENETIC, SUBSTANTIVE (alt: (1990) pxx), SUCCESSOR (alt: (1791) xpx), UTENSIL

(xpx > xxp)   AVANT-GARDE

5.13.14   4-syllable words:

Stress has remained *unchanged* in:

(pxxx)   CELIBACY, LEGISLATOR, OPERATOR, VENTILATOR

(xpxx)   ACADEMY (alt: (1791) pxpx), ADVERTISEMENT (alt: (1791) xxpx), CAPILLARY, CONSECUTIVE, DIOCESAN, GEOGRAPHY (alt: (1990) pxx), SUPERFLUOUS, TOPOGRAPHY

(xxpx)   INTUMESCENCE

(xxxp)   INOPPORTUNE (alt: (1990) xpxx)

Stress has moved *forwards* in:

(pxxx > xpxx)   ACCEPTABLE, ACCEPTABLY, ACCESSORY, COMMENDABLE, CONSISTORY, CONTROVERSY (alt: (1990) pxxx), COROLLARY, DISPUTABLE (alt: (1990) pxxx), EXEMPLARY, EXIGENCY (alt: (1990) pxxx), EXQUISITELY (alt: (1990) pxxx), FORMIDABLY (alt: (1990) pxxx), HOSPITABLY (alt: (1990) pxxx), JUDICATURE (alt: (1990) pxxx), MISCELLANY (alt: (1990) pxxx)

(xpxx > xxpx)   UNTOWARDLY

Stress has moved *backwards* in:

(xxxp > xpxx)	INOPPORTUNE (alt: (1990) xxxp)
(xxpx > xpxx)	ADVERTISEMENT (alt: (1791) xpxx), CO-ADJUTOR
(xxpx > pxxx)	ADVERTISING, AMPHITHEATRE, COMMENTATOR, DANDELION, GLADIATOR, MEDIATOR, MODERATOR, PROCURATOR, RAGAMUFFIN, UNDERTAKER
(xpxx > pxx[x])	AERIAL, DEMONSTRABLY (alt: (1990) xpxx), EXECUTER, GEOGRAPHY (alt: (1990) xpxx),

5.13.15 *5-syllable words:*

Stress has remained *unchanged* in:

(xxpxx)	APHRODISIAC, ARISTOCRACY, HYPOCHONDRIAC
(xpxxx)	COMMENDATORY (alt: (1990) xxpxx), EXHORTATORY, EXPURGATORY, IRREPARABLE, ILLUSTRATIVELY (alt: (1990) pxxxx), INDISPUTABLE (alt: (1990) xxpxx), INEXPLICABLE (alt: (1990) xxpxx)

Stress has moved *forwards* in:

(pxxxx > xpxxx)	DESPICABLENESS (alt: (1990) pxxxx), LABORATORY
(pxxxx > xxpxx)	DEPRECATORY (alt: (1990) pxxxx), DESPICABLENESS (alt: (1990) pxxxx)
(xpxxx > xxpxx)	COMMENDATORY (alt: (1990) xpxxx), INDISPUTABLE (alt: (1990) xpxxx), INDISSOLUBLY, INEXPLICABLE (alt: (1990) xpxxx)

Stress has moved *backwards* in:

(xxxpx > xpxxx)	ADMINISTRATOR
(xpxxx > pxxxx)	ILLUSTRATIVELY (alt: (1990) xpxxx)

5.13.16 *6-syllable words:*

None of the words in Walker (HYPOCHONDRIACAL, PACIFICATORY, and SACRIFICATORY) occurs in Wells. However, an examination of the stress patterns for them in other dictionaries shows very little change, with the exception of Ogilvie (1880), who has pxxpxx for HYPOCHONDRIA-CAL. PACIFICATORY is xpxxxx in Walker and the other dictionaries, except for Knowles (1835) who has xpxpxx, and *EPD*1 (1917), which has an alternative pxxxxx pattern. For SACRIFICATORY, the only divergence from Walker (xpxxxx) is Knowles (1835), with pxxpxx. One may tentatively conclude, then, that the pattern xxxpxx has remained largely constant over 200 years, and that xpxxxx has remained reasonably constant, but with the possibilities of first-syllable and/or fourth-syllable stress.

5.14   Intonation and rhythm

5.14.1

Only a handful of publications in the eighteenth and nineteenth centuries attempt an analysis of the intonational and rhythmical patterns of English.[147] Of these, the most perceptive was Joshua Steele's *Essay towards Establishing the Melody and Measure of Speech* (1775), later revised and re-issued under the title of *Prosodia Rationalis* (1779).[148] From it – see the reproductions in figure 5.2 – one can establish a considerable amount of information about the suprasegmental features of two eighteenth-century speakers: Joshua Steele, born in 1700, and the actor David Garrick, born in 1717; there is even sufficient detail for a comparison to be made with today's patterns. The first reproduction in figure 5.2 shows the intonation and rhythm used by Steele himself in reading the first few words from Hamlet's monologue. By means of a bass musical stave which notates quarter-tones, not just semi-tones and tones, the pitch of the syllables, as well as their lengths, the duration of silent pauses, the occurrence and degree of stress and the degree of loudness of each syllable can be notated.[149] The thick diagonal lines in the middle represent the pitch changes. In the second reproduction, Garrick's pronunciation is notated (but without any indication of the absolute pitch values). A comparison of the two shows differences in the pitch movements of certain syllables, in the timing of silences between syllables, and in the degree of stress on the word is. The third reproduction shows three different versions of the same sentence; note the differences in the positioning of the nuclear syllable in the intonation group in the first two sentences, and, in the third sentence, the two nuclear syllables DO and SO. Comparing the intonations and rhythms of the various examples in the book reveals no substantial differences between late eighteenth-century English intonation and today's intonation.[150]

The comments on intonation by John Walker, especially in his *Elements of Elocution* (1781), are important, although the amount of detail that he presents is, compared with that in Steele, fairly slim: see, for example, his examples of 'inflexions' in Walker 1781.I: opp. 143.[151] The reproductions from Smart (1819: 54, 101–3) in figure 5.2 show a noticeable simplification of the syllable-by-syllable analysis of Steele. James Chapman's schema for

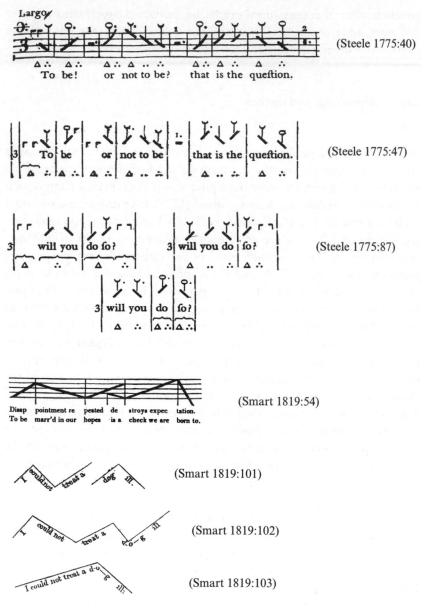

Figure 5.2 Intonation and rhythm

the analysis of intonation and rhythm (Chapman 1819), based as it is on Steele's analysis of 1775/1779, deserves attention, not only for the examples he gives, but, like Steele, for his exposition of the theory that should underpin the description of intonation and rhythm.

5.14.2

Sweet, in 1877, singled out the *Elocutionary Manual* of 1852 of Alexander Melville Bell as containing the best guide to English intonation so far published (Sweet 1877: 93–6). In a section headed *Inflexion* (pp. 55–68), Bell describes (and notates) the main features of English intonation, which later, twentieth-century phoneticians have since developed. Sweet summarises the current state of knowledge by setting up three primary 'forms' or 'inflections' (level, rising, falling tones; glide-tones; and a variety of compound tones). He admits, however, that 'the whole relation of tone to language has as yet been only imperfectly studied' (1877: 95).

5.14.3

For Grandgent, the characteristic features of English intonation were the use of an 'exceedingly high pitch' (with abrupt transitions from falsetto to bass), together with the rise–fall (which 'gives to the English accent now a deprecatory, now a peculiarly supercilious effect'). By comparison, the use of 'high and middle tones', as well as the fall and the fall-rise were the commonest intonation patterns in America (Grandgent 1895: 467).

5.14.4

A comparison of the descriptions and notations in the works from Walker to Sweet, and in Grandgent, can do little more than confirm the existence of intonation patterns still used in RP and GenAm. Attempts to draw conclusions about the direction and speed of any intonation patterns from the end of the eighteenth to the end of the nineteenth centuries from this inevitably restricted set of published data are inappropriate.

5.15   Voice qualities

5.15.1

There are very few direct comments on voice quality (in the sense of a quasi-permanent auditory colouring of speech; cf. Laver 1994: 397–427).

Herries (1773: 117) recommended speakers to adopt a certain 'roundness and openness' of speech; his prescription to achieve this was 'depressing tongue and jaw, and enlarging the cavity of the mouth in the pronunciation of vowels'. Sweet notes that for 'English' speakers, 'partial closure of the mouth (i.e. by raising the jaw), together with nasality, is a common characteristic (Sweet 1877: 98).

5.15.2

In the USA, a clearer image of certain late eighteenth-century voice qualities comes from Webster (1789.II: 106), and one which bears strong similarities to the description of voice qualities in Sweet (1877). Webster remarks on the 'drawling nasal manner of speaking . . . [among the yeomanry of New England]', which he attributes to their 'not opening the mouth sufficiently. Hence words are drawled out in a careless lazy manner, or the sound finds a passage thro the nose' (Webster 1789.II: 108). More generally, he castigates 'that drawling, whining cant that distinguishes a certain class of people; and too much pains cannot be taken to reform the practice. Great efforts should be made by teachers of schools, to make their pupils open the teeth, and give a full clear sound to every syllable' (Webster 1789.II: 108–9).

5.16   Conclusions

5.16.1

The nineteenth century in Britain was the period during which phonological and phonetic changes, begun before the end of the eighteenth century, were taking wider hold: the diphthongisation of /oː/ and /eː/; the centralling and backing of /aː/; the redistribution of the pairs /æ/ and /aː/, /ɒ/ and /ɔː/ before certain fricatives and nasals; the transition from rhoticity to non-rhoticity (with intermediate varieties of semi-rhoticity); the consolidation of /ɜː/ and the temporary emergence of /ɔə/; the centralling of unaccented vowels; and alterations in certain lexical stress patterns.

In America, the changes were fewer, and involved mainly the diphthongisation of /oː/ and /eː/; some centralling and backing of /aː/; some redistribution of /æ/, /aː/, and /ɔː/ before certain fricatives and nasals; and some centralling of unaccented vowels.

By the beginning of the twentieth century, RP at least was largely very similar to what its late twentieth-century successor has turned out to be.

The social mechanisms that have contributed to this relatively stable period in English linguistic history, and, conversely, to the relatively major changes during the eighteenth century (and sometimes the second half of the seventeenth century) amongst a much smaller population, have still to be fully explored.

5.16.2

Much additional research is required before a full picture emerges of the precise sociolinguistic and stylistic changes that English has undergone over the past 200 and more years. A more detailed understanding of the precise social backgrounds and interests of the eighteenth-century orthoepists and of their interaction with one another would, perhaps, allow a more definitive analysis to be made of their publications. A comprehensive comparison of the pronunciations listed in dictionaries, grammarbooks, spellers, etc. would create an historical 'pronouncing dictionary' database of English covering the eighteenth, nineteenth and twentieth centuries (cf. Sundby 1976).

An analysis of the extant recordings of speakers born during the nineteenth century, especially towards the beginning – Tennyson and Gladstone, for example, were both born in 1809 – could certainly help to reveal more about the *phonetic* features of various 'educated' idiolects.[152]

5.16.3

The data considered in this chapter has, in the main, dealt with 'educated' speech. In what ways has the size of the population and the shifting social patterns that resulted from, e.g., urbanisation, especially during the mid- to late nineteenth century, contributed to linguistic change? To what extent has 'educated London' speech differed from RP? Certainly, the narrowing of focus by British twentieth-century phoneticians onto RP, to the relative exclusion of the other 'educated', but non-RP, accents compares unfavourably with the position taken by nineteenth-century phoneticians such as Ellis and Sweet, and by twentieth-century phoneticians in the USA. The British public-school system and its association with RP has indirectly contributed to a lessening of professional interest, until relatively recently, in the non-dialectal speech of the majority of the inhabitants of the British Isles.

This, in turn, raises questions about the degree to which the real substance of British English over the last 200 and more years the 'social' and 'regional' standards and the manifold varieties of 'non-standard' speech – has been investigated. In this connection too, the issue of the development and operation of social styles of speech (e.g. 'polite', 'educated', 'vulgar') needs to be addressed (cf. Mugglestone 1995).

5.16.4

The relationship between the forms of English described in this chapter and ex-colonial varieties of English requires thorough investigation. For example, the fronter, [aː]-ish realisations of the vowel in HEART, etc., in southern English English of the late eighteenth and early nineteenth centuries have their counterparts in, for example, present-day Northern English English and Australian English. Some of the lexical stress patterns of the later eighteenth century (e.g. ADVER'TISEMENT) have their counterparts in several forms of present-day Scottish English and American English. It is tempting to suggest that, by listening to certain late twentieth-century regional accents of English, one can achieve a more realistic awareness of how particular features of southern English English would have sounded at various stages during the last 200 or more years.[153] Kenyon, for example, goes so far as to state that 'American pronunciation is today [1946] what Southern British was in 1800–50' (Kenyon 1946: 167).

5.16.5

Although little has been said here about the motivations for the sound-changes that have been discussed, a tacit assumption has been that socially inferior forms of speech (e.g. Cockney) have contributed to – if not directly stimulated – the alterations in at least some of the more socially elevated forms: cf. Dobson 1968: 945, 975, Wells 1982: 104–05. This hypothesis, if it can be further substantiated and refined, has important implications for a sociolinguistic theory of sound-change.

NOTES

1 The terms are taken from Wells (1982: 72–81). The theoretical stance of this chapter is that an older, philological approach to the description of sounds and the changes they undergo, which would analyse the sounds of the eighteenth century onwards simply as reflexes of ME vowel and consonant phonemes from some 400 and more years earlier (see e.g. Horn & Lehnert 1954) can fail to capture all of the data synchronically – especially if the

sound in question has no historical antecedent in Middle English. Wells's accent-differentiation framework has been employed instead. Diachronic changes are thus viewed as alterations to one or more of the four strands of the framework, not merely as a change from one 'sound' to another.

2 See section 5.10.5 of this chapter and *CHEL* V, for references to the same phenomenon in twentieth-century Irish and Caribbean English.

3 See also the comments by the Arabist, Francis Newman, on the differences between educated English in the 1870s and in the earlier nineteenth century (Newman 1878).

4 His *Rhetorical Grammar* (1780) is an appendix to the *General Dictionary*. Other authors (e.g. Walker and Kenrick) also published works with the title *Rhetorical Grammar*.

5 Books on spelling and reading for school-children (e.g. Murray, L. 1800, Anon. 1817) are also of use. On these, see e.g. Michael 1993.

6 Many orthoepical works, especially reissues, were published anonymously.

7 The need for an agreed method for identifying vowels was recognised as early as 1860. The American linguist, Samuel Haldeman writes that 'vowels cannot be described intelligibly until there is a scale or apparatus by which the exact amount of throat or lip aperture may be indicated' (Haldeman 1860: 77).

8 Thomas Batchelor was born and lived in Bedfordshire. James Buchanan, though born possibly in Scotland, was a schoolmaster in Surrey. James Elphinston, born in Edinburgh, moved to London at the age of 32. Stephen Jones was born and lived in London. William Kenrick was born in Hertfordshire. James Malcolm was born in Philadelphia, but left for London whilst still a schoolboy. William Mitford was born in London, educated in Surrey and Oxford, and lived near Southampton and was an MP in the House of Commons. Lindley Murray was born in Pennsylvania, but moved to York (England) at the age of 18, spending the rest of his life in England. Robert Nares was born in York and moved later to London (and Oxford). Samuel Pegge was educated at Cambridge, and later lived in London. Edward Search (the *nom-de-plume* of Abraham Tucker) was born in London and educated in Hertfordshire and Oxford; he later lived in Surrey. Granville Sharp, born in Durham, moved to London at the age of 15. Thomas Sheridan, though born in Dublin, was educated in London for a short time during his teens. He moved back to Dublin, but later returned to London as an actor. Benjamin Smart lived in London and taught elocution there. Thomas Steele, though born in Dublin, lived in London for many years. John Walker spent most of his life in London (see also 5.4.7). (Much of this information derives from entries in the *Dictionary of National Biography* and/or from remarks in the works of the individual authors.)

9 Later, in the 1880s, when the phonetic notation to be used in the *OED* was being prepared, the phonetician James Lecky reminded James Murray, the dictionary's editor, to notate 'real, living speech', not the 'formal, fictitious or antiquated orthoepy' of the earlier dictionaries (cf. MacMahon 1985: 77).

10 'Jeder Kenner dieser Materie wird einräumen müssen, daß die wahren Grund-
sätzen der Aussprache des Englischen auf einer ganz andern Basis ruhen, als
jener Orthoepist [= Walker] ihr zu geben gesucht hat' (Voigtmann 1846: 166).

11 Keble composed 'Sun of my soul, thou Saviour dear', from which this
example is taken, in November 1820, at the age of 28. Hymns have tended
to be a underused source of information on changes (and fashions) in
English pronunciation.

12 Cf. Connolly 1981: 403 on nineteenth-century Ulster rhymes as a potential
source of information on contemporary regional pronunciations.

13 Further information about Thornton is given in fn. 45.

14 But amateurish commentaries have continued: 'There are few subjects on
which educated Americans are so ready to pass judgment and give advice on
the basis of so little sound knowledge as the pronunciation of the language
we use' (Kenyon 1946: 3).

15 An exception is Gildon & Brightland's *Grammar of the English Tongue* (1711),
which specifically refers to the work of John Wallis and Francis Lodwick.

16 See in particular the lengthy 'Principles of English Pronunciation' included
in the *Critical Pronouncing Dictionary*.

17 Cf. also the comments on James Brady's 'phonemic intuition' in his
French–English dictionary of 1756 (Popp 1989: 54).

18 This topic is reviewed by Sheldon 1946.

19 A later example of Court speech still being regarded as the automatic norm
was: 'pronunciation most used by men of education at Court . . . the best
authority . . . the only standard we can refer to' (Telonicus 1798: 569). This is
a quotation from Sheridan's *Course of Lectures on Elocution* (1762: 45).

20 For those 'who are not so fortunate to possess a polite London utterance', he
was, of course, able to recommend his *Practical Grammar of English
Pronunciation* (Smart 1819: 41)!

21 Cf. Ellis 1869: 624–30.

22 Note similarly the wide degree of variability between two educated speakers that
Montgomery discussed, nearly forty years later (Montgomery 1910: 46–51).

23 See also the phonetic transcriptions of their respective accents in Ellis 1874:
1206–07.

24 A more geographically circumscribed definition was 'der mir geläufige
Londoner dialect, wie er in gebildeten kreisen gesprochen wird' (1885: iii).

25 According to Wyld, the replacement of earlier /n/ by /ŋ/ took place in the
1820s and 1830s (Wyld 1913: 21). See also 5.10.14.

26 He later refers to it as *mainstream* RP (Gimson 1989: 88).

27 British visitors to North America in the eighteenth century had also been
struck by the widespread uniformity of pronunciation, compared with the
situation in the British Isles: see Read 1933/1980: 20–3.

28 See also the extracts from various writers on the question of standard and
correct pronunciations in *Webster* (Gove 1971: 40a–41a).

29 Two changes have been made to the phoneme symbols in Wells 1990, to aid the comparison of RP and GenAm. Instead of /e/ DRESS and /ɒː/ THOUGHT, the symbols /ε/ and /ɔː/ have been used.

30 Note in this connection the comment by Kenyon (1946: 211) about 'observation of this sound [being] difficult' in twentieth-century American speech.

31 A /ɪu/ diphthong remains in present day New England accents: i.e. it is felt by native speakers to be a single vowel unit, not a sequence of /j/ and /uː/. Webster's accent was New England.

32 The possibility of the contrast being additionally dependent on a different rhythmical structure of the two sentences is not discussed by Kenyon. See also the different notations of the /juː/ sequence in the words MISUSED and ABUSED in OED1.

33 There is some evidence, albeit ambiguous, to suggest that, at an earlier stage in the history of some forms of English English, one of the reflexes of later ME /iː/ may have been /ɪi/, which was separate from both /eː/ deriving from ME /εː/, and /iː/ deriving from ME /eː/ (Dobson 1968: 662). If such a phoneme had ever existed, and if its realisation had been [ɪ] rather than [ɪi] (at least in some contexts), then it appears to have been lost from the system after about the end of the seventeenth century.

34 In the first (1791) and second (1797) editions, the wording is different: Walker grouped the vowel of EIGHT, WEIGHT, etc. with that of DEIGN, etc. It is not known what caused him to change his mind for the 1802 edition.

35 The comment by Horn/Lehnert (1954: 329) that 'andere Sprachlehrer' made the distinction cannot be substantiated.

36 Wells refers to it as 'BATH raising'.

37 For Ellis's own pronunciations of BAD, MAN, and GLAD – all with a short [æ] – see Ellis 1874: 1169, 1171, 1173.

38 See Fudge (1977) for a detailed discussion of [æ] and [æː] in a Southern English English idiolect. The existence of an extra phoneme has been noted too for some forms of American and Australian speech (see references in Fudge 1977).

39 Neumann 1924: 36.

40 This remark is not in the original, 1791, edition.

41 The key symbol is (ǫ̇), which occurs in words such as SOFT and COST, and which is glossed as being 'of medial or doubtful length'. Murray, the first editor of the OED1, set up six symbols associated with the two phonemes /ɒ/ and /ɔː/. Of these, (ǫ̇) is used for OFTEN, but (ǭ̇), in ORPHAN. ((ǭ̇), is also used for SOUGHT, but (ǭ̇), in NAUGHT.) It should be borne in mind that Murray's notational set was not intended to notate only RP, but other educated British accents as well. Furthermore, his own accent was Scottish, whose phonology and phonetics with respect to words like CROSS, GOT, WALK, THORN, WRATH, was crucially different from that of RP (see MacMahon 1985).

42 See the discussion of North-East English and Scottish pronunciations as 'modified standards' in the eighteenth century in Beal (1994). On Spence, see Shields (1974).

43 Even in today's RP, there are few minimal pairs with which to demonstrate its existence. Reference to stress patterns and different vowel qualities is usually required. Alexander Melville Bell instances the minimal pair 'Men shun him' and 'Mention him' (see Ellis 1874: 1162), but his accent was modified Scottish English, not English English.

44 He refers, during the course of his discussion of unaccented syllables, to the '[ə]-[ʌ] phoneme' in twentieth-century English, dating back to the late seventeenth century (Dobson 1968: 920).

45 Thornton's accent is not easy to determine. He was born in the West Indies in 1759 of English parents and lived there until the age of five when he moved to England. He studied medicine at Edinburgh, subsequently graduating MD from Aberdeen at the age of 25. He returned to America when he was 27, remaining there for the rest of his life (see Kimball 1936). From the examples he quotes in his 'Cadmus' (Thornton 1793), he seems to have had, in addition to /ʌ/ doing duty for /ʌ/ and /ə/, a tenuous /æ/≠/aː/ distinction (CALM has /aː/, but YARN and DARK have /æ/). /ʌ/ also occurs in LENGTH (1793: 286) and VERY; /ɒ/ in NO, GO, COST, OPEN; and /uː/ in TOOK, HOOK, WOULD – the latter even with /l/ (1793: 285); the word JURY has /ʊ/, not /uː/ as one would have expected; and SPECIAL (1793: 290) has /æ/ in the last syllable, not /ʌ/.

46 On Buchanan, see Ellis 1874: 1050, Sheldon 1938: 260. On Herries, see Scott 1928: 474. If this John Herries were the author of the *Elements of Speech* (1773), then he would have been aged about 83 when it appeared. Another, younger John Herries, who matriculated at Edinburgh University in 1765 and 1767 (i.e. when he was in his teens or early 20s) is the more likely author (Edinburgh University Archives). On Smith (*c*.1750–*c*.1829), see Scott 1928: 494.

47 See, for example, the title of the 1795 work, together with the comments on the phonotactics of #Cj— and #C— in New England and the southern states (1795: 25).

48 Such a phonemic contrast is not to be confused with the use of /uː/≠/juː/ (THROUGH≠THREW) in certain Welsh, north-of-England and American accents (cf. Wells 1982: 206, 385–6).

49 I am grateful to John Local (University of York, England) for the information about the contrast in and around Tyneside.

50 See also the commentary by Ekwall 1975: 47–50.

51 The conflation of /ʊə/, /ɔə/ and /ɔː/ is regarded by Nicklin as a feature of 'careless speakers of Standard English' (1920: 44). He instances the developing homophony of POOR, PORE, POUR, and PAWER.

52 In place of /ɜr/, one could write /ər/.

53 Cf. also the later remark by Nicklin (1920: 50): 'The writer can recall a discussion in which for nearly a quarter of an hour one speaker of Standard English endeavoured by iteration and emphasis to make clear to three others a difference which he supposed himself to make between the sounds he used for *fir* and *fur*.'

54 Sweet considered that Bell's scheme derived from 'artificial elocutionary habits' (Sweet 1877: 111).

55 Thomas Hallam later responded to his questionnaire, with the result that the unaccented vowels of 'educated English' form a major part of his diary data; see MacMahon 1983 and references therein. For example, Hallam concluded that, for the vowel corresponding to <i> in CALAMITY, about 57 per cent of his 'educated speakers' used /ə/, about 28 per cent /ɪ/, whilst the remaining 14 per cent varied between /ɪ/ and /ə/.

56 Similar attention to the fine detail of the pronunciation of unaccented vowels can be found in the twentieth century, in Jones's discussion of the qualities and distribution of several distinct allophones of /ə/ (Jones, D. 1960: 91–4). Note, though, that Dobson (1968: 920) saw no point in attempting to identify or explain their historical antecedents.

57 An explanation for the difference between the two unstressed vowels in the first pair could be the operation of a word-prosody of 'darkness', resulting in all the segments following the initial /k/ being 'darker' than those following the initial /m/ (cf. Kelly 1995).

58 These transcriptions are deliberately phonetic, not phonemic.

59 Wells (1990a: 476) uses [i] for [ɪ], [iː], 'or something intermediate or indeterminate' in weak syllables.

60 Both Walker and Ellis stressed this word on the second syllable.

61 The comment by Dobson (1968: 918) that in twentieth-century English, 'unstressed [ɪ] always tends to be laxer . . . and . . . is often lowered to [ɇ] [=IPA [e]]' raises questions about Dobson's interpretation of the phonetics of /ɪ/ – above CV2 [e], or raised and retracted from it? It therefore cannot be taken at face value.

62 Murray's reply has not survived.

63 Walker uses <ḙ> for the vowel in e.g. METRE, but <ḛe> for the vowel in SEA and the syllable-final unstressed vowels in PROFILE and INVALID. Dyche (1805: 82) also notes that 'at the end of words [y] is commonly sounded like *ee*, as in *Normandy, formerly, liberty*'. Whether anything specific can be read into his use of 'commonly' is not clear.

64 In the 1791 edition, the vowel is /ʌɪ/, subsequently changed in all the later editions to /ɪ/.

65 Ellis (1874: 1162) notes that the recent pronunciation of MADAM as ['mædæm'] is used by 'shopwomen'. By contrast, the pronunciation of the word by 'servant girls' in the phrases YES, MADAM, or NO, MADAM is [m̩m̩] (1874: 1167).

66 'Careful speakers, especially clergymen, insist on . . . -*i*l [= IPA [-ęl]]' (Ellis 1874: 1164).
67 His transcription of FAR is a matter of lexical incidence, not of vowel change dependent on stress.
68 The term is taken from Wells 1982: 203–06.
69 The data used in this analysis is as follows:

ɒr

AWARD (Nares 1784), CORD (Elphinston 1790, Mackintosh 1799, Gilchrist 1824), CORN (Mackintosh 1799), DWARF (Elphinston 1790), FORM [= FIGURE] (Smart 1842), FORTUNE (Duponceau 1818), FORTY (Elphinston 1790), GORGE (Carrol 1795), LORD (Sharp 1777), MORTAL (Duponceau 1818), NORTH (Carrol 1795), ORCHARD (Duponceau 1818), SHORT (Thornton 1793), WAR (Kenrick 1784, Elphinston 1790, Hornsey 1807).

ɔːr

BORN (Herries 1773), CORD (Sheridan 1781, Anon 1812, Angus 1830), CORE (Henslowe 1840), EXHORT (Johnston 1764), FORK (Hornsey 1807, Anon 1812, Angus 1830), GEORGE (Sheridan 1781), LORD (Sheridan 1781, Fulton 1826), LORE (Henslowe 1840), MORE (Henslowe 1840), NORTH (Fulton 1826), ORB (Angus 1830), SHORT (Sheridan 1781, Fulton 1826), SORT (Angus 1830), STORK (Hornsey 1807), SWARTH (Hornsey 1807), WAR (Fogg 1792, Harvey 1793, Adams 1794), WARD (Henslowe 1840), WARM (Barrie 1794, Fulton & Knight 1800), WARN (Barrie 1794, Fulton & Knight 1800).

70 For details of the current distribution of /æ/ and /ɑː/ in RP, see Wells 1982: 232–3.
71 Grandgent 1893b: 7. This comparison involves data which are not strictly comparable: 58 speakers from one part of the GenAm. area, but 'all' GenAm. speakers as represented by Wells 1990a. See also the other numerical categories calculated by Grandgent and his comment that 'it appears that in the North every word in the list is variable'.
72 In Scottish English, the phrase would be /ɪv kors/.
73 Cf. Wells 1982: 236.
74 One notes the absence from Sweet's list of a pronunciation containing the older 'fashionable' /ɡj-/ sequence. By the late nineteenth century, a <gyell> pronunciation was considered 'illiterate' (Mugglestone 1995: 234). See also section 5.10.5.
75 Spence 1775 and Knowles 1837 give BUM as /bʌm/ and BOMB as /bɒm/.
76 On his varied linguistic background, see fn. 45.
77 The standard work on the subject (Thurot 1881–3) is unhelpful in that it concentrates mainly on orthographic matters and makes very little attempt to discuss the material in phonetic terms.
78 Görlach, however, regards the diphthongal pronunciation as being the norm since at least the *beginning* of the eighteenth century (1991: 70).

79 Confusion also arises in later editions, e.g. 1819: 27, 1838: 21, which quote FÉE and ÉPÉE. Comparisons with the pronunciation of French, Italian and German words abound in the literature – especially French: cf. Sharp 1767: 4, Sharp 1777: 8, 23; Nares 1784: 3; Smith 1795: 9; Mackintosh, Mackintosh & Mackintosh 1799: opp. 47; Henslowe 1840: 16.

80 Wells 1982: 210.

81 Most discussions of the actual quality of a diphthong fail to mention that a bi-literal symbol such as IPA [eɪ] omits a considerable amount of information, which in the case of the change of /eː/ to /eɪ/ is relevant: the time spent by the tongue on its trajectory from starting-point to end-point; the speed of accel-eration and deceleration; and the precise starting- and end-points. Notations which give more information than IPA does can be found in the works of Ellis. He utilizes notations such as (*ⁱ̈*), (*eⁱ*), (*eeⁱ*) (cf. Ellis 1874: 1108–12).

82 Presumably he meant the French grave <è>.

83 Care is needed when interpreting Thornton's accent: see fn. 45.

84 See Eustace 1969: 77.

85 Ellis 1874: 1106. For the interpretation of (ɛ), see Eustace 1969: 77.

86 James Brady too, in his French–English dictionary of 1756, makes it clear that English /æ/ was not the same as either French <a> or <è> (Popp 1989: 139).

87 Ekwall (1975: 15) dismisses, without explanation, the possibility of any other realisation of /æ/ than [æ]. He even finds fault with Walker's description (1791)!

88 See fn. 45.

89 Note the later comment by Ellis that (*a*) [= IPA [ɑ]] 'is now lost in English, but is heard in Scotch' (Ellis 1869: 593).

90 On Ellis's Palaeotype notation, and the difficulties surrounding its interpre-tation, see Eustace 1969.

91 Ekwall (1975: 23) opts for [æː] – but with the proviso that it was 'usually a front' vowel.

92 Note that Ekwall's translator, A. Ward, uses [a] for IPA [ɑ] (more accurately, [ɐ], MKCM) (Ekwall 1975: xv).

93 Eustace 1969 maintains that the position of Ellis's (a) in relation to the Visible Speech scheme (i.e. IPA [ʌ]) was 'very wrong' (Eustace 1969: 77), but admits that an 'obvious explanation' is not forthcoming. He believes in any case that Ellis's (a) was [ɐ]. Either way, one is dealing with a vowel sound which lies towards the bottom-right corner of the CV chart, whereas seventy or more years earlier, at the end of the eighteenth century, the articulation had been further forward, towards the bottom-left area of the CV chart.

94 There is a crucial ambiguity in Ellis's notation. Does one read (aah) as (a) fol-lowed by (ah), in which case it transliterates into IPA as [ʌɐ]; or as (ahah) [= IPA [ɐː]? I have taken it in the latter sense, solely because Ellis does not draw attention to any diphthongal quality in the sound.

95 His background was mixed. He was born in 1760 in France and learned English from British soldiers garrisoned in his home-town of St. Martin. At the age of 17, he sailed for America, eventually becoming a lawyer in Philadelphia. See Knott (1930) for further details.

96 See also the discussion of /ɒː/≠/ɔː/above, section 5.5.10.

97 Jones's partial comparison of the starting-point with that of the French vowel in LE is further evidence of a more centralised starting-point (Jones, D. 1909: 87).

98 Montgomery's notation *nɒu* is equivalent to IPA [nʌʊ].

99 See also section 5.6.7.

100 See MacMahon 1985: 81–3.

101 Herries was Scottish by birth (and probably upbringing) – see fn. 46 – and this may have a bearing on what sort of English he was describing. A current Scottish pronunciation of TIDE would be [tʌid], and of TIED [taed].

102 It is noteworthy that the new edition of the *Shorter OED* (Brown 1993) uses /ʌɪ/, not /aɪ/.

103 Cf. Wells 1990a: 136.

104 It must be remembered too that Sharp came from Durham, in the North of England, and he may well be quoting examples of his own speech; see fn. 8.

105 See also the very similar remarks in Elphinston 1766: 4, 1790: 49, as well as in Buchanan 1766: xviii, Herries 1773: 41, Sharp 1777: 3, Sheridan 1781: 21–2, Perry 1793: xvii, Barrie 1794: 4, Odell 1806: 15, and Knowles 1837: 7.

106 See fn. 95.

107 Consonants do not attract the same analytical attention in the orthoepical literature as vowels – for reasons to do with the greater isomorphism between their phonetic values and the equivalent orthographic symbols.

108 Loss of /ʍ/ was due to pressure from 'vulgar' speech: see Dobson 1968: 945, 975.

109 Western (1902: 25) regards it as infrequent in normal speech, but more frequent when reading aloud. On the other hand, True & Jespersen (1897: *passim*) use it consistently.

110 In this same passage, Ellis draws attention to a third pronunciation: [ʍw-] alongside [ʍ] and [w].

111 James Murray was advised to keep it in the *OED* (MacMahon 1985: 77) – sure evidence that *some* speakers were no longer using it.

112 Cf. Jespersen 1909/1961: 374, Ward, I.C. 1945: 151; Jones, D. 1960: 208 ('In the South the more usual pronunciation . . . is **wɔt, witʃ**, etc., though the use of ʍ or **hw** is sometimes taught as being more 'correct'); Gimson 1980: 215–16 ('Among RP speakers . . . especially males – the use of /ʍ/ as a phoneme has declined rapidly (though it is often taught as the correct form in verse-speaking)'); Wells 1982: 228–9 ('Present-day RP usage could be described as schizophrenic').

113 /f/ LOCH, Sharp 1767; /f/ LOUGH Sharp 1767, Spence 1775; /k/LOCH Spence 1775, Sheridan 1781, Nares 1784, Smith 1795, Smart 1836; /k/ LOUGH Sheridan 1781, Carrol 1795, Smart 1836.

114 Further examples (albeit associated with syllable-boundaries) can be found amongst the variant spellings of certain surnames: see e.g. the entries for BROCKLEBANK, BUTLIN, MUTLOW, PRITLOVE, ROUTLEDGE, and SHERCLIFF in Reaney (1991). I am grateful to Carole Hough (University of Glasgow) for drawing my attention to this.

115 Personal observations.

116 See also section 5.5.3 above.

117 Wells's 'Early Yod Dropping' (1982: 206–7) clearly lasted longer than the early years of the eighteenth century.

118 'In Dr Webster's view, [the best speakers] give a slight softening between the vowel and the consonant, pronouncing *rude* in a less broad and open manner than *rood*' (Webster 1847: lxxxiv).

119 Ellis comments that 'the pronunciation of the stage is inclined to be archaic, except in the modernest imitations of everyday life' (Ellis 1869: 23). In this connection, note the reference to the archaic (and rhotic) pronunciation of BOURNE as [buːrn] by Sir Herbert Beerbohm Tree (1852–1917) in 1906 (Eustace 1969: 63).

120 *EPD*1 has only /kaɪnd/. It lives on, albeit very sporadically, in some forms of late twentieth-century English English and Scottish English. In Irish English, its use is more widespread. See *CHEL* V.

121 Walker had died in 1807.

122 Melville Bell, however, continued to teach the /kj-/ and /gj-/ pronunciations to his students of elocution (Horn 1905: 42).

123 He does, however, let slip the opposite view, in 1874, that GUIDANCE 'has very frequently (gj), even from young speakers' (Ellis 1874: 1161).

124 The identity of the Earl of Harrowby cannot be determined precisely. He was either Dudley Francis Stuart Ryder (1831–1900) or Henry Dudley Ryder (1836–1900).

125 Similarly, Brady had noted thirty years earlier, in 1756, that English syllable-final /r/ 'est tellement adoucie qu'elle devient presque muette' (Popp 1989: 165–6).

126 See also Emerson R. H. (1993).

127 He contrasts this with the total absence of post-vocalic /r/ 'amongst the vulgar in London' in words like FAR, HARD, CORD, LORD – 'an extreme which must be avoided as carefully as the strong trill of the *r* in an improper place' (Smart 1836: vii). Cf. also C. Jones's view that there is some evidence from this period to suggest that '[r] vocalization . . . was considerably stigmatized' (Jones C. 1989: 300).

128 Similarly, Duponceau draws attention to the fact that the /eː/ in FAME and FAIR (in American speech) were 'evidently dissimilar' (Duponceau 1818: 232).

129 On Hallam and his observations of educated and dialect speech, see MacMahon 1983.

130 Cf. also the dogmatic statement by Country Rector (1890) that he could 'find a distinct and additional movement of the tongue in the words containing the R'.

131 For a survey of mainly nineteenth-century views on intrusive /r/, from 1849 to 1907, see Jespersen 1909/1961: 371–2.

132 See Mugglestone (1995: 107–59) for a detailed discussion of the social implications of /h/-ful and /h/-less pronunciations in England during the nineteenth century.

133 Dobson classes the pronunciation [-ntʃ] 'a ModE development', without being more specific (Dobson 1968: 1002).

134 Discussion of this topic is hindered by uncertainty over the *phonetic* values of the 'letters'. In BENCH, for example, is a respelling such as <nsh> to be read as: [nʃ], [nʔʃ], [nn̩ʃ] (i.e. with laryngealisation of the second part of [n]); and is <ntsh> [ntʃ], [nn̩tʃ] or [nʔtʃ]? The ambiguity in whether to interpret <ntsh> as indicating a postalveolar plosive after the <n> (hence a <t> in the respelling) or some other phonetic activity (e.g. laryngealisation of the preceding [n]) may invalidate the conclusions set out here.

135 Fogg (1792) quotes /n/ in MORNING and STOCKINGS.

136 Jespersen (1909: 297) notes that, despite the change in spelling from 'Bristow' to 'Bristol' in the seventeenth century, the /l/-less pronunciation predominated until at least the late eighteenth century; see also Ekwall 1975: 65. The wider issue of intrusive /l/ in the speech of the Bristol area is discussed by Wells 1982: 344–5.

137 Noteworthy in this connection is the detailed discussion of word-final /t/ by Ellis (1874: 1111–2), which touches on the mechanisms of aspirated release and glottalised release, but makes no mention of [ʔ] by itself as a possible allophone. He does, nevertheless, refer, cryptically, to the 'phonetic mysteries, which are far from having been yet fully revealed' surrounding word-final /t/— this in connection primarily with syllabification in Danish. See also his later comments on word-initial [ʔ] in various Yorkshire dialects (1889: 317) – again suggesting that, had the glottal plosive existed naturally in RP towards the end of the nineteenth century, Ellis would have commented on it.

138 Cf., however, Sheridan's comment that 'this letter has always the same sound' (Sheridan 1781: 34), and Smith's 'R has uniformly one sound, as in the English word *rear*' (Smith 1795: xliii). Note, however, Walker's comment that 'there is a distinction in the sound of this letter, scarcely ever noticed by any of our writers on the subject; and that is the rough and smooth *r* (Walker 1791: 50). For an early seventeenth-century comment by Thomas Hayward on different realisations of /r/, see Dobson 1968: 324, 946.

139 Walker writes *baa* in place of *laad* – a misprint.

140 This description is similar to that in Sheridan (1781: 34).

141 Although he was described on the 1795 titlepage as 'living in Camberwell' (i.e. close to London), other evidence shows that his background was Scottish: see e.g. Scott 1928: 494.

142 See Eustace 1969: 61–6 for a detailed exposition and discussion of the variety of [r]-like sounds and symbols used by Ellis. Some of these, e.g. Ellis's 'vocal *r*', and 'vocal murmur', were probably rhotacised sounds. Similarly, of the two sorts of /r/ realisation mentioned by Comstock & Mair (1874), the second, the 'smooth' one, is also likely to have been rhotacised (Comstock & Mair 1874: 16–17).

143 The description of American /r/ by Day (1843: 450) deliberately leaves open the question of the position and activity of the tip of the tongue, once the 'essential position' is established of the posterior part of the tongue being in contact with the upper teeth or gums.

144 Confirmation of an earlier fricative pronunciation may come from the typical South African pronunciation nowadays of /r/ as a fricative, not an approximant – on the assumption that an earlier (i.e. eighteenth and early nineteenth century) British pronunciation lies behind some of the phonological and phonetic features of modern South African English. A similar line of argument can be offered for the occurrence of the 'bunched /r/' in American English, with a possible antecedent being the use of this articulation in earlier forms of British English.

145 ABDOMEN, ACADEMY, ACCEPTABLE, ACCEPTABLY, ACCESS, ACCESSARY, ACCESSORY, ACETOSE, ACUMEN, ADMINISTRATOR, ADVERTISE, ADVERTISEMENT, ADVERTISER, ADVERTISING, AERIAL, ALCOVE, ALLY, ALMOST, AMPHITHEATRE, ANCHOVY, ANNEX, APHRODISIAC, ARBUTUS, ARCHDUKE, ARISTOCRACY, ARISTOCRAT, AVANT-GARDE, BALCONY, BELLES LETTRES, BITUMEN, BOMBAST, CANINE, CAPILLARY, CAPRICE, CARBINE, CELIBACY, CEMENT, CEMENT (V), CHAMPAIGN (open country), CHAMPAIGN (wine), COADJUTOR, COMMENDATORY, COMMENDABLE, COMMENDATORY, COMMENTATOR, COMMODORE, COMMONWEALTH, COMPENSATE, COMPLAISANCE, COMPROMISE, COMPROMISING, CONCORDANCE, CONFESSOR, CONFISCATE, CONSECUTIVE, CONSISTORY, CONSTRUE, CONSTRUED, CONSUMMATE, CONTEMPLATE, CONTRARY, CONTROVERSY, COQUETRY, COROLLARY, CORRIDOR, DANDELION, DECOROUS, DEHORTATORY, DEMONSTRABLY, DEMONSTRATE, DEPRECATORY, DESPICABLE, DESPICABLENESS, DIOCESAN, DISPUTABLE, ELONGATE, ENERVATE, ENTERPRISE, ENTERPRISING, ENVELOPE, EXCAVATE, EXCAVATED, EXECUTER, EXEMPLARY, EXHORTATORY, EXIGENCY, EXPURGATORY, EXQUISITE, EXQUISITELY, FINANCIER, FLORIN, FORMIDABLY, GEOGRAPHY, GLADIATOR, GRIMACE, HOSPITABLE, HOSPITABLY, HYPOCHONDRIAC, HYPOCHONDRIACAL, ILLUSTRATE, ILLUSTRATIVELY, IMBECILE, IMPRECATORY, INCULCATE, INDISPUTABLE,

INDISSOLUBLE, INDISSOLUBLY, INEXPERT, INEXPLICABLE, INN HOLDER, INOPPORTUNE, INTERSTICE, INTUMESCENCE, IRREPARA- BLE, JUDICATURE, KORAN, LABORATORY, LANDAU, LEGISLATOR, MAGNETISE, MATADOR, MEDIATOR, MENAGERIE, MISCELLANY, MISHAP, MODERATOR, MULTIPLICATE, OBDURATE, OPERATOR, ORCHESTRA, ORCHESTRE, PACIFICATORY, PANTHEON, PEREMPTO- RILY, PEREMPTORINESS, PEREMPTORY, PERFECT (V), PERFECTED, PREDICAMENT, PRETEXT, PROCURATOR, PROFILE, PROMULGATE, QUADRUPLE, QUINTESSENCE, RAGAMUFFIN, RECOGNISE, RECOG- NISING, RECUSANT, REMONSTRATE, RENDEZVOUS, RESEARCH, RESERVOIR, RETINUE, SACRIFICATORY, SACRIFICING, SALINE, SATELLITE, SCRUTINISE, SHERBET, SINISTER, SPLENETIC, SUBSTAN- TIVE, SUCCESSOR, SUPERFLUOUS, SUPERVISE, SUPERVISING, SUR- CHARGE, SURVEY, TOPOGRAPHY, TOUPEE, TRAVERSE, TRAVERSE, TURMOIL, UNDERTAKER, UNTOWARD, UNTOWARDLY, UTENSIL, VAGARY, VENTILATOR, VERTIGO, VIBRATE.

146 Ideally, a dataset is required which takes full account of the various morpho- logical features and diachronic lexical sources which have contributed to the numerous lexical stress patterns of English (cf. the typology of such a dataset in Kingdon 1958). Furthermore, the accuracy of some of the data to be examined here cannot be fully guaranteed. For instance, it is noteworthy that *OED*2 (1992) quotes far more cases of alternative stress-patterns which are identical to pre-1945 patterns, than any of the other dictionaries from 1945 onwards. This may have more to do with the automatic 'translation' of Murray's phonetic notation for *OED*1 into IPA for *OED*2 (cf. MacMahon 1985), than the results of any survey of late twentieth-century stress patterns. An example is ILLUSTRATE: up to about 1850, the pattern was xpx; by 1908, it was both pxx and xpx; since 1917, the stressing has been only pxx – with the exception of *OED*2, which, in 1992, has xpx. The latter is the same as *OED*1's stress-pattern of the word from no later than 1899.

147 Even then, the brief remarks in, for example, Herries 1773 and Odell 1806 are indicative rather than substantive.

148 See further Abercrombie 1965.

149 The pitch of A_4 in the 1770s was approximately 425 Hz; cf. with today's 440 Hz. Consequently, all the pitch values in Steele 1775/1779 should be lowered by about a semi-tone to reproduce as accurately as possible the physical qual- ities of Steele's and Garrick's intonation.

150 A caveat must be that Steele was born in Ireland and moved later to London. Garrick was brought up in Staffordshire and moved to London at the age of twenty. Given the relatively sparse examples that exist of intonation gener- ally in the published literature, it is not possible to determine the extent to which their rhythm and intonation may have differed from that of educated native Londoners.

151 Vol. II contains a few more examples. Walker makes no attempt to systematise the description of intonation. Note, however, the view of Faber 1987: 31, who argues that Walker's 'genius [in the description of intonation] and the scale of his contribution are not sufficiently recognised'. Faber maintains that Walker anticipated 'in many ways' the concept of the nucleus, that he described all the nuclear tones and that he introduced the tonetic marks for rising and falling tones. (One can, of course, already see elements of Walker's analysis in Steele (1775).)

152 Cylinder recordings exist of the speech of Alfred, Lord Tennyson (1809–92), William Gladstone (1809–98), Robert Browning (1812–89), George, 2nd Duke of Cambridge (1819–1904), William Booth (1829–1912), Arthur Peel (1829–1912), Robert Cecil, 3rd Marquess of Salisbury (1830–1903), Charles Haddon Spurgeon (1834–92), and Sir Henry Irving (1838–1905). For an analysis of a recording of Gladstone, see Eustace 1969: 74.

153 It cannot be assumed, of course, that 'regional' accents (within Britain at least) will automatically have been more conservative, and hence have altered less over the last two centuries than RP has.

FURTHER READING

The major scholarly study of the period between late Middle English and the early eighteenth century is Dobson (1968); occasionally, it also touches on matters to do with later eighteenth-century pronunciations. Horn & Lehnert (1954), though much less detailed than Dobson, brings the description of both British and American English pronunciations forward in the twentieth century. Specifically for American English from the mid-eighteenth to the early twentieth century, the second volume of Krapp (1925) is recommended. Jespersen (1909/1961) is an accessible text, and includes much useful commentary on late nineteenth-century pronunciation. Briefer summaries of the period can be found in Ekwall (1975) and Görlach (1991). Wells's *tour de force* of current English pronunciation world-wide (1982) includes several discussions of phonological changes from Middle English onwards. Mugglestone (1995) is an important study of various aspects of the sociophonetics of nineteenth-century British English.

6 ENGLISH GRAMMAR AND USAGE

Edward Finegan

6.1. Introduction

The codification of English usage, not by an official academy but by a disparate band of independent entrepreneurs, constitutes the story of this chapter. It is a story of increasing knowledge about language in general and English in particular, of competition between prescriptive and descriptive ideals of grammar and lexicography in the market-place and of a shifting role for the place of speech and writing in codifying the language. It is also a story of the influence of piety, morality, discipline and social politics on the evaluation of English usage as the language was codified and the codifications disseminated over the last two centuries. The focus throughout is on Britain, but the interactions between Britons and Americans and the intertwined scholarship and international markets for English-language grammars and dictionaries make a tidy separation of the British and American stories impracticable. Following section 6.1, the discussion is divided into three periods. Section 6.2 concentrates on the years roughly from the mid-eighteenth century to the introduction of comparative historical linguistics into Britain around 1830, section 6.3 the period from 1830 to 1930 so as to encompass the entire scope of planning and producing the *Oxford English Dictionary*, and section 6.4 the span from the completion of the *OED* to the close of the millennium. The chronological subdivisions are somewhat arbitrary in that the patterns examined do not start or end on particular dates, but the periods serve as convenient frames for focusing on notable trends. Section 6.5 offers some conclusions and prospects. (American views of grammar and usage are reported in volume VI.)

6.1.1 Latin yields to English in Britain

Latin played an important role in the intellectual life of Britain for some time after the Reformation had muted its voice in the religious life of the nation. Although English increasingly encroached on the already limited territory of the classical language, Latin by no means vanished from Britain. Especially in matters of philosophy and science, writers surprisingly often preferred the classical tongue. In the seventeenth century even grammars of English appeared in Latin, as with Wallis's influential *Grammatica Linguae Anglicanae* (1653) and Cooper's (1685) later work of the same title. In other fields, too, writing continued in Latin well into the eighteenth century: Newton employed it not only for *Principia Mathematica* (1687) but also for *Arithmetica Universalis* (1707). As well, the Royal Society's *Philosophical Transactions* contain occasional pieces in Latin as late as 1775. Further, in the last decades of the eighteenth century English-language writers sometimes quoted and occasionally composed paragraphs in Latin, more often than not on title pages and dedications, to be sure, but apparently confident that many readers would find the code transparent and the content illuminating. Even in the nineteenth century some university lecturing in Latin could be heard, and an occasional Ph.D. dissertation was submitted in the traditional language of learning.

By 1700, of course, the tide of writing in Latin had ebbed and by 1776 had receded so definitively that the elocutionist Thomas Sheridan, writing in 1780 (Preface), could say of the classical languages that they are 'fallen into utter disuse... Nay so totally are they gone out of fashion, that in order to avoid the imputation of pedantry, no gentleman must let it appear in conversation, that he ever had the least tincture of those studies.' Still, for centuries it had been Latin that was referenced by expressions like 'grammar school' and 'the study of grammar', and only grudgingly and incompletely in the course of the eighteenth century did the study of English grammar emerge from the shadows of the classical tongue. By then the place of English in the intellectual life of Britain had become a matter of some pride, though it was a neglected school subject, as Joseph Priestley's (1761: ix) mid-century comments indicate:

> it is not much above a century ago, that our native tongue seemed to be looked upon as below the notice of a classical scholar; and men of learning made very little use of it, either in conversation or in writing: and even since it hath been made the vehicle of knowledge of all kinds, it hath not found its way into the schools appropriated to language, in proportion to its growing importance . . .

The disproportionately small place of English in the schools was to be corrected on both sides of the Atlantic in the course of the century to follow. Writing in a newly independent United States of America, Noah Webster

(1789: 18) acknowledged that 'The English tongue . . . has attained to a considerable degree of purity, strength and elegance, and been employed, by an active and scientific nation, to record almost all the events and discoveries of ancient and modern times', and he busied himself codifying the language of the new nation in his spellers, grammars, and dictionaries.

6.1.2 Vernacular regulation and academies

Well before the eighteenth century entered its final quarter, English had extended its robust reach into every domain of use. Bolstered in vocabulary and syntax to meet an extensive set of literary, legal, commercial, and scientific demands, it had become 'the vehicle of knowledge of all kinds', as Priestley put it, and had been employed 'to record almost all the events and discoveries of ancient and modern times', as Webster wrote. Nor could anyone using English doubt its strength and adaptability or its potential for eloquence. Despite such patent vigour, however, there remained a distinct perception that not all was well with the vernacular and a nettlesome concern that it was inadequately regulated. Compared with the classical language it had displaced in science and philosophy and compared even with certain Continental vernaculars, English appeared uncultivated – unpolished, unrefined, unstable, and unregulated. As a consequence writers felt uncertain about aspects of its use.

By contrast the Italians had established an academy for the cultivation and regulation of their vernacular in 1582, and by 1635 the French had done likewise for theirs. Calls for an English academy had been voiced by Dryden and Defoe, among others, but not until a century after Italy's Accademia della Crusca had published its monolingual Italian dictionary was the best-known call for an English academy given voice. In 1712 Jonathan Swift addressed *A Proposal for Correcting, Improving and Ascertaining the English Tongue* to the Lord High Treasurer:

> I do here . . . complain . . . that our Language is extremely imperfect; that its daily Improvements are by no means in proportion to its daily Corruptions; that the Pretenders to polish and refine it, have chiefly multiplied Abuses and Absurdities; and, that in many Instances, it offends against every Part of Grammar . . .
>
> What I have most at Heart is, that some Method should be thought on for *ascertaining* and *fixing* our Language for ever, after such Alterations are made in it as shall be thought requisite.   (1712: 8,31)

Thus did Swift lament the imperfections, corruptions, abuses, and absurdities of the vernacular, and he urged formation of a society to alter it where necessary and then to stabilise it.

For various reasons Swift's proposal was never to be honoured and among the reasons was suspicion of an official body to rule over the language. Discussing the French Academy's lack of success, John Fell (1784: x–xi) observed that 'the republic of letters is a true republic, in its disregard to the arbitrary decrees of usurped authority'. Of Britain he added that 'Our critics are allowed to petition, but not to command: and why should their powers be enlarged? The laws of our speech, like the laws of our country, should breathe a spirit of liberty: they should check licentiousness, without restraining freedom.' Priestley (1761: vii) had expressed a similar sentiment in noting that the idea of an academy was 'not only unsuitable to the genius of a *free nation*, but in itself ill calculated to reform and fix a language', and he further deemed an academy superfluous because 'the best forms of speech will, in time, establish themselves by their own superior excellence'. Preferring the 'slow and sure' decisions of time to the 'often hasty and injudicious' decisions of synods, Priestley argued that a language that 'many persons have leisure to read and write' would eventually reach 'all the perfection' of which it was capable, much as manufactured goods are perfected when they are in demand.

Whereas Priestley professed respect for the efficient workings of what might be called a linguistic market-place, his contemporaries generally shared Swift's concern that the market-place was corrupting the language by propagating 'Abuses and Absurdities'. Thus, although Britain did not establish a language academy, it was not because Swift's pessimistic view was unique or even uncommon: conventional wisdom held that English lacked adequate codification and that 'its daily Improvements [were] by no means in proportion to its daily Corruptions'. Rather, many influential Britons believed that English would suffer from the official linguistic constraints of an academy, although they remained persuaded that, academy or not, the language needed taming and its unruly improvements reining in. While many, including Dr Johnson, shared Priestley's distaste for an official academy, his view that English would reach perfection without assistance was not widely shared, and analysts by the score – Priestley among them – enlisted their grammars and dictionaries in pursuit of what they feared an otherwise elusive goal.

6.1.3 Grammars, dictionaries, and handbooks

In 1700 a score of English grammars existed, and scores more appeared by 1800. Several English dictionaries, slight by later standards, also existed in 1700, and substantial ones including Dr Johnson's were to follow in the next hundred years. Thus, in the eighteenth century the regulation and codification of English fell to independent entrepreneurs: grammarians and lexicographers operating in a market-place unfettered by guidelines, unsanctioned by imprimatur, and unencumbered by official meddling. Then in the nineteenth century, besides grammars and dictionaries aplenty, including a beginning for the grand *Oxford English Dictionary*, prescriptive handbooks of lexical and grammatical usage also flourished, as the battle between prescriptivists and descriptivists was joined. In the twentieth century, grammar books with distinctly descriptivist underpinnings have been compiled, and the *OED* completed, updated, integrated, and computerised so that it is now available in a mammoth set of twenty volumes or a single saucer-sized compact disc. *The Oxford English Dictionary on CD-ROM* is emblematic of the impressive power of the new technologies available at the close of the millennium, when machine-readable corpora of English-language texts and computer programs for exploring the linguistic usage captured in those texts have enhanced the character of reliable information about English usage world-wide.

For all that, though, there remains uncertainty in many quarters as to what is right and wrong in English usage, grammar, and lexicography, and sometimes strident disagreement about how best to address such matters. Echoing nineteenth-century convictions, there is also a resurrected sense that if only English grammar were taught properly in the schools, splendid social and moral benefits would shower like manna from heaven upon the citizens of righteous English-speaking communities.

6.2 First period: mid-eighteenth century–1830

Particularly since the introduction of printing at Westminster in the late fifteenth century, the wider functions of English have fostered a vernacular adept at carrying out the high and low affairs of Britain and its colonies. In the extension of English into new domains throughout Britain's English-speaking centres of learning, commerce, and government, however, there also had arisen a perplexing diversity of linguistic expression. Not only in regional and social dialects but in situational registers, competing forms of English prompted concern about correct usage. Observers fretted about variant forms and continuing innovation. Underlying the unease was an assumption that, far from enhancing a language, alternative ways of expressing things was potentially harmful. In this environment, entrepreneurs set about to *ascertain* the language by determining its correct forms and to *fix* it or give it permanent form by *codifying* it in dictionaries and grammars.

6.2.1   *Selecting a variety to be standardised*

In his 1712 proposal Swift had observed that were it not for familiarity with the English of the Bible and Common Prayer Book, 'we should hardly be able to understand any Thing that was written among us an hundred Years ago'. Expressing the concern of many writers that a too fluid language would soon leave the written word incomprehensible, he noted that the Bible and the Book of Common Prayer, because they were 'perpetually read in Churches', had served as 'a kind of Standard for Language, especially to the common People'. In referring to 'a kind of Standard', Swift pointed to what would remain a perennial challenge for grammarians and lexicographers: identifying appropriate models of English to codify. He also pointed to the role of books in providing a standard.

In 1776 the Scottish rhetorician George Campbell published *The Philosophy of Rhetoric*, a work of scope and substance that included discussion of 'grammatical purity'. For Campbell, the best-known rhetorician of his age, what gave 'law to language' was *use*. Like many of his contemporaries, Campbell understood language to be 'purely a species of fashion' and words to carry meanings by virtue of a tacit agreement among speakers and writers, as Locke had proposed at the end of the seventeenth century. Drawing an important distinction between the practice of grammar and the practice of verbal criticism, Campbell restricted grammarians to the task of description: 'It is not the business of grammar, as some critics seem preposterously to imagine, to give law to the fashions which regulate our speech'.

In 1776, however, the challenge facing grammarians who took usage as the basis for grammatical description was in choosing *whose* usage and *which kind* of usage to describe. '[I]f use be . . . a matter of such consequence, it will be necessary . . . to ascertain precisely what it is', Campbell (1776: 141) said and, in an oft echoed phrase, proposed 'reputable, national, and present use' as the basis for establishing a standard language. *Present* use he distinguished from *obsolete*, recognising that the relevant chronological scope differs across different forms of composition. *National* he opposed not only to *provincial* and *foreign* use but to *professional styles* as well. *Reputable* use he identified in theory as 'the practice of those who have had a liberal education, and are therefore presumed to be best acquainted with men and things' (1776: 143). (Apologetically, he offered that if this last characterisation implied 'any deference to the practice of the great and rich, it is not ultimately because they are greater and richer than others, but because, from their greatness and riches, they are imagined to be wiser and more knowing'.) In practice Campbell (1776: 144–5) settled on 'authors of reputation' – on the modes of language that are 'authorized as good by the writings of a great number, if not the majority, of celebrated authors'. In balancing theoretical considerations with practical ones, Campbell's views are typical of those that informed late eighteenth-century opinion about the role of usage in ascertaining and codifying English. He raised questions about the central criteria for ascertaining correctness and establishing a standard: the roles of writing and speaking; the choice of models; and the distinct responsibilities of grammarians and critics.

6.2.2   History and scope of grammar

The earliest English grammars had appeared only in the late sixteenth century, and the field expanded somewhat in the seventeenth century, but by 1700 only twenty-one English grammars had been published (Michael 1970: 151). In the eighteenth century, interest in regularising the vernacular had sufficiently increased that British and American entrepreneurs – clerics and teachers, scientists and lawyers – faced a demand so voluminous that some grammars sold by the hundreds of thousands. The success of Robert Lowth (1710–87) prompted popularisers and interpreters such as John Ash, whose *Grammatical Institutes* (1763) promoted itself as an 'easy introduction' to Lowth's (1762) work. The most successful interpreter was Lindley Murray (1745–1826), an American who had retired to England after a successful career as a lawyer and merchant and whose *English Grammar* (1795), prepared initially for a girls' school in York, eventually saw more than 300 editions on both sides of the Atlantic. Other contributors included the distinguished natural scientist Joseph Priestley (1733–1804), whose *Rudiments of English Grammar* (1761) appeared a few months before Lowth's work and was superior to it in many ways but failed to achieve its popularity. The impressive *Essay on Grammar* (1765) by William Ward, master of a grammar school in York, comprised a speculative treatise of almost 300 pages and a somewhat smaller practical grammar. Despite its mammoth proportions, Ward's *Essay* found a sufficient market to be reissued three times before the century was out, and the practical grammar was abridged for separate publication. In America no grammar was more popular than the Englishman Thomas Dilworth's (1751) *New Guide to the*

English Tongue, which was published in Philadelphia in 1747, seven years after its initial appearance in London. It was Dilworth's grammar that Webster had used as a schoolboy and aimed to displace when as a school-master he wrote the second part of his *Grammatical Institute* (1784).

'Grammar' carried several senses in eighteenth-century Britain. Besides philosophical, speculative, and universal grammar as rooted in the Port Royal tradition (see Padley 1988), the term also referred to the structure of particular languages. In the latter sense it typically referenced Latin but came increasingly to include and eventually to mean English grammar. A distinction was drawn, as by Lowth (1762: 1), between particular and universal grammar: 'The Grammar of any particular Language, as the English Grammar, applies those common principles [of Universal Grammar] to that particular language, according to the established usage and custom of it'. Grammar typically comprised four levels: orthography, etymology, syntax, and prosody (e.g. Fisher 1750; Johnson 1755; Priestley 1761; Ward 1765; Murray 1795; Cobbett 1823; Webster 1828). To cite Priestley's characterisations of these levels (though the words were not original with him), orthography is 'the art of combining letters into syllables, and syllables into words'; etymology 'the deduction of one word from another, and the various modifications by which the meaning of the same word is diversified'; syntax 'the proper construction of words, or the method of joining them together in sentences'; and prosody 'the rules of pronunciation, and of versification'. Reflecting the influence of Latin, English grammars of the period concentrated particularly on etymology, which included inflectional morphology and occasional elements of word derivation, as well as the analysis of historical roots, though this last was little pursued in school grammars.

Grammars of the second half of the eighteenth century and the first half of the nineteenth are relatively uniform in aim and scope. As defined by Johnson (1755) and Priestley (1761: 1), grammar is 'the art of using words properly'; by Lowth (1762: 1), 'the art of rightly expressing our thoughts by words'; by Fell (1784: 1), 'the Art of Speaking and Writing the English Language, agreeably to the established usage of the best and most approved Speakers and Writers'; by Murray (1795: 1), 'the art of speaking and writing the English language with propriety'. Generally it was conceded that one studied grammar in order to 'learn to speak and write properly and correctly' (Fisher 1750: 1). As Cobbett (1823: 4) succinctly put it, 'Grammar . . . teaches us *how to make use of words* . . . in a proper manner'. Thus, notions of 'propriety' – proper, right, agreeable, correct – defined the study of English in the late eighteenth and early nineteenth centuries.

If Priestley (1761: v) sought as well 'to give the youth of our nation an insight into the fundamental principles of their own language', that goal set him apart from his contemporaries. For nearly all grammarians the study of English had practical rather than intellectual motivation.

The utilitarian philosophy underlying the study of English grammar finds striking exemplification in the grammar of William Cobbett. Cobbett (1762–1835) was born in England and died there but resided in North America from time to time. In 1817, following imprisonment in England, he returned to New York and a short while later published a grammar, drafted as a series of letters to his son. (The grammar has been republished several times and saw three editions even in the 1980s.) As a soldier Cobbett had schooled himself by memorising sections of Lowth's grammar, and he subsequently became a noted writer on agricultural and political subjects. He explained the importance of grammar to his son and the 'soldiers, sailors, apprentices and plough-boys' he was also addressing:

> In order to obtain the co-operation, the concurrence, or the consent, of others, we must communicate our thoughts to them. The means of this communication are *words*; and grammar teaches us *how to make use of words...*
>
> But ... my dear son, there is one motive, which ... ought ... to be strongly felt ... in an extraordinary degree: I mean, that desire, which every man, and especially every young man, should entertain to be able to assert with effect the rights and liberties of his country ... you will find, that tyranny has no enemy so formidable as the pen.   (1823: 4)

As for providing insight into the fundamental principles of language, as Priestley had intended for grammar, Cobbett spurned such inutility as a waste of time for his labouring readers, as illustrated by his analysis of derived forms like *thankful* and *thankless*:

> of what *use* to us to enter on, and spend our time in, inquiries of mere curiosity? It is for monks, and for Fellows of English Colleges, who live by the sweat of other people's brows, to spend their time in this manner, and to call the results of their studies *learning*; for you, who will have to earn what you eat and what you drink and what you wear, it is to avoid every thing that tends not to real utility.   (1823: 55)

Cobbett saw grammar as a political and economic tool to be used for fighting oppression. In this his aims and motivation differed notably from the pious aims of many predecessors and contemporaries, though he shared with them a belief in the utility of knowing grammar.

6.2.3   The doctrine of correctness

Present-day analysts routinely distinguish between prescriptive and descriptive approaches to grammar and sometimes contrast eighteenth-century prescriptivism with twentieth-century descriptivism. This distinction corresponds roughly to the one made by Campbell between grammar and verbal criticism. Descriptivism aims to characterise actual usage; prescriptivism aims to evaluate actual usage and to make recommendations based on any of a number of possible criteria. But the distinction is in some ways an exaggerated one. For one thing, the act of descriptively recording and disseminating particular language varieties or language forms tends in itself to prescribe their use. Grammars or dictionaries of '*the* English language' tend to compel adherence among all who would lay claim to speaking or writing English. For another, at least since the time of Priscian, grammar has been conventionally defined as the art of speaking and writing correctly or properly, as Fisher, Johnson, Priestley, Lowth, Murray, and Cobbett continued to define it. Historically, then, the *raison d'être* of grammar has been prescription (Michael 1970: 189), and today's pedagogical grammars inevitably remain prescriptive to a greater or lesser degree (Quirk 1968). Further, even descriptivists elect which aspects of grammar and lexicon to codify, skirting aspects of usage that they may regard as controversial or unsettled. Finally, it is noteworthy that in the final quarter of the twentieth century many publishers and learned societies, even societies of linguists (usually the staunchest antagonists of prescription) have proscribed certain nominal and pronominal usages, in pursuit of egalitarian social goals rather than the religious or moral goals acceptable in an earlier age. Despite Campbell's exhortations, pure description of language use is a recent and more abstruse enterprise than prescription, and it is carried out by and for scholars typically treating languages remote from their own and often lacking traditions of literacy. The simple fact seems to be that scholars of diverse stripes sometimes experience difficulty writing pure descriptions of their own language.

Eighteenth-century English grammarians have been characterised as subscribing to a 'doctrine of correctness' (Leonard 1929). Simply put, this doctrine claims that every expression is either correct or incorrect and that alternative expressions for the same meaning or function cannot both be correct. In attempting to regulate the vernacular and limit variation in linguistic form, a general inclination prevailed to regard variant forms for the same meaning or function as unacceptable. Priestley (1761: 47) recognised that 'of the vast number of synonymous terms in which every cultivated language abounds, no two of them convey precisely the same idea', but his point was not widely appreciated, and common practice betrayed many a grammarian's discomfort with variant usages. Even Priestley (1761: vi) allowed that 'language, to answer the intent of it, which is to express our thoughts with certainty in an intercourse with one another, must be fixed and consistent with itself', and his 'must' suggests some leeway for analysts to make alterations and eliminate inconsistencies.

6.2.4   *The authority of custom and the role of analogy*

A profession of faith in the supreme authority of usage graces most eighteenth-century and early nineteenth-century grammars and rhetorics. Illustrative is Campbell's (1776: 140–1) definition of grammar as:

> a collection of general observations methodically digested, and comprising all the modes previously and independently established, by which the significations, derivations, and combinations of words in that language are ascertained. It is of no consequence . . . to what causes originally these modes or fashions owe their existence, to imitation, to reflection, to affectation, or to caprice; they no sooner obtain and become general, than they are laws of the language, and the grammarian's only business is to note, collect, and methodize them . . .
>
> Only let us rest in these as fixed principles, that use, or the custom of speaking, is the sole original standard of conversation, as far as regards the expression, and the custom of writing is the sole standard of style . . . that to the tribunal of use, as to the supreme authority, and consequently, in every grammatical controversy, the last resort, we are entitled to appeal from the laws and the decisions of grammarians; and that this order of subordination ought never, on any account, to be reversed.

In determining grammatical correctness, then, for Campbell and for many others 'the supreme authority' and 'the last resort' was 'the tribunal of use'. But, as we saw in section 6.2.1, in elaborating the notion of 'use' or 'custom' Campbell endorsed 'reputable custom' – the usage of 'celebrated authors' and not that of *general* use. The position of Bishop Lowth was more regulated. Despite a perfunctory nod in the direction of custom, he judged its guidance inadequate: 'Much practice in the polite world, and a general acquaintance with the best authors . . . will hardly be sufficient'. Only knowledge of the rules of grammar would ensure proper and accurate expression, and even 'our best Authors for want of some rudiments of this kind have sometimes fallen into mistakes, and been guilty of palpable errors in point of Grammar'. Lowth so discounted the role of custom or usage and so elevated 'the rules of grammar' that he could say about particular features (in this instance about the phrase *by observing* instead of *by* THE *observing*) that 'there are hardly any of our Writers, who have not fallen into this inaccuracy'. Given a milieu in which usage was placed on a theoretical pedestal only to be ignored in practice, it is no surprise to find Lowth (1762: 121) judging certain phrases 'somewhat defective', though 'pretty common and authorised by Custom'. For him, custom was expressly subordinate to the rules of grammar.

Even Priestley, more faithful to the authority of usage than any of his contemporaries, allowed the practice of 'good authors' only a limited role where different authors exhibited different practices. For him analogy ranked higher than usage: 'since good authors have adopted different forms of speech, and in a case that admits of no standard but that of *custom*, one authority may be of as much weight as another; the *analogy of language* is the only thing to which we can have recourse, to adjust these differences' (1761: vi). (By analogy he meant the parallel between an expression and some established general pattern or paradigm.) Like other grammarians of the time, Priestley denied that differing usages could be equally acceptable even when used by equally reputable authors. Despite his conviction that the best forms of speech would establish themselves by their own superiority, his practice permitted an intervening role for analogical reasoning. In principle custom ranked highest in deciding questions of grammar, but when custom offered competing patterns, as it often did, he invoked analogy to exclude all but one. Only where analogy could not resolve an issue because existing patterns supported more than one preference could it be left to time to settle the issue.

In deciding particular points, other grammarians also deferred to analogy and sometimes to logic and sometimes to the history of a word (what might be called its 'etymologic'). In practice, if not always in theory, grammarians of this period shared a disposition to reject alternative usages as equally correct. If *shall* is right in this usage, *will* must be wrong; if *among* serves several, *between* must be limited to two, as its etymology might be taken to dictate.

6.2.5   Latin grammar influences English grammar

Despite the triumph of English in all domains of use, Latin grammar continued to cast a long shadow over the grammatical analysis of the vernacular. In part the influence of Latin followed from its being perceived as an exemplar of universal grammar par excellence; it was only natural, then, that grammarians were inclined to impose the Procrustean bed of Latin structure on their analyses of English. Some grammarians objected strongly, though. Webster alleged that certain grammars were little more than translations of Latin ones: the declensions and conjugations of Latin had been erased, as it were, leaving their English equivalents laid out on the page as fully as they had been as glosses to the Latin paradigms. Grammars of English thus wound up exhibiting paradigms that better exemplified the inflected nominal and verbal systems of the classical language than its own inflectionally reduced declensions and conjugations. Such classical paradigms disguised English structures in Latin garb and provided sometimes deliberate, sometimes unwitting insight into the structure of the classical tongue while obscuring the character of the vernacular one.

As an illustration consider that in the second quarter of the eighteenth century John Stirling had laid out the English adjective *wise* in a paradigm with no fewer than thirty-six cells, representing six cases in three genders, both singular and plural. In that paradigm all thirty-six occurrences of *wise* were, of course, identical. The thirty-six cells represented possible inflectional variants of the Latin paradigm. They had no relation to English and might as well have been 136. To represent the English facts, just one cell would be needed. As late as 1780, Wells Egelsham declined the invariant English article for both case and number (Michael 1987: 318–9). Even the largely original grammar by Ward (1765: 336) presents English noun paradigms that assign the customary names of the six Latin cases, as shown:

	Singular	Plural
Nominative	the king	the kings
Genitive	of the king	of the kings
	the king's	
Dative	to the king	to the kings
Accusative	the king	the kings
Vocative	o king	o kings
Ablative	by the king	by the kings

Such a format suited Latin nouns, which can be inflected for several cases in the singular and plural (theoretically yielding up to twelve different forms – *rex, regis, regi, regem*, etc. – although the various declensions had merged some case endings). It does not make sense, though, for English with only four (written) noun forms (*king, king's, kings, kings'*). The Latin paradigm justified twelve entries for up to twelve noun forms. By the same logic, English required a mere four because its nouns distinguish singulars from plurals (*child/children*) and possessive (or 'genitive') case from a general unmarked form (*child's/child* and *children's/children*). The somewhat more diverse system of English pronouns (with three case forms as in the first-person singular *I, mine, me* and plural *we, ours, us*) would match the Latin paradigm better but not well. Doubtless the germination of English nominal, verbal, and adjectival paradigms in the gardens of Latin morphological analysis and the contemporary understanding of universal and particular grammar helps account for the assertion heard even to the present day that nothing illuminates English grammar like the study of Latin. The observation made by a young schoolmaster toward the end of the eighteenth century has had echoes at the end of the twentieth:

> We are apt to be surprised, that men who made the languages their principal study . . . should not discover that the Grammar of one language would not answer for another; but our wonder will cease when we reflect, that the English nation at large have, till very lately, entertained the idea that our language was incapable of being reduced to a system of rules; and that even now many men of much classical learning warmly contend that the only way of acquiring, a grammatical knowledge of the *English Tongue*, is first to learn a *Latin Grammar*. That such a stupid opinion should ever have prevailed in the English nation – that it should still have advocates – nay that it should still be carried into practice, can be resolved into no cause but the amazing influence of habit upon the human mind.
>
> (Webster 1784: 3)

Increasingly, though, observers on both sides of the Atlantic successfully resisted imposing Latin structure on the analysis of English.

A by-product of modelling English grammars on Latin exemplars that met less resistance was the practice of exercises in 'false syntax', which offered made-up examples for analysis and correction. Used routinely in the teaching of Latin, where the case inflections on nouns served to express grammatical relations such as subject and direct object, the practice of exhibiting fanciful specimens of false syntax in native language instruction is credited to Fisher (1750). Among a kind she called 'promiscuous' can be found sentences like those below, which violate rules of agreement or concord or doubly mark the superlative degree of the adjective:

> The minister preaches, but sinners hears not.
> Thou and me is both accused of the same fault.
> The men drink heartily, and eats sparingly.
> Prudent men forsees evil, but the simple pass on and is punished.
> The lyon is accounted the most strongest and most generous of all brute creatures.

Such 'promiscuous' examples of 'false syntax' larded many grammars but struck at least one contemporary as bizarre. Not surprisingly it was Priestley (1761: xi), who observed that he would have included such examples if they did not 'make so uncouth an appearance in print'. For the most part, though, grammarians shared Murray's (1795: iv-v) influential view that 'a proper selection of faulty composition is more instructive to the young grammarian, than any rules and examples of propriety that can be given'. From the earliest influential grammars, then, pupils were required to judge fictitious sentences as to which rule they violated and then to recast them in conformity to its dictates.

6.2.6 Writing and speech

Lowth (1762: 2) judged letters the 'first principles' of words, and in an age when recorded speech was unimaginable and writing alone promised permanence, it was perhaps only natural that the written word served as the model for speaking. Today, scholars view speech as fundamental, as the ground of writing. In the eighteenth century the relationship between these modes of expression was understood differently, and orthography, now discarded as a branch of grammar, was then an integral part of it.

Although the relationship between speech and writing was generally agreed by grammarians and lexicographers of the period, it did not much concern them. Few perceived the matter as starkly as Thomas Sheridan (1762: 7), who noted that:

> we have in use two different kinds of language, which have no sort of affinity between them, but what custom has established; and which are communicated thro' different organs . . . But these two kinds of language are so early in life associated, that it is difficult ever after to separate them; or not to suppose that there is some kind of natural connection between them.

The difficulty of dissociating speech and writing showed itself in grammar after grammar. Typical was Fisher (1750: 5), who not only did not keep letters and sounds distinct but saw writing as underlying speech: 'A vowel is a letter, which, without the help of any other letter joined to it, doth, by itself, denote a perfect sound, and often alone makes a perfect syllable'. For Fisher as for most there were the traditional alphabetic vowels *a, e, i, o, u* (and sometimes *y*), each with two realisations, a long and a short.

Written language provided models of usage in theory and in practice for most eighteenth-century codifiers. Even those who might have wished to rely on speech would have been obliged to do so from memory or notes made in haste, thereby subjecting their citations to contest in ways in which written ones would not be. Moreover, reliance on speech would have given codifiers excessive latitude in choosing authorities. With Lowth (1762: 52) grammarians were on safer ground citing as 'great authorities' Milton, Dryden, Addison, Prior, and Pope, whose written usage could be verified. Thus, with respect to lexicon, morphology, and syntax, the consensus held that *written* English was to be codified.

With respect to pronunciation, there was no consensus. A great deal about eighteenth-century views can be learned from Defoe's report of a visit he made to a schoolroom in Somerset, where a pupil was reading aloud from the Bible:

> I observed also the Boy read it out with his Eyes still on the Book, and his Head, like a mere Boy, moving from Side to Side, as the Lines reached cross the Columns of the Book: His Lesson was in the *Canticles of Solomon*; the Words these;
>
> 'I have put off my Coat; how shall I put it on? I have washed my Feet; how shall I defile them?' The Boy read thus, with his Eyes, as I say, full on the Text: 'Chav a doffed my Coot; how shall I don't? Chav a washed my Feet; how shall I moil 'em?'
>
> How the dexterous Dunce could form his Mouth to express so readily the Words (which stood right printed in the Book) in his Country Jargon, I could not but admire. (From Tucker: 1961. 61–2)

Defoe's astonishment (as *admire* here suggests) underscores his view that pronunciation ought to be based upon spelling and that spelling should be independent of local pronunciations. Some codifiers, Johnson among them, promoted spelling pronunciations: 'the best rule is, to consider those as the most elegant speakers who deviate least from the written words'. But standards varied greatly.

6.2.7   Dialects

Knowledge of dialect variation in the eighteenth and early nineteenth centuries was incidental and unsystematic. Regional differences were recognised, and here and there in grammars and rhetorics appeared mention of country jargon, Irish brogue, American accents, jouring (as Defoe called the speech of Somerset), and others, and comments were almost invariably unfavorable. In the preface to his *General Dictionary* of 1780, Sheridan observed that 'not only the natives of Ireland, Scotland, and Wales, who speak English, and are taught to read it, pronounce it differently, but each county in England has its peculiar dialect, which infects not only their speech, but their reading also'. Sheridan's metaphorical 'infection' reveals his disdain for regional dialects, much as Defoe's description revealed his (see Ihalainen 1994 for views of dialects during this period). Even the title pages of some grammars alluded to the disfavoured status of certain regional or national varieties, though preoccupation with dialects was more prevalent in America, where xenophobic fear of contamination by other tongues was greater than in Britain. Besides regional dialects, social dialects were also recognised but, again, not systematically. Cockney was known, and occasional reference made to the language of 'lower orders'.

6.2.8   Language and morality

At this stage any explicit link between morality and dialect such as later characterised Victorian Britain remained muted. Still, a generalised association between language use and morality did exist and is not surprising, given the pious dispositions and religious employments so common among grammarians and rhetoricians of the age. Some were high-ranking clerics or prelates and many experienced a sense of divine presence in their lives. Even some of the nonclerics wrote on religious as well as grammatical subjects: for example, Fisher on *The Child's Christian Education* and Murray on *The Power of Religion on the Mind, in Retirement, Affliction and at the Approach of Death* (already in its sixth edition when his grammar appeared in 1795). Among the clerics can be counted Swift, Lowth, and Priestley. Equally telling, the contents of the grammars exhibit what by today's standards must be deemed excessively pious sentiments. Often the examples of false syntax constituted mini-sermons: besides grammatical points they provided moral lessons and pious exhortation. Priestley (1761: 65), who expressly sought to provide insight into linguistic principles, nevertheless chose passages 'calculated for the use of youth, tending both to lead them into a just and manly taste in composition, and also to impress their minds with the sense of what is rational, useful, and ornamental in their temper, and conduct in life'. Like many others he included scriptural passages, not for their grammatical aptness alone but for their 'excellent moral uses' as well. Murray, in his preface, claimed to have 'no interest' in the grammar but 'endeavouring to promote the cause of learning and virtue' and said he had been 'studious ... not only to avoid all examples and illustrations which might have an improper effect on the minds of youth; but also to introduce, on many occasions, such as have a moral and religious tendency'.

Significantly, then, and not only for Murray, 'learning and virtue' were intertwined, and the perception did not lag far behind that the language of the lower classes lacked both – for grammarians tended to view variant usages not merely as different but as faulty and corrupt. If writers and speakers were seen as 'guilty' of 'faults', as using 'improper' forms, and as displaying 'great impropriety' and 'barbarous corruption', to cite a few of Bishop Lowth's epithets, the link that Murray established between 'learning and virtue' left the uneducated and the poor in a decidedly precarious moral position.

6.2.9 Stylistic and register variation

Some codifiers showed a sensitivity to the appropriateness of expressions in different circumstances. Campbell refers to 'professional dialects', such as commercial idiom and medical cant. Priestley (1761: 50–1), in an unusual chapter called 'Observations on style', noted about sentence-final prepositions:

> It is often really diverting to see with what extreme caution words of such frequent occurrence as *of* and *to* are prevented from fixing themselves in the close of a sentence; though that be a situation they naturally incline to, where they favour the easy fall of the voice, in a familiar cadence; and from which nothing but the solemnity of an address from the pulpit ought to dislodge them; as in any other place they often give too great a stiffness and formality to a sentence.

With a clear grasp of the different functions that speech and writing typically serve, Priestley (1761: 45–6) noted that 'The use of writing, as of speaking, is to express our thoughts with certainty and perspicuity. But as *writing* is a permanent thing, it is requisite that *written* forms of speech have a greater degree of precision and perspicuity than is necessary in *colloquial* forms, or such as very well answer the purpose of common conversation.' He added that 'The ease of conversation seems, in some cases, to require a relaxation of the severer laws of Grammar . . . . For instance, who, in common conversation, would scruple to say, "*who is this for*'''; or *where learnt . . . thou this*; rather than, *whom is this for*; or, *where learnedst thou this*.' In a similar vein, Horne Tooke (1798: 232) discussed the preference in legal discourse for repeating nouns rather than using pronouns. Expressing sentiments that have lost none of their pertinence two centuries later, he observed that 'legal instruments . . . have always been, and always must be, remarkably more tedious and prolix than any other writings, in which the same clearness and precision are not equally important. . . . In common discourse we save time by using the short substitutes HE and SHE and THEY and IT;

and . . . they answer our purpose very well . . . But this substitution will not be risqued in a legal instrument . . .' Despite such sporadic comments, however, little was known about the systematic relations of one style or register to another, and no established framework of language varieties existed in which to situate the codification of grammar and lexicon.

6.2.10   *Horne Tooke and the* Diversions of Purley

Exercising extraordinary influence on the study of usage in the nineteenth century was the philosophical grammar of John Horne Tooke (1736–1812), first published in 1786. Called the *Diversions of Purley*, it took the form of a conversation among William Tooke (owner of an estate called Purley, where the conversation occurs), John Horne Tooke himself, and Richard Beadon (Bishop of Gloucester and a guest at Purley). *ΕΠΕΑ ΠΤΕΡΟΕΝΤΑ* ('on winged words'), as the *Diversions* is actually titled, constitutes a lengthy and imaginative speculative treatise about the relation of words to things and to other words. The conversation serves as a platform for Horne Tooke's central notion that nouns and verbs are the basic parts of speech, all words in other classes arising merely as abbreviations of them.

Early in the discussion at Purley, Horne Tooke tells his interlocutors, 'I consider [Grammar] as absolutely necessary in the search after philosophical truth . . . And I think it no less necessary in the most important questions concerning religion and civil society' (1798: 5). Herein lies the importance of Horne Tooke, for he argues that grammar – in particular etymology – is essential to the pursuit of philosophical, religious, and civic truths. He adds that he found it 'impossible to make many steps in the search after *truth* and the nature of *human understanding*, of *good* and *evil*, of *right* and *wrong*, without well considering the nature of language', which he thought 'inseparably connected with them' (1798: 12). Admitting disagreement with 'all those who with such infinite labour and erudition have gone before me on this subject' (1798: 14), he reviewed the relationship between signs and the things they signify and sketched how various philosophical approaches have led to differences in the numbers and kinds of the parts of speech before and since the time of Aristotle. Crucially for his theory, Horne Tooke argued that words are not always signs of things or ideas but often represent other words, as shorthand would. 'The first aim of Language was to *communicate* our thoughts: the second, to do it with *dispatch*', and the chief cause of the variety of words is to enable the tongue to keep pace with the mind by use of 'winged' words (1798: 27–9). These 'abbreviations' constitute the pivotal notion of Horne Tooke's theory of language, and the *Diversions of Purley* details his derivation of English words from their original, unabbreviated roots.

To illustrate the argument that informs the *Diversions*, consider its fanciful derivation of the preposition *by* from the Old English imperative verb form *byð* of *beon* or of *beneath* from the imperative verb *be* compounded with the (lost) noun *neath*, which in turn Horne Tooke related to *nether* and *nethermost* (1798: 405–6). *Under*, with the same meaning as *beneath*, he derived from *on neder* (1798: 408), while *head* and *heaven* are 'evidently the past participles of the verb to *Heave*'; indeed, 'the names of all abstract relation . . . are taken either from the adjectived common names of objects, or from the participles of common verbs' (1798: 453). Horne Tooke thus endeavoured to show that some particular noun or verb can be found at the origin of every word and that each word has a core meaning, namely the sense attached to its original noun or verb. Ridiculing the two dozen meanings offered for the preposition *from* in Johnson's *Dictionary*, Horne Tooke argues that in all instances *from* 'continues to retain invariably one and the same single meaning', namely 'beginning'.

Unaware of the philological ferment around him (see section 6.3.1), Horne Tooke's etymologies are speculative associations, not philological reconstructions. In fact, he insulated his philosophy from empirical constraints both in theory and in practice. Because his theory preceded his etymologies, the former could not be challenged by questioning the latter: 'it was general reasoning *a priori*, that led me to the particular instances; not particular instances to the general reasoning'.

> This Etymology, against whose fascination you would have me guard myself, did not occur to me till many years after my system was settled: and it occurred to me suddenly, in this manner; – 'If my reasoning concerning these conjunctions is well founded, there must then be in the original language from which the English (and so of all other languages) is derived, literally *such* and *such* words bearing precisely *such* and *such* significations.' – I was the more pleased with this suggestion, because I was entirely ignorant even of the Anglo-saxon and Gothic characters: and the experiment presented to me a mean, either of disabusing myself from error . . . or of obtaining a confirmation sufficiently strong to encourage me to believe . . . that I had really made a discovery.
>
> (1798: 131–2)

Given contemporary widespread interest in the relationship between words and the mind, Horne Tooke's metaphysical approach to language won the day. All Britain seemed inclined to agree that he had made a genuine discovery, and fascination with the number and nature of the parts of speech held centre stage in the philological theatre of Britain (and exerted influence in North America, as well). Horne Tooke's concerns and speculative methods engaged the more philosophical grammarians and some prominent lexicographers for decades after the turn of the century, and preoccupation with his etymologies insulated Britain from the incipient comparative and historical linguistics that was stimulating solid philological learning particularly in Germany and Scandinavia. Today, a linguistically trained reader finds nothing of etymological value in the *Diversions*. But on the positive side the book helped dislodge belief in the direct, non-arbitrary connection between words and things that James Harris had argued for in *Hermes*, a much admired grammar that Lowth called 'the most beautiful and perfect example of analysis . . . since the days of *Aristotle*'. On the negative side, and more to our purposes, Horne Tooke's approach to etymology – utterly fanciful though it was – exercised a profound decades-long influence on linguistic thinking generally and views of English usage in particular, as we shall see in section 6.3.

6.2.11   Samuel Johnson's Dictionary

It is not within the scope of this chapter to discuss in detail the contributions made by Samuel Johnson (1755) or Noah Webster (1828) in their dictionaries. The initial publication of Johnson's dictionary preceded the period under discussion here, and Webster is treated in volume VI. Still, the importance of these lexicographers requires brief mention.

In the codification of English during the eighteenth century the publication of Johnson's dictionary stands out above all other events, and a good deal has been written about both the lexicographer and his lexicon (cf. Sledd & Kolb 1955; Reddick 1996). Germane here is the fact that Johnson relied heavily on citations of actual usage in arriving at and illustrating his definitions. Among its 40,000 entries, the dictionary's impressive 114,000 citations signal a significant advance in lexicography and a noteworthy commitment to the centrality of usage in ascertaining and codifying the language. By way of illustration, part of the entry for *between* from Johnson's *Dictionary of the English Language* (1755) is provided below:

> 6. *Between* is properly used of two, and *among* of more; but perhaps this accuracy is not always preserved.

While Johnson provides no citations for this particular use, for other senses and uses he provides citations from Pope, Bacon, Locke, and others.

Not everyone regarded Johnson's use of citations favourably, and among those who judged them excessive was Webster, who criticised them in the introduction to his *American Dictionary* (1828) some seventy years later:

> One of the most objectionable parts of Johnson's Dictionary . . . is the great number of passages cited from authors, to exemplify his definitions. Most English words are so familiarly and perfectly understood, and the sense of them so little liable to be called in question, that they may be safely left to rest on the authority of the lexicographer, without examples . . .
>
> In most cases, one example is sufficient to illustrate the meaning of a word; and this is not absolutely necessary, except in cases where the signification is a deviation from the plain literal sense, a particular application of the term; or in a case, where the sense of the word may be doubtful, and of questionable authority. Numerous citations serve to swell the size of a Dictionary, without any adequate advantage.

In the two decades needed to prepare his *American Dictionary*, much of Webster's energy attended etymology. Although he disavowed Horne Tooke and denied him any influence on the 1828 dictionary, he had earlier credited him with 'discovery of the true theory of the construction of language' and had accepted the likelihood that 'the *noun* or substantive is the principal part of speech . . . from which most words are originally derived' (1789: 182). Etymology is an aspect of the story of correctness that is far more significant than many accounts indicate, and we consider it further in the following sections.

6.3 Second period: 1830–1930

We focus here on the century between 1830 and 1930, with scope to examine the *OED* from inspiration to publication. Genuine knowledge of the new philological learning started in Britain around 1830 and is manifest in the *New English Dictionary on Historical Principles*, whose actual publication stretched from 1884 to 1928. Examining a century-long period inevitably encompasses distinct, even contradictory trends, and alongside the broad, soundly empirical and gentle scholarship of the *OED* and other philological learning lies the narrow, fanciful and sometimes strident pedantry of some Victorian handbooks. Alongside the triumph of usage in the citations and analysis of the *OED*, the nineteenth century witnessed its practical and theoretical repudiation in contemporary handbooks and school grammars. Whereas actual usage was given a place of honour in the dictionary, it was rejected as valid evidence of acceptability by prescriptive grammarians and handbook compilers. The story of those contrasts and of the attendant rivalries among scholarly and popular grammarians occupies us in this section.

6.3.1   The new philology

We return briefly to 1786 to examine a philological event of great significance. We have already examined Horne Tooke's *Diversions of Purley*, first published that year in London. Here we visit the Asiatic Society of Bengal and a lecture delivered there by a resident English judge exceptionally well versed in oriental languages. In words often repeated since, William Jones announced that he found Sanskrit to bear a 'stronger affinity' to the Latin and Greek languages 'than could possibly have been produced by accident; so strong indeed, that no philologer could examine them all three, without believing them to have sprung from some common source which, perhaps, no longer exists'. Jones also supposed that Gothic, Celtic, and Persian belonged to the same family. On the Continent, where Jones already enjoyed a reputation as a translator and poet, his hypothesis of an Indo-European family of languages was greeted with excitement and launched the impressive historical and comparative philology of the nineteenth century (see Pedersen 1959). In Britain the story was otherwise: Jones was virtually ignored, while Horne Tooke remained the rage.

It lies beyond our scope to trace the development of linguistic science stemming from Jones's recognition of Indo-European, but the negligible impact his important and provocative hypothesis had in the English-speaking world for almost half a century is remarkable. Whereas the Indo-European hypothesis stirred scholarly and Romantic interest and excitement elsewhere, it caused hardly a ripple in Britain, where language study remained speculative and continued to find philosophical and theological employment. Interest in language for its own sake continued to find Britain's soil infertile. In keeping with Johnson's observation in the preface to his dictionary that 'words are the daughters of the earth ... things ... the sons of heaven', Britain kept its eyes on the sons of heaven. 'Language is only the instrument of science, and words ... but the signs of ideas', Johnson continued, highlighting in 'instruments' and 'signs' the determination in Britain to see through language to the world that lay behind it. For almost half a century after 1786, it was not the comparative approach of Jones but the speculations of Horne Tooke that captured the British philological imagination. Indeed, the *Diversions of Purley* is 'of fundamental importance in the history of linguistic thought, and its influence in the first

half of the nineteenth century . . . profound', as Alston notes in his introduction to the facsimile edition of the work. What has not been sufficiently
noted is the depth and duration of that influence on views of English usage
nor how Horne Tooke's philosophical ideas were transformed into theological ones in the grammars and handbooks of the nineteenth century. We
turn to those effects in section 6.3.3. First we examine the origins of the
Oxford English Dictionary.

6.3.2   The new dictionary of the Philological Society

The most significant event in the codification of English during the nineteenth century was, of course, the compilation of the *New English Dictionary*,
whose grounding can be traced to the Philological Society, founded in
London in 1842. By the mid-1850s members of the Society had come to
recognise certain deficiencies in the dictionaries of Samuel Johnson and
Charles Richardson, the latter a disciple of Horne Tooke. Consequently, to
plan a lexicon that would supplement the existing dictionaries, a committee
comprising F. J. Furnivall, Richard Chenevix Trench, and Herbert Coleridge
undertook in 1857 to collect 'words and idioms hitherto unregistered'. Later
that year, however, Trench, dean of Westminster at the time, a great admirer
of Horne Tooke, and an enormously popular writer himself, presented two
papers to the Philological Society in which he successfully argued that a
supplement would not adequately remedy the 'deficiencies in our English
dictionaries'. Instead, he proposed an entirely new work that would provide
a historical treatment for *every* word of English literature.

In his presentations Trench articulated a revolutionary kind of dictionary
– one that would provide a comprehensive historical inventory of English.
He recognised from the first that a dictionary maker is 'an historian of [the
language], not a critic. The *delectus verborum* . . . on which nearly everything in
style depends, is a matter with which *he* [the dictionary maker] has no
concern'; further, he flatly rejected the notion that a dictionary should function as a standard of the language: 'It is nothing of the kind' (1857: 4–5), he
said, and plainly indicated his rationale for 'impartial hospitality':

> Where [the lexicographer] counts words to be needless, affected, pedan-
> tic, ill put together, contrary to the genius of the language, there is no
> objection to his saying so; on the contrary, he may do real service in this
> way: but let their claim to belong to our book-language be the humblest,
> and he is bound to record them, to throw wide with an impartial hospital-
> ity his doors to them, as to all other. A Dictionary is an historical monu-
> ment, the history of a nation contemplated from one point of view, and

the wrong ways into which a language has wandered, or attempted to wander, may be nearly as instructive as the right ones in which it has travelled: as much may be learned, or nearly as much, from its failures as its successes, from its follies as from its wisdom. . . . It is . . . for those who use a language to sift the bran from the flour, to reject that and retain this.   (1857: 5–8)

Two points should be underscored. The first is the echo of the eighteenth and earlier nineteenth centuries' admiration for the pedagogical benefits of 'false syntax'. Trench's claim that 'the wrong ways into which a language has wandered . . . may be nearly as instructive as the right ones' echoes that of predecessors like Murray (1795: iv–v): 'a proper selection of faulty composition is more instructive to the young grammarian than any rules and examples of propriety that can be given'. The second point is the exclusive focus on the written word, on 'our book-language'. Central to Trench's radical reconception of a dictionary were actual citations illustrative of use; in fact, he saw 'no difference between a word absent from a Dictionary, and a word there, but unsustained by an authority' (1857: 7n.), and he criticised Webster for having skimped on citations: 'Even if Webster were in other respects a better book, the almost total absence of illustrative quotations would deprive it of all value in my eyes' (1857: 7).

Persuaded of the sorry state of English lexicography and of the necessity for a corporate corrective, the Philological Society supported Trench's proposal and committed itself to making a New English Dictionary. In the prospectus announcing its plan, the Society allowed that 'England does not possess a Dictionary worthy of her language' and ventured that it is impossible for such a work to be written 'as long as lexicography is confined to the isolated efforts of a single man' (Coleridge 1859: 8). It also wholeheartedly endorsed Trench's principle of lexical inclusion:

the first requirement of every lexicon is, that it should contain *every word occurring in the literature of the language it professes to illustrate*. We entirely repudiate the theory, which converts the lexicographer into an arbiter of style, and leaves it in his discretion to accept or reject words according to his private notions of their comparative elegance or inelegance.

(Coleridge 1859: 2–3)

According to Aarsleff (1983), part of the Society's motivation in undertaking the dictionary was to halt the speculative etymologies of Horne Tooke and his disciple Charles Richardson, whose dictionary largely incorporated the speculative etymologies from the *Diversions of Purley* into an alphabetised list. Recognising at last that fanciful etymological reconstructions had kept empirical philology from bearing fruit in Britain, the Society undertook to provide the sure philological footing that existed on the Continent for other languages. In Aarsleff's (1983: 165) view, 'The new dictionary is unthinkable . . . without the complete departure from the powerful Tooke tradition, from philological speculation, from random etymologizing, and from the notion that the chief end of language study is the knowledge of the mind'.

From its inception the dictionary project experienced difficulties, starting with Coleridge's death at the age of thirty shortly after he was appointed first editor. Furnivall succeeded him and established the Early English Text Society and the Chaucer Society, without whose volumes of Old English and Middle English texts the envisioned dictionary could not have made adequate progress. But the dictionary project itself slowed so much during Furnivall's editorship that the Society's contract with the publisher lapsed. The project was also hindered by a persistent inability of its managers to grasp the magnitude of the undertaking and the resources needed to complete it. Fifteen years after the project's inception, A. J. Ellis was so discouraged at the lack of progress that in his 1874 presidential address to the Philological Society he expressed doubts about a learned society's ability to compile a dictionary.

Fortunately in 1879 James A. H. Murray became editor after another publisher had invited him to organise a dictionary that would compete with those of Webster and Joseph Worcester (1859), American works that were popular in Britain at the time. Failing to agree to terms with Macmillan, Murray was recruited instead to edit the Philological Society's New English Dictionary, and Oxford University Press agreed to publish it, providing substantial financial and logistical support over the ensuing decades (Burchfield 1987: 15). But even in 1879, two decades after the Society had announced its plan, unrealistic projections continued to plague the project. For example, the agreement with Oxford called for a work of between six and seven thousand pages, but *The New English Dictionary on Historical Principles* eventually required more than sixteen thousand pages. Moreover, the project consumed another half century, even with Henry Bradley, William A. Craigie, and C. T. Onions ultimately joining Murray as editors with responsibility for particular letters and with independent staffs. By time the letter *Z* appeared in 1928, more than forty-four years after the letter *A*, so much additional information had been uncovered about the lexicon of the earlier letters that a supplementary volume was needed to bring all letters to comparable standing.

Like all dictionaries, the *Oxford English Dictionary*, as it was renamed after its completion, is a product of its time, and its strengths and weaknesses reflect its intellectual and social milieu. Its scholarly etymologies reflected the philological learning that had finally arrived in Britain in the 1830s and provided an eloquent and definitive rebuttal to the philosophical etymologies inspired by Horne Tooke. Its definitions and sense differentiations were subtler by far than in any earlier dictionary, a direct result of the extensive reliance on citations of actual usage. Once completed the dictionary offered a stellar monument to the language it described. On the other hand, the final corrected copy of the work emerged from Victorian England, where even distinguished scholarship sometimes averted its gaze from taboo matters, in this case ignoring words and senses that risked offending contemporary sensibilities. It is no task of the lexicographer to select the 'good words' of the language, Trench had warned, but the editors of the *OED* made selections. They excluded some infamous four-letter words, moving directly from *fucivorous* to *fuco'd*, for example, although they entered other 'Anglo-Saxonisms', such as those between *shisham* and *shiver*, alleging however that these words are 'not now in decent use', the same judgement made of *fart*. More significantly (because subtler and not nearly so familiar to readers), the editors ignored certain word senses, such as the sexual one Shakespeare sometimes intended to convey with the verb *die*, thus leaving inquiring minds to seek a more candid report in Partridge's *Shakespeare's Bawdy* or the like. Given the social mores of the time, the editors may not have viewed their exclusions as a form of prescriptive lexicography, but in these delicate matters they surely were just that.

With respect to the orthodox questions of usage, those lexical and grammatical matters so troubling (as we shall see) to the refined tastes of Victorian and Edwardian Britain, the *OED* was more faithful to its descriptive commitments, although, following the lead suggested by Trench, its editors were not shy about signalling the status of debatable usages. *Donate* is marked 'chiefly U.S.' and readers are told about the conjunction *like* that it is 'Now generally condemned as vulgar or slovenly, though examples may be found in many recent writers of standing'. About *banister*, a word impugned by contemporary handbooks, the *OED* reported: 'though condemned by Nicholson as "improper", by Stuart (*Dict. Archit.* 1830) and Gwilt as "vulgar", the term had already taken literary rank, and has now acquired general acceptance'. As is to be expected from a descriptive dictionary, debatable words and usages are faithfully entered and citations provided so as to make the historical record complete. Provided below, by way of illustration, is part of the entry on *between*. In its entirety the entry runs to more than a page; cited here is the point debated by grammarians and handbook writers as to whether or not the word is used solely in reference to two objects:

> V. 19. In all senses, *between* has been, from its earliest appearance, extended to more than two. In OE. and ME. it was so extended in sense 1, in which AMONG is now considered better. It is still the only word available to express the relation of a thing to many surrounding things severally and individually, *among* expressing a relation to them collectively and vaguely: we should not say 'the space lying among the three points,' or 'a treaty among three powers,' or 'the choice lies among the three candidates in the select list,' or 'to insert a needle among the closed petals of a flower.' **971** *Blickl. Hom.* 229 þa apostoli wæron æt-somne; and hie sendon hlot him betweonum. *c* **1175** *Lamb. Hom.* 61 And cristes wille bo us bitwon. *c* **1205** LAY. 26936 Heo . . sweoren heom bitwænen [*c* **1250** bitwine] þat heo wolden. *a* **1225** *Ancr. R.* 358 In unkuðe londe, & in unkuðe earde, bitwhen unðeode. *c* **1250** *Gen. & Ex.* 1601 And wulde noȝt ðat folc bi-twen Herberȝed . . ben. *a* **1300** *Cursor M.* 10244 Ga heþen, he said, fra vs bituin. *c* **1380** *Sir Ferumb.* 1255 By-twenc hymcn þanne euerechon: þay lift vp þat bodi faste. *a* **1400** *Cov. Myst.* 352, I xalle telle ȝow why In ȝoure erys prevyly Betweyn us thre. **1755** JOHNSON *Dict., Between* is properly used of two, and *among* of more: but perhaps this accuracy is not always preserved. **1771** JOHNSON in *Boswell* (1826) II. 127, I . . hope, that, between publick business, improving studies, and domestick pleasures, neither mclancholy nor caprice will find any place for entrance. **1828** SOUTHEY *Ess.* (1832) II. 436 Between the prior, the boatmen, and a little offering to St. Patrick, he had not as much money left, etc. **1885** J. COWPER in *N. & Q.* Ser. VI. XII. 148/2 There were six, who collected between them 15*s.* 4*d.*

The *OED* indicates not only that *between* has from its beginning been used for more than two but also, in what seems almost an endorsement, that it is 'the only word available to express the relation of a thing to many surrounding things severally and individually, *among* expressing a relation to them collectively and vaguely'. In anticipation of a point to be discussed in section 6.4.1 below, it is useful to highlight an expression the entry cites as representing what a speaker would *not* say, namely 'a treaty among three powers'.

The tale of the *OED*'s compilation in human and scholarly costs is rehearsed elsewhere (Murray 1977), but one observation may be made here. The task of compiling a competent historical dictionary with reliable etymologies and 1.8 million citations of literary usage required Herculean effort over a period of seventy years by dozens of dedicated editors and subeditors, as well as volunteer readers by the thousands on both sides of the Atlantic. Whatever the shortcomings of Johnson, Webster, Worcester, and other entrepreneurial lexicographers preceding the *OED*, to denigrate their efforts in comparison to it would be to overlook the staggering corporate resources of texts, readers, editors, and publishers that made the scope and quality of the *OED* possible. As private and entrepreneurial as the *OED* assuredly was, its initiation and sponsorship by the Philological Society and its sustained support by Oxford University Press constitute the equivalent in English language scholarship of the official dictionaries compiled by the Continental academies, all of whose considerable accomplishments are dwarfed by the grand *Oxford English Dictionary*.

6.3.3   Richard Chenevix Trench and fossilised ethics

The nineteenth-century cloudburst of knowledge about linguistic evolution that Jones instigated with the Indo-European hypothesis helped prompt popular enthusiasm about language matters. Partly as a result of the new science (and partly as a continuation of forces set in motion in the eighteenth century), handbooks of usage and other popular treatments proliferated.

We can trace much of the enthusiasm for discussions about language in both Britain and America to the influence of Richard Chenevix Trench (1807–86), the central figure in launching the *OED*. Decades before the first fascicles of *OED* eventually appeared, Trench's books stirred popular linguistic interest. A great admirer of Horne Tooke, Trench subscribed to the prevailing British view that language study, rather than being useful in itself, served higher goals. If Horne Tooke's interests were philosophical, those of his disciple, later to become Archbishop of Dublin, were decidedly moral and theological. Borrowing both words and metaphor, Trench (1852: 6) described language as "'like amber in its efficacy to circulate the electric spirit of truth [and] in embalming and preserving the relics of ancient wisdom'", and he held up for examination such treasures of wisdom as could be uncovered by speculative etymology. Though well aware by mid-century of Horne Tooke's philosophical and etymological 'shortcomings', Trench (1852: 5) remained doggedly enamoured:

> Whatever may be Horne Tooke's shortcomings, whether in occasional details of etymology, or in the philosophy of grammar, or in matters more serious still, yet, with all this, what an epoch in many a student's intellectual life has been his first acquaintance with *The Diversions of Purley*.

As with contemporary philology in general, Trench focused on words rather than on sentences or texts, and wherever he looked his goal was moral truth: 'not in books only . . . but often also in words contemplated singly, there are boundless stores of moral and historic truth' (1852: 9). Viewing language as fossilised poetry, fossilised ethics, and fossilised history, he lauded the benefits of seeking after a word's 'etymology or primary meaning' (1852: 12). Following his friend Herbert Coleridge, he noted that 'few modes of instruction [are] more useful or more amusing than that of accustoming young people to seek for the etymology or primary meaning of the words they use [for] more knowledge of more value may be conveyed by the history of a word than by the history of a campaign' (1852: 12–13). In short, for Trench, 'Many a single word . . . is itself a concentrated poem, having stores of poetical thought and imagery laid up in it. Examine it', he recommended, 'and it will be found to rest on some deep analogy of things natural and things spiritual' (1852: 14). He urged teachers and students to purify their native language '"from the corruptions which time brings upon all things . . . and to endeavor to give distinctness and precision to whatever in it is confused, or obscure, or dimly seen"' (1852: 6–7). For Trench, then, words were assuredly not a species of fashion; rather, they possessed a core meaning and were connected to natural or spiritual things: words embodied moral truth.

To exemplify his approach to language as fossilised poetry, Trench analysed the phrase *dilapidated fortune*. Given that *lapidary* and *dilapidated* are related to the Latin word for stone, he mused about the original coiner of the phrase: 'what an image must have risen up before his mind's eye of some falling house or palace, stone detaching itself from stone, till all had gradually sunk into desolation and ruin' (1852: 14). A second illustration drew out the hidden meaning of *sierra*: 'Many a man had gazed . . . at the jagged and indented mountain ridges of Spain, before one called them 'sierras' or 'saws' . . . but that man coined his imagination into a word, which will endure as long as the everlasting hills which he named' (1852: 15).

Thus for Trench, as earlier for Horne Tooke, at the heart of the matter was the origin of words, about which, as about the human race itself, there were the competing views of evolution and the Garden of Eden. Trench argued that if human beings had evolved and human language with them, language would be a mere accident of human nature and might be expected not to exist among all peoples. But since no tribe lacking language was known to exist, the evolutionary, or 'orang-outang', theory of language must be wrong. That left the view of language as God-given, like reason itself. Trench (1852: 23–4) concluded that God had given Adam the 'power of naming' rather than a full-blown language, for in Genesis 'it is not God who imposed the first names on the creatures, but Adam . . . at the direct suggestion of his Creator'. Thus Genesis provides 'the clearest intimation of the origin, at once divine and human, of speech' (1852: 24), and the record of language would be a record of man's 'greatness and of his degradation, of his glory and of his shame' (1852: 38).

> It needs no more than to open a dictionary . . . and we shall find abundant confirmation of this sadder and sterner estimate of man's moral and spiritual condition. How else shall we explain this long catalogue of words, having all to do with sin, or with sorrow, or with both? . . . We may be quite sure that they were not invented without being needed, that they have each a correlative in the world of realities. I open the first letter of the alphabet; what means this 'ah,' this 'alas,' these deep and long-drawn sighs of humanity, which at once we encounter there? And then presently follow words such as these: 'affliction,' 'agony,' 'anguish,' 'assassin,' 'atheist,' 'avarice,' and twenty more . . . And indeed . . . it is a melancholy thing to observe how much richer is every vocabulary in words that set forth sins, than in those that set forth graces . . .
>
> And our dictionaries, while they tell us much, yet will not tell us all. How shamefully rich is the language of the vulgar everywhere in words which are not allowed to find their way into books, yet which live as a sinful oral tradition on the lips of men, to set forth that which is unholy and impure . . . How much wit, how much talent, yea, how much imagination must have stood in the service of sin, before it could have a nomenclature so rich, so varied, and often so Heaven-defying as it has.
>
> (1852: 38–41)

Trench knew of course the converse of his approach to fossilised ethics. Indeed, the other side of the coin, with its potential for improving the language, motivated much that followed among the amateur philologians of the late nineteenth and early twentieth centuries:

> I should greatly err, if I failed to bring before you the fact that the parallel process of purifying and ennobling has also been going forward, especially, through the influences of Divine faith working in the world; which, as it has turned *men* from evil to good, or lifted them from a lower earthly goodness to a higher heavenly, so has it in like manner elevated, purified, and ennobled a multitude of the words which they employ, until these which once expressed only an earthly good, express now a heavenly . . .
>
> Let us now proceed to contemplate some of the attestations for God's truth, and then some of the playings into the hands of the devil's falsehood, which may be found to lurk in words. (1852: 45–7)

From numerous examples we cite just one:

> there are those who will not hear of great pestilences being God's scourges of men's sins; who fain would find out natural causes for them, and account for them by the help of these. I remember it was thus with too many during both our fearful visitations from the cholera. They may do so, or imagine that they do so; yet every time they use the word 'plague', they implicitly own the fact which they are endeavoring to deny; for 'plague' means properly and according to its derivation, 'blow', or 'stroke'; and was a title given to these terrible diseases, because the great universal conscience of men, which is never at fault, believed and confessed that these were 'strokes' or 'blows' inflicted by God on a guilty and rebellious world. With reference to such words so used we may truly say: *Vox populi, vox Dei*, The voice of the people is the voice of God …
>
> How deep an insight into the failings of the human heart lies at the root of many words; and if only we would attend to them, what valuable warnings many contain against subtle temptations and sins! (1852: 48–9)

With its eloquent linking of language and morality, Trench's *On the Study of Words* was popular enough to warrant a second British edition within months, an American edition within a year, and all told some fifty-odd editions by 1910. These lectures found great favour among the reading public, including even a far-away California schoolmaster who edited them for classroom use (see Trench 1877). The published lectures, coupled with his popular *English, Past and Present* (1855), made Trench's work 'the major British work on language in the 1850s', according to Crowley (1989: 52). Aarsleff (1983: 234–5) believes that Trench's two books 'did far more than any previous publication to make language study popular', and he credits that popularity for the ability of the *OED* to enlist readers world-wide and sustain interest in the decades-long dictionary project.

Trench's popularity also sustained aspects of the speculative approach to language, though now in a guise scarcely resembling the philosophical etymologies of the *Diversions of Purley*. Trench's expressed sentiments reveal the spirit motivating him in launching the new historical dictionary: it would make available the great truths hidden in every etymology and provide 'boundless stores of moral and historic truth'. In his extraordinarily influential work Trench managed to merge the 'lecturer's desk with a pulpit', as his biographer put it, and to express a thoroughgoing 'strain of Victorian moralism' apparent even in a chapter title like 'On the morality in words' (Bromley 1959: 230).

On the Continent, Rask and Grimm were seeking to keep philology focused on language itself; in Britain the study of language was sustained by ulterior motives. We noted such motives in Johnson, Fisher, Lowth, and Murray in the eighteenth century and in Cobbett in the early nineteenth century. We see them continuing now at mid-century with Trench, ironically the person most responsible for inspiring the radically empiricist *OED*.

6.3.4 The influence of Horne Tooke and Dean Trench

Also much influenced by Horne Tooke was another notable, Max Müller, an Oxford Sanskritist and popular lecturer on comparative philology. In his *Lectures on the Science of Language*, initially delivered at the Royal Institution of Great Britain in 1861 and 1863, Müller (1874: 355) said he regarded 'no books . . . so instructive to the student of language' as Locke's *Essay* and Horne Tooke's *Diversions of Purley*, but in his lectures one hears most distinctly the echoes of Horne Tooke's disciple Trench.

> Language . . . has marvels of her own, which she unveils to the inquiring glance of the patient student. There are chronicles below her surface; there are sermons in every word. Language has been called sacred ground, because it is the deposit of thought. We cannot tell as yet what language is. It may be a production of nature, a work of human art, or a divine gift. . . . If it be the gift of God, it is God's greatest gift; for through it God spake to man and man speaks to God in worship, prayer, and meditation.
>
> (1862: 12–13)

This is perhaps not a surprising sentiment for a Sanskritist, but for a comparative philologist working in Britain three-quarters of a century after Jones had formulated his Indo-European hypothesis and an admirer of Locke's *Essay*, it is remarkable testimony to the profound influence of Horne Tooke and Dean Trench.

At about the time that Trench was urging a new dictionary upon the Philological Society and Müller was gravely focusing on rightness and wrongness in linguistic usage, other commentators were calling issues of linguistic propriety to the attention of large audiences and doing so not in the reverential tones of Trench and Müller but in what can with some irreverence be described as antic trans-Atlantic philological bickering. Such exchanges highlight two significant nineteenth-century linguistic themes. The first is the link between language usage and morality, whose basis we have now traced through Trench, where it was explicit, to Horne Tooke's notion of original core meaning. The second is the relationship between social or national identity on the one hand and linguistic practice on the other, also with a basis in Trench and bolstered by Romantic ideals linking nation and language. It is ironic that Horne Tooke's materialist philosophy linking words and things should have led to a connection between usage and morality, as it did in Trench and some of the popular language commentators in Britain and America. With respect to nation and language, it is noteworthy that the individuality and closeness to the ground celebrated by Romantic idealism should have been transformed (as we shall see) into condemnations of nations on the basis of folk etymologies.

One noted populariser of these themes was Henry Alford, dean of Canterbury. In a series of lectures initially addressed to a church literary association, Dean Alford lambasted the English used in America. Published afterwards as magazine pieces and then a book called *A Plea for the Queen's English*, Alford's views helped revive a prominent eighteenth-century refrain, alleging 'what every one who values our native tongue in its purity must feel: that most of the grammars, and rules, and applications of rules, now so commonly made for our language, are in reality not contributions towards its purity, but main instruments of its deterioration' (1864: xiv). Alford forged a link between language use and character whose validity was readily accepted at the time, strengthened by the web Trench had woven between language and ethics. By way of illustrating the bond between the language and morals of a nation, Alford (1864: 6) targeted the 'deterioration which our Queen's English has undergone at the hands of the Americans':

> Look at those phrases which so amuse us in their speech and books; at their reckless exaggeration, and contempt for congruity; and then compare the character and history of the nation – its blunted sense of moral obligation and duty to man; its open disregard of conventional right where aggrandizement is to be obtained; and . . . its reckless and fruitless maintenance of the most cruel and unprincipled war in the history of the world.

Foregoing comment on the principles at stake in Abraham Lincoln's Civil War, we focus on the link between conduct and language – between 'reckless exaggeration' and 'contempt for congruity' and a 'blunted sense of moral obligation and duty to man'. There was fear among many observers at the time, by no means all of them in Britain, that American linguistic abuses were undermining the English language and threatening to undermine morals more widely. In fact, the notion that language and morality went hand in glove pervaded popular discussion of English in the mid-nineteenth century. The connection between the views of Alford and

Trench is clear: if in the etymologies of words can be uncovered the fossilised ethics of a nation, then current language usage reveals national ethics in formation. Alford, dean of Canterbury, following Trench, dean of Westminster, maintained that the lexicon of a nation and the morality of its people were inextricably intertwined.

In America, too, such views found favour. In lectures delivered in New York City in the fall and winter of 1858–9, George Perkins Marsh (1860: 37) took Trench's etymological forays further than fossil ethics and argued that 'the forms of language . . . are natural and necessary products of the organization, faculties, and condition of men'. Forging a bond between morality and language, Marsh (1860: 649) proclaimed: 'To deny that language is susceptible of corruption, is to deny that races or nations are susceptible of depravation; and to treat all its changes as normal, is to confound things as distinct as health and disease'. He drew a distinction between natural linguistic changes, which stem from 'the character of speech', and 'Mere corruptions . . . which arise from extraneous or accidental causes'. The latter should be 'detected, exposed, and if not healed, at least prevented from spreading beyond their source, and infecting a whole nation':

> To pillory such offences, to point out their absurdity, to detect and expose the moral obliquity which too often lurks beneath them, is the sacred duty of every scholar, of every philosophic thinker, who knows how nearly purity of speech, like personal cleanliness, is allied with purity of thought and rectitude of action. (1860: 644–5)

Marsh (1860: 649) expressed disdain for linguists and grammarians, whose putative ignorance he saw 'as a frequent cause of the corruption of language', and among those he most disagreed with was the prolific British writer Robert Gordon Latham. For Latham's claim that '*in language whatever IS is right*', he was judged by Marsh (1860: 645) to have confounded 'the progress of natural linguistic change, which is inevitable, and the deterioration arising from accidental or local causes, which may be resisted'. Marsh continued:

> the theory which I am combating, forgets that language . . . is of itself an informing vital agency, and that, so truly as *language* is what man has made it, just so truly *man* is what language has made him. The deprevation of a language is not merely a token or an effect of the corruption of a people, but corruption is accelerated, if not caused by the perversion and degradation of its consecrated vocabulary . . . When . . . popular writers in vulgar irony apply to vicious and depraved objects, names or epithets set apart by the common consent of society to designate the qualities or the acts which constitute man's only claim to reverence and affection,

they both corrupt the speech, and administer to the nation a poison more subtle and more dangerous . . . than the bitterest venom with which the destructive philosophy has ever assailed the moral or the spiritual interests of humanity.

Besides the moral degradation of language, accidental circumstances . . . often corrupt language philologically, by introducing violations of grammar, or of other proprieties of speech, which a servile spirit of imitation adopts, and which, at last, supersede proper and idiomatic forms of expression. . . . Changes of this sort are not exemplifications of the general laws of language, any more than the liability to be smitten with pestilence through infection is an exemplification of the normal principles of physiology; and therefore a language thus affected is as properly said to be corrupted, as a person who has taken a contagious malady to be diseased. (Marsh 1860: 647–8)

In a final example linking language, philology, and morality, Marsh (1860: vi) alludes to the announced dictionary of the Philological Society as 'a work of prime necessity to all the common moral and literary interests of the British and American people'.

Mining the same xenophobic vein, another American asked whether anything could 'be more significant of the profound degradation of a people than the abject character of the complimentary and social dialect of the Italians, and the pompous appellations with which they dignify things in themselves insignificant' (Mathews 1876: 61). Given such chauvinistic thinking, it is not surprising that the French too fared poorly, accused among other things of promoting bribery by the mere act of referring to it as *pot-de-vin*. Following the logic of Trench, the argument rests on the literal interpretation of *pot-de-vin* as 'jug of wine': an alluring thing enhances whatever its name attaches to, in this case enticing speakers to offer and accept bribes. In this increasingly widespread form of amateur etymological morality we see Horne Tooke's notion of an original core meaning combined with Trench's fossil ethics now transplanted to North America. In utter disregard of Locke's view of language as conventional, many commentators viewed words as linked to things by a natural bond. On both sides of the Atlantic, the seeds of Trench's and Alford's approach found fertile soil in the Romantic ideals that coupled nation and language.

As we saw in section 6.2, eighteenth-century grammarians often endorsed the force of usage in theory even as they ignored it in practice. By the mid-nineteenth century profoundly altered attitudes are suggested in the etymological morality modelled by Dean Trench, Dean Alford, and others.

Horne Tooke's philosophy had combined with Trench's theology to undermine even the theoretical authority of usage. Usage, it was now widely thought, reflected moral corruption, and, it was suspected, even caused it.

6.3.5   Ipse dixit *pronouncements*

With ethics and fanciful etymology victorious, commentators proceeded to a new plateau of prescription, and their handbooks served as platforms for pronouncements lacking explicit rationales. They propagated pronouncements made with authority no better than the writer's say-so and for that reason were called *ipse dixit* pronouncements after the Latin for 'he himself said it'. With no manifest inclination to justify many of their prescripts, these masters of dogma broadcast their linguistic condemnations and their prescriptions for linguistic correctness in magazine pieces and handbooks that the educated public eagerly embraced.

A seeming obsession with putative errors of usage had so taken hold that handbooks of verbal criticism multiplied in Britain and America, some carrying patently puristic titles such as *Errors in the Use of English* (Hodgson 1886) or *Modern English Literature: Its Blemishes and Defects* (Breen 1857) or *Bad English* (Moon 1869). That the puristic function of these volumes was valued is documented by an assistant examiner to Her Majesty's Civil Service Commission, whose *Every-day Errors of Speech* (Meredith 1877: 115) cites a letter from a friend who had seen advance pages of the book: 'I am absolutely filled with astonishment to see how many simple words I have been mispronouncing all my life, and would have kept on mispronouncing to the end of my days, if my thoughts had not been directed to them'.

The analyses of other authors underscore the continuing appeal of etymology, real and imagined, as an honoured criterion for linguistic propriety. W. B. Hodgson, professor of political economy at the University of Edinburgh according to the title page of his *Errors in the Use of English* (1886), invokes etymology to show how certain words have been used erroneously and to point to their 'true' meanings:

> *Verbal* (from Lat. *verbum*, 'a word') means 'couched in words,' spoken or written as the case may be, and is not synonymous with *oral*, 'delivered by word of mouth' (Lat. *os, oris*, 'a mouth'), seeing that it is as impossible to pen as it is to utter a sentence without the use of words. Yet writers of standing have often confounded these two words, thereby obliterating the separate functions of each. What the true functions of *verbal* are may be gathered from our first ten examples; what they are not is illustrated in the twelve that follow. (1886: 66)

Of the twenty-two citations he then offers, the majority illustrate 'errone-ous use' by writers such as Fielding, Trollope, Bulwer Lytton, and H. M. Commissioners on Capital Punishment. As a standard of correctness ety-mology outweighed frequent usage, as with the 'much-abused preposition' *between*, whose 'fundamental notion' is duality and 'which can not therefore correctly be employed with more than two objects of reference' (1886: 130). Etymology triumphs even over near universal usage: concerning prepositions 'Some blunders . . . seem . . . now to be almost universal' (1886: 127); concerning number agreement with relative pronouns (e.g. 'One of the most valuable *books* that *has* appeared in any language') 'this error . . . is oftener committed than avoided', an achievement Hodgson (1886: 164ff.) documents with pages of examples, several 'committed' by other philolo-gists.

The American Thomas Embley Osmun, using the pseudonym Alfred Ayres under which he had earlier edited Cobbett's grammar, compiled two popular handbooks. In one (1882) he listed some 3500 frequently mispro-nounced words from *Aaron* and *abdomen* to *zoological* and *Zunz*, and in the other (1897) examined 'the right and the wrong use of words and . . . other matters of interest to those who would speak and write with propriety'. Characteristically, he says of *donate* merely that it is 'looked upon by most champions of good English as . . . an abomination'; of *real* that it is 'often vulgarly used in the sense of . . . *very*; thus, *real* nice, *real* pretty, *real* angry, *real* cute, and so on'. Concerning the shortened form *gents* he says: 'Of all vulgarisms, this is perhaps the most offensive' and asks, 'If we say *gents*, why not say *lades*?' *Kids* is a 'vile contraction', *lunch* an 'inelegant abbreviation', and *nicely* the 'very quintessence of popinjay vulgarity' when used for *well*. *Only* he judged 'more frequently misplaced than any other word in the lan-guage'. In its entirety the entry on *overly* says simply: 'This word is now used only by the unschooled'. Such ipse dixit-isms are characteristic of the kinds of advice that overflowed from the handbooks of the time. They are characteristically absolute, often unsubstantiated, and typically baseless.

Even more than the handbook writers, school grammarians revelled in rivalry and found as much fault with the rules, writing, and methods of their competitors as with faulty grammar and usage themselves. We pass lightly over the school grammars of this and the following period because by about the middle of the nineteenth century handbooks and dictionaries had become so important a forum for debating language correctness and the role of usage, displacing grammars in this respect. Little in the treat-ment of usage in school grammars was not played out in bolder colours in the handbooks and dictionaries.

6.3.6   Reactions against false philology

By the 1860s and 1870s the empirical findings of comparative philology were coming to be well understood on both sides of the Atlantic, and while writers unfamiliar with or unpersuaded by the findings continued their fanciful analyses, knowledgeable commentators objected strongly to the amateur etymologising. The most vigorous objection to the 'false philology' of the etymological marauders came from Fitzedward Hall, an expatriate American who had taught in India for years before taking up a post teaching Indian jurisprudence and Sanskrit at King's College, London. In *Recent Exemplifications of False Philology* (1872) and *Modern English* (1873), Hall (1873: xiii) took to task what he called the 'motley cluster of philologists, semi-philologists, and entire philologasters', and with a knowledge of English literary usage greatly enhanced by his reading for the Philological Society's new dictionary, he exposed the error of the speculative claims of the amateurs around him. Thus, a decade before the first fascicle of the *OED*'s letter *A* was published, Hall could marshall ammunition from the entire alphabet and fire volley after volley into the speculative armour of the 'philologasters' and amateur etymologists. He delighted in exhibiting 'specimens of such erroneous conclusions as one is sure to be landed in, from electing, in philology, assumption and divination, in preference to investigation and induction' (1873: x).

Hall's exemplifications were pointed, logically argued, and amply illustrated. Occasionally they attempted to be witty, as in this instance, discussing the third edition of Max Müller's *Lectures on the Science of Language*:

> we are informed that, 'in fact, "*very* pleased" and "*very* delighted" are Americanisms which may be heard even in this country' . . . The phrases just named become, however, in Professor Müller's fourth edition, simply 'expressions which may be heard in many drawing-rooms'. That they should be felt to deserve promotion from, it might be, Whitechapel of the Seven Dials, to decent society, as soon as they were discovered not to bear the brand of Americanisms, was, all things considered, only to be expected. They are heard, we are told, 'in many drawing-rooms'. And there they were heard, without question, four or five generations ago. Sir William Jones wrote '*very* concerned', in 1760; and Gibbon '*very* unqualified', in 1762.   (1873: 54–5)

More typically, Hall's barbs were excessive and dull, and his technically devastating observations proved to be rhetorical duds. He understood that 'Language may be at once perfectly correct and ludicrously inappropriate', but he failed to keep his own prose supple and his vocabulary accessible enough to win him an audience. Enlisted on behalf of etymology and historical usage, his torturous syntax and opaque lexicon (*parvanimities, catachresis, nummulary*) made for distinctly unappetising philological fare. Reviewers judged *False Philology* 'an exhibition of arrogance, of pompous pretence, and of literary brutality' and described its author as writing 'like a braggart, a bully, and a blackguard', epithets Hall (or his publisher) apparently took pride in, as one may infer from the fact that the reviews containing the comments were reprinted in the back matter of Hall's *Modern English* a year later. If style and substance combined to minimise Hall's appeal, as George McKnight (1928: 538) figured, many other well-informed commentators since then have also tried and failed to establish the validity of usage as the sole determinant in language correctness.

Indeed, following Dean Trench the language shamans of the late nineteenth century proclaimed the intrinsic goodness or badness of linguistic form – and that conviction persists in much educated opinion to the present day. In the face of such entrenched beliefs, it has proved difficult for scholars to make inroads by marshalling the relevant facts of usage. Still, as the fascicles of the *OED* started appearing in 1884, it became increasingly clear that the prescriptions of the handbooks were greatly at odds with the facts of recorded usage. By the turn of the century, scholarly opinion pronounced most handbooks embarrassingly out of touch with the facts of usage and even 'grotesque in their ignorance' (Matthews 1901: 212). The discrepancy between the descriptivists' facts and the prescriptivists' ideals of usage continues to the present day.

6.3.7   Speech and writing

By the end of the nineteenth century the phonetic sciences were maturing in Britain, having been established by A. J. Ellis (whose comments as head of the Philological Society we noted earlier) and Henry Sweet, the rough model for Professor Henry Higgins in Shaw's 'Pygmalion', which was produced in 1916. With advances in phonetics came renewed discussion of the roles of speaking and writing as norms for English usage. While Britain excelled in the scientific aspects of phonetic description, American scholars such as Brander Matthews eloquently argued the case for speech over writing as the norm. President of the Modern Language Association, chairman of the Simplified Spelling Board, and professor of English at Columbia University, Matthews was also a drama critic upon whom the power of the theatre and the eloquence of the spoken word exercised a profound influence. He shared his learned colleagues' judgement about the centrality of usage but disagreed sharply with those who argued for writing as the basis for correctness: 'The real language of a people is the spoken word, not the written. Language lives on the tongue and in the ear; there it was born, and there it grows'; the English language belongs 'to the peoples who speak it' (1901: 71, prefactory note).

As noted earlier, the consensus of opinion has usually maintained that, for both theoretical and practical reasons, written usage should serve as the basis for linguistic correctness and as citations in dictionaries, grammars, and handbooks of usage. Inevitably, perhaps, the argument that placed writing and especially literary usage at the pinnacle was perceived as élitist, for literacy and literature do not belong equally to all social levels. Whereas the American Thomas Lounsbury (1908: 97) had dismissed 'the man in the street' because he had 'no direct influence upon the preservation . . . of any word or phrase', Matthews (1921: 9) viewed language as 'governed not by elected representatives but by a direct democracy, by the people as a whole assembled in town-meeting'. Somewhat reminiscent of Priestley's views about academies and the perfectibility of English, Matthews (1901: 212) noted that 'In language, as in politics, the people at large are in the long run better judges of their own needs than any specialist can be'.

Likewise disenchanted with a literary standard for English usage was George Philip Krapp (1909: 14), another American who judged it 'a false standard of values to assume that the test of highest excellence is to be found only in printed and written words'. Following Matthews, he pointed to living speech as 'the real guide to good grammar', and citing Walt Whitman and echoing the preface to *Lyrical Ballads* he articulated a view of language that had 'its bases broad and low, close to the ground'. Similar Romantic sentiments and democratic commitments are apparent in Krapp's comment that the 'final decisions [of language] are made by the masses, people nearest the concrete, having most to do with actual land and sea' (1909: 328–9). Echoing a metaphor used by Priestley, Krapp argued that 'the grammarian has no more power of legislating in the rules of grammar than the scientist has in the physical laws of nature' (1909: 322).

More than anyone else in Britain or America, Krapp rationalised notions of English not as a monolithic unity nor as '*the* English language' but as a collection of functionally and socially related varieties. Analysts before him recognised differences between spoken and written varieties and among the dialects of social groups, but none had clearly looked at different kinds of varieties along conceptually distinct axes. Krapp articulated a distinction between good English, which is effective and appropriate and 'hits the mark', and standard or conventional English. He criticised the notion of an absolute or uniform standard of linguistic correctness and argued icono-clastically that progress depended upon 'individual initiative': 'The true road towards community sympathy, towards community efficiency, in language as in all other social institutions, is through the recognition of the value, of the right, even of the duty, of individual variation based on the principle of truth to individual character and environment' (1908: 26). At the same time he also acknowledged that in 'self-defense, every person is compelled to take account of the social demands and penalties' involved in using particular language varieties (1927: 175–6).

6.3.8. Fowler and 'Fowler'

In 1926, after decades of disagreement about the role of usage in deciding matters of linguistic correctness, Henry W. Fowler (1858–1933) brought out his now famous *Dictionary of Modern English Usage*. Collaborating earlier with his brother Francis George Fowler, Henry W. Fowler had compiled *The Concise Oxford Dictionary* (1911) and *The Pocket Oxford Dictionary* (1925). From work on these projects, he gained impressive lexicographical experi-ence and familiarity with the resources of the *OED* and nurtured a gift for analysing English in ways that were to hold great popular appeal.

Modern English Usage lacks a preface laying out Fowler's views, but its entries make clear his intent to offer to sophisticated readers guidance about how to honour the name of good usage. Serviceable enough for writers seeking an acceptable choice, *MEU* holds most appeal for those seeking the best choice. Not shy about expressing his personal prefer-ences, Fowler larded his entries with examples of usages to be admired or avoided by aspirants to a higher linguistic calling. His entries are warm and famously engaging, neither strident nor saccharine, and they prompt reflection on the character of English as much as they offer conclusions about its usage.

Focusing on a couple of the items that remain troublesome at the end of the twentieth century, we note Fowler's observations that it is 'nonsense' to call anything *more, most,* or *very unique*. About *like* as a conjunction, as in *Unfortunately few have observed like you have done*, he wrote that 'Every illiterate person uses this construction daily' but that in the *OED*'s judgement this usage is 'Now generally condemned as vulgar or slovenly, though examples may be found in many recent writers of standing'. In his two-part discus-sion, the first sets the record straight by relying principally on the *OED*'s citations and then offers readers a choice:

The reader who has no instinctive objection to the construction can now decide for himself whether he shall consent to use it in talk, in print, in both, or in neither; he knows that he will be able to defend himself if he is condemned for it, but also that, until he has done so, he will be condemned. It remains to give a few newspaper examples so that there may be no mistake about what the 'vulgar or slovenly' use in its simplest form is.

The second part of the entry – 'intended for those who decide against the conjunctional use . . . & are prepared to avoid also some misuses of a less easily recognizable kind' – offers advice of a distinctly nobler standard than mere usage.

MEU characterises *between* as 'a sadly ill-treated word', especially when its objects are joined by a word other than *and* ('Societies with a membership between one thousand *to* five thousand') because *and* is 'the one & only right connexion', even if 'writers indulge in all sorts of freaks', the more 'exceptional & absurd' of which Fowler amply exemplifies. Concerning *between you and I*, it is described in the entry for *I* as 'a piece of false grammar not sanctioned . . . even by colloquial usage', but in the entry for *between* Fowler acknowledges that it is often said, and he speculates (perplexingly, given his acquaintance with the historical record) that the phrase may result 'from a hazy remembrance of hearing *you & me* corrected in the subjective'. In evaluating the prepositional use of *due to*, Fowler writes: 'Under the influence of analogy, [it] is often used by the illiterate as though it had passed, like *owing to*, into a mere compound preposition. In all the examples below *owing* would stand, but *due* . . . is impossible'; and he illustrates with sentences like 'Some articles have increased in price, due to the increasing demand'. Of *who* and *whom* he writes: 'The interrogative *who* is often used in talk where grammar demands *whom*, as in *Who did you hear that from?*'. The opposite 'mistake' – using *whom* instead of *who* – 'is a bad one, but fortunately so elementary that it is nearly confined to sports-reporters & patrons of the *as-to* style . . . & needs no discussion'. He adds that 'The relative *who* now & then slips in for *whom*, giving the educated reader a shock'.

To this day, three-quarters of a century after its initial publication in 1926, connoisseurs consult 'Fowler' on the finer points of usage, much as ordinary citizens consult 'the dictionary' for guidance about spellings, meanings, and pronunciations. In 1983 *MEU* was revised by Ernest Gowers under the original title and in 1996 by Robert Burchfield as *The New Fowler's Modern English Usage* (Fowler 1996). As the name 'Webster' is synonymous with dictionary in some parts of the English-speaking world, 'Fowler' continues to mean honoured handbook of usage throughout.

6.4   Third period: 1930–present

With completion of the *OED* in 1928 and a four-volume *Supplement* in 1986 (Burchfield 1972–86), as well as a second edition integrating the whole in 1989, the twentieth century witnessed the maturation of an extraordinary monument to lexicographical description. But the second half of the century has also seen a strong reaction against pure description and a growing sense that complete description should encompass the facts not only of usage but of evaluation as well. In part the final seven decades of the century can be characterised as a continuation of trends started by the *OED*'s editors in surveying and reporting recorded usage, but it also continued Fowler's practice of combining the facts of usage with interpretive comments about appropriateness and even elegance. Along with more complex and more complete information about the facts of usage than was available earlier in the century, the practice of offering evalution has continued and spread to some erstwhile strictly descriptive reference works. Building on techniques like those employed by turn-of-the-century dialect geographers in collecting data about regional variation (cf. Ihalainen 1994), later researchers surveyed *perceptions* of usage and *opinions* about it and incorporated their findings into handbooks, grammars, and dictionaries. At century's end it seems clear that machine-readable corpora and computer-assisted analysis will enhance, if not revolutionise, the study of written and spoken English usage.

6.4.1   *Surveys of usage and surveys of opinion*

Surveys of English usage examine the practice usually of writers and sometimes of speakers. The great monument to this approach to lexicography is the *OED*, whose printed quotations come from a multi-million citation collection garnered from a systematic examination of all English literature by a veritable army of readers. (Eighty-nine crowded pages of the *OED* list its quoted books.) As noted in section 6.3.2 the Early English Text Society and the Chaucer Society were founded in the nineteenth century precisely to provide mines of Old and Middle English texts for the Philological Society's new dictionary. The use of citations was not new, though, when Trench proposed a new dictionary to be based on them nor even when Johnson relied on his personal reading and the assistance of his amanuenses to provide tens of thousands of citations for his 1755 dictionary. Citations are the *sine qua non* of reliable, respectable lexicography. Moreover, during the twentieth century surveys of usage have been undertaken for grammatical analyses as well. For example, Otto Jespersen

(1909–49) relied on a collection of citations for his monumental grammar, while Charles C. Fries (1940, 1952) examined some 3,000 letters addressed to a branch of the US government and a corpus of spoken conversation as the basis for his grammars.

Two types of surveys of linguistic opinion have also been developed in this century. In the United States under the aegis of the National Council of Teachers of English, Sterling Leonard (1932) sent ballots containing hundreds of usage items to several juries (linguists, business people, teachers), asking them to report 'your observation of what is actual usage rather than your opinion of what usage should be'. He found that usage as observed by educated respondents outpaced the recommendations for good usage in handbooks and grammars. Subsequently, researchers compared these observations with actual usage as recorded in the newly completed *OED*. Focusing on 121 items whose status Leonard deemed 'disputable', Marckwardt and Walcott (1938) found fifty recorded in literary usage (e.g. 'A treaty . . . *between the four* powers', '*One* rarely likes to do as *he* is told', '*Neither* of your reasons *are* really valid') and an additional fifty-six in good colloquial usage or American literary usage. Of thirty-eight items Leonard labelled 'illiterate', thirteen were recorded in the *OED* as occurring in literary or standard colloquial use. As Leonard had documented the conservatism of textbook dogma in contrast to educated observation, Marckwardt and Walcott demonstrated the conservatism of educated observation as compared to recorded usage.

In the UK a research team at the University of Newcastle (Mittins *et al.* 1970) combined a survey of respondents' estimates of 'the favourableness or otherwise of their spontaneous reaction' to selected usage items with a compendium of published opinions about the items. With more than 450 respondents considering fifty items in situations of formal and informal speech and writing the Newcastle team assembled some 91,000 judgements, of which 58 per cent represented rejections and only 41 per cent acceptances. In the Newcastle survey the highest overall rate of acceptance (86 per cent) was accorded to 'He did not do *as* well as the experts had expected' (cf. '. . . *so* well . . .'), while at the opposite extreme 'The process is *very unique*' had the lowest rate (11 per cent). The item designed to assess reaction to *between* applied to more than two items ('The agreement *between* the four powers') had an acceptance rate of 57 per cent, although fewer than half the teachers and examiners among the respondents judged it acceptable. Recall that the *OED* identified 'a treaty *among* three powers' as an expression speakers would not be inclined to say. The Newcastle team found it 'not easy to imagine' that most of those rejecting '*between* the four powers' (60 per cent in formal writing, 53 per cent in formal speech) would themselves write or say '*among* the four powers', as their rejection of the item might be taken to entail. Usage items with lower rates of acceptance included the split infinitive ('He refused *to even think* of it') at only 40 per cent and the use of *less* for *fewer* ('*less* road accidents') at 35 per cent. Items with acceptance ratings under 20 per cent included the dangling participle and the perennially perplexing conjunctive *like*, here in place of *as if* ('It looked *like* it would rain'). The researchers noted often contradictory judgements and 'indications of pedantry, of prejudice, of readiness to pontificate, and of unrealistic conservatism' in both the published and elicited comments. One might quarrel with a methodology that relies on respondents' having to intuit 'spontaneous reactions' to usage items in four imagined situations, but by coupling current opinion and published assessments the Newcastle study highlighted the continuing conservatism of educated attitudes to usage in the second half of the century and showed for Britain what had been earlier demonstrated for America.

The three studies just examined surveyed opinion among professional groups or compared opinions to published records of usage or other opinion. The *OED* provided a reliable record of the usages that Leonard had investigated, while published comment provided the Newcastle researchers with a set of opinions about the acceptability of usages that respondents had been asked to judge. To ascertain actual usage, lexicographers have more recently established collections of machine-readable texts as the basis for aspects of usage such as spelling, capitalisation, part of speech, and word senses, as well as for labelling aspects of status (region, register, etc.). As noted earlier, though, the persuasive use of citation evidence in grammars and dictionaries relies on the premise that usage is the principal or exclusive determinant of correctness in language, for reliance on records of actual usage carries an implicit suggestion that linguistic practices constitute a legitimate norm of correctness. This is, of course, the basis of the descriptivist position.

Since the mid-nineteenth century, however, many journalists and much of the educated public have questioned the validity and desirability of strict description as the sole basis for deciding questions of usage. If, in tacit acknowledgement of that fact, twentieth-century descriptivists have mostly taken care to avoid Latham's (1848) provocative claim that in language 'whatever *is* is right', not all have done so, and educators, journalists, and public figures have tended to perceive a flagrantly permissive philosophy in certain grammatical and lexicographical descriptions. *Leave Your Language Alone!* (Hall 1950), the much ballyhooed title of a book by a descriptive linguist, encapsulated what descriptive grammarians and lexicographers had been suspected of urging, and the publication of *Webster's Third New International Dictionary* (1961) a decade later confirmed the perception and became an international *cause célèbre* with its boldly trumpeted descriptivism. Reinforcing the impression were comments like one in *The Random House Dictionary of the English Language* (McDavid 1966: xxi) that 'Essentially, in the usage of native speakers, whatever is, is right; but some usages may be more appropriate than others, at least socially'. However defensible, even sensible, such a comment seemed to descriptive linguists, the philosophy underlying it struck a raw nerve among many educated readers and journalists. It seemed to threaten the health not only of the English language but of acceptable social and moral standards as well. Many twentieth-century commentators have found a permissive view of language anathema and vociferously condemned it. The putative permissivism of descriptive lexicographers and grammarians was taken by many as a slap in the face to dedicated teachers, hard-working copy editors (and even exasperated parents struggling to cope with unruly teenagers). Descriptive linguistics has been equated with grammar-to-the-winds permissivism and viewed as symptomatic of a contagious disregard of time-honoured principles of discipline and righteous living.

Reaction has been strong against descriptivism and the attack it was perceived as mounting against good English. As one emblem of it, an American publishing company sought to buy out the G. & C. Merriam Company, intending to suppress its infamous *Third*. Failing that, the publisher that saw itself as guardian of the language instead produced *The American Heritage Dictionary of the English Language* (1969). To counterbalance what its editors saw as descriptivism gone astray, the *AHD* incorporated 'usage notes' reporting the opinions of a conservative usage panel that had been polled for its views of scores of disputed or controversial usage items, such as *between* ('the correct preposition when only two persons or things serve as objects'), *hopefully* (as used to mean 'it is to be hoped' or 'let us hope', it is 'still not accepted by a substantial number of authorities on grammar and usage' and was judged acceptable by only 44 per cent of the Usage Panel), *shall* and *will*, and other predictable matters. Usage notes, though not a usage panel, have proved popular, and other dictionaries now incorporate them, including *The Concise Oxford Dictionary* and even Merriam-Webster's collegiate dictionaries. The usage notes of *The Concise Oxford* (8th edition 1990) are 'not to prescribe usage but to alert the user to a difficulty or controversy attached to particular uses'. The usage 'paragraphs' in *Webster's Ninth New Collegiate Dictionary* (1983: 19) are appended to:

terms that are considered to present problems of confused or disputed usage. A usage paragraph typically summarizes the historical background of the item and its associated body of opinion, compares these with available evidence of current usage, and often adds a few words of suitable advice for the dictionary user.

As with the *OED*'s use of citations, usage notes do not lack precedent in so far as modern dictionaries typically interpret their findings with labels indicating geographical distribution and status. The labels assess or evaluate reported usages – in the case of the *OED*, for example, as 'American' or 'vulgar' or 'illiterate' and in the case of *The Concise Oxford* as 'British' or 'US' or 'formal' or 'colloquial' or 'jocular' or 'offensive' or 'disputed'. Even the Merriam-Webster Company, much maligned for its sparse application of usage labels in the *Third*, had not entirely abandoned them. Indeed, usage labels remain an orthodox element of a word's description. What is remarkable about the *AHD*, then, is not that it incorporated usage notes but that its editors polled the *opinions* of a jury empanelled specifically for that purpose, and it heralded a wider practice of describing not only actual usage but opinion about it as well.

6.4.2   *Popular reaction against descriptivism*

Following the publication of *Webster's Third New International Dictionary* in 1961, a surprisingly virulent reaction to linguistic descriptivism found expression in the United States. By the 1980s in Britain, following a period of cultural, social and political ferment, educational authorities had grown uneasy about the state of knowledge of English in the schools, and conservative commentators and public figures expressed concern that schools had become lax in enforcing standards of good English. Even the Prince of Wales voiced his negative assessment of the situation. In some of those expressions of concern the familiar link between English usage on the one hand and social and moral values on the other is apparent. For example, John Rae, a former public school headmaster, wrote a piece that appeared under the title 'The Decline and Fall of English Grammar' (*Observer* 7 February 1982). Referring to the influence of descriptivism on school curricula he said:

> The overthrow of grammar coincided with the acceptance of the equivalent of creative writing in social behaviour. As nice points of grammar were mockingly dismissed as pedantic and irrelevant, so was punctiliousness in such matters as honesty, responsibility, property, gratitude, apology and so on. (Cited in Cameron 1995: 94)

A few years later a radio comment by Norman Tebbit MP signalled similar concerns and expressly linked standards for good English to criminal activity:

> If you allow standards to slip to the stage where good English is no better than bad English, where people turn up filthy at school . . . all these things tend to cause people to have no standards at all, and once you lose standards then there's no imperative to stay out of crime.

> (Cited in Cameron 1995: 94)

Cameron portrays the 'grammar controversy of the 1980s and early 1990s' as having 'deep and tangled' political roots in which 'Grammar was made to symbolize . . . a commitment to traditional values as a basis for social order, to "standards" and "discipline" in the classroom, to moral certainties rather than moral relativism and to cultural homogeneity rather than pluralism' (1995: 111–2). The chords struck in the comments of Rae, Tebbit, and many others, echo familiar themes in the history of grammar and usage. From its early days grammar was seen as a matter of propriety and, at least since the eighteenth century, it has been affiliated with pious sentiments and righteous living. In the mid-nineteenth century Dean Trench linked English usage with ethics in his influential works, and since that time words have been widely viewed in Britain and America as having true and false senses and right and wrong uses. Language has been viewed as a mirror of community standards and community ethics. The comments of Rae, Tebbit, and others, then, reflect a common and long-standing conviction that grammar and ethics are intertwined and that negligence of the points of usage and of grammatical analysis can lead to a diminution of social and ethical responsibility.

6.4.3   Computerised corpora of English language texts

Using new technologies that became more readily available in the 1960s, large-scale collections of English texts have been compiled in machine-readable form, making computerised analysis possible. The 'Brown Corpus' contains 500 texts of 2,000 words each from fifteen genres of writing published in the United States in 1961. British English has the parallel London–Oslo/Bergen ('LOB') Corpus. These one-million-word corpora are available in plain-text and grammatically tagged machine-readable versions, and published studies report the frequency and distribution of words and word classes in the corpora and across their fifteen genres (see Francis & Kučera 1982; Johansson & Hofland 1989). Reliable comparisons are thus possible between British and American writing published at mid-century. The Brown and LOB corpora, as well as more recent larger corpora, can provide valuable lexical information and illustration of written English, and they have been exploited to that end. Corpora of spoken English also exist, notably the London–Lund Corpus of British English (see Svartvik & Quirk 1980), and others are in development for national varieties of English world-wide (see Greenbaum 1996). For current English the British National Corpus is a 100-million-word collection of about 3,200 written and 850 spoken texts, the latter comprising about 10 per cent of the corpus, the former including fiction, newspaper articles, and academic books, as well as unpublished letters, memoranda, and school and university essays. The promise of such corpora is signalled by the BNC's being identified in *The Concise Oxford Dictionary of Current English* (1995: vii) as the most significant among a large body of corpus and citation evidence used in its compilation. Exceeding the BNC in size but with limited accessibility is the COBUILD corpus and the Bank of English, joint projects of Collins Publishers and Birmingham University (see Sinclair 1987), and these too have provided a basis for dictionaries and grammars.

Besides corpora of twentieth-century English, machine-readable collections of historical texts have been compiled, notably the Helsinki Corpus and ARCHER (see Kytö, Rissanen & Wright 1994). Such historical corpora provide valuable information about actual historical language usage – principally genre-based, but also reflecting some social and regional differences. The mammoth undertaking by hundreds of readers manually drafting citation slips for the editors of the *OED* has now evolved into an electronic process after several decades of experience with computers and machine-readable corpora, and there is every reason to expect significant improvement in our understanding of English usage and in the dictionaries and grammars describing that usage.

6.5   Conclusions and prospects

Looking back over two centuries of views towards propriety and correctness in English usage, some patterns are discernible. From its seventeenth- and eighteenth-century foundations, the study of English grammar has had lobbyists who regarded usage as the highest or only determinant of correctness and others who subordinated it to other considerations – Latin, logic, etymologic, analogic, and personal preference, among them. Among those espousing usage as the basis for correctness in language (and that would include many eighteenth-century grammarians and lexicographers), probably most have found it unpalatable to accept alternative usages as equally good and have instead expressed preference for one variant or another.

During the eighteenth century, when grammar started to emerge from philosophy and when the influence of Latin waned, grammarians analysed English because they perceived it to be in need of codification as compared to the classical tongue and the Continental vernaculars. During the nineteenth century, however, fanciful etymologies were enlisted in support of inquiry into philosophical truth. When Trench transmuted Horne Tooke's philosophical etymologies into theological inquiries, he provided a compelling basis for viewing linguistic expression as fossilised ethics, a veritable window on past morality and immorality alike. It was then only a short step to viewing contemporary usage through ethical lenses and trying to shape it to what were imagined its best and most ethical forms. The nineteenth century was an era of moral and ethical philology, and ironically Dean Trench, the prime propagator of such a perspective, was also the catalyst responsible for instigating the Philological Society's *New English Dictionary*. Once published, the *OED* with its massive record of facts about English usage forever made the ethical analysis of grammar and lexicon difficult, though the ethical analysis of language use (quite a different matter) remains strong at the end of the twentieth century.

The study of English usage in the twentieth century has been sharply constrained by the citations reported in the *OED* and other bodies of recorded usage. The survey system that emerged strongly during the century helped create an impressive monument of scholarship. The same social scientific tenor of the time has given rise to surveys of opinion – about what people write and say as well as about reactions to it.

Coupled with interpretive opinion as reports of usage now commonly are, twentieth-century approaches to usage have increasingly come to balance the facts of usage with discussion of opinion about suitability, appropriateness, and alternatives. The availability of corpora of English-language texts and of computational facilities for exploring them is expected to produce increasingly better descriptions of English usage for diverse dialects and registers. If past is prelude, it is clear that the twenty-first century will see even the most descriptive dictionaries and grammars incorporating evaluation of usages as part of their descriptions.

FURTHER READING

6.1.   Strands of the story told here are well documented elsewhere. Jones (1953) details the triumph of English prior to the eighteenth century. The collection by Stein & Tieken-Boon van Ostade (1993) provides insight as to the processes of standardisation in the seventeenth and eighteenth centuries. Michael (1970) describes British grammatical traditions in Latin and English before 1800, emphasising categorisations of the parts of speech, the central component of contemporary grammatical analysis. The character and origin of standard languages in Europe is discussed by Joseph (1987), while general discussions of the issues discussed in this chapter can be found in Milroy & Milroy (1991), and the story of American prescriptivism in Finegan (1980) and Baron (1982). Bailey (1991) provides an informative historical overview of 'Images of English'. Tucker (1961), Bolton (1966), Bolton & Crystal (1969), and Crowley (1991) are collections of important documents of the period.

6.2.   Leonard (1929) provides a detailed account of the eighteenth-century doctrine of correctness. Michael (1987) tells the story of the teaching of English, particularly in Britain, from the sixteenth through the nineteenth centuries. Landau (1984) provides an overview of English dictionaries from the beginning, while Stein (1985) provides details about early dictionaries. Valuable discussions of Johnson's dictionary can be found in Reddick (1996) and Sledd & Kolb (1955).

6.3.   Aarsleff (1983) provides an intellectual backdrop to much of our story in his analysis of language study in England between 1780 and 1860 and is particularly helpful in understanding Horne Tooke and Dean Trench. The human side of the making of the *OED* is engagingly told in the biography of Murray by his granddaughter K. M. E. Murray (1977). Mugglestone (1995) discusses the standardisation of pronunciation and accent during the nineteenth century, a topic which we have not taken up in this chapter.

6.4.   Crowley (1989) is a critical study of the standardisation of English, attending especially to issues of social justice; Cameron (1995) directly and provocatively discusses various forms of 'verbal hygiene'. Sledd & Ebbitt (1962) is a collection of published reviews of *Webster's Third New International Dictionary*, while Morton (1994) puts the war of words over the *Third* into perspective. Gilman (1989) and Peters (1995) are exemplary models of modern usage dictionaries, the latter based in part on the findings of certain corpora.

   Information about existing English language corpora can be found in Johansson & Hofland (1989), while information about the availability of both modern English and historical English corpora is available via the Internet from ICAME (International Computer Archive of Modern and Medieval English, maintained by the Norwegian Computing Centre for the Humanities) at <http://www.hd.uib.no/icame.html>. The British National Corpus was compiled by a consortium comprising Oxford University Press, Addison-Wesley Longman and Larousse Kingfisher Chambers, as well as the British Library's Research and

Innovation Centre, the Oxford University Computing Services, and Lancaster University's Centre for Computer Research on the English Language; consult <http: //info.ox.ac.uk/bnc/whatbnc.html>. Greenbaum (1996) discusses the International Corpus of English, and current information can be found at <http: //www.ucl.ac.uk/english-usage/ice.htm>; the journal *World Englishes* (1995, 15: 1) is devoted to the 'ICE' project.

7 LITERARY LANGUAGE

Sylvia Adamson

7.1 Introduction

7.1.1 *The two revolutions*

(1) Every revolution in poetry is apt to be, and sometimes to announce itself as, a return to common speech. That is the revolution which Wordsworth announced in his prefaces and he was right . . . and the same revolution was due again something over a century later. (Eliot 1942)

T. S. Eliot, like many other commentators, identifies two revolutions in the history of poetic language since 1776. The 'revolution which Wordsworth announced in his prefaces', conventionally known as the Romantic revolution, is commonly dated from the collaborative production of *Lyrical Ballads* by Wordsworth and Coleridge in 1798. The second revolution – Modernism – has its equivalent landmark publication in Eliot's own *The Waste Land* of 1922, though the movement began over a decade earlier, with the arrival in London of Eliot's mentor Ezra Pound in 1908 and the impact of the first exhibition of Post-Impressionist painting in 1910.

In the years between 1910 and 1922, Eliot, Pound, and other members of their circle were anxious to stress the stylistic gulf dividing them from their nineteenth-century predecessors and to represent Modernism as a counter-revolution *against* Romanticism. But in (1), reviewing events from the retro-perspective of the 1940s, Eliot emphasises instead the common ground between the two movements and defines this as 'a return to common speech'. It's a definition that may seem paradoxical to those who share the belief, voiced by Larkin in (2), that Modernism fosters élitist and difficult forms of writing which *remove* literature from common speech:

(2)   It seems to me undeniable that up to this century literature used
        language in the way we all use it, painting represented what
        anyone with normal vision sees . . . The innovation of
        'modernism' in the arts consisted of doing the opposite.

                                                        (Larkin 1983)

In this chapter I shall attempt to resolve the paradox and show how (1) and
(2) can be reconciled as accounts of stylistic history. But there are some
preliminary questions to consider: (i) how is 'a return to common speech'
to be defined and linguistically characterised? (ii) can it be detected in literary genres outside poetry?

7.1.2   Quantifying stylistic change

These questions are addressed by Biber & Finegan (1989), in a paper which
is also an important pilot study for the application of quantificational
methods to historical stylistics. Taking samples from three non-poetic
genres – fiction, essays, letters – Biber & Finegan find that, during the
period covered by this volume, all genres show a marked shift from **literate**
to **oral** styles. What makes their findings relevant here is that they define *oral
style* as the form of language canonically associated with **conversation**
(Biber 1988: 37) and this corresponds both with the way Eliot defines the
term *common speech* in his 1942 essay and with the model for poetry proposed
by Wordsworth in the advertisement to *Lyrical Ballads* (see (4a) below).

The linguistic characterisation offered by Biber & Finegan for the
difference between literate and oral is summarised in table 7.1, where the features above the dotted line are associated with literate styles and the features
below it with oral styles. But the presence of the line does not mean that we
are dealing with discrete stylistic options. Rather, table 7.1 represents a continuum along which texts are classed as *more* or *less* oral or literate on the basis
of the relative density in their language of the feature cluster associated with
each polarity. The arrangement of features in three columns marks the
further recognition that orality is a complex notion: conversational speech
has a number of distinct situational characteristics, each of which correlates
with a distinct set of linguistic features. As Biber puts it 'in terms of its situational characteristics, stereotypical speech is interactive, and dependent on
shared space, time and background knowledge . . . in terms of its linguistic
characteristics, stereotypical speech is structurally simple, fragmented, concrete and dependent on exophoric (situation-dependent) reference' (Biber
1988: 37). Accordingly, column A lists the features that reflect the purpose

Table 7.1. *Linguistic features associated with literate and oral styles (adapted from Biber & Finegan 1989: 491)*

Literate Styles		
A (edited & informational)	**B** (context-independent)	**C** (abstract)
1. nouns	6. WH-relatives on object position	11. conjuncts
2. word-length	7. **pied-piping**	12. agentless passives
3. prepositions	8. WH-relatives on subject position	13. past participle adverbial clauses
4. high type/token ratio	9. phrasal co-ordination	14. BY-passives
5. attributive adjectives	10. nominalisations	15. past participle **WHIZ deletion**
		16. other adverbial subordinators
17. private verbs	40. time adverbials	
18. THAT-deletion	41. place adverbials	
19. contractions	42. other adverbs	
20. present-tense		
21. 2nd-person pronouns		
22. DO as pro-verb		
23. analytic negation		
24. demonstratives		
25. emphatics		
26. 1st-person pronouns		
27. IT		
28. BE as main verb		
29. causative subordination		
30. discourse particles		
31. indefinite pronouns		
32. hedges		
33. amplifiers		
34. sentence relatives		
35. WH-questions		
36. possibility modals		
37. nonphrasal co-ordination		
38. WH-complement clauses		
39. final prepositions		
A (unedited & interactive)	**B** (context-dependent)	**C** (non-abstract)
	Oral Styles	

(For further guidance on the interpretation of the parameters and features in Table 7.1., see Biber 1988: 101–120.)

of the speaker/writer (i.e. whether informative or interactive) and the conditions of production (i.e. whether edited or on-line); column B reflects the degree of context-dependency; and column C reflects the degree of abstractness. It is assumed that a maximally oral style, like 'stereotypical speech', is – or will appear to be – simultaneously interactive, unedited, context-dependent and non-abstract. But the separation of these characteristics allows the analyst to register the fact that different genres, for example, may select or foreground different aspects of orality.

By computational and statistical methods (described in full in Biber 1988) a text can be given a score on each of the three parameters, thus allowing stylistic comparisons to be made between texts or groups of texts (such as the works of particular authors, periods, genres). Figure 7.1 shows the result of this process applied to Biber & Finegan's corpus in respect of the parameter of column B (the level of context-dependent reference). It provides a clear picture both of differences between genres and of a concerted shift in all of them towards the oral end of the continuum; interestingly, too, the rate of shift depicted is at least consonant with Eliot's perception of a renewed or additional impetus towards 'common speech' style in the early twentieth century.

I have not however adopted Biber & Finegan's methods in this chapter (although I shall make use of the feature-list of table 7.1). There are two reasons for this decision. The first is purely practical. Although there are many literary anthologies in both printed and electronic format, there is at present no collection of texts that would be universally accepted as a representative corpus of English literature for the modern period; indeed, the principles on which such a corpus might be constructed have yet to be debated. But there are also objections in principle to using quantitative methods for the kind of history I am writing here. Figure 7.1 may show the outcome of 'a return to common speech', but it does not explain the *motives* or *mechanisms* of the shift. And in aggregating the contribution of linguistic features to achieve an orality score, it obscures the contribution of any individual feature. In a history of literary style, some features may have a special significance because of their role as **style-markers** or the part they play in **stylisation**; and it is not clear that either of these issues can be addressed by a quantificational approach.

7.1.3   *Style-markers and stylisation*

Those who consciously class themselves as writers are normally working within some conscious conception of a stylistic ideal, whether it has a name

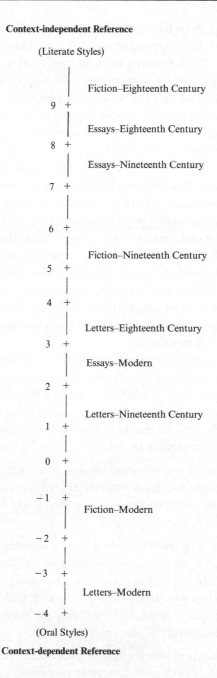

Context-independent Reference

(Literate Styles)

Figure 7.1 Level of context-dependent reference in three genres across three centuries (adapted from Biber & Finegan 1989: 502) (as in **imagism** or **free indirect style**) or whether it is seen simply as a way of writing to be cultivated or avoided (as in the wish to write 'like Boswell' rather than 'like Johnson'). In these images of a style, individual linguistic features may acquire a particular salience, so that they become **style-markers**. Like **stereotype** features of a language-variety, they are, in public perception, detached from the complex of features with which they naturally co-occur and turned into an epitome or emblem of the style as a whole. The passive construction has this status for scientific writing, latinate vocabulary for Johnsonese. The historical importance of style-markers is that they are likely to become the primary target both for writers imitating the stylistic ideal they represent and for those revolting against it. And within the developmental history of a style, they are often the features that undergo **stylisation**. In this process (described more fully in Adamson 1994a: 75–81) a linguistic feature is simultaneously generalised and conventionalised in the discourse type in which it occurs, with the result that it may increase in frequency but simultaneously alter in function or value. To illustrate the process in action, I'll look briefly at one of the features which travels the path from style-marking to stylisation in the period covered by this volume, **parenthesis**.

By *parenthesis*, I mean the simultaneous interruption of the syntactic structure of sentence and the semantic structure of topic. Such interruptions are typical of unplanned, unedited discourse and hence occur frequently in conversational speech, as in (3a) (adapted and abbreviated from Biber 1988: 10). An amateur beer-maker is comparing his home-made product to commercial brands:

(3a)   I mean when you get used to that beer, which at its best is
         simply, you know, superb (It really is (You know, I've really got it
         now, really, you know, got it to a T and mm) oh, there's no,
         there's no comparison.

As Biber notes (Biber 1988: 11), the speaker interrupts the syntactic sequence *when you get used to that beer there's no comparison* with interpolated comments that shift the topic from the quality of his beer to his own prowess in beer-making. Compare this with (3b), in which the writer similarly interrupts a sentence describing the contents of a picture with a parenthetical eulogy of the art of painting:

(3b)   The meek intelligence of those dear eyes
         (Blest be the art that can immortalize,
         The art that baffles time's tyrannic claim
         To quench it) here shines on me still the same.   (Cowper 1798)

It's very evident that the parenthesis in (3b) is accompanied by relatively few of the other features which are associated with oral styles in table 7.1 and which co-occur with the parenthesis in (3a). For example, compared with (3a), (3b) has a high ratio of nouns to pronouns, a greater average word-length, and several attributive adjectives (*meek, dear, tyrannic*) (table 7.1, items 1, 2, 5); it has none of (3a)'s private verbs (*know, mean*), contractions (*it's, I've*), emphatics (*really, simply*) or second-person pronouns (table 7.1, items 17, 19, 21, 25). An overall computation of its feature cluster would place (3b) very much towards the literate end of the continuum. Not surprisingly, its style does not strike most modern readers as 'conversational'. Yet this is precisely the term that came first to the mind of Cowper's contemporaries and passages such as (3b) provided the stylistic model for the new Romantic genre of the **conversation poem** (discussed in 7.6.4 below).

The explanation for this disparity of perception is that parenthesis had a particular salience for Cowper and his contemporaries because of its relation to a dominant stylistic ideal of the eighteenth century, commonly known as 'perspicuity' (see Adamson, *CHEL* III, forthcoming). In the late-century reformulations of this ideal by Campbell (1776) and Blair (1783), particularly as codified and popularised by Murray (1795), a high value was placed on unity and connectedness in discourse, so that parenthesis, which threatened these qualities, was stigmatised as a peculiarly transgressive construction. Murray's 'third rule for preserving the unity of sentences', which he italicises for emphasis, is '*keep clear of all unnecessary parentheses* [because] their effect is extremely bad': their use represents 'the perplexed method of disposing of some thought which a writer wants judgment to introduce in its proper place' (Murray 1795: 200). But by the same token, parenthesis could be converted into a positively-valued style-marker for an opposing ideal, one which rated associationism above logic, the expression of emotion above the disposition of thought, or spontaneous above pre-planned discourse. It is for this reason that Cowper's parenthesis, encased though it is in the features of a literate style, could act as a standard-bearer for the oral revolution announced in Wordsworth's prefaces.

In (3c–d), we see how two later phases in this revolution affected the role of parenthesis:

(3c)   It was your own wine, sir, the good champagne,
         (I took it for Catawba, – you're so kind)
         Which put the folly in my head!   (Browning 1864)

(3d)   a hollow muscular organ which, by contracting vigorously, keeps
up the
     (to have the heart
       (a whorl of green bracts at the base
       (ling,
she is known as   (Olson 1960)

The conversational effect of (3c) rests not on isolated style-markers but on a general style-shift: parenthesis appears, as it does in (3a), as one of a cluster of oral features, co-occurring with, for instance, second-person pronouns, contractions (*you're*), emphatics (*so*). Compared with (3b), literate features have been reduced: Browning uses fewer nouns than Cowper and shorter word-length. Although he retains the iambic pentameter, it has lost the obtrusive couplet rhyme of (3b) and the poet's aim seems to be to push poetic metre in the direction of conversational rhythms. In (3d), this process is taken further, the iambic pentameter has gone, the frequency of parenthesis itself has increased and, as in (3a), each parenthesis marks a cumulative side-shifting of topic. And yet the overall effect of parenthesis in (3d) is *not* more conversational than (3c) – indeed, many readers might see it as justifying Larkin's judgment in (2) that Modernism 'consists of doing the opposite'. This is because parenthesis has a different value in Olson's style than in Cowper's or Browning's. In (3b), parenthesis is a **style-marker**, a token representative of natural conversational language disrupting the artificial literary structures of sentence and couplet: in (3c), parenthesis is simply one of a cluster of features that locate the text at a certain level of orality; in (3d), what we see is the **stylisation** of parenthesis. A century and a half after Cowper, topic-shift, interrupted syntax, associative connections, instead of challenging a dominant stylistic ideal have themselves crystallised into a new ideal, and parenthesis, the formal feature which epitomises these qualities, has effectively *replaced* couplet and sentence as the structural principle of the poetry. As Olson's typography signals, it is foregrounded as a device of art and conventionalised into a form that removes it from its conversational origins.

7.1.4   *Romantic v. Modernist orality*

Setting (3a–d) alongside one another also throws light on the question raised in section 7.1.1 about the relation between the two revolutions. What is clear first of all is that none of the literary texts is *very* like the transcribed conversation of (3a). Even restricting the grounds of comparison to parenthesis, none of (3b–d) has an instance of the purely pragmatic parentheticals *I mean* and *you know* which pepper the text of (3a). Nor would we find a comparable density of this feature in the most colloquial of modern dramatists. In one sense, then, there is never 'a return to common speech' in literature; all literary representations are idealisations. The discrepancy between Eliot's view in (1) and Larkin's in (2) simply indicates a difference between Romantic and Modernist idealisations of orality.

Broadly speaking, the Romantic revolution was naturalist in its aims. Selecting features of conversational language made salient by their exclusion from the highly literate styles of the mid- to late eighteenth century, Wordsworth, Coleridge, and their successors attempted to create the illusion that written language was in fact a transcript of oral language. Like perspective painting, which sets out to create the illusion that an opaque, two-dimensional canvas is a transparent window on a three-dimensional world, Romantic conversational writing set out to overcome its own textuality and allow readers to as it were hear or overhear the voice of 'a man speaking to men'. (3b) shows the tentative beginnings of this project; (3c) illustrates how the illusion was made progressively more realistic; and Larkin in (2) testifies to the ongoing success of the Romantic revolution by his very failure to realise that using language 'in the way we all use it' is not the permanent and natural condition of literature, but a stylistic ideal that evolved at a particular historical moment.

The 'innovation of Modernism' put Romantic illusionism in question, by exposing the fact that a poem is not a conversation (or more generally that writing is not speech) in the same way that Post-Impressionist painting exposed the fallacy of supposing that a canvas could act as a window. But just as much of the art produced by the Post-Impressionists and their successors gains its effects not by discarding traditional illusionist techniques but by dislocating or intensifying them (as in the multiple perspectives of Braque's cubism, or the real-life still-lifes of Duchamp's *objets trouvés*) so Modernist writing typically works by radicalising the techniques of Romantic orality – as when Olson makes a structural principle out of interrupted structure. There is a sense in which Eliot and Larkin are both right if their claims are applied to (3d). Of the three literary excerpts I have reviewed, Olson's topic-skipping may well be the most naturalistic in reproducing the associative leaps and self-interruptions we all practise when we talk to ourselves or to an intimate friend, but put in writing and addressed to a public audience, it strikes many readers as a perversely difficult form of communication.

The following sections will tell the story of the two revolutions in terms of the style-markers and changing stylistic ideals which underlie the drift to orality quantified by Biber & Finegan. The discussion will cover changes in language-variety (7.2), versification (7.3), syntax (7.4) and metaphor (7.5), in each case showing how Romantics and Modernists in turn distanced themselves from the stylistic practices of their predecessors and how those who inherit both revolutions have perpetuated or reconciled their differences; finally (in 7.6), I will offer an account of some special techniques that have developed in the literature of our period from the initial Romantic enterprise of representing a speaking voice in a printed text.

7.2   Breaking the Standard

7.2.1   Introduction

(4)   a. The majority of the following Poems are to be considered as experiments. They were written chiefly with a view to ascertain how far the language of conversation in the middle and lower classes of society is adapted to the purposes of poetic pleasure.

(Advertisement to *Lyrical Ballads* 1798)

b. He Do the Police in Different Voices

(Working title for *The Waste Land* 1919–21)

For Wordsworth, poetic revolution begins with the overthrow of 'what is usually called poetic diction' (Wordsworth [1802]: 66, 79, 88–93). His primary target was the view that poetry should be written in a specialised variety of English, deviating from contemporary spoken language in features of lexis, grammar, and idiom, and justified in its deviations by precedents in the literary usage of Spenser, Milton or Pope. This is poetic diction as practised and advocated by Gray, who 'thought his language more poetical as it was more remote from common use' (Johnson 1783: iv.461). But in attacking Gray, Wordsworth was led to confront a less extreme but more deeply entrenched ideal of poetic diction as a 'system of words at once refined from the grossness of domestic use, and free from the harshness of terms appropriated to particular arts [i.e. trades or professions]' (Johnson 1783: ii. 117). On this view, which came with the authority of Addison as well as Johnson, poetic diction is achieved not by eliminating the language of the day but by editing it to remove colloquialisms, regionalisms, jargon and whatever else offends against the current standard of 'polite' and 'refined' usage. In other words, Literary English is Standard English in evening dress. Hence the dictum attributed to Adam Smith: 'it is the duty of the poet to write like a gentleman' (*European Magazine* 20, 1791: 135). What made Wordsworth's position controversial was his rejection of this duty. In proposing to replace Gray's 'curiously elaborate' diction with 'a selection of the real language of men', he defined a 'real language' as one grounded in colloquial speech and open to non-Standard varieties, such as the conversation of the 'lower classes' cited in (4a) or the 'low and rustic' speakers cited in the Preface (Wordsworth [1802]: 56–7, 60–1, 67–8).

The second step is not, of course, an inevitable consequence of the first. Coleridge, for example, while condemning 'laborious and florid' styles, did not favour the use of non-Standard varieties, considering 'rustic life (above all *low* and rustic life) especially unfavourable to the formation of a human diction' (Coleridge [1817]: i.25, ii.40–57); and modern critics have sometimes doubted whether Wordsworth himself followed the more radical course that his Preface recommends. But its polemic proved influential, and, as a result, one difficulty in describing the literary language of the modern period is the absence of a unitary literary norm. Post-Romantic literature opens itself to include the varieties of English spoken by many different groups, whether defined by ethnic or regional origin, social class, age, gender, or trade; and, unlike the literature of the period covered by *CHEL* III (forthcoming), it increasingly treats these varieties not merely as comic relief or aberrations from a literary Standard, but as legitimate competitors for its status and functions. To complicate matters further, some varieties that began the period as regional or non-Standard dialects (such as Irish, American or Jamaican English) have since developed into independent national Standards, each the medium of a distinctive literary tradition, and each with its own non-Standard varieties seeking literary recognition, as in the case of Black English Vernacular in America.

It is impossible to do even summary justice to this proliferation of literary languages in the space at my disposal here. For the sake of coherence, I will concentrate my discussion on some of the general issues involved in breaking the literary hegemony of a Standard variety and take as my illustrative case-study the Standard variety which was crystallising in London as our period opened. Until the end of the nineteenth century this was the main linguistic reference-point for literary rebels and reactionaries in all English-speaking cultures and in some it has remained a target (in one sense or other of the term) until the present day.

7.2.2   The representation of non-Standard varieties

The Romantic revolt against the Literary Standard did not result in a return to the situation of the Medieval period, when a literary work might be written in whatever regional variety its author happened to speak. With very few exceptions, modern writers command a Standard variety of the language, which has been disseminated in a more codified form, and (through the State school system) on a wider scale than ever before. Even at the beginning of our period, Burns, while publishing poems in his native Ayrshire dialect, used Standard English in informal private letters. For him, and for all subsequent writers, written English is canonically Standard English and any writer choosing an alternative variety faces the problem of devising an appropriate orthography to represent it. (3a), for instance, shows the difficulties of segmenting the flow of on-line utterance by means of a punctuation system designed to signal the structure of written sentences. This problem is even more acute when it comes to representing accent.

The most common method is to use non-Standard spelling. In its most skeletal form, known as **eye-dialect**, this is little more than a way of signalling 'non-Standardness' since the spellings have no phonetic implications that would in fact distinguish non-Standard from Standard pronunciations (as when *grate* is used for *great*, *sez* for *says*, or *would of* for *would've*). As many commentators have noted, the effect of eye-dialect is always derogatory: the forms are read as mis-spellings and the character whose speech they represent somehow acquires the social stigma attached to illiteracy. Slightly more strenuous uses of orthography attempt to evoke a specific variety by selecting one or two **stereotype** features and making them stand for the whole. Cockney, for instance, established as the primary non-Standard urban dialect by the popularity of Pierce Egan's Tom and Jerry, in the 1820s, is commonly represented by a selection of vowel sounds (indicated by spelling *boiled* as *biled*, *out* as *aht*), the omission of initial /h/ and/or its hypercorrected insertion (*'as your 'orse 'ad any Hoats?*), and, especially in early examples, the v-w interchange (*vot a wery fine Vellington boot*). Like eye-dialect, however, this method is commonly associated with comic, satirical or reductive portrayals. Attempts to go beyond stereotype necessarily involve a more systematic effort to bend the spelling system into a phonetic representation. The advantages and difficulties of this procedure are revealed by Shaw's attempt to render Cockney in *Pygmalion*, and by the rueful commentary he attached to it:

(5)   Ow, eez ye-ooa san, is e? Wal, fewd dan y'de-ooty bawmz a
        mather should, eed now bettern to spawl a pore gel's flahrzn
        than ran awy athaht pyin. Will ye-oo py me f'them? (Here, with
        apologies, this desperate attempt to represent her dialect without
        a phonetic alphabet must be abandoned as unintelligible outside
        London.)   (Shaw 1914)

Shaw's democratising intentions are clear. Whereas forms like *on 'is 'orse with
'is 'awk in 'is 'and* acknowledge in their very orthography that the author
believes the initial /h/ should really be there, Shaw's spelling attempts to
put Standard and non-Standard pronunciation on the same level. For
example, *eez* (rather than *'e's*) represents simultaneously the non-Standard
'dropped h', the Standard but colloquial contraction of *he is* to *he's*, and the
final voiced fricative, which is both colloquial and formal, Standard and
non-Standard, since in this instance the sound-systems of **RP** and Cockney
equally deviate from the /s/ implied by the conventional spelling of *is*.
Nevertheless, Shaw's admission of defeat is justified. For one thing, his
pursuit of notational accuracy on the phonetic level leads to a loss of structural information on the lexico-grammatical level, as when *fewd* stands for
'if you had' or *bawmz* for 'by him as'. In these circumstances, reading
becomes more like an act of deciphering. Furthermore – and this is the
crucial objection – in the absence of a dialect-neutral phonetic alphabet,
(5) is significantly more 'unintelligible' for readers who speak a non-
Standard variety (whether or not they live 'outside London'). For instance,
the spelling *now*, with which Shaw tries to capture the Cockney pronunciation of *know* as /nau/, is likely to evoke the sound-sequence /na:/ for a
Cockney reader and /nu:/ for a Scottish reader. In other words, Shaw's
sound-spelling correspondences assume an audience composed of speakers of Standard British English; and this implicit alliance between author
and reader necessarily generates social condescension towards the non-
Standard group whose speech is represented.

A sense of distaste for this kind of social 'placing' is already evident at
the beginning of our period in Godwin's refusal to attempt a phonetic-
spelling rendition of the speech of Hector, the Negro jailer in *St Leon*
(1799) whom he wishes to present as a natural philosopher; and the steady
growth of radical-democratic sentiment has clearly played its part in bringing about the relative recessiveness of this method of dialect representation in the twentieth-century. Modern writers more commonly rely on
stereotypes of lexis or idiom to evoke the variety intended, as in this
example from *The Waste Land*, where the change of scene to a lower-class

London pub is signalled by the stereotypically Cockney name, *Lil*, the colloquial passive *got [Verb]ed* (for *was [Verb]ed*) and the then recent slang abbreviation for *demobilized* (the earliest *OED* citation of *demob* is dated 1920):

(6)   When Lil's husband got demobbed, I said –   (Eliot 1922)

As the manuscript of this section of the poem shows, Eliot rejected the idea of representing *something* as *somethink* with the comment 'I want to avoid trying [to] show pronunciation by spelling', whereas he accepted suggestions for lexical or grammatical indicators of variety, revising, for instance, (7a) to (7b):

(7)   a. Its *that medicine* I took, *in order to* bring it off
        b. It's *them pills* I took, *to* bring it off

In drama, it is possible to make the sound patterns of non-Standard speech a key feature of its representation without the stigmatising and alienating effects involved in an orthographic rendering. Wesker, for instance, made no attempt to represent accents in the published text of *The Kitchen* (1960), but instead provided introductory notes of instruction for the actors (e.g. 'Raymond is an Italian who speaks almost perfect English but with an accent'). And in the late twentieth century, the extension of performance art through radio, television, film and sound recording has led to a blossoming in the non-satiric representation of non-Standard accents, for example Manchester in *Coronation Street* (1960–) and Liverpool in *Brookside* (1982–). The immense popularity of these non-Standard soap operas and their great longevity (compared with most of their Standard-based rivals) may suggest that modern audiences share Wordsworth's equation of non-Standard speech with the 'real language' of 'real situations'.

The desire to break away from the Standard has encountered problems of function as well as – and partly in consequence of – its problems of form. Dialect writing is most readily accepted in lyric poetry, which by virtue of its brevity can be written in non-Standard forms without over-taxing its readers: Burns's *Poems, Chiefly in the Scottish Dialect* (1786) found admirers even in Southern England and provided both the empirical grounding for Wordsworth's theories and also a model for the use of English dialects by poets such as Clare (Northamptonshire), Barnes (Dorset) and Lawrence (Nottingham). The novel, however, presents more difficulties; its greater length and wider readership favour the use of the most generally intelligible variety. Edgeworth, who carried Wordsworth's revolution into the novel by using a non-Standard speaking (Irish) narrator for *Castle Rackrent* (1800), included far fewer dialect markers than Burns and apologised for those few. Most subsequent novelists have accepted a convention by which non-Standard varieties are confined to dialogue and, even there, are reserved for minor characters, leaving the narrator (and commonly the main protagonists) to speak Standard. The absurdities that often result – such as Dickens's workhouse orphan, Oliver Twist, using a Standard he can scarcely have heard – indicate the imperiousness of the convention. With the progressive acceptance of non-Standard varieties as inherently valid forms of language, it might be expected that they would gradually penetrate narrative itself, a tendency which some contemporaries detected (and deplored) in Dickens:

(8)   catching the infection from his own actors, he adopts their forms
        of expression, and offends the shade of Lindley Murray with
        such barbarisms as 'It had not been painted or papered, hadn't
        Todgers, past the memory of man'   (*North British Review* 1845)

The 'barbarism' here is the tag-topicalisation (*hadn't Todgers*) and what has drawn Dickens into it is his use of **free indirect style**, a technique which, by blurring the distinction between the voices of character and narrator, has promoted a diffusion of non-Standard forms from dialogue to narrative. But until the late twentieth century, consistent non-Standard narration remains rare, even in first-person novels where the distinction between character-language and narrator-language cannot apply. The earlier emergence of a more radical tradition in American writing – with Twain's *Huckleberry Finn* (1884) as its landmark publication – suggests that the class attitudes evident in (8) continued to play a part in inhibiting the development of a full non-Standard literature in England.

7.2.3   *The uses of non-Standard varieties: from naturalism to metaphor*

For all the limitations and constraints I have noted, however, the representation of the varieties of English has served a wide range of important functions in the literature of our period. These may be divided into two major groups: **naturalistic** and **metaphorical**.

The prime naturalistic function of non-Standard language is as the tool of **social realism**, a mode of writing which first established itself in the Romantic period and continues to flourish. In this respect, *Coronation Street* stands at the end of a tradition of documentary fiction which stretches back through Henry Green's portrait of Birmingham (in *Living* 1929), Lawrence's of Nottingham (in *Sons and Lovers* 1913) and Gaskell's of

Manchester (in *Mary Barton* 1848 and *North and South* 1855) to those Romantic novelists who aimed at providing a historical chronicle of the lives and language of particular communities: Ireland in the case of Edgeworth, the west of Scotland in the case of Galt. This function of dialect, though less commonly, appears in poetry too, as in Tennyson's Lincolnshire monologues, *Northern Farmer Old Style* and *Northern Farmer New Style* (1869), which record changes in Victorian rural values, or in Harrison's *The School of Eloquence* (1978) and *v* (1985), which explore the cultural and linguistic rift that divides an educated Standard-speaking Yorkshireman from his working-class origins.

But in cases where the writer is documenting the speech of a group to which he himself belongs, or aspires to belong, social realism may modulate into what Le Page and Tabouret-Keller (1985) call **acts of identity**, the use of a variety to express solidarity with a national, local or ethnic group. The growth of intra-national nationalism in the twentieth century has promoted this tendency: in the early century, the Scots dialect of MacDiarmid's poetry and Grassic Gibbon's novels was politically expressive rather than representationally accurate; in the late century, a form of Jamaican creole has been similarly adopted by British Black writers, such as Linton Kwesi Johnson, in order to preserve and foster not only a distinctive variety, but also a racial and cultural identity; and the Cockney used by punk-rock singers of the late 1970s was a gesture of defiance directed against not only the Standard variety of the middle class but also the American idiom which had dominated post-war pop in Britain.

Finally among the uses of non-Standard English that I have called naturalistic comes a form of literary **code-switching** which closely models, although often in a stylised way, the normal functions of code-switching in a speech community. Writers, that is, switch from Standard to non-Standard, either between or within works, to reflect changes of genre or express changes of attitude. Burns's *Halloween*, for instance, uses Scottish dialect for the poem itself but Standard English for the explanatory prose of the preface and footnotes; *The Cotter's Saturday Night* switches from the Standard English of the first stanza, a formal apostrophe to its dedicatee (9a), to 'simple Scottish' when the topic changes to the Cotter and his family and the genre changes to narrative (9b); and *Address to the Deil* switches code within the apostrophe itself (10) to mark the shift in attitude from (mock-heroic) reverence to impudent familiarity:

(9)   a. My lov'd, my honor'd, much respected friend,
            No mercenary Bard has homage pays;

b. The expectant *wee-things*, toddlan, stacher through
   To meet their *Dad*, wi' flichterin noise and glee.

(Burns 1786; original italics)

(10)   O Thou, whatever title suit thee!
        Auld Hornic, Satan, Nick, or Clootie   (Burns 1786)

Similar patterns are found in the novel, particularly where writers attempt
the realistic characterisation of bi-dialectal speakers. In Achebe's *A Man of
the People*, Chief Nanga switches from Standard English to Nigerian pidgin,
trying the language first of authority then of jocular solidarity in his effort
to win round the narrator (whose girlfriend he has just spent the night
with):

(11)   'Don't be childish, Odili,' he said paternally. 'After all she is not
        your wife. What is all this nonsense . . . If you like I can bring
        you six girls this evening. You go do the thing sotay you go beg
        say you no want again. Ha, ha, ha, ha!'   (Achebe 1966)

Since, however, in all such cases the non-Standard idiom is consciously
adopted by an author trained to write, if not to speak, in Standard, and is
often used in contrast with that Standard, there is almost inevitably a **metaphorical** element in its use: the message it conveys is not merely 'this is
my/our/their kind of speech' but 'this kind of speech has such-and-such
connotations deriving from the characteristics of its speakers'. In
Lawrence's *Lady Chatterley's Lover* (1928), the regional dialect used by the
gamekeeper, Mellors, is a natural option as far as the character is concerned,
but within the overall design of the novel it also stands for his natural
sensuality, as opposed to the impotence of Sir Clifford Chatterley and the
inhibitions of his wife. This kind of metaphorisation is not peculiar to literature. As sociolinguists have found, there are strong correlations in folk
mythology between, for instance, non-Standard urban varieties and physical toughness or Standard varieties and high intelligence. Metaphorical uses
in literature simply exploit and extend such correlations. In general, rural
dialects (in Hardy's novels, for example) represent pre-industrial values,
both positive (natural vigour, gnomic wisdom, knowledge of nature) and
negative (narrow-mindedness and stupidity); urban dialects, and especially
Cockney, may represent, as in Dickens's Sam Weller, a combination of
shrewdness and sincerity, or as in *The Waste Land*, uncultured nastiness. Not
that examples need be confined to regional or class dialects. For it is in the
metaphorical use of varieties that the language of other social groupings,

defined by profession, age, gender etc., plays a major role in the literature of our period, particularly in the twentieth century. The language of science, for instance, generally represented by the stereotype features of passive constructions and nominalisations, is frequently used as an image of either precise thinking or emaciated feeling.

7.2.4 *Polyvocalism and Modernism*

(12)   HAIL, Muse! *et cetera* . . .   (Byron 1821)

In this famous opening to Canto III of *Don Juan*, Byron like Wordsworth is attacking the use of poetic diction, but, unlike Wordsworth, he attacks it by subversion rather than avoidance. Beginning with one of the invocatory openings that English writers had inherited from classical epic, he immediately interrupts himself with the *etcetera* formula of a business letter or inventory. The juxtaposition exposes the equally formulaic nature of the poetic invocation and destructively implies that epic poets are engaged in a commercial venture like the tradesmen they affect to despise and that poetic diction is nothing but a professional jargon. Structurally, (12) resembles (10) or (11), but in (12) the metaphorical function of code-switching has virtually displaced naturalism. Neither the epic nor the business variety is *used*; each is, rather, *quoted*. And Byron's selection of the most instantly recognisable marker of each variety prompts the reader to interpret the result as stereotype and the aim as satire.

This type of code-switching, used sporadically through the nineteenth century, was stylised at the beginning of the twentieth into the technique of **polyvocalism**, that mixing of varieties which is one of the hallmarks of Modernism. As (4b) indicates, the Modernists turned code-switching into a principle of construction, like the topic-skipping discussed in section 7.1.3, and one of the features that makes (3d) instantly recognisable as a Modernist text is that Olson accompanies his topic-shifts with variety-shifts, cutting from the language of textbook definition (*a hollow muscular organ* . . .) to colloquial cliché (*to have the heart*). The most influential early exponents of polyvocalism, Joyce in the novel and Eliot and Pound in poetry, present their readers with elaborate collages, juxtaposing regional dialects and foreign languages, religious and administrative varieties, formal style and slang. Their divergence from nineteenth-century naturalism can be gauged by setting Eliot's working title for *The Waste Land* (4b) alongside Dickens's use of the same words in *Our Mutual Friend* (1865). There *he do the police in different voices* occurs as part of the dialogue and its non-Standard grammar is part of the class-characterisation of its speaker, Betty Higden. Eliot deracinates it from this indexical function. Like Byron's *Hail Muse*, (4b) is quotative (doubly so, since it evokes both a particular variety and a specific literary precedent) and metaphoric (it stands for the breaking of the Standard). And although Eliot abandoned this title, its implicit manifesto is carried through in *The Waste Land* and other Modernist works. Standard English is typically present in such texts, but it is demoted from the role of narrative continuo so that neither it nor any alternative variety can be taken as the vehicle of authorial viewpoint or authoritative statement. (13) below provides a small-scale illustration:

(13)   Tunicled functionaries signify and clear-voiced heralds cry
         and leg it to a safe distance:
         leave fairway for the Paladins, and Roland throws a kiss —
         they've nabbed his batty for the moppers-up
             and Mr Jenkins takes them over   5
         and don't bunch on the left
         for Christ's sake.

             Riders on pale horses loosed
         and vials irreparably broken
         an' Wat price bleedin' Glory   10
         Glory
         Glory Hallelujah . . .   (David Jones 1937)

Here Jones offers snapshots of the 1914–18 war in a collage of varieties: the language of traditional epic (evoked by the latinate vocabulary of the first three words and the nomenclature of the *Chanson de Roland* in 1.3); barrack-room Cockney (represented lexically in 1.4 and orthographically in 1.10); the Bible (the images of 11.8–9 are from the Book of Revelation); and the Battle Hymn of the Republic (directly quoted in 11.11–12). Each way of speaking epitomises a way of seeing and their sequence presents a kaleidoscope of mutually critical evaluations of war: chivalric, stoical, apocalyptic, cynical, celebratory.

Even writers of the anti-Modernist schools follow similar practices, though in more cautious form:

(14)   Ah, were I courageous enough
         To shout *Stuff your pension!*
         But I know, all too well, that's the stuff
         That dreams are made on   (Larkin 1955)

Unlike (13), code-switching here can be interpreted naturalistically as self-deflating modulations of tone in a single speaker or discourse. But the pattern has metaphoric significance too. In the poem as a whole, the values of bourgeois conformity are opposed to those both of low-life drop-outs and of high-minded intellectuals and poets, and in this stanza their conflict is expressed by code-switching from the educated Standard variety of lines 1 and 3 (its conservatism signalled by the markedly formal use of sub-junctive and inversion for the conditional – *were I* instead of *if only I was*) to the demotic abuse of *stuff your pension* in line 2 and the Shakespearean conclusion *the stuff that dreams are made on* (quoted from *The Tempest* 4.i. 156–7). The paradoxical alliance of demotic and poetic forms of rebellion is foregrounded by their common use of *stuff*, which works as a kind of cross-varietal pun.

And although the staple variety in (14) remains Standard English, the validity of that variety is put in question by the values with which it is asso-ciated: it appears as the voice of timid conservatism, grey rather than neutral, restrictive rather than refined. This vision of Standard English as the lowest common denominator rather than the highest common factor, particularly common among twentieth-century writers, provides another motive for varietal eclecticism: a desire to revitalise the medium of literary discourse.

7.2.5 *Enriching the literary language 1: latinity and taboo*

For most of its history as a literary language, English has enriched its expressive repertoire by borrowing from culturally more prestigious lan-guages, notably French in the Middle Ages (see *CHEL* II) and Latin in the Renaissance (see *CHEL* III, forthcoming). In the modern period, as English itself increasingly took on the role of a major world language, writers were less likely to acknowledge the cultural hegemony of foreign languages; and one result of the Romantic advocacy of common speech was a widespread rejection of previous borrowings, especially the latinate lexis associated with the grand style of Milton's poetry and Johnson's prose. The changing attitude to the latinate is illustrated in (15 a–c) below:

(15)   a. if I reprehend any thing in this world, it is the use of my
           oracular tongue, and a nice derangement of epitaphs!

                                                          (Sheridan 1775)

        b. 'Under the impression,' said Mr Micawber, 'that your
           peregrinations in this metropolis have not as yet been extensive,

and that you might have some difficulty in penetrating the arcana of the Modern Babylon in the direction of the City Road – in short,' said Mr Micawber, in another burst of confidence, 'that you might lose yourself . . . ' (Dickens 1850)

c. Millions of peasants are robbed of their farms and sent trudging along the roads with no more than they can carry: this is called *transfer of population* or *rectification of frontiers*

(Orwell 1946)

Whereas Mrs Malaprop, the speaker of (15a), is ridiculous because she cannot manage vocabulary derived from the classical languages, Mr Micawber in (15b) is ridiculous precisely because he can. Dickens's satire of him echoes Macaulay's criticism of Johnson for avoiding 'strong plain words' in favour of unnatural bombast, and both form part of a strenuous campaign in favour of 'Saxon-English' which, by the end of the nineteenth century, had largely succeeded in driving latinate vocabulary out of the literary lexicon. By the mid-twentieth century, it was being evicted from its refuge in academic and administrative discourse by those who, like Orwell in (15c), regarded it as the servant of euphemism and political deceit. And by the late twentieth century the fate of latinate English was probably sealed when Latin lost its privileged place in the school curriculum. The consequence for literature has been a narrowing of vocabulary range and a loss of expressive contrast between 'plain' and 'elevated' language.

One solution has been to extend the range in the opposite direction, including levels of vocabulary which the eighteenth century had regarded as too 'low' for use in serious literature. Byron, sanctioned by the genre of satire, incorporated oaths and obscenities into the varietal mixture of *Don Juan*, but other writers were slow to follow his lead. In 1913, Shaw evidently calculated that the audience of *Pygmalion* would find it shocking to hear a well-dressed, RP-speaking character say 'not bloody likely' (and they did), and, as late as 1937, Jones, though including *bleedin' glory* in (13), complained in the preface to *In Parenthesis* that he had been 'hampered by the convention of not using impious and impolite words'. The trial of Penguin books in 1960 on obscenity charges for publishing the unexpurgated version of Lawrence's *Lady Chatterley's Lover* (written in 1928) marked a major watershed as much for the permissible language of literature as for its permissible contents. So whereas in (14) Larkin marks *stuff your pension* as quotative (and something he would *not* say), in (16a), written after Penguin's acquittal, he incorporates a 'four-letter word' into the repertoire of the narrative voice itself:

(16a)   Groping back to bed after a piss
        I part thick curtains, and am startled by
        The rapid clouds, the moon's cleanliness   (Larkin 1974)

Compare a similar moment in Wordsworth:

(16b)   when the deed was done,
        I heard among the solitary hills
        Low breathings coming after me, and sounds
        Of undistinguishable motion   (Wordsworth 1805)

Both writers use a change in **register** to represent the shift from ordinary to extraordinary experience. But Larkin's formality-scale begins lower (with *piss*) and Wordsworth's extends higher, with the polysyllabic latinate *undistinguishable motion*, which continues the Miltonic association of the latinate and the sublime. The only polysyllable in (16a) – *cleanliness* – though not a common word or used in its commonest sense, still qualifies as 'plain English' in being composed out of the basic native derivational morphemes *ly* + *ness*.

7.2.6   *Enriching the literary language 2: borrowing and inventing*

For writers who wish to avoid both the latinate and the taboo, the main resource has been to substitute internal for external borrowing, enriching the literary repertoire from previously non-literary varieties of English itself. One of Burns's early admirers, responding to his claim to be 'illiterate' in Latin and Greek, suggested that his intermingling of Scottish and Standard varieties gave him an alternative route to '*copia verborum*' – the term used by Renaissance writers for the richness of language achieved by classical borrowing (Low 1974: 8–9). Subsequent writers, even when highly literate in the classics, have also preferred intra-linguistic borrowings. Morris resurrected obsolete words and forms (such as *burg, glaive, eyen, tomorn*) and was praised by linguistic nationalists for showing 'how copious . . . an almost purely Teutonic diction may be' (Oliphant 1873: 319); Hopkins drew eclectically on regional words and the technical terms of traditional trades, such as *reeve* (from naval vocabulary) and *sillion* (from ploughing); and MacDiarmid first pursued what he called the 'Doric economy of expressiveness' of Scots lexis such as *yow-trummle, watergaw, onding*, then turned in his later poetry to the resources of the technical terminology of chemistry, geology and botany, as Olson does in (3d) with the cluster of *whorl, bract, ling*. The general motivation for all these experiments has been to find forms of expression that are strange without being foreign, or metaphorical without being unrealistic. Both factors are at work in the title of Hopkins's *The Windhover*, a dialect word which, though less common than its Standard synonym *kestrel*, is both more English (by virtue of being Anglo-Saxon rather than French in origin) and more expressive (in that it is descriptive rather than simply denominative).

Borrowing of this sort is not confined to lexis. Milroy suggests that one of Hopkins's grammatical tics, omitting the definite article, is an expressive device borrowed from Lancashire speakers, such as the youth who, he recorded in 1872, 'dropped or slurred the article' when 'he began to speak quickly or descriptively' (Milroy 1977: 89). Similarly, Synge's use of Gaelic-influenced idioms and syntax – often interpreted as an assertion of Irish nationalism – is explained by himself in more purely aesthetic terms, as an attempt to create an expressive language as 'rich and copious' as that of Elizabethan poetic drama. In the preface to *Playboy of the Western World* (1907), he echoes Wordsworth's preface to *Lyrical Ballads* in claiming to have found in the speech of the 'Irish peasantry' a language that is simultaneously natural (unlike the verbal contortions of Symbolist writers) and, through its violations of Standard norms, imaginative. The effects he achieves (in (17a) for example) may be compared with the effects created in late twentieth-century writing by Achebe, for instance, who deliberately uses **calques** from Ibo syntax and idiom (as in (17b)) to enrich the repertoire of International Standard English (Traugott & Pratt 1980: 389).

(17) a. It's that you'd say surely if you seen him and he after drinking for weeks, rising up in the red dawn, or before it maybe, and going out into the yard as naked as an ash-tree in the moon of May.   (Synge 1907)

b. 'Has your wife been in the hospital a long time?' I asked. '*Since three weeks*. But *her body has not been hers* since the beginning of the rainy season.'
'God will hear our prayers,' I said.
'*He holds the knife and He holds the yam*.'   (Achebe 1966)

Twentieth-century writers have progressively felt less need to appeal to philology or dialectology to authenticate such experiments and some have undertaken to invent an entire new form of English. This is particularly common in one of the major genres of the century: science fiction (or fantasy writing more generally). Whereas in early heterocosmic fictions by Wells or Conan Doyle, time travellers take – and sometimes implausibly find – Standard English as the medium of discourse in their new worlds, later examples of the genre offer a range of alternative varieties, such as Newspeak in Orwell's *1984* (1949), Neanderthal in Golding's *The Inheritors* (1955), 'nadsat', the Russo-English of 'space-age hooligans' in Burgess's *A Clockwork Orange* (1962) and post-holocaust Cockney in Hoban's *Riddley Walker* (1980). Often more is involved than a delight in exotic forms. Halliday argues, for instance, that the unusual patterns of transitivity in Lok's language in *The Inheritors* encode a pre-modern understanding of cause–effect relations (Halliday 1981: 325–360) and Laadan, the language constructed by Elgin for *Native Tongue* (1984), was deliberately designed to show that 'if women had a language adequate to express their perceptions, it might reflect a quite different reality than that perceived by men' (Elgin 1988: 3). The paradigm case for such experiments is to be found, I believe, in the language of children's literature, the genre which occupied in the nineteenth century the place held by science fiction in the twentieth.

7.2.7   The logic of non-Standard English

The eighteenth-century prescriptive grammarians who were the arbiters of the emerging Standard were motivated by the desire to make the language not only stable but rational, and the belief that Standard English is in fact more logical than non-Standard dialects remains deeply rooted in folk mythology. As recently as the 1960s, Labov found it necessary to demonstrate that a speaker of Black English Vernacular could argue as cogently as a Standard speaker (Labov 1969). It was largely the presumption of conceptual gaps and rational deficiencies in 'low and rustic' speech that made Coleridge reject the more radical part of Wordsworth's poetic programme (Coleridge [1817]: ii.52–5). And yet elsewhere Coleridge himself expresses interest in varieties of language that, in comparison to educated Standard English, were not simply deficient but deviant in their reasoning. The two varieties he chooses are Irish English and children's language.

The feature of Irish English that attracted Coleridge's attention was the kind of self-contradictory statement known as an **Irish bull**, for example:

(18)　　a.　Follow me, sir, I'm right behind you.
　　　　b.　No English hen ever laid a fresh egg.
　　　　c.　I was a fine child but they changed me.
　　　　d.　Whatever you say, say nothing.

Largely ridiculed by earlier writers, or cited as a sign of the mental inferiority of Irish speakers, the bull was rehabilitated by the Edgeworths (1802), who like Coleridge, stressed its affinities with the workings of the poetic imagination. (18c) for instance exploits the ambiguity of the term *I* (self-as-speaker and self-as-referent) to unsettle apparently rational notions of the persistence of personal identity. For Coleridge, it is this power to disrupt norms of reasoning that links the Irish bull to the anomalies and contradictions found in children's language – in which it is possible to speak in opposites or issue an imperative in relation to past time (Ricks 1993: 187–91).

The importance of children's language as a model for the Wordsworthian school was noted by contemporaries and Jeffrey coupled it with their interest in lower-class varieties in claiming that their style was derived from 'plebeian nurseries'. Its virtue, for Wordsworth, lay in combining the simplicity of vocabulary and syntax which he found in 'low and rustic' speakers with a visionary violation of the standard logico-linguistic categories of experience. The most notable example in *Lyrical Ballads* is the 'idiot boy' who conflates the categories of night and day in:

(19)   The cocks did crow to-whoo, to-whoo,
         And the sun did shine so cold.   (Wordsworth 1798)

but the apparently rational 'little Maid' in *We are Seven* poses an equal challenge to the assumptions of her adult interlocutor when she questions the categorial distinction between life and death by insisting that she still has six siblings even though two of them have died.

The encounter between adult and child reasoning becomes a recurrent motif in nineteenth-century literature, but in early examples, as in Wordsworth's case, the narrating voice is typically adult and employs standard logic as well as Standard English. It is only towards the end of the century that children are cast in the role of narrator, as in the novels of Nesbit. But from the mid-century, the non-Standard semantics of children's language had been exploited on a large scale in works written *for* children by Lear and Carroll, often subversively parodying the moral and practical inductions into adult values purveyed by previous children's literature. Compare, for example:

(20)   a. 'Tis the Voice of the *Sluggard*. I hear him complain
            You have wak'd me too soon, I must slumber again.
                                          (Watts 1715; original italics)

         b. 'Tis the voice of the lobster; I heard him declare,
            'You have baked me too brown, I must sugar my hair.'
                                          (Carroll 1865)

The emergence of **nonsense writing** as a distinct genre promoted the stylisation of semantic deviance: in particular, the use of anomalous combination, which occurs at the syntactic level in (19) and (20b), extends to the lexical and phonological level, producing: *treacle-well, star-bespringled, slithy, borascible, ipwergis*, and even *mhruxian*.

Modernism brought a diffusion of such techniques to adult genres, most notoriously in the wholesale adoption into Joyce's *Finnegans Wake* of **portmanteau** words coined on the same principles as *slithy* and *borascible* (e.g. *athemisthued, blasphorous*). The element of nonsense-technique has also been noted in Hopkins (Sonstroem 1967) and critics have argued for the influence of Carroll and Lear on Eliot (and hence on surrealist poets of the 1930s, such as Gascoyne and Dylan Thomas) and for the influence of the Irish bull on Beckett (and hence on the absurdist novel and drama of the later twentieth century) (Sewell 1962; Ricks 1993: 153–203). Many of these later writers make explicit the challenge to established categories of thought and social ordering which are implicit in earlier practice. Auden, for instance, who celebrates Lear's nonsense as a land of escape from the 'Terrible Demon' of bourgeois adult reality, adopts the techniques of nonsense – nursery rhyme stanza and semantic anomalies – to create a scenario that threatens the comforts and conventions on which that 'reality' rests.

(21)   The glacier knocks in the cupboard,
         The desert sighs in the bed,
         And the crack in the tea-cup opens
         A lane to the land of the dead.

         Where the beggars raffle the bank-notes,
         And the Giant is enchanting to Jack,
         And the Lily-White Boy is a roarer,
         And Jill goes down on her back   (Auden 1937)

7.3   Breaking the pentameter

7.3.1   Introduction

(22)   a. When this Verse was first dictated to me I consider'd a
         Monotonous Cadence like that used by Milton & Shakspeare &
         all writers of English Blank Verse, derived [i.e. detached] from
         the modern bondage of Rhyming; to be a necessary and
         indispensible part of Verse. But I soon found that in the mouth

of a true Orator such monotony was not only awkward, but as much a bondage as rhyme itself. I therefore have produced a variety in every line, both of cadences & number of syllables. Every word and every letter is studied and put into its fit place: the terrific numbers are reserved for the terrific parts the mild & gentle, for the mild & gentle parts, and the prosaic, for inferior parts: all are necessary to each other. Poetry Fetter'd, Fetters the Human Race. (Blake 1820)

b. (to break the pentameter, that was the first heave)

(Pound 1948)

For both Blake and Pound, poetic revolution begins with a revolution in metre, a repudiation of the **syllabo-tonic** tradition of versification established in the Renaissance. Both epitomise this *ancien régime* in the **iambic pentameter**, the verse-form that, in the period since 'Milton and Shakespeare', had come to occupy the position of a metrical norm in English poetry.

Eighteenth-century metrics were essentially mathematical, as seen in the common use of the term 'numbers' for rhythm and in Johnson's definition of *versification* as 'the arrangement of a certain number of syllables according to certain laws' (Johnson 1755: sig.N1*v*). The laws generally prescribed for the iambic pentameter were that an abstract pattern, for which 'the ingenious Mr Mason' devised the now familiar schema:

(23)   ti-TUM ti-TUM ti-TUM ti-TUM ti-TUM

should be realised as transparently as possible in linguistic material – ideally as a sequence of ten syllables with stressed syllables occurring *only* in TUM positions, though not necessarily in *all* TUM positions. This conceptualisation profoundly influenced the way in which the iambic pentameter was composed and performed in the eighteenth century. Writers aiming at a verse-style that would be judged 'harmonious' produced a high proportion of lines like (24), in which the distribution of stressed syllables falls naturally into the pattern of (23):

(24)   the CURfeu TOLLS the KNELL of PARTing DAY (Gray 1751)

and the more irregular practice of earlier periods was often re-interpreted to fit the same pattern. When we see the scansion that Monboddo proposed for the first line of *Paradise Lost*:

(25)   of MANS first DISoBEdience AND the FRUIT

we can understand why Blake in (22a) describes Milton's cadence as 'monotonous'.

One indication of changing attitudes appears when Joshua Steele draws on his study of English intonation to contest the scansion of (25). He proposes instead:

(26)   of MANS FIRST disoBEdience and the FRUIT

and justifies his analysis on the grounds that poetic rhythm reflects the natural emphases of speech and that 'our sense of *rhythmus* [is] much more *instinctive* than *rational*' (Steele 1775: 76–8, 166–7). From the turn of the century, these ideas were taken up more widely as Romantic writers, rejecting the calculation implied by mathematical models, looked for metrical theories more consonant with an ideal of poetry as a form of discourse organised by passion rather than reason. Coleridge was an influential spokesman:

(27)   Physicians assert that each passion has its proper pulse. – So it
         was with metre when rightly used. A state of excitement
         produced is, in truth, an analogy of the language of strong
         passion – not that strong passion always speaks in metre, but it
         has a language more measured than is employed in common
         speaking.   (Coleridge 1811)

Here metre is organically related to the speaker; it imitates the regularities of passionate speech. Later theorists developed the implications of Coleridge's medical analogy and there have been many attempts to ground metre in the regularities of human biology – the tempo of the heartbeat, for example, or the rhythm of breathing.

In terms of metrical practice, these views ultimately result in attempts to create verse-forms in which such regularities are structural, as in Frost's proposal to base metre on intonation patterns ('sentence-sounds', as he called them) or Olson's claim that his lines (as in (3d)) correspond to breath-units (Scully 1966: 50–53, 271–282). But for the immediate heirs of eighteenth-century poetics, the first priority was to break the dominance of the iambic pentameter. What we find in Romantic and Victorian poets is a variety of formal experiments which have in common the subversion of what had become the pentameter's salient features: the iambic foot; the five-stress line; and finally, rhyme, that 'modern bondage' resisted by Milton, which eighteenth-century practice, under the influence of Dryden and Pope, had made central to the ideal of 'English Heroic Verse'.

7.3.2   The iambic foot

The foot as a unit of metre can be seen as a stylisation of the foot of ordinary speech, that is, a stressed syllable associated with a variable number of unstressed syllables and perceived to occur at roughly isochronous intervals in the utterance. In the case of the iambic foot (ti-TUM in Mason's schema) the stylisation is a doubly unnatural one, since the foot of conversational English frequently contains more than one unstressed syllable and, on the most plausible analysis, the stressed syllable occupies initial rather than final position. The new naturalism in nineteenth-century metrics generated experiments that attempted to match metre to speech rhythm by varying the length of the metrical foot and/or reversing its stress pattern. A variable foot is in effect the 'new principle' that Coleridge announced for *Christabel*:

(28)   the metre of the Christabel is not, properly speaking, irregular,
        though it may seem so from its being founded on a new
        principle: namely, that of counting in each line the accents, not
        the syllables. Though the latter may vary from seven to twelve,
        yet in each line the accents will be found to be only four.

                                                            (Coleridge 1816)

The effects Coleridge was aiming at may be judged from the poem's opening lines:

(29)   'Tis the middle of night by the castle clock,
        And the owls have awaken'd the crowing cock;
        Tu–whit!–Tu–whoo!
        And hark, again! the crowing cock,
        How drowsily it crew.

The influence of *Christabel* appears intermittently through the nineteenth century, for example, in Shelley's *Sensitive Plant* (1820) and Browning's *Flight of the Duchess* (1845), and towards the end of the century, Coleridge's 'new principle' was rediscovered by Hopkins as the basis for his own 'sprung rhythm'. The practice found its major academic theorist in Guest, whose *History of English Rhythms* (first published 1838, more influentially re-issued under the aegis of Skeat in 1878) showed that the new principle was in effect a reappearance of the old principle of **accentual prosody** which had regulated the practice of Old and Middle English poetry and, he argued, had continued as an underground resistance movement throughout the period of the syllabo-tonic tradition, which he identified as 'the rhythm of the foreigner'. Metre was thus drawn into the nationalist movement in philology, with the consequence that poets like Morris and Hopkins, who replaced latinate with Anglo-Saxon in vocabulary (see 7.2.5–7.2.6 above), also experimented with the **alliterative metre** of *Beowulf* (which Morris translated) and *Piers Plowman*. The complex and systematic patterns of these historical precedents are not closely imitated (indeed, before Sievers 1893, they were imperfectly understood), but the flavour of their versification is captured by using alliteration to foreground some of the stressed syllables in the line (as in (30a–b)). In later experiments, the form is at once more knowingly and more metaphorically used: by Pound as an indigenous equivalent of Homeric epic verse (30c), by Auden and Wilbur as a metrical image of primitive heroism in sardonic counterpoint with modern lifestyles, whether effete as in (30d) or sordid as in (30e):

(30)   a. The *s*ails of the *s*torm of *b*attle adown the *b*ickering *b*last

(Morris 1876)

       b. Thou art *l*ightning and *l*ove, I found it, a *w*inter and *w*arm

(Hopkins 1875 publ. 1918)

       c. *T*omb hideth *t*rouble. The blade is *l*ayed *l*ow   (Pound 1912)

       d.   . . . *l*ightning at noonday
           *S*wiftly *s*tooping to the *s*ummer-house   (Auden 1948)

       e. An *a*xe *a*ngles
                 from my neighbor's *a*shcan   (Wilbur 1961)

In another strand of nineteenth-century poetics, the practice of the variable foot was justified from classical prototypes. The **hexameter** was particularly favoured, Coleridge's experimental *Hymn to the Earth* (1799) being followed by large-scale works such as Southey's *Vision of Judgment* (1821), Longfellow's *Evangeline* (1847), Clough's *Amours de Voyage* (1858) and Kingsley's *Andromeda* (1858). The similarity in effect between this and the experiments in accentual prosody can be seen in (31), an example of what Clough called his 'Anglo-savage hexameters':

(31)   ARchi/TECtural/BEAUty in/APPli/CAtion to/WOmen

(Clough 1848)

The model is the Virgilian hexameter, which utilises three of the foot-types of classical metrics: **spondee** (TUM-TUM), **dactyl** (TUM-ti-ti) and **trochee** (TUM-ti). The Anglo-savage equivalent is created by substituting syllable stress for syllable length in the realisation of the foot and permitting a trochee where Latin verse would require a spondee. The structure of (31) is thus trochee, dactyl, dactyl, trochee, dactyl, trochee. In terms of the effect, what is striking is the way in which the repeated, if slight, variation in foot length together with the consistent use of stress-initial foot-types in place of the stress-final iamb (ti-TUM) is enough to distance the sound from the familiar pattern of (23–24) and create an approximation to the rhythms of prose, as in (32a), or conversational speech, as in (32b):

(32)   a. They, too, swerved from their course; and, entering the Bayou
        of Plaquemine,
      Soon were lost in a maze of sluggish and devious waters,
      Which, like a network of steel, extended in every direction.

                              (Longfellow 1847)

    b. Take off your coat to it, Philip, cried Lindsay, outside in the
        garden . . .
      Take off your coat to it, Philip.
                    Well, well, said Hewson, resuming;
      Laugh if you please at my novel economy; listen to this,
        though   (Clough 1848)

The hexameter features one elongation of the foot that achieved a special status in the nineteenth century, the **dactyl**, a tri-syllabic foot in which the stressed syllable is followed by two unstressed syllables (TUM-ti-ti). This, or its stress-final counterpart, the **anapaest** (ti-ti-TUM), is widely used to vary iambic rhythms (as in *Christabel*), and sometimes appears as the metrical base-form itself, giving rise to what is often known as **triple metre**. In the eighteenth century, triple metre was largely associated with burlesque or with songs, but Cowper extended its range in his plaintive *The Poplar-field* (1785), and in the nineteenth century it encroaches on the territory of the iambic pentameter when it is made the vehicle of epic narrative, as in Byron's anapaestic *Destruction of Semnacherib* (33a), or of lyric elegy, as in Hardy's dactylic *The Voice* (33b):

(33)   a. For the Angel of Death spread his wings on the blast,
      And breathed in the face of the foe as he pass'd;
      And the eyes of the sleepers wax'd deadly and chill

                              (Byron 1815)

    b. Woman much missed, how you call to me, call to me,
      Saying that now you are not as you were
      When you had changed from the one who was all to me

                              (Hardy 1914)

As these examples show, triple metre is more monotonous and less conversational than iambic metre. Its popularity in the nineteenth century – unparalleled in any other period of literature – is therefore remarkable and must suggest that, for some poets at least, the imperative to break the iambic pentameter took priority over the desire to re-create the sound-patterns of speech. Triple metre is the perfect antidote to iambics, since its principle of construction – that every third syllable *must* carry a stress – means it is continually breaking one of the basic rules of metricality for iambic metre: that a **stress maximum** must *not* fall on an odd-numbered syllable. This happens in every line of (33a), for instance, where stress maxima occur in line 1 on syllable 3 (*ANG*); in line 2 on syllable 5 (*FACE*); in line 3 on syllable 3 (*EYES*). It's worth noting in this context that the opening line of the consciously revolutionary *Christabel* (34a) announces its departure from the iambic norm in the same way, by employing a stress maximum on syllable 3 (or, in traditional terminology, by replacing the expected initial iamb with an anapaestic foot); similarly, Pound boasts of breaking the pentameter (34b) in a twelve-syllable line with stress maximum on syllable 5 – in the middle of the word *pentameter*.

(34) a. 'Tis the MIDDle of night by the castle clock
   b. to break the penTAmeter, that was the first heave

7.3.3 The five-stress line

To avoid the pentameter's five-stress line, poets in our period have experimented with both shorter and longer options. Three influential precedents for these experiments appeared in the 1760s, though their main effects were felt in the following century. Initially, all were associated with the image of primitive rural language invoked by Wordsworth and with the notion that poetry was a natural form of utterance in early stages of a language or society.

The most popular of the short-line verse-forms **ballad metre** – quatrain stanzas, alternating 4 and 3 stress lines and rhyming on lines 2 and 4, as in (21) – derived its prestige for the Romantics from its role as the vehicle of traditional folk poetry, children's nursery rhymes and popular hymns. Folk-ballads surviving in oral tradition were published in collections such as Percy's *Reliques of Ancient English Poetry* (1765) and their importance as a model is acknowledged both in the title of *Lyrical Ballads* and in the choice of Coleridge's *The Rime of the Ancyent Marinere* as the opening poem of the first edition. Ballad influence continues through to the late nineteenth century, with Kipling's *Barrack-room Ballads* (1892) and Wilde's *Ballad of Reading Gaol* (1898), and can be detected in the twentieth century in the work of both Modernists and traditionalists. In many of these modern examples, the form is metaphorised, being used as a metrical image of pastoral continuity or child-like simplicity, set in ironic counterpoint with its subject-matter, whether the rural decay of Housman's *Shropshire Lad* (1896) or the urban depravity depicted by Auden in (21). Or else both form and content are radicalised: for Blake, Dickinson and Christina Rossetti in the nineteenth century and for Stevie Smith in the twentieth, the ballad provided a starting-point and precedent for more experimental short-line quatrains in which irregular metre (varying both number and placement of stresses) is combined with visionary or revisionary – contents. The process can be seen in action in the contrast between the first and second stanzas of (35):

(35)   I asked a thief to steal me a peach,
         He turnd up his eyes;
         I ask'd a lithe lady to lie her down,
         Holy & meek she cries.

         As soon as I went
         An angel came
         He wink'd at the thief
         And smild at the dame   (Blake 1791–2)

On the side of elongating the pentameter, the influential work again appeared in the 1760s with Macpherson's enormously famous, largely bogus, translations of ancient Gaelic writing by 'Ossian son of Fingal', which provided an inspiration and model for Blake's Prophetic Books and set the pattern for later long-line verse from Whitman in the nineteenth century to poets of the late twentieth:

(36)   a. Shadows of Prophecy shiver along by the lakes and the rivers
            and mutter across the ocean, France rend down thy
            dungeon   (Blake *c.* 1790)

         b. The sniff of green leaves and dry leaves, and of the shore and
            darkcolored sea-rocks, and of hay in the barn
                                                       (Whitman 1855)

         c. I remember the first time, out of a bush in the darkness, a
            nightingale's piercing cries and gurgles startled the depths
            of my soul   (Lawrence 1921)

d. a lost battalion of platonic conversationalists jumping down
    the stoops off fire escapes off windowsills off Empire State
    out of the moon   (Ginsberg 1956)

e. He adored the desk, its brown-oak inlaid with ebony, assorted
    prize pens, the seals of gold and base metal into which he
    had sunk his name.   (Hill 1971)

Though these can all be classed as long lines, it would be difficult to call
them metred in any sense that could be reflected in a structural description
and some of them seem designed to blur the boundaries between poetry
and prose (a reminder that the **prose-poem** became an established genre
in this period, the term itself first attested in the *OED* as 1842). More conservative versions of the long line in the nineteenth century draw on precedents in the classical tradition (like the hexameter), or the longer options in
the syllabo-tonic tradition, such as **alexandrines** (as in Browning's *Fifine at
the Fair*, 1872) or **fourteeners** (as in Macaulay's *Lays of Ancient Rome*, 1842).
Despite the variety of provenance, many of these long lines converge in
practice on a six-stress norm, and this has other structural consequences.
For whereas the iambic pentameter can be contained in a single intonation
contour or tone-group, the six-stress line tends to promote a strong medial
pause, producing what Hopkins described as 'the deep natural monotony'
of a structure with 'middle pause and equal division'; his and his period's
preoccupation with such structures may reflect not only a desire to escape
from the pentameter, but also a perception that structural monotony may
be needed to maintain regularity over against a longer line and/or a variable foot. A bi-partite line is a feature not only of the alexandrine but also
of the accentual verse of Old and Middle English which Hopkins and
others took as their model.

For the nineteenth century at least, the model of the long bi-partite line
was further endorsed by the third of the metrical influences emanating
from the mid-eighteenth century, the Bible, which at that point gained a
new, and specifically poetic, status from Lowth's assimilation of the Old
Testament to primitive poetics (in his *Lectures on the Sacred Poetry of the
Hebrews*, published in Latin in 1753 and in English in 1787). Wordsworth,
taking his cue from Lowth, cites the Bible as an example of what the language of ordinary speech could achieve under the influence of inspired
passion, and Coleridge concedes that in so far as rustic speech might
become the source of poetry it would do so because rustic speakers were
imbued with the language of the Bible and the liturgy (Coleridge [1817]:
ii.44). What the Bible provided was a model of metre founded on the

principle of lexical and syntactic repetition, as Hopkins put it, a 'figure of sense' rather than the figure of sound which is the basis of the iambic pentameter. But when the principle is put into practice it has its own characteristic sound pattern, producing more often than not a bi-partite line of approximately equi-stressed halves:

(37) There the wicked cease from troubling; and there the weary be at rest.
      There the prisoners rest together; they hear not the voice of the oppressor.
      The small and great are there; and the servant is free from his master.

This style was directly imitated by Blake (38a), by the immensely popular Victorian moral versifier, Martin Tupper in *Proverbial Philosophy* (1838, '42, '67, '76) and by Eliot in some of the Choruses from *The Rock* (38b), and it can be felt behind much long-line verse of the period, notably Whitman in the nineteenth century and Lawrence in the twentieth.

(38) a. They cannot smite the wheat, nor quench the fatness of the earth.
         They cannot smite with sorrows, nor subdue the plow and spade.
         They cannot wall the city, nor moat round the castle of princes.   (Blake 1793)

      b. I have given you hands which you turn from worship,
         I have given you speech, for endless palaver,
         I have given you my Law, and you set up commissions.
                                                          (Eliot 1934)

7.3.4   *Rhyme*

Rhyme is not a necessary concomitant of the iambic pentameter – as witness the **blank verse** of Shakespeare and Milton – but Dryden and Pope had established the **heroic couplet** as the dominant type of the iambic pentameter for the eighteenth century and Pope had perfected the use of rhyme as the instrument of reason, using it to foreground similarities and antitheses of meaning or to clinch the point of an argument (Wimsatt 1970). Hence rhyme was included in the general Romantic distrust of formal artifice. Indeed a preference for blank verse over couplets is one marker of those eighteenth century works which, on other grounds, are classed as the precursors of Romanticism, notably Thomson's *The Seasons* (1730), Young's *Night Thoughts* (1742) and Cowper's *The Task* (1785).

Like line-length, rhyme can be subverted by either under-performing or over-performing, and the period is fertile in experiments that do something less or more than perfect rhyming. On the less side, Blake and Whitman experimented with unrhymed long lines as in (36a–b), and Arnold with unrhymed lyrics, thus anticipating the main **free verse** forms of the twentieth century; Browning expressed an interest in **eye-rhymes** such as *warp/harp*, *death/beneath*, *word/sword* and Barrett Browning sometimes used **half-rhyme** (e.g. *faith/death*, *noon/sewn/gown*), devices employed more systematically by, for instance, Owen and Gurney in the first half of the twentieth century and Larkin and Hill in the second. Half-rhyme has always been common in ballads and popular song. The tentativeness of nineteenth-century writers in adopting it for serious poetry may owe something to the critical storm which met Keats's *Endymion* in 1818 (and in popular mythology hastened his death). Keats provoked the storm by choosing to subvert the salient features of the heroic couplet within the couplet form itself, using what critics derided as 'loose, nerveless versification, and Cockney rhymes' as part of a conscious revolt against the practices of Pope.

(39)   a. Nor do we merely feel these essences
           For one short hour; no, even as the trees . . .

       b. Young companies nimbly began dancing
          To the swift treble pipe, and humming string.   (Keats 1818)

(39a) is a half-rhyme /iz/-/iːz/, and both (a) and (b) violate the norm of Popean couplets by rhyming a stressed with an unstressed syllable, a pattern that occurs repeatedly in the poem (for instance *tenement/intent*, *press/weariness*, *breath/witnesseth*). It was not until the twentieth century that this type of rhyme was fully habilitated. It is used by Lawrence and Gurney, features prominently in Marianne Moore's poetry (with rhymes such as *we/unnecessary*, *surliness/less*, *all/external*, *dead/repeated*, *the/sea*) and becomes increasingly popular in the second half of century. Concealed rhyme of this sort – especially where the spelling provides no signal of its occurrence – creates the illusion of a natural speech which falls into rhyme almost accidentally and the prominence of the rhyme is left to be determined in performance. Those reading section 7.2.5, for instance, are unlikely to have noticed the rhyme in Larkin's *piss/cleanliness* (16a) without previous knowledge of the poem.

At the other extreme, rhyme can be heightened and foregrounded by being extended across 2 or 3 syllables, a device which draws attention to the ingenuity of the poet and/or the artificiality of the convention. Byron set the fashion with such notorious rhymes as:

(40)   But – Oh! ye lords of ladies inte*llectual,*
         Inform us truly, have they not hen-*peck'd you all?*   (Byron 1819)

and his followers include Browning in the nineteenth century (*leaps, ache/keepsake; unit/soon hit*) and in the twentieth Auden (*tenmen/wen men*) and Stevie Smith (*illfed/Wilfred*). These largely satiric uses could be seen as a natural extension of the eighteenth-century association between poly-syllabic rhyming and burlesque. But in the nineteenth century, at least, such rhymes also appear in non-satiric writing as a natural concomitant of the extension of triple metre to serious contexts, as when Hardy rhymes *call to me* with *all to me* in (33b). In (41), Hopkins alternates trisyllabic and disyl-labic rhymes:

(41)   This very very day came down to us after a boon he on
         My late being there begged of me, overflowing
                 Boon in my bestowing,
         Came, I say, this day to it – to a First Communion.
                                                     (Hopkins 1879/1918)

There is no sign that this is intended as a burlesque or debunking move. It should perhaps be interpreted as an attack on the closed line rather than on rhyme in itself, since one effect of polysyllabic rhyming is to move the stress back from the line-end, forming a major contrast with eighteenth-century practice where stress and line-end largely coincide and a **feminine** (i.e. unstressed) ending is a very rare variant. In this respect, much polysyllabic rhyming performs the same function as the final trochaic foot of the hexa-meter in (31–32).

In eighteenth-century couplets, the line-end was marked by a battery of phonological features: in addition to stress and rhyme there was a pause. Pause is more a matter of performance than the other two, but eighteenth-century poets promoted its occurrence by making the line-end coincide with the boundary of a (usually major) syntactic unit. This feature, too, shows a progressive weakening in the modern period through increasing use of **enjambement**. Where the Romantics do use couplets, enjambement provides an undercurrent of subversion, a metrical figure for 'the overflow of powerful feelings' which is central to a Wordsworthian definition of poetry. Keats developed the term 'straddled lines' to describe the practice:

(42)   A thing of beauty is a joy for ever:
         Its loveliness increases; it will never
         Pass into nothingness; but still will keep
         A bower quiet for us, and a sleep . . .   (Keats 1818)

Here the auxiliary–verb sequence (*will . . . pass*) straddles lines 2–3 and the verb–object relation (*keep/a bower*) discourages a pause between lines 3 and 4. A comparison with (41) shows how the technique became progressively radicalised during the nineteenth century, Hopkins straddles lines 2–3 with an adjective–noun sequence (*overflowing-boon*) and lines 1–2 with preposition–noun phrase (*on/my late being there*). The reader faces the choice of preserving the tone-group of normal speech or the metrical unit of the line. Such an extreme instance of the conversational challenging the metrical becomes common among later nineteenth-century poets in a way not seen since late Shakespeare, and in his practice it is counterbalanced by the persistence of the iambic pentameter as a metrical norm. In (41), not one of the lines is construable as an iambic pentameter. The foregrounded rhyme may be in part a compensatory method of demarcating the line-unit. It's notable that many of the nineteenth century's most experimental metrists in terms of stress-placement and line-length retain the marker of rhyme, as Christina Rossetti does, for instance, in *Goblin Market* (1862), a poem whose rhythms Ruskin judged to be unpublishably irregular.

7.3.5   *Conservatism and experimentalism in modern poetry*

With all these nineteenth-century experiments going on, why did Pound claim that the pentameter remained to be broken by Modernism? One reason may be the relative timidity of nineteenth-century polemics, which tended to conceal the radicalness of metrical experimentation by affiliating it to, for instance, classical precedent. But in any case, it would be misleading to suggest that all nineteenth-century verse was experimental in the ways described here. Much adhered to the syllabo-tonic tradition and even to the iambic pentameter. Wordsworth, who for the nineteenth century was the most influential voice in the Romantic revolution, was himself metrically conservative and although experimenting with new metrics in, for instance, *The White Doe of Rylstone* (1815), chose blank verse for nearly all his large-scale work. The belated publication of *The Prelude* in 1850 re-established the authority of iambic pentameter and set the metrical precedent for the major public epics of the mid-Victorian period: Barrett Browning's *Aurora Leigh* (1857), Tennyson's *Idylls of the King* (1859),

Browning's *The Ring and the Book* (1868). It is, however, important to note that the iambic pentameter that emerges at the end of the nineteenth century is very different from the form in which it was practised in the eighteenth. Though its abstract pattern remains essentially that of Mason's schema, it shows the same progressive loss of transparency between abstract pattern and linguistic realisation in mid- to late nineteenth-century practice as it underwent between Gascoigne and Donne in the Renaissance (Freeman 1968; Tarlinskaya 1973; Kiparsky 1977). It's possible, therefore, to see some of Eliot's free verse practice as continuing rather than repudiating the blank verse practice of late nineteenth-century poets. For if Wordsworth was metrically less radical than Coleridge, Eliot was less radical than Pound and he retains the iambic pentameter as what he calls 'the ghost behind the arras' behind much of his free verse, producing sequences like:

(43)   I that was near your heart was removed therefrom
         To lose beauty in terror, terror in inquisition.
         I have lost my passion: why should I need to keep it
         Since what is kept must be adulterated?
         I have lost my sight, smell, hearing, taste and touch:
         How should I use it for your closer contact?   (Eliot 1920)

This passage flirts with the 5-stress/10-syllable ideal of iambic pentameter blank verse; indeed lines 4 and 6 with an eleventh unstressed syllable are acceptable instantiations of Mason's schema in (23). But Eliot almost pedantically avoids a full instantiation: lines with five stresses (e.g. i have LOST my PASSion; WHY should i NEED to KEEP it) have too many syllables to be classed as iambic pentameter, while the lines closer to ten syllables have less than five stresses and carefully avoid distributing them in a strict ti-TUM sequence (e.g. HOW should i USE them for your CLOser CONtact). What is more, out of the six lines in this extract, only two end with a stressed syllable and one of those includes a stress maximum on an odd-numbered syllable (MOVED on syllable 9 of line 1), as if Eliot was fearful of lapsing into the style Pound stigmatised as 'too penty'.

Eliot's metrical effects in (43) come very close to those of poets such as Frost and Edward Thomas, usually regarded as belonging to a different and more traditionalist school of poetry. What Pound's version of Modernism offered instead was a technique that radicalised nineteenth-century innovations. This is partly a matter of using them in combination, whereas nineteenth-century poets were liable to balance experimentalism in one area with a compensatory conservatism in another. Many of the techniques discussed in sections 7.3.2–7.3.4 are brought together in the following brief poem:

(44)   The black panther treads at my side,
        And above my fingers
        There float the petal-like flames.

        The milk-white girls
        Unbend from the holly-trees,
        And their snow-white leopard
        Watches to follow our trace.   (Pound 1916)

The first stanza consciously poses a problem for syllabo-tonic metrics by **varying syllable and stress-count** in every line. The second stanza gestures towards the **ballad quatrain** but radicalises it by reducing the stresses to two per line and varying their placement. Only line 4 of the poem approximates to iambic rhythm (the MILK-white GIRLS); in the rhyming lines **triple metre** comes more to the fore (unBEND from the HOLly-trees; WATCHes to FOLLow our TRACE). **Syntactic patterning** seems as important as stress-patterning: the first stanza falls into a **chiasmus** pattern in which the Subject–Verb–Locative Adverbial of line 1 is echoed and reversed in the Locative Adverbial–Verb–Subject of lines 2–3; and in the second stanza the lines alternate matching syntactic units – Subject (line 1) Predicate (line 2) Subject (line 3) Predicate (line 4) – forming a grammatical equivalent to the a–b–a–b rhyme scheme of the traditional quatrain (here invoked in ghostly form by the **half-rhyme** on *trees/trace*). None of these features is unprecedented, but they are rarely found together in a nineteenth-century poem.

Where Modernist metrics makes a distinctive *addition* to the technical repertoire it inherits is in its use of **typography**. In one respect the increased importance of typography is a purely contingent development. If all phonological features demarcating the line as a unit are removed, only typography remains. In (45) for instance, Feinstein's enjambement, like Hopkins's, places line-endings in the middle of **phonological words**, but since, unlike Hopkins, she excludes rhyme, the only marker of the line as a unit is its lay-out on the page:

(45)   Suppose I took out a slender ketch from
        under the spokes of Palace pier tonight to
        catch a sea going fish for you   (Feinstein 1971)

There are also more positive reasons for this development. As poets move from attacking the iambic pentameter to constructing an alternative basis for metre, those who choose the units of conversational rhythm face the problem that the length of the foot and more particularly the **tone-unit** is a matter of performance. The opening line of *Christabel*, for instance, can be read as a single tone-unit or as two (*tis the middle of night/ /by the castle clock*). Typography can provide a set of performance instructions by signalling where the boundaries are intended to fall. That is the basis of the 'new measure' announced by William Carlos Williams, and his influence can be seen in Feinstein's lineation in (45) or Olson's in (3d).

In **concrete poetry**, it is avowedly the visual values of typography that matter. The Romantic revolution largely resisted the condition of textuality in pursuit of the Wordsworthian concept of poetry as speech, but one strand of the Modernist revolution reinstates and exploits that condition in a way not seen since the seventeenth century, as in Dylan Thomas's lozenge-shaped *Vision and Prayer* (1945) or Ian Hamilton Finlay's pear-shaped *Au Pair Girl* (1964). But the typographic experimentalism of twentieth-century poetry is too widespread to be explained by literary nostalgia. This rediscovery of the expressive potential of print should rather be attributed to the invention of the typewriter, which gave every poet command over a personal printing-press, providing the resources not only to notate speech sounds (as capitals for shouts or variable spacing for pauses) but also to create visual effects that resist translation into speech, as when Pound's *Papyrus* uses ellipsis marks to imitate the ragged edge of a fragmentary document.

(46)   Spring . . .
         Too long . . .
         Gongula . . .   (Pound 1916)

By the second half of the century such practices had been accepted even by conservative writers. Larkin, for instance, entitles one of his 1964 poems *MCMXIV* as a reminder both of the Roman numerals chiselled on civic memorials to the generation lost in the First World War and of the Roman values of civic self-sacrifice that died with them. But these allusions are available only to the eye; they are lost when the title is read out as 'nineteen fourteen'.

At the other extreme of contemporary metrics, the conversational model gives way to music rather than pictorialism, as in the use of jazz rhythms and jazz accompaniments, pioneered by Vachel Lindsay and Langston Hughes in the 1920s and popularised by Beat poets such as Ferlinghetti and Kerouac in the late 1950s. In the same spirit, more recent writers have built poems out of reggae rhythms, as in (47):

(47) Shock-black bubble-doun-beat bouncing
      rock-wise tumble-doun sound music;
      foot-drop find drum, blood story,
      bass history is a moving
                    is a hurting black story.   (Johnson 1975)

Late twentieth-century writers of Afro-Caribbean descent have felt as
much fettered by the iambic pentameter as Blake did, seeing it as a verse-
form that reflected their continued bondage to Euro-centric literary
history, instead of expressing the culture that had developed in their West
Indian transplantation. As Brathwaite put it: 'The hurricane does not roar
in pentameters. And that's the problem: how do you get a rhythm which
approximates the *natural* experience, the *environmental* experience?'
(Brathwaite 1984: 10). One response has been to turn, as Johnson does in
(47), to the rhythm of reggae and a poetry whose instantiation depends on
music-accompanied performance. Brathwaite locates the inspiration for
this movement in Modernism and the jazz rhythms he hears in Eliot's more
experimental poetry, but its origins go back to Romanticism too: its choice
of reggae/calypso as a model echoes Wordsworth's revaluation of the
'vulgar ballad' while its emphasis on the physicality of dance/performance
updates Coleridge's grounding of metre in body rhythm.

7.4 The breaking of hypotaxis

7.4.1 *Introduction*

(48) a. A close reasoner and a good writer in general may be known
      by his pertinent use of connectives. Read that page of Johnson;
      you cannot alter one conjunction without spoiling the sense.
                                                       (Coleridge 1833)

      b. Italy went to rot, destroyed by rhetoric, destroyed by the
      periodic sentence and by the flowing paragraph . . . For when
      words cease to cling close to things, kingdoms fall.
                                                       (Pound 1916)

In his *Philosophy of Rhetoric* (1776), Campbell defines and explains a syntactic
ideal that English imitators of the classics had pursued through most of the
preceding three centuries, the **periodic sentence**: 'A period is a complex
sentence, wherein the meaning remains suspended till the whole is finished.
The connexion consequently is so close between the beginning and the
end, as to give rise to the name *period*, which signifies circuit' (Campbell

1776: ii.339). As English writers were aware, Quintilian had advised Roman orators that the best way to keep the meaning suspended was to postpone the verb to the end of the sentence. This is difficult to achieve in a language with the relatively fixed SVO word order of English and in late eighteenth-century practice the effect of suspension is most commonly created by using a complex sentence in which a subordinate clause either *precedes* the main clause or *intervenes* between its subject and predicate. Both of these sentence types figure in the heavily periodic opening of Boswell's *The Life of Samuel Johnson*. In (49a), the subject (*To write the life*) has a deferred predicate (*is an arduous . . . task*); in (49b), several subordinate clauses (the reiterated conditional *Had Dr Johnson written . . . had he employed . . .*) precede the main clause (*the world would probably have had . . .*).

(49)   a. To write the life of him who excelled all mankind in writing the lives of others, and who, whether we consider his extraordinary endowments, or his various works, has been equalled by few in any age, is an arduous, and may be reckoned in me a presumptuous task.

          b. Had Dr Johnson written his own Life, in conformity with the opinion which he has given, that every man's life may be best written by himself; had he employed in the preservation of his own history, that clearness of narration and elegance of language in which he has embalmed so many eminent persons, the world would probably have had the most perfect example of biography that was ever exhibited.   (Boswell 1791)

But what we also see in (49) is a form that the spirit has gone out of. The suspended main clause is not here the instrument of dramatic dénouement, as Campbell envisaged ('You defer the blow a little, but it is solely that you may bring it down with greater weight'); it seems, rather, a method of establishing the dignity of the subject-matter or the adequacy of the author. Like Gray's poetic diction, Boswell's periodic sentence has lost its specific expressive functions and become a formality marker. And by the time (49) was published, the style it exemplifies was receiving the same critical reappraisal we have seen in the case of poetic diction and iambic pentameter. Cowper expresses the new mood in (50), classing *rounded periods* together with heroic couplets (*the morris-dance of verse*) and rejecting both as the enemies of *sentiment, sense*, and *truth*.

(50)   Thus, all success depending on an ear,
          And thinking I might purchase it too dear,

If sentiment were sacrific'd to sound,
And truth cut short to make a period round,
I judg'd a man of sense could scarce do worse,
Than caper in the morris-dance of verse.   (Cowper 1782)

But, like many late eighteenth-century writers, Cowper provides no solution for the stylistic problem he perceives. Despite his protestations, he writes (50) in regular, rhymed, end-stopped iambic couplets and he employs all the salient features of periodic sentence construction, postponing his main clause (*I judged . . .*) until late in the structure and making it the climax of a series of clauses whose subordinate status is signalled either by an explicit subordinator (*if*) or by participial verb forms (*thinking . . .* ; *all success depending . . .*).

Among Cowper's Romantic successors, opposition to the periodic sentence intensified. To those who valued 'low and rustic' language, (49) and (50) epitomised a style modelled on Ciceronian Latin, whose mastery depended on the privileges of a classical education. To those who valued the 'language of conversation', they epitomised written rather than spoken discourse. The formal features of a periodic sentence imply that the ideas it expresses have been pre-analysed into a hierarchy of importance (reflected in the main clause–subordinate clause contrast) and a causal chain (reflected in connectives like *thus* and *if* in (50)). Above all, the principle of suspension implies that the ending has been foreseen before the first word is set down. Periodic style leaves no room for the interruptions, digressions and new directions of spontaneous speech. Hence the breaking of a periodic sentence becomes an important figure in Romantic syntax:

(51)   a.   If this
        Be but a vain belief, yet, oh! how oft,
        In darkness, and amid the many shapes
        Of joyless day-light . . .
        How oft, in spirit, have I turned to thee
        O sylvan Wye! Thou wanderer through the wood
        How often has my spirit turned to thee!

                                        (Wordsworth 1798)

        b. Springing from the bed, and throwing herself upon me – her
        piercing shrieks–   (Hays 1796)

Both extracts begin with the characteristic signals of periodic construction, the subordinating conjunction in (a) and the participial clause in (b). But the expectations they raise are frustrated, the periods never rounded. Instead they are interrupted, by an exclamative in (a) and a complete suspension of the discourse in (b), as if premeditated rational argument had been blown off-course by 'the spontaneous overflow of powerful feelings'.

Underlying such frontal attacks on the periodic sentence is a more widespread shift in attitudes to connectivity, or, in syntactic terms, to the conventions governing clause-combining. The periodic sentence was salient because it was the most highly crafted exemplar of the most highly valued option for clause-combining in the eighteenth century, a form of **hypotaxis** in which clauses are linked in a relationship of dependency and dependency is canonically signalled by explicit subordinating conjunctions. It was a commonplace of eighteenth-century criticism – inherited from Locke and echoed by Coleridge in (48a) – to equate a 'good writer' with a 'close reasoner' and to see a 'pertinent use of connectives' as the index of both. But what is notable in (48a) is that Coleridge himself *avoids* connectives both between sentences and between the component clauses of his second sentence. Where Cowper in (50) uses a conditional construction, signalled by the subordinator *if,* Coleridge simply juxtaposes an imperative with a declarative and leaves the conditional relation between them to be inferred (i.e. [if you] *read that page of Johnson* [you will see that] *you cannot alter one conjunction*). This is a common method of expressing conditionals in spoken discourse and its use here is one of the features that makes Coleridge's representation of 'table-talk' more naturalistic than Cowper's. More generally, (48a) exemplifies the type of clause-combining known as **parataxis**, in which linkage is signalled by simple juxtaposition (supplemented in speech by intonation) or by co-ordinating conjunctions: *and, but.* This was the option which increasingly challenged hypotaxis when the Romantics' speech-based model for literature began to shape stylistic norms. But the transition from hypotactic to paratactic styles was gradual and complex; as (48a) and (50) suggest, opinion and practice often pulled in opposite directions and, as later examples will show, by the time the issue was decided in favour of parataxis, its problems were as evident as its virtues.

7.4.2   From hypotaxis to parataxis

An early and consciously controversial example of the extended use of parataxis is Mackenzie's *The Man of Feeling* (1771). As his introduction makes clear, the novel is designed to frustrate the eighteenth-century reader who looks for close reasoning: 'I could never find the author in one strain for two chapters together: and I don't believe there's a single syllogism from beginning to end'. It anticipates the Romantic genre of **the fragment**, by purporting to be 'scattered chapters, and fragments of chapters' and its syntax is often similarly disconnective:

(52)   You remember old Trusty, my shag house-dog; I shall never
         forget it while I live; the poor creature was blind with age, and
         could scarce crawl after us to the door; he went however as far as
         the gooseberry-bush; that you may remember stood on the left
         side of the yard; he was wont to bask in the sun there: when he
         had reached that spot, he stopped; we went on: I called to him;
         he wagged his tail, but did not stir: I called again; he lay down: I
         whistled, and cried Trusty; he gave a short howl, and died!

                                                              (Mackenzie 1771)

Where subordinating conjunctions appear, they are temporal rather than logical (*while* and *when* rather than *if*), but Mackenzie prefers co-ordinators (*but/and*) to subordinators and quite commonly he has no connective at all. His basic unit of composition is the independent simplex declarative clause.

The style of (52) was not unusual in private communications in the eighteenth century – Boswell, for instance, prefers it to the style of (49) when writing letters to his friend, Temple. And even for public literature, most eighteenth-century grammarians had sanctioned the use of short sentences and the omission of connectives in the context of simple narratives and/or strong feelings. In that sense, Mackenzie is working within the constraints of his period's accepted stylistic ideals: his innovation, as his title implies, is to make simple narratives of strong feeling the substance of a whole novel. As our period goes on, the style exemplified by (52) extends its range of contexts, becoming the **unmarked** form for much late twentieth-century writing.

For most of the nineteenth century, however, parataxis remains the **marked** option and carries the connotations of one or more of its original contexts: powerful feeling, intimate registers, and/or uneducated varieties (e.g. rustics and children). From the 1790s it also acquired political overtones when Romantic radicals, such as Godwin and Hazlitt, adopted the short sentence style as the medium for arguing the case for constitutional reform. In the aftermath of the French Revolution, what Hazlitt saw as a democratic style (the 'broken English' of 'common elliptical expressions' and 'popular modes of construction') struck others as dangerously subversive. It does not appear in the prose-writing of the more reactionary Romantics, such as Coleridge (who deplored 'the present anglo-gallican fashion of unconnected, epigrammatic periods') and its general diffusion was inhibited until well after the defeat of Napoleon in 1815.

These early restrictions in genre are matched by a conservatism in form. Mackenzie, for example, composes (52) in the spirit of the periodic sentence: he uses punctuation to link a much more extensive series of clauses than could be held together by intonation; he organises them into a set of parallel or contrastive pairs (*he stopped – we went on / I called – he wagged / I called – he lay down / I whistled – he . . . howled*); and he plots the sequence to lead up to a final climax (*and died!*). Similarly, in (53), we find Macaulay rejecting Johnson's latinate style in a sentence of apparently latinate form: it is divided (as Macaulay's punctuation indicates) into four 'members' (the recommended norm for the Ciceronian periodic sentence); it uses the classical devices of parallel construction and incremental length; and it is designed to produce a 'rounded' paradox in which a *learned* language finally turns out to be one in which *nobody thinks*:

(53) All [Johnson's] books are written in a learned language, — in a language which nobody hears from his mother or his nurse, — in a language in which nobody ever quarrels, or drives bargains, or makes love, — in a language in which nobody ever thinks.

(Macaulay 1831)

Yet the basic composition of (53) looks forward rather than back, both in the way its 'members' are ordered and in the way they are connected. The ordering imitates the topic-comment procedures of spontaneous talk, in which the main point rather than being suspended first comes first and modifications or elaborations are tacked on as they occur to the mind. And the method of connection is **apposition**: the last three members of the sentence are all in apposition to the final phrase of the first member, offering explanatory reformulations of what is meant by *learned*. This is a pattern that dominates later prose style. Where the long composite sentence survives in the modern period, its constructional relations are typically closer to parataxis than to hypotaxis – there is an increase, that is, in clause-types based on juxtaposition (e.g. appositive, parenthetical and tag clauses) at the expense of clause-types based on subordination (e.g. complement and adverbial clauses).

The class of **relative clauses** includes both hypotactic and paratactic variants, in the forms known respectively as **restrictive** and **non-restrictive** relatives. The surviving representative of hypotaxis in (53) is the restrictive relative clause, which appears in each of the last three members. In a construction like *a language* **which nobody hears from his mother** the relative clause (here printed in bold-face) has the logical function of limiting the denotative scope of the head noun it modifies (here *language*) and syntactically it is best analysed as a constituent of the same noun phrase. A non-restrictive relative (such as *Johnson's language,* **which nobody else speaks**) is used to provide additional information about a referent that has already been specified. Its function is descriptive rather than defining and syntactically it may be best analysed as a separate noun phrase in apposition to its antecedent. For this reason some commentators have called it the **appositive relative**. Relative clauses of this type occur freely in spoken language (in (3a) for instance, we find *you get used to that beer,* **which is simply superb**) and are a conspicuous feature of fifteenth-century curial prose and its sixteenth-century descendants (see Adamson, *CHEL* III, forthcoming). But by the early eighteenth century they had lost currency in literary usage and the restrictive relative predominates in the influential style of Addison. The resurgence of parataxis in the nineteenth century brought a revival of the appositive relative. In the novels of Dickens and Thackeray, for instance, it provides a syntactic counterpart of the Victorian 'baggy-monster' plot construction deplored by James, in which all the events in the panoramic survey are simultaneously independent and interlinked. In the following (admittedly extreme) example, Dickens uses chained non-restrictive relatives (introduced by *who* in line 4 and *whom* in line 10) to digress from one story-line to another and in each case the relative clause is the mechanism for converting an incidental figure in one episode into the main protagonist of the next.

(54)   It was not unpleasant to remember, on the way thither, that Mrs. MacStinger resorted to a great distance every Sunday morning, to attend the ministry of the Reverend Melchisedech Howler, **who,** having been one day discharged from the West India Docks on a false suspicion (got up expressly against him by the general enemy) of screwing gimlets into puncheons, and applying his lips to the orifice, had announced the destruction of the world for that day two years, at ten in the morning, and opened a front parlour for the reception of ladies and gentlemen of the Ranting persuasion, **upon whom,** on the first occasion of their assemblage, the admonitions of the Reverend Melchisedech had produced so powerful an effect, that, in their rapturous performance of a sacred jig, which closed the service,

the whole flock broke through into a kitchen below, and disabled
a mangle belonging to one of the fold.   (Dickens 1848)

Despite the importance of paratactic construction here, Dickens, like
Macaulay, flirts with the salient features of periodic style, in the extreme
length of the whole and in the periodic structure of the first relative clause
(lines 4–8), where, like Cowper in (50), he postpones the main verb (*had
announced*) until after the long participial construction (*having been* . . .). But
whereas for the eighteenth century, length and suspension of sense normally
contributed towards elevation, in many nineteenth-century examples, they
are used for comic bathos, matching the way that the other salient feature of
Johnson's 'learned language', its latinate lexis, is deflated in the speech of
Micawber (15b). Hence (54) culminates in the disabling of a mangle.

Although appositive relatives are paratactic in being non-dependent,
they share with their hypotactic counterparts, restrictive relatives, the use
of an explicit connective (*who/whom*). In twentieth-century writing, their
place is frequently taken by a type of juxtapositional construction which
dispenses with such signals, the **free modifier**. Described as 'the very main-
stay of modern fiction' (Tufte 1971: 159), it occurs in a variety of forms.
The most common are illustrated in (55) below, in the italicised participle
clause (*walking heel-and-toe*), adverb (*insultingly*), prepositional phrase
(*like* . . .), and **absolute construction** (*the red shafts* . . . *twitching*).

(55)   The gypsy was walking out toward the bull again, walking heel-
         and-toe, insultingly, like a ballroom dancer, the red shafts of the
         banderillos twitching with his walk.
                            (Hemingway 1925; in Christensen 1967: 35)

Characteristically, free modifiers are set off from the main clause by
commas and they are 'free' in two senses: their syntactic position is unfixed
and the modifier-head relationship is unspecified and often unspecific. Free
modifiers occur also in eighteenth-century periodic styles (in (50) for
instance we find *all success depending* . . . and *thinking* . . .); but there they
canonically *precede* the main clause and their semantic relation to it is taken
to be the same as adverbial clauses of time, cause, condition, concession
(in (50) the relation is both temporal and causal). In modern usage, typified
by (55), free modifiers are more commonly positioned *after* the main clause
and their function is more often adjectival: they add descriptive details to
the scenario sketched in the main clause. The sentence sequence below
illustrates the way in which this type of sentence combines with the short
simplex declarative in much late twentieth-century prose:

(56)   I picked up my log basket and went towards the cottage and,
         as I did so, the wind gusted off the Fen towards the apple tree,
         taking the last of the leaves, the last remaining apples, and
         leaving the branches bare.
         I shivered. The year had turned again. It was winter.
         I went inside quickly, and closed the door.

                                                        (Susan Hill 1982)

As in (52), the only subordinating conjunction in this sequence is a temporal adverbial (**as** *I did so*). Otherwise the cluster of simplex declaratives
is varied by co-ordinate constructions (here dominated by *and*) and free
modifiers positioned after the main clause (*taking* . . . ; *leaving* . . .).

The most speech-like and the most disruptive of juxtapositional
constructions is the **parenthesis,** in which a formally distinct and self-
complete clause or clause group is inserted into another. Used in speech for
digressions or asides, parentheses in written language carry the implication
that the writer has neither premeditated his thoughts nor revised his text.
Hence Dr Johnson, as Boswell tells us, disapproved of their use and
avoided them in his own writings. On the same grounds Coleridge
defended parentheses as the sign of 'impassioned' eloquence and an
organic rather than an artificial style: 'They . . . present the thought
growing, instead of a mere *Hortus siccus*' (cited in Ricks 1984: 310). For evidence of the salience of parenthesis at the end of the eighteenth century,
we may return to (3b) and to Cowper. Unwilling as he was to violate his
period's stylistic ideals of couplet and hypotactic syntax, he used the parenthesis to push against their formal constraints, disrupting the neat correspondences of verse unit and syntactic unit with the (apparent)
improvisations of table-talk. Constructions like (3b) are not unprecedented
in eighteenth-century couplet writing, but by increasing the 'frequency and
regularity of this device', Cowper gave it the status of stylistic innovation
(Brown 1948: 132–4).

If the periodic sentence epitomised the virtues of hypotaxis for the
eighteenth century, the parenthesis, as the most extreme form of parataxis,
has had an equivalent importance since the beginning of the nineteenth. As
well as being a device of naturalism, used, as in (3c), to create the illusion of
authentic speech, it has also become an aesthetico-moral ideal, just as periodic construction was for Renaissance writers and their classical mentors
(Adamson *CHEL* III, forthcoming). Hence its stylisation by Olson in (3d).
Where the period symbolised the virtues of unity and completeness, the
parenthesis celebrates digression as a mode of discovery and the aside as

the index of feeling and truth. Some of these implications appear in David Jones's explanation of the title of his poem on the First World War:

(57) **This writing is called 'In Parenthesis' because I have written it in a kind of space between** – *I dont know between quite what – but as you turn aside to do something,* **and because for us amateur soldiers** (*and especially for the writer, who was not only amateur, but grotesquely incompetent, a knocker-over of piles, a parade's despair*) **the war itself was a parenthesis** – *how glad we thought we were to step outside its brackets at the end of '18* – **and also because our curious type of existence here is altogether in parenthesis.** (Jones 1937; my typeface)

In this long sentence there is an interplay between hypotactic and paratactic strategies of clause-combining and the values they most commonly represent. The section printed in boldface consists of a set of co-ordinated clauses, all subordinated to the initial main clause by the conjunction *because*. Jones uses this hypotactic clause group to present a rational justification of his project and an orderly vision of the relationship between his poem, the war, and the general human condition. But his exposition is continually disrupted by parentheses (here italicised) and the interpolated material – hedges, personal memories – works against the main statement, alerting us to the fact that in both personal and cultural history the war turned out to be not a momentary interruption but a defining experience. Correspondingly, the work that Jones offers under the title *In Parenthesis* turns out to be a 40,000-word epic.

7.4.3   *The information deficit*

One important product of the shift from hypotaxis to parataxis is an information deficit. When parataxis occurs in speech, intonation normally tells us where the links are, and information about the nature of the link is often supplied by the context of speech and the shared knowledge of the speech participants. In a hypotactic style of writing much of this information is carried instead by explicit connectives. In (57), for instance, *because* signals that the following clause is to be construed syntactically as subordinate and semantically as causal. By removing connectives, paratactic writing creates potentially serious problems of intelligibility.

One solution, particularly exploited in early examples, is the use of punctuation to replace intonation both as a linking device (comma, semicolon, colon) and as a foregrounding device (exclamation mark, dash, brackets). In (52), for example, Mackenzie uses the colon and semicolon to mark equivalents of major and minor tone group boundaries, while the exclamation mark after *he died* designates this as not just the final event of the series but its climax. In equivalent twentieth-century styles, the linking role of colon and semi-colon is likely to be replaced by *and* in the early century or paragraphing in the late century. Both techniques appear in (56) where the first three main clauses are linked together by and (*I picked . . . and went . . . and . . . the wind gusted*) and the next three by paragraph member-ship (*I shivered . . . winter*).

But although Mackenzie and Hill have solved the problem of marking linkage, the information deficit persists in that the *nature* of the links has to be inferred by the reader: are the actions of man and dog in (52) or woman and weather in (56) to be construed as parallel? sequential? or causally related? Hypotactic writing would specify, for instance, 'he stopped *although* we went on', '*because* I called, he wagged his tail'. If such connectives seem superfluous here it is because Mackenzie has adopted the principle of **iconic ordering**, in which the sequence of clauses reflects the posited sequence of events so that his text gives the impression of being a trans-parent window on a world. In hypotactic writing it is possible to vary clause order, since the explicit connective allows, for instance, a cause-and-effect sequence to be expressed either in iconic order (*because I called, he wagged his tail*) or non-iconic (*he wagged his tail because I called*). To the opponents of hypotaxis, its ability to avoid iconic ordering is part of its regrettable abstractness, the dislocation it permits between the order of language and the order of experience, or, as Pound puts it in (48b), its failure to make words 'cling close to things'. But the range of effects made available by iconic ordering is quite limited. Even in its most obvious manifestation, the event-to-event sequencing of linear narrative, it can never be continuous because information will always be required which it cannot accommodate. Hence Mackenzie's simple narrative has to be interrupted to incorporate background information about the gooseberry-bush (*that you may remember stood on the left side of the door; he was wont to bask in the sun there*). And as soon as iconic ordering is disrupted the relation between elements becomes vague or ambiguous. In (52) are we to infer that Trusty stops by the goose-berry bush *because* he 'was wont to bask in the sun there'? And how are we to construe the sequence in the middle paragraph of (56)? Does it mean: 'I shivered [because] the year had turned again'? or 'I shivered [and there-fore realised that] the year had turned again'?

Such limitations mean that iconic ordering is seldom in itself sufficient to give coherence even in a narrative sequence. In non-narrative genres, which do not lend themselves to iconic ordering, other solutions are needed to solve the problems of information deficit. For many modern writers, the most important replacement for connectives has been the device of lexical or structural **repetition**.

In eighteenth-century stylistics, repetition had been disfavoured, being regarded as a form of redundancy. Its status changed with the translation into English in 1787 of Lowth's *Lectures on the Sacred Poetry of the Hebrews*, which demonstrated the importance of repetition as a structural principle in the poetic books of the Bible (where, as discussed in 7.3.3, parallelism of syntax takes the place of metre). Wordsworth, taking up Lowth's point, singled out for particular praise a passage from the Song of Deborah (58) in which syntactic repetition is coupled with a high degree of lexical repetition. It is this combination that creates a sublime style from simple language:

(58)   At her feet he bowed, he fell, he lay down: at her feet, he bowed, he fell; where he bowed, there he fell down dead.

Such repetitions, he claims, are part of a natural rather than an artificial rhetoric because they are the outcome and index of feeling:

> an attempt is rarely made to communicate impassioned feelings without something of an accompanying consciousness of the inadequateness of our own powers, or the deficiencies of language. During such efforts there will be a craving in the mind, and as long as it is unsatisfied the speaker will cling to the same words, or words of the same character
>
> (Wordsworth 1800)

More recent commentators have also argued that repetition is the primary rhetorical device of spoken language. Tannen, for instance, takes it as the basis for her concept of 'a poetics of talk' (Tannen 1989: 36–97) and even the brief conversational extract of (3a) supports her analysis. The speaker organises his discourse by a strategy of incremental repetition and the repeated motifs give his speech both rhythm and emphasis: *it really is . . . I've really got it . . . got it to a T; there's no, there's no comparison*. As literature became increasingly oral in style, writers similarly turned to repetition as a structural and expressive resource. In paratactic sequences, it acts both as a mode of cohesion and a foregrounding device. In (51a), for instance, when hypotaxis breaks down, incremental repetition takes over, holding the paragraph together and sounding the keynotes of the feeling: *how oft . . . how oft . . . how often; in spirit . . . my spirit; turned to thee . . . turned to thee*. In (52), Mackenzie supplements iconic ordering with structural repetition, using the recurrent

'I [verb]ed-he [verb]ed' pattern to establish the man–dog relationship as an important theme of this episode. In (53), Macaulay combines structural with lexical repetition. The reiterated words emphasise the point that Johnson writes *nobody's language* and the structural parallelism ensures that all the juxtaposed relative clauses are interpreted in apposition to the first restrictive modifier, *learned*.

It is this mutual reinforcement of semantic, lexical, and structural repetition that makes Macaulay's style seem over-emphatic to many readers in the late twentieth century – a response that reflects a continuing trend through the period to prise them apart or play off one form of repetition against another. In (55), for instance, Hemingway uses a string of free modifiers, but their internal structure is markedly different; and where he repeats the base-form *walk*, he varies its morphology and its syntactic category (*was walking, walking, his walk*). In (56) the repetition is still further attenuated. Like the half-rhymes of modern poetry, Hill's recurrences are contrived to seem accidental: repetition of sound does not entail repetition of lexeme (*leaves/leaving*) and semantic repetition is concealed by formal variation: *the year had turned = it was winter*. Only one full repetition remains (*last/last*) to sound the theme that might prompt the reader to find the others.

7.4.4   The syntax of Modernism

In Modernism, the information deficit staved off or compensated for by these devices is foregrounded and the resulting disconnection thematised. In (59a), for example, Waugh exploits the fragmenting potential of Mackenzie's short-sentence narrative style: apart from the placing of the second sentence, the sequence seems arbitrary and the continual change of subject (five subjects in as many sentences) draws attention to the social dislocations which the novel describes. As (59b) shows, it requires very little adaptation to turn this style into the vehicle of absurdism.

(59)   a. She was out of bed and out of the room. Brittling followed. Miss Holloway collected the cheques and papers. The young man on the ladder dabbed away industriously. Josephine rolled to the head of the bed and stared up at him.   (Waugh 1938)

b. Snow in patches lay on the ground still. Pia wrapped cabbage leaves around chopped meat. She was still wearing her brown coat. Willie's cheque was still in the pocket. It was still Sunday.
(Barthelme 1968)

The difference is that whereas Waugh neither promotes nor blocks a reading in terms of coherent narrative, Barthelme does both. By using the temporal adverb *still*, he asks his reader to relate the events reported here to a past inception or a future change, and by repeating *still* in four of the five sentences, he encourages us to look for other similarities or connections between them. Yet neither 'snow' nor 'Sunday' has been mentioned in the narrative before and neither the weather nor the day of the week has anything to do with the 'brown coat' or 'Willie's check'.

The short-sentence style is radicalised in its form too, by the extensive use of elliptical constructions, verbless clauses, or phrases instead of clauses. Dickens opens *Bleak House* (1853) with a sequence of this kind, but its more widespread use is initiated by Joyce in *Ulysses*:

(60)   She folded the card into her untidy bag and snapped the catch.
         Same blue serge dress she had two years ago, the nap
         bleaching. Seen its best days. Wispish hair over her ears. And that
         dowdy toque, three old grapes to take the harm out of it. Shabby
         genteel. She used to be a tasty dresser. Lines round her mouth.
         Only a year or so older than Molly.   (Joyce 1922)

Verbless, phrase-based units such as these are highly characteristic of spoken discourse. As the discovery of Boswell's private papers has shown, the phrase rather than the clause was also the norm for self-addressed jottings at the start of our period. But before the twentieth century, such constructions appear only sporadically in published writing, usually as a marker of strong feeling in exclamative poetry or polemical prose, or in the naturalistic representation of colloquial speech in novels. And in one sense Joyce, like Mackenzie, works within the constraints he inherits, using a full sentence form for the framing narrative of the opening sentence in (60) and elliptical forms to characterise the mental speech of his protagonist. But by avoiding inverted commas, Joyce blurs the boundary between quotative and non-quotative components of his text, and by increasing the proportion of text given over to the character's variety he transfers to it many of the narrative functions of description and exposition. He thus paves the way for the phrase-unit to replace the clause-unit as the medium of narration itself, and for the associative leaps of a stream-of-consciousness to become the principle of connectivity. The use of a similar style in Modernist poetry seems designed to foreground its potential difficulties, baffling the reader's ability to reconstruct either syntax or message or the train of thought that might hold the parts together. Pound's *Papyrus*, for example, stands at the end of the Romantic fragment genre and pushes to an extreme the technique of Mackenzie's fragmenting style.

(61)   Spring . . .
         Too long . . .
         Gongula.   (Pound 1916)

Free modifiers were another modern practice that underwent radicalisation in Modernism. In the following example, Eliot exploits the fact that what a free modifier modifies has to be inferred by the reader:

(62)   Here are the years that walk between, bearing
         Away the fiddles and the flutes, restoring
         One who moves in the time between sleep and waking, wearing

         White light folded, sheathed about her, folded.   (Eliot 1930)

The verse structure here foregrounds the participial clauses that are acting as free modifiers (*bearing* . . . , *restoring* . . . , *wearing* . . .) and makes them appear to be structurally identical. But whereas the clauses headed by *bearing* and *restoring* both modify *the years that walk* in the main clause, the clause headed by *wearing* modifies *one who moves* in the immediately preceding clause, as readers belatedly discover in the last line, when they encounter *her* rather than 'them'. Eliot has set up what psycholinguists call a 'garden path' construction by combining – or confusing – two strategies of juxtapositional linkage which the nineteenth-century examples, (53) and (54), keep distinct. In Macaulay's appositional series, all appositives relate back to the same initial element, *a learned language*; in Dickens's series, each appositive relative relates to the noun phrase that immediately precedes it: *the Reverend Melchisedech Howler,* **who** . . . *ladies and gentlemen of the Ranting persuasion, upon* **whom** . . .

The following example further exposes the tenuous nature of juxtaposition as a connective principle by exploiting the structural similarity between an appositional series (whose items are semantically related) and a list (whose items are only contingently related):

(63)   I Tiresias, though blind, throbbing between two lives,
         Old man with wrinkled female breasts, can see
         At the violet hour, the evening hour that strives
         Homeward, and brings the sailor home from sea,
         The typist home at teatime, clears her breakfast, lights
         Her stove, and lays out food in tins.   (Eliot 1922)

This passage opens with a set of noun phrases that are clearly to be construed as appositional: *I/ Tiresias/ old man . . .* ; and closes with a set of verb phrases that are equally obviously intended as a list: *clears . . . , lights . . . , lays out . . .* In between are elements whose status is more ambiguous. Is *the evening hour* in apposition to the lexically similar *violet hour*, or is it the direct object of *can see?* Is *the typist home at teatime* in apposition to *the sailor home from the sea* (and thus to be interpreted as a literal gloss on a metaphorical expression) or is it a separate but parallel object of *brings?* Alternatively, is it the object not of *brings* but of *can see?* The plot of the poem (and the evidence of its manuscripts) suggests that the intended reading of this passage is probably 'I . . . can see . . . the typist [who] . . . clears her breakfast'; but this has to be sifted out from other possibilities encountered along the garden path.

The process of sifting is made more difficult by another feature of Modernist disconnective syntax, the omission of the relative pronoun linking *the typist* to the verbs of which it is the subject. This kind of construction occurs quite commonly in Early Modern English (e.g. *I have a brother ' is condemn'd to die; and get praise to him ' would take it in hand; the assent ' is given them is produced another way*), but it had pretty well been eliminated from formal written English by the eighteenth century's drive towards full and explicit constructions and by 1900 it was largely confined to THERE sentences in informal or non-Standard speech (e.g. *there was a bloke ' came in the pub last night; there's one thing ' bothers me*) (see Rissanen *CHEL* III forthcoming and Denison this volume 3.6.5.2). Its reintroduction into the syntax of twentieth-century poetry, which extends it well beyond its contemporary range, can be explained in a number of ways: as a hypercorrection towards colloquialism; as an archaism, a conscious echoing of Elizabethan usage; or as part of the deliberate courting of difficulty in Modernist aesthetics. Milroy, describing Hopkins's practice favours the first two explanations; Hamilton, describing Eliot and Auden, opts for the third (Milroy 1977: 114; Hamilton 1949: 46–8). In (63) the ambiguity of construction suits Eliot's theme, as outlined in his footnote to these lines: the first subject, *Tiresias*, imperceptibly slides into the second subject, *the typist*, in a movement corresponding to the way in which each character 'melts into' or 'is not wholly distinct from' the rest, and all are united in Tiresias. But in many examples in Auden the motivation is less clear. Hamilton cites (64), for instance, as 'wantonly obscure':

(64)   The song, the varied action of the blood
         Would drown the warning from the iron wood
         Would cancel the inertia of the buried

                                        (Auden 1930; in Hamilton 1949: 47–8)

Line 1 contains two noun phrases in apposition and it is tempting to read the two verb phrases of lines 2 and 3 as appositional also. But this tempting garden path leads to the semantic impasse of a self-contradiction in which *the song* both causes and cancels inertia. It is more likely that the verb phrase of line 3 should be taken as a relative clause modifying *the warning* of line 2, to give the reading: 'the song . . . would drown the warning [which] . . . would cancel the inertia'. What makes the misreading possible is the omission of the linking subject relative *which*; but what makes it almost inevitable is that the second two lines have parallel constructions and identical opening words. In other words, in (64) as in (62) and (59b), the principles of structural and lexical repetition, which in earlier writing compensated for the disconnections of juxtapositional syntax, have themselves been converted into instruments of confusion.

7.5   The problem of metaphor

7.5.1   Introduction

(65)   a. The Reader will find that personifications of abstract ideas rarely occur in these volumes; and, I hope, are utterly rejected as an ordinary device to elevate the style, and raise it above prose. I have proposed to myself to imitate, and, as far as is possible, to adopt the very language of men; and assuredly such personifications do not make any natural or regular part of that language   (Wordsworth 1802)

b. Don't use such an expression as 'dim lands of *peace*'. It dulls the image. It mixes an abstraction with the concrete. It comes from the writer's not realising that the natural object is always the *adequate* symbol   (Pound 1913)

Figurative language had occupied a problematic position in the stylistic repertoire of eighteenth-century writers, ever since it was branded as a language of falsehood by Locke, speaking for philosophy, Addison, speaking for literary criticism, and Sprat, speaking for the scientists of the Royal Society (see Adamson, *CHEL* III, forthcoming). **Metaphor** became the paradigm case of the problem: as the figure of speech that by definition involves talking about one referent or field of reference in terms of another (as *the lion roars* for *the king threatens*), it was seen as a perverse avoidance of plain, literal expressions. Wordsworth's Preface appears to open the door for its rehabilitation by setting up Poetry as the antithesis of

'Matter of Fact, or Science'; but the continued and increasing prestige of the natural sciences in the following two centuries put persistent pressure on literature to meet their criteria of empirical content and descriptive precision. Both Romantics and Modernists typically accept this demand. Wordsworth himself regards it as a claim of excellence that 'there is in these poems little falsehood of description' and this is echoed by Pound's emphasis on 'objectivity and again objectivity' in the representation of 'the natural object'. In their forms of description, therefore, both schools favour concrete and particular terms over abstractions. Both, however, distinguish the concrete particular of poetic discourse from the kind of literal factual description which Wordsworth satirises in *Peter Bell*:

(66)   A primrose by a river's brim
         A yellow primrose was to him,
         And it was nothing more.   (Wordsworth 1819)

For Wordsworth, as for Pound in (65b), the 'natural object' must be recognised as a 'symbol', the primrose must mean something more than the fact of its own existence.

These demands create a set of interlocking problems for the language of modern literature. How can the fictional be described so as to appear empirically real? How can empirical reality be described so as to acquire symbolic value? And how can symbolic description be made to appear a 'natural and regular part' of the 'very language of men'?

7.5.2   The pathetic fallacy

The 'personification of abstract ideas', which Wordsworth condemns in (65a), had become a dominant figure in eighteenth-century poetry largely because it minimises the falsification involved in metaphor: replacing *an old man* with *Age*, for example, can be seen as a form of generalisation rather than substitution. In the passage below, the personification of *Ease* and *Health* exemplifies the type of device that Wordsworth 'utterly rejected' in his predecessors:

(67)   And oft as EASE and HEALTH retire
         To breezy Lawn, or Forest deep,
         The Friend shall view yon whit'ning Spire,
         And 'mid the varied Landscape weep.   (Collins 1749)

And yet it is not difficult to find personifications in Wordsworth's own poetry. For example:

(68)   ... from behind that craggy Steep, till then
         The bound of the horizon, a huge Cliff,
         As if with voluntary power instinct,
         Uprear'd its head ...
                                                and still,
         With measur'd motion, like a living thing,
         Strode after me.
                                        (Wordsworth 1805)

In terms of linguistic strategy, the figurative expressions used in (68) and (67) are at first sight very similar. Both could be described as a breach of normal **selectional restrictions**, by which a verb that canonically co-occurs with human or animate subjects (e.g. *retire* in (67), *strode* in (68)) is put in construction with a non-animate subject, which is thereby re-interpreted as having animate attributes. There are two crucial differences, however. First, where Collins replaces the expected animate subject with an abstract noun (*Ease, Health*), Wordsworth opts for a concrete noun (*Cliff*). Second, although he uses capitalisation to highlight and endorse the cliff's personified status, he adds an epistemic hedge – *as if* – overtly acknowledging that a *huge Cliff... strode after me* should not be taken to imply actual 'voluntary power' in the natural object. The second difference is as important as the first. For the personification of a 'natural object' is quite common in eighteenth-century poetry, as in (69), for instance, where Pope combines a non-animate subject (*trees*) with a verb which normally selects an animate subject (*crowd*) and uses an animate adjective (*lagging*) to modify (and hence personify) the non-animate *wind*.

(69)   a. How could thy soul ...
            Outfly the nimble sail, and leave the lagging wind?
         b. Trees, where you sit, shall crowd into a shade
                                        (Pope; as quoted in Ruskin 1856)

These are the examples cited by Ruskin when comparing Pope unfavourably with his Romantic successors. What he objects to is that Pope has no adequate psychological motivation for deviating from plain description and without such justification, (69a) looks like an ornamental avoidance of more literal expressions (e.g. that the soul moved more quickly than the wind) and (69b) appears like 'simple falsehood, uttered by hypocrisy; definite absurdity, rooted in affectation, and coldly asserted in the teeth of nature and fact' (Ruskin [1856]: 216). By contrast, the falsification involved in (68) is justified by its psychological verisimilitude. Wordsworth's breach of selectional restrictions encodes a recategorisation of the world brought about by the transforming perspective of powerful feeling. The passage, that is, records a double perception: the past self (a child rowing across a lake in a stolen boat) sees the mountain move in pursuit of him; the qualifying *as if* interposes the perspective of the present, narrating self, who knows that the apparent movement resulted from the progressive change in the rower's angle of vision and that its apparent menace was the product of a guilty imagination.

It is this transformation of literal description under the influence of emotion that Ruskin names **the pathetic fallacy** (where *pathetic* means 'the product of feeling'). He diagnoses it as the dominant form of metaphor in the nineteenth century, and judges it to be a virtue or a vice on the plausibility of the transformed description and the strength of feeling that motivates it. An instance he particularly praises is from Tennyson's *Maud* (1855):

(70)　　　　　　For a great speculation had fail'd;
　　　And ever he mutter'd and madden'd, and ever wann'd with
　　　　　despair;
　　　And out he walk'd, when the wind like a broken worldling wail'd,
　　　And the flying gold of the ruin'd woodlands drove thro' the air.
　　　　　　　　　　　　　　(Tennyson; as quoted in Ruskin 1856)

The personification of the wind effected by *the wind . . . wail'd* is plausible both empirically (because the noise made by the wind can actually be mistaken for a human voice) and psychologically (because the speaker of the poem is thinking about his father's bankruptcy and suicide). Similarly the *flying gold* and *ruined woodland* of the second line are motivated empirically (leaves blown from the trees in autumn) and psychologically ('a great speculation had fail'd'). The modification to Wordsworth's technique (which makes (70) more typically Victorian than Romantic) is that the transforming perspective is attributed to a character within the poem rather than to the self of the poet. In part, this reflects a growing interest in entertaining alternative perspectives on experience (analogous to the use of alternative varieties described in 7.2). But also, like Wordsworth's epistemic hedge, it expresses a refusal to back the ontological claims of the metaphoric transfer. As Tennyson warns his reader, the poem's descriptions may represent the misperceptions of a morbid imagination.

The same could be said of *Mariana*, a key poem for later developments in the practice of metaphor:

(71)　　With blackest moss the flowerplots
　　　Were thickly crusted, one and all,

The rusted nails fell from the knots
  That held the peach to the gardenwall.
The broken sheds looked sad and strange,
  Unlifted was the clinking latch,
    Weeded and worn the ancient thatch
Upon the lonely moated grange.
    She only said 'My life is dreary,
      He cometh not,' she said;
    She said 'I am aweary, aweary;
      I would that I were dead!'   (Tennyson 1830)

As in (68) and (70), elements of the landscape carry human emotions: the *sheds* are described as *sad*, the *grange* as *lonely*; and, as in (68) and (70), these descriptions are given epistemic hedges, here by the choice of *looked* rather than *were* in line 5. But what (71) adds to previous examples is that many of the details – moss-encrusted flowerplots, rusted nails, weeded (i.e. weedy) thatch – are described as fully naturalistic concrete particulars, that is, without any breach of selectional restrictions. Instead, Tennyson sets up a semantic correspondence between the human terminology of the refrain *dreary/aweary/dead* and the non-human lexical set of the verse *rusted/broken/worn*, which may prompt us to read one as the reflection of the other. In this version of the pathetic fallacy, it is the reader who supplies the transforming perspective on the scene, by accepting the option to interpret the dilapidated garden as a symbol of Mariana's state.

7.5.3   *The synecdochic detail*

The description of a location (such as a grange) in terms of its component details (flower-plots, sheds, rusty nail, clinking latch) is a technique associated with the description of empirical reality in **documentary journalism** and **travel writing**. Both genres blossomed in the nineteenth century and their descriptive methods were widely adopted, especially in the novel, as a device of illusionism, a means of giving a fictional world the same solidity as places described in Murray's guidebooks or Mayhew's newspaper reports. In (72) below, for example, the greater elaboration of the noun phrases, compared with those in (71), provides the circumstantial detail that persuades us we could actually find the location described.

(72)   In such a neighbourhood, beyond Dockhead in the Borough of
       Southwark, stands Jacob's Island, surrounded by a muddy ditch,
       six or eight feet deep and fifteen or twenty wide when the tide is

in ... At such times, a stranger, looking from one of the wooden
bridges thrown across it at Mill-lane, will see ... Crazy wooden
galleries common to the backs of half-a-dozen houses, with
holes from which to look upon the slime beneath; windows
broken and patched, with poles thrust out on which to dry the
linen that is never there; rooms so small, so filthy, so confined,
that the air would seem too tainted even for the dirt and squalor
which they shelter ... dirt-besmeared walls and decaying
foundations; every repulsive lineament of poverty, every
loathsome indication of filth, rot, and garbage   (Dickens 1838)

But the description goes beyond what is needed for simple verisimilitude; as in *Mariana*, there is a semantic consonance in the description of the
concrete particulars that relates them all to the general conclusion
expressed in the abstract terms of the last phrases. Each one is a 'lineament
of poverty' or an 'indication of filth'. In this, they conform to Coleridge's
definition of the symbol:

(73)   *a sign included in the Idea, which it represents*: ex.gr. an actual *part*
         chosen to represent the *whole*, as a lip with a chin prominent is a
         Symbol of Man ... by which definition the Symbolical is
         distinguished *toto genere* from the Allegoric and Metaphorical
                                                          (Coleridge 1825)

Coleridge is here developing a strand of eighteenth-century thought which
saw **metonymy** as a more truthful and natural figure than metaphor.
Although both figures operate by talking about one referent in terms of
another, the displacing terms in metonymy are drawn from the same field
of reference, which means that the **vehicle** is more transparent to the
tenor (as when *king* is figured by the metonymic *palace* rather than the meta-
phorical/allegorical *lion*). Furthermore, many of the relations on which
metonymic transfer is founded (such as cause and effect, container and
contained, act and agent, object and attributes) represent the natural
association of ideas recognised in Hartleyan psychology and this in turn is
because they represent the relations in which objects are encountered in
experience (as opposed to the abstract resemblances on which metaphor
depends). **Synecdoche**, the figure described by Coleridge and the only one
of the metonymic relations distinguished by a special title, is a particularly
powerful form of the figure since 'the name of a *part* of a thing will suggest
the idea of the *whole* with greater clearness and strength than the name of
the whole itself' and the specific instance has greater impact than the

'general and comprehensive term' it exemplifies (Priestley 1777: 233). The illustration Priestley offers – *give us this day our daily bread* – is particularly interesting since, like the description of the rusted nails in (71) or the broken windows in (72), the form of words contains no breach of selectional restrictions (unlike synecdoches such as *the hands threatened to mutiny; the strings came in late*) so that the form of the figurative matches the form of the literal. The result is to turn synecdoche into a figure of interpretation rather than a figure of speech: the reader must choose to read the request for bread as a general request for providential aid.

The task of the writer, then, is to encourage the interpretative act by which a concrete detail is read as synecdochic and hence symbolic. In nineteenth-century writing, this is typically done by foregrounding one detail through repetition or, as in (71) and (72), by accumulating details and foregrounding the semantic consonances between them. Often the 'general and comprehensive term' is also present in the text (like *poverty* in (72)) and often the relation between the two is somewhere made explicit, as in (74) below, where Maria Bertram, inspecting the estate of her future husband, remarks:

(74)   But unluckily that iron gate, that Ha, Ha, give me a feeling of
         restraint and hardship. I cannot get out, as the starling said.

                                                              (Austen 1814)

The gate and ha-ha act as a double synecdoche: they stand for the whole estate of Sotherton (of which they are a part and which Maria will acquire on her marriage) and they are instances of a state of 'restraint', which is what Maria fears her marriage will entail.

Those who continue the symbolist-realist tradition in the twentieth century are less likely to offer such explicit guidance. In Orwell's *A Hanging* (1931), for instance, the superintendent's stick acquires a complex symbolic status, but it does so *only* by being brought recurrently to the foreground of the narrative (Lodge 1977: 108, 113–4). But in much twentieth-century writing, the nineteenth-century synthesis of realist concrete detail and symbolic value breaks apart, with symbolist writers moving away from metonymy towards metaphor and realist writers describing component details in such a way that they refuse to act as synecdoches, as in (75):

(75)   Not till about
         One-twenty on the sunlit Saturday
         Did my three-quarters-empty train pull out,
         All windows down, all cushions hot, all sense
         Of being in a hurry gone.   (Larkin 1964)

Here Larkin rejects the expectations of the *Mariana* tradition. The details serve *only* the function of realism; each one seems too specific to be symbolic (*one-twenty, three-quarters-empty*) and (unlike (72)) no common semantic feature links them to each other or to the abstract terms with which the series concludes. Larkin's message seems to be that the one-twenty on Saturday was a train to him and it was nothing more. In (76) O'Hara also resists general symbolism, but in this case by returning the synecdochic detail to its psychological origins in the contingent associations of private experience. What gives the details of (76) coherence and meaning is that they are what 'I' happened to be doing on the day he learned the news of Billie Holiday's death. Hence the poem's title: *The Day Lady Died.*

(76)   and for Mike I just stroll into the PARK LANE
        Liquor Store and ask for a bottle of Strega and
        then I go back where I came from to 6th Avenue
        and the tobacconist in the Ziegfeld Theatre and
        casually ask for a carton of Gauloises and a carton
        of Picayunes, and a NEW YORK POST with her face on it

                                          (O'Hara 1964)

7.5.4   *Metaphor in Modernism*

By the end of the nineteenth century, the pathetic fallacy had, like personification at the end of the previous century, become associated with stock and stigmatised forms. The one Pound attacks in (65b) is the equative *of*, which arbitrarily couples the natural object noun (*lands*) with a noun denoting its symbolic value (*peace*). This construction is widespread in the nineteenth century, from Wordsworth's *fields of sleep* through Arnold's *sea of faith* and *sea of life*, and continues into the early twentieth with Lawrence's *ship of death*, Yeats's *rag and bone shop of the heart* and Auden's *seas of pity* and *ranches of isolation*. The **transferred epithet** (such as *ruined woodlands* in (70), *sad . . . sheds, lonely . . . grange* in (71)), became equally notorious, being used promiscuously (like Harvey's Sauce according to Lewis Carroll), and without meeting Ruskin's criterion that the transfer should be empirically and psychologically plausible.

In Modernist writing, by conscious contrast, adjectives are few and those there are tend to be simply visual. This tendency is most strongly developed in **Imagism**, a movement that sought, as Pound indicates in (65b), to represent natural objects without appearing to predetermine their symbolic status. For example:

(77)   so much depends
          upon

          a red wheel
          barrow

          glazed with rain
          water

          beside the white
          chickens   (Williams 1923)

Williams's wheelbarrow is, like Tennyson's sheds in (71), an ordinary object.
But instead of employing transferred epithets to invest it with 'pathetic' significance, Williams simply informs his readers that it *has* significance (*so
much depends on . . .*) and leaves them to infer what that might be. Colour
adjectives represent it as a visual percept rather than an object reclassified
by conception and the perceiver is uncharacterised (unlike Wordsworth's
guilty child in (68) or Tennyson's grieving Mariana in (71)). We can read it
as a synecdochic detail, but are given no help in deciding what it might be
a part or an instance of. As with the *objets trouvés* of Post-Impressionist art,
the symbolic status of the object rests only on its deracination from any
context of use; grammatically there is no figurative transformation at all,
apart from the use of *glazed* to hint at the analogy with painted objects. But
the typography compensates for this. Whatever the metrical function of
Williams's lineation (see 7.3.5 above), in the poetic tradition that descends
from Williams it plays a crucial role in realigning the components of a sentence and a scene, encouraging a symbolic reading of what could otherwise
be taken as a literal description. The symbolic status of Wordsworth's primrose could be similarly established by re-lineating (66):

          A primrose
          by

          a river
          's brim

          a yellow
          prim

          rose was
          to him

   In another influential example of Imagist technique, Pound creates the
symbol by juxtaposition:

(78)   The apparition   of these faces   in the crowd:
          Petals   on a wet, black   bough.   (Pound 1913)

Compared with *Papyrus* (61), the elliptical forms here seem designed not to baffle but to draw readers into the process of creating a metaphor, tempting them to supply an equative link between the lines and to infer both the grounds and the significance of the equation. But apart from the word-spacing, there is no attempt to transform the natural objects (faces or petals) by linguistic deviation in the form of their description.

But Pound has not merely rejected the grammatical basis of the pathetic fallacy, he has also, if (78) is read as a metaphor, reversed the direction of transfer. Where the pathetic fallacy predicates human properties of non-human objects, in (78) faces become petals in a metaphor that dehumanises the human. This rejection or reversal of pathetic fallacy also occurs in cases where writers retain its technique of breaking selectional restrictions, for example:

(79)   a. My self-possession gutters   (Eliot 1917)

         b. The force that through the green fuse drives the flower
                                                        (Dylan Thomas 1933)

         c. The glacier knocks in the cupboard   (Auden 1937)

(79a) and (b) oppose pathetic fallacy very ostentatiously, (a) by a *de*-humanising construction that transfers properties from the anticipated subject of *gutters* (a candle? small fire?) on to *my self-possession* and (b) by selecting a Wordsworthian natural object, *the flower*, but re-categorising it in terms drawn from the field of technology (the flower here *explodes* into bloom). (79c) retains the form of an animising metaphor – a natural object noun in construction with a verb that normally takes a human subject – but the result is not pathetic fallacy but surrealism because it cannot be construed in terms of any plausible real-world scenario.

7.5.5   *Colloquial figures 1: simile*

The problem of how to reconcile figurative language with plain fact is paralleled by the problem of how to reconcile it with plain speech. One way of addressing both problems at once is to use **simile** rather than metaphor. In many accounts, metaphor is defined as an elliptical simile so that (79a), for instance, is said to be equivalent to 'my self-possession is like a guttering candle'. The difference is that the simile version involves no breach of syntactic norms and presents no bar to literal construal. As Davidson puts it 'most metaphorical sentences are patently false just as all similes are trivially true' (Davidson 1984: 258). Similes therefore protect the truth claims of figurative language and it's noticeable that in (68) and (70) both Wordsworth and Tennyson use simile to accompany the metaphor and make its comparative basis explicit (*like a living thing, like a . . . wordling*). At the same time, the simile formula – *A is like B* – foregrounds the transition from one field of reference to another and so converts metaphor from a poetic product into a psychological process (seeing a likeness) and a kind of speech act (which can be made explicit, as it is by Browning in 'I liken his Grace to an acorned hog'). The differences between metaphor and simile are strikingly demonstrated in (80), where Byron opens with a complex metaphor in the first line and then explicates it in a series of similes.

(80)   The evaporation of a joyous day
       Is like the last glass of champagne, without
       The foam . . .
       Or like a system coupled with a doubt;
       Or like a soda bottle when its spray
       Has sparkled and let half its spirit out;
       Or like a billow left by storms behind . . .
       Or like an opiate which brings troubled rest,
       Or none; or like – like nothing that I know
       Except itself; – such is the human breast;
       A thing, of which similitudes can show
       No real likeness   (Byron 1824)

At one level, this passage expresses the positivist assumption that figurative language can tell us nothing about the world of things. At another level, it justifies the activity of making 'similitudes' as an index of the creative energy of the mind that produces them. The (apparently) spontaneous attempts to find a satisfactory analogue make the metaphorical formulation of the first line (in which vehicle and tenor are syntactically fused) appear over-crafted, or, in Wordsworth's terms, a mere 'device to elevate the style and raise it above prose'.

It is not surprising, then, that simile very often takes the place of metaphor in consciously realist prose and anti-poetic poetry. In writers of the 1930s, for example, highly elaborated or surprising similes are counterpointed with the careful descriptivism of documentary (81a) or novel (b) or the abstract terms of political debate (c):

(81)   a. Cellarshops where the lamps burn all day, under the shadow of topheavy balconied facades, dirty plaster frontages embossed with scroll-work and heraldic devices. The whole district is like this: street leading into street of houses *like monumental safes crammed with the tarnished valuables and second-hand furniture of a bankrupt middle class.* (Isherwood 1939; in Lodge 1977: 199–200)

b. Congratulate me, he seemed to be saying, and his humorous friendly shifty eyes raked her *like the headlamps of a second-hand car which had been painted and polished to deceive.*

(Greene 1935; in Lodge 1977: 201)

c. When there is a gap between one's real and one's declared aims, one turns as it were instinctively to long words and exhausted idioms, *like a cuttlefish squirting out ink.*

(Orwell 1946)

What is particularly striking in (81c) is that Orwell's metaphor (*exhausted idioms*) is itself an exhausted idiom, whereas his concluding simile is individual and inventive. This generalises into a pattern for his whole essay: the metaphors are usually conventional (e.g. *stale phrases, debased language, worn-out metaphors*) and the similes always creative (e.g. *like the sections of a pre-fabricated hen-house, like cavalry horses answering the bugle, like tea-leaves blocking a sink*).

The influence of Orwell was strong on the Movement writers and may help to account for the prominence given to simile in their work. When Larkin, for example, wishes to modulate from the matter-of-fact realism of (75) to a Wordsworthian intimation of something beyond the facts, he concludes with a simile rather than a metaphor:

(82)   We slowed again,
And as the tightened brakes took hold, there swelled
A sense of falling, *like an arrow-shower*
Sent out of sight, somewhere becoming rain   (Larkin 1964)

But in this instance, the surprising and inexplicable nature of the comparison links Larkin with the Modernists and their Postmodernist descendants, in whom Byron's use of simile as the index of speaker creativity is radicalised:

(83)   a.   Let us go then, you and I,
When the evening is spread out against the sky
Like a patient etherised upon a table   (Eliot 1915)

> b. The creek was *like 12,845 telephone booths in a row with high Victorian ceilings and all the doors taken off and all the backs of the booths knocked out.* (Brautigan 1972; in Lodge 1977: 236)

In the light of the text that follows it, (83a) can be read as another instance of psychologically explicable pathetic fallacy (the speaker projects onto the landscape his fears of being socially dissected). But compared with Tennyson in (70), Eliot both postpones his explanation and reduces the empirical resemblance on which his metaphoric transfer rests: alongside 'the wind is like a wailing worldling', the claim that 'the evening is like a spreadeagled patient' may appear surreal or perverse. (83b) intends to appear nothing else. It could have been written to illustrate Davidson's point that similes are only trivially true because anything can be likened to anything. Rather than conferring symbolic status on the natural object (the creek) it stands as a celebration of its own inventiveness – or a satire on the simile as a figure of speech.

7.5.6 Colloquial figures 2: the cliché-metaphor

If simile has often been used as the marker of colloquial creativity, the opposite effect seems at first sight to be the aim of an even more widely used device, the cliché-metaphor. The word *cliché* itself was borrowed from the specialist vocabulary of printing in the 1890s as a pejorative term for a predictable collocation whose use implies lack of originality or independent thought in the user. A preference for cliché was associated with 'journalese' in writing and the 'lowbrow' in conversation, and one continuing use of cliché in literature has been as a register marker for the (usually satiric) representation of those varieties. But it has had a more complex and far-reaching role in twentieth-century texts than such an account would imply. Even in the 1890s, Wilde, acting as spokesman for aestheticism, distanced himself from what the aesthetes saw as the banality of ordinary usage not by avoiding cliché but by producing variations on it, so that the cliché, as in (84), becomes both the butt and the mechanism of the wit:

(84)   a. [of a woman flirting with her own husband] It is simply washing one's clean linen in public.
   b. [of a woman recently widowed] I hear her hair has turned quite gold from grief.
   c. in married life three is company and two none.   (Wilde 1899)

What makes cliché relevant to the problem of reconciling metaphor with a colloquial poetics is that many clichés are in fact metaphors (e.g. *to wash dirty linen in public, to stretch a point, to catch a cold, the ivory tower, the grass roots, food for thought*) but unlike 'personifications of abstract ideas', they assuredly do form a natural and regular part of colloquial language and so carry no taint of poetese. Their disadvantage is that they have been so regularly used that they have all to varying degrees undergone semantic bleaching. One definition offered for cliché in general is 'the supersedure of meaning by function' (Zijderveld 1979) and in ordinary conversation the cliché-metaphor typically conveys a message without drawing attention to the non literal status of its form of expression, becoming what another cliché-metaphor calls a **dead metaphor**. To make use of the resources of dead metaphor a writer will therefore need techniques for resuscitating some element of the original meaning.

Varying its form of words, as Wilde does in (84a), is one such technique; another is repetition, as in (85):

(85)   . . . Please, will you
          Give us a light?
          Light
          Light   (Eliot 1931)

The first lines of this group – initially construed as a request for a match or the use of a cigarette lighter – represent what Eliot sees as the automated language of routine activities and lower class speakers; and the metaphorisation of *light* to mean 'a source of ignition' instead of 'a source of illumination' is very old and very dead indeed. But the effect of repetition is to take the cliché out of its functional context, revive the original meaning of *light*, and retrospectively endow the request with a metaphysical significance grounded in traditional Christian metaphors (such as the *Light of the World; lighten our darkness, O Lord*). Eliot has created a kind of pun across demotic and religious varieties and in the process revitalised the formulaic language of both.

A third common procedure is to collocate clichés. Even in ordinary speech, this has the power to revive their metaphorical force, sometimes creating humorous effects unintended by the speaker (e.g. *I smell a rat . . . but I'll nip him in the bud; we must grasp the nettle and bite the bullet*). In literature, too, collocating clichés is a common device of comedy. But it can be used to produce effects that are not simply comic:

(86)   Practice dwindling. A mighthavebeen. Losing heart. Gambling.
         Debts of honour. Reaping the whirlwind. Used to get good
         retainers from D. and T. Fitzgerald. Their wigs to show their grey

matter. Brains on their sleeve like the statue in Glasnevin . . .
Funny the way these newspaper men veer about when they get
wind of a new opening. Weathercocks. Hot and cold in the same
breath . . . Go for one another baldheaded in the papers and then
all blows over. Hailfellow well met the next moment.

(Joyce 1922)

Here Joyce represents the stream-of-consciousness of his 'ordinary' hero,
Bloom, as a stream of clichés. But unlike (84) or (85) the effect is not to
stigmatise or satirise this class of speaker or this form of language. The
passage seems rather to demonstrate (as Freud did in contemporary
psychological theory) that cliché promotes as well as inhibits thought and
that the ordinary mind in the process of thinking puns effortlessly – and
creatively – across functional, metaphorical, and literal meanings. For
example, *reaping the whirlwind* initiates a whole series of wind metaphors (*get
wind of, weathercocks, [blow] hot and cold, all blows over*); the phrase *grey matter* sits
between *wigs* and *brains*, and is poised between literal and metaphorical
applications to each; and the mention of *wigs* triggers the use of the cliché-
metaphor *baldheaded* later in the paragraph, while simultaneously preparing
the reader to see its (comic) literal potential.

In later twentieth-century texts there is less use of variation, repetition,
and collocation to foreground the double-valued cliché. Perhaps because
punning across the different meanings of a cliché has become a well-established feature of the language of journalism and advertising, writers seem
to rely more on the reader's power to recognise a cliché from its form of
words and to determine from the context of use which of its meanings
apply (functional, literal, metaphorical or all three).

(87)   a. Quietly they wade the disturbed shore;
          Gather the dead as the first dead scrape home

       b. Naked, as if for swimming, the martyr
          Catches his death in a little flutter
          Of plain arrows   (Geoffrey Hill 1959; in Ricks 1984: 362–3)

In (87a), Hill invites us first to reject the conventional meaning of the
cliché *scrape home* ('achieve a narrow victory') in favour of a more literal
sense (in which corpses rasp on the beach as they're pulled ashore) but
then to re-evaluate that decision (maybe the dead *have* achieved some kind
of victory?). In (b) *catch his death* (conventionally meaning 'get a severe
cold') shows a double shift: we realise first that a literal interpretation of
death is appropriate and then that *catch* can be a purposive action (just as

some martyrs' deaths are not so much passively suffered as actively pursued).

What we see in the sequence from (84) to (87) is evidence of a progressive upward revaluation of cliché-metaphor in the literature of the twentieth century. Among commentators on cliché, too, the hostility of early and mid-century accounts (such as Partridge 1940, Orwell 1946) has given way to more sympathetic studies in cognitive linguistics (Lakoff & Johnson 1980) and literary criticism (McLuhan 1970, Ricks 1984: 356–68). One of the turning-points for both theory and practice was Davie's *Purity of Diction in English Poetry* (1952). In what became a manifesto statement for the Movement group of writers, Davie, like Wordsworth and Pound before him, addresses the problem of metaphor and argues that the *restraint* of metaphor is the key to achieving a style which maintains both the continuities of the literary tradition and the common-ground between literature and 'the very language of men'. While the attempt to reform metaphor by conscious innovation produces deviant language and difficult literature, a writer can preserve and promote 'purity of diction' (in literary and non-literary usage alike) by making readers recognise – and re-cognise – new meanings in old metaphors, or even old meanings that have become overlaid or overlooked.

7.6   Self-expression and self-representation

7.6.1   *Introduction*

(88)   a. . . . here must I remain   (Coleridge 1800)
        b.   I am here
              Or there, or elsewhere.   (Eliot 1943)

In what remains the standard account of the Romantic revolution, Abrams (1953) uses the difference between a mirror and a lamp as a metaphor for the change in poetic orientation that took place at the end of the eighteenth century, when a predominantly mimetic theory (in which poetry, like a mirror, reflects the external world) gave way to a predominantly expressive theory (in which, like a lamp, it projects the poet's inner self). Coleridge encapsulated this idea in a pair of terms that his influence made central to subsequent debate when he drew a distinction between 'the *objective* poetry of the ancients and the *subjective* mood of the moderns' (Abrams 1953: 235–244,375). One effect of the deepening subjective mood in modern literature has been to shift the balance in its use of subjective and objective forms of language.

In one sense, all forms of language are subjective. Apart from fixed formulae, any set of words is chosen and any choice of words is influenced by, and therefore expresses, its speaker's attitudes, beliefs or social identity (as in the difference between calling a building a *house* or a *habitation*). But the expressions that are subjective in the technical sense intended here are those whose definition requires mention of the **sujet de l'énonciation** or **locutionary agent** (the *I* of the current speech-act). Considered in this light, *house, habitation*, and even *bijou residence*, are all objective by comparison to *here* (defined by the *OED* as 'the place where the person speaking is'). Primary members of the subjective class are **deictic**, **epistemic**, and **emotive** expressions. **Deictics** describe objects/events in terms of their spatio-temporal relation to the person speaking (e.g. *here, yonder, this, in front, come, bring, now, ago, tomorrow, soon*); **epistemics** express their speaker's current state of knowledge (in adverbs such as *perhaps* or *probably* and modal auxiliaries such as *may* or *might*); **emotive** terms include exclamative constructions, interjections (*oh, alas, damn*), and affective and evaluative adjectives (*charming, hideous, dear*). (In table 7.1, subjective language is represented by items 20–1, 24–6, 30, 32–3, 36.)

During the eighteenth century, an objectivising, generalising style had become the goal in most forms of public discourse, prompting writers to look for ways of eliminating, minimising or conventionalising the use of subjective features. In scientific writing, for instance, the impulse towards objective description led to the gradual emergence of the passive, which linguistically emancipates an experiment from its author's personal experience (by converting, for instance, 'I saw the liquid boil' to 'the liquid was seen to boil'). The equivalent impulse in literature shapes the language of poems such as the *Ode occasion'd by the death of Mr Thomson* (1749), in which Collins gives public expression to his private grief by generalising his feelings into personified abstractions, such as *Pity* and *Remembrance*, and by objectifying himself into 'he whose heart in sorrow bleeds' or 'the friend' (as in (67) above).

While the following two centuries largely continued the objectivising trend for scientific discourse, the Romantics' insistence on an absolute genre division between 'Poetry and Matter of Fact, or Science' (Wordsworth [1802]: 69) promoted a different line of development for literature. A notable feature of the period since 1776 is the emergence of genres and styles that use subjective elements of language in novel or heightened ways.

7.6.2   The language of affect: interjections and affective adjectives

Interjections such as *oh* or *ah* are the purest type of expressive language, having no referential content at all. Regarded by eighteenth-century linguistic philosophers as the most basic and universal part of speech, 'VOICES OF NATURE, rather than Voices of *Art*, expressing those Passions and natural Emotions, which spontaneously arise in the human Soul' (Harris 1771: 290), the interjection was bound to become stylistically salient when poetry was re-defined as 'the spontaneous overflow of powerful feelings'. Hence Wordsworth's choice of *oh!* to mark the moment when natural passion breaks through the rational artifice of the periodic sentence in (51a). Blake's use of *ah* in (89) is even more radical.

(89)   Ah Sun-flower! weary of time,
         Who countest the steps of the Sun   (Blake 1794)

The poem prolongs the postmodification of *sun-flower* for a further six lines, in a manner typical of periodic construction (see 7.4.1). But in breach of the expectations it creates, there is no culminating main verb and no proposition is made. In a sense, all that is predicated of the sun-flower is the emotion it evokes, expressed in the opening *ah*, which here illustrates Ward's claim that an interjection may be 'equivalent to a full sentence . . . either of the indicative or the imperative or the optative mood' (Ward 1765: 445).

In pre-Romantic literary tradition, a vocative *O* (collocated with a following noun phrase) had been borrowed from Latin in early Middle English and had been frequent since the Renaissance in poetry that echoed the forms of classical apostrophe; but free-standing exclamatory *O* (increasingly differentiated by the spelling <oh> had been more commonly associated with the discourse of religious enthusiasm, where it typically signalled the sudden advent of either remorse or revelation. Both in syntax and in function the latter provides the more important precedent for the Romantic use of interjection. As witness Southey's gibe at the 'throbs and throes and ahs and ohs' of evangelical preaching, religious exclamation was revitalised in the Romantic period and religious connotations colour many poetic examples, including the opening line of *The Prelude*:

(90)   *Oh* there is *blessing* in this gentle breeze   (Wordsworth 1805)

This line also illustrates how the interjection extended its genre range, taking in not only lyric poetry (traditionally an expressive genre) but epic (traditionally descriptive and narrative). Where Milton began *Paradise Lost* with a statement of its topic 'Of man's first disobedience', Wordsworth announces the more subjective orientation of his rival epic by opening with *Oh*, thus grounding the poem in a representation of the sound of its author's voice and in the emotion of which that sound is the index. In prose genres, too, the interjection extends its range, passing from dialogue to narrative in the novel and from essay to biography and history in non-fictional prose. And in both prose and poetry, as the interjection increases in frequency and diffuses across genres, it generalises into a wider exclamative modality. This may take the form of chained exclamative constructions as in (94a–b) or, as in (95a–b), the exclamation mark may be used to create nonce exclamatives out of declaratives or noun phrases, thereby pressing canonically propositional and referential structures into the service of the emotive function of language.

(91)   a. What melancholy charm steals o'er mind!
          What hallow'd tears the rising rapture greet!

                                         (Radcliffe 1791)

    b. *How* they shone! moving like fine-broken starlight through the purple leaves. How they shone!   (Ruskin 1889; original italics)

(92)   a. And yet at bottom it is not the King dying, but the Man!

                                          (Carlyle 1837)

    b. Span of youth! Ever-pushed elasticity! Manhood balanced and florid and full!
       My lovers suffocate me!   (Whitman 1855)

Affective adjectives (e.g. *ugly*, *darling*, *atrocious*) form a semantically distinct subset of their word class. Although like descriptive adjectives (such as *black*, *square*, *wooden*) they may appear as premodifiers or complements of a noun (*a **darling** child*, *the house is **ugly***), they do not convey information about the inherent properties of the object being referred to, such as its shape (*square*), colour (*black*), or material (*wooden*); instead, they express the response it evokes in the speaker, whether aesthetic (*ugly*) or emotional (*darling*). Historically, the set of affective adjectives has been gradually enlarged by the **subjectivisation** of descriptive adjectives (such as *horrid*, which originally meant 'bristling') and there is some evidence to suggest that this process was particularly active – or particularly salient – at the end of the eighteenth century. In *Northanger Abbey*, for instance, Austen correctly notes that *nice*, commonly used in the early eighteenth century to mean 'precise' or 'fastidious', had subjectivised to acquire the affective sense 'pleasing to me'. Austen herself uses this modern sense in her correspondence, welcoming 'a nice long letter' and admiring 'a nice-looking woman', but in *Northanger Abbey* through the ironic voice of Henry Tilney she expresses the conservative view that she associates with disciples of Johnson and Blair:

(93)   'But now, really, do you not think *Udolpho* the nicest book in the world?' . . . 'Very true,' said Henry, 'and this is a very nice day, and we are taking a very nice walk, and you are two very nice young ladies. Oh! it is a very nice word indeed! – it does for every thing. Originally perhaps it was applied only to express neatness, propriety, delicacy, or refinement; – people were nice in their dress, in their sentiments, or their choice. But now every commendation on every subject is comprised in that one word.'

                                                                        (Austen 1818)

In the larger discussion in which this exchange is embedded Austen seems to suggest that the subjectivisation of such popular eighteenth-century colloquialisms as *nice* and *amazingly* is parallel to (or even promoted by) the increased currency of affective language in contemporary literature. Specifically, she draws attention to the prominent role played by the more sensational members of the *nice* class (such as *shocking, horrible, dreadful*) in the genre of **Gothic fiction**. The following paragraph of *The Mysteries of Udolpho* typifies the style, with Radcliffe combining *tremendous, dreadful*, and *awful* to convey the affective power of a landscape whose actual properties are concealed by darkness and distance:

(94)   But soon, even this light faded fast, and the scenery assumed a more *tremendous* appearance, invested with the obscurity of twilight . . . and the vale, which far, far below had opened its *dreadful* chasm, the eye could not longer fathom. A melancholy gleam still lingered on the summits of the highest Alps . . . seeming to make the stillness of the hour more *awful*.

                                                                        (Radcliffe 1794)

In Romantic poetry, too, affective adjectives provided an important resource for those conscious of a discrepancy between subjective response and objective evidence, especially if they shared Hazlitt's view that a poet's primary duty is to represent not the object in itself but 'the impression which the object under the influence of passion makes on the mind' (cited Prynne 1988: 137). In some cases affect is the *only* property predicated of the external world, as in (95), where the inverted word order draws attention to this fact:

(95)   a. Ah! close the scene, – ah! close – for *dreadful* is the sight.

                                                                        (Coleridge 1790/1834)

b. *Fair* are the woods and *beauteous* is the spot

(Wordsworth 1805)

c. *sweet* is the night air! (Arnold 1867)

As one index of the new prominence of affective adjectives in Romantic poetry, we may note that, on figures derived from the *English Poetry Database*, whereas Keats uses *sweet* 250 times in 151 poems and Shelley uses it 444 times in 312 poems, Pope's 304 poems contain only 86 instances, none of them involving a construction like (95c).

7.6.3 *Subjective time: present progressive and present perfect*

Since tense is a deictic category, the expression of time is always in some sense subjective. But during the course of the eighteenth century the development and codification of the modern aspectual system made it possible to choose between more and less speaker-oriented forms. By 1776 the contrast between progressive and simple verb forms had been grammaticalised (see Denison, this volume) and grammarians of the period recognise a distinction in the present tense between the simple present (e.g. *he walks*) as the appropriate form of 'gnomologic' propositions or habitual events and the progressive present (e.g. *he is walking*) as the form oriented to the 'real now' of current experience or current speech (Harris 1771: 124–5; Pickbourn 1789: 20–7). Poets of the generation immediately preceding the Romantics make very little use of this contrast, either because the progressive was still regarded as too colloquial for poetic use or because eighteenth-century poetics favoured the representation of typical scenes and general truths, for which the simple present was the more appropriate form. Romantic poets, by contrast, embraced both colloquial diction and immediate personal experience and there was a corresponding leap in the incidence of present progressives. Whereas Thomson uses the present progressive once in 11,487 lines and Collins not at all, the ratio for Wordsworth is 1 per 150 lines and for Coleridge 1 : 154, rising in the next generation to 1 : 115 for Keats and 1 : 89 for Shelley (Wright 1974: 576). However, the extra syllables of the progressive, compared to the simple present, make it more awkward to handle in many metrical patterns, and it is always less common in verse than in prose. For the nineteenth century, at least, the progressive remains very much the marked form of the pair, occurring typically at structurally salient points (openings, transitions, conclusions) or in local contrast with the simple present to mark moments of enhanced experiential intensity. In Wordsworth's *The Solitary Reaper*, for example, the simple present is used to catalogue the girl's activities (*cuts, binds, sings*), giving way to the progressive (*is overflowing*) after the interjection that marks the transition from percept to affect, from matter of fact to matter of experience.

(96)   Alone she *cuts*, and *binds* the grain,
        And *sings* a melancholy strain;
        O listen! for the Vale profound
        Is overflowing with the sound   (Wordsworth 1807)

A similar option was available in the expression of past time by the contrast between simple past (e.g. *he walked*) and present perfect (e.g. *he has walked*). Not fully systematised in 1600, this opposition had become established by the end of the eighteenth century and was described by the period's grammarians in essentially modern terms. Functionally, the simple past was recognised as the canonical tense of history; it places events within a neutral chronological record. In Brittain's account (Brittain 1788: 101), it is 'narrative', whereas the present perfect is 'assertive', centred on the speaker rather than the event and, as Murray puts it, conveying 'an allusion to the present time' (Murray 1795: 42–3). For this reason, the present perfect is the tense of *memory* rather than the tense of record and is used by Romantic writers to express 'the affective presence of past experience' (Boyd & Boyd 1977: 6). Its contrast in meaning with the simple past is exploited in (97):

(97)   O Wedding-guest! this soul *hath been*
        Alone on a wide wide sea:
        So lonely '*twas*, that God himself
        Scarce *seeméd* there to be   (Coleridge 1798)

All the verbs here (*hath been, was, seemed*) refer to the same time and event in the past, but the use of the present perfect for the first of them intimates that 'this soul' is still in the grip of the isolating experiences it has undergone. The speaker is reporting not only a past event but also a current existential condition and its continuing affective power is confirmed, as in (96), by the collocation of the subject-oriented aspect with an explicit interjection.

Although there are signs that the aspectual values associated with the progressive and perfect may be shifting or being eroded in the present century (see Adamson forthcoming; Denison this volume), the expressive contrasts represented by (96) and (97) are still operative for many twentieth-century writers. In (98), for example, which continues the text given in

(76), O'Hara switches from the simple present of catalogued activities –
the *I stroll, ask, go back, ask* of (76) – to the present progressive of experiential immediacy as the poem finally records his reaction to the news of
Billie Holiday's death.

(98)   and I *am sweating* a lot by now and thinking of
           leaning on the john door in the 5 SPOT
           while she whispered a song along the keyboard   (O'Hara 1964)

In (99) Pound draws on the present perfect as part of a complex temporal
layering which contrasts the eternal present of a story (which 'ends' but can
always be repeated), the real-life existence of its protagonists (whose
actions – *won, stole, kept* – are now over and fixed in a definite historical past
that is cut off from the present), and his own attempts to relive the lost past,
now themselves past, but alive in his memory as an affect and a kind of
achievement.

(99)   I *have seen* the ruind 'Dorata' . . .
           I h*ave thought* of the second Troy . . .
           He *won* the lady
           Stole her away for himself, *kept* her against armed force:
           So *ends* that story . . .
           I *have walked* over these roads;
           I *have thought* of them living.   (Pound 1916)

7.6.4   *Conversation poem and dramatic monologue*

But Abrams's image of the poet as a radiant lamp is in part a misleading
one. In most English Romantics, the discourse of egocentric expressiveness is checked, not only by a concern for empirical verifiability in the language of description (discussed in 7.5) but also by a desire to imitate
language as 'really spoken', coupled with a recognition that the situation of
speech is characteristically dialogic rather than monologic. Though
Wordsworth defines poetry as 'the spontaneous overflow of powerful feelings', he defines the poet as 'a man speaking to men' (Wordsworth [1802]:
62; 82; 70–1). Conversation is a model of discourse invoked by other
Romantic writers too and it is institutionalised in two new genres in the
period: the **conversation poem**, and its descendant, the **dramatic monologue**. Both attempt to create the illusion of an overheard or transcribed
conversation, using techniques whose literary precedents lie in
Shakespeare's drama and Donne's dramatic lyrics. Nor is the dialogic effect

confined to new genres, though it is most explicitly foregrounded in them: lyric poetry in general shows an increasing tendency to situate expressive utterance in an implicitly conversational context, as when Arnold begins *To Marguerite* (1852) with 'Yes!', as though it was the second turn in a dialogue.

The system of **deixis** provides the strongest evidence for claims that conversation is the fundamental form of language, with its special nomenclature for conversational participants (*I-you*) and its verbal equivalents of pointing gestures for picking out objects in their spatio-temporal environment (*this* v. *that*; *here* v. *there*). All these terms acquire referential content from the specifics of particular conversational contexts but in themselves they encode relationship without assigning reference. It is this combination of properties that accounts for their power when used in poetry. Because they *encode* rather than *describe* relationship, they can do so very economically, and because they require referential construal, they draw the reader in as an active collaborator in constructing a plausible physical and interpersonal scenario. Conversation poems are thus conversational in two respects: they imitate the forms of reference that typify conversation and canonically differentiate it from written discourse; and they give the reader the role of a conversational partner, an active interpreter of the text.

The advantages and difficulties of deictic reference show themselves in the first line of one of the earliest conversation poems:

(100)   a. Well, they are gone and here must I remain   (Coleridge 1800)

The opposition between *they . . . gone* and *I . . . here* gives the reader the means of inferring the spatial relations between the speaker and *they*; the modal auxiliary *must* conveys the speaker's sense of constraint; the discourse marker *well* suggests his mood of rueful resignation. But who are *they* and *I*? Where is *here*? What caused the constraint? In this instance, such questions are answered by the prefatory note (100b), in which Coleridge supplies objective reference-points:

(100)   b. In the June of 1797, some long-expected Friends paid a visit
            to the Author's Cottage; and on the morning of their arrival he
            met with an accident,which disabled him from walking during
            the whole time of their stay. One evening, when they had left
            him for a few hours, he composed the following lines, in the
            Garden Bower.

As the comparison with (a) demonstrates, a gain in explicitness in (b) is paid for by increased length and reduced reader-involvement: the reader of (b) is informed, not stimulated to infer.

The more famous successor to the conversation poem is the dramatic monologue, regarded by many critics as the most important genre innovation of post-Romantic literature. Its emergence may be seen in part as a response to the problems of verisimilitude encountered by the earlier genre in which (as in (100a) above) the poet appears to be simultaneously speaking to an interlocutor who shares his spatio-temporal location and writing to a general public who don't. Paradoxically, the dramatic monologue, by opting for a fully fictionalised speaker, becomes more realistic. The poet adopts the role of the neutral transcriber/reporter of a conversation whose 'I' is unaware of a public audience: the actual print and the posited speech of the poem are thereby divided and separately naturalised rather than being, as in the conversation poem, artificially and confusingly ascribed to a single source. Linguistically, the only difference between conversation poem and dramatic monologue is that the latter pushes further towards conversational naturalism, drawing more heavily on those forms which encode interactions with an addressee: second person pronouns, interrogatives, imperatives, address-forms and discourse markers such as *well, in fact, of course* (which might be seen as the dialogic, interactive equivalent of the monologic, expressive interjection). Building on the precedent of the conversation poem, the mid-nineteenth-century dramatic monologue can also demand more complex acts of inference from its readers. The stylistic development of the form may be gauged by setting Coleridge's first line (100a) alongside one of Browning's openings:

(101)   a. Now, don't sir! Don't expose me! Just this once!
         This was the first and only time, I'll swear   (Browning 1864)

The first line here encodes social rather than physical relations: the imperative, converted to a plea by the coaxing *now*, and the speaker's self-subordination to the addressee, expressed both in the choice of address-form (*sir*), and in the evocation of child language (*just this once*). The proximal-distal combination of *this was* in the second line allows us to infer that the utterance is prompted by an event in the very recent past and we will have already inferred that it is an event shameful to the speaker if we are alert to the presuppositions of *expose* (compared with, say, *betray* or *give me away*). But what is the shameful event? Instead of Coleridge's lengthy exposition, the later poet offers as preface only the title: *Mr Sludge 'the Medium'*, again inviting us to exert ourselves to draw conclusions from the connotations of the name and the denotation of the profession. A later extract from the same poem shows other developments in technique:

(101)   b. You'll tell?

> Go tell, then! Who the devil cares
> What such a rowdy chooses to . . .

> Aie – aie – aie!

This exemplifies what Browning elsewhere calls 'the printed voice'. All the resources of textuality – punctuation, page layout – are recruited to support the illusion of realistic (that is, situated and interactive) speech. The typographic dislocation of the first iambic pentameter seems to allow space for the interlocutor's reply (presumably, along the lines of 'you bet I'll tell'), and the ellipsis accompanying the break in the second line (*chooses to* . . .) seems to represent his physical intervention. The concluding *aie – aie – aie!* can be seen as a similar advance on Romantic technique, in this case pushing the interjection in the direction of the non-verbal sounds used in human communication (other examples in Browning include *Grrr!* and *ugh! ugh!*).

7.6.5   *Empathetic narrative*

Psychologically what is involved in the shift from the autobiographical 'I' of the conversation poem to the fictional 'I' of dramatic monologue is a modulation from egocentricity to empathy, an attempt to see the world from another speaker's point of view. The imperative towards empathy is a powerful force in Romantic ideology and it finds another linguistic expression in the main stylistic innovation in the period's main prose genre, the novel. This is the emergence of **empathetic narrative**. It too can be seen as the solution to a technical problem in its genre, arising from the fact that narration and event typically occupy different time-zones. In the simple case, events in a novel are reported by an omniscient narrator (existing in a here and now) but experienced by a participating character (existing in a there and then); yet, paradoxically, it is the quality of that distanced experience that the reader is normally invited to share. To resolve the paradox, eighteenth-century novelists had experimented with forms which diminish the gap between report and experience, for example, first person narration (in which reporter and participant are the same person) and the epistolary novel (in which reporting time and event time are closely contemporaneous). But in both cases, to retain verisimilitude, events are narrated retrospectively and in written form. What empathetic narrative provides is a technique for incorporating the character's (supposed) thoughts, words or perceptions in such a way that events seem to be narrated through a filter of the narratee's immediate experience of them.

(102)   a. but Mr. Knightley had walked in then, soon after tea, and dissipated every melancholy fancy. Alas! Such delightful proofs of Hartfield's attractions, as those sort of visits conveyed, might shortly be over . . . The prospect before her now was threatening to a degree that could not entirely be dispelled . . . How was it to be endured?   (Austen 1816)

          b. Now he was the one dying by the wayside where no good Samaritan would halt. Though it was perplexing there should be this sound of laughter in his ears, of voices: ah, he was being rescued at last. He was in an ambulance shrieking through the jungle itself, racing uphill past the timberline toward the peak – and this was certainly one way to get there!   (Lowry 1947)

These passages exemplify what has been characterised as 'dual voice' narration (Pascal 1977). Its linguistic basis is the use of a special narrative tense (the **epic preterite** or **was–now paradox**) in which events are described simultaneously in terms appropriate to a narrator for whom they are distant (hence the past tense) and to a character for whom they are part of current experience (hence the proximal deictic adverbials e.g. *shortly* and *now* in (102a), *now* in (b)). Other subjective expressions are interpreted, like the adverbials, as anchored in the character's subjectivity rather than the author's. The epistemics (the modal auxiliary *might* in (a), the adverb *certainly* in (b)) represent the characters' current state of knowledge; the emotive/affective expressions represent their feelings (in the interjections *alas* (a) and *ah* (b) and in the affective adjectives *delightful* and *threatening* (a), *perplexing* (b)); and the concluding question in (a) is read as self-addressed by the character rather than posed by Austen to her reader.

Sentences of this type occur sporadically in pre-Romantic novels and it has been suggested that a more sustained empathetic narrative was developed in the first person form by Bunyan in the seventeenth century (Adamson 1994a). But there is general agreement that Austen is the first novelist to use the third person form illustrated here as the staple style for a whole narrative, though an influential predecessor is clearly Radcliffe, who, in passages such as (94), uses affective adjectives (*tremendous, dreadful*) and deictic expressions (*this, below*) to represent the emotional and physical viewpoint of a focal character. In the following century, Austen's innovation gradually established itself as a dominant style of narration, the preferred form for Trollope, James, Hemingway, and many others.

As it diffuses, empathetic narrative undergoes some formal changes, most notably in its methods of realising the character's 'now'. There has been an increasing tendency to replace the explicit adverbial by progressive or perfect aspect. Essentially this is an extension of the subjective functions of aspect (described in 7.6.3) in which the progressive represents experiential immediacy and the perfect represents memory, the difference being that in empathetic narrative the tense is past and the aspect is oriented towards the character's 'now' rather than the narrator's. A past perfect is used in (102a) and a past progressive in (102b): their effect in prompting us to read the passages as an expression of the character's consciousness can be gauged by contrasting them with simple past-tense forms, which are more likely to be interpreted as an authorial report of event:

(103)   a. Mr Knightley had walked in then (from 102a)
        b. Mr Knightley walked in then

(104)   a. he was being rescued at last (from 102b)
        b. he was rescued at last

A second major development in the form of empathetic narrative (as a comparison between (102a) and (102b) suggests) has been an increasing tendency for the idiom of such narratives to reflect the norms of the character's rather than the narrator's speech-variety. Sporadic examples can be found in nineteenth-century novels (as in Dickens's lapse into 'barbarism' in (8) above); but Joyce is the main innovator in this respect. As far as I know, *A Portrait of the Artist as a Young Man* (1916) is the first full-length attempt at an empathetic narrative conducted largely in the speech variety of its focal character, its lexis and syntax changing as he moves from childhood (105a) through adolescence (105b):

(105)   a. Rody Kickham was a decent fellow but Nasty Roche was a stink. Rody Kickham had greaves in his number and a hamper in the refectory. Nasty Roche had big hands. He called the Friday pudding dog-in-the-basket

        b. To him she would unveil her soul's shy nakedness, to one who was but schooled in the discharging of a formal rite rather than to him, a priest of the eternal imagination, transmuting the daily bread of experience into the radiant body of everliving life.

        (Joyce 1916)

7.6.6   Deconstructing the self

The Modernists reacted in two ways to the subjective language they inherited: they rejected it and they subverted it. Simple rejection focused on the
direct expression of emotion. Writers influenced by Pound's insistence on
'objectivity' studiously avoided affective adjectives, interjections and
exclamatives, so that, with some exceptions – notably Ginsberg's influential revival of the style of (92b) in Part II of *Howl* (1956) – the language of
affect discussed in 7.6.2 is primarily a nineteenth-century phenomenon. To
the forms described in 7.6.3–7.6.5, the response was more complex and has
much in common with the Post-Impressionist response to perspective.
Whereas nineteenth-century writers had attempted to overcome the condition of textuality to create the illusion of a personality speaking through
the printed page, with a credible voice and a coherent viewpoint, the
Modernists took over the techniques on which this illusion was constructed and deconstructed them.

Not that the Romantics weren't already aware of the problems implicit in
the relativistic and shifting nature of deictic reference, as appears in Keats's
La Belle Dame sans Merci (1820). The poem offers a stark opposition between
the dismal lakeside where the speaker of the poem tells his story and the 'elfin
grot' where he enjoyed the Belle Dame. And the distance between the two is
emphasised by the repeated reference to the lakeside as *here* and the grot as
there. Yet when Keats supplies a translation of these deictic terms into objective locations, we find that both *here* and *there* are glossed as 'on the cold hill
side'. The distance between them, that is, is purely subjective, the knight's
journey from one to the other purely internal. William Allingham's *The Witch
Bride* (1850), a literary descendant of *La Belle Dame*, makes the same point
with affective adjectives, as it narrates how 'A *fair* witch crept to a young man's
side' only to become 'a thing more *frightful* than mouth may say' and finally
'the *foul* Witch-Bride'. No information beyond emotional attitude is conveyed
and it is not necessary to suppose that the bride underwent any physical transformation at all. The problem of communication that this creates is acknowledged by James, who, like Austen in (93), draws attention to the opacity of
affective terms in the following exchange from *The Ambassadors*:

(106)   'How does she do her hair?'
         He laughed out. *'Beautifully.'*
         'Ah, that doesn't tell me.'   (James 1903)

On the whole, the predominantly illusionist bias of nineteenth-century
writing means that these potential problems with subjective reference are

recognised in order to be overcome, as, for example, when Coleridge provides (100b) to contextualise (100a); but in much Modernist writing, they are foregrounded *as* problems. In Pound's *A Girl*, for example:

(107)   Tree you are,
          Moss you are,
          You are violets with wind above them.
          A child – *so* high – you are,
          And all this is folly to the world   (Pound 1912; original italics)

Here '*so* high' is a gestural deictic which cannot be translated into actual size without its accompanying hand movement – to which as readers of a text we of course have no access. It functions therefore as a peculiarly forcible reminder that the reader is in the world *outside* the poem, excluded from whatever we might posit as the world within or behind the text. The deictic *this* of the last line reinforces the message. What does it refer to? Is it the events reported in the poem – perhaps, in a naturalistic interpretation, a game of metamorphosis being played between speaker and girl? or is it the poem itself?

In (108), Ashbery writes an updated version of (100a), but suppresses the explanation:

(108)   This is where we are spending our vacation. A nice restful spot.
          Real camp life. Hope you are feeling fine.   (Ashbery 1975)

For the frustrated reader demanding a referent for *this*, *we*, *you*, Ashbery's collaborator Brainard supplies an illustration – but only to emphasise the problem: it shows the front of an envelope with stamp, address, and post-mark all in various ways blurred or erased. The point being made is that the 'real language' of 'real situations' is often uninterpretable when taken out of its context of utterance. The apparent naturalism of the tradition repre-sented by (100)–(101) is exposed as careful artifice.

The opacity and relativity of deictic reference are recruited as part of a general strategy of Modernism that Winters calls *pseudo-reference* (1960: 40–57, 86–88), which involves the invocation of a non-existent plot or context. Hamilton (1949) points out the role played in its effects by the def-inite article, in such lines as:

(109)   *The* person in *the* Spanish cape
          Tries to sit on Sweeney's knees . . .

          The silent man in mocha brown
          Sprawls at the window sill and gapes   (Eliot 1918)

The scene described is intentionally mysterious, but for those purposes '*a* person in *a* Spanish cape' or '*a* silent man' would have served just as well. What the definite article adds is the implication that the reader ought to be able to identify the intended referent (as any real conversational partner would). Technically, Eliot is doing no more than Wordsworth does in referring to '*the* grain' and '*the* vale' in (96). The difference is that all readers have some stored memory of cornfields and valleys which can be accessed to enable them to (re)construct the scene Wordsworth posits; the definite article thus functions, as it does in conversation, as a world-sharing gesture, an invitation to supply an appropriate referent. But in (109) Eliot's noun phrases are too specific for referents to be supplied from a reader's general experience and because information necessary to their construal is withheld, the effect is as of a rebuff. The world-sharing gesture becomes a means of reminding readers that they are excluded from the 'world' from which the poem is presumed to originate; it suggests that the discourse is really addressed to some more adequate reader who could identify its referents.

An even more extreme deconstruction of subjective reference involves what might be called **the Escher effect**. This occurs when, as in some of M. C. Escher's pictures, the normal cues of perspective are deployed not to build up a naturalistic coherent viewpoint, but to construct multiple and contradictory perspectives. The effect may be of simple paradox, as with Bunting's *then is now* or Eliot's *I am here/ Or there, or elsewhere* in (88b), or it may be more radical. In (110), for instance, the oscillation of tense – *holds/asked, is/was* – frustrates attempts to construct a coherent narrative sequence for events or a coherent location for their narrator:

(110)   He *holds* a key in his right hand.
         'Please,' he *asked* willingly.
         He *is* thirty years old.
         That *was* before

         We could drive hundreds of miles
         At night through dandelions.   (Ashbery 1962)

The juxtaposition of such deictically incompatible fragments matches the juxtaposition of dialectally incompatible fragments in (12) and similarly subverts our attempts to recognise a speaker in the poem. The illusion of coherent spatio-temporal identity disintegrates alongside the illusion of coherent social identity.

The Modernist novel witnesses similar disturbances of perspective. As poets dismantled the assumed world of the conversation poem and dramatic monologue, so novelists seem to have become discontented with the representation of a unified, developing consciousness which underlies the technique of empathetic narrative. Woolf and Lawrence, for instance, prefer to cut between different perspectives, often in successive sentences or clauses, as in (111), where the shift in viewpoint is most clearly registered in the affective terms: the sequence *prig, how charming, so nice* represents the way Hutton feels about Clarissa; but *divinely* represents the way she feels about him.

(111)   She was rather a prig. But how charming to look at! She made her house so nice, if it weren't for her Professors. Clarissa had half a mind to snatch him off and set him down at the piano in the back room. For he played divinely.

(Woolf 1925; in Ehrlich 1990: 100)

As the Modernists experimented with more extreme versions of (111), the style represented by (102) became increasingly associated with fiction labelled as 'lowbrow' (a term that came into use around the same time as *cliché*). But in the 1960s it enjoyed a revival, starting in America with the **New Journalism**, a form of writing that, like the work of the Movement group in England, attempted to bridge the divisions that had grown up between highbrow and lowbrow and between subjective fictions and 'matter of fact'. Works such as Capote's *In Cold Blood* (1965), which the author described as 'the non-fiction novel', and Mailer's *The Armies of the Night* (1968), subtitled 'history as a novel, the novel as history' pioneered the genre, whose stylistic aims were described as follows:

(112)   It just might be possible to write journalism that would . . . read like a novel . . . This was the sincerest form of homage to The Novel and to those greats, the novelists, of course. Not even the journalists who pioneered in this direction doubted for a moment that the novelist was the reigning literary artist, now and forever. All they were asking for was the privilege of dressing up like him . . . until the day when they themselves would work up the nerve and go into the shack and try it for real.   (Wolfe 1975)

Wolfe is here writing as a New Journalist and the passage exemplifies the style it advocates. Like (102a–b), it combines past tense with temporal references appropriate to the narratees' 'now': the proximal deictic adverb *now* in *now and forever* and the main clause past progressive of *all they were asking*. In addition, the epistemic stance of *it just might be possible* reflects the

677

modest aspirations with which the narratees started; and their speech-variety is echoed in *go into the shack and try it for real.* What differentiates (112) from (102) or (105) is that the focalised consciousness is that of a group rather than an individual. This is not an absolute innovation. Empathetic narrative had been used occasionally in the nineteenth-century English novel to represent the voice of a community, in the novels of George Eliot, for instance, or Hardy. But these communal voices were never the main protagonists and their representation often showed signs of the general nineteenth-century tendency to stigmatise non-Standard varieties. The New Journalism represents a conscious effort to empathise with the perspective of particular (often socially marginalised, non-Standard speaking) groups.

In some late twentieth-century fiction, the practices of New Journalism blend with the legacy of Modernist deconstruction, as in (113):

(113)   Annie-Belle will bake bread, tramp the linen clean and cook the
          beans and bacon; this lily of the West had not spare time enough
          to pause and consider the lilies of the field, who never do a
          hand's turn. No, sir. A woman's work is never done and she
          became a woman early.

          The gaunt paterfamilias would drive them into town to church
          on Sundays with the black Bible on his knee . . . and Annie-Belle,
          at thirteen, fourteen, increasingly astonished at and rendered shy
          by her own lonely flowering. Fifteen. How pretty she was
          growing! They came to pray in God's house that, like their own,
          was built of split logs. Annie-Belle kept her eyes down; she was a
          good girl. They were good children. The widower drank,
          sometimes, but not much . . .

          The Minister's wife made sure Annie-Belle knew a thing or
          two when she judged it about time the girl's bleeding started.

                                                                    (Carter 1988)

The narrative here roots itself in the idiom of 'the West' (*a hand's turn; no, sir; knew a thing or two*) but not in any individual consciousness. Who, for example, thinks or says *no, sir?* or exclaims *How pretty she was growing?* who passes the judgment *they were good children?* This generalising of narrative empathy is typical of New Journalism's attempt to represent what Wolfe calls 'the *downstage voice*, as if characters downstage from the protagonist . . . were talking' (1975: 32). But, as in a Modernist text, the voice represented is not a consistent one, being disrupted by far from home-spun phrases, such as *gaunt paterfamilias* and *rendered shy by her own lonely flowering.* And (113) aligns itself with experiments like (110) in the disruption of temporal perspective in its first sentence, which switches disconcertingly from *will bake* to *had* to *who never do*, thus breaking the consistent **was–now** convention of empathetic narrative, which had survived from Austen to Woolf.

7.7 Coda: the two revolutions and the literary common core

Like Eliot in (1), I have treated 'the two revolutions' as successive events in the history of literary style. But for most of the twentieth century they have also been competing synchronic options. Working alongside the early Modernists were writers who were developing Romantic techniques in more straightforward ways, to produce an ever greater degree of naturalism in the representation of a localised, personalised voice while making it speak from the frame of traditional forms and conventions. The conservative poetry of Hardy's *Late Lyrics* and Frost's *New Hampshire* appeared within a year of Eliot's *The Waste Land*, and even as Joyce was writing *Ulysses*, the novels of Arnold Bennett and Sherwood Anderson were perpetuating the narrative styles that he was dismantling. Though Modernists claimed that a new era had begun (in 1910 according to Woolf or 1921 according to Pound), by the 1930s many writers were taking their stylistic models from these non-Modernist moderns instead. Lodge (1977) interprets subsequent literary history as a cyclical oscillation between modes of writing that had polarised at the century's start. Fowler considers the darker possibility of a permanent schism in which 'literature may split into two separate developments: one "high", international, cerebral and difficult; the other "low", insular, anti-academic and readable' (Fowler 1987: 377).

Both sides of this division have been claimed as the true 'common core' language for contemporary literature. Apologists for Modernism argue that the 'synthetic idiom' of *Ulysses* and *The Waste Land* 'helped establish a potential independence of literary "English" from any nation' by creating a style that could be used by anglophone writers everywhere (Kenner 1987: 4). Anti-Modernists point out that an *international* style is not the same as a *universal* style. Larkin's attack on Pound's polyvocalism in (2) parallels Macaulay's attack on Johnson's neo-classical latinity in (53) for being a language that nobody speaks and that only an élite can write or read. For Larkin, as for Macaulay, the plain English tradition – established by Wordsworth and Cobbett and continued by Hardy and Orwell – is the true common core style, in the sense of being the most democratic. What neither side in this debate would contest is Fowler's claim that these options are mutually incompatible, that literary English is 'split'.

As intimated by Fowler's use of the term 'insular', it has become common, too, to align this split with the Atlantic divide and to project a growing divergence between English and American styles of writing, with America providing the conditions – in its system of small presses and campus poets – to foster ongoing experimentalism, while England, with a centralised literary establishment dominated by large publishing houses looking for mass markets, aims at the 'anti-academic and readable'. This divergence has been actively promoted in England by the influential Movement group and their successors. From the late 1950s onwards, these writers have branded Modernism as an American import and pursued the idiom of the Wordsworthian tradition in a conscious assertion of *English*ness, seeking to establish a national literary style as a defensive gesture against the internationalising of their language and the Americanising of their culture. When Modernist works are written by English writers, they now tend to be classed as untypical or unEnglish. Hence perhaps the omission of Bunting and Tomlinson from the *Short Oxford History of English Literature* (Sanders 1994), the deletion of Feinstein from the 6th edition of the *Norton Anthology of English Literature* (the 4th edition having noted her 'verbal adventurousness'), and my own use of predominantly American examples to illustrate late Modernism in this chapter. It is not surprising that Donald Davie should have detected a 'silent conspiracy which now unites all the English poets from Robert Graves down to Philip Larkin, and all the critics, editors and publishers too, the conspiracy to pretend that Pound and Eliot never happened' (cited in Kenner 1987: 5).

But, though widely accepted, the pictures painted by Fowler and Kenner are, I believe, too stark. They assume that the divisions they detect are categorial and constant. Whereas, as I've tried to show here, there is considerable common ground in technical terms between 'high' and 'low' versions of speech-based styles. This makes it easy, and not uncommon, for a writer to shift from one mode to another during the course of a career, usually, as in the case of Lowell and Hill, from conservatism towards Modernism, though Eliot to some extent moved in the other direction. And once we turn from a synchronic to a diachronic analysis, further qualifications begin to show. In many cases, what is 'difficult' to one generation becomes 'readable' to the next and techniques gradually diffuse from 'high' and 'low' genres of writing. That is, after all, what happened with the Romantic revolution. Larkin's belief (in 2) that the styles it produced had always been the norm for the language of literature is simply a tribute to the Romantics' long-term success in changing the norm they inherited and in creating, as Wordsworth put it, 'the taste by which [they could] be relished'. It now requires an effort to recapture the shock that Cowper's parenthesis (3b) gave his contemporaries; rhythms that *The Quarterly Review* found uncouth and inharmonious in Keats looked natural and easy when they were used by Frost; and the narrative style that was innovative in Austen became the commonplace of twentieth-century popular romance. A similar process has been in train for the innovations of Modernism. The polyvocalism of Eliot and Jones (as in 13) finds echoes in the work of the anti-Modernist Larkin (as in 14); the mixed idioms and intercut perspectives of 'high' Modernist narrative (as in 105 and 111) have been grafted on to the 'low' genre of journalism (as in 112); and, as a sign of styles to come, free verse and the disconnective syntax of haiku, which were experimental and iconoclastic forms for Pound in (78), are now part of the standard repertoire of schoolchildren.

FURTHER READING

The second half of Fowler's *History of English Literature* (1987: 199–378) complements this chapter by providing an introduction to the history of genres; to place these formal developments in the wider context of literary and cultural change, see Sanders 1994 (for the English tradition) and Spiller *et. al.* 1974 (for the American tradition). Brief general introductions to the literature of the modern period and to many of the individual authors cited in this chapter are included in the *Norton Anthology of English Literature* (vol. ii) and the *Norton Anthology of American Literature* (2 vols.), both of which offer a good selection of representative texts and useful bibliographies of the relevant literary criticism.

An excellent introduction to the synchronic study of literary language can be obtained by reading Traugott & Pratt 1980 alongside Leech 1969 (for poetry) and Leech & Short 1981 (for prose fiction). There are no comparably broad-based introductions to historical stylistics, though the subject has been broached by Stephens & Waterhouse 1990 and Bradford 1993 has supplied a companion volume focusing on change in poetic genres; Gordon 1966 remains the best introductory overview of the development of prose. Though methodologically outdated, the pioneering statistically based histories of style by Miles (1964, 1967) are still suggestive in their results and impressive in their scope. Detailed studies of the language of individual authors can be found in Deutsch's *Language Library* series and Macmillan's *The Language of Literature* series.

The additional reading suggested in relation to the separate sections of this chapter is necessarily very selective and those wishing to pursue particular topics further should consult the extensive bibliographies provided by Bailey & Burton 1968, Bennett 1986, and the annual updates in the journal *Style*.

7.1   The standard introduction to the topic of orality and literacy is Ong 1982; more detailed consideration of some of the linguistic questions involved will be found in Tannen 1982 and Biber 1988. The drift towards orality in modern prose styles is quantified by Biber & Finegan 1989; the concept of stylisation is discussed and exemplified in Adamson 1994a: 75–81. For a (witty and provocative) literary critic's account of the aftermath of the Modernist revolution, see Kenner 1975 (on American writers) and Kenner 1987 (on English writers). To pursue the parallels with events and controversies in the history of art, see the later chapters of E. H. Gombrich's *The Story of Art* and *Art and Illusion* (both published by Phaidon).

7.2   For a historical overview of the changing role of non-Standard language in English literature, see Blake 1981; the more radical tradition that succeeds Twain in America is described by Bridgman 1966. Ch. 8 and ch. 9 of Traugott & Pratt 1980 introduce many of the theoretical and practical issues raised by the literary representation of language-varieties and there is a useful section on dialect in literature in Williamson & Burke 1971, which includes the seminal paper by Ives, 'A Theory of Literary Dialect'. The problem of orthographic representation is considered by Cole 1986 and Preston 1985; and some of the particular problems associated with the novel as a genre are covered by Page 1973, Tulloch 1985 and by Fowler 1983, who also considers the merging of naturalistic and metaphorical functions in variety-mixing. The chapter on Diction in Nowottny 1962 provides a helpful starting-point for the study of polyvocalism in poetry. The role of internal borrowing and calquing as a means of enriching the literary languages is illustrated in Part 2 of Milroy 1977, in Allsopp 1992 and Zabus 1991. On the invented languages of science fiction-fantasy, see Barnes 1975 and Meyers 1980. Children's literature is discussed in Otten & Schmidt 1989 and Stephens 1992 and nonsense in Lecercle 1994 (for Victorian writers) and Rieke 1992 (for Modernists).

7.3   For historical overviews of changes in English versification, see Tarlinskaya 1976 and Brogan 1981 and, for the post-Romantic period specifically, Wesling 1985. For changes in metrical theory, see Fussell 1954, for the eighteenth century, and Omond 1921 for the nineteenth; twentieth-century theoretical positions are represented in Scully 1966 (essays by poets) and Kiparsky & Youmans 1989 (essays by linguists). Historical accounts of specific forms include Piper 1969 on the heroic couplet, Tarlinskaya 1987 on iambic metres and Hascall 1974 on triple metre. The influence of Biblical models is discussed in Kugel 1981. For twentieth-century developments, see Steele 1990 on free verse and Solt 1968 on concrete poetry. The modern fate of rhyme is considered in Wesling 1980.

7.4   The grammatical features that typify spoken language are introduced briefly in Brown & Yule 1983: 14–19 and Crystal 1980 and discussed extensively in Biber 1988. In discussing the relation between parataxis and hypotaxis, I have started from a nineteenth-century viewpoint in which hypotaxis includes all forms of dependency and parataxis all forms of adjacency. As the examples in this section reveal, the distinction is not as simple as that and the classification of clause-combining strategies is still a matter of debate. Useful discussions of the main issues involved (and of the main constructions considered in this chapter) can be found in ch. 10 of Matthews 1981 and ch. 7 of Hopper & Traugott 1993. The stylistic prominence of the free modifier in the modern period is discussed by Christensen 1967 and the role of parenthesis by Ricks 1984: 292–318 and Lennard 1991; Meyer 1992 offers a detailed account of apposition in contemporary English. At a more introductory level, the stylistic functions of simple and complex sentences are discussed in ch. 7 of Leech & Short 1981, which also covers the topics of iconicity and cohesion. The most comprehensive study of techniques of cohesion is Halliday & Hasan 1976. The particular importance of repetition in oral styles has recently been recognised, as in Tannen 1989 and the essays collected in Fischer 1994 and Johnstone 1994. Some of the syntactic sources of difficulty in Modernist writing are illuminated by Dillon 1978, which discusses the processing problems associated with a range of constructions.

7.5   Ch. 9 of Leech 1969 provides a good introduction to the linguistic descrip tion of metaphor, which can be pursued at more advanced level in Levin 1977 and Brooke-Rose 1965. The question of historical change in figurative language is introduced in ch. 6 of Stephens & Waterhouse 1990 and Lodge 1977 shows how the contrast between metaphor and metonymy can be made the basis of typology of modern writing and of an explanatory account of stylistic change in the novel. On the 'imagery' of conversation, see ch. 5 of Tannen 1989 and on the metaphors of everyday language, see Lakoff & Johnson 1980. Literary uses of cliché and dead metaphor are well discussed by Ricks 1984: 80–88, 356–368.

7.6   For literary-critical approaches to the topic of self-representation, see Shaw & Stockwell 1991. On various aspects of its linguistic form, see the following: Prynne 1988 for a fuller discussion of the Romantic interjection; Wright 1974 and Adamson forthcoming for the role of the progressive in poetry; Boyd & Boyd 1977 for the present perfect in poetry; and Fleischman 1990 for the changing role of tense in narration. The classic literary account of the dramatic monologue is given by Langbaum 1957 and a later study more attentive to its linguistic form is Griffiths 1988. Much has been written on free indirect style and on that point of view more generally but very little about its historical development; a helpful introductory account, covering both the form of free indirect style and its evolution across the nineteenth century, is provided by Pascal 1977 and some comparisons with earlier and later practice are included in Adamson 1994a and 1994b. For the most compendious study of the style, see Fludernik 1993, and for the most controversial, see Banfield 1982, whose linguistic and historical account remains profitably challenging.

KEY TO THE NUMBERED EXAMPLES

The text of the numbered examples follows that of the editions given here, except for the italicisations, which are mine, unless otherwise indicated.

1   From *The Music of Poetry* (W. P. Ker Memorial lecture delivered in the University of Glasgow, 24 February 1942). Glasgow: Jackson, Son & Company, 1942: 16.

2   From *Required Writing*. London: Faber & Faber, 1983: 72.

3b   From 'On the Receipt of My Mother's Picture out of Norfolk'. In *Poems*. London: J. Johnson, 1798, vol. 1: 244–5.

3c   From 'Mr Sludge, "The Medium"'. In *Dramatis Personae*. London: Chapman and Hall, 1864: 171.

3d   From 'Tyrian Businesses'. In *The Maximus Poems*. London: Cape Goliard Press, 1960.

4a   From *Lyrical Ballads, with a Few Other Poems*. London: J. and A. Arch, 1798: i. Also in Mason 1992: 34.

4b   From *The Waste Land: a Facsimile and Transcript*, ed. V. Eliot. London: Faber and Faber, 1971: 4ff.

5   From Act 1 of *Pygmalion*. In *Everybody's Magazine*, vol. 31, no. 5, November 1914: 578 (first performed 1913).

6   From *The Waste Land*. New York: Boni and Liveright, 1922: 22.

7a   As 4b, p. 13.

7b   As 6, p. 25.

8   In *Dickens* (The Critical Heritage), ed. P. Collins. London: Routledge & Kegan Paul, 1971: 188.

9a   From 'The Cotter's Saturday Night'. In *Poems Chiefly Written in the Scottish Dialect*. Kilmarnock: John Wilson, 1786: 124.

9b   Ibid. p. 126.

10   From 'Address to the Deil'. As 9a, p. 55.

11   From ch. 7 of *A Man of the People*. London: Heinemann, 1966: 81.

12   From Canto III of *Don Juan*. London: T. Davison, 1821: 3.

13   From *In Parenthesis*. London: Faber and Faber, 1937: 160.

14   From 'Toads'. In *The Less Deceived*. Hessle: the Marvell Press, 1955: 30.

15a   From Act III, Scene 3 of *The Rivals*. London: John Wilkie, 1775: 48.

15b   From ch. 11 of *David Copperfield*. London: Bradbury and Evans, 1850: 113.

15c   From 'Politics and the English Language'. In *Horizon* 76, April 1946: 261.

16a   From 'Sad Steps'. In *High Windows*. London: Faber and Faber, 1974: 32.

16b   From Book 1 of *The Prelude*. In *The Thirteen-Book Prelude*, ed. M. L. Reed. Ithaca: Cornell University Press 1991: 115 (see Reed's introduction for a discussion of the status of the text and its date of composition).

17a   From Act 1 of *The Playboy of the Western World*. Dublin: Maunsel, 1907: 21.

17b   As 11; from ch. 9, p. 102.

18 No single source; 18c is discussed both by Edgeworth & Edgeworth 1802 and by Coleridge [1817].

19 From 'The Idiot Boy'. As 4a, p. 179.

20a From 'The Sluggard'. In *Divine Songs, Attempted in Easy Language for the Use of Children*. London: M. Lawrence, 1715: 46.

20b From ch. 10 of *Alice's Adventures in Wonderland*. London: Macmillan and Co., 1866: 157.

21 From 'Song' ['As I walked out one evening']. In *The New Statesman and Nation*, 15 January, 1938: 82.

22a From the prefatory address 'To the Public'. In *Jerusalem*. London: W. Blake, 1820:3 (title plate dated 1804).

22b From Canto LXXXI. In *The Pisan Cantos*. New York: James Laughlin, 1948: 96.

23 Adapted from the version given in Priestley 1777: 299.

24 From *An Elegy Written in a Country Church Yard* 4th edn. London: Dodsley, 1751:5 (typography adapted).

25 Steele 1775: 76 (typography adapted).

26 Ibid. p. 77.

27 From the lecture of 24 November 1811. In *Lectures 1808–1819 on Literature*, ed. R. A. Foakes. *The Collected Works* 5 (Bollingen Series 75). Princeton: Princeton University Press, 1987, vol. 1: 222.

28 From the preface to *Christabel; Kubla Khan; The Pains of Sleep*, 2nd edn. London: John Murray, 1816: vii.

29 From 'Christabel'; as 28, p. 3.

30a From *The Story of Sigurd the Volsung*. London: Ellis and White, 1876 (Book 1, line 6).

30b From 'The Wreck of the Deutschland'. In *Poems*, ed. R. Bridges. London: Humphrey Milford, 1918: 14 (written in 1875).

30c From 'The Seafarer'. In *Ripostes*. Boston: Small, Maynard & Co., 1913: 30 (London edn. 1912).

30d From *The Age of Anxiety*. London: Faber & Faber, 1948: 42.

30e From 'Junk'. In *Advice to a prophet, and other poems*. New York: Harcourt, Brace & World, 1961: 15.

31 From Section 2 of *The Bothie of Toper-na-Fuosich*. Oxford: Frank Macpherson; London: Chapman and Hall, 1848: 14.

32a From *Evangeline: A Tale of Acadie*. London: H. G. Clarke & Co., 1848: 87 (US edn. 1847).

32b As 31, pp. 10–11.

33a From 'The Destruction of Semnacherib'. In *Hebrew Melodies*, London: John Murray, 1815: 47.

33b From 'The Voice'. In *Satires of Circumstance*. London: Macmillan and Co., 1914: 109 (poem dated December 1912).

34a As 29.

34b   As 22b.

35   Item N114 from *The Notebook of William Blake: a photographic and typographic facsimile*, ed. D. V. Erdman. Oxford: Clarendon Press, 1973.

36a   From 'A Song of Liberty'. Plate 25 in *The Marriage of Heaven and Hell*. London: W. Blake, *c*. 1790.

36b   From *Leaves of Grass*. Brooklyn, New York: [W. Whitman], 1855: 13.

36c   From 'Tortoise Shout'. In *Tortoises*. New York: Thomas Seltzer, 1921: 48.

36d   From Part 1 of 'Howl'. In *Howl and Other Poems*. San Francisco: City Lights Books, 1956: 10.

36e   From Hymn X ('Offa's Laws') of *Mercian Hymns*. London: Deutsch, 1971.

37   *The Book of Job* 3.17–19 (Authorised Version).

38a   From Plate 11 of *America A Prophecy*. Lambeth: W. Blake, 1793.

38b   From *The Rock*. London: Faber & Faber, 1934: 29.

39a   From Book 1 of *Endymion: A Poetic Romance*. London: Taylor and Hessey, 1818: 4.

39b   Ibid. p. 18.

40   From Canto 1 of *Don Juan*. London: Thomas Davison, 1819: 14.

41   From 'The Bugler's First Communion' (written in 1879). As 30b, p. 44.

42   As 39a, p. 3.

43   From Gerontion. In *Poems*. New York: Alfred A. Knopf, 1920: 15.

44   'Heather'. In *Lustra*. London: Elkin Matthews, 1916: 45.

45   From 'Anniversary'. In *The Magic Apple Tree*. London: Hutchinson, 1971: 9.

46   'Papyrus'. As 44, p. 46.

47   From 'Reggae Sounds'. In *Dread Beat and Blood*. London: Bogle-L'Ouverture Publications, 1975: 56.

48a   Entry for 15 May 1833. In *Specimens of the Table Talk of the late Samuel Taylor Coleridge*, ed. H. N. Coleridge. London: John Murray, 1835, vol.2: 185.

48b   From *Gaudier-Brzeska, A Memoir*. London: John Lane. The Bodley Head, 1916: 136.

49a–b   From *The Life of Samuel Johnson LL.D*. London: Charles Dilly, 1791, vol.1: 1.

50   From 'Table Talk'. In *Poems*. London: J. Johnson, 1782: 27.

51a   From 'Lines written a few miles above Tintern Abbey'. As 4a, p. 204.

51b   From ch. 26 of *Memoirs of Emma Courtney*. London: G. G. & J. Robinson, 1796, vol. II: 211.

52   From ch. 34 of *The Man of Feeling*. 2nd edn. London: T. Cadell, 1771: 180–1.

53   From a review of Croker's edition of Boswell's *Life of Johnson*. In the *Edinburgh Review*, CVII, September 1831: 36.

54   From ch. 15 of *Dombey and Son*. London: Bradbury and Evans, 1848: 147.

55   From 'The Undefeated'; text as in Christensen 1967: 35.

56   From *The Magic Apple Tree*. London: Hamish Hamilton, 1982: 199.

57   As 13, p. xv.

58   From *The Book of Judges* 5.27; quoted in a note to 'The Thorn' appended to *Lyrical Ballads with other poems*. London: T. N. Longman and O. Rees, 1800, vol. i: [213–4]. Also in Mason 1992: 39.

59a   From ch. 1 of *Scoop*. London: Chapman & Hall, 1938: 7.

59b   From 'Edward and Pia'. In *Unspeakable Practices, Unnatural Acts*. New York: Farrar, Strauss and Giroux, 1968: 80.

60   From episode 8 ['the Lestrygonians'] of *Ulysses*. Paris: Shakespeare and Co., 1922: 151.

61   As 46.

62   From *Ash-Wednesday*. London: Faber and Faber, 1930: 16.

63   As 6, p. 31–2.

64   From poem IV ['A Free One']. In *Poems*. London: Faber & Faber, 1930: 43.

65a   From the preface to *Lyrical Ballads*. London: T. N. Longman and O. Rees, 1802: xvii–xviii. Also in Mason 1992: 65.

65b   From 'A Few Don'ts by an Imagiste'. *Poetry* 1.6, 6 March 1913.

66   From *Peter Bell*. London: Longman, Hurst, Rees, Orme and Brown, 1819: 19.

67   From *Ode occasion'd by the death of Mr Thomson*. London: R. Manby and H. S. Cox, 1749: 6.

68   As 16b, p. 116–7.

69a   From 'Of the Pathetic Fallacy'. In Ruskin [1856]: 207.

69b   Ibid. p. 216.

70   Ibid. p. 219.

71   From 'Mariana'. In *Poems, Chiefly Lyrical*. London: Effingham Wilson, 1830: 14.

72   From ch. 48 of *Oliver Twist*. London: Richard Bentley, 1838, vol. 3: 239–41.

73   From *Aids to Reflection*. London: Taylor & Hessey, 1825: 254.

74   From ch. 10 of *Mansfield Park*. London: T. Egerton, 1814, vol. 1: 206.

75   From 'The Whitsun Weddings'. In *The Whitsun Weddings*. London: Faber and Faber, 1964: 21.

76   From 'The Day Lady Died'. In *Lunch Poems*. San Francisco: City Lights Books, 1964: 27 (poem dated 1959).

77   ['The Red Wheelbarrow']. In *Spring and All*. Dijon: Contract Publishing Co., 1923: 74.

78   'In a Station of the Metro'. In *Poetry* II.1, April 1913: 12.

79a   From 'Portrait of a Lady'. In *Prufrock and Other Observations*. London: The Egoist, 1917: 22.

79b   Title and first line of one of the *Eighteen Poems*. London: The Fortune Press, 1934: 13.

79c   As 21.

80   From Canto XVI of *Don Juan*. London: Thomas Davison, 1824: 65–6.

81a   From *Goodbye to Berlin*; text as in Lodge 1977: 199–200.
81b   From *England Made Me*; text as in Lodge 1977: 201.
81c   As 15c, p. 262.
82   As 75, p. 23.
83a   From 'The Love Song of J. Alfred Prufrock'. In *Poetry* VI.3, June 1915: 130.
83b   From *Trout Fishing in America*; text as in Lodge 1977: 236.
84a   From *The Importance of Being Earnest*. London: Leonard Smithers and Co., 1899: 17 (first performed 1895).
84b   Ibid. p. 22.
84c   Ibid. p. 18.
85   From *Triumphal March*. London: Faber and Faber, 1931: [3].
86   From episode 7 ['Aeolus'] of *Ulysses*; as 60, p. 121.
87a   From 'The Guardians'. In *For the Unfallen*, 1959; text as in Ricks 1984: 362–3.
87b   From 'The Martyrdom of St Sebastian'; as 87a.
88a   From 'This Lime-Tree Bower My Prison'. In *The Annual Anthology*, ed. R. Southey. London: T. N. Longman and O. Rees, 1800, vol. 2: 140.
88b   From *Four Quartets*. New York: Harcourt, Brace and Co., 1943: 12.
89   From 'Ah! Sun-flower'. Plate 43 in *Songs of Experience*. London: W. Blake, 1794.
90   As 16b, p. 107.
91a   From 'Night'. In ch. 5 of vol. 1 of *The Romance of the Forest*. London: T. Hookham & Carpenter, 1791: 208.
91b   From *Praeterita*. Orpington, Kent: George Allen, 1889, vol. 3: 181.
92a   From *The French Revolution*. London: James Fraser, 1837, vol. 3: 148–9.
92b   As 36b, p. 50.
93   From ch. 14 of vol. 1 of *Northanger Abbey*. In *Northanger Abbey and Persuasion*. London: John Murray, 1818: 254.
94   From ch. 12 of vol. 4 of *The Mysteries of Udolpho*. London: G. G. and J. Robinson, 1794: 227.
95a   From 'Progress of Vice'. In *The Poetical Works of S. T. Coleridge*. London: William Pickering, 1834, vol. 1: 53 (written 1790).
95b   From Book 5 of *The Prelude*. As 16b, p. 172.
95c   From 'Dover Beach'. In *New Poems*. London: Macmillan & Co., 1867: 112.
96   From 'The Solitary Reaper'. In *Poems in Two Volumes*. London: Longman, Hurst, Rees and Orme, 1807, vol. 2: 11.
97   From Part 7 of 'The Rime of the Ancyent Marinere'. As 4a, p. 49.
98   As 76.
99   From 'Provincia Deserta'. As 44, p. 63–4.
100a–b As 88a.
101a   As 3c, p. 171.

101b   Ibid. p. 172.

102a   From ch. 48 of *Emma*. London: John Murray, 1816, vol. 3: 228.

102b   From ch. 12 of *Under the Volcano*. London: Jonathan Cape, 1947: 394.

105a   From ch. 1 of *A Portrait of the Artist as a Young Man*. New York: B. W. Huebsh, 1916: 3.

105b   Ibid. from ch. 5, p. 259–60.

106   From ch. 1 of Book 2 of *The Ambassadors*. London: Methuen and Co., 1903: 50.

107   From 'A Girl'. As 30c, p. 21.

108   From *The Vermont Notebook* (with J. Brainard). Santa Barbara: Black Sparrow Press, 1975: 88–9.

109   From 'Sweeney Among the Nightingales'. In *Little Review* 5, September 1918: 10.

110   From 'They Dream Only of America'. In *The Tennis Court Oath*. Middletown, Connecticut: Wesleyan University Press, 1962: 13.

111   From *Mrs Dalloway*; text as in Ehrlich 1990: 100.

112   Wolfe 1975: 21–2.

113   From 'John Ford's *'Tis Pity She's a Whore'*, Granta 25, Autumn 1988: 181–2 (reprinted in *American Ghosts and Old World Wonders*. London: Chatto & Windus, 1993).

KEY TO THE CITED AUTHORS

Achebe, Chinua, 1930–
Addison, Joseph, 1672–1719
Allingham, William, 1824–89
Anderson, Sherwood, 1876–1941
Ashbery, John, 1927–
Arnold, Matthew, 1822–88
Auden, W(ystan) H(ugh), 1907–73
Austen, Jane, 1775–1817
Barnes, William, 1801–86
Barrett (Browning), Elizabeth, 1806–61
Beckett, Samuel, 1906–89
Bennett, Arnold, 1867–1931
Blake, William, 1757–1827
Boswell, James, 1740–95
Brautigan, Richard, 1935–84
Browning, Robert, 1812–89
Bunting, Basil, 1900–85
Burgess, Anthony, 1917–93
Burns, Robert, 1759–96
Byron, George Gordon, Lord, 1788–1824

Capote, Truman, 1924–84
Carlyle, Thomas, 1795–1881
Carroll, Lewis, (C. L. Dodgson) 1832–98
Carter, Angela, 1940–92
Clare, John, 1793–1864
Clough, Arthur Hugh, 1819–61
Cobbett, William 1762–1835
Coleridge, Samuel Taylor, 1772–1834
Collins, William, 1721–59
Conrad, Joseph, 1857–1924
Cowper, William, 1731–1800
Davie, Donald, 1922–95
Dickens, Charles 1812–70
Dickinson, Emily, 1830–86
Donne, John, 1572?–1631
Doyle, Sir Arthur Conan, 1859–1930
Dryden, John, 1631–1700
Edgeworth, Maria, 1767–1849
Egan, Pierce, 1772–1849
Elgin, Suzette Haden, 1936–
Eliot, George (M. A. Evans) 1819–80
Eliot, T(homas) S(tearns), 1888–1965
Feinstein, Elaine, 1930–
Ferlinghetti, Lawrence, 1919–
Finlay, Ian Hamilton, 1925–
Frost, Robert, 1875–1963
Galt, John, 1779–1839
Gascoigne, George, 1542–77
Gascoyne, David, 1916–
Gaskell, Elizabeth, 1810–65
Gibbon, Lewis Grassic (J. L. Mitchell) 1901–35
Ginsberg, Allen, 1926–97
Godwin, William, 1756–1836
Golding, William, 1911–93
Gray, Thomas, 1716–71
Green, Henry (H. V. Yorke) 1905–73
Greene, Graham, 1904–91
Gunn, Thom, 1929–
Gurney, Ivor, 1890–1937
Hardy, Thomas, 1840–1928
Harrison, Tony, 1937–
Hays, Mary, 1760–1843
Hazlitt, William, 1778–1830

Hemingway, Ernest, 1898–1961
Herbert, George, 1593–1633
Hill, Geoffrey, 1932–
Hill, Susan, 1942–
Hoban, Russell, 1925–
Hopkins, Gerard Manley, 1844–89
Housman, A(lfred) E(dward), 1859–1936
Hughes, Langston, 1902–67
Hughes, Ted, 1930–
Isherwood, Christopher, 1904–86
James, Henry, 1843–1916
Johnson, Linton Kwesi, 1952–
Johnson, Samuel, 1709–84
Jones, David, 1895–1974
Joyce, James, 1882–1941
Keats, John, 1795–1821
Kerouac, Jack, 1922–69
Kingsley, Charles, 1819–75
Kipling, Rudyard, 1865–1936
Larkin, Philip, 1922–85
Lawrence, D(avid) H(erbert), 1885–1930
Lear, Edward, 1812–88
Lindsay, Vachel, 1879–1931
Longfellow, Henry Wadsworth, 1807–82
Lowell, Robert, 1917–77
Lowry, Malcolm, 1909–57
Macaulay, Thomas Babington, Lord, 1800–59
MacDiarmid, Hugh (C. M. Grieve), 1892–1978
Mackenzie, Henry, 1745–1831
Macpherson, James, 1736–96
Mailer, Norman, 1923–
Milton, John, 1608–74
Moore, Marianne, 1887–1972
Morris, William, 1834–96
Nesbit, Edith, 1858–1924
O'Hara, Frank, 1926–66
Olson, Charles, 1910–70
Orwell, George (E. A. Blair), 1903–50
Owen, Wilfred, 1893–1918
Pope, Alexander, 1688–1744
Pound, Ezra, 1885–1972
Radcliffe, Ann, 1764–1823
Rossetti, Christina, 1830–94

Ruskin, John, 1819–1900
Shakespeare, William, 1564–1616
Shaw, George Bernard, 1856–1950
Shelley, Percy Bysshe, 1792–1822
Sheridan, Richard Brinsley, 1751–1816
Smith, Stevie, 1902–71
Southey, Robert, 1774–1843
Spenser, Edmund, c.1552–99
Swinburne, Algernon, 1837–1909
Synge, J(ohn) M(illington), 1871–1909
Tennyson, Alfred, Lord, 1809–92
Thackeray, William Makepeace, 1811–63
Thomas, Dylan, 1914–53
Thomas, Edward, 1878–1917
Thomson, James, 1700–48
Tomlinson, Charles, 1927–
Trollope, Anthony, 1815–82
Tupper, Martin, 1810–89
Twain, Mark (S. L. Clemens), 1835–1910
Watts, Isaac, 1674–1748
Waugh, Evelyn, 1903–66
Wells, H(erbert) G(eorge), 1866–1946
Wesker, Arnold, 1932–
Whitman, Walt, 1819–92
Wilbur, Richard, 1921–
Wilde, Oscar, 1854–1900
Williams, William Carlos, 1883–1963
Wolfe, Tom, 1930–
Woolf, Virginia, 1882–1941
Wordsworth, William, 1770–1850
Young, Edward, 1683–1765

GLOSSARY OF LINGUISTIC TERMS

For fuller definitions of linguistic terms, see D. Crystal's *A Dictionary of Linguistics and Phonetics*, 3rd rev. edn. (Oxford: Blackwell, 1991) or P. Matthews's *A Concise Dictionary of Linguistics* (Oxford: Clarendon Press, 1997); for stylistic terms see K. Wales's *A Dictionary of Stylistics* (London: Longman, 1990).

abbreviation A short form of a word or other expression; specifically, a short written form representing the pronunciation of the full form; the process of so shortening a form.

ablaut reduplication See **consonantal reduplication**.

abstraction A change in the reference of a word from something more material or specific to something less material or more general (cf. **concretion**).

accentual metre A verse-design prescribing a stress-pattern rather than a syllable-count.

acronym A written short form of a word or other expression pronounced according to the normal rules of spelling.

acronomy The process of forming **acronyms**.

adaptation The process of forming a **loanword** with relatively greater changes from its foreign **etymon** (cf. **adoption**).

adjunct An optional modifier, most often an **adverbial** or adverbial clause.

adoption The process of forming a loanword with only minimal changes from its foreign etymon (cf. **adaptation**).

adverbial One of the chief functional elements of clauses, along with subject and object, predicative complement, and predicator (verbal group), and most often filled by the categories adverb phrase, prepositional phrase or clause.

affective adjectives A sub-class of adjectives specifying the attitude of the speaker rather than an attribute of the NP's referent, e.g. *a **nice** book*; *a **hideous** idea*.

affix A **bound morpheme** that generally is used only in combination with a **base morpheme**.

affixing or affixation The formation of a **composite word** by the use of an **affix**.

agentive A semantic role that involves instigation and volition; an agentive NP is the doer of an action.

alexandrine The standard verse-line of French neo-classical poetry. The term was borrowed into English to refer to the **iambic hexameter**.

alien word A **foreign word**.

alliterative metre An **accentual metre** in which the verse-design also prescribes that some of the stressed syllables **alliterate** (i.e. have the same initial consonant).

alphabetism A written short form of a word or other expression pronounced by the names of the letters with which it is written.

amelioration A change in the reference of a word to a referent more highly regarded than its older referent (cf. **pejoration**).

anaphoric Referring back to some constituent already mentioned (the antecedent).

aphesis The omission of an initial unstressed syllable from an expression.

apodosis The consequent (main) clause of a conditional construction; the subordinate or *if*-clause is the **protasis**.

apposition Adjacency of two constituents with the same function and reference and without any overt linking element.

appositive In **apposition**.

argument A constituent which plays a part in the semantic structure of a verb – subject, object, etc. – usually obligatory, and possibly subject to selectional restrictions imposed by the verb. Thus in *The Pope kissed the ground on his arrival*, the NPs *the Pope* and *the ground* are arguments of **kiss**, while *his arrival* is not.

assimilation The change of a sound by becoming identical with or more like a neighbouring sound.

attributive Modifying a **head** noun within NP, and contrasted with **predicative**.

backformation The shortening of a word by omitting an **affix** or what is taken to be an affix.

bahuvrihi compound An **exocentric compound** (from Sanskrit '[having] much rice').

ballad metre A four-line stanza composed of alternating four-beat and three-beat lines with a rhyming pattern *abab* or *abcb*. Also known as **common metre**.

base morpheme A **free morpheme** or a **bound morpheme** to which **affixes** can be added to form words.

bestowal The conscious act of name-giving, as opposed to the evolution of a referring expression into a name.

blank verse Verse written in unrhymed **iambic pentameter**.

blend A word formed by combining **etyma** while omitting part of at least one of its etyma.

borrowing A **loanword**; the process of forming loanwords.

bound morpheme A **morpheme** that cannot be used alone as a word, but must be combined with another.

calque A form of **borrowing** in which a word or phrase from one language is translated part-by-part into another, e.g. Eng. *skyscraper* (Sp. *rascacielos*, Ger. *Wolkenkratzer*). Also known as **loan translation**.

catenative A lexical (nonauxiliary) verb with another verb in its complement.

chiasmus A pattern in which elements are repeated in the reverse order, e.g. /xx/; *abba*; *John kissed Mary, Mary kissed John*.

clang association A change in **reference** by which one word acquires the **referent** of another word to which it is similar in sound.

clipping The **shortening** of a spoken or written form, specifically without phonological motive.

clitic A form which is syntactically equivalent to a word but which is phonologically attached to a neighbouring word.

collocate Habitually co-occur, not necessarily with any syntactic relation.

commutation Intersubstitutability.

commute Can be substituted one for another.

complementary See **distribution**.

complementiser A constituent which acts as introducer of an embedded clause and whose content, when lexically filled, is roughly equivalent to a subordinating conjunction in traditional terminology.

composing The process of forming a **composite word**, specifically either **compounding** or **affixing**.

composite word A word formed by combining **etyma**.

compound A word formed from two or more **base morphemes**.

compounding The formation of **compounds**.

concord The formal relationship between units whereby the form of one word requires a corresponding form in another, specifically the present-tense verbal ending *-(e)s* in agreement with a 3 SG subject.

concrete poetry Used from the 1950s to refer to a type of poetry in which visual appearance makes an essential contribution to the meaning.

concretion A change in the **reference** of a word from something less material or specific to something more material or less general (cf. **abstraction**).

conjunct An **adverbial** which links a clause to the preceding context, e.g. *furthermore, nonetheless*.

consonantal reduplication A **reduplication** of consonants with variation of the stressed vowel, such as *fiddle-faddle*.

contrastive See **distribution**.

conversion The process of making a **shift** in part of speech; a word so shifted.

co-ordination The process or product of linking linguistic units of equal status, usually by means of a **co-ordinating** conjunction *and, but, or*.

copula A linking verb, typically a verb of being, e.g. *This is a glossary*.

copulative compound A **compound** that combines two words, either of which might be used alone in the same construction as the compound, such as *secretary-treasurer*.

counterfactual Hypothetical and already ruled out by the known course of events, as in the conditional sentence *If Cambridge had been bombed flat in the War, it wouldn't be such a big tourist attraction*.

creation A word not based on other words, that is, with no **etyma**.

dactyl A metrical **foot** of three syllables patterned long-short-short or (as is more commonly the case in English metres) stress-unstress-unstress e.g. *HAPPily*; *CALL to me*.

deictic Of an item reflecting the orientation of discourse participants in time and space, normally with reference to the speaker, **deixis**, along a **proximal** (towards-speaker) versus **distal** (away-from-speaker) axis, e.g. *I:you*; *this:that*; present:past.

derivation The history of a word; or the pattern or structure of a word; or the study of either of those.

determiner The cover term for articles (*a, the*), demonstratives (*this, that*) and quantifiers (*few, three*).

diachronic Historical.

disjunct An **adverbial** which conveys the speaker's comment on the rest of the sentence, e.g. initial *Frankly* or *Understandably*.

distal See **deictic**.

distribution There are two important types of distribution: (a) complementary distribution, where the **environment** in which the two elements may occur consists of two disjoint sets, each associated with only one element; and (b) contrastive distribution, where the environment consists of two overlapping sets.

do-support The introduction of *do* as a 'dummy' auxiliary, e.g. in the interrogative and negative sentences in the following pairs: *They often go to Paris/Do they often go to Paris?*; *We received your parcel/We did not receive your parcel.*

durative Use of verbs or clauses describing events that involve a period of time.

dvandva compound A **copulative compound** (from Sanskrit 'two-two').

echoic word A word whose sound suggests its referent.

elision A spoken short form of a word or other expression resulting from the omission of some sounds for phonological reasons; specifically by **aphesis**, **syncope**, or **assimilation**.

ellipsis The omission of one or more words from an expression, as the **shortening** of a compound noun to one of its components.

embedded Used of a clause syntactically subordinate to some other clause and therefore included within it.

empathetic deixis The re-centring of **deixis** on an entity or person other than the speaker. See Lyons 1977: 677.

empathetic narrative A narrative style in which forms of **empathetic deixis** are systematically employed.

enclitic A **clitic** which follows its host.

endocentric compound A **compound**, one of whose elements is logically substitutable for the whole compound, such as *redbird* = a bird (cf. **exocentric compound**).

enjamb(e)ment In poetry, the continuation of a syntactic unit across the metrical boundary created by a line-end.

environment The linguistic context relevant to the use or selection of some form.

epic preterite A translation of *Episches Praeteritum*, the term used for the **was–now paradox** by Hamburger (1973).

epistemic A term referring to the semantics of probability, possibility and belief, as in *They must be married* in the sense *(From what is known to me) I conclude that they are married.*

etymology The history of a word; the study of word histories.

etymon (plural, **etyma)** A **vocabulary** element that is the source of another word.

exocentric compound A **compound** neither of whose elements is logically substitutable for the whole compound, such as *pickpocket* ≠ a pocket, but rather someone who picks pockets (cf. **endocentric compound**).

extraction A linguistic process which relates a constituent outside a clause to an apparent gap inside it, as where *who* in *Who did you want me to invite [φ]?* corresponds to the missing object of *invite* (and in a transformational generative grammar is analysed as having been moved from that site).

eye-dialect The representation of non-standard speech by non-standard spellings which do not indicate a genuine difference in pronunciation e.g. <*wimmin*> for *women.*

eye-rhyme A rhyme based on similarity of spelling not sound e.g. *plaid/paid; sword/word.* The deliberate use of eye-rhyme is a feature of post eighteenth-century poetry; apparent instances in earlier poetry are usually the result of an intervening sound-change.

folk etymology A process of **word formation** that involves reinterpreting the structure of a word or the identity of its parts, often with a consequent change in the word's shape, as *bridegroom* 'bride's man' was reinterpreted and remodelled as *bride + groom.*

foot A unit of rhythm normally consisting of a stressed syllable and its satellite(s).

foreign word A **loanword** by **adoption** that is markedly foreign in appearance or use.

formation word derivation.

fourteener A poetic line of fourteen syllables in **iambic** metre.

free indirect style An anglicisation of *style indirect libre* the term introduced by Bally (1912), originally to refer to a style of speech-reporting which combines features of **direct speech** (not subordinated to a reporting clause) and **indirect speech** (back-shifted tense). Sometimes used of **empathetic narrative** more generally.

free modifier A modifying element structurally detached from its head.

free morpheme A **morpheme** that is capable of being used alone as a word.

free verse An anglicisation of *vers libre*, used especially in the early twentieth century to refer to experimental poetry not conforming to traditional metrical patterns.

generalisation An increase in the number of sorts of things a word refers to (cf. **specialisation**).

generic A common noun, as opposed to a **trade name** or **proprietary name**.

grammaticalisation The process whereby a device developed for stylistic or topicalisation purposes or an element of full referential meaning comes to be employed as the regular grammatical exponent of a particular category. In English the change in use of the progressive form of verbs from a stylistic device to an expression of duration is an example of grammaticalisation.

Great Vowel Shift A series of sound changes in the fifteenth and sixteenth centuries affecting nearly all the long vowels in Standard English: fully described in volume II.

h-dropping The absence of /h/ in the pronunciation of words like *hat* (rendered as /æt/) in some regional forms of English.

half-rhyme An umbrella term for various kinds of matched sound-sequences which relax the criteria for **full-rhyme** (identity in the last stressed vowel and all succeeding sounds). Also known as **off-rhyme** or **para-rhyme**.

head The central or essential element in a larger unit, e.g. *man* in *the large man*.

heroic couplet A pair of rhymed **iambic pentameter** lines.

hexameter A verse line consisting of six metrical **feet**. The standard metre of epic in Latin poetry, where it is composed of **dactyls** and **spondees** in prescribed combination. Imitated by English writers with various degrees of adaptation, e.g. substituting stress for length in realisations of the foot and **trochee** for **spondee** in realisations of the line.

higher clause, verb The highest clause of a sentence is the independent or main clause, and lower or subordinate clauses are **embedded** within a higher clause. Thus in *Max knew him to be a fraud*, the higher clause is the one whose verb is *knew*, the lower clause is *him to be a fraud*, with verb *be*.

hybrid compound A **compound** whose parts originally derive from different languages.

hyperbole A change in **reference** caused by exaggeration (cf. **litotes**).

hypercorrection The term used to refer to the production of anomalous forms through the faulty imitation of prestige norms and their extension to inappropriate **environments**. For example, the dropping of initial /h/ in many dialects leads some speakers to add it to words which do not have it etymologically, as in *hable* 'able', *Hamsterdam* 'Amsterdam'.

hypotaxis A term used by late nineteenth-century grammarians (in contrast to **parataxis**) to refer to forms of clause-combining that involve dependency; sometimes used more specifically to refer to the presence of subordinating conjunctions such as *if, when, so that*, e.g. *he left when I arrived.*

iamb A metrical **foot**, consisting of a short syllable followed by a long syllable or (as is more commonly the case in English metres) an unstressed syllable followed by a stressed syllable, e.g. *beGIN; to DRINK; the GIN.*

iambic hexameter In English prosody, a line based on the pattern of six **iambs**. More commonly known as **alexandrine**.

iambic pentameter In English prosody, a line based on the pattern of five **iambs**. The standard metre for **blank verse** and **heroic couplets**, it is the functional equivalent of the French **alexandrine** or the classical **hexameter**.

iconicity A formal resemblance between some aspect of a linguistic expression and the object or event which it denotes or refers to, e.g. *moo* resembles its denotatum in sound; *I came, I saw, I conquered* matches clause-order to the chronological order of the actions described.

innovative borrowing The process of joining words imitated from another language into a combination that does not occur in that language.

ISV International Scientific Vocabulary, words formed in recent times and found in slightly varying forms in several languages, whose exact history is difficult or impossible to reconstruct.

lexeme The minimal distinctive unit in the lexical system and the abstract unit underlying a set of grammatical variants; hence close to popular notions of a word. The forms *sing, sings, sang*, and *singing* all belong to the lexeme *sing*; and the forms *rose tree, beech tree, tree diagram* are lexical units which are related through the lexeme *tree*. The head words in a dictionary are usually lexemes.

lexical-incidental Referring to the occurrence (or incidence) of a particular phoneme in a particular word (hence lexical). For example, ECONOMICS may be pronounced with either /iʔ/ or /ɛ/ as its first phoneme; individual speakers vary in their choice. Elsewhere in the vocabulary, no such choice exists: e.g. EKE and ECHO must be pronounced with /iʔ/ and /ɛ/ respectively as their first phoneme.

lexicalised Of an element or construction which has acquired the status of a **lexeme**.

lexicography The recording of **vocabulary** in a dictionary, or the study of such recording.

lexicology The study of **vocabulary** in any of its aspects.

loan clipping A **loanword** or morpheme that is a **clipping** of its foreign **etymon**.

loan translation See **calque**.

loanword A word formed by imitating a word from another language, that is, a word with a non-English **etymon**.

locutionary agent A term introduced by Lyons (1977) to avoid possible ambiguities in the term *the speaker*. It designates the occupant of the *I*-role in a given (written or spoken) utterance. The French term **sujet de l'énonciation** is sometimes used instead.

lytotes A change in the **reference** of a word to a new **referent** in some way opposite to its older referent, or by understatement or euphemism (cf. **hyperbole**).

marked See **unmarked**.

metaphor Used generally of non-literal forms of reference; more specifically, a figure of speech in which one topic (sometimes known as the **tenor**) is described (and hence interpreted) in terms of another (sometimes known as the **vehicle**), on the basis of some resemblance between the two, e.g. *a filly* for 'a young woman'; *to plough the sea* for 'to sail'.

metonymy A non-literal form of reference in which something is designated by the name of something else with which it is associated, e.g. *a skirt* for 'a woman'; *the press* for 'newspapers'.

modality A term referring to attitudes to obligation, necessity, truth, and belief which in PDE are usually restricted to auxiliary verbs such as *can*.

mood The cover term for indicative, subjunctive and imperative. The choice may be controlled by specific constructions or by the semantic function of expressing doubt, hypothesis or unreality.

morpheme A meaningful form (sequence of sounds) in a language that cannot be divided into smaller meaningful forms.

morphology The structure and form of words, either in terms of inflections (*inflectional morphology*) or word formation (*derivational morphology*).

native development A word derived from an earlier word in the same language by phonological or semantic change.

neologism A new word, an innovation in **vocabulary**.

neology The making of **neologisms**; the study of that process.

NICE An acronym for the four environments of <u>N</u>egation, <u>I</u>nversion, <u>C</u>ode (= post-verbal ellipsis), <u>E</u>mphasis which distinguish **operators** from all other verbs.

non-restrictive relative clause See **relative clause**.

onomastic reference Reference unmediated by the meaning of the whole or the elements identifiable in the referring expression; as in the case of *Redhill* identifying a particular town in some discourse without appeal to the notions 'red' or 'hill'.

onomasticon The list or dictionary of names associated with some language or dialect or idiolect, but arguably not strictly PART of that language.

onomatisation Becoming a proper name; i.e. losing sense, and becoming institutionalised to some degree.

onomatopoeic word An **echoic word**.

operator A verb which can appear in **NICE** contexts: in PDE a modal, BE, or certain uses of DO and HAVE.

orthoepical Relating to the rules by which a spelling form is regularly pronounced.

paradigm The set of forms belonging to a single word or grammatical category. *Conjugation* refers to the paradigm of a verb; *declension* refers to the paradigm of a noun, adjective or pronoun.

paradigmatic See **syntagmatic**.

parataxis The opposite of **hypotaxis**; clause-linkage without subordination and typically without overt conjunctions, e.g. *she stays, I go*; *I arrived, he left*; **co-ordination** is often classed as a paratactic construction, e.g. *I arrived and he left*.

parenthesis Occurs when a syntactic sequence is interrupted by the insertion of a word, phrase or sentence; sometimes classed as a type of **parataxis**, e.g. *I arrived (did you see me?) in a taxi*.

particle An invariant item with grammatical function which usually cannot be easily classified within the traditional parts of speech. Used here especially for the originally spatial prepositions and/or adverbs like *at, away, in, off, up* which form part of group-verbs.

pejoration A change in the **reference** of a word to a **referent** less highly regarded than its older referent (cf. **amelioration**).

periodic sentence A **hypotactic** construction in which the main clause is interrupted or delayed.

periphrasis Phrasal as opposed to inflectional expression of case, mood or temporal relations. Thus *of the man* is the periphrastic counterpart of *man's*. The term is used more loosely to refer to any structure where several words are found where one would suffice.

phonestheme A sound or usually combination of sounds that suggest a meaning, at least vaguely, such as the *gl-* in *gleam, glint, glitter, glow*.

phonological word A unit of phonology, which may be distinct from the word as a unit of syntax, e.g. *I'm* is a phonological word, so, in some accounts, are the following: *to go*; *the time*.

phonotactics The freedoms and constraints on the occurrence of allophones or phonemes in a syllable or word; a more general term than 'structural'.

pied-piping A term formerly used in generative grammar, particularly to refer to constructions such as *from where did they come?* or *the man on whom they relied*, where both the preposition and its following noun phrase appear at the front of the clause (as opposed to **preposition-stranding** constructions, such as *where did they come from?* or *the man they relied on*).

polyvocalism Variety mixing within a text, where each variety is associated with a value or a viewpoint; also known as **polyphony**.

pragmatics The relationship between a word or other expression and its users, specifically limitations on the use of an expression with respect to formality, social acceptability, geographical distribution, historical status, and the like.

predicate A term in syntax referring to all the obligatory elements in a sentence apart from the subject, e.g. the bracketed constituents in *John [gave Mary a kiss] last week*.

predicative A constituent co-referential with a preceding NP and predicating some property of it, e.g. *Jim was <u>a happy man</u>, The suggestion made Jim <u>a happy man</u>*.

proprietary name A **trade name**, to which the owner has legal rights.

protasis See **apodosis**.

proximal See **deictic**.

raising A term used in certain linguistic analyses to refer to the phenomenon whereby a constituent of a subordinate clause becomes part of the superordinate clause.

realia The **referents** of words.

realisational Referring to the allophonic realisation of a phoneme. For example, the pronunciation of LEVEL, with clear or dark /l/s, is a matter of realisation; there are no systemic implications.

reduplication A **compound** consisting of parts that are identical in whole (*hush-hush*) or in part (*fiddle-faddle, hootchy-kootchy*).

reference The process by which a word stands for a thing (or **referent**).

referent The thing (object or event or quality) that a word stands for.

register A variety of language which is defined according to the social situation in which it is employed, e.g. formal vs. informal.

relative clause A clause that modifies the head of a noun phrase. A restrictive relative clause also restricts the referential scope of the phrase (e.g. *the man who came in was my father*), a non-restrictive relative clause supplies additional, non-defining information (e.g. *my father, who just came in, wants to meet you*).

resultative A clause or element whose meaning includes the notion of change, with focus on the result.

rhyming reduplication A **compound** whose components rhyme, such as *hootchy-kootchy*.

rhotacised Produced with a hollowing in the centre line of the tongue, and with the back of the tongue raised towards the soft palate. Many American pronunciations of /r/ involve rhotacisation.

rhotic An accent is 'rhotic' if the phoneme /r/ can occur in three phonological contexts: pre-vocalic (e.g. /rɛd/), pre-consonantal (e.g. /faʔrm/), and pre-pausal (e.g. /kaʔr/). Most speakers of American English are rhotic; most speakers of British English are non-rhotic. Note that some phonetics texts use 'rhotic' as a general term for /r/ sounds; it is *not* used this way in chapter 5.

right dislocation A construction in which a constituent is moved to final position, leaving a pronoun copy in its normal place, e.g. *He's good, that student*.

RP (Received Pronunciation) An accent of English identified by Daniel Jones as characteristic of educated speakers in the southern parts of Britain; a prestige norm in England for much of the twentieth century.

S-curve The shape of graph often seen when replacement of one linguistic form by another is plotted over time: slow onset, rapid central phase, slow completion.

selectional restrictions Semantic constraints on the ability of lexical items to combine within a given grammatical context without producing anomaly (or metaphor), e.g. **transferred epithet** and the **was–now paradox** both violate normal **selectional restrictions**.

semantic Pertaining to the meaning of words and **morphemes**.

semantic loan The use of the meaning of a word in another language for an English word of similar form or other uses.

shift A word derived from another word by changing its part of speech, its sense, the order of its sounds, or its range of use; the process of forming such a word.

shortening A word formed by omitting part of an **etymon**; the process of forming such a word.

simile A type of **metaphor** in which the **tenor-vehicle** comparison is made explicit, e.g. *my love is like a red, red rose*.

slang Language that is informal, deliberately unconventional, and indicative of self-identified membership in a particular social group.

specialisation A decrease in the number of sorts of things a word refers to (cf. **generalisation**).

spondee A metrical **foot** consisting of two long syllables or (as is more commonly the case in English poetry) two stressed syllables, e.g. *BIG BANG*, *PIGS FLY*.

stative Applied to verbs which express a state or condition, e.g. *be, know, mean*, etc., as opposed to dynamic or nonstative verbs, e.g. *change, grow, run (I am running)*, etc.

stereotype A linguistic feature which in popular belief typifies a variety (whether or not it does so in actual usage) e.g. the interjection *Begorra* is a stereotype of Hiberno-English, the pronunciation of *earl* as *oil* a stereotype of Brooklyn speech.

stock The list of institutionalised names forming part of the onomasticon.

stress maximum A term used by Halle and Keyser (see Freeman 1981: 206–24) to refer to a stressed syllable flanked by unstressed syllables in the same syntactic unit, e.g. the capitalised syllables in: *a PITy*; *to KILL them*; *with KINDness*.

structural Referring to the freedoms and constraints on the occurrence of phonemes in a syllable or word. For example, the difference between rhotic and non-rhotic accents is one of structure.

style-marker A linguistic feature whose use is consciously associated with a particular style, e.g. latinate vocabulary is a style-marker of Johnsonese.

stylisation The process by which a pattern of linguistic choices becomes conventionalised.

substratum A linguistic variety or set of forms which has influenced the structure or use of a more dominant variety or language within a community.

sujet de l'énonciation See **locutionary agent**.

syllabo-tonic metre A verse-design that prescribes both stress-pattern and syllable count e.g. **iambic pentameter**.

synchronic Descriptive without reference to history.

syncope The omission of a medial sound or syllable because of lack of stress.

syncretism The merger of two distinct inflectional forms into one, such as the earlier subjective *ye* and objective *you* under the undifferentiated form *you*.

synecdoche A type of **metonymy** in which the part stands for the whole, e.g. *a pair of ragged claws* for 'a crab'.

syntagm A group of words which are syntactically related, often though not always forming a constituent.

syntagmatic A term referring to the co-occurrence or combination within the string of words of co-ordinated discourse. It contrasts with **paradigmatic**, which refers to the choice available to replace a single item in the discourse.

systemic Referring to the system (=list) of phonemes, or, more specifically, to the number of phonemes in a system. A systemic difference between RP and GenAm. is that RP has the phonemes /ac/,/a?/, and /p/ in its system, whereas GenAm. has only /ac/ and /a?/.

tag question An interrogative consisting of **operator** and pronoun, appended to a clause, often with the opposite polarity, e.g. *It'll be raining, won't it?, John hasn't arrived, has he?*

tatpurusha compound An **endocentric compound** (from Sanskrit 'that person').

tenor See **metaphor**.

tone-unit A stretch of utterance unified and demarcated by features of intonation and interpreted as a unit of information; it may or may not correspond to a phrase or sentence as indicated by the punctuation marks of written language.

trade name The commercial name of a product.

transferred epithet The use of a literally anomalous modifier (usually an adjective), e.g. *he smoked a meditative pipe; April is the cruellest month.*

transparent etymology Etymology may have the specific sense of 'transparent etymology', which may be accessed during linguistic processing, but is not necessarily so accessed.

trochee A metrical **foot** consisting of a long syllable followed by a short syllable or (as is more commonly the case in English poetry) a stressed syllable followed by an unstressed syllable, e.g. *LISTen; SINGing; FIELDmice.*

unmarked Used of the default or 'unless' choice in a binary system, and typically morphologically simpler, more general in meaning, more frequent; opposed to **marked**.

usage pragmatics; in Britain often more generally also including the syntactic use of an expression; in America usually more specifically the social restrictions on the use of an expression.

vehicle See **metaphor**.

vocabulary The stock of words or **morphemes** in a language.

was–now paradox The collocation of past-tense verb (e.g. *was*) with non-past-time adverbial (e.g. *now*), the stylistic hallmark of **empathetic narrative** but semantically anomalous when decontextualised, e.g. *tomorrow was Monday; he now knew the truth.*

WHIZ-deletion A term formerly used in generative grammar to refer to the conversion of a relative clause into a post-modifying phrase through the omission of a relative pronoun and its associated verb, e.g. *the man [who is] standing next to me.*

word formation The pattern or structure of a word, or the process by which a word has come into existence.

BIBLIOGRAPHY

1 Introduction

Abercrombie, D. (1963). *Problems and Principles in Language Study*. 2nd edn. London: Longman.

(1965). *Studies in Phonetics and Linguistics*. London: Oxford University Press.

Alford, H. (1864). *The Queen's English: a Manual of Idiom and Usage*. London: Longman and Green.

(1864). *A Plea for the Queen's English*.

Algeo, J. (1988a). A computer corpus for a dictionary of Briticisms. In Kytö, Ihalainen & Riissanen (eds.), 45–59.

(1988b). British and American Grammatical Differences. *International Journal of Lexicography* 1: 1–31.

(ed.) (forthcoming). *English in North America: origins and development. The Cambridge History of the English Language*, vol. VI. Cambridge: Cambridge University Press.

Algeo, J. & A. Algeo (1993). Among the new words. *American Speech* 68: 253–62.

Anderson, B. (1991). *Imagined Communities. Reflections on the Origin and Spread of Nationalism*. London: Verso. Revised edn.

Ashcroft, B., Griffiths, G. & H. Tiffin (1989). *The Empire Writes Back: Theory and Practice in Post-colonial Literatures*. London: Routledge.

Auerbach, E. (1968). *Mimesis*. Princeton, NJ: Princeton University Press.

Ayto, J. (1983). English: failures of language reforms. In Fodor, I. & C. Hagège (eds.), *Language Reform. History and Future*, vol. I. Hamburg: Helmut Buske Verlag, 85–100.

Bailey, C-J. N. & K. Maroldt (1977). The French lineage of English. In Meisel, Jürgen (ed.), *Pidgins – Creoles – Languages in Contact*. Tübingen: Narr, 21–53.

Bailey, R. W. (1991). *Images of English*. Ann Arbor: University of Michigan Press.

Baker, S. J. (1945). *The Australian Language*. Melbourne: Sun Books.

Baron, D. (1990). *The English-Only Question. An Official Language for Americans*. New Haven: Yale University Press.

Bauer, L. (1993). Progress with a Corpus of New Zealand English and some early results. In Souter, C. & E. Atwell (eds.) *Corpus-Based Computational Linguistics*. Amsterdam: Rodopi. 1–10.

Baugh, A. C. & T. Cable (1993). *A History of the English Language*. 4th edn. London: Routledge.

Beier, A. L. & R. Finlay (eds.) (1986). *London 1500–1700. The Making of the Metropolis*. London: Longman.

Bell, A. (1982). This isn't the BBC: colonialism in New Zealand English. *Applied Linguistics* 3: 246–58.

Beloff, M. (1938). *Public Order and Public Disturbances, 1660– 1714*. London.

Bhabha, H. K. (ed.) (1990). *Nation and Narration*. London: Routledge.

Biber, D. & E. Finegan (1989). Drift and the evolution of English style: a history of three genres. *Language* 65: 487–517.

Blake, N. F. (1992). Translation and the history of English. In Rissanen, Ihalainen, Nevalainen & Taavitsainen (eds.), 3–24.

Brathwaite, E. K. (1984). *The History of the Voice: the Development of Nation Language in Anglophone Caribbean Poetry*. London: New Beacon Books.

Brookman, J. (1993). Britain's lost literary horizons. *Times Higher Education Supplement*, 12 February.

Burchfield, R. W. (1989). *The English Language*. Oxford: Oxford University Press.

(ed.) (1994). *English in Britain and Overseas: Origins and Development. The Cambridge History of the English Language*, vol. V. Cambridge: Cambridge University Press.

Cameron, D. & J. Bourne (1988). No common ground: Kingman, Grammar and the Nation. *Language and Education* 2: 147–60.

Chambers, J. K. 1992. Dialect acquisition. *Language* 68: 673–705.

Chambers, J. K. & P. Trudgill (1980). *Dialectology*. Cambridge: Cambridge University Press.

Chapman, R. W. (1932). Oxford English. *Society for Pure English*, 4, no. 37.

Clyne, M. (ed.) (1992). *Pluricentric Languages Differing Norms in Different Languages*. Berlin: Mouton de Gruyter.

Cobbett, W. (1818). *A Grammar of the English Language*. London.

Collins, P. & P. Peters (1988). The Australian Corpus Project. In Kytö, Ihalainen & Rissanen (eds.), 103–20.

Cooper, C. (1995). *Noises in the Blood. Orality, Gender, and the 'Vulgar' Body of Jamaican Culture*. Durham: Duke University Press.

Corfield, P. J. (1991). Class by name and number in eighteenth century Britain. In Corfield (ed.), 101–49.

(ed.) (1991). *Language, History and Class*. Oxford: Blackwell.

Crowley, T. (ed.) (1991). *Proper English? Readings in Language, History and Cultural Identity*. London: Routledge.

Daly, M. (1987). *Webster's First New Intergalactic Wickedary of the English Language Conjured by Mary Daly in Cahoots with Jane Caputi*. Boston: Beacon Press.

De Quincey, T. (1890). The English Language. In Masson, D. (ed.), *Collected Writings New and Enlarged*. 14 vols. Edinburgh. Vol. XIV: 146–61.

Delbridge, A. (1990). Australian English now. In Ricks, C. & L Michaels (eds.), *The State of the Language*. Berkeley: University of California Press, 66–76.

Department of Education and Science (DES) (1985). *Education for all*. (The Swann Report on the Education of Children from Ethnic Minority Groups) London: HMSO.

(1988). Report of the Committee of Inquiry into the Teaching of the English Language (The Kingman Report). London: HMSO.

Duff, A. (1990). *Once Were Warriors*. Auckland: Tandem Press.

Ellis, A. J. (1869). *On Early English Pronunciation*. London: Early English Text Society.

Enright, D. J. (1989). Tide of pollution that engulfs our language. *The Observer* 24 December.

Fallon, P. & D. Mahon (eds.) (1990). *The Penguin Book of Contemporary Irish Verse*. Harmondsworth: Penguin.

Ferguson, C. F. & S. B. Heath (eds.) (1981). *Language in the USA*. Cambridge: Cambridge University Press.

Fowler, H. W. (1906). *The King's English*. Oxford: Oxford University Press.

Gates, H. L. , Jr. (1992). African American criticism. In Greenblatt, S. & G. Gunn (eds.) (1992), *Redrawing the Boundaries. The Transformation of English and American Literary Studies*. New York: The Modern Language Association, 303–19.

Gerritsen, M. & D. Stein (eds.) (1992). *Internal and External Factors in Syntactic Change*. Berlin: Mouton de Gruyter.

Giegerich, H. J. (1992). *English Phonology. An Introduction*. Cambridge: Cambridge University Press.

Gimson, A. C. (1980). *An Introduction to the Pronunciation of English*. 3rd edn. London: Edward Arnold.

Gordon, G. (1970). *The Status Areas of Edinburgh. A Historical Analysis*. Ph.D. thesis. University of Edinburgh.

Graham, G. F. (1869). *A Book About Words*. Chapter XIII Slang Words and Americanisms. Reprinted in Crowley, T. (ed.) (1991), *Proper English? Readings in Language, History and Cultural Identity*. London: Routledge, 159–70.

Gramsci, A. (1985). *Selections from Cultural Writings*. (Eds. D. Forgacs & G. Nowell Smith; trans. W. Boelhower.) London: Lawrence & Wishart.

Greaves, W. (1989). Selling English by the pound. *The Times* October 24: 14.

Greenbaum, S. (1990). Whose English? In Ricks, C. & L. Michaels (eds.), *The State of the Language*. Berkeley: University of California Press, 15–23.

Grillo, R. D. (1989). *Dominant Languages. Language and Hierarchy in Britain and France*. Cambridge: Cambridge University Press.

Harris, J. (1984). Syntactic variation and dialect divergence. *Journal of Linguistics* 20: 303–27.

(1991). Conservation vs. substratal transfer in Irish English. In Trudgill & Chambers (eds.), 191–212.

Harris, M. (1987). Developing one's Haspirations. *Daily Telegraph*. December 23:14.

Hobsbawm, E. J. (1987). *The Age of Empire, 1875–1914*. London: Weidenfeld & Nicholson.

Holmes, J. (1995). Glottal stops in New Zealand English: an analysis of variants of word final /t/. *Linguistics* 33: 433–65.

Honey, J. (1988). *The Language Trap: Race, Class and the 'Standard Language' Issue in British Schools*. London: National Council for Educational Standards.

(1989). *Does Accent Matter? The Pygmalion Factor*. Boston: Faber and Faber.

Hon. H. H. (1866). *Poor Letter H. Its Use and Abuse*. London: John F. Shaw and Co. (40th edn.)

Hulme, K. (1983). *The Bone People*. Auckland: Hodder & Stoughton.

Ihimaera, W. (1987). *The Matriarch*. Auckland: Heinemann.

Jameson, F. (1986). Third-World literature in the era of multinational capitalism. *Social Text* 15: 65–88.

Johnson, S. (1755). *A Dictionary of the English Language*. 2 vols. London.

Jones, C. (1993). Scottish Standard English in the late eighteenth century. *Transactions of the Philological Society* 91: 95–131.

Jones, D. (1917). *An English Pronouncing Dictionary*. London: Dent.

Kachru, B. (ed.) (1980). *The Other Tongue*. Oxford: Pergamon.

Kallen, J. L. (1994), English in Ireland. In Burchfield (ed.), 148–97.

Kelman, J. (1994). *How Late it was, How Late*. London: Secker and Warburg.

Kilpiö, M. (1995). The verb *To Be* from Old to Early Modern English. In Rissanen, M. *et al.* (1995), *English in Transition. Diachronic Studies in Variation*. Berlin: Mouton de Gruyter.

Kincaid, J. (1996). *The Autobiography of My Mother*. New York: Farrar Straus, Giroux.

Kloss, H. (1967). Abstand languages and Ausbau languages. *Anthropological Linguistics* 9: 29–41.

(1978). *Die Entwicklung neuer germanischer Kultursprachen seit 1800*. Düsseldorf: Schwann.

Kytö, M. (1991). *Variation and Diachrony, with Early American English in Focus*. Frankfurt: Peter Lang.

Kytö, M., O. Ihalainen & M. Rissanen (eds.) (1988). *Corpus Linguistics, Hard and Soft*. Amsterdam: Rodopi.

Labov, W. (1966). *The Social Stratification of English in New York City*. Washington, DC: Centre for Applied Linguistics.

(1991). The boundaries of a grammar: inter-dialectal reactions to positive *anymore*. In Trudgill & Chambers (eds.), 273–88.

Lass, R. (forthcoming). Phonology and morphology. In Lass, R. (ed.), *The Cambridge History of the English Language. Volume III 1476–1776*. Cambridge: Cambridge University Press.

Leitner, G. (1982). The consolidation of 'Educated Southern English' as a model in the early 20th century. *International Review of Applied Linguistics* 20: 91–107.

(1984). Australian English or English in Australia – linguistic identity or dependence in broadcast language. *English World Wide* 5: 55–85.

Le Page, R. B. & A. Tabouret-Keller (1985). *Acts of Identity. Creole-based Approaches to Language and Ethnicity*. Cambridge: Cambridge University Press.

McAfee, A. (1994). Judges split as Kelman wins Booker. *Financial Times*. October 12: 12.

Macaulay, R. K. S. (1988). RP R.I.P. *Applied Linguistics* 9: 115–24.

McClure, J. D. (1994). English in Scotland. In Burchfield (ed.), 23–94.

McCrum, R., W. Cran & R. MacNeil (1986). *The Story of English*. New York: Viking Penguin Inc.

McLuhan, M. (1989). *The Global Village: Transformations in World Life and Media in the 21st Century*. Oxford: Oxford University Press.

Marshall, D. (1982). *Industrial England 1776–1851*. (2nd edn) London.

Matthews, B. (1900). The future literary centre of the English Language. *Bookman* 12: 238–42.

Mencken, H. L. (1919). *The American Language*. Knopf: New York.

Miller, G. M. (ed.) (1971). *BBC Pronouncing Dictionary of English Names*. London: Oxford University Press.

Milroy, J. (1992). *Linguistic Variation and Change*. Oxford: Blackwell.

Milroy J. & L. Milroy (1985). Linguistic change, social network, and speaker innovation. *Journal of Linguistics* 21: 339–84.

Milroy, L. (1984). Comprehension and context: successful communication and communicative breakdown. In Trudgill, P. (ed.), *Applied Sociolinguistics*. London: Academic Press, 7–33.

Mitchell, A. G. (1946). *The Pronunciation of English in Australia*. Sydney: Angus and Robertson.

Molee, E. (1888). *Plea for an American Language, or Germanic-English*. Chicago: John Anderson and Company.

Morris, M. (ed.) (1988). *Jean Binta Breeze Riddym Ravings and Other Poems*. London: Race Today Publications.

Mudrooroo [Narogin] (1990). *Writing from the Fringe. A Study of Modern Aboriginal Literature*. Melbourne: Hyland House.

Mugglestone, L. (1995). '*Talking Proper.' The Rise of Accent as Social Symbol*. Oxford: Oxford University Press.

Murray, J. A. H. (1900). *The Evolution of English Lexicography: The Romanes Lecture*. Oxford. (1970. College Park, MD: McGrath)

Neale, A. V. & H. R. E. Wallis (eds.) (1955). *The Boke of Chyldren by Thomas Phaire*. Edinburgh: E. & S. Livingstone.

Newbolt, H. (1921). The teaching of English in England. Extracts reprinted in Crowley (ed.) (1991), 193–206.

Nordberg, B. (ed.) (1994). *The Sociolinguistics of Urbanisation: The Case of the Nordic Countries*. Berlin: Mouton de Gruyter.

Osselton, N. E. (1984). Informal spelling systems in Early Modern English 1500–1800. In Blake, N. F. & C. Jones (eds.), *English Historical Linguistics: Studies in Development*. Sheffield: The Centre for English Cultural Tradition and Language, 123–137.

Paine, T. (1791). *The Rights of Man*. (ed. H. Collins. (1969). Harmondsworth: Penguin)

Pedersen, H. (1931). *The Discovery of Language: Linguistic Science in the Nineteenth Century*. (Trans. J. W. Spargo (1959). Bloomington: Indiana University Press)

Penelope, J. (1990). *Speaking Freely. Unlearning the Lies of The Fathers' Tongues*. Oxford: Pergamon.

Phillips, K. C. (1984). *Language in Victorian England*. Oxford: Blackwell.

Preisler, B. (1995). Standard English in the world. *Multilingua* 14: 341–62.

Quirk, R., S. Greenbaum, G. Leech & J. Svartvik (1985). *A Comprehensive Grammar of the English Language*. London: Longman.

Ramson, W. S. (ed.) (1988). *The Australian National Dictionary: a Dictionary of Australianisms in Historical Perspective*. Melbourne: Oxford University Press.

Read, A. W. (1933). British recognition of American speech in the eighteenth century. *Dialect Notes* 6: 313–34. (Reprinted in Dillard, J. L. (1980), *Social Perspectives on American English*. The Hague: Mouton, 15–35.)

Rissanen, M., O. Ihalainen, T. Nevalainen & I. Taavitsainen (eds.) (1992). *History of Englishes. New Methods and Interpretations in Historical Linguistics*. Berlin: Mouton de Gryuter.

Romaine, S. (1982). *Socio-Historical Linguistics. Its Status and Methodology*. Cambridge: Cambridge University Press.

(1984a). The sociolinguistic history of t/d deletion. *Folia Linguistica Historica* 5: 221–55.

(1984b). On the problem of syntactic variation and pragmatic meaning in sociolinguistic theory. *Folia Linguistica* 18: 409–39.

(1991). Introduction. In Romaine, S. (ed.), *Language in Australia*. Cambridge: Cambridge University Press, 1–24.

(1995). Birds of a different feather: Tok Pisin and Hawai'i Creole English as literary languages. *The Contemporary Pacific. A Journal of Island Affairs* 7: 81–123.

(1996). Internal vs. external factors in socio-historical explanations of change: a fruitless dichotomy? In Ahlers, J., L. Bilmes, J. S. Guenter, B. A. Kaiser & J. Namkung (eds.), *Proceedings of the Twenty-First Annual Meeting of the Berkeley Linguistics Society. General Session and Parasession on Historical Issues in Sociolinguistics/Social Issues in Historical Linguistics*. Department of Linguistics. University of California, Berkeley, 478–91.

(1997a). The British heresy in ESL revisited. In Eliasson, S. & E. H. Jahr (eds.), *Language and its Ecology*. Berlin: Mouton de Gruyter, 417–32.

(1997b). Forgetting and remembering: Novels and nations. 11th Pacific History Association Conference and Twenty First Annual University of Hawai'i Pacific Islands Studies Conference. History, Culture and Power in the Pacific. To appear in *Ethnohistory*.

(forthcoming). English in Contact with other Languages. In Algeo (ed.) (forthcoming).

Rosewarne, D. (1994). Estuary English; Tomorrow's RP? *English Today* 37: 3–8.

Ross, A. S. C. (1956). U and non-U. Reprinted in Mitford, N. (ed.) (1980). *Noblesse Oblige*. London: Futura, 11–38.

Said, E. W. (1993). Culture and Imperialism. New York: Alfred A. Knopf.

Sapir, E. (1921). *Language. An Introduction to the study of speech*. New York: Harcourt, Brace.

Seton-Watson, H. (1977). *Nations and States. An Enquiry into the Origins of Nations and the Politics of Nationalism*. Boulder, CO: Westview Press.

Shattuck, J. & M. Wolff (eds.) (1982). Introduction. *The Victorian Periodical Press. Samplings and Soundings*. Toronto: University of Toronto Press.

Shaw, G. B. (1916). *Pygmalion*. New York: Brentano.

Simon, J. (1980). *Paradigms Lost. Reflections on Literacy and Its Decline*. New York: Clarkson N. Potter, Inc.

Singh, G. (ed.) (1983). *Collected Essays. D. Q. Leavis*. Vol. I: *The Englishness of the English Novel*. Cambridge: Cambridge University Press.

Smith, L. J. (1994). 'The prize will be useful. I'm skint'. *The Times*. October 13.

Snow, C. P. (1959). *The two cultures: and a second look*. New York: Mentor.

Spender, D. (1980). *Man Made Language*. London: Routledge.

Stead, C. K. (1985). Keri Hulme's *The Bone People* and the Pegasus Award for Maori Literature. *Ariel* 16: 178–88.

Steiner, G. (1975). Why English? Presidential Address delivered to the English Association. London.

Strang, B. M. H. (1970). *A History of English*. London: Methuen.

Sweet, H. (1890). *A Primer of Spoken English*. Oxford.

Treglown, J. (ed.) (1988). *The Lantern Bearers and Other Essays by Robert Louis Stevenson*. New York: Farrar Straus Giroux.

Trench, D. [Richard Chevenix] (1855). *English Past and Present*. Five lectures. London: John W. Parker and Son.

Trudgill, P. (1974). *The Social Differentiation of English in Norwich*. Cambridge: Cambridge University Press.

   (1981). On the limits of passive 'competence': sociolinguistics and the polylectal grammar controversy. In Crystal, D. (ed.), *Linguistic Controversies: Festschrift for F. R. Palmer*. London: Arnold.

   (1986). *Dialects in Contact*. Oxford: Blackwell.

Trudgill, P. & J. Hannah (1982). *International English. A Guide to Varieties of Standard English*. London: Edward Arnold.

Trudgill, P. & J. K. Chambers (eds.) (1991). *Dialects of English. Studies in Grammatical Variation*. Harlow: Longman.

Tulloch, G. (1989). Review of *The Good News Bible*. Australian Bicentennial Edition. *English World Wide* 10: 178–9.

Watt, I. (1957). *The Rise of the Novel. Studies in Defoe, Richardson and Fielding*. Berkeley and Los Angeles: University of California Press.

Webster, N. (1788). *American Spelling Book*. Middletown, CT: William H. Niles. (1831 edn.)

(1789). *Dissertations on the English Language*. Boston: Thomas.

(1806). *A Compendious Dictionary of the English Language*. Sidney's Press. (Facsimile edition 1970 edn. by P. P. Gove. Bounty Books.)

(1828). *An American Dictionary of the English Language*. New York: Converse.

Weinreich, U., W. Labov, & M. Herzog (1968). Empirical foundations for a theory of language change. In Lehmann, W. P. & Y. Malkiel (eds.), *Directions in Historical Linguistics*. Austin: University of Texas Press, 95–189.

Wells, J. C. (1982). *Accents of English*, 3 vols. Cambridge: Cambridge University Press.

Wendt, A. (1973). *Sons for the Return Home*. Auckland: Longman Paul.

(1978). *Leaves of the Banyan Tree*. Auckland: Longman Paul.

Williams, G. A. (1989). *Artisans and Sans-Culottes: Popular Movements in France and Britain during the French Revolution*. Routledge: London.

Willinsky, J. (1994). *Empire of Words. The Reign of the OED*. Princeton, NJ: Princeton University Press.

Wrightson, K. (1991). Estates, degrees, and sorts: changing perceptions of society in Tudor and Stuart England. In Corfield (ed.), 30–52.

Wyld, H. C. (1906). *The Place of the Mother Tongue in National Education*. London: Murray.

(1920). *A History of Modern Colloquial English*. 3rd edn. Oxford: Blackwell..

(1927). *A Short History of English*. 3rd edn. London: John Murray.

(1934). *The Best English: a Claim for the Superiority of Received Standard English*. Society for Pure English, tract 39. Oxford: Clarendon Press.

2 Vocabulary

Adams, V. (1973). *An Introduction to Modern English Word-Formation*. London: Longman.

Aitchison, J. (1987). *Words in the Mind: an Introduction to the Mental Lexicon*. Oxford: Blackwell.

Algeo, J. (1971). The voguish uses of *non. American Speech* 46: 87–105.

(1975). The acronym and its congeners. *First LACUS Forum 1974*, ed. Adam Makkai and Valerie Becker Makkai, 217–34. Columbia, SC: Hornbeam.

(1977). Blends, a structural and systemic view. *American Speech* 52: 47–64.

(1978). The taxonomy of word making. *Word* 29: 122–31.

(1980). Where do all the new words come from? *American Speech* 55: 264–77.

(1990). American Lexicography. In *Wörterbücher • Dictionaries • Dictionnaires: International Encyclopedia of Lexicography*, ed. F. J. Hausmann, O. Reichmann, H. E. Wiegand & L. Zgusta, 1987–2009. Berlin: de Gruyter.

Algeo, J. & A. S. Algeo (eds.) (1991). *Fifty Years 'Among the New Words': A Dictionary of Neologisms*, 1941–1991. New York: Cambridge University Press.

Among the new words. (1941–). Ed. D. L. Bolinger, I. W. Russell, M. G. Porter, J. Algeo, A. S. Algeo & W. Glowka. *American Speech* 16– .

Aronoff, M. (1976). *Word Formation in Generative Grammar.* Cambridge, MA: MIT Press.

Ayto, J. (1989–90). *The Longman Register of New Words.* 2 vols. Harlow, Essex: Longman.

Bailey, R. W. (ed.) (1978). *Early Modern English: Additions and Antedatings to the Record of English Vocabulary, 1475–1700.* Hildesheim: Georg Olms.

Barber, C. (1964). *Linguistic Change in Present-Day English.* Edinburgh: Oliver & Boyd.

Barnhart, C. L. & D. K. Barnhart (eds.) (1982–). *The Barnhart Dictionary Companion: A Quarterly to Update General Dictionaries.* Cold Spring, NY: Lexik House.

Barnhart, C. L. & R. K. Barnhart (eds.) (1988). *World Book Dictionary.* Chicago: World Book.

Barnhart, C. L., S. Steinmetz & R. K. Barnhart (1973). *The Barnhart Dictionary of New English since 1963.* Bronxville, NY: Barnhart.

(1980). *The Second Barnhart Dictionary of New English.* Bronxville, NY: Barnhart.

Barnhart, D. K. (1987). *The Barnhart Dictionary Companion Index (1982–1985).* Cold Spring, NY: Lexik House.

(1994). *The Barnhart New-Words Concordance.* Cold Spring, NY: Lexik House.

Barnhart, R. K. & S. Steinmetz (eds.) (1988). *The Barnhart Dictionary of Etymology.* Bronx, NY: H. W. Wilson.

Barnhart, R. K. & S. Steinmetz, with C. L. Barnhart (1990). *The Third Barnhart Dictionary of New English.* New York: H. W. Wilson.

Bauer, L. (1983). *English Word-Formation.* Cambridge: Cambridge University Press.

Beale, P. (ed.) (1984). *A Dictionary of Slang and Unconventional English.* By Eric Partridge. London: Routledge & Kegan Paul.

Beard, R. (1976). Once more on the analysis of ed-adjectives. *Journal of Linguistics* 12: 155–7.

Biese, Y. M. (1941). *Origin and Development of Conversions in English.* Annales Academiae Scientiarum Fennicae, ser. B, vol. 45, no. 2. Helsinki: Suomalainen Tiedeakatemia.

Boase-Beier, J. (1987). *Poetic Compounds: The Principles of Poetic Language in Modern English Poetry.* Tübingen: Max Niemeyer.

Bolinger, D. L. (1937–40). The living language. *Words: A Periodical Devoted to the Study of the Origin, History, and Etymology of English Words* 3–6. Los Angeles, CA.

Brown, R. W. (1956). *Composition of Scientific Words.* Rev. edn. Washington: Smithsonian Institution Press.

Burchfield, R. W. (1972–86). *A Supplement to the Oxford English Dictionary.* 4 vols. Oxford: Clarendon.

Butler, S. (ed.) (1990). *The Macquarie Dictionary of New Words.* Macquarie University: Macquarie Library.

Cannon, G. (1987). *Historical Change and English Word-Formation.* New York: Peter Lang.

Cartsensen, B. (1968). Zur Systematik und Terminologie Deutsch-Englischer Lehnbeziehungen. *In Wortbildung, Syntax, und Morphologie: Festschrift zum 60. Geburtstag von Hans Marchand*, ed. H. E. Brekle & L. Lipka, 32–45. The Hague: Mouton.

Cassidy, F. G. & J. Hall (eds.) (1985–) *Dictionary of American Regional English*. Vols. 1–. Cambridge, MA: Belknap.

Chapin, P. G. (1967). *On the Syntax of Word-Derivation in English*. Bedford, MA: Mitre Corp.

Chapman, R. L. (1986). *New Dictionary of American Slang*. New York: Harper and Row.

Clark, E. V. & H. H. Clark (1979). When nouns surface as verbs. *Language* 55: 767–811.

Derolez, R. (1972). Two new dictionaries [Finkenstaedt, Leisi, Wolff 1970; Lehnert 1971]. *English Studies* 53: 144–52.

Downing, P. (1977). On the creation and use of English compound nouns. *Language* 53: 810–42.

Ellegård, A. (1963). *English, Latin, and Morphemic Analysis*. Gothenburg Studies in English 15. Göteborg: University of Gothenburg.

Finkenstaedt, T., E. Leisi & D. Wolff (1970). *A Chronological English Dictionary Listing 80,000 Words in Order of Their Earliest Known Occurrence*. Heidelberg: Carl Winter.

Finkenstaedt, T. & D. Wolff (1973). *Ordered Profusion: Studies in Dictionaries and the English Lexicon*. Heidelberg: Carl Winter.

Flexner, S. B. (ed.) (1987). *The Random House Dictionary of the English Language*. 2nd edn., unabridged. New York: Random House.

Foster, B. (1968). *The Changing English Language*. London: Macmillan.

Gilman, E. W. (ed.) (1989). *Webster's Dictionary of English Usage*. Springfield, MA: Merriam-Webster.

Gove, P. B. (ed.) (1961). *Webster's Third New International Dictionary of the English Language*. Springfield, MA: Merriam-Webster.

Halle, M. (1973). Prolegomena to a theory of word formation. *Linguistic Inquiry* 4: 3–16.

Hatcher, A. G. (1951). *Modern English Word-Formation and Neo-Latin*. Baltimore: Johns Hopkins Press.

Haugen, E. (1950). The analysis of linguistic borrowing. *Language* 26: 210–31.

Hawkins, R. E. (ed.) (1984). *Common Indian Words in English*. Delhi: Oxford University Press.

Hirtle, W. H. (1969). -Ed adjectives like 'verandahed' and 'blue-eyed'. *Journal of Linguistics* 6: 19–36.

Hofland, K. & S. Johansson (1982). *Word Frequencies in British and American English*. Bergan: Norwegian Computing Centre for the Humanities.

Hudson, R. A. (1975). Problems in the analysis of ed-adjectives. *Journal of Linguistics* 11: 69–72.

Jespersen, O. (1942). *A Modern English Grammar on Historical Principles*, vol. 6, *Morphology*. London: Allen & Unwin, reprinted 1961.

Johansson, S. (1978). *Some Aspects of the Vocabulary of Learned and Scientific English*. Gothenburg Studies in English 42. Göteborg: University of Gothenburg.

Johansson, S. & K. Hofland (1989). *Frequency Analysis of English Vocabulary and Grammar*. 2 vols. Oxford: Clarendon.

Klein, E. (1966–7). *A Comprehensive Etymological Dictionary of the English Language*. 2 vols. Amsterdam: Elsevier, one-volume reprint 1971.

Koziol. H. (1972). *Handbuch der englischen Wortbildungslehre*. Heidelberg: Carl Winter.

Kruisinga, E. (1932). *A Handbook of Present-Day English*. Part II, *English Accidence and Syntax* 3. 5th edn. Groningen: Noordhoff.

Kurath, H. & S. M. Kuhn (eds.) (1954–). *Middle English Dictionary*. Ann Arbor: University of Michigan Press.

Kurian, G. T. (1993). *Timenglish: The Words of Time*. Baldwin Place, NY: Word Almanac.

Lees, R. B. (1960). *The Grammar of English Nominalizations*. Reprint, The Hague: Mouton, 1968.

Lehnert, M. (1971). *Rückläufiges Wörterbuch der englischen Gegenwartssprache*. Leipzig: VEB Verlag Enzyklopädie.

Leith, D. (1983). *A Social History of English*. London: Routledge & Kegan Paul.

Lerner, S. & G. S. Belkin. (1993). *Trash Cash, Fizzbos, and Flatliners: A Dictionary of Today's Words*. Boston: Houghton Mifflin. Reprinted as *A Dictionary of New Words* (New York: Barnes and Noble, 1995).

Levi, J. N. (1978). *The Syntax and Semantics of Complex Nominals*. New York: Academic.

Lieber, R. (1981). *On the Organization of the Lexicon*. Bloomington: Indiana University Linguistics Club.

Lighter, J. E. (1994–). *Random House Historical Dictionary of American Slang*. Vols. 1–. New York: Random House.

Lindelöf, U. (1938). *English Verb-Adverb Groups Converted into Nouns*. Commentationes Humanarum Litterarum, vol. 9, no. 5. Helsingfors: Societas Scientiarum Fennica.

Ljung, M. (1970). *English Denominal Adjectives: A Generative Study of the Semantics of a Group of High-Frequency Denominal Adjectives in English*. Gothenburg Studies in English 21. Göteborg: University of Gothenburg.

(1974). *A Frequency Dictionary of English Morphemes*. Stockholm: AWE/Gebers.

(1976). -Ed adjectives revisited. *Journal of Linguistics* 12: 159–68.

Malkiel, Y. (1993). *Etymology*. Cambridge: Cambridge University Press.

Marchand, H. (1969). *The Categories and Types of Present-Day English Word-Formation*. 2nd edn. Munich: C. H. Beck.

Matthews, P. H. (1974). *Morphology: An Introduction to the Theory of Word-Structure*. Cambridge: Cambridge University Press.

McMillan, J. B. (1980). Infixing and interposing in English. *American Speech* 55: 163–83.

Meus, V. (1975). Review of *Ordered Profusion*, by T. Finkenstaedt and D. Wolff. *English Studies* 56: 181–3.

Meys, W. J. (1975). *Compound Adjectives in English and the Ideal Speaker-Listener.* Amsterdam: North-Holland.

Mish, F. C. (1976). *6,000 Words: A Supplement to Webster's Third New International Dictionary.* Springfield, MA: Merriam-Webster.

(1983). *9,000 Words: A Supplement to Webster's Third New International Dictionary.* Springfield, MA: Merriam-Webster.

(1986). *12,000 Words: A Supplement to Webster's Third New International Dictionary.* Springfield, MA: Merriam-Webster.

Morris, W. (ed.) (1969). *American Heritage Dictionary of the English Language.* New York: American Heritage.

Mort, S. (1986). *Longman Guardian New Words.* Harlow, Essex: Longman.

Morton, H. C. (1994). *The Story of 'Webster's Third': Philip Gove's Controversial Dictionary and Its Critics.* New York: Cambridge University Press.

Murray, E. (1977). *Caught in the Web of Words: James Murray and the Oxford English Dictionary.* New Haven, CT: Yale University Press.

Murray, J. A. H., H. Bradley, W. A. Craigie & C. T. Onions. 1884–1933. *The Oxford English Dictionary.* 2nd edn., prepared by J. A Simpson and E. S. C. Weiner. 20 vols. Oxford: Clarendon, 1989.

Neufeldt, V. (ed.) (1988). *Webster's New World Dictionary of American English.* 3rd college edn. New York: Webster's New World.

Neuhaus, H. J. (1971). Towards a diachronic analysis of vocabulary. *Cahiers de lexicologie* 18: 29–42.

Norrick, N. R. (1987). Semantic aspects of comparative noun-adjective compounds. In *Neuere Forschungen zur Wortbildung und Historiographie der Linguistik: Festgabe für Herbert E. Brekle zum 50. Geburtstag*, 145–54. Tübingen: Narr.

Onions, C. T. (1966). *The Oxford Dictionary of English Etymology.* New York: Oxford University Press.

Pennanen, E. V. (1966). *Contributions to the Study of Back-Formation in English.* Acta Academiae Socialis, ser. A, vol. 4. Tampere: Julkaisija Yhteiskunnallinen Korkeakoulu.

(1971). *On the Introduction of French Loan-Words into English.* Acta Universitatis Tamperensis, ser. A., vol. 38. Tampere: Tampereen Yliopsisto.

(1972). Current views of word-formation. *Neuphilologische Mitteilungen* 73: 292–308.

(1982). Remarks on syntagma and word-formation. *Folia Linguistica* 16: 241–61.

Pfeffer, J. A. (1987). *Deutsches Sprachgut im Wortschatz der Amerikaner und Engländer.* Tübingen: Max Niemeyer.

Pound, L. (1914). *Blends: Their Relation to English Word Formation.* Anglistische Forschungen 42. Heidelberg: Carl Winter.

Praninskas, J. (1968). *Trade Name Creation: Processes and Patterns.* The Hague: Mouton.

Quirk, R., S. Greenbaum, G. Leech & J. Svartvik (1985). *A Comprehensive Grammar of the English Language*. London: Longman.

Rao, G. S. (1954). *Indian Words in English*. Oxford: Clarendon.

Ruhl, C. (1989). *On Monosemy: A Study in Linguistic Semantics*. Albany: State University of New York Press.

Schäfer, J. (1980). *Documentation in the 'O.E.D.': Shakespeare and Nash as Test Cases*. Oxford: Clarendon.

Serjeantson, M. S. (1935). *A History of Foreign Words in English*. London: Routledge & Kegan Paul.

Seymour, R. K. (1968). *A Bibliography of Word Formation in the Germanic Languages*. Durham, NC: Duke University Press.

Simpson, J. (1988). The new vocabulary of English. In *Words for Robert Burchfield's Sixty-Fifth Birthday*, ed. E. G. Stanley & T. F. Hoad, 143–52. Cambridge: D. S. Brewer.

Simpson, J. & E. Weiner (1993). *Oxford English Dictionary Additions Series*. 2 vols. Oxford: Clarendon.

Soukhanov, A. H. (1995). *Word Watch: The Stories behind the Words of Our Lives*. New York: Holt.

Starnes, D. T. & G. E. Noyes (1946). *The English Dictionary from Cawdrey to Johnson, 1604–1755*. Chapel Hill: University of North Carolina Press.

Stein, G. (1973). *English Word-Formation over Two Centuries*. Tübingen: Narr.

(1977). The place of word-formation in linguistic description. In *Perspektiven der Wortbildungsforschung*, ed. Herbert E. Brekle and Dieter Kastovsky, 219–35. Bonn: Bouvier.

(1984). Champers, preggers, starkers: *-ers* in present-day English. In *Navicula Tubingensis: Studia in Honorem Antonii Tovar*, ed. F. J. Oroz Arizcuren, 353–57. Tübingen: Narr.

Svartvik, J. (ed.) (1996). *Words: Proceedings of an International Symposium, Lund, 25–26 August 1995, organized under the auspices of the Royal Academy of Letters, History and Antiquities*. Stockholm: Kungl. Vitterhets Historie och Antikvitets Akademien.

Thorén, B. (1959). *8000 ord för 8 års engelska*. Malmö: Gleerups.

Thorndike, E. L. & I. Lorge (1944). *The Teacher's Word Book of 30,000 Words*. New York: Teachers College, Columbia University, 3rd printing 1959.

Thun, N. (1963). *Reduplicative Words in English: A Study of Formations of the Types 'Tick-tick', 'Hurly-burly', and 'Shilly-shally'*. Lund: Carl Bloms.

Trench, R. C. (1851). *On the Study of Words*. 2nd edn. New York: Redfield, 1852.

(1855). *English, Past and Present*. 9th edn. London: Macmillan, 1875.

Wall, C. E. & E. Przebienda (eds.) (1969–70). *Words and Phrases Index*. 4 vols. Ann Arbor, MI: Pierian.

Warren, B. (1978). *Semantic Patterns of Noun-Noun Compounds*. Gothenburg Studies in English 41. Göteborg: University of Gothenburg.

Williams, R. (1976). *Keywords: A Vocabulary of Culture and Society*. New York: Oxford University Press.

Willinsky, J. (1994). *Empire of Words: The Reign of the OED*. Princeton, NJ: Princeton University Press.

Words and meanings, New. 1944–76. Ed. D. L. Bolinger, I. W. Russell, R. L. Chapman, S. Potter & the G. and C. Merriam staff. *Britannica Book of the Year*. Chicago: Encyclopaedia Britannica.

Zandvoort, R. W. (1969). *A Handbook of English Grammar*. 5th edn. London: Longmans.

3 Syntax

Aarts, B. (1998). Binominal Noun Phrases in English. *Transactions of the Philological Society* 96: 117–58.

Adamson, S. (1994). From empathetic deixis to empathetic narrative: stylisation and (de-)subjectivisation as processes of language change. *Transactions of the Philological Society* 92: 55–88.

Adamson, S., V. A. Law, N. Vincent & S. Wright (eds.) (1990). *Papers from the 5th International Conference on English Historical Linguistics: Cambridge, 6–9 April 1987*. (Current Issues in Linguistic Theory 65.) Amsterdam and Philadelphia: John Benjamins.

Aijmer, K. & B. Altenberg (eds.) (1991). *English Corpus Linguistics: Studies in Honour of Jan Svartvik*. London and New York: Longman.

Akmajian, A., R. A. Demers & R. M. Harnish (1979). *Linguistics: an introduction to language and communication*. Cambridge MA and London: MIT Press.

Algeo, J. (1992). British and American mandative constructions. In Blank (1992: 599–617).

Allen, R. L. (1966). *The Verb System of Present-Day American English*. (Janua Linguarum, series practica, 24.) The Hague and Paris: Mouton.

Allerton, D. J. (1995). Problems of Modern English grammar IV: findings. *English Studies* 76: 81–90.

Anderson, J. (1993). Parameters of syntactic change: a notional view. In Jones (1993: 1–42).

Arnaud, R. (1983). On the progress of the progressive in the private correspondence of famous British people (1800–1880). In Jacobson (1983: 83–94).

Austin, F. O. (1980). A crescent-shaped jewel of an island: appositive nouns in phrases separated by *of*. *English Studies* 61: 357–66.

   (1985). Relative *which* in late 18th-century usage: the Clift family correspondence. In R. Eaton, O. Fischer, W. Koopman & F. van der Leek (eds.), *Papers from the 4th International Conference on English Historical Linguistics: Amsterdam, 10–13 April 1985*. (Current Issues in Linguistic Theory 41.) Amsterdam and Philadelphia: John Benjamins, 15–29.

van der Auwera, J. (1984) More on the history of subject contact clauses in English. *Folia Linguistica Historica* 5: 171–84.

   (1985). Relative *that* – a centennial dispute. *Journal of Linguistics* 21: 149–79.

Bache, C. (1978). *The Order of Premodifying Adjectives in Present-Day English*. Odense University Press.

Baker, C. L. (1995). Contrast, discourse prominence, and intensification, with special reference to locally free reflexives in British English. *Language* 71: 63–101.

Ball, C. N. (1994). Relative pronouns in *it*-clefts: the last seven centuries. *Language Variation and Change* 6: 179–200.

(1996). A diachronic study of relative markers in spoken and written English. *Language Variation and Change* 8: 227–58.

Barber, C. (1964). *Linguistic Change in Present-Day English*. Edinburgh and London: Oliver and Boyd.

(1985). Linguistic Change in Present-Day English. In S. Backman & G. Kjellmer (eds.), *Papers on Language and Literature: Presented to Alvar Ellegård and Erik Frykman*. (Gothenburg Studies in English 60.) Gothenburg: Acta Universitatis Gothoburgensis, 36–45.

Bauer, L. (1990). Two points of English grammar. *Leeds Working Papers in Linguistics and Phonetics* 5: 19–23.

Biber, D. (1988). *Variation across Speech and Writing*. Cambridge: Cambridge University Press.

Biber, D. & E. Finegan (1987). An initial typology of English text types. In J. Aarts & W. Meijs (eds.), *Corpus Linguistics II: New Studies in the Analysis and Exploitation of Computer Corpora*. (Costerus new series 57.) Amsterdam: Rodopi, 19–46.

(1992). The linguistic evolution of five written and speech-based genres from the 17th to the 20th centuries. In Rissanen, Ihalainen, Nevalainen & Taavitsainen (eds.), 688–704).

Biber, D., E. Finegan, D. Atkinson, A. Beck, D. Burges & J. Burges (1994). The design and analysis of the ARCHER corpus: a progress report [A Representative Corpus of Historical English Registers]. In Kytö, Rissanen & Wright (1994: 3–6).

Blank, C. (ed.) (1992). *Language and Civilization: a Concerted Profusion of Essays and Studies in Honour of Otto Hietsch*. 2 vols. Frankfurt-on-Main, Berne, New York and Paris: Peter Lang.

Blyth, C., jr., S. Recktenwald & J. Wang (1990). 'I'm like, "Say what?!"': a new quotative in American oral narrative. *American Speech* 65: 215–27.

Bodelsen, C. A. (1974[1936/7]). The expanded tenses in Modern English: an attempt at an explanation. In A. Schopf (ed.), *Der englische Aspekt*. (Wege der Forschung 253.) Darmstadt: Wissenschaftliche Buchgesellschaft, 144–62.

Bodine, A. (1975). Androcentrism in prescriptive grammar: singular 'they', sex-indefinite 'he' and 'he or she'. *Language in Society* 4: 129–46.

Bolinger, D. (1977). *Meaning and Form*. (English Language Series 11.) London: Longman.

(1979). The jingle theory of double *-ing*. In D. Allerton, E. Carney & D.

Holdcroft (eds.), *Function and Context in Linguistic Analysis; a Festschrift for William Haas.* Cambridge University Press, 41–56.

(1992). Shifts of attachment. In Blank (1992: 594–98).

Boyland, J. T. (1998). A corpus study of *would* + *have* + past-participle in English. In Hogg & van Bergen (eds.), 1-17.

Brainerd, B. (1989[1993]). The contractions of *not*: a historical note. *Journal of English Linguistics* 22: 176–96

Breivik, L. E. (1983). *Existential 'There': a Synchronic and Diachronic Study,* 1st edn. (Studia Anglistica Norvegica 2.) Bergen: Department of English, University of Bergen. 2nd edn. (1990). Oslo: Novus.

Brinton, L. J. (1988). *The Development of English Aspectual Systems: Aspectualizers and Post-verbal Particles.* (Cambridge Studies in Linguistics 49.) Cambridge University Press.

(1994). The differentiation of statives and perfects in early Modern English: the development of the conclusive perfect. In Stein & Tieken Boon van Ostade (1994: 135–70).

Brook, G. L. (1970). *The Language of Dickens.* (The Language Library.) London: André Deutsch.

Brown, P. &. S. C. Levinson (1987). *Politeness: Some Universals in Language Usage.* (Studies in Interactional Sociolinguistics 4.) Cambridge: Cambridge University Press.

Bublitz, W. (1992). Transferred negation and modality. *Journal of Pragmatics* 18: 551–77.

Butler, M. (1981). *Romantics, Rebels and Reactionaries: English Literature and its Background 1760–1830.* Oxford: Oxford University Press.

Butters, R. R. (1983). Syntactic change in British English propredicates. *Journal of English Linguistics* 16: 1–7.

Carden, G. & D. Pesetsky (1977). Double-verb constructions, markedness, and a fake co-ordination. *Papers from the 13th Regional Meeting of the Chicago Linguistic Society* 13: 82–92.

Chapman, C. (1998). A subject-verb agreement hierarchy: evidence from analogical change in modern English dialects. In Hogg & van Bergen (1998), 35–44.

Charleston, B. M. (1941). *Studies on the Syntax of the English Verb.* (Schweizer Anglistische Arbeiten [11].) Bern: Francke.

Cheshire, J. (1982). *Variation in an English Dialect: A Sociolinguistic Study.* Cambridge: Cambridge University Press.

Christophersen, P. (1939). *The Articles: A Study of their Theory and Use in English.* Copenhagen: Munksgaard.

Clark, J. W. (1975). *The Language and Style of Anthony Trollope.* (The Language Library.) London: André Deutsch.

Coates, J. (1983). *The Semantics of the Modal Auxiliaries.* London: Croom Helm.

Coates, R. (1989). A solution to the *must of* problem. *York Papers in Linguistics* 14: 159–67.

Collins, P. (1988). The semantics of some modals in contemporary Australian English. *Australian Journal of Linguistics* 8: 261–86.

Corbett, G. (1991). *Gender.* (Cambridge Textbooks in Linguistics.) Cambridge: Cambridge University Press.

Curme, G. O. (1912). A history of the English relative constructions. *Journal of English and Germanic Philology* 11: 10–29, 180–204, 355–80.

Curry, K. (1984). *The Contributions of Robert Southey to the 'Morning Post'.* Alabama: University of Alabama Press.

Davies, E. (1986). *The English Imperative.* London: Croom Helm.

Dekeyser, X. (1975). *Number and Case Relations in 19th century British English: a Comparative Study of Grammar and Usage.* (Bibliotheca Linguistica, Series Theoretica.) Antwerp and Amsterdam: De Nederlandsche Boekhandel.

(1984). Relativizers in Early Modern English: a dynamic quantitative study. In Fisiak (1984: 61–87).

(1986). English contact clauses revisited: a diachronic approach. *Folia Linguistica Historica* 7: 107–20.

Denison, D. (1981). Aspects of the history of English group-verbs: with particular attention to the syntax of the Ormulum. Diss. D.Phil., University of Oxford.

(1984). On *get it over with. Neophilologus* 68: 271–7.

(1985). Some observations on *being teaching. Studia Neophilologica* 57: 157–9.

(1992). Counterfactual *may have.* In M. Gerritsen & D. Stein (eds.), *Internal and External Factors in Syntactic Change.* (Trends in Linguistics/Studies and Monographs 61.) Berlin and New York: Mouton de Gruyter, 229–56.

(1993a). *English Historical Syntax: Verbal Constructions.* (Longman Linguistics Library.) London and New York: Longman.

(1993b). Some recent changes in the English verb. In Gotti (1993: 15–33).

(1994). A corpus of late Modern English prose. In Kytö, Rissanen & Wright (1994: 7–16).

(1996). The case of the unmarked pronoun. In D. Britton (ed.), *English Historical Linguistics 1994: Papers from the 8th International Conference on English Historical Linguistics (8.ICEHL, Edinburgh, 19–23 September 1994).* (Current Issues in Linguistic Theory 135.) Amsterdam and Philadelphia: John Benjamins, 287–99.

Dennis, L. (1940). The progressive tense: frequency of its use in English. *Publications of the Modern Language Association of America* 55: 855–65.

Dillard, J. L. (1992). *A History of American English.* London and New York: Longman.

Downing, A. (1996). The semantics of *get*-passives. In R. Hasan, C. Cloran & D. Butt (eds.) *Functional Descriptions.* (Current Issues in Linguistic Theory 121.) Amsterdam and Philadelphia PA: John Benjamins, 179–205.

Duffley, P. [J] (1992a). The use of the verb *dare* in blends between the modal and main verb constructions. *Canadian Journal of Linguistics* 37: 1–16.

(1992b). *The English Infinitive.* (English Language Series 19.) London and New York: Longman.

(1994). *Need* and *dare*: the black sheep of the modal family. *Lingua* 94: 213–43.

Elsness, J. (1989). The English present perfect: has it seen its best days? In L. E. Breivik, A. Hille & S. Johansson (eds.) *Essays on English Language in Honour of Bertil Sundby.* Oslo: Novus, 95–106.

Emonds, J. (1986). Grammatically deviant prestige constructions. In M. Brame, H. Contreras & F. Newmeyer (eds.), *A Festschrift for Sol Saporta.* Seattle: Noit Amrofer, 93–129.

Erdmann, P. (1980). On the history of subject contact-clauses in English. *Folia Linguistica Historica* 1: 139–70.

Fanego, T. (1996). The gerund in Early Modern English: evidence from the Helsinki Corpus. *Folia Linguistica Historica* 17: 97–152.

Fillmore, C. J. (1990). Epistemic stance and grammatical form in English conditional sentences. *Papers from the 26th Regional Meeting of the Chicago Linguistic Society* 26: 137–62.

Finegan, E. & D. Biber (1995). *That* and zero complementisers in Late Modern English: exploring ARCHER from 1650–1990. In B. Aarts & C. Meyer (eds.), *The Verb in Contemporary English.* Cambridge: Cambridge University Press, 241–57.

Fischer, O. (1990). Syntactic change and causation: developments in infinitival constructions in English. Diss. Ph.D., University of Amsterdam [(Amsterdam Studies in Generative Grammar 2)].

(1991). The rise of the passive infinitive in English. In Kastovsky (1991: 141–88). [Also in Fischer (1990: 151–217) with paragraph numbering 1 higher.]

(1992). Syntax. In N. Blake (ed.) *The Cambridge History of the English Language,* vol. II, *1066–1476.* Cambridge: Cambridge University Press, 207–408.

(1994). The development of quasi-auxiliaries in English and changes in word order. *Neophilologus* 78: 137–64.

Fisiak, J. (ed.) (1984). *Historical Syntax.* (Trends in Linguistics/Studies and Monographs 23.) Paris and The Hague: Mouton.

Foster, B. (1970). *The Changing English Language.* Harmondsworth: Penguin.

Fridén, G. (1948). *Studies on the Tenses of the English Verb from Chaucer to Shakespeare: with Special Reference to the Late Sixteenth Century.* (Essays and Studies on English Language and Literature 2.) Uppsala: Uppsala University English Institute.

Furness, N. A. (1992). Signs and sins of the times? Some recurrent issues in current English usage. In Blank (1992: 645–58).

Geerts, G., W. Haeseryn, J. de Rooij & M. C. van den Toorn (1984). *Algemene nederlandse Spraakkunst.* Groningen: Wolters-Noordhoff.

Gotti, M. (ed.) (1983). *English Diachronic Syntax.* (Collana Blu, 20.) Milan: Guerini. [Proceedings of the Vth national congress of history of the English language.]

Goyvaerts, D. L. (1968). An introductory study on the ordering of a string of adjectives in Present-Day English. *Philologica Pragensia* 11: 12–28.

Granger, S. (1983). The '*Be + Past Participle' Construction in Spoken English: with Special Emphasis on the Passive*. (North-Holland Linguistic Series 49.) Amsterdam, New York and Oxford: North-Holland.

Greenbaum, S. & R. Quirk (1990). *A Student's Grammar of the English language*. London: Longman.

Greenbaum, S., G. Leech & J. Svartvik (eds.) (1980). *Studies in English Linguistics: for Randolph Quirk*. London and New York: Longman.

Halliday, M. A. K. (1980). On being teaching. In Greenbaum, Leech & Svartvik (1980: 61–64).

Harris, M. (1981). It's I, it's me: further reflections. *Studia Anglica Posnaniensia* 13: 17–20.

(1986). English *ought (to)*. In Kastovsky & Szwedek (1986: I 347–58).

Hench, A. L. (1937). A survival of *it is = there is*. English Studies 19: 209.

Henry, A. (1995). *Belfast English and Standard English: Dialect Variation and Parameter Setting*. (Oxford Studies in Comparative Syntax.) Oxford and New York: Oxford University Press.

Hirtle, W. & C. Bégin (1990). TO BE in the progressive: a new use. *Canadian Journal of Linguistics* 35: 1–11.

Hogg, R. M. & L. van Bergen (eds.) (1998). *Historical Linguistics 1995*, vol. 2, *Germanic*. (Current Issues in Linguistic Theory.) Amsterdam and Philadelphia: John Benjamins.

Hopper, P. J. & E. C. Traugott (1993). *Grammaticalization*. (Cambridge Textbooks in Linguistics.) Cambridge: Cambridge University Press.

Huddleston, R. (1977). Past tense transportation in English. *Journal of Linguistics* 13: 43–52.

(1980). Criteria for auxiliaries and modals. In Greenbaum, Leech & Svartvik (1980: 65–78).

(1984). *Introduction to the Grammar of English*. (Cambridge Textbooks in Linguistics.) Cambridge: Cambridge University Press.

(1994). The contrast between interrogatives and questions. *Journal of Linguistics* 30: 411–39.

Huddleston, R. & G. K. Pullum (in prep.). *The Cambridge Grammar of English*. Cambridge: Cambridge University Press.

Hudson, R. (1995). Does English really have case? *Journal of Linguistics* 31: 375–92.

Jacobson, S. (ed.) (1983). *Papers from the Second Scandinavian Symposium on Syntactic Variation: Stockholm, May 15–16, 1982*. (Stockholm Studies in English 57.) Stockholm: Almqvist & Wiksell.

Jacobsson, B. (1994). Nonrestrictive relative *that*-clauses revisited. *Studia Neophilologica* 66: 181–95.

Jespersen, O. (1894). *Progress in Language: with Special Reference to English*. London and New York: Sonnenschein.

(1909–49). *A Modern English Grammar on Historical Principles.* 7 vols. Heidelberg: Carl Winters Universitätsbuchhandlung. [Also published by Ejnar Munksgaard, Copenhagen; reprinted by George Allen & Unwin, London, 1961.]

Jones, C. (ed.) (1993). *Historical Linguistics: Problems and Perspectives.* London and New York: Longman.

Jørgensen, E. (1984). 'Ought': present or past tense? *English Studies* 65: 550–4.

Jucker, A. H. (1992). *Social Stylistics: Syntactic Variation in British Newspapers.* Berlin: Mouton de Gruyter.

Karpf, F. (1933). Die erlebte Rede im Englischen. *Anglia* 57: 225–76.

Kastovsky, D. (ed.) (1991). *Historical English Syntax.* (Topics in English Linguistics 2.) Berlin and New York: Mouton de Gruyter.

Kastovsky, D. & A. Szwedek (eds.) (1986). *Linguistics across Historical and Geographical Boundaries: in Honour of Jacek Fisiak on the Occasion of his Fiftieth Birthday.* 2 vols. (Trends in Linguistics/Studies and Monographs 32.) Berlin, New York and Amsterdam: Mouton de Gruyter.

Kato, K. & R. R. Butters (1987). American instances of propredicate *do. Journal of English Linguistics* 20: 212–6.

Kilby, D. (1984). *Descriptive Syntax and the English Verb.* London, Sydney and Dover NH: Croom Helm.

Kirk, J. M. (1985). Linguistic atlases and grammar: the investigation and description of regional variation in English syntax. In J. M. Kirk, S. Sanderson & J. D. A. Widdowson (eds.), *Studies in Linguistic Geography: the Dialects of English in Britain and Ireland.* London: Croom Helm, 130–56.

Kjellmer, G. (1986). 'Us Anglos are a cut above the field': on objective pronouns in nominative contexts. *English Studies* 67: 445–9.

Klein, W. (1992). The present perfect puzzle. *Language* 68: 525–52.

Klemola, J. & M. Filppula (1992). Subordinating uses of *and* in the history of English. In Rissanen, Ihalainen, Nevalainen & Taavitsainen (1992: 310–18).

Knowles, G. O. (1973). Scouse: the urban dialect of Liverpool. Diss. Ph.D., University of Leeds.

Kortmann, B. (1992). *Free Adjuncts and Absolutes in English: Problems of Control and interpretation.* London and New York: Routledge.

Kroch, A. S. (1981). On the role of resumptive pronouns in amnestying island constraint violations. *Papers from the 17th Regional Meeting of the Chicago Linguistic Society* 17: 125–35.

Kytö, M. (1991a). *Can (could)* vs. *may (might)*: regional variation in Early Modern English? In Kastovsky (1991: 233–89).

(1991b). *Variation and Diachrony, with Early American English in Focus: Studies on CAN/MAY and SHALL/WILL.* (Bamberger Beiträge zur Englischen Sprachwissenschaft/University of Bamberg Studies in English Linguistics 28.) Frankfurt am Main: Peter Lang.

(1997). *Be/have* + past participle: the choice of the auxiliary with intransitives from Late Middle to Modern English. In M. Rissanen, M. Kytö & K. Heikkonen (eds.), *English in Transition: Corpus-based Studies in Linguistic Variation and Genre Styles* (Topics in English Linguistics, 23). Berlin and New York: Mouton de Gruyter, 17–85.

Kytö, M. & M. Rissanen (1993). 'By and by enters [this] my artificiall foole': searching syntactic construction in the Helsinki Corpus. In M. Rissanen, M. Kytö & M. Palander-Collin (eds.), *Early English in the Computer Age: Explorations through the Helsinki Corpus.* (Topics in English Linguistics 11.) Berlin and New York: Mouton de Gruyter, 253–66.

Kytö, M., M. Rissanen & S. Wright (eds.) (1994). *Corpora across the Centuries: Proceedings of the First International Colloquium on English Diachronic Corpora, St Catharine's College Cambridge, 25–27 March 1993.* (Language and Computers. Studies in Practical Linguistics 11.) Amsterdam and Atlanta GA: Rodopi.

Kytö, M. & S. Romaine (1997). Competing forms of adjective comparison in Modern English: what could be more quicker and easier and more effective? In T. Nevalainen & L. Kahlas-Tarkka (eds.), *To Explain the Present: Studies in the Changing English Language.* Helsinki: Société Néophilologique, 329–52.

Labov, W. (1972). *Language in the Inner City: Studies in the Black English Vernacular.* Philadelphia: University of Pennsylvania Press.

Lakoff, G. (1987). *Women, Fire, and Dangerous Things: What Categories Reveal about the Mind.* University of Chicago Press.

Langacker, R. W. (1991). *Foundations of Cognitive Grammar*, vol 2, *Descriptive application.* Stanford University Press.

Larson, R. K. (1985). Bare-NP adverbs. *Linguistic Inquiry* 16: 595–621.

Lehmann, C. (1991). Grammaticalization and related changes in contemporary German. In Traugott & Heine (1991: 493–535).

Leisi, E. (1964). *Das heutige Englisch: Wesenszüge und Probleme*, 3rd edn. Heidelberg: Carl Winter Universitätsverlag.

Leonard, S. A. (1929). *The Doctrine of Correctness in English Usage 1700–1800.* (University of Wisconsin Studies in Language and Literature 25.) Madison WI: University of Wisconsin.

LINGUIST (1900–). Discussion list moderated by A. Aristar and H. Dry.

Maling, J. M. (1983). Transitive adjectives: a case of categorial reanalysis. In F. Heny & B. Richards (eds.), *Linguistic Categories: Auxiliaries and Related Puzzles*, vol. 1. (Synthese Language Library 19.) Dordrecht: Reidel, 253–89.

Melchers, G. (1983). 'It's a sweet thing, is tea-cake' – a study of tag statements. In Jacobson (1983: 57–66).

Mencken, H. L. (1963). *The American Language.* 4th edn., abridged by Raven I. McDavid, jr. London: Routledge & Kegan Paul.

Meyer, M. (1992). *Das englische Perfekt: grammatischer Status, Semantik und Zusammenspiel mit dem Progressive.* (Linguistische Arbeiten 277.) Tübingen: Niemeyer.

Miller, J. (1988). *That*: a relative pronoun? Sociolinguistics and syntactic analysis. *Edinburgh Studies in the English Language* 1: 113–19.

Milroy, J. (1993). On the social origins of language change. In Jones (1993: 215–36).

Milroy, L. (1987). *Language and Social Networks*, 2nd edn. (Language in Society 2.) Oxford: Blackwell.

Montgomery, M. (1989). The standardization of English relative clauses. In J. B. Trahern, jr. (ed.), *Standardizing English: Essays in the History of Language Change: in honor of John Hurt Fisher*. (Tennessee Studies in Literature 31.) Knoxville TN: University of Tennessee Press, 113–38.

Mossé, F. (1938). *Histoire de la forme périphrastique 'être + participe présent' en germanique*, vol. 2, *Moyen-anglais et anglais moderne*. (Collection Linguistique, La Société Linguistique de Paris 43.) Paris: C. Klincksieck.

(1947). *Esquisse d'une histoire de la langue anglaise*. (Les langues du monde 2.) Lyon: Edition I.A.C.

Murray, L. (1795). *English Grammar: Adapted to the Different Classes of Learners*. York: Wilson, Spence, and Mawman. [Reprinted by Scolar Press, Menston (English Linguistics 1500–1800 106), 1968.]

Nakamura, F. (1981). Observations on the language of Samuel Pepys's 'Diary': some peculiarities in the use of the progressive. *Persica* 8: 137–57.

(1991). On the historical development of the activo-passive progressive: 'the house is building'. In S. Chiba (ed.), *Aspects of English Philology and Linguistics (Festschrift Offered to Dr Masatomo Ukaji on his Sixtieth Birthday)* Tokyo: Kaitakusha, 121–43.

Nehls, D. (1974). *Synchron-diachrone Untersuchungen zur Expanded Form im Englischen: eine struktural-funktionale Analyse*. (Linguistische Reihe 19.) Munich: Max Hueber Verlag.

Nevalainen, T. (1991). *BUT, ONLY, JUST: Focusing Adverbial Change in Modern English 1500–1900*. (Mémoires de la Société Néophilologique de Helsinki 51.) Helsinki: Société Néophilologique.

Ohlander, S. (1986). Question-orientation versus answer-orientation in English interrogative clauses. In Kastovsky & Szwedek (1986: II 963–82).

Orton, H., S. Sanderson & J. Widdowson (eds.) (1978). *The Linguistic Atlas of England*. London: Croom Helm.

Palmer, F. R. (1988). *The English Verb*. 2nd edn. London: Longman.

(1990). *Modality and the English Modals*. 2nd edn. London: Longman.

Parker, F. (1976). Language change and the passive voice. *Language* 52: 449–60.

Phillips, K. C. (1970). *Jane Austen's English*. (The Language Library.) London: André Deutsch.

(1978). *The Language of Thackeray*. (The Language Library.) London: André Deutsch.

(1984). *Language and Class in Victorian England*. Oxford: Blackwell.

Pinker, S. (1994). *The Language Instinct: the New Science of Language and Mind*. London: Allen Lane, The Penguin Press.

Plank, F. (1984). The modals story retold. *Studies in Language* 8: 305–64.

Platt, J., H. Weber & M. L. Ho (1984). *The New Englishes.* London: Routledge & Kegan Paul.

Poussa, P. (1992). Pragmatics of *this* and *that.* In Rissanen, Ihalainen, Nevalainen & Taavitsainen (1992: 401–17).

Poutsma, H. (1914–29). *A Grammar of Late Modern English,* (part I) 2nd edn., (part II) 1st edn. Groningen: Noordhoff.

Pullum, G. K. (1992). English nominal gerund phrases as noun-phrases with verb phrase heads. In R. Tracy (ed.), *Who Climbs the Grammar-tree.* (Linguistische Arbeiten 281.) Tübingen: Niemeyer, 435–64.

Quirk, R. (1957). Relative clauses in educated spoken English. *English Studies* 38: 97–109.

Quirk, R., S. Greenbaum, G. Leech & J. Svartvik (1985). *A Comprehensive Grammar of the English Language.* London and New York: Longman.

Radford, A. (1988). *Transformational Grammar: A First Course.* (Cambridge Textbooks in Linguistics.) Cambridge: Cambridge University Press.

Reuter, O. R. (1936). *On continuative relative clauses in English: a feature of English style and syntax ascribed to Latin influence.* (Commentationes Humanarum Litterarum 9.3.) Helsingfors: Societas Scientarum Fennica.

Rickford, J. R., T. A. Wasow, N. Mendoza-Denton & J. Espinoza (1995). Syntactic variation and change in progress: loss of the verbal coda in topic-restricting *as far as* constructions. *Language* 71: 102–31.

Rissanen, M. (1984). The choice of relative pronouns in 17th century American English. In Fisiak (1984: 417–35).

(1991a). On the history of *that*/zero as object-clause links in English. In K. Aijmer & B. Altenberg (eds.), *English Corpus Linguistics: Studies in Honour of Jan Svartvik.* London and New York: Longman, 272–89.

(1991b). Spoken language and the history of *do*-periphrasis. In Kastovsky (1991: 321–42).

(1993). Aspects of the development of the noun phrase in English. In Gotti (1993: 35–54).

(1997). The pronominalization of *one.* In M. Rissanen, M. Kytö & K. Heikkonen (eds.), *Grammaticalization at Work: Studies of Long-term Developments in English.* (Topics in English Linguistics, 24.) Berlin and New York: Mouton de Gruyter, 87–143.

(forthcoming). Syntax. In Lass, R. (ed.) (forthcoming), *The Cambridge History of the English Language,* vol. III, *1476–1776.* Cambridge: Cambridge University Press.

Rissanen, M., O. Ihalainen, T. Nevalainen & I. Taavitsainen (eds.) (1992). *History of Englishes: New Methods and Interpretations in Historical Linguistics.* (Topics in English Linguistics 10.) Berlin and New York: Mouton de Gruyter.

Romaine, S. (1982). *Socio-Historical Linguistics: its Status and Methodology.* (Cambridge Studies in Linguistics 34.) Cambridge: Cambridge University Press.

Romaine, S. & D. Lange (1991). The use of *like* as a marker of reported speech and thought: a case of grammaticalization in progress. *American Speech* 66: 227–79.

Ross, J. R. (1972). Doubl-ing. *Linguistic Inquiry* 3: 61–86.

Rydén, M. (1979). *An Introduction to the Historical Study of English Syntax*. Stockholm: Almqvist & Wiksell.

Rydén, M. & S. Brorström (1987). *The 'Be/Have' Variation with Intransitives in English: with Special Reference to the Late Modern Period*. (Stockholm Studies in English 70.) Stockholm: Almquist & Wiksell International.

Scheffer, J. (1975). *The Progressive in English*. (North-Holland Linguistic Series 15.) Amsterdam and Oxford: North-Holland.

Seppänen, A. & G. Kjellmer (1995). The dog that's leg was run over: on the genitive of the relative pronoun. *English Studies* 76: 389–400.

Shopen, T. (1971). Caught in the act: an intermediate stage in a would-be historical process providing syntactic evidence for the psychological reality of paradigms. *Papers from the 7th Regional Meeting of the Chicago Linguistic Society* 7: 254–63.

Shorrocks, G. (1992). Case assignment in simple and coordinate constructions in Present-Day English. *American Speech* 67: 432–44.

Simon-Vandenbergen, Anne-M. (1983). 'Subjunctive' *MAY*: a fossilizing pattern. *Studia Anglica Posnaniensia* 16: 71–6.

(1984). Deontic possibility: a diachronic view. *English Studies* 65: 362–5.

Simpson, J. A. & E. S. C. Weiner (1992). *The Oxford English Dictionary: CD-ROM version*. 2nd edn. Oxford: Oxford University Press.

Smith, O. (1984). *The Politics of Language, 1791–1819*. Oxford: Clarendon Press.

Sørensen, K. (1980). From postmodification to premodification. In S. Jacobson (ed.), *Papers from the Scandinavian Symposium on Syntactic Variation: Stockholm, May 18–19, 1979*. (Stockholm studies in English 52.) Stockholm: Almqvist & Wiksell, 77–84.

Stageberg, N. C. (1965). *An Introductory English Grammar*. New York, etc: Holt, Rinehart & Winston.

Stein, D. & I. Tieken-Boon van Ostade (eds.) (1994). *Towards a Standard English 1600–1800*. (Topics in English Linguistics 12.) Berlin and New York: Mouton de Gruyter.

Stockwell, R. P. (1984). On the history of the verb-second rule in English. In Fisiak (1984: 575–92).

Strang, B. M. H. (1970). *A History of English*. London: Methuen.

(1982). Some aspects of the history of the *be + ing* construction. In J. Anderson (ed.), *Language Form and Linguistic Variation: Papers Dedicated to Angus McIntosh*. (Current Issues in Linguistic Theory 15.) Amsterdam: John Benjamins, 427–74.

Sundby, B. (1983). Syntactic variation in the context of normative grammar. In Jacobson (1983: 123–34).

Sundby, B., A. K. Bjørge & K. E. Haugland (1991). *A Dictionary of English Normative Grammar 1700–1800*. (Studies in the History of the Language Sciences 63.) Amsterdam and Philadelphia: John Benjamins.

Swan, T. (1988). *Sentence Adverbials in English: a Synchronic and Diachronic Investigation.* Oslo: Novus.

(1990). The development of sentence adverbs in English. In E. H. Jahr & O. Lorentz (eds.), *Tromsø Linguistics in the Eighties.* (Tromsø Studies in Linguistics 11.) Oslo: Novus Press, 369–88.

Sweet, H. (1898). *A New English Grammar: Logical and Historical,* vol. 2, *Syntax,* Oxford: Clarendon Press.

Thompson, S. A. & A. Mulac (1991). A quantitative perspective on the grammaticization of parentheticals in English. In Traugott & Heine (1991: 313–29).

Thrasher, R. H., jr. (1974). Shouldn't ignore these strings: a study of conversational deletion. Diss. Ph.D., University of Michigan, Ann Arbor MI.

Tieken-Boon van Ostade, I. (1987). *The Auxiliary 'Do' in Eighteenth-century English: a Sociohistorical-linguistic Approach.* Dordrecht: Foris.

Tieken-Boon van Ostagde, I. (1994). Standard and non-standard pronominal usage in English, with special reference to the eighteenth century. In Stein & Tieken-Boon van Ostade (1994: 217–42).

Traugott, E. C. (1972). *A History of English Syntax: a Transformational Approach to the History of English Sentence Structure.* New York: Holt, Rinehart & Winston.

(1992). Syntax. In R. M. Hogg (ed.) *The Cambridge History of the English Language,* vol. I, *The Beginnings to 1066.* Cambridge University Press, 168–289.

(1997). Subjectification and the development of epistemic meaning: the case of *promise* and *threaten.* In T. Swan & O. J. Westvik (eds.), *Modality in Germanic Languages: Historical and Comparative Perspectives.* Berlin: Mouton de Gruyter, 185–210.

Traugott, E. C. & B. Heine (eds.) (1991). *Approaches to Grammaticalization,* vol 2, *Focus on Types of Grammatical Markers.* (Typological Studies in Language 19.) Amsterdam and Philadelphia: John Benjamins.

Trudgill, P. (1984). Standard English in England. In P. Trudgill (ed.), *Language in the British Isles.* Cambridge University Press, 32–44.

Underhill, R. (1988). *Like* is, like, focus. *American Speech* 63: 234–46.

Vanneck, G. (1958). The colloquial preterite in modern American English. *Word* 14: 237–42.

Varantola, K. (1983). Premodification vs. postmodification and chain compound structures. In Jacobson (1983: 75–82).

(1984). *On Noun Phrase Structures in Engineering English.* (Annales Universitatis Turkuensis ser. B, 168.) Turku: University of Turku.

Visser, F. T. (1963–73). *An Historical Syntax of the English Language.* 4 vols. Leiden: E. J. Brill.

Wald, B. (1983). Referents and topic within and across discourse units: observations from current vernacular English. In F. Klein-Andreu (ed.), *Discourse Perspectives on Syntax.* New York: Academic Press, 91–116.

Wales, K. (1996). *Personal Pronouns in Present-Day English.* (Studies in English Language.) Cambridge University Press.

Warner, A. [R.] (1982). *Complementation in Middle English and the Methodology of Historical Syntax: a Study of the Wyclifite Sermons.* London and Canberra: Croom Helm.

(1985). *The Structuring of English Auxiliaries: a Phrase Structure Grammar.* Bloomington IN: Indiana University Linguistics Club.

(1986). Ellipsis conditions and the status of the English copula. *York Papers in Linguistics* 12: 153–72.

(1990). Reworking the history of English auxiliaries. In Adamson, Law, Vincent & Wright (1990: 537–58).

(1993). *English Auxiliaries: Structure and History.* (Cambridge Studies in Linguistics 66.) Cambridge University Press.

(1995). Predicting the progressive passive: parametric change within a lexicalist framework. *Language* 71: 533–57.

Wekker, H. C. (1987). Points of Modern English syntax LXIX. *English Studies* 68: 456–63.

Wood, M. (1994). *Radical satire and print culture, 1790–1822.* Oxford: Clarendon Press.

van der Wurff, W. (1989[1991]). A remarkable gap in the history of English syntax. *Folia Linguistica Historica* 9: 117–59.

(1990). The easy-to-please construction in Old and Middle English. In Adamson, Law, Vincent & Wright (1900: 519–36).

(1992). Syntactic variability, borrowing, and innovation. *Diachronica* 9: 61–85.

(1993). Gerunds and their objects in the Modern English period. In J. van Marle (ed.), *Historical Linguistics 1991: Papers from the 10th International Conference on Historical Linguistics, Amsterdam, August 12–16, 1991.* (Current Issues in Linguistic Theory 107.) Amsterdam: John Benjamins, 363–75.

Youmans, G. (1986). Any more on *anymore*? Evidence from a Missouri dialect survey. *American Speech* 61: 61–75.

Zwicky, A. M. (1977). Hierarchies of person. *Papers from the 13th Regional Meeting of the Chicago Linguistic Society*, 13: 714–33.

(1991). Systematic versus accidental phonological identity. In F. Plank (ed.) *Paradigms: the Economy of Inflection.* (Empirical Approaches to Language Typology 9.) Berlin and New York: Mouton de Gruyter, 113–31.

Zwicky, A. M. & G. K. Pullum (1983). Cliticization versus inflection: English *n't*. *Language* 59: 502–13.

4 Onomastics

Place-name sources (gazetteers and topographical works)

Anderson, J. P. (1881). *The book of British Topography.* London: Satchell. (Reprinted Amsterdam: Theatrum Orbis Terrarum (1967).)

Brabner, J. H. F. (ed.) (1894–5). *The Comprehensive Gazetteer of England and Wales.* London: Mackenzie.

Coulet du Gard, R. & D. C. Western. (1981). *The Handbook of American Counties, Parishes, and Independent Cities.* Newark (DE): Editions des deux mondes.

Hudson, E. (ed.) (1957). *Commercial Gazetteer of Great Britain.* London: Geographia.

Lewis, S. (1837–49). *Topographical Dictionary of England/Ireland/Scotland/Wales,* various editions. London: Lewis & Co.

Mason, O. (1977). *Gazetteer of Britain.* Edinburgh: John Bartholomew.

Ordnance Survey (1982). *Ordnance Survey Atlas of Great Britain.* Southampton/Feltham: Ordnance Survey.

Parliamentary Gazetteer of England and Wales (1847). London: Fullarton.

Post Office (1976). *Postal Addresses and Index to Postcode Directories.* London: The Post Office.

Wilson, J. M. (1870). *Imperial Gazetteer.* London: Fullarton.

For other sources, see section 4.1.

Secondary sources

Algeo, J. (1973). *On Defining the Proper Name.* Gainsville (FL): Florida University Press.
   (1986). From Classic to Classy: Changing Fashions in Street Names. In Harder (1986), 230–45.

Algeo, J. & A. Algeo (1983). Bible Belt Onomastics Revisited. *Names* 31: 103–16.

Armstrong, G. H. (1930). *The Origin and Meaning of Place-Names in Canada.* Toronto: Macmillan of Canada.

Baldwin, L. M. & M. Grimaud (1992). How New Naming Systems Emerge: the Prototypical Case of Columbus and Washington. *Names* 40: 153–66.

Barry, H. III & A. S. Harper (1982). Evolution of Unisex Names. *Names* 30: 15–22.
   (1993). Feminization of Unisex Names from 1960 to 1990. *Names* 41: 228–38.

Berry, M. (1987). The Functions of Place-names. *Leeds Studies in English* 18 (*Studies in Honour of Kenneth Cameron*): 71–88.

Binns, A. L. (1981). Hull fishermen's place-names. *Nomina* 5: 20–7.

Black, K. (1996). Afro-American naming traditions. *Names* 44: 105–18, with an afterword by Cleveland E. Evans, 119–26.

Boddewyn, J. (1986). The names of U.S. industrial corporations: a study in change. In Harder (1986), 146–59.

Brett, D. (1985). The use of telephone directories in surname studies. *The Local Historian* 16: 392–404.

Busse, T. V. (1983). Nickname usage in an American high school. *Names* 31: 300–6.

Campbell, J. C. (1991). Stream generic terms as indicators of historical settlement patterns. *Names* 39: 333–65.

Carroll, J. M. (1984). The name game: creative and practical names for a building. *Language and Speech* 27: 99–114.

Carter, R. (1987) The placing of names: sequencing in narrative openings. *Leeds Studies in English* 18 (*Studies in honour of Kenneth Cameron*): 89–100.

Clark, C. (1981). Nickname-creation: some sources of evidence, 'naive' memoirs especially. *Nomina* 5: 83–94.

Coates, R. (1980). A phonological problem in Sussex placenames. *Beiträge zur Namenforschung* (neue Folge) 15: 299–318.

(1984). Coldharbour – for the last time? *Nomina* 8: 73–8.

(1990). English proper names since 1776: a theoretical and historical survey. *Cognitive Science Research Reports* (University of Sussex) 175.

Cole, T. M. (1992). Placenames in Paradise: Robert Marshall and the naming of the Alaska wilderness. *Names* 40: 99–116.

Cottle, B. (1983). *Names*. London: Thames and Hudson.

Cox, B. (1994). *English Inn and Tavern Names*. Nottingham: Centre for English Name Studies, University of Nottingham.

Cutler, A., J. McQueen & K. Robinson (1990). Elizabeth and John: sound patterns of men's and women's names. *Journal of Linguistics* 26: 471–82.

Dillard, J. L. (1976). *Black Names*. The Hague: Mouton.

On the grammar of Afro-American naming practices. In Harder (1986), 310–7. Reprinted from *Names* 16 (1968): 230–7.

Duggan, D. A., A. A. Cota & K. L. Dion (1993). Taking thy husband's name: what might it mean? *Names* 41: 87–102.

Dunkling, L. A. (1977). *First Names First*. London: Dent.

Dunkling, L. A. & W. Gosling (1991). *The Book of First Names*. 3rd edn. London: Dent.

Dunkling, L. A. & G. Wright (1994). *Pub Names of Britain*. 2nd edn. London: Dent.

Ecclestone, M. (1989). The diffusion of English surnames. *The Local Historian* 19: 63–70.

Ellis, A. & M. Beechley (1954). Emotional disturbance in children with peculiar given names. *Journal of Genetic Psychology* 85: 337–9.

Fairclough, G. T. (1986). New light on old Zion. In Harder (1986), 89–99. Reprinted from *Names* 8 (1960).

Feinman, S. & A. S. Slater. (1985). Gender and the phonology of North American first names. *Sex Roles* 13: 429–40.

Field, J. (1972). *English Field-names: a Dictionary*. Newton Abbot: David and Charles.

(1977). Derogatory field-names. *Journal of the English Place-Name Society* 8: 19–25.

(1979). Progress in field-name research. *The Local Historian* 13: 388–96.

(1987a). Crops for man and beast. *Leeds Studies in English* 18 *(Studies in honour of Kenneth Cameron)*: 157–71.

(1987b). The use of names of distant places in English field nomenclature. In Eichler, E. *et al.* (eds.), *Der Eigenname in Sprache und Gesellschaft*. Leipzig: Karl-Marx-Universität, vol. III: 63–7.

(1993). *A History of English Field-Names*. Harlow: Longmans.

FitzHugh, Terrick V. H. (1988). *The Dictionary of Genealogy*. 2nd edn. Sherborne: Alphabooks.

Forster, K. (1980). *A Pronouncing Dictionary of English Place-Names.* London: Routledge and Kegan Paul.

Goepel, J. (1983). *How I chose Crawley Street-names.* Crawley: Crawley Museum Society.

Goff, J. H. (1975). *Placenames of Georgia* (ed. by F. L. Utley & M. R. Hamperley). Athens: University of Georgia.

Green, E. (1982). Naming and mapping the environments of early Massachusetts. *Names* 30: 77–92.

Gulley, H. E. (1995). British and Irish toponyms in the South Atlantic states. *Names* 43: 85–102.

Guppy, H. B. (1890). *The Homes of Family Names in Great Britain.* London: Harrison. [Reprinted Baltimore (1968).]

Hamilton, W. B. (1978). *Macmillan Book of Canadian Place-Names.* Toronto: Macmillan.

Hanks, P. (1993). The present-day distribution of surnames in the British Isles. *Nomina* 16: 79–98.

Harder, K. B. (1982). Dickens and his list of names. *Names* 30: 33–41.

(ed.) (1986). *Names and their Varieties.* Lanham (MD): University Press of America.

Harris, H. C. W. (1969). *Housing Nomenclature in Bristol.* Bristol: Corporation of Bristol P. and S. Dept.

Hartmann, A. A., R. C. Nicoley & J. Hurley (1968). Unique personal names as a social adjustment factor. *Journal of Social Psychology* 75: 107–10.

Hattersley-Smith, G. (1980). *The History of Place-Names in the Falkland Islands Dependencies (South Georgia and the South Sandwich Islands).* Cambridge: British Antarctic Survey (Scientific Report 101).

(1989). *The History of Place-Names in the British Antarctic Territory.* Cambridge: British Antarctic Survey (Scientific Report 113).

Hixon, R. & H. Hixon (1980). *The Place Names of the White Mountains.* Camden (ME): Down East Books.

Huden, J. C. (1962). *Indian Place-Names of New England.* New York: Museum of the American Indian (Heye Foundation).

Johnston, J. B. (1934). *The Place-Names of Scotland,* 3rd edn. London: John Murray.

Josling, J. F. (1980). *Change of Name.* 12th edn. London: Oyez.

Kingsbury, S. E. (1981). Sets and name duplication in the Upper Peninsula of Michigan. *Names* 29: 303–12.

Koegler, K. (1986). A farewell to arms: The 'greening' of American apartment names. *Names* 34: 46–61.

Lasker, G. W. & B. E. Kaplan (1983). English Place-name Surnames Tend to Cluster Near the Place Named. *Names* 31: 167–77.

Lassiter, M. (1983). *Our Names, Our Selves.* London: Heinemann.

Lawson, E. D. (1971). Semantic differential analysis of men's first names. *Journal of Psychology* 78: 229–40.

(1973). Men's first names, nicknames and short names – a semantic differential analysis. *Names* 21: 22–7.

(1974). Women's first names – a semantic differential analysis. *Names* 22: 52–8.

(1980). First names on the campus: a semantic differential analysis. *Names* 28: 69–83.

(compiler) (1985). *Personal Names and Naming: an Annotated Bibliography.* Westport (CT): Greenwood Press.

(1987). Psychological dimensions of men's names: a semantic differential analysis. In Eichler, E. Sass & H. Walther (eds.), *Der Eigenname in Sprache und Gesellschaft.* Leipzig: Karl-Marx-Universität, vol. III: 143–8.

(1992). Onomastics journals: how many and where? *The Serials Librarian* 21: 99–138.

Lawson, E. D. & L. M. Roeder (1986). Women's full first names, short names and affectionate names: a semantic differential analysis. *Names* 34: 175–84.

Leaver, R. (1990). Families on the move: personal mobility and the diffusion of surnames. *The Local Historian* 20: 65–72.

Leighly, J. (1986). Biblical place-names in the United States. In Harder (1986), 291–304.

Lyons, J. (1977). *Semantics*, vols. I and II. Cambridge: Cambridge University Press.

Mac Aodha B. S. (1993). Some commemorative British place-names in Dublin City. *Nomina* 16, 71–7.

(1995). The nature of Irish pub-names. *Nomina* 18: 63–75.

Matthews, C. M. (1972). *Place-Names of the English-speaking World.* London: Weidenfeld and Nicolson.

McClure, P. (1981a). Nicknames and petnames: linguistic forms and social contexts. *Nomina* 5: 63–76.

(1981b). Review of Morgan *et al.* (1979) *Nomina* 5: 121–3.

McKinley, R. A. (1989). *A History of British Surnames.* Harlow: Longmans.

Milbauer, J. A. (1996). Physical generic toponyms in Oklahoma. *Names* 44: 205–24.

Miles, J. C. (1979). The naming of private houses in Britain since 1700. Unpublished M.Litt dissertation, University of Bristol.

(1982). *The House Names Book: Ackybotha to Zeelust.* London: Unwin.

Miller, M. R. (1983). *Place-Names of the Northern Neck of Virginia from John Smith's 1606 Map to the Present.* Richmond (VA): Virginia State Library.

Morgan, J. C. O'Neill & R. Harré (1979). *Nicknames: their Origins and Social Consequences.* London: Routledge & Kegan Paul.

Murray, T. E. (1997). Attitudes towards married women's surnames: evidence from the American Midwest. *Names* 45: 163–83.

Nicolaisen, W. F. H. (1980). Onomastic dialects. *American Speech* 55: 36–45.

(1983). An onomastic vernacular in Scottish literature. In McClure, J. D. (ed.) *Scotland and the Lowland Tongue. Studies in the Language and Literature of Lowland Scotland in Honour of David D. Murison.* Aberdeen: Aberdeen University Press, 209–18.

Nienaber, P. J. (1972). *Suidafrikaanse Pleknaamwoordeboek.* 2nd edn. Cape Town: Suid-Afrikaanse Boekensentrum.

Noreen, R. S. (1965). Ghetto worship: a study of Chicago store front churches. *Names* 13: 19–38.

Paustian, P. R. (1978). The evolution of naming practices among American Blacks. *Names* 26: 177–91.

Pelham, R. A. (1964). The concept of Wessex. In Monkhouse, F. J. (ed.) *Survey of Southampton and its Region*. Southampton: Southampton University Press for the British Association for the Advancement of Science, 169–76.

Phillimore, W. P. W. & E. A. (eds.) (1905). *An Index to Change of Name, 1760–1901*. London: Phillimore & Co.

PNLi = Cameron, K. (1985). *The Place-Names of Lincolnshire*, part I. Nottingham: English Place-Name Society (vol. 58).

PNMx = Gover, J. E. B., Mawer, A. H. & F. M. Stenton, with S. J. Madge (1942). *The Place-Names of Middlesex (apart from the City of London)*. Cambridge: Cambridge University Press (English Place-Name Society vol. 18).

PNNf = Sandred, K. I. & B. Lindström (1989). *The Place-Name of Norfolk*, part I. Nottingham: English Place-Name Society (vol. 61).

Porteous, J. D. (1985). Place loyalty. *The Local Historian* 16: 343–5.

Powell, M. S. & S. D. Powell (1990). Bibliography of place-name literature, United States and Canada, 1980–1988. *Names* 38: 49–141.

Pyles, T. (1986). Bible Belt onomastics, or some curiosities of anti-Pedobaptist nomenclature. In Harder (1986), 72–88. Reprinted from *Names*.

Raper, P. E. (1987). *Dictionary of Southern African Place-Names*. Johannesburg: Lowry.

Raup, H. F. (1982). An overview of Ohio place names. *Names* 30: 49–54.

Read, W. A. (1984). *Indian Place-Names in Alabama*. Revised edition by James B. McMillan. University (AL): University of Alabama.

Reaney, P. H. (1960). *The Origin of English Place-Names*. London: Routledge & Kegan Paul.

Reed, A. W. (1973). *The Story of New Zealand Place-Names*. 2nd edn. Wellington: A. H. and W. A. Reed.

Robson, J. M. (1988). Surnames and Status in Victorian England. *Queen's Quarterly* 95: 642–61.

Rohe, R. (1988). Toponymy and the U.S. Land Survey in Wisconsin. Names 36: 43–50.

Room, A. (1980). *Place-name Changes since 1900: a World Gazetteer*. London: Routledge & Kegan Paul.

(1983). *A Concise Dictionary of Modern Place-Names in Great Britain and Ireland*. Oxford: Oxford University Press.

(1989). *Dictionary of World Place-Names Derived from British Names*. London: Routledge & Kegan Paul.

(1992). *The Street Names of England*. Stamford: Paul Watkins.

(1993). *The Naming of Animals*. Jefferson, NC: McFarland.

Scherr, A. (1986). Change-of-name petitions of the New York courts: an untapped source in historical onomastics. *Names* 34, 284–302.

Sealock, R. B., M. M. Sealock & M. S. Powell (compilers) (1982). *Bibliography of Place-Name Literature: United States and Canada.* 3rd edn. Chicago: American Library Association.

Seary, E. R. (1982). A short survey of the place-names of Newfoundland. In B. S. MacAodha (ed.) *Topothesia: Aistí in Onóir T. S. Ó Máille.* Galway: RTCOG: 144–57.

Smith, E. C. (compiler) (1950–1). Personal names: an annotated bibliography. *Bulletin of the New York Public Library* 54–55. (Reprinted Detroit: Gale (1966).)

(1950). *The Story of our Names.* New York: Harper.

Spittal, J. & J. Field (1990). *A Reader's Guide to Place-Names in the British Isles.* Stamford: Paul Watkins. [2nd edn. forthcoming.]

Stewart, G. R. (1945). *Names on the Land: a Historical Account of Place-naming in the United States.* New York: Random House (4th edn. San Francisco: Lexikus (1982).)

(1970). *A Concise Dictionary of American Place-Names.* Oxford: Oxford University Press.

Stronks, J. B. (1964). Chicago store front churches: 1964. *Names* 12: 127–8.

Titterton, J. (1990). Pinpointing the origin of a surname. *The Local Historian* 20: 3–8.

Walasek, R. A. (1983). The nature of electric utility company names. *Names* 31: 197–206.

Wilhelm, A. E. (1988). Pretty is as pretty says: the rhetoric of beauty-salon names. *Names* 36: 61–8.

Withycombe, E. G. (1977). *The Oxford Dictionary of English Christian Names.* 3rd edn. Oxford: Oxford University Press.

Zelinsky, W. (1967). Classical town names in the United States. *Geographical Review* 57: 463–95.

Zweigenhaft, R. L. (1983). Unusual First Names: a Positive Outlook. *Names* 31: 258–70.

5 Phonology

Abercrombie, D. (1965). Steele, Monboddo and Garrick. In *Studies in Phonetics and Linguistics.* London: Oxford University Press, 35–44.

Adams, J. (1794). *Euphonologia linguae Anglicanae, et mirum sonarum artificium, regulis conformium, rejecto nudae exceptionis effugio, facta cum Gallica contentione, et lusus literarii libera vagatione, etc.* London: R. White.

Afzelius, J. A. (1908). *A Concise Pronouncing Dictionary of English.* Stockholm: P. A. Norstedt & Söners Förlag.

Alexander, H. (1939). What is happening to English ou?. *Le Maître Phonétique,* avril–juin, 22–3.

Andrews, E. F. (1896). Common sense in the pronunciation of English. *Chautaquan* 22: 595–7.

Angus, W. (1800). *A Pronouncing Vocabulary of the English Tongue.* Glasgow: D. Niven. (1830) *An English Spelling and Pronouncing Vocabulary, on a new plan.* Glasgow: A. Young. (Nineteenth edn.)

Anon. (1784). *A General View of English Pronunciation.* Edinburgh. (Ascribed to William Scott: see the re-print, Menston: Scolar Press, 1968.)

(1790). *A Caution to Gentlemen Who Use Sheridan's Dictionary* . . . London.

(1796). *A Pronouncing Dictionary of the English Language, In Which the Meaning of Every Word is Clearly Explained, and the Sound of Every Syllable Distinctly Shown* . . . London: J. W. Myers.

(1797). *A Vocabulary of Such Words in the English Language as are of Dubious or Unsettled Accentuation; in which the pronunciation of Sheridan, Walker, and other orthoepists is compared.* London: F. & C. Rivington; *et al.*

(1812). *The Child's Preceptor; or a short and easy guide to spelling and reading the English language.* London: B. Crompton.

(1813). *Difficult Pronunciation, with Explanations of the Words* . . . London: T. Rutt.

(1817). *Errors of Pronunciation and Improper Expressions, Used Frequently, and Chiefly by the Inhabitants of London, to which are added, those in similar use, chiefly by the inhabitants of Paris.* London: printed for the author.

(1830). *The Juvenile Reader's Assistant* . . . *Chiefly Selected From Walker's Rhetorical Grammar.* Maldon: P. H. Youngman.

Ash, J. (1775/1795). *The New and Complete Dictionary of the English Language, to which is Prefixed, a Comprehensive Grammar.* London: E. & C. Dilly, and R. Baldwin.

Ausonius (1798). Criterion of pronunciation. *Gentleman's Magazine* 68: 290–1.

Barrie, A. (1792). *The Only Sure Guide to the English Tongue, or, New Pronouncing Spelling Book upon the Same Plan as Perry's Royal Standard English Dictionary.* Worcester, MA: I. Thomas.

(1794). *A Spelling and Pronouncing Dictionary of the English Language.* Edinburgh: A. Barrie.

Batchelor, T. (1809). *An Orthoëpical Analysis of the English Tongue; or, An Essay on the Nature of its Simple and Combined Sounds; etc.* London: Diddier & Tebbet. [See also Zettersten, A. (1974).]

Bauer, L. (1994). *Watching English Change: an introduction to the study of linguistic change in standard Englishes in the twentieth century.* London & New York: Longman.

Beal, J. (1993). Lengthening of *a* in eighteenth-century English: a consideration of evidence from Thomas Spence's *Grand Repository of the English Language* and other contemporary pronouncing dictionaries. *Newcastle & Durham Working Papers in Linguistics* I: 2–17.

(1994). The Jocks and Geordies: modified standards in eighteenth-century pronouncing dictionaries. *Newcastle & Durham Working Papers in Linguistics* II: 1–22.

Beattie, J. (1783). Of accent. Its nature and use. Standard of pronunciation. In *The Theory of Language. Dissertations Moral and Critical.* London: W. Strahan, 231–502.

Bell, A. M. (1867). *Visible Speech: The Science of Universal Alphabetics* . . . London: Simpkin, Marshall & Co.

Benezet, A. (1779). *The Pennsylvania Spelling-Book, or, Youth's Friendly Instructor and Monitor . . .* 2nd edn. Philadelphia: J. Crukshank.

Boag, J. (1853). *The Imperial Lexicon of the English Language . . .* Edinburgh: A. Fullerton & Co.

Bridges, R. (1919). *On English Homophones.* Oxford: Clarendon Press.

Bronstein, A. J. (1949). The vowels and diphthongs of the nineteenth century. *Speech Monographs* 16, ii: 227–42.

—— (1954). Nineteenth-century attitudes towards pronunciation. *Quarterly Journal of Speech,* XL: 417–21.

—— (1960). *The Pronunciation of American English.* New York: Appleton-Century-Crofts.

Brown, L. (ed.) (1993). *The New Shorter Oxford English Dictionary on Historical Principles.* Oxford: Clarendon Press.

Buchanan, J. (1766). *Essay towards Establishing a Standard for an Elegant and Uniform Pronunciation of the English Language, throughout the British Dominions, as Practised by the Most Learned and Polite Speakers.* London: E. & C. Dilly.

C——, A. C. (1829–30). Stray thoughts on language. *Gentleman's Magazine* [1829] 99 (I): 494–6; (II) 120–4, 317–20, 591–4; [1830] 100 (I): 308–10, 501–3; (II): 393–6.

Carrol, J. (1795). *The American Criterion of the English Language; containing the elements of pronunciation in five sections. For the use of English schools and foreigners.* London: S. Green.

Catford, J. C. (1988). *A Practical Introduction to Phonetics.* Oxford: Clarendon Press.

Chance, F. (1872). The pronunciation of initial cl and gl in English. *Notes and Queries,* 17 August 1872, 123–4.

Chapman, J. (1819). *The Music, or Melody and Rhythmus of the English Language.* Edinburgh: Michael Anderson.

Chomsky, N. & M. Halle (1968). *The Sound Pattern of English.* New York: Harper and Row.

Coleman, H. O. (1911). Individual peculiarities. *Le Maître Phonétique* juillet–aôut: 108–10.

Comstock, A. & J. A. Mair. (1874). *The Model Elocutionist: A Manual of Instruction in Vocal Gymnastics.* London: W. Collins.

Connolly, R. I. (1981). *An Analysis of Some Linguistic Information Obtained from Eighteenth and Nineteenth-Century Ulster Poetry.* Unpublished Ph.D. thesis, Queen's University of Belfast.

Cooley, A. J. (1861). *A Dictionary of the English Language Exhibiting the Orthography, Pronunciation and Definition of Words.* London & Edinburgh: W. and R. Chambers.

Country Rector, A (1890). Modern English pronunciation. Letter to *The Times* 27 December 1890: 11.

Craig, J. (1848). *A New Universal, Etymological, Technological and Pronouncing Dictionary of the English Language.* London: H. G. Collins.

Danielsson, B. (1948). *Studies on the Accentuation of Polysyllabic Latin, Greek, and Romance Loan-Words in English*. Stockholm: Almqvist & Wiksell.

Day, H. N. (1843). English phonology. *American Biblical Repository* 10: 432–54.

De Witt, E. M. (1925). *Euphon English in America*. London: J. M. Dent & Sons Ltd.

Dobson, E. J. (1968). *English Pronunciation 1500–1700*. 2 vols. 2nd edn. Oxford: Oxford University Press.

Duponceau, P. S. (1818). English phonology, or An essay towards an analysis and description of the component sounds of the English language. *Transactions of the American Philosophical Society* (n.s.) 1: 228–64.

Dyche, T. (rev. Smith, T.) (1805). *A Guide to the English Tongue* . . . London: Scatcherd & Letterman.

Earnshaw, C. (1818). *The Pronouncing Instructer [sic]*. Leeds: Edward Baines.

Eastlake, C. L. (1902). Changes in the pronunciation of English. *Nineteenth Century* 52: 992–1001.

Eijkman, L. P. H. (1909). Notes on English pronunciation. *Die Neueren Sprachen* 17: 443–5.

Ekwall, E. (1975). *A History of Modern English Sounds and Morphology*. Oxford: Basil Blackwell.

Ellis, A. J. (1869/1870/1874/1889). *On Early English Pronunciation,* vols. I–V. London: Asher Co. & Trübner & Co.

Elphinston, J. (1765). *The Principles of the English Language Digested; or, English Grammar Reduced to Analogy*, vol. 1. London: J. Bettenham.

  (1786–7). *Propriety Ascertained in Her Picture; or, Inglish Speech and Spelling Rendered Mutual Guides,* 2 vols. London: J. Walter. [Vol. 1 is undated, but datable to 1786; vol. 2 is dated 1787.]

  (1790). *Inglish Orthoggraphy Epittomized* . . . London: W. Ritchardson.

Emerson, O. F. (1892). The 'Guide to Pronunciation' again. *Modern Language Notes* 7: 388–92.

Emerson, R. H. (1993). The distribution of eighteenth-century prerhotic *o*-phonemes in Walker's *Critical Pronouncing Dictionary*. *American Speech* 68,ii: 115–38.

*EPD*1: see Jones, D. (1917).

*EPD*14: see Gimson, A. C. (1977).

Eustace, S. S. (1969). The meaning of the Palaeotype in A. J. Ellis's *On Early English Pronunciation 1869–89*. *Transactions of the Philological Society* 1969 (publ. 1970): 31–79.

Faber, D. (1987). *Some Problems of English Nucleus Placement*. Unpublished Ph.D. thesis, University of Manchester.

Fogg, P. W. (1792). *Elementa Anglicana, or, The principles of English grammar displayed and exemplified, in a method entirely new*. Stockport: J. Clarke.

Fudge, E. K. (1977). Long and short [æ] in one Southern British speaker's English. *Journal of the International Phonetic Association* 7: 55–65.

Fuhrken, G. E. (1932). *Standard English Speech: a compendium of English phonetics for foreign students*. Cambridge: Cambridge University Press.

Fulton, G. (1826). *A Pronouncing Vocabulary*. Edinburgh: Oliver & Boyd.

Fulton, G. & G. Knight, (1800). *A Pronouncing Spelling Book*. Edinburgh: P. Hill.

Gilchrist, J. (1824). *The Etymologic Interpreter; or an Explanatory and Pronouncing Dictionary of the English Language*. London: R. Hunter.

Gildon, C. & J. Brightland, (1711). *A Grammar of the English Tongue*. London: J. Brightland.

Gimson, A. C. (1962/1970/1980/1989/1994). *An Introduction to the Pronunciation of English*. London: E. Arnold.

(1964). Phonetic change and the RP vowel system. In Abercrombie, D. *et al.* (eds.) *In Honour of Daniel Jones*. London: Longmans, Green and Co. Ltd., 131–6.

(1977). *Everyman's English Pronouncing Dictionary*. 14th edn. London: Dent. [*EPD*14]

Görlach, M. (1991). *Introduction to Early Modern English*. Cambridge: Cambridge University Press.

Gove, P. B. (ed.) (1971). *Webster's Third International Dictionary of the English Language*. Springfield, MA: G. & C. Merriam Co.

Grandgent, C. H. (1891–2). Notes on American pronunciation. *Modern Language Notes* 6: 82–7, 458–67; 7: 183–4.

(1893a). American pronunciation again. *Modern Language Notes* 8: 273–82.

(1893b). *Off and On*. Phonetic Section of the Modern Language Association of America.

(1895). English in America. *Die Neueren Sprachen* 2: 443–67, 520–8.

H—, F. C. (1872). Pronunciation of initial *cl* and *gl* in English. *Notes & Queries* 14 September 1872: 209.

Haldeman, S. S. (1860). *Analytic Orthography*. Philadelphia: J. B. Lippincott Co.

Hare, J. C. *et al.* (1832–3). On English orthography. *Philological Museum* 1: 640–78; 2: 243–6.

Henslowe, W.-H. (1840). *The Phonarthron, Or, Natural System of the Sounds of Speech; a Test of Pronunciation for All Languages*. London: J. G. F. & J. Rivington.

Henton, C. G. (1983). Changes in the vowels of received pronunciation. *Journal of Phonetics* 11: 353–71.

Herries, J. (1773). *The Elements of Speech*. London: E. & C. Dilly.

Honey, J. (1991). Talking proper: schooling and the establishment of English 'Received Pronunciation'. In Nixon, G. & J. Honey, (eds.), *An Historic Tongue: Studies in English Linguistics in Memory of Barbara Strang*. London & New York: Routledge, 209–27.

Horn, W. (1905). *Untersuchungen zur neuenglischen Lautgeschichte*. Strassburg: K. J. Trübner.

Horn, W. & M. Lehnert, (1954). *Laut und Leben. Englische Lautgeschichte der neueren Zeit (1400–1950)*. 2 vols. Berlin: Deutscher Verlag der Wissenschaften.

Hornsey, J. (1809). *The Pronouncing Expositor; or, New Spelling Book*. London: Longman.

Jameson, R. S. (1828). *A Dictionary of the English Language by Johnson and Walker.* 2nd edn. London: W. Pickering.

Jespersen, O. (1909/1961). *A Modern English Grammar on Historical Principles, Vol. I Pt. 1: Sounds and Spellings.* Heidelberg: C. Winter. [1961 reprint: London: George Allen & Unwin Ltd., Copenhagen: Ejnar Munksgaard]

Johnson, S. (1755). *A Dictionary of the English Language.* London: W. Strahan.

Johnston, W. (1764). *A Pronouncing and Spelling Dictionary . . . Together with an Introduction, and an Appendix, Containing Many New and Useful Observations on the Sounds of the Letters . . .* London: W. Johnston.

Jones, C. (1989). *A History of English Phonology.* London & New York: Longman.

(1993). Scottish Standard English in the late eighteenth century. *Transactions of the Philological Society* 91,i: 95–131

Jones, D. (1909). *The Pronunciation of English. I. Phonetics. II. Phonetic Transcription.* Cambridge: Cambridge University Press.

(1917). *An English Pronouncing Dictionary (on Strictly Phonetic Principles).* London, Toronto, New York: J. M. Dent; E. P. Dutton. [*EPD*1]

(1958). *The Pronunciation of English.* 4th edn. Cambridge: Cambridge University Press.

(1960). *An Outline of English Phonetics.* 9th edn. Cambridge: W. Heffer Sons.

(1962). *An Outline of English Phonetics.* 9th edn. [with further alterations]. Cambridge: W. Heffer Sons.

Juul, A., Nielsen, H. F. & K. Sørensen, (eds.) (1988). Editors' introduction. In *Degeneration on Air?* Copenhagen: Landscentralen for Undervisningsmidler, ix-xxxi.

Kelly, J. (1995). Consonant-associated resonance in three varieties of English. In Lewis, J. W. (ed.) *Studies in General and English Phonetics: essays in honour of Professor J. D. O'Connor.* London & New York: Routledge, 335–49.

Kemp, J. A. (1972). *John Wallis: Grammar of the English Language: with an Introductory Grammatico-Physical Treatise on Speech, (or on the Formation of all Speech Sounds:) a new edition with translation and commentary.* London: Longman.

Kenrick, W. (1773). *A New Dictionary of the English Language, to Which is Prefixed, a Rhetorical Grammar . . .* London: J. & F. Rivington.

(1784). *A Rhetorical Grammar of the English Language . . .* London: R. Cadell & W. Longman.

Kenyon, J. (1946). *American Pronunciation,* 9th edn. Ann Arbor, MI: G. Wahr.

Kimball, F. (1936). Thornton, William. In *Dictionary of American Biography.* London: H. Mitford & OUP; New York: C. Scribner's Sons, vol. XVIII, 504–7.

Kingdon, R. (1958). *The Groundwork of English Stress.* London: Longman.

Knott, H. W. H. (1930). Du Ponceau, Pierre Étienne. In *Dictionary of American Biography,* vol. V. London: H. Mitford & OUP; New York: C. Scribner's Sons, 525–6.

Knowles, J. (1835). *A Pronouncing and Explanatory Dictionary of the English Language . . .* London: De Porquet & Cooper.

Knowles, J. (1837). *A Pronouncing and Explanatory Dictionary of the English Language* . . . 4th edn. London: Simpkin, Marshall & Co.

Krapp, G. P. (1919). *The Pronunciation of Standard English in America.* New York: Oxford University Press.

(1925). *The English Language in America.* 2 vols. New York: Century Co.

Kurath, H. (1928). *American Pronunciation.* London: Oxford University Press.

Kurath, H. & McDavid, R. I. Jr. (1961). *The Pronunciation of English in the Atlantic States, Based upon the Collections of the Linguistic Atlas of the Eastern United States.* Ann Arbor: The University of Michigan Press.

Ladefoged, P. & I. Maddieson, (1996). *The Sounds of the World's Languages.* Oxford: Blackwell.

Laver, J. (1994). *Principles of Phonetics.* Cambridge: Cambridge University Press.

Lepsius, R. (1863). *Standard Alphabet for Reducing Unwritten Languages and Foreign Graphic Systems to a Uniform Orthography of European Letters.* 2nd edn. London: Williams & Norgate.

Lloyd, R. J. (1894). Standard English. *Die Neueren Sprachen* II: 52–3.

Lounsbury, T. R. (1903). The standard of pronunciation in English. *Harper's Magazine* 107: 261–8, 575–82.

LPD: see Wells, J. C. (1990).

Luckombe, P. (1771). *The History and Art of Printing.* London: J. Johnson.

MacCarthy, P. A. D. (1945). *An English Pronouncing Vocabulary.* Cambridge: W. Heffer.

Mackintosh, D. and His Two Daughters (1797). *A Plain, Rational Essay on English Grammar: the main object of which is to point out a plain, rational and permanent standard of pronunciation* . . . Boston: Manning & Loring.

MacMahon, M. K. C. (1983). Thomas Hallam and the study of dialect and educated speech. *Transactions of the Yorkshire Dialect Society* 83: 19–31.

(1985). James Murray and the phonetic notation in the *New English Dictionary.* *Transactions of the Philological Society* 72–112.

Martin, J. P. A. (1889). [Letter to the Editor] *Le Maître Phonétique,* septembre–octobre: 83.

Max Müller, F. (1891). *The Science of Language,* vol. II. London: Longmans, Green, & Co.

Mencken, H. L. (1937). *The American Language. An Inquiry into the Development of English in the United States.* New York: Alfred A. Knopf.

Michael, I. (1993). *Early Textbooks of English: a guide.* Swansea: Colloquium on Textbooks, Schools and Society.

Millward, C. M. (1989). *A Biography of the English Language.* Forth Worth: Holt, Rinehart & Winston, Inc.

Mitford, W. (1804). *An Inquiry into the Principles of Harmony in Language, and of the Mechanism of Verse, Modern and Antient.* 2nd edn. London: Cadell & Davies.

Montgomery, M. (1910). *Types of Standard Spoken English and Its Chief Local Variants. Twenty-Four Phonetic Transcripts from British Classical Authors of the XIXth Century.* Strassburg: K. J. Trübner.

Mugglestone, L. C. (1988). *Studies in the Pronunciation of Standard English in the Late eighteenth and nineteenth Centuries according to the Evidence of Contemporary Writers on the Language.* Unpublished D.Phil. thesis, University of Oxford.

(1991). The fallacy of the Cockney rhyme: from Keats and earlier to Auden. *Review of English Studies* 42: 57–66.

(1995). *'Talking Proper': the rise of accent as social symbol.* Oxford: Clarendon Press.

Murray, J. A. H. (ed.) (1888–1928). *A New English Dictionary on Historical Principles.* Oxford: Clarendon Press. [*OED*1]

Murray, L. (1800). *English Grammar Adapted to the Different Classes of Learners.* 6th edn. York: T. Wilson & R. Spence.

Nares, R. (1784). *Elements of Orthoepy, Containing a Distinct View of the Whole Analogy of the English Language so Far as it Relates to Pronunciation, Accent, and Quantity.* London: T. Payne & Son.

Neumann, J. H. (1924). *American Pronunciation According to Noah Webster (1783).* Unpublished Ph.D. thesis, Columbia University.

Newman, F. W. (1878). The English language as spoken and written. *Contemporary Review* 31: 689–706.

Nicklin, T. (1920). *Standard English Pronunciation, with some notes on accidence and syntax.* Oxford: Clarendon Press. [The title on the cover is *The Sounds of Standard English.*]

Nohlgren, R. (1981). *English Pronunciation According to Peter Moberg (1801 ff.) and Other Swedes before 1900.* Stockholm: Almqvist & Wiksell International.

Nuttall, P. A. (1863). *The Standard Pronouncing Dictionary of the English Language.* London: Routledge, Warne, & Routledge.

Observator (1789). Thoughts on English orthography. *Gentleman's Magazine* 59: 601–02.

Odell, J. (1806). *An Essay on the Elements, Accents, Prosody, of the English Language . . .* London: Lackington, Allen & Co.

*OED*1: see Murray, J. A. H. (ed.) (1888–1928).

*OED*2: see Simpson, J. A. & E. S. C. Weiner (eds.) (1992).

Ogilvie, J. (1880). *The Imperial Dictionary of the English Language . . .* London: Blackie & Son.

Perry, W. (1775). *The Royal Standard English Dictionary . . .* Edinburgh: D. Willison.

(1793). *The Royal Standard English Dictionary . . .* 8th edn. Edinburgh: D. Willison.

Phipson, E. (1895). [Corrections.] *Le Maître Phonétique.* Décembre: 217.

Pickering, J. (1828). English orthoepy [Review of *Johnson's English Dictionary, as Improved by Todd . . . edited by Joseph E. Worcester.* Boston: Examiner Press]. *American Quarterly Review* 4: 191–214.

Pitman Dictionary of the English Language, The (1949). London: Sir Isaac Pitman & Sons Ltd.

Pointon, G. (1988). The BBC and pronunciation: a short history. In Juul, A., Nielsen, H. F. & K. Sørensen (eds.), *Degeneration on Air?* Copenhagen: Landscentralen for Undervisningsmidler, 41–50.

Popp, M. (1989). *Die englische Aussprache im 18. Jahrhundert im Lichte englisch-französischer Zeugnisse. Teil I. Das Dictionnaire de la Prononciation angloise 1756.* Heidelberg: Carl Winter Universitätsverlag.

Porter, S. (1892). A review of Dr. Emerson's criticism of 'Guide to Pronunciation'. *Modern Language Notes* 8: 235–42.

Prator, C. H. (1951). *Manual of American English Pronunciation for Adult Foreign Students.* Berkeley: University of California Press.

Prator, C. H. & B. W. Robinett (1972). *Manual of American English Pronunciation.* 3rd edn. New York: Holt, Rinehart & Winston.

R—, E. S. (1872). Pronunciation of initial cl and gl in English. *Notes & Queries* 14 September 1872: 209.

Ramsaran, S. (1990). RP: fact *and* fiction. In Ramsaran, S. (ed.), *Studies in the Pronunciation of English. A commemorative volume in honour of A. C. Gimson.* London: Routledge, 178–90.

Read, A. W. (1933/1980). British recognition of American speech in the eighteenth century. *Dialect Notes* VI, 1933. Reprinted in J. L. Dillard, (ed.) (1980), *Perspectives on American English.* The Hague, Paris, New York: Mouton Publishers, 15–35.

Reaney, P. H. (1991). *A Dictionary of English Surnames* 3rd edn. rev. R. M. Wilson. Oxford: Oxford University Press.

Rippmann, W. (1906). *The Sounds of Spoken English.* London: J. M. Dent & Co.

Rohlfing, H. (1984). *Die Werke James Elphinstons (1721–1809) als Quellen der englischen Lautgeschichte. Eine Analyse orthoepistischer Daten.* Heidelberg: Carl Winter Universitätsverlag.

Rush, J. (1827/1855). *The Philosophy of the Human Voice; Embracing its Physiological History* . . . Philadelphia: J. Maxwell; 4th edn. 1855.

Scott, H. (1928). *Fasti Ecclesiae Scoticanae: the succession of ministers in the Church of Scotland from the Reformation,* vol. VII. Edinburgh: Oliver and Boyd.

Search, E. (1773). *Vocal Sounds.* London: T. Jones.

Sergeant, L. (1872). Pronunciation of initial cl and gl in English. *Notes & Queries* 14 September: 209–10.

Sharp, G. (1767). *A Short Treatise on the English Tongue: being an attempt to render the reading and pronunciation of the same more easy to foreigners.* London: R. Horsfield & I. Allix.

Sheldon, E. K. (1938). *Standards of English Pronunciation According to the Grammarians and Orthoepists of the 16th, 17th, and 18th Centuries.* Unpublished Ph.D. dissertation, University of Wisconsin.

(1946). Pronouncing systems in eighteenth-century dictionaries. *Language* 22: 27–41.

(1947). Walker's influence on the pronunciation of English. *Publications of the Modern Language Association* 62: 130–46.

Sheridan, T. (1756). *British Education, Or the source of the disorders of Great Britain; being an essay towards proving, that the immorality, ignorance, and false taste, which so gener-*

ally prevail, are the natural and necessary consequences of the present defective system of education, with an attempt to shew, that a revival of the art of speaking, and the study of our own language, might contribute, in a great measure, to a cure of those evils. London: R. & J. Dodsley.

(1762). *A Course of Lectures on Elocution.* London: W. Strahan.

(1780). *A General Dictionary of the English Language. The Main Object of Which, is, to Establish a Plain and Permanent Standard of Pronunciation. To Which is Prefixed a Rhetorical Grammar.* London: J. Dodsley, C. Dilly & J. Wilkie.

(1781). *A Rhetorical Grammar of the English Language, Calculated solely for the Purposes of Teaching Propriety of Pronunciation, and Justness of Delivery, in That Tongue, by the Organs of Speech.* Dublin: Price, W. and H. Whitestone; Sleater, Sheppard, G. Burnet, R. Cross, Flin, Stewart, Mills, Wilkinson, Exshaw, Perrin, Byrne.

(1786). *Elements of English: Being a New Method of Teaching the Whole Art of Reading both with Regard to Pronunciation and Spelling.* Pt. I. London: C. Dilly.

Shields, A. (1974). Thomas Spence and the English language. *Transactions of the Philological Society* 1974: 33–64.

Simpson, J. A. & E. S. C. Weiner (eds.) (1992). *The Oxford English Dictionary [2nd ed.] on Compact Disc.* Oxford: Oxford University Press; New York: Clarendon Press. [*OED*2]

Smalley, D. S. (1855). *The American Phonetic Dictionary of the English Language.* London: F. Pitman; Cincinnati: Longley Brothers.

Smart, B. H. (1810). *A Practical Grammar of English Pronunciation on Plain and Recognised Principles Calculated to Assist in Removing Every Objectionable Peculiarity of Utterance, Arising either from Foreign, Provincial, or Vulgar Habits, etc.* London: J. Richardson.

(1819). *The Theory of Elocution, Exhibited in Connexion with a New and Philosophical Account of the Nature of Instituted Language.* London: J. Richardson.

(1836). *Walker Remodelled: A New Critical Pronouncing Dictionary of the English Language.* London: T. Cadell.

(1842). *The Practice of Elocution*, 4th edn. London: Longman, Brown, Green, & Longmans.

(1849). *Manual of Rhetoric: with exercises for the improvement of style or diction, subjects for narratives, familiar letters, school orations, &c. : being one of two sequels to 'Grammar on Its True Basis'.* London: Longman, Brown, Green, & Longmans.

Smith, W. (1795). *An Attempt to Render the Pronunciation of the English Language More Easy to Foreigners.* London: T. Gillet.

Soames, L. (1899). *Introduction to English, French, and German Phonetics with Reading Exercises.* New edn. London: Swan Sonnenschein & Co. Ltd.

Spence, T. (1775). *The Grand Repository of the English Language.* Newcastle upon Tyne: T. Saint.

Spurrell, W. (1850). *Geiriadur Cynaniaethol Seisoneg a Chymraeg . . . (An English–Welsh Pronouncing Dictionary . . .).* Caerfyrddin: W. Spurrell.

Stearns, E. J. (1858). *A Practical Guide to English Pronunciation for the Use of Schools.* Boston: Crosby, Nichols & Company.

Steele, J. (1775). *An Essay towards Establishing the Melody and Measure of Speech to be Expressed and Perpetuated by Peculiar Symbols.* London: J. Almon. [See next entry.]

(1779). *Prosodia Rationalis: or An Essay towards Establishing the Melody and Measure of Speech to be Expressed and Perpetuated by Peculiar Symbols.* London: J. Nichols. [See previous entry.]

Storm, J. [unpublished]. Letter to J. A. H. Murray, 12 April 1888, Murray Papers.

Storm, J. F. B. (1879). *Engelsk Filologi. Anvisning til et Videnskabeligt Studium af det Engelske Sprog for Studerende, Lærere og Viderekomne. I. Det Levende Sprog.* Kristiania: A. Cammermeyer.

Strang, B. M. H. (1970). *A History of English.* London: Methuen.

Sundby, B. (1976). *English Pronunciation 1500–1800: Report Based on the DEMEP Symposium and Editorial Meeting at Edinburgh, 23–26 October 1974.* Stockholm : School of English, Stockholm University; Almqvist & Wiksell International.

Sweet, H. [unpublished]. Letter to Alois Brandl, 5 Jan. 1882, Universitäts- und Stadtbibliothek Köln.

[unpublished]. Letter to A. H. Sayce, 3 April 1880, Oxford University Library: Bod.MS. Eng.Lett.d.64.

[unpublished]. Letters to Johan Storm, Universitetsbiblioteket i Oslo, MS. 8° 2402.JIII, JVI.

(1877). *A Handbook of Phonetics, Including a Popular Exposition of the Principles of Spelling Reform.* Oxford: Clarendon Press.

(1880–1). Sound-notation. *Transactions of the Philological Society:* 177–232.

(1882). *Elementary Sounds of English. A paper read Nov. 1881.* London: privately printed.

(1885). *Elementarbuch des Gesprochenen Englisch: Grammatik, Texte und Glossar.* Oxford: Clarendon Press; Leipzig: T. O. Weigel.

(1888). *A History of English Sounds from the Earliest Period with Full Word-Lists.* Oxford: Clarendon Press.

(1890a). *A Primer of Spoken English.* Oxford: Clarendon Press.

(1890b). *A Primer of Phonetics.* Oxford: Clarendon Press.

(1899). *The Practical Study of Languages. A Guide for Teachers and Learners.* London: J. M. Dent & Co.

(1908). *The Sounds of English. An Introduction to Phonetics.* Oxford: Clarendon Press.

Telonicus (1798). Criterion of pronunciation. *Gentleman's Magazine* 68: 567–9.

Thornton, W. (1793). Cadmus, or, A treatise on the elements of written language, illustrating, by a philosophical division of speech, the power of each character, thereby mutually fixing the orthography and orthoepy. *Transactions of the American Philosophical Society* 3: 262–319. Re-issued as a separate publication, Philadelphia: R. Aitken & Son, 1793.

Thurot, C. (1881–3). *De la prononciation française depuis le commencement du XVIe siècle d'après les témoignages des grammariens.* 2 vols. Paris: Imprimérie Nationale.

Tolman, A. H. (1887). The pronunciation of initial *cl* and *gl* in English words. *Modern Language Notes* 2,vi: 442–3.

True, E. T. & O. Jespersen (1897). *Spoken English: everyday talk with phonetic transcription.* 4th edn. Leipzig: O. R. Reisland.

Viëtor, W. (1904). *Elemente der Phonetik des Deutschen, Englischen und Französischen.* 5te Aufl. Leipzig: O. R. Reisland.

Voigtmann, [C. G.] (1846). Beiträge zur Lehre von der Aussprache des Englischen. *Archiv* 1: 166–83, 314–26.

Wagner, P. (1899). *Die Sprachlaute des Englischen nebst Anhang: Englische Eigennamen. Ein Hilfsbuch für den Schul- und Privatunterricht.* 2. Aufl. Stuttgart: P. Neff.

Walker, J. (1774). *A General Idea of a Pronouncing Dictionary of the English Language on a Plan Entirely New, with Observations on Several Words that are Variously Pronounced* . . . London: T. Becket.

(1775). *A Dictionary of the English Language, Answering at Once the Purposes of Rhyming, Spelling and Pronouncing.* London: T. Becket.

(1785). *A Rhetorical grammar, or, Course of Lessons in Elocution.* London: J. Robinson.

(1791). *A Critical Pronouncing Dictionary and Expositor of the English Language* . . . London: G. G. J. & J. Robinson, & T. Cadell.

(1806). *A Critical Pronouncing Dictionary and Expositor of the English Language* . . . 4th edn. London: A. Miller.

(1819a). *A Critical Pronouncing Dictionary and Expositor of the English Language* . . . 21st edn. London: T. Cadell & W. Davies.

(1819b). *A Rhyming Dictionary: answering at the same time, the purposes of spelling and pronouncing the English language, a plan not hitherto attempted.* London: T. Cadell & W. Davies.

(1838). *A Critical Pronouncing Dictionary and Expositor of the English Language* . . . Edinburgh: Peter Brown.

Wallis, J. (1653). *Grammatica Linguae Anglicanae.* Oxford: L. Lichfield.

Ward, A. (1952). *Some Problems in the English Orthoepists 1750–1809.* Unpublished B.Litt. thesis, University of Oxford.

Ward, I. C. (1945). *The Phonetics of English.* Cambridge: W. Heffer & Sons Ltd.

Webster, N. (1783). *The American Spelling Book, Being the first part of A Grammatical Institute of the English Language.* Hartford: Hudson & Goodwin.

(1787). *The American Spelling Book, Being the first part of A Grammatical Institute of the English Language.* 6th edn. Hartford: Hudson & Goodwin.

(1789). *Dissertations on the English Language: With Notes, Historical and Critical. To which is added, by way of an appendix, an essay on a reformed mode of spelling with Dr. Franklin's arguments on that subject.* Boston: I. Thomas & Co.

(1828). *An American Dictionary of the English Language.* New York: S. Converse.

(rev. Goodrich, C. A.) (1847). *A Dictionary of the English Language: Intended to Exhibit . . . The Orthography and Pronunciation of Words, as Sanctioned by Reputable Usage, and Where this Usage is Divided, as Determinable by a Reference to the Principles of Analogy . . .* London: Black, Young & Young.

Wells, J. C. (1982). *Accents of English.* 3 vols. Cambridge: Cambridge University Press.

(1990a). *Longman Pronunciation Dictionary.* Harlow: Longman. [*LPD*]

(1990b). A phonetic update on RP. *Moderna Språk,* 84, i: 3–9.

Western, A. (1902). *Englische Lautlehre für Studierende und Lehrer,* 2te gänzlich umgearbeitete Auflage. Leipzig: Reisland.

Whitney, W. D. (1875). The elements of English pronunciation. In *Oriental and Linguistic Studies. Second series.* London: Trübner & Co., 200–76.

Wright, J. (1905). *The English Dialect Grammar.* Oxford: Henry Frowde.

Wrocklage, E. (1943). *Der Lautstand der englischen Sprache um 1800 nach John Walker's Critical Pronouncing Dictionary (1791–1806).* Unpublished doctoral dissertation, University of Berlin.

Wyld, H. C. (1913). *Evolution in English Pronunciation. A public lecture delivered at the University of Liverpool . . .* Liverpool: University of Liverpool Press.

(1914). *A Short History of English . . .* London: J. Murray.

Xanthus, (1826). Remarks on pronunciation. *U. S. Literary Gazette* 3: 378–85; 4: 436–43.

Yeomans, J. (1759). *The Abecedarian or, Philosophic Comment upon the English Alphabet, Setting Forth the Absurdities in the Present Custom of Spelling.* London: J. Coote.

Zettersten, A. (1974). *A Critical Facsimile Edition of Thomas Batchelor: An Orthoëpical Analysis of the English Language and An Orthoëpical Analysis of the Dialect of Bedfordshire (1809).* Lund: C. W. K. Gleerup.

6 English Grammar and Usage

Primary sources and texts

Alford, H. (n.d.) [1864]. *A Plea for the Queen's English: Stray Notes on Speaking and Spelling.* Repr. from 2nd London edn. New York: Dick & Fitzgerald.

Ash, J. (1763). *Grammatical Institutes.* 4th edn. London. [E. L. 9, 1967]

Ayres, A. (1897) [1881]. *The Verbalist: a Manual Devoted to Brief Discussions of the Right and the Wrong Use of Words.* Rev. edn. New York: Appleton.

(1882) [1880]. *The Orthoëpist: a Pronouncing Manual.* New York: Appleton.

Breen, H. H. (1857). *Modern English Literature: Its Blemishes and Defects.* London: Longman, Brown, Green & Longmans.

Brown, G. (1853) [1823]. *The Institutes of English Grammar.* New York: S. Wood.

Burchfield, R. W. (ed.) (1972–86). *A Supplement to the Oxford English Dictionary.* 4 vols. Oxford: Clarendon Press.

Campbell, G. (1776). *The Philosophy of Rhetoric.* Ed. L. F. Bitzer. Carbondale: Southern Illinois University Press (1963).

Cobbett, W. (1818). *A Grammar of the English Language. The 1818 New York first edition with passages added in 1819, 1820, and 1823.* Ed. C. C. Nickerson & J. W. Osborne (1983). Amsterdam: Rodopi.

Cobbett, W. (1823). *A Grammar of the English Language.* With an introduction by Robert Burchfield. (1984). Oxford: Oxford University Press.

(1832). *A Grammar of the English Language.* Facsimile reproduction with introductions by C. Downey and F. Aarts. (1986). Delmar, NY: Scholars' Facsimiles and Reprints.

Cooper, C. (1685). *Grammatica Linguae Anglicanae.* [E. L. 86, 1968]

Coleridge, H. (1859). *Proposal for the Publication of a New English Dictionary, by the Philological Society.* London: Trübner.

Dilworth, T. (1751) [1740]. *A New Guide to the English Tongue.* London: Kent. [E. L. 4, 1967]

Fell, J. (1784). *An Essay towards an English Grammar.* London: Dilly. [E.L. 16, 1967]

Fisher, A. (1750). *A New Grammar.* Newcastle upon Tyne. [E. L. 130, 1968]

Fowler, H. W. (1926). *A Dictionary of Modern English Usage.* Oxford: Oxford University Press. [2nd edn. rev. by E. Gowers. 1965]

(1996). *The New Fowler's Modern English Usage.* Rev. by R. W. Burchfield. Oxford: Oxford University Press.

Fries, C. C. (1940). *American English Grammar* (National Council of Teachers of English: Monograph No. 10). New York: Appleton-Century-Crofts.

Fries, C. C. (1952). *The Structure of English.* New York: Harcourt, Brace.

Greaves, P. (1594). *Grammatica Anglicana.* [E. L. 169, 1969]

Hall, F. (1872). *Recent Exemplifications of False Philology.* New York: Scribner, Armstrong. (1873). *Modern English.* New York: Scribner, Armstrong.

Hall, R. A., Jr. (1950). *Leave Your Language Alone!* Ithaca, NY: Linguistica.

Hodgson, W. B. (1886). *Errors in the Use of English.* American rev. edn. New York: D. Appleton and Company. [First published Edinburgh, 1882]

Horne Tooke, J. (1798). *EπEA πTEPOENTA. Or, The Diversions of Purley,* I. 2nd edn. London. [E. L. 127, 1968] [1st edn. 1786]

Hudson, K. (1977). *The Dictionary of Diseased English.* London: Macmillan.

Jespersen, O. (1909–49). *A Modern English Grammar on Historical Principles.* 7 vols. London: Allen & Unwin.

Johnson, S. (1755). *A Dictionary of the English Language.* 2 vols. London: W. Strahan.

Krapp, G. P. (1908). *The Authority of Law in Language.* (University Studies, University of Cincinnati, Series II, Vol. IV, No. 3.)

Krapp, G. P. (1909). *Modern English: Its Growth and Present Use.* New York: Scribner's. (1927). *The Knowledge of English.* New York: Holt.

Latham, R. G. (1848). *The English Language.* 2nd edn. London.

Leonard, S. A. (1932). *Current English Usage* (National Council of Teachers of English: Monograph No. 1). Chicago: Inland.

Lowth, R. (1762). *A Short Introduction to English Grammar*. London. [E. L. 18, 1967]

Marckwardt, A. H. & F. G. Walcott. (1938). *Facts About Current English Usage* (National Council of Teachers of English: Monograph No. 7). New York: Appleton-Century-Crofts.

Marsh, G. P. (1860). *Lectures on the English Language*. New York: Scribner's.

Mathews, W. (1876). *Words; Their Use and Abuse*. Chicago.

Matthews, B. (1901). *Parts of Speech: Essays on English*. New York: Scribner's.

(1921). *Essays on English*. New York: Scribner's.

Meredith, L. P. (1877). *Every-day Errors of Speech*. Rev. by T. H. L. Leary. London: William Tegg.

Mittins, W. H., M. Salu, M. Edminson & S. Coyne (1970). *Attitudes to English Usage*. London: Oxford University Press.

Moon, G. W. (1869). *The Bad English of Lindley Murray and Other Writers on the English Language*. 3rd edn. London.

Morris, W. (ed.) (1969). *The American Heritage Dictionary of the English Language*. Boston: American Heritage & Houghton Mifflin.

Müller, M. (1862). *Lectures on the Science of Language*. From 2nd London edn., rev. New York: Scribner's.

(1874). *Lectures on the Science of Language*. Second series. New York: Scribner, Armstrong.

Murray, L. (1795). *English Grammar, Adapted to the Different Classes of Learners*. York. [E. L. 106, 1968]

Partridge, E. (1969). *Shakespeare's Bawdy*. Rev. edn. New York: Dutton.

Priestley, J. (1761). *The Rudiments of English Grammar*. London: Griffiths. [E. L. 210, 1969]

Richardson, C. (1836). *A New Dictionary of the English Language*. London: William Pickering.

(1854). *On the Study of Language: An Exposition of 'ΕπΕΑ πΤΕΡΟΕΝΤΑ, or the Diversions of Purley, by John Horne Tooke.'*. London: George Bell.

Sheridan, T. (1762). *A Course of Lectures on Elocution*. London: W. Strahan. [E. L. 129, 1968]

Sheridan, T. (1780). *A General Dictionary of the English Language*. London: J. Dodsley. [E. L. 50, 1967]

Swift, J. (1712). *A Proposal for Correcting, Improving and Ascertaining the English Tongue*. London. [E. L. 213, 1969]

Trench, R. C. (1852) [1851]. *On the Study of Words*. [From 2nd London edn.] New York: Redfield.

(1855). *English, Past and Present*. London: Parker.

(1857). *On Some Deficiencies in our English Dictionaries. Being the Substance of Two Papers Read before the Philological Society, Nov. 5, and Nov. 19, 1857*. 2nd edn. 1860. London: Parker.

(1877). *Suplée's Trench on Words*. New York: Widdleton.

Wallis, J. (1653). *Grammatica Linguae Anglicanae*. Oxonia: Excudebat. Leon. Lichfield. Veneunt apud Tho. Robinson. [E. L. 142, 1969]

Ward, W. (1765). *An Essay on Grammar*. London: Horsfield. [E. L. 15, 1967]

Webster, N. (1784). *A Grammatical Institute, of the English Language, Comprising, An Easy, Concise, and Systematic Method of Education, Designed for the Use of English Schools in America*. Part II. Hartford: Hudson & Goodwin. [E. L. 90, 1968]

(1789). *Dissertations on the English Language*. Boston: Isaiah Thomas and Company. [Scolar Press Facsimile, 1967]

(1828). *An American Dictionary of the English Language*. New York: Converse.

Worcester, J. E. (1859). *A Dictionary of the English Language*. London: Sampson Low.

Secondary sources

Aarsleff, H. (1983) [1967]. *The Study of Language in England, 1780–1860*. Minneapolis: University of Minnesota Press.

Bailey, R. W. (1991). *Images of English*. Ann Arbor: University of Michigan Press.

Baron, D. (1982). *Grammar and Good Taste*. New Haven: Yale University Press.

Bolton, W. F. (ed.) (1966). *The English Language: Essays by English and American Men of Letters, 1490–1839*. Cambridge: Cambridge University Press.

Bolton, W. F. & D. Crystal (eds.) (1969). *The English Language: Essays by Linguists and Men of Letters, 1858–1964*. Cambridge: Cambridge University Press.

Bromley, J. (1959). *The Man of Ten Talents: a Portrait of Richard Chenevix Trench 1807–86. Philologist, Poet, Theologian, Archibishop*. London: SPCK.

Burchfield, R. W. (1987). *The Supplement to the Oxford English Dictionary: the End of the Alphabet*. In Bailey, R. W. (ed.), *Dictionaries of English: Prospects for the Record of our Language*. Ann Arbor: University of Michigan Press, 11–21.

Cameron, D. (1995). *Verbal Hygiene*. London and New York: Routledge.

Crowley, T. (1989). *Standard English and the Politics of Language*. Urbana: University of Illinois Press. [= *The Politics of Discourse: the Standard Language Question in British Cultural Debates*. Basingstoke: Macmillan Education.]

Crowley, T. (1991). *Proper English? Readings in Language, History and Cultural Identity*. London and New York: Routledge.

Finegan, E. (1980). *Attitudes toward English Usage*. New York and London: Teachers College Press, Columbia University.

Francis, W. N. & H. Kucera. (1982). *Frequency Analysis of English Usage: Lexicon and Grammar*. Boston: Houghton Mifflin.

Gilman, E. W. (ed.) (1989). *Webster's Dictionary of English Usage*. Springfield: Merriam-Webster.

Greenbaum, S. (ed.) (1996). *Comparing English Worldwide: the International Corpus of English*. Oxford: Clarendon Press.

Ihalainen, O. (1994). The Dialects of England since 1776. In Burchfield, R. (ed.), *The Cambridge History of the English Language*, vol. V. Cambridge: Cambridge University Press, 197–274.

Johansson, S. & K. Hofland (1989). *Frequency Analysis of English Vocabulary and Grammar: Based on the LOB Corpus.* 2 vols. Oxford: Clarendon Press.

Jones, R. F. (1953). *The Triumph of the English Language: a Survey of Opinions concerning the Vernacular from the Introduction of Printing to the Restoration.* Stanford: Stanford University Press.

Joseph, J. E. (1987). *Eloquence and Power: the Rise of Language Standards and Standard Languages.* New York: Blackwell.

Kytö, M., M. Rissanen & S. Wright (eds.) (1994). *Corpora across the Centuries: Proceedings of the First International Colloquium on English Diachronic Corpora.* Amsterdam and Atlanta: Rodopi.

Landau, S. I. (1984). *Dictionaries: the Art and Craft of Lexicography.* Cambridge: Cambridge University Press.

Leonard, S. A. (1929), *The Doctrine of Correctness in English Usage, 1700–1800.* Repr. New York: Russell & Russell, 1962.

McDavid, R. I., Jr. (1966). Usage, Dialects, and Functional Varieties. In Stein, J. (ed.), *The Random House Dictionary of the English Language – The Unabridged Edition.* New York: Random House, xix–xxi.

McKnight, G. H. (1928). *Modern English in the Making.* New York: Appleton.

Michael, I. (1970). *English Grammatical Categories and the Tradition to 1800.* Cambridge: Cambridge University Press.

(1987). *The Teaching of English from the Sixteenth Century to 1870.* Cambridge: Cambridge University Press.

Milroy, J. & L. Milroy (1991). *Authority in Language: Investigating Language Prescription and Standardisation.* 2nd edn. London and New York: Routledge.

Morton, H. C. (1994). *The Story of* Webster's Third*: Philip Gove's Controversial Dictionary and Its Critics.* Cambridge: Cambridge University Press.

Mugglestone, L. (1995). *'Talking Proper': the Rise of Accent as Social Symbol.* Oxford: Clarendon Press.

Murray, K. M. E. (1977). *Caught in the Web of Words.* New Haven: Yale University Press.

Padley, G. A. (1988). *Grammatical Theory in Western Europe, 1500–1700: Trends in Vernacular Grammar II.* Cambridge: Cambridge University Press.

Pedersen, H. (1959). *The Discovery of Language; Linguistic Science in the Nineteenth Century.* Trans. J. W. Spargo. Bloomington: Indiana University Press. [Originally published 1931.]

Peters, P. (1995). *The Cambridge Australian English Style Guide.* Cambridge: Cambridge University Press.

Quirk. R. (1968). From Descriptive to Prescriptive: an Example. In Quirk, R., *Essays on the English Language: Medieval and Modern.* Bloomington: Indiana University Press, 109–13.

Reddick, A. (1996). *The Making of Johnson's Dictionary, 1746–1773.* Rev. edn. Cambridge: Cambridge University Press.

Sinclair, J. M. (ed.) (1987). *Looking Up.* London: Collins ELT.

Sledd, J. H. & W. R. Ebbitt (eds.) (1962). *Dictionaries and* That *Dictionary*. Chicago: Scott, Foresman.

Sledd, J. H. & G. J. Kolb. (1955). *Dr. Johnson's Dictionary: Essays in the Biography of a Book*. Chicago: University of Chicago Press.

Stein, D. & I. Tieken-Boon van Ostade (eds.) (1993). *Towards a Standard English 1600–1800*. Berlin: Mouton de Gruyter.

Stein, G. (1985). *The English Dictionary before Cawdrey*. Tübingen: Max Niemeyer.

Sundby, B., A. K. Bjørge, & K. E. Haugland (1991). *A Dictionary of English Normative Grammar 1700–1800*. Amsterdam: John Benjamins.

Svartvik, J. & R. Quirk (eds.) (1980). *A Corpus of English Conversation*. Lund: C. W. K. Gleerup.

Treble, H. A. & G. H. Vallins (1936). *An ABC of English Usage*. Oxford: Clarendon Press.

Tucker, S. I. (1961). *English Examined*. Cambridge: Cambridge University Press.

7 Literary Language

Abrams, M. H. (1953). *The Mirror and The Lamp*. Oxford: Oxford University Press.

Adamson, S. M. (1994a). From empathetic deixis to empathetic narrative: stylisation and (de)subjectivisation as processes of language-change. *Transactions of the Philological Society* 92.1: 55–88. Reprinted in D. Stein & S. Wright (eds.) (1995), *Subjectivity and Subjectivisation*. Cambridge: Cambridge University Press, 195–224.

(1994b). Subjectivity in narration: empathy and echo. In M. Yaguello (ed.), *Subjecthood and Subjectivity*. Paris: Ophrys.

(forthcoming). The code as context: language change and (mis)interpretation. In K. Malmkjaer & J. Williams (eds.), *Context in Language Learning and Language Understanding*. Cambridge: Cambridge University Press.

Allsopp, R. (1992). What would they know of English who only English know?: the contribution of Caribbean creoles to the expressive resources of the English language. In J. H. Hall (ed.), *Old English and New: Studies in Language and Linguistics in Honor of Frederic G. Cassidy*. New York: Garland, 143–55.

Bailey, R. W. & D. M. Burton (1968). *English Stylistics: A Bibliography*. Cambridge MA: MIT Press.

Bally, C. (1912). Le style indirect libre en français moderne. *Germanisch-Romanische Monatsschrift*, 4: 549–56, 597–606.

Banfield, A. 1982. *Unspeakable Sentences: Narration and Representation in the Language of Fiction*. London: Routledge.

Barnes, M. E. (1975). *Linguistics and Language in Science Fiction-Fantasy*.

Bennett, J. R. (1986). *A Bibliography of Stylistics and Related Criticism, 1967–83*. New York: Modern Languages Association of America.

Biber, D. (1988). *Variation across Speech and Writing*. Cambridge: Cambridge University Press.

Biber, D. & E. Finegan (1989). Drift and the evolution of English style: a history of three genres. *Language* 65: 487–517.

Blair, H. (1783). *Lectures on Rhetoric and Belles Lettres*. 3 vols. Dublin: Whitestone, Colles *et al.*

Blake, N. (1981). *Non-standard Language in English Literature*. London: André Deutsch.

Boyd, J. & Z. Boyd. (1977). The perfect of experience. *Studies in Romanticism*, 16.1: 3–13.

Bradford, R. (1993). *A Linguistic History of English Poetry*. London: Routledge.

Brathwaite, E. K. (1984). *A History of the Voice: the Development of Nation Language in Anglophone Caribbean Poetry*. London: New Beacon.

Bridgman, R. (1966). *The Colloquial Style in America*. New York: Oxford University Press.

Brittain, L. (1788). *Rudiments of English Grammar*. Louvain: L. J. Urban.

Brogan, T. V. F. (1981). *English Versification 1570–1980*. Baltimore: John Hopkins.

Brooke-Rose, C. (1965). *A Grammar of Metaphor*. London: Secker and Warburg.

Brown, W. C. (1948). *The Triumph of Form: a Study of the Later Masters of the Heroic Couplet*. Chapel Hill: University of North Carolina Press.

Brown, G. & G. Yule (1983). *Discourse Analysis*. Cambridge: Cambridge University Press.

Campbell, G. 1776. *The Philosophy of Rhetoric*. London.

Christensen, F. (1967). *Notes Toward a New Rhetoric*. New York: Harper & Row.

Cole, R. W. (1986). Literary representation of dialect: a theoretical approach to the artistic problem. *The USF Language Quarterly* 14: 3–8.

Coleridge, S. T. (1817). *Biographia Literaria*. In J. Engell & W. J. Bate (eds.) (1983), *The Collected Works* 7. i–ii. (Bollingen Series 75). Princeton: University Press.

Crystal, D. (1980). Neglected grammatical factors in conversational English. In S. Greenbaum, G. Leech & J. Svartvik (eds.), *Studies in English Linguistics*. London: Longman.

(1991). *A Dictionary of Linguistics and Phonetics*. 3rd rev. edn. Oxford: Blackwell.

Davidson, D. 1984. What metaphors mean. In *Inquiries into Truth and Interpretation*, Oxford: Clarendon Press, 245–64.

Dillon, G. L. (1978). *Language Processing and the Reading of Literature: Toward a Model of Comprehension*. Bloomington: Indiana University Press.

Edgeworth, R. L. & M. Edgeworth (1802). *Essay on Irish Bulls*. London.

Ehrlich, S. (1990). *Point of View: a Linguistic Analysis of Literary Style*. London: Routledge.

Elgin, S. H. (1988). *A First Dictionary and Grammar of Laadan*. Ed. D. Martin. Madison, Wisconsin: Society for the Furtherance and Study of Fantasy and Science Fiction.

Fischer, A. (ed.) (1994). *Repetition*. Tübingen: Narr.

Fleischman, S. (1990). *Tense and Narrativity: from Medieval Performance to Modern Fiction*. London: Routledge.

Fludernik, M. (1993). *The Fictions of Language and the Languages of Fiction: the Linguistic Representation of Speech and Consciousness*. London: Routledge.

Fowler, A. (1987). *A History of English Literature*. Oxford: Blackwell.

Fowler, R. (1983). Polyphony and problematic in *Hard Times*. In R. Giddings (ed.), *The Changing World of Charles Dickens*. New York: Barnes and Noble.

Freeman, D. C. (1968). On the primes of metrical style. *Language and Style* 1: 63–101.
(ed.) (1981). *Essays in Modern Stylistics*. London: Methuen.

Fussell, P. (1954). *Theory of Prosody in Eighteenth-Century England*. (Connecticut College Monographs) New London, Connecticut: Connecticut College.

Gordon, I. A. (1966). *The Movement of English Prose*. London: Longman.

Griffiths, E. P. (1988). *The Printed Voice*. Oxford: Clarendon Press.

Halliday, M. A. K. (1981). Linguistic function and literary style: an enquiry into the language of William Golding's *The Inheritors*. In D. C. Freeman (ed.) (1981), 325–60.

Halliday, M. A. K. & R. Hasan (1976). *Cohesion in English*. London: Longman.

Hamburger, K. (1973). The Logic of Literature (tr. by M. J. Rose). Bloomington & London: Indiana University Press.

Hamilton, G. R. (1949). *The Tell-Tale Article: a Critical Approach to Modern Poetry*. London.

Harris, J. (1771). *Hermes, or A Philosophical Inquiry Concerning Universal Grammar*. 3rd rev. edn. London: John Nourse.

Hascall, D. L. (1974). Triple meter in English verse. *Poetics* 12: 49–71.

Hopper, P. & E. C. Traugott. (1993). *Grammaticalization*. Cambridge: Cambridge University Press.

Johnson, S. (1755). *A Dictionary of the English Language*. London: J. & P. Knapton *et al.*
(1783). *Lives of the Poets*. London: C. Bathurst *et al.*

Johnstone, B. (ed.) (1994). *Repetition in Discourse: Interdisciplinary Perspectives*. Norwood NJ: Ablex.

Kenner, H. (1975). *A Homemade World: the American Modernist Writers*. New York: Alfred A. Knopf.
(1987). *A Sinking Island: the Modern English Writers*. London: Barrie and Jenkins.

Kiparsky, P. (1977). The rhythmic structure of English verse. *Linguistic Inquiry* 8: 189–247.

Kiparsky, P. & G. Youmans (eds.) (1989). *Phonetics and Phonology 1: Rhythm and Meter*. London: Academic Press.

Kugel, J. L. (1981). *The Idea of Biblical Poetry: Parallelism and its History*. New Haven: Yale University Press.

Labov, W. (1969). The logic of nonstandard English. In *Georgetown Monographs on Language and Linguistics*, 22. Washington DC: Georgetown University Press. Reprinted as ch. 5 of W. Labov (1972), *Language in the Inner city*. Philadelphia: University of Pennsylvania Press.

Lakoff, G. & M. Johnson (1980). *Metaphors We Live By*. Chicago: Chicago University Press.

Langbaum, R. (1957). *The Poetry of Experience*. London: Chatto & Windus.

Lecercle, J.-J. (1994). *Philosophy of Nonsense: the Intuitions of Victorian Nonsense Literature*. London: Routledge.

Leech, G. N. (1969). *A Linguistic Guide to English Poetry*. London: Longman.

Leech, G. N. & M. H. Short (1981). *Style in Fiction*. London: Longman.

Le Page, R. B. & A. Tabouret-Keller (1985). *Acts of Identity*. Cambridge: Cambridge University Press.

Lennard, J. (1991). *But I Digress: the Exploitation of Parentheses in English Printed Verse*. Oxford: Clarendon Press.

Levin, S. (1977). *The Semantics of Metaphor*. Baltimore and London: John Hopkins.

Lodge, D. (1977). *The Modes of Modern Writing*. London: Edward Arnold.

Low, D. (ed.) (1974). *Burns* (The Critical Heritage). London: Routledge & Kegan Paul.

Lyons, J. (1977). *Semantics*. Cambridge: Cambridge University Press.

Mason, M. (ed.) (1992). *Lyrical Ballads* (Longman Annotated Texts). London: Longman.

Matthews, P. (1981). *Syntax*. Cambridge: Cambridge University Press.

(1997). *The Concise Oxford Dictionary of Linguistics*. Oxford: Oxford University Press.

Meyer, C. F. (1992). *Apposition in Contemporary English*. Cambridge: Cambridge University Press.

Meyers, W. E. (1980). *Aliens and Linguistics: Language Study and Science Fiction*. Athens: University of Georgia Press.

Miles, J. (1964). *Eras and Modes in English Poetry*. Revised edition. Berkeley: University of California Press.

(1967). *Style and Proportion: The Language of Prose and Poetry*. Boston: Little, Brown and Co.

Milroy, J. (1977). *The Language of Gerard Manley Hopkins* (The Language Library). London: André Deutsch.

Murray, L. (1795). *English Grammar*. York: Wilson, Spence and Mawman.

Nowottny, W. (1962). *The Language Poets Use*. London: Athlone Press.

Oliphant, T. L. K. (1873). *The Sources of Standard English*. London: Macmillan.

Omond, T. S. (1921). *English Metrists*. Oxford: Clarendon Press.

Ong, W. J. (1982). *Orality and Literacy: the Technologizing of the Word*. London: Routledge.

Otten, C. F. & G. D. Schmidt (eds.) (1989). *The Voice of the Narrator in Children's Literature: Insights from Writers and Critics*. London: Greenwood Press.

Page, N. (1973). *Speech in the English Novel.* London: Macmillan.

Pascal, R. (1977). *The Dual Voice: free indirect style and its functioning in the nineteenth century European novel.* Manchester: Manchester University Press.

Pickbourn, J. (1789). *A Dissertation on the English Verb.* London: J. Davies.

Piper, W. B. (1969). *The Heroic Couplet.* Cleveland: Case Western Reserve University Press.

Preston, D. R. (1985). The Li'l Abner syndrome: written representations of speech. *American Speech* 60: 328–36.

Priestley, J. (1777). *A Course of Lectures on Oratory and Criticism.* London: J. Johnson.

Prynne, J. (1988). English poetry and emphatical language. *Proceedings of the British Academy* 74: 135–69.

Ricks, C. B. (1984). *The Force of Poetry.* Oxford: Clarendon Press.

(1993). *Beckett's Dying Words.* (The Clarendon Lectures 1990.) Oxford: Clarendon Press.

Rieke, A. (1992). *The Sense of Nonsense.* Iowa: University of Iowa Press.

Ruskin, J. (1856). *Modern Painters III.* Volume 5 of E. T. Cook & A. Wedderburn (eds.) (1904), *The Works of John Ruskin.* London: George Allen.

Sanders, A. (1994). *The Short Oxford History of English Literature.* Oxford: Clarendon Press.

Scully, J. (1966). *Modern Poets on Modern Poetry.* London and Glasgow: Collins/Fontana.

Sewell, E. (1962). Lewis Carroll and T. S. Eliot as nonsense poets. In H. Kenner (ed.), *T. S. Eliot.* (Twentieth Century Views series.) New Jersey: Prentice Hall, 65–72.

Shaw, P. & P. Stockwell (eds.) (1991). *Subjectivity and Literature from the Romantics to the Present Day.* London: Pinter Publishers.

Sievers, E. (1893). *Altergermanische Metrik.* Halle: Max Niemeyer.

Solt, M. E. (ed.) (1968). *Concrete Poetry. A World View.* Bloomington: Indiana University Press.

Sonstroem, D. (1967). Making earnest of game: G. M. Hopkins and nonsense poetry. *Modern Language Quarterly* 28 (June).

Spiller, R. E., W. Thorp, T. H. Johnson, H. S. Canby, R. M. Ludgwig & W. M. Gibson. *A Literary History of the United States.* 4th rev. edn. New York: Macmillan.

Steele, J. (1775). *An Essay towards Establishing the Melody and Measure of Speech.* London: J. Almon, 76.

Steele, T. (1990). *Missing Measures: Modern Poetry and the Revolt against Meter.* Fayetteville: University of Arkansas Press.

Stephens, J. (1992). *Language and Ideology in Children's Fiction.* Harlow: Longman.

Stephens, J. & R. Waterhouse (1990). *Literature, Language and Change: from Chaucer to the Present.* London: Routledge.

Tannen, D. (ed.) (1982). *Spoken and Written Language: Exploring Orality and Literacy.* Norwood NJ: Ablex.

(1989). *Talking voices: repetition, dialogue, and imagery in conversational discourse.* Cambridge: Cambridge University Press.

Tarlinskaya, M. (1976). *English Verse: Theory and History.* The Hague: Mouton.

(1987). Meter and mode: English iambic pentameter, hexameter, and septameter and their period variations. *Style* 21: 400–26.

Traugott, E. C. & M. L. Pratt (1980). *Linguistics for Students of Literature.* New York: Harcourt Brace Jovanovich.

Tufte, V. (1971). *Grammar as Style.* New York: Holt, Rinehart & Winston.

Tulloch, G. (1985). The search for a Scots narrative voice. In M. Görlach (ed.) *Focus On: Scotland.* Amsterdam: Benjamins, 159–80.

Wales, K. (1990). *A Dictionary of Stylistics.* London: Longman.

Ward, W. (1765). *An Essay on Grammar.* London.

Wesling, D. (1980). *The Chances of Rhyme: Device and Modernity.* Berkeley: University of California Press.

(1985). *The New Poetries: Poetic Form since Coleridge and Wordsworth.* Lewisburg: Bucknell University Press.

Williamson, J. & V. M. Burke (eds.) (1971). *A Various Language: Perspectives on American Dialects.* New York: Holt, Rinehart and Winston.

Wimsatt, W. K. (1970). One relation of rhyme to reason. In *The Verbal Icon.* London: Methuen, 153–66. (First published 1954, Lexington: University of Kentucky.)

Winters, Y. (1960). *In Defense of Reason.* London: Routledge & Kegan Paul.

Wolfe, T. (1975). *The New Journalism.* London: Pan. (First published 1973, New York: Harper & Row.)

Wordsworth, W. (1802). Preface and Appendix to 3rd edition of *Lyrical Ballads* (page references to the text as printed in Mason 1992).

Wright, G. T. (1974). The lyric present: simple present verbs in English poems. *PMLA* 89, 563–79.

Zabus, C. (1991). *The African Palimpsest: Indigenization of Language in the West African Europhone Novel.* Amsterdam: Rodopi.

Zijderveld, A. C. (1979). *On Clichés.* London: Routledge & Kegan Paul.

INDEX

Index

English compared, 30–1; borrowing, 25–6, 78, 79–80, 82, 357, 363; core common to British English and, 6, 22–48; dictionaries, 9–10, 57, 58, 66, 556, 557, 582–3; in EFL, 28; as independent of British English, 9–10; innovativeness, 32, 68, 73; international influence, 1, 16–17, 24–5, 28, 31, 38; literary language, 599, 680–1; modality, 33; neologisms, 4, 25–6, 363; noun phrases, 96–7, 99, 101, 105, 130; *OED* citations, 29, 31; past, simple, 192; phonology, 15, 35–40, 376, 380, 381, 396–408, 521, 522, (consonants), 468, 469, 473, 486, 487, 491–2, 533n144, (intonation and rhythm), 519, (regional accents), 15, 39, 401, 521, (voice qualities), 520, (vowel phonotactics), 438, 440, 444, (vowel realisations), 451, 453, 458–9, 459–60, 462, (vowel system), 403–4, 405, 406, 407–9, 411, 412, 525n38, (*see also under* standard *below*); politeness strategies, 101; pseudo coordination of adverbial clauses, 311; regional varieties, 15, 39, 40, 401, 521; semantic change, 10; sentence-initial conjuncts, 242; slang, 58; spelling, 9–10, 22–3; standard, 6, 28, 39, 552, (phonology), 396, 397–8, 399, 400, 402–3; subordinate interrogative clauses, 246; *see also* Americanisms; General American; United States

American Indian languages, 25–6, 78, 357, 363

Americanisms in British English, 16–17, 23, 31, 118; false, 32–3; rejection, 7, 25–6, 52

American Standard Code for Information Exchange (ASCII), 12–13

amongst see *between*

amplifiers, 591

analogy and usage, 546–7, 585

And as sentence opener, 256

Anderson, Sherwood, 295, 679

Andrews, Eliza, 401

Anglo-Saxon, 3, 49, 74, 618; 'Saxon English' movement, 609, 617–18

Angus, W., 470, 471, 472, 494–512 *passim*; on vowels, 413, 434, 436, 437, 445, 447, 528n69

Anson, George, 472

Antarctica, 339

any-body/-one/-thing, 104–6

anymore, positive, 34

APEC (Alliance for the Preservation of English in Canada), 55

apostrophe, 120–1, 155

APPEAR, 231–2, 258

apposition: contact clauses in, 259; literary language, 635, 644–5; relative clauses, 636

Arabic, 27, 78

ARCHER corpus, 95, 585

army officers, 53

Arnold, Matthew, 624, 653, 666, 669

articles, 118; definite, 33–4, 611, 675–6

Artin, Edward, 403

as as relative marker, 282

ASCII (American Standard Code for Information Exchange), 12–13

ash (runic letter and phonetic symbol), 70–1

Ash, John, 492, 542

Ashbery, John, 675, 676

Asiatic Society of Bengal, 558

aspect, 34–5, 92, 666; *see also* progressives

Auden, W. H., 614, 645–6, 653, 655; versification, 618, 621, 625

Austen, Jane, 9, 94; composite sentences, 257, 262, 264, 269, 283, 294, 302, 303; elements of clause, 214, 224, 227, 229–30, 232; noun phrase, 99, 101, 108, 111, 119–20; self-expression, 262, 664–5, 672, 681; structure of clause, 243, 248, 262; synecdoche, 652; verbal group, 136, 148, 195, 204, (declaratives), 237, 239, 240, (ellipsis), 198, 199, 200, (modal verbs), 168, 174, 177, (progressive), 144, 147, 155

Australia, 5, 12, 27, 40

Australian Broadcasting Corporation, 38

Australian English, 27, 29, 30–1, 83, 242; onomastics, 336, 338, 339, 348, 354, 356; phonology, 11, 28, 38, 39–40, 473, 522, 525n38; standard, 10–11, 28, 30

auxiliaries, 92, 131, 132, 193–206; affirmatives, 194–5; contraction, 136; Dutch, with infinitive, 141; invariance, 210–11; LET in imperatives, 252–4; negatives, 195–8; nonfinite verbal groups, 203–6; post-verbal ellipsis and emphasis, 198–202; questions and other inversions, 198; *see also* BE; DO; GET; HAVE; *and under* passive

Ayres, Alfred (*pseud.* of Thomas Embley Osmun), 573

babytalk, 75

backformation, 72–3

backshifting, 133–4, 178, 179, 261

back-spellings, 366

Bailey, Nathan, 25

Baker, Kenneth, 50

Baker, Robert, 113

Baker, S. J., 10–11

ballad metre, 620–1, 628, 630

Bank of English, 585

Barnes, William, 602

Barnhart, C. L. and D. K., 77–9, 82–3

Baron, Dennis, 32–3

Barrie, A., 412, 414, 434, 435, 437, 438, 445, 528n69

Barrie, Sir J. M., 158, 274, 344

Barthelme, Donald, 642–3

Index

Batchelor, Thomas, 376, 381, 406, 448, 450
bathos, comic, 637
Bauer, L., 461–2, 473
Baum, L. Frank, 213, 238, 302, 304
BBC, *see* British Broadcasting Corporation
BE: contractions, 120, 196, 197; copula/non-
  copula uses, 7; DO periphrasis with, 203, 252;
  identifying, with subject *it*, 212; inflection,
  134, 161; main verb, literate/oral styles, 591;
  modal use, 171, 174, 202, 209–10; passive
  auxiliaries, 132, 181, 206; perfects, 35,
  135–43; post-verbal ellipsis, 200–1;
  progressive, 143–60, 155, 156, 194, 206, 207,
  208; and right dislocation, 237; subjunctives,
  161, 162–3
Beat poets, 629
Beattie, James, 385–6
Beckett, Samuel, 614
Bedfordshire accent, 448
BEGIN + infinitive in complement, 187
Belfast, 17
Bell, Alexander Melville, 380, 491, 519, 531n122;
  vowels, 419, 452, 460, 463
Bell, Gertrude, 94; composite sentences, 259,
  264, 278, 294, 306, 307, 309, 322n77;
  declarative clauses, 242; interrogatives, 247;
  elements of clause, 214, 215, 216, 218; noun
  phrase, 102, 124; verbal group, 135, 139, 146,
  186, 191, (modal verbs), 165, 171, 176
Benezet, Anthony, 414
Bengali loanwords, 78
Bennett, Arnold, 283, 284, 679
Bennett, Louise, 40
between/amongst, 547, 563, 573, 578, 580–1, 582
Biber, D. & Finegan, E., 590–2
Bible: Garden of Eden, 565–6; names derived
  from, 340, 341, 356, 357; prosody, 622–3,
  641; translations, 22, 30, 52
Birmingham University, 585
Black anglophone personal names, 344, 347
Black English Vernacular, 212, 599, 612
Black Muslim movement, 347
Blackmore, R. D., 170, 250, 258, 340
Blake, William, 8, 252, 276, 663; versification,
  614–15, 621, 623, 624
blank verse, 623–4
blends, 60, 85, 86, 87; names, 333, 344, 365
Boag, J., 494–512 *passim*
Booker Prize for fiction, 41–2
borrowing, 3–4, 25–6, 76–88; adoption and
  adaptation, 60; hybrid compounds, 76;
  innovative, 76; literary language, 608–9,
  610–11; loan clipping, 76; loan translations,
  76; naturalized/non-naturalized, 60;
  onomastics, 332, (personal names), 340, 341,
  342–3, 345, (place-names), 352, 356, 357,
  359–60, 361; recent neologisms, 82–8;

semantic change, 82; semantic loans, 76;
  sources of loanwords, 77–9; *see also individual
  source languages, especially* French; Greek; Indic
  languages; Italian; Latin
Boston, Mass., 15, 398
Boswell, James, 631, 634, 643
bourgeoisie, *see* middle classes
Bradley, Henry, 561
Brady, James, 524n17, 531n125
Brathwaite, Edward Kamau, 43, 630
Breeze, Jean Binta, 43
Bridges, Robert, 25, 415
Brightland, J., 450, 459, 524n15
Britain, L., 667
Britain, *see individual aspects throughout index*
Briticisms, 31–2
British Broadcasting Corporation, 36–7, 37–8,
  394–5
British Council, 23–4
British English: innovativeness, 32, 68, 73; core
  common to American English and, 6, 22–48;
  see also individual aspects throughout index
British National Corpus, 585
Bronstein, A. J., 403
Brontë, Charlotte, 184, 266, 269
Brown, R. W., 81
Brown Corpus of American English, 30–1, 62,
  584–5
Browning, Elizabeth Barrett, 624, 626
Browning, Robert, 101, 162, 252, 656; dramatic
  monologues, 670–1; parenthesis, 595, 596,
  597; versification, 617, 622, 624, 625, 627
Buchanan, James, 376, 471; on vowels, 412, 413,
  436, 437, 445–9 *passim*
Buddhism, 82
Bulwer-Lytton, Edward, 213, 239, 248;
  adverbials, 126, 234, 297, 299, 300; noun
  phrase, 100, 104, 112, 126; verbal group, 143,
  163, 196, 223
Bunting, Basil, 676, 680
Bunyan, John, 672
Burchfield, Robert, 24, 29, 578
Burgess, Anthony, 612
Burney, Fanny, 105, 138, 232
Burns, Robert, 600, 602, 604–5, 610
business, language of, 13, 538
but that/what, 257–8, 282–3
Byron, George Gordon, 6th Baron, 606, 609,
  619, 625, 656, 657

Cable News Network (CNN), 38
Cajun French, 363
California, 55, 486, 487
Cambridge University, 386, 393–4
Camden, William, 351
Campbell, George, 541–2, 545, 546, 553, 595,
  630–1

764

Index

Hawai'i, 27, 42–3, 79
Hays, Mary, 632
Hazlewood, C. H., 196, 236, 239, 244, 254, 275, 298, 305
Hazlitt, William, 634, 665
head, 96
Head-Driven Phrase Structure Grammar, 157
Heaney, Seamus, 41
Heavy-NP Shift, 238–9
Hebrew loanwords, 78
hedges, 591
Helsinki Corpus, 585
Hemingway, Ernest, 637, 642, 673
Henslowe, W. H., 449, 457–8, 474, 528n69
Henton, C. G., 461
her, 269
heroic couplet, 623, 624
Herries, J., 412, 520, 526n46; on vowels, 413, 435, 444, 446, 528n69, (realisations), 455, 456, 458, 459, 461, 463, 465
hexameter, 618–19, 622
Hiberno-English, *see* Irish English
Hill, Geoffrey, 622, 624, 660–1, 680
Hill, Susan, 642, 638, 640
Hindi loanwords, 78, 81
historical status, change in word's, 70–1
historic present, 191
history of language, external, 6–22
Hoban, Russell, 612
Hodges, Richard, 471
Hodgson, W. B., 572–3
homosexuals' surnames, 350
hopefully, 234, 582
Hopkins, Gerard Manley, 610, 611, 614, 645; versification, 617, 618, 622, 623, 625, 626, 628
Horn, W., 452, 471
Hornsey, J.: on consonants, 468, 470, 471, 477–8, 481, 483, 485; on vowels, 413, 417, 418, 433–7 *passim*, 445, 528n69
house-names, 352, 370–1
Housman, A. E., 621
How/What about?, 247–8
How come?, 198, 247
Hughes, Langston, 629
Hulme, Keri, 41, 47
hybrid compounds, 76
hymns, 379–80
hyperbole, 69
hypercorrection, 426, 600, 601, 645; to subjective case, 109, 110–11, 247, 270, 278, 578
hypocoristic naming, 336–7, 344–5, 347
hypotaxis, 22, 633–42; *see also* subordinate clauses

iambic verse, 615, 617–20, 620–3, 626–7
Ibo, 611

iconic ordering, 640–1
idealised language, 22
identity, acts of, 42–3, 604; *see also* national identity and language
idiom in literature, 601–2, 673, 681
Ignatius, Fr. (Joseph Lycester Lyne), 475
Ihimaera, Witi, 47
Imagism, 594, 653–5
immigrants into Britain, 55
imperatives, 162, 249–54, 670
imperialism, *see* colonies, former; empire, British
Inclosure Awards, 334
India, 27, 29, 33, 42, 48–9
Indic loanwords, 78, 81–2
indirect style, 261–2, 594, 603
Indo-European languages, 558, 564
Indonesian loanwords, 78
Industrial Revolution, 11, 13, 15
infinitives, 184–8, 265–8, 291–3; split, 116, 205–6, 242, 581
inflection, *see* morphology
-ing ending, 204–5, 208, 265–7; *see also* gerunds
inheritance, and surnames, 348, 349
initialism, 71
innovation, 540–1, 577; American/British comparison, 32, 68, 73; innovative borrowing, 76; literary language, 611–12, 680–1
insecurity, linguistic, 19, 55–6, 383
Intelsat III, 12
INTEND, 266
intensifying adverbs, 126–7
interference, native language, 32–3
interjections, 662–4, 671, 672, 674
International English, 26, 61
International Phonetic Alphabet, 382, 422–3
Internet, 12
interrogatives, 2, 245–9, 670; *wh*-, 237, 245, 246–7, 247–8, 261, 591; *see also* questions
intonation and rhythm, 517–19, 639
introduction, formulas of, 101
Inuit, 364
invention, *see* innovation
inversion, subject-auxiliary, 235–7, 245, 254–5, 287, 608; NICE property, 193–4, 198
IPA (International Phonetic Alphabet), 382, 422–3
ipse dixit pronouncements, 572–3
Ireland: Gaelic, 54, 611; Irish bull, 612–13, 614; literature, 5, 41, 599, 602–3, 604, 612–13, 614; no local standard, 5; onomastics, 353, 354, 362, 371; phonology, 39–40, 444, 468, 469, 489; Plantation, 353, 362; syntax, 34–5, 246, 273
Iroquoian, 363
Isherwood, Christopher, 657
it, 120, 212–13, 225–7, 228, 591
Italian, 78, 340, 449, 538; borrowed plurals as count singulars, 100

Index

Index

Lehnert, M., 452
Leonard, Sterling, 580
Leopold, Prince, 472, 475
Lepsius, Richard, 462, 490
less/fewer, 124, 155, 581
LET, 162, 174–5, 252–4
letters, 18, 94, 145, 593, 600, 634; epistolary novel, 145, 671; official, 21
Lewis, Meriwether, 364
lexical-incidental features *see under* consonant phonotactics; vowel phonotactics
lexical stress, 492–517
lexicon, *see* vocabulary
like: conjunction, 71, 562, 577–8, 581; focusing adverbial, 242; transitive adjective, 128–9
Lindsay, Vachel, 629
lingua franca, English as technological, 12–13
Linguistic Association of Great Britain, 53
linguistics, comparative and historical, 16, 49, 81; development, 18th/19th-century, 556, 558–9, 562, 564, 567, 574–5; influence of Horne Tooke, 556, 558–9, 568; 'Saxon English' movement, 609, 617–18
Linguistic Society of America, 53
literacy, mass, 17–18, 21
literature, 589–692; affect, 602, 662–6, 674; American, 599, 680–1; authenticity, 43–4, 47; centre-margin relationship, 46; colonial and postcolonial, 5, 40–8, 599, 604; common core, 40–8, 679–81; deixis, 662, 669, 672, 674–5; emotive expressions, 662; epistemics, 662, 672; foregrounding devices, 639–40, 652; metaphor, 646–61, (cliché-metaphor), 658–61, (Modernism), 653–5, (pathetic fallacy), 647–50, 654–5, 658, (simile), 655–8, (synecdoche), 650–3; and national identity, 47; nonsense writing, 613–14; oral styles, 22, 589–602, 635; and oral tradition, 43, 47; self-expression and self-representation, 43, 661–79, (conversation poem and dramatic monologue), 595, 668–71, (deconstructing the self), 674–9, (empathetic narrative), 671–3, 677–9, 681, (language of affect), 602, 662–6, 674, (subjective time), 666–8; style-markers and stylisation, 592–6, 597, 614, 631, 638; syntax, 538, 630–46, (hypotaxis-parataxis shift), 633–9, (information deficit in shift), 639–42, (Modernist), 642–6; varieties of language, 598–614, (metaphorical functions), 605–6, (naturalistic functions), 603–5, (New Journalist style), 678, (problems of function), 602–3, (representation of non-standard), 600–3, (standard), 599, 600, 612–14, (use of non-standard), 603–6, 606–8, 673; verbs, 150–8, 666–7, 667–8, 673; vocabulary, 538, 609–10; *see also individual authors,* children's books; Imagism; Modernism; typography; parenthesis;

polyvocalism; repetition; Romanticism; versification; *and under* adjectives; apposition; borrowing; innovation; Ireland; Latin; onomastics; punctuation; relative clauses
litotes, 70
Liverpool dialect, 197, 602
Lloyd, Richard, 393, 487
loanwords, *see* borrowing
LOB (London-Oslo/Bergen) Corpus, 30–1, 62, 584–5
Locke, John, 541, 568, 571, 633, 646
Lodge, D., 679
Lodwick, Francis, 524n15
logic, 585, 612–14, 633
London: central role in linguistic change, 15, 18–19; court speech, 383, 386; development, 13, 15, 366; phonology, 403–4, 412, 451, 475, (as standard), 15, 377, 383, 385–6, 387, 389, 392, (vernacular), 15, 18–19, 412, (*see also* Cockney); social composition, 14, 17; street names, 366
London-Lund Corpus, 585
London-Oslo/Bergen Corpus, *see* LOB Corpus
Longfellow, Henry Wadsworth, 238, 618, 619
Longman Pronunciation Dictionary (J. C. Wells), 494–512 *passim*
Lounsbury, Thomas, 380, 401, 576
'lowbrow', 658, 677
Lowell, Robert, 680
Lowry, Malcolm, 672
Lowth, Robert, 8, 542, 544, 552, 553, 568; on Biblical prosody, 622, 641; conception of grammar, 543, 545, 546–7; written language as norm, 550, 551
Luckombe, Philip, 379, 468
Lyne, Joseph Lycester (Fr. Ignatius), 475

Macaulay, Thomas Babington, 609, 622, 635, 642, 644–5, 679
MacCarthy, P. A. D., 494–512 *passim*
McDavid, R. I. Jr., 473
MacDiarmid, Hugh (C. M. Grieve), 604, 610
McEnroe, John, 135
Mackenzie, Henry, 633–4, 635, 640, 641–2
Mackintosh, D., and His Two Daughters: on consonants, 482, 483, 484; on vowels, 414, 434, 436, 437, 445, 449, 452, 453, 528n69
Macmillan publishers, 561
Macpherson, James, 621
Mailer, Norman, 677
Malayo-Polynesian loanwords, 78
Malcolm, James, 523n8
Manchester, 14, 602, 603–4
many; quasi-nominal use, 125
Maori literature, 43–5, 47
Marlowe, Christopher, 2, 128
Marsh, George Perkins, 157, 570–1

Index

Index

neologisms, recent, 58, 79, 82–8, 344

Nesbit, E.: composite sentences, 255, 260, 262, 263, 265, 268, 272, 312, (adverbials), 296, 304, 305, (relatives), 277, 281, 282, 288, 290; elements of clause, 226, 228, 213–14, 219; noun phrases, 116, 118, 121, 126, 127, (pronouns), 104, 107–8, 110, 111, 316n19; structure of clause, 236, 239, 241, 242, 244, 254; verbal groups, 141, 182, 197, 199, 202, 203, 205, (modals), 165, 171, 173, 175, 180, (past time), 142, 191, 192

network English, 39

networks, social, 16, 17, 154

Neuberger, Rabbi Julia, 41

never, 197, 250

New England phonology, 398, 400, 459

new Englishes, 98, 246

New York Times, 53

New Zealand, 19, 23, 27, 31, 38, 192; literature, 40, 43–5, 46; phonology, 19, 28, 38, 39–40; place-names, 354, 356

Newbolt Report (1921), 50, 51

Newcastle-upon-Tyne, 417, 580–1

Newman, F. W., 432, 468, 470, 523n3

Newman, J. H., 155

Newton, Isaac, 465, 537

next, transitive adjective, 128–9

nice, affective adjective, 664–5

NICE properties, 193–4, 195–8, 202

Nicklin, T., 415

nicknames, 336–7, 344–5, 347

Nightingale, Florence, 342

Nobel Prize for Literature, 41

no-body/-one/-thing, 104–6

nominal clauses, 256–74; contact clauses, 256–7, 258–9, 591; finite, 257–64, (links introducing), 257–61, (subjunctive in), 262–4; nonfinite, 265–74, (complementation with *-ing* vs *to*-infinitive), 265–7, (gerunds), 268–72, (indirect object + *to*-infinitive), 267–8, (raising), 272–4; relative, 274, 285–6

nominalisations, 591, 606

none, 115, 122–3

nonfinite clauses: adverbial, 305–10; nominal, 265–74; relative, 291–3; voice in, 184–8

nonsense writing, 613–14

nor, 255–6

Norfolk dialect, 18, 20, 405, 476

Northamptonshire dialect, 409, 602

Northcote, Stafford, 475

Northern English English, 406, 522, 526n48

Norwegian loanwords, 78

Norwich dialect, 18, 20

Nottingham, 602, 603

noun phrases, 92, 96–130; attributive nouns, 129–30; adjectives in, 113–14, 125–9; determiners, 114–25; noun as head, 96–100;

postmodification, 130; pronouns as head, 100–13

nouns: attributive, 129–30; collective, 99; count/noncount, 96–8, 124–5; formation, 68, 73, 75; as head of NP, 96–100; Horne Tooke's speculative etymology, 554, 557; and literate/oral styles, 591, 595; morphology, 92, 548–9; number concord, 99–100

novel, 40, 41; absurdist, 614; epistolary, 145, 671; first person narration, 145, 671; grammaticalization of progressive and, 144–5; Modernist, 676–9; and national identity, 47

NPs, *see* noun phrases

number concord, 95, 99–100, 121–3, 213–14, 580

numbers as postdeterminers, 123

Nuttall, P. Austin, 389

O, exclamatory/vocative, 663

objective case, 107–8, 109–11, 268–70

objectivity, literary, 646, 647, 661–2, 674

objects, 215–28; contact clauses, 258–9; direct, 237–8, 239; group-verbs, 221–5; indefinite, anticipatory and anaphoric *it*, 225–8; indirect, 217–19, 238, 239, 267–8; placement, 237–9; prepositional, 220–1, 238; reflexive and reciprocal use of verbs, 216–17; topicalisation, 237–8; transitive and intransitive verbs, 215–16

obligation, verbs of, 170–1, 171–2

obscenities, 562, 209–10

OCCUR, 258

Odell, J., 410–11, 413, 431, 432, 436, 437, 457, 463

OED, *see* Oxford English Dictionary

of: equative, 646, 653; stressed form of enclitic *'ve*, 142

OFFER, 267–8

official status of English, 55

Ogilvie, J., 494–512 *passim*, 516

O'Hara, Frank, 653, 668

Okri, Ben, 41

Old English, 3, 49, 62, 74, 291; *see also* Anglo-Saxon

Olson, Charles, 596, 597, 606, 610, 616, 629, 638

one, anaphoric pronoun, 101–2, 102–3, 114

Onions, C. T., 561

only, 241–2

onomastics, 330–72; aliasing, 349, 351; categories other than people or places, 338, 370–1; definition of terms, 330–2; English-transmitted names, 332, 336; Gaelic influence, 343, 348, 361; grammatical changes, 331; individuals or families commemorated by, 341, 342, 357–9; Latin influence, 340, 357, 362–3; literary, 338, 339, 342, 352, 371;

Index

Index

Steele, Thomas, 21, 523n8
Steiner, George, 41
stem, bare, 211
stereotype features, 594, 600, 601–2
Sterne, Laurence, 9, 314n15
Stevenson, Robert Louis, 54, 282
Stirling, John, 548
Storm, J., 425, 439, 440, 462, 479
Strang, B. M. H., 120, 144–5, 492
stream-of-consciousness writing, 643, 659–60
Streatfeild, Noel, 111, 122, 149, 173, 202, 245, 290
street-names, 334, 338, 339, 365–70
stress, lexical, 492–517
structure, phonological *see under* consonant
  phonemes; vowel phonemes
style, 17, 390, 394; literary marking, 592–6, 631;
  and phonology, 387–8, 390, 394
stylisation, literary, 592–6, 597, 614, 638
subconscious, 89
subject, 212–15
subjective case in non-subject position, 107–8,
  109–11, 270, 578
subjective language, literary, 661–2, 674
subjunctive, 160–4, 262–4, 294; conditional,
  294, 608; imperative, 162, 252; negation, 162,
  198
subjuncts, 233–4
subordinate clauses, 256–312; *see also* hypotaxis
  and individual types of clause
such as determiner, 116, 117–18
Suffolk dialect, 15
suggestions, progressives in, 188
superlative NPs, quantifiers before, 115–16
surnames, 337, 348–50, 371; changing of, 344,
  347, 348–9, 349–50; as given names, 341; as
  place-names, 358–9, 361
surrealism, 614, 655
Survey of English Place-Names, 335–6, 350
surveyors and place-names, 335, 364
suspension of meaning, 630–1, 632, 639
Swann Report (1985), 50
swear words, 562, 609–10
Sweden, Swedish, 23, 27, 78
sweet, 666
Sweet, Henry, 19–20, 380, 392, 521, 575; on
  consonants, 467–8, 470–9 *passim*, 483–8
  passim, 491; on voice qualities, 520; phonetic
  notation, 382; on vowels, 407, 411, 413, 414,
  420, 421, 425–6, 431–2, 439–44 *passim*,
  448–52 *passim*, 456, 457, 460–7 *passim*
Swift, Jonathan, 10, 13, 340, 538–9, 541, 552
syllabic consonants, 432
symbolism, 651, 652–3, 654
synecdochic detail, 650–3
Synge, J. M., 5, 611
syntax, 92–329; change, 2, 92–3, 95; composite
  sentences, 255–312; data, 94–5, 323–6; 18th-

century conception, 543, 551; elements of
  clause, 212–35; false, exercises in, 549–50,
  552, 560; Latin and Greek influence, 21;
  literary language, 630–46, (Modernist); 642–6,
  681, (shift from hypotaxis to parataxis),
  633–42; noun phrase, 92, 96–130; onomastic,
  331, 339, 352, 359; structure of clause,
  235–55; verbal group, 130–212; word order,
  92; *see also individual structures and parts of speech*

t/d, dropping of final, 19
taboo vocabulary, 609–10
tag clauses, 635
tag-topicalism, 603
Tamil loanwords, 81
Tartt, Donna, 141, 169, 173, 177, 242, 288, 310
Taylor, Tom & Reade, Charles, 196, 202, 212,
  257, 288
Taylor, John, the Water-poet, 354
Tebbit, Norman MP, 584
technology, language of, 12–13, 80
telecommunications, 12–13
television, 12, 16–17, 18, 38, 602, 603
Telford, Shropshire, 353
temporal clauses, 304
Tennyson, Alfred, 1st Baron, 306, 394, 521, 604,
  626; figurative language, 649–50, 654, 656
tense, 160, 132–5, 210, 211–12
terriers (catalogues of landholdings), 334
/th/-/v/ change, 18
Thackeray, William Makepeace, 53, 227, 269,
  292, 636
that: adjective premodifier, 127; clause
  connective, 257–60; in compound
  conjunctions, 294; deletion, 591; relative
  marker, 278–80, 284, 285
Thatcher, Margaret, Baroness, 38, 51
theology, 564–8, 559
there, 95, 187, 213–14, 281
THINK, 259, 261
Thiong'o, Ngugi wa, 42
this, new-, 118
Thomas, Dylan, 614, 629, 655
Thomas, Edward, 627
Thomson, James, 624, 666
Thornton, William, 376, 380, 526n45; on
  vowels, 411, 435, 436, 445, 446, 447, 449,
  452–8 *passim*, 461, 528n69
thou, 106, 134, 157, 161, 249
Tiffin, William, 405
time, expression of, 188–93
Time magazine, 58
Times, The, 29, 53, 337
Tithe Awards, 334–5
titles, personal, 53
to infinitive marker, 204, 205–6, 266
Tok Pisin, 42–3

THE CAMBRIDGE HISTORY
OF THE ENGLISH LANGUAGE

GENERAL EDITOR Richard M. Hogg

VOLUME I *The Beginnings to 1066*
EDITED BY Richard M. Hogg

EDITED BY Roger Lass

1   Introduction
    ROGER LASS

2   Semantics and lexis
    TERTTU NEVALAINEN

3   Pholology and morphology
    ROGER LASS

4   Orthography and punctuation
    VIVIAN SALMON

5   Dialectology
    MANFRED GÖRLACH

6   Syntax
    MATTI RISSANEN

7   Literary language
    SYLVIA ADAMSON

    Glossary of linguistic terms
    Bibliography
    Index

Regional dialects
LEE PEDERSON

Contact with other languages
SUZANNE ROMAINE

Spelling
RICHARD L. VENEZKY